SOCIAL PSYCHOLOGY

Eighth Edition

Advisory editorial board

Eighth Edition

SOCIAL PSYCHOLOGY

Michael A. Hogg
Claremont Graduate University

Graham M. Vaughan
University of Auckland

Harlow, England • London • New York • Boston • San Francisco • Toronto • Sydney • Dubai • Singapore • Hong Kong
Tokyo • Seoul • Taipei • New Delhi • Cape Town • São Paulo • Mexico City • Madrid • Amsterdam • Munich • Paris • Milan

Pearson Education Limited
KAO Two
KAO Park
Harlow CM17 9NA
United Kingdom
Tel: +44 (0)1279 623623
Web: www.pearson.com/uk

First published 1995 (print)
Second edition published 1998 (print)
Third edition published 2002 (print)
Fourth edition published 2005 (print)

Fifth edition published 2008 (print)
Sixth edition published 2011 (print)
Seventh edition published 2014 (print and electronic)
Eighth edition published 2018 (print and electronic)

© Pearson Education Limited 1995, 1998, 2002, 2005, 2008, 2011 (print)
© Pearson Education Limited 2014, 2018 (print and electronic)

ISBN: 978-1-292-09045-0 (print)
         978-1-292-09050-4 (PDF)
         978-1-292-18245-2 (ePub)

British Library Cataloguing-in-Publication Data
A catalogue record for the print edition is available from the British Library

Library of Congress Cataloging-in-Publication Data
Names: Hogg, Michael A., 1954–author. | Vaughan, Graham M., author.
Title: Social Psychology / Michael A. Hogg, Claremont Graduate University,
  Graham M. Vaughan, University of Auckland.
Description: Eighth Edition. | New York : Pearson, [2018] | Revised edition
  of the authors' Social psychology, 2014.
Identifiers: LCCN 2017028310 | ISBN 9781292090450 (Print) | ISBN 9781292090504 (PDF) |
  ISBN 9781292182452 (ePub)
Subjects: LCSH: Social psychology.
Classification: LCC HM1033 .H64 2018 | DDC 302—dc23
LC record available at https://lccn.loc.gov/2017028310

10 9 8 7
22 21

Print edition typeset in 10/12 Sabon MT Pro by iEnergizer Aptara®, Ltd.
Printed by CPI Group (UK) Ltd, Croydon CR0 4YY

NOTE THAT ANY PAGE CROSS REFERENCES REFER TO THE PRINT EDITION

Brief contents

Contents

3   Attribution and social explanation   82

12 Aggression 468

Preface

This is the eighth edition of our *Social Psychology*. The original idea to write a European social psychology text was born in Oxford in 1992 from meetings with Farrell Burnett, who was then psychology editor at Harvester Wheatsheaf. We decided to write the text because we felt there was a need for a comprehensive social psychology text written specifically for university students in Britain and continental Europe. Such a text, we felt, should approach social psychology from a European rather than American perspective not only in terms of topics, orientation and research interests but also in terms of the style and level of presentation of social psychology and the cultural context of the readership. However, a European text cannot ignore or gloss over American social psychology – so, unlike other European texts, we located mainstream American social psychology within the framework of the text, covered it in detail and integrated it fully with European work. We intended this to be a self-contained and comprehensive coverage of social psychology. You would not need to switch between American and European texts to understand social psychology as a truly international scientific enterprise – an enterprise in which European research now has a significant and well-established profile. The first edition was published in 1995 and was widely adopted throughout Europe.

Subsequent editions followed fast upon earlier editions – no sooner did one edition appear than, it seemed, we were hard at work preparing the next. The second edition was written while Graham Vaughan was a visiting Fellow of Churchill College at Cambridge University and Michael Hogg was a visiting Professor at Princeton University. It was published early in 1998 and launched at the 1998 conference of the Social Section of the British Psychological Society at the University of Kent. It was a relatively modest revision aimed primarily at improving layout and presentation, though the text and coverage were updated, and we raised the profile of some applied topics in social psychology.

The third edition was published in 2002. It was a major revision to accommodate significant changes in the field since the first edition. The structure and approach remained the same, but some chapters were dropped, some completely reworked, others amalgamated and some entirely new chapters written. In addition, the text was updated and the layout and presentation significantly improved. Such a large revision involved substantial input from our Advisory Editorial Board and from lecturers around Britain and Europe, and many meetings in different places (Bristol, Glasgow and Thornbury) with Pearson Education, our publishers.

The fourth edition was published in 2005. We expanded our Editorial Board to include seventeen leading European social psychologists to represent different aspects of social psychology, different levels of seniority and different nations across Europe. However, the key change was that the book was now in glorious full-colour. We also took a rather courageous step – the sleeve just showed empty chairs, no people at all; quite a departure for a social psychology text. Auckland harbour was the venue for initial planning of the fourth edition, with a series of long meetings in London, capped by a productive few days at the Grand Hotel in Brighton.

The fifth edition, published in 2008, was a very substantial revision with many chapters entirely or almost entirely rewritten. We liked the 'empty chairs' sleeve for the fourth edition so decided to continue that theme but be a bit more jolly – so the sleeve showed those Victorian-style bathing booths that used to be common at British and French beach resorts. Initial planning took place at our favourite writing retreat (Noosa, just north of Brisbane in Australia) and then a string of long meetings with the Pearson team in Bristol, London, Birmingham and even Heathrow. We returned to Noosa to finalise plans and the actual writing was done in Auckland and Los Angeles.

The sixth edition, published in 2011, was again a relatively significant revision in which we thoroughly updated material to reflect changes in the field and renamed and repositioned some chapters. We also recruited members of Mike's Social Identity Lab at Claremont to meticulously check the references. The text was planned and set in motion over a week in November 2007 when Graham and Mike holed up in Mike's new home in the Santa Monica Mountains just outside Los Angeles. There were many subsequent meetings with the Pearson team in London, of which two are particularly memorable; one where we adjourned to a nearby lunch venue and did not resurface until late afternoon, and another where we ventured to the 'posh' Carluccio's in Covent Garden and our editor, Janey Webb, almost missed her flight to Stockholm. The edition was written in late 2009 and early 2010 while Mike was in Los Angeles and Graham was in Auckland.

The seventh edition, published in 2014, was intended to be a light revision but we got carried away – we ended up including over 250 new references and expanding our Advisory Editorial Board to twenty-two scholars from across Europe. The initial planning meeting with the Pearson crew (Janey Webb and Tim Parker) was in London in February 2010 during Britain's big freeze. Mike then visited Graham in Auckland in December 2011 to finalize planning and start writing – it rained torrentially and blew a gale continuously. A year later, in December 2012, Mike had a final meeting with Neha and Janey from Pearson in a pub outside Bristol – and yes, once again it was freezing cold. So, we like to consider the seventh edition as a victory over climate change. The actual writing was done in the second half of 2012 and start of 2013 while Mike was in Los Angeles and San Francisco and Graham was in Auckland.

The eighth edition

In preparing this eighth edition we focused on significantly updating material to reflect important advances in the field (there are over 250 new references) but have not made dramatic changes. We have retained the structure and approach of previous editions, and the text is framed by the same scientific and educational philosophy as before. We have improved the narrative throughout; significantly rewritten large portions of text for greater accessibility; updated real-world examples and provided new figures, boxes and photos. Specific more significant changes include:

- Updated and expanded coverage of affect and emotion, including a new section on emotion regulation.
- Updated and expanded coverage of rumour, and new inclusion of gossip.
- Expanded discussion of societal attributions.
- More on self-awareness and identity fusion.
- The attitude-behaviour section is heavily revised and restructured, and has additional material on health and on the IAT.
- A whole new section on morality has been introduced.
- Coverage of group deviants and marginal members has been rewritten and updated.
- Discussion of trust and leadership has been updated and extended.
- Discussion of ambivalent sexism and of discrimination against sexual minorities has been updated and expanded

- Significant update and extension of radicalization, social dilemmas, intergroup emotions, intergroup anxiety and intergroup contact.

- The aggression and prosocial chapters have been heavily updated and revised for accessibility – with new material on volunteering and martyrdom.

- Discussion of relationships has been updated and expanded with new material, especial on attachment styles and intimate relationships on the web.

- There is expanded and new material on the linguistic category model, on deception, and on CMC and social media-based communication.

- There is new material on face-saving, the tightness–looseness of cultures, and a broadened discussion of multicultural societies and how to manage them.

To prepare this eighth edition we obtained feedback on the seventh edition from our Editorial Board, and as many of our colleagues and postgraduate and undergraduate students as we could find who had used the text as teacher, tutor or student. We are enormously grateful for this invaluable feedback – we see our text as a genuine partnership between us as authors and all those who use the text in different capacities. We are also indebted to our wonderful publishing team at Pearson in scenic Harlow – Neha Sharma and Natalia Jaszczuk oversaw the early planning stages and then our long-time editor Janey Webb returned to see it all through. Our post-submission team was Melanie Carter and Emma Marchant, who oversaw the final stages of production of the text. We were sustained and energised by their enthusiasm, good humour, encouragement and wisdom, and were kept on our toes by their timeline prompts, excellent editing and fearsome perceptiveness and efficiency.

To start the process, Mike met with Neha in London in December 2013 – off Trafalgar Square, just around the corner from St. Martin-in-the-Fields where Nelson Mandela's commemoration service was being held at the time. There was another London meeting, with Natalia, in 2014, and then Natalia and Mike met again in Birmingham in March 2016, at Aston University and Browns in the Bull Ring. The final publisher meeting was particularly memorable; it was with Janey in a pub in Mike's home village of Westbury-on-Trym in Bristol on June 23, 2016 – the day of the Brexit vote. The writing itself was done during 2016 while Graham was in Auckland and Mike bounced between his homes in Los Angeles and San Francisco and spent time in Rome as a visiting research professor at Sapienza Università di Roma.

How to use this text

This eighth edition is an up-to-date and comprehensive coverage of social psychology as an international scientific enterprise, written from the perspective of European social psychology and located in the cultural and educational context of people living in Britain and Europe. However, in this world of cheap travel and the Internet, we are all heavily exposed to different cultural, scientific and educational milieu – the text will not seem out of place in social psychology courses in other parts of the world.

The text has a range of pedagogical features to facilitate independent study. At the end of Chapter 1 we outline important primary and review sources for finding out more about specific topics in social psychology. Within chapters some material appears in boxes – typically six or more boxes per chapter. We have designed these boxes to reflect the fact that social psychology is a dialectical basic and applied science in which the development and empirical testing of theory informs our understanding of the world around us and our own everyday life, which in turn feeds back into theory development. To do this we have labelled boxed material as: (a) *Research classic* (focuses on and describes a classic, highly cited piece of conceptual or empirical research); (b) *Research highlight* (focuses on and highlights a specific relevant piece of conceptual or empirical research); (c) *Our world* (focusses your attention on the outside world of social issues and sociopolitical and historical events – showing or hinting at how social psychology can help understand it; and (d) *Your life* (focuses your attention on phenomena in your own everyday life – showing or hinting at how social psychology can help understand them).

Each chapter opens with a table of contents and some questions inviting you to consider your own views on topics within the chapter before you learn what the science has to say, and closes with a detailed summary of the chapter contents, a list of key terms, some guided questions, and a fully annotated list of further reading. At the end of each chapter, we also have a section called 'Literature, film and TV'. Social psychology is part of everyday life – so, not surprisingly, social psychological themes are often creatively and vividly explored in popular media. The 'Literature, film and TV' section directs you to some classic and contemporary works we feel have a particular relevance to social psychological themes.

As with the earlier editions, the text has a logical structure, with earlier chapters flowing into later ones. However, it is not essential to read the text from beginning to end. The chapters are carefully cross-referenced so that chapters or groups of chapters can be read independently in almost any order.

However, some chapters are better read in sequence. For example, it is better to read Chapter 5 before tackling Chapter 6 (both deal with aspects of attitudes), Chapter 8 before Chapter 9 (both deal with group processes), and Chapter 10 before Chapter 11 (both deal with intergroup behaviour). It may also be interesting to reflect back on Chapter 4 (the self) when you read Chapter 16 (culture). Chapter 1 describes the structure of the text, why we decided to write it and how it should be read – it is worthwhile reading the last section of Chapter 1 before starting later chapters. Chapter 1 also defines social psychology, its aims, its methods and its history. Some of this material might benefit from being reread after you have studied the other chapters and have become familiar with some of the theories, topics and issues of social psychology.

The primary target of our text is the student, although we intend it to be of use also to teachers and researchers of social psychology. We will be grateful to any among you who might take the time to share your reactions with us.

Michael Hogg, Los Angeles
Graham Vaughan, Auckland
February 2017

Social Psychology, Eighth Edition

Supporting resources

- Complete, downloadable Instructor's Manual, which presents chapter summaries, key terms and teaching ideas including essay questions, discussion topics, class exercises and a list of films that illustrate social psychological concepts.
- Downloadable PowerPoint slides with key figures from the text.

These lecturer resources can be downloaded from the lecturer web site at **www.pearsoned.co.uk/hogg** by clicking on the Instructor Resource link next to the cover. All instructor-specific content is password protected.

About the authors

Michael Hogg was educated at Bristol Grammar School and Birmingham University and received his PhD from Bristol University. Currently Professor of Social Psychology and Chair of the Social Psychology Program at Claremont Graduate University in Los Angeles, and an Honorary Professor of Social Psychology at the University of Kent, he is also a former President of the Society of Experimental Social Psychology. He has taught at Bristol University, Princeton University, the University of Melbourne and the University of Queensland, and is a Fellow of numerous scholarly societies including the Association for Psychological Science, the Society for Personality and Social Psychology, and the Society for the Psychological Study of Social Issues. He was the 2010 recipient of the Carol and Ed Diener Award in Social Psychology from the Society for Personality and Social Psychology. His research interests are group behaviour, intergroup relations, and self and social identity; with a specific interest in uncertainty and extremism, and processes of

influence and leadership. In addition to publishing about 350 scientific books, chapters and articles, he is foundation editor with Dominic Abrams of the journal *Group Processes and Intergroup Relations*, an associate editor of *The Leadership Quarterly*, and a past associate editor of the *Journal of Experimental Social Psychology*. Two of his books are citation classics, *Rediscovering the Social Group* (1987) with John Turner and others, and *Social Identifications* (1988) with Dominic Abrams. Recent books include the *Encyclopedia of Group Processes and Intergroup Relations* (2010) with John Levine, and *Extremism and the Psychology of Uncertainty* (2012) with Danielle Blaylock.

Graham Vaughan has been a Fulbright Fellow and Visiting Professor at the University of Illinois at Champaign-Urbana, a Visiting Lecturer and a Ford Foundation Fellow at the University of Bristol, a Visiting Professor at Princeton University, a Visiting Directeur d'Etudes at the *Maison des Science de l'Homme,* Paris, a Visiting Senior Fellow at the National University of Singapore, a Visiting Fellow at the University of Queensland and a Visiting Fellow at Churchill College, Cambridge. As Professor of Psychology at the University of Auckland, he served twelve years as Head of Department. He is an Honorary Fellow and past President of the New Zealand Psychological Society, and a past President of the Society of Australasian Social Psychologists. Graham Vaughan's primary areas of interest in social psychology are attitudes and attitude development, group processes and intergroup relations, ethnic relations and identity, culture and the history of social psychology. He has published widely on these topics. His 1972 book, *Racial Issues in New Zealand*, was the first to deal with ethnic relations in that country. Recent books include *Essentials of Social Psychology* (2010) with Michael Hogg.

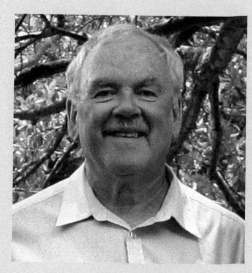

Acknowledgements

The publisher would like to thank the following for their kind permission to reproduce the following:

(Key: L – left; R – right)

Image credits

Action Plus Sports Images: Neil Tingle 256; **Alamy Images:** 360b 140, Agencja Fotograficzna Caro 666, Christina Kennedy 593, Cultura RM 301, David Pearson 662, Don Tonge 133, Foto Arena LTDA 438, Les Gibbon 366, Mandoga Media 320, Martin Dalton 92, Martin Thomas Photography 624, Martyn Evans 194, Mary Ann Alwan 325, Michael Seaman 540, OZSHOTZ 7, Paul Baldesare 560, Peter Titmuss 477, Phanie 185, Picture Partners 166, Reuters 124, 170, 506, Richard Levine 454, The Photolibrary Wales 608, Travel Pictures 111, Xinhua 618, YAY Media AS 135, ZUMA Press, Inc. 337, nagelestock.com 82; **Asset Library:** 123rf.com/Pearson Education Ltd 53, ampyang. Shutterstock/Pearson Education Ltd 51, Andresr. Shutterstock/Pearson Education Ltd 297, Andrey Popov. 123rf.com/Pearson Education Ltd 15, Andrey_Popov. Shutterstock/Pearson Education Ltd 388, Blend Images. Shutterstock/Pearson Education Ltd 30, chaoss. Shutterstock/Pearson Education Ltd 570, Corepics VOF. Shutterstock/Pearson Education Ltd 292, Creativa Images. Shutterstock/Pearson Education Ltd 219, Darren Baker. 123rf.com/Pearson Education Ltd 633, dolgachov. 123rf.com/Pearson Education Ltd 88, Dragon Images. Shutterstock/Pearson Education Ltd 280, Evlakhov Valeriy. Shutterstock/Pearson Education Ltd 544, Gareth Boden/Pearson Education Ltd 68, Gelpi JM. Shutterstock/Pearson Education Ltd 615L, Hung Chung Chih. Shutterstock/Pearson Education Ltd 426, iko. Shutterstock/Pearson Education Ltd 616, James Michael Dorsey. Shutterstock/Pearson Education Ltd 638, Jules Selmes. Pearson Education Ltd/Pearson Education Ltd 209, Katherine00. Shutterstock/Pearson Education Ltd 250, Kolett. Shutterstock/Pearson Education Ltd 565, Kzenon. Shutterstock/Pearson Education Ltd 670, lenetstan. Shutterstock/Pearson Education Ltd 653, Lisa Payne Photography. Pearson Education Ltd 59L, Malyugin. Shutterstock/Pearson Education Ltd 94, Miriam Doerr. Shutterstock/Pearson Education Ltd 504, Monkey Business Images. Shutterstock/Pearson Education Ltd 21, 223, 496, 516, O Driscoll Imaging. Shutterstock/Pearson Education Ltd 511, oliveromg. Shutterstock/Pearson Education Ltd 315, PathDoc. Shutterstock/Pearson Education Ltd 330, Piotr Wawrzyniuk. Shutterstock/Pearson Education Ltd 152, Pressmaster. Shutterstock/Pearson Education Ltd 327, Ronald Sumners. Shutterstock/Pearson Education Ltd 143, SasinTipchai. Shutterstock/Pearson Education Ltd 84, stockbroker. 123rf.com/Pearson Education Ltd 394, StockLite. Shutterstock/Pearson Education Ltd 615R, StraH. Shutterstock/Pearson Education Ltd 265, Suzanne Clouzeau. Pearson Education, Inc. 524, Tinxi. Shutterstock/Pearson Education Ltd 121, Triff. Shutterstock/Pearson Education Ltd 9, Wavebreak Media Ltd. 123rf.com/Pearson Education Ltd 274, wavebreakmedia. Shutterstock/Pearson Education Ltd 177, 349; **DK Images:** Neil Lukas 42; **Getty Images:** AWelshLad 581R, Albert L. Ortega 309, Anne-Christine Poujoulat/AFP 381, Art Media/Print

Collector 197, Atlantide Phototravel/Corbis/VCG 247, Bloomberg 344, Bryn Lennon 28L, Carl Court/Stringer 412, Catherine Ivill – AMA 200, Chris Falkenstein 59R, Christopher Robbins 627, Colin Anderson/Stockbyte 238, D-Ozen 218, Desmond Kwande/Stringer 402, Dmitry Astakhov/AFP 243, Eric Feferberg/AFP 28R, Franc & Jean Shor/National Geographic 648, Francisco Cruz/SuperStock 284, Fuse 421, HelpingHandPhotos 548, John Borthwick/Lonely Planet Images 64, Jonathan Kantor/Photodisc 32, Lisa Valder 576, Louai Beshara/AFP 667, Mark Dadswell 436, Mike Kemp 2, Mladen Antonov 463, Noorullah Shirzada/AFP 500, Patrick Hertzog/AFP 355, Pornchai Kittiwongsakul/AFP 228, Ralph A. Clevenger 475, Stanislav Solntsev 480, Stockbyte 71, VisitBritain/Britain on View 447, Walter Hodges/Stone 289, asiseeit 596; **Graham Vaughan:** 276, 407, 604; **PA Images:** ABACA 160; **Photofusion:** Paul Doyle 586; **Reuters Pictures:** Adnan Abidi 660, Andrew Kelly 261; **Rex Features:** Lehtikuva Oy/Rex/Shutterstock 99, Lionsgate TV/Netflix/Kobal/REX/Shutterstock 147, PB/KMLA/Rex/Shutterstock 485; **Science Photo Library:** TEK Image 372; **Shutterstock:** ART production 468, Chintung Lee 116, Creatista 554, Everett Collection 360, Ivanko80 176, JLOrtin 457, John Gomez 102, Monkey Business Images 622, a9photo 211, mountainpix 533, Rave NIK 258, Roman Mikhailiuk 451, s_bukley 334, spass 579, szefei 527; **Thinkstock/Getty Images:** Gina Smith 546, Hemera 148, Jupiter Images 581L.

Text credits

Figure 8.13 from Socialization in small groups: temporal changes in individual-group relations, *Advances in Experimental Social Psychology*, vol. 15, pp. 137–192 (Moreland, R. L. & Levine, J. M., 1982), with permission from Richard Moreland and John Levine; Figure 11.5 from The effect of threat upon interpersonal bargaining, *Journal of Abnormal and Social Psychology*, vol. 61, pp. 181–189 (Deutsch, M. & Krauss, R. M., 1960), American Psychological Association, reprinted with permission; Figure 13.1 from Some neo-Darwinian decision rules for altruism: weighing cues for inclusive fitness as a function of the biological importance of the decision, *Journal of Personality and Social Psychology*, vol. 67, pp. 773–789 (Burnstein, E., Crandall, C. & Kitayama, S., 1994), with permission from Eugene Burnstein; Figure 14.2 from The evolutionary psychology of facial beauty, *Annual Review of Psychology*, vol. 57, pp. 199–226 (Rhodes, G., 2006), reproduced with permission from the *Annual Review of Psychology*, Volume 57 © 2006 by Annual Reviews, http://www.annualreviews.org, and Gillian Rhodes; Figure 14.9 from *The Triangle of Love* (Sternberg, R. J., 1988), with permission from Robert J. Sternberg; Figure 15.2 from The intergroup model of second language acquisition, *Journal of Multilingual and Multicultural Development*, vol. 3, pp. 17–40 (Giles, H. & Byrne, J. L., 1982), reprinted by permission of the publisher (Taylor & Francis Ltd, http://www.tandfonline.com); Figure 15.7 from *Responses to Touch as an Index of Sex Role Norms and Attitudes* (Heslin, R., 1978), American Psychological Association, reprinted with permission.

Guided tour

Each chapter opens with a short guide to what will be covered. ➤

◀ **Research classic** boxes summarise classic research studies, highlighting their continuing relevance and discussing new developments.

Our world boxes highlight examples of social psychology in action, putting social psychological principles into familiar, our world contexts. Clear and concise definitions of key terms can be found in the margins and the glossary at the end of the text.

Research highlight sections emphasise the wider relevance of social psychology and give detailed examples of contemporary research and practice.

Each chapter is richly illustrated with diagrams and photographs.

At the end of each chapter the **Summary** pulls the key points together to help you consolidate your knowledge and understanding.

Examples of **literature, film and TV** offer the chance to explore key social psychological concepts through popular culture and media.

Guided questions present typical essay-style questions.

Learn more sections at the end of chapters provide annotated further reading lists, guiding you towards the right resources to help you deepen your understanding and prepare for essays and assignments.

38   CHAPTER 1   INTRODUCING SOCIAL PSYCHOLOGY

Summary

- Social psychology is the scientific investigation of how the thoughts, feelings and behaviour of individuals are influenced by the actual, imagined or implied presence of others. Although social psychology can also be described in terms of what it studies, it is more useful to describe it as a way of looking at human behaviour.
- Social psychology is a science. It employs the scientific method to study social behaviour. Although this involves a variety of empirical methods to collect data to test hypotheses and construct theories, experimentation is usually the preferred method as it is the best way to learn what causes what. Nevertheless, methods are matched to research questions, and methodological pluralism is highly valued.
- Social psychological data are usually transformed into numbers, which are analysed by statistical procedures. Statistics allow conclusions to be drawn about whether a research observation is a true effect or some chance event.
- Social psychology is enlivened by debate over the ethics of research methods, the appropriate research methods for an understanding of social behaviour, the validity and power of social psychology theories, and the type of theories that are properly social psychological.
- Although having origins in nineteenth-century German folk psychology and French crowd psychology, modern social psychology really began in the United States in the 1920s with the adoption of the experimental method. In the 1940s, Kurt Lewin provided significant impetus to social psychology, and the discipline has grown exponentially ever since.
- Despite its European origins, social psychology was quickly dominated by the United States – a process accelerated by the rise of fascism in Europe during the 1930s. However, since the late 1960s, there has been a rapid and sustained renaissance of European social psychology, driven by distinctively European intellectual and sociohistorical priorities to develop a more *social* social psychology with a greater emphasis on collective phenomena and group levels of analysis. European social psychology is now well established as an equal but complementary partner to the United States in social psychological research.

Key terms

Archival research	Evolutionary psychology	Neo-behaviourism
Behaviour	Evolutionary social psychology	Operational definition
Behaviourism	Experimental method	Positivism
Case study	Experimental realism	Radical behaviourist
Cognitive theories	Experimenter effects	Reductionism
Confirmation bias	External validity	Science
Confounding	fMRI	Social neuroscience
Correlation	Hypotheses	Social psychology
Data	Independent variables	Statistical significance
Demand characteristics	Internal validity	Statistics
Dependent variables	Laboratory	Subject effects
Discourse	Level of explanation	*t* test
Discourse analysis	Metatheory	Theory
Double-blind	Mundane realism	*Völkerpsychologie*

GUIDED QUESTIONS   39

Literature, film and TV

The Beach
The 1997 Alex Garland novel (also the 2000 eponymous film starring Leonardo DiCaprio). Backpackers in Thailand drop out to join a group that has set up its own normatively regimented society on a remote island. They are expected to submerge their own identity in favour of the group's identity. This dramatic book engages with many social psychological themes having to do with self and identity, close relationships, norms and conformity, influence and leadership, and conflict and cooperation. The book could be characterised as *Apocalypse Now* (Francis Ford Coppola's legendary 1979 war movie) meets *Lord of the Flies* (William Golding's classic 1954 novel about a group of boys marooned on an island).

War and Peace
Leo Tolstoy's (1869) masterpiece on the impact of society and social history on people's lives. It does a wonderful job of showing how macro- and micro-levels of analysis influence one another, but cannot be resolved into one another. It is a wonderful literary work of social psychology – how people's day-to-day lives are located at the intersection of powerful interpersonal, group and intergroup processes. Other classic novels of Leo Tolstoy, Emile Zola, Charles Dickens and George Eliot

accomplish much the same social psychological analysis.

Les Misérables
Victor Hugo's (1862) magnum opus and classic literary masterpiece of the nineteenth century. It explores everyday life and relationships against the background of conventions, institutions and historical events in Paris over a 17-year period (1815–1832). Those of you who enjoy musicals will know that it has been adapted into an eponymous 2012 musical film directed by Tom Hooper and starring Hugh Jackman (as the central character, Jean Valjean), Russell Crowe, Anne Hathaway and Amanda Seyfried.

Gulliver's Travels
Jonathan Swift's 1726 satirical commentary on the nature of human beings. This book is relevant to virtually all the themes in our text. The section on Big-Endians and Little-Endians is particularly relevant to Chapter 11 on intergroup behaviour. Swift provides a hilarious and incredibly full and insightful description of a society that is split on the basis of whether people open their boiled eggs at the big or the little end – relevant to the minimal group studies in Chapter 11 but also to the general theme of how humans can read so much into subtle features of their environment.

Guided questions

1 What do social psychologists study? Can you give some examples of interdisciplinary research?
2 Sometimes experiments are used in social psychological research. Why?
3 What do you understand by levels of explanation in social psychology? What is meant by reductionism?
4 If you or your lecturer were to undertake research in social psychology, you would need to gain ethical approval. Why is this, and what criteria would need to be met?
5 If the shock level 'administered' in Milgram's obedience study had been 150 volts instead of the maximum 450 volts, would this have made the experiment more ethical?

514   CHAPTER 12   AGGRESSION

psychopathic adolescent who murders his father and sister and then commits a cold-blooded massacre at his school – using a bow and arrows. This is a harrowing and disturbing movie, and of course relevant to the seemingly endless litany of school and university campus massacres in the USA – for example the 2012 Sandy Hook elementary school massacre in the US of 20 six-year-olds and 6 adults,

and the 2007 Virginia Tech University massacre of 32 people. The film addresses the interplay of inherited behaviour, mental health and family relationships in the emergence of cold-blooded aggression expressed through school killings most often by adolescents and young adults.

Guided questions

1 What is the *frustration–aggression hypothesis*? Does it help explain the origins of aggression?
2 Can children really learn quite quickly how to be aggressive?
3 Does the incidence of aggression vary in relation to gender or culture?
4 Does viewing television violence make people more aggressive?
5 In what ways can the tendency to aggress be reduced?

Learn more

Anderson, C. A., & Huesmann, L. R. (2007). Human aggression: A social-cognitive view. In M. A. Hogg & J. Cooper (Eds.), *The SAGE handbook of social psychology: Concise student edition* (pp. 259–287). London: SAGE. Comprehensive and accessible overview of research on human aggression, by two of the world's leading aggression researchers.

Baron, R. A., & Richardson, D. R. (1994). *Human aggression* (2nd ed.). New York: Plenum. A heavily cited source for research on human aggression.

Berkowitz, L. (1993). *Aggression: Its causes, consequences and control.* Philadelphia, PA: Temple University Press. Another work by an authority in the field with a good coverage of the topic.

Buford, B. (1993). *Among the thugs.* New York: Vintage. An insider's perspective on the world of English football 'hooligans' in British and other European settings. The work is compelling – one reviewer described it as 'A *Clockwork Orange* comes to life'.

Bushman, B. J., & Huesmann, L. R. (2010). Aggression. In S. T. Fiske, D. T. Gilbert, & G. Lindzey (Eds.), *Handbook of social psychology* (5th ed., Vol. 2, pp. 833–863). New York: Wiley. Currently the most up-to-date, detailed and comprehensive coverage of theory and research on all aspects of and perspectives on human aggression.

Campbell, A. (1993). *Men, women, and aggression.* New York: HarperCollins. A discussion of sex, gender and aggression.

Glick, R. A., & Roose, S. P. (Eds.) (1993). *Rage, power, and aggression.* New Haven, CT: Yale University Press. A collection of chapters reviewing research, theory and clinical perspectives on the origins, nature and development of aggression.

Goldstein, A. P. (1994). *The ecology of aggression.* New York: Plenum. As the title suggests, the focus is on how aggression can be influenced by ecological factors, which can be both physical and social.

Krahé, B. (2013). *The social psychology of aggression* (2nd ed.). New York: Psychology Press. Up-to-date and authoritative text on the social psychology of aggression by one of the world's leading aggression researchers.

Chapter 1
Introducing social psychology

Chapter contents

What do *you* think?

1   Would it ever be ethical to conceal the true purpose and nature of a psychology experiment from someone volunteering to take part?

2   How complete an explanation of social behaviour do you think evolution or neuroscience provides?

3   Social psychology texts often convey the impression that social psychology is primarily an American discipline. Do you have a view on this?

What is social psychology?

Social psychology
Scientific investigation of
how people's thoughts,
feelings and behaviour are
influenced by the actual,
imagined or implied
presence of others.

Social psychology is 'the scientific investigation of how the thoughts, feelings and behaviours of individuals are influenced by the actual, imagined or implied presence of others' (G. W. Allport, 1954a, p. 5). What does this mean? What do social psychologists actually do, how do they do it and what do they study?

Social psychologists are interested in explaining *human* behaviour and generally do not study animals. Animal research sometimes identifies processes that generalise to people (e.g. social facilitation – **see Chapter 8**), and certain principles of social behaviour may be general enough to apply to humans and, for instance, other primates (e.g. Hinde, 1982). But, as a rule, social psychologists believe that the study of animals does not take us very far in explaining human social behaviour, unless we are interested in evolutionary origins (e.g. Neuberg, Kenrick, & Schaller, 2010; Schaller, Simpson, & Kenrick, 2006).

Behaviour
What people actually do
that can be objectively
measured.

Social psychologists study **behaviour** because behaviour can be observed and measured. Behaviour refers not only to obvious motor activities (such as running, kissing and driving) but also to more subtle actions such as a raised eyebrow, a quizzical smile or how we dress, and, critically important in human behaviour, what we say and what we write. In this sense, behaviour is publicly verifiable. However, behaviour serves a communicative function. What a behaviour means depends on the motives, goals, perspective and cultural background of the actor and the observer (**see Chapter 15**).

Social psychologists are interested not only in behaviour, but also in feelings, thoughts, beliefs, attitudes, intentions and goals. These are not directly observable but can, with varying degrees of confidence, be inferred from behaviour and may influence or even determine behaviour. The relationship between these unobservable processes and overt behaviour is in itself a focus of research; for example, in research on attitude–behaviour correspondence (**see Chapter 5**) and research on prejudice and discrimination (**see Chapter 10**). Unobservable processes are also the psychological dimension of behaviour, as they occur within the human brain. However, social psychologists almost always go one step beyond relating social behaviour to underlying psychological processes – they almost always map psychological aspects of behaviour onto fundamental cognitive processes and structures in the human mind and sometimes to neuro-chemical processes in the brain (**see Chapter 2**).

What makes social psychology *social* is that it deals with how people are affected by other people who are physically present (e.g. an audience – **see Chapter 8**) or who are imagined to be present (e.g. anticipating performing in front of an audience), or even whose presence is implied. This last influence is more complex and addresses the fundamentally social nature of our experiences as humans. For instance, we tend to think with words; words derive from language and communication; and language and communication would not exist without social interaction (**see Chapter 15**). Thought, which is an internalised and private activity that can occur when we are alone, is thus clearly based on implied presence. As another example of implied presence, consider that most of us do not litter, even if no one is watching and even if there is no possibility of ever being caught. This happens because people, as members of a society, have constructed and internalised a social convention or norm that proscribes littering. Such a norm implies the presence of other people and influences behaviour even in their absence (**see Chapters 7 and 8**).

Science
Method for studying nature
that involves the collecting
of data to test hypotheses.

Theory
Set of interrelated concepts
and principles that explain a
phenomenon.

Data
Publicly verifiable
observations.

Social psychology is a **science** because it uses the scientific method to construct and test theories. Just as physics has concepts such as electrons, quarks and spin to explain physical phenomena, social psychology has concepts such as dissonance, attitude, categorization and identity to explain social psychological phenomena. The scientific method dictates that no **theory** is 'true' simply because it is logical and seems to make sense. On the contrary, the validity of a theory is based on its correspondence with fact. Social psychologists construct theories from **data** and/or previous theories and then conduct empirical research, in which data are collected to test the theory (see 'Scientific method' and Figure 1.2).

Social psychology and its close neighbours

Social psychology sits at the crossroads of a number of related disciplines and subdisciplines (see Figure 1.1). It is a subdiscipline of general psychology and is therefore concerned with explaining human behaviour in terms of processes that occur within the human mind. It differs from individual psychology in that it explains *social* behaviour, as defined in the previous section. For example, a general psychologist might be interested in perceptual processes that are responsible for people overestimating the size of coins. However, a social psychologist might focus on the fact that coins have value (a case of implied presence, because the value of something generally depends on what others think), and that perceived value might influence the judgement of size. A great deal of social psychology is concerned with face-to-face interaction between individuals or among members of groups, whereas general psychology focuses on people's reactions to stimuli that do not have to be social (e.g. shapes, colours, sounds).

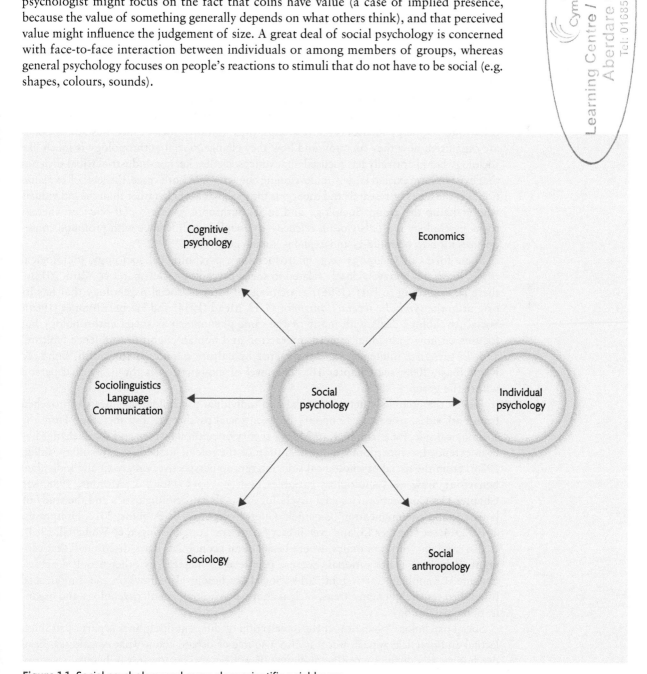

Figure 1.1 Social psychology and some close scientific neighbours
Social psychology draws on a number of subdisciplines in general psychology and has connections with other disciplines, mostly in the social sciences.

The boundary between individual and social psychology is approached from both sides. For instance, having developed a comprehensive and hugely influential theory of the individual human mind, Sigmund Freud set out, in his 1921 essay 'Group psychology and the analysis of the ego', to develop a social psychology. Freudian, or psychodynamic, notions have left an enduring mark on social psychology (Billig, 1976), particularly in the explanation of prejudice (**see Chapter 10**). Since the late 1970s, social psychology has been strongly influenced by cognitive psychology. It has employed its methods (e.g. reaction time) and its concepts (e.g. memory) to explain a wide range of social behaviours. Indeed, this approach to social psychology, called social cognition (**see Chapter 2**), is the dominant approach in contemporary social psychology (Fiske & Taylor, 2013; Moskowitz, 2005; Ross, Lepper, & Ward, 2010), and it surfaces in almost all areas of the discipline (Devine, Hamilton, & Ostrom, 1994). In recent years, neuroscience (the study of brain biochemistry; Gazzaniga, Ivry, & Mangun, 2013) has also influenced social psychology (Lieberman, 2010; Todorov, Fiske, & Prentice, 2011).

Social psychology also has links with sociology and social anthropology, mostly in studying groups, social and cultural norms, social representations, and language and intergroup behaviour. Sociology focuses on how groups, organisations, social categories and societies are organised, how they function and how they change. Social anthropology is much like sociology but historically has focused on 'exotic' societies (i.e. non-industrial tribal societies that exist or have existed largely in developing countries). In both cases, the level of explanation (i.e. the focus of research and theory) is the group as a whole rather than the individuals who make up the group. Sociology and social anthropology are *social sciences* whereas social psychology is a *behavioural science* – a disciplinary difference with profound consequences for how one studies and explains human behaviour.

Some forms of sociology (e.g. microsociology, psychological sociology, sociological psychology) are, however, closely related to social psychology (Delamater & Ward, 2013) – there is, according to Farr (1996), a sociological form of social psychology that has its origins in the *symbolic interactionism* of G. H. Mead (1934) and Herbert Blumer (1969). Social psychology deals with many of the same phenomena as social anthropology but focuses on how individual human interaction and human cognition influence 'culture' and, in turn, are influenced or constructed by culture (Heine, 2016; Smith, Bond, & Kağitçibaşi, 2006; **see Chapter 16**). The level of explanation is the individual person within the group.

Just as the boundary between social and individual psychology has been approached from both sides, so has the boundary between social psychology and sociology. From the sociological side, for example, Karl Marx's theory of cultural history and social change has been extended to incorporate a consideration of the role of individual psychology (Billig, 1976). From the social psychological side, intergroup perspectives on group and individual behaviour draw on sociological variables and concepts (Hogg & Abrams, 1988; **see Chapter 11**). Contemporary social psychology also abuts sociolinguistics and the study of language and communication (Gasiorek, Giles, Holtgraves, & Robbins, 2012; Holtgraves, 2010, 2014; **see Chapter 15**) and even literary criticism (Potter, Stringer, & Wetherell, 1984). It also overlaps with economics, where behavioural economists have 'discovered' that economic behaviour is not rational, because people are influenced by other people – actual, imagined or implied (Cartwright, 2014). Social psychology also draws on and is influenced by applied research in many areas, such as sports psychology, health psychology and organisational psychology.

Social psychology's location at the intersection of different disciplines is part of its intellectual and practical appeal. But it is also a source of debate about what constitutes social psychology as a distinct scientific discipline. If we lean too far towards individual cognitive processes, then perhaps we are pursuing individual psychology or cognitive psychology. If we lean too far towards the role of language, then perhaps we are being scholars of language and communication. If we overemphasise the role of social structure in intergroup relations, then perhaps we are being sociologists. The issue of exactly what constitutes social psychology fuels a vigorous metatheoretical debate (i.e. a debate about what sorts of theory are appropriate for social psychology), which forms the background to the business of social psychology (see the section 'Theories in social psychology').

Topics of social psychology

One way to define social psychology is in terms of what social psychologists study. Because this text is a comprehensive coverage of the main phenomena that social psychologists study, and have studied, social psychology can be defined by the contents of this and other publications that present themselves as social psychology texts. A brief look at the contents of this text will give a flavour of the scope of social psychology. Social psychologists study an enormous range of topics, including conformity, persuasion, power, influence, obedience, prejudice, prejudice reduction, discrimination, stereotyping, bargaining, sexism and racism, small groups, social categories, intergroup relations, crowd behaviour, social conflict and harmony, social change, overcrowding, stress, the physical environment, decision making, the jury, leadership, communication, language, speech, attitudes, impression formation, impression management, self-presentation, identity, the self, culture, emotion, attraction, friendship, the family, love, romance, sex, violence, aggression, altruism and prosocial behaviour (acts that are valued positively by society).

One problem with defining social psychology solely in terms of what it studies is that social psychology is not properly differentiated from other disciplines. For example, 'intergroup relations' is a focus not only of social psychologists but also of political scientists and sociologists. The family is studied not only by social psychologists but also by clinical psychologists. What makes social psychology distinct is a combination of *what* it studies, *how* it studies it and what *level of explanation* is sought.

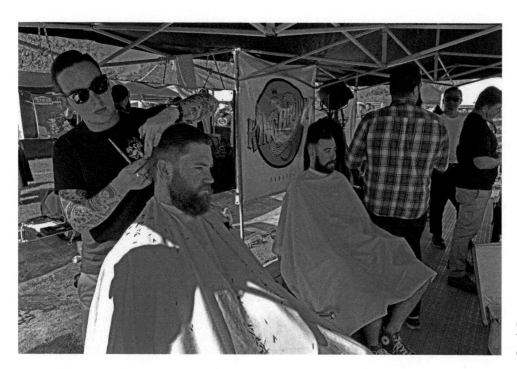

Conformity
Tats and beards are now *de rigeur*.

Research methods

Scientific method

Social psychology employs the scientific method to study social behaviour (Figure 1.2). It is the *method* – not the people who use it, the things they study, the facts they discover or the explanations they propose – that distinguishes science from other approaches to knowledge. In this respect, the main difference between social psychology and, say, physics, chemistry or biology is that the former studies human social behaviour, while the others study non-organic phenomena and chemical and biological processes.

Hypotheses
Empirically testable predictions about what co-occurs with what, or what causes what.

Science involves the formulation of **hypotheses** (predictions) on the basis of prior knowledge, speculation and casual or systematic observation. Hypotheses are formally stated predictions about what may cause something to occur; they are stated in such a way that they can be tested empirically to see if they are true. For example, we might hypothesise that ballet dancers perform better in front of an audience than when dancing alone. This hypothesis can be tested empirically by measuring and comparing their performance alone and in front of an audience.

Strictly speaking, empirical tests can falsify hypotheses (causing the investigator to reject the hypothesis, revise it or test it in some other way) but not prove them (Popper, 1969). If a hypothesis is supported, confidence in its veracity increases and one may generate more finely tuned hypotheses. For example, if we find that ballet dancers do indeed perform better in front of an audience, we might then hypothesise that this occurs only when the dancers are already well-rehearsed; in science-speak we have hypothesised that the effect of the presence of an audience on performance is conditional on (moderated by) amount of prior rehearsal. An important feature of the scientific method is replication: it guards against the possibility that a finding is tied to the circumstances in which a test was conducted. It also guards against fraud.

The alternative to science is dogma or rationalism. Something is true because one simply believes it to be true, or because an authority (e.g. the ancient philosophers, religious

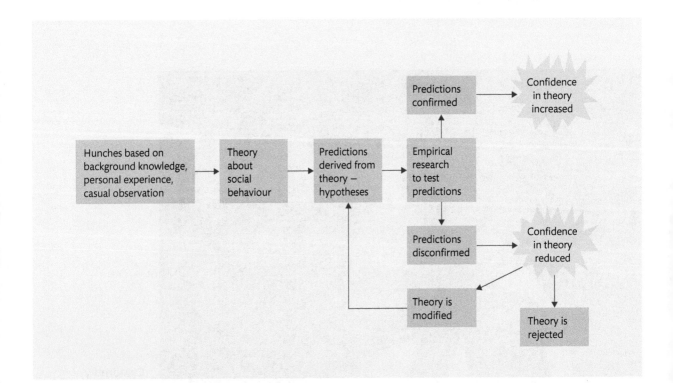

Figure 1.2 A model of the scientific method used by social psychologists

scriptures, charismatic leaders) says it is so, or because one simply believes it to be true. Valid knowledge is acquired by pure reason and grounded in faith and conviction: for example, by learning well, and uncritically accepting and trusting, the pronouncements of authorities. Even though the scientific revolution, championed by such people as Copernicus, Galileo and Newton, occurred in the sixteenth and seventeenth centuries, dogma and rationalism still exist as influential alternative paths to knowledge.

As a science, social psychology has at its disposal an array of different methods for conducting empirical tests of hypotheses (Crano & Brewer, 2015). There are two broad types of method, *experimental* and *non-experimental*: each has advantages and limitations. The choice of an appropriate method is determined by the nature of the hypothesis under investigation, the resources available for doing the research (e.g. time, money, research participants) and the ethics of the method. Confidence in the validity of a hypothesis is enhanced if the hypothesis has been confirmed a number of times by different research teams using different methods. Methodological pluralism helps to minimise the possibility that the finding is an artefact of a particular method, and replication by different research teams helps to avoid **confirmation bias**, which occurs when researchers become so personally involved in their own theories that they lose objectivity in interpreting data (Greenwald & Pratkanis, 1988; Johnson & Eagly, 1989).

Confirmation bias
The tendency to seek, interpret and create information that verifies existing explanations for the cause of an event.

Experiments

An experiment is a hypothesis test in which something is done to see its effect on something else. For example, if I hypothesise that my car greedily guzzles too much petrol because the tyres are under-inflated, then I can conduct an experiment. I can note petrol consumption over an average week; then I can increase the tyre pressure and again note petrol consumption over an average week. If consumption is reduced, then my hypothesis is supported. Casual experimentation is one of the commonest and most important ways in which people learn about their world. It is an extremely powerful method because it allows us to identify the causes of events and thus gain control over our destiny.

Not surprisingly, systematic experimentation is the most important research method in science. Experimentation involves *intervention* in the form of *manipulation* of one or more **independent variables**, and then measurement of the effect of the treatment (manipulation)

Independent variables
Features of a situation that change of their own accord or can be manipulated by an experimenter to have effects on a dependent variable.

Brain imaging
Social neuroscientists are using new techniques, such as fMRI, to establish correlates, consequences and causes of social behaviour.

Dependent variables
Variables that change as a consequence of changes in the independent variable.

on one or more focal **dependent variables**. In the example above, the independent variable is tyre inflation, which was manipulated to create two experimental conditions (lower versus higher pressure), and the dependent variable is petrol consumption, which was measured on refilling the tank at the end of the week. More generally, independent variables are dimensions that the researcher hypothesises will have an effect and that can be varied (e.g. tyre pressure in the present example, and the presence or absence of an audience in the ballet-dancing example). Dependent variables are dimensions that the researcher hypothesises will vary (petrol consumption or quality of the ballet dancer's performance) as a consequence of varying the independent variable. Variation in the dependent variable is *dependent* on variation in the independent variable.

Social psychology is largely experimental, in that most social psychologists would prefer to test hypotheses experimentally if at all possible, and much of what we know about social behaviour is based on experiments. Indeed, one of the most enduring and prestigious scholarly societies for the scientific study of social psychology is the *Society of Experimental Social Psychology*.

A typical social psychology experiment might be designed to test the hypothesis that violent television programmes increase aggression in young children. One way to do this would be to assign twenty children randomly to two conditions in which they individually watch either a violent or a non-violent programme, and then observe the amount of aggression expressed immediately afterwards by the children while they are at play. Random assignment of participants (in this case, children) reduces the chance of systematic differences between the participants in the two conditions. If there were any systematic differences, say, in age, sex or parental background, then any significant effects on aggression might be due to age, sex or background rather than to the violence of the television programme. That is, age, sex or parental background would be *confounded* with the independent variable. Likewise, the television programme viewed in each condition should be identical in all respects except for the degree of violence. For instance, if the violent programme also contained more action, then we would not know whether subsequent differences in aggression were due to the violence, the action or both. The circumstances surrounding the viewing of the two programmes should also be identical. If the violent programmes were viewed in a bright red room and the non-violent programmes in a blue room, then any effects might be due to room colour, violence or both. It is critically important in experiments to avoid **confounding**: the conditions must be identical in all respects except for those represented by the manipulated independent variable.

Confounding
Where two or more independent variables covary in such a way that it is impossible to know which has caused the effect.

We must also be careful about how we measure effects: that is, the dependent measures that assess the dependent variable. In our example, it would probably be inappropriate, because of the children's age, to administer a questionnaire measuring aggression. A better

Box 1.1 Our world
Radicalization and the slaughter of innocents

Radicalization has become a burning concern around the globe. It is identified as a significant way in which largely isolated individuals become indoctrinated and inspired by terrorist ideologies and then embark on some appalling slaughter of innocents. Examples are countless: for example, the July 2011 terrorist act in Norway where Anders Behring Breivik killed 77 people mainly at a summer camp, and the July 2016 attack where Mohamed Lahouaiej-Bouhlel drove a truck at people celebrating Bastille Day on the Promenade des Anglais in Nice and killed 86.

What is the social psychology of radicalization and how would you set about researching it? What causes would you investigate – and how significant are psychological causes relative to socio-economic causes? Could you do laboratory or field experiments? Perhaps the only options are non-experimental – a case study or archival research?

Consider this issue in the light of our discussion in this chapter of the nature of social psychology and its research methods.

technique would be unobtrusive observation of behaviour; but then, what would we code as 'aggression'? The criterion would have to be sensitive to changes: in other words, loud talk or violent assault with a weapon might be insensitive, as all children talk loudly when playing (there is a *ceiling effect*), and virtually no children violently assault one another with a weapon while playing (there is a *floor effect*). In addition, it would be a mistake for whoever records or codes the behaviour to know which experimental condition the child was in: such knowledge might compromise objectivity. The coder(s) should know as little as possible about the experimental conditions and the research hypotheses.

The example used here is of a simple experiment that has only two levels of only one independent variable – called a one-factor design. Most social psychology experiments are more complicated than this. For instance, we might formulate a more textured hypothesis that aggression in young children is increased by television programmes that contain *realistic* violence. To test this hypothesis, a two-factor design would be adopted. The two factors (independent variables) would be (1) the violence of the programme (low versus high) and (2) the realism of the programme (realistic versus fantasy). The participants would be randomly assigned across four experimental conditions in which they watched (1) a non-violent fantasy programme, (2) a non-violent realistic programme, (3) a violent fantasy programme or (4) a violent realistic programme. Of course, independent variables are not restricted to two levels. For instance, we might predict that aggression is increased by moderately violent programmes, whereas extremely violent programmes are so distasteful that aggression is actually suppressed. Our independent variable of programme violence could now have three levels (low, moderate, extreme).

The laboratory experiment

The classic social psychology experiment is conducted in a **laboratory** in order to control as many potentially confounding variables as possible. The aim is to isolate and manipulate a single aspect of a variable, an aspect that may not normally occur in isolation outside the laboratory. Laboratory experiments are *intended* to create artificial conditions. Although a social psychology laboratory may contain computers, wires and flashing lights, or even medical equipment and sophisticated brain imaging technology, often it is simply a room containing tables and chairs. For example, our ballet hypothesis could be tested in the laboratory by formalising it to one in which we predict that someone performing any well-learnt task performs that task more quickly in front of an audience. We could unobtrusively time individuals, for example, taking off their clothes and then putting them back on again (a well-learnt task), either alone in a room or while being scrutinised by two other people (an audience). We could compare these speeds with those of someone dressing up in unusual and difficult clothing (a poorly learnt task). This method was actually used by Markus (1978) when she investigated the effect of an audience on task performance (**see Chapter 8 for details**).

Social psychologists have become increasingly interested in investigating the bio-chemical and brain activity correlates, consequences and causes of social behaviour. This has generated an array of experimental methods that make social psychology laboratories look more like biological or physical science laboratories. For example, a psychologist studying how interaction with other people may make us feel anxious and stressed might measure changes in our level of the hormone cortisol in our saliva (e.g. Blascovich & Seery, 2007; Townsend, Major, Gangi, & Mendes, 2011). Research in social neuroscience using functional Magnetic Resonance Imaging (**fMRI**) has become popular. This involves participants being placed in a huge and very expensive magnetic cylinder to measure their electro-chemical brain activity (Lieberman, 2010; Todorov, Fiske, & Prentice, 2011).

Laboratory experiments allow us to establish cause–effect relationships between variables. However, laboratory experiments have a number of drawbacks. Because experimental conditions are artificial and highly controlled, particularly social neuroscience experiments, laboratory findings cannot be generalised directly to the less 'pure' conditions that exist in the 'real' world outside the laboratory. However, laboratory findings address *theories* about human social behaviour, and, on the basis of laboratory experimentation, we can generalise

Laboratory
A place, usually a room, in which data are collected, usually by experimental methods.

fMRI (functional Magnetic Resonance Imaging)
A method used in social neuroscience to measure where electrochemical activity in the brain is occurring.

External validity or Mundane realism
Similarity between circumstances surrounding an experiment and circumstances encountered in everyday life.

Internal validity or Experimental realism
Psychological impact of the manipulations in an experiment.

Subject effects
Effects that are not spontaneous, owing to demand characteristics and/or participants wishing to please the experimenter.

Demand characteristics
Features of an experiment that seem to 'demand' a certain response.

Experimenter effects
Effects produced or influenced by clues to the hypotheses under examination, inadvertently communicated by the experimenter.

Double-blind
Procedure to reduce experimenter effects, in which the experimenter is unaware of the experimental conditions.

these theories to apply to conditions other than those in the laboratory. Laboratory experiments are intentionally low on **external validity** or **mundane realism** (i.e. how similar the conditions are to those usually encountered by participants in the real world) but should always be high on **internal validity** or **experimental realism** (i.e. the manipulations must be full of psychological impact and meaning for the participants) (Aronson, Ellsworth, Carlsmith, & Gonzales, 1990).

Laboratory experiments are susceptible to a range of biases. There are **subject effects** that can cause participants' behaviour to be an artefact of the experiment rather than a spontaneous and natural response to a manipulation. Artefacts can be minimised by carefully avoiding **demand characteristics** (Orne, 1962), *evaluation apprehension* and *social desirability* (Rosenberg, 1969). Demand characteristics are features of the experiment that seem to 'demand' a particular response: they give information about the hypothesis and inform helpful and compliant participants about how to react to confirm the hypothesis. Participants are thus no longer naive or *blind* regarding the experimental hypothesis. Participants in experiments are real people, and experiments are real social situations. Not surprisingly, participants may want to project the best possible image of themselves to the experimenter and other participants present. This can influence spontaneous reactions to manipulations in unpredictable ways. There are also **experimenter effects**. The experimenter is often aware of the hypothesis and may inadvertently communicate cues that cause participants to behave in a way that confirms the hypothesis. This can be minimised by a **double-blind** procedure, in which the experimenter is unaware of which experimental condition they are running.

Since the 1960s, laboratory experiments have tended to rely on psychology undergraduates as participants (Sears, 1986). The reason is a pragmatic one – psychology undergraduates are readily available in large numbers to come to a physical laboratory on campus. In most major universities, there is a research participation scheme, or 'subject pool', where psychology students act as experimental participants in exchange for course credits or as a course requirement. Critics have often complained that this over-reliance on a particular type of participant may produce a somewhat distorted view of social behaviour – one that is not easily generalised to other sectors of the population. In their defence, experimental social psychologists point out that theories, not experimental findings, are generalised, and that replication and methodological pluralism ensures that social psychology is about people, not just about psychology students.

The field experiment

Social psychology experiments can be conducted in more naturalistic settings outside the laboratory. For example, we could test the hypothesis that prolonged eye contact is uncomfortable and causes 'flight' by having an experimenter stand at traffic lights and either gaze intensely at the driver of a car stopped at the lights or gaze nonchalantly in the opposite direction. The dependent measure would be how fast the car sped away once the lights changed (Ellsworth, Carlsmith, & Henson, 1972; **see Chapter 15**). Field experiments have high external validity and, as participants are usually completely unaware that an experiment is taking place, are not reactive (i.e. no demand characteristics are present). However, there is less control over extraneous variables, random assignment is sometimes difficult, and it can be difficult to obtain accurate measurements or measurements of subjective feelings (generally, overt behaviour is all that can be measured).

Non-experimental methods

Systematic experimentation tends to be the preferred method of science, and indeed it is often equated with science. However, there are all sorts of circumstances where it is simply impossible to conduct an experiment to test a hypothesis. For instance, theories about planetary systems and galaxies can pose a real problem: we cannot move planets around to see what happens! Likewise, social psychological theories about the relationship between biological sex and decision-making are not amenable to experimentation, because we cannot manipulate biological sex experimentally and see what effects emerge. Social psychology also confronts ethical issues that can proscribe experimentation. For instance, hypotheses about the effects on self-esteem of being a victim of violent crime are not easily tested experimentally – we would not be able to assign participants randomly to two conditions and then subject one group to a violent crime and see what happened.

Where experimentation is not possible or appropriate, social psychologists have a range of non-experimental methods from which to choose. Because these methods do not involve the manipulation of independent variables against a background of random assignment to condition, it is almost impossible to draw reliable causal conclusions. For instance, we could compare the self-esteem of people who have been victims of violent crime with those who have not. Any differences could be attributed to violent crime but could also be due to other uncontrolled differences between the two groups. We can only conclude that there is a **correlation** between self-esteem and being the victim of violent crime. There is no evidence that one causes the other (i.e. being a victim may lower self-esteem or having lower self-esteem may increase the likelihood of becoming a victim). Both could be *correlated* or co-occurring effects of some third variable, such as chronic unemployment, which independently lowers self-esteem *and* increases the probability that one might become a victim. In general, non-experimental methods involve the examination of correlation between naturally occurring variables and as such do not permit us to draw causal conclusions.

Correlation
Where changes in one variable reliably map on to changes in another variable, but it cannot be determined which of the two variables *caused* the change.

Archival research

Archival research is a non-experimental method that is useful for investigating large-scale, widely occurring phenomena that may be remote in time. The researcher assembles data collected by others, often for reasons unconnected with those of the researcher. For instance, Janis (1972) used an archival method to show that overly cohesive government decision-making groups may make poor decisions with disastrous consequences because they adopt poor decision-making procedures (called 'groupthink'; **see Chapter 9**). Janis constructed his theory on the basis of an examination of biographical, autobiographical and media accounts of the decision-making procedures associated with, for example, the 1961 Bay of Pigs fiasco, in which the United States futilely tried to invade Cuba. Other examples of archival research include Fogelson's (1970) archival analysis of the 1960s urban riots in the United States and Simonton's (1980) archival and secondary data analyses of battles (**see Chapter 8**).

Archival research
Non-experimental method involving the assembly of data, or reports of data, collected by others.

Archival methods are often used to make comparisons between different cultures or nations regarding things such as suicide, mental health or child-rearing strategies. Archival research is not reactive, but it can be unreliable because the researcher usually has no control over the primary data collection, which might be biased or unreliable in other ways (e.g. missing vital data). The researcher has to make do with whatever is there.

Case studies

The **case study** allows an in-depth analysis of a single case (either a person or a group) or a single event. Case studies often employ an array of data collection and analysis techniques involving structured, open-ended interviews and questionnaires and the observation of behaviour. Case studies are well suited to the examination of unusual or rare phenomena that could not be created in the laboratory: for instance, bizarre cults, mass murderers or disasters. Case studies are useful as a source of hypotheses, but findings may suffer from researcher or subject bias (the researcher is not blind to the hypothesis, there are demand characteristics and participants suffer evaluation apprehension), and findings may not easily be generalised to other cases or events.

Case study
In-depth analysis of a single case (or individual).

Qualitative research and discourse analysis

Closely related to case studies is a range of non-experimental methodologies that analyse largely naturally occurring behaviour in great detail. Among these are methods that meticulously unpack **discourse**, what people say to whom and in what context, in order to identify the underlying narrative that may reveal what people are thinking, what their motivations are and what the discourse is intended to do. **Discourse analysis** (Augoustinos & Tileaga, 2012; Edwards, 1997; Potter & Wetherell, 1987; Wetherell, Taylor, & Yates, 2001) draws on literary criticism and the notion that language is a performance (e.g. Hall, 2000) and is often grounded in a generally critical orientation towards mainstream social psychology (cf. Billig, 2008). Discourse analysis is both a language-based and communication-based methodology and approach to social psychology (**see Chapter 15**) that has proven particularly useful in a number of areas, including the study of prejudice (e.g. Van Dijk, 1987; Verkuyten, 2010).

Discourse
Entire communicative event or episode located in a situational and socio-historical context.

Discourse analysis
A set of methods used to analyse text – in particular, naturally occurring language – in order to understand its meaning and significance.

Survey research

Another non-experimental method is data collection by *survey*. Surveys can involve structured interviews, in which the researcher asks participants a number of carefully chosen questions and notes the responses, or a questionnaire, in which participants write their own responses to written questions. In either case the questions can be open-ended (i.e. respondents can give as much or as little detail in their answers as they wish) or closed-ended (where there is a limited number of predetermined responses, such as circling a number on a nine-point scale). For instance, to investigate immigrant workers' experiences of prejudice, one could ask respondents a set of predetermined questions and summarise the gist of their responses or assign a numerical value to their responses. Alternatively, respondents could record their own responses by writing a paragraph or by circling numbers on scales in a questionnaire.

Surveys can be used to obtain a large amount of data from a large sample of participants; hence generalisation is often not a problem. However, like case studies and qualitative methods, this method is subject to experimenter bias, subject bias and evaluation apprehension. Anonymous and confidential questionnaires may minimise experimenter bias, evaluation apprehension and some subject biases, but demand characteristics may remain. In addition, poorly constructed questionnaires may obtain biased data due to 'response set' – that is, the tendency for some respondents to agree unthinkingly with statements or to choose mid-range or extreme responses.

Field studies

The final non-experimental method is the field study. We have already described the field experiment: the field study is essentially the same but without any interventions or manipulations. Field studies involve the observation, recording and coding of behaviour as it occurs. Most often, the observer is non-intrusive by not participating in the behaviour, and 'invisible' by not influencing the ongoing behaviour. For instance, one could research the behaviour of students in the student cafeteria by concealing oneself in a corner and observing what goes on. Sometimes 'invisibility' is impossible, so the opposite strategy can be used – the researcher becomes a full participant in the behaviour. For instance, it would be rather difficult to be an invisible observer of gang behaviour. Instead, you could study the behaviour of a street gang by becoming a full member of the gang and surreptitiously taking notes (e.g. Whyte, 1943; **see Chapter 8**). Field studies are excellent for investigating spontaneously occurring behaviour in its natural context but are particularly prone to experimenter bias, lack of objectivity, poor generalisability and distortions due to the impact of the researcher on the behaviour under investigation. Also, if you join a gang, there is an element of personal danger!

Data and analysis

Social psychologists love data and are eager to collect it in any way they can. Recently, the Internet has provided a new opportunity for data collection that is becoming increasingly popular because it is an inexpensive, fast and efficient way to collect data from a large and

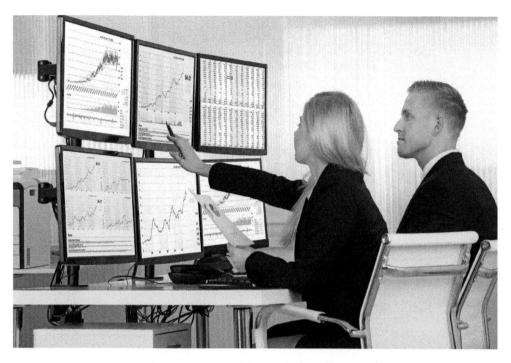

Statistics
Social psychological data and often quantitative, requiring statistical analysis to find patterns that give meaning to numbers.

diverse population. One particularly popular web-based resource is Amazon's Mechanical Turk (MTurk), which, if used carefully, allows a range of methods that can generate high-quality data (Buhrmeister, Kwang, & Gosling, 2011; Mason & Suri, 2012; Paolacci & Chandler, 2014; Paolacci, Chandler, & Ipeirotis, 2010).

Research provides data, which are analysed to draw conclusions about whether hypotheses are supported. The type of analysis undertaken depends on at least:

- *The type of data obtained* – for example, binary responses such as 'yes' versus 'no', continuous variables such as temperature or response latency, defined positions on nine-point scales, rank ordering of choices and open-ended written responses (text).

- *The method used to obtain data* – for example, controlled experiment, open-ended interview, participant observation, archival search.

- *The purposes of the research* – for example, to describe in depth a specific case, to establish differences between two groups of participants exposed to different treatments, to investigate the correlation between two or more naturally occurring variables.

Overwhelmingly, social psychological knowledge is based on statistical analysis of quantitative data. Data are obtained as, or are transformed into, numbers (i.e. quantities), and these numbers are then compared in various formalised ways (i.e. by **statistics**). For example, to decide whether women are more friendly interviewees than are men, we could compare transcripts of interviews of both men and women. We could then code the transcripts to count how often participants made positive remarks to the interviewer, and compare the mean count for, say, twenty women with the mean for twenty men. In this case, we would be interested in knowing whether the difference between men and women was 'on the whole' greater than the difference among men and among women. To do this, we could use a simple statistic called the *t* **test**, which computes a number called the *t* statistic that is based on both the difference between the women's and men's mean friendliness scores and the degree of variability of scores within each sex. The larger the value of *t*, the larger the between-sex difference relative to within-sex differences.

The decision about whether the difference between groups is psychologically significant depends on its **statistical significance**. Social psychologists adhere to an arbitrary convention: if the obtained value of *t* has less than a 1-in-20 (i.e. 0.05) probability of occurring by

Statistics
Formalised numerical procedures performed on data to investigate the magnitude and/or significance of effects.

t test
Procedure to test the statistical significance of an effect in which the mean for one condition is greater than the mean for another.

Statistical significance
An effect is statistically significant if statistics reveal that it, or a larger effect, is unlikely to occur by chance more often than 1 in 20 times.

CASE 1. *A significant difference*: The *t* statistic is relatively large because the difference between means is large and the variation within sex groups is small.

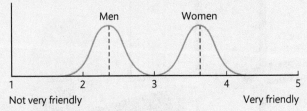

CASE 2. *Not a significant difference*: The *t* statistic is relatively small because, although the difference between means is still large, the variation within sex groups is much larger.

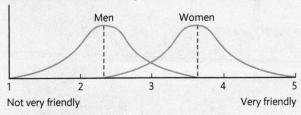

CASE 3. *A significant difference*: The *t* statistic is large because, although the difference between means is smaller, the variation within sex groups is small.

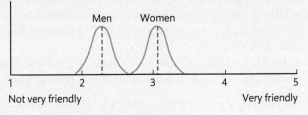

Figure 1.3 Distribution of friendliness scores for twenty male and twenty female interviewees: Using the *t* statistic

chance (that is, if we randomly selected 100 groups of ten males and ten females, only five times or fewer would we obtain a value of *t* as great as or greater than that obtained in the study), then the obtained difference is statistically significant and there really is a difference in friendliness between male and female interviewees (see Figure 1.3).

The *t* test is very simple. However, the principle underlying the *t* test is the same as that underlying more sophisticated and complex statistical techniques used by social psychologists to test whether two or more groups differ significantly. The other major method of data analysis used by social psychologists is correlation, which assesses whether the co-occurrence of two or more variables is significant. Again, although the example below is simple, the underlying principle is the same for an array of correlational techniques.

To investigate the idea that rigid thinkers tend to hold more politically conservative attitudes (Rokeach, 1960; **see Chapter 10**) we could have thirty participants answer a questionnaire measuring cognitive rigidity (dogmatism: a rigid and inflexible set of attitudes) and political conservatism (e.g. endorsement and espousal of right-wing political and social policies). If we rank the thirty participants in order of increasing dogmatism and find that conservatism also increases, with the least dogmatic person being the least conservative and the most dogmatic the most conservative, then we can say that the two variables are positively correlated (see Figure 1.4, in which dots represent individual persons, positioned with respect to their scores on both dogmatism and conservatism scales). If we find that conservatism systematically decreases with increasing dogmatism, then we say that the two variables

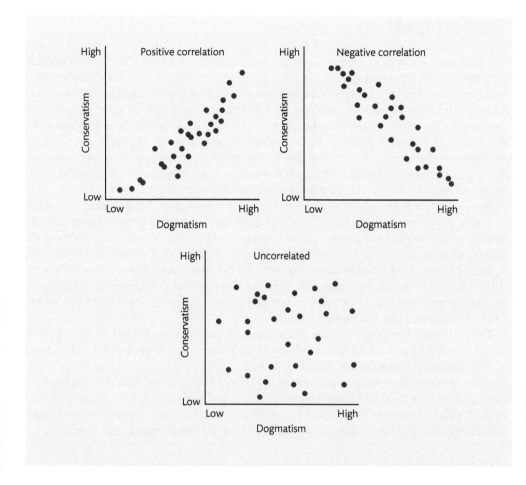

Figure 1.4 Correlation between dogmatism and conservatism for thirty respondents: Using Pearson's correlation coefficient

are negatively correlated. If there seems to be no systematic relationship between the two variables, then they are uncorrelated – there is zero correlation. A statistic can be calculated to represent correlation numerically: for instance, the statistical measure known as Pearson's r varies from −1 for a perfect negative to +1 for a perfect positive correlation. Depending on, among other things, the number of persons, we can also know whether the correlation is statistically significant at the conventional 5 per cent level.

Although statistical analysis of quantitative data is the bread and butter of social psychology, some social psychologists find that this method is unsuited to their purposes and prefer a more *qualitative* analysis. For example, analysis of people's explanations for unemployment or prejudice may sometimes benefit from a more discursive, non-quantitative analysis in which the researcher tries to unravel what is said in order to go beyond surface explanations and get to the heart of the underlying beliefs and reasons. One form of qualitative analysis is *discourse analysis* (e.g. Augoustinos & Tileaga, 2012; Potter & Wetherell, 1987; Tuffin, 2005; Wetherell, Taylor, & Yates, 2001). Discourse analysis treats all 'data' as 'text' – that is, as a communicative event that is replete with multiple layers of meaning but that can be interpreted only by considering the text in its wider social context. For example, discourse analysts believe that we should not take people's responses to attitude statements in questionnaires at face value and subject them to statistical analysis. They believe, instead, that we should interpret what is being communicated. This is made possible only by considering the response as a complex conjunction of social-communicative factors embedded in both the immediate and wider socio-historical context. However, discourse analysis is more than a research method: it is also a systematic critique of 'conventional' social psychological methods and theories (see the subsection 'Positivism and post-positivism' later in this chapter).

Research ethics

As researchers, social psychologists confront important ethical issues. Clearly, it is unethical to fake data or to report results in a biased or partial manner that significantly distorts what was done, what was found and how the hypotheses and theory under examination now fare. As in life, scientists do sometimes cheat, and this not only impedes scientific progress and damages the reputation of the discipline, but it has dreadful career and life consequences for those involved. However, cheating is very rare and equally rare across both the psychological and biomedical sciences (Stroebe, Postmes, & Spears, 2012). In the case of social psychology, the largely team-based nature of research helps prevent scientists, who are all under enormous pressure to publish, take, to put it euphemistically, scientific shortcuts.

Research ethics is also about treatment of research participants. For instance, is it ethical to expose experimental participants to a treatment that is embarrassing or has potentially harmful effects on their self-concept? If such research is important, what are the rights of the person, what are the ethical obligations of the researcher and what guidelines are there for deciding? Although ethical considerations surface most often in experiments (e.g. Milgram's (1974) obedience studies; **see Chapter 7**), they can also confront non-experimental researchers. For example, is it ethical for a non-participant observer investigating crowd behaviour to refrain from interceding in a violent assault?

To guide researchers, the American Psychological Association established, in 1972, a set of ethical principles for conducting research involving humans, which was revised and updated in 2002 (American Psychological Association, 2002). These principles are reflected in the ethics codes of national societies of psychology in Europe. Researchers design their studies with these guidelines in mind and then obtain official approval from a university or departmental research ethics committee. Five ethical principles in particular have received the most attention: protection from harm, right to privacy, deception, informed consent and debriefing.

Physical welfare of participants

Clearly it is unethical to expose people to physical *harm*. For example, the use of electric shocks that cause visible burning would be difficult to justify. However, in most cases, it is also difficult to establish whether non-trivial harm is involved and, if so, what its magnitude is and whether debriefing (see the 'Debriefing' section later in this chapter) deals with it. For instance, telling experimental participants that they have done badly on a word-association task may have long-term effects on self-esteem and could therefore be considered harmful. On the other hand, the effects may be so minor and transitory as to be insignificant.

Box 1.2 Your life
Do research ethics apply to hypotheses you test in everyday life?

We often conduct social psychology research in our own everyday lives. For example, you might want to confirm your hypothesis that your best friend values your friendship above other friendships. To test this hypothesis, you decide to set up little challenges for him, such as going with you to watch a golf tournament – you absolutely love golf, but he finds it about as exciting as watching paint dry. If he goes with you and tries to look engaged – hypothesis supported. If he drops out at the last minute, or he goes but tries to spoil it for you by looking miserable and grumbling incessantly – hypothesis disconfirmed. Is it ethical to conduct this piece of research?

Of course, we do this kind of private 'research' all the time to learn about our world. We do not think of it in terms of research ethics. Maybe we should? After all, you could argue that the welfare of the 'participant' is put at risk, and you have used deception by not explaining the hypothesis you are testing. What do you think – do principles of research ethics apply to everyday hypothesis testing that we use to understand our day-to-day life?

Respect for privacy

Social psychological research often involves invasion of *privacy*. Participants can be asked intimate questions, can be observed without their knowledge and can have their moods, perceptions and behaviour manipulated. It is sometimes difficult to decide whether the research topic justifies invasion of privacy. At other times, it is more straightforward – for example, intimate questions about sexual practices are essential for research into behaviour that may put people at risk of contracting HIV and developing AIDS. Concern about privacy is usually satisfied by ensuring that data obtained from individuals are entirely *confidential*: that is, only the researcher knows who said or did what. Personal identification is removed from data (rendering them *anonymous*), research findings are reported as means for large groups of people, and data no longer useful are usually destroyed.

Use of deception

Laboratory experiments, as we have seen, involve the manipulation of people's cognition, feelings or behaviour in order to investigate the spontaneous, natural and non-reactive effect of independent variables. Because participants need to be naive regarding hypotheses, experimenters commonly conceal the true purpose of the experiment. A degree of *deception* is often necessary. Between 50 and 75 per cent of experiments published prior to the mid-1980s involved some degree of deception (Adair, Dushenko, & Lindsay, 1985; Gross & Fleming, 1982). Because the use of deception seems to imply 'trickery', 'deceit' and 'lying', it has attracted a frenzy of criticism – for example, Baumrind's (1964) attack on Milgram's (1963, 1974) obedience studies (see **Chapter 7**). Social psychologists have been challenged to abandon controlled experimental research in favour of role playing or simulations (e.g. Kelman, 1967) if they cannot do experiments without deception.

This is probably too extreme a request, as social psychological knowledge has been enriched enormously by classic experiments that have used deception (many such experiments are described in this text). Although some experiments have used deception that seems excessive, in practice the deception used in the overwhelming majority of social psychology experiments is trivial. For example, an experiment may be introduced as a study of group decision-making when in fact it is part of a programme of research into prejudice and stereotyping. In addition, there has been no evidence of any long-term negative consequences of the use of deception in social psychology experiments (Elms, 1982), and experimental participants themselves tend to be impressed, rather than upset or angered, by cleverly executed deceptions, and they view deception as a necessary withholding of information or a necessary ruse (Christensen, 1988; Sharpe, Adair, & Roese, 1992; Smith, 1983). How would you address the first 'What do *you* think?' question at the beginning of this chapter?

Informed consent

A way to safeguard participants' rights in experiments is to obtain their *informed consent* to participate. In principle, people should give their consent freely (preferably in writing) to participate on the basis of full information about what they are consenting to take part in, and they must be entirely free to withdraw without penalty from the research whenever they wish. Researchers cannot lie or withhold information in order to induce people to participate, nor can they make it 'difficult' to say 'no' or to withdraw (i.e. via social pressure or by exercise of personal or institutionalised power). In practice, however, terms such as 'full information' are difficult to define, and, as we have just seen, experiments often require some deception so that participants remain naive.

Debriefing

Participants should be fully *debriefed* after taking part in an experiment. Debriefing is designed to make sure that people leave the laboratory with an increased respect for and understanding of social psychology. More specifically, debriefing involves a detailed explanation of the experiment and its broader theoretical and applied context. Any deceptions are explained and justified to the satisfaction of all participants, and care is taken to make sure that the effects of manipulations have been undone. However, strong critics of deception (e.g. Baumrind, 1985) believe that no amount of debriefing puts right what they consider to be the fundamental wrong of deception that undermines basic human trust.

Social psychologists often conduct and report research into socially sensitive phenomena, or research that has implications for socially sensitive issues: for example, stereotyping, prejudice and discrimination (**see Chapters 10, 11 and 15**). In these cases, the researcher must be especially careful that both the conducting and reporting of research are done in a way that is not biased by personal prejudices and not open to public misinterpretation, distortion or misuse. For example, early research into sex differences in conformity found that women conformed more than men. This finding is, of course, fuel to the view that women are more dependent than men. Later research discovered that men and women conform equally, and that whether one conforms or not depends largely on how much familiarity and confidence one has with the conformity task. Early research used tasks that were more familiar to men than to women, and many researchers looked no further because the findings confirmed their assumptions (**Chapters 7 and 10**).

Theories and theorising

According to Van Lange (2013), a good theory should reveal the truth, describe specifics in terms of more general abstracted principles, make an advance on existing theory and be framed in such a way that it speaks to and is applicable to the real world. In some aspects, this echoes Lewin's earlier promotion of full cycle research, in which basic research develops theory, and applied research, which involves the application of theory to social issues, mutually reinforce each other (e.g. Lewin, 1951; Marrow, 1969).

Social psychologists construct, test and apply theories of human social behaviour. A social psychological theory is an integrated set of propositions that explains the causes of social behaviour, generally in terms of one or more social psychological processes. Theories rest on explicit assumptions about social behaviour and contain a number of defined concepts and formal statements about the relationship between concepts. Ideally, these relationships are causal ones that are attributed to the operation of social and/or psychological processes. Theories are framed in such a way that they generate hypotheses that can be tested empirically. Social psychological theories vary greatly in terms of their rigour, testability and generality. Some theories are short-range mini-theories tied to specific phenomena, whereas others are broader general theories that explain whole classes of behaviour. Some even approach the status of 'grand theory' (such as evolutionary theory, Marxism, general relativity theory and psychodynamic theory) in that they furnish a general perspective on social psychology.

Social identity theory (e.g. Tajfel & Turner, 1986; **see Chapters 4 and 11**) is a good example of a relatively general mid-range social psychological theory. It explains how the behaviour of people in groups relates to their self-conception as group members. The theory integrates a number of compatible (sub)theories that deal with and emphasise (see Abrams & Hogg, 2010; Hogg, 2006):

- intergroup relations and social change;
- motivational processes associated with group membership and group behaviour;
- social influence and conformity processes within groups;
- cognitive processes associated with self-conception and social perception.

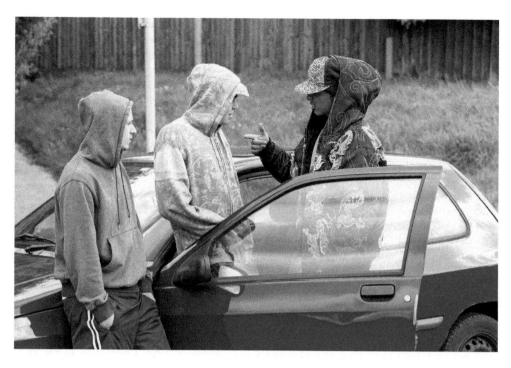

Social identity
Hoodies belong to groups too. They dress to emphasise group membership and social identity.

These, and other associated processes, operate together to produce group behaviour, as distinct from interpersonal behaviour. This theory generates testable predictions about a range of group phenomena, including stereotyping, intergroup discrimination, social influence in groups, group cohesiveness, social change and even language and ethnicity.

Theories in social psychology

Theories in social psychology can generally be clustered into types of theory (Van Lange, Kruglanski, & Higgins, 2012), with different types of theory reflecting different *metatheories*. Just as a theory is a set of interrelated concepts and principles that explain a phenomenon, a **metatheory** is a set of interrelated concepts and principles about which theories or types of theory are appropriate. Some theories can be extended by their adherents to account for almost the whole of human behaviour – the 'grand theories' mentioned above. In this section, we discuss several major types of theory that have had an impact on social psychology.

Metatheory
Set of interrelated concepts and principles concerning which theories or types of theory are appropriate.

Behaviourism

Behaviourist or learning perspectives derive from Ivan Pavlov's early work on conditioned reflexes and B. F. Skinner's work on operant conditioning. **Radical behaviourists** believe that behaviour can be explained and predicted in terms of reinforcement schedules – behaviour associated with positive outcomes or circumstances grows in strength and frequency. However, more popular with social psychologists is **neo-behaviourism**, which invokes unobservable intervening constructs (e.g. beliefs, feelings, motives) to make sense of behaviour.

The behaviourist perspective in social psychology produces theories that emphasise the role of situational factors and reinforcement/learning in social behaviour. One example is the *reinforcement–affect model of interpersonal attraction* (e.g. Lott, 1961; **Chapter 14**): people grow to like people with whom they associate positive experiences (e.g. we like people who praise us). Another, more general example is *social exchange theory* (e.g. Kelley & Thibaut, 1978; **Chapter 14**): the nature of social interactions depends on people's evaluation of the rewards and costs involved. *Social modelling* is another broadly behaviourist

Radical behaviourist
One who explains observable behaviour in terms of reinforcement schedules, without recourse to any intervening unobservable (e.g. cognitive) constructs.

Neo-behaviourist
One who attempts to explain observable behaviour in terms of contextual factors and unobservable intervening constructs such as beliefs, feelings and motives.

perspective: we learn vicariously by imitating behaviour that we see others being reinforced for (e.g. Bandura, 1977; **Chapter 12**). Finally, *drive theory* (Zajonc, 1965; **Chapter 8**) explains how the strength of a learned response influences whether we perform a task better or worse in front of an audience.

Cognitive psychology

Cognitive theories
Explanations of behaviour in terms of the way people actively interpret and represent their experiences and then plan action.

Critics have argued that behaviourist theories exaggerate how passive people are as recipients of external influences. **Cognitive theories** redress the balance by focusing on how people's cognitive processes and cognitive representations actively interpret and change their environment. Cognitive theories have their origins in Kurt Koffka and Wolfgang Köhler's Gestalt psychology of the 1930s, and in many ways, social psychology has always been fundamentally cognitive in its perspective (Landman & Manis, 1983; Markus & Zajonc, 1985). One of social psychology's earliest cognitive theories was Kurt Lewin's (1951) field theory, which dealt, in a somewhat complicated manner, with how people's cognitive representations of features of the social environment produce motivational forces to behave in specific ways. Lewin is generally considered the father of experimental social psychology.

In the 1950s and 1960s, cognitive consistency theories dominated social psychology (Abelson et al., 1968). These theories assumed that cognitions about ourselves, our behaviour and the world, which are contradictory or incompatible in other ways, produce an uncomfortable state of cognitive arousal that motivates us to resolve the cognitive conflict. This perspective has been used to explain attitude change (e.g. Aronson, 1984; **Chapter 6**). In the 1970s, attribution theories dominated social psychology. Attribution theories focus on how people explain the causes of their own and other people's behaviour, and on the consequences of causal explanations (e.g. Hewstone, 1989; **Chapter 3**). Finally, since the late 1970s, social cognition has been the dominant perspective in social psychology. It subsumes a number of theories specifying how cognitive processes (e.g. categorization) and cognitive representations (e.g. schemas) influence and are influenced by behaviour (e.g. Fiske & Taylor, 2013; **Chapter 2**).

Neuroscience and biochemistry

Social neuroscience
Exploration of brain activity associated with social cognition and social psychological processes and phenomena.

A more recent development of social cognition is a focus on neurological and biochemical correlates of social behaviour. Called **social neuroscience**, or social cognitive neuroscience, this approach rests on the view that because psychology happens in the brain, cognition must be associated with electro-chemical brain activity (e.g. Harmon-Jones & Winkielman, 2007; Lieberman, 2010; Ochsner, 2007; Ochsner & Lieberman, 2001; Todorov, Fiske, & Prentice, 2011; **see Chapter 2**). Social neuroscience uses brain imaging methodologies, for example fMRI, to detect and locate brain activity associated with social thinking and social behaviour. This general idea that we are biological entities and that therefore social behaviour has neuro- and biochemical correlates surfaces in other theorising that focuses more on biochemical markers of social behaviour – for example, measures of the hormone cortisol in people's blood or saliva as a marker of stress (see Blascovich & Seery, 2007).

Evolutionary social psychology

Evolutionary social psychology
An extension of evolutionary psychology that views complex social behaviour as adaptive, helping the individual, kin and the species as a whole to survive.

Evolutionary psychology
A theoretical approach that explains 'useful' psychological traits, such as memory, perception or language, as adaptations through natural selection.

Another theoretical development is **evolutionary social psychology** (Caporael, 2007; Kenrick, Maner, & Li, 2005; Neuberg, Kenrick, & Schaller, 2010; Schaller, Simpson, & Kenrick, 2006; Simpson, & Kenrick, 1997). Drawing on nineteenth-century Darwinian theory (Darwin, 1872) and modern **evolutionary psychology** and sociobiology (e.g. Wilson, 1975, 1978), evolutionary social psychologists argue that much of human behaviour is grounded in the ancestral past of our species. Buss and Reeve (2003, p. 849) suggest that evolutionary processes have shaped 'cooperation and conflict within families, the emergence of cooperative alliances, human aggression, acts of altruism . . .'. These behaviours had survival value for the species and so, over time, became a part of our genetic make-up.

A biological perspective can be pushed to extremes and used as a sovereign explanation for most, even all, behaviour. However, when the human genome had finally been charted in 2003, researchers felt that the 20,000–25,000 genes and 3 billion chemical base pairs making up human DNA were insufficient to account for the massive diversity of human behaviour – context and environment play a significant role (e.g. Lander et al., 2001). This is, of course, where social psychology steps in. Nevertheless, evolutionary social psychology has relevance for several topics covered in this text – for example, leadership (**Chapter 9**), aggression (**Chapter 12**), prosocial behaviour (**Chapter 13**), interpersonal attraction (**Chapter 14**) and non-verbal and human spatial behaviour (**Chapter 15**).

Personality and individual differences

Social psychologists have often explained social behaviour in terms of enduring (sometimes innate) personality differences between people. For instance, good leaders have charismatic personalities (**Chapter 9**), people with prejudiced personalities express prejudice (**Chapter 10**) and people who conform too much have conformist personalities (**Chapter 7**). In general, social psychologists now consider personality and differences in personality to be at best a partial explanation, at worst an inadequate re-description, of social phenomena. There are at least two reasons for this:

1 There is actually very little evidence for stable personality traits. People behave in different ways at different times and in different contexts – they are influenced by situation and context.

2 If personality is defined as behavioural consistency across contexts, then rather than being an explanation of behaviour, personality is something to be explained. Why do some people resist social and contextual influences on behaviour? What is it about their interpretation of the context that causes them to behave in this way?

Overall, most contemporary treatments of personality see personality as interacting with many other factors to impact behaviour (e.g. Funder & Fast, 2010; Snyder & Cantor, 1998).

Collectivist theories

Personality and individual difference theories can be contrasted with collectivist theories. Collectivist theories focus on people as a product of their location in the matrix of social categories and groups that make up society. People behave as they do not because of personality or individual predispositions, but because they internalise group norms that influence behaviour in specific contexts. An early collectivist viewpoint was William McDougall's (1920) theory of the 'group mind' (**Chapter 11**). In groups, people change the way they think, process information and act, so that group behaviour is quite different from interpersonal behaviour – a group mind emerges.

More recently, this idea has been significantly elaborated and developed by European social psychologists who emphasise the part played by the wider social context of intergroup relations in shaping behaviour (e.g. Tajfel, 1984). Of these, social identity theory is perhaps the most developed (Tajfel & Turner, 1986; **Chapter 11**). Its explanation of the behaviour of people in groups is strongly influenced by an analysis of the social relations between groups. Collectivist theories adopt a 'top-down' approach, in which individual social behaviour can be properly explained only with reference to groups, intergroup relations and social forces. Individualistic theories, in contrast, are 'bottom-up': individual social behaviour is constructed from individual cognition or personality.

Many social psychological theories contain elements of two or more different perspectives, and these and other perspectives often merely lend emphasis to different theories. Metatheory does not usually intentionally reveal itself with prodigious fanfare (but see Abrams & Hogg, 2004).

Social psychology in crisis

Social psychology occurs against a background of metatheoretical contrasts, which from time to time come to the fore to become the focus of intense public debate. For example, in the late 1960s and early 1970s, many social psychologists felt the discipline had reached a crisis that seriously eroded people's confidence in the discipline (e.g. Elms, 1975; Israel & Tajfel, 1972; Rosnow, 1981; Strickland, Aboud, & Gergen, 1976). There were two principal concerns:

1 Social psychology was overly *reductionist* (i.e. by explaining social behaviour mainly in terms of individual psychology, it failed to address the essentially social nature of the human experience).

2 Social psychology was overly *positivistic* (i.e. it adhered to a model of science that was distorted, inappropriate and misleading).

Reductionism and levels of explanation

Reductionism
Explanation of a phenomenon in terms of the language and concepts of a lower level of analysis, usually with a loss of explanatory power.

Reductionism is the practice of explaining a phenomenon with the language and concepts of a lower level of analysis. Society is explained in terms of groups, groups in terms of interpersonal processes, interpersonal processes in terms of intrapersonal cognition, cognition in terms of neuropsychology, neuropsychology in terms of biology, and so on. A problem of reductionist theorising is that it can leave the original scientific question unanswered. For example, the act of putting one's arm out of the car window to indicate an intention to turn can be explained in terms of muscle contraction, or nerve impulses, or understanding of and adherence to social conventions, and so on. If the **level of explanation** does not match the level of the question, then the question remains effectively unanswered.

Level of explanation
The types of concepts, mechanisms and language used to explain a phenomenon.

Although a degree of reductionism can strengthen theorising, too great a degree can create an explanatory gap. Social psychology has been criticised for being inherently reductionist because it tries to explain social behaviour purely in terms of asocial intrapsychic cognitive and motivational processes (e.g. Moscovici, 1972; Pepitone, 1981; Sampson, 1977; Taylor & Brown, 1979). The recent trends towards social cognitive neuroscience and evolutionary social psychology, explaining behaviour in terms of neural activity and genetic predisposition, can be criticised on the same grounds (cf. Dovidio, Pearson, & Orr, 2008). How would you now address the second 'What do *you* think?' question at the beginning of this chapter?

Reductionism can be a particular problem for explanations of group processes and intergroup relations. By viewing these phenomena exclusively in terms of personality, interpersonal relations or intrapsychic processes, social psychology may leave some of their most important aspects incompletely explained – for example, prejudice, discrimination, stereotyping, conformity and group solidarity (Billig, 1976; Hogg & Abrams, 1988; Turner & Oakes, 1986). Worse, reductionist explanations of societally constructed perceptions and behaviours can have undesirable sociopolitical consequences. Fine has levelled this charge at social neuroscience; arguing that some fMRI research reinforces gender stereotypes (Fine, 2010).

Willem Doise (1986; Lorenzi-Cioldi & Doise, 1990) has suggested that one way around this problem is to accept the existence of different levels of explanation but to construct theories that formally integrate (Doise uses the French term 'articulate') concepts from different levels (see Box 1.3). This idea has been adopted by many social psychologists (see Tajfel, 1984). One of the most successful attempts may be social identity theory (e.g. Tajfel & Turner, 1986; **see Chapter 11**), which articulates individual cognitive processes, social interactive processes and large-scale social forces to explain group behaviour. Doise's ideas have also been employed to reinterpret group cohesiveness (Hogg, 1992, 1993), attribution theories (Hewstone, 1989) and social representations (e.g. Doise, Clémence, &

Box 1.3 Research classic
Levels of explanation in social psychology

I Intrapersonal

Analysis of psychological processes to do with people's representation and organisation of their experience of the social environment (e.g. research on cognitive balance).

II Interpersonal and situational

Analysis of interindividual interaction within circumscribed situations. Social positional factors outside the situation are not considered. The focus is on the dynamics of relations between specific individuals at a specific time and in a specific situation (e.g. some attribution research, research using game matrices).

III Positional

Analysis of interindividual interaction in specific situations, but with the role of social position (e.g. status, identity) outside the situation taken into consideration (e.g. some research into power and social identity).

IV Ideological

Analysis of interindividual interaction that considers the role of general social beliefs, and of social relations between groups (e.g. some research into social identity, social representations and minority influence; studies considering the role of cultural norms and values).

Source: Taken from material in Hogg (1992, p. 62) and based on Lorenzi-Cioldi and Doise (1990, p. 73) and Doise (1986, pp. 10–16).

Lorenzi-Cioldi, 1993; Lorenzi-Cioldi & Clémence, 2001). Organisational psychologists have also advocated articulation of levels of analysis – they use the term cross-level research (Wilpert, 1995; see also Haslam, 2004).

Positivism and post-positivism

Positivism is the non-critical acceptance of scientific method as the only way to arrive at true knowledge. Positivism was introduced in the early nineteenth century by the French mathematician and philosopher Auguste Comte and was enormously popular until the end of that century. The character Mr Gradgrind in Charles Dickens's 1854 novel *Hard Times* epitomises positivism: science as a religion. A more contemporary one-dimensional stereotype of positivism is embodied by geeky, nerd-like characters such as "Doc" in the *Back to the Future* movies and Sheldon and friends in the phenomenally popular TV series *The Big Bang Theory*.

Social psychology has been criticised for being positivistic (e.g. Gergen, 1973; Henriques et al., 1984; Potter, Stringer, & Wetherell, 1984; Shotter, 1984). It is argued that because social psychologists are ultimately studying themselves, they cannot achieve the level of objectivity of, say, a chemist studying a compound or a geographer studying a landform. Since complete objectivity is unattainable, scientific methods, particularly experimental ones, are simply not appropriate for social psychology. Social psychology can only masquerade as a science – it cannot be a true science. Critics argue that what social psychologists propose as fundamental causal mechanisms (e.g. categorization, attribution, cognitive balance, self-concept) are only 'best-guess' concepts that explain some historically and culturally restricted data – data that are subject to unavoidable and intrinsic bias. Critics also feel that by treating humans as objects or clusters of variables that can be manipulated experimentally, we are not only cutting ourselves off from a rich reservoir of subjective or introspective data, but we are also dehumanising people.

These criticisms have produced some quite radical post-positivism alternatives to traditional social psychology. Examples include social constructionism (Gergen, 1973), humanistic psychology (Shotter, 1984), ethogenics (Harré, 1979), discourse analysis or discursive psychology (Augoustinos & Tileaga, 2012; Edwards, 1997; Potter & Wetherell, 1987), critical

Positivism
Non-critical acceptance of science as the only way to arrive at true knowledge: science as religion.

psychology (Billig, 2008) and poststructuralist perspectives (Henriques et al., 1984). There are differences among these alternatives, but they share an emphasis on understanding people as whole human beings who are constructed historically and who try to make sense of themselves and their world. Research methods tend to emphasise in-depth subjective analysis (often called *deconstruction*) of the relatively spontaneous accounts that people give of their thoughts, feelings and actions. Subjectivity is considered a virtue of, rather than an impediment to, good research. The fact that discursive psychology is fundamentally incommensurate with 'mainstream' social psychology has more recently worried some scholars and led them to advocate a degree of rapprochement (e.g. Rogers, 2003; Tuffin, 2005).

However, most mainstream social psychologists respond to the problem of positivism in a less dramatic way, which does not involve diluting or abandoning the scientific method. Instead, they deal with the pitfalls of positivism by being rigorous in the adoption of best-practice scientific methods of research and theorising (e.g. Campbell, 1957; Jost & Kruglanski, 2002; Kruglanski, 1975; Turner, 1981a). For example, **operational definitions** of social psychological concepts (e.g. aggression, altruism, leadership) are critical – a key feature of positivism is that scientific concepts be defined in a concrete manner that allows them to be measured. In addition, as scientists, we should be mindful of our own subjectivity and should acknowledge and make explicit our biases. We should also be sensitive to the pitfalls of reductionism and, where appropriate, articulate different levels of analysis (as discussed earlier). We should also recognise that experimental participants are real people who do not throw off their past history and become unidimensional 'variables' when they enter the laboratory. Culture, history, socialisation and personal motives are all present in the laboratory – experiments are social situations (Tajfel, 1972). Finally, attention should be paid to language, as that is perhaps the most significant way in which people represent the world, think, plan action and manipulate the world around them (**Chapter 15**). Language is also the epitome of a social variable: it is socially constructed and internalised to govern individual social cognition and behaviour.

Operational definition
Defines a theoretical term in a way that allows it to be manipulated or measured.

Historical context

Social psychology is not a static science. It has a history, and it is invaluable to consider a science in its proper historical context in order to understand its true nature. Here we give an overview of the history of social psychology. Although ancient forms of social and political philosophy considered such questions as the nature–nurture controversy, the origins of society and the function of the state, it was mostly a speculative exercise devoid of fact gathering (Hollander, 1967). An empirical approach to the study of social life did not appear until the latter part of the nineteenth century.

Social psychology in the nineteenth century

Anglo-European influences

An influential precursor to the development of social psychology as an independent discipline was the work of scholars in Germany known as the *folk psychologists*. In 1860, a journal devoted to *Völkerpsychologie* was founded by Steinthal and Lazarus. It contained both theoretical and factual articles. In contrast to general psychology (elaborated later by Wundt) which dealt with the study of the individual mind, folk psychology, which was influenced by the philosopher Hegel, dealt with the study of the *collective* mind. This concept of collective mind was interpreted in conflicting ways by Steinthal and Lazarus, meaning on the one hand a societal way of thinking within the individual and on the other a form of super-mentality that could enfold a whole group of people.

Völkerpsychologie
Early precursor of social psychology, as the study of the collective mind, in Germany in the mid- to late nineteenth century.

This concept, of a *group mind*, became, in the 1890s and early 1900s, a dominant account of social behaviour. An extreme example of it can be found in the work of the French writer Gustav LeBon (1896/1908), who argued that crowds often behave badly because the behaviour of the individual is controlled by the group mind. The English psychologist William McDougall (1920) even wrote an entire book, entitled *The Group Mind*, as an explanation of collective behaviour. Much later, Solomon Asch (1951) observed that the wider issue that such writers confronted had not gone away: to understand the complexities of an individual's behaviour, we need to view the person in the context of group relations.

Early texts

At the dawn of the twentieth century, there were two social psychology texts, by Bunge (1903) and Orano (1901). Because they were not in English, they received little attention in Britain and the United States. Even earlier, an American, Baldwin (1897/1901), touched on social psychology in a work that dealt mainly with the social and moral development of the child. A book by the French sociologist Gabriel Tarde (1898) had clear implications for the kind of data and the level of explanation that social psychology should adopt. He adopted a bottom-up approach, which was offered in debate with Emile Durkheim. Whereas Durkheim argued that the way people behave is determined by social laws that are fashioned by society, Tarde proposed that a science of social behaviour must derive from the psychology of the individual. His conception of social psychology is closer in flavour to most current thinking than any of the other early texts (Clark, 1969).

The two early texts that caught the attention of the English-speaking world were written by McDougall (1908) and the American sociologist E. A. Ross (1908). Neither looks much like a modern social psychology text. The central topics of McDougall's book, for example, were the principal instincts, the primary emotions, the nature of sentiments, moral conduct, volition, religious conceptions and the structure of character. Compare these with the chapter topics of the present text.

The rise of experimentation

In 1924, Floyd Allport published a highly influential textbook; it set an agenda for social psychology that was quickly and enduringly followed by many teachers in psychology departments for years to come. Following the manifesto for psychology as a whole laid out by the behaviourist John Watson (1913), Allport argued that social psychology would flourish only if it became an experimental science. The challenge was taken up by Gardner Murphy and Lois Murphy (1931/1937), who published a text proudly entitled *Experimental Social Psychology*. Not all of the studies reviewed were true experiments, but the authors' intentions for the discipline were clear.

Although earlier texts had not shown it, the closing decade of the nineteenth century had set an agenda in which social psychology would be inextricably entwined with the broader discipline of general psychology. As such, social psychology's subsequent development reflects the way in which psychology was defined and taught in university departments of psychology, particularly in the United States which rapidly replaced Germany as the leading nation for psychological research. Just as the psychological laboratory at Leipzig founded by Wilhelm Wundt in 1879 had provided an experimental basis for psychology in Germany, the laboratories set up at American universities did likewise in the United States. In the period 1890–1910, the growth of laboratories devoted to psychological research was rapid (Ruckmick, 1912). Thirty-one American universities established experimental facilities in those twenty years. The subject taught in these departments was clearly defined as an experimental science. In the United States, therefore, it is not surprising that social psychology should quite early on view the **experimental method** as a touchstone. By the time Allport produced his 1924 text, this trend was well established.

Experimental method
Intentional manipulation of independent variables in order to investigate effects on one or more dependent variables.

Social facilitation
These pictures represent an idea that caught Triplett's attention. Gold medalist Bradley Wiggins completed in the time trial and the road race at the London Olympics. Would he ride faster when competing alone or with others? Why?

When was social psychology's first experiment?

This is a natural question to ask, but the answer is clouded. One of the oldest psychological laboratories was at Indiana University. It was here that Norman Triplett (1898) conducted a study that is often cited as social psychology's first experiment – an experiment on social facilitation (**see Chapter 8**). Allport (1954a) suggested that what Wundt did in Leipzig for experimental psychology, Triplett did in Indiana for a scientific social psychology. However, a different picture emerges in the literature of the time.

Triplett was a mature teacher who returned to postgraduate study to work on his master's thesis, published in 1898. His supervisors were two experimental psychologists, and the research was conducted in a laboratory that was one of the very best in the world. His interest had been stimulated by popular wisdom that competitive cyclists go faster when racing or being paced than when riding alone. Cycling as an activity had increased dramatically in popularity in the 1890s and had spectacular press coverage. Triplett listed explanations, some quite entertaining, for superior performance by cyclists who were racing or being paced:

- The pacer in front provided suction that pulled the following rider along, helping to conserve energy; or else the front rider provided shelter from the wind.

- A popular 'brain worry' theory predicted that solitary cyclists did poorly because they worried about whether they were going fast enough. This exhausted their brain and muscles, numbing them and inhibiting motor performance.

- Friends usually rode as pacers and no doubt encouraged the cyclists to keep up their spirits.

- In a race, a follower might be hypnotised by the wheels in front and so rode automatically, leaving more energy for a later, controlled burst.

- A dynamogenic theory – Triplett's favourite – proposed that the presence of another person racing aroused a 'competitive instinct' that released 'nervous energy', similar to the modern idea of arousal. The sight of movement in another suggested more speed, inspired greater effort, and released a level of nervous energy that an isolated rider cannot achieve alone. The energy of the cyclist's movement was in proportion to the idea of that movement.

In the most famous of Triplett's experiments, schoolchildren worked in two conditions, alone and in pairs. They worked with two fishing reels that turned silk bands around a drum. Each reel was connected by a loop of cord to a pulley two metres away, and a small flag was attached to each cord. To complete one trial, the flag had to travel four times around the pulley. Some children were slower and others faster in competition, while others were little affected. The faster ones showed the effects of both 'the arousal of their competitive instincts and the idea of a faster movement' (Triplett, 1898, p. 526). The slower ones were overstimulated and, as Triplett put it, 'going to pieces'!

In drawing on the *dynamogenic theory* of his day, Triplett focused on ideo-motor responses – that is, one competitor's bodily movements acted as a stimulus for the other competitor. Essentially, Triplett highlighted *non-social* cues to illustrate the idea of movement being used as a cue by his participants.

The leading journals in the decade after Triplett's study scarcely referred to it. It was catalogued in general sources, but not under any headings with a 'social' connotation. Clearly, Triplett was neither a social psychologist nor considered to be one. If we adopt a revisionist view of history, then the spirit of his experiment emerges as a precursor to the study of social facilitation. The search for a founding figure, or a first idea, is not a new phenomenon in the history of science or, indeed, in the history of civilisation. The Triplett study has the trappings of an origin myth. There were other, even earlier, studies that might just as easily be called the 'first' in social psychology (Burnham, 1910; Haines & Vaughan, 1979). Vaughan and Guerin (1997) point out that sports psychologists have claimed Triplett as one of their own.

Later influences

Social psychology's development after the early impact of **behaviourism** was guided by a number of other important developments, some of which came from outside mainstream psychology.

Behaviourism
An emphasis on explaining observable behaviour in terms of reinforcement schedules.

Attitude scaling

One of these developments was the refinement of methods for constructing scales to measure attitudes (Bogardus, 1925; Likert, 1932; Thurstone, 1928; **see Chapter 5**). Some of this research was published in sociology journals. This is unsurprising – sociologists have often championed approaches to social psychology that are critical of an exclusively individual-behaviour level of analysis. There is still a branch of social psychology called sociological social psychology (e.g. Delamater & Ward, 2013; see Farr, 1996), and in the context of attitudes, Thomas and Znaniecki (1918) defined social psychology as the scientific study of attitudes rather than of social behaviour (**see Chapter 5**).

Studies of the social group

Groups have always been a core focus of social psychology (**see Chapters 8, 9 and 11**). Kurt Lewin, considered the 'father' of experimental social psychology, put much of his energy into the study of group processes (Marrow, 1969). For example, one of Lewin's imaginative studies was an experiment on the effect of leadership style on small-group behaviour (Lewin, Lippitt, & White, 1939; **see also Chapter 9**), and by 1945 he had founded a research centre devoted to the study of group dynamics (which still exists, in a different guise and now at the University of Michigan).

Groups have also been a focus of industrial psychologists. A well-known study carried out in a factory setting showed that work productivity can be influenced more by the psychological properties of the work group and the degree of interest that management shows in its workers (Roethlisberger & Dickson, 1939) than by mere physical working conditions. A significant outcome of research of this kind was consolidation of an approach to social psychology in which theory and application can develop together. Indeed, Lewin is often quoted as saying 'there is nothing so practical as a good theory'. He was a passionate advocate of what he called 'full cycle' research, where basic and applied research each inform one another.

Popular textbooks

The 1930s marked a burgeoning of the study of social psychology and thus the publication of influential textbooks. Carl Murchison (1935) produced the first handbook, a weighty tome that proclaimed that here was a field to be taken seriously. A later expanded edition of the Murphy and Murphy text (1931/1937) summarised the findings of more than 1,000 studies, although it was used mainly as a reference work. Perhaps the most widely used textbook of the time was written by LaPiere and Farnsworth (1936). Another by Klineberg (1940) was also popular; it featured contributions from cultural anthropology and emphasised the role played by culture in the development of a person's personality. Just after the Second World War, Krech and Crutchfield (1948) published an influential text that emphasised a *phenomenological approach* to social psychology; that is, an approach focusing on how people actually experience the world and account for their experiences.

In the 1950s and thereafter, the number of textbooks appearing on bookshelves increased exponentially. For obvious historical and demographic reasons (the legacy of the Second World War and a current population of 325 million English speakers), most texts have been and still are published in the United States. Although these texts mainly report American-based research and ideas, this has very noticeably changed over the past decade or so – European-based research and ideas are now an integral part of the reported science throughout this text. However, American texts are, understandably, written for American students at American institutions and can seem culturally alien to people living in Europe, Australasia and so forth. We like to think that the text you are now reading redresses this cultural leaning.

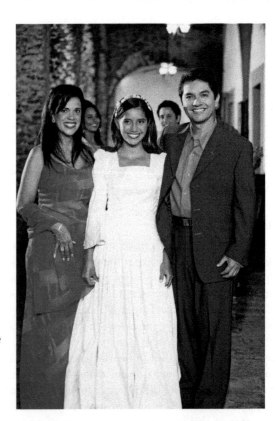

Role transition
Birthdays can mark important life changes in Latin America, quinceañera marks a fifteen-year-old girl's transition from childhood to womanhood – an opportunity to be 'grown up'!

Famous experiments

A number of social psychology experiments stand out as having an enduring fascination for teachers and students alike. They have also had a wider impact across psychology and other disciplines, and some have entered popular culture. We will not go into detail about these studies here, as they are described in later chapters.

Muzafer Sherif (1935) conducted an experiment on *norm formation,* which caught the attention of psychologists eager to pinpoint what could be 'social' about social psychology (**Chapter 7**). Solomon Asch (1951) demonstrated the dramatic effect that *group pressure* can have in persuading a person to conform (**Chapter 7**). Muzafer and Carolyn Sherif (Sherif & Sherif, 1953) examined the impact that competition for resources can have on intergroup conflict (**Chapter 11**). Leon Festinger (1957) supported his theory of *cognitive dissonance* by showing that a smaller reward can change attitudes more than can a larger reward (Festinger & Carlsmith, 1959), a finding that annoyed orthodox reinforcement theorists of the time (**Chapters 5 and 6**). The term cognitive dissonance is now used (generally inaccurately) in everyday conversation. Stanley Milgram's (1963) study of *destructive obedience* highlighted the dilemma facing a person ordered by an authority figure to perform an immoral act, a study that became a focus of critics who questioned the future of the experimental method in social psychology (**Chapter 7**). Henri Tajfel (1970; Tajfel, Billig, Bundy, & Flament, 1971) conducted a watershed experiment to show that merely being categorized into groups was sufficient to generate *intergroup discrimination* (**Chapter 11**).

Finally, Phillip Zimbardo (1971) set up a simulated prison in the basement of the Stanford University psychology department to study *deindividuation* and the reality of and extremity of *roles* (**Chapter 8**). This study has caught the imagination of a reality-TV-oriented society; to the extent that two prominent British social psychologists, Alex Haslam and Stephen Reicher, were commissioned as consultants on a 2002 BBC TV programme re-running the experiment (Reicher & Haslam, 2006). There is even a 2015 Hollywood-style movie called *The Stanford Prison Experiment* that dramatises the experiment in the form of a thriller.

Famous programmes

One way of viewing the development of a discipline is to focus on social networks and ask 'Who's who?' and then 'Who influenced whom?' Looked at in this way, the group-centred research of the charismatic Kurt Lewin (Marrow, 1969) had a remarkable impact on other social psychologists in the United States. One of his students was Leon Festinger, and one of Festinger's students was Stanley Schachter. The latter's work on the cognitive labelling of emotion is a derivative of Festinger's notion of social comparison (i.e. the way in which individuals use other people as a basis for assessing their own thoughts, feelings and behaviour).

There have been other groups of researchers whose research programmes have had an enduring impact on the discipline. Circumstances surrounding the Second World War focused the attention of two research groups. Inspired by the possibility that the rise of German autocracy and fascism resided in the personality and child-rearing practices of a nation, one group studied the *authoritarian personality* (Adorno, Frenkel-Brunswik, Levinson, & Sanford, 1950) – embarking on an ambitious cross-cultural study of authoritarianism in the United States (**Chapter 10**). Another group studied attitude change. The Yale *attitude change* programme, led by Carl Hovland, developed and tested theories explaining how techniques and processes of persuasion and propaganda could change people's attitudes (Hovland, Janis, & Kelley, 1953; see **Chapter 6**).

John Thibaut and Harold Kelley (1959) developed an approach to the study of interpersonal relationships, based on an economic model of *social exchange* (**Chapter 14**). This

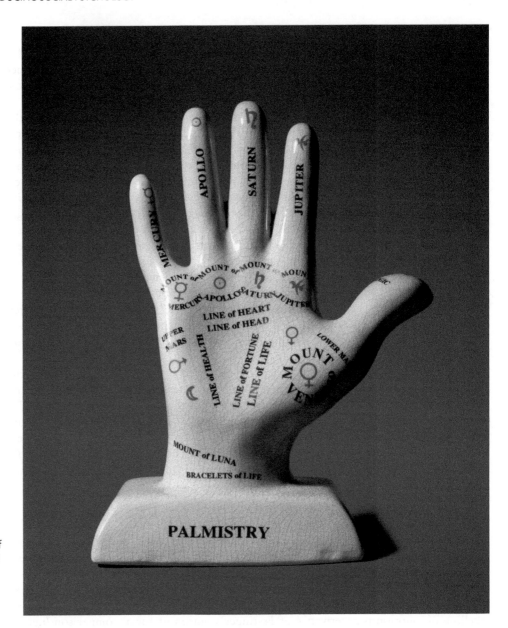

Attribution
People try to make sense of their lives in many different ways. We can try palmistry, or more mundanely examine the immediate causes of our experiences.

approach has had an enormous impact in social psychology, beyond the study of close relationships. For example, Morton Deutsch's (Deutsch & Krauss, 1960) applied the exchange principle to interpersonal bargaining. Once again, the long arm of Lewin is evident – all of these scholars (Thibaut, Kelley, Deutsch) were Lewin's students.

The modern period has been dominated by cognitive approaches. Ned Jones (Jones & Davis, 1965) launched *attribution theory* by focusing attention on the ordinary person's ideas about causality (**Chapter 3**). Darley and Latané (1968) researched *prosocial behaviour* by introducing an innovative cognitive model to explore how people interpret an emergency and sometimes fail to help a victim (**Chapter 13**).

Early work on social perception by Fritz Heider (1946) and Solomon Asch (1946) was transformed in the 1970s into contemporary *social cognition* (**see Chapter 2**). Some key players in this transformation were Walter Mischel (Cantor & Mischel, 1977), who explored how perceived behaviour traits can function as prototypes, and Richard Nisbett and Lee Ross (1980), who explored the role of cognitive heuristics (mental short-cuts) in social thinking.

The journals

Journals are critical in science. They are overwhelmingly the main forum for scientists to exchange ideas and communicate ideas and findings. Early journals that were important up to the 1950s were the *Journal of Abnormal and Social Psychology* and the *Journal of Personality*. A sociological journal, *Sociometry*, also catered for social psychological work.

From the 1960s, there was increased demand for outlets. This reflected not only growth in the number of social psychologists around the world but also a demand for regional and sub-disciplinary representation. The *Journal of Abnormal and Social Psychology* divided into two, one part devoted to abnormal psychology and the other titled the *Journal of Personality and Social Psychology* (founded in 1965). *Sociometry* was re-titled *Social Psychology Quarterly* (1979) to reflect more accurately its social psychological content. Anglo-European interests were represented by the *British Journal of Social and Clinical Psychology* (1963) (which split in about 1980 to spin off the *British Journal of Social Psychology*), and the *European Journal of Social Psychology* (1971).

Further demand for journals dedicated to experimental research was met by the *Journal of Experimental Social Psychology* (1965) and then in 1975 by the *Personality and Social Psychology Bulletin*. Other journals devoted to social psychology include the *Journal of Applied Social Psychology* (1971), *Social Cognition* (1982), the *Journal of Language and Social Psychology* (1982) and the *Journal of Social and Personal Relationships* (1984). Over the past twenty years, these journals have been joined by others, including *Personality and Social Psychology Review*, *Social Psychological and Personality Science*, *Group Processes and Intergroup Relations*, *Self and Identity*, *Group Dynamics* and *Social Influence*.

From the perspective of articles published, there was an explosion of interest in social psychology during the decade bridging the 1960s and the 1970s. Since then, publication has accelerated. In the past decade or so, we have witnessed a journal crisis in social psychology, and psychology more generally. There is so much published that the task of deciding what to read is overwhelming. One important criterion is the quality of the journal (i.e. its impact factor and the calibre of its editorial board), but there are now so many journals and such huge volume of articles submitted that the editorial review process that is essential to quality is creaking under the load. This, in conjunction with the massive potential of electronic access to research, has led to a fiery debate about alternative forms of scientific communication and publication (Nosek & Bar-Anan, 2012).

Social psychology in Europe

Although, as our historical overview has shown, social psychology and psychology as a whole were born in Europe, America quickly assumed leadership in terms not only of concepts but also of journals, books and organisations. One significant cause of this shift in hegemony was the rise of fascism in Europe in the 1930s. Take Germany, for example; in 1933, Jewish professors were dismissed from the universities, and from then through the end of the Second World War the names of Jewish authors were expunged from university textbooks in the name of National Socialism and to promulgate Aryan doctrine (Baumgarten-Tramer, 1948). This led, during the immediate pre-war period, to a massive exodus of

European social psychologists and other scholars to the United States. By 1945, social psychology in Europe had been decimated, particularly when compared with the rapid development of the field in the United States. The continent was destroyed by six years of war and little European social psychology remained.

From 1945 into the 1950s, the United States provided resources (e.g. money and academic links) to (re-)establish centres of European social psychology. Although partly a scientific gesture, this was also part of a wider Cold War strategy to provide an intellectual environment in Western Europe to combat the encroachment of communism. These centres were linked to the United States rather than to one another. In fact, there were very few links among European social psychologists, who were often unaware of one another and who tended instead to have lines of communication with American universities. Europe, including Britain, was largely an outpost of American social psychology. In the period from 1950 to the end of the 1960s, social psychology in Britain was largely based on American ideas. Likewise, in The Netherlands, Germany, France and Belgium, most work was influenced by American thinking (Argyle, 1980).

Europe slowly rebuilt its infrastructure, and European social psychologists gradually became more conscious of the hegemony of American ideas and of intellectual, cultural and historical differences between Europe and America. At that time the recent European experience was of war and conflict within its boundaries (the 1914–18 First World War, then the 1936–9 Spanish Civil war morphed into the 1939–45 Second World War, which morphed immediately into the Cold War), while America's last major conflict within its own borders was its 1861–5 Civil War. Not surprisingly, Europeans considered themselves to be more concerned with intergroup relations and groups, while Americans were perhaps more interested in interpersonal relations and individuals. Europeans pushed for a more *social* psychology. There was a clear need for better communication channels among European scholars and some degree of intellectual and organisational independence from the United States.

The first step along this road was initiated in the early 1950s by Eric Rinde in Norway, who, in collaboration with the American David Krech, brought together several American and more than thirty European social psychologists to collaborate on a cross-national study of threat and rejection. The wider goal was to encourage international collaboration and to increase training facilities for social scientists in Europe. Building on this project, the next step was a *European conference on experimental social psychology* organised by John Lanzetta and Luigi Petrullo, both from the United States, held in Sorrento in 1963. Among the twenty-eight participants were five Americans and twenty-one Europeans from eight countries. The organising committee (Mulder, Pages, Rommetveit, Tajfel and Thibaut) was also charged with preparing a proposal for the development of experimental social psychology in Europe.

It was decided to hold a second European conference and a summer school (held later in Leuven in 1967). The conference was held in Frascati in 1964, and it elected a 'European planning committee' (G. Jahoda, Moscovici, Mulder, Nuttin and Tajfel) to explore further a formal structure for European social psychology. A structure was approved at the third European conference, held in 1966 at Royaumont near Paris; thus was formally born the *European Association of Experimental Social Psychology* (EAESP). Moscovici was the foundation president, and there were approximately forty-four members.

EAESP, which was renamed the *European Association of Social Psychology* (EASP) in 2008, has been the enormously successful focus for the development of European social psychology for over fifty years, and it currently has about 1,200 members. Most members by far are from The Netherlands, the United Kingdom and Germany (in that order), followed by Italy, France and then the United States. It is a dynamic and integrative force for social psychology that for many years now has reached outside Europe with strong links with the leading international social psychology organisations (*Society for Personality and Social Psychology, Society of Experimental Social Psychology, Society for the Psychological Study of Social Issues*) – its last triennial conference, the eighteenth general meeting held in Granada in July 2017 (the previous five conferences were held in San Sebastián, Würzburg, Opatija, Stockholm and Amsterdam) had close to 1,500 delegates from about 50 countries across Europe and the rest of the world.

European journals and textbooks have provided additional focus for European social psychology. The *European Journal of Social Psychology* was launched in 1971 and the *European Review of Social Psychology* in 1990 – both are considered among the most prestigious social psychology journals in the world. The EASP is also a partner in publication of the now highly impactful journal *Social Psychological and Personality Science*, launched in 2010.

Textbooks used in Europe have largely been American or, more recently, European adaptations of American books. But there have been notable European texts, probably beginning with Moscovici's *Introduction à la Psychologie Sociale* (1973), followed by Tajfel and Fraser's *Introducing Social Psychology* (1978) and then Moscovici's *Psychologie Sociale* (1984). Aside, of course, from our own – dare we say fabulous – text (first published in 1995 and now in its eighth edition), the most recent other European texts are Hewstone, Stroebe and Jonas's *An Introduction to Social Psychology* (2012), now in its fifth edition; and Sutton and Douglas's *Social Psychology* (2013).

Since the early 1970s, then, European social psychology has undergone a powerful renaissance (Doise, 1982; Jaspars, 1980, 1986). Initially, it self-consciously set itself up in opposition to American social psychology and adopted an explicitly critical stance. However, since the late 1980s, European social psychology, although not discarding its critical orientation, has attained substantial self-confidence and international recognition. Its impact on American social psychology, and thus on international perspectives, is significant and acknowledged (e.g. Hogg & Abrams, 1999). Moreland, Hogg and Hains (1994) documented how an upsurge in research into group processes (as evidenced from publication trends over the previous twenty years in the three major American social psychology journals) was almost exclusively due to European research and perspectives. It is, perhaps, through work on social representations (**Chapter 3**), social identity and intergroup behaviour (**Chapter 11**), minority influence (**Chapter 7**) and, more recently, social cognition (**Chapter 2**) that Europe has had and continues to have its most visible and significant international impact. Now reconsider your response to the third 'What do *you* think?' question posed at the start of this chapter.

Europe is a continent of many languages and a historical diversity of national emphases on different aspects of social psychology: for example, social representations in France, political psychology and small-group processes in Germany, social justice research and social cognition in The Netherlands, social development of cognition in French-speaking Switzerland, goal-oriented action in German-speaking Switzerland, and applied and social constructionist approaches in Scandinavia. A 2010 international benchmarking review of British psychology identified British social psychology as being strongly invested in research on social identity, prejudice and discrimination, attitudes, health behaviour, and discourse analysis and critical psychology. A great deal of research is published in national social psychology journals. However, in recognition of the fact that English is the global language of science, European social psychologists publish in English so that their ideas might have the greatest impact both internationally and within Europe: most major European journals, series and texts publish in English.

Historically, two figures have particularly shaped European social psychology: Henri Tajfel and Serge Moscovici. Tajfel (1974), at the University of Bristol, revolutionised how we think about intergroup relations. His *social identity theory* focused on how a person's identity is grounded in belonging to a group, and how such *social* identity shapes intergroup behaviour. It questioned Sherif's argument that an objective clash of interests was the necessary ingredient for intergroup conflict (**Chapter 11**). Moscovici (1961), at the Maison des

Sciences de l'Homme in Paris, resuscitated an interest in the work of the nineteenth-century sociologist Durkheim with his idea of social representations (**Chapter 3**). In addition, he initiated a radical new interpretation of conformity processes – developing an entirely new focus on how minorities can influence majorities and thus bring about social change (**Chapter 7**).

About this text

We have written this introductory text, now in its eighth edition, to reflect European social psychology as an integral part of contemporary social psychological science. We smoothly integrate American and European research but with an emphasis that is framed by European, not American, scientific and sociohistorical priorities. Students of social psychology in Britain and Europe tend to use a mixture of American and European texts. American texts are comprehensive, detailed and well produced, but are pitched too low for British and European universities, do not cover European topics that well and, quite understandably, are grounded in the day-to-day cultural experiences of Americans. European texts, which are generally edited collections of chapters by different authors, address European priorities but tend to be idiosyncratic, uneven and less well produced, and incomplete in their coverage of social psychology. Our text satisfies the need for a single comprehensive introduction to social psychology for British and European students of social psychology.

Our aim has been to write an introduction to social psychology for undergraduate university students of psychology. Its language caters to intelligent adults. However, since it is an *introduction*, we pay careful attention to accessibility of specialist language (i.e. scientific or social psychological jargon). It is intended to be a comprehensive introduction to mainstream social psychology, with no intentional omissions. We cover classic and contemporary theories and research, generally adopting a historical perspective that most accurately reflects the unfolding of scientific inquiry. The degree of detail and scope of coverage are determined by the scope and intensity of undergraduate social psychology courses in Britain and Europe. We have tried to write a text that combines the most important and enduring features of European and American social psychology. As such, this can be considered an international text, but one that specifically caters for the British and European intellectual, cultural and educational context.

Many social psychology texts separate basic theory and research from applied theory and research, generally by exiling to the end of the book 'applied' chapters that largely address health, organisations, justice or gender. Much like Kurt Lewin's view that there is nothing so practical as a good theory, our philosophy is that basic and applied research and theory are intertwined or best treated as intertwined: they are naturally interdependent. Thus, applied topics are interwoven with basic theory and research. Currently, some significant areas of application of social psychology include human development (e.g. Bennett & Sani, 2004; Durkin, 1995), health (e.g. Rothman & Salovey, 2007; Stroebe, 2011; Taylor, 2003), gender (e.g. Eagly, Beall, & Sternberg, 2005), organisations (e.g. Haslam, 2004; Thompson & Pozner, 2007), law and criminal justice (e.g. Kovera & Borgida, 2010; Tyler & Jost, 2007), political behaviour (e.g. Krosnick, Visser, & Harder, 2010; Tetlock, 2007) and culture (e.g. Heine, 2010, 2016; Smith, Bond, & Kağitçibaşi, 2006). The latter, culture, is now an integral part of contemporary social psychology (**see Chapter 16**); and language and communication (e.g., Holtgraves, 2010), which is central to social psychology but is often treated as an application, has its own chapter (**Chapter 15**).

The text is structured so that Chapters 2 to 5 deal with what goes on in people's heads – cognitive processes and cognitive representations, including how we conceive of ourselves and how our attitudes are structured. Chapter 6 continues the attitude theme but focuses on how attitudes change and how people are persuaded. This leads directly into Chapter 7, which discusses more broadly how people influence one another. Because groups play a key role in social influence, Chapter 7 flows logically into Chapters 8 and 9, which deal with group processes including leadership. Chapters 10 and 11 broaden the discussion of groups to consider what happens between groups – prejudice, discrimination, conflict and intergroup behaviour. The sad fact that intergroup behaviour so often involves conflict invites a discussion of human aggression, which is dealt with in Chapter 12.

Lest we become disillusioned with our species, Chapter 13 discusses how people can be altruistic and can engage in selfless prosocial acts of kindness and support. Continuing the general emphasis on more positive aspects of human behaviour, Chapter 14 deals with interpersonal relations, including attraction, friendship and love, but also with breakdowns in relationships. At the core of interpersonal interaction lies communication, of which spoken language is the richest form: Chapter 15 explores language and communication. Chapter 16 discusses the cultural context of social behaviour – an exploration of cultural differences, cross-cultural universals and the significance of culture in contemporary society.

Each chapter is self-contained, although integrated into the general logic of the entire text. There are plentiful cross-references to other chapters, and at the end of each chapter are references to further, more detailed coverage of topics covered by the chapter. We also suggest classic and contemporary literature, films and TV programmes that deal with subject matter that is relevant to the chapter topic.

Many of the studies referred to in this text can be found in the social psychology journals that we have already noted in the historical section – check new issues of these journals to learn about up-to-date research. In addition, there are three social psychology journals that are dedicated to scholarly state-of-the-art summaries and reviews of topics in social psychology: *Advances in Experimental Social Psychology*, *Personality and Social Psychology Review* and *European Review of Social Psychology*. Topics in social psychology are also covered in general psychology theory and review journals such as *Annual Review of Psychology*, *Psychological Bulletin* and *Psychological Review*.

For a short general introduction to social psychology, see Hogg's (2000a) chapter in Pawlik and Rosenzweig's (2000) *International Handbook of Psychology*. For a stripped-down simple introductory European social psychology text that focuses on only the very essentials of the subject, see Hogg and Vaughan's (2010) *Essentials of Social Psychology*. In contrast, the most authoritative and detailed sources of information about social psychology are undoubtably the current handbooks of social psychology, of which there are four: (1) Fiske, Gilbert and Lindzey's (2010) *Handbook of Social Psychology*, which is currently in its fifth edition; (2) Hogg and Cooper's (2007) *The SAGE Handbook of Social Psychology: Concise Student Edition*; (3) Kruglanski and Higgins's (2007) *Social Psychology: Handbook of Basic Principles*, which is in its second edition; and (4) Hewstone and Brewer's four-volume *Blackwell Handbook of Social Psychology*, each volume of which is a stand-alone book with a different pair of editors: *Intraindividual Processes* by Tesser and Schwartz (2001), *Interpersonal Processes* by Fletcher and Clark (2001), *Group Processes* by Hogg and Tindale (2001) and *Intergroup Processes* by Brown and Gaertner (2001).

A wonderful source of shorter overview pieces is Baumeister and Vohs's (2007) two-volume, 1,020-page *Encyclopedia of Social Psychology* – there are more than 550 entries written by an equal number of the leading social psychologists from around the world. Also keep your eyes out for Hogg's similarly comprehensive but more recent *Oxford Encyclopedia of Social Psychology* that is due to be published in 2017 or 2018. Two other, more topic-specific encyclopedias are Reis and Sprecher's (2009) *Encyclopedia of Human Relationships* and Levine and Hogg's (2010) *Encyclopedia of Group Processes and Intergroup Relations*. Finally, Hogg's (2003) *SAGE Benchmarks in Psychology: Social Psychology* is a four-volume edited and annotated collection of almost 80 benchmark research articles in social psychology – it contains many of the discipline's most impactful classic works. The volumes are divided into sections with short introductions.

Summary

- Social psychology is the scientific investigation of how the thoughts, feelings and behaviour of individuals are influenced by the actual, imagined or implied presence of others. Although social psychology can also be described in terms of what it studies, it is more useful to describe it as a way of looking at human behaviour.

- Social psychology is a science. It employs the scientific method to study social behaviour. Although this involves a variety of empirical methods to collect data to test hypotheses and construct theories, experimentation is usually the preferred method as it is the best way to learn what causes what. Nevertheless, methods are matched to research questions, and methodological pluralism is highly valued.

- Social psychological data are usually transformed into numbers, which are analysed by statistical procedures. Statistics allow conclusions to be drawn about whether a research observation is a true effect or some chance event.

- Social psychology is enlivened by debate over the ethics of research methods, the appropriate research methods for an understanding of social behaviour, the validity and power of social psychology theories, and the type of theories that are properly social psychological.

- Although having origins in nineteenth-century German folk psychology and French crowd psychology, modern social psychology really began in the United States in the 1920s with the adoption of the experimental method. In the 1940s, Kurt Lewin provided significant impetus to social psychology, and the discipline has grown exponentially ever since.

- Despite its European origins, social psychology was quickly dominated by the United States – a process accelerated by the rise of fascism in Europe during the 1930s. However, since the late 1960s, there has been a rapid and sustained renaissance of European social psychology, driven by distinctively European intellectual and sociohistorical priorities to develop a more *social* social psychology with a greater emphasis on collective phenomena and group levels of analysis. European social psychology is now well established as an equal but complementary partner to the United States in social psychological research.

Key terms

Archival research	Evolutionary psychology	Neo-behaviourism
Behaviour	Evolutionary social psychology	Operational definition
Behaviourism	Experimental method	Positivism
Case study	Experimental realism	Radical behaviourist
Cognitive theories	Experimenter effects	Reductionism
Confirmation bias	External validity	Science
Confounding	fMRI	Social neuroscience
Correlation	Hypotheses	Social psychology
Data	Independent variables	Statistical significance
Demand characteristics	Internal validity	Statistics
Dependent variables	Laboratory	Subject effects
Discourse	Level of explanation	*t* test
Discourse analysis	Metatheory	Theory
Double-blind	Mundane realism	*Völkerpsychologie*

Literature, film and TV

The Beach

The 1997 Alex Garland novel (also the 2000 eponymous film starring Leonardo DiCaprio). Backpackers in Thailand drop out to join a group that has set up its own normatively regimented society on a remote island. They are expected to submerge their own identity in favour of the group's identity. This dramatic book engages with many social psychological themes having to do with self and identity, close relationships, norms and conformity, influence and leadership, and conflict and cooperation. The book could be characterised as *Apocalypse Now* (Francis Ford Coppola's legendary 1979 war movie) meets *Lord of the Flies* (William Golding's classic 1954 novel about a group of boys marooned on an island).

War and Peace

Leo Tolstoy's (1869) masterpiece on the impact of society and social history on people's lives. It does a wonderful job of showing how macro- and micro-levels of analysis influence one another, but cannot be resolved into one another. It is a wonderful literary work of social psychology – how people's day-to-day lives are located at the intersection of powerful interpersonal, group and intergroup processes. Other classic novels of Leo Tolstoy, Emile Zola, Charles Dickens and George Eliot accomplish much the same social psychological analysis.

Les Misérables

Victor Hugo's (1862) magnum opus and classic literary masterpiece of the nineteenth century. It explores everyday life and relationships against the background of conventions, institutions and historical events in Paris over a 17-year period (1815–1832). Those of you who enjoy musicals will know that it has been adapted into an eponymous 2012 musical film directed by Tom Hooper and starring Hugh Jackman (as the central character, Jean Valjean), Russell Crowe, Anne Hathaway and Amanda Seyfried.

Gulliver's Travels

Jonathan Swift's 1726 satirical commentary on the nature of human beings. This book is relevant to virtually all the themes in our text. The section on Big-Endians and Little-Endians is particularly relevant to Chapter 11 on intergroup behaviour. Swift provides a hilarious and incredibly full and insightful description of a society that is split on the basis of whether people open their boiled eggs at the big or the little end – relevant to the minimal group studies in Chapter 11 but also to the general theme of how humans can read so much into subtle features of their environment.

Guided questions

1 What do social psychologists study? Can you give some examples of interdisciplinary research?

2 Sometimes experiments are used in social psychological research. Why?

3 What do you understand by levels of explanation in social psychology? What is meant by reductionism?

4 If you or your lecturer were to undertake research in social psychology, you would need to gain ethical approval. Why is this, and what criteria would need to be met?

5 If the shock level 'administered' in Milgram's obedience study had been 150 volts instead of the maximum 450 volts, would this have made the experiment more ethical?

Learn more

Allport, G. W. (1954). The historical background of modern social psychology. In G. Lindzey (Ed.), *Handbook of social psychology* (Vol. 1, pp. 3–56). Reading, MA: Addison-Wesley. Classic and often-cited account of the history of social psychology, covering the formative period up to the 1950s.

Aronson, E., Ellsworth, P. C., Carlsmith, J. M., & Gonzales, M. H. (1990). *Methods of research in social psychology* (2nd ed.). New York: McGraw-Hill. Detailed, well-written and now-classic coverage of research methods in social psychology.

Crano, W. D., & Brewer, M. B. (2015). *Principles and methods of social research* (3rd ed.). New York: Routledge. A detailed but very readable overview of research methods in social psychology.

Dawkins, R. (2011). *The magic of reality: How we know what's really true.* London: Bantam Press. Ethologist and evolutionary biologist Richard Dawkins argues that science does indeed aim to uncover what is real – whether it be an earthquake, a supernova, DNA or the nature of jealousy.

Denzin, N. K., & Lincoln, Y. S. (Eds.) (2011). *The SAGE handbook of qualitative research* (4th ed.). Thousand Oaks, CA: SAGE. This academic bestseller is considered the gold standard for qualitative research methods.

Ellsworth, P. C., & Gonzales, R. (2007). Questions and comparisons: Methods of research in social psychology. In M. A. Hogg & J. Cooper (Eds.), *The SAGE handbook of social psychology: Concise student edition* (pp. 24–42). London: SAGE. A concise and readable overview of how one moves from research question to research itself in social psychology, and how one makes choices about methods.

Farr, R. M. (1996). *The roots of modern social psychology: 1872–1954.* Oxford, UK: Blackwell. A scholarly and provocative discussion of the intellectual roots of modern social psychology. Farr is a renowned historical commentator on social psychology.

Goethals, G. R. (2007). A century of social psychology: Individuals, ideas, and investigations. In M. A. Hogg & J. Cooper (Eds.), *The SAGE handbook of social psychology* (pp. 3–23). London: SAGE. A very readable, comprehensive and inclusive coverage of the history of social psychology.

Howell, D. C. (2010). *Statistical methods for psychology* (8th ed.). Belmont, CA: Duxbury. Highly respected and often-used basic introduction to psychological statistics. With the usual equations and formulae that we all love so much, it is also easy to read.

Jones, E. E. (1998). Major developments in five decades of social psychology. In D. T. Gilbert, S. T. Fiske, & G. Lindzey (Eds.), *The handbook of social psychology* (4th edn, Vol. 1, pp. 3–57). Boston, MA: McGraw-Hill. This treatment recaps and moves on from Allport's (1954) treatment, covering the period from 1935 to 1985. In addition to classical developments, it also covers the growth of research on social comparison, cognitive dissonance, attitude change, conformity, person perception and attribution.

Rosnow, R. L., & Rosenthal, R. (1997). *People studying people: Artifacts and ethics in behavioral research.* New York: Freeman. An introduction to notable biases that can distort research on human behaviour. There is also coverage of ethical issues.

Ross, L., Lepper, M., & Ward, A. (2010). History of social psychology: Insights, challenges, and contributions to theory and application. In S. T. Fiske, D. T. Gilbert, & G. Lindzey (Eds.), *Handbook of social psychology* (5th ed., Vol. 1, pp. 3–50). New York: Wiley. The most recent overview and account of the history of social psychology.

Sansone, C., Morf, C. C., & Panter, A. T. (Eds.) (2004). *The SAGE handbook of methods in social psychology.* Thousand Oaks, CA: SAGE. At over 550 pages and 22 chapters, this is a comprehensive coverage of quantitative and qualitative research methods in social psychology, including discussion of research ethics, programme development, cultural sensitivities, and doing interdisciplinary and applied research.

Tabachnik, B. G., & Fidell, L. S. (2013). *Using multivariate statistics* (6th ed.). Boston, MA: Pearson. The acknowledged 'bible' for doing, interpreting and reporting multivariate statistics in psychology.

Van Lange, P. A. M., Kruglanski, A. W., & Higgins, E. T. (Eds.) (2013). *Handbook of theories of social psychology*. Thousand Oaks, CA: SAGE. All the major theories in social psychology are here, described clearly and concisely by experts in the theory or by the theorists themselves.

Chapter 2
Social cognition and social thinking

Chapter contents

What do *you* think?

1 You have been interviewed for a job. Your possible future boss, Ms Jones, has decided that you are intelligent, sincere and helpful. However, you did not laugh at one of her jokes – she may suspect you don't have a sense of humour! How would she form an overall impression of you?

2 John's hair is multi-coloured and the colours change every couple of weeks. Would others spot him immediately at a student–staff meeting in your psychology department? What about at a board meeting of your capital city's largest accountancy firm?

3 Aaron comes to mind rather differently for Julie and Rosa. Julie remembers him mostly when she thinks of the various lawyers whom she knows. Rosa thinks about his quirky smile and his knowledge of best-selling novels. Why might their memories differ in these ways?

4 During her first, 2008, candidacy for the US presidency, Hillary Clinton once claimed she ran with her head down to escape sniper fire at a Bosnian airport, when in fact she was greeted very peacefully. 'I misremembered,' she later explained. Was she lying, or was her memory unreliable? What affects how accurately eyewitnesses recall events?

Social psychology and cognition

As we learned in Chapter 1, social psychology studies 'how human thought, feeling and behaviour is influenced by and has influence on other people'. Within this definition, thought plays a central role: people think about their social world, and on the basis of thought they act in certain ways. However, when social psychologists talk about thought, they typically use the more technical term 'cognition'. In everyday conversation, we tend to use thought and cognition interchangeably; however, the two terms are used a little differently by social psychologists. *Thought* is the internal language and symbols we use – it is often conscious, or at least something we are or could be aware of. *Cognition* is broader; it also refers to mental processing that can be largely automatic. We are unaware of it and only with some effort notice it, let alone capture it in language or shared symbols. Cognition acts a bit like a computer program or operating system: it operates automatically in the background, running all the functions of the computer.

Cognition and thought occur within the human mind. They are the mental activities that mediate between the world out there and what people subsequently do. Their operation can be inferred from what people do and say – from people's actions, expressions, sayings and writings. If we can understand cognition, we may gain some understanding of how and why people behave the way they do. **Social cognition** is an approach in social psychology that focuses on how cognition is affected by wider and more immediate social contexts and on how cognition affects our social behaviour.

Social cognition
Cognitive processes and structures that influence and are influenced by social behaviour.

During the 1980s, there was an explosion in social cognition research. According to Taylor (1998), during social cognition's heyday 85 per cent of submissions to the *Journal of Personality and Social Psychology*, social psychology's flagship journal, were social cognition articles. Social cognition remains the dominant perspective on the explanation of social behaviour (e.g. Dijksterhuis, 2010; Fiske & Taylor, 2013; Macrae & Quadflieg, 2010; Moskowitz, 2005). It has taught us much about how we process and store information about people, and how this information affects how we perceive and interact with others. It has also taught us new methods and techniques for conducting social psychological research – methods and techniques borrowed from cognitive psychology, and more recently neuroscience (Gazzaniga, Ivry, & Mangun, 2013; Todorov, Fiske, & Prentice, 2011), and then refined for social psychology. Social cognition has had, and continues to have, an enormous impact on social psychology (Devine, Hamilton, & Ostrom, 1994).

A short history of cognition in social psychology

Wilhelm Wundt (1897) was one of the founders of modern empirical psychology. He used self-observation and introspection to gain an understanding of cognition (people's subjective experience), which he believed to be the main purpose of psychology. This methodology became unpopular because it was not scientific. Data and theories were idiosyncratic, and because they were effectively autobiographical, they were almost impossible to refute or generalise.

Because psychologists felt that theories should be based on publicly observable and replicable data, there was a shift away from studying internal (cognitive) events towards external, publicly observable events. The ultimate expression of this change in emphasis was American **behaviourism** of the early twentieth century (e.g. Skinner, 1963; Thorndike, 1940; Watson, 1930) – cognition became a dirty word in psychology for almost half a century. Behaviourists focused on overt behaviour (e.g. a hand wave) as a response to observable stimuli in the environment (e.g. an approaching bus), based on past punishments and rewards for the behaviour (e.g. being picked up by the bus).

Behaviourism
An emphasis on explaining observable behaviour in terms of reinforcement schedules.

By the 1960s, psychologists had begun to take a fresh interest in cognition. This was partly because behaviourism seemed terribly cumbersome and inadequate as an explanation of human language and communication (see Chomsky, 1959); some consideration of how people represent the world symbolically and how they manipulate such symbols was needed. Moreover, the manipulation and transfer of information was beginning to dominate the world: information processing became an increasingly important focus for psychology (Broadbent, 1985; Wyer & Gruenfeld, 1995). This development continued with the computer revolution, which has encouraged and enabled psychologists to model or simulate highly complex human cognitive processes. The computer has also become a metaphor for the human mind, with computer software/programs standing in for cognition. Cognitive psychology, sometimes called cognitive science, re-emerged as a legitimate scientific pursuit (e.g. Anderson, 1990; Neisser, 1967).

In contrast to general psychology, social psychology has almost always been notably cognitive (Manis, 1977; Zajonc, 1980). This emphasis can be traced at least as far back as Kurt Lewin, who is often referred to as the father of experimental social psychology. Drawing on **Gestalt psychology**, Lewin (1951) believed that social behaviour is most usefully understood as a function of people's perceptions of their world and their manipulation of such perceptions. Cognition and thought were placed centre stage in social psychology. The cognitive emphasis in social psychology has had at least four guises (Jones, 1998; Taylor, 1998): cognitive consistency, naive scientist, cognitive miser and motivated tactician.

After the Second World War, in the 1940s and 1950s, there was a frenzy of research on attitude change that produced theories sharing an assumption that people strive for **cognitive consistency**: that is, people are motivated to reduce discrepancies between their various cognitions because such discrepancies are aversive (e.g. Abelson et al., 1968; Festinger, 1957; Heider, 1958; **see also Chapters 5 and 6**). Consistency theories lost some popularity in the 1960s as evidence accumulated that people are actually remarkably tolerant of cognitive inconsistency – however, they are still influential (Gawronski & Strack, 2012).

In its place there arose in the early 1970s a **naive scientist** model; people need to attribute causes to behaviour and events in order to render the world a meaningful place in which to act. This model underpins the **attribution** theories of behaviour that dominated social psychology in the 1970s (**see Chapter 3**). The naive scientist model assumes that people are basically rational in making scientific-like cause–effect analyses. Any errors or biases that creep in are departures from normality that can be traced to limited or inaccurate information and to motivations such as self-interest.

In the late 1970s, however, it became clear that even in ideal circumstances people are not very careful scientists at all. The 'normal' state of affairs is that people are limited in their capacity to process information and take numerous cognitive short-cuts: they are **cognitive misers** (Nisbett & Ross, 1980; Taylor, 1981). The various errors and biases associated with social thinking are not motivated departures from some ideal form of information processing but are intrinsic to social thinking. Motivation is almost completely absent from the cognitive miser perspective. However, as this perspective has matured, the importance of motivation has again become evident (Gollwitzer & Bargh, 1996; Showers & Cantor, 1985) – the social thinker has become characterised as a **motivated tactician**:

> a fully engaged thinker who has multiple cognitive strategies available and chooses among them based on goals, motives, and needs. Sometimes the motivated tactician chooses wisely, in the interests of adaptability and accuracy, and sometimes . . . defensively, in the interests of speed or self-esteem.
>
> Fiske & Taylor (1991, p. 13)

The most recent development in social cognition is **social neuroscience**, sometimes called cognitive neuroscience or social cognitive neuroscience (Harmon-Jones & Winkielman, 2007; Lieberman, 2010; Todorov, Fiske, & Prentice, 2011). Social neuroscience is largely a methodology in which cognitive activity can be monitored by the use of functional Magnetic Resonance Imaging (fMRI), which detects and localises electrical activity in the brain associated with cognitive activities or functions. In this way, different parts of the brain 'light up' when people are, for example, thinking positively or negatively about friends or strangers or

Gestalt psychology
Perspective in which the whole influences constituent parts rather than vice versa.

Cognitive consistency
A model of social cognition in which people try to reduce inconsistency among their cognitions, because they find inconsistency unpleasant.

Naive psychologist (or scientist)
Model of social cognition that characterises people as using rational, scientific-like, cause–effect analyses to understand their world.

Attribution
The process of assigning a cause to our own behaviour, and that of others.

Cognitive miser
A model of social cognition that characterises people as using the least complex and demanding cognitions that are able to produce generally adaptive behaviours.

Motivated tactician
A model of social cognition that characterises people as having multiple cognitive strategies available, which they choose among on the basis of personal goals, motives and needs.

Social neuroscience
Exploration of brain activity associated with social cognition and social psychological processes and phenomena.

social categories, or when they are attributing causality to different behaviours. Social neuroscience is now widely applied to social psychological phenomena – for example, interpersonal processes (Gardner, Gabriel, & Diekman, 2000), attributional inference (Lieberman, Gaunt, Gilbert, & Trope, 2002), prejudice and dehumanisation (Harris & Fiske, 2006), the experience of being socially excluded (Eisenberger, Lieberman, & Williams, 2003) and even religious conviction (Inzlicht, McGregor, Hirsh, & Nash, 2009).

Forming impressions of other people

We are very quick to use personality traits when we describe other people, even those whom we have just met (Gawronski, 2003). People spend an enormous amount of time thinking about other people. We form impressions of the people we meet, have described to us or encounter in the media. We communicate these impressions to others, and we use them as bases for deciding how we will feel and act. Impression formation and person perception are important aspects of social cognition (Schneider, Hastorf, & Ellsworth, 1979). However, the impressions we form are influenced by some pieces of information more than others.

What information is important?

Configural model
Asch's Gestalt-based model of impression formation, in which central traits play a disproportionate role in configuring the final impression.

Central traits
Traits that have a disproportionate influence on the configuration of final impressions, in Asch's configural model of impression formation.

Peripheral traits
Traits that have an insignificant influence on the configuration of final impressions, in Asch's configural model of impression formation.

According to Solomon Asch's (1946) **configural model**, in forming first impressions we latch on to certain pieces of information, called **central traits**, which have a disproportionate influence over the final impression. Other pieces of information, called **peripheral traits**, have much less influence. Central and peripheral traits are ones that are more or less intrinsically correlated with other traits, and therefore more or less useful in constructing an integrated impression of a person. Central traits influence the meanings of other traits and the perceived relationship among traits; that is, they are responsible for the integrated configuration of the impression.

To investigate this idea, Asch had students read one of two lists of seven adjectives describing a hypothetical person (see Figure 2.1). The lists differed only slightly – one contained the word *warm* and the other the word *cold*. Participants then evaluated the target person on a number of other bipolar evaluative dimensions, such as generous/ungenerous, happy/unhappy, reliable/unreliable. Asch found that participants who read the list containing *warm* generated a much more favourable impression of the target than did those who read the list containing the trait *cold*. When the words *warm* and *cold* were replaced by *polite* and *blunt*, the difference in impression was far less marked. Asch argued that warm/cold is a central trait dimension that has more influence on impression formation than polite/blunt, which is a peripheral trait dimension. Subsequent research has confirmed that warmth is indeed a fundamental dimension of social perception and impression formation (Cuddy, Fiske, & Glick, 2008; Fiske, Cuddy, & Glick, 2007; Kervyn, Yzerbyt, & Judd, 2010). Warmth is also closely connected to how a person can become attached to another (Williams & Bargh, 2008; also **see Chapter 14**).

Asch's experiment was replicated in a naturalistic setting by Harold Kelley (1950), who ended his introduction of a guest lecturer with: 'People who know him consider him to be a rather *cold* [or very *warm*] person, *industrious, critical, practical* and *determined*.' The lecturer gave identical lectures to a number of classes, half of which received the *cold* and half the *warm* description. After the lecture, the students rated the lecturer on a number of dimensions. Those who received the *cold* trait rated the lecturer as more *unsociable, self-centred, unpopular, formal, irritable, humourless* and *ruthless*. They were also less likely to ask questions and to interact with the lecturer. This seems to support the Gestalt view that impressions are formed as integrated wholes based on central cues.

However, critics have wondered how people decide that a trait is central. Gestalt theorists believe that the centrality of a trait rests on its intrinsic degree of correlation with other traits.

- Intelligent

- Skilful

- Industrious

- ▪

The empty space
contains either:

Warm or Cold
or
Polite or Blunt

- Determined

- Practical

- Cautious

% assigning additional traits as function of focal trait inserted:

Additional traits	Focal traits inserted in the list			
	Warm	Cold	Polite	Blunt
Generous	91	8	56	58
Wise	65	25	30	50
Happy	90	34	75	65
Good-natured	94	17	87	56
Reliable	94	99	95	100

Figure 2.1 Impressions of a hypothetical person, based on central and peripheral traits

Asch (1946) presented participants with a seven-trait description of a hypothetical person in which either the word **warm** or **cold**, or **polite** or **blunt**, appeared. The percentage of participants assigning other traits to the target was markedly affected when **warm** was replaced by **cold**, but not when **polite** was replaced by **blunt**.

Source: Based on Asch (1946).

Others have argued that centrality is a function of context (e.g. Wishner, 1960; Zanna & Hamilton, 1972). In Asch's experiment, warm/cold was central because it was distinct from the other trait dimensions and was semantically linked to the response dimensions. People tend to employ two main and distinct dimensions for evaluating other people: good/bad social, and good/bad intellectual (Rosenberg, Nelson, & Vivekanathan, 1968), or what Fiske and colleagues call warmth and competence (Cuddy, Fiske, & Glick, 2008; Fiske, Cuddy, & Glick, 2007). Warm/cold is clearly good/bad social, and so are the traits that were used to evaluate the impression (*generous, wise, happy, good-natured, reliable*). However, the other cue traits (*intelligent, skilful, industrious, determined, practical, cautious*) are clearly good/bad intellectual.

Biases in forming impressions

Primacy and recency

The order in which information about a person is presented can dramatically affect the subsequent impression. Asch (1946), in another experiment, used six traits to describe a hypothetical person. For half the participants, the person was described as *intelligent, industrious, impulsive, critical, stubborn* and *envious* (i.e. positive traits first, negative traits last). The order of presentation was reversed for the other group of participants. Asch found a **primacy** effect: the traits presented first disproportionately influenced the final impression, so that the

Primacy
An order of presentation effect in which earlier presented information has a disproportionate influence on social cognition.

person was evaluated more favourably when positive information was presented first than when negative information was presented first. Perhaps early information acts much like central cues, or perhaps people simply pay more attention to earlier information.

Recency
An order of presentation effect in which later presented information has a disproportionate influence on social cognition.

A recency effect can also emerge, where later information has more impact than earlier information. This might happen when you are distracted (e.g. overworked, bombarded with stimuli, tired) or when you have little motivation to attend to someone. Later, when you learn, for example, that you may have to work with this person, you may attend more carefully to cues. However, all other things being equal, primacy effects are more common (Jones & Goethals, 1972) – first impressions really do matter.

Positivity and negativity

In the absence of information to the contrary, people tend to assume the best of others and form a positive impression (Sears, 1983). However, any negative information attracts our attention and looms large in our subsequent impression – we are biased towards negativity (Fiske, 1980). Furthermore, once formed, a negative impression is much more difficult to change in the light of subsequent positive information than is a positive impression in the light of subsequent negative information (e.g. Hamilton & Zanna, 1974). We may be particularly sensitive to negative information for two reasons:

1   The information is unusual and distinctive – unusual, distinctive or extreme information attracts attention (Skowronski & Carlston, 1989).

2   The information indirectly signifies potential danger, so its detection has survival value for the individual and ultimately the species.

Personal constructs and implicit personality theories

Personal constructs
Idiosyncratic and personal ways of characterising other people.

George Kelly (1955) has suggested that individuals develop their own idiosyncratic ways of characterising people. These personal constructs can, for simplicity, be treated as sets of bipolar dimensions. For example, I might consider *humour* the single most important organising principle for forming impressions of people, while you might prefer *intelligence*. We have different personal construct systems and would form different impressions of the same person. Personal constructs develop over time as adaptive forms of person perception and so are resistant to change.

Implicit personality theories
Idiosyncratic and personal ways of characterising other people and explaining their behaviour.

We also develop our own implicit personality theories (Bruner & Tagiuri, 1954; Schneider, 1973; Sedikides & Anderson, 1994), *lay theories of personality* (Plaks, Levy, & Dweck, 2009) or *philosophies of human nature* (Wrightsman, 1964). These are general principles concerning what sorts of characteristics go together to form certain types of personality. For instance, Rosenberg and Sedlak (1972) found that people assumed that intelligent people are also friendly but not self-centred. Implicit personality theories are widely shared within cultures but differ between cultures (Markus, Kitayama, & Heiman, 1996). But, like personal constructs, they are resistant to change and can be idiosyncratically based on personal experiences (Smith & Zárate, 1992).

Physical appearance counts

Although we would probably like to believe that we are way too sophisticated to be swayed in our impressions by mere physical appearance, research suggests this is not so. Because appearance is often the first information we have about people, it is very influential in first impressions, and, as we have seen above, primacy effects are influential in enduring impressions (Park, 1986). This is not necessarily always a bad thing – appearance-based impressions can be surprisingly accurate (Zebrowitz & Collins, 1997). One of the most immediate appearance-based judgements we make is whether we find someone physically attractive or not. Research confirms that we tend to assume that physically attractive people are 'good' (Dion, Berscheid, & Walster, 1972) – they are interesting, warm, outgoing, socially skilled and have what the German poet Friedrich Schiller (1882) called an 'interior beauty, a spiritual and moral beauty'.

Physical attractiveness has a marked impact on affiliation, attraction and love (**see Chapter 14**) but can also affect people's careers. For example, a study by Heilman and Stopeck (1985) found that attractive male executives were considered more able than less attractive male executives. Attractive female executives were considered less able than less attractive female executives; participants suspected that attractive females had been promoted because of their appearance, not their ability (**see Chapter 10**). More specific data come from research on the relationship between height and income and weight and income – in most Western countries, taller men (and to some extent women) and lighter women are considered more attractive. A meta-analysis of forty-five different studies involving 8,500 British and American participants found that someone who is 6 feet (1.83 m) tall earns, on average, nearly $166,000 more during a thirty-year career than someone who is 5 feet 5 inches (1.65 m) – even controlling for gender, age and weight (Judge & Cable, 2004). Another study, of weight (excluding obese weights) and income conducted in Germany and the United States, found that as a woman's weight increased, her income decreased; whereas for men, the relationship was the other way around (Judge & Cable, 2011).

Stereotypes

Impressions of people are also strongly influenced by widely shared assumptions about the personalities, attitudes and behaviours of people based on group membership; for example, ethnicity, nationality, sex, race and class. These are **stereotypes** (discussed in this chapter **and in detail in Chapters 3, 10 and 11**). One of the salient characteristics of people we first meet is their category membership (e.g. ethnicity), and this information generates a stereotype-consistent impression. Haire and Grune (1950) found that people had little difficulty composing a paragraph describing a 'working man' from stereotype-consistent information, but enormous difficulty incorporating one piece of stereotype-inconsistent information – that the man was *intelligent*. Participants ignored the information, distorted it, took a very long time and even promoted the man from worker to supervisor.

Stereotype
Widely shared and simplified evaluative image of a social group and its members.

Social judgeability

People form impressions to make judgements about other people: whether they are mean, friendly, intelligent, helpful and so forth. People are unlikely to form impressions and make judgements if the target is deemed not to be **socially judgeable** in the specific context; that is, if there are social rules (norms, conventions, laws) that proscribe making judgements (Leyens, Yzerbyt, & Schadron, 1992; Yzerbyt, Leyens, & Schadron, 1997; Yzerbyt, Schadron, Leyens, & Rocher, 1994). However, if the target is deemed to be socially judgeable, then judgements are more polarised and are made with greater confidence the more socially judgeable the target is considered to be. One implication is that people will not make stereotype-based judgements if conventions or legislation proscribe such behaviour as 'politically incorrect', but they will readily do so if conventions encourage and legitimise such behaviour.

Social judgeability
Perception of whether it is socially acceptable to judge a specific target.

Cognitive algebra

Impression formation involves the sequential integration of pieces of information about a person (i.e. traits emerging over time) into a complete image. The image is generally evaluative, and so are the pieces of information themselves. Imagine being asked your impression of a person you met at a party. You might answer: 'He seemed very friendly and entertaining – all in all, a nice person.' The main thing we learn from this is that you formed a positive/favourable impression. Impression formation is very much a matter of evaluation, not description. **Cognitive algebra** is an approach to the study of impression formation that focuses on how we assign positive and negative valence to attributes and how we then

Cognitive algebra
Approach to the study of impression formation that focuses on how people combine attributes that have valence into an overall positive or negative impression.

Table 2.1 Forming an impression by summation, averaging or weighted averaging

	Summation All traits weighted 1	Averaging All traits weighted 1	Weighted averaging	
			Potential 'friend' weighting	Potential 'politician' weighting
Initial traits				
Intelligent (+2)			2	3
Sincere (+3)			3	2
Boring (−1)			3	0
Initial impression	+4.0	+1.33	+3.33	+4.00
Revised impression on learning that the person is also *humorous* (+1)	+5.0	+1.25	(weight = 1) +2.75	(weight = 0) +3.00
Final impression on learning that the person is also *generous* (+1)	+6.0	+1.20	(weight = 2) +2.60	(weight = 1) +2.60

combine these pluses and minuses into a general evaluation (Anderson, 1965, 1978, 1981). There are three principal models of cognitive algebra: summation, averaging and weighted averaging (see Table 2.1).

Summation

Summation refers to a process where the overall impression is the cumulative sum of each piece of information. Say that we have a mental rating scale that goes from −3 (very negative) to +3 (very positive), and that we assign values to specific traits such as *intelligent* (+2), *sincere* (+3) and *boring* (−1). If we met someone who had these characteristics, our overall impression would be the sum of the constituents: $(+2 + 3 − 1) = +4$ (see Table 2.1). If we now learn that the person was *humorous* (+1), our impression would improve to +5. It would improve to +6 if we then learn that the person was also *generous* (+1). Every bit of information counts, so to project a favourable impression, you should present every facet of yourself that was positive, even marginally positive. In this example, you would be wise to conceal the fact that you were *boring*; your impression on others would now be $(+2 + 3 + 1 + 1) = +7$.

Averaging

Averaging
A method of forming positive or negative impressions by averaging the valence of all the constituent attributes.

Averaging is a process where the overall impression is the cumulative average of each piece of information. So, from the previous example, our initial impression would be $(+2 + 3 − 1)/3 = +1.33$ (see Table 2.1). The additional information that the person was *humorous* (+1) would actually worsen the impression to +1.25: $(+2 + 3 − 1 + 1)/4 = +1.25$. It would deteriorate further to +1.20 with the information that the person was *generous* (+1): $(+2 + 3 − 1 + 1 + 1)/5 = +1.20$. So, to project a favourable impression, you should present only your single very best facet. In this example, you would be wise to present yourself as sincere, and nothing else; your impression on others would now be +3.

Weighted averaging

Weighted averaging
Method of forming positive or negative impressions by first weighting and then averaging the valence of all the constituent person attributes.

Although research favours the averaging model, it has some limitations. The valence of separate pieces of information may not be fixed but may depend on the context of the impression-formation task. Context may also influence the relative importance of pieces of information and thus weight them in different ways in the impression. These considerations led to the development of a **weighted averaging** model. For example (see Table 2.1), if the target person was being assessed as a potential friend, we might assign relative weights to *intelligent, sincere* and *boring* of 2, 3 and 3. The weighted average would be +3.33: $((+2 \times 2) + (+3 \times 3) + (−1 \times 3))/3 = +3.33$.

Making an impression
She really wants this job and has been short-listed for interview. Should she highlight ALL of her positive qualities or just the very best?

If the person was being assessed as a potential politician, we might assign weights of 3, 2 and 0 to arrive at a weighted average of +4: $((+2 \times 3) + (+3 \times 2) + (-1 \times 0))/3 = +4.00$. Table 2.1 shows how additional information with different weighting might affect the overall impression. (Refer to the first 'What do *you* think' question at the beginning of this chapter. Suggest different ways that Ms Jones might form her overall impression of you.)

Weights reflect the perceived importance of pieces of information in a particular impression-formation context. They may be determined in a number of ways. For instance, we have seen that negative information (e.g. Kanouse & Hanson, 1972) and earlier information (the primacy effect, discussed above) may be weighted more heavily. Paradoxically, we may now have come full circle to Asch's central traits. The weighted averaging model seems to allow for something like central traits, which are weighted more heavily in impression formation than are other traits. The difference between Asch and the weighted averaging perspective is that for the latter, central traits are simply more salient and heavily weighted information; while for Asch, central traits actually influence the meaning of surrounding traits and reorganise the entire way we view the person. Asch's perspective retains the descriptive or qualitative aspect of traits and impressions, whereas cognitive algebra focuses only on quantitative aspects and suffers accordingly.

More recent developments in social cognition have tended to supplant central traits with the more general concept of cognitive schema (Fiske & Taylor, 2013), and with the more modern idea that warmth and competence are perennially central organising principles in social perception (Cuddy, Fiske, & Glick, 2008; Fiske, Cuddy & Glick, 2007). Warmth and competence evaluations can have quite textured effects – for example, in the case of competence, future competence (potential) may attract more favourable evaluations and outcomes than past competence (achievement) (Tormala, Jia, & Norton, 2012).

Social schemas and categories

A **schema** is a 'cognitive structure that represents knowledge about a concept or type of stimulus, including its attributes and the relations among those attributes' (Fiske & Taylor, 1991, p. 98). It is a set of interrelated cognitions (e.g. thoughts, beliefs, attitudes) that allows us quickly to make sense of a person, situation, event or location on the basis of limited information. Certain cues activate a schema. The schema then 'fills in' missing details.

For example, imagine you are visiting Paris. Most of us have a place schema about Paris, a rich repertoire of knowledge about what one does when in Paris – sauntering along

Schema
Cognitive structure that represents knowledge about a concept or type of stimulus, including its attributes and the relations among those attributes.

boulevards, sitting in parks, sipping coffee at pavement cafés, browsing through bookshops or eating at restaurants. The reality of life in Paris is obviously more gritty and diverse, yet this schema helps you interpret events and guide choices about how to behave. While in Paris you might visit a restaurant. Arrival at a restaurant might invoke a 'restaurant schema', which is a set of assumptions about what ought to take place (e.g. someone ushers you to a table, you study the menu, someone takes your order, you eat, talk and drink, you pay the bill, you leave). An event schema such as this is called a **script** (see the section 'Scripts' below). While at the restaurant, your waiter may have a rather unusual accent that identifies him as English – this would engage a whole set of assumptions about his attitudes and behaviour. A schema about a social group, particularly if it is widely shared, is a stereotype (**Chapters 10, 11 and 15**).

Once invoked, schemas facilitate top-down, concept-driven or theory-driven processing, as opposed to bottom-up or data-driven processing (Rumelhart & Ortony, 1977). We tend to fill in gaps with prior knowledge and preconceptions rather than seek information gleaned directly from the immediate context. The concept of cognitive schema first emerged in research by Bartlett (1932) on non-social memory, which focused on how memories are actively constructed and organised to facilitate understanding and behaviour. It also has a precedent in Asch's (1946) *configural model* of impression formation (discussed earlier in this chapter), Heider's (1958) *balance theory* of person perception (**see Chapters 3 and 5**) and, more generally, in Gestalt psychology (Brunswik, 1956; Koffka, 1935). These approaches all assume that simplified and holistic cognitive representations of the social world act as relatively enduring templates for the interpretation of stimuli and the planning of action.

The alternative to a schema approach is one in which perception is treated as an unfiltered, veridical representation of reality (e.g. Mill, 1869); impression formation is, as discussed earlier, the cognitive algebra of trait combination (e.g. Anderson, 1981); and memory is laid down passively through the repetitive association of stimuli (e.g. Ebbinghaus, 1885).

Types of schemas

There are many types of schemas. They all influence encoding (internalisation and interpretation) of new information, memory of old information and inferences about missing information. The most common schemas, some of which have been used as examples above, are person schemas, role schemas, event schemas or scripts, content-free schemas and self-schemas.

Person schemas

Person schemas are knowledge structures about specific individuals. For example, you may have a person schema about your best friend (e.g. that she is kind and intelligent but is silent in company and would rather frequent cafés than go mountain-biking), or about a specific politician, a well-known author or a next-door neighbour.

Role schemas

Role schemas are knowledge structures about role occupants: for example, airline pilots (they fly the plane and should not be seen swigging whisky in the cabin) and doctors (although often complete strangers, they are allowed to ask personal questions and get you to undress). Although role schemas apply to **roles** (i.e. types of function or behaviour in a group; **see Chapter 8**), they can sometimes be better understood as schemas about social groups, in which case if such schemas are shared, they are social stereotypes (**Chapters 10 and 11**).

Scripts

Schemas about events are generally called scripts (Abelson, 1981; Schank & Abelson, 1977). We have scripts for attending a lecture, going to the cinema, having a party, giving a presentation or eating out in a restaurant. For example, people who often go to football matches

Script
A schema about an event.

Roles
Patterns of behaviour that distinguish between different activities within the group, and that interrelate to one another for the greater good of the group.

have a very clear script for what happens both on and off the pitch. This makes the entire event meaningful. Imagine how you would fare if you had never been to a football match and had never heard of football (**see Box 3.2 in Chapter 3**, which describes one such scenario). It is the lack of relevant scripts that often causes the feelings of disorientation, frustration and lack of efficacy encountered by sojourners in foreign cultures (e.g. new immigrants; **see Chapter 16**).

Content-free schemas

Content-free schemas do not contain rich information about a specific category but rather a limited number of rules for processing information. Content-free schemas might specify that if you like John and John likes Tom, then, in order to maintain balance, you should also like Tom (see balance theory, Heider, 1958; **discussed in Chapter 6**). Or, they might specify how to attribute a cause to someone's behaviour (e.g. Kelley's (1972b) idea of causal schemata, **discussed in Chapter 3**).

Self-schemas

Finally, people have schemas about themselves. They represent and store information about themselves in a similar but more complex and varied way than information about others. Self-schemas form part of people's concept of who they are, the self-concept; they are **discussed in Chapter 4**, which deals with self and identity.

Categories and prototypes

To apply schematic knowledge, you first need to categorise a person, event or situation as fitting a particular schema. Building on early work by the philosopher Ludwig Wittgenstein (1953), cognitive psychologists believe that people cognitively represent categories as **fuzzy sets** of attributes called **prototypes**, and that instances of the category have a

Fuzzy sets
Categories are considered to be fuzzy sets of features organised around a prototype.

Prototype
Cognitive representation of the typical/ideal defining features of a category.

Categories as fuzzy sets
What is a university lecturer? Hmm. Well, how much do I know about him? Or her? Let me check *Box 2.1 Your life* for some clues.

Family resemblance
Defining property of
category membership.

family resemblance to one another and to the category prototype (e.g. Cantor & Mischel, 1977, 1979; Mervis & Rosch, 1981; Rosch, 1978). Instances within a category are not identical but differ in varying degree from one another and from the prototype, which is the standard against which family resemblance is assessed and category membership decided (see Box 2.1).

Consider the category *concert* – concerts vary enormously in music (heavy metal, classical quartet), venue (open field, concert hall), audience size (small pub, Glastonbury festival), duration (couple of hours, many days) and so forth, but they do have a distinctive family resemblance to one another and to a prototype that is a fuzzy set of attributes rather than a list of criterial attributes (even the fact that that there is music is not a defining attribute – operas, ballets and even lifts also have music).

Although prototypes can represent the average/typical category member, this may not always be the case (Chaplin, John, & Goldberg, 1988). Under some circumstances, the prototype may be the typical member (e.g. the typical environmentalist), while under other circumstances, the prototype may be an extreme member (the most radical environmentalist). Extreme prototypes may prevail when social categories are in competition (e.g. environmentalists versus developers): this analysis is used to explain how people conform to more extreme or polarised group norms (e.g. Abrams, Wetherell, Cochrane, Hogg, & Turner, 1990; Gaffney, Rast, Hackett, & Hogg, 2014; see Chapter 7).

Categories are organised hierarchically – less inclusive categories (few members and attributes) are nested beneath/within more inclusive categories (more members and more attributes); see Figure 2.2. Generally, people rely on intermediate-level categories more than very inclusive or very exclusive categories. These basic-level categories are neither too broad nor too narrow; they are what Brewer calls optimally distinctive (Brewer, 1991; Leonardelli, Pickett, & Brewer, 2010). For instance, most of us are more likely to identify something as a car than as a vehicle (too inclusive) or a BMW convertible (too exclusive).

Basic-level categories are the default option, but they may not actually be that common in social perception, where contextual and motivational factors dominate the choice of level of

Box 2.1 Your life
Categories are fuzzy sets organised around prototypes

Here is a short exercise to illustrate the nature of categories as fuzzy sets:

1 Consider the category 'university lecturer'. Whatever comes immediately to mind is your prototype of a university lecturer – most likely it will be a set of characteristics and images.

2 Keep this in mind, or write it down. You may find this more difficult than you anticipated – prototypes can become frustratingly nebulous and imprecise when you try to document them.

3 Now picture all the university lecturers you can think of. These will be lecturers who have taught you in large lecture halls or small classes, lecturers you have met after classes, in their offices, or lecturers just seen lurking around your psychology department. Also include lecturers whom you have read about in books and newspapers, or seen in movies or on television.

These are all instances of the category 'university lecturer'.

4 Which of these instances is most prototypical? Do any fit the prototype perfectly, or are they all more or less prototypical? Which of these instances is least prototypical? Is any so non-prototypical that it has hardly any family resemblance to the rest? You should discover that there is an enormous range of prototypicality (the category is relatively diverse, a fuzzy set containing instances that have family resemblance) and that no instance fits the prototype exactly (the prototype is a cognitive construction).

5 Finally, compare your prototype with those of your classmates. You may discover a great deal of similarity; your prototype is shared among students. Prototypes of social groups (e.g. lecturers) that are shared by members of a social group (e.g. students) can be considered social stereotypes.

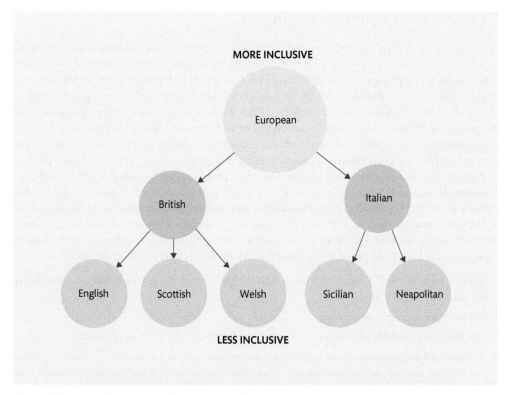

Figure 2.2 Categories organised by level of inclusiveness
Categories are organised hierarchically so that less inclusive (smaller) categories are nested beneath more inclusive (larger) categories.

categorization (Brewer, 1991; Cantor & Kihlstrom, 1987; Hampson, John, & Goldberg, 1986; Turner, 1985).

In addition to representing categories as abstractions (i.e. prototypes), people may represent categories in terms of specific concrete instances they have encountered (i.e. **exemplars**; Smith & Zárate, 1992). For example, Europeans may represent the category 'American' in terms of Barack Obama, or perhaps Donald Trump.

To categorise new instances, people sometimes use exemplars rather than prototypes as the standard. Brewer (1988) suggests that as people become more familiar with a category, they shift from prototypical to exemplar representation, and Judd and Park (1988; see also Klein, Loftus, Trafton, & Fuhrman, 1992) suggest that people use both prototypes and exemplars to represent groups to which they belong, but only exemplars to represent outgroups. Social psychologists are still not certain about the conditions of use of prototypes versus exemplars (Fiske & Neuberg, 1990; Linville, Fischer, & Salovey, 1989; Park & Hastie, 1987), or about the advisability of blurring the distinction between abstraction-based prototypes and instance-based exemplars in so-called 'blended' models of category representation (Hamilton & Sherman, 1994).

As well as representing categories as prototypes or as exemplars, we can also represent them as **associative networks** of attributes such as traits, beliefs or behaviour that are linked emotionally, causally or by mere association (e.g. Wyer & Carlston, 1994).

Once a person, event or situation is categorized, a schema is invoked. Schemas and prototypes are similar and indeed are often used interchangeably. One way to distinguish them is through how they are organised. Prototypes are relatively nebulous, unorganised fuzzy representations of a category; schemas are highly organised specifications of features and their interrelationships (Wyer & Gordon, 1984).

Exemplars
Specific instances of a member of a category.

Associative network
Model of memory in which nodes or ideas are connected by associative links along which cognitive activation can spread.

Categorization and stereotyping

Stereotypes are widely shared generalisations about members of a social group (Leyens, Yzerbyt, & Schadron, 1994; Macrae, Stangor, & Hewstone, 1996). They are essentially schemas of social groups; simplified images that are often derogatory when applied to out-groups and are often based on, or create, clearly visible differences between groups (e.g. in terms of physical appearance; Zebrowitz, 1996). Box 2.2 describes a study by Linssen and Hagendoorn (1994) of Europeans' stereotypes of northern and southern European nations. In another study, of central and eastern European nations, Poppe and Linssen (1999) showed that geographical features become attached in an evaluative way to national stereotypes.

Stereotypes and stereotyping are central aspects of prejudice and discrimination (**see Chapter 10**) and of intergroup behaviour as a whole (**see Chapter 11**). First described scientifically by Walter Lippman (1922), stereotypes were treated as simplified mental images that act as templates to help to interpret the bewildering diversity of the social world. Decades of research on the content and form of stereotypes have produced a number of clear findings (Brigham, 1971; Katz & Braly, 1933; Oakes, Haslam, & Turner, 1994; Tajfel, 1978):

- People are remarkably ready to characterise large human groups in terms of a few fairly crude common attributes.
- Stereotypes are slow to change.
- Stereotypes generally change in response to wider social, political or economic changes.
- Stereotypes are acquired at an early age, often before the child has any knowledge about the groups that are being stereotyped (but other research suggests that some stereotypes crystallise later in childhood, after age 10; Rutland, 1999).
- Stereotypes become more pronounced and hostile when there is social tension and conflict between groups, and then they are extremely difficult to modify.
- Stereotypes are not inaccurate or wrong; rather, they serve to make sense of particular intergroup relations.

Perceptual accentuation

Although stereotypes have usually been thought to be associated with social categories (e.g. Allport, 1954b; Ehrlich, 1973), it was Henri Tajfel (1957, 1959) who first specified how the *process* of categorization might be responsible for stereotyping. Tajfel reasoned that in making judgements on some focal dimension, people rely on any other peripheral dimension

---

Box 2.2 Research highlight
Students' stereotypes of northern and southern European nations

During December 1989 and January 1990, Hub Linssen and Louk Hagendoorn (1994) distributed a questionnaire to 277 sixteen-and eighteen-year-old school pupils in Denmark, England, The Netherlands, Belgium, Germany, France and Italy. The pupils indicated what percentage of each national group they thought had each of twenty-two characteristics. These characteristics clustered into four general dimensions:

1 **dominant** – e.g. proud, assertive, aggressive;
2 **efficient** – e.g. industrious, scientific, rich;

3 **empathic** – e.g. helpful, friendly;
4 **emotional** – e.g. enjoying life, religious.

There was a sharp north/south distinction, with southern European nations being considered more emotional and less efficient than northern European nations. These stereotypes were independent of other differences between northern and southern European nations (e.g. size, political power, social organisation).

Source: Based on Linssen and Hagendoorn (1994).

that might help (see also Bruner & Goodman, 1947). This is an absolutely basic feature of how the mind makes sense of the world. For example, if a red wine is coloured white or a white wine coloured red (using a tasteless and odourless colouring agent), then people use the colour of the wine to help them judge the taste – they report they are tasting a white or red wine, respectively (Goode, 2016).

Another example: if you had to judge the length of a series of lines (focal dimension), and you knew that all lines labelled A were bigger than all lines labelled B (peripheral dimension), then you might use these labels to help your judgement. Tajfel and Wilkes (1963) tested this idea. They had participants judge the length of a series of lines presented one at a time, a number of times and in varying order. There were three conditions: (1) the lines were randomly labelled A or B; (2) all the shorter lines were labelled A and all the longer ones B and (3) there were no labels. Participants appeared to use the information in the second condition to aid judgement and tended to underestimate the average length of A-type lines and overestimate the average length of B-type lines. The relevance of this experiment to social stereotyping becomes clear if, for example, you substitute singing ability for line length and Welsh/English for the A/B labels. Because people might believe that the Welsh sing particularly beautifully (i.e. a social stereotype exists), the categorization of people as Welsh or English produces a perceptual distortion on the focal dimension of singing ability: that is, categorization produces stereotyping.

This, and a number of other experiments with physical and social stimuli (see Doise, 1978; Eiser, 1986; Eiser & Stroebe, 1972; McGarty & Penny, 1988; McGarty & Turner, 1992; Taylor, Fiske, Etcoff, & Ruderman, 1978; Tajfel, 1981a), have confirmed Tajfel's (1957, 1959) **accentuation principle**:

- The categorization of stimuli produces a perceptual accentuation of intra-category similarities and inter-category differences on dimensions believed to be correlated with the categorization.
- The accentuation effect is enhanced where the categorization has importance, relevance or value to the participant.

A third condition can be added. Research by Corneille, Klein, Lambert and Judd (2002) has shown that the accentuation effect is most pronounced when people are uncertain about the dimension of judgement. Accentuation was greater for Belgians making length judgements in inches and Americans making length judgements in centimetres (unfamiliar units), than Belgians using centimetres and Americans using inches (familiar units).

The accentuation principle lies at the core of Tajfel's work on intergroup relations and group membership, which has fed into the subsequent development by John Turner and his associates of **social identity theory** and **self-categorization theory** (e.g. Hogg & Abrams, 1988; Tajfel & Turner, 1986; Turner, 1982; Turner, Hogg, Oakes, Reicher, & Wetherell, 1987; also see Abrams & Hogg, 2010; Hogg, 2006); these theories are described in **Chapter 11**. However, Tajfel (1981a) felt that although categorization might account for the process of stereotyping as a context-dependent perceptual distortion of varying strength, it could not explain the origins of specific stereotypes about specific groups.

Beyond accentuation

Stereotypes are not only consensual beliefs held by members of one group about members of another group; they are also more general *theories* (Von Hippel, Sekaquaptewa, & Vargas, 1995) or social representations (Farr & Moscovici, 1984; Lorenzi-Cioldi & Clémence, 2001; **see also Chapters 3 and 5**) of the attributes of other groups. To flesh out our understanding of stereotypes, we may need to go beyond cognitive processes alone and:

- re-incorporate analysis of the content of specific stereotypes (Hamilton, Stroessner, & Driscoll, 1994) (see Box 2.3),
- understand how stereotypes are formed, represented and used in language and communication (Maass, 1999; Maass & Arcuri, 1996), and

Accentuation principle
Categorization accentuates perceived similarities within and differences between groups on dimensions that people believe are correlated with the categorization. The effect is amplified where the categorization and/or dimension has subjective importance, relevance or value.

Social identity theory
Theory of group membership and intergroup relations based on self-categorization, social comparison and the construction of a shared self-definition in terms of ingroup-defining properties.

Self-categorization theory
Turner and associates' theory of how the process of categorizing oneself as a group member produces social identity and group and intergroup behaviours.

Box 2.3 Research highlight
Analysis of the content of stereotypes provides evidence of different kinds of prejudice

Susan Fiske and her colleagues argue in their *stereotype content model* that social perception is organised along two distinct dimensions, warmth (or sociability) and competence (Cuddy, Fiske, & Glick, 2008; Fiske, Cuddy, & Glick, 2007; Fiske, Cuddy, Glick, & Xu, 2002; Fiske, Xu, Cuddy, & Glick, 1999) – people, and thus the social groups they belong to, can be viewed positively as warm and competent, negatively as cold and incompetent, or ambivalently as warm and incompetent or cold and competent.

Ambivalent outgroup stereotypes are quite common. *Paternalistic prejudice* occurs when a group is viewed as incompetent but warm – the group may be liked but not respected. For example, stereotypes of African Americans may derogate them as incompetent but at the same time compliment them as being athletic, musical and rhythmic (Czopp & Monteith, 2006). Likewise, stereotypes of women can characterise them negatively as incompetent but positively as nurturing and attractive (as measured by the Ambivalent Sexism Inventory) – this is called *benevolent sexism* as it evokes protectiveness in males who subscribe to traditional sex role stereotypes (Glick & Fiske, 1996; **see the discussion of sexism in Chapter 10**).

Envious prejudice occurs when a group is viewed as cold but competent – the group may be respected and admired but not liked. For example, stereotypes of Jews may derogate them for being greedy but admire them for being clever (Glick, 2002), and stereotypes of Asian Americans (measured by a Scale of Anti-Asian American Stereotypes) may admire them for being intelligent and industrious but dislike them for being unsociable outside their family network (Lin, Kwan, Cheung, & Fiske, 2005).

Nicolas Kervyn and his colleagues (Kervyn, Yzerbyt, & Judd, 2010) have also identified an intriguing compensation effect involving the warmth and competence dimensions. When people judge two targets (individuals or groups) and they think of one target more positively on, say, the competence dimension, they are then likely to judge the other target more positively on the warmth dimension. They give this example:

> In college, students who work diligently and get straight As are seen as nerds. Everyone tries to copy their notes and summaries but no one invites them to parties. In sharp contrast, a girl who is on the cheerleading squad will be invited to at least three different parties every Friday night, but she will have a hard time finding a group to work with for her major assignment.
>
> Kervyn, Yzerbyt and Judd (2010, pp. 155–156)

- consider the social functions of stereotypes and the sociohistorical context of relations between groups (Tajfel, 1981a; see also Hogg & Abrams, 1988; Leyens, Yzerbyt, & Schadron, 1994; Oakes, Haslam, & Turner, 1994) – this idea is pursued **in Chapters 3 and 11**.

Although stereotypes have inertia, they are not static. They respond to social context and to people's motives. Immediate or enduring changes in social context (e.g. whom one compares oneself with, and for what purpose) affect the nature of the stereotype and how it is expressed (e.g. Oakes, Haslam, & Turner, 1994). Generally speaking, stereotypes persist if they are readily accessible to us in memory (probably because we use them a great deal and they are self-conceptually important) and they seem to make good sense of people's attitudes and behaviour (i.e. they neatly fit 'reality'). Changes in accessibility or fit will change the stereotype.

Motivation plays an important role because stereotypical thinking serves multiple purposes. In addition to helping with cognitive parsimony and the reduction of self-uncertainty (Hogg, 2007b, 2012), stereotypes can clarify social roles (Eagly, 1995), power differentials (Fiske, 1993b) and intergroup conflicts (Robinson, Keltner, Ward, & Ross, 1995), and they can justify the status quo (Jost & Banaji, 1994; Jost & Kramer, 2002; Jost & Van der Toorn, 2012) or contribute to a positive sense of ingroup identity (Hogg & Abrams, 1988).

How we use, acquire and change schemas

Using schemas

People, situations and events possess so many features that it may not be immediately obvious which features will be used as a basis of categorization and, consequently, which schemas will apply (see Figure 2.3). For instance, Carla is a British female Catholic from Aberdeen who is witty, well read, not very sporty and works as an engineer. What determines which cues serve as a basis for categorization and schema use?

Because people rely on basic-level categories that are neither too inclusive nor too exclusive (Mervis & Rosch, 1981; Rosch, 1978; see the previous section), they initially access subtypes rather than superordinate or subordinate categories (e.g. career woman, not woman or lawyer; Ashmore, 1981; Pettigrew, 1981), and they access social stereotypes and role schemas rather than trait schemas (e.g. politician, not intelligent). People are also more likely to use schemas that are cued by easily detected features, such as skin colour, dress or physical appearance (Brewer & Lui, 1989; Zebrowitz, 1996), or features that are distinctive in a particular context, such as a single man in a group of women. Accessible schemas that are habitually used or salient in memory (Bargh, Lombardi, & Higgins, 1988; Bargh & Pratto, 1986; Wyer & Srull, 1981), and schemas that are relevant to oneself in that context, are more likely to be invoked. So, for example, a racist (someone for whom race is important, salient in memory and habitually used to process person information) would tend to use racial schemas more than someone who was not racist. Finally, people tend to cue mood-congruent schemas (Erber, 1991) and schemas that are based on earlier rather than later information (i.e. a primacy effect; see earlier in this chapter).

These fairly automatic schema-cueing processes are functional and accurate enough for immediate interactive purposes. They have *circumscribed accuracy* (Swann, 1984). Sometimes, however, people need to use more accurate schemas that correspond more

Commonly used schemas
Social settings can invoke many schemas. Is a Mother someone who is in the home, playing with a chlid, and perhaps thinking about cooking dinner? Or maybe she is doing something rather dangerous - like climbing big rocks!

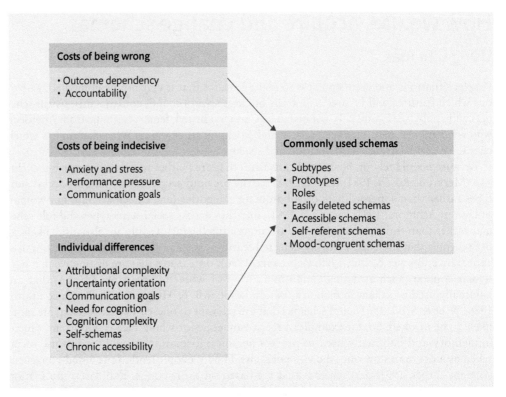

Figure 2.3　Some major influences on commonly used schemas

Some schemas are more commonly used than others, and their use is influenced by a range of individual and information-processing factors.

closely to the data at hand, in which case there is a shift from theory-driven cognition towards data-driven cognition (Fiske, 1993a; see Figure 2.3). If the costs of being wrong are increased, people are more attentive to data and may use more accurate schemas.

The costs of being wrong can be important where people's outcomes (i.e. rewards and punishments) depend on the actions or attitudes of others (Erber & Fiske, 1984; Neuberg & Fiske, 1987). Under these circumstances, people probe for more information, attend more closely to data, particularly to schema-inconsistent information, and generally attend more carefully to other people. The costs of being wrong can also be important where people need to explain or justify their decisions or actions. Under these circumstances, there is greater vigilance and attention to data and generally more complex cognition, which may improve accuracy (Tetlock & Boettger, 1989; Tetlock & Kim, 1987).

If the costs of being indecisive are high, people tend to make a quick decision or form a quick impression; indeed, any decision or impression, however inaccurate, may be preferable to no decision or impression, so people rely heavily on schemas. Performance pressure (i.e. making a judgement or performing a task with insufficient time) can increase schema use. For example, in one study, time pressure caused men and women with conservative sex-role attitudes to discriminate against female job applicants and women with more progressive sex-role attitudes to discriminate against male applicants (Jamieson & Zanna, 1989).

Distraction and anxiety can also increase the perceived cost of indecisiveness and cause people to become more reliant on schematic processing (Wilder & Shapiro, 1989). When one has the task of communicating information to others (e.g. formal presentations), it becomes more important to be well organised, decisive and clear, and thus it is more important to rely on schemas (Higgins, 1981). This may particularly be the case when one is communicating about something technical (scientific mode) rather than telling a story that requires rich description and characterisation (narrative mode) (Zukier, 1986).

People can be aware that schematic processing is inaccurate, and in the case of schemas of social groups undesirable, because it may invoke derogatory stereotypes. Consequently, they can deliberately try not to be over-reliant on schemas. Although this can have some success, it is often rather insignificant against the background of the processes described in this chapter (Ellis, Olson, & Zanna, 1983). However, there are some *individual differences* that may influence the degree and type of schema use:

- *Attributional complexity* – people vary in the complexity of their explanations of other people (Fletcher, Danilovics, Fernandez, Peterson, & Reeder, 1986).

- *Uncertainty orientation* – people vary in their interest in gaining information versus remaining uninformed but certain (Sorrentino & Roney, 1999).

- *Need for cognition* – people differ in how much they like to think deeply about things (Cacioppo & Petty, 1982).

- *Need for cognitive closure* – people differ in how quickly they need to tidy up cognitive loose ends and move to a decision or make a judgement (Kruglanski & Webster, 1996).

- *Cognitive complexity* – people differ in the complexity of their cognitive processes and representations (Crockett, 1965).

People also differ in the sorts of schema they have about themselves (Markus, 1977; see earlier in this chapter). In general, attributes that are important in our self-schema are also important in the schematic perception of others (Markus, Smith, & Moreland, 1985). Individual differences in the chronic **accessibility** (i.e. frequent use, ease of remembering) of schemas can also quite obviously impact schema use for perceiving others. For instance, Battisch, Assor, Messé and Aronoff (1985) conducted a programme of research showing that people differ in terms of their habitual orientations to others in social interaction (some being more dominant and controlling, some more dependent and reliant), and that this influences schematic processing.

Accessibility
Ease of recall of categories or schemas that we already have in mind.

Two types of schema that have been extensively researched, and on which people differ, are gender and political schemas. People tend to differ in terms of the traditional or conservative nature of their gender or sex-role schemas (Bem, 1981), and this influences the extent to which they perceive others as being more or less masculine or feminine (**see Chapter 10**). Political schemas appear to rest on political expertise and knowledge, and their use predicts rapid encoding, focused thought and relevant recall (Fiske, Lau, & Smith, 1990; Krosnick, 1990).

Acquiring schemas

We can acquire schemas second-hand: for example, you might have a lecturer schema based only on what you have been told about lecturers. In general, however, schemas are constructed, or at least modified, from encounters with category instances (e.g. exposure to individual lecturers in literature, the media or face-to-face). *Schema acquisition* and *development* involve a number of processes:

- Schemas become more abstract, less tied to concrete instances, as more instances are encountered (Park, 1986).

- Schemas become richer and more complex as more instances are encountered: greater experience with a particular person or event produces a more complex schema of that person or event (Linville, 1982).

- With increasing complexity, schemas also become more tightly organised: there are more and more complex links between schematic elements (McKiethen, Reitman, Rueter, & Hirtle, 1981).

- Increased organisation produces a more compact schema, one that resembles a single mental construct that can be activated in an all-or-nothing manner (Schul, 1983).

- Schemas become more resilient – they are better able to incorporate exceptions rather than disregard them because they might threaten the validity of the schema (Fiske & Neuberg, 1990).

- All things being equal, this entire process should make schemas generally more accurate, in the sense of accurately mapping social reality.

Changing schemas

Because schemas *appear* to be accurate, they impart a sense of order, structure and coherence to a social world that would otherwise be highly complex and unpredictable. Because of this, schemas do not easily change (Crocker, Fiske, & Taylor, 1984). People are very resistant to information that undermines a schema: they generally disregard the information or reinterpret it. For example, Ross, Lepper and Hubbard (1975) allowed participants to form impressions of a target individual on the basis of information that the target made good decisions or poor decisions (getting either 24 or 10 items correct out of a total of 25). Although participants were then told that the information was false, they maintained their impressions – predicting that, on average on a subsequent task, the target would get 19 or 14.5 items correct.

Trial lawyers in the United States take advantage of this. They introduce inadmissible evidence, which the judge immediately instructs the jury to disregard. But, of course, an impression formed from inadmissible evidence will not vanish just because the judge has instructed jurors to disregard it. The impression lingers (Thompson, Fong, & Rosenhan, 1981).

People think a lot about their schemas, marshalling all sorts of supportive evidence (Millar & Tesser, 1986). People also protect their schemas by relying uncritically on their own earlier judgements – they justify and rationalise by using prior judgements, which are in turn based on even earlier judgements. The original basis of a particular schema is lost in the mists of time and is rarely unearthed, let alone critically re-examined (Schul & Burnstein, 1985).

However, schemas do change if they are really inaccurate. For example, a schema that characterised lions as cuddly, good-natured and playful pets as seen in a fun TV programme would, if you encountered one on foot in the wild, change rather dramatically – assuming that you survived the encounter! Rothbart (1981) has studied how social categorization works and suggested three ways in which schemas can change:

Bookkeeping
Gradual schema change through the accumulation of bits of schema-inconsistent information.

1 **Bookkeeping** – slow change in the face of accumulating evidence.

2 **Conversion** – sudden and massive change once a critical mass of disconfirming evidence has accumulated.

Conversion
Sudden schema change as a consequence of gradual accumulation of schema-inconsistent information.

3 **Subtyping** – schemas morph into a subcategory to accommodate disconfirming evidence.

Research favours the subtyping model (Weber & Crocker, 1983; **see Chapter 11 for a discussion of stereotype change**). For example, a woman who believes that men are violent might, through encountering many who are not, form a subtype of non-violent men to contrast with violent men.

Subtyping
Schema change as a consequence of schema-inconsistent information, causing the formation of subcategories.

Schema change may also depend on the extent to which schemas are either *logically* or *practically* disconfirmable (Reeder & Brewer, 1979) compared with ones that cannot be disconfirmed at all. A schema that is logically disconfirmable is relatively easily changed by counter-evidence: if my schema of a stranger is that he is *honest,* then evidence that he has cheated is very likely to change my schema (honest people do not cheat). Schemas that can be disconfirmed in practice are also relatively easily changed: they are ones for which the likelihood of encountering discrepant instances is relatively high – for example, *friendliness,* because it is often displayed in daily life (Rothbart & Park, 1986). There is less opportunity to display *cowardice,* for example, so a *cowardly* schema is less likely to be disconfirmed in practice.

Social encoding

Social encoding refers to the way in which external social stimuli are represented in the mind of the individual. There are at least four key stages (Bargh, 1984):

1 *Pre-attentive analysis* – an automatic and non-conscious scanning of the environment.

2 *Focal attention* – once noticed, stimuli are consciously identified and categorized.

3 *Comprehension* – stimuli are given meaning.

4 *Elaborative reasoning* – the stimulus is linked to other knowledge to allow for complex inferences.

Social encoding depends markedly on what captures our attention. In turn, attention is influenced by salience, vividness and accessibility.

Salience

Attention-capturing stimuli are salient stimuli. In social cognition, **salience** refers to the property of a stimulus that makes it stand out relative to other stimuli. Consider the second 'What do *you* think' at the start of this chapter. For example, a single male is salient in an all-female group but not salient in a sex-balanced group; a woman in the late stages of pregnancy is salient in most contexts except at the obstetrician's clinic; and someone wearing a bright T-shirt is salient at a funeral but not on the beach. Salience is 'out there' – a property of the stimulus domain. People can be salient because:

Salience
Property of a stimulus that makes it stand out in relation to other stimuli and attract attention.

- they are novel (single man, pregnant woman) or figural (bright T-shirt) in the immediate context (McArthur & Post, 1977);

- they are behaving in ways that do not fit prior expectations of them as individuals, as members of a particular social category or as people in general (Jones & McGillis, 1976); or

- they are important to your goals, they dominate your visual field or you have been told to pay attention to them (Erber & Fiske, 1984; Taylor & Fiske, 1975; see Figure 2.4).

Salient people attract attention and, relative to non-salient people, tend to be considered more influential in a group. They are also more personally responsible for their behaviour and less influenced by the situation, and they are generally evaluated more extremely (McArthur, 1981; Taylor & Fiske, 1978; see Figure 2.4). Because we attend more to salient people, they dominate our thoughts and, consequently, increase the coherence (i.e. organisation and consistency) of our impressions. People do not necessarily recall more about salient people; rather, they find it easier to access a coherent impression of the person. For example, imagine you generally do not like very tall men. If you now go to a party where one particularly tall man stands out, you may feel very negative about him and feel that he dominated conversation and was relatively uninfluenced by others. Although you will not necessarily recall much accurate information about his behaviour, you will have formed a fairly coherent impression of him as a person.

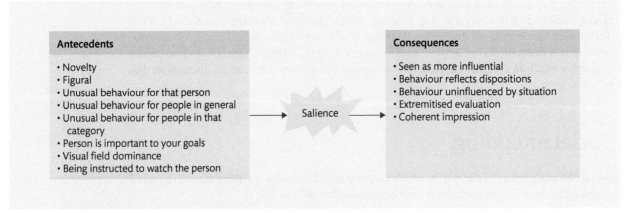

Figure 2.4 Some antecedents and consequences of social salience
For social cognition, salience is mainly a property of the stimulus in relation to other stimuli in the social context. It has predictable consequences for perception, thought and behaviour.

Vividness

Vividness
An intrinsic property of a stimulus on its own that makes it stand out and attract attention.

While salience is a property of the stimulus in relation to other stimuli in a particular context, **vividness** is an intrinsic property of the stimulus itself. Vivid stimuli are ones that are:

- emotionally attention-grabbing (e.g. a terrorist attack);
- concrete and image-provoking (e.g. a gory and detailed description of a terrorist attack); or
- close to you in time and place (e.g. a very recent terrorist attack in your city) (Nisbett & Ross, 1980).

Vivid stimuli ought to attract attention just like salient stimuli and ought, therefore, to have similar social cognitive effects. However, research has not confirmed this (Taylor & Thompson, 1982). Vividly presented information (e.g. through direct experience or colourful language accompanied by pictures or videos) may be more entertaining, though not more persuasive, than pallidly presented information. Apparent effects of vividness can

Standing out
Salient stimuli capture our attention. Hare Krishnas have come to Moscow and show interest in a little boy. Who is more salient to you?

often be attributed to other factors that co-occur with vividness. For example, vivid stimuli may convey more information, and thus it may be the information and not the vividness that influences social cognition.

Accessibility

Attention is often directed not so much by stimulus properties 'out there' but by the accessibility, or ease of recall, of categories or schemas that we already have in our heads (Higgins, 1996). **Priming** occurs when we become conscious of features of a stimulus domain that are highly accessible in memory; they come easily to mind and are useful in making sense of the intrinsically ambiguous nature of social information. They are categories that we often use, have recently used and are consistent with current goals, needs and expectations (Bruner, 1957, 1958). For example, people who are very concerned about sex discrimination (i.e. it is an accessible category) may find that they see sexism almost everywhere: it is readily primed and used to interpret the social world. Some categories are chronically accessible; they are habitually primed in many contexts (Bargh, Lombardi, & Higgins, 1988), and this can have pervasive effects. Bargh and Tota (1988) suggest that depression may be attributed in part to chronic accessibility of negative self-schemas.

Research on accessibility exposes people to cues that prime particular categories. This is done in such a way that people do not consciously detect the cue/category link. Participants then interpret ambiguous behaviour (Higgins, Bargh, & Lombardi, 1985). Participants could be exposed to words such as *adventurous* or *reckless* and then be asked to interpret behaviour such as 'shooting rapids in a canoe'. The interpretation of the behaviour would be different depending on the category primed by the cue word. For example, studies in the United States have shown that racial categories can be primed by words relating to African Americans. White participants so primed interpreted ambiguous behaviour as being more hostile and aggressive, which is consistent with racial stereotypes (Devine, 1989).

Once primed, a category tends to encode stimuli by interpreting them in a *category-consistent* manner. This is particularly true of ambiguous stimuli. However, when people become aware that a category has been primed, they often contrast stimuli with the category: they interpret them in a *category-incongruent* manner (Herr, Sherman, & Fazio, 1983; Martin, 1986). For example, gender is often an accessible category that is readily primed and used to interpret behaviour (Stangor, 1988); but if you knew that gender had been primed, you might make a special effort to interpret behaviour in a non-gendered way.

Priming
Activation of accessible categories or schemas in memory that influence how we process new information.

Memory for people

Social behaviour relies significantly on how we store information about other people and therefore what we remember about them (Fiske & Taylor, 2013; Martin & Clark, 1990; Ostrom, 1989b). Social psychological approaches to person memory draw on cognitive psychological theories of memory and mainly adopt what is called an associative network or *propositional* model of memory (e.g. Baddeley, Eysenck, & Anderson, 2009). The general idea is that we store *propositions* (e.g. 'The student reads the book', 'The book is a social psychology text', 'The student has a ponytail') consisting of nodes or ideas (e.g. book, ponytail, student, reads) that are linked by relationships between ideas. The links are *associative* in so far as nodes are associated with other nodes (e.g. *student* and *ponytail*), but some associative links are stronger than others. Links become stronger the more they are activated by cognitive rehearsal (e.g. recalling or thinking about the propositions), and the more different links there are to a specific idea (i.e. alternative retrieval routes), the more likely it is to be recalled.

Recall is a process where nodes become activated and the activation spreads to other nodes along established associative links: for example, the node *student* activates the node *ponytail* because there is a strong associative link. Finally, a distinction is made between *long-term memory*, which is the vast store of information that can potentially be brought to mind, and *short-term memory* (or working memory), which is the much smaller amount of information that you actually have in consciousness, and is the focus of your attention, at a specific time.

This sort of memory model has been applied to person memory. In terms of our general impression of someone, we are more likely to recall information that is inconsistent rather than consistent with our impression (Hastie, 1988; Srull & Wyer, 1989; Wyer & Carlston, 1994). This is because inconsistent information attracts attention and generates more cognition and thought, and this strengthens linkages and retrieval routes. However, better recall of inconsistent information does not occur when:

- we already have a well-established impression (Fiske & Neuberg, 1990);
- the inconsistency is purely descriptive and not evaluative (Wyer & Gordon, 1982);
- we are making a complex judgement (Bodenhausen & Lichtenstein, 1987);
- we have time afterwards to think about our impression (Wyer & Martin, 1986).

Contents of person memory

Consider your best friend. An enormous amount of detail comes to mind – her likes and dislikes, her attitudes, beliefs and values, her personality traits, the things she does, what she looks like, what she wears, where she usually goes. This information varies in terms of how concrete and directly observable it is: it ranges from appearance, which is concrete and directly observable, through behaviour, to traits that are not directly observable but are based on inference (Park, 1986). Cutting across this continuum is a general tendency for people to cluster together features that are positive and desirable and, separately, those that are negative and undesirable.

Most person-memory research concerns *traits*. Traits are stored in the usual propositional form ('Mary is mean and nasty') but are based on elaborate inferences from behaviour and situations. The inference process rests heavily on making causal attributions for people's behaviour (**see Chapter 3**). The storage of trait information is organised with respect to two continua: social desirability (e.g. *warm*, *pleasant*, *friendly*) and competence (e.g. *intelligent*, *industrious*, *efficient*; see Cuddy, Fiske, & Glick, 2008; Fiske, Cuddy, & Glick, 2007). Trait memories can be quite abstract and can colour more concrete memories of behaviour and appearance.

Behaviour is usually perceived as purposeful action, so memory for behaviour may be organised with respect to people's goals: the behaviour 'Michael runs to catch the bus' is stored in terms of Michael's goal to catch the bus. In this respect, behaviour, although more concrete and observable than traits, also involves some inference – inference of purpose (Hoffman, Mischel, & Mazze, 1981).

Memory for *appearance* is usually based on directly observable concrete information ('Boris has unruly yellow hair and a large face') and is stored as an analogue rather than a proposition. In other words, appearance is stored directly, like a picture in the mind, which retains all the original spatial information rather than as a deconstructed set of propositions that have symbolic meaning. Laboratory studies reveal that we are phenomenally accurate at remembering faces: we can often recall faces with 100 per cent accuracy over very long periods of time (Freides, 1974). However, we tend to be less accurate at recognising the faces of people who are of a different race from our own (Malpass & Kravitz, 1969). One explanation

Box 2.4 Our world
Eyewitness testimony is often highly unreliable

On 22 July 2005, two weeks after the 7 July London bombings and the day after the 21 July failed bombing, a Brazilian electrician who had been under surveillance by the police entered Stockwell tube station in London dressed in a bulky winter coat. It was a hot midsummer's day. Plain-clothes police followed him into the station and ordered him to stop. Instead, he ran – vaulting barriers and jumping on to a tube. The police brought him to the ground and shot him five times in the head. There were many witnesses – they gave very different accounts of what had happened. According to the *Guardian* (23 July 2005, p. 3) one eyewitness reported that the man had been pursued by three plain-clothes police, and that there were five shots; another reported ten policemen armed with machine guns and that there were six to eight shots; another reported shots from a 'silencer gun'; another reported twenty cops carrying big black guns; another reported that the man had a bomb belt with wires, and that there were two shots.

Different people witnessing the same event can see very different things, especially when the situation is fast-moving, confusing and frightening. Eyewitness testimony can be highly unreliable. (Reflect on the fourth 'What do *you* think?' question at the beginning of this chapter. Perhaps Hillary Clinton was not actually lying.)

---

of this is that we simply pay less attention to, or process more superficially, outgroup faces (Devine & Malpass, 1985). Indeed, superficial encoding undermines memory for faces in general, and one remedy for poor memory for faces is simply to pay more attention (Wells & Turtle, 1988).

We are also remarkably inaccurate at remembering appearances in natural contexts where eyewitness testimony is required: for example, identifying or describing a stranger we saw commit a crime (Kassin, Ellsworth, & Smith, 1989; Loftus, 1996). This is probably because witnesses or victims often do not get a good, clear look at the offender: the offence may be frightening, unexpected, confusing and over quickly, and the offender may be glimpsed only through a dirty car window or may wear a mask or some other disguise. More broadly, eyewitness testimony, even if confidently given, should be treated with caution (see Box 2.4). However, eyewitness testimony is more accurate if certain conditions are met (Shapiro & Penrod, 1986; see Box 2.5).

Box 2.5 Our world
Factors that make eyewitness testimony more accurate

Although eyewitness testimony is often unreliable, there are various ways to improve its accuracy.

The witness:

- mentally goes back over the scene of the crime to reinstate additional cues;
- has already associated the person's face with other symbolic information;
- was exposed to the person's face for a long time;
- gave testimony a very short time after the crime;
- is habitually attentive to the external environment;
- generally forms vivid mental images.

The person:

- had a face that was not altered by disguise;
- was younger than 30 years old;
- looked dishonest.

Source: Based on Shapiro and Penrod (1986); Valentine, Pickering and Darling (2003); Wells, Memon and Penrod (2006).

Person memory
How accurately do you think you might describe these robbers? How many were there? What age were they, and what were they wearing? Do an Internet check on the reliability of *eyewitness testimony*.

Organisation of person memory

In general, we remember people as a cluster of information about their traits, behaviour and appearance. However, we can also store information about people in a very different way: we can cluster people under attributes or groups. Social memory, therefore, can be organised by *person* or by *group* (Pryor & Ostrom, 1981; see Figure 2.5). In most settings, the preferred mode of organisation is by person because it produces richer and more accurate person memories that are more easily recalled (Sedikides & Ostrom, 1988). (Recall that Julie and Rosa have different memories of Aaron in the third 'What do *you* think?' question.) Organisation by person is particularly likely when people are significant to us because they are familiar, real people with whom we expect to interact across many specific situations (Srull, 1983).

Organisation by group membership is likely in first encounters with strangers: the person is pigeonholed, described and stored in terms of stereotypical attributes of a salient social category (e.g. age, ethnicity, sex; **see Chapter 10**). Over time, the organisation may change to one based on the person. For example, your memory of a lecturer you have encountered only a few times lecturing on a topic you are not very interested in will most likely be organised in terms of the stereotypical properties of the group 'lecturers'. If you should to get to know this person a little better, you might find that your memory gradually or suddenly becomes reorganised in terms of the lecturer as a distinct individual person.

There is an alternative perspective on the relationship between person-based and group-based person memory, and that is that they can coexist as essentially distinct forms of representation (Srull & Wyer, 1989; Wyer & Martin, 1986). These distinct forms of representation may be associated with different sorts of identity that people may have, based on either interpersonal relationships or group memberships. This idea is consistent with *social identity theory*, which is a theory of group behaviour as something quite distinct from interpersonal behaviour (e.g. Hogg & Abrams, 1988; Tajfel & Turner, 1986; **see Chapter 11**).

Using person memory

It is not unreasonable to assume that in making social judgements we draw upon person memory. In fact, it appears that sometimes we do but sometimes we do not. Hastie and Park (1986) integrated findings from a large number of studies to conclude that, by default, people tend to form impressions of people *on-line*: that is, they rely disproportionately on incoming data, which are assimilated by schemas to produce an impression. There is little correlation

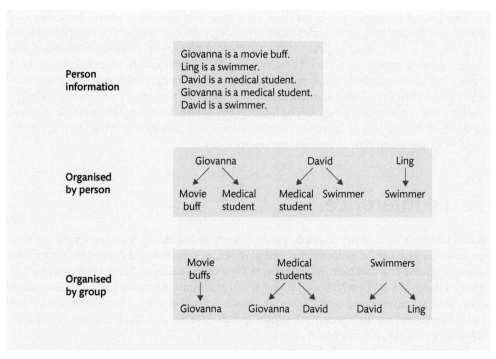

Figure 2.5 Person memory organised by person or by group

We can organise information about people in two quite different ways. We can cluster attributes under individual people, or we can cluster people under attributes or groups.

Source: Based on Fiske and Taylor (1991).

between memory and judgement. It is more unusual for people to draw on memory and make *memory-based* judgements, but when they do there is a stronger correlation between memory and judgement. Whether people make on-line or memory-based judgements or impressions is influenced by people's goals and purposes in the interaction or judgement task.

Box 2.6 Your life
Goals and their effects on person memory

What you remember about people in your life depends very much on what you need or want to remember about them – that is, your interaction and memory goals. Think of how your memory goals differ when the other person is a bank teller, a movie star, a close friend, or a lover. Social psychologists have identified a number of social interaction goals and how they affect your memory for other people.

Goal	Effect
Comprehension	Limited memory
Memorising	Variable memory, organised in an ad hoc manner, often by psychologically irrelevant categories
Forming impressions	Good memory, organised by traits
Empathising	Good memory, organised by goals
Comparing with oneself	Excellent memory, organised by psychological categories (traits or goals)
Anticipated interaction	Excellent, well-organised memory, type of organisation not yet clear
Actual interaction	Variable memory, depending on concurrent goal

Source: Based on Fiske and Taylor (1991).

The general principle is that recall of information about other people improves as the purpose of the interaction becomes more psychologically engaging and less superficial (Srull & Wyer, 1986, 1989; Wyer & Srull, 1986). Psychologically engaging interactions entail information processing at a deeper level that involves the elaboration of more complex and more varied links between elements, and consequently a more integrated memory (Greenwald & Pratkanis, 1984). Paradoxically, then, instructing someone to memorise another person (psychologically not very engaging) will be less effective than asking someone to form an impression, which in turn will be less effective than asking someone to empathise. Box 2.6 shows a number of goals and how they affect person memory.

Social inference

Social inference is, in many respects, the core of social cognition. It addresses the inferential processes (which can be quite formal and abstract, or intuitive and concrete) that we use to identify, sample and combine information to form impressions and make judgements. There are two distinct ways in which we process social information: (a) we can rely automatically on general schemas or stereotypes in a top-down deductive fashion; or (b) we can deliberatively rely on specific instances in a bottom-up inductive fashion. This distinction surfaces in different guises throughout social cognition.

We have already discussed the distinction between Asch's configural model (impressions are based on holistic images) and Anderson's cognitive algebra model (impressions are based on integration of pieces of information). More recently, Brewer (1988, 1994) has proposed a dual-process model that contrasts relatively automatic category-based processing of social information with more deliberate and personalised attribute-based processing. Closely related is Fiske and Neuberg's (1990; Fiske & Dépret, 1996) continuum model, which makes a similar distinction between schema-based and data-based inferences.

From research into attitudes come two other related distinctions (Eagly & Chaiken, 1998; **see Chapter 6 for details**). Petty and Cacioppo's (1986b) elaboration-likelihood model distinguishes between *central route processing*, where people carefully and deliberately consider information, and *peripheral route processing*, where people make rapid top-of-the-head decisions based on stereotypes, schemas and other cognitive short-cuts. Almost identical is Chaiken's (Bohner, Moskowitz, & Chaiken, 1995; Chaiken, Liberman, & Eagly, 1989) heuristic–systematic model: people process information carefully and systematically, or they automatically rely on cognitive heuristics.

Generally, social cognition researchers have studied inferential processes in comparison with ideal processes, called **normative models**, which produce the best possible inferences. Collectively, these normative models are known as **behavioural decision theory** (Einhorn & Hogarth, 1981). The intuitive strategies of social inference involve a range of biases and errors, which produce suboptimal inferences – inferences that fall short of those described by the principles of behavioural decision theory (e.g. Fiske & Taylor, 2013; Nisbett & Ross, 1980).

Normative models
Ideal processes for making accurate social inferences.

Behavioural decision theory
Set of normative models (ideal processes) for making accurate social inferences.

Departures from normality

Gathering and sampling social information

The first stage in making an inference involves gathering data and sampling information from those data. In doing this, people rely too heavily on schemas. This can cause them to overlook information that is potentially useful, or to exaggerate the importance of information that is misleading. For example, members of selection committees believe they are assessing candidates objectively on the basis of information provided by the candidate.

Departures from normality
If we rely too heavily on schemas, we may ignore interesting details, attend too closely to misleading information, or even worse!

However, what often happens is that person schemas are quickly, and often unconsciously, activated and used as the basis for candidate assessment. This reliance on person schemas is referred to as 'clinical judgement' and, although by no means all bad, it can produce suboptimal inferences and judgements (Dawes, Faust, & Meehl, 1989).

People can also be overly influenced by extreme examples and small samples (small samples are rarely representative of larger populations; this is called the *law of small numbers*); and they can be inattentive to biases in samples and to how typical a sample is of its population. For example, in Europe there is substantial media coverage of hate speech by radical 'Islamists' who promote anti-Western violence and terrorism. From this, some people seem happy to infer that all 1.6 billion Muslims in the world behave like this. However, this inference is flawed – it is based on unrepresentative information (most mass media present extreme, not ordinary, cases) that portrays a small sample of atypical Muslims behaving in an extreme manner.

Regression

Individual instances are often more extreme than the average of the population from which they are drawn: over a number of instances, there is a **regression** to the population mean. For example, a restaurant you have just visited for the first time may have been truly excellent, causing you to extol its virtues to all your friends. However, the next time you go, it turns out to be mediocre. On the next visit, it is moderately good, and on the next fairly average. This is an example of regression. The restaurant is probably actually moderately good, but this would not become apparent from one visit: a number of visits would have to be made. The way to control for regression effects in forming impressions is to be conservative and cautious in making inferences from limited information (one or a few cases or instances). However, people tend not to do this: they are generally ignorant of regression and do not control for it in forming impressions and making judgements (Kahneman & Tversky, 1973).

People can, however, be induced to make more conservative inferences if the initial information is made to seem less diagnostic by the presence of other information. For example, knowing that Hans kicks cats may generate an extreme and negative impression of him: kicking cats is relatively diagnostic of being a nasty person. However, if this piece of information is *diluted* (Nisbett, Zukier, & Lemley, 1981) by other information that he is a committed conservationist who writes poetry, collects antiques, drives a hybrid and cares for his

Regression
Tendency for initial observations of instances from a category to be more extreme than subsequent observations.

infirm mother, the impression is likely to become less extreme, because the tendency to use the diagnosis 'he kicks cats' is weakened.

Base-rate information

Base-rate information is general information, usually factual and statistical, about an entire class of events. For instance, if we knew that only 5 per cent of university lecturers gave truly awful lectures, or that only 7 per cent of social security recipients preferred being on the dole to working, this would be base-rate information. Research shows that people chronically underuse this information in making inferences, particularly when more concrete anecdotal cases exist (Bar-Hillel, 1980; Taylor & Thompson, 1982). So, on the basis of vivid and colourful media exposés of dull lecturers or social security cheats, people tend to infer that these are stereotypical properties of the parent categories, even if they have the relevant base-rate information to hand.

The main reason that base-rate information is ignored is not so much that it is pallid and uninteresting in comparison with vivid individual instances, but rather that people often fail to see the relevance of base-rate information, relative to other information, to the inference task (Bar-Hillel, 1980). People increase their use of base-rate information when it is made clear that it is more relevant than other information (e.g. case studies) to the inferential task.

Covariation and illusory correlation

Judgements of covariation are judgements of how strongly two things are related. They are essential to social inference and form the basis of schemas (schemas, as we saw earlier, are beliefs about the covariation of behaviour, attitudes or traits). To judge covariation accurately – for example, the relationship between hair colour and how much fun one has – we should consider the number of blondes having fun and not having fun, and the number of brunettes having fun and not having fun. The scientific method provides formal statistical procedures that we could use to assess covariation (**Chapter 1**).

However, in making covariation judgements, people fall far short of normative prescriptions (Alloy & Tabachnik, 1984; Crocker, 1981). In general, this is because they are influenced by prior assumptions (i.e. schemas) and tend to search for or recognise only schema-consistent information: people are generally not interested in disconfirming their cherished schemas. So, in assessing the relationship between hair colour and fun, people may have available the social schema that 'blondes have more fun', and instances of blondes who have fun will come to mind much more readily than blondes who are having a miserable time or brunettes who are having a ball.

When people assume that a relationship exists between two variables, they tend to overestimate the degree of correlation or see a correlation where none actually exists. This phenomenon, called **illusory correlation**, was demonstrated by Chapman (1967), who presented students with lists of paired words such as *lion/tiger, lion/eggs, bacon/eggs, blossoms/notebook* and *notebook/tiger*. The students then had to recall how often each word was paired with each other word. Although every word was paired an equal number of times with every other word, participants overestimated meaningful pairings (e.g. *bacon/eggs*) and distinctive pairings (e.g. *blossoms/notebook* – words that were much longer than all the other words in the list).

Chapman reasoned that there are two bases for illusory correlation: **associative meaning** (items are seen as belonging together because they 'ought' to, on the basis of prior expectations) and **paired distinctiveness** (items are thought to go together because they share some unusual feature).

Distinctiveness-based illusory correlation may help to explain stereotyping, particularly negative stereotypes of minority groups (Hamilton, 1979; Hamilton & Sherman, 1989; Mullen & Johnson, 1990; **see also Chapter 11**). Hamilton and Gifford (1976) had participants recall statements describing two groups, A and B. There were twice as many statements about group A as there were about group B, and there were twice as many positive as

Base-rate information
Pallid, factual, statistical information about an entire class of events.

Illusory correlation
Cognitive exaggeration of the degree of co-occurrence of two stimuli or events, or the perception of a co-occurrence where none exists.

Associative meaning
Illusory correlation in which items are seen as belonging together because they 'ought' to, on the basis of prior expectations.

Paired distinctiveness
Illusory correlation in which items are seen as belonging together because they share some unusual feature.

negative statements about each group. Participants erroneously recalled that more negative statements (the less common statements) were paired with group B (the less common group). When the experiment was replicated but with more negative than positive statements, participants now overestimated the number of positive statements paired with group B.

In real life, negative events are distinctive because they are perceived to be rarer than positive events (Parducci, 1968), and minority groups are distinctive because people often have relatively few contacts with them. Thus, the conditions for distinctiveness-based illusory correlation are met. There is also evidence for an associative-meaning basis to negative stereotyping of minority groups: people have preconceptions that negative attributes go with minority groups (McArthur & Friedman, 1980).

Although illusory correlation may be involved in the formation and use of stereotypes, its role may be limited to situations where people make memory-based rather than on-line judgements (McConnell, Sherman, & Hamilton, 1994) – after all, they have to remember distinctiveness or associative information in order to make illusory correlations.

More radically, it can be argued that stereotypes are not 'illusory' at all. Rather, they are rational, even deliberate, constructs that differentiate ingroups from outgroups in ways that evaluatively favour the ingroup (Leyens, Yzerbyt, & Schadron, 1994; McGarty, Haslam, Turner, & Oakes, 1993; Oakes, Haslam, & Turner, 1994). Stereotypical differences are functionally adaptive to the stereotyper – they are 'real', and the process of stereotyping is one in which these differences are automatically (and strategically; for example, through rhetoric) accentuated as a consequence of categorizing oneself as a member of one of the groups.

Heuristics

We have now seen how bad we are, in comparison with standards from behavioural decision theory, at making inferences. Perhaps the reason for this is that we have limited short-term memory available for online processing but enormous capacity for long-term memory – using the analogy of a computer, the former is RAM, random access memory, and the latter hard-drive capacity. It pays, then, to store information schematically in long-term memory and call up schemas to aid inference. Social inference is therefore likely to be heavily theory/schema-driven, with the consequence that it is biased towards conservative, schema-supportive inferential practices. Despite doing this, and being so poor at social inference, human beings seem to muddle through. Perhaps the process is adequate for most of our inferential needs most of the time, and we should study these 'adequate' rather than optimal processes in their own right.

With just this idea in mind, Tversky and Kahneman (1974; Kahneman & Tversky, 1973) detail the sorts of cognitive short-cut, called heuristics, that people use to reduce complex problem-solving to simpler judgemental operations. The three key heuristics are: (1) representativeness, (2) availability and (3) anchoring and adjustment.

Heuristics
Cognitive short-cuts that provide adequately accurate inferences for most of us most of the time.

Representativeness heuristic

In deciding how likely it is that a person or an event is an instance of one category or another, people often simply estimate the superficial resemblance of the instance to a typical or average member of the category. The representativeness heuristic is a relevance judgement that disregards base-rate information, sample size, quality of information and other normative principles. Nevertheless, it is fast and efficient and produces inferences that are accurate enough for our purposes most of the time. For example, consider the following information: 'Steve is very shy and withdrawn, invariably helpful, but with little interest in people, or in the world of reality. A meek and tidy soul, he has a need for order and structure, and a passion for detail' (Tversky & Kahneman, 1974). The representativeness heuristic would quickly lead to the inference that Steve is a librarian rather than, say, a farmer, surgeon or trapeze artist, and in general that would probably be correct.

Representativeness heuristic
A cognitive short-cut in which instances are assigned to categories or types on the basis of overall similarity or resemblance to the category.

Availability heuristic

The **availability heuristic** is used to infer the frequency or likelihood of an event on the basis of how quickly instances or associations come to mind. Where instances are readily available, we tend to inflate frequencies. For example, exposure to many media reports of violent Muslim extremists will make that information available and will tend to inflate our estimate of the overall frequency of violent Muslims. Similarly, in forming an impression of Paul, who has short hair, wears big boots and carries a cane, you might overestimate the likelihood that he will be violent because you have just seen the film *A Clockwork Orange*.

Under many circumstances, availability is adequate as a basis for making inferences – after all, things that come to mind easily are probably fairly plentiful. However, availability is subject to bias, as it does not control for such factors as idiosyncratic exposure to unusual samples.

Anchoring and adjustment

In making inferences we often need a starting point – an anchor – from which, and with which, we can adjust subsequent inferences (e.g. Wyer, 1976). **Anchoring and adjustment** is a heuristic that ties inferences to initial standards. So, for example, inferences about other people are often anchored in beliefs about ourselves: we decide how intelligent, artistic or kind someone else is with reference to our own self-schema. Anchors can also come from the immediate context. For example, Greenberg, Williams and O'Brien (1986) found that participants in a mock jury study who were instructed to contemplate the harshest verdict first used this as an anchor from which only small adjustments were made. A relatively harsh verdict was delivered. Participants instructed to consider the most lenient verdict first likewise used this as an anchor, subsequently delivering a relatively lenient verdict.

Improving social inference

Social inference is not optimal. We are biased, we misrepresent people and events and we make mistakes. However, many of these shortcomings may be more apparent than real (Funder, 1987). Social cognition and social neuroscience experiments may provide unnatural contexts, for which our inference processes are not well suited. Intuitive inference processes may actually be well suited to everyday life. For example, on encountering a pit bull terrier in the street, it might be very adaptive to rely on availability (media coverage of attacks by pit bull terriers) and to flee automatically rather than adopt more time-consuming normative procedures: what is an error in the laboratory may not be so in the field.

Nevertheless, inferential errors can sometimes have serious consequences. For example, negative stereotyping of minority groups and suboptimal group decisions may be partly caused by inferential errors. In this case, there may be something to be gained by considering ways in which we can improve social inference. The basic principle is that social inference will improve to the extent that we become less reliant on intuitive inferential strategies. This may be achieved through formal education in scientific and rational thinking as well as in statistical techniques (Fong, Krantz, & Nisbett, 1986; Nisbett, Krantz, Jepson, & Fong, 1982).

Affect and emotion

Social cognition focuses on thinking rather than feeling, but in recent years there has been an 'affective revolution' (e.g. Forgas, 2006; Forgas & Smith, 2007; Haddock & Zanna, 1999; Keltner & Lerner, 2010; Wetherell, 2012). Research has asked how feelings (affect, emotion, mood) influence and are influenced by social cognition.

Typically, in the absence of strong emotion-evoking events, people are in a mildly good mood and feel happy. The reason for this is evolutionary – behaviours associated with a good mood are ones that promote self-protective and reproductive success (Diener,

Kanazawa, Suh, & Oishi, 2015). However, when more marked emotion-evoking events occur, things change. Different situations (funeral, party) evoke different emotions (sad, happy), but also the same situation (examination) can evoke different emotions (threat, challenge) in different people (weak student, competent student).

Antecedents of affect

People process information about the situation and their hopes, desires and abilities, and on the basis of these cognitive *appraisals*, different affective reactions and physiological responses follow. Because affective response (emotion) is, fundamentally, a mode of action readiness tied to appraisals of harm and benefit, the appraisal process is continuous and largely automatic (see Box 2.7).

Based on a distinction between simple primary and more complex secondary appraisals, research has shown that primary appraisals related to whether something is good/bad, or perhaps harmless/dangerous, occur in the amygdala. This is the part of the 'old brain' responsible for fast, autonomic system-related emotional reactions that have clear survival value (Baxter & Murray, 2002; Russell, 2003).

Hence, primary appraisals generate emotions blindingly quickly, well before conscious recognition of the target of the appraisal (Barrett, 2006). For example, people with a snake phobia showed physiological signs of terror even when they saw photos of snakes so quickly that the images could not even be recognised (Öhman & Soares, 1994). Furthermore, when people focus on negative rather than positive stimuli, brain activity may be particularly fast (Ito, Larsen, Smith, & Cacioppo, 1998).

Secondary appraisals generate more complex emotions and more slowly. For example, envy is a complex emotion where we feel we have missed out on something pleasant and valuable, but others did not. How envious we feel is markedly influenced by the

---

Box 2.7 Research highlight
How we decide when to respond affectively

According to Richard Lazarus and Craig Smith, affective response rests on seven appraisals, which can be framed as questions that people ask themselves in particular situations. There are two sets of appraisal dimensions, primary and secondary, that are relevant to all emotions.

Primary appraisals

1 How relevant (important) is what is happening in this situation to my needs and goals?
2 Is this congruent (good) or incongruent (bad) with my needs or goals?

Secondary appraisals

These appraisals relate to accountability and coping.

1 How responsible am I for what is happening in this situation?
2 How responsible is someone or something else?

3 Can I act on this situation to make or keep it more like what I want?
4 Can I handle and adjust to this situation however it might turn out?
5 Do I expect this situation to improve or to get worse?

Together, these seven appraisal dimensions produce a wide array of affective responses and emotions. For example, if something were important and bad and caused by someone else, we would feel anger and be motivated to act towards the other person in a way that would fix the situation. If something were important and bad, but caused by ourselves, then we would feel shame or guilt and be motivated to make amends for the situation.

Source: Lazarus (1991); Smith and Lazarus (1990).

counterfactual appraisal that "it could have been me" and is felt more strongly if the desired outcome that we missed out on was almost achieved (Van den Ven & Zeelenberg, 2015).

Jim Blascovich and his colleagues have proposed a *biopsychosocial model of arousal regulation* to describe how challenge and threat motivate performance and create approach and avoidance-related emotions (Blascovich, 2008; Blascovich & Tomaka, 1996). When people feel there is a demand on them, they appraise their resources for dealing with the demand – if perceived resources equal or exceed the demand, people experience a feeling of challenge that motivates approach-related emotions and behaviours (fight); if perceived resources are inadequate to meet the demand, people experience a feeling of threat that motivates avoidance-related emotions and behaviours (flight).

Consequences of affect

Affect-infusion model
Cognition is infused with affect such that social judgements reflect current mood.

Affect, emotion and mood infuse and therefore influence thinking, judgement and behaviour. The **affect-infusion model** describes the effects of mood on social cognition, with the prediction that affect infusion occurs only where people process information in an open and constructive manner that involves active elaboration of stimulus details and information from memory (Forgas, 1994, 1995, 2002).

According to Forgas, there are four distinct ways in which people can process information about one another:

- *Direct access* – they directly access schemas or judgements stored in memory.
- *Motivated processing* – they form a judgement on the basis of specific motivations to achieve a goal or to 'repair' an existing mood.
- *Heuristic processing* – they rely on various cognitive short-cuts or heuristics.
- *Substantive processing* – they deliberately and carefully construct a judgement from a variety of informational sources.

Current mood states do not influence judgements involving direct access or motivated processing, but they do affect judgements involving heuristic processing or substantive processing. In the latter cases, cognition is infused with affect such that social judgements reflect current mood, either indirectly (affect primes target judgement) or directly (affect acts as information about the target). For example, under heuristic processing, mood may itself be a heuristic that determines response – being in a bad mood would produce a negative reaction to another person (i.e. mood-congruence). Under substantive processing, the more we deliberate, the greater the mood-congruence effect.

Affect influences social memory and social judgement – for example, people tend to recall current mood-congruent information more readily than current mood-incongruent information, and judge others and themselves more positively when they themselves are in a positive mood. In line with the affect–infusion model, the effect of mood on self-perception is greater for peripheral than central aspects of self – peripheral aspects are less firmly ensconced and therefore require more elaboration and construction than central aspects (e.g. Sedikides, 1995). Stereotyping is also affected by mood. Being in a good mood can increase reliance on stereotypes when group membership is not very relevant (Forgas & Fiedler, 1996), but negative affect can encourage people to correct hastily made negative evaluations of outgroups (Monteith, 1993).

One concrete consequence of affect infusion is the effect of emotion on decision-making. Typically, we think that emotion is anathema to good decision-making because it injects irrationality into the process. Zeelenberg and colleagues intriguingly argue the opposite, that emotions help decision-making by prioritising and focusing attention and setting behavioural goals (Zeelenberg, Nelissen, Breugelmans, & Pieters, 2008). Emotions are not just a matter of valence (good vs. bad); each emotion is quite distinctive with a different cognitive component that represents meaning and embodies goals that specify and motivate action. For example, regret, disappointment, guilt and shame are all affectively negative but they each have different subjective meanings and encourage different decisions and subsequent actions.

Emotion regulation

People do not always express their emotions. For example, collectivist societies disapprove of overt emotional expression (**see Chapter 16**) – however, context can override this. A set of five archival studies of the expression of pride by Olympic and national contest athletes confirmed the general cultural difference (Chinese medallists expressed less pride than Americans) but also found that this only happened when Chinese outperformed non-Chinese. When Chinese outperformed Chinese, they did not express pride – whereas Americans always expressed pride irrespective of who they outperformed (Van Osch, Zeelenberg, & Breugelmans, 2016).

This raises the wider question of how and when we regulate the expression of our emotions – if your goal is to remain calm, how do you inhibit expression of your feelings of anger or anxiety? Research converges on the idea that people regulate their emotions, and they do this to advance their own goals (Gross, 2014, 2015; Koole, 2009). For example, someone might decide not to show their anger in a particular situation, in order to cope with the situation (instrumental goal) or to feel happy (hedonic goal).

Webb and colleagues adopt an action control perspective that focuses on self-regulation (Webb, Schweiger Gallo, Miles, Gollwitzer, & Sheeran, 2012). Failure to regulate emotions results from difficulties with the self-regulatory tasks of identifying the need to regulate, deciding whether and how to regulate and enacting a regulation strategy. People can effectively surmount these difficulties by forming implementation intentions or engaging in 'if-then' planning.

Beyond cognition and neuroscience

Although research on affect and emotion has come a long way in recent years, a number of questions remain and some critical issues have been raised. For example, self-report measures of people's appraisals of a stimulus may be unreliable (Parkinson & Manstead, 1992), as they are based on semantics and influenced by communicative motivations and goals. As a result, we need to know more about how primary appraisals are tied to the valence, novelty, salience or intensity of a stimulus. We also need to understand how primary appraisals give rise to conscious experiences (Keltner & Lerner, 2010).

Social cognition research on affect and emotion, which is what we have discussed in this chapter, tends to focus on cognitive processes, and increasingly on the underlying neuroscience of basic primary emotions. However, affect and emotion are critical aspects of group life and of intergroup relations – there is now a growing literature on collective and intergroup emotions which we discuss **in Chapter 11** (e.g. Goldenberg, Halperin, Van Zomeren, & Gross, 2016; Iyer & Leach, 2008; Mackie, Maitner, & Smith, 2009).

Margaret Wetherell (2012) has similarly worried that the contemporary social psychology of affect and emotion is too tied to exploration of cognitive and neurological processes associated with simple or basic emotions. She reminds us that our emotional life is significantly impacted by a vast range of complex and nuanced emotions that may be much more closely tied to language and semantics embedded in everyday discourse. Emotions, both felt and expressed, serve to communicate with others and to 'get things done'.

Where is the 'social' in social cognition?

Social psychology has always described the cognitive processes and structures that influence and are influenced by social behaviour, and there is no doubt that modern social cognition, which really emerged only in the late 1970s, has made enormous advances in this direction.

However, some critics have wondered if social cognition has been *too* successful. It may have taken social psychology too far in the direction of cognitive psychology, and more recently neuroscience, while it has diverted attention from many of social psychology's traditional topics. There has been a worry that there may not be any 'social' in social cognition (Kraut & Higgins, 1984; Markus & Zajonc, 1985; Moscovici, 1982; Zajonc, 1989).

Many of the social cognitive processes and structures that are described seem to be little affected by social context and seem more accurately to represent *asocial* cognition operating on social stimuli (i.e. people). In this respect, critics have characterised social cognition as **reductionist** (**see Chapter 1**) and have focused on three main areas of concern: (1) a failure to deal properly with language and communication, which are two fundamentally social variables, (2) a failure to deal with processes of human interaction and (3) a failure to articulate cognitive processes with wider interpersonal, group and societal processes. However, there are exceptions; for example, Maass and Arcuri's (1996) research on language and stereotyping (**see Chapter 15**), and self-categorization research on collective self and group behaviour (Turner, Hogg, Oakes, Reicher, & Wetherell, 1987; **see Chapter 11**). Recently, there has been a more systematic attempt to (re-)socialise social cognition (e.g., Abrams & Hogg, 1999; Levine, Resnick, & Higgins, 1993; Moskowitz, 2005; Nye & Bower, 1996; Wyer & Gruenfeld, 1995).

One strand of social cognition has, however, moved in the opposite direction towards greater reductionism – in the guise of social neuroscience (e.g., Harmon-Jones & Winkielman, 2007; Lieberman, 2010; Ochsner, 2007; Ochsner & Lieberman, 2001). Social neuroscience, which focuses on brain correlates of behaviour, would seem to suffer all the problems of traditional social cognition, but even more so – mapping complex social behaviour on to localised electrical and chemical activity in the brain.

Although advocates for social neuroscience see much of value and a central contribution to social psychology in this particular form of reductionism, many other social psychologists are wary, wondering how knowledge of what part of the brain 'lights up' can help us understand complex social behaviours such as negotiation, social dilemmas and conformity. For example, Fine (2010) has used the term 'neurosexism' to register concern that reductionist tendencies in social neuroscience and fMRI studies of gender differences may reinforce gender stereotypes. For a discussion of pros and cons of social neuroscience in explaining group processes and intergroup relations, see Prentice and Eberhardt (2008).

Reductionism
Explanation of a phenomenon in terms of the language and concepts of a lower level of analysis, usually with a loss of explanatory power.

Summary

- Social cognition refers to cognitive processes and structures that affect and are affected by social context. It is assumed that people have a limited capacity to process information and are cognitive misers who take all sorts of cognitive short-cuts; or they are motivated tacticians who choose, on the basis of their goals, motives and needs, among an array of cognitive strategies.

- The overall impressions we form of other people are dominated by stereotypes, unfavourable information, first impressions and idiosyncratic personal constructs. In forming impressions of other people, we weight components and then average them in complex ways; or certain components may influence the interpretation and meaning of all other components and dominate the resulting impression.

- Schemas are cognitive structures that represent knowledge about people, events, roles, the self and the general processing of information. Once invoked, schemas bias all aspects of information processing and inference in such a way that the schema remains unassailed.

- Categories are fuzzy sets of features organised around a prototype. They are hierarchically structured in terms of inclusiveness in such a way that less inclusive categories are subsets of broader, more inclusive categories. The process of categorization accentuates perceived intra-category similarities and inter-category differences on dimensions that a person believes are correlated with the categorization. This accentuation effect is the basis for stereotyping, but it requires consideration of intergroup relations to provide a full explanation.

- In processing information about other people, we tend to rely on schemas relating to subtypes, stereotypes, current moods, easily detected features, accessible categories and self-relevant information. However, people are less dependent on schemas when the cost of making a wrong inference is increased, when the cost of being indecisive is low, and when people are aware that schematic processing may be inaccurate.

- Schemas become more abstract, complex, organised, compact, resilient and accurate over time. They are hard to change but can be modified by schema-inconsistent information, mainly through the formation of subtypes.

- The encoding of information is heavily influenced by the salience of stimuli and by the cognitive accessibility of existing schemas.

- We remember people mainly in terms of their traits but also in terms of their behaviour and appearance. They can be cognitively stored as individual people, or as category members.

- The processes we use to make inferences fall far short of ideal. Our schemas dominate us, we disregard regression effects and base-rate information, and we perceive illusory correlations. We rely on cognitive short-cuts (heuristics) such as representativeness, availability, and anchoring and adjustment, rather than on optimal information-processing techniques.

- Affect and emotion are cognitively underpinned by appraisals of accountability and our needs, goals and capacity to deal with a demand in a particular situation. In turn, affect influences social cognition – it infuses social cognition only where people process information in an open and constructive manner that involves active elaboration of stimulus details and information from memory.

- Social cognition has been criticised for being too cognitive and for not properly relating cognitive processes and structures to language, social interaction and social structure, consequently failing to address many topics of central concern to social psychology. This situation has improved in recent years; however, social neuroscience may fall prey to these limitations in an even bigger way.

Key terms

Accentuation principle	Conversion	Reductionism
Accessibility	Exemplars	Regression
Affect–infusion model	Family resemblance	Representativeness heuristic
Anchoring and adjustment	Fuzzy sets	Roles
Associative meaning	Gestalt psychology	Salience
Associative network	Heuristics	Schema
Attribution	Illusory correlation	Script
Availability heuristic	Implicit personality theories	Self-categorization theory
Averaging	Motivated tactician	Social cognition
Base-rate information	Naive psychologist (or scientist)	Social identity theory
Behavioural decision theory	Normative models	Social judgeability
Behaviourism	Paired distinctiveness	Social neuroscience
Bookkeeping	Peripheral traits	Stereotype
Central traits	Personal constructs	Subtyping
Cognitive algebra	Primacy	Summation
Cognitive consistency	Priming	Vividness
Cognitive miser	Prototype	Weighted averaging
Configural model	Recency	

Literature, film and TV

The Reader

A 2008 film directed by Stephen Daldry and starring Ralph Fiennes, Jeanette Hain and David Kross. A teenage boy, Michael, in post-Second World War Germany develops a passionate relationship with an older woman, Hanna, which profoundly affects him. Hanna suddenly disappears, but reappears eight years later in Michael's life when she is on trial for war crimes. The impression of Hanna that Michael has cherished for so long is dramatically and upsettingly turned upside down. One way in which Michael deals with this is by focusing on a positive aspect of his former impression of her – her vulnerability in one aspect of her life.

Billy Elliot

A 2000 film by Stephen Daldry, and with Julie Walters. Set in a north of England mining town against the backdrop of the very bitter 1984 miners' strike. Billy Elliot is an 11-year-old boy who rejects the traditional male activity of boxing – preferring to become a ballet dancer. The film shows what happens when people violate social scripts and behave out of role in counter-stereotypical ways.

The King's Speech

A 2010 historical drama directed by Tom Hooper and starring Colin Firth, Geoffrey Rush and Helena Bonham Carter.

The film focuses on the developing relationship between King George VI (played by Firth) and his Australian speech therapist Lionel Logue (played by Rush), who is given the task of curing the King's stutter. This was a very significant and urgent task given the historical backdrop of Nazi Germany preparing for war and the British monarchy rocked by scandal surrounding the abdication of Edward VIII. A key theme of the film is the clash of cultural, professional and status-related expectations at a time of great social and technological change that mark the relationship between George VI and Logue.

Erin Brockovich

Steven Soderbergh's 2000 biographical film, starring Julia Roberts as Erin Brockovich. In 1993, Brockovich was an unemployed single mother of three who ended up working for a lawyer, Ed Masry (played by Albert Finney). She persuaded Masry to let her take the lead in a class action suit against a huge Californian energy company (Pacific Gas and Electricity Company – PG&E) for contaminating the groundwater with highly carcinogenic hexavalent chromium. Brockovich successfully persuaded 634 plaintiffs to join the suite and was able to win the case – the judge ordered PG&E to pay a colossal settlement of $333 million. Throughout this entire process, Brockovich confronts and overcomes an array of gender, marital status, educational and socio-economic stereotypes.

Guided questions

1 You have heard the saying that people sometimes 'judge a book by its cover'. Use this maxim as a springboard to outline how we form our first impressions of another person.

2 Are *schemas* and *stereotypes* the same thing? If not, how do they differ?

3 Why are stereotypes slow to change?

4 How reliable is eyewitness testimony? Apply what you know about *person memory* to this issue.

5 Can thinking be affected by our moods?

Learn more

Devine, P. G., Hamilton, D. L., & Ostrom, T. M. (Eds.) (1994). *Social cognition: Impact on social psychology*. San Diego: Academic Press. Leading experts discuss the impact that social cognition has had on a wide range of topics in social psychology.

Dijksterhuis, A. (2010). Automaticity and the unconscious. In S. T. Fiske, D. T. Gilbert, & G. Lindzey (Eds.), *Handbook of social psychology* (5th ed., Vol. 1, pp. 228–267). New York: Wiley. Detailed and comprehensive coverage of perhaps the core of social cognition – automatic cognitive processes.

Fiske, S. T., & Taylor, S. E. (2013). *Social cognition: From brains to culture* (2nd ed.). Los Angeles: Sage. Most recent edition of Fiske and Taylor's classic social cognition text – it is comprehensive, detailed and well written, and it also covers recent developments in social neuroscience.

Forgas, J. P., & Smith, C. A. (2007). Affect and emotion. In M. A. Hogg & J. Cooper (Eds.), *The SAGE handbook of social psychology: Concise student edition* (pp. 146–175). London: SAGE. Comprehensive and readable overview of what we know about the social cognitive antecedents and consequences of people's feelings.

Hamilton, D. L. (Ed.) (2004). *Social cognition: Essential readings*. New York: Psychology Press. An edited collection of classic publications in social cognition. The book has an introductory overview chapter and shorter introductory chapters for each section.

Keltner, D., & Lerner, J. S. (2010). Emotion. In S. T. Fiske, D. T. Gilbert, & G. Lindzey (Eds.), *Handbook of social psychology* (5th ed., Vol. 1, pp. 317–352). New York: Wiley. Up-to-date and very detailed overview of what we know about affect and emotion.

Lieberman, M. D. (2010). Social cognitive neuroscience. In S. T. Fiske, D. T. Gilbert, & G. Lindzey (Eds.), *Handbook of social psychology* (5th ed., Vol. 1, pp. 143–193). New York: Wiley. Up-to-date and very detailed overview of social neuroscience from one of its leading researchers.

Macrae, C. N., & Quadflieg, S. (2010). Perceiving people. In S. T. Fiske, D. T. Gilbert, & G. Lindzey (Eds.), *Handbook of social psychology* (5th ed., Vol. 1, pp. 428–463). New York: Wiley. Comprehensive coverage of what we know about person perception – how we form and use our cognitive representations of people.

Moskowitz, G. B. (2005). *Social cognition: Understanding self and others*. New York: Guilford. A relatively recent comprehensive social cognition text that is written in an accessible style as an introduction to the topic.

Todorov, A., Fiske, S. T., & Prentice, D. A. (2011) *Social neuroscience: Towards understanding the underpinnings of the social mind*. New York: Oxford University Press. Comprehensive discussion of the neural bases of cognition.

Chapter 3
Attribution and social explanation

6 Weiner's (1979, 1985) attributional theory; and

7 Deschamps's (1983), Hewstone's (1989) and Jaspars's (Hewstone & Jaspars, 1982, 1984) intergroup perspective.

We discuss the first six of these below and then deal with intergroup attribution by itself in greater detail later in the chapter.

How people attribute causality

People as naive psychologists

Fritz Heider (1958) believed it was important for social psychologists to study people's naive, or common sense, psychological theories, because such theories influenced ordinary people's everyday perceptions and behaviour. For example, people who believe in astrology are likely to have different expectations and to act in different ways from those who do not. Heider believed that people are intuitive psychologists who construct causal theories of human behaviour, and because such theories have the same form as scientific social psychological theories, people are actually intuitive or **naive psychologists**.

Heider based his ideas on three principles:

1 Because we feel that our own behaviour is motivated rather than random, we look for the causes for other people's behaviour in order to discover their motives. The search for causes does seem to pervade human thought, and it can be difficult to explain or comment on something without using causal language. Heider and Simmel (1944) demonstrated this in an ingenious experiment. People who were asked to describe the movement of abstract geometric figures described them as if they were humans with intentions to act in certain ways. Nowadays, we can witness the same phenomenon in people's often highly emotional ascription of human motives to computer-generated figures. People's pervasive need for causal explanation reveals itself most powerfully in the way that almost all societies construct an origin myth, an elaborate causal explanation for the origin and meaning of life that is often a centrepiece of a religion.

2 Because we construct causal theories in order to be able to predict and control the environment, we tend to look for stable and enduring properties of the world around us. We try to discover personality traits and enduring abilities in people, or stable properties of situations, that cause behaviour.

3 In attributing causality for behaviour, we distinguish between personal factors (e.g. personality, ability) and environmental factors (e.g. situations, social pressure). The former are examples of an **internal (or dispositional) attribution** and the latter of an **external (or situational) attribution**. So, for example, it might be useful to know whether someone you meet at a party who seems aloof and distant is an aloof and distant person or is acting like that because that person is not enjoying the party. Heider believed that because internal causes, or intentions, are hidden from us, we can only infer their presence if there are no clear external causes. However, as we see later, people tend to be biased in preferring internal to external attributions even in the face of evidence for external causality. It seems that we readily attribute behaviour to stable properties of people. Scherer (1978), for example, found that people made assumptions about the stable personality traits of complete strangers simply on the basis of hearing their voices on the telephone.

Heider identified the major themes and provided the insight that forms the blueprint for all subsequent, more formalised, theories of attribution.

Naive psychologist (or scientist)
Model of social cognition that characterises people as using rational, scientific-like, cause–effect analyses to understand their world.

Internal (or dispositional) attribution
Process of assigning the cause of our own or others' behaviour to internal or dispositional factors.

External (or situational) attribution
Assigning the cause of our own or others' behaviour to external or environmental factors.

From acts to dispositions

Correspondent inference
Causal attribution of behaviour to underlying dispositions.

Ned Jones and Keith Davis's (1965; Jones & McGillis, 1976) theory of **correspondent inference** explains how people infer that a person's behaviour corresponds to an underlying disposition or personality trait – how we infer, for example, that a friendly action is due to an underlying disposition to be friendly. People like to make correspondent inferences (attribute behaviour to underlying disposition) because a dispositional cause is a stable cause that makes people's behaviour predictable and thus increases our own sense of control over our world.

To make a correspondent inference, we draw on five sources of information, or cues (see Figure 3.1):

1 *Freely chosen* behaviour is more indicative of a disposition than is behaviour that is clearly under the control of external threats, inducements or constraints.

Non-common effects
Effects of behaviour that are relatively exclusive to that behaviour rather than other behaviours.

Outcome bias
Belief that the outcomes of a behaviour were intended by the person who chose the behaviour.

2 Behaviour with effects that are relatively exclusive to that behaviour rather than common to many behaviours (i.e. behaviour with **non-common effects**) tells us more about dispositions. People assume that others are aware of non-common effects and that the specific behaviour was performed intentionally to produce the non-common effect – this tendency has been called **outcome bias** (Allison, Mackie, & Messick, 1996). So, for example, if a person has to choose between behaviour A and behaviour B, and both produce roughly the same effects (i.e. no non-common effects) or a very large number of different effects (i.e. many non-common effects), the choice tells us little about the person's disposition. However, if the behaviours produce a small number of different effects (i.e. few non-common effects – e.g. behaviour A produces only terror and behaviour B produces only joy), then the choice does tell us something about that person's disposition.

3 *Socially desirable* behaviour tells us little about a person's disposition, because it is likely to be controlled by societal norms. However, socially undesirable behaviour is generally counter-normative and is thus a better basis for making a correspondent inference.

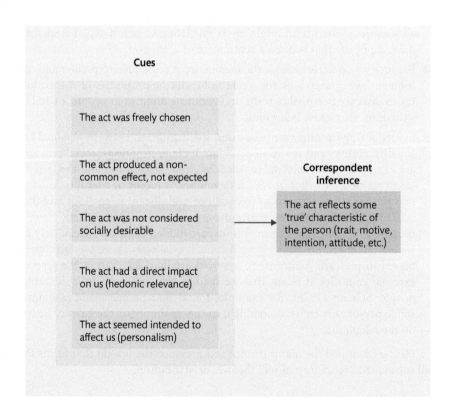

Figure 3.1 How we make a correspondent inference

To make an inference that a person's behaviour corresponds to an underlying disposition, we draw on five sources of information.

4 We make more confident correspondent inferences about others' behaviour that has important consequences for ourselves: that is, behaviour that has **hedonic relevance.**

5 We make more confident correspondent inferences about others' behaviour that seems to be directly intended to benefit or harm us: that is, behaviour that is high in **personalism.**

Experiments testing correspondent inference theory provide some support. Jones and Harris (1967) found that American students making attributions for speeches made by other students tended to make more correspondent inferences for freely chosen socially unpopular positions, such as freely choosing to make a speech in support of Cuba's president at the time, Fidel Castro.

In another experiment, Jones, Davis and Gergen (1961) found that participants made more correspondent inferences for out-of-role behaviour, such as friendly, outer-directed behaviour by someone who was applying for an astronaut job, in which the required attributes favour a quiet, reserved, inner-directed person.

Correspondent inference theory has some limitations and has declined in importance as an attribution theory (Hewstone, 1989; Howard, 1985). For instance, the theory holds that correspondent inferences depend significantly on the attribution of intentionality, yet unintentional behaviour (e.g. careless behaviour) can be a strong basis for a correspondent inference (e.g. that the person is a careless person).

There is also a problem with the notion of non-common effects. Correspondent inference theory maintains that people assess the commonality of effects by comparing chosen and non-chosen actions, while research shows that people simply do not attend to non-occurring behaviours and so would not be able to compute the commonality of effects accurately (Nisbett & Ross, 1980; Ross, 1977). More generally, although we may correct dispositional attributions in the light of situational factors, this is a rather deliberate process, whereas correspondent inferences themselves are relatively automatic (Gilbert, 1995).

People as everyday scientists

The best-known attribution theory is Harold Kelley's (1967, 1973) **covariation model.** In trying to discover the causes of behaviour, people act much like scientists. They identify what factor covaries most closely with the behaviour and then assign to that factor a causal role. The procedure is similar to that embodied by the statistical technique of analysis of variance (ANOVA), and for this reason Kelley's model is often referred to as an ANOVA model. People use this covariation principle to decide whether to attribute behaviour to internal dispositions (e.g. personality) or external environmental factors (e.g. social pressure).

In order to make this decision, people assess three classes of information associated with the co-occurrence of a certain action (e.g. laughter) by a specific person (e.g. Tom) with a potential cause (e.g. a comedian):

1 **Consistency information** – does Tom always laugh at this comedian (high consistency) or only sometimes laughs at this comedian (low consistency)?

2 **Distinctiveness information** – does Tom laugh at everything (low distinctiveness) or only at the comedian (high distinctiveness)?

3 **Consensus information** – does everyone laugh at the comedian (high consensus) or is it only Tom who laughs (low consensus)?

Where consistency is low, people **discount** the potential cause and search for an alternative (see Figure 3.2). If Tom sometimes laughs and sometimes does not laugh at the comedian, then presumably the cause of the laughter is neither the comedian nor Tom but some other covarying factor: for example, whether or not Tom smoked marijuana before listening to the comedian, or whether or not the comedian told a funny joke (see McClure, 1998, for a review of the conditions under which discounting is most likely to occur). Where

Hedonic relevance
Refers to behaviour that has important direct consequences for self.

Personalism
Behaviour that appears to be directly intended to benefit or harm oneself rather than others.

Covariation model
Kelley's theory of causal attribution – people assign the cause of behaviour to the factor that covaries most closely with the behaviour.

Consistency information
Information about the extent to which a behaviour Y always co-occurs with a stimulus X.

Distinctiveness information
Information about whether a person's reaction occurs only with one stimulus, or is a common reaction to many stimuli.

Consensus information
Information about the extent to which other people react in the same way to a stimulus X.

Discount
If there is no consistent relationship between a specific cause and a specific behaviour, that cause is discounted in favour of some other cause.

Consensus information
Everyone in this audience is reacting in the same way to stand-up comedian. Clearly, his routine has worked!

consistency is high, and distinctiveness and consensus are also high, one can make an external attribution to the comedian (the cause of Tom's laughter was the comedian); but where distinctiveness and consensus are low, one can make an internal attribution to Tom's personality (Tom laughed at the comedian because Tom tends to laugh a lot).

McArthur (1972) tested Kelley's theory by having participants make internal or external attributions for a range of behaviours, each accompanied by one of the eight possible configurations of high or low consistency, distinctiveness and consensus information. Although

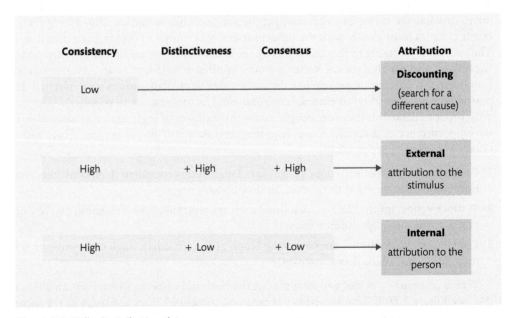

Figure 3.2 Kelley's attribution theory
Kelley's covariation model states that people decide what attributions to make after considering the (a) consistency and (b) distinctiveness of a person's behaviour, and (c) the degree of consensus among other observers in their reaction to the person's behaviour.

the theory was generally supported (see review by Kassin, 1979), there was a tendency for people to underuse consensus information. There are also some general issues to consider:

- Just because people can use pre-packaged consistency, distinctiveness and consensus information to attribute causality (the case in experimental tests of Kelley's model) does not mean that in the normal course of events they do.
- There is evidence that people are actually very bad at assessing covariation – they are poor statisticians (Alloy & Tabachnik, 1984).
- There is no guarantee that people are using the covariation principle – they may attribute causality to the most salient feature or to whatever causal agent appears to be similar to the effect (Nisbett & Ross, 1980).
- If people do attribute causality on the basis of covariance or correlation, then they certainly are *naive* scientists (Hilton, 1988) – covariation is not causation.

Another drawback of the covariation model is that consistency, distinctiveness and consensus information require multiple observations. Sometimes we have this information: we may know that Tom does indeed laugh often at almost anything (low distinctiveness), and that others do not find the comedian particularly amusing (low consensus). At other times, we may have incomplete information or even no information from multiple observations. How do we now attribute causality?

To deal with this, Kelley (1972b) introduced the notion of **causal schemata** – beliefs or preconceptions, acquired from experience, about how certain kinds of cause interact to produce a specific effect. One such schema is that a particular effect requires at least two causes (called the 'multiple necessary cause' schema): for example, someone with a drunk-driving record must have drunk a certain amount of alcohol and have been in control of a vehicle. Although the notion of causal schemata does have some empirical support (Kun & Weiner, 1973) and does help resolve attributional problems raised by the case of a single observation, it is by no means uncritically accepted (Fiedler, 1982).

Causal schemata
Experience-based beliefs about how certain types of causes interact to produce an effect.

Extensions of attribution theory

Explaining our emotions

Causal attribution may play a role in how we experience emotions (Schachter, 1964, 1971; for review, see Reisenzein, 1983). Emotions have two distinct components: an undifferentiated state of physiological *arousal*, and *cognitions* that label the arousal and determine which emotion is experienced. Usually the arousal and label go hand-in-hand and our thoughts can generate the associated arousal (e.g. identifying a dog as a Rottweiler may produce arousal that is experienced as fear). Sometimes, however, there is initially unexplained arousal that could be experienced as different emotions, depending on what kind of attributions we make for what we are experiencing. This intriguing possibility of 'emotional lability' was the focus of a classic study by Schachter and Singer (1962) – see Box 3.1 and Figure 3.3.

For a time, the most significant potential of Schachter's work was the possibility that it might be applied in therapy (Valins & Nisbett, 1972). If emotions depend on what cognitive label is assigned, through causal attribution to undifferentiated arousal, then it might, for example, be possible to transform depression into cheerfulness simply by reattributing arousal. A paradigm was devised to test this idea – called the misattribution paradigm (Valins, 1966). People who feel anxious and bad about themselves because they attribute arousal internally are encouraged to attribute arousal to external factors. For example, someone who is shy can be encouraged to attribute the arousal associated with meeting new people to ordinary environmental causes rather than to personality deficiencies and thus no longer feel shy. A number of experiments used this type of intervention with some success (e.g. Olson, 1988; Storms & Nisbett, 1970).

Box 3.1 Research classic
Context can affect how we label an emotion

In the late nineteenth century, the famous psychologist William James turned the usual account of how we experience an emotion on its head. As ordinary folk, we might believe that our mental images cause the body to react and thus define our feelings as an emotion. However, James argued that the body first responds automatically to a stimulus, and then we interpret our bodily responses on the basis of what is going on around us: if we see a bear, we run, and a little later, our pounding heart tells us that we are afraid.

One of Stanley Schachter's experiments dealing with 'emotional lability' brought this idea into the laboratory and gave it an attributional flavour (Schachter & Singer, 1962). Male students were given an injection of either adrenalin (the drug epinephrine), or a placebo (salt water) that provided a control condition. Students who had been administered the drug were then allocated to one of three conditions: (1) they were correctly informed that this would cause symptoms of arousal (e.g. rapid breathing, increased heart rate), (2) they were given no explanation

or (3) they were misinformed that they might experience a slight headache and some dizziness. All participants then waited in a room with a confederate to complete some paperwork. For half the participants, the confederate behaved euphorically (engaging in silly antics and making paper aeroplanes), and for the other half angrily (ripping up the papers and stomping around).

Schachter and Singer predicted that the 'drug-uninformed' participants would experience arousal and would search for a cause in their immediate environment (see Figure 3.3). The behaviour of the confederate would act as the salient cue, encouraging participants in the 'euphoric' condition to feel euphoric and those in the 'angry' condition to feel angry. The emotions of the other two drug groups and the control group would be unaffected by the behaviour of the confederate: the control participants had experienced no arousal from the drug, and the correctly informed and misinformed participants already had an explanation for their arousal. The results of the experiment largely supported these predictions.

However, initial enthusiasm for emotional lability and the clinical application of misattribution waned in the light of subsequent criticisms (Buchanan & Seligman, 1995; Forsterling, 1988; Reisenzein, 1983).

- Emotions may be significantly less labile than was originally thought (Maslach, 1979). Environmental cues are not readily accepted as bases for inferring emotions from unexplained arousal, and because unexplained arousal is intrinsically unpleasant, people have a propensity to assign it a negative label.

- The misattribution effect is unreliable, short-lived and largely restricted to laboratory studies (Parkinson, 1985). It is not clear that it is mediated by an attribution process, and in any case it is also restricted to a limited rage of emotion-inducing stimuli.

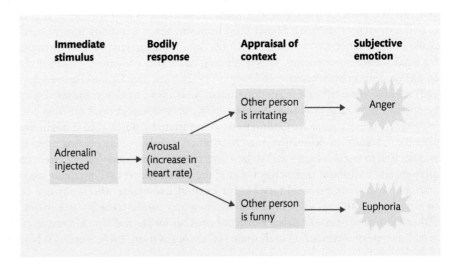

Figure 3.3 Attributing a likely cause to an experimentally induced emotion

The more general idea that cognition, particularly cognitive appraisals of the surrounding situation, plays an important role in generation and experience of emotion has, however, fed into the contemporary revival of research on affect and emotion (e.g. Blascovich, 2008; Forgas, 2006; Forgas & Smith, 2007; Haddock & Zanna, 1999; Keltner & Lerner, 2010; **see Chapter 2**). Indeed, attribution theory was the conceptual springboard for the later exploration of the concept of appraisal (e.g. Lazarus, 1991).

Attributions for our own behaviour

One significant implication of treating emotion as cognitively labelled arousal is the possibility that people make more general attributions for their *own* behaviour. This idea has been elaborated by Daryl Bem (1967, 1972) in his **self-perception theory**. (Because this is an account of how people construct their self-concept, **we describe it in Chapter 4** which explores the nature of self and identity.)

Self-perception theory
Bem's idea that we gain knowledge of ourselves only by making self-attributions: for example, we infer our own attitudes from our own behaviour.

Task performance attributions

Another extension of attribution theory focuses on the causes and consequences of the attribution people make for how well they and others perform on a task – for example, success or failure in an examination (Weiner, 1979, 1985, 1986). In making an achievement attribution, we consider three performance dimensions:

1 *Locus* – is the performance caused by the actor (internal) or by the situation (external)?
2 *Stability* – is the internal or external cause a stable or unstable one?
3 *Controllability* – to what extent is future task performance under the actor's control?

These produce eight different types of explanation for task performance (see Figure 3.4). For example, failure in an examination might be attributed to 'unusual hindrance from others' (the top right-hand box in Figure 3.4) if the student was intelligent (therefore, failure is external)

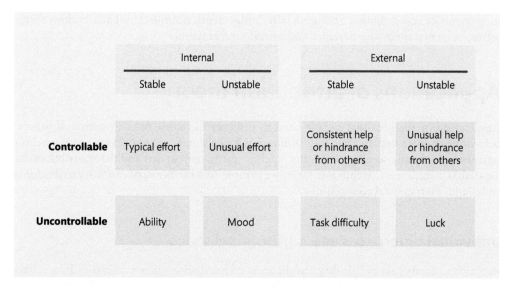

Figure 3.4 Achievement attributions as a function of locus, stability and controllability
How we attribute someone's task achievement depends on:

• *Locus* – is the performance caused by the actor (internal) or the situation (external)?
• *Stability* – is the internal or external cause a stable or unstable one?
• *Controllability* – to what extent is future task performance under the actor's control?

Achievement attribution
'Will these Reality TV stars attribute success to internal (personal) factors or to external (situational) factors?'

and was disturbed by a nearby student sneezing from hay fever (unstable and controllable, because in future examinations the sneezing student might not be present or have taken an anti-histamine, and/or one could choose to sit in a place away from the sneezing student).

According to Weiner, people first determine whether someone has succeeded or failed and accordingly experienced positive or negative emotion. They then make a causal attribution for the performance, which produces more specific emotions (e.g. pride for doing well due to ability) and expectations that influence future performance.

This idea is relatively well supported by experiments where participants are provided with performance outcomes and locus, stability and controllability information, often under role-playing conditions (e.g. De Jong, Koomen, & Mellenbergh, 1988; Frieze & Weiner, 1971). However, critics have suggested that controllability may be less important than was first thought and have wondered to what extent people outside controlled laboratory conditions really analyse achievement in this way. Subsequently, Weiner (1995) has placed an emphasis on judgements of responsibility. On the basis of causal attributions, people make judgements of responsibility, and these latter judgements, not the causal attributions themselves, influence affective experience and behavioural reactions.

Applications of attribution theory

Application of the idea that people need to discover the cause of their own and others' behaviour in order to plan their own actions has had a significant impact on social psychology. We have already seen two examples – achievement attributions and the reattribution of arousal as a therapeutic technique. Here, we explore two further applications: attributional styles and interpersonal relationships.

Individual differences and attributional styles

Attributional style
An individual (personality) predisposition to make a certain type of causal attribution for behaviour.

Research suggests that people differ in the sorts of attributions they make; they have different **attributional styles**. This is because they differ in the amount of control they feel they have over the reinforcements and punishments they receive (Rotter, 1966). *Internals* believe they have significant personal control over their destiny – things happen because they make them happen. *Externals* are more fatalistic – they believe that they have little control over what happens to them; things simply occur by chance, luck or the actions of powerful external agents. To measure people's locus of control, Rotter devised a twenty-nine-item scale. This scale has been used to relate locus of control to a range of behaviours, including political beliefs, achievement behaviour and reactions to illness. One problem with the scale is that it may measure not a unitary construct (i.e. a single personality dimension) but, rather, a number of relatively independent beliefs to do with control (Collins, 1974).

The notion of individual differences in attributional style, a tendency for individuals to make particular kinds of causal inference rather than others, over time and across different situations, has sponsored the development of a number of questionnaires to measure attributional style (Metalsky & Abramson, 1981). Of these, the attributional style questionnaire or ASQ (Peterson et al., 1982; Seligman, Abramson, Semmel, & Von Baeyer, 1979) is perhaps the most widely known. It measures the sorts of explanation that people give for aversive (i.e. unpleasant) events on three dimensions: internal/external, stable/unstable and global/specific. The global/specific dimension refers to how wide or narrow a range of effects a cause has – 'the economy' is a global explanation for someone being made redundant, whereas the closing of a specific company is a specific explanation. People who view aversive events as being caused by internal, stable, global factors have a 'depressive attributional style' (i.e. the glass is half empty), which may promote helplessness and depression and may have adverse health consequences (Abramson, Seligman, & Teasdale, 1978; Crocker, Alloy, & Kayne, 1988).

Another, slightly different scale, called the attributional complexity scale (ACS), has been devised by Fletcher et al. (1986) to measure individual differences in the complexity of the attributions that people make for events.

The idea that attributional style is a personality trait is not without problems: for instance, the ASQ and the ACS provide only limited evidence of cross-situational individual consistency in causal attribution (e.g. Cutrona, Russell, & Jones, 1985). Also not without problems is the link between attributional style, learnt helplessness and clinical depression. Although more than 100 studies involving about 15,000 participants confirm an average correlation of 0.30 between attributional style and depression (Sweeney, Anderson, & Bailey, 1986), this does not establish causation – it is a correlation where one factor explains 9 per cent of variance in the other.

More useful are studies that show that attributional style measured at one time predicts depressive symptoms at a later date (Nolen-Hoeksma, Girgus, & Seligman, 1992), but again causality is not established. Causality is difficult to establish because it is of course unethical to induce clinical depression in experimental settings. We are largely left with experimental evidence from studies of transitory mood, which is a rather pale analogue of depression. Is it justified to generalise from feelings about doing well or poorly on a trivial laboratory task to full-blown clinical depression?

Interpersonal relationships

Attributions play an important role in interpersonal relationships (see Chapter 14); particularly close relationships (e.g. friendship and marriage) where people *communicate* attributions, for example to explain, justify or excuse behaviour and to attribute blame and instil guilt (Hilton, 1990).

Interpersonal relationships typically go through three basic phases: formation, maintenance and dissolution (Harvey, 1987; see also Moreland and Levine's (1982; Levine & Moreland, 1994) model of group socialisation in Chapter 8). During the formation stage, attributions reduce ambiguity and facilitate communication and an understanding of the relationship (Fincham, 1985). In the maintenance phase, the need to make attributions wanes because stable personalities and relationships have been established. The dissolution phase is characterised by an increase in attributions in order to regain an understanding of the relationship.

A not-uncommon feature of interpersonal relationships is attributional conflict (Horai, 1977), where partners proffer divergent causal interpretations of behaviour and disagree

Attributing blame
Couples sometimes cannot agree on what is cause and what is effect. For example, does nagging cause withdrawal or withdrawal cause nagging?

over what attributions to adopt. Often partners cannot even agree on a cause–effect sequence, one exclaiming, 'I withdraw because you nag', the other, 'I nag because you withdraw'. Research mainly on heterosexual couples has shown that attributional conflict is strongly associated with relationship dissatisfaction (Kelley, 1979; Orvis, Kelley, & Butler, 1976; Sillars, 1981).

Most research has focused on the role of attributions in heterosexual marital satisfaction (e.g. Fincham & Bradbury, 1991; Fletcher & Thomas, 2000; Noller & Ruzzene, 1991), with the aim of distinguishing between distressed and non-distressed spouses in order to provide therapy for dysfunctional marital relationships. Correlational studies (e.g. Fincham & O'Leary, 1983; Holtzworth-Munroe, & Jacobson, 1985) reveal that happily married (or non-distressed) spouses tend to credit their partners for positive behaviour by citing internal, stable, global and controllable factors to explain them. Negative behaviour is explained away by ascribing it to causes viewed as external, unstable, specific and uncontrollable. Distressed couples behave in exactly the opposite way.

While women fairly regularly think in causal terms about the relationship, men do so only when the relationship becomes dysfunctional. In this respect, and contrary to popular opinion, men may be the more diagnostic barometers of marital dysfunction – when men start analysing the relationship, alarm bells should ring!

Do attributional dynamics produce dysfunctional marital relationships, or do dysfunctional relationships distort the attributional dynamic? This key causal question has been addressed by Fincham and Bradbury (1987; see overview by Hewstone, 1989), who measured responsibility attributions, causal attributions and marital satisfaction in 39 married couples on two occasions 10–12 months apart. Attributions made on the first occasion were found reliably to predict marital satisfaction 10–12 months later, but only for wives.

Another longitudinal study (although over only a two-month period) confirmed that attributions do have a causal impact on subsequent relationship satisfaction (Fletcher, Fincham, Cramer, & Heron, 1987). Subsequent, more extensive and better-controlled longitudinal studies have replicated these findings for both husbands and wives (Fincham & Bradbury, 1993; Senchak & Leonard, 1993).

Attributional biases

The attribution process is clearly subject to bias: for example, it can be biased by personality, biased by interpersonal dynamics or biased to meet communication needs. We do not approach the task of attributing causes for behaviour in an entirely dispassionate, disinterested and objective manner, and the cognitive mechanisms that are responsible for attribution may themselves be subject to imperfections that make them suboptimal.

As evidence of attributional biases and 'errors' accumulated, there was a shift of perspective. Instead of viewing people as naive scientists or even statisticians (in which case biases were largely considered a theoretical nuisance), we now think of people as **cognitive misers** or **motivated tacticians** (Moskowitz, 2005; Fiske & Taylor, 2013; **see Chapter 2**). People use cognitive short-cuts (called heuristics) to make attributions that, although not always accurate or correct, are quite satisfactory and adaptive. Sometimes the choice of short-cut and choice of attribution can also be influenced by personal motives.

Biases are entirely adaptive characteristics of ordinary, everyday social perception (Fiske & Taylor, 2013; Nisbett & Ross, 1980; Ross, 1977). In this section, we discuss some of the most important attributional biases.

Correspondence bias and the fundamental attribution error

One of the best-known attribution biases is **correspondence bias** – a tendency for people to over-attribute behaviour to stable underlying personality dispositions (Gilbert & Malone, 1995) (see Box 3.2). This bias was originally called the **fundamental attribution error**. Although the correspondence bias and fundamental attribution errors are not identical (Gawronski, 2004), the terms are often used interchangeably – the change in the preferred label mainly reflects evidence that this bias or error may not be quite as 'fundamental' as originally thought (see 'Cultural and developmental factors').

The fundamental attribution error, originally identified by Ross (1977), is a tendency for people to make dispositional attributions for others' behaviour, even when there are clear external/environmental causes. For example, in the Jones and Harris (1967) study mentioned earlier, American participants read speeches about Cuba's President Fidel Castro ostensibly written by fellow students. The speeches were either pro-Castro or anti-Castro, and the writers had ostensibly either freely chosen to write the speech or been instructed to do so. Where there was a choice, participants not surprisingly reasoned that those who had written a pro-Castro speech were in favour of Castro, and those who had written an anti-Castro speech were against Castro – an internal, dispositional attribution was made (see Figure 3.5).

However, a dispositional attribution was also made even when the speech-writers had been *instructed* to write the speech. Although there was overwhelming evidence for an exclusively external cause, participants largely disregarded this and still preferred a dispositional explanation – the fundamental attribution error. (Bearing these points in mind, how would

Cognitive miser
A model of social cognition that characterises people as using the least complex and demanding cognitions that are able to produce generally adaptive behaviours.

Motivated tactician
A model of social cognition that characterises people as having multiple cognitive strategies available, which they choose among on the basis of personal goals, motives and needs.

Correspondence bias
A general attribution bias in which people have an inflated tendency to see behaviour as reflecting (corresponding to) stable underlying personality attributes.

Fundamental attribution error
Bias in attributing another's behaviour more to internal than to situational causes.

Box 3.2 Our world
Correspondence bias in election campaigns

People's inherent tendency to fall prey to the correspondence bias can be exploited by the political process. In the 2016 US presidential election, the Republican Party spun information about the past behaviour of the Democratic contender, Hillary Clinton, to paint a picture of her as an untrustworthy and unlikable person – Donald Trump, the Republican contender, repeatedly used the term 'crooked Hillary'. The Democratic Party, in turn, drew attention to Trump's behaviour (his tweets and campaign speeches), to paint a picture of him as an unstable, thin-skinned narcissist dangerously unsuited to the presidency.

In both cases the partisan electorate seemed more comfortable focusing on the flawed personality of the opposing presidential contender than on the more complex policy landscape of the party the contender represented. When an election 'gets personal' by focusing on and overinflating or falsely creating an opponent's personal failings, it plays right into the hands of the correspondence bias and ultimate attribution error.

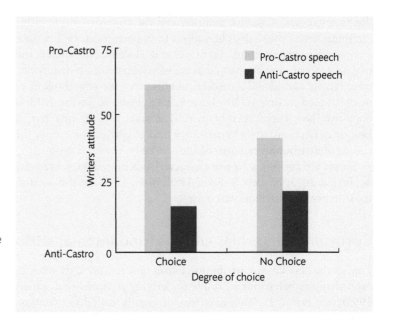

Figure 3.5 The fundamental attribution error: Attributing speech writers' attitudes on the basis of their freedom of choice in writing the speech

- Students who freely chose to write a pro- or an anti-Castro speech were attributed with a pro- or anti-Castro attitude respectively.
- Although less strong, this same tendency to attribute the speech to an underlying disposition (the fundamental attribution error) prevailed when the writers had no choice and were simply instructed to write the speech.

Source: Based on data from Jones and Harris (1967).

you account for the different views held by Helen and Lewis? See the first 'What do *you* think' question.)

The fundamental attribution error, or correspondence bias, has been demonstrated repeatedly both inside and outside the social psychology laboratory (Gawronski, 2004; Gilbert, 1998; Jones, 1979, 1990; Nisbett & Ross, 1980). Correspondence bias may also be responsible for a number of more general explanatory tendencies: for example, people's tendency to attribute road accidents to the driver rather than to the vehicle or the road conditions (Barjonet, 1980); and some people's tendency to attribute poverty and unemployment to the person rather than to social conditions (see the discussion of the key term 'Belief in a just world' later in this chapter).

Pettigrew (1979) has suggested that the fundamental attribution error may emerge in a slightly different form in intergroup contexts where groups are making attributions about ingroup and outgroup behaviour – he calls this the *ultimate attribution error* (see the 'Intergroup Attribution' section later in this chapter). Correspondence bias and the fundamental attribution error are closely related to two other biases: the *outcome bias* (e.g. Allison, Mackie, & Messick, 1996), where people assume that a person behaving in some particular way intended all the outcomes of that behaviour; and **essentialism** (Haslam, Rothschild, & Ernst, 1998; Medin & Ortony, 1989), where behaviour is considered to reflect underlying and immutable, often innate, properties of people or the groups they belong to.

Essentialism can be particularly damaging when it causes people to attribute stereotypically negative attributes of outgroups to essential and immutable personality attributes of members of that group (e.g. Bain, Kashima, & Haslam, 2006; Haslam, Bastian, Bain, & Kashima, 2006; Haslam, Bastian, & Bissett, 2004). There is evidence that groups can use essentialism strategically to discriminate against outgroups (Morton, Hornsey, & Postmes, 2009). For example, the stereotype of an outgroup as being laid-back, liberal and poorly educated becomes more pernicious if these attributes are considered immutable, perhaps genetically induced, properties of the group's members – the people themselves are considered to have personalities that are immutably lazy, immoral and stupid.

Different explanations of the correspondence bias have been proposed. They include:

1 *Focus of attention.* The actor's behaviour attracts more attention than the background; it is disproportionately salient in cognition, stands out as the figure against the situational background and is therefore over-represented causally (Taylor & Fiske, 1978). Thus, the actor

Essentialism
Pervasive tendency to consider behaviour to reflect underlying and immutable, often innate, properties of people or the groups they belong to.

and the actor's behaviour form what Heider (1958) called a 'causal unit'. This explanation makes quite a lot of sense. Procedures designed to focus attention away from the actor and on to the situation increase the tendency to make a situational rather than dispositional attribution (e.g. Rholes & Pryor, 1982). When people really want to find out about a situation from a person's behaviour, they focus on the situation and are less likely to leap to a dispositional attribution – the correspondence bias is muted or reversed (e.g. Krull, 1993).

2 *Differential forgetting.* Attribution requires the representation of causal information in memory. There is evidence that people tend to forget situational causes more readily than dispositional causes, thus producing a dispositional shift over time (e.g. Moore, Sherrod, Liu, & Underwood, 1979; Peterson, 1980). Other studies show the opposite effect (e.g. Miller & Porter, 1980), and Funder (1982) has argued that the direction of shift depends on the focus of information processing and occurs immediately after the behaviour being attributed.

3 *Linguistic facilitation.* One rather interesting observation by Nisbett and Ross (1980) is that the construction of the English language makes it relatively easy to describe an action and the actor in the same terms, but more difficult to describe the situation in the same way. For example, we can talk about a kind or honest person, and a kind or honest action, but not a kind or honest situation. The English language may facilitate dispositional explanations (Brown & Fish, 1983; Semin & Fiedler, 1991).

Cultural and developmental factors

The correspondence bias was originally called the fundamental attribution error because it was considered an automatic and universal outcome of perceptual experience and cognitive activity (e.g. McArthur & Baron, 1983). However, there is evidence that both developmental factors and culture may affect the correspondence bias. For example, in Western cultures, young children explain action in concrete situational terms and learn to make dispositional attributions only in late childhood (Kassin & Pryor, 1985; White, 1988). Furthermore, this developmental sequence itself may not be universal. Hindu Indian children do not drift towards dispositional explanations at all, but rather towards increasingly situational explanations (Miller, 1984). We return to this point later when we discuss particular cultural and developmental differences in how children make attributions (see Figure 3.7).

These differences quite probably reflect different cultural norms for social explanation, or more basic differences between Western and non-Western conceptions of self – the autonomous and independent Western self and the interdependent non-Western self (Chiu & Hong, 2007; **see Chapters 4 and 16**). The correspondence bias is a relatively ubiquitous and socially valued feature of Western cultures (Beauvois & Dubois, 1988; Jellison & Green, 1981), but, although present, it is less dominant in non-Western cultures (Fletcher & Ward, 1988; Morris & Peng, 1994).

As noted earlier, the fundamental attribution error is not as fundamental as was originally thought. In many ways, it may be a normative way of thinking (**see discussion of norms in Chapters 7 and 8**). This is one reason why Gilbert and Malone (1995) recommend that the term 'correspondence bias' be used in preference to the term 'fundamental attribution error'. Indeed, according to Gawronski (2004), the two constructs are subtly different: technically, he argues, the fundamental attribution error is the tendency to underestimate the impact of situational factors; and the correspondence bias is the tendency to draw correspondent dispositional inferences from behaviour that is constrained by the situation.

The actor–observer effect

Imagine the last time a shop assistant was rude to you. You probably thought, 'What a rude person!' although perhaps put less politely – in other words, you made an internal attribution to the shop assistant's enduring personality. In contrast, how did you explain the last

Actor-observer effect
Tendency to attribute our own behaviours externally and others' behaviours internally.

time *you* snapped at someone? Probably not in terms of your personality; more likely in terms of external factors such as time pressure or stress. The **actor-observer effect** (or the self–other effect) is really an extension of the correspondence bias. It refers to the tendency for people to attribute others' behaviour internally to dispositional factors and their own behaviour externally to environmental factors (Jones & Nisbett, 1972).

Research has provided substantial evidence for this effect (Watson, 1982), and some extensions and qualifications. For example, not only do we attribute others' behaviour more dispositionally than our own, but we also consider their behaviour to be more stable and predictable than our own (Baxter & Goldberg, 1988). The valence of the behaviour also matters. People make more dispositional attributions for socially desirable than socially undesirable behaviour, irrespective of who the actor is (e.g. Taylor & Koivumaki, 1976), and actors are more dispositional in attributing positive behaviour and more situational in attributing negative behaviour than are observers (e.g. Chen, Yates, & McGinnies, 1988).

The actor–observer effect can be inverted if someone knows their behaviour is dispositionally caused. For example, you may 'adopt' an injured hedgehog knowing that you are a sucker for injured animals and you have often done this sort of thing in the past (Monson & Hesley, 1982). Finally, the actor–observer effect can be erased or reversed if the actor is encouraged to take the role of the observer regarding the behaviour to be attributed, and the observer the role of the actor. Now the actor becomes more dispositional and the observer more situational (e.g. Frank & Gilovich, 1989).

There are two main explanations for the actor–observer effect:

1 *Perceptual focus.* This explanation is almost identical to the 'focus of attention' explanation for the correspondence bias described earlier in this chapter. For the observer, the actor and the actor's behaviour are figural against the background of the situation. However, actors cannot 'see' themselves behaving, so the background situation assumes the role of figure against the background of self. The actor and the observer quite literally have different perspectives on the behaviour and therefore explain it in different ways (Storms, 1973). Perceptual salience does indeed seem to play an important role in causal explanation. For example, McArthur and Post (1977) found that observers made more dispositional attributions for an actor's behaviour when the actor was strongly illuminated than when dimly illuminated.

2 *Informational differences.* Another reason why actors tend to make external attributions and observers internal ones is that actors have a wealth of information to draw on about how they have behaved in other circumstances. They may actually know that they behave differently in different contexts and thus quite accurately consider their behaviour to be under situational control. Observers are not privy to this autobiographical information. They see the actor behaving in a certain way in one context, or a limited range of contexts, and have no information about how the actor behaves in other contexts. It is therefore not an unreasonable assumption to make a dispositional attribution. This explanation, first suggested by Jones and Nisbett (1972), does have some empirical support (Eisen, 1979; White & Younger, 1988).

The false consensus effect

Kelley (1972a) identified consensus information as being one of the three types of information that people used to make attributions about others' behaviour (see earlier in this chapter). One of the first cracks in the naive scientist model of attribution was McArthur's (1972) discovery that attributors in fact underused or even ignored consensus information (Kassin, 1979).

Subsequently, it became apparent that people do not ignore consensus information but rather provide their own consensus information. People see their own behaviour as typical and assume that, under similar circumstances, others would behave in the same way.

The false consensus effect
This mid-winter arctic dipper discovers an attributional bias. Who else would swim here before breakfast?

Ross, Greene and House (1977) first demonstrated this **false consensus effect**. They asked students if they would agree to walk around campus for 30 minutes wearing a sandwich board carrying the slogan 'Eat at Joe's'. Those who agreed estimated that 62 per cent of their peers would also have agreed, while those who refused estimated that 67 per cent of their peers would also have refused.

Well over 100 studies testify to the robust nature of the false consensus effect (Marks & Miller, 1987; Mullen, Atkins, Champion, Edwards, Hardy, Story, & Vanderklok, 1985; Wetzel & Walton, 1985). The effect exists for a number of reasons:

- We usually seek out similar others and so should not be surprised to find that other people are similar to us.

- Our own opinions are so salient to us, at the forefront of our consciousness, that they eclipse the possibility of alternative opinions.

- We are motivated to ground our opinions and actions in perceived consensus in order to validate them and build a stable world for ourselves.

The false consensus effect is stronger for important beliefs, ones that that we care a great deal about (e.g. Granberg, 1987), and for beliefs about which we are very certain (e.g. Marks & Miller, 1985). In addition, external threat, positive qualities, the perceived similarity of others and minority group status also inflate perceptions of consensus (e.g. Sanders & Mullen, 1983; Sherman, Presson, & Chassin, 1984; Van der Pligt, 1984).

False consensus effect
Seeing our own behaviour as being more typical than it really is.

Self-serving biases

In keeping with the motivated tactician model of social cognition (Fiske & Taylor, 1991) discussed earlier in this chapter (**also see Chapter 2**), attribution is influenced by our desire for a favourable image of ourselves (**see Chapter 4**). We make attributions that satisfy **self-serving biases**. Overall, we take credit for our positive behaviours and successes as reflecting who we are and our intention and effort to do positive things (the *self-enhancing bias*). At the same time, we explain away our negative behaviours and failures as being due

Self-serving biases
Attributional distortions that protect or enhance self-esteem or the self-concept.

to coercion, normative constraints and other external situational factors that do not reflect who we 'really' are (the *self-protecting bias*). This is a robust effect that holds across many cultures (Fletcher & Ward, 1988).

Self-serving biases are clearly ego-serving (Snyder, Stephan, & Rosenfield, 1978). However, Miller and Ross (1975) suggest there is also a cognitive component, particularly for the self-enhancing aspect. People generally expect to succeed and therefore accept responsibility for success. If they try hard to succeed, they associate success with their own effort, and they generally exaggerate the amount of control they have over successful performances. Together, these cognitive factors might encourage internal attribution of success. Overall, it is most likely both cognitive and motivational factors have a role (Anderson & Slusher, 1986; Tetlock & Levi, 1982) and they are difficult to disentangle from one another (Tetlock & Manstead, 1985; Zuckerman, 1979).

Self-enhancing biases are more common than self-protecting biases (Miller & Ross, 1975) – partly because people with low self-esteem tend not to protect themselves by attributing their failures externally; rather, they attribute them internally (Campbell & Fairey, 1985). Both of these forms of bias can be muted by a desire not to be seen to be boasting over our successes and lying about our failures (e.g. Schlenker, Weingold, & Hallam, 1990) – but they are not totally extinguished (Riess, Rosenfield, Melburg, & Tedeschi, 1981). One self-serving bias which most of us have exploited from time to time is **self-handicapping**, a term described by Jones and Berglas:

> The self-handicapper, we are suggesting, reaches out for impediments, exaggerates handicaps, embraces any factor reducing personal responsibility for mediocrity and enhancing personal responsibility for success.

> Jones and Berglas (1978, p. 202)

People self-handicap in this way when they anticipate failure, whether in their job performance, in sport, or even in therapeutic settings when being 'sick' allows one to drop out of life. What a person often will do is intentionally and publicly make external attributions for a poor showing even before it happens. Check the experiment about choosing between drugs in Box 3.3 and Figure 3.6.

Another instance of self-serving attribution surfaces when attribution of responsibility (Weiner, 1995) is influenced by an outcome bias (Allison, Mackie, & Messick, 1996). People tend to attribute greater responsibility to someone who is involved in an accident with large rather than small consequences (Burger, 1981; Walster, 1966). For example, we would attribute greater responsibility to the captain of a super-tanker that spills millions of litres of oil than to the captain of a charming little fishing boat that spills only a few litres, although the degree of responsibility may actually be the same.

This effect quite probably reflects the tendency for people to cling to an **illusion of control** (Langer, 1975) by believing in a *just world* (Furnham, 2003; Lerner, 1977). People like to believe that bad things happen to 'bad people' and good things to 'good people' (i.e. people get what they deserve), and that people have control over and responsibility for their outcomes. This attributional pattern makes the world seem a controllable and secure place in which we can determine our own destiny.

Belief in a just world can result in a pattern of attribution where victims are deemed responsible for their misfortune – poverty, oppression, tragedy and injustice all happen because victims deserve it. Examples of the just world hypothesis in action are such views as the unemployed are responsible for being out of work, and rape victims are responsible for the violence against them. Another example is the belief, still held by some people, that the 6 million Jewish victims of the Holocaust were responsible for their own fate – that they deserved it (Davidowicz, 1975). Refer back to the second 'What do *you* think?' question. Just world beliefs are also an important component of many religious ideologies (Hogg, Adelman, & Blagg, 2010).

Self-handicapping
Publicly making advance external attributions for our anticipated failure or poor performance in a forthcoming event.

Illusion of control
Belief that we have more control over our world than we really do.

Belief in a just world
Belief that the world is a just and predictable place where good things happen to 'good people' and bad things to 'bad people'.

Box 3.3 Your life
Self-handicapping: Explaining away your failure

Imagine that you are waiting to take an examination in a subject you find difficult and that you fully anticipate failing. You might well make sure that as many people as possible know that you have done no revision, are not really interested in the subject and have a mind-numbing hangover to boot. Your subsequent failure is thus externally attributed without it seeming that you are making excuses to explain away your failure.

To investigate this idea, Berglas and Jones (1978) had introductory psychology students try to solve some problems where the problems were either solvable or not solvable. They were told that they had done very well, and

before continuing with a second problem-solving task, they were given the choice of taking either a drug called 'Actavil', which would ostensibly improve intellectual functioning and performance, or 'Pandocrin', which would have the opposite effect. As predicted, those students who had succeeded on the solvable puzzles felt confident about their ability and so chose Actavil in order to improve further (see Figure 3.6). Those who had succeeded on the not-solvable puzzles attributed their performance externally to luck and chose Pandocrin in order to be able to explain away more easily the anticipated failure on the second task.

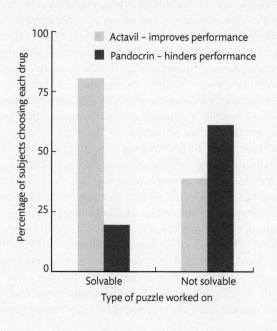

Figure 3.6 Self-handicapping: Choosing a drug depends on a puzzle's solvability

- Students who had done well on a solvable puzzle could attribute their performance internally (e.g. to ability): anticipating an equally good performance on a second similar task, they chose a performance-enhancing drug, Actavil, rather than a performance-impairing drug, Pandocrin.
- Students who had done well on a not-solvable puzzle could only attribute their performance externally (e.g. to luck): with the prospect of an equivalent performance on the second task they chose the performance-impairing drug, as the self-handicapping option.

Source: Based on data from Berglas and Jones (1978).

Belief in a just world may also be responsible for self-blame. Victims of traumatic events such as incest, debilitating illness, rape and other forms of violence can experience a strong sense that the world is no longer stable, meaningful, controllable or just. One way to reinstate an illusion of control is, ironically, to take some responsibility for the event (Miller & Porter, 1983).

Intergroup attribution

Attribution theories are concerned mainly with how people make dispositional or situational attributions for their own and others' behaviour and the sorts of bias that distort this process. The perspective is tied to interpersonal relations: people as unique individuals make attributions

Intergroup attribution

Black Lives Matter is an international movement of political activists whose belief system incorporates social change (see Chapter 11). Their outgroup is huge and amorphous – whites, governments, police and security forces.

Intergroup attribution
Process of assigning the cause of one's own or others' behaviour to group membership.

Ethnocentrism
Evaluative preference for all aspects of our own group relative to other groups.

Ultimate attribution error
Tendency to attribute bad outgroup and good ingroup behaviour internally, and to attribute good outgroup and bad ingroup behaviour externally.

for their own behaviour or the behaviour of other unique individuals. However, there is another attributional context – intergroup relations – where individuals as group members make attributions for the behaviour of themselves as group members and others as either ingroup or outgroup members (Deschamps, 1983; Hewstone, 1989; Hewstone & Jaspars, 1982, 1984).

Examples of **intergroup attribution** abound. One example is the attribution of national economic and social malaise to immigrant minorities (e.g. Middle Eastern and North African refugees in Europe, Eastern Europeans in the United Kingdom and Mexicans in the United States). Another is the explanation of behaviour in terms of stereotypical properties of a person's group membership – for example, attributions for performance that are consistent with gender or racial stereotypes (Inzlicht & Schmader, 2011).

Intergroup attributions serve two functions, the first relating to ingroup bias and the second to self-esteem. Extending our discussion of self-serving attributional biases to intergroup relations, **ethnocentrism** can be viewed as an ingroup-serving bias. Socially desirable (positive) behaviour by ingroup members and socially undesirable (negative) behaviour by outgroup members are internally attributed to dispositions, and negative ingroup and positive outgroup behaviour are externally attributed to situational factors (Hewstone & Jaspars, 1982; Hewstone, 1989, 1990). This tendency is more prevalent in Western than in non-Western cultures (Fletcher & Ward, 1988) and is common in team sports contexts, where the success of one's own team is attributed to internal stable abilities rather than effort, luck or task difficulty – we are skilful, they were lucky. This *group-enhancing* bias is stronger and more consistent than the corresponding *group-protective* bias (Mullen & Riordan, 1988; Miller & Ross, 1975).

Pettigrew (1979) has described a related bias, called the **ultimate attribution error**. This is an extension of Ross's (1977) fundamental attribution error that focuses on attributions for outgroup behaviour. Pettigrew argued that negative outgroup behaviour is dispositionally attributed, whereas positive outgroup behaviour is externally attributed or explained away so that we preserve our unfavourable outgroup image. The ultimate attribution error refers to attributions made for outgroup behaviour only, whereas broader intergroup perspectives focus on ingroup attributions as well.

Taylor and Jaggi (1974) conducted an early study of intergroup attributions in southern India against a background of intergroup conflict between Hindus and Muslims. Hindu participants read vignettes describing Hindus or Muslims acting in a socially desirable way (e.g. offering shelter from the rain) or socially undesirable way (e.g. refusing shelter) towards them and then chose one of a number of explanations for the behaviour. The results were as predicted. Hindu participants made more internal attributions for socially desirable than socially undesirable acts by Hindus (ingroup). This difference disappeared when Hindus made attributions for Muslims (outgroup).

Hewstone and Ward (1985) conducted a more complete and systematic follow-up, with Malays and Chinese in Malaysia and Singapore. Participants made internal or external attributions for desirable or undesirable behaviour described in vignettes as being performed by Malays or by Chinese. In Malaysia, Malays showed a clear ethnocentric attribution bias – they attributed a positive act by a Malay more to internal factors than a similar act by a Chinese, and a negative act by a Malay less to internal factors than a similar act by a Chinese (see Figure 3.7). The ingroup enhancement effect was much stronger than the outgroup derogation effect. The Chinese participants showed no ethnocentric bias – instead, they showed a tendency to make similar attributions to those made by Malays. In Singapore, the only significant effect was that Malays made internal attributions for positive acts by Malays.

Hewstone and Ward explain these findings in terms of the nature of intergroup relations in Malaysia and Singapore. In Malaysia, Malays are the clear majority group and Chinese an ethnic minority. Furthermore, relations between the two groups were tense and relatively conflictual at the time, with Malaysia pursuing a policy of ethnic assimilation. Both Malays and Chinese generally shared an unfavourable **stereotype** of Chinese and a favourable stereotype of Malays. In contrast, Singapore has been ethnically more tolerant. The Chinese are in the majority, and ethnic stereotypes are markedly less pronounced.

Stereotype
Widely shared and simplified evaluative image of a social group and its members.

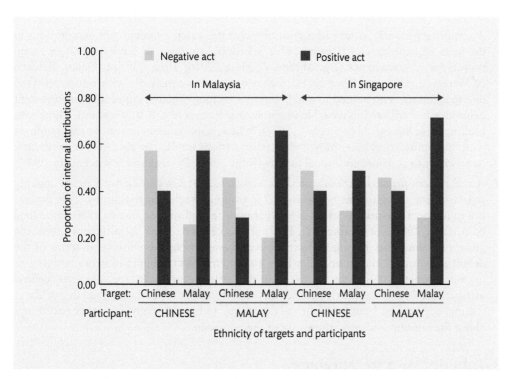

Figure 3.7 Internal attribution of positive and negative acts by Malays or Chinese as a function of attributor ethnicity

Malays showed an ethnocentric attributional bias in which a positive act was more internally attributed to a Malay than a Chinese, and a negative act less internally attributed to a Malay than a Chinese: the effect was more pronounced in Malaysia, where Malays are the dominant group and Chinese the ethnic minority, than in Singapore. Chinese did not show an ethnocentric attribution bias.

Source: Based on data from Hewstone and Ward (1985).

Level of explanation
The types of concepts, mechanisms and language used to explain a phenomenon.

The takeaway message from this analysis is that ethnocentric attribution is not a universal tendency that reflects asocial cognition; rather, it depends on intergroup dynamics in a sociohistorical context. The sorts of attribution that group members make about ingroup and outgroup behaviour are influenced by the nature of the relations between the groups.

This is consistent with Hewstone's (1989) argument that a fuller analysis of attribution, more accurately described as social explanation, requires a careful articulation (i.e. theoretical integration or connection) of different **levels of explanation** (see Doise, 1986; **see also Chapter 1**). In other words, we need to know how individual cognitive processes, interpersonal interactions, group membership dynamics and intergroup relations all affect, are affected by and are interrelated with one another.

Further evidence for ethnocentric intergroup attributions comes from studies of interracial attitudes in educational settings in the United States (Duncan, 1976; Stephan, 1977); from studies of inter-ethnic relations between Israelis and Arabs (Rosenberg & Wolfsfeld, 1977) and between Hindus and Muslims in Bangladesh (Islam & Hewstone, 1993); and from studies of race, sex and social class-based attributions for success and failure (Deaux & Emswiller, 1974; Feather & Simon, 1975; Greenberg & Rosenfield, 1979; Hewstone, Jaspars, & Lalljee, 1982).

More recently, Mackie and Ahn (1998) found that the *outcome bias*, the assumption that the outcomes of behaviour were intended by the person who chose the behaviour, is affected by whether the actor is a member of your group or not, and whether the outcome was desirable or not. Mackie and Ahn found that there was an outcome bias in the case of an ingroup member and a desirable outcome but not when the outcome was undesirable.

At least two processes may be responsible for ethnocentric intergroup attributions:

1 *A cognitive process:* Social categorization generates category-congruent expectations in the form of expectancies (Deaux, 1976), schemas (e.g. Fiske & Taylor, 1991) or group prototypes or stereotypes (e.g. Abrams & Hogg, 2010; Turner, Hogg, Oakes, Reicher, & Wetherell, 1987; **see Chapter 11**). Behaviour that is consistent with our stereotypes or expectancies is attributed to stable internal factors, whereas expectancy-inconsistent behaviour is attributed to unstable or situational factors (e.g. Bell, Wicklund, Manko, & Larkin, 1976; Rosenfield & Stephan, 1977). When people explain behaviour that confirms their expectancy, they may simply rely on dispositions implied by a stereotype, with little or no effort to consider additional factors (Kulik, 1983; Pyszczynski & Greenberg, 1981).

2 *A self-esteem process:* People's need for secure self-esteem can be nurtured by making self-favouring comparisons between their ingroup and relevant outgroups. This process is a fundamental aspect of **social identity theory** (e.g., Tajfel & Turner, 1986; also Hogg & Abrams, 1988; **see Chapter 11**). Because people derive their social identity from the groups to which they belong (a description and evaluation of themselves in terms of the defining features of the group), they have a vested interest in maintaining or obtaining an ingroup profile that is more positive than that of relevant outgroups. The ethnocentric attributional bias quite clearly satisfies this aim: it internally attributes good things about the ingroup and bad things about the outgroup, and it externally attributes bad things about the ingroup and good things about the outgroup.

Social identity theory
Theory of group membership and intergroup relations based on self-categorization, social comparison and the construction of a shared self-definition in terms of ingroup-defining properties.

Attribution and stereotyping

Societal and intergroup attribution processes significantly influence and are influenced by the stereotypes we have of groups in society. Stereotyping is not only an individual cognitive activity (**see Chapter 2**); it can also serve ego-defensive functions (making one feel good in contrast to others) and social functions (allowing one to fit in with other people's world views) (Snyder & Miene, 1994).

Groups invoke and accentuate existing stereotypes in order to attribute large-scale distressing events to the actions of specific outgroups – that is, scapegoats (Tajfel, 1981a).

For instance, during the 1930s in Germany, the Jews were blamed for the economic crisis of the time. It was politically expedient to invoke the 'miserly Jew' stereotype to explain in simplistic terms the lack of money: there is no money because the Jews are hoarding it. Closer to home, stereotypes of immigrants as sponging on the state were invoked by "leavers" in the run-up to the June 2016 referendum that voted for Britain to leave the European Union. Stereotypes may also be invoked to justify actions committed or planned against an outgroup (e.g. Crandall, Bahns, Warner, & Schaller, 2011). For instance, a group might develop a stereotype of an outgroup as dull-witted, simple, lazy and incompetent in order to explain or justify the economic and social exploitation of that group.

Social knowledge and societal attributions

People do not wake up every morning and causally reconstruct their world anew. In general, we rely on well-learnt causal scripts (Abelson, 1981) and general causal schemata. We stop, think and make causal attributions only when events are unexpected or inconsistent with expectations (e.g. Hastie, 1984; Langer, 1978; Pyszczynski & Greenberg, 1981), when we are in a bad mood (Bohner, Bless, Schwarz, & Strack, 1988), when we feel a lack of control (Liu & Steele, 1986) or when attributions are occasioned by conversational goals: for example, when we want to offer a particular explanation or justification of behaviour to someone (Hewstone & Antaki, 1988; Lalljee, 1981; Tetlock, 1983). Usually, we rely on a wealth of acquired and richly textured cultural knowledge that automatically explains what is going on around us. This knowledge resides in cultural beliefs, social stereotypes, collective ideologies and **social representations** (see Box 3.4).

Social representations

One way in which cultural knowledge about the causes of things may be constructed and transmitted is described by Moscovici's theory of social representations (e.g. Farr & Moscovici, 1984; Lorenzi-Cioldi & Clémence, 2001; Moscovici, 1961, 1981, 1988; Purkhardt,

Social representations
Collectively elaborated explanations of unfamiliar and complex phenomena that transform them into a familiar and simple form.

Box 3.4 Your life
A very strange custom: The cultural context of causal attribution

Gün Semin tells a fictitious story about a Brazilian aborigine who visits Rio de Janeiro and then returns home to his tribe deep in the Amazonian rainforest to give an account of the visit (Semin, 1980, p. 292).

> On particular days more people than all those you have seen in your whole lifetime roam to this huge place of worship, an open hut the size of which you will never imagine. They come, chanting, singing, with symbols of their gods and once everybody is gathered the chanting drives away all alien spirits. Then, at the appointed time the priests arrive wearing colourful garments, and the chanting rises to war cries until three high priests, wearing black, arrive. All priests who were running around with sacred round objects leave them and at the order of the high priests begin the

religious ceremony. Then, when the chief high priest gives a shrill sound from himself they all run after the single sacred round object that is left, only to kick it away when they get hold of it. Whenever the sacred object goes through one of the two doors and hits the sacred net the religious followers start to chant, piercing the heavens, and most of the priests embark on a most ecstatic orgy until the chief priest blows the whistle on them.

This is, of course, a description of a football match by someone who does not know the purpose or rules of the game. It illustrates an important point. For your explanations to be meaningful they need to be grounded in a wider and more general interpretative framework that constitutes your socially acquired cultural knowledge.

1995). (**See Chapter 5 for a discussion of the relationship between social representations and attitudes.**) Social representations are understandings shared among group members. They emerge through informal everyday communication. They transform the unfamiliar and complex into the familiar and straightforward, and they therefore provide a common-sense framework for interpreting our experiences.

An individual or a specialist interest group develops a sophisticated, non-obvious, technical explanation of a commonplace phenomenon (e.g. explaining mental illness in terms of biological or social factors rather than spiritual forces). This attracts public attention and becomes widely shared and popularised (i.e. simplified, distorted and ritualised) through informal discussion among non-specialists. It is now a social representation – an accepted, unquestioned common-sense explanation that ousts alternatives to become the orthodox explanation.

Moscovici originally focused on the development of the theory of psychoanalysis, but his analysis is just as applicable to other formal theories and complex phenomena that have been transformed and simplified to become part of popular consciousness: for example, evolution, relativity, dietary and health theories, Marxism and climate change. The theory of social representations has come under some criticism, often for the rather imprecise way in which it is formulated (e.g. Augoustinos & Innes, 1990). Nonetheless, it does suggest how ordinary social interaction in society constructs common-sense or 'naive' causal theories that are widely used to explain events (Heider, 1958). As the world becomes increasingly complex the relevance of a social representations perspective becomes very appealing – for example, to help explain how the enormously complex dynamics surrounding the emergence and appeal of terrorist groups such as DAISH, Al-Qaeda and the Taliban is boiled down to a misleadingly simplistic conflict between Islam and the West.

One source of criticism of social representations has been that it is difficult to know how to analyse social representations quantitatively. This problem has now largely been resolved. Appropriate quantitative techniques have been developed (Doise, Clémence, & Lorenzi-Cioldi, 1993), and practical descriptions of methodology have been published (Breakwell & Canter, 1993). These methods include qualitative and quantitative analyses of interviews, questionnaires, observational data and archival material. A good example of this methodological pluralism is Jodelet's (1991) classic description of social representations of mental illness in the small French community of Ainay-le-Chateau, in which questionnaires, interviews and ethnographic observation were all used.

Social representations, like norms (**see Chapters 7 and 8**), tend to be grounded in groups and differ from group to group such that intergroup behaviour can often revolve around a clash of social representations (Lorenzi-Cioldi & Clémence, 2001). For example, in Western countries, attitudes and behaviour that promote healthy lifestyles are associated with higher social status, and health promotion messages tend to come from middle-class professional groups (Salovey, Rothman, & Rodin, 1998). A social representations analysis suggests that these messages are relatively ineffective in promoting healthy lifestyles for non-middle-class people because they are inconsistent with the wider representational framework of a good life for such people.

The European Union (EU) provides fertile ground for social representations research (e.g. Chryssochoou, 2000) that connects with the study of European identity dynamics (e.g. Cinnirella, 1997; Huici, Ros, Cano, Hopkins, Emler, & Carmona, 1997). The EU is, in many ways, a prototypical social representation – a relatively new and technical idea that has its roots in complex economic matters such as free trade and subsidies. But the EU is now an accepted and commonplace part of European discourse which often emphasises more emotive issues of national and European identity – although the recent global and European economic and immigration crises have refocused attention on the nature of national borders and national identity and on economic and trade issues associated with the single currency and the concept of a European Central Bank.

Rumour and gossip

Social representations are constructed in a way that resembles how rumours develop and are communicated (Allport & Postman, 1947; DiFonzo & Bordia, 2007). One of the earliest studies of rumour was conducted by Allport and Postman (1945), who found that if experimental participants described a photograph to someone who had not seen the photo, and then this person described it to another person, and so on, only 30 per cent of the original detail remained after five retellings. Allport and Postman identified three processes associated with rumour transmission:

1 *Levelling* – the rumour quickly becomes shorter, less detailed and less complex.
2 *Sharpening* – certain features of the rumour are selectively emphasised and exaggerated.
3 *Assimilation* – the rumour is distorted in line with people's pre-existing prejudices, partialities, interests and agendas.

More naturalistic studies have found rather less distortion as a consequence of rumour transmission (e.g. Caplow, 1947; Schachter & Burdeck, 1955).

Whether or not rumours are distorted, and even whether rumours are transmitted at all, seems to depend on how anxious those who hear the rumour are (Buckner, 1965; Rosnow, 1980). Uncertainty and ambiguity increase anxiety and stress, which lead people to seek out information to rationalise anxiety, which in turn enhances rumour transmission. (Check the third 'What do *you* think?' question. Here is one reason why Rajna wanted to pass a rumour on.) Whether a rumour is distorted or becomes more precise depends on whether people approach the rumour with a critical or uncritical orientation. In the former case the rumour is refined, while in the latter (which often accompanies a crisis) the rumour is distorted.

Rumours always have a source, and often this source purposely elaborates the rumour for a specific reason. The stock market is a perfect context for rumour elaboration – and, of course, the consequences for ordinary people's everyday lives can be enormous. At the end of the 1990s, rumour played a significant role in inflating the value of 'dot-com' start-up companies, which then crashed in the NASDAQ meltdown early in 2000. More recently, there was enormous build-up and hype surrounding the launching of Facebook as a public company on the stock market in May 2012 – Facebook shares lost 25 per cent of their value in the two weeks following the launch. Rumour also played a significant role in the global stock market crash at the end of 2008 and beginning of 2009 (the market lost more than half its value), and in reports about Greek economic collapse that depressed the stock market in August 2011 and May 2012.

Another reason why rumours are purposely elaborated is to discredit individuals or groups. An organisation can spread a rumour about a competitor in order to undermine the competitor's market share (Shibutani, 1966), or a group can spread a rumour to blame another group for a widespread crisis. A good example of this is the fabrication and promulgation of conspiracy theories, which we discuss in the next subsection.

But first, what about gossip? Gossip is informal talk, usually but not necessarily malicious, behind the back of absent third parties (Foster, 2004; also see Baumeister, Zhang, & Vohs, 2004; Smith, 2014). In this respect it is narrower than rumour – rumour is about issues of significance to a group (a possible round of lay-offs) whereas gossip is about the personal characteristics of an absent other (a colleague's embarrassing sexual escapades). Gossip polices normative practices by vilifying those who violate norms; increases cohesion among those who are included in the circle of gossip; and empowers those who spread the gossip by making them appear to be 'in the loop', privy to secret information and superior to the victims of the gossip. In these respects, gossip serves a very clear social representational function, but of course, gossiping is also for many people just great fun.

Conspiracy theories

Conspiracy theory
Explanation of widespread, complex and worrying events in terms of the premeditated actions of small groups of highly organised conspirators.

Conspiracy theories are simplistic and exhaustive causal theories that attribute widespread natural and social calamities to the intentional and organised activities of certain social groups that are seen as conspiratorial bodies set on ruining and then dominating the rest of humanity (Graumann & Moscovici, 1987). These groups are also perceived to be highly entitative (distinct, homogenous, inward looking – see **Chapter 8**), even cliquish (Grzesiak-Feldman & Suszek, 2008).

One of the best-documented conspiracy theories is the myth, dating from the Middle Ages, of the Jewish world conspiracy (Cohn, 1966), which surfaces periodically and often results in massive systematic persecution. Other conspiracy theories include the belief that immigrants are intentionally plotting to undermine the economy, that homosexuals are intentionally spreading HIV and that witches (in the Middle Ages) and DAISH (most recently) are behind virtually every world disaster you care to mention (e.g. Cohn, 1975). Research suggests that it is people who are personally willing to conspire who tend to endorse conspiracy theories most readily (Douglas & Sutton, 2011).

Conspiracy theories wax and wane in popularity. They were particularly popular from the mid-seventeenth to the mid-eighteenth century:

> Everywhere people sensed designs within designs, cabals within cabals; there were court conspiracies, backstairs conspiracies, ministerial conspiracies, factional conspiracies, aristocratic conspiracies, and by the last half of the eighteenth century even conspiracies of gigantic secret societies that cut across national boundaries and spanned the Atlantic.

> Wood (1982, p. 407)

The accomplished conspiracy theorist can, with consummate skill and breath-taking versatility, explain even the most arcane and puzzling events in terms of the devious schemes and inscrutable machinations of hidden conspirators. Billig (1978) believes it is precisely this that makes conspiracy theories so attractive – they are incredibly effective at reducing uncertainty (Hogg, 2007b, 2012). They provide a causal explanation in terms of enduring dispositions that can explain a wide range of events, rather than complex situational factors that are less widely applicable. Furthermore, worrying events become controllable and easily remedied because they are caused by small groups of highly visible people rather than being due to complex sociohistorical circumstances (Bains, 1983).

Not surprisingly, conspiracy theories are almost immune to disconfirming evidence. For example, in December 2006, the outcome of a three-year, 3.5-million-pound enquiry into the death in 1997 of Princess Diana was reported – although there was absolutely no evidence that the British Royal Family conspired with the British government to have her killed to prevent her from marrying an Egyptian Muslim, this conspiracy theory still persists. There are also conspiracy theories about the 9/11 terrorist attacks in the United States in 2001 – some Americans are absolutely convinced it was the doing of the US government, and in parts of the Muslim world, many people believe it was perpetrated by Israel (Lewis, 2004). A recent conspiracy theory has it that President Barack Obama is not only black, and presumably not white, but not really an American at all! (See Box 3.5.)

Societal attributions

The emphasis on attributions as social knowledge surfaces in research on people's explanations for large-scale social phenomena. In general, this research supports the view that causal attributions for specific phenomena are located within and shaped by wider, socially constructed belief systems.

For example, Catholics and non-Catholic Christians have subtly different attributional styles when explaining social phenomena and, in particular, the religious notion of

Box 3.5 Our world
Barack Obama is black and not really an American

Why is Barack Obama – the child of a Midwestern mother 'white as milk' and a Kenyan father 'black as pitch' (Obama, 2004, p. 10) – considered an African American, but never White?

Halberstadt, Sherman and Sherman (2011, p. 29)

This is an example of *hypodescent* – a tendency to categorise children whose parents come from different status groups, usually ethnic, into the subordinate group. Jamin Halberstadt and his colleagues have argued that hypodescent is a bias in the way we compare and classify features of majority and minority group members, and the importance that we give to distinctive features of the minority. **(See Chapter 2 for a detailed discussion of salient or attention-capturing stimuli.)**

In the case of Obama, the bias of hypodescent has been elaborated into a conspiracy myth. In the United States, a full quarter of adult Americans, mainly right-wing social and religious conservatives, are 'birthers'. They believe that Obama was not born in America and thus was ineligible to be president, and that there was a Democratic conspiracy to conceal this.

Even though there is overwhelming and incontrovertible proof that Obama was born in Hawaii (his official birth certificate was made public in 2008 and again in April 2011), birthers were not fazed. A 13 May 2011 Gallup poll showed that 23 per cent of Republican supporters remained birthers. Conspiracy theorists are tenacious. As it became increasingly difficult to sustain the belief that Obama was foreign-born, some birthers became 'schoolers' who believe that because Obama is black there is no way he could have gained entry to Harvard without cheating and receiving special favours, and that – wait for it – the Democrats have a conspiracy going to conceal this as well.

'salvation' (Li, Johnson, Cohen, Williams, Knowles, & Chen, 2014). Catholics are extrinsically motivated and explain people's behaviour, plight and ultimately salvation in terms of external factors (including ritual, the Pope, priests), whereas non-Catholic Christians are intrinsically motivated and proffer explanation in terms of internal factors in the form of personally internalised religious tenets (e.g. the protestant work ethic – Furnham, 1984; Weber, 1930).

Socioeconomic status and political ideology also influence attribution and social explanation. For example, research on explanations for poverty has shown that both the rich and the poor tend to explain poverty in terms of poor people's behaviour rather than the situation that those people find themselves in (e.g. Feagin, 1972; Feather, 1974). This individualistic tendency is weaker among people with a more left-wing or liberal ideology and people living in developing countries where poverty is widespread (Pandey, Sinha, Prakash, & Tripathi, 1982).

Explanations for wealth tend to depend on political affiliation. In Britain, Conservatives often ascribe it to positive individual qualities of thrift and hard work, while Labour supporters attribute it to the unsavoury individual quality of ruthless determination (Furnham, 1983). Not surprisingly, there are also cross-cultural differences: for example, individualistic explanations are very common in Hong Kong (Forgas, Morris, & Furnham, 1982; Furnham & Bond, 1986).

Similarly, explanations given for unemployment are influenced by people's wider belief and value systems (**Chapter 5**). For example, Australian students preferred societal over individualistic explanations for unemployment; nominating defective government, social change and economic recession as more valid causes of unemployment than lack of motivation and personal handicap (Feather, 1985; see also Feather & Barber, 1983; Feather & Davenport, 1981). However, students who were politically more conservative placed less emphasis on societal explanations. Studies conducted in Britain show the same thing – societal explanations are more prominent than individualistic explanations, and that there is general agreement between employed and unemployed respondents (Furnham, 1982; Gaskell & Smith, 1985; Lewis, Snell, & Furnham, 1987).

Other research has focused on people's explanations for riots (**social unrest, collective behaviour and riots are discussed in detail in Chapter 11**). Riots are enormously complicated phenomena where there are both proximal and distal causes – a specific event or action might trigger the riot, but only because of the complex conjunction of wider conditions. For instance, the proximal cause of the 1992 Los Angeles riots was the acquittal of white police officers charged with the beating of a black motorist, Rodney King (see Box 11.1); however, this alone would have been unlikely to promote a riot without the background of racial unrest and socio-economic distress in the United States at the time.

As with explanations of poverty, wealth and unemployment, people's explanations for a specific riot are influenced by their sociopolitical perspective (e.g. Litton & Potter, 1985; Reicher, 1984, 2001; Reicher & Potter, 1985; Schmidt, 1972). Conservative members of the establishment tend to identify deviance, or personal or social pathology, while people with more liberal social attitudes tend to identify social circumstances.

For example, Schmidt (1972) analysed printed media explanations of the spate of riots that occurred in American cities during 1967. The explanations could be classified on three dimensions: (a) legitimate–illegitimate, (b) internal–external cause, and (c) institutional–environmental cause. The first two dimensions were strongly correlated, with legitimate external causes (e.g. urban renewal mistakes, slum conditions) going together and illegitimate internal causes (e.g. criminal intent, belief that violence works) going together. Media sources on the political right tended to identify illegitimate internal causes, whereas those classified as 'left–centre' (i.e. liberal) emphasised legitimate external causes.

Finally, Sniderman, Hagen, Tetlock and Brady (1986) investigated people's explanations for racial inequality and their preferences for different government policies. They used a national sample of whites in the United States (in 1972) and focused on the influence of level of education. They found that less-educated whites employed an 'affect-driven' reasoning process. They started with their (mainly negative) feelings about blacks, then proceeded directly to advocate minimal government assistance. Having done this, they 'doubled back' to fill in the intervening link to justify their advocacy – namely that blacks were personally responsible for their own disadvantage. In contrast, better-educated whites adopted a 'cognition-driven' reasoning process where they reasoned both forwards and backwards. Their policy recommendations were based on causal attributions for inequality, and in turn their causal attributions were influenced by their policy preference.

Culture's contribution

Attribution and social explanation is not only affected by religious ideology, sociopolitical values, educational status, group membership and ethnicity, but also, perhaps unsurprisingly, by culture. People from different cultures often make very different attributions, make attributions in different ways or approach the entire task of social explanation in different ways (Chiu & Hong, 2007; Heine, 2016; Smith, Bond, & Kağitçibaşi, 2006). Consequently, the potential for cross-cultural interpersonal misunderstanding is enormous.

For example, the Zande people of West Africa have a dual theory of causality, where common-sense proximal causes operate within the context of witchcraft as the distal cause (Evans-Pritchard, 1937; see also Jahoda, 1979). This is, ironically, not really that different from moderate Christians' belief in the proximal operation of scientific principles within the context of God as the distal cause. For the Zande, an internal–external distinction would make little sense.

Culture and attribution
Is the puppet responsible for its own actions? Easterners are less likely than Westerners to make dispositional attributions about people – let alone puppets!

Another example: Lévy-Bruhl (1925) reported that the natives of Motumotu in New Guinea attributed a pleurisy epidemic to the presence of a specific missionary, his sheep, two goats and, finally, a portrait of Queen Victoria. Although initially quite bizarre, these sorts of attribution are easily explained as social representations. How much more bizarre are they than, for example, the postulation in physics of other universes and hypothetical particles shaped like strings or membranes as part of a unified theory to explain the origin and structure of the cosmos (Hawking, 1988; Hawking & Mlodinow, 2010)? Horgan exclaimed that 'This isn't physics any more. It's science fiction with mathematics' (Horgan, 2011, p. B7).

One area of cross-cultural attribution research is the correspondence bias (discussed earlier in this chapter). We have seen that in Western cultures, people tend to make dispositional attributions for others' behaviour (Gilbert & Malone, 1995; Ross, 1977), and that such dispositional attributions become more evident over ontogeny (e.g. Pevers & Secord, 1973). In non-Western cultures, however, people are less inclined to make dispositional attributions (Carrithers, Collins, & Lukes, 1986; Morris & Peng, 1994). This is probably partly a reflection of the more pervasive and all-enveloping influence of social roles in more collectivist non-Western cultures (Fletcher & Ward, 1988; Jahoda, 1982) and partly a reflection of a more holistic world view that promotes context-dependent, occasion-bound thinking (Shweder & Bourne, 1982).

To investigate further the role of culture in dispositional attributions, Miller (1984) compared middle-class North Americans and Indian Hindus from each of four age groups (adults, and 15-, 11- and 8-year-olds). Participants narrated prosocial and antisocial behaviour and gave their own spontaneous explanations of the causes of this behaviour. Miller coded responses to identify the proportion of dispositional and contextual attributions that participants made. Among the youngest children there was little cross-cultural difference (see Figure 3.8). As age increased, however, the two groups diverged, mainly because the Americans increasingly adopted dispositional attributions. For context attributions, the results were reversed.

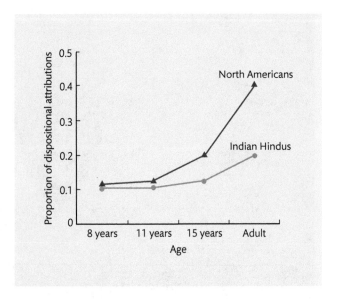

Figure 3.8 Dispositional attributions as a function of age and cultural background

North Americans and Indian Hindus initially do not differ in the proportion of dispositional attributions made for behaviour. However, by the age of 15, there is a clear difference that strengthens in adulthood, with Americans being significantly more dispositional than Indians in their attributions.

Source: Based on data from Miller (1984).

The important lesson this study teaches us is that cultural factors have a significant impact on attribution and social explanation. (**We return to the role of culture in social behaviour in Chapter 16.**)

Summary

- People are naive psychologists seeking to understand the causes of their own and other people's behaviour.
- Much like scientists, people consider consensus, consistency and distinctiveness information in deciding whether to attribute behaviour internally to personality traits and dispositions, or externally to situational factors.
- The attributions that we make can have a profound impact on our emotions, self-concept and relationships with others. There may be individual differences in propensities to make internal or external attributions.
- People are actually poor scientists when it comes to making attributions. They are biased in many different ways, the most significant of which are a tendency to attribute others' behaviour dispositionally and their own behaviour externally, and a tendency to protect the self-concept by externally attributing their own failures and internally attributing their successes.
- Attributions for the behaviour of people as ingroup or outgroup members are ethnocentric and based on stereotypes. However, this bias is affected by the real or perceived nature of intergroup relations.
- Stereotypes may originate in a need for groups to attribute the cause of large-scale distressing events to outgroups that have (stereotypical) properties that are causally linked to the events.
- People resort to causal attributions only when there is no readily available social knowledge (e.g. scripts, causal schemata, social representations, cultural beliefs) to explain things automatically.
- Social representations are simplified causal theories of complex phenomena that are socially constructed through communication contextualised by intergroup relations. Rumour and gossip may play a key role in social representations.

- Conspiracy theories are one particularly bizarre but sadly prevalent type of causal theory that often persists in the face of overwhelming evidence that the theory is wrong.
- People's world views and identity in society (e.g., religion, wealth, politics, culture) significantly impact how they make attributions and explain social phenomena (e.g. poverty, unemployment, riots).

Key terms

Actor–observer effect	Discount	Motivated tactician
Attribution	Distinctiveness information	Naive psychologist (or scientist)
Attributional style	Essentialism	Non-common effects
Belief in a just world	Ethnocentrism	Outcome bias
Causal schemata	External (or situational) attribution	Personalism
Cognitive miser	False consensus effect	Self-handicapping
Consensus information	Fundamental attribution error	Self-perception theory
Consistency information	Hedonic relevance	Self-serving bias
Conspiracy theory	Illusion of control	Social representations
Correspondence bias	Intergroup attributions	Social identity theory
Correspondent inference	Internal (or dispositional) attribution	Stereotype
Covariation model	Level of explanation	Ultimate attribution error

Literature, film and TV

JFK

A 1991 film by Oliver Stone. It stars Kevin Costner as a New Orleans district attorney who reopens the case to find out who really assassinated JFK on 22 November 1963, in Dallas, and what the process/plot behind it was. This is a wonderful encounter with conspiracy theories and people's need to construct a causal explanation, however bizarre, of a disturbing event. The film also stars Tommy Lee Jones and Sissy Spacek.

Going Clear: Scientology and the Prison of Belief

A multi-award-winning 2015 documentary directed by Alex Gibney, based on an earlier 2013 book by Lawrence Wright, which, with the aid of archive footage, dramatic reconstructions and interviews describes the origins, history and nature of L. Ron Hubbard's Church of Scientology. The film documents the awful lengths to which a group can go to protect its ideology and world view – any divergence is seen as heresy or blasphemy, and is severely and cruelly punished in order to make sure that everyone believes in the group's explanation of the nature of things.

Macbeth

Shakespeare's 1606–7 tragedy in which three witches prophesise a string of evil deeds committed by Macbeth during his bloody rise to power, including the murder of the Scottish king Duncan. The causal question is whether the prophecy caused the events – or whether was there some other complex of causes. For those of you who prefer films, Justin Kurzel has directed a highly acclaimed 2015 film version of Macbeth that stars Michael Fassbender in the title role and Marion Cotillard as Lady Macbeth.

Legally Blonde

A 2001 award-winning comedy directed by Robert Luketic and starring Reese Witherspoon. Witherspoon plays Elle Woods, a stereotypically breathless self-confident blonde southern California sorority girl. This sounds pretty much one of a million such films, but this one is actually funny, relatively clever and has more going on. It is a nice vehicle for exploring the way that people construct someone's personality from the way they appear and behave, and then it can be difficult for the target to break free of the pigeonhole. Elle, like most people, is more complex and less superficial than her appearance and some of her behaviour lead one to think. But as she tries to be taken seriously as a law student and a person, she finds that those around her continually construct her personality on the basis of superficial cues.

Guided questions

1   What is meant by *locus of control*? How does locus of control affect the way we invoke effort, ability, fate and chance to explain behaviour, and how might this influence our own success in life?

2   Do attribution processes create problems in close relationships, or vice versa?

3   Sometimes our mental short-cuts lead us into error. One such error is the *correspondence bias*. What is this bias, how is it produced and how can it be combatted?

4   What is meant by self-handicapping? Provide a real-world setting in which it can be applied.

5   The term *conspiracy theory* has entered everyday language. Can social psychology help us understand what purpose these theories serve, and even combat them?

Learn more

Fiske, S. T., & Taylor, S. E. (2013). *Social cognition: From brains to culture* (2nd ed.) Los Angeles: Sage. Most recent edition of Fiske and Taylor's classic social cognition text – it is comprehensive, detailed and well written, and it also covers the recent developments in social neuroscience.

Fletcher, G., & Fincham, F. D. (Eds.) (1991). *Cognition in close relationships*. Hillsdale, NJ: Erlbaum. A collection of leading scholars contributes detailed chapters on attribution and other sociocognitive approaches to close relationships.

Hewstone, M. (1989). *Causal attribution: From cognitive processes to collective beliefs*. Oxford: Blackwell. A comprehensive and detailed coverage of attribution theory and research, which also includes coverage of European perspectives that locate attribution processes in the context of society and intergroup relations.

Hilton, D. J. (2007). Causal explanation: From social perception to knowledge-based causal attribution. In A. W. Kruglanski & E. T. Higgins (Eds.), *Social psychology: Handbook of basic principles* (2nd ed., pp. 232–253). New York: Guilford. A comprehensive coverage of research on causal attribution processes and social explanation.

Macrae, C. N., & Quadflieg, S. (2010). Perceiving people. In S. T. Fiske, D. T. Gilbert, & G. Lindzey (Eds.), *Handbook of social psychology* (5th ed., Vol. 1, pp. 428–463). New York: Wiley. Comprehensive coverage of what we know about person perception – how we form and use our cognitive representations of people.

Moskowitz, G. B. (2005). *Social cognition: Understanding self and others*. New York: Guilford. A relatively recent comprehensive social cognition text that is written in an accessible style as an introduction to the topic.

Smith, E. R. (1994). Social cognition contributions to attribution theory and research. In P. G. Devine, D. L. Hamilton, & T. M. Ostrom (Eds.), *Social cognition: Impact on social psychology* (pp. 77–108). San Diego, CA: Academic Press. A focused coverage of social cognitive dimensions of attribution processes.

Trope, Y., & Gaunt, R. (2007). Attribution and person perception. In M. A. Hogg, & J. Cooper (Eds.), *The SAGE handbook of social psychology: Concise student edition* (pp. 176–194). London: SAGE. A relatively recent, comprehensive and above all readable overview of attribution research.

Weary, G., Stanley, M. A., & Harvey, J. H. (1989). *Attribution*. New York: Springer-Verlag. A discussion of applications of attribution theory and the operation of attribution processes in clinical settings and everyday life outside the laboratory.

Chapter 4
Self and identity

Chapter contents

What do *you* think?

1   To what extent is your identity unique, distinguishing you from all other human beings?

2   Would you accept that you are overwhelmingly driven to look good in other people's eyes?

3   Manfred asks: if people generally want to feel good about themselves, have those with low self-esteem failed in their quest? Clarify this apparent anomaly for Manfred.

4   Andrea has found out that you are studying social psychology. She asks your advice for presenting herself in the best possible light to others. Can you give her some tips?

Who are you?

Take a look in your wallet. You will find cards that have your name on them, and probably a rather gruesome photograph of yourself. What happens when you meet someone? Very early on you discover each other's name, and soon after that you establish such things as their occupation, their attitudes and what they like to do. You also try to identify mutual acquaintances. In more formal contexts, people sometimes display their identity by donning a uniform, whipping out a flashy business card or wearing one of those often embarrassing name/role badges. In the brave new world of the Internet, people can of course construct and nurture, courtesy of Facebook and other social media, limitless more or less truthful selves and identities.

Your identity and your self-concept underpin your everyday life. Knowing who you are allows you to know what you should think and do and how others might think of and treat you; and knowing who others are allows you to predict what they think and what they do. Knowing our identity regulates and structures how we interact with others, and in turn, identities are grounded in social interaction and the structure of society.

Many scholars believe that it is reflexive thought – that is, the ability to think about ourselves thinking – that separates us from almost all other animals. Reflexive thought means that we can think about ourselves, about who we are, how we would like to be and how we would like others to see us. Humans have a highly developed sense of self, and self and identity are fundamental parts of being human. We should not be surprised that social psychologists in particular have become intrigued with the self.

In this chapter, we explore the self – where it comes from, what it looks like and how it influences thought and behaviour. Because self and identity are cognitive **constructs** that influence social interaction and perception, and that are themselves influenced by society, the material in this chapter connects to virtually all other chapters in the text. The self is an enormously popular focus of research (e.g. Leary & Tangney, 2003; Sedikides & Brewer, 2001; Swann & Bosson, 2010). Ashmore and Jussim (1997) reported 31,000 social psychological publications on the self over a two-decade period to the mid-1990s. There is now an International Society for Self and Identity and a scholarly journal imaginatively entitled *Self and Identity*.

Constructs
Abstract or theoretical concepts or variables that are not observable and are used to explain or clarify a phenomenon.

Self and identity in historical context

The self is, historically, a relatively new idea (Baumeister, 1987). In medieval society, social relations were fixed and stable and legitimised in religious terms. People's lives and identities were mapped out according to their position in the social order – by ascribed attributes such as family membership, social rank, birth order and place of birth. In many ways, what you saw was what you got, so the idea of a complex individual self lurking underneath it all was superfluous and difficult to imagine.

All this started to change in the sixteenth century, and the change has gathered momentum ever since. The forces for change included:

- *Secularisation* – the idea that fulfilment occurs in the afterlife was replaced by the idea that you should actively pursue personal fulfilment in this life.

- *Industrialisation* – people were increasingly seen as units of production that moved from place to place to work and thus had a portable personal identity that was not locked into static social structures such as the extended family.

- *Enlightenment* – people felt that they could organise and construct different, better, identities and lives for themselves by overthrowing orthodox value systems and oppressive regimes (e.g. the French and American revolutions of the late eighteenth century).

- *Psychoanalysis* – Freud's theory of the human mind crystallised the notion that the self was unfathomable because it lurked in the gloomy depths of the unconscious (see the 'Psychodynamic self' section).

Psychoanalysis challenged the way we think about self and identity: it attributes behaviour to complex dynamics that are hidden deep within the person's sense of who they are. Earlier in the text (**see Chapter 3; also see Chapter 5**), we explored the theory of social representations – a theory that invoked psychoanalysis as an example of how a novel idea or analysis can entirely change the way that people think about their world (e.g. Moscovici, 1961; see Lorenzi-Cioldi & Clémence, 2001).

Together, these and other social, political and cultural changes caused people to think about self and identity as complex and problematic. Theories of self and identity propagated and flourished in this fertile soil.

Psychodynamic self

Freud (e.g. 1921) believed that unsocialised and selfish libidinal impulses (the *id*) are repressed and kept in check by internalised societal norms (the *superego*), but that, from time to time and in strange and peculiar ways, repressed impulses surface. Freud's view of the self is one in which you can only truly know yourself, or indeed others, when special procedures, such as hypnosis or psychotherapy, are employed to reveal repressed thoughts. His ideas about self, identity and personality are far-reaching in social psychology: for example, Adorno, Frenkel-Brunswik, Levinson and Sanford's (1950) influential authoritarian personality theory of prejudice is a psychodynamic theory (**see Chapter 10**).

Individual versus collective self

Freud, like many other psychologists, viewed the self as very personal and private – the high point of individuality: something that uniquely describes an individual human being. When someone says '*I am* . . .' they are describing what makes them different from all other human beings. But think about this for a moment. 'I am British', 'I come from Bristol', 'I am a social psychologist' – these are all descriptions of my*self*, but they are also descriptions of many other people's selves (there are 64 million Britons, over 440,000 people currently living in Bristol, and many thousands of social psychologists). So the self can also be a shared or collective self – a 'we' or 'us'.

Social psychologists have argued long and hard for more than a century over what to make of this – is the self an individual or a collective phenomenon? The debate has created polarised camps, with advocates of the individual self and advocates of the collective self slogging it out in the literature. It is fair to say that the advocates of the individual self have tended to prevail. This is largely because social psychologists have considered groups to be made up of individuals who interact with one another rather than of individuals who have a collective sense of shared identity. Individuals interacting in aggregates is the focus of social psychology as a behavioural science, whereas groups as collectives is the focus of social sciences, such as sociology and political science (**see Chapters 1 and 11**).

This perspective on groups, summed up by Floyd Allport's legendary proclamation that 'There is no psychology of groups which is not essentially and entirely a psychology of individuals' (Allport, 1924, p. 4), has made it difficult for the collective self to thrive as a research topic.

Collective self

It was not always like this. In the early days of social psychology, things were very different (see Farr, 1996; Hogg & Williams, 2000). Wilhelm Wundt was the founder of psychology as an experimental science, and he proposed that social psychology was the study of:

> those mental products which are created by a community of human life and are, therefore, inexplicable in terms merely of individual consciousness since they presuppose the reciprocal action of many.

> Wundt (1916, p. 3)

Wundt's social psychology dealt with collective phenomena, such as language, religion, customs and myth, which, according to Wundt, could not be understood in terms of the psychology of the isolated individual. Emile Durkheim (1898), one of the founding fathers of sociology, was influenced by Wundt's interest in collective life and also maintained that collective phenomena could not be explained in terms of individual psychology.

The view that the self draws its properties from groups is shared by many other early social psychologists: for example, early theorists of collective behaviour and the crowd (e.g. LeBon, 1908; Tarde, 1901; Trotter, 1919; **see also Chapter 11**). Notably, William McDougall, in his book *The Group Mind* (McDougall, 1920), argued that out of the interaction of individuals there arose a 'group mind', which had a reality and existence that was qualitatively distinct from the isolated individuals making up the group. There was a collective self that was grounded in group life. Although phrased in rather quaint old-fashioned language, this idea has a direct line of descent to subsequent experimental social psychology which confirms that human interaction has emergent properties that endure and influence other people: for example, Muzafer Sherif's (1936) research on how norms emerge from interaction and are internalised to influence behaviour, and some of Solomon Asch's (1952) research on conformity to norms.

Since the early 1980s there has been a revival of interest in the notion of a collective self, largely initiated by European research on the emergence of social representations out of social interaction (e.g. Farr & Moscovici, 1984; Lorenzi-Cioldi & Clémence, 2001; **see Chapters 3, 5, 7 and 8**), and on the role of social identity in group processes and intergroup behaviour (e.g. Tajfel & Turner, 1986; also see Hogg, 2006; Hogg & Abrams, 1988; **discussed later in this chapter but covered fully in Chapter 11**).

Symbolic interactionist self

Another twist to the idea of the collective self is recognition that the self emerges and is shaped by social interaction. Early psychologists such as William James (1890) distinguished between self as stream of consciousness, 'I', and self as object of perception, 'me'. In this way, reflexive knowledge is possible because 'I' can be aware of 'me', and people can therefore know themselves. However, this is not to say that people's self-knowledge is particularly accurate. People tend to reconstruct who they are without being aware of having done it (Greenwald, 1980), and in general, although people may be aware of who they are in terms of their attitudes and preferences, they are rather bad at knowing how they arrived at that knowledge (Nisbett & Wilson, 1977).

Symbolic interactionism
Theory of how the self emerges from human interaction, which involves people trading symbols (through language and gesture) that are usually consensual and represent abstract properties rather than concrete objects.

Nevertheless, people do have a sense of 'me', and according to **symbolic interactionism**, the self arises out of human interaction (Mead, 1934; see also Blumer, 1969). G. H. Mead believed that human interaction is largely symbolic. When we interact with people, it is mainly in terms of words and non-verbal cues that are rich with meaning because they symbolise much more than is superficially available in the behaviour itself (**see Chapter 15**). Mead believed that society influences individuals through the way individuals think about themselves, and that self-conception arises and is continually modified through interaction between people. This interaction involves symbols that must have shared meaning if they are to be communicated effectively. If you say to your friend 'let's eat out tonight', you both know what this means and that it opens up a variety of choices that each of you know about.

Interacting effectively also rests on being able to take the role of the other person. This of course entails 'looking in from outside' and seeing oneself as others do – as a social *object*, 'me', rather than a social *subject*, 'I' (cf. Batson, Early, & Salvarani, 1997). Because others often view us as representatives of a category (e.g. a student), the 'me' is probably more often seen as a collective 'me' – we might even think of it as 'us'. The representations, or views, that our society has of the world are traded through interacting symbolically with

The looking glass self
According to G.H. Mead, our self-concept derives from seeing ourselves as others see us. Is the broken mirror a metaphor for her self-concept?

others. We are effective only if we can take the role of the other and thus see ourselves as others (ultimately, society) do. In this way, we construct a self-concept that reflects the society we live in; we are socially constituted.

Symbolic interactionism offers a quite sophisticated and complex model of how the self is formed. And yet it generates a very straightforward prediction. Because forming our concept of self comes from seeing ourselves as others see us (the idea of the **looking-glass self**), how we view ourselves should be closely shadowed by how others view us. Shrauger and Schoeneman (1979) reviewed sixty-two studies to see if this was true. What they found was that people did *not* tend to see themselves as others saw them but instead saw themselves as they *thought* others saw them. For a more recent example of research on the looking-glass self, see Box 4.1 and Figure 4.1.

One implication of the idea that people do not see themselves as others see them, but instead see themselves as they think others see them, is that we do not actually take the role of the other in constructing a sense of self. An alternative reading is that the communication process in social interaction is noisy and inaccurate. It is influenced by a range of

Looking-glass self
The self derived from seeing ourselves as others see us.

Box 4.1 Research highlight
Public versus private self-presentation

Dianne Tice (1992) conducted an experiment where undergraduate students were asked to act as 'stimulus persons' for postgraduate clinical psychology trainees. Their task was to use an intercom system to answer verbal questions in a way that would reflect an aspect of their personality. Effectively, they were to describe themselves so that they would come across as either consistently emotionally stable (implying not responsive) or emotionally responsive in different situations.

There were two experimental conditions: (a) a private condition where the students believed no one was watching them, and (b) a public condition where they believed a clinical psychology trainee was closely monitoring their

behaviour. (This was a ruse, since there was no one actually monitoring the students.) In the next phase, they were asked to rate themselves in terms of how responsive they really were. They made their ratings on a 25-point scale ranging from 1 (stable = not responsive) to 25 (responsive).

Tice intended the public condition to be the one that would engage the looking-glass self. As predicted, subsequent descriptions of self were more radically altered under public conditions than private conditions (see Figure 4.1) – suggesting that the students did not see themselves as others saw them, but instead as they *thought* others saw them.

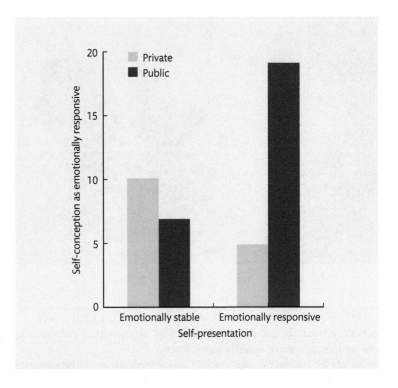

Figure 4.1 Conceiving of oneself as emotionally stable or emotionally responsive, as a function of public or private self-presentation

- People were instructed to present themselves as either less emotionally responsive (i.e. more stable) or more emotionally responsive.
- Next, they rated their 'true' level of emotional responsiveness on a 25-point scale, ranging from a low score (less emotionally responsive) to a high score (more emotionally responsive).
- When they believed that their earlier behaviour had been public, their self-conception moved in the direction of their action: closer to a score of 1 for those who had been less emotionally responsive, or closer to a score of 25 for those who had been more emotionally responsive.

Source: Based on data from Tice (1992), Study 1.

self-construal motivations (motives to view others, and be viewed by them, in particular ways) that conspire to construct an inaccurate image of others and what they think about us. People are mostly unaware of what other people really think of them (Kenny & DePaulo, 1993), perhaps fortunately so. A sage person once said, 'if you really want to hear how much people like you, you'd better listen to what they say at your funeral!'

As we discover in this chapter, our concept of self is linked to how we go about enhancing our self-image. People normally overestimate their good points, overestimate their control over events and are unrealistically optimistic – Sedikides and Gregg (2007) call this the *self-enhancing triad*.

Self-awareness

If the truth be known, you do not spend all your time thinking about yourself. Self-awareness comes and goes for different reasons and has an array of consequences. Although I am sure you can all think of people who appear to think only of themselves almost all the time (we discuss narcissism later in this chapter)!

In their book *A Theory of Objective Self-Awareness*, Shelley Duval and Robert Wicklund (1972) argued that self-awareness is a state in which you are aware of yourself as an object, much as you might be aware of a tree or another person. When you are objectively self-aware, you make comparisons between how you actually are and how you would like to be – an ideal, a goal or some other standard. The outcome of this comparison is often a sense that you have shortcomings, along with negative emotions associated with this recognition. People then try to overcome their shortcomings by bringing the self closer into line with ideal standards. This can be very difficult, leading people to give up trying and thus feel even worse about themselves.

Objective self-awareness is generated by anything that focuses your attention on yourself as an object: for example, being in front of an audience (**see Chapter 6**) or catching your image in a mirror. Indeed, a very popular method for raising self-awareness in laboratory studies is actually to place participants in front of a mirror. Charles Carver and Michael

Scheier (1981) introduced a qualification to self-awareness theory, in which they distinguished between two types of self that you can be aware of:

1 the *private self* – your private thoughts, feelings and attitudes;
2 the *public self* – how other people see you, your public image.

Private self-awareness leads you to try to match your behaviour to your internalised standards, whereas public self-awareness is oriented towards presenting yourself to others in a positive light.

Being self-aware can be very uncomfortable. We all feel self-conscious from time to time and are only too familiar with how it affects our behaviour – we feel anxious, we become tongue-tied, or we make mistakes on tasks. We can even feel slightly paranoid (Fenigstein, 1984). However, sometimes being self-aware can be a terrific thing, particularly on those occasions when we have accomplished a great feat. In early December 2003, having won the Rugby World Cup, the England team paraded through London and ended up in Trafalgar Square in front of three-quarters of a million people – standing in an open-topped bus, the team looked freezing but certainly did not suffer from the crowd's adulation.

Self-awareness can also make us feel good when the standards against which we compare ourselves are not too exacting: for example, if we compare ourselves against standards derived from 'most other people' or from people who are less fortunate than ourselves (Taylor & Brown, 1988; Wills, 1981). Self-awareness can also improve introspection, intensify emotions and improve performance of controlled effort-sensitive tasks that do not require undue skill, such as checking over an essay you have written.

The opposite of being objectively self-aware is being in a state of reduced objective self-awareness. Because elevated self-awareness can be stressful or aversive, people may try to avoid this state by drinking alcohol, or by more extreme measures such as suicide (Baumeister, 1991). Reduced self-awareness has also been identified as a key component of **deindividuation**, a state in which people are blocked from awareness of themselves as distinct individuals, fail to monitor their actions and can behave impulsively. Reduced self-awareness may be implicated in the way that crowds behave and in other forms of social unrest. Read how this comes about in both small groups and crowd settings in **Chapters 11 and 12**.

Deindividuation
Process whereby people lose their sense of socialised individual identity and engage in unsocialised, often antisocial, behaviours.

Self-awareness is about being *aware* of self. However, recent research suggests that the same effect of trying to match one's behaviour to standards can be obtained by unconsciously focusing *attention* on self. Silvia and Phillips (2013) report two studies where self-awareness was primed not by usual explicit mirror method but by subliminal first-name priming. The effects were the same; suggesting that self-awareness can be primed subliminally and is therefore not a deliberative awareness phenomenon but an automatic attention phenomenon. Silvia and Phillips suggest perhaps talking more about self-focused *attention* than self-awareness.

Self-knowledge

When people are self-aware, what are they aware of? What do we know about ourselves, and how do we gain a sense of who we are? Self-knowledge is constructed in much the same way and through many of the same processes as we construct representations of other people. **We looked at some of these general processes when we discussed social thinking and attribution in Chapters 2 and 3.**

Self-schemas

Earlier (**see Chapter 2**) we saw how information about other people is stored in the form of a **schema**. We cognitively store information about the self in a similar but more complex and varied way – as separate context-specific nodes where different contexts activate

Schema
Cognitive structure that represents knowledge about a concept or type of stimulus, including its attributes and the relations among those attributes.

An ideal self
'Wow! So how do
I look?'

different nodes and thus, effectively, different aspects of self (Breckler, Pratkanis, & McCann, 1991; Higgins, Van Hook, & Dorfman, 1988). You are probably now itching to ask, 'So . . . where in the brain *is* the self?' Well, research suggests that no single brain system or area of the brain is, of itself, responsible for one's sense of self. Instead, the experience of self emerges from widely distributed brain activity across the medial prefrontal and medial precuneus cortex of the brain (e.g. Saxe, Moran, Scholz, & Gabrieli, 2006).

The self-concept is neither a singular, static, lump-like entity nor a simple averaged view of the self – it is complex and multi-faceted, with a large number of discrete self-schemas (Markus, 1977; Markus & Wurf, 1987). People tend to have clear conceptions of themselves (i.e. self-schemas) on some dimensions but not others – i.e. they are schematic on some but aschematic on others. People are self-schematic on dimensions that are important to them, on which they think they are extreme and on which they are certain the opposite does not hold. For example, if you think you are sophisticated, and being sophisticated is important to you, then you are self-schematic on that dimension – it is part of your self-concept. If you do not think you are sophisticated, and if this does not bother you, then being *sophisticated* is not one of your self-schemas.

Most people have a complex self-concept with a relatively large number of discrete self-schemas. Patricia Linville (1985, 1987; see 'Many selves, multiple identities' in this chapter) has suggested that this variety helps to buffer people from the negative impact of life events by making sure that there are always self-schemas from which they can derive a sense of satisfaction. People can be quite strategic in how they use their self-schemas – Linville used a colourful phrase to describe what we usually do: 'don't put all your eggs in one cognitive basket'.

Self-schemas that are rigidly compartmentalised have disadvantages (Showers, 1992). If some self-schemas are very negative and some are very positive, events may cause extreme mood swings according to whether a positive or negative self-schema is primed. Generally, more integrated self-schemas are preferable. For example, if James believes that he is a wonderful cook but an awful musician, he has compartmentalised self-schemas – contexts that prime one or the other self-schema will produce very positive or very negative moods. Contrast this with Sally, who believes she is a reasonably good cook but not a great musician. She has self-schemas where the boundaries are less clear – context effects on mood will be less extreme.

Self-schemas influence information processing and behaviour in much the same way as schemas about other people (Markus & Sentis, 1982): self-schematic information is more readily noticed, is overrepresented in cognition and is associated with longer processing time. Self-schemas do not only describe how we are. Markus and Nurius (1986) have suggested that we have an array of possible selves – future-oriented schemas of what we would like to become, or what we fear we might become. For example, a postgraduate student may have future selves as a university lecturer or a rock musician.

Another perspective is offered by Higgins's (1987) **self-discrepancy theory**. Higgins suggests that we have three types of self-schema:

1 *actual self* – how we currently are;
2 *ideal self* – how we would like to be;
3 *'ought' self* – how we think we should be.

The ideal self and the ought self are 'self-guides', but they mobilise different types of self-related behaviours. The same goal – for example, prosperity – can be constructed as an ideal (we strive to be prosperous) or an 'ought' (we strive to avoid not being prosperous). Discrepancies between actual and ideal or 'ought' motivate change to reduce the discrepancy – in this way we engage in **self-regulation**. (**In Chapter 13 we discuss self-regulation in the context of close relationships**.) Furthermore, these self-discrepancies make us emotionally vulnerable. When we fail to resolve an actual–ideal discrepancy, we feel dejected (e.g. disappointed, dissatisfied, sad); when we fail to resolve an actual–ought discrepancy, we feel agitated (e.g. anxiety, threat, fear). Read how Higgins and his colleagues tested self-discrepancy theory in Box 4.2 and Figure 4.2.

Regulatory focus theory

Self-discrepancy theory and the general notion of self-regulation have been elaborated into **regulatory focus theory** (Higgins, 1997, 1998). Higgins proposes that people have two separate self-regulatory systems, termed promotion and prevention, which are concerned with the pursuit of different types of goals.

- The *promotion system* is concerned with the attainment of one's hopes and aspirations – one's *ideals*. It generates sensitivity to the presence or absence of positive events. People in a promotion focus adopt *approach strategic means* to attain their goals. For example, promotion-focused students would seek ways to improve their grades, find new challenges and treat problems as interesting obstacles to overcome.

- The *prevention system* is concerned with the fulfilment of one's duties and obligations – one's *oughts*. It generates sensitivity to the presence or absence of negative events. People in a prevention focus use *avoidance strategic means* to attain their goals. For example, prevention-focused students would avoid new situations or new people and concentrate more on avoiding failure than on achieving the highest possible grade.

Some people are habitually more approach-focused and others more prevention-focused – it is an individual difference that can arise during childhood (Higgins & Silberman, 1998). A promotion focus can arise if children are habitually hugged and kissed for behaving in a desired manner (a positive event) and love is withdrawn as a form of discipline (absence of a positive event). A prevention focus can arise if children are encouraged to be alert to potential dangers (absence of a negative event) and punished and shouted at when they behave undesirably (a negative event). Against the background of individual differences, regulatory focus can also be influenced by the immediate context, for example by structuring the situation so that people focus on prevention or on promotion (Higgins, Roney, Crowe, & Hymes, 1994).

Research shows that people who are promotion-focused are especially likely to recall information relating to the pursuit of success by others (Higgins & Tykocinski, 1992).

Self-discrepancy theory
Higgins's theory about the consequences of making actual – ideal and actual – 'ought' self-comparisons that reveal self-discrepancies.

Self-regulation
Strategies that we use to match our behaviour to an ideal or 'ought' standard.

Regulatory focus theory
A promotion focus causes people to be approach-oriented in constructing a sense of self; a prevention focus causes people to be more cautious and avoidant in constructing a sense of self.

Box 4.2 Research classic
Self-discrepancy theory: the impact of using self-guides

Tory Higgins and his colleagues measured self-discrepancy by comparing the differences between attributes of the *actual* self with those of either the *ideal* self or those of the *'ought'* self (Higgins, Bond, Klein, & Strauman, 1986).

They administered questionnaires to identify students who were either high in both kinds of discrepancies or else low in both. Several weeks later, the same students participated in an experiment in which emotions that reflected dejection or agitation were measured, both before and after a priming procedure. For their 'ideal' prime they were asked to discuss their own and their parents' hopes for them; for their 'ought' prime they discussed their own and their parents' beliefs about their duties and obligations.

It was hypothesised that an actual–ideal discrepancy would lead to feeling dejected (but not agitated), whereas an actual–'ought' discrepancy would lead to feeling agitated (but not dejected). These predictions were supported, as the results in Figure 4.2 show.

Figure 4.2 Priming the ideal self can lead to dejection, whereas priming the 'ought' self can lead to agitation

People with a high actual–ideal and actual–ought self-discrepancy experienced:

- an increase in dejection but not agitation emotions after being primed to focus on their *ideal self*, and

- an increase in agitation but not dejection emotions after being primed to focus on their *'ought' self*.

Source: Based on Higgins, Bond, Klein and Strauman (1986), Experiment 2.

Lockwood and her associates found that people who are promotion-focused look for inspiration to positive role models who emphasise strategies for achieving success (Lockwood, Jordan, & Kunda, 2002). Such people also show elevated motivation and persistence on tasks that are framed in terms of gains and non-gains (Shah, Higgins, & Friedman, 1998). People who are prevention-focused behave quite differently – they recall information relating to the avoidance of failure by others, are most inspired by negative role models who highlight strategies for avoiding failure, and exhibit motivation and persistence on tasks that are framed in terms of losses and non-losses.

Regulatory focus theory has also been explored in the context of intergroup relations and how people feel about and behave towards their ingroup and relevant outgroups (e.g. Jonas, Sassenberg, & Scheepers, 2010; **see Chapter 11**). For example, studies have shown that in intergroup contexts, a measured or manipulated promotion focus strengthens positive emotion-related bias and behavioural tendencies towards the ingroup, while a prevention focus strengthens more negative emotion-related bias and behavioural tendencies against the outgroup (Shah, Brazy, & Higgins, 2004).

Inferences from our behaviour

One of the most obvious ways to learn about who you are is to examine your private thoughts and feelings about the world – knowing what you think and feel about the world is a very useful clue to the sort of person you are.

However, when these internal cues are weak, we may make inferences about ourselves from what we do – our behaviour. This idea underpins Daryl Bem's **self-perception theory** (Bem, 1967, 1972). Bem argues that we make attributions not only for others' behaviour (**see Chapter 3**) but also for our own, and that there is no essential difference between self-attributions and other-attributions. Furthermore, just as we form an impression of someone else's personality by making internal dispositional attributions for their behaviour, so we form a concept of who we are not by introspection but by being able to attribute our own behaviour internally. So, for example, I know that I enjoy eating curry because, if given the opportunity, I eat curry of my own free will and in preference to other foods, and not everyone likes curry – I am able to make an internal attribution for my behaviour.

How we perceive ourselves can also be based on simply imagining ourselves behaving in a particular way (Anderson & Godfrey, 1987). For example, sports psychologist Caroline van Gyn and her colleagues divided runners into two groups; one group practised power training on exercise bikes, the other did not. Half of each group used imagery (i.e. also imagined themselves sprint training), whereas the others did not. Of course, the sweaty business of power training itself improved subsequent performance; but, remarkably, those who imagined themselves sprint training did better than those who did not. The researchers concluded that imagery had affected self-conception, which in turn produced performance that was consistent with that self-conception (Van Gyn, Wenger, & Gaul, 1990).

Self-attributions have implications for motivation. If someone is induced to perform a task by either enormous rewards or fearsome penalties, task performance is attributed externally and thus motivation to perform is reduced. If there are minimal or no external factors to which performance can be attributed, we cannot easily avoid attributing performance internally to enjoyment or commitment, so motivation increases. This has been called the **overjustification effect** (see Figure 4.3), for which there is now substantial evidence (Deci & Ryan, 1985).

For example, Mark Lepper and his colleagues had nursery-school children draw pictures. Some of the children drew of their own free will, while the rest were induced to draw with the promise of a reward, which they were subsequently given. A few days later, the children were unobtrusively observed playing; the children who had previously been rewarded for drawing spent half as much time drawing as did the other group. Those who had received no extrinsic reward seemed to have greater intrinsic interest in drawing (Lepper, Greene, & Nisbett, 1973).

A review by John Condry (1977) concludes that introducing external rewards may backfire by reducing motivation and enjoyment of a task that was previously intrinsically motivated. The educational implications are obvious. Parents love to tell their children stories, and they encourage the young ones to enjoy stories by learning to read themselves. However, if reading is accompanied by rewards, the children's intrinsic joy is put at risk. So, is it possible for rewards to play any useful role? The answer is yes. The trick is to reduce reliance on rewards that are *task-contingent* and make more use of those that are *performance-contingent*. Even a task that people find boring can be enlivened when they shift their attention to features of their performance (Sansone, Weir, Harpster, & Morgan, 1992). Consider how you look for ways to maintain interest in a monotonous physical fitness programme, especially when you have to exercise alone. You could, of course, listen to music or watch television. However, a performance-contingent strategy is to set targets using measures such as 'distance' covered on an exercycle, checking your heart rate and how many calories you expended.

Self-perception theory
Bem's idea that we gain knowledge of ourselves only by making self-attributions: for example, we infer our own attitudes from our own behaviour.

Overjustification effect
In the absence of obvious external determinants of our behaviour, we assume that we freely choose the behaviour because we enjoy it.

Figure 4.3 The overjustification effect

One's motivation to perform a task can be reduced, and performance of the task impaired, if there are obvious external causes for task performance – an overjustification effect that is reversed if performance can be internally attributed.

Social comparison and self-knowledge

Social comparison (theory)
Comparing our behaviours and opinions with those of others in order to establish the correct or socially approved way of thinking and behaving.

Are you intelligent? How do you know? Although we can learn about ourselves through introspection and self-perception, we can also learn about ourselves by comparing ourselves with other people. This simple truth lies at the core of Festinger's (1954) **social comparison theory**, which describes how people learn about themselves through comparisons with others (see also Suls & Wheeler, 2000; Wheeler, 1991). People need to be confident about the validity of their perceptions, attitudes, feelings and behaviour, and because there is rarely an objective measure of validity, people ground their cognitions, feelings and behaviour in those of other people. In particular, they seek out similar others to validate their perceptions and attitudes, which can, to some extent, be read as meaning that people anchor their attitudes and self-concept in the groups to which they feel they belong.

When it comes to performance, we try to compare ourselves with people who are slightly worse than us – we make downward social comparisons which deliver an evaluatively positive self-concept (Wills, 1981). Often, however, our choices are limited: for example, younger siblings in families often have no option but to compare themselves with their more competent older brothers and sisters. Indeed, upward comparison may sometimes have a harmful effect on self-esteem (Wood, 1989).

Self-evaluation maintenance model
People who are constrained to make esteem-damaging upward comparisons can underplay or deny similarity to the target, or they can withdraw from their relationship with the target.

How can we avoid this? According to Abraham Tesser's (1988) **self-evaluation maintenance model**, we try to downplay our similarity to the other person or withdraw from our relationship with that person. Medvec and her colleagues conducted an intriguing study along these lines (Medvec, Madley, & Gilovich, 1995). They coded the facial expressions of medal winners at the 1992 Olympic Games in Barcelona and found that the bronze medallists expressed noticeably more satisfaction than the silver medallists! Medvec and colleagues argued that silver medallists were constrained to make unfavourable upward comparisons with gold medallists, whereas bronze medallists could make self-enhancing downward comparisons with the rest of the field, who received no medal at all.

Downward comparisons also occur between groups. Groups try to compare themselves with inferior groups in order to feel that 'we' are better than 'them'. Intergroup relations are largely a social comparison-based struggle for evaluative superiority of one's own group over relevant outgroups (see Hogg, 2000c; Hogg & Gaffney, 2014; Turner, 1975). Because we tend to describe and evaluate ourselves in terms of groups we belong to, this process enhances self-evaluation and self-esteem (Tajfel & Turner, 1986 – **see Chapter 11**).

Sport provides a perfect context in which the outcome of this process can be seen. Few Portuguese will not have felt enormously positive when their team beat France, the host nation, in the finals of the 2016 UEFA European Championship. Bob Cialdini and his colleagues have referred to this phenomenon as 'basking in reflected glory', or **BIRGing** (Cialdini et al., 1976). To illustrate the effect, they conducted experiments in which they raised or lowered self-esteem via feedback on a general knowledge test; and student participants were then, seemingly incidentally, asked about the outcome of a recent football game. Participants who had had their self-esteem lowered tended to associate themselves with winning and not with losing teams – they tended to refer to the teams as 'we' in the former case and as 'they' in the latter.

BIRGing
Basking in Reflected Glory; that is, name-dropping to link yourself with desirable people or groups and thus improve other people's impression of you.

Many selves, multiple identities

It is probably inaccurate to characterise the self as a single undifferentiated entity. In his book *The Concept of Self,* Kenneth Gergen (1971) depicts the self-concept as containing a repertoire of relatively discrete and often quite varied identities, each associated with a distinct body of knowledge. These identities have their origins in the array of different social relationships that form, or have formed, the anchoring points for our lives, ranging from close personal relationships with friends and family, through relationships and roles defined by work groups and professions, to relationships defined by ethnicity, race, nationality and religion.

As we noted earlier, we differ in *self-complexity* (Linville, 1985). Some of us have a more diverse and extensive set of selves than do others – people with many independent aspects of self have higher self-complexity than people with only a few, relatively similar, aspects of self. The notion of self-complexity is given a slightly different emphasis by Marilynn Brewer and her colleagues (Brewer & Pierce, 2005; Roccas & Brewer, 2002), who focus on self that is defined in group terms (social identity) and the relationship among identities rather than the number of identities people have. People have a complex social identity if they have discrete social identities that do not share many attributes, and a simple social identity if they have overlapping social identities that share many attributes.

Grant and Hogg (2012) have recently suggested and shown empirically that the effect, particularly on group identification and group behaviours, of the number of identities one has and their overlap may be better explained in terms of the general property of social identity prominence – how subjectively prominent, overall and in a specific situation, a particular identity is in one's self-concept.

Types of self and identity

Social identity theorists (Tajfel & Turner, 1986) have argued that there are two broad classes of identity that define different types of self:

1 **social identity**, which defines self in terms of group memberships;
2 **personal identity**, which defines self in terms of idiosyncratic traits and close personal relationships.

Social identity
That part of the self-concept that derives from our membership in social groups.

Personal identity
The self defined in terms of unique personal attributes or unique interpersonal relationships.

Table 4.1 Self and self-attributes as a function of level of identity (social versus personal) and type of attributes (identity versus relationship)

	Identity attributes	Relationship attributes
Social identity	*Collective self*	*Collective relational self*
	Attributes shared with others that differentiate the individual from a specific outgroup, or from outgroups in general.	Attributes that define how the self as an ingroup member relates to specific others as ingroup or outgroup members.
Personal identity	*Individual self*	*Individual relational self*
	Attributes unique to self that differentiate the individual from specific individuals, or from other individuals in general.	Attributes that define how the self as a unique individual relates to others as individuals.

Now check the first 'What do *you* think' question.

Brewer and Gardner (1996) asked the question 'Who is this "We"?' and distinguished three forms of self:

1 *Individual self* – based on personal traits that differentiate the self from all others.

2 *Relational self* – based on connections and role relationships with significant others.

3 *Collective self* – based on group membership that differentiates 'us' from 'them'.

More recently it has been proposed that there are four types of identity (Brewer, 2001; Chen, Boucher, & Tapias, 2006):

1 *Person-based social identities* – emphasising the internalisation of group properties by individual group members as part of their self-concept.

2 *Relational social identities* – defining the self in relation to specific other people with whom one interacts in a group context – corresponding to Brewer and Gardner's (1996) relational identity and to Markus and Kitayama's (1991) 'interdependent self'.

3 *Group-based social identities* – equivalent to social identity as defined above.

4 *Collective identities* – referring to a process whereby group members not only share self-defining attributes but also engage in social action to forge an image of what the group stands for and how it is represented and viewed by others.

The relational self is interesting. Although in one sense it is an interpersonal form of self, it can also be considered a particular type of collective self. For example, East Asian cultures define groups in terms of networks of relationships (Yuki, 2003), and women place greater importance than men on their relationships with others in their groups (Seeley, Gardner, Pennington, & Gabriel, 2003; see also Baumeister & Sommer, 1997; Cross & Madson, 1997). East Asians and women are often considered to be more collectivist than Western Europeans and men, respectively.

Table 4.1 shows one way in which different types of self and self-attributes could be classified according to level of identity (social versus personal) and type of attributes (identity defining versus relationship defining).

Contextual sensitivity of self and identity

Evidence for multiple selves comes from research where contextual factors are varied to discover that people describe themselves and behave differently. For example, Russell Fazio and his colleagues were able to get participants to describe themselves in very different ways by asking them loaded questions that made them search through their stock of self-knowledge for information that presented the self in a different light (Fazio, Effrein, & Falender, 1981).

Other researchers have found, time and time again, that experimental procedures that focus on group membership lead people to act very differently from procedures that focus on individuality and interpersonal relationships. Consider 'minimal group' studies in which participants are either (a) identified as individuals or (b) explicitly categorized, randomly or by some minimal or trivial criterion as group members (Tajfel, 1970; see Diehl, 1990, **and Chapter 11**). A consistent finding is that being categorized makes people discriminate against an outgroup, conform to ingroup norms, express attitudes and feelings that favour the ingroup, and indicate a sense of belonging and loyalty to the ingroup. Furthermore, these effects of minimal group categorization are generally very fast and automatic (Otten & Wentura, 1999).

The idea that we have many selves, and that contextual factors bring different selves into play, has a number of ramifications. Social constructionists have suggested that the self is entirely situation-dependent. An extreme form of this position argues that we do not carry self-knowledge around in our heads as cognitive representations at all; rather, we construct disposable selves through talk (e.g. Potter & Wetherell, 1987; **see the discussion of discourse analysis in Chapters 1 and 15**). A less extreme version has been proposed by Penny Oakes (e.g. Oakes, Haslam, & Reynolds, 1999), who does not emphasise the role of talk but still maintains that self-conception is highly context-dependent. A middle way is to argue that people do have cognitive representations of the self that they carry in their heads as organising principles for perception, categorization and action, but that these representations are temporarily or more enduringly modified by situational factors (e.g. Abrams & Hogg, 2001; Turner, Reynolds, Haslam, & Veenstra, 2006).

In search of self-coherence

That we have many selves needs to be placed in perspective. Although we may have a diversity of relatively discrete selves, we also have a quest: to find and maintain a reasonably integrated picture of who we are. Self-conceptual coherence provides us with a continuing theme for our lives – an 'autobiography' that weaves our various identities and selves together into a whole person. People who have highly fragmented selves (e.g. some people with schizophrenia, amnesia or Alzheimer's disease) find it extraordinarily difficult to function effectively.

People use many strategies to construct a coherent sense of self (Baumeister, 1998). Here are some that you may have used yourself:

- Restrict your life to a limited set of contexts. Because different selves come into play as contexts keep changing, you will protect yourself from self-conceptual clashes.

- Keep revising and integrating your 'autobiography' to accommodate new identities. Along the way, get rid of any worrisome inconsistencies. In effect, you are rewriting your history to make it work to your advantage (Greenwald, 1980).

- Attribute changes in the self externally to changing circumstances, rather than internally to fundamental changes in who you are. This is an application of the **actor–observer effect** (Jones and Nisbett, 1972; **see also Chapter 3**).

Actor–observer effect
Tendency to attribute our own behaviours externally and others' behaviours internally.

We can also develop a self-schema that embodies a core set of attributes that we feel distinguishes us from all other people – that makes us unique (Markus, 1977; see 'Self-schemas' discussed earlier in this chapter). We then tend to recognise these attributes disproportionately in all our selves, providing thematic consistency that delivers a sense of a stable and unitary self (Cantor & Kihlstrom, 1987).

In summary, people find ways to construct their lives such that their self-conceptions appear steady and coherent.

Social identity theory

Social identity theory
Theory of group membership and intergroup relations based on self-categorization, social comparison and the construction of a shared self-definition in terms of ingroup-defining properties.

Because **social identity theory** is a theory of both self and identity, and group and intergroup behaviour, we say a little about it here, but we **discuss it fully in Chapter 11** (see Abrams & Hogg, 2010; Hogg, 2006; Hogg & Abrams, 1988, 2003).

Social identity theory has its origins in research by Henri Tajfel on social categorization, intergroup relations, social comparison, and prejudice and stereotyping (e.g. Tajfel, 1969, 1974) – often called the *social identity theory of intergroup relations* (Tajfel & Turner, 1986). Later developments by John Turner and his associates specified the role of social categorization of self and others to broaden the theory to understand group behaviour more generally (Turner, Hogg, Oakes, Reicher, & Wetherell, 1987) – called the *social identity theory of the group,* or **self-categorization theory**.

Self-categorization theory
Turner and associates' theory of how the process of categorizing oneself as a group member produces social identity and group and intergroup behaviours.

Personal identity and social identity

As noted above, social identity theorists propose the existence of two broad classes of identity that define different types of self: (1) *social identity,* which defines the self in terms of group memberships (e.g. one's ethnicity), and (2) *personal identity,* which defines the self in terms of idiosyncratic personal relationships and traits (e.g. one's relationship with one's romantic partner, or being witty). We have as many social identities as there are groups that we feel we belong to, and as many personal identities as there are interpersonal relationships we are involved in and clusters of idiosyncratic attributes that we believe we possess.

Social identity, our main focus in this section, is associated with group and intergroup behaviours such as ethnocentrism, ingroup bias, group solidarity, intergroup discrimination, conformity, normative behaviour, stereotyping and prejudice. Social identity can be a very important aspect of our self-concept. For example, Citrin, Wong and Duff (2001) describe a study in which 46 per cent of Americans reported that they felt being an American, a social identity, was the most important thing in their life. In contrast, personal identity is associated with positive and negative close interpersonal relationships and with idiosyncratic personal behaviour.

Processes of social identity salience

In any given situation, our sense of self and associated perceptions, feelings, attitudes and behaviour rests on whether social or personal identity, and which specific social or personal identity, is the psychologically salient basis of self-conception. The principle that governs social identity salience hinges on the process of social categorization (Oakes, 1987) and on people's motivation to make sense of and reduce uncertainty about themselves and others (Hogg, 2012), and to feel relatively positive about themselves (e.g. Abrams & Hogg, 1988) – see Figure 4.4.

People use limited perceptual cues (what someone looks like, how they speak, what attitudes they express, how they behave) to categorise other people. Generally, we first 'try out' categorizations that are readily accessible to us because we often use them, because they are important to us or perhaps because they are glaringly obvious in the situation. The categorization brings into play all the additional schematic information we have about the category. This information is cognitively stored as a **prototype**, which describes and prescribes the attributes of the category in the form of a fuzzy set of more or less related attributes, rather than a precise checklist of attributes.

Prototype
Cognitive representation of the typical/ideal defining features of a category.

Meta-contrast principle
The prototype of a group is that position within the group that has the largest ratio of 'differences to ingroup positions' to 'differences to outgroup positions'.

Category prototypes accentuate similarities within groups, but they also accentuate differences between groups – they obey what is called the **meta-contrast principle**. As such, group prototypes usually do not identify average or typical members or attributes, but ideal members or attributes. The content of a group prototype may also vary from situation to situation. For example, Britishness will probably be slightly different in a situation where one is interacting with other 'Brits' than a situation where one is interacting with Americans. Category attributes in memory interact with situational factors to generate the

Social identity salience
The wearing of the kilt is a mark of nationalism, commitment to the cause and a resolve to act in unison in times of stress.

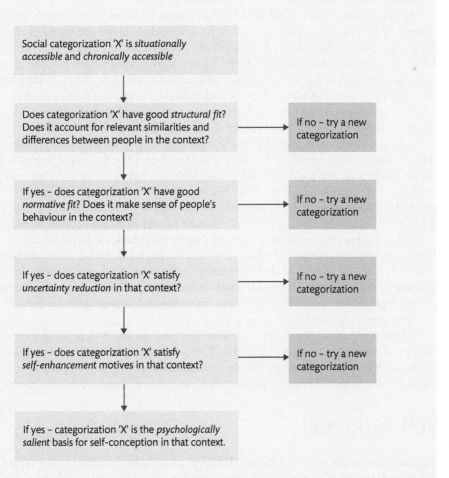

Figure 4.4 Social identity theory's model of the sequence through which a particular self-conception becomes psychologically salient in a specific context

situation-specific prototype. Category attributes stored in memory act as an anchor that ensures the integrity of the core identity and imposes limits on the amount and type of influence situation can have on the prototype (Van Bavel & Cunningham, 2010).

Ultimately, if the categorization fits, in that it accounts for similarities and differences between people satisfactorily (called *structural fit*), and it makes good sense of why people are behaving in particular ways (called *normative fit*), then the categorization becomes psychologically salient as the basis of categorizing self and others.

Consequences of social identity salience

When a categorization becomes psychologically salient, people's perception of themselves and others becomes *depersonalised*. This means that people no longer consider themselves or others as unique multidimensional persons but as more or less complete embodiments of the category prototype – they are viewed through the relatively narrow lens of a group membership that is defined by the specific ingroup or outgroup prototype. Swann and colleagues have suggested that when this process is extreme, identity fusion arises such that one's personal identity becomes fused with the group and thus with social identity (Swann, Jetten, Gomez, Whitehouse, & Bastian, 2012); and then, because there is no prototype-based differentiation of self within the group, behavior can become extreme (Swann, Gómez, Seyle, Morales, & Huici, 2009).

In addition to the transformation of self-conception into social identity, people also think, feel, believe and behave in terms of the relevant prototype. The process produces the range of behaviour we characteristically associate with people in groups and with the way groups treat each other, a theme that recurs throughout this text.

The actual nature of the behaviour (what people think and do) depends on the specific content of the relevant prototype, and on people's beliefs about the status of their group in society and about the nature of the relations between groups (Tajfel & Turner, 1986; see Ellemers, 1993; Hogg & Abrams, 1988). Group status is important because groups define social identity and social identity defines our self-concept; thus, the evaluative implications of a specific group (the status, prestige and regard in which it is held) reflect the esteem in which others hold us, and they influence the esteem in which we hold ourselves, our self-esteem (Crocker & Major, 1994; **see the discussion of social stigma in Chapter 10**).

So, people strive for membership in prestigious groups, or they strive to protect or enhance the prestige and esteem of their existing group. How they do this is influenced by their understanding of the nature of the status relations between their group and a specific outgroup – is it permeable, is it stable, is it legitimate? If the group's evaluation in society is generally unfavourable and you feel you can pass into a more prestigious group, you might try to leave the group entirely; however, this can be very difficult, because in reality the psychological boundaries between groups can be impermeable or impassable. For example, various immigrant groups in Britain may find it difficult to 'pass' as British because they simply do not look British or they are readily 'given away' by subtle clues in their accent. If 'passing' is not possible, people can try to make sure that the attributes that do define their group are positive ones, or they can focus attention on less prestigious groups, in comparison with which they will look rather good.

Groups can sometimes recognise that the entire basis on which their group is considered low status is illegitimate, unfair and unstable. If this recognition is tied to feasible strategies for change, then groups will compete directly with one another to gain the upper hand in the status stakes – a competition that can range from rhetoric and democratic process to terrorism and war.

Self-motives

Because selves and identities are critical reference points for leading a well-adapted life, people are enthusiastically motivated to secure self-knowledge. Entire industries are based on this search for knowledge, ranging from personality tests to dubious practices such as astrology and palmistry. However, people do not go about this search in a dispassionate way; they have preferences for what they would like to know about themselves and can be dismayed when the quest unearths things they did not expect or did not want to find.

Social psychologists have identified three classes of motive that interact to influence self-construction and the search for self-knowledge:

- *self-assessment* motivates pursuit of valid information about self;
- *self-verification* motivates pursuit of information that is consistent with our own self-image;
- *self-enhancement* motivates pursuit of information that makes us look good.

Self-assessment and self-verification

The first motive is a simple desire to have accurate and valid information about oneself – there is a **self-assessment** motive (e.g. Trope, 1986). People strive to find out the truth about themselves, regardless of how unfavourable or disappointing the truth may be.

But people also like to engage in a quest for confirmation – to confirm what they already know about themselves they seek out self-consistent information through a **self-verification** process (e.g. Swann, 1987). So, for example, people who have a negative self-image will actually seek out negative information to confirm the worst. Although the 'self' in self-verification was originally viewed as the idiosyncratic personal self, research shows that self-verification can also occur at the group level. People seek information and behave in ways aimed at verifying their social identity (Chen, Chen, & Shaw, 2004).

Self-enhancement

Above all else, we like to learn good things about ourselves – we seek new favourable knowledge about ourselves as well as revise pre-existing but unfavourable views of ourselves. We are guided by a **self-enhancement** motive (e.g. Kunda, 1990). This motive to promote

Self-assessment
The motivation to seek out new information about ourselves in order to find out what sort of person we really are.

Self-verification
Seeking out information that verifies and confirms what we already know about ourselves.

Self-enhancement
The motivation to develop and promote a favourable image of self.

Self-affirmation theory
'Way to go, man!'

self-positivity has a mirror motive, self-protection, which fends off self-negativity. Research suggests that self-enhancement functions operate routinely and relatively globally, but that self-protection functions are usually occasioned only by an event or series of events that threatens a specific self-related interest (Alicke & Sedikides, 2009).

Self-affirmation theory
The theory that people reduce the impact of threat to their self-concept by focusing on and affirming their competence in some other area.

One manifestation of the self-enhancement motive is described by **self-affirmation theory** (Sherman & Cohen, 2006; Steele, 1988). People strive publicly to affirm positive aspects of who they are; this can be done blatantly by boasting or more subtly through rationalisation or dropping hints. The urge to self-affirm is particularly strong when an aspect of one's self-esteem has been damaged. So, for example, if someone claims you are a lousy artist, you might retort that while that might be true, you are an excellent dancer. Self-affirmation rests on people's need to maintain a global image of themselves as being competent, good, coherent, unitary, stable, capable of free choice, capable of controlling important outcomes and so on. Ultimately, we like to be viewed as moral beings – and so we engage in a range of behaviours aimed at establishing and even asserting our moral credentials (Merritt, Effron, Fein, Savitsky, Tuller, & Monin, 2012; Monin & Miller, 2001). Box 4.3 describes research by Claude Steele (1975) in which self-affirmation processes were studied in the context of religious adherence.

Which motive is more fundamental and more likely to prevail in the pursuit of self-knowledge – self-assessment, self-verification or self-enhancement? In a series of six experiments, Constantine Sedikides (1993) pitted the three motives against one another. He used a self-reflection task where participants can ask themselves more or less diagnostic questions focusing on different aspects of themselves – the asking of more diagnostic questions indicates greater self-reflection, and the focus of self-reflection differs depending on what self-motive is operating:

- *Self-assessment* – greater self-reflection on *peripheral* than central traits of self, whether the attribute is desirable or not, indicates a drive to find out more about self (people already have knowledge about traits that are central for them).

- *Self-verification* – greater self-reflection on *central* than on peripheral traits, whether the attribute is positive or not, indicates a drive to confirm what one already knows about oneself.

Box 4.3 Research classic
Self-affirmation in Salt Lake City

Claude Steele (1975) reported a study in Salt Lake City in which Mormon women who were at home during the day were telephoned by a female researcher posing as a community member. The researcher asked the women if they would be willing to list everything in their kitchen to assist the development of a community food cooperative; those who agreed would be called back the following week. Because community cooperation is a very strong ethic among Mormons, about 50 per cent of women agreed to this time-consuming request.

In addition to this baseline condition, there were three other conditions in the study arising from a previous call, two days earlier, by an entirely unrelated researcher posing as a pollster. In the course of this previous call, the pollster mentioned in passing that it was common knowledge that, as members of their community, they were either:

- un-cooperative with community projects (a direct *threat* to a core component of their self-concept), or
- un-concerned about driver safety and care (a *threat* to a relatively irrelevant component of their self-concept), or
- cooperative with community projects (*positive reinforcement* of their self-concept).

Consistent with self-affirmation theory, the two threats greatly increased the probability that women would subsequently agree to help the food cooperative – about 95 per cent of women agreed to help. Among women who had been given positive reinforcement of their self-concept, 65 per cent agreed to help the cooperative.

Box 4.4 Your life
Techniques to enhance or protect positive aspects of the self

You may have noticed how people (perhaps you!) are inclined to boost themselves. Think about all the ways you might do this . . . then read on. Here are some of the tricks that people get up to – do they seem familiar to you?

- They take credit for their successes but deny blame for their failures (e.g. Zuckerman, 1979); this is one of the self-serving biases (**see Chapter 3**).
- They forget failure feedback more readily than success or praise (e.g. Mischel, Ebbesen, & Zeiss, 1976).
- They accept praise uncritically but receive criticism sceptically (e.g. Kunda, 1990).

- They try to dismiss interpersonal criticism as being motivated by prejudice (e.g. Crocker & Major, 1989).
- They perform a biased search of self-knowledge to support a favourable self-image (e.g. Kunda & Sanitoso, 1989).
- They place a favourable spin on the meaning of ambiguous traits that define self (e.g. Dunning, Meyerowitz, & Holzberg, 1989).
- They persuade themselves that their flaws are widely shared human attributes but that their qualities are rare and distinctive (e.g. Campbell, 1986).

- *Self-enhancement* – greater self-reflection on *positive* than on negative aspects of self, whether the attribute is central or not, indicates a drive to learn positive things about self (**see Box 4.4**).

Sedikides found that self-enhancement was strongest, with self-verification a distant second and self-assessment an even more remote third. The desire to think well of ourselves reigns supreme; it dominates both the pursuit of accurate self-knowledge and the pursuit of information that confirms self-knowledge. (Does this apply to you? See the second 'What do *you* think?' focus question.)

Because self-enhancement is so important, people have developed a formidable repertoire of strategies and techniques to pursue it. People engage in elaborate self-deceptions to enhance or protect the positivity of their self-concepts (Baumeister, 1998). It has even been suggested that the name-letter effect, where people prefer letters that occur in their own name over those that do not, reflects self-esteem and can actually be used as an indirect measure of self-esteem (Hoorens, 2014).

Self-esteem

Why are people so strongly motivated to think well of themselves – to self-enhance? Research suggests that people generally have a rosy sense of self – they see, or try to see, themselves through 'rose-tinted spectacles'. For example, people who are threatened or distracted often display what Del Paulhus and Karen Levitt (1987) called *automatic egotism* – a widely favourable self-image. In their review of a link between illusions and a sense of well-being, Shelley Taylor and Jonathon Brown (1988) concluded that people normally overestimate their good points, overestimate their control over events and are unrealistically optimistic. Sedikides and Gregg (2003) call these three characteristics of human thought *the self-enhancing triad*.

For example, a study conducted in an American setting found that very low-achieving students (in the bottom 12 per cent) thought they were relatively high achievers (in the top 38 per cent) (Kruger & Dunning, 1999). According to Patricia Cross (1977), your lecturers show positivity bias too, with 94 per cent convinced that their teaching ability is above average! The tendency to overestimate our good points is well documented in research (Brown, 2012; Guenther & Alicke, 2010; Williams & Gilovich, 2012) and is referred to as the *above-average-effect*. See Box 4.5 and Figure 4.5 for an applied example of this bias among young drivers.

Box 4.5 Our world
Self-enhancement in young drivers

How able and cautious young drivers think they are predicts how optimistic they are about avoiding a crash. Another factor is . . . perceived luck in avoiding crashes!

Can people accurately judge how good they are as drivers? Niki Harré and her colleagues addressed this question in a study of self-enhancement bias and crash optimism in young drivers (Harré, Foster, & O'Neill, 2005). More than three hundred male and female technical institute students (aged 16–29 years) compared their driving attributes to their peers on a series of ten items.

Each item was responded to on a seven-point scale that ranged from 1 (*much less*) to 7 (*much more*) with the midpoint 4 labelled *about the same*. Factor analysis showed that the ten items reflected two underlying dimensions: perceived driving ability (e.g. 'Do you think you are more or less *skilled* as a driver than other people your age?') and perceived driving caution (e.g. 'Do you think you are more or less *safe* as a driver than other people your age?')

A self-enhancement bias was found on both scales and all items. The results for the *skilled* and *safe* items are shown in Figure 4.5. Most rated themselves as above

average or well above average, both on skill and safety. Although there was no age difference, the genders did differ: in comparison to their peers, men gave themselves slightly higher skill ratings while women gave themselves slightly higher safety ratings.

Crash-risk optimism was also measured. These young drivers estimated the likelihood of being involved in a crash, again relative to their peers. Perceived ability and perceived caution were significant predictors of crash-risk optimism, in combination with another measure – believing that luck would help them avoid crashes!

Harré and her colleagues noted that their study was not designed to identify which young drivers are biased, since to do so would require measuring a person's actual skill and actual safety when driving. Nevertheless, these drivers had an overly optimistic view of themselves. Other research suggests that optimistic drivers may, for example, ignore safety messages because they do not believe they are relevant (Walton & McKeown, 1991). This is a concern, given that safe-driving campaigns are a major strategy for reducing the road toll.

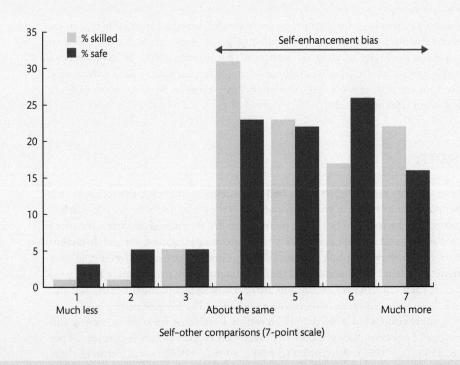

Figure 4.5 Self-enhancement bias: Rating one's driving as above average

- Young drivers compared attributes of their individual driving behaviour (skilled, safe) with their peers.
- Most showed a self-enhancement bias, using above-average ratings of 5, 6 or 7.

Source: Based on data from Harré, Foster and O'Neill (2005).

Box 4.6 Our world
Threats to your self-concept can damage your health: ways of coping

There are three major sources of threat to our self-concept, and all can affect our sense of self-worth:

1 *Failures* – ranging from failing a test, through failing a job interview, to a marriage ending in divorce.
2 *Inconsistencies* – unusual and unexpected positive or negative events that make us question the sort of person we are.
3 *Stressors* – sudden or enduring events that may exceed our capacity to cope, including bereavement, a sick child and over-commitment to work.

Threats to our self-concept not only arouse negative emotions that can lead to self-harm and suicide, they also contribute to physical illness (Salovey, Rothman, & Rodin, 1998). They can affect our immune responses, nervous system activity and blood pressure. For example, one study found that when people were reminded of significant self-discrepancies, the level of natural killer cell activity in their bloodstream decreased (Strauman, Lemieux, & Coe, 1993). These cells are important in defending the body against cancers and viral infections.

There are several ways in which people try to cope with self-conceptual threats:

- *Escape* – people may remove themselves physically from the threat situation. When people who had done poorly on an intelligence and creativity task were asked to wait in another room equipped with a mirror and video camera (to heighten self-awareness), they fled the scene much more quickly than participants who had done well on the task (Duval & Wicklund, 1972).

- *Denial* – people may take alcohol or other drugs, or engage in risky 'just for kicks' behaviour. This is not a particularly constructive coping mechanism, since it can create additional health problems.
- *Downplay the threat* – this is a more constructive strategy, either by re-evaluating the aspect of self that has been threatened or by reaffirming other positive aspects of the self (Steele, 1988). For example, Taylor (1983) found that breast cancer patients who were facing the possibility of death often expressed and reaffirmed what they felt were their most basic self-aspects – some quit dead-end jobs, others turned to writing and painting, and others reaffirmed important relationships.
- *Self-expression* – this is a very effective response to threat. Writing or talking about one's emotional and physical reactions to self-conceptual threats can be an extraordinarily useful coping mechanism. It reduces emotional heat, headaches, muscle tension and pounding heart, and it improves immune system functioning (Pennebaker, 1997). Most benefits come from communication that enhances understanding and self-insight.
- *Attack the threat* – people can directly confront threat by discrediting its basis ('This is an invalid test of my ability'), by denying personal responsibility for the threat ('The dog ate my essay'), by setting up excuses for failure before the event (on the way into an exam, announcing that you have a terrible hangover - **self-handicapping** (Berglas, 1987; **see Chapter 3**) or by taking control of the problem directly, such as seeking professional help or addressing any valid causes of threat.

People who fail to exhibit these biases can tend towards depression and some other forms of mental illness (e.g. Tennen & Affleck, 1993). Thus, a self-conceptual positivity bias, based on positive illusions, is psychologically adaptive. Box 4.6 describes some health aspects of self-esteem and self-conception.

However, a breathlessly inflated sense of how wonderful one is, is nauseatingly gushy. It is also maladaptive, as it does not match reality. Although feeling good about oneself is important, it needs to be balanced by a degree of self-conceptual accuracy (Colvin & Block, 1994). Generally, the self-conceptual positivity bias is small enough not to be a serious threat to self-conceptual accuracy (Baumeister, 1989), and people suspend their self-illusions when important decisions need to be made (Gollwitzer & Kinney, 1989). Nevertheless, a positive self-image and associated self-esteem is a significant goal for most people most of the time.

The pursuit of **self-esteem** is an adaptive and global human pursuit that persists throughout one's life (e.g. Wagner, Gerstorf, Hoppmann, & Luszcz, 2013). However, how one pursues self-esteem differs across individuals, groups and the life span. One notable difference is between cultures (Falk & Heine, 2015). For example, although Japanese society stresses communality and interconnectedness and engages in self-criticism, research suggests that

Self-handicapping
Publicly making advance external attributions for our anticipated failure or poor performance in a forthcoming event.

Self-esteem
Feelings about and evaluations of oneself.

this is simply a different way of satisfying self-esteem – in Western countries, self-esteem is more directly addressed by overt self-enhancement (Kitayama, Markus, Matsumoto, & Norasakkunkit, 1997). According to Mark Leary and his colleagues, self-esteem is a reflection of successful social connectedness (Leary, Tambor, Terdal, & Downs, 1995), as we see in the next subsection.

Self-esteem and social identity

As we have seen above (**see also Chapters 10 and 11**), self-esteem is closely associated with social identity – by identifying with a group, that group's prestige and status in society attaches to one's self-concept. Thus, all things being equal, being identified as belonging to the group of obese people is less likely to generate positive self-esteem than being identified as belonging to the group of Olympic athletes (Crandall, 1994). However, there is a general caveat: members of stigmatised groups are generally extremely creative at avoiding the self-esteem consequences of **stigma** (Crocker & Major, 1989; Crocker, Major, & Steele, 1998; **see Chapter 10**).

In practice, and consistent with social comparison theory (see earlier in this chapter **and also Chapter 11**), there can be several outcomes when self-esteem is tied to social identity. These depend on the perceived status of comparison outgroups relative to our own group. Take the example of Jesse Owens: he was the star athlete at the 1936 Berlin Olympics, the winner of four gold medals. As a member of the US team he was triumphant in demonstrating the athletic superiority of the United States over Germany against the backdrop of Hitler's white supremacist notion of the Master Race. Jesse Owens was less happy on his return home, where, as an African American, he was just another member of a disadvantaged minority.

Ethnicity and race are significant sources of social identity-related self-esteem. Studies have shown that members of ethnic minorities often report perceptions of lowered self-esteem, but only when making inter-ethnic or inter-racial comparisons with dominant groups (e.g. Cross, 1987).

Stigma
Group attributes that mediate a negative social evaluation of people belonging to the group.

Self-esteem
She wants to look like this. How close is she to her goal?

Some of the original and classic research on ethnic identity and self-worth was done in the United States in the 1930s and 1940s and was restricted to studies of African American and white American children (see Box 4.7). Later work focused on other non-white minorities such as Native Americans, 'Chicanos', Chinese and French Canadians (see review by Aboud, 1987), New Zealand Maori (e.g. Vaughan, 1978a), and indigenous Australians (Pedersen, Walker, & Glass, 1999). Consistently, children from non-white minorities showed clear outgroup preference and wished they were white themselves.

Although pre-adolescent children from an ethnic minority might prefer to be members of the ethnic majority, this effect gradually declines with age (see Box 11.3 for an example). It is probable that young, disadvantaged children experience a conflict between their actual and ideal selves (see Box 4.2). As they grow older, they can rectify this in different ways:

- They can avoid making self-damaging intergroup comparisons (**see Chapter 11**).

- They can join with other ingroup members in a quest to establish more equal status relative to the majority group (**again see Chapter 11**).

- They can identify or develop ingroup characteristics, such as their language and culture, which provide a sense of uniqueness and positivity (**see Chapter 15**).

Box 4.7 Research classic
Depressed self-esteem and ethnic minority status

Research on children's ethnic identity has a long history in social psychology. Some of the earliest studies were conducted by two African Americans, Kenneth and Mamie Clark (1939a, 1939b, 1940). The Clarks showed young African American children pairs of black and white dolls, probing for the children's ethnic identity and ethnic preference. Independently, Horowitz (1936, 1939) used a different method – sketches of black and white people – to test white children's awareness of differences between ethnic groups and attitudes towards blacks. Mary Goodman (1946, 1952), who worked with the social psychologist Gordon Allport at Harvard University, studied ethnic awareness and attitudes among white and African American nursery-school children in more detail. She extended the Clarks' method by including a doll play technique to allow the children to project attitudes towards their ethnic ingroup and outgroup.

These investigations used different samples from different American states, at slightly different periods and with an extensive range of tests. Their results consistently showed that when making ethnic comparisons:

- White children preferred white children.
- African American children preferred white children.
- African American children had lower self-esteem.

Goodman referred to the main effect as 'White over Brown'. A wider recognition of the impact of these studies led to Kenneth Clark appearing as a witness in a landmark case in the US Supreme Court – *Brown* v *Topeka Board of Education* (1954) – in which he testified that black children's self-esteem was extensively damaged over time. Flowing from this case, the legal decision to outlaw school segregation was instrumental in helping to legitimise the civil rights movement in the United States (Goodman, 1964).

Despite later claims that the 'doll studies' were methodologically flawed (Hraba, 1972; Banks, 1976), an analysis of the trends in ethnic identity studies carried out in other countries pointed to at least two stable patterns (Vaughan, 1986):

1 Ethnic minorities that are disadvantaged (educationally, economically, politically) are typified by lowered self-esteem when intergroup comparisons are made.
2 Social change in the status relationship between ethnic groups leads to a significant improvement in minority pride and individuals' feelings of self-worth.

With respect to the second pattern, Hraba and Grant (1970) documented a phenomenon in African American children called 'Black is Beautiful', following the success of the American Black Power movement in the late 1960s. (**Social stigma and self-esteem are discussed in detail in Chapter 10, and the processes underlying social change are discussed in Chapter 11.**)

Individual differences

We all know people who seem to hold themselves in very low regard and others who seem to have a staggeringly positive impression of themselves. Do these differences reflect enduring and deep-seated differences in self-esteem; and are such differences the causes, consequences or merely correlates of other behaviours and phenomena?

One view that has become somewhat entrenched, particularly in the United States, is that low self-esteem is responsible for a range of personal and social problems such as crime, delinquency, drug abuse, unplanned pregnancy and underachievement in school. This view has spawned a huge industry, with accompanying mantras, to boost individual self-esteem, particularly in childrearing and school contexts. However, critics have argued that low self-esteem may be a product of the stressful and alienating conditions of modern industrial society, and that the self-esteem 'movement' is an exercise in rearranging deck chairs on the *Titanic* that merely produces selfish and narcissistic individuals.

So, what is the truth? First, research suggests that individual self-esteem tends to vary between moderate and very high, not between low and high. Most people feel relatively positive about themselves – at least university students in the United States do (Baumeister, Tice, & Hutton, 1989). However, lower self-esteem scores have been obtained from Japanese students studying in Japan or the United States (Kitayama, Markus, Matsumoto, & Norasakkunkit, 1997; **see also Chapter 16**).

Even if we focus on those people who have low self-esteem, there is little evidence that low self-esteem causes the social ills that it is purported to cause. For example, Baumeister, Smart and Boden (1996) searched the literature for evidence for the popular belief that low self-esteem causes violence (**see also Chapter 12**). They found quite the opposite. Violence was associated with high self-esteem; more specifically, violence seems to erupt when individuals with high self-esteem have their rosy self-images threatened.

However, we should not lump together all people who hold themselves in high self-esteem. Consistent with common sense, some people with high self-esteem are quietly self-confident and non-hostile, whereas others are thin-skinned, arrogant, conceited and overly assertive (Kernis, Granneman, & Barclay, 1989). These latter individuals also feel 'special' and superior to others, and they actually have relatively volatile self-esteem – they are **narcissistic** (Back, Küfner, Dufner, Gerlach, Rauthmann, & Denissen, 2013). Colvin, Block and Funder (1995) found that it was this latter type of high-self-esteem individual who was likely to be maladjusted in terms of interpersonal problems. Some personality theorists see narcissism as often going together with Machiavellianism and psychopathy to produce what is ominously referred to as personality's 'dark triad' (Paulhus & Williams, 2002) – leaders who have these attributes are particularly destructive (**see Chapter 9**).

Narcissistic individuals may also be more prone to aggression – specifically, according to the threatened egotism model, if they feel that their ego has been threatened (Baumeister, Smart, & Boden, 1996). Bushman and Baumeister (1998) conducted a laboratory experiment to test this idea. After writing an essay, student participants received an evaluation of the essay which was either an 'ego threat' or an 'ego boost'. Later, they were given the opportunity to act aggressively against the person who had offended them. Self-esteem did not predict aggression, but narcissism did – narcissistic individuals were more aggressive towards people who they felt had provoked and offended them. An interesting extension to this idea has focused on group-level narcissism, collective narcissism, and shown how narcissistic groups (e.g., narcissistic ethnic groups, religions or nations) that experience a status threat are more likely than non-narcissistic groups to resort to collective violence (Golec de Zavala, Cichocka, Eidelson, & Jayawickreme, 2009).

Overall, research into self-esteem as an enduring trait provides quite a clear picture of what people with high and low self-esteem are like (Baumeister, 1998; see Table 4.2). There are two main underlying differences associated with trait self-esteem (Baumeister, Tice, & Hutton, 1989; Campbell, 1990): (1) self-concept confusion – high self-esteem people have a

Narcissism
A personality trait that is volatile, comprising self-love and an inflated or grandiose view of oneself.

Terror management theory
Everyone dies. People buffer fear of their own death by elevating their self-esteem.

more thorough, consistent and stable stock of self-knowledge than do low self-esteem people; (2) motivational orientation – high self-esteem people have a self-enhancing orientation in which they capitalise on their positive features and pursue success, whereas low self-esteem people have a self-protective orientation in which they try to remedy their shortcomings and avoid failures and setbacks. (Knowing this, you might want to learn a bit more about Manfred. See the third 'What do *you* think?' question.)

In pursuit of self-esteem

Why do people pursue self-esteem? This may seem a silly question – obviously, self-esteem makes you feel good. There is of course some truth here, but there are causality issues to be addressed – being in a good mood, however caused, may create a rosy glow that distorts the esteem in which people hold themselves. So, rather than self-esteem producing happiness, feeling happy may inflate self-esteem.

Fear of death

One intriguing, and somewhat gloomy, reason given for why people pursue self-esteem is that they do so in order to overcome their fear of death. Greenberg, Pyszczynski and Solomon (1986; Greenberg, Solomon, & Pyszczynski, 1997; Pyszczynski, Greenberg, & Solomon, 1999, 2004; Solomon, Greenberg, & Pyszczynski, 1991) developed this idea in their **terror management theory**. They argue that the inevitability of death is the most

Terror management theory
The notion that the most fundamental human motivation is to reduce the terror of the inevitability of death. Self-esteem may be centrally implicated in effective terror management.

Table 4.2 Characteristics of people with high and low self-esteem

High self-esteem	Low self-esteem
Persistent and resilient in the face of failure	Vulnerable to impact of everyday events
Emotionally and affectively stable	Wide swings in mood and affect
Less flexible and malleable	Flexible and malleable
Less easily persuaded and influenced	Easily persuaded and influenced
No conflict between wanting and obtaining success and approval	Want success and approval but are sceptical of it
React positively to a happy and successful life	React negatively to a happy and successful life
Thorough, consistent and stable self-concept	Sketchy, inconsistent and unstable self-concept
Self-enhancement motivational orientation	Self-protective motivational orientation

fundamental threat that people face, and thinking about our own death produces 'paralysing terror' – fear of dying is thus the most powerful motivating factor in human existence. Self-esteem, however achieved, is part of a defence against that threat.

Through high self-esteem, people can escape from the anxiety that would otherwise arise from continual contemplation of the inevitability of their own death – the drive for self-esteem is grounded in terror associated with dying. High self-esteem makes people feel good about themselves – they feel immortal, and positive and excited about life. One way to elevate self-esteem to protect against fear of death is to acquire symbolic immortality by identifying with and defending cultural institutions and their associated world view – cultural institutions survive long after we are dead.

To support this analysis, Greenberg and his colleagues conducted three experiments in which participants did or did not receive success and positive personality feedback (manipulation of self-esteem) and then either watched a video about death or anticipated painful electric shocks (Greenberg et al., 1992). They found that participants who had had their self-esteem raised had lower physiological arousal and reported less anxiety (see Figure 4.6).

Another factor that may buffer death anxiety is humility. Pelin Kesebir (2014) conducted five studies in which *humility*, as an individual difference or personality trait, or as a temporary state induced by priming, buffered fear of death. Kesebir's explanation is that humility is a virtue that embodies forgivingness, generosity and helpfulness, which stands in contrast to being neurotic and narcissistic. The humble person is less self-focused. People with high self-esteem may respond to the thought of death by acting defensively or even aggressively (Bushman & Baumeister, 1998); a person with humility may be blessed with 'existential anxiety buffer'.

Self-esteem as a 'sociometer'

Another reason why people pursue self-esteem is that it is a reliable index, or internal monitor, of social acceptance and belonging. In this respect, self-esteem has been referred to as a 'sociometer'. Leary and his colleagues have shown that self-esteem is quite strongly correlated (at about 0.50) with reduced anxiety over social rejection and exclusion (e.g. Leary &

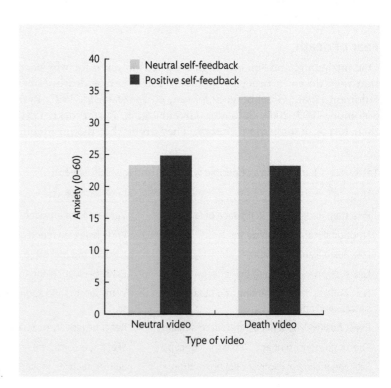

Figure 4.6 Anxiety as a function of positive or neutral self-esteem feedback and of having viewed a death video

People felt more anxious (on a 0–60 scale) after watching an explicit video about death if their self-esteem had not previously been elevated through positive feedback, than if their self-esteem had previously been elevated.

Source: Based on data from Greenberg et al. (1992), Experiment 1.

Kowalski, 1995), and there is strong evidence that people are pervasively driven by a need to form relationships and to belong (e.g. Baumeister & Leary, 1995; **also, the consequences of social ostracism are discussed in Chapter 8 and social isolation in Chapter 14**). Leary feels that having high self-esteem does not mean that we have conquered our fear of death, but rather that we have conquered the threat of loneliness and social rejection.

Leary and colleagues conducted a series of five experiments to support their view (Leary, Tambor, Terdal, & Downs, 1995). They found that high self-esteem participants reported greater inclusion in general and in specific real social situations. They also found that social exclusion from a group for personal reasons depressed participants' self-esteem.

Other critics of terror management theory worry that the theory is unfalsifiable and over-stretched because it tries to explain all of human behaviour in terms of a single motive (Martin & Van den Bos, 2014). Yet others suggest more specifically that high self-esteem may be a response to overcoming existential uncertainty or uncertainty about who we are and our place in the world, rather than overcoming fear associated with dying (Hohman & Hogg, 2011, 2015; Van den Bos, 2009).

Self-presentation and impression management

Selves are constructed, modified and played out in interaction with other people. Since the self that we project has consequences for how others react, we try to control the self that we present. In *The Presentation of Self in Everyday Life,* the sociologist Erving Goffman (1959) likened this process of **impression management** to theatre, where people play different roles for different audiences. Hundreds of studies show that people behave differently in public than in private (Leary, 1995).

There are two classes of motive for self-presentation: strategic and expressive. Research by Mark Snyder (1974) into individual differences in **self-monitoring** suggests that high self-monitors adopt strategic self-presentation strategies because they typically shape their behaviour to project the impression they feel their audience or the situation demands, whereas low self-monitors adopt expressive self-presentation strategies because their behaviour is less responsive to changing contextual demands.

Impression management
People's use of various strategies to get other people to view them in a positive light.

Self-monitoring
Carefully controlling how we present ourselves. There are situational differences and individual differences in self-monitoring.

Strategic self-presentation

Building on classic work by Jones (1964), Jones and Pittman (1982) identified five strategic motives:

1 *self-promotion* – trying to persuade others that you are competent;

2 *ingratiation* – trying to get others to like you;

3 *intimidation* – trying to get others to think you are dangerous;

4 *exemplification* – trying to get others to regard you as a morally respectable individual; and

5 *supplication* – trying to get others to take pity on you as helpless and needy.

The behaviour that represents the operation of these motives is fairly obvious (**see Chapter 6 on persuasion tactics**). In fact, ingratiation and self-promotion service two of the most common goals of social interaction: to get people to like you and to get people to think you are competent (Leary, 1995). As we saw earlier (**Chapter 2**), warmth and competence are the two most fundamental and pervasive dimensions on which we form impressions of people (e.g. Cuddy, Fiske, & Glick, 2008; Fiske, Cuddy, & Glick, 2007). Research into ingratiation shows that ingratiation has little effect on an observer's liking for you but a big effect on the target – flattery can be hard to resist (Gordon, 1996). (Use Box 4.8 to help advise Andrea. See the fourth 'What do *you* think?' question.)

Box 4.8 Your life
Some tips on how to present yourself so that others like you

Think about what you might do to get others to like you. We all like to be liked, but it can be quite a challenge to know how best to do this. Fortunately, social psychology has some very reliable answers.

The key to getting people to like you through strategic self-presentation is to be relatively subtle so that it does not look too obviously like ingratiation. According to Ned Jones (1990), there are four principal strategies you should adopt:

1 Agree with people's opinions (similarity enhances attraction – **see Chapter 13**), but make it credible (a) by balancing agreement on important issues with disagreement on trivial issues and (b) by balancing forceful agreement with weak disagreement.

2 Be selectively modest (a) by making fun of your standing on unimportant issues and (b) by putting yourself down in areas that do not matter very much.

3 Try to avoid appearing too desperate for others' approval. Try to get others to do the strategic self-presentation for you and, if it is left up to you, use the strategy sparingly and do not use it under conditions where it would be expected.

4 Basking in reflected glory really does work. Make casual references to your connections with winners, and only make links with losers when such links cannot be turned against you.

Source: Based on Jones (1990).

Expressive self-presentation

Self-presentation
A deliberate effort to act in ways that create a particular impression, usually favourable, of ourselves.

Strategic **self-presentation** focuses on manipulating others' perceptions of you. In contrast, expressive self-presentation involves demonstrating and validating our self-concept through our actions – the focus is more on oneself than on others (Schlenker, 1980). But we are not unrealistic: we usually seek out people whom we believe are likely to validate who we are. The expressive motive for self-presentation is a strong one. A particular identity or self-concept is worthless unless it is recognised and validated by others – it is of little use to me if I think I am a genius but no one else does. Identity requires *social validation* for it to persist and serve a useful function.

For example, research by Nicholas Emler and Steve Reicher (1995) has shown that delinquent behaviour among boys is almost always performed publicly or in forms that can be publicly verified, because its primary function is identity validation – validation of possession of a delinquent reputation. There is little point in being a closet delinquent. Other research confirms that people prefer social situations that allow them to act in ways that are consistent with their self-concept (e.g. Snyder & Gangestad, 1982), and they prefer partners who agree with their own self-images (Swann, Hixon, & de la Ronde, 1992).

Social validation of expressed behaviour also seems to be implicated in self-concept change. Refer back to Tice's experiment in Figure 4.1, where she asked her participants to act as if they were either emotionally stable or emotionally volatile. Half of them performed the behaviour publicly and half privately. They all then completed ratings of what they believed their 'true self' was like. Tice found that only publicly performed behaviour was internalised as a description of their self. What is important in self-concept change is that other people perceive you in a particular way – this is social validation. It is not enough for you, and only you, to perceive yourself in this way (Schlenker, Dlugolecki, & Doherty, 1994).

The self-conceptual consequences of public behaviour have additional support from a programme of research by Snyder (1984; **see Figure 10.10**). Observers were led to believe that a target stranger they were about to meet was an extrovert. Snyder then monitored what happened. The expectation constrained the target to behave as an extrovert would. In turn, this confirmed the expectation and strengthened the constraint, leading the target to believe that he or she really was an extrovert.

Identity on display
Sometime soon they will dress in their civvies and walk outside. It will be hard work to feel good on the 'inside' as well.

This process where expectations create reality can have a nicely positive outcome – called the Michelangelo phenomenon (Drigotas, Rusbult, Wieselquist, & Whitton, 1999; Rusbult, Finkel, & Kumashiro, 2009 – **also see Chapter 14**). In close relationships, the partners often view each other positively and have positive expectations of one another – and these positive expectations guide each person towards their ideal selves. If I affirm your ideal self, you increasingly come to resemble your ideal self – and vice versa. Of course, the opposite can also happen – if the relationship is dysfunctional and each person can only see the bad in the other.

Cultural differences in self and identity

We discuss culture and cultural differences fully in Chapter 16. As far as self and identity are concerned, however, there is one pervasive finding. Western cultures such as Western Europe, North America and Australasia tend to be individualistic, whereas most other cultures, such as those found in Southern Europe, Latin America, Asia and Africa, are collectivist (Triandis, 1989; also see Chiu & Hong, 2007; Heine, 2016; Oyserman, Coon, & Kemmelmeier, 2002). The anthropologist Geertz puts it beautifully:

> The Western conception of the person as a bounded, unique, more or less integrated, motivational and cognitive universe, a dynamic centre of awareness, emotion, judgement, and action organized into a distinctive whole and set contrastively both against other such wholes and against a social and natural background is, however incorrigible it may seem to us, a rather peculiar idea within the context of the world's cultures.

Geertz (1975, p. 48)

Markus and Kitayama (1991) describe how people in individualistic cultures have an independent self, whereas people in collectivist cultures have an interdependent self. Although, in both cases, people seek a coherent sense of who they are, the independent self is grounded in a view of the self as autonomous, separate from other people and revealed through one's inner thoughts and feelings. The interdependent self is grounded in one's connection to and relationships with other people. It is expressed through one's roles and relationships. 'Self . . . is defined by a person's surrounding relations, which often are derived from kinship networks and supported by cultural values such as filial piety, loyalty, dignity,

Interdependent self
Women from traditional
collectivist cultures have strong
family connections, are non-
confrontational, and often dress
demurely in public settings.

Table 4.3 Differences between independent and interdependent selves

	Independent self	Interdependent self
Self-definition	Unique, autonomous individual, separate from context, represented in terms of internal traits, feelings, thoughts and abilities.	Connected with others, embedded in social context, represented in terms of roles and relationships.
Self-structure	Unitary and stable, constant across situations and relationships.	Fluid and variable, changing across situations and relationships.
Self-activities	Being unique and self-expressive, acting true to your internal beliefs and feelings, being direct and self-assertive, promoting your own goals and your difference from others.	Belonging, fitting in, acting appropriately to roles and group norms, being indirect and non-confrontational, promoting group goals and group harmony.

Source: Based on Markus and Kitayama (1991).

and integrity' (Gao, 1996, p. 83). Table 4.3 shows the ways in which independent and inter-dependent selves differ. **We return to this cultural difference in the self in Chapter 16.**

From a conceptual review of the cultural context of self-conception, Vignoles, Chryssochoou and Breakwell (2000) conclude that the need to have a distinctive and integrated sense of self is probably universal. However, self-distinctiveness means something quite different in individualist and collectivist cultures. In one it is the isolated and bounded self that gains meaning from separateness, whereas in the other it is the relational self that gains meaning from its relations with others.

Consistent with our historical analysis of conceptions of the self at the beginning of this chapter, the most plausible account of the origins of individualist and collectivist cultures, and the associated independent and interdependent self-conceptions, is probably in terms of economic activity. Western cultures have, over the past two hundred to three hundred years, developed an economic system based on labour mobility. People are units of production that are expected to move from places of low labour demand to places of high labour demand – they are expected to organise their lives, their relationships and their self-concepts around mobility and transient relationships.

Independence, separateness and uniqueness have become more important than connectedness and the long-term maintenance of enduring relationships – these values have become enshrined as key features of Western culture. Self-conceptions reflect cultural norms that codify economic activity.

Summary

- The modern Western idea of the self has gradually crystallised over the past two hundred years as a consequence of a number of social and ideological forces, including secularisation, industrialisation, enlightenment and psychoanalysis. As a recent science, social psychology has tended to view the self as the essence of individuality.

- In reality, there are many different forms of self and identity. The three most important are the collective self (defined in terms of attributes shared with ingroup members and distinct from outgroup members), the individual self (defined in terms of attributes that make one unique relative to other people) and the relational self (defined in terms of relationships that one has with specific other people).

- People experience different selves in different contexts, yet they also feel that they have a coherent self-concept that integrates or interrelates all these selves.

- People are not continuously consciously aware of themselves. Self-awareness can sometimes be very uncomfortable and at other times very uplifting – it depends on what aspect of self we are aware of and on the relative favourability of that aspect.

- Self-knowledge is stored as schemas. We have many self-schemas, and they vary in clarity. In particular, we have schemas about our actual self, our ideal self and our 'ought' self. We often compare our actual self with our ideal and 'ought' selves – an actual–ideal self-discrepancy makes us feel dejected, whereas an actual–ought self-discrepancy makes us feel anxious. The way in which we construct and regulate our sense of self is influenced by the extent to which we are prevention- or promotion-focused.

- People construct a concept of self in a number of ways in addition to introspection. They can observe what they say and what they do, and if there are no external reasons for behaving in that way, they assume that the behaviour reflects their true self. People can compare themselves with others to get a sense of who they are – they ground their attitudes in comparisons with similar others but their behaviour in comparison with slightly less well-off others. The collective self is also based on downward comparisons, but with outgroup others.

- The collective self is associated with group memberships, intergroup relations and the range of specific and general behaviour that we associate with people in groups.

- Self-conception is underpinned by three major motives: self-assessment (to discover what sort of person you really are), self-verification (to confirm what sort of person you are) and self-enhancement (to discover what a wonderful person you are). People are overwhelmingly motivated by self-enhancement, with self-verification a distant second and self-assessment bringing up the rear. This is probably because self-enhancement services self-esteem, and self-esteem is a key feature of self-conception.

- Some people have generally higher self-esteem than others. High self-esteem people have a clear and stable sense of self and a self-enhancement orientation; low self-esteem people have a less clear self-concept and a self-protective orientation.

- People pursue self-esteem for many reasons, one being that it is a good internal index of social integration, acceptance and belonging. It may indicate that one has successfully overcome loneliness and social rejection. To protect or enhance self-esteem, people carefully manage the impression they project. They can do this strategically (manipulating others' images of the self) or expressively (behaving in ways that project a positive image of the self).

- Individualist Western cultures emphasise the independent self, whereas other (collectivist) cultures emphasise the interdependent self (the self defined in terms of one's relations and roles relative to other people).

Key terms

Actor-observer effect
BIRGing
Constructs
Deindividuation
Impression management
Looking-glass self
Meta-contrast principle
Narcissism
Overjustification effect
Personal identity
Prototype

Regulatory focus theory
Schema
Self-affirmation theory
Self-assessment
Self-categorization theory
Self-discrepancy theory
Self-enhancement
Self-esteem
Self-evaluation maintenance
    model
Self-handicapping

Self-monitoring
Self-perception theory
Self-presentation
Self-regulation
Self-verification
Social comparison (theory)
Social identity
Social identity theory
Stigma
Symbolic interactionism
Terror management theory

Literature, film and TV

Invisible Man

Ralph Ellison's 1947 novel about how black people in the United States are 'invisible' to white people. It shows the consequences of ostracism or denial of identity and existence.

The Departed

Starring Leonardo DiCaprio, Matt Damon and Jack Nicholson, this is a dramatic and violent 2006 film about Irish American organised crime in Boston. But it is also a study of the strain of nourishing multiple identities and living an all-consuming double life – Billy Costigan is an undercover cop who has infiltrated the mob, and Colin Sullivan is a hardened criminal who has infiltrated the police.

Deadpool

A 2016 superhero film based on Marvel Comics and starring Ryan Reynolds as Wade Wilson. Wilson is terribly disfigured with burn-like scars over his body by a (malicious) attempt to cure his cancer. His appearance is changed, and people respond with disgust to who he is, so he responds by assuming an alter ego, Deadpool, and becoming a masked vigilante tracking down the person, Ajax, who did this to him. This film can be read to confront issues of identity, self-assessment, self-verification and self enhancement that are discussed in this chapter.

Eat Prey Love

A 2010 romantic comedy-drama directed by Ryan Murphy, starring Julia Roberts and also featuring Javier Bardem and Viola Davis. This is essentially an 'in search of self' odyssey in which Elizabeth Gilbert, Roberts's character, has it all and is then thrown into identity turmoil by divorce. She is lost and confused and unclear about who she is, so she embarks on a mid-life quest for self-discovery, travelling to three very different cultures – Italy, India and Indonesia. She discovers the true pleasure of food in Italy, the power of spirituality in India, and the inner peace and balance of true love in Indonesia.

Guided questions

1   Do you have a looking-glass self? How and why might you present yourself differently in public and in private?

2   If the way you actually are is different from the way you would like to be, or how you think you should be, how might this be revealed?

3   What are the usual ways that people try to enhance their sense of self-worth?

4   How could threats to your sense of self-worth damage your health?

5   What does it mean to say that you are objectively aware of yourself?

Learn more

Abrams, D., & Hogg, M. A. (2001). Collective identity: Group membership and self-conception. In M. A. Hogg & R. S. Tindale (Eds.), *Blackwell handbook of social psychology: Group processes* (pp 425–460). Oxford, UK: Blackwell. Detailed discussion and overview of the relationship between the self-concept and group membership, with an emphasis on the collective self and social identity.

Baumeister, R. F. (Ed.) (1993). *Self-esteem: The puzzle of low self-regard*. New York: Plenum. An edited collection of chapters from most of the leading self-esteem researchers, each describing and over-viewing their research programme and general conclusions.

Baumeister, R. F. (Ed.) (1999). *The self in social psychology*. Philadelphia, PA: Psychology Press. A detailed overview of theory and research on self and identity organised around reprints of twenty-three key and classic publications on the self. There is an integrative introductory chapter and short introductory pieces to each set of readings. This is an excellent resource for the study of self and identity.

Leary, M. R., & Tangney, J. P. (Eds.) (2012). *Handbook of self and identity* (2nd ed.). New York: Guilford. A completely up-to-date and wide-ranging selection of scholarly chapters from leading scholars of self and identity.

Oyserman, D. (2007). Social identity and self-regulation. In A. W. Kruglanski & E. T. Higgins (Eds.), *Social psychology: Handbook of basic principles* (2nd ed., pp. 432–453). New York: Guilford. Detailed and up-to-date coverage of research on self and identity, with a particular emphasis on collective identity.

Sedikides, C., & Gregg, A. P. (2007). Portraits of the self. In M. A. Hogg & J. Cooper (Eds.), *The SAGE handbook of social psychology: Concise student edition* (pp. 93–122). London: SAGE. A detailed but accessible overview of research and theory on self and identity. Sedikides is one of the world's leading self researchers.

Swann, W. B., Jr, & Bosson, J. K. (2010) Self and identity. In S. T. Fiske, D. T. Gilbert, & G. Lindzey (Eds.), *Handbook of social psychology* (5th ed., Vol. 1, pp. 589–628). New York: Wiley. Comprehensive and up-to-date coverage of the literature on self and identity – in the most recent edition of the authoritative handbook of social psychology.

Chapter 5
Attitudes

Chapter contents

What do *you* think?

1 The word *attitude* has many different everyday meanings. For example, it can refer to the posture a hunting dog assumes when indicating the presence of prey, or a football coach may despair about a player who has an 'attitude problem'. Is the term worth keeping in our psychological dictionary if it has different everyday meanings?

2 Citizens sometimes say that paying research companies to assess people's political attitudes is a waste of money. One poll may contradict another carried out at the same time, and poll predictions of actual voting have not always been very reliable – a case in point is the 23 June 2016 Brexit vote in the United Kingdom. Is there any use, therefore, in trying to link people's attitudes to people's behaviour?

3 Rita polls people's attitudes and believes she knows what makes them tick. Her advice to psychologists is: if you want to find out what people's attitudes are, ask them! Is she right?

4 People can sometimes be unaware of or conceal their attitudes – how can we reveal these hidden attitudes?

Structure and function of attitudes

A short history of attitudes

Attitude is not only a word that is part of everyday language but has also been called social psychology's most indispensable concept. In the 1935 *Handbook of Social Psychology*, which was highly influential at the time, Gordon Allport wrote:

> The concept of attitudes is probably the most distinctive and indispensable concept in contemporary American social psychology. No other term appears more frequently in the experimental and theoretical literature.
>
> Allport (1935, p. 798)

In the historical context in which Allport was writing, his view is not remarkable. Others, such as Thomas and Znaniecki (1918) and Watson (1930), had previously equated social psychology and attitude research – actually defining social psychology as the scientific study of attitudes! The early 1930s also witnessed the earliest questionnaire-based scales to measure attitudes. According to Allport, an attitude is:

> a mental and neural state of readiness, organised through experience, exerting a directive or dynamic influence upon the individual's response to all objects and situations with which it is related.
>
> Allport (1935, p. 810)

Allport was not to know that such a fashionable concept would become the centre of controversy in the decades ahead. For example, a radical behavioural view would emerge to argue that an attitude is merely a figment of the imagination – people invent attitudes to explain behaviour that has already occurred. In charting the history of attitude research in social psychology, McGuire (1986) identified three main phases separated by periods of waning interest:

1 A concentration on attitude measurement and how these measurements related to behaviour (1920s and 1930s).
2 A focus on the dynamics of change in a person's attitudes (1950s and 1960s).
3 A focus on the cognitive and social structure and function of attitudes and attitude systems (1980s and 1990s).

The word 'attitude' is derived from the Latin *aptus*, which means 'fit and ready for action'. This ancient meaning refers to something that is directly observable, such as a boxer in a boxing ring. Today, however, attitude researchers view 'attitude' as a psychological construct that, although not directly observable, precedes behaviour and guides our choices and decisions for action.

Attitude research in psychology and the social sciences has generated enormous interest and probably thousands of studies covering almost every conceivable topic about which attitudes might be expressed. During the 1960s and 1970s, attitude research entered a period of pessimism and decline. To some extent, this was a reaction to concern about the apparent lack of relationship between expressed attitudes and overt behaviour.

However, during the 1980s, attitudes again became a centre of attention for social psychologists, stimulated by cognitive psychology's impact on social psychology (see reviews by Olson & Zanna, 1993; Tesser & Shaffer, 1990). This resurgence focused on how information processing and memory, and affect and feelings affect attitude formation and change (Haddock & Zanna, 1999; Lieberman, 2000; Murphy, Monahan, & Zajonc, 1995), on attitude strength and accessibility, on how attitudes relate to behaviour (Ajzen, 2001) and on implicit measures of attitude (Crano & Prislin, 2006; Fazio & Olson, 2003). Most recently there has been a focus on biochemical dimensions of attitude phenomena (Blascovich & Mendes, 2010) and on neural activity associated with attitudes (Stanley, Phelps, & Banaji, 2008).

Here, we take the view that attitudes are basic to and pervasive in human life. Without having attitudes, people would have difficulty in construing and reacting to events, in trying to make decisions and in making sense of their relationships with other people in everyday life. Attitudes continue to fascinate researchers and remain a key, if sometimes controversial, part of social psychology. Let us now look at the anatomy of an attitude.

Attitude structure

A very basic psychological question to ask about attitudes is whether they are a unitary construct or whether they have a number of different components.

One component

Early **one-component attitude models** define an attitude as 'the affect for or against a psychological object' (Thurstone, 1931, p. 261) and 'the degree of positive or negative affect associated with some psychological object' (Edwards, 1957, p. 2). How simple can you get – do you like the object or not? With hindsight, it can be argued that the dominant feature of affect became the basis of a more sophisticated sociocognitive model proposed by Pratkanis and Greenwald (1989) (see the next section).

One-component attitude model
An attitude consists of affect towards or evaluation of the object.

Two components

Allport (1935) favoured a **two-component attitude model**. To Thurstone's 'affect' Allport added a second component – a state of mental readiness. Mental readiness is a predisposition that influences how we decide what is good or bad, desirable or undesirable, and so on. An attitude is therefore private and externally unobservable. It can only be inferred by examining our own mental processes introspectively, or by making inferences from what we say and do. You cannot see, touch or physically examine an attitude; it is a hypothetical construct.

Two-component attitude model
An attitude consists of a mental readiness to act. It also guides evaluative (judgemental) responses.

Three components

A third view is the **three-component attitude model**, which has its roots in ancient philosophy:

> The trichotomy of human experience into thought, feeling, and action, although not logically compelling, is so pervasive in Indo-European thought (being found in Hellenic, Zoroastrian and Hindu philosophy) as to suggest that it corresponds to something basic in our way of conceptualisation, perhaps . . . reflecting the three evolutionary layers of the brain, cerebral cortex, limbic system, and old brain.
>
> McGuire (1989, p. 40)

Three-component attitude model
An attitude consists of cognitive, affective and behavioural components. This threefold division has an ancient heritage, stressing thought, feeling and action as basic to human experience.

The three-component model of attitude was particularly popular in the 1960s and 1970s (e.g. Breckler, 1984; Krech, Crutchfield, & Ballachey, 1962; Ostrom, 1968; Rosenberg & Hovland, 1960). Himmelfarb and Eagly (1974) described an attitude as a relatively enduring organisation of beliefs about, and feelings and behavioural tendencies towards, socially significant objects, groups, events or symbols. This definition not only included the three components but also emphasised that attitudes are:

- relatively *permanent*: they persist across time and situations; a momentary feeling is not an attitude;
- limited to *socially significant* events or objects;

- *generalisable* and capable of abstraction. If you drop a book on your toe and find that it hurts, this is not enough to form an attitude, because it is a single event in one place and at one time. But if the experience makes you dislike books or libraries, or clumsiness in general, then that dislike is an attitude.

Attitudes, then, are made up of (a) thoughts and ideas, (b) a cluster of feelings, likes and dislikes and (c) behavioural intentions. Despite the appeal of the 'trinity', this model presents a problem by prejudging a link between attitude and behaviour (Zanna & Rempel, 1988), itself a thorny and complex issue that is detailed later in this chapter. Suffice to say that most modern definitions of attitude involve both belief and feeling structures and are concerned with how, if each can indeed be measured, the resulting data may help predict people's actions. (Based on what you have read so far, try to answer the first 'What do *you* think?' question.)

Attitude functions

Presumably attitudes exist because they are useful – they serve a purpose, they have a function. The approaches we have considered so far make at least an implicit assumption of purpose. Some writers have been more explicit. Katz (1960), for example, proposed that there are various kinds of attitude, each serving a different function, such as:

- knowledge;
- instrumentality (means to an end or goal);
- ego-defence (protecting one's self-esteem);
- value-expressiveness (allowing people to display values that uniquely identify and define them).

Schema
Cognitive structure that represents knowledge about a concept or type of stimulus, including its attributes and the relations among those attributes.

Stereotype
Widely shared and simplified evaluative image of a social group and its members.

Cognitive consistency theories
A group of attitude theories stressing that people try to maintain internal consistency, order and agreement among their various cognitions.

Cognition
The knowledge, beliefs, thoughts and ideas that people have about themselves and their environment. May also refer to mental processes through which knowledge is acquired, including perception, memory and thinking.

An attitude saves cognitive energy, as we do not have to figure out 'from scratch' how we should relate to a particular object or situation (Smith, Bruner, & White, 1956). This function parallels the utility of a **schema** or **stereotype** and fits the cognitive miser or motivated tactician models of contemporary social cognition (e.g. Fiske & Taylor, 2013; **see Chapter 2**).

Overall, the main function of any kind of attitude is a utilitarian one: that of object appraisal (Fazio, 1989). This should hold regardless of whether the attitude has a positive or negative valence (i.e. whether our feelings about the object are good or bad). Merely possessing an attitude is useful because it provides an orientation towards the attitude object. For example, having a negative attitude towards snakes (believing they are dangerous) is useful if we cannot differentiate between safe and deadly varieties. However, for an attitude truly to fulfil this function, it must be accessible. We develop this last point later in the chapter when we discuss the relationship between attitudes and behaviour.

Cognitive consistency

In the late 1950s and 1960s, **cognitive consistency theories** (see Gawronski & Strack, 2012) dominated social psychology, and their emphasis on **cognition** dealt a fatal blow to simplistic reinforcement explanations (e.g. by learning theorists such as Thorndike, Hull and Skinner) in social psychology (Greenwald, Banaji, Rudman, Farnham, Nosek, & Mellott, 2002). The best known of these theories was cognitive dissonance theory (Cooper, 2007; Festinger, 1957), which, because of its importance in explaining attitude change, **we deal with in Chapter 6**. Another early example was balance theory.

As well as specifying that beliefs are the building blocks of attitude structure, consistency theories focused on inconsistencies among people's beliefs. The theories differ in how they define consistency and inconsistency, but they all assume that people find inconsistent beliefs aversive. Two thoughts are inconsistent if one seems to contradict the other, and such a state of mind is bothersome. This disharmony is known as *dissonance*. Consistency theories argue that people are motivated to change one or more contradictory beliefs so that the belief system as a whole is in harmony. The outcome is restoration of consistency.

Balance theory

The consistency theory with the clearest implications for attitude structure is Fritz Heider's **balance theory** (Heider, 1946; also see Cartwright & Harary, 1956). Heider's ideas were grounded in Gestalt psychology, an approach to perception popular in Germany in the early twentieth century and applied by Heider to interpersonal relations. Gestalt psychologists believed that the human mind is a person's 'cognitive field', and it comprises interacting forces that are associated with people's perceptions of people, objects and events.

Balance theory focuses on the P–O–X unit of the individual's cognitive field. Imagine a triad consisting of three elements: a person (P), another person (O), and an attitude, object or topic (X). A triad is consistent if it is balanced, and balance is assessed by counting the number and types of relationships between the elements. For instance, P liking X is a positive (+) relationship, O disliking X is negative (−), and P disliking O is negative (−).

There are eight possible combinations of relationships between two people and an attitude object, four of which are balanced and four unbalanced (Figure 5.1). A triad is balanced if there is an odd number of positive relationships and can occur in a variety of ways. If P likes O, O likes X and P likes X, then the triad is balanced. From P's point of view, balance theory acts as a divining rod in predicting interpersonal relationships: if P likes the object X, then any compatible other, O, should feel the same way. Likewise, if P already likes O, then O will be expected to evaluate object X in a fashion similar to P. By contrast, if P likes O, O likes X and P dislikes X, then the relationship is unbalanced. The principle of consistency that underlies balance theory means that in unbalanced triads, people may feel tense and be motivated to restore balance. Balance is generally restored in whatever way requires the least effort. So, in the last example, P could decide not to like O or to change his or her opinion about X, depending on which is the easier option.

Unbalanced structures are usually less stable and more unpleasant than balanced structures. However, in the absence of contradictory information, people assume that others will like what they themselves like. Further, we often prefer to agree with someone else – or, in balance-theory language, P and O seek structures where they agree rather than disagree about how they evaluate X (Zajonc, 1968). Again, people do not always seek to resolve inconsistency. Sometimes they organise their beliefs so that elements are kept isolated and are resistant to change (Abelson, 1968). For example, if P likes opera and O does not, and if P and O like each other, P may decide to isolate the element of opera from the triad by listening to opera when O is not present.

Overall, research on balance theory has been extensive and mostly supportive (Gawronski & Strack, 2012). For a recent example of an attitude-focused study in this tradition, see Gawronski, Walther and Blank (2005).

Cognition and evaluation

The one-component attitude model, described above, treats affect (Thurstone, 1931) or evaluation (e.g. Osgood, Suci, & Tannenbaum, 1957) as the core component of an attitude. This simple idea resurfaces in a more complicated guise in Pratkanis and Greenwald's (1989)

Balance theory
According to Heider, people prefer attitudes that are consistent with each other over those that are inconsistent. A person (P) tries to maintain consistency in attitudes to, and relationships with, other people (O) and elements of the environment (X).

Figure 5.1 Examples of balanced and unbalanced triads from Heider's theory of attitude change

In the balanced triads the relationships are consistent, in the unbalanced triads they are not.

Sociocognitive model
Attitude theory highlighting an evaluative component. Knowledge of an object is represented in memory along with a summary of how to appraise it.

sociocognitive model, where an attitude is defined as 'a person's evaluation of an object of thought' (p. 247). An attitude object (see Figure 5.2) is represented in memory by:

- an object label and the rules for applying that label;
- an evaluative summary of that object; and
- a knowledge structure supporting that evaluation.

For example, the attitude object we know as a 'shark' may be represented in memory as a really big fish with very sharp teeth (*label*); that lives in the sea and eats other fish and sometimes people (*rules*); is scary and best avoided while swimming (*evaluative summary*); and is a scientifically and fictionally well-documented threat to our physical well-being (*knowledge structure*). However, despite the cognitive emphasis, it was the evaluative component that Pratkanis and Greenwald highlighted.

The evaluative dimension of attitudes is of course a central focus of research on prejudice, where the key problem is that members of one group harbour negative attitudes towards members of another group (Dovidio, Glick, & Rudman, 2005; Jones, 1996; **see Chapter 10**). In the attitude literature, various terms have been used almost interchangeably in denoting this evaluative component, such as 'affect', 'evaluation', 'emotion' and 'feeling', suggesting an urgent need for the terminology to be tidied up and standardised (Breckler & Wiggins, 1989a, 1989b). Recent research on affect and emotion (**discussed in Chapter 2**) has helped sort some of this out by focusing on the role of cognitive appraisals of stimuli in people's experience of affect and emotion (e.g. Blascovich, 2008, Lazarus, 1991; also see

Figure 5.2 The sociocognitive model of attitude structure and function

This theory draws on research in social cognition and studies of memory. Just as physical objects or even people can be represented in memory, so too can an attitude object.

Source: Based on Pratkanis and Greenwald (1989).

Keltner & Lerner, 2010). When we apply this idea to the study of an attitude, we can distinguish between *affect* (an emotional reaction to an attitude object) and *evaluation* (particular kinds of thought, belief and judgement about the object).

Decision-making and attitudes

Do we perform cognitive algebra?

Information processing approaches emphasise how complex it is to acquire knowledge and to form and change our attitudes. According to **information integration theory** (Anderson, 1971, 1981; **see Chapter 2**), we use **cognitive algebra** to construct our attitudes from information we receive about attitude objects. People are sophisticated problem-solvers and vigilant evaluators of new information. How we receive and combine this information provides the basis for attitude structure. The salience of some items and the order in which they are received become important determinants of the way in which they are processed. As new information arrives, people evaluate it and combine it with existing information stored in memory. For example, a warning from health authorities that a certain brand of food may cause serious illness may lead people to re-evaluate their attitude, change their behaviour and not eat that brand again.

In Norman Anderson's approach, we acquire and re-evaluate attitudes by using cognitive algebra. We 'mentally' average out the values attached to discrete bits of information that are collated and stored in memory about an attitude object. Ordinary people habitually use such mathematics: for example, if you think a friend is shy, energetic and compassionate, your overall attitude is an average of the evaluations you attach to those traits. You would calculate a different average for another friend who was outgoing, energetic and charismatic.

Attitudes and automatic judgements

As a challenge to classical attitude theory, Patricia Devine (1989) suggested that people's attitudes are underpinned by implicit and automatic judgements of which they are unaware. Because these judgements are automatic and unconscious, they are less influenced by *social*

Information processing
The evaluation of information; in relation to attitudes, the means by which people acquire knowledge and form and change attitudes.

Information integration theory
The idea that a person's attitude can be estimated by averaging across the positive and negative ratings of the object.

Cognitive algebra
Approach to the study of impression formation that focuses on how people combine attributes that have valence into an overall positive or negative impression.

desirability bias (i.e. how others might react). They should therefore be a more reliable measure of a person's 'true' attitudes and may even be more closely related to what people actually do (Schwarz, 2000).

Others are more cautious and warn that implicit measures may be as dependent on context as explicit measures (attitudes), but in different ways (Glaser & Banaji, 1999). Implicit measures correlate only weakly with both explicit self-reports and overt behaviour (Hilton & Karpinski, 2000), and correlations between implicit and explicit measures of intergroup attitudes are generally low (Dovidio, Kawakami, & Beach, 2001). In considering developments in attitude theory, Van der Pligt and de Vries (2000) proposed a decision-making strategy continuum, which ranges from intuition at one end to controlled information processing (e.g. Anderson, 1971) at the other.

Dispute over the best way to characterise attitudes continues and shows little sign of abating. Is an attitude a directive and organised state of readiness (Allport), an outcome of algebraic calculation (Anderson) or an automatic judgement (Devine)?

Can attitudes predict behaviour?

Why study attitudes if scientists disagree about how best to define them? One answer is that attitudes may be useful for predicting what people will do – maybe if we change people's attitudes, we might be able to change their behaviour. Perhaps with tongue in cheek, Crano and Prislin (2006) have written: 'Because attitudes predict behaviour, they are considered the crown jewel of social psychology' (p. 360). As we shall see, a number of behavioural scientists have questioned this assumption.

For instance, Gregson and Stacey (1981) found only a small positive correlation between people's attitudes and their reported alcohol consumption. Furthermore, there was no evidence of any benefits in focusing on attitude change rather than on economic incentives to control alcohol use (e.g. avoiding fines, increasing taxes). This sort of finding has caused some critics to question the utility of the concept of attitude: if attitude measures bear no relation to what people actually do, then what is the use of the concept? Even a very early and oft-cited study of ethnic attitudes by LaPiere (1934) revealed a glaring inconsistency between what people do and what they say (see Box 5.1; **see also Chapter 10**).

Attitudes and behaviour
This voter is under surveillance. Will her selection reflect her own view, or might it be constrained by a prevailing norm?

Box 5.1 Research classic
Do attitudes really predict behaviour?

The sociologist Richard LaPiere (1934) was interested in the difference between prejudiced attitudes towards Chinese in general and discriminatory behaviours towards a Chinese couple in particular. In the early 1930s, anti-Asian prejudice was quite strong among Americans. LaPiere embarked on a 10,000-mile sightseeing tour of the United States, accompanied by two young Chinese friends. They visited 66 hotels, caravan parks and tourist homes and were served in 184 restaurants. As they went from place to place, LaPiere was concerned that his friends might not be accepted but, as it turned out, they were refused service only once.

Six months after their trip, LaPiere sent a questionnaire to all the places they had visited, asking, 'Will you accept members of the Chinese race as guests in your establishment?'

Of the 81 restaurants and 47 hotels that replied, 92 per cent said that they would *not* accept Chinese customers! Only 1 per cent said they would accept them, and the remainder checked 'Uncertain, depends on circumstances'. These written replies from the erstwhile hosts directly contradicted the way they had actually behaved.

This study was not, of course, scientifically designed – perhaps the people who responded to the letters were not those who dealt face-to-face with the Chinese couple; they might have responded differently in writing if they had been told that the couple was educated and well dressed; attitudes may have changed in the six months between the two measures. Nevertheless, the problem that LaPiere had unearthed provided an early challenge to the validity of the concept of attitude.

Following LaPiere's study, which vividly called into question the predictive utility of questionnaires, researchers have used more sophisticated methods to study the attitude–behaviour relationship but still found relatively low correspondence between questionnaire measures of attitudes and measures of actual behaviour. After reviewing this research, Wicker (1969) concluded that the correlation between attitudes and behaviour is seldom as high as 0.30 (which, when squared, indicates that only 9 per cent of the variability in a behaviour is accounted for by an attitude). In fact, Wicker found that the average correlation between attitudes and behaviour was only 0.15. This finding was seized upon during the 1970s as damning evidence – the attitude concept is worthless since it has little predictive power. A sense of despair settled on the field (Abelson, 1972). Nevertheless, attitudes are still being researched (Banaji & Heiphetz, 2010; Fazio & Olson, 2007), and the topic commands two chapters of this text.

What gradually emerged was that attitudes and overt behaviour are not related in a one-to-one fashion, and not all behaviours can be predicted accurately from verbally expressed attitudes. There are conditions that promote or disrupt the correspondence between having an attitude and behaving (Doll & Ajzen, 1992; Smith & Stasson, 2000). For example, attitude–behaviour consistency can vary according to:

- how accessible an attitude is (see 'Attitude Accessibility' later in this chapter);
- whether an attitude is expressed publicly, say in a group, or privately, such as when responding to a questionnaire;
- how strongly someone identifies with a group for which the attitude is normative.

Let us now look at research that has explored why attitude–behaviour correspondence is often weak, and what factors may strengthen the correspondence.

Beliefs, intentions and behaviour

Martin Fishbein (1967a, 1967b, 1971) agrees with Thurstone (1931) that the basic ingredient of an attitude is affect. However, if you measure an attitude purely on a unidimensional bipolar evaluative scale (such as good/bad), you cannot reliably predict how a person

Table 5.1 A young man's hypothetical attitude towards contraceptive use: the strength and value of his beliefs

Attribute	Man's belief about woman using pill						Man's belief about man using condom					
	Strength of belief		Value of belief			Result	Strength of belief		Value of belief			Result
Reliability	0.90	×	+2		=	+1.80	0.70	×	−1		=	−0.70
Embarrassment	1.00	×	+2		=	+2.00	0.80	×	−2		=	−1.60
Side effects	0.10	×	−1		=	−0.10	1.00	×	+2		=	+2.00
Outcome						+3.70						−0.30

The strength of a belief, in this example, is the probability (from 0 to 1) that a person thinks that the belief is true. The value of a belief is an evaluation on a bipolar scale (in this case, ranging from +2 to −2).

will later behave. Better prediction depends on an account of the interaction between attitudes, beliefs and behavioural intentions, and the connections of all of these with subsequent actions.

In this equation, we need to know both how strong and how valuable a person's beliefs are: some beliefs will carry more weight than others in relation to the final act. For example, the strength or weakness of a person's religious convictions may be pivotal in their decision-making processes regarding moral behaviour – moral norms may play a very important role in attitude–behaviour relations (Manstead, 2000). Without this information, prediction of behaviour is a hit-or-miss affair.

Consider the example in Table 5.1. A young, heterosexually active man might believe, strongly or not, that certain things are true about two forms of contraception, the pill and the condom. *Belief strength* (or expectancy) has a probability estimate, ranging from 0 to 1, regarding the truth; for example, he may hold a very strong belief (0.90) that the pill is a highly reliable method of birth control. Reliability of a contraceptive is a 'good' thing, so his *evaluation* (or value) of the pill is +2, say, on a five-point scale ranging from −2 to +2. Belief strength and evaluation interact, producing a final rating of +1.80. (Like Anderson, Fishbein's view incorporates the idea that people are able to perform cognitive algebra.)

Next, the young man might be fairly sure (0.70) that the condom is less reliable (−1), a rating of −0.70. Likewise, he thinks that using a condom is potentially embarrassing in a sexual encounter. His further belief that using a condom has no known side effects is not sufficient to offset the effects of the other two beliefs. Check the hypothetical algebra in Table 5.1. Consequently, the young man's intention to use a condom, should he possess one, may be quite low. Only by having all of this information could we be fairly confident about predicting his future behaviour.

This approach to prediction also offers a method of measurement, the expectancy–value technique. In subsequent work with his colleague Icek Ajzen, Fishbein developed the *theory of reasoned action*, which we discuss fully later in this section, to link beliefs to intentions to behaviour (Ajzen & Fishbein, 1980; Fishbein & Azjen, 1974). One important observation made by this research was that behavioural predictions can be improved if the measures of attitudes are specific rather than general.

Specific attitudes

Ajzen and Fishbein believed that attitude research suffered from either trying to predict specific behaviours from general attitudes or vice versa, so that low correlations were to be expected. This is, in essence, what LaPiere did. Ajzen and Fishbein believed that behaviour was better predicted by measuring attitudes that were very specific to the behaviour.

An example of a specific attitude predicting specific behaviour would be a student's attitude towards a psychology exam predicting how diligently he or she studies for that exam. In contrast, an example of a general attitude predicting a general class of behaviour would be attitudes towards psychology as a whole, predicting the behaviour generally relevant to learning more about psychology, such as reading magazine articles or talking with your tutor. How interested you are in psychology generally is not likely to be predictive of how well you prepare for a specific psychology exam.

In a two-year longitudinal study by Davidson and Jacard (1979), women's attitudes towards birth control were measured at different levels of specificity and used as predictors of their actual use of the contraceptive pill. The measures, ranging from very general to very specific, were correlated as follows with actual pill use (correlations in brackets): 'Attitude towards birth control' (0.08), 'Attitude towards birth control pills' (0.32), 'Attitude towards using birth control pills' (0.53) and 'Attitude towards using birth control pills during the next two years' (0.57). Thus, this last measure was the most highly correlated with actual use of the contraceptive pill. It indicates quite clearly that the closer the question was to the actual behaviour, the more accurately the behaviour was predicted. (See Kraus, 1995, for a **meta-analysis** of attitudes as predictors of behaviour.)

General attitudes

However, general attitudes can sometimes predict behaviour – but only if we adopt a **multiple-act criterion** (Fishbein & Ajzen, 1975). The idea here is that general attitudes predict multiple behaviours (acts) much better than they predict a specific single behaviour, because single behaviours are usually affected by many factors. For example, the specific behaviour of participating in a paper-recycling programme on a given day is a function of many factors, even the weather. Yet a person engaging in such behaviour may claim to be 'environmentally conscious', a general attitude. Environmental attitudes are no doubt one determinant of this behaviour, but they are not the only, or even perhaps the major, one.

Reasoned action

These ideas having to do with the specificity of attitudes and behaviours were expanded and integrated into a far-reaching theory of the attitude–behaviour relationship – the **theory of reasoned action** (Ajzen & Fishbein, 1980; Fishbein & Ajzen, 1974). The theory encapsulates three processes of beliefs, intention and action, and it includes the following components:

- *Subjective norm* – a product of what the person thinks others believe. Significant others provide direct or indirect information about 'what is the proper thing to do'.
- *Attitude towards the behaviour* – a product of the person's beliefs about the target behaviour and how these beliefs are evaluated (refer back to the cognitive algebra in Table 5.1). Note that this is an attitude towards behaviour (such as taking a birth control pill in Davidson and Jacard's study), not towards the object (such as the pill itself).
- *Behavioural intention* – an internal declaration to act.
- *Behaviour* – the action performed.

Usually, an action will be performed if (1) the person's attitude is favourable; and (2) the social norm is also favourable. In early tests of the theory, Fishbein and his colleagues (Fishbein & Coombs, 1974; Fishbein & Feldman, 1963) gave participants a series of statements about the attributes of various attitude objects: for example, political candidates. The participants estimated *expectancies* – that is, how likely it was that the object (candidate) possessed the various attributes – and gave the attributes a *value*. These expectancies and values were then used to predict the participants' feelings towards the attitude object, assessed by asking the participants how much they liked or disliked that object. The correlation between the scores and the participants' feelings was high. Other research reported that

---

Meta-analysis
Statistical procedure that combines data from different studies to measure the overall reliability and strength of specific effects.

Multiple-act criterion
Term for a general behavioural index based on an average or combination of several specific behaviours.

Theory of reasoned action
Fishbein and Ajzen's theory of the relationship between attitudes and behaviour. A specific attitude that has normative support predicts an intention to act, which then predicts actual behaviour.

when people's voting intentions were later compared with how they actually voted, the correlations were as follows:

- A correlation of 0.80 in the 1976 American presidential election (Fishbein, Ajzen, & Hinkle, 1980); and

- A correlation of 0.89 in a referendum on nuclear power (Fishbein, Bowman, Thomas, Jacard, & Ajzen, 1980).

Overall if you know someone's very specific behavioural intentions, then you are effectively almost there in terms of predicting what they will actually do – their behaviour. Meta-analyses of relevant research suggest this is the case but that some hurdles remain, for example, to do with behavioural opportunities (Gollwitzer & Sheeran, 2006; Webb & Sheeran, 2006).

Planned behaviour

The theory of reasoned action emphasises not only the rationality of human behaviour but also the belief that the behaviour is under the person's conscious control: for example, 'I know I can stop smoking if I really want to'. However, some actions are less under people's control than others.

This prompted Ajzen (1989; Ajzen & Madden, 1986) to extend the theory of reasoned action to consider the role of behavioural control. Perceived behavioural control is a person's belief, based on past experience and present obstacles, that it is easy or difficult to perform a behaviour. For example, students, not surprisingly, want to get A-grades in their courses: A-grades are highly valued by the students (attitude), and they are the grades that their family and friends want them to get (subjective norm). However, prediction of actually getting an A will be unreliable unless the students' perceptions of their own abilities are taken into account.

Ajzen has argued that perceived behavioural control can relate to either the behavioural intention or to the behaviour itself. He referred to this theory as the **theory of planned behaviour**. In a subsequent meta-analysis, Richard Cooke and Pascal Sheeran (2004) have claimed that the theory of planned behaviour is 'probably the dominant account of the relationship between cognitions and behaviour in social psychology' (p. 159; also see Ajzen & Fishbein, 2005). The two theories, of reasoned action and planned behaviour, are not in conflict. The concepts and the way in which they are linked in each theory are shown in Figure 5.3. How would you apply these theories to answer the second 'What do *you* think?' question?

In one study, Beck and Ajzen (1991) started with students' self-reports of how dishonest they had been in the past. The behaviours sampled included exam cheating, shoplifting and telling lies to avoid completing written assignments – behaviours that were quite often reported. They found that measuring the perception of control that students thought they had over these behaviours improved the accuracy of prediction of future behaviour, and, to some extent, the actual performance of the act. This was most successful in the case of cheating, which may well be planned in a more deliberate way than shoplifting or lying.

In another study, Madden, Ellen and Ajzen (1992) measured students' perceptions of control in relation to nine behaviours. These ranged from 'getting a good night's sleep' (quite hard to control) to 'taking vitamin supplements' (quite easy to control). The results were calculated to compare predictive power by squaring the correlation coefficient (i.e. r^2) between each of the two predictors (sleep and vitamins) and each of the outcomes (intentions and actions). Perceived control improved the prediction accuracy for both intentions and actions, and this improvement was substantially effective in predicting the action itself. These effects are evident in the steep gradient of the two lower lines in Figure 5.4, an outcome that has been confirmed in an independent study using a wide range of thirty behaviours (Sheeran, Trafimow, Finlay, & Norman, 2002).

Theory of planned behaviour
Modification by Ajzen of the theory of reasoned action. It suggests that predicting a behaviour from an attitude measure is improved if people believe they have control over that behaviour.

Figure 5.3 A comparison of the theory of reasoned action (TRA) and the theory of planned behaviour (TPB)

The solid lines show the concepts and links in the original theory of reasoned action; the dotted lines show an addition introduced in the theory of planned behaviour.

Source: Based on Ajzen and Fishbein (1980); Madden, Ellen and Ajzen (1992).

In critically evaluating both the theories of reasoned action and planned behaviour, Tony Manstead and Dianne Parker (1995) argued that the inclusion of 'perceived behavioural control' in the theory of planned behaviour is an improvement on the original theory. In a meta-analysis by Armitage and Conner (2001), perceived behavioural control emerged as a significant variable that accounted for up to 20 per cent of prospective actual behaviour.

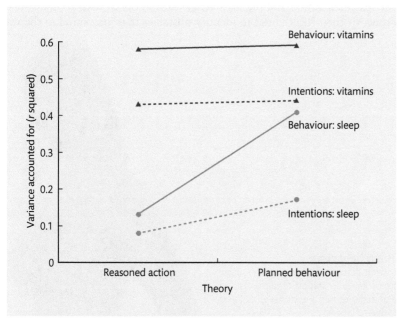

Figure 5.4 Theories of reasoned action and planned behaviour compared: The effect of including perceived behavioural control as a variable

Source: Based on data from Madden, Ellen and Ajzen (1992).

The theory of planned behaviour has also been used to predict anti-nuclear intentions or behaviour from anti-nuclear attitudes (Fox-Cardamone, Hinkle, & Hogue, 2000), and to predict driver behaviour in Britain (e.g. Conner, Lawton, Parker, Chorlton, Manstead, & Stradling, 2007; Parker, Manstead, & Stradling, 1995). Regarding driver behaviour, studies have measured both the intentions of drivers and their behaviours, such as speeding, cutting in, weaving recklessly and illegal overtaking on the inside lanes of a motorway. The study by Conner and his colleagues also measured actual behaviour – in a driving simulator and real on-road driving caught on a discreet camera. They found that the theory of planned behaviour can provide a basis for developing interventions designed to reduce speeding on the roads. The tendency to speed is based partly upon a driver's intentions to speed and partly on the absence of a moral norm not to speed, itself a thorny and complex issue that is dealt with later in this chapter (see section 'Beliefs, intentions and behaviour').

Aside from the usual variable associated with the theories of reasoned action and planned behaviour, people's *moral values* may play a role in determining action (e.g. Gorsuch & Ortbergh, 1983; Manstead, 2000; Pagel & Davidson, 1984; Schwartz, 1977). For example, if you wanted to know whether someone would donate money to charity, you would do well to find out whether acting charitably is a priority in their lives. In this specific context, Maio and Olson (1995) found that general altruistic values predicted charitable behaviour (donating to cancer research), but only where the context emphasised the *expression* of one's values. Where the context emphasised rewards and punishments (i.e. a utilitarian emphasis), values did not predict donating.

Habit is also a predictor of future behaviour. An action can become relatively automatic (discussed later in this chapter), and can operate independently of processes underlying the theory of planned behaviour. Trafimow (2000) found that male and female students who were in the habit of using condoms reported that they would continue to do so on the next occasion. In effect, habitual condom users do not 'need' to use reasoned decisions, such as thinking about what their attitudes are or about what norms are appropriate. A theory of planned behaviour study of binge drinking (Norman & Conner, 2006) found that how students viewed their drinking history could predict their future behaviour. For example, if Bill believes he is a binge drinker, he will attend less to his attitude towards alcohol abuse and will also feel that he has less control over how much he drinks.

Promoting healthy behaviour

Both the theories of reasoned action and planned behaviour have been used to understand people's attitudes towards their health, and to identify obstacles that may stand in the way

Planned behaviour
The promotion of a healthy practice, such as breast self-examination, requires that a woman believes that she knows what to do and what to look for.

of healthy attitudes translating into healthy lifestyles (Conner, Norman, & Bell, 2002; Stroebe, 2011). For example, Debbie Terry and her colleagues (Terry, Gallois, & McCamish, 1993) have studied safe sex behaviour as a response to the threat of contracting HIV (see Box 5.2). Specifically, the target behaviour included monogamous relationships, non-penetrative sex and the use of condoms. All of the variables shown in Figure 5.3 can be applied in this setting. In the context of practising safe sex, the particular variable of perceived behavioural control needs to be accounted for, particularly where neither of the sex partners may be fully confident of controlling the wishes of the other person. One practical question is the degree of control that a woman might perceive she has about whether a condom will be used in her next sexual encounter.

Another theory, related to the theories of reasoned action and planned behaviour, that focuses on how people can protect their health, maintain better practices and avoid risky behaviour is **protection motivation theory** (see Box 5.3 and Figure 5.5). Taken together, all three theories share the idea that motivation towards protection results from a perceived threat and the desire to avoid potential negative outcomes (Floyd, Prentice-Dunn, & Rogers, 2000).

Protection motivation theory
Adopting a healthy behaviour requires cognitive balancing between the perceived threat of illness and one's capacity to cope with the health regimen.

Health issues to which these theories have been applied include HIV prevention (Smith & Stasson, 2000), condom use and safer sex behaviour (Sheeran & Taylor, 1999), alcohol consumption (Conner, Warren, Close, & Sparks, 1999), smoking (Godin, Valois, Lepage, & Desharnais, 1992) and healthy eating (Conner, Norman, & Bell, 2002).

Healthy lifestyles may not just be a matter of individual attitudes translating into individual behaviours, as is the focus of the theories of reasoned action and planned behaviour.

Box 5.2 Our world
Reasoned action, planned behaviour and safe sex

The theories of reasoned action and planned behaviour have proved useful in understanding and promoting responsible sexual behaviour

Social psychologists have increasingly turned their attention to promoting health practices such as avoiding the abuse of alcohol, tobacco and other substances; promoting dental hygiene; vaccinating against infectious diseases; participating in cervical smear tests; and using sunscreen products (**see also Chapter 6**).

Another sphere of application has been the promotion of contraceptive practices to avoid unwanted pregnancies. Health professionals have also been concerned about the spread of HIV and contraction of AIDS. (**We noted in Chapter 2 that some people tend to underestimate the riskiness of their sexual practices.**)

In this context, social psychologists have mounted a concerted campaign of research promoting condom use, safe sex and monogamous relationships. Several researchers have explicitly recognised Fishbein and Ajzen's (Fishbein & Ajzen, 1974; Ajzen & Fishbein, 1980) theory of reasoned action as a model that helps to account for variability in people's willingness to practise safe sex (see Terry, Gallois, & McCamish, 1993). One feature of this work has been to focus on establishing how much people feel they can actually exert control over their health. A woman with

this sense of control is more likely to wear a seat belt, examine her breasts, use a contraceptive, have sex in an exclusive relationship and discuss her partner's sexual and intravenous drug-use history.

Apart from a sense of control, other factors such as perceptions of condom proposers (those who initiate condom use), as well as the expectations and experience of safe sex, are implicated in initiating safe sex (Hodges, Klaaren, & Wheatley, 2000). Coupled with these factors, cultural background also plays a role in the gender and sexuality equation. For example, Conley, Collins and Garcia (2000) found that Chinese Americans reacted more negatively than European Americans to the female condom proposer. Furthermore, Japanese Americans perceived the female condom proposer to be less sexually attractive than did the Chinese or European Americans (**see also Chapter 16**).

A problem with practising safe sex with one's partner is that it is not a behaviour that comes completely under one individual's *volitional control*, whereas going for a run usually is. The theory of reasoned action, together with its extension, the theory of planned behaviour (see Figure 5.3), provides a framework for psychologists and other health professionals to target particular variables that have the potential to encourage safe sex as well as other health behaviour.

Box 5.3 Our world
Can we protect ourselves against major diseases?

According to statistics from the US Centers for Disease Control and Prevention, heart disease and cancer were by far the leading causes of death in the United States in 2014 (1.2 million deaths), a statistic that prevails in most Western nations. It is well known that preventive behaviour for both diseases includes routine medical examinations, regular blood pressure readings, exercising aerobically for at least twenty minutes three times per week, eating a well-balanced diet that is low in salt and fat, maintaining a healthy weight and not smoking. It is a major challenge for health psychologists to find a model of health promotion that is robust enough to encourage people to engage in these preventative behaviours.

According to Floyd, Prentice-Dunn and Rogers (2000), protection motivation theory has emerged as just such a model. The model was developed initially to explain the effects of fear-arousing appeals on maladaptive health attitudes and behaviour, and it was derived from Fishbein's theories of expectancy-value and reasoned action. Other components built into protection motivation theory included the effects of intrinsic and extrinsic reward (related to social learning theory) and Bandura's (1986, 1992) concept of self-efficacy, which in turn is closely related to that of *perceived behavioural control* in the theory of planned behaviour (Ajzen, 1998).

From their meta-analysis of sixty-five studies and more than twenty health issues, Floyd, Prentice-Dunn and

Rogers argue that adaptive intentions and behaviour are facilitated by:

- an increase in the perceived severity of a health threat;
- the vulnerability of the individual to that threat;
- the perceived effectiveness of taking protective action; and
- self-efficacy.

In considering why Joe, for example, might either continue to smoke or decide to quit, protection motivation theory specifies two mediating cognitive processes:

1 *Threat appraisal* – smoking has intrinsic rewards (e.g. taste in mouth, nicotine effect) and extrinsic rewards (e.g. his friends think it's cool). These are weighed against the extent to which Joe thinks there is a severe risk to his health (e.g. after reading the latest brochure in his doctor's waiting room) and that he is vulnerable (e.g. because a close relative who smoked died of lung cancer).
2 *Coping appraisal* – Joe takes into account response efficacy (whether nicotine replacement therapy might work) and **self-efficacy** (whether he thinks he can adhere to the regime).

The trade-off when Joe compares his appraisals of threat and coping determines his level of protection motivation and whether he decides to quit smoking (see Figure 5.5).

Figure 5.5 Mediating cognitive processes in protection motivation theory

This theory, which grew from health promotion research, argues that adoption of healthy behavioural practices depends on several cognitive processes that lead people to balance health threats and the capacity to cope with a health regime.

Source: Based on Floyd, Prentice-Dunn and Rogers (2000).

Self-efficacy
Expectations that we have about our capacity to succeed in particular tasks.

Healthy lifestyles may also be a matter of identity, where healthy behaviour is normative of a group that one identifies strongly with as a key part of who one is in society (Jetten, Haslam, & Haslam, 2012). For example, Grant and colleagues found that healthy adults who identified strongly with an exercise-defined referent group reported higher levels of physical activity, and this was because they felt they would actually be able to do the exercise and would gain benefits from it (Grant, Hogg, & Crano, 2015).

Overall, social psychology has enormous potential for application to public health. However, many believe that this potential has not yet been fully realised, citing social psychology's sub-disciplinary specialisation, poor connection to other disciplines, research methodology and publication practices, among other things, as obstacles (Klein, Shepperd, Suls, Rothman, & Croyle, 2015).

Attitude accessibility

Attitudes are represented in memory (Olson & Zanna, 1993), and accessible attitudes are those that can be recalled from memory more easily and can therefore be expressed more quickly (Eagly & Chaiken, 1998). Accessible attitudes exert a strong influence on behaviour (Fazio, 1986) and are associated with greater attitude–behaviour consistency (Doll & Ajzen, 1992). They are also more stable, more selective in judging relevant information and more resistant to change (Fazio, 1995). There is some evidence that affective evaluations are faster than cognitive evaluations, suggesting that more evaluative attitudes are more accessible in memory (Verplanken & Aarts, 1999; Verplanken, Hofstee, & Janssen, 1998).

Most studies of attitude accessibility focus on highly accessible attitudes, drawing on Fazio's (1995) model of attitudes as an association in memory between an object and an evaluation. The rationale behind Fazio's model is that an attitude is 'handy' or functional and useful for the individual to the extent that it can be automatically activated in memory. The likelihood of automatic activation depends on the strength of the association between the object and the evaluation (Bargh, Chaiken, Govender, & Pratto, 1992). Strong object–evaluation associations should therefore be highly functional because they help us make decisions.

Although the ideas behind attitude accessibility are intuitively appealing and supported by some research (e.g. Fazio, Ledbetter, & Towles-Schwen, 2000), there is also some evidence that implicit measures (as object–evaluation associations) correlate only weakly with explicit self-reports, what people actually say (Hilton & Karpinski, 2000). We return to this later in this chapter when we examine how attitudes are measured.

As well as facilitating decision-making, accessible attitudes orientate visual attention and categorization processes (Roskos-Ewoldsen & Fazio, 1992; Smith, Fazio, & Cejka, 1996), and free up resources for coping with stress (Fazio & Powell, 1997). How might accessible attitudes affect the way we categorise? Smith, Fazio and Cejka (1996) showed that, when choosing from a number of possible categories to describe an object, we are more likely to select an accessible one. For example, when participants rehearsed their attitudes towards dairy products, yoghurt was more likely to cue as a *dairy product*. On the other hand, if attitudes towards health food were experimentally enhanced, and therefore made more accessible in memory, yoghurt was more likely to cue as a *health food* (Eagly & Chaiken, 1998).

Fazio's studies confirmed earlier findings that perceptions of stimuli will probably be biased in the direction of a person's attitude (Lambert, Solomon, & Watson, 1949; Zanna, 1993). However, he also showed that costs are associated with highly accessible attitudes. Recall that accessible attitudes are stable over time. Thus, if the object of an attitude changes, accessible attitudes towards that object may function less well (Fazio, Ledbetter, & Towles-Schwen, 2000). Accessibility can produce insensitivity to change – we have become set in our ways. Consequently, someone who feels negatively about a particular attitude object may not be able to detect if the 'object' has changed for better or perhaps worse (see Box 5.4).

Box 5.4 Research highlight
Accessible attitudes can be costly

There may be costs associated with highly accessible attitudes. Fazio, Ledbetter and Towles-Schwen (2000) tested this idea in several experiments using computer-based morphing. Twenty-four same-sex digital facial photographs were paired so that one image in each pair was relatively attractive and one was not, based on earlier data. Five morphs (composites) of the images of each pair were created that varied in attractiveness determined by the percentage (e.g. 67 / 33, 50 / 50, 13 / 87) that each image contributed to a morph.

In part 1 of an experimental sequence, participants 'formed' attitudes that were either highly accessible (HA) or less accessible (LA). HA participants verbally rated how attractive each morph was, whereas LA participants verbally estimated the morph's probable physical height.

Part 2 involved the detection of change in an image. Participants were told that they would see more faces, some of which were different photographs of people they had already seen, and they were to choose both quickly and accurately whether each image was the same or different from those seen earlier. HA participants were slower to respond than LA participants and also made more errors than LA participants. In an experimental variation, they also noticed less change in a morphed image.

All attitudes are functional and accessible attitudes even more so, since they usually deal with objects, events and people that are stable. However, if the attitude object changes over time, then a highly accessible attitude may become dysfunctional – it is stuck in time.

Another way to conceptualise accessibility is in the language of *connectionism*. An accessible attitude is a cognitive node in the mind that is well connected to other cognitive nodes (thorough learning and perhaps conditioning), and so the focal attitude can be activated in many different ways and along many different cognitive paths. According to Frank Van Overwalle and Frank Siebler:

> This allows a view of the mind as an adaptive learning mechanism that develops accurate mental representations of the world. Learning is modeled as a process of online adaptation of existing knowledge to novel information . . . the network changes the weights of the connections with the attitude object so as to better represent the accumulated history of co-occurrences between objects and their attributes and evaluations.

Van Overwalle and Siebler (2005, p. 232)

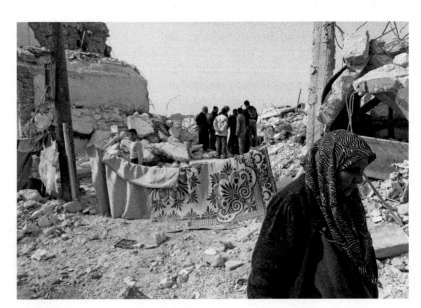

Attitude strength
If your village had been bombed into oblivion, how might you feel?

Van Overwalle and Siebler suggest that a connectionist approach is consistent with: (1) dual-process models of attitude change (**see Chapter 6**), and (2) the notion of algebraic weights placed on beliefs, introduced by Fishbein (see the example in Table 5.1).

Attitude strength and direct experience

Do strong attitudes guide behaviour? The results of a study of attitudes towards Greenpeace suggest so (Holland, Verplanken, & Van Knippenberg, 2002). People with very positive attitudes towards Greenpeace were much more likely to make a donation to the cause than those with weak positive attitudes.

Almost by definition, strong attitudes must be highly accessible. They come to mind more readily and influence behaviour more than weak attitudes. Attitudes are evaluative associations with objects, and associations can vary in strength from 'no link' (i.e. a non-attitude), to a weak link, to a strong link. Only an association that is strong allows the **automatic activation** of an attitude (Fazio, 1995; Fazio, Blascovich, & Driscoll, 1992; Fazio & Powell, 1997; Fazio, Sanbonmatsu, Powell, & Kardes, 1986; see Figure 5.6).

Direct experience of an object and having a vested interest in it (i.e. something with a strong effect on your life) make the attitude more accessible and strengthen its effect on behaviour. For example, people who have had a nuclear reactor built in their neighbourhood will have stronger and more clearly defined attitudes regarding the safety of nuclear reactors. These people will be more motivated by their attitudes – they may be more involved in protests or more likely to move house.

As another example, consider attitudes towards doctor-assisted suicide (Haddock, Rothman, Reber, & Schwarz, 1999). As subjective experience with this form of dying increased – its certainty, intensity and importance – the corresponding attitude about doctor-assisted suicide became stronger. It became more certain, intense and important.

Automatic activation
According to Fazio, attitudes that have a strong evaluative link to situational cues are more likely to come automatically to mind from memory.

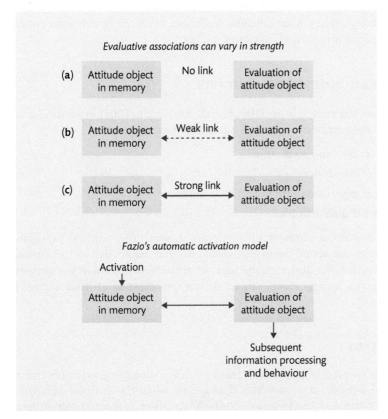

Figure 5.6 When is an attitude accessible?
A stronger attitude is more accessible than a weaker attitude. It can be automatically activated and will exert more influence over behaviour.

The more often you *think* about an attitude, the more likely it is to resurface and influence your behaviour through easier decision-making (Fazio, Blascovich, & Driscoll, 1992). Powell and Fazio (1984) were able to make an attitude more accessible simply by asking on six different occasions what people's attitudes were as opposed to asking them only once. Accessing general attitudes can affect behaviour in specific situations. If the general attitude is never accessed, it cannot affect behaviour. Therefore, the activation step of Fazio's model is critical, since only activated attitudes can guide subsequent information processing and behaviour. Think of a sports coach priming a team by asking the question 'Which is the greatest team?', demanding a shouted response of 'We are!' and repeating this scenario a number of times before the match begins.

In addition to the role of strength, an attitude becomes more accessible as direct experience with the attitude object increases. Attitudes formed through actual experience are more consistently related to behaviour (Doll & Ajzen, 1992; Regan & Fazio, 1977). Suppose Mary has participated in several psychology experiments but William has only read about them. We can predict Mary's willingness to participate in the future more accurately than William's (Fazio & Zanna, 1978). Another example: your attitude towards UFOs is far less likely to predict how you will act should you encounter one (!) than your attitude towards lecturers is likely to predict your lecture room behaviour. Likewise, it would be reassuring to think that those people who had been caught driving with excessive blood alcohol levels would be less likely to drink and drive in the future. Unfortunately, this is not always the case.

Therefore, although direct experience seems appealing as an influence on attitude accessibility, establishing its actual effectiveness is a difficult task. We consider the role of direct experience again in the context of attitude formation in a later section of this chapter.

Apart from attitude accessibility and direct experience with the attitude object, issues such as attitude salience, ambivalence, consistency between affect and cognition, attitude extremity, affective intensity, certainty, importance, latitudes of rejection and non-commitment are common themes in attitude research that fall under the general rubric of 'attitude strength'. Not surprisingly, attitude strength may consist of many related constructs rather than just one (Krosnick, Boninger, Chuang, Berent, & Carnot, 1993). Although some dimensions of attitude strength are strongly related, most are not.

Reflecting on the attitude–behaviour link

Let us take stock of what research tells us (Glassman & Albarracín, 2006). As attitudes are being *formed*, they correlate more strongly with a future behaviour when:

- the attitudes are *accessible* (easy to recall);
- the attitudes are *stable over time*;
- people have had *direct experience* with the attitude object;
- people *frequently report* their attitudes.

The attitude–behaviour link is stronger when relevant information – such as persuasive arguments – is relevant to the actual behaviour, one-sided and supportive of the attitude object, rather than two-sided. We deal with the topic of attitude formation in the next section and the role of persuasive arguments as part of our treatment of attitude change in **Chapter 6**.

Moderator variable
A variable that qualifies an otherwise simple hypothesis with a view to improving its predictive power (e.g. A causes B, but only when C (the moderator) is present).

Moderator variables

Although it is difficult to predict single acts from general attitudes, prediction can be improved by considering **moderator variables** that specify when the attitude–behaviour relationship is stronger or weaker. Moderators include the situation, personality, habit, sense of control and direct experience. The attitude itself can also act as a moderator – for example, an attitude that expresses a person's self-concept and central values has stronger attitude–behaviour correspondence than one that simply maximises rewards and minimises punishments (Verplanken & Holland, 2002; Maio & Olson, 1994). Ironically, moderator variables may turn out to be more powerful predictors of an action than the more general, underlying attitude. We consider two cases.

Situational variables

Aspects of the situation, or context, can cause people to act in a way that is inconsistent with their attitudes (Calder & Ross, 1973). Weak attitudes are particularly susceptible to context (Lavine, Huff, Wagner, & Sweeney, 1998), and in many cases, social norms that are contextually salient overwhelm people's underlying attitudes. For instance, if university students expect each other to dress in jeans and casual clothes, these expectations represent a powerful norm for how students dress on campus.

Norms have always been considered important in attitude–behaviour relations, but they have generally been separated from attitudes: attitudes are 'in here' (private, internalised cognitive constructs), norms are 'out there' (public, external pressures representing the cumulative expectations of others). This view of norms has been challenged by social identity theory (**see Chapter 11**), which sees no such distinction – attitudes can be personal and idiosyncratic, but much more typically they are a normative property of a group, and group identification causes one to internalise the group's normative properties, including its attitudes, as an aspect of self (e.g. Abrams & Hogg, 1990a; Hogg & Smith, 2007; Turner, 1991; **see Chapter 7**).

This idea has been applied to attitude–behaviour relations to argue that attitudes are more likely to express themselves as behaviour if the attitudes and associated behaviour are normative properties of a contextually salient social group with which people identify (Hogg & Smith, 2007; Terry & Hogg, 1996; Terry, Hogg, & White, 2000). To test this, Terry and Hogg (1996) conducted two longitudinal questionnaire studies of students' intentions to take regular exercise and to protect themselves from the sun. These intentions were stronger when participants identified strongly with a self-relevant student peer group whom participants believed took regular exercise or habitually protected themselves from the sun (Figure 5.7).

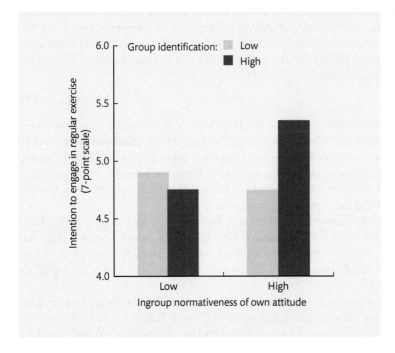

Figure 5.7 The role of norms and group identification in attitude–behaviour consistency

Students expressed a stronger intention to engage in regular exercise when they felt their attitudes towards exercise were normative of a student peer group with which they identified strongly.

Source: Based on data by Terry and Hogg (1996).

Individual differences

Social psychologists tend to be divided into two camps – those who prefer situational explanations of social behaviour and those who prefer personality and individual difference explanations (Ross & Nisbett, 1991). Although this distinction has become less stark in recent years (Funder & Fast, 2010) it nevertheless has influenced attitude research. For example, Mischel (1968) argued that situational characteristics were more reliable predictors of behaviour than were personality traits (see also the weak correlations reported between personality measures and leadership in **Chapter 9**). Whereas Bem and Allen (1974) and Vaughan (1977) have shown that people who were consistent in their *answers* on a personality scale were more likely to be consistent in their *behaviour* across a variety of relevant situations than people who gave variable answers. For example, a high scorer on an extraversion–introversion scale would be more likely to behave in an extroverted manner and a low scorer in an introverted manner, across different social settings. On the other hand, those who were variable (mid-range scorers) in their answers on the scale would not behave consistently.

It is therefore useful to know how people's behavioural *habits* are related to their *degree of control* over the behaviour (Langer, 1975; Petty & Cacioppo, 1981; Triandis, 1980; Verplanken, Aarts, Van Knippenberg, & Moonen, 1998) – the study of habits has experienced a recent revival (see Neal, Wood, Labrecque, & Lally, 2012; Wood & Neal, 2007). Triandis (1977) proposed a model similar to Fishbein and Ajzen's, which included a habit factor to reflect the number of times a person had performed a particular action in the past. Smoking, for instance, is habitual for many people and is often partly due to a physiological and/or psychological dependency. Thus, the behaviour of smokers may bear little relationship to their attitudes towards cigarettes. Oskamp (1984) reported that about 70 per cent of smokers agreed that 'smoking is one of the causes of lung cancer', and that 'cigarette smoking causes disease and death'.

From a review of research on 'habit', Bas Verplanken and Henk Aarts (1999) concluded that the relationship between attitudes and behaviour and between intentions and behaviour were near zero when habits were strong but sizeable when habits were weak. However, psychologists are fiercely vigilant in protecting their theories! In this instance, Ajzen (2002) does not see an inconsistency between habitual behaviour and planned behaviour:

> The theory of planned behavior [and of reasoned action] does not propose that individuals review their behavioral, normative, and control beliefs prior to every enactment of a frequently performed behavior. Instead, attitudes and intentions – once formed and well-established – are assumed to be activated automatically and to guide behavior without the necessity of conscious supervision.
>
> Ajzen (2002, p. 108)

Mood as a moderator variable may be considered both a situational and a personality variable. Carolyn Semmler and Neil Brewer (2002) examined the effects of trial-induced mood on how jurors processed information and made decisions. They found that being sad did not affect a juror's judgement, despite an increase in irrelevant thought. However, angry jurors actually reported more irrelevant thoughts, detected fewer inconsistencies in the witness's testimony and judged the defendant more harshly.

If we replace 'mood' with terms like 'affect' and 'emotion', we invoke part of the three-component model of attitude structure discussed earlier. In this wider context, there has been considerable research into affect-based evaluations of an attitude object (e.g. 'I hate broccoli, but I love ice cream') especially in the context of persuasion and advertising (**see Chapter 6**).

Cognitive biases, one of which is self–other discrepancy (**see Chapter 4**), are also moderators of attitude–behaviour correspondence. Angela Paglia and Robin Room (1999) studied what more than 800 people expected to happen when they drank alcohol and also how readily available they thought alcohol should be. They found that support for tighter control over alcohol availability stems partly from what people expect to happen, both from their own drinking and from the drinking of others. There was a distinct self–other discrepancy: people expect alcohol to affect others more adversely than themselves! Furthermore, the greater the bias, the greater the support for alcohol restriction.

Finally, some people are more focused than others on what has been called their *self-identity* – their sense of who they are as defined by the roles they occupy in society; although similar to social identity (**see Chapter 11**), self-identity is more focused on roles than on group membership (Terry, Hogg, & White, 1999; **also see Chapter 4**). Self-identity has been viewed as an influence on people's intentions to act, which is a component of the theory of planned behaviour, discussed earlier (Hagger & Chatzisarantis, 2006). In one study, people were more likely to express an intention to donate blood if being a blood donor was an important part of their self-identity (Charng, Piliavin, & Callero, 1988).

Forming attitudes

Attitudes are learnt as part of the socialisation process (Fishbein & Ajzen, 1975; McGuire, 1969; Oskamp, 1977). They develop through direct experiences or vicariously through interactions with others, or they are a product of cognitive processes and thought. Social psychologists have been focusing mainly on basic psychological processes that underlie **attitude formation** rather than exploring how particular classes of attitude develop. The study of these processes usually involves laboratory experiments rather than survey or public opinion research.

Attitude formation
The process of forming our attitudes, mainly from our own experiences, the influences of others and our emotional reactions.

Behavioural approaches

Effects of direct experience

Attitudes are often formed through direct experience with attitude objects. There are several explanations for how this happens: mere exposure, classical conditioning, operant conditioning, social learning and self-perception.

Direct experience provides information about the attributes of an object, which shapes our beliefs and how much we like or dislike the object (Fishbein & Ajzen, 1975). Even a mildly traumatic experience can trigger a negative attitude (Oskamp, 1977; Sargant, 1957) and make certain beliefs more salient than others. If your first visit to the dentist is painful, you may conclude that dentists hurt rather than help you, despite their friendly smile.

Mere exposure to an object on several occasions is likely to affect how we evaluate it – the **mere exposure effect** (Zajonc, 1968). The first time you hear a new song, you may neither strongly like nor dislike it; but with repetition, your response in one direction or the other is likely to strengthen. However, the effect of continued repeated exposure diminishes. For example, increased liking for photos of people levelled off after about ten exposures (Bornstein, 1989). Mere exposure has most impact when we lack information about an issue. Sitting MPs, for example, usually have an advantage over other candidates in an election, simply because their names are more familiar.

Mere exposure effect
Repeated exposure to an object results in greater attraction to that object.

Classical conditioning

Repeated association may cause a formerly neutral stimulus to elicit a reaction that was previously elicited only by another stimulus. In the specific case of **evaluative conditioning**, the degree of *liking* for an object will change when the object is consistently paired with other stimuli that are either positive or negative (De Houwer, Thomas, & Baeyens,

Evaluative conditioning
A stimulus will become more liked or less liked when it is consistently paired with stimuli that are either positive or negative.

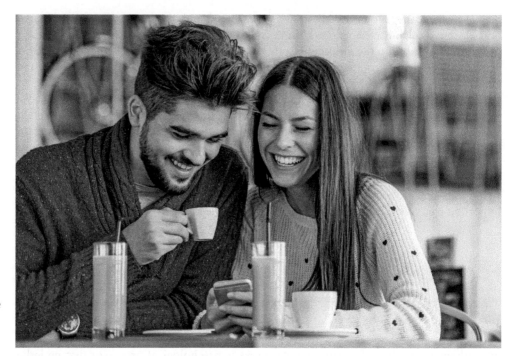

Classical conditioning
A relaxed setting induces a good mood. It is an easy step to associate this mood with someone who is immediately present, increasing mutual liking.

2001; Jones, Olson, & Fazio, 2010). For example, children initially have no political party preference but later vote as young adults for a specific party after years of exposure to a parent who has been an enthusiastic supporter of that party – a classically conditioned response has become the basis of a subsequent political attitude. A wide variety of attitudes may be formed in this way through classical conditioning (Zanna, Kiesler, & Pilkonis, 1970).

The evaluative conditioning effect is incredibly robust – it has been documented in over 250 studies (Hofmann, De Houwer, Perugini, Baeyens, & Crombez, 2010). One issue, however, is the extent of awareness that is required for evaluative conditioning – can it occur subliminally as an automatic process, or does it require the person to be aware of the co-occurrence? Decisive evidence either way is limited (Krosnick, Betz, Jussim, & Lynn, 1992; Olson & Fazio, 2002). A recent review concludes that the question remains unresolved, partly because it is very difficult to research subliminal evaluative conditioning, but that some aspect of automaticity has been confirmed (Sweldens, Corneille, & Yzerbyt, 2014).

Classical conditioning can be a powerful, even insidious, form of attitude learning. In one study, participants who were provided with soft drinks while they read a persuasive message were more persuaded by what they read than those who were not provided with soft drinks (Janis, Kaye, & Kirschner, 1965). In another study, participants who listened to pleasant guitar music as an accompaniment to persuasive messages presented as folk songs were more persuaded than those who did not listen to the guitar music (Galizio & Hendrick, 1972). The positive feelings associated with the soft drinks or with guitar music became associated, via classical conditioning, with the persuasive messages.

Spreading attitude effect
A liked or disliked person (or attitude object) may affect not only the evaluation of a second person directly associated with the second person but also others merely associated with the second person.

An interesting corollary of this line of research is the **spreading attitude effect**. Eva Walther (2002) gives this example: Mary is at a conference where she notices Peter and Paul talking. She barely knows either one – they are affectively neutral. Then she sees Peter talking with Marc, someone she dislikes. First, Peter is now less likeable (evaluative conditioning); second, Paul is also less likeable (the spreading attitude effect). Peter's bad company has had a ripple effect on someone merely associated with him (in this case, Paul).

Instrumental conditioning

Behaviour that is followed by positive consequences is reinforced and is more likely to be repeated, whereas behaviour that is followed by negative consequences is not. For example, parents use verbal reinforcers to encourage acceptable behaviour in their children – quiet, cooperative play wins praise. There have been several studies of the effects of positive reinforcement on prosocial *behaviour*, such as rewarding children when they behave generously – see the study by Rushton and Teachman (1978) for an example (**Chapter 13, Figure 13.3**). However, when the children fight, a reward is withheld or a punishment such as scolding is introduced. Instrumental learning can be accelerated or slowed by the frequency, temporal spacing and magnitude of the reinforcement (Kimble, 1961). When parents reward or punish their children, they are shaping their *attitudes* on many issues, including religious or political beliefs and practices.

Adults' attitudes can also be shaped by verbal reinforcers. Chester Insko (1965) showed that students' responses to an attitude survey had been influenced by an apparently unrelated telephone conversation which took place a week earlier, in which particular opinions were 'rewarded' by the interviewer responding with the reinforcer 'good'.

Both classical and instrumental conditioning emphasise the role of direct reinforcers in how behaviour is acquired and maintained. This is relevant to attitudes if we define them as types of behaviour, and it becomes fairly straightforward if they are operationalised as an *evaluative response* (Fishbein, 1967a; Osgood, Suci, & Tannenbaum, 1957).

Observational learning

Attitude formation can also be treated as a social learning process that does not depend on direct reinforcers, but involves a process of **modelling** (Bandura, 1973 – **see also Chapters 12 and 14**). Modelling involves observation: people learn new responses, not by directly experiencing positive or negative outcomes but by observing the outcomes of others' responses. If a significant other expresses an attitude or behaves in a way that attracts a favourable response, then you will be more likely to acquire that attitude or behaviour. In this way, ethnic attitudes can be instilled in otherwise naive children if the models are significant adults

Modelling
Tendency for a person to reproduce the actions, attitudes and emotional responses exhibited by a real-life or symbolic model. Also called *observational learning*.

Observational learning
'So that's how you chop vegetables!' Young children model their behaviour on significant adults.

in their lives. This can be seen in children who use ethnic slurs and insults, and who claim to hate a certain ethnic group, but who are unable correctly to define the group or have no factual knowledge about its members (Allport, 1954b; see also Chapter 11).

Cognitive development

Attitude formation can also, of course, be viewed as a cognitive process where, according to cognitive consistency theories (e.g. balance and cognitive dissonance, treated in Chapter 6), we build connections (balanced or consonant) between more and more cognitive elements (e.g. beliefs). As the number of related elements increases, it is more likely that a generalised concept – an attitude – is being formed. Similarly, information integration theory would view attitude learning as a process in which more and more items of information about an attitude object have been integrated (say, by averaging their weights).

A difference between cognitive and behavioural approaches is the relative weight that each gives to internal events versus external reinforcement. Although social cognition is the dominant paradigm in social psychology (Chapters 2 and 3), we should not ignore some advantages of behavioural approaches. The latter are linked to the study of learning and often deal directly with developmental data (generated from studies of animals or children). Thus, learning theories continue to appeal to social psychologists who study attitude acquisition.

Self-perception theory
Bem's idea that we gain knowledge of ourselves only by making self-attributions; for example, we infer our own attitudes from our own behaviour.

One interesting approach with both a behavioural and a perceptual flavour is Bem's (1972) self-perception theory (see Chapter 4 for details). Bem proposed that people acquire knowledge about what kind of person they are, and thus their attitudes, by examining their own behaviour and asking: 'Why did I do that?' A person may act for reasons that are not obvious and then determine their attitude from the most readily available cause. For example, if you often go for long walks, you may conclude that 'I must like them, as I'm always doing that'. Bem's theory suggests that people act, and form attitudes, without much deliberate thinking.

Sources of learning

One of the most significant sources of your attitudes is the actions of other people around you. However, you can also learn attitudes from books, the media and the Internet.

Parents and peers

Attitudes are quickly acquired early in life, so one of the most significant sources of a person's attitudes is their parents, and then their peer group. For children, their parents are a powerful influence, involving all the kinds of learning mentioned earlier (classical conditioning, instrumental conditioning and observational learning). The correlation between the *specific* attitudes of parents and their children is generally positive, but it is also surprisingly weak; the correlation is stronger for *broad* attitudes (Connell, 1972).

Jennings and Niemi (1968) found a 0.60 correlation between high-school children's preferences for a particular political party and their parents' choices, and a correlation of 0.88 between parents' and children's choices of religion. Of course, such correlations may be constrained by parental opposition, a common experience of adolescents. Many high-school pupils deliberately adopt, or appear to adopt, attitudes that are inconsistent with those of their parents, perhaps to be contrary but probably also because they are forging a new identity and associated attitudes that conform to their increasingly important peer groups (Tarrant, 2002). In a longitudinal study of values, Kasser, Koestner and Lekes (2002) found strong links between childhood environmental factors, such as parenting, and later adult values. Restrictive parenting at age five was reflected in higher conformity values and lower self-directed values in adulthood. Values are discussed later in this chapter.

Mass media and the Internet

The mass media strongly influence attitudes, and there is little question that visual media, particularly television, play an important part in attitude formation in children, particularly when attitudes are not strongly held (Goldberg & Gorn, 1974). A study by Chaffee, Jackson-Beeck, Durall and Wilson (1977) showed that, before age seven, American children got most of their political information from television and that this affected their views on politics and political institutions (Atkin, 1977; Rubin, 1978).

Among adults, MacKay and Covell (1997) reported a relationship between viewing sexual images of women in advertisements and holding attitudes sympathetic to sexual aggression (**see also Chapter 12**). Overall, the impact of television on adults as opposed to children is less clear-cut; however, an extensive statistical analysis of changes in Americans' racial attitudes over the last half-century revealed that media coverage does more than reflect public opinion – it has helped shape it (Kellstedt, 2003). Long periods of liberalism have been followed by periods of conservatism, and these eras have responded to cues in the American media.

The impact of commercials on children's attitudes is well known. For example, Atkin (1980) found that children who watched a lot of television were twice as likely as those who watched a little to believe that sugar-coated sweets and cereals were good for them. In the same study, two-thirds of a group of children who saw a circus strong man eat a breakfast cereal believed it would make them strong too! These findings are of particular concern in the light of murders committed by young children (e.g. the murder in Liverpool in 1993 of 2-year-old James Bulger by two 10-year-old boys) and carried out in ways similar to those portrayed in certain films. Media effects on aggression are discussed in **Chapter 12**.

What is missing from much of this older research is the role of the Internet in attitude learning. As research accumulates (e.g. Bargh & McKenna, 2004; Green & Carpenter, 2011; Wallace, 1999), one thing we do know – no surprises here – is that people overwhelmingly learn and fine-tune their attitudes by searching the Internet. However, we also know that the Internet is a convenient source of information to support and consolidate one's existing attitudes rather than change attitudes or acquire new ones. Liberals go to liberal web sites, conservatives to conservative web sites and so forth.

Concepts related to attitudes

Values

Although this is a chapter about attitudes, your specific attitudes are often framed by your wider set of **values** (e.g. Bernard, Maio, & Olson, 2003; Maio, 2010; Rohan, 2000). Values and attitudes are similar in some ways but differ in important other ways and are usually measured differently. Attitudes are measured to reflect favourability towards an object, whereas values are rated for their importance as guiding principles in life. So, for example, an early measure of values focused on how important six broad values were to people (Allport & Vernon, 1931):

Values
A higher-order concept thought to provide a structure for organising attitudes.

1 *theoretical* – an interest in problem solving, the basis of how things work;

2 *economic* – an interest in economic matters, finance and money affairs;

3 *aesthetic* – an interest in the arts, theatre, music and so on;

4 *social* – a concern for one's fellows, a social welfare orientation;

5 *political* – an interest in political structures and power arrangements;

6 *religious* – a concern with theology, the afterlife and morals.

Milton Rokeach (1973) later suggested that values should be conceived less in terms of interests or activities and more as preferred goals (end-states). He distinguished between *terminal values* (e.g. equality and freedom) and *instrumental values* (e.g. honesty and ambition). A terminal value, such as equality, could significantly affects someone's attitudes on racial issues, which is just what Rokeach found. From this viewpoint, a value is a higher-order concept that influences more specific attitudes. For example, measuring values can help to predict people's attitudes to the unemployed (Heaven, 1990), to industrial action (Feather, 2002) and to beliefs in a just world (Feather, 1991). When values are primed, we are more likely to make choices consistent with our values. For example, if information enhances our thoughts about the environment, we are more likely to behave in an environmentally friendly way (Verplanken & Holland, 2002).

Himmelweit, Humphreys and Jaeger (1985) conducted a longitudinal study, spanning almost a quarter of a century, of social psychological influences on voting in Britain. They found that specific attitudes were usually poor predictors, while broader sociopolitical values and party identifications were much better predictors. In another large-scale study by Hewstone (1986), this time of attitudes of French, Italian, German and British students towards European integration, general value orientation changes were seen to have some influence on changed attitudes towards integration.

According to Norman Feather (1994), values are general beliefs about desirable behaviour and goals, with an 'oughtness' quality about them. They both transcend attitudes and influence the form that attitudes take. Values offer standards for evaluating actions, justifying opinions and conduct, planning behaviour, deciding between different alternatives, engaging in social influence and presenting the self to others. Within the person, they are organised into hierarchies, and their relative importance may alter during a lifetime. Value systems vary across individuals, groups and cultures.

Feather (2002) tested some of these principles in the context of an industrial dispute. They found that people not involved in the dispute made judgements of the quality of the behaviour (e.g. procedural fairness) of both the employer and the union that were based on values such as authority, wealth, power, equality and being prosocial. Others have explored the way that entire cultures can be characterised and differentiated by their underlying value systems (e.g. Hofstede, 1980; Schwartz, 1992; Schwartz et al., 2012; **see Chapter 16**).

Can values predict behaviour? If the target behaviour is a specific act, it is very unlikely, given that a value is an even more general concept than an attitude. Although Bardi and Schwartz (2003) found correlations between some values and self-reported congruent behaviour (e.g. traditionalism and observing traditional holiday customs), they did not collect actual behavioural data.

Ideology

Ideology
A systematically interrelated set of beliefs whose primary function is explanation. It circumscribes thinking, making it difficult for the holder to escape from its mould.

Ideology overlaps to some extent with the term 'value'. Ideologies are integrated and widely shared systems of beliefs, usually with a social or political reference, that serve an explanatory function (Thompson, 1990). They also frame more specific values, attitudes and behavioural intentions (e.g. Crandall, 1994). Most familiar to us are the religious and sociopolitical ideologies that divide societies and underpin the world's most intransigent intergroup conflicts (**see Chapters 10 and 11**).

Ideologies can maintain the status quo – making the state of things as they are seem perfectly natural (the naturalistic fallacy), justifying and legitimising the status quo (Jost & Hunyadi, 2002; Jost & van der Toorn, 2012; Major, Quinton, & McCoy, 2002), and enhancing hierarchical social relations (e.g. Sidanius, Levin, Federico, & Pratto, 2001; Sidanius & Pratto, 1999). However, they can also challenge the status quo – viewing it as unnatural, illegitimate and so forth.

Philip Tetlock (1989) has proposed that terminal values, such as those described by Rokeach (1973), underlie many *political ideologies*. For example, Machiavellianism as an ideology, named after Machiavelli (a sixteenth-century Florentine diplomat), is the notion that craft and deceit are justified in pursuing and maintaining power in the political world (Saucier, 2000). Ideologies can vary as a function of two characteristics:

1 They may assign different priorities to particular values: traditionally, we might expect liberals and conservatives to rank 'individual freedom' and 'national security' in opposite ways.

2 Some ideologies are pluralistic and others monistic. A pluralistic ideology can tolerate a conflict of values: for example, neoliberalism as a pluralistic ideology emphasises economic growth and also a concern with social justice. A monistic ideology will be quite intolerant of conflict, seeing issues in starkly simplistic terms (see the discussion of authoritarianism in **Chapter 10**). An example of a monistic ideology is Manicheism – the notion that the world is divided between good and evil principles.

Michael Billig (1991) has suggested that much of our everyday thinking arises from what he calls ideological dilemmas. Teachers, for example, face the dilemma of being an authority and yet encouraging equality between teacher and student. When conflict between values arises, it can trigger a clash of attitudes between groups. For example, Katz and Hass (1988) reported a polarisation of ethnic attitudes in a community when values such as communalism and individualism clashed.

Ideology, particularly more orthodox ideology, has also been implicated in societal extremism. Ideology, because of its all-embracing explanatory function, provides an immensely comforting buffer against uncertainty; uncertainty about what to think, what to do, who one is and ultimately the nature of existence (Hogg, 2012, 2014; Hogg, Kruglanski, & Van den Bos, 2013; Martin & Van den Bos, 2014; Solomon, Greenberg, Pyszczynski, & Pryzbylinski, 1995; Van den Bos, 2009). People will go to great lengths to protect and promote their ideology and the group that defines it. One reason why religious ideologies are so powerful and enduring, and why religious fundamentalism arises, is precisely because organised religions are uncertainty-reducing groups that have sophisticated ideologies that define one's self and identity and normatively regulate both secular and existential aspects of life (Hogg, Adelman, & Blagg, 2010).

According to **terror management theory** (e.g. Greenberg, Solomon, & Pyszczynski, 1997; Pyszczynski, Greenberg, & Solomon, 1999; Solomon, Greenberg, & Pyszczynski, 1991), people may also subscribe to an ideology and defend their world view in order to buffer themselves against paralysing terror over what happens to them as they die. Numerous studies have shown that making a person's own death salient leads to worldview defence. However, critics have worried that the theory is too broad to be falsifiable (Martin & Van den Bos, 2014) and underplays the role played by uncertainty about the afterlife (Hohman & Hogg, 2011, 2015).

Terror management theory
The notion that the most fundamental human motivation is to reduce the terror of the inevitability of death. Self-esteem may be centrally implicated in effective terror management.

Social representations

Social representations (discussed fully in **Chapter 3**) are somewhat similar to ideologies in how they relate to attitudes. First described by Serge Moscovici (1961) and based on earlier work by the French sociologist Emile Durkheim on 'collective representations', social representations refer to the way that people elaborate simplified and shared understandings of their world through social interaction (Deaux & Philogene, 2001; Farr & Moscovici, 1984; Lorenzi-Cioldi & Clémence, 2001; Moscovici, 1981, 1988, 2000; Purkhardt, 1995).

Moscovici believed that people's attitudes and beliefs are shaped by what other people believe and say and are shared with other members of one's community:

> Our reactions to events, our responses to stimuli, are related to a given definition, common to all the members of the community to which we belong.
>
> Moscovici (1983, p. 5)

Social representations
Collectively elaborated explanations of unfamiliar and complex phenomena that transform them into a familiar and simple form.

Expectancy-value model
Direct experience with an attitude object informs a person how much that object should be liked or disliked in the future.

Semantic differential
An attitude measure that asks for a rating on a scale composed of bipolar (opposite) adjectives. (Also a technique for measuring the connotative meaning of words or concepts.)

Thurstone scale
An 11-point scale with 22 items, 2 for each point. Each item has a value ranging from very unfavourable to very favourable. Respondents check the items with which they agree. Their attitude is the average scale value of these items.

Likert scale
Scale that evaluates how strongly people agree/disagree with favourable/unfavourable statements about an attitude object. Initially, many items are tested. After item analysis, only those items that correlate with each other are retained.

Acquiescent response set
Tendency to agree with items in an attitude questionnaire. This leads to an ambiguity in interpretation if a high score on an attitude questionnaire can be obtained only by agreeing with all or most items.

Unidimensionality
A Guttman scale consists of a single (low to high) dimension. It is also cumulative; that is, agreement with the highest-scoring item implies agreement with all lower-scoring items.

Guttman scale
A scale that contains either favourable or unfavourable statements arranged hierarchically. Agreement with a strong statement implies agreement with weaker ones; disagreement with a weak one implies disagreement with stronger ones.

Thus, specific attitudes are framed by, and embedded within, wider representational structures, which are in turn grounded in social groups. In this sense, attitudes tend to reflect the society or groups in which people live their lives.

This view on attitudes reflects a broader 'top-down' perspective on social behaviour, which has been a hallmark of European social psychology (see Chapter 1). It prompted the American social psychologist William McGuire (1986) to observe that 'the two movements serve mutually supplementary uses' in that the European concept of collective representations highlights how *alike* group members are, while the American individualist tradition highlights how *different* they are (see also Tajfel, 1972).

Social representations may influence the evaluative tone of attitudes 'nested' within them. If the evaluative tone of the overarching representation changes, so does the evaluative tone of nested attitudes, and vice versa (Moliner & Tafani, 1997). Social representations also embody causal beliefs that influence the embedded attitudes. Consider, for example, a study of how Muslim and Christian students in the United Kingdom represented the second Iraq war, which started in 2003, focusing on causal networks used by each group as explanations of the conflict (Rafiq, Jobanuptra, & Muncer, 2006). Muslims and Christians agreed that there were causal links (sometimes bi-directional) between racism, religious prejudice and the history of conflict in the Middle East; however, Christians were more likely than Muslims to believe that the war was connected with a hunt for terrorist cells in Iraq – a reason consistently emphasised by then US president G. W. Bush.

Measuring attitudes

Attitude scales

How should we measure attitudes; explicitly or implicitly? Some forms of attitude measurement can be completely explicit: people are simply asked to agree or disagree with various statements about their beliefs. Particularly in the early days of attitude research, in the 1930s, it was assumed that explicit measures would get at people's real beliefs and opinions. The US media used opinion polls (in particular, the Gallup Poll) to predict election results and to discover what election candidates believed and how they might act. The result was frenzied development of attitude questionnaires. Several scales that were technically sophisticated for their time were developed by Thurstone, Likert, Guttman and Osgood, and are briefly described in Box 5.5.

A key challenge was to move beyond scales that simply summed scores across items, and to devise scales that optimised the fit between a single item and a specific behaviour. Fishbein and Ajzen (1974) met this challenge by measuring both the evaluative and belief component of an attitude. They developed the **expectancy-value model**, where each contributing belief underlying an attitude is weighted by the strength of its relationship to the attitude object. The main elements of this model were described earlier in this chapter (see also Table 5.1). Despite some criticisms (see Eagly & Chaiken, 1993), this technique has had predictive success in a variety of settings – in marketing and consumer research (Assael, 1981), politics (Bowman & Fishbein, 1978), family planning (Vinokur-Kaplan, 1978), classroom attendance (Fredericks & Dossett, 1983), seat-belt wearing (Budd, North, & Spencer, 1984), preventing HIV infection (Terry, Gallois, & McCamish, 1993), and how mothers feed their infants (Manstead, Proffitt, & Smart, 1983).

Using attitude scales today

Combinations of the Likert scale and the **semantic differential** have been used successfully to measure quite complex evaluations. For example, voters can be asked to evaluate various issues using a semantic differential scale. Then, using a Likert scale, they can be asked how

Box 5.5 Research classic
Attitude scales

An enormous volume of research on people's attitudes towards social and political issues was stimulated by the development of four early attitude scales.

Thurstone scale

When Thurstone (1928) published his landmark paper 'Attitudes can be measured', his approach was based on psychophysical scaling in experimental psychology. In a study of attitudes towards religion, more than 100 statements of opinion ranging from extremely favourable to extremely hostile were collected, statistically analysed and refined as a scale (Thurstone & Chave, 1929). Participants then classified the statements into eleven categories on a favourable–unfavourable continuum. Their responses were used to select a final scale of twenty-two items, two for each of the eleven points on the continuum, using items with the strongest inter-judge agreement. Such a scale can then be used to measure other people's attitudes towards the issue. On a Thurstone scale, a person's attitude score is calculated by averaging the scale values of the items endorsed.

Likert scale

A Thurstone scale is tedious to construct, so Likert (1932) developed a technique that produces a reasonably reliable attitude measure with relative ease – a Likert scale. Respondents use a five-point response scale to indicate how much they agree or disagree with each of a series of statements. The points use labels such as 'strongly agree', 'agree', 'undecided', 'disagree' and 'strongly disagree', ranging numerically from 5 to 1.

A person's score is summed across the statements and the total used as an index of the person's attitude. Typically, responses to questions will not correlate equally with the total score. Those that do not correlate well are considered unreliable and dropped. Any ambiguous items – those that do not differentiate between people with differing attitudes – are dropped. The remainder constitute the final scale and, when the responses are summed, measure a person's attitude.

Where possible, items are selected so that for half of the items 'agree' represents a positive attitude, and for the other half it represents a negative attitude. The scoring of the latter set of items is reversed (i.e. 5 becomes 1, 4 becomes 2, etc.) before the item scores are summed. This procedure controls acquiescent response set, a bias that otherwise could affect a variety of psychometric (such as personality) scales.

Guttman scale

A score on Thurstone and Likert scales does not have a unique meaning because two persons could receive the same score (averaged or summed) yet endorse quite different items. Guttman (1944) tried a different approach – a single, unidimensional trait can be measured by a set of statements that are ordered along a continuum ranging from least extreme to most extreme. Such a scale possesses unidimensionality. The statements vary from those that are easy to endorse to those that few people might endorse. Items on a Guttman scale are cumulative: acceptance of one item implies that the person accepts all other items that are less extreme. We could then predict a person's response to less extreme statements by knowing the most extreme item they will accept. Consider these items relating to the topic of inter-ethnic social contact – *I would accept people who are members of the immigrant ethnic group 'X':* . . . (1) *into my country* . . . (2) *into my neighbourhood* . . . (3) *into my house*. Agreement with (3) implies agreement with (1) and (2). Agreement with (2) implies agreement with (1), but not necessarily with (3). In practice, it is very difficult to develop a perfect unidimensional scale, which suggests that people respond on multiple dimensions rather than a single dimension.

Osgood's semantic differential

Osgood (Osgood, Suci, & Tannenbaum, 1957) avoided using opinion statements altogether by focusing on the connotative meaning that people give to a word or concept. Studies of connotative meanings of words show that one of the major underlying dimensions is evaluation – the goodness or badness implied by the word. The word 'friend' tends to be thought of as *good* and the word 'enemy' as *bad*. According to Osgood, this evaluative dimension corresponds to our definition of an attitude. We should therefore be able to measure attitudes by having people rate a particular concept on a set of evaluative semantic scales. The concept of 'nuclear power' could be measured by responses on several evaluative (seven-point) scales (e.g. *good/bad, nice/nasty, pleasant/unpleasant, fair/unfair, valuable/worthless*). An attitude score is averaged across the scales used. Osgood scales do not require writing attitude-relevant questions, and their reliability increases as more semantic scales are used. A disadvantage is that the measure can be too simple: it deals with evaluative meanings of a concept but not with opinions, which of course are the meat of the other classic scales.

they think each candidate stands on particular issues. Combining the two measures enables us to predict for whom they will vote (Ajzen & Fishbein, 1980).

The Likert scale has also contributed significantly to many modern questionnaires that start from the premise that the attitude being measured may have many underlying dimensions. The availability of powerful computer programs means that researchers are likely to choose from a variety of multivariate statistical methods such as factor analysis to analyse the underlying structure of questionnaire data. Likert tested for unidimensionality in a fairly simple way by calculating item–total score correlations. In contrast, factor analysis starts from a matrix of correlations between all pairs of items making up the questionnaire scale. One then estimates whether a single general factor (or dimension), or more than one factor, is required to explain the variance in the respondents' pattern of responses to the questionnaire. For example, your attitudes towards your country's possession of nuclear weapons might depend on your reactions to war, nuclear contamination and relationships with other countries. Each of these might be measured on a different dimension, and so the questionnaire could comprise several subscales (see Oppenheim, 1992).

Sometimes, factor analysis reveals substructures underlying a set of items that can be both interesting and subtle. In the development of a scale designed to measure 'sexism towards women', Glick and Fiske (1996) found evidence for two subscales – 'hostile sexism' and 'benevolent sexism' – pointing to covert ambivalence in their participants (see **Chapter 10**).

The development of a reliable attitude questionnaire rests on a whole range of methodological considerations – for example, even something as simple as the order in which questions are presented can affect responses. (To learn about questionnaire construction, see: Crano & Brewer, 2015; Oppenheim, 1992; Schwarz, 1996; Schwarz & Strack, 1991.)

Physiological measures

Attitudes, particularly ones that have a strong evaluative or affective component, can also be measured indirectly by monitoring physiological indices such as skin resistance (Rankin & Campbell, 1955), heart rate (Westie & DeFleur, 1959) and pupil dilation (Hess, 1965). Does your heart beat faster each time a certain person comes close? If so, we might surmise you have an attitude of some intensity!

Physiological measures have one big advantage over self-report measures: people may not realise that their attitudes are being assessed and, even if they do, they may not be able to control their responses. This is why a polygraph or 'lie detector' is sometimes used in criminal investigations. Another physiological measure of attitudes that focuses more on whether the attitude is associated with avoidance-related feelings of threat or approach-related feelings of challenge is cortisol level in the blood or saliva (Blascovich & Tomaka, 1996; see discussion of affect and emotion in **Chapter 2**). Cortisol has been used as an indicator of stress level: (a) when people's identity was under threat (Townsend, Major, Gangi, & Mendes, 2011); and (b) when people might be concerned about appearing prejudiced in an inter-racial encounter (Trawalter, Adam, Chase-Lansdale, & Richeson, 2012).

However, physiological measures also have drawbacks, since most are sensitive to variables other than attitudes (Cacioppo & Petty, 1981; also see Blascovich & Mendes, 2010; Blascovich & Seery, 2007). For example, skin resistance can change in the presence of novel or incongruous stimuli that may have nothing to do with the attitude in question. Similarly, heart rate is sensitive to task requirements – problem-solving tasks raise heart rate, while vigilance tasks (such as watching a VDU screen) usually lower it. Further, these measures provide limited information: they can indicate intensity of feeling but not direction. Two, totally opposed people who feel equally strongly about an issue cannot be distinguished.

One measure that can distinguish between positive and negative attitudes is facial expression. Building on Darwin's suggestion that different facial expressions are used to convey

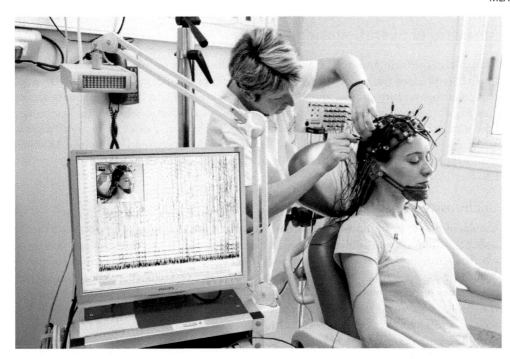

Social neuroscience
Electrical activity in the brain may inform us of the nature and strength of a person's attitude.

different emotions (**see Chapter 15**), Cacioppo and his colleagues (Cacioppo & Petty, 1979; Cacioppo & Tassinary, 1990) have mapped facial muscle movements onto underlying attitudes. They reasoned that people who agreed with a speech they were listening to would display facial movements different from those of people who disagreed with the speech. To test this, they recorded the movements of specific facial muscles (associated with smiling or frowning) before and during a speech that advocated a conservative or a liberal view – either stricter or more lenient university regulations regarding alcohol or hall-of-residence visiting hours. Before the speech, different patterns of muscle movement were associated with agreement compared with disagreement. These differences became more pronounced when people actually listened to the speeches. Thus, facial muscle movements were a useful way of distinguishing people with favourable attitudes on a topic from those with unfavourable attitudes.

If attitudes, as internal states, can be inferred from external physiological indices such as heart rate and facial expression, why not take this one stage further and measure electrical activity in the brain? This idea underpins **social neuroscience** (e.g. Harmon-Jones & Winkielman, 2007; Lieberman, 2010; Ochsner, 2007; Todorov, Fiske, & Prentice, 2011; **see Chapter 2**), and in the context of attitude measurement, the intensity and form of electrical activity and where it occurs in the brain should give an indication of what the attitude is.

Social neuroscience
Exploration of brain activity associated with social cognition and social psychological processes and phenomena.

For example, Levin (2000) investigated racial attitudes by measuring event-related brain potentials (ERPs) that indicate electrical activity when we respond to different stimuli. An ERP waveform includes several components, each signifying different types of processing. In Levin's study, where white participants viewed a series of white and black faces, an ERP component indicated that white faces received more attention – suggesting that participants were processing their racial ingroup more deeply and the racial outgroup more superficially. This is consistent with other experimental evidence that people tend to perceptually differentiate ingroup members more than outgroup members – called the **relative homogeneity effect** (**see Chapter 11**). In addition, participants who were more prejudiced as measured by an explicit attitude measure showed greater ingroup evaluative (Ito, Thompson, & Cacioppo, 2004).

Relative homogeneity effect
Tendency to see outgroup members as all the same, and ingroup members as more differentiated.

Measures of overt behaviour

We can also measure and infer attitudes by recording what people do. Sometimes, what they really do does not accord with what they *say* they do. For example, people's verbal reports of behaviours such as smoking, calories consumed and dental hygiene practices may not correspond very well to their actual physical condition. However, if we do not take what is said at face value but instead consider the entire discursive event (what is said, how it is said, what non-verbal cues accompany the words, and the context in which it all happens), we can do a better job of inferring behaviour from what people say (**see Chapter 15**).

Unobtrusive measures

Unobtrusive measures
Observational approaches that neither intrude on the processes being studied nor cause people to behave unnaturally.

Counts of empty beer and whisky bottles in dustbins are examples of **unobtrusive measures** of attitudes towards alcohol in your neighbourhood, while chemists' records show which doctors prescribe new drugs. Bodily traces and archival records can furnish evidence of people's attitudes (Webb, Campbell, Schwartz, & Sechrest, 1969). In a museum, the number of prints made by noses or fingers on a display case might show how popular the display was – and the height of the prints might indicate the viewers' ages! Public records and archival information can yield evidence about past and present community attitudes – for example, the ebb and flow of authoritarianism and changes in prejudice (Simonton, 2003).

Changes in sex-role attitudes might be reflected in the roles of male and female characters in children's books. Library book withdrawals of fiction, not non-fiction, declined when television was introduced – suggesting one effect of television on people's behaviour. Will a book or play be more popular if it receives a favourable review? Download statistics also give an indication of trends in viewing preferences. These kinds of data are increasingly available in a world where our every choice is monitored by web-based tracking systems that can even target advertisements at us based on our past behaviour.

Non-verbal behaviour (see **Chapter 15**) can also be used as an unobtrusive measure of people's attitudes. For example, people who like each other tend to sit closer together – so physical distance can be measured as an index of 'social distance' and tolerance of intimacy (Bogardus, 1925). Strangers in a waiting room who sit far apart from members of particular other groups are perhaps indicating intergroup antipathy, or maybe they are simply anxious about how to interact with a specific outgroup (Stephan & Stephan, 2000). Interpersonal distance can also measure fear. In one study (Webb, Campbell, Schwartz, & Sechrest, 1969), adults told ghost stories to young children seated in a circle. The size of the circle of children grew smaller with each successive scary story!

Overall, however, unobtrusive measures are probably not as reliable as self-reported attitudes. Their value is that their limitations are different from those of standard measures. A researcher who wanted to be more confident of valid results would use both types and then correlate the data.

Bogus pipeline technique
A measurement technique that leads people to believe that a 'lie detector' can monitor their emotional responses, thus measuring their true attitudes.

We have discussed unobtrusive measures of behaviour in this section. Is it possible to have an obtrusive measure that will work? One instance is the **bogus pipeline technique** (Jones & Sigall, 1971), which is designed to convince participants that they cannot hide their true attitudes. People are connected to a machine said to be a lie detector and are told that it measures both the strength and direction of emotional responses, thus revealing their true attitudes and implying that there is no point in lying. Participants usually find this deception convincing and are less likely to conceal socially unacceptable attitudes, such as racial prejudice (Allen, 1975; Quigley-Fernandez, & Tedeschi, 1978), and socially undesirable or potentially embarrassing behaviours such as drinking in excess, snorting cocaine and having frequent oral sex (Tourangeau, Smith, & Rasinski, 1997). So, take care when you trial psychological equipment at the next university open day! In a study of whites' attitudes towards African Americans, Nier (2005) used the bogus pipeline technique to compare implicit and explicit attitude measures (see the next section). He reported similar results for both measures. This suggests that the tendency to make a socially desirable response on matters of race rather than reveal one's 'true', potentially negative, attitude was reduced.

Measuring covert attitudes

Two terms have been used in this and related literature: 'implicit' and 'unobtrusive'. Although both methods are designed to measure attitudes, John Kihlstrom (2004) has made a conceptual distinction. Although it does not have a major impact on the discussion that follows, Kihlstrom argues that an unobtrusive method assesses an attitude that people are aware of but may be unwilling to reveal, whereas an implicit method assesses an attitude that people are not actually aware of.

Social psychologists have trialled a variety of implicit (or unobtrusive) measures to circumvent people's tendency to conceal their underlying attitudes by responding in socially desirable ways (Crosby, Bromley, & Saxe, 1980; Devine, 1989; Gregg, Seibt, & Banaji, 2006). We discuss three methods: detecting bias in language use, the priming of attitudes, and the implicit association test (IAT).

Bias in language use

Anne Maass and her colleagues (Franco & Maass, 1996; Maass, 1999; Maass, Salvi, Arcuri, & Semin, 1989) have found that there are positive ingroup and negative outgroup biases in the way that language is used. People are more likely to talk in abstract than concrete terms about undesirable characteristics of an outgroup, and vice versa for desirable characteristics. Consequently, the ratio of abstract to concrete language usage, in relation to desirable versus undesirable characteristics, could be used as an index of prejudiced attitudes towards a particular group. Other techniques have involved the detailed analysis of discourse to reveal hidden attitudes (Van Dijk, 1987, 1993; see Chapter 15) and likewise of non-verbal communication (Burgoon, Buller, & Woodall, 1989; see Chapter 15). (What do you think of Rita's view of measuring attitudes in the third 'What do *you* think?' question?)

Attitude priming

Fazio and his colleagues (Fazio, Jackson, Dunton, & Williams, 1995) used **priming** to explore how we make a judgement more quickly when an underlying attitude is congruent with a 'correct' response. While looking at a series of photos of black and white people, participants decided by pressing a button whether an adjective (from a series of positive and negative adjectives) that followed very quickly after a particular image was 'good' or 'bad'. White participants were slower in rating a positive adjective as good when it followed a black image, and black participants were slower in rating a positive adjective as good when it followed a white image.

Kawakami, Young and Dovidio (2002) used a similar rationale to explore how stereotypic judgements follow when a social category is invoked. Student participants were either in a primed group or a control (non-primed) group. There were two phases:

1 *Priming the category 'elderly'*. A series of photographs of two different age groups, elderly people and college-age people, were shown to the primed group in random order on a computer screen, one at a time for 250 milliseconds. Each photograph was followed by the word *old?* and participants responded yes/no on either of two buttons.

Priming
Activation of accessible categories or schemas in memory that influence how we process new information.

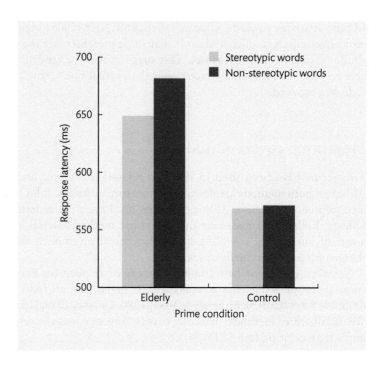

Figure 5.8 Priming the category 'elderly' can activate stereotypes

- The category 'elderly' was primed by having participants choose whether people in a series of photographs were old or not.
- The primed participants then decided whether word strings were real words or non-words. Half of the real words were age-stereotypic.

Source: Based on data from Kawakami, Young and Dovidio (2002).

2 *Activation of stereotypes.* Both groups were shown a list of strings of words (anagrams) and non-words and asked to respond yes/no if the word string was a real word or not. The real words were either age-stereotypic (e.g. serious, distrustful, elderly, pensioner) or not age-stereotypic (e.g. practical, jealous, teacher, florist).

There were two significant effects in the response latencies (time taken to respond), shown in Figure 5.8. First, the primed group took longer overall to respond than the control group. It is likely that the concept *elderly* activates a behavioural representation in memory of people who are mentally and physically slower than the young. The participants unwittingly slowed down when they responded. Second, the primed group (but not the control group) were a little quicker in responding to age-stereotypic words.

Implicit association test

In a similar way to attitude priming, Tony Greenwald and his colleagues (Greenwald, Banaji, Rudman, Farnham, Nosek, & Mellott, 2002; Greenwald, McGhee, & Schwartz, 1998; also see Kihlstrom, 2004) developed the **implicit association test** (IAT) using a computer display coupled with responding on a keyboard. They wanted to reveal underlying negative inter-ethnic attitudes, for example, by comparing the response latencies of American Japanese with American Koreans. The Japanese responded more quickly when a Japanese name was paired with a pleasant word, and the Koreans did the same when a Korean name was paired with a pleasant word. (Reflect on the fourth 'What do *you* think?' question at the beginning of this chapter). For a recent review of the use of the IAT in measuring prejudice against sexual minorities, see Herek and McLemore (2013). The IAT has become enormously popular as a reliable way to measure socially undesirable underlying attitudes. However, over the years, various concerns over its validity have been raised; see Box 5.6 for details.

Implicit association test
Reaction-time test to measure attitudes – particularly unpopular attitudes that people might conceal.

Box 5.6 Research highlight
The implicit association test

Social psychologists have created an ingenious solution to the problem of measuring underlying attitudes in contexts where people may want to conceal what they really think – the implicit association test (IAT) (Greenwald, McGhee, & Schwartz, 1998).

Based on the assumption that attitudes are associative mental networks and that associations are stronger if the attitude exists than if it doesn't, it follows that people will more quickly link concepts that are related than those that are not. So, if you dislike property developers, you will more quickly respond 'yes' to the word 'nasty' and 'no' to the word 'nice' than if you do not have a negative attitude towards developers. The IAT has participants press different keys on a keyboard or button box to match concepts (e.g. Algerian, lazy). What happens is that, where an attitude exists, the reaction is much faster when the concepts share a response key than when they do not.

The IAT has become remarkably popular in recent years as an indirect technique for measuring prejudice in liberal Western societies such as the United States (**see Chapter 10**). Its proponents have argued that it is internally consistent and to an extent correlated with other measures of prejudice and implicit attitudes (Cunningham, Preacher, & Banaji, 2001; Greenwald, Banaji, Rudman, Farnham, Nosek, & Mellott, 2002). However, it has met with some criticism. In their review of implicit measures in social cognition research, Fazio and Olson (2003) noted that much of the data relating to the IAT is based on 'known-groups' – people who differ in an expected way by favouring their ingroup in preference to a particular outgroup: for example, East Germans compared with West Germans, Japanese

Americans compared with Korean Americans, or Jewish compared with Christian respondents. Fazio and Olson asked for more convincing evidence that the IAT has predictive validity (i.e. can IAT responses predict actual behaviour?). Fiedler, Messner and Bluemke (2006) have added methodological concerns about the IAT.

Greenwald and his associates responded with a meta-analysis of 122 studies comparing the predictive validity of both self-report and IAT measures (Greenwald, Poehlmann, Uhlmann, & Banaji, 2009). They surmised that studies would differ in social sensitivity, and that those that were highly sensitive were likely subject to **impression management**. They concluded that: (a) the attitude domains reviewed varied considerably in social sensitivity from high (e.g. attitudes towards African Americans) to low (e.g. attitudes towards yoghurt); (b) within a socially sensitive domain, the predictive validity of IAT measures was clearly superior to that of self-report measures.

In response, further concerns about the IAT's predictive validity have been raised in a rival, large-scale meta-analysis of studies of intergroup bias conducted by Frederick Oswald and his associates (Oswald, Mitchell, Blanton, Jaccard, & Tetlock, 2013). They reported low correlations between the IAT and explicit measures of intergroup bias – in particular, explicit measures of inter-racial and inter-ethnic bias. They argued that the IAT, now a highly researched indirect measure of attitude, should surely predict behaviour in inter-racial and inter-ethnic settings better than this.

However, when all is said and done, the IAT remains a useful research tool – albeit, with some limitations.

Concluding thoughts

Attitudes have typically been viewed as having three components: cognitive, affective and behavioural. Traditional questionnaire research uses belief items to measure the degree of affect (like or dislike) towards an attitude object. A well-researched questionnaire is usually based on a quantitative scale involving statistical analysis. Older questionnaire data were often not checked against real behavioural outcomes (such as the result of an election). More recently, there has been a shift towards the use of implicit measures, in order to uncover what people may try to conceal and to understand how attitudes are structured and how they function. Implicit measures of attitudes may have some way to go to yield consistently valid and reliable findings. But if we let Greenwald and colleagues have the last word about the IAT, this currently most popular implicit measure is a clear winner when an attitude topic is socially sensitive.

Impression management
People's use of various strategies to get other people to view them in a positive light.

We should also remember that failure to detect an attitude does not necessarily imply that it does not exist; the way we have chosen to measure it may limit our capacity to unearth it. Furthermore, an attitude may 'reemerge' after a period of time. Consider the very public expressions of anti-immigrant and racist attitudes in recent years by national figures in a number of countries. In the case of race, has an attitude re-emerged that was more prevalent in years gone by, or is it an overt expression of a commonly held attitude that has been 'suppressed' by liberal norms promoting social equality? **Chapter 10** confronts some of these issues.

Summary

- Attitudes have been a major interest of social psychologists for many years. They have been described as the most important concept in social psychology.

- Theories of attitude structure agree that attitudes are lasting, general evaluations of socially significant objects (including people and issues). Some emphasise that attitudes are relatively enduring organisations of beliefs and behavioural tendencies towards social objects.

- Attitude structure has been studied mostly from a cognitive viewpoint. Balance theory and the theory of cognitive dissonance (**see Chapter 6**) suggest that people strive to be internally consistent in their attitudes and beliefs.

- The link between attitudes and behaviour has been a source of controversy. The apparently poor predictive power of attitude measures led to a loss of confidence in the concept of attitude itself. Fishbein argued that attitudes can indeed predict behaviour. However, if the prediction concerns a specific act, the measure of attitude must also be specific.

- The interrelated theories of reasoned action and planned behaviour emphasise the need to relate a specific act to a measure of the intention to perform that act. Other variables that affect the predicted behaviour are norms provided by other people and the extent to which the individual has control over the act.

- A strong attitude has a powerful evaluative association with the attitude object. It is more accessible in memory and more likely to be activated and the related behaviour performed. A more accessible attitude can involve a cost; high accessibility can lead to insensitivity to change in the attitude object.

- Attitudes that are accessible are more likely to be acted on.

- The prediction of behaviour from an attitude can be improved partly by accounting for moderator variables (situational and personality factors).

- Attitudes are learnt. They can be formed by direct experience, by conditioning, by observational learning and by drawing inferences from our own behaviour (self-perception).

- Parents and the mass media are powerful sources of attitude learning in children – peers and the Internet quickly become important as well.

- A value is a higher-order concept that can play a guiding and organising role in relation to attitudes. Ideology and social representations are other related concepts.

- Measuring attitudes is both important and difficult. Traditional attitude scales of the 1930s are less frequently used today. While the response format of many modern measures is still based on the old Likert scale, the data are analysed by sophisticated statistical programs.

- A variety of physiological and behavioural indexes, both explicit and implicit, have been used to measure attitudes. The implicit association test has proved particularly popular and has gained traction when a more valid measure of a socially sensitive topic is required. Brain imaging technology is also being used to record neural processes correlated with implicit attitudes.

Key terms

Acquiescent response set	Information integration theory	Semantic differential
Attitude	Information processing	Social neuroscience
Attitude formation	Likert scale	Social representations
Automatic activation	Mere exposure effect	Sociocognitive model
Balance theory	Meta-analysis	Spreading attitude effect
Bogus pipeline technique	Modelling	Stereotype
Cognition	Moderator variable	Terror management theory
Cognitive algebra	Multiple act criterion	Theory of planned behaviour
Cognitive consistency theories	One-component attitude model	Theory of reasoned action
Evaluative conditioning	Priming	Three-component attitude model
Expectancy–value model	Protection motivation theory	Thurstone scale
Guttman scale	Relative homogeneity effect	Two-component attitude model
Ideology	Schema	Unidimensionality
Implicit association test	Self-efficacy	Unobtrusive measures
Impression management	Self-perception theory	Values

Literature, film and TV

1984

George Orwell's 1949 novel about life in a fictional totalitarian regime, based on Stalin's Soviet Union. The book shows how such a regime controls all aspects of human existence and has a particular emphasis on the crucial role of ideology and control of information. Through the creation of a new language, 'Newspeak', the regime is able to manipulate thought and thus how people view the world. The book touches on the relationship between language and thought (**see Chapter 15**), and how language constrains and reflects what we can easily think about.

The Office

A BBC TV series, first broadcast in 2001, in which David Brent (played by Ricky Gervais) and Gareth Keenan (played by Mackenzie Crook) are both prejudiced in old-fashioned and modern ways. Their antics are acutely embarrassing, and a wonderful illustration of how prejudiced attitudes reveal themselves in behaviour – all played out in a suburban British office environment. The US adaptation which stars Steve Carell first aired in 2005 and ran for nine seasons and 2,101 episodes – it was, and remains, phenomenally popular.

To Kill a Mockingbird

The 1960 Pulitzer Prize-winning novel by Harper Lee. Set in the American Deep South of the 1930s, this novel explores racial injustice, prejudiced attitudes and, through the eyes of a 10-year-old child, Scout, the erosion of innocence. Scout's father, Atticus Finch, is a moral hero who embodies the highest human values of compassion, integrity and tolerance in his struggle against racial prejudice. This heart-warming novel is not only relevant to this chapter on attitudes, but also to **Chapter 10** which explores prejudice more fully.

Pride and Prejudice

Jane Austen's classic 1813 novel about life and love in the genteel rural society of the day. The focal characters are Elizabeth and Darcy. One of the key features of this society is the possibility of misunderstanding based on the fact that there are strong normative pressures that inhibit the expression of one's true attitudes. The six-episode 1995 BBC mini-series adaptation of the book is a classic – Colin Firth's Mr Darcy in a wet shirt has become an unforgettable British TV moment.

Guided questions

1   What we do does not always follow from what we think. Why not?

2   What is the theory of *planned behaviour*? How can it be used to improve the predictive power of an attitude measure? Give an example from research.

3   Discuss the meaning of attitude accessibility and attitude strength. Illustrate your answer.

4   How are attitudes learnt?

5   Outline the connections between attitudes, values and ideology. Give an example of each.

Learn more

Banaji, M. R., & Heiphetz, L. (2010). Attitudes. In S. T. Fiske, D. T. Gilbert, & G. Lindzey (Eds.), *Handbook of social psychology* (5th ed., Vol. 1, pp. 353–393). New York: Wiley. An up-to-date, comprehensive and detailed discussion of attitude research.

Eagly, A. H., & Chaiken, S. (2005). Attitude research in the 21st century: The current state of knowledge. In D. Albarracin, B. T. Johnson, & M. P. Zanna (Eds.), *The handbook of attitudes* (pp. 742–767). Mahwah, NJ: Erlbaum. Another excellent review from two of the leading attitude researchers.

Fazio, R. H., & Olson, M. A. (2007). Attitudes: Foundations, functions, and consequences. In M. A. Hogg & J. Cooper (Eds.), *The SAGE handbook of social psychology: Concise student edition* (pp. 123–45). London: SAGE. A nicely readable yet detailed overview of attitude theory and research.

Gawronski, B., & Strack, F. (Eds.) (2012). *Cognitive consistency: A fundamental principle in social cognition*. New York: Guilford Press. An up-to-date collection of 21 chapters on all aspects of cognitive consistency written by leading social psychologists.

Kihlstrom, J. F. (2004). Implicit methods in social psychology. In C. Sansone, C. C. Morf, & A. T. Panter (Eds.), *The SAGE handbook of methods in social psychology* (pp. 195–212). Thousand Oaks, CA: SAGE. A survey of methods used to assess people's unconscious (or implicit) attitudes, beliefs, and other mental states.

Maio, G. R., & Haddock, G. (2010). *The psychology of attitudes and attitude change*. London: SAGE. A mid- to upper-level text dedicated to the science of attitudes – written by two leading attitude researchers.

Oppenheim, A. N. (1992). *Questionnaire design, interviewing and attitude measurement* (2nd ed.). London: Pinter. A well-illustrated and comprehensive guide with easy-to-follow examples.

Robinson, J. P., Shaver, P. R., & Wrightsman, L. S. (Eds.) (1991). *Measures of personality and social psychological attitudes*. New York: Academic Press. A sourcebook of scales that have been used in social psychology and the study of personality.

Schwarz, N. (1996). Survey research: Collecting data by asking questions. In G. R. Semin, & K. Fiedler (Eds.), *Applied social psychology* (pp. 65–90). London: SAGE. A brief bird's-eye view of questionnaire design; with examples.

Terry, D. J., & Hogg, M. A. (Eds.) (2000). *Attitudes, behavior, and social context: The role of norms and group membership*. Mahwah, NJ: Erlbaum. A collection of chapters discussing attitudes and attitude phenomena from the perspective of group norms, group membership and social identity.

Chapter 6
Persuasion and attitude change

Chapter contents

What do *you* think?

1   Someone offers you what you believe is a fair price for your prized racing bike. After they have checked their bank balance, the would-be purchaser reduces the offer by 15 per cent, saying that's all they can afford. Could such a tactic work?

2   You have just joined the army. Along with other cadets you listen to an amazing talk by an officer skilled in the use of survival techniques in difficult combat conditions. Among other things, he asks you to eat some fried grasshoppers. 'Try to imagine this is the real thing! You know, you might have to do this to save your life one day', he says. Despite your first reaction, you go ahead and eat them. Would you end up liking the delicacy more if the officer's style of presentation was warm and friendly or cold and distant?

Attitudes, arguments and behaviour

Earlier (**see Chapter 5**), we saw that although the relationship between attitudes and behaviour is generally weak, under the right circumstances people's attitudes certainly can predict what people say and do. So, if you should want to influence someone's behaviour, it certainly is worthwhile trying first to influence their attitudes. This belief lies, of course, at the heart of political propaganda and commercial advertising, which seek to change people's attitudes in order to persuade them to support and vote for candidates and policies, and to buy products.

In this chapter we explore the cognitive dynamics of attitude change and how individuals can change other individuals' attitudes. We also explore how discrepancies between attitudes and behaviour, rather than being an embarrassment to attitude theory, actually engage the very processes through which **attitude change** can occur. In subsequent chapters (**Chapters 7, 8 and 9**) we focus on how attitudes are configured by group norms and how group processes can change group norms and people's attitudes.

The persuasion and attitude change literature is enormous (Albarracín & Vargas, 2010; Maio & Haddock, 2010; Visser & Cooper, 2007) – there are thousands of studies and a daunting variety of theories and perspectives. In our coverage, we focus on two general orientations. The first concentrates on people's use of arguments to convince others that a change of mind, and perhaps of behaviour, is needed. Research has focused on the nature, source and target of the persuasive message. Obvious areas of application relate to political propaganda and advertising.

The second orientation focuses on the behaviour of the target person. By getting someone to behave in a certain way, we may actually be able to change their underlying attitudes. This path to attitude change is the focus of **cognitive dissonance**, one of the consistency theories of attitudes referred to earlier in the text (see **Chapter 5**).

Whereas the first orientation starts from the premise that you reason with people to change how they think and act, the second orientation eliminates reasoning. Simply persuade others to act differently, even if you have to use trickery; later they may come to *think* differently (i.e. change their attitude) and should then continue acting the way you want.

Attitude change
Any significant modification of an individual's attitude. In the persuasion process this involves the communicator, the communication, the medium used and the characteristics of the audience. Attitude change can also occur by inducing someone to perform an act that runs counter to an existing attitude.

Cognitive dissonance
State of psychological tension produced by simultaneously having two opposing cognitions. People are motivated to reduce the tension, often by changing or rejecting one of the cognitions. Festinger proposed that we seek harmony in our attitudes, beliefs and behaviours and try to reduce tension from inconsistency among these elements.

Persuasive communication

The receptive powers of the masses are very restricted, and their understanding is feeble. On the other hand, they quickly forget. Such being the case, all effective propaganda must be confined to a few bare essentials and those must be expressed as far as possible in stereotyped formulas. These slogans should be persistently repeated until the very last individual has come to grasp the idea that has been put forward. If this principle be forgotten and if an attempt be made to be abstract and general, the propaganda will turn out ineffective; for the public will not be able to digest or retain what is offered to them in this way. Therefore, the greater the scope of the message that has to be presented, the more necessary it is for the propaganda to discover that plan of action which is psychologically the most efficient.

Hitler, *Mein Kampf* (1933)

Has there ever been a more dramatic, mesmerising and chilling communicator than Adolf Hitler? His massive audiences at the Nazi rallies of the 1930s and 1940s may not have been so impressed had they known what he thought of them. The extreme case of Hitler, but also of other demagogues, connects the study of persuasive communication to leadership (see **Chapter 9**), rhetoric (e.g. Billig, 1991, 1996), and social mobilisation and crowd behaviour (see **Chapter 11**).

13·MÄRZ 1938
EIN VOLK EIN REICH
EIN FÜHRER

Persuading the masses
Hitler felt that the content of an effective public message needed to be simple. Slogans were a key ingredient of Nazi propoganda.

Research on the relationship between **persuasive communication** and attitude change is, however, generally more narrowly focused and has been most thoroughly applied to advertising and marketing (Johnson, Pham, & Johar, 2007) on the assumption that behavioural change 'obviously cannot occur without [attitude change] having taken place' (Schwerin & Newell, 1981, p. 7).

Persuasive communication
Message intended to change an attitude and related behaviours of an audience.

Social psychologists have long been interested in persuasion and what makes persuasive messages effective. Systematic investigation began towards the end of the Second World War, at a time when President Roosevelt was concerned that Americans, after being victorious in Europe, would lose the will to fight on against Japan. Carl Hovland was contracted by the US War Department to investigate how propaganda could be used to rally support for the American war effort – as it already had for the German cause by Hitler and the Nazi Party.

After the war, Hovland continued this work at Yale University in the first coordinated research programme focusing on the social psychology of persuasion. Research funding was again geopolitically motivated, this time by the Cold War – the United States's perception of threat from the Soviet Union, and its 'wish to justify its ways to the classes and win the hearts and minds of the masses' (McGuire, 1986, p. 99). The main features of this research programme were outlined in the research team's book, *Communication and Persuasion* (Hovland, Janis, & Kelley, 1953). They suggested that the key to understanding why people attend to, understand, remember and accept a persuasive message is to study the characteristics of the person presenting the message, the contents of the message and the characteristics of the receiver of the message.

The general model of the Yale approach, shown in Figure 6.1, is still used as the basis of contemporary *communications theory* in marketing and advertising (see Belch & Belch, 2012). Hovland, Janis and Kelley asked, 'Who says what to whom and with what effect?' and studied three general variables involved in persuasion:

1 the communicator, or the source (who);

2 the communication, or message (what);

3 the audience (to whom).

They also identified four steps in the persuasion process: attention, comprehension, acceptance and retention. This research programme spanned nearly three decades and produced an enormous quantity of data. Box 6.1 is a summary, with a real-life flavour, of the main findings. If you were planning to make a public campaign as persuasive as possible, there are points to bear in mind: some communicators, message strategies and speech styles are more effective than others; and the nature of the audience needs to be accounted for.

Not all findings from the Yale research programme have endured. Baumeister and Covington (1985) found that people with high self-esteem are just as easily persuaded as those with low self-esteem, but they do not want to admit it. When persuasion does occur, people may even deny it. Bem and McConnell (1970) reported that when people do succumb to persuasion, they conveniently fail to recall their original opinion.

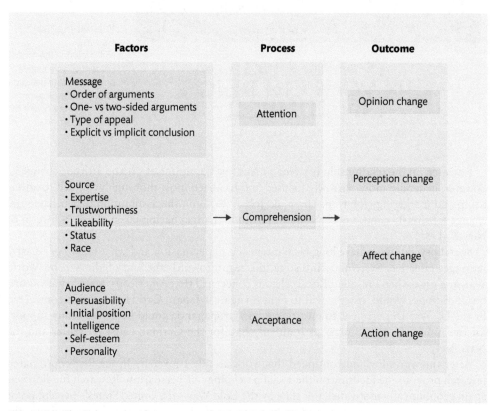

Figure 6.1 The Yale approach to communication and persuasion

In this classic research, various message, source and audience factors were found to affect the extent that people can be persuaded. See Box 6.1 for details of such message factors.

Source: Based on Janis and Hovland (1959).

Box 6.1 Your life
Persuasive communications can change attitudes

We all like to have things our own way; to be able to persuade people to change their attitudes to see the world the way we do. But how would you construct a communication so that it is persuasive? Lots of factors are involved. Fortunately (for political propaganda, consumer advertising and, of course, you) social psychologists have learned a great deal about those factors that one should consider in making a communication persuasive.

WHO: source factors

- *Expertise* – experts are more persuasive than non-experts. The same arguments carry more weight when delivered by someone who seems to know all the facts (Hovland & Weiss, 1952).
- *Popularity and attractiveness* – these factors make communicators more effective (Kiesler & Kiesler, 1969).
- *Speech rate* – communicators who speak rapidly are more persuasive than those who speak slowly. Rapid speech gives an impression of 'I know what I'm talking about' (Miller, Maruyama, Beaber, & Valone, 1976).

WHAT: message factors

- *Perceived manipulation* – we are more easily persuaded when we think the message is not deliberately intended to manipulate us (Walster & Festinger, 1962).
- *Linguistic power* – a message in a powerless linguistic style (frequent hedges, tag questions, hesitations) is less persuasive than one in a powerful linguistic style. A powerless style gives a negative impression of both the arguments and the speaker (Blankenship & Holtgraves, 2005).
- *Fear* – messages that arouse fear can be very effective. For example, to stop people smoking we might show them pictures of cancerous lungs (Leventhal, Singer, & Jones, 1965).

TO WHOM: audience factors

- *Self-esteem* – people with low self-esteem are persuaded more easily than people with high self-esteem (Janis, 1954; but see Baumeister & Covington, 1985).
- *Distraction* – people are sometimes more susceptible to persuasion when they are distracted than when paying full attention, at least when the message is simple (Allyn & Festinger, 1961).
- *Age* – people in the 'impressionable years' are more susceptible to persuasion than those who are older (Krosnick & Alwin, 1989).
- *When the argument in a message is of high quality* – those who are high self-monitors are persuaded more by someone who is an attractive person; those who are low self-monitors are persuaded more by an expert (Evans & Clark, 2012).

The persuasion process is a series of steps in which the audience has at least to pay attention to the communicator's message, understand the content and think about what was said (Eagly & Chaiken, 1984). The audience's thoughts are critical in this process (Petty & Cacioppo, 1981); the message will ultimately be accepted if it arouses favourable thoughts, but rejected if the recipients argue strongly against it in their minds.

People are not oblivious to persuasion attempts. We can hardly avoid commercial advertising, public education programmes and political propaganda. Perhaps not surprisingly, most people believe they are less likely to be influenced than others by advertisements; a phenomenon called the **third-person effect** ('You and I are not influenced, but they are'). For example, if we see a mundane product being advertised by using attractive models in an exotic setting, we assume that we (and those like us) are wiser than others to the tricks of the advertising industry. In reality, we are just as susceptible. Julie Duck and her associates have conducted a series of studies of the third-person effect in the context of political advertising and AIDS prevention messages (see Duck, Hogg, & Terry, 2000).

Third-person effect
Most people think that they are less influenced than others by advertisements.

In the next three sections, we look at each of the three links in the persuasion chain: the communicator, the message and the audience. In any given context all three of course operate, and some of the studies in these sections do indeed analyse more than one of these three variables at a time to find that they often interact: for example, whether an argument should present a one-sided or a two-sided case can depend on how intelligent the audience is.

The communicator

The Yale communication programme showed early on that there is a group of variables relating to characteristics of the source (communicator) that significantly affect how acceptable we find a message. Great expertise, good physical looks and extensive interpersonal and verbal skills make a communicator more effective (Triandis, 1971). We are also more influenced by people we feel familiar, close and attracted to, and by people with power and control over the kinds of reinforcement we might receive. In all of these cases, such sources of influence have the best chance of persuading us to change our attitudes and behaviour.

Source credibility

The credibility of the communicator affects the acceptability of persuasive messages. But attractiveness, likeability and similarity also play a very significant role. Source *attractiveness* is exploited mercilessly by the advertising industry. For example, the actor George Clooney has been used extensively in TV commercials around the world advertising Martini, Nespresso and Toyota, and iconic rock stars such as David Bowie and Bon Jovi have famously been used to advertise sake and Advil, respectively. The assumption of these advertising campaigns is that attractive, popular and likeable spokespersons are persuasive and therefore instrumental in enhancing consumer demand for a product. Attitude research generally supports this assumption (Chaiken, 1979, 1983).

Attractiveness also significantly influences the political process – people tend to prefer and vote for attractive candidates over less attractive candidates, even if the latter are objectively far better qualified for the job (Wänke, 2015) For example, a study of the 2004 congressional election in the United States found that almost 70% of the outcomes could be attributed to voters' inferences of competence based on facial attractiveness (Todorov, Mandisodza, Goren, & Hall, 2005).

Similarity plays a role because we like people who are similar to us and are therefore more persuaded by similar than dissimilar others: for example, a member of your peer group should be more persuasive than a stranger. However, it is not quite this simple (Petty & Cacioppo, 1981). When the focus of persuasion is a matter of taste or judgement (e.g. who was Italy's greatest football player of all time?), similar sources are accepted more readily than dissimilar sources. But when the focus is a matter of fact (e.g. at which Olympic Games did your country win its greatest number of gold medals?), dissimilar sources do better (Goethals & Nelson, 1973).

Source credibility
When Jürgen Klopp speaks even Adam Lallana listens.

No single communication variable can be treated in isolation. What works best in the persuasion process is an interaction of three categories of variables ('communication language' terms are given in brackets):

1 The **source** (sender) – from whom does the communication come?

2 The **message** (signal) – what medium is used, and what kinds of argument are involved?

3 The **audience** (receiver) – who is the target?

Source
The point of origin of a persuasive communication.

Message
Communication from a source directed to an audience.

Audience
Intended target of a persuasive communication.

For example, a study by Stephen Bochner and Chester Insko (1966) focused on source *credibility* in combination with the discrepancy between the opinion of the target and that of the source. Bochner and Insko predicted that an audience would pay more attention to a more credible communicator, and that there would be more room for attitude change when the target's opinion was more discrepant from that of the source.

Participants were students who were initially asked how much sleep was required to maintain one's health. Most said eight hours. They were then exposed to two sources of opinion that varied in expertise and therefore credibility. One was a Nobel Prize-winning physiologist with expertise in sleep research (higher credibility) and the other a YMCA instructor (lower credibility). Discrepancy was manipulated as the amount of disagreement between the student opinion and that of the source. If the source said that five hours was enough, the discrepancy was three hours with respect to the typical view of eight hours: the pressure to shift should be higher than if the discrepancy was only one hour. However, what would happen if the source said that two hours was sufficient? Look at the results in Figure 6.2.

More opinion change occurred at moderate levels of difference between the students and the source. It seems that extreme discrepancy is not a good tactic in influencing a target. The

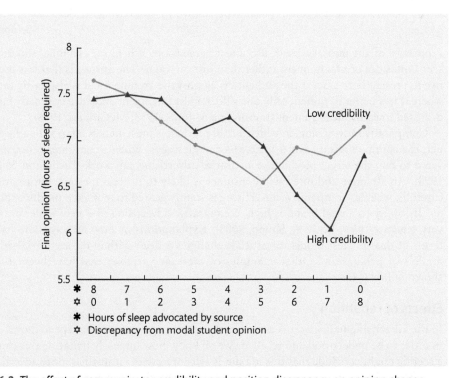

Figure 6.2 The effect of communicator credibility and position discrepancy on opinion change

As a position adopted in a message becomes increasingly discrepant from what most people would accept, a more credible communicator becomes more effective in inducing opinion change.

Source: Based on data from Bochner and Insko (1966).

audience will resist if the difference is too great and may look for ways to discredit the communicator ('They don't know what they are talking about!'). However, this discrepancy effect was affected by the credibility of the source. It was the expert who induced the greatest amount of change, and this took place when discrepancy was marked. In Bochner and Insko's study, the change was greatest when the highly credible source advocated one hour of sleep and students had suggested eight hours, a discrepancy of seven hours.

Interaction effects in research point to nuances in the way that one or more variables can determine a given outcome, and one example of this relates to source credibility. When a message is simple, i.e. it does not require much elaboration or thought processing, source credibility acts as a heuristic: 'this person is famous, so what they say must be true'. However, a more complex message requires more elaboration or thought processing.

In this context, Zakary Tormala and his associates have found that source credibility has more than one role and its capacity to persuade is 'all in the timing'. People's thinking became more confident when the identity of the source followed the message; but their thinking became more favourable when the identity of the source preceded the message (Tormala, Briñol, & Petty, 2007).

In an Italian study of political speeches, Michela Menegatti and Monica Rubini (2013) reported interaction (or combination) effects of source and audience variables. When the speaker and the audience have politically similar views (e.g. both have left-wing or both have right-wing views), the message has more impact and is more likely to be abstract than concrete. An adept politician knows that abstract statements work well when the audience is sympathetic, whereas concrete statements invite closer scrutiny. Recall how Hitler used slogans to great effect at mass rallies of his supporters.

The message

> An important idea not communicated persuasively is like having no idea at all.
>
> Bernbach (2002)

Properties of the message itself also affect persuasion. When, for example, should we present both sides of an argument rather than just our own? The answer is that it is more effective to present both sides if the audience is against the argument but is also fairly intelligent, whereas it is better to present only one side if a less intelligent audience is already favourably disposed towards the argument (Lumsdaine & Janis, 1953; McGinnies, 1966).

Comparative advertising, in which a rival product is presented as inferior to a target product, is a common instance of using two-sided messages. When a consumer is not very motivated to buy the target product, comparative advertising can work (Pechmann & Esteban, 1994). An attentive and interested consumer is likely to process message information quite carefully, whereas comparative advertising is simply geared to making a product appear better. If loyalty to a rival brand is high, comparative advertising of a new target brand is not very effective (Nye, Roth, & Shimp, 2008). Explanations of how messages are handled in terms of dual-process models of attitude change are dealt with in the section 'Dual-process models of persuasion'. Other examples of message variables that have been studied are shown in Box 6.1.

Effects of repetition

In the advertising industry, it is a maxim that a message needs to be repeated over and over in order to be understood and recalled. We all know how intensely irritating this can be, and a sceptic might conclude that this maxim is self-interested – it justifies more advertising and thus boom times for advertising agencies. If we believe the advertising industry, however, this is not a major motive. According to Ray (1988), the main goal is to strive for repetition minimisation: that is, to have the maximum impact with the minimum exposure and therefore the most cost-effective expenditure. Television advertising exposure reinforces preferences more than it motivates brand choices; and the optimum exposure rate is two to three times a week (Tellis, 1987).

In general, the issue of message repetition invites, as we shall see below, examination of the way in which information is processed and of how memory works. Somewhat more startling is a finding that simple repetition of a statement gives it the *ring of truth* (Arkes, Boehm, & Xu, 1991; Moons, Mackie, & Garcia-Marques, 2009)! Repeated exposure to an object clearly increases familiarity with that object. Repetition of a name can make that name seem famous (Jacoby, Kelly, Brown, & Jasechko, 1989). (Note also that an increase in familiarity between people can increase interpersonal liking; see **Chapter 14**.) However, there is a catch to the use of repetition, identified in a study of TV and Internet advertising: it may not work very well with a totally new product and may even become decreasingly effective. Even a little brand familiarity helps (Campbell & Keller, 2003).

Another variable that affects attitude change is fear. Fear has been used by the media to induce people to obey the law or to care for their health, and in the 2016 US presidential election, fear was almost the entire persuasion strategy of the Republican presidential nominee Donald Trump.

Does fear work?

Fear-arousing messages may enhance persuasion – but how fearful can a message become and still be effective? Many agencies in our community use forms of advertising and persuasion that are intended to frighten us into complying with their advice or admonitions. Health workers may visit the local school to lecture children on how 'smoking is dangerous to your health'. To drive the point home, they might show pictures of a diseased lung. Television advertising may remind you that 'if you drink, don't drive' and perhaps try to reinforce this message with graphic scenes of carnage on the roads. In the late 1980s, a legendary advertising campaign associated the Grim Reaper with unsafe sexual practices and the likelihood of contracting HIV. Does this work? The answer is a mixed one.

An early study by Janis and Feshbach (1953) had three different experimental conditions under which participants were encouraged to take better care of their teeth. In a low-fear condition, they were told of the painful outcomes of diseased teeth and gums, and suggestions were made about how to maintain good oral health. In a moderate-fear condition, the warning about oral disease was more explicit. In a high-fear condition, they were told that the disease could spread to other parts of the body, and very unpleasant visual slides were presented showing decayed teeth and diseased gums. Participants reported their current dental habits and were followed up one week later. Janis and Feshbach found an inverse relationship between degree of (presumed) fear arousal and change in dental hygiene practices. The low-fear participants were taking the best care of their teeth after one week, followed by the moderate-fear group and then the high-fear group.

Leventhal, Watts and Pagano (1967) reported a conflicting result from a study of how a fearful communication might aid in persuading people to stop smoking. The participants were volunteers who wanted to give up smoking. In a moderate-fear condition, the participants listened to a talk with charts illustrating the link between death from lung cancer and the rate at which cigarettes were used. In a high-fear condition, they also saw a graphic film about an operation on a patient with lung cancer. Their results showed a greater willingness to stop smoking among people in the high-fear condition.

How do we explain the discrepancy between these results? Both Janis (1967) and McGuire (1969) suggested that an inverted U-curve hypothesis might account for the conflicting results (see Figure 6.3). McGuire proposed two parameters that might control the way we respond to a persuasive message, one involving comprehension and the other involving the degree to which we yield to change. The more we can understand what is being presented to us and can conceive of ways to put this into effect, the more likely we are to go along with a particular message.

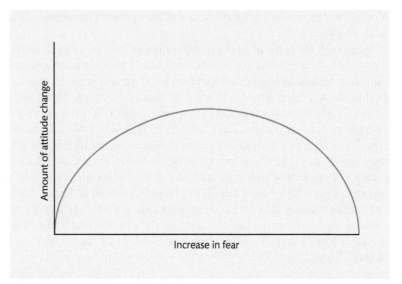

Figure 6.3 The inverted U-curve relationship between fear and attitude change

The amount of attitude change increases as a function of fear up to a medium level of arousal. At high levels of fear, however, there is a fall-off in attitude change. This could be due to lack of attention to the stimulus, or to the disruptive effects of intense emotion, or both.

According to Keller and Block (1995), and in line with dual-process models of information processing (see **Chapters 2 and 5**), people who are not particularly frightened may not be motivated to attend to the message because the message does not spell out sufficiently the harmful consequences of the behaviour. As fear increases, so does arousal, interest and attention to what is going on. However, a very frightening presentation of an idea may arouse so much anxiety, even a state of panic, that we become distracted, miss some of the factual content of the message and are unable to process the information properly or know what to do.

What we do not know is whether the high-fear condition in the Janis and Feshbach study aroused more fear than the same condition in the Leventhal, Watts and Pagano study. If it did, then a curvilinear relationship might fit the data. In any event, there may be a limit to the effectiveness of fear-arousing messages. Disturbing TV images, for example, may distract people from the intended message or, even if the message is attended to, may so upset people that the entire episode is avoided.

In the context of health behaviour, and according to *protection motivation theory* (see **Chapter 5**), fear appeals should reduce dangerous health practices if they include an effective presentation of how to cope with the danger (see Wood, 2000, for a review). Witte, Berkowitz, Cameron and McKeon (1998), for example, combined a fear appeal with the promotion of self-protective behaviours in a campaign to reduce the spread of genital warts.

Whether a scary message achieves its goals is probably determined by a trade-off between the perception of danger (*threat appraisal*) and whether people believe they can carry out the corrective behaviour (*coping appraisal*; see **Figure 5.5 in Chapter 5**). The underlying idea is consistent with Blascovich's biopsychosocial model of challenge and threat (Blascovich, 2008; Blascovich & Tomaka, 1996; see **Chapter 2**) – a demand can be perceived as a threat if one feels one does not have the resources to cope, and a challenge if one feels one does have the resources to cope.

The nature of threat appraisal was examined in a German study of stress-related illness (Das, de Wit, & Stroebe, 2003). In this study, it was assumed that ordinary people in a health-risk setting ask themselves two questions ('How vulnerable am I?' and 'How severe is the risk?'), and risk following long-term stress could range from fairly mild (e.g. fever or cold hands and feet) to very severe (e.g. stomach ulcers or heart disease). Once it was accepted there was even a mild risk (the second question), people were more likely to follow a health recommendation provided they believed they were very vulnerable to a threat (the first question). This suggests that impactful messages about risky health practices should pinpoint the matter of *vulnerability* to a greater degree than simply severity.

There is further twist to understanding the effect of fearful messages. If the fear is so extreme that it makes us aware of our own death and mortality, then terror management processes may come into play. According to **terror management theory** (Greenberg, Solomon, & Pyszczynski, 1997; Pyszczynski, Greenberg, & Solomon, 1999; see **Chapter 4**) thoughts of our own death create 'paralysing terror'. This makes us seek symbolic immortality, which we achieve by identifying with and psychologically defending cultural institutions and ideologies that we subscribe to. Fear-laden messages may lead to ideological conviction and zealous identification with groups, rather than to attitude and behaviour change related to the focus of the message.

Terror management theory
The notion that the most fundamental human motivation is to reduce the terror of the inevitability of death. Self-esteem may be centrally implicated in effective terror management.

Facts versus feelings

We noted earlier (**Chapter 5**) that a distinction is commonly drawn between belief and affect as components of an attitude (e.g. Haddock & Zanna, 1999). In the advertising industry, a related distinction is made between *factual* and *evaluative* advertising. The former involves claims of fact and is thought to be objective, whereas the latter involves opinion and is subjective. A factually oriented advertisement is high on information and is likely to emphasise one or more attributes among the following: price, quality, performance, components or contents, availability, special offer, taste, packaging, guarantees or warranties, safety, nutrition, independent research, company-sponsored research or new ideas. However, the simple recall of facts from an advertisement does not guarantee a change in the brand purchased. Furthermore, if there is factual content in a message, it is important for people to be able to assimilate and understand the general conclusion of the message (Albion & Faris, 1979; Beattie & Mitchell, 1985).

In contrast, evaluative advertising means that instead of conveying facts or objective claims, the message is couched in such a way that it is intended to make the consumer feel generally 'good' about the product. Although evaluation and affect/emotion are not the same thing (see **Chapter 2**), they are certainly related, and a common method in evaluative advertising is to capitalise on the *transfer of affect*, which itself is based on learning by association (Gawronski & Bodenhausen, 2011). For example, we have all been entertained by (evaluative) advertising that uses humour. How effective is this? Well, perhaps unsurprisingly, very effective. Research confirms that repeated pairing of a novel brand with brand-unrelated humour crates a positive attitude towards the brand – we like the product (Strick, Holland, Van Baaren, Van Knippenberg, & Dijksterhuis, 2013).

The distinction between facts and feelings does not imply that a given advertisement contains only factual or only evaluative material. On the contrary, marketing strategy favours using both approaches in any advertisement. A consumer can be led to *feel* that one product is superior to another by subtle associations with music or colour, or through the use of humour or attractive models. The same consumer can be led to *believe* that the product is a better buy because it is a better value for money.

Another question is whether the kind of appeal (facts versus feelings) should fit the basis on which an attitude is held (Petty & Wegener, 1998). According to Edwards (1990), if the underlying attitude is emotional (affect-based), then the appeal should be as well; but if the attitude is centred on beliefs (cognition-based), then a factual appeal should work better. Millar and Millar (1990) argue for a mismatch: for example, using a factual appeal when the attitude is emotional. However, the attitude objects used in research by Edwards (e.g. photographs of strangers, a fictitious insecticide) were unknown to the participants, whereas those used by Millar and Millar were well known (a list of drinks actually generated by the participants) so participants could counter with effective arguments.

The medium and the message

Chaiken and Eagly (1983) compared the relative effects on an audience of presenting messages in video, audio and written forms. This has obvious implications for advertising. Which has more impact on the consumer: television, radio or printed media? It depends. If the message is simple, as much advertising is, the probable answer is: video is more impactful than audio, and audio is more impactful than written.

A moderating variable is how easy or difficult the audience finds the message to comprehend. If the points of a message require considerable processing by the target, a written medium is likely to be best. Readers have the chance to go back at will, mull over what is being said and then read on. If the material is quite complex, then newspapers and magazines can come into their own. However, there is an interesting interaction with the difficulty of the message. Look at the difference in effectiveness between various media in Figure 6.4. When the message was easy to comprehend, Chaiken and Eagly found that a videotaped presentation brought about most opinion change. When the message was difficult, however, opinion change was greatest when the material was written. Only recently has research included a focus on computer-mediated attitude change (e.g. Sassenberg & Boos, 2003 – see **Chapter 15**).

Framing a message

The way in which a message is framed or slanted can have subtle effects on its meaning, and therefore on whether it is accepted. For example, if the issue of 'affirmative action' is presented as 'equal opportunity' rather than 'reverse discrimination', people view it more favourably (Bosveld, Koomen, & Vogelaar, 1997). In their review of how to promote health-related behaviour, Rothman and Salovey (1997) found that message framing plays an important role. If the behaviour relates to detecting an illness, such as breast self-examination, the message should be framed in terms of preventing loss; but if the behaviour leads to a positive outcome, such as taking regular exercise, the message should be framed in terms of gain.

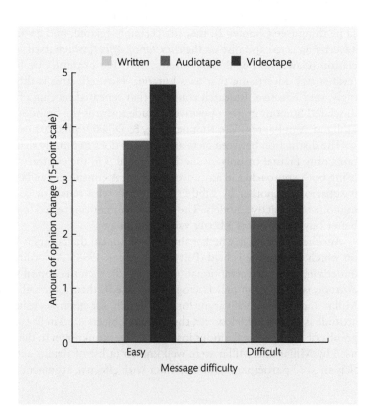

Figure 6.4 Effects of source modality and message difficulty on opinion change

Using sound or a visual image rather than the printed word makes an easily understood message more acceptable. However, a difficult message profits from using a written document.

Source: Based on Chaiken and Eagly (1983).

The sleeper effect

A persuasive message should have its greatest impact just after it is presented. It is counterintuitive to think that its power might increase with the passage of time, and yet this is precisely what the **sleeper effect** suggests (Kelman & Hovland, 1953). An early finding in the Yale attitude change programme (Hovland, Lumsdaine, & Sheffield, 1949) was that films promoting more positive attitudes among American soldiers towards their British allies in the Second World War became more effective well after they had been viewed.

Kelman and Hovland reasoned that we initially associate the conclusion of a message with: (1) the quality of its argument, and (2) other cues, such as the credibility of its source. Of these, memory of the argument becomes more enduring as time goes by. Take the part played by source credibility as it interacts with our views on how much sleep we need each night, discussed earlier (see Figure 6.2). Were we to take a measure of the impact of an extreme message about a month later, the sleeper effect predicts that the less credible source would probably be as persuasive as the more credible source: the message survives, but the source does not.

Although the reliability of the sleeper effect has long been questioned (e.g. Crano & Prislin, 2006; Gillig & Greenwald, 1974), the effect has been replicated under quite strict conditions (e.g. Pratkanis, Greenwald, Leippe, & Baumgardner, 1988), and a recent meta-analysis by Kumkale and Albarracín (2004) identifies the conditions under which the effect is most robust. See Box 6.2 for an experimental example that applies to the world of politics.

The sleeper effect has some resemblance to the phenomena of latent influence and conversion in the minority influence literature (Moscovici, 1980; for a review see Martin & Hewstone, 2008;

Sleeper effect
The impact of a persuasive message can increase over time when a discounting cue, such as an invalid source, can no longer be recalled.

Box 6.2 Our world
Delayed impact of a negative political attack

The curious case of the exploding lie detector

A context ripe for the operation of the sleeper effect is a political campaign. Parties often resort to messages that attack an opponent. These are built around specific, easily remembered content, such as Joe Black 'has been caught lying', 'is corrupt' or 'yet again has been cheating on his wife'. Campaigns of this nature are often disliked by the public and can alienate potential voters. The real-world response to an attack is to mount a defence. A direct, defensive message – typical in a political context – becomes the 'discounting cue' found in many laboratory sleeper-effect studies. A discounting cue is intended to undermine either the credibility of the source or the content of the attack message, or both, and to suppress the impact of the attack.

Ruth Ann Lariscy and Spencer Tinkham (1999) tested for a sleeper effect among registered voters in the American state of Georgia. A political advertisement was professionally produced in a real-world political format, including subtle humour. It featured two fictitious candidates running for the US Congress in Kentucky, with 'Pat Michaels' as the sponsor of the advertisement and 'John Boorman' as his opponent.

A voice-over lists Boorman's claims about his military record in Vietnam, his tax policy and his heartfelt concern for Kentuckians. With each claim, a lie detector that is visually central in the sequences shows wild swings on a graph – lie, lie, lie! At the mention of Boorman's care for Kentucky, the detector finally explodes.

Following the attack advertisement were Boorman's direct and defensive advertisements, arriving almost immediately or else after a delay. These were designed to suppress the impact of the original message by refuting Michaels's attacks and discounting his credibility. Michaels's credibility was designed to be at its lowest when the defensive messages were immediate.

To reduce confusion with real-world candidates in their own state, the voters in Georgia were asked to assume that they were voting in Kentucky. During a telephone callback made one week after the attack advertisement and repeated six weeks later, they were asked which candidate they would endorse. When Michaels's credibility was lowest, only 19.6 per cent of participants were prepared to vote for him. After a delay of six weeks, however, support for Michaels had risen to an astonishing 50 per cent. Behold the sleeper effect – the exploding lie detector had done its job: 'negative advertising is not only damaging, it can wreak havoc that lasts until election day' (Lariscy & Tinkham, 1999, p. 26).

Source: Lariscy and Tinkham (1999).

see **Chapter 7**). Groups that hold a minority view can, if they adopt the right behavioural style (Mugny, 1982) and are not rejected outright as an outgroup (Crano & Seyranian, 2009), be quite effective in changing the attitudes of the majority. Typically, however, there is initial resistance and the attitude change comes later in the form of a sudden conversion.

The audience

Self-esteem

In their 1950s studies, Hovland and his colleagues had noted that a distracted audience is more easily persuaded than one that is paying full attention, provided the message is simple; and that people with low self-esteem are more susceptible than those with high self-esteem (see Box 6.1). McGuire (1968) suggested that the relationship between persuasibility and self-esteem is actually curvilinear: that is, it follows an inverted U-curve of the kind shown in Figure 6.3 (substituting 'self-esteem' for 'fear'). This curve suggests that people with either low or high self-esteem are less persuasible than those with moderate self-esteem. He reasoned that those with low self-esteem would be either less attentive or else more anxious when processing a message, whereas those with high self-esteem would be less susceptible to influence, presumably because they are generally more self-assured. Research generally confirms this curvilinear relationship (Rhodes & Wood, 1992). As an aside, McGuire has also proposed a similar curvilinear relationship between intelligence and persuasibility.

Men and women

Another consistent, but controversial, finding is that women are more easily persuaded than men (Cooper, 1979; Eagly, 1978). Crutchfield (1955) was the first to report this, when he found that women were more conforming and susceptible to social influence than men. One explanation of this was that women are socialised to be cooperative and non-assertive and are therefore less resistant than men to attempts to influence them (Eagly, Wood, & Fishbaugh, 1981). Sistrunk and McDavid (1971) favoured another explanation – women are more easily influenced than men, but only when the topic is one with which men are more familiar. When the topic is female-oriented, men are more influenced than women (see **Chapters 7 and 10**).

The consistent gender difference found in persuasibility was due to a methodological bias. The persuasive messages used in attitude research had typically dealt with male-oriented topics, and the researchers were usually male. If the topics had not been gender-biased, the male–female differences would not have been found. Subsequent research has addressed this bias (e.g. Eagly & Carli, 1981) and supported the topic-familiarity explanation.

Carli (1990) investigated gender differences in both the audience and the source. Participants heard a recorded message read by either a man or a woman, who spoke either tentatively or assertively. When the reader was female and tentative rather than assertive, male listeners were more easily persuaded than female listeners. In contrast, male readers were equally influential in each condition. This suggests that gender-related persuasiveness is a complex interaction of who is speaking, who is listening and whether the message is delivered in a sex-stereotyped way.

Covell, Dion and Dion (1994) investigated the effectiveness of tobacco and alcohol advertising as a function of gender and generation. The participants were male and female adolescents and their mothers and fathers. They rated the image and the quality of the advertised products and showed a preference for image-oriented over quality-oriented advertising. A gender difference was restricted to the adolescents, among whom females showed an even stronger preference for image-oriented advertising. Covell, Dion and Dion suggested that when advertisements target adolescents and feature alcohol and tobacco, young women might be particularly attentive to image-oriented messages and judge drinking and smoking to be more desirable.

In general, gender differences in attitude change mirror gender differences in social influence in small groups (see **Chapter 7**; also see the review by Carli, 1990).

Individual differences

Men and women may not differ in persuasibility, but are there other differences between people that make some more easily persuaded than others? Research has focused on individual differences in *need for cognition* (Haugtvedt & Petty, 1992), *need for closure* (Kruglanski & Webster, 1996; Kruglanski, Webster, & Klem, 1993), *need to evaluate* (Jarvis & Petty, 1995), *preference for consistency* (Cialdini, Trost, & Newsom, 1995) and *attitude importance* (Zuwerink & Devine, 1996). People who score high on these needs and preferences are less likely to be persuaded than those who score low, with the exception of need for closure where the relationship is the reverse. However, the relationship between personality variables and persuasion is not simple. In almost all cases, social context acts as a **moderator variable** that influences the personality–persuasibility relationship.

Moderator variable
A variable that qualifies an otherwise simple hypothesis with a view to improving its predictive power (e.g. A causes B, but only when C (the moderator) is present).

Age

Do people become more, or less easily persuaded as they get older? There are five possibilities, which can be framed as hypotheses (Tyler & Schuller, 1991; Visser & Krosnick, 1998):

1 *Increasing persistence* – susceptibility to attitude change is high in early adulthood but decreases gradually across the life span; attitudes reflect the accumulation of relevant experiences (a negative linear line).

2 *Impressionable years* – core attitudes, values and beliefs are crystallised during a period of great plasticity in early adulthood (an S-curve).

3 *Life stages* – there is a high susceptibility during early adulthood and later life, but a lower susceptibility throughout middle adulthood (a U-curve).

4 *Lifelong openness* – individuals are to some extent susceptible to attitude change throughout their lives.

5 *Persistence* – most of an individual's fundamental orientations are established firmly during pre-adult socialisation; susceptibility to attitude change thereafter is low.

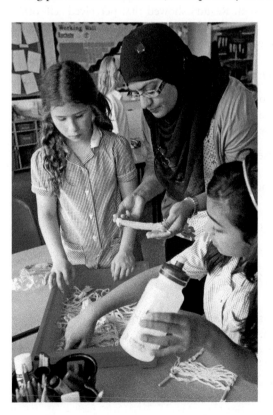

The impressionable years
Respected adults, such as this teacher, are enormously influential in the development of young children's attitudes.

Which of these hypotheses is most accurate remains an open question. Tyler and Schuller's (1991) field study of attitudes towards the government supports the *lifelong openness* hypothesis: that is, age is generally irrelevant to attitude change. On the other hand, Visser and Krosnick's (1998) laboratory experiments support the *life stages* hypothesis. Rutland's (1999) research on the development of prejudice shows that negative attitudes towards ethnic and national outgroups only crystallise in later childhood (around age 10).

Other variables

There are at least two other audience variables that relate to the persuasion process.

> **Disconfirmation bias**
> The tendency to notice, refute and regard as weak, arguments that contradict our prior beliefs.

1 *Prior beliefs* affect persuasibility. There is evidence for a **disconfirmation bias** in argument evaluation. Arguments that are incompatible with prior beliefs are scrutinised longer, are subjected to more extensive refutational analyses and are judged weaker than arguments compatible with prior beliefs. Furthermore, the magnitude of a disconfirmation bias is greater if prior beliefs are accompanied by emotional conviction (Edwards & Smith, 1996). Even if arguments contain only facts, prior beliefs affect whether factual information is considered at all. In a political controversy over the stranding of a Soviet submarine near a Swedish naval base in 1981, the contending sides were most unwilling to accept facts introduced by each other into the debate, querying whether they were relevant and reliable (Lindstrom, 1997). The disconfirmation bias is evident daily in media political discussions. For example, the disaster of the *Kursk*, a Russian submarine that sank in the Barents Sea in 2000, and the refusal of Western help in the rescue mission, sparked a similar debate to that in 1981.

2 *Cognitive biases* are important in both attitude formation and change (see **Chapter 3** for an overview). For example, Duck, Hogg and Terry (1999) demonstrated the *third-person effect* in media persuasion (discussed earlier). According to this bias, people believe that they are less influenced than others by persuasion attempts. Students' perceptions of the impact of AIDS advertisements on themselves, students (ingroup), non-students (outgroup) and people in general were examined. Results showed that perceived self–other differences varied with how strongly students identified with being students. Those who did not identify strongly as students (low identifiers) exhibited the third-person effect, while those who did identify strongly (high identifiers) were more willing to acknowledge impact on themselves and the student ingroup.

In closing, we should emphasise that in practice, the three major categories of variables dealt with – source, message and audience – interact. For example, whether one would choose to employ an expert source to deliver a message can depend on the target group:

> A guiding principle in both marketing research and in persuasion theory is to 'know your audience' . . . marketers realize that a key to capturing a significant portion of the market share is to target one's product to those who are most likely to want or need it.
>
> Jacks and Cameron (2003, p. 145)

Let us now focus on exactly how the persuasion process works.

Dual-process models of persuasion

The key question here is, how do we process a message and its content? The answer is provided by dual-process models of persuasion. There are two variants, one proposed by Petty and Cacioppo (e.g. Petty & Cacioppo, 1986a, 1986b) and one by Chaiken (e.g. Chaiken, 1987; Chaiken, Liberman, & Eagly, 1989). They have elements in common. Both invoke two processes and draw on social cognition research on memory (see **Chapter 2**), and both deal with persuasion cues. Sometimes it may not be the quality and type of the persuasion cues

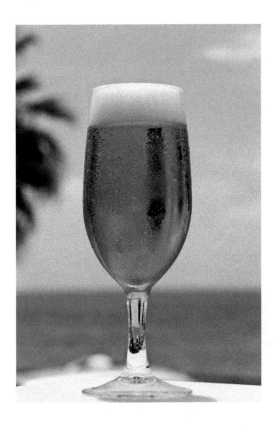

Peripheral cues in advertising
According to Homer Simpson, 'beer is so much more than just a breakfast drink'. Consumers, however, are more susceptible to stimuli that induce a good mood and a healthy first!

that matter, but rather the quantity of message processing that underlies attitude change (Mackie, Worth, & Asuncion, 1990). After more than twenty years of research, are these theories still relevant?

> Without question, the dual-process models remain today's most influential persuasion paradigms, as they have been since their inception. In these models, source and message may play distinct roles that, in concert with motivation and ability to process information, determine the outcomes of persuasive interactions.
>
> Crano and Prislin (2006, p. 348)

Elaboration–likelihood model

According to Richard Petty and John Cacioppo's **elaboration–likelihood model** (ELM), when people receive a persuasive message, they think about the arguments it makes. However, they do not necessarily think deeply or carefully, because that requires considerable cognitive effort. People are cognitive tacticians who are motivated to expend valuable cognitive capital only on issues that are important to them (see **Chapter 2**). Persuasion follows two routes, depending on whether people expend a great deal or very little cognitive effort on the message.

If the arguments of the message are followed closely, a *central route* is used. We digest the arguments in a message, extract a point that meets our needs and indulge mentally in counter-arguments if we disagree with some of them. If the central route to persuasion is to be used, the points in the message need to be put convincingly, as we will be required to expend considerable cognitive effort – that is, to work hard – on them. For example, suppose your doctor told you that you needed major surgery. The chances are that you would take a considerable amount of convincing, that you would listen carefully to what the doctor says, read what you could about the matter and even seek a second medical opinion. On the other hand,

Elaboration–likelihood model
Petty and Cacioppo's model of attitude change: when people attend to a message carefully, they use a central route to process it; otherwise they use a peripheral route. This model competes with the heuristic–systematic model.

Figure 6.5 The elaboration–likelihood model of persuasion
Source: Based on Petty and Cacioppo (1986b).

when arguments are not well attended to, a *peripheral route* is followed. By using peripheral cues, we act in a less diligent fashion, preferring a consumer product on a superficial whim, such as an advertisement in which the product is used by an attractive model. The alternative routes available according to the elaboration–likelihood model are shown in Figure 6.5.

Heuristic–systematic model

Heuristic–systematic model
Chaiken's model of attitude change: when people attend to a message carefully, they use systematic processing; otherwise they process information by using heuristics, or 'mental short-cuts'. This model competes with the elaboration–likelihood model.

Shelley Chaiken's **heuristic–systematic model** (HSM) deals with the same phenomena using slightly different concepts, distinguishing between *systematic* processing and heuristic processing. Systematic processing occurs when people scan and consider available arguments. In the case of heuristic processing, we do not indulge in careful reasoning but instead use cognitive heuristics, such as thinking that longer arguments are stronger. Persuasive messages are not always processed systematically. Chaiken has suggested that people will sometimes employ cognitive heuristics to simplify the task of handling information.

You will recall that heuristics are simple decision rules or 'mental short-cuts', the tools that cognitive misers and motivated tacticians use. So, when we are judging the reliability of a message, we resort to such truisms as 'statistics don't lie' or 'you can't trust a politician' as an easy way of making up our minds. As previously discussed, this feature of judgement is actively exploited by advertising companies when they try to influence consumers by portraying their products as supported by scientific research or expert opinion. For instance, washing detergents are often advertised in laboratory settings, showing technical equipment and authoritative-looking people in white coats.

At what point would we switch from heuristic to systematic processing? People seem to have a *sufficiency threshold* (Petty & Wegener, 1998): heuristics are used as long as they satisfy our need to be confident in the attitude that we adopt, but when we lack sufficient confidence we switch to more effortful systematic processing.

The role of cognition is fundamental in handling a persuasive message, but how well we concentrate on the content of a message can be affected by something as transient as our *mood*. Diane Mackie, for example, has shown that merely being in a good mood changes the way we attend to information (Mackie & Worth, 1989; see also Petty, Schuman, Richman, & Stratham, 1993). For example, background music is a widely used advertising ploy to engender a mellow feeling. There is a sneaky reason behind this – feeling 'good' makes it difficult for us to process a message systematically. When time is limited, which is typical of TV advertising, feeling really good leads us to flick on to autopilot, i.e. to use a peripheral route (ELM) or heuristic processing (HSM).

Think again about how advertisers present everyday merchandise: cues like feel-good background music have an additional and longer-term 'benefit' (Gorn, 1982). Marketing strategists George Belch and Michael Belch (2012) noted that, through classical conditioning, a product repeatedly associated with a good mood can become evaluated positively – in time, in the absence of music or other positive contextual cues (Gawronski & Bodenhausen, 2011; Strick, Holland, Van Baaren, Van Knippenberg, & Dijksterhuis, 2013).

However, people who are already happy do not always scrutinise messages superficially. If the message content is in line with our attitudes (therefore congruent with our already good mood), then being happy as well leads to more extensive processing (Wegener, Petty, & Smith, 1995). What is involved here is an interaction between two of the three major persuasion factors noted in the Yale programme: a supportive message and a happy audience.

In addition, feeling 'good' makes it difficult to process a message systematically. When time is limited, such as when we watch a TV advertisement, feeling really good can make us more susceptible to peripheral heuristic processing. Bohner, Chaiken and Hunyadi (1994) induced either a happy or a sad mood in students who then heard arguments that were strong, weak or ambiguous. All arguments were attributed to a highly credible source. When the message was unambiguous, sad participants were more easily influenced when they used heuristic processing. The effects of a sad mood have also been studied in a mock court setting (Semmler & Brewer, 2002). When jurors feel sad, their accuracy (i.e. systematic processing) in detecting witness inconsistencies and their perceptions of witness reliability and a defendant's culpability is improved.

As a reminder that social processes can be complex, consider a study by Chaiken and Maheswaran (1994): systematic processing can be eroded when certain variables interact (see Box 6.3).

Box 6.3 Research highlight
Systematic processing can be undermined

A study by Chaiken and Maheswaran (1994) dealt with complex interactions between source and message variables, as well as task importance, in relation to whether people use heuristic or systematic processing. In New York, students were asked to rate a new telephone-answering machine in an experiment with three independent variables:

1 *Task importance.* Some students believed that their opinion would weigh heavily, since sample size was small, in whether the machine would be distributed throughout New York; other students thought that their opinion would merely contribute to a much larger sample of New Yorkers and would not alter the outcome very much.
2 *Source credibility.* The product description was supposedly written by either a high-credibility source (Consumer Reports) or a low-credibility source (the sales staff of K-mart).
3 *Message type.* A pretest established eight product features, four of which were important (e.g. could take different cassette types, screening of incoming calls) and four unimportant (e.g. colour range, special bolts for a wall). The important-to-unimportant ratio of these features was varied to create messages that were strong (4:2), ambiguous (3:3) or weak (2:4).

The findings for the students showed:

- For the unimportant task (their opinion did not count for much), the machine was rated in terms of the credibility of the source – heuristic processing was used – regardless of whether the message was strong, ambiguous or weak.
- For the important task (their opinion really counted), the machine was rated in terms of message content – systematic processing was used – provided the message was clearly strong or clearly weak. Source credibility did not affect these ratings.
- However, source credibility did play a role when the task was important but the message was ambiguous. Both systematic and heuristic processing were used.

Source: Chaiken and Maheswaran (1994).

In summary, when people are motivated to attend to a message and to deal with it *thoughtfully*, they use a central route to process it according to the ELM (Petty and Cacioppo) or process it systematically according to the HSM (Chaiken). When attention is reduced so that people become cognitively *lazy*, they use a peripheral route (Petty and Cacioppo) or resort to heuristics – simple decision rules (Chaiken).

Compliance

Compliance
Superficial, public and transitory change in behaviour and expressed attitudes in response to requests, coercion or group pressure.

The terms compliance and conformity are often used interchangeably. From a scientific point of view, however, they are different. **Compliance**, which we discuss in this chapter, refers to a surface *behavioural* response to a *request by another individual*; whereas conformity, which we discuss in **Chapter 7**, refers to the influence of a group upon an individual that usually produces more enduring internalised changes in one's attitudes and beliefs (see Hogg, 2010). Because compliance is more closely associated with behaviour, and conformity with attitudes, the compliance–conformity distinction engages with the attitude–behaviour relationship we discussed earlier (**Chapter 5**; see Sheeran, 2002). Compliance is also more closely associated with individuals having some form of power over you (French & Raven, 1959; see Fiske & Berdahl, 2007)

We are confronted daily with demands and requests. Often they are put to us in a straightforward and clear manner, such as when a friend asks you to dinner, and nothing more is requested. At other times, requests have a 'hidden agenda': for example, an acquaintance invites you to dinner to get you into the right mood to ask you to finance a new business venture. The result is often the same – we comply. So, what influences how compliant we are, and why are we more influenced on some occasions than others? Generally, people influence us when they use effective tactics or have powerful attributes.

Tactics for enhancing compliance

Persuading people to comply with requests to buy certain products has been the cornerstone of many economies. It is not surprising, therefore, that over the years many different tactics have been devised to enhance compliance. Salespeople, especially, have designed and refined many indirect procedures for inducing compliance, as their livelihood depends on it. We have all come across these tactics, which typically involve strategic self-presentation designed to elicit different emotions that compel you to comply (see **Chapter 4**).

Jones and Pittman (1982) describe five such strategies and emotions: *intimidation* is an attempt to elicit fear by getting others to think you are dangerous; *exemplification* is an attempt to elicit guilt by getting others to regard you as a morally respectable individual; *supplication* is an attempt to elicit pity by getting others to believe you are helpless and needy; *self-promotion* is an attempt to elicit respect and confidence by persuading others that you are competent; and *ingratiation* is simply an attempt to get others to like you in order to secure compliance with a subsequent request. These last two, self-promotion and ingratiation, service two of the most common goals of social interaction: to get people to think you are competent and to get people to like you (Leary, 1995) – competence and warmth are the two most basic dimensions on which we evaluate people (Cuddy, Fiske, & Glick, 2008; Fiske, Cuddy, & Glick, 2007).

Ingratiation
Strategic attempt to get someone to like you in order to obtain compliance with a request.

Ingratiation

Ingratiation (Jones, 1964) is a particularly common tactic. A person attempts to influence others by first agreeing with them and getting them to like him or her. Next, various requests are made. You would be using ingratiation if you agreed with other people to appear similar to them or to make them feel good, made yourself look attractive, paid compliments, dropped names of those held in high esteem or physically touched them. However, ingratiation that is transparent can backfire, leading to the 'ingratiator's dilemma': the more obvious it is that an ingratiator will profit by impressing the target person, the less likely it is that the tactic will succeed (see Gordon, 1996, for a meta-analysis).

Invoking the **reciprocity principle** is another tactic, based on the social principle that 'we should treat others the way they treat us'. If we do others a favour, they feel obliged to reciprocate. Regan (1971) showed that greater compliance was obtained from people who had previously received a favour than from those who had received none. Similarly, *guilt arousal* produces more compliance. People who are made to feel guilty are more likely to comply with a later request: for example, to make a phone call to save native trees, to agree to donate blood, or at a university to participate in an experiment (Carlsmith & Gross, 1969; Darlington & Macker, 1966; Freedman, Wallington, & Bless, 1967).

Have you had your car windscreen washed while waiting at traffic lights? If the cleaner washes it before you can refuse, there is subtle pressure on you to pay for the service. In some cities (e.g. in Portugal), people might guide you into parking spaces that one could have easily located, and then ask you for money. These are real-life examples of persuasion to give money that involves activation of the reciprocity principle.

Multiple requests

Another very effective tactic is the use of **multiple requests**. Instead of a single request, a two-step procedure is used, with the first request functioning as a set-up or softener for the second, real request. Three classic variations are the foot-in-the-door, the door-in-the-face and low-balling tactics (see Figure 6.6; for a recent review, see Cialdini & Goldstein, 2004).

The **foot-in-the-door tactic** builds on the assumption that if someone agrees to a small request, they will be more willing to comply with a later large request. Some salespeople use this approach. At first, they might call you to ask just a few questions 'for a small survey that we are doing' and then entice you to join 'the hundreds of others in your area' who subscribe to their product.

In a study by Freedman and Fraser (1966), people were contacted at home and pitched a ludicrously large request of allowing six people to make a thorough inventory of all their

Reciprocity principle
This is sometimes called the reciprocity norm, or 'the law of doing unto others what they do to you'. It can refer to an attempt to gain compliance by first doing someone a favour, or to mutual aggression, or to mutual attraction.

Multiple requests
Tactics for gaining compliance using a two-step procedure: the first request functions as a set-up for the second, real request.

Foot-in-the-door tactic
Multiple-request technique to gain compliance, in which the focal request is preceded by a smaller request that is bound to be accepted.

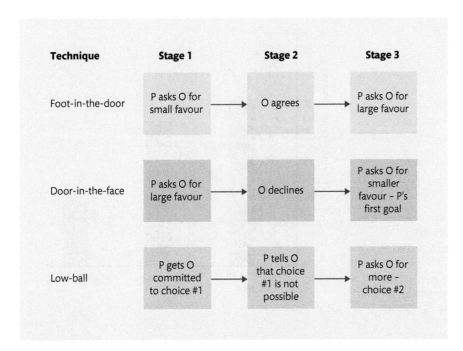

Figure 6.6 Three classic techniques for inducing compliance

household items. Only 22 per cent agreed. However, a subset of people who had previously been contacted to answer a few simple questions about the kind of soap they used at home were much more willing to comply – 53 per cent agreed.

The foot-in-the-door tactic may not always work. If the initial request appears too small or the second too large, the link between the requests breaks down (Foss & Dempsey, 1979; Zuckerman, Lazzaro, & Waldgeir, 1979). Nevertheless, a review by Saks (1978) suggested that if the technique is tuned carefully, people can even be induced to act as donors for organ and tissue transplants.

In a refinement of the tactic, people agreed to a series of graded requests rather than jumping from a small to a large request. They were presented with two preliminary requests, increasingly demanding, prior to an ultimate request (Goldman, Creason, & McCall, 1981; Dolinski, 2000). This has proved more effective than the classic foot-in-the-door technique. Think of this, perhaps, as the two-feet-in-the-door technique! Graded requests occur often when someone asks someone else out on a 'date'. At first, a prospective partner might not agree to go out with you on a date but might well agree to go with you to study in the library. Your next tactic is to request another meeting, and eventually a proper date.

In a Polish field experiment, Dariusz Dolinski (2000) arranged for a young man to ask people in the city of Wroclaw for directions to Zubrzyckiego Street. There is no such street. Most said they did not know, although a few gave precise directions! Further down the street, the same people were then asked by a young woman to look after a huge bag for five minutes while she went up to the fifth floor in an apartment building to see a friend. A control group was asked to look after the bag, but not for the street directions. Compliance with the second, more demanding request was higher in the experimental group (see Figure 6.7; also see **Chapter 14** for discussion of altruism).

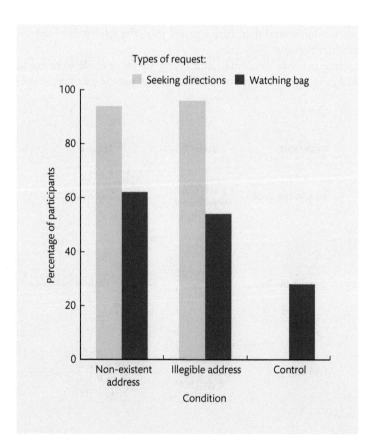

Figure 6.7 The foot-in-the-door technique: Compliance with an impossible request followed by a possible request

Percentage of participants who answered 'I do not know' when asked about a non-existent or illegible address and of those who then complied with the request to keep an eye on the confederate's bag.

Source: Based on data from Dolinski (2000), Experiment 2.

There is good evidence across a variety of studies that the foot-in-the-door technique actually works, but what psychological process could account for it? A likely candidate is provided by Bem's (1967) self-perception theory (DeJong, 1979; see **Chapter 4**). By complying with a small request, people become committed to their behaviour and develop a picture of themselves as 'giving'. The subsequent large request compels them to appear consistent. Dolinski explained his results in the same way. In trying to help a stranger, although unsuccessfully, his participants would have inferred that they were altruistic. They were therefore more susceptible to a later influence – even if that request was more demanding.

Similarly, Cialdini and Trost (1998) explain the effect in terms of the principle of *self-consistency*. We try to manage our self-concept in such a way that if we are charitable on one occasion, then we should be charitable again on the second occasion. Gorassini and Olson (1995), however, are sceptical that something as dramatic as self-conceptual change mediates the effect. Instead, they proposed an explanation with fewer assumptions. The foot-in-the-door tactic alters people's interpretation of situations that activate attitudes enhancing compliance. The self is left out of the loop.

What happens if an attempt to get a foot in the door fails? Common sense suggests that this should reduce the likelihood of future compliance. Surprisingly, the opposite strategy, the **door-in-the-face tactic**, can prove successful (Cialdini, Vincent, Lewis, Catalan, Wheeler, & Darby, 1975; Patch, 1986). Here a person is asked a large favour first and a small request second. Politicians especially are masters of this art. To illustrate, say that the government warns the media that student fees will need to go up 30 per cent. Are you angry? Later, however, it announces officially that the increase will 'only' be 10 per cent – the actual figure planned. You probably feel relieved and think 'that's not so bad', and consequently are more accepting.

Door-in-the-face tactic
Multiple-request technique to gain compliance, in which the focal request is preceded by a larger request that is bound to be refused.

Cialdini and colleagues (1975) tested the effectiveness of this tactic by approaching students with a huge request: 'Would you serve as a voluntary counsellor at a youth offenders' centre two hours a week for the next two years?' Virtually no one agreed. However, when the researchers then made a considerably smaller request, 'Would you chaperone a group of these offenders on a two-hour trip to the zoo?' 50 per cent agreed. When the second request was presented alone, less than 17 per cent complied. For the tactic to be effective, the researchers noted that the final request should come from the same person who made the initial request. According to them, participants perceive the scaled-down request as a concession by the influencer, and consequently they feel pressure to reciprocate. If some other person were to make the second request, reciprocation would not be necessary.

According to Cialdini, the door-in-the-face technique may well capitalise on a contrast effect: just as lukewarm water feels cool when you have just had your hand in hot water, a second request seems more reasonable and acceptable when it is contrasted with a larger request. This procedure is prevalent in sales settings. Suppose you tell an estate agent that you would like to spend quite a lot of hard-earned money on a small flat and she shows you a few run-down and overpriced examples. Then the higher-priced flats (the ones she really wants to show you!) look like extremely good bargains. In doing this, the estate agent has used the door-in-the-face tactic.

The other multiple-request technique used in similar situations is the **low-ball tactic** (check the first 'What do *you* think?' question) (see Box 6.4). Here the influencer changes the rules halfway and manages to get away with it. Its effectiveness depends on inducing the customer to agree to a request before revealing certain hidden costs. It is based on the principle that once people are committed to an action, they are more likely to accept a slight increase in the cost of that action. This tendency for people to stick with decisions is also captured in the notion of *sunk costs* (Fox & Hoffman, 2002), where once a course of action is decided on, people will continue to invest in it even if the costs increase dramatically.

Low-ball tactic
Technique for inducing compliance in which a person who agrees to a request still feels committed after finding that there are hidden costs.

Low-ball
After consulting with his boss a salesman tells a keen buyer that the quoted price for a new car no longer includes certain attractive 'extras'.

Box 6.4 Your life
Buying an airline ticket – low-balling raised to an art form

Think of the last time you bought an airline ticket. We are all very familiar with low-balling – airlines have raised this to an art form. You go to an airline web site and discover to your delight that they have a really cheap and convenient flight to your holiday destination. So you start the tedious online process of booking. Near the end of the long process where you are doing the payment piece, you discover there is an extra charge for baggage, an extra charge for food and drink, an extra charge for entertainment, an extra charge to reserve a seat to avoid the stampede at the gate and so forth. This is a classic example of low-balling. Another everyday example is when someone asks, 'Could you do me a favour?' and you agree before actually knowing what will be expected of you.

Just how effective low-balling can be was demonstrated by Cialdini, Cacioppo, Bassett and Miller (1978). They asked half their participants to be in an experiment that began at 7 a.m. The other half were asked first to commit to participating in an experiment and then were informed that it would start at 7 a.m. The latter group had been low-balled and complied more often (56 per cent) than the control group (31 per cent) and also tended to keep their appointments.

Studies of compliance show when and how compliance occurs. Sometimes our decision to comply may be rational: we weigh the pros and cons of our action. However, we often act before we think. According to Langer, Blank and Chanowitz (1978), much compliance is due to **mindlessness**: we agree without giving it a thought. Langer and her colleagues conducted experiments in which people were asked to comply with requests with little or no justification. In one, a person about to use a photocopier was interrupted by an experimenter, who requested priority use for: (1) no reason, (2) a non-informative reason ('I have to make copies') or (3) a justified reason ('I'm in a rush'). They found that as long as the request was small, people were likely to agree, even for a spurious reason. There was lower compliance when there was no reason.

Mindlessness
The act of agreeing to a request without giving it a thought. A small request is likely to be agreed to, even if a spurious reason is provided.

Action research

At about the time that Hovland and his associates were studying attitude change in the US Army, the expatriate German psychologist Kurt Lewin was undertaking another piece of practical wartime research on the home front for a civilian government agency. With the aim of conserving supplies at a time of food shortages and rationing, he tried to convince American housewives to feed their families unusual but highly nutritious foods, such as beef hearts and kidneys, rather than steak or roast beef.

Lewin believed that attitude change could best be achieved if people were actively engaged in the change process rather than just being passive targets of persuasion. He referred to this involvement of the participants in the actual research process, and its outcome, as **action research**. Lewin demonstrated that an active discussion among 'housewives' about how best to present beef hearts and other similar foods to their families was much more effective than merely giving them a persuasive lecture presentation. Thirty-two per cent of the women in the discussion group went on to serve the new food, compared with only 3 per cent in the lecture group (Lewin, 1943).

The emphasis on action by participants fitted in with parts of the attitude change programme of Hovland and his associates. For instance, Janis and King (1954) investigated the effects of role-playing by their participants. They found that those who gave a speech arguing against something that they believed in (i.e. acted out a role) experienced greater attitude change than when they listened passively to a speech arguing against their position.

This early study of counter-attitudinal behaviour foreshadowed the subsequent development by Festinger, who was one of Lewin's students, of cognitive dissonance theory (discussed in the next section). A key premise of cognitive dissonance is that people actively organise their cognitions and will change them to make them consistent with what they are feeling or with how they are acting (Festinger, 1980).

More recently, action research has played a role, although not as great a role as some would hope (Klein, Shepperd, Suls, Rothman, & Croyle, 2015), in addressing community

Action research
The simultaneous activities of undertaking social science research, involving participants in the process and addressing a social problem.

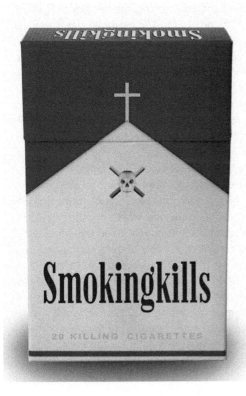

Action research
Involving a participant in the research process can be effective. Would a smoker buy this brand? And smoke what is inside?

health issues relating to smoking, sun exposure and risky sexual practices. For example, prompted by the fact that Australia has the highest incidence of melanoma in the world, Hill and his colleagues (Hill, White, Marks, & Borland, 1993) conducted a three-year study on changing attitudes and behaviour related to sun exposure, called the SunSmart health promotion programme. This campaign was called SLIP! SLOP! SLAP! ('slip on a shirt, slop on some sunscreen, slap on a hat'), and was conducted via an array of media over three successive summers throughout the state of Victoria in southern Australia. Hill and associates found a significant change among 4,500 participants in sun-related behaviour over this period. There was:

- a drop in those reporting sunburn – 11 to 7 per cent;
- an increase in hat wearing – 19 to 29 per cent;
- an increase in sunscreen use – 12 to 21 per cent;
- an increase in body area covered by clothing – 67 to 71 per cent.

These changes in behaviour were associated with attitude change. Agreement declined with items such as 'A suntanned person is more healthy' and 'There is little chance I'll get skin cancer'. Action research methods have also been used to reduce smoking (see Box 6.5) and to promote healthy sexual behaviour. A study conducted in France with 1,400 patients living with HIV or AIDS found that respondents reported that information provided in the mass media helped them to manage their sexual life by using condoms and avoiding secondary infection (Peretti-Watel, Obadia, Dray-Spira, Lert, & Moatti, 2005).

Box 6.5 Our world
Quit smoking: Anti-smoking campaigns

Anti-smoking campaigns have had some success in changing a habit that is very resistant to change

Smoking has become deeply unfashionable in most Western countries over the past thirty years or so, yet its incidence remains disappointingly high (approximately one in five British adults still smoke, 20 per cent). But compare this with a whopping two out of three East and South East Asian males (66 per cent) and rising, with more than 285 million of China's 1.4 billion people smoking every single day. Even legislation against smoking in shared public spaces (e.g., work, restaurants, pubs, public transport) has had limited success when measured by a decline in the percentage of people who still smoke. In these countries, the highest rates of smoking tend to be found among people in the 20–29 age group, teenage women and working-class ('lower blue-collar') groups.

Smokers are usually well informed about illnesses related to smoking, such as lung cancer, emphysema and heart disease. Despite this knowledge, current smokers tend to underestimate the risk of dying from smoking when compared with former smokers and those who have never smoked. This bias in risk perception has also been reported for those who engage in risky sexual practices.

Anti-smoking campaigns have used a wide variety of media and techniques to discourage smoking (Hill, White, Marks, & Borland, 1993). For example, one campaign adopted a television commercial and poster, while another used a direct-mail approach, along with radio advertisements. Various celebrities have helped by performing at places of work and by recording verbal messages. A classic, two-sided argument technique has been tried by providing counter-arguments for several commonly held self-exempting beliefs: that is, notions applied to exonerate oneself from the habit.

Target groups have varied. One campaign aimed to reach women, who outnumber men in the under-18 smokers' group, stressing the benefits of not smoking with respect to health, beauty and fitness. Another used baby stickers. Another campaign highlighted the benefits of a smoke-free workplace in major clothing chain stores, supplemented by radio and television advertisements. Nowadays, there is a socially supportive context to quit, and the recognition that passive smoking is dangerous may help some in the future to quit permanently.

How can quitting be connected to the smoker's *intention to quit*? Giving up the habit can be traced through several stages. According to Biener and Abrams (1991), the 'contemplation ladder' suggests that a person moves from thought to action thus:

1   I'm taking action to quit – for example, cutting down (top of ladder).
2   I'm starting to think about how to change my smoking patterns.
3   I think I should quit, but I'm not quite ready.

4   I think I should consider quitting some day.
5   I have no thought of quitting (bottom of ladder).

Clearly, quitting is not an overnight decision. The journey from having an unfavourable attitude towards smoking, to intending to quit, to actually quitting is impacted by all the moderators described by research on the attitude-behaviour relationship (for example, the theories of planned behaviour and reasoned action – see **Chapter 5**).

Cognitive dissonance and attitude change

People can change their minds and, as you know, they do. A compelling account of how this happens is provided by cognitive dissonance theory. Its core premise is that cognitive dissonance is an unpleasant state of psychological tension generated when a person has two or more cognitions (bits of information) that are inconsistent or do not fit together. Cognitions are thoughts, attitudes, beliefs or states of awareness of behaviour. For example, if someone believes that monogamy is an important feature of their marriage and yet is having an extra-marital affair, they may experience guilt and discomfort (dissonance). One of a family of **cognitive consistency theories** (Gawronski & Strack, 2012), it was developed by Leon Festinger (1957) and became the most studied topic in social psychology during the 1960s (see Cooper, 2007).

Festinger proposed that we seek harmony in our attitudes, beliefs and behaviour and try to reduce tension from inconsistency between these elements. People will try to reduce dissonance by changing one or more of the inconsistent cognitions (e.g. in the case of the person having an extramarital affair, 'What's wrong with a little fun if no one finds out?'), by looking for additional evidence to bolster one side or the other ('My partner doesn't understand me'), or by derogating the source of one of the cognitions ('Fidelity is a construct of religious indoctrination'). The maxim appears to be: *The greater the dissonance, the stronger the attempts to reduce it.* Experiencing dissonance leads people to feel physiologically 'on edge' – as evidenced by changes in the electrical conductivity of the skin that can be detected by a polygraph.

For dissonance to lead to attitude change, two sets of attitudes need to be in conflict (see Box 6.6). Because dissonance is unpleasant, people tend to avoid exposure to ideas that produce it. According to the **selective exposure hypothesis**, people are remarkably choosy when potentially dissonant information is on the horizon. Exceptions are when their attitude is either: (1) very strong, and they can integrate or argue against contrary information, or (2) very weak, and it seems better to discover the truth now and then make appropriate attitudinal and behavioural changes (Frey, 1986; Frey & Rosch, 1984).

For example, Frey and Rosch (1984) gave participants written profiles on the basis of which they had to form an attitude about whether to terminate or continue the employment of a 'manager'. Half the participants were told that their attitude was reversible (they could change their mind later on) and half that their attitude was irreversible. Then they selected as many bits of additional information as they wished from a pool containing five items of consonant information (in support of their attitude) and five items of dissonant information (in opposition to their attitude). Participants chose more consonant than dissonant information, and the effect was greatly magnified in the irreversible condition (see Figure 6.8).

Cognitive consistency theories
A group of attitude theories stressing that people try to maintain internal consistency, order and agreement among their various cognitions.

Selective exposure hypothesis
People tend to avoid potentially dissonant information.

Box 6.6 Our world
The impact of student exchange on national stereotypes

Student exchanges provide a wonderful opportunity for sojourners to confront their stereotypic attitudes about other nations with new information gleaned from personal experience in a foreign country. From a cognitive dissonance perspective, one would expect (or hope) that pleasant personal experiences would conflict with ingrained negative attitudes towards a foreign nation, and would arouse cognitive dissonance, which, under the circumstances, could only be resolved by changing the initial attitude.

This idea is illustrated in a study by Stroebe, Lenkert and Jonas (1988) of American students on one-year exchanges in Germany and France. They found that in the case of sojourners in Germany, reality matched existing attitudes, and consequently there was no dissonance and no attitude change. Sojourners in France, however, found that realities were less pleasant than pre-existing attitudes led them to believe. There was dissonance, and consequently they departed from France with changed attitudes – unfortunately, changed for the worse. These findings are consistent with other research on sojourners' attitudes (e.g. Klineberg & Hull, 1979), and they foreshadow the complexity of the impact of direct contact with an outgroup on people's stereotypes (see **Chapter 11**).

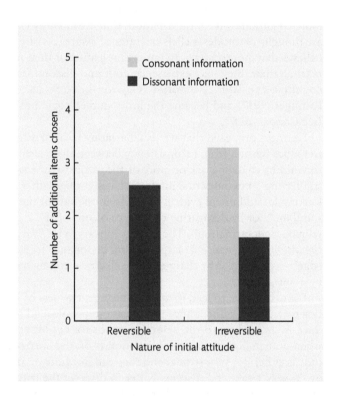

Figure 6.8 Selection of consonant and dissonant information as a function of attitude irreversibility

Source: Based on data from Frey and Rosch (1984).

A virtue of cognitive dissonance theory is that it is stated in a broad and general way. It is applicable in many situations, particularly ones involving attitude or behaviour change. For instance, it has been used to understand:

- people's feelings of regret and changes of attitude after making a decision;
- their patterns of exposing themselves to and searching for new information;
- reasons why people seek social support for their beliefs;
- attitude change in situations where lack of support from fellow ingroup members acted as a dissonant cognition;

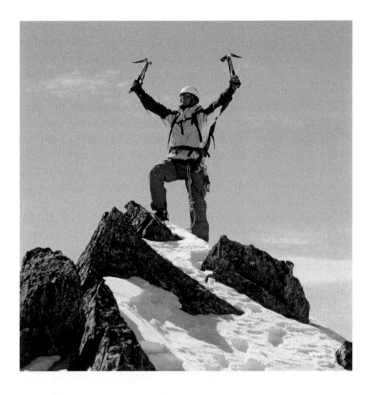

Effort justification
Was the monstrous effort to reach the summit of Kala Pattar worth it? This trekker's celebration provides the answer. Everest may have to wait.

- attitude change in situations where a person has said or done something contrary to their customary beliefs or practice; and
- attitude change to rationalise hypocritical behaviour (Stone & Fernandez, 2008; Stone, Wiegand, Cooper, & Aronson, 1997).

A particularly appealing feature of dissonance theory is that it can generate non-obvious predictions about how people make choices when faced with conflicting attitudes and behaviours (Insko, 1967). Dissonance research adopts one of three different research paradigms (Worchel, Cooper, & Goethals, 1988): effort justification, induced compliance and free choice. Let us see how these differ.

Effort justification

Now here is a surprise. The moment you choose between alternatives, you invite a state of dissonance. Suppose you need some takeaway food tonight. You make the momentous decision to get Indian food rather than Chinese food. You keep mulling over the alternatives even after making your choice. Tonight's the night for a curry – you can taste it in your mouth already! The curry will be evaluated more favourably, or perhaps Chinese food becomes less attractive, or maybe both – and tomorrow is another day. The way the **effort justification** paradigm works is shown in Figure 6.9.

Effort justification
A special case of cognitive dissonance: inconsistency is experienced when a person makes a considerable effort to achieve a modest goal.

Figure 6.9 The general model of the effort justification paradigm

An early classic study of effort justification had female students volunteer to take part in a group discussion about sex (Aronson & Mills, 1959). They were told that before they could join a group, they must first pass a screening test for their capacity to speak frankly. Those who agreed were assigned to one of two conditions. In the severe condition, they were given a list of obscene words and explicit sexual descriptions to read aloud; in the mild condition, they were to read words that included some such as 'petting' and 'prostitution'. After being initiated, they listened over headphones to a group discussion with a view to joining in during the following week. What they heard was tame – far short of embarrassing. The discussion was in fact a recording where the participants had been primed to mumble incoherently and be plain boring. As well as the severe and mild initiation conditions, there was a control condition where the participants did not undergo the screening experience.

The hypothesis was that the severe condition would cause some distress to the participants. Yet they *had* volunteered to participate, and the act of volunteering for embarrassment should cause dissonance. The outcome would be increased liking for the chosen option (to participate in the discussion group), because the choice had entailed suffering. To make this sequence consonant, participants would need to rate the group discussion as more interesting than it really was. The hypothesis was confirmed. Those who went through the severe initiation thought that both the group discussion and the other group members were much more interesting than did those in the mild or control conditions (see Figure 6.10).

Later studies have shown that effort justification is a useful device to induce behavioural changes relating to phobias and alcohol abuse. For example, Cooper and Axsom (1982) studied women participants who felt they needed help to lose weight and were willing to try a 'new experimental procedure'. They were required to come to a laboratory, where they were weighed and the procedure was explained to them.

In a high-effort condition, the women participated in a variety of time-consuming and effortful tasks, including reading tongue-twisters aloud for a session lasting forty minutes. These tasks required psychological effort rather than physical exercise. When the effort was low, the tasks were shorter and easier. In a control condition, the volunteers did not participate in any tasks at all but were simply weighed and asked to report again at a later date. The high-effort and low-effort groups came to the laboratory for five sessions over a period of three weeks, at which point they were weighed again. The results are shown in Figure 6.11.

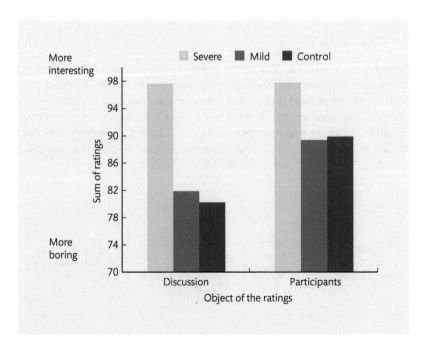

Figure 6.10 Interest in a group discussion as a function of the severity of the initiation procedure

Some degree of 'suffering' makes a voluntary activity seem more attractive.

Source: Based on data from Aronson and Mills (1959).

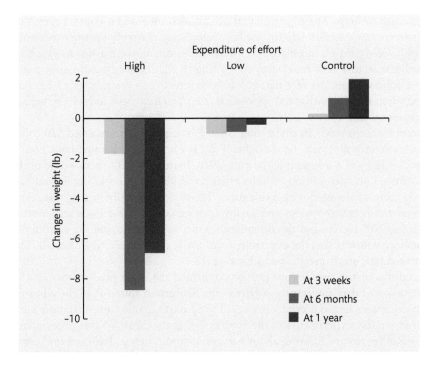

Figure 6.11 Change in weight among overweight women after expending psychological effort

You may think that physical effort should reduce weight. This study suggests that mental effort is an important ingredient in a programme's effectiveness.

Source: Based on data from Cooper and Axsom (1982).

Cooper and Axsom were encouraged to find that the weight loss in the high-effort group was not just an artefact of the interest shown in the women during the time of the five-week study. The participants were contacted again after six months and after one year and agreed to be weighed again. The weight loss was much more marked after time had elapsed. After six months, a remarkable 94 per cent of the high-effort group had lost some weight, while only 39 per cent of the low-effort group had managed to do so.

Induced compliance

Sometimes people are induced to act in a way that is inconsistent with their attitudes. An important feature of the **induced compliance** paradigm is that the inducement should not be so strong that people feel they have been forced against their will. Festinger and Carlsmith (1959) carried out an often-cited experiment in which students who had volunteered to participate in a psychology experiment were asked to perform an extremely boring task for an hour, believing that they were contributing to research on 'measures of performance'.

Imagine that you are the volunteer and that in front of you is a board, on which there are several rows of square pegs, each peg sitting in a square hole. You are asked to turn each peg a quarter of a turn to the left and then a quarter of a turn back to the right. When you have finished turning all the pegs, you are told to start all over again, repeating the sequence over and over for twenty minutes. (This was not designed to be fun!) When the twenty minutes are up, the experimenter tells you that you have finished the first part, and you can now start on the second part, this time taking spools of thread off another peg board and placing them all back on again, and again, and again. Finally, the mind-numbing jobs are over.

At this point, the experimenter lets you in on a secret: you were a control participant, but you can now be of 'real' help. It seems that a confederate of the experimenter has failed to show up. Could you fill in? All you have to do is tell the next person that the tasks are really interesting. The experimenter explains that he was investigating the effects of preconceptions on people's work on a task. Later, the experimenter offers a monetary incentive if you would be willing to be on call to help again at some time in the future. Luckily, you are never called.

In the Festinger and Carlsmith study, participants in one condition were paid the princely sum of $1 for agreeing to cooperate in this way, while others in a second condition were

Induced compliance
A special case of cognitive dissonance: inconsistency is experienced when a person is persuaded to behave in a way that is contrary to an attitude.

paid $20 for agreeing to help. The experimental design also included a control group of participants who were not asked to tell anyone how interesting the truly boring experience had been, and they were paid no incentive. On a later occasion, all were asked to rate how interesting or otherwise this task had been. According to the induced compliance paradigm, dissonance follows from the fact that you have agreed to say things about what you have experienced when you know that the opposite is true. You have been induced to behave in a *counter-attitudinal* way.

The variation in incentive adds an interesting twist. Participants who received $20 could explain their lie to themselves with the thought, 'I did it for the $20. It must have been a lousy task, indeed' – $20 was a tidy sum in the mid-1950s. In other words, there would probably be no dissonance in this condition. On the other hand, those who told the lie and had been paid only $1 were confronted with a dilemma: 'I have done a really boring task, then told someone else that it is interesting, and finally even agreed to come back and do this again – for a measly $1!' Herein lies the dissonance. One way of reducing the continuing arousal is to convince yourself that the experiment was really quite interesting after all. The results of this now-classic study are shown in Figure 6.12.

The interest ratings of the two reward groups confirmed the main predictions. The $1 group rated the task as fairly interesting, whereas the $20 group found it slightly boring (while control participants found it even more so). The $1 participants were also more willing to take part in similar experiments in the future. The main thrust of this experiment, which is to use a smaller reward to bring about a larger attitude change, has been replicated several times. To modify an old saying: 'If you are going to lead a donkey on, use a carrot, but make it a small one if you want the donkey to enjoy the trip.'

Talking of carrots brings us to consider eating fried grasshoppers. An intriguing experiment carried out in a military setting by Zimbardo and his colleagues (Zimbardo, Weisenberg, Firestone, & Levy, 1965) tackled this culinary question. The participants were asked to comply with the aversive request to eat grasshoppers by an authority figure whose interpersonal style was either positive (warm) or negative (cold). According to the induced compliance variant of cognitive dissonance, **post-decisional conflict** (and consequent attitude change) should be greater when the communicator is negative – how else could one justify voluntarily behaving in a counter-attitudinal way? Read what happened in this study in Box 6.7, and check the results in Figure 6.13.

Post-decisional conflict
The dissonance associated with behaving in a counter-attitudinal way. Dissonance can be reduced by bringing the attitude into line with the behaviour.

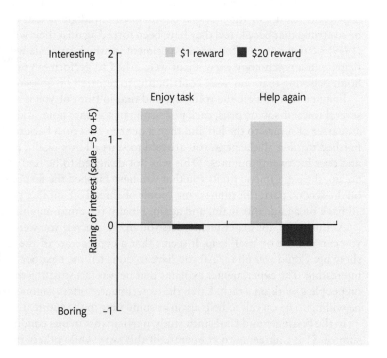

Figure 6.12 The effect of incentives on evaluating a boring task in an induced-compliance context
One of social psychology's counter-intuitive findings: Commitment to return to repeat a boring task is maximised, as is dissonance, by offering a minimal reward.

Source: Based on data from Festinger and Carlsmith (1959).

Box 6.7 Research classic
To know grasshoppers is to love them

Attitude change following induced compliance

Consider the second 'What do *you* think?' question at the beginning of the chapter. This scenario, involving young military cadets, was actually researched by Phil Zimbardo and his colleagues (Zimbardo, Ebbesen, & Maslach, 1977). They had an officer in command suggest to the cadets that they might eat a few fried grasshoppers, and mild social pressure was put on them to comply. A questionnaire about food habits administered earlier had revealed that all the cadets thought there were limits to what they should be expected to eat, and that a meal of fried grasshoppers was one such limit. However, the officer gave them a talk about modern soldiers in combat conditions being mobile and, among other things, being ready literally to eat off the land. After his talk, the cadets were each given a plate with five fried grasshoppers and invited to try them out.

A critical feature of the experiment was how the request was made. For half the cadets the officer was cheerful, informal and permissive. For the other half, he was cool, official and stiff. There was also a control group who gave two sets of food ratings but were never induced, or given the chance to eat grasshoppers. The social pressure on the experimental participants had to be subtle enough for them to feel they had freely chosen whether or not to eat the grasshoppers. An order to eat would not arouse dissonance, because a cadet could then justify his compliance by saying 'He made me do it'. Furthermore, the cadets who listened to the positive officer might justify complying by thinking 'I did it as a favour for this nice guy'. However, those who might eat the grasshoppers for the negative officer could not justify their behaviour in this way. The resulting experience should be dissonance, and the easy way of reducing this would be to change their feelings about grasshoppers as a source of food.

As it turned out, about 50 per cent of the cadets actually ate some grasshoppers. Those who complied ate, on average, two of the five hoppers sitting on their plate. The results in Figure 6.13 show the percentage of participants who changed their ratings of liking or disliking grasshoppers as food. Note that in both the negative and positive officer conditions, eaters were more favourable and non-eaters less favourable, suggesting that a degree of self-justification was required to account for an act that was voluntary but aversive. However, the most interesting result concerned the negative officer condition. This is the case in which dissonance should be maximal and, in line with the theory, it was here that the biggest change towards liking the little beasties was recorded.

Source: Based on Zimbardo, Ebbesen and Maslach (1977); Zimbardo, Weisenberg, Firestone and Levy (1965).

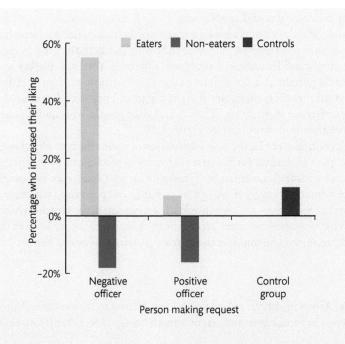

Figure 6.13 Military cadets' liking for fried grasshoppers as food, as a function of the interpersonal style of an officer

As with Figure 6.12, here is another counter-intuitive outcome: Complying with an unpleasant request can seem more attractive when the person making the request is less attractive (see also Box 6.7).

Source: Based on data from Zimbardo, Weisenberg, Firestone and Levy (1965).

Induced compliance
Eating insects in a military training exercise in a Thai jungle may be more frequent and lots of fun these days. Would you like to join in?

Inducing people to act in opposition to their attitudes is not easy and often requires a subtle approach. Counter-attitudinal actions with foreseeable negative consequences, such as being quoted in the media saying that smoking is not harmful, requires an intricate inducement; whereas actions with less serious or negative consequences, such as voting anonymously that smoking is harmless, may be less difficult to bring about. However, once people have been induced to act counter-attitudinally, the theory predicts that dissonance will be strong and that they will seek to justify their action (Riess, Kalle, & Tedeschi, 1981).

Free choice

Suppose that your choices between alternative courses of action are fairly evenly balanced, and that you are committed to make a decision. This applies to many everyday situations: whether to buy this product or that; go to this tourist spot or another for a holiday; take this job offer or some other one. Based on Festinger's (1964) blueprint of the process of conflict in decision-making, the pre-decision period is marked by uncertainty and dissonance, and the post-decision period by relative calm and confidence.

Dissonance reduction after free choice may also be a feature of betting. Once a person has made a choice between decision alternatives, dissonance theory predicts that the person making a bet will become more confident about a successful outcome. Younger, Walker and Arrowood (1977) interviewed people at a Canadian national exposition who were either about to bet or had just placed their bets on games such as bingo and wheel of fortune, and asked them to rate their confidence in winning. They found that people who had already made their bet were more confident of winning (see Figure 6.14).

However, dissonance reduction may not be the only explanation of these effects of free choice. Other research contrasts people's preference for intuitive over rational predictions of outcomes, using the **representativeness heuristic** (Kahneman & Tversky, 1973; see **Chapter 2**). For example, we are less confident of winning a lottery if we opt to exchange our purchased ticket for a new ticket. Intuitively, it does not feel right – the cognitive load of assessing the competing choice probabilities is excessive. Why, we sometimes even 'refrain from changing checkout lines at the grocery store or from switching answers on multiple choice tests' (Risen & Gilovich, 2007, p. 21)!

Representativeness heuristic
A cognitive short-cut in which instances are assigned to categories or types on the basis of overall similarity or resemblance to the category.

The role of self

According to Aronson (e.g. Aronson, 1999), *self-consistency* is central to dissonance. People strive for a view of themselves as moral and competent human beings (Merritt, Effron, Fein,

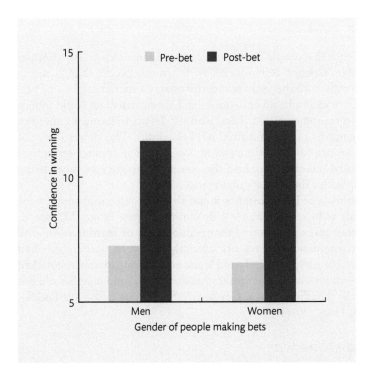

Figure 6.14 Degree of confidence in winning before and after making a bet

Making a commitment reduces dissonance. When we make a bet, we 'had better believe' we have just increased our chances of winning!

Source: Based on data from Younger, Walker and Arrowood (1977).

Savitsky, Tuller, & Monin, 2012). Counter-attitudinal behaviour is inconsistent with this view, and is therefore distressing and motivates change, particularly among people who think relatively highly of themselves (i.e. they have higher self-esteem).

This idea that self-consistency is crucial for dissonance is taken up in a slightly different guise by **self-affirmation theory** (Steele, 1988; Steele, Spencer, & Lynch, 1993; also see Sherman & Cohen, 2006). If your self-concept is evaluatively challenged in one domain, then you can rectify the problem by publicly making positive statements about yourself in another domain. For example, if your competence as a scholar is challenged, you might emphasise (affirm) that you are a wonderful cook and a great athlete. From a dissonance perspective, negative behaviours are particularly threatening to one's sense of self. People who have high self-esteem can respond via self-affirmation – they experience no dissonance. However, people who have low self-esteem and are therefore less able to self-affirm do experience dissonance. Here, there is a conflict: Aronson (self-consistency) predicts greater dissonance under high self-esteem, whereas Steele (self-affirmation) predicts greater dissonance under low self-esteem (see Tesser, 2000).

Stone (2003) has suggested that these contradictions involving self-esteem can be accounted for by recasting an explanation in terms of *self-standards*. When we evaluate our actions to judge if they are good or sensible rather than bad or foolish, we use personal (individualised) standards or normative (group, or cultural) standards as yardsticks. The standards operating at a given time are those that are readily or chronically accessible in memory. If we believe we have acted foolishly, dissonance will probably occur; but self-esteem will not enter the equation unless a personal standard has been brought to mind.

Overall, dissonance research involving the self, self-concept and self-esteem remains fluid, although this much seems agreed:

> contemporary views of the self in dissonance have at least one common bond – they all make important assumptions about how people assess the meaning and significance of their behavior.
>
> Stone and Cooper (2001, p. 241)

Self-affirmation theory
The theory that people reduce the impact of threat to their self-concept by focusing on and affirming their competence in some other area.

Vicarious dissonance

There is some intriguing evidence that people can experience dissonance vicariously (Cooper & Hogg, 2007; Norton, Monin, Cooper, & Hogg, 2003). When two people share a strong bond, such as identifying strongly with the same group, dissonance experienced by one person may be felt by the other. For example, an anti-smoking TV advertisement could induce dissonance in viewers who witness someone 'like them' who also knows smoking is unhealthy smoking a cigarette (i.e. engaging in counter-attitudinal behaviour). The viewer does not actually have to behave counter-attitudinally. If the viewer does engage in counter-attitudinal behaviour, there may be a rebound effect because the common category member being observed provides social support for the viewer's dissonance.

Research by Blake McKimmie and his colleagues found that ingroup social support for counter-attitudinal behaviour reduces dissonance (McKimmie, Terry, Hogg, Manstead, Spears, & Doosje, 2003). Other researchers found that endorsement of ingroup normative attitudes to do with pro-environmental behaviours strengthened when participants had observed an ingroup member acting hypocritically and when an outgroup member remarked negatively on the hypocrisy – endorsement was weakest when an outgroup member did not appear to notice the hypocrisy (Gaffney, Hogg, Cooper, & Stone, 2012; also see Focella, Stone, Fernandez, Cooper, & Hogg, 2016).

Alternative views to dissonance

Cognitive dissonance theory has had a chequered history in social psychology (see Visser & Cooper, 2003). Festinger's original ideas have been refined. Dissonance was not as easy to create as Festinger originally believed, and in some cases other theories (e.g. self-perception theory, discussed next) may provide a better explanation of attitude change than cognitive dissonance. Despite this, cognitive dissonance theory remains one of the most widely accepted explanations of attitude change and much other social behaviour. It has generated well over 1,000 empirical studies and will probably continue to be an integral part of social psychological theory for many years (Beauvois & Joule, 1996; Cooper, 2007; Cooper & Croyle, 1984; Joule & Beauvois, 1998).

Self-perception theory

Self-perception theory
Bem's idea that we gain knowledge of ourselves only by making self-attributions: for example, we infer our own attitudes from our own behaviour.

Some have suggested that attitude change does not come about through the processes proposed by dissonance theory and that some of the results of dissonance experiments can be explained by **self-perception theory** (Bem, 1972; see **Chapter 4**). Research comparing the two theories suggests that both help in understanding attitude and behaviour change, but dissonance and self-perception processes operate in different domains (Fazio, Zanna, & Cooper, 1977).

To understand the domain of applicability of each theory, imagine that there are latitudes of attitude acceptance and rejection around your attitudes (Sherif & Sherif, 1967). If you are in favour of keeping the drinking age at 18, you might also agree to 17 or 19. There is a latitude of acceptance around your position. Alternatively, there is also a latitude of rejection: you might definitely oppose a legal drinking age of either 15 or 21. Mostly we act within our own latitudes of acceptance. Sometimes we may go outside them: for instance, when we pay twice the amount for a dinner at a restaurant than we planned. If you feel you chose freely, you will experience dissonance.

When your actions fall within your range of acceptance, self-perception theory best accounts for your response. So, if you had been willing to pay up to 25 per cent more than your original budget, there is no real conflict: 'I suppose I was willing to pay that little bit more.' However, when you find yourself acting outside your previous range of acceptance, dissonance theory gives a better account of your response. We reduce our dissonance only by changing our attitude: 'I paid twice what I had budgeted, but that's okay because I thought the food was fantastic' (Fazio, Zanna, & Cooper, 1977). Thus, attitudes may be changed either through a self-attributional process such as self-perception or through attempts to reduce the feeling of cognitive dissonance.

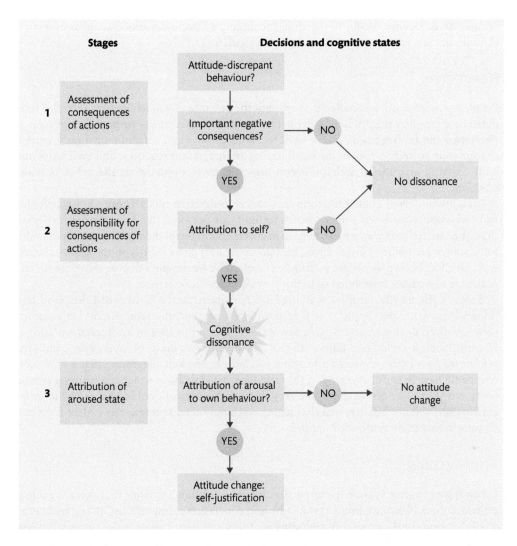

Figure 6.15 A revised cognitive dissonance model of attitude-discrepant behaviour

Source: Based on Cooper and Fazio (1984).

A new look at cognitive dissonance

Joel Cooper and Russell Fazio (1984), in their *new look* model, countered some of the objections to cognitive dissonance theory. One controversy was how to retain and defend the concept of attitude when a person's observed behaviour and beliefs are in contradiction. According to Cooper and Fazio, when behaviour is counter-attitudinal, we try to figure out what the consequences might be. If these are thought to be negative and fairly serious, we must then check to see if our action was voluntary. If it was, we then accept responsibility, experience arousal from the state of dissonance that follows and bring the relevant attitude into line, so reducing dissonance. This revision, shown in Figure 6.15, also includes attributional processes, in terms both of whether we acted according to our free will and of whether external influences were more or less important.

The new look model is supported by considerable evidence (Cooper, 1999), but so is the traditional cognitive dissonance theory that focuses on inconsistency rather than behavioural consequences (e.g. Harmon-Jones, 2000).

Resistance to persuasion

Our discussion so far has mainly focused on factors that change our attitudes, very often unconsciously. Yet, far more attempts at persuasion fail than ever succeed. When we feel strongly about an issue, we can be very stubborn in resisting attempts to change our position

(Zuwerink & Devine, 1996). Research has focused on three main processes of resistance to attitude change: reactance, forewarning and inoculation.

Reactance

Reactance
Brehm's theory that people try to protect their freedom to act. When they perceive that this freedom has been curtailed, they will act to regain it.

People are more easily persuaded if they think the message is not deliberately intended to be persuasive (see Box 6.1). Where a deliberate persuasion attempt is suspected, a process of **reactance** can be triggered. Think back to an occasion when someone obviously tried to change your attitudes. You might recall having an unpleasant reaction, and even hardening your existing attitude – perhaps becoming even more opposed to the other person's position.

Jack Brehm (1966) coined the term 'reactance' to describe this process – a psychological state we experience when someone tries to limit our personal freedom. Research suggests that when we feel this way, we can engage in covert counter-argument and attempts to undermine source credibility (Silvia, 2006), and go on to shift more overtly in the opposite direction, an effect known as *negative attitude change*. The treatment a doctor recommends to a patient is sometimes responded to in this way (Rhodewalt & Strube, 1985).

Some of you may be familiar with the biblical story set in the Garden of Eden. God said, 'I forbid you to eat that apple'. Eve (egged on by the serpent) thought, 'Right! Let's see how it tastes.' Brad Bushman and Angela Stack (1996) tested this idea in an interesting study of warning labels for television films with violent content. Two kinds of labels were compared: (a) *tainted fruit* labels, in which a warning is relatively low-key, suggesting that a film's content could have harmful effects; and (b) *forbidden fruit* labels, in which the warning is more overt and seems like censorship – the very thing that a network could be anxious to avoid. Perhaps you will not be surprised that strong warnings increase interest in violent films, and viewers in this study responded in kind.

Forewarning

Forewarning
Advance knowledge that one is to be the target of a persuasion attempt. Forewarning often produces resistance to persuasion.

Forewarning is prior knowledge of persuasive intent – telling someone that you are going to influence them. When we know this in advance, persuasion is less effective (Cialdini & Petty, 1979; Johnson, 1994), especially regarding attitudes and issues we consider important (Petty & Cacioppo, 1979). When people are forewarned, they have time to rehearse counter-arguments that can be used as a defence. From this point of view, forewarning can be thought of as a special case of inoculation. A meta-analysis of research on forewarning by Wood and Quinn (2003) concluded that forewarning produces resistance (a boomerang effect) among people who are highly involved in the issue, but slight agreement with the persuasive message among those who are less involved.

Inoculation

Inoculation
A way of making people resistant to persuasion. By providing them with a diluted counter-argument, they can build up effective refutations to a later, stronger argument.

> The Chinese Communists have developed a peculiar brand of soul surgery which they practice with impressive skill – the process of 'thought reform'. They first demonstrated this to the American public during the Korean conflict . . . And more recently we have seen . . . Western civilians released from Chinese prisons, repeating their false confessions, insisting upon their guilt, praising the 'justice' and 'leniency' which they have received, and expounding the 'truth' and 'righteousness' of all Communist doctrine.
>
> R. J. Lifton (1956); cited in Bernard, Maio and Olson (2003, p. 63)

As the term suggests, **inoculation** is a form of protection. In biology, we can inject a patient with a weakened or inert form of disease-producing germs to build resistance to a more powerful form. In social psychology, we might seek an analogous method to provide a defence against persuasive ideas (McGuire, 1964). The technique of inoculation, described as 'the grandparent theory of resistance to attitude change' (Eagly & Chaiken, 1993, p. 561), is initiated by exposing a person to a weakened counter-attitudinal argument.

Bill McGuire and his associates (e.g. McGuire & Papageorgis, 1961; Anderson & McGuire, 1965) became interested in the technique following reports of 'brainwashing' of American soldiers imprisoned by Chinese forces during the Korean War of the early 1950s. Some of these soldiers made public statements denouncing the US government and saying they wanted to remain in China when the war ended. McGuire reasoned that these soldiers were mostly inexperienced young men who had not previously been exposed to attacks on the American way of life and were not forearmed with a defence against Marxist ideology.

McGuire applied the biological analogy of inoculation to persuasive communications, distinguishing two kinds of defence:

1 *Supportive defence* – this is based on attitude bolstering. Resistance could be strengthened by providing additional arguments that back up the original beliefs.

2 *Inoculation defence* – this employs counter-arguments and may be more effective. A person learns what the opposition's arguments are and then hears them demolished.

Inoculation at the outset poses a threat, since a counter-argument is an attack on one's attitude (Insko, 1967). The inoculation defence capitalises on the advantage of a two-sided presentation, discussed earlier in relation to characteristics of a persuasive message. In general terms, this defence starts with a weak attack on the person's position, as a strong one might be fatal! The person can then be told that the weak argument is not too strong and should be easy to rebut, or else an argument is to be provided that deals directly with the weak attack. Increased resistance to persuasion develops because we become motivated to defend our beliefs, and we acquire some skill in doing this.

McGuire and Papageorgis (1961) put both forms of defence to the test. Students were asked to indicate their agreement on a fifteen-point scale with a series of truisms relating to health beliefs, such as:

• It's a good idea to brush your teeth after every meal if at all possible.

• The effects of penicillin have been, almost without exception, of great benefit to mankind.

• Everyone should get a yearly chest X-ray to detect any signs of TB at an early stage.

• Mental illness is not contagious.

Before the experiment began, many of the students thoroughly endorsed these propositions, scoring 15 on the 15-point response scale. They were then subjected to defences and attacks on these health beliefs in the form of essays offering arguments for or against the truisms. Students who were in the defence groups were in either (a) a *supportive* defence group (they received support for their position) or (b) an *inoculation* defence group (their position was subjected to a weak attack, which was then refuted). There were also two control groups, one in which the students were neither attacked nor defended, and another that read essays that strongly attacked the truisms but none defending them.

Not surprisingly, control participants who had been neither attacked nor defended continued to show the highest level of acceptance of the truisms. The crucial findings, shown in Figure 6.16 were:

• Students equipped with a supportive defence were a little more resistant to an attack when compared with the control group who had been attacked without any defence (compare the data in columns 2 and 4).

• Students who had been inoculated were substantially strengthened in their defence against a strong attack compared with the same control group (compare the data in columns 1 and 4).

Inoculation is clearly a strong defence against persuasion (also see Jacks & Cameron, 2003), particularly when the audience is to be exposed to a new argument. By having to deal

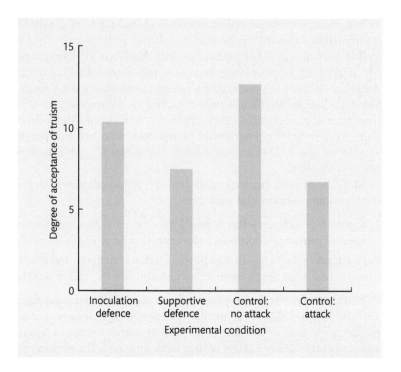

Figure 6.16 Degree of acceptance of health truisms in modes of reading and writing as a function of supportive and inoculation defences

One of the best forms of defence against counter-arguments is to be exposed to small doses of these arguments.

Source: Based on data from McGuire and Papageorgis (1961).

with a mild earlier attack on their position, they will be better equipped to innovate when a stronger one is mounted. However, McGuire (1964) notes that although a supportive defence is weaker, it should not be ignored. Defence is most effective when attacks on one's position are well understood, so that established and rehearsed supportive arguments can be called up. For example, try persuading committed visitors to your door that they are in error when they are intent on telling you about the wonders of their religion. The chances are that they have heard your counter-arguments before.

Inoculation has been used in some kinds of advertising. An example is issue/advocacy advertising, where a company protects consumer loyalty from 'attitude slippage' by issuing media releases on controversial issues (see Burgoon, Pfau, & Birk, 1995). For example, a chemical company may issue a statement about environmental pollution in order to inoculate its consumers against allegations of environmental misconduct from competing companies, or from other 'enemies' such as a local green party. This practice is now widespread: an alcohol company may fund alcohol research and alcohol-moderation campaigns, and a fashion company may support the protection of wildlife and the fight against child labour.

Attitude accessibility and strength

Other variables that influence people's resistance to persuasion are attitude *accessibility* and attitude *strength*. Accessible attitudes come to mind more easily and are likely to be stronger (see **Chapter 5**). When applied to the study of resistance, Michael Pfau and his colleagues confirmed what we might expect. An attitude that is accessible and strong is more resistant to persuasion (Pfau, Compton, Parker, et al., 2004; Pfau, Roskos-Ewoldsen, Wood, et al., 2003). In the case of inoculation, the initial threat to one's attitude makes the attitude more accessible, and even more so if we form counter-arguments. Success in resisting persuasion can then rebound on the persuader by strengthening the target's initial attitude (Tormala & Petty, 2002), even when the message was strong (Tormala & Petty, 2004a) or came from an expert source (Tormala & Petty, 2004b).

To be effective, a persuasive message must impact the real-life behavioural decisions that people later make – their *post-message behaviour*. Consider campaigns directed at risky behaviour, such as trying to dissuade young people from drinking alcohol. Albarracín, Cohen and Kumkale (2003) found that warnings about health and injury were not effective in promoting abstinence. A message such as 'just say no' to offers of alcohol may not stand much chance at the next teenage party. Young people who indulge in a 'trial' drink will immediately be in conflict – experience dissonance – between their behaviour and the content of the message. One outcome could be a weakening of the very attitude that the message was designed to support.

Research on resistance to persuasion has grown over the last decade or so and been applied to a range of persuasion domains (see Knowles & Linn, 2004). McGuire's original research was triggered by wartime brainwashing in the 1950s. However, what was happening in Korea was actually an attempt to induce value conversion rather than merely change attitudes. This, of course, resonates today not only with what happens in religious cults that essentially brainwash their members to subscribe to the cult's ideology (Bernard, Maio, & Olson, 2003), but also the process of radicalization that instils a world view to inspire terrorists to commit appalling atrocities against innocent people (King & Taylor, 2011). Effective inoculation or defence against value conversion may involve different or additional resources to those that work for attitudes (cf. Maio, 2010).

Summary

- The Yale research programme was an influential study of communication and persuasion. It focused on three classes of factors: the source of a message (*who* factors), the message itself (*what* factors) and the audience (*to whom* factors).

- A well-researched communicator variable is source credibility, and a well-researched message variable is fear-based appeals. The sleeper effect is a phenomenon where some messages gain impact after the passage of time.

- Social psychological research on persuasion and attitude change has had a significant influence on two areas of our everyday life – commercial advertising and political propaganda.

- There are two main models of how a persuasive message is learnt. Petty and Cacioppo's elaboration–likelihood model proposes that when people attend to a message carefully, they use a central route to process it; otherwise they use a peripheral route. Chaiken's heuristic–systematic model suggests that people use systematic processing when they attend to a message carefully; otherwise they use heuristic processing. The models are not in conflict.

- There are many techniques to induce another person to comply with our requests: these include ingratiation, reciprocity and guilt arousal. There are also multiple-request techniques (foot-in-the-door, door-in-the-face and low-balling), in which a first request functions as a set-up for the second, real, request.

- Festinger's cognitive dissonance theory explains attitude change in terms of conflict between a person's beliefs, and discrepancy between behaviour and underlying attitudes, and behaviour and self-conception. There are three ways in which dissonance is brought about: effort justification, induced compliance and free choice.

- Reactance is an increase in resistance to persuasion when the communicator's efforts to persuade are obvious. Techniques for building up resistance include forewarning and inoculation. In recent years, manufacturing companies have used inoculating media releases to shore up consumer loyalty.

- Defensive strategies against attacks on peoples' wider ideologies and value systems may require different or additional cognitive and social resources to those involved in defending against attacks on specific attitudes.

Key terms

Action research
Attitude change
Audience
Cognitive consistency theories
Cognitive dissonance
Compliance
Disconfirmation bias
Door-in-the-face tactic
Effort justification
Elaboration–likelihood model
Foot-in-the-door tactic

Forewarning
Heuristic–systematic model
Induced compliance
Ingratiation
Inoculation
Low-ball tactic
Message
Mindlessness
Moderator variable
Multiple requests
Persuasive communication

Post-decisional conflict
Reactance
Reciprocity principle
Representativeness heuristic
Selective exposure hypothesis
Self-affirmation theory
Self-perception theory
Sleeper effect
Source
Terror management theory
Third-person effect

Literature, film and TV

Frost/Nixon

In the summer of 1977, ex-president Richard Nixon, three years after being forced from office in disgrace for the Watergate scandal, decides to put the record straight and repair his legacy through a televised interview. He chooses the breezy young jet-setting British interviewer David Frost. What follows, in this 2009 film, is an exercise in persuasion and attitude change as Nixon (played by Frank Langella) cleverly seems to prevail over Frost (played by Michael Sheen) for most of the interview and surrounding events.

The Godfather trilogy: 1901–80

All three *Godfather* movies together (1992), directed by Francis Ford Coppola and with stars such as Marlon Brando, Al Pacino, Robert Duvall, James Caan, Robert de Niro, Diane Keaton, Andy Garcia and even the young Sofia Coppola. A trilogy about the persuasive power exerted by the Mafia through fear, and the actual, implied or imagined presence of the Godfather.

Pride

This 2014 film, directed by Matthew Warchus, is based on a true story surrounding the 1984 miners' strike in the United Kingdom. A group of London-based lesbian and gay rights activists raise money to support families in South Wales affected by the strike. This spawned a wider campaign – Lesbians and Gays Support the Miners – which initially seemed an inconceivable alliance given the prevailing homophobic attitudes of the time. However, attitudes gradually changed over time to build a strong bond of respect and tolerance between the two groups. This heart-warming film highlights the challenge of changing people's attitudes, especially when social change looms and people's attitudes are grounded in deep-seated fears and prejudices. The film is also relevant to our discussion of minority influence in Chapter 7 and of prejudice in Chapter 10.

The Motorcycle Diaries

A beautifully filmed and highly absorbing 2004 biopic (in Spanish with English subtitles) chronicling the 1952 road trip, initially by motorcycle, through South America by 23-year-old Ernesto Guevara (played by Gael Garcia Bernal) and his friend Alberto Granado (played by Rodrigo de la Serna). The trip is initially a hedonistic expression of youth, but through their encounters with grinding poverty and with disadvantage, injustice and oppression, Guevara's attitudes, world view and life priorities are gradually transformed. The trip (which Guevara himself documented in a memoir/travelogue) was the catalyst for Ernesto's transformation into the now-legendary Marxist revolutionary Che Guevara.

Guided questions

1   The university doctor wants your classmate Joseph to stop smoking. She thinks she might ask him to look at a large jar containing a chemical solution and a diseased lung. Why might this not work very well?

2 How effective is it to use fear as the basis of a persuasive message?

3 The sleeper effect has been described as unreliable. Do you think it still has some validity?

4 Describe any one *multiple-request tactic* for gaining compliance. Can you think of an everyday example of its use?

5 If your aim were to 'inoculate' someone against a forthcoming propaganda campaign, how would you go about it?

Learn more

Albarracín, D., & Vargas, P. (2010). Attitudes and persuasion: From biology to social responses to persuasive intent. In S. T. Fiske, D. T. Gilbert, & G. Lindzey (Eds.), *Handbook of social psychology* (5th ed., Vol. 1, pp. 394–427). New York: Wiley. Detailed and authoritative discussion of persuasion, which also covers literature on biochemical and brain science dimensions.

Banaji, M. R., & Heiphetz, L. (2010). Attitudes. In S. T. Fiske, D. T. Gilbert, & G. Lindzey (Eds.), *Handbook of social psychology* (5th ed., Vol. 1, pp. 353–393). New York: Wiley. An up-to-date, comprehensive and detailed discussion of attitude research, which also covers processes of attitude change, with detailed coverage of recent social neuroscience research.

Belch, G. E., & Belch, M. A. (2012). *Advertising and promotion: An integrated marketing communications perspective* (9th ed.). New York: McGraw-Hill. A well-known textbook that uses a communications theory approach (source, message, receiver) to explore how consumer attitudes and behaviour can be changed. It is rich with examples and illustrations of advertisements.

Bohner, G., Moskowitz, G. B., & Chaiken, S. (1995). The interplay of heuristic and systematic processing of social information. *European Review of Social Psychology, 6*, 33–68. An in-depth overview of the heuristic–systematic model of social information processing, which links attitude change more broadly to social influence.

Johnson, E. J., Pham, M. T., & Johar, G. V. (2007). Consumer behavior and marketing. In A. W. Kruglanski, & E. T. Higgins (Eds.), *Social psychology: A handbook of basic principles* (2nd ed., pp. 869–887). New York: Guilford Press. This detailed chapter also discusses persuasion and attitude change in the area of consumer behaviour.

Knowles, E. S., & Linn, J. A. (Eds.) (2004). *Resistance and persuasion.* Mahwah, NJ: Erlbaum. A discussion of persuasion with a particular emphasis on resistance to persuasion.

Maio, G. R., & Haddock, G. (2007). Attitude change. In A. W. Kruglanski, & E. T. Higgins (Eds.), *Social psychology: Handbook of basic principles* (2nd ed., pp. 565–586). New York: Guilford. Comprehensive coverage of what we know about processes of attitude change.

Maio, G. R., & Haddock, G. (2010). *The psychology of attitudes and attitude change.* London: SAGE. A mid- to upper-level text dedicated to the science of attitudes – written by two leading attitude researchers.

Rothman, A. J., & Salovey, P. (2007). The reciprocal relation between principles and practice: Social psychology and health behaviour. In A. W. Kruglanski, & E. T. Higgins (Eds.), *Social psychology: A handbook of basic principles* (2nd ed., pp. 826–849). New York: Guilford Press. Detailed overview of social psychological processes in the context of health; including coverage of heath attitudes and behaviour.

Visser, P. S., & Cooper, J. (2007). Attitude change. In M. A. Hogg, & J. Cooper (Eds.), *The SAGE handbook of social psychology: Concise student edition* (pp. 197–218). London: SAGE. A comprehensive and accessible overview of theory and research on attitude change.

Zimbardo, P. G., & Leippe, M. R. (1991). *The psychology of attitude change and social influence.* New York: McGraw-Hill. A detailed look at attitudes and social influences in society, with particular attention to persuasion, influence and change. Well illustrated with relevant examples.

Chapter 7
Social influence

Chapter contents

What do *you* think?

1   While serving in the army on combat duty, Private Jones is ordered to set booby traps in a neighbourhood that is also used as a playground by small children. Although he feels very distressed about doing this, he sees that other members of his unit are already obeying the order. What is Private Jones likely to do, and how will he feel about it? What factors might make it easier for him to disobey this order?

2   Tom entered an elevator with several people already in it. Like them, he positioned himself to face the door. At the next floor, a few more people entered, and stood immediately in front of him. As the elevator moved off, they all turned to face the rear. Tom thought this was strange, even stupid. Why did they do this? Should he do the same?

3   While playing Trivial Pursuit®, Sarah simply agrees with Paul and John when they decide which plane first broke the sound barrier. They say she is a typical conformist female. What do you say?

4   Aleksei and Ivan work for a large multinational corporation. They agree that many conditions of their employment are highly exploitative. Aleksei wants to take the corporation on, but Ivan exclaims, 'How can we possibly succeed? There are only two of us up against the system!' What tips would you give Aleksei and Ivan to improve their chance of success?

Types of social influence

Social psychology was defined by Gordon Allport (1954a) as 'an attempt to understand and explain how the thoughts, feelings, and behaviours of individuals are influenced by the actual, imagined, or implied presence of others' (p. 5). This widely accepted and often quoted definition of social psychology (see **Chapter 1**) identifies a potential problem for the study of **social influence** – how does the study of social influence differ from the study of social psychology as a whole? There is no straightforward answer. Instead, we will look at the kinds of issues that are researched by social psychologists who claim to be studying social influence.

Social life involves a great deal of argument, conflict and controversy, where individuals or groups try to change the thoughts, feelings and behaviour of others by persuasion, argument, example, command, propaganda or force. People can be quite aware of influence attempts and can form impressions of how affected they and other people are by different types of influence (see **Chapter 6**).

Social life is also characterised by **norms**: that is, by attitudinal and behavioural uniformities among people, or what Turner (1991) has called 'normative social similarities and differences between people' (p. 2). One of the most interesting sets of issues in social influence, perhaps even in social psychology, is how people construct norms, how they conform to or are regulated by those norms, and how those norms change. Since norms are very much group phenomena, we discuss their structure, their origins and some of their effects later in the text (**Chapter 8**), reserving for this chapter discussion of the processes of conformity and resistance to norms.

Leaders play a central role in the development of norms and, more broadly, in processes of influence and persuasion. Leadership is clearly an influence process (Hogg, 2010), but it is also a group process because norms are properties of groups; and where there are leaders, there are followers. For this reason, and because leadership is so central to the human condition, we discuss leadership in detail later in the text (see **Chapter 9**).

Compliance, obedience, conformity

We are all familiar with the difference between yielding to direct or indirect pressure from a group or an individual, and being genuinely persuaded. For example, you may simply agree publicly with other people's attitudes, comply with their requests or go along with their behaviour, yet privately not feel persuaded at all. On other occasions, you may privately change your innermost beliefs in line with their views or their behaviour. This has not gone unnoticed by social psychologists, who find it useful to distinguish between coercive **compliance** on the one hand and persuasive influence on the other (Box 7.1).

Some forms of social influence produce public compliance – an outward change in behaviour and expressed attitudes in response to a request from another person, or as a

Social influence
Process whereby attitudes and behaviour are influenced by the real or implied presence of other people.

Norms
Attitudinal and behavioural uniformities that define group membership and differentiate between groups.

Compliance
Superficial, public and transitory change in behaviour and expressed attitudes in response to requests, coercion or group pressure.

Box 7.1 Your life
Where shall we go to eat?

You are sitting around with your friends discussing where to go to eat. You have your heart set on Lebanese, but they are all into Indian. A spirited debate ensues, and in the end, you find yourself agreeing that Indian is the way to go. What has happened here? Did you simply cave in to pressure – you were coerced, and still much prefer Lebanese but complied to keep the peace? Or did you feel persuaded in such a way that Indian seemed exactly what you'd like, and on reflection, this group that you belong to more often than not goes out for Indian food? Would the outcome or associated feelings about the decision have been different if the group was not one that you felt deeply grounded in? This chapter discusses the difference between behavioural compliance and more deep-seated persuasion that produces attitude change.

consequence of persuasion or coercion. As compliance does not reflect internal change, it usually persists only while behaviour is under surveillance. For example, children may obey parental directives to keep their room tidy, but only if they know that their parents are watching! An important prerequisite for coercive compulsion and compliance is that the source of social influence is perceived by the target of influence to have power; power is the basis of compliance (Moscovici, 1976).

However, because evidence for internal mental states is gleaned from observed behaviour, it can be difficult to know whether compliant behaviour does or does not reflect internalisation (Allen, 1965) – although some recent neuroscience experiments have begun to chart brain activity differences associated with compliant behaviour versus more deep-seated cognitive changes (cf. Berns, Chappelow, Zink, Pagnoni, Martin-Skurski, & Richard, 2005). People's strategic control over their behaviour for self-presentation and communication purposes can amplify this difficulty. Research into compliance with direct requests has generally been conducted within an attitude-change and persuasion framework (see **Chapter 6**).

In contrast to compliance, other forms of social influence produce private acceptance and internalisation. There is subjective acceptance and conversion (Moscovici, 1976), which produces true internal change that persists in the absence of surveillance. Conformity is based not on power but rather on the subjective validity of social norms (Festinger, 1950): that is, a feeling of confidence and certainty that the beliefs and actions described by the norm are correct, appropriate, valid and socially desirable. Under these circumstances, the norm becomes an internalised standard for behaviour, and thus surveillance is unnecessary. In making determinations about the validity and self-relevance of group norms, we often turn to leaders we trust as members of our group – and this can cause us to perceive them as having charisma (e.g., Platow, Van Knippenberg, Haslam, Van Knippenberg, & Spears, 2006) and power (Turner, 2005).

Some time ago, Harold Kelley (1952) made a valuable distinction between reference groups and membership groups. **Reference groups** are groups that are psychologically significant for people's attitudes and behaviour, either in the positive sense that we seek to behave in accordance with their norms, or in the negative sense that we seek to behave in opposition to their norms. **Membership groups** are groups to which we belong (which we are *in*) by some objective criterion, external designation or social consensus.

A positive reference group is a source of conformity (which will be socially validated if that group also happens to be our membership group), while a negative reference group that is also our membership group has enormous coercive power to produce compliance. For example, if I am a student but I despise all the attributes of being a student, and if I would much rather be a lecturer because I value lecturer norms so much more, then 'student' is my membership group and is also a negative reference group, while 'lecturer' is a positive reference group but not my membership group. I will comply with student norms but conform to lecturer norms.

The general distinction between coercive compliance and persuasive influence is a theme that surfaces repeatedly in different guises in social influence research. The distinction maps on to a general view in social psychology that two quite separate processes are responsible for social influence phenomena. Thus, Turner and colleagues refer to traditional perspectives on social influence as representing a **dual-process dependency model** (e.g. Turner, 1991). This dual-process approach is currently perhaps most obvious in Petty and Cacioppo's (1986b) elaboration–likelihood model and Chaiken's (Bohner, Moskowitz, & Chaiken, 1995) heuristic–systematic model of attitude change (see **Chapter 6**; Eagly & Chaiken, 1993).

Power and influence

Compliance tends to be associated with power relations, whereas conformity is not. Compliance is affected not only by the persuasive tactics that people use to make requests but also by how much power the source of influence is perceived to have. **Power** can be interpreted as the capacity or ability to exert influence; and influence is power in action. For example, John French and Bert Raven (1959) identified five bases of social power, and

Reference group
Kelley's term for a group that is psychologically significant for our behaviour and attitudes.

Membership group
Kelley's term for a group to which we belong by some objective external criterion.

Dual-process dependency model
General model of social influence in which two separate processes operate – dependency on others for social approval and for information about reality.

Power
Capacity to influence others while resisting their attempts to influence.

1 Reward power	The ability to give or promise rewards for compliance
2 Coercive power	The ability to give or threaten punishment for non-compliance
3 Informational power	The target's belief that the influencer has more information than oneself
4 Expert power	The target's belief that the influencer has generally greater expertise and knowledge than oneself
5 Legitimate power	The target's belief that the influencer is authorised by a recognised power structure to command and make decisions
6 Referent power	Identification with, attraction to or respect for the source of influence

Figure 7.1 There are many different sources of power that people can access to persuade others
Source: Based on Raven (1965).

Raven (1965, 1993) later expanded this to six: reward power, coercive power, informational power, expert power, legitimate power and referent power (see Figure 7.1).

Because it is almost a truism in psychology that the power to reinforce or punish people should influence behaviour, there have been virtually no attempts to demonstrate reward and coercive power (Collins & Raven, 1969). One problem is that reinforcement formulations, particularly of complex social behaviour, find it difficult to specify in advance what are rewards and what are punishments, yet find it very easy to do so after the event. Thus, reinforcement formulations tend to be unfalsifiable, and it may be more useful to focus on the cognitive and social processes that cause specific individuals in specific contexts to treat some things as reinforcement and others as punishment.

While information may have the power to influence, it is clearly not true that all information has such power. If we were earnestly to tell you that we had knowledge that pigs really do fly, it is very unlikely that you would be persuaded. For you to be persuaded, other influence processes would also have to be operating: for instance, the information might have to be perceived to be consistent with normative expectations, or coercive or reward power might have to operate.

However, information can be influential when it originates from an expert source. Bochner and Insko (1966) provided a nice illustration of expert power. They found that participants more readily accepted information that people did not need much sleep when the information was attributed to a Nobel Prize-winning physiologist than to a less prestigious source. The information lost the power to influence only when it became intrinsically implausible – stating that almost no sleep was needed (see Figure 6.2 in **Chapter 6**).

Legitimate power rests on authority and is probably best illustrated by a consideration of obedience (see the next section, 'Obedience to authority'). Referent power may operate through a range of processes (see also Collins & Raven, 1969), including consensual validation, social approval and group identification (all of which are discussed in the section on conformity later in this chapter). Focusing on legitimacy and power, Galinsky and his colleagues have pursued a line of research showing, among other things, that people who believe they have legitimate power are more likely to take action to pursue goals – they feel empowered (Galinsky, Gruenfeld, & Magee, 2003), and that people who do not feel their power is legitimate or associated with status can be extremely destructive (Fast, Halevy, & Galinsky, 2012).

In addition to power as the ability to influence, there are other perspectives on social power (Fiske & Berdahl, 2007; Keltner, Gruenfeld, & Anderson, 2003; Ng, 1996). For example, Fiske (1993b; Fiske & Dépret, 1996; Goodwin, Gubin, Fiske, & Yzerbyt, 2000) presents a social cognitive and attributional analysis of power imbalance within a group (see **Chapter 9**). Serge Moscovici (1976) actually contrasts power with influence, treating them as two different processes. Power is the control of behaviour through domination that produces compliance and submission: if people have power, in this sense, they do not need influence; and if they can influence effectively, they need not resort to power. There is also a significant literature on intergroup power relations (e.g. Hornsey, Spears, Cremers, & Hogg, 2003; Jost & Major, 2001; also see **Chapter 11**).

Power can also be thought of as a role within a group that is defined by effective influence over followers: that is, as a leadership position. However, as we shall see in **Chapter 9**, the relationship between power and leadership is not clear-cut. Some leaders certainly do influence by the exercise of power through coercion – they are the all-too-familiar autocratic or dictatorial leaders who may cajole and use ideological methods to keep their power elite in line, but most certainly exercise raw power over the masses (e.g. Moghaddam, 2013). However, most leaders influence by persuasion and by instilling their vision in the rest of the group. Groups tend to permit their leaders to be idiosyncratic and innovative (Abrams, Randsley de Moura, Marques, & Hutchison, 2008; Hollander, 1985), and they see their leaders as being charismatic (Avolio & Yammarino, 2003) and, in many cases, as having legitimate authority (Tyler, 1997).

Legitimate
You may want the leader of a powerful nation to have expertise, charisma, and to be greeted with respect. Does a buffed pose do it for you?

Leadership researchers typically distinguish leadership from power (e.g. Chemers, 2001; Lord, Brown, & Harvey, 2001). Leadership is a process of influence that enlists and mobilises others in the attainment of collective goals; it imbues people with the group's attitudes and goals and inspires them to work towards achieving them. Leadership is not a process that requires people to exercise power over others in order to gain compliance or, more extremely, in order to coerce or force people. Leadership may actually be more closely associated with conformity processes than power processes, and power may be social construct rather than a cause of effective leadership (Hogg, 2010; Hogg & Van Knippenberg, 2003; Hogg, Van Knippenberg, & Rast, 2012a; Reid & Ng, 1999).

John Turner (2005) has critiqued traditional perspectives on power and influence. The traditional perspective is that power resides in control of resources and is the basis of influence that psychologically attaches people to groups. In contrast, Turner argues that attachment to and identification with a group is the basis of influence processes. Those who are influential are invested with power, and power allows control of resources. Turner's approach is a social identity analysis (see **Chapter 11**). It invokes social identity theory's conceptualisation of influence in groups (e.g. Turner, 1981b; see the section 'Social identity and self-categorization' in this chapter) and of leadership in groups (e.g. Hogg & Van Knippenberg, 2003; see the section 'Social identity and leadership' in **Chapter 9**).

Obedience to authority

In 1951 Solomon Asch published the results of a now-classic experiment on conformity, in which student participants conformed to incorrect judgements of line lengths made by a numerical majority (see later in this chapter for details). Some critics were soundly unimpressed by this study: the task, judging line length, was trivial, and there were no significant consequences for conforming or resisting.

Stanley Milgram (1974, 1992) was one of these critics; he tried to replicate Asch's study, but with a task that had important consequences attached to the decision to conform or remain independent. He decided to have experimental confederates apparently administer electric shocks to another person to see whether the true participant, who was not a confederate, would conform. Before being able to start the study, Milgram needed to run a control group to obtain a base rate for people's willingness to shock someone *without* social pressure from confederates. For Milgram, this almost immediately became a crucial question in its own right. In fact, he never actually went ahead with his original conformity study, and the control group became the basis of one of social psychology's most dramatic research programmes.

A larger social issue influenced Milgram. Adolf Eichmann was the Nazi official most directly responsible for the logistics of Hitler's 'Final Solution', in which 6 million Jews were systematically slaughtered. Hannah Arendt (1963) reported his trial in her book *Eichmann in Jerusalem*, bearing the riveting subtitle *A Report on the Banality of Evil*. This captures a scary finding, one that applied to Eichmann and later to other war criminals who have been brought to trial. These 'monsters' may not have been monsters at all. They were often mild-mannered, softly spoken, courteous people who repeatedly and politely explained that they did what they did not because they hated Jews (or Muslims, etc.) but because they were ordered to do it – they were simply obeying orders. Looks can, of course, be deceiving. Peter Malkin, the Israeli agent who captured Eichmann in 1960, discovered that Eichmann knew some Hebrew words, and he asked:

> 'Perhaps you're familiar with some other words,' I said. '*Aba. Ima.* Do those ring a bell?'
> 'Aba, Ima,' he mused, trying hard to recall. 'I don't really remember. What do they mean?'
> 'Daddy, Mommy. It's what Jewish children scream when they're torn from their parents' arms.' I paused, almost unable to contain myself. 'My sister's boy, my favorite playmate, he was just your son's age. Also blond and blue-eyed, just like your son. And you killed him.'

Genuinely perplexed by the observation, he actually waited a moment to see if I would clarify it. 'Yes,' he said finally, 'but he was Jewish, wasn't he?'

Malkin and Stein (1990, p. 110)

Milgram brought these strands together in a series of experiments with the underlying premise that people are socialised to respect the authority of the state (Milgram, 1963, 1974; also see Blass, 2004). If we enter an **agentic state**, we can absolve ourselves of responsibility for what happens next. Participants in his experiments were recruited from the community by advertisement and reported to a laboratory at Yale University to take part in a study of the effect of punishment on human learning. They arrived in pairs and drew lots to determine their roles in the study (one was the 'learner', the other the 'teacher'). See Box 7.2 for a description of what happened next, and check how the shock generator looked in Figure 7.2.

Agentic state
A frame of mind thought by Milgram to characterise unquestioning obedience, in which people as agents transfer personal responsibility to the person giving orders.

Factors influencing obedience

Milgram (1974) conducted eighteen experiments, in which he varied different parameters to investigate factors influencing obedience. In all but one experiment the participants were 20- to 50-year-old males, not attending university, from a range of occupations and socio-economic levels. In one study in which women were the participants, exactly the same level of obedience was obtained as with male participants. In an attempt to see if twenty-first-century Americans would be obedient like their 1970s counterparts, Burger (2009) conducted a partial replication of the original Milgram studies (a full replication was not possible due to research ethics concerns – see the next subsection on 'The ethical legacy of Milgram's experiments'). Burger discovered only slightly lower levels of obedience than in the original 1970s studies.

Milgram's experiment has been replicated in Italy, Germany, Australia, Britain, Jordan, Spain, Austria and The Netherlands (Smith, Bond, & Kağitçibaşi, 2006). Complete obedience ranged from over 90 per cent in Spain and The Netherlands (Meeus & Raaijmakers, 1986), through over 80 per cent in Italy, Germany and Austria (Mantell, 1971), to a low of 40 per cent among Australian men and only 16 per cent among Australian women (Kilham & Mann, 1974). Some studies have also used modified settings: for example, Meeus and Raaijmakers (1986) used an administrative obedience setting where an 'interviewer' was required to harass a 'job applicant'.

One reason why people continue to administer electric shocks may be that the experiment starts very innocuously with quite trivial shocks. Once people have committed themselves to a course of action (i.e. to give shocks), it can be difficult subsequently to change their minds. The process, which reflects the psychology of sunk costs in which once committed to a course of action people will continue their commitment even if the costs increase dramatically (Fox & Hoffman, 2002), may be similar to that involved in the foot-in-the-door technique of persuasion (Freedman & Fraser, 1966; see **Chapter 6**).

A significant factor in obedience is *immediacy of the victim* – how close or obvious the victim is to the participant. Milgram (1974) varied the level of immediacy across a number of experiments. We have seen above that 65 per cent of people 'shocked to the limit' of 450 V when the victim was unseen and unheard except for pounding on the wall. In an even less immediate condition in which the victim was neither seen nor heard at all, 100 per cent of people went to the end. The baseline condition (the one described in detail earlier) yielded 62.5 per cent obedience. As immediacy increased from this baseline, obedience decreased: when the victim was visible in the same room, 40 per cent obeyed to the limit; and when the teacher actually had to hold the victim's hand down on to the electrode to receive the shock, obedience dropped to a still frighteningly high 30 per cent.

Immediacy may prevent dehumanisation of the victim (cf. Haslam, 2006; Haslam, Loughnan, & Kashima, 2008), making it easier to view a victim as a living, breathing person like oneself and thus to empathise with their thoughts and feelings. Hence, pregnant women

Box 7.2 Research classic
Milgram's procedure in an early study of obedience to authority

Together with the experimenter in the Yale laboratory, there was a teacher (the real participant) and a learner (actually, a confederate).

The learner's role was to learn a list of paired associates, and the teacher's role was to administer an electric shock to the learner every time the learner gave a wrong associate to the cue word. The teacher saw the learner being strapped to a chair and having electrode paste and electrodes attached to his arm. The teacher overheard the experimenter explain that the paste was to prevent blistering and burning, and overheard the learner telling the experimenter that he had a slight heart condition. The experimenter also explained that although the shocks might be painful, they would cause no permanent tissue damage.

The teacher was now taken into a separate room housing a shock generator (see Figure 7.2). He was told to administer progressively larger shocks to the learner every time the learner made a mistake – 15 V for the first mistake, 30 V for the next mistake, 45 V for the next and so on. An important feature of the shock generator was the descriptive labels attached to the scale of increasing voltage. The teacher was given a sample shock of 45 V, and then the experiment commenced.

The learner got some pairs correct but also made some errors, and very soon the teacher had reached 75 V, at which point the learner grunted in pain. At 120 V the learner shouted out to the experimenter that the shocks were becoming painful. At 150 V the learner, or now more accurately the 'victim', demanded to be released from the experiment, and at 180 V he cried out that he could stand it no longer. The victim continued to cry out in pain at each shock, rising to an 'agonised scream' at 250 V. At 300 V the victim ceased responding to the cue words; the teacher was told to treat this as a 'wrong answer'.

Throughout the experiment, the teacher was agitated and tense, and often asked to break off. To such requests, the experimenter responded with an ordered sequence of replies proceeding from a mild 'please continue', through 'the experiment requires that you continue' and 'it is absolutely essential that you continue', to the ultimate 'you have no other choice, you must go on'.

A panel of 110 experts on human behaviour, including 39 psychiatrists, were asked to predict how far a normal, psychologically balanced human being would go in this experiment. These experts believed that only about 10 per cent would exceed 180 V, and no one would obey to the end. These predictions, together with the actual and the remarkably different behaviour of the participants are shown schematically in Figure 7.3).

In a slight variant of the procedure described above, in which the victim could not be seen or heard but pounded on the wall at 300 V and 315 V and then went silent, almost everyone continued to 255 V, and 65 per cent continued to the very end – administering massive electric shocks to someone who was not responding and who had previously reported having a heart complaint!

The participants in this experiment were quite normal people – forty 20- to 50-year-old men from a range of occupations. Unknown to them, however, the entire experiment involved an elaborate deception in which they were always the teacher, and the learner/victim was actually an experimental stooge (an avuncular-looking middle-aged man) who had been carefully briefed on how to react. No electric shocks were actually administered apart from the 45 V sample shock to the teacher.

Note: See extracts from Milgram's work at http://www.panarchy.org/milgram/obedience.html.

Figure 7.2 Milgram's shock generator

Participants in Milgram's obedience studies were confronted with a 15–450 Volt shock generator that had different descriptive labels, including the frighteningly evocative 'XXX', attached to the more impersonal voltage values.
Source: Milgram (1974).

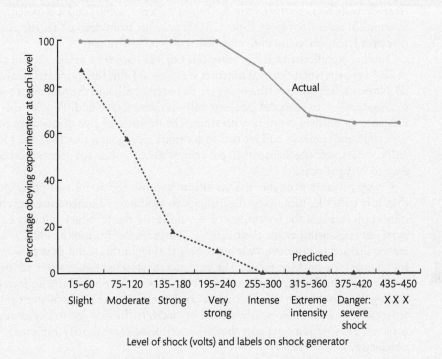

Figure 7.3 Predicted versus actual levels of shock given to a victim in Milgram's obedience-to-authority experiment

'Experts' on human behaviour predicted that very few normal, psychologically balanced people would obey orders to administer more than a 'strong' electric shock to the 'incompetent' learner in Milgram's experiment – in actual fact 65 per cent of people were obedient right to the very end, going beyond 'danger: severe shock', into a zone labelled 'XXX'.

Source: Based on data from Milgram (1974).

Obedience to authority
This guard's uniform symbolises complete unquestioning obedience to the British Monarch as a legitimate authority.

express greater commitment to their pregnancy after having seen an ultrasound scan that clearly reveals body parts (Lydon & Dunkel-Schetter, 1994); and it is easier to press a button to wipe out an entire village from 12,000 metres or from deep under the ocean in a submarine than it is to shoot an individual enemy from close range.

Another significant factor is *immediacy of the authority figure*. Obedience was reduced to 20.5 per cent when the experimenter was absent from the room and relayed directions by telephone. When the experimenter gave no orders at all, and the participant was entirely free to choose when to stop, 2.5 per cent still persisted to the end. Perhaps the most dramatic influence on obedience is group pressure. The presence of two disobedient peers (i.e. others who appeared to revolt and refused to continue after giving shocks in the 150–210 V range) reduced complete obedience to 10 per cent, while two obedient peers raised complete obedience to 92.5 per cent.

Group pressure probably has its effects because the actions of others help to confirm that it is either legitimate or illegitimate to continue administering the shocks. Another important factor is the legitimacy of the authority figure, which allows people to abdicate personal responsibility for their actions. For example, Bushman (1984, 1988) had confederates, dressed in uniform, neat attire or a shabby outfit, stand next to someone fumbling for change for a parking meter. The confederate stopped passers-by and 'ordered' them to give the person change for the meter. Over 70 per cent obeyed the uniformed confederate (giving 'because they had been told to' as the reason) and about 50 per cent obeyed a confederate who was either neatly attired or shabbily dressed (generally giving altruism as a reason). These studies suggest that mere emblems of authority can create unquestioning obedience.

Milgram's original experiments were conducted by lab-coated scientists at prestigious Yale University, and the purpose of the research was quite clearly the pursuit of scientific knowledge. What would happen if these trappings of legitimate authority were removed? Milgram ran one experiment in a run-down inner-city office building. The research was ostensibly sponsored by a private commercial research firm. Obedience dropped, but to a still remarkably high 48 per cent.

Milgram's research addresses one of humanity's great failings – the tendency for people to obey orders without first thinking about (1) what they are being asked to do and (2) the consequences of their obedience for other living beings. However, obedience can sometimes be beneficial: for example, many organisations would grind to a halt or would be catastrophically dysfunctional if their members continually, painstakingly negotiated orders (think about an emergency surgery team, a flight crew, a commando unit). (Now consider the first 'What do *you* think?' question.) However, the pitfalls of blind obedience, contingent on immediacy, group pressure, group norms and legitimacy, are also many. For example, American research has shown that medication errors in hospitals can be attributed to the fact that nurses overwhelmingly defer to doctors' orders, even when metaphorical alarm bells are ringing (Lesar, Briceland, & Stein, 1977).

In another study focusing on organisational obedience, 77 per cent of participants who were playing the role of board members of a pharmaceutical company advocated continued marketing of a hazardous drug merely because they felt that the chair of the board favoured this decision (Brief, Dukerich, & Doran, 1991).

Before closing this section on obedience, it is worth noting that reservations have been expressed over the connection between destructive obedience as Milgram conceived it on one hand, and the Holocaust itself on the other. Cialdini and Goldstein (2004), in their review of social influence research, have pointed out that:

- Milgram's participants were troubled by the orders they were given, whereas many of the perpetrators of Holocaust atrocities obeyed orders willingly and sometimes sadistically.
- Although the Nazi chain of command and the experimenter in Milgram's studies had apparent legitimate authority, the experimenter had expert authority as well.

Reicher, Haslam and Smith (2012) take a slightly different tack that draws on the social identity theory of leadership (e.g. Hogg, Van Knippenberg, & Rast, 2012b). Drawing on Milgram's findings across his various studies, they reinterpret the results as reflecting group-membership-based leadership rather than obedience to an authority figure. The participants are in an uncertain and stressful situation where they need guidance about what to do – they need leadership. Whether they administer strong shocks or not is a matter not of obeying or disobeying the experimenter, but of whether the conditions of the experiment encourage identification with the experimenter and the scientific community that the experimenter represents, or with the learner and the general community that the learner represents.

The ethical legacy of Milgram's experiments

One enduring legacy of Milgram's experiments is the heated debate that it stirred up over research ethics (Baumrind, 1964; Rosnow, 1981). Recall that Milgram's participants really believed they were administering severe electric shocks that were causing extreme pain to another human being. Milgram was careful to interview and, with the assistance of a psychiatrist, follow up with the more than 1,000 participants in his experiments. There was no evidence of psychopathology, and 83.7 per cent of those who had taken part indicated that they were glad, or very glad, to have been in the experiment (Milgram, 1992, p. 186). Only 1.3 per cent were sorry or very sorry to have participated.

The ethical issues really revolve around three questions concerning the ethics of subjecting experimental participants to short-term stress:

1 Is the research important? If not, then such stress is unjustifiable. However, it can be difficult to assess the 'importance' of research objectively.

2 Is the participant free to terminate the experiment at any time? How free were Milgram's participants? In one sense, they were free to do whatever they wanted, but it was never made explicit to them that they could terminate whenever they wished – in fact, the very purpose of the study was to persuade them to remain!

3 Does the participant freely consent to being in the experiment in the first place? In Milgram's experiments the participants did not give fully informed consent: they volunteered to take part, but the true nature of the experiment was not fully explained to them.

This raises the issue of deception in social psychology research. Kelman (1967) distinguishes two reasons for deceiving people. The first is to induce them to take part in an otherwise unpleasant experiment. This is, ethically, a highly dubious practice. The second reason is that in order to study the automatic operation of psychological processes, participants need to be naive regarding the hypotheses, and this often involves some deception concerning the true purpose of the study and the procedures used. The fallout from this debate has been a code of ethics to guide psychologists in conducting research. The principal components of the code are:

* participation must be based on fully informed consent;

* participants must be explicitly informed that they can withdraw, without penalty, at any stage of the study;

* participants must be fully and honestly debriefed at the end of the study.

A modern university ethics committee would be unlikely to approve the impressively brazen deceptions that produced many of social psychology's classic research programmes of the 1950s, 1960s and early 1970s. What is more likely to be endorsed is the use of minor and harmless procedural deceptions enshrined in clever cover stories that are considered essential to preserve the scientific rigour of much experimental social psychology. The main ethical requirements in all modern research involving human participants are also discussed in Chapter 1, and see the American Psychological Association's (2002) Code of Ethics at **http://www.apa.org/ethics/code2002.html**.

Conformity

The formation and influence of norms

Conformity
Deep-seated, private and enduring change in behaviour and attitudes due to group pressure.

Although social influence is often reflected in compliance with direct requests and obedience to authority, social influence can also operate in a less direct manner, through **conformity** to social or group norms. For example, Floyd Allport (1924) observed that people in groups gave less extreme and more conservative judgements of odours and weights than when they were alone. It seemed as if, in the absence of direct pressure, the group could cause members to converge and thus become more similar to one another.

Muzafer Sherif (1936) explicitly linked this convergence effect to the development of *group norms*. Proceeding from the premise that people need to be certain and confident that what they are doing, thinking or feeling is correct and appropriate, Sherif argued that people use the behaviour of others to establish the range of possible behaviour: we can call this the **frame of reference**, or relevant *social comparative context*. Average, central or middle positions in such frames of reference are typically perceived to be more correct than fringe positions; thus, people tend to adopt them. Sherif believed that this explained the origins of social norms and the associated convergence that accentuates consensus within groups.

Frame of reference
Complete range of subjectively conceivable positions on some attitudinal or behavioural dimension, which relevant people can occupy in a particular context.

Autokinesis
Optical illusion in which a pinpoint of light shining in complete darkness appears to move about.

To test this idea, he conducted a now-classic study using **autokinesis** (see Box 7.3 and Figure 7.4 for details), in which small groups making estimates of physical movement quickly converged over a series of trials on the mean of the group's estimates and remained influenced by this norm even when they later made estimates alone.

The origins, structure, function and effects of norms are discussed later (see **Chapter 8**). However, it is worth emphasising that normative pressure is one of the most effective ways to change people's behaviour. For example, we noted earlier (see **Chapter 6**) that Kurt Lewin (1947) tried to encourage American housewives to change the eating habits of their families – specifically to eat more offal (beef hearts and kidneys). Three groups of thirteen to seventeen housewives attended an interesting factual lecture that, among other things, stressed how valuable such a change in eating habits would be to the war effort (it was 1943). Another three groups were given information but were also encouraged to talk among themselves and arrive at some kind of consensus (i.e. establish a norm) about buying the food.

A follow-up survey revealed that the norm was far more effective than the abstract information in causing change in behaviour: only 3 per cent of the information group had changed their behaviour, compared with 32 per cent of the norm group. Subsequent research confirmed that the norm, not the attendant discussion, was the crucial factor (Bennett, 1955).

Conformity and group acceptance
All groups have norms. These women know how to dress for a 'girls' night out.

Yielding to majority group pressure

Like Sherif, Solomon Asch (1952) believed that conformity reflects a relatively rational process in which people construct a norm from other people's behaviour in order to determine correct and appropriate behaviour for themselves. Clearly, if you are already confident and certain about what is appropriate and correct, then others' behaviour will be largely

Box 7.3 Research classic
Sherif's autokinetic study: The creation of arbitrary norms

Muzafer Sherif (1936) believed that social norms emerge in order to guide behaviour under conditions of uncertainty. To investigate this idea, he took advantage of a perceptual illusion – the autokinetic effect. Autokinesis is an optical illusion where a fixed pinpoint of light in a completely dark room appears to move: the movement is actually caused by eye movement in the absence of a physical frame of reference (i.e. objects). People asked to estimate how much the light moves find the task very difficult and generally feel uncertain about their estimates. Sherif presented the point of light a large number of times (i.e. trials) and had participants, who were unaware that the movement was an illusion, estimate the amount the light moved on each trial. He discovered that they used their own estimates as a frame of reference: over a series of 100 trials they gradually focused

on a narrow range of estimates, with different people adopting their own personal range, or norm (see session 1 in Figure 7.4a, when participants responded alone).

Sherif continued the experiment in further sessions of 100 trials on subsequent days, during which participants in groups of two or three took turns in a random sequence to call out their estimates. Now the participants used each other's estimates as a frame of reference and quickly converged on a group mean, so that they all gave very similar estimates (see sessions 2–4 in Figure 7.4a).

This norm seems to be internalised. When participants start and then continue as a group (sessions 1–3 in Figure 7.4b), the group norm is what they use when they finally make autokinetic estimates on their own (session 4 in Figure 7.4b).

Note: The results shown in Figure 7.4 are based on two sets of three participants who made 100 judgements on each of four sessions, spread over four different days.

- ■ The experimental context used the autokinetic phenomenon.
- ■ In condition (a), individuals 1, 2 and 3 started alone and settled on a personal norm.
- ■ Later in groups, they gradually converged on a group norm.
- ■ In condition (b), individuals 4, 5 and 6 started in groups and converged on a group norm.
- ■ Later when alone, they used their group norm, now internalised, as a personal guide.

Figure 7.4 Experimental induction of a group norm
Source: Based on data from Sherif (1936).

irrelevant and thus not influential. In Sherif's study, the object being judged was ambiguous: participants were uncertain, so a norm arose rapidly and was highly effective in guiding behaviour. Asch argued that if the object of judgement was entirely unambiguous (i.e. one would expect no disagreement between judges), then disagreement, or alternative perceptions, would have no effect on behaviour: people would remain entirely independent of group influence.

To test this idea, Asch (1951, 1956) created another classic experimental paradigm. Students, participating in what they thought was a visual discrimination task, seated themselves around a table in groups of seven to nine. They took turns in a fixed order to call out publicly which of three comparison lines was the same length as a standard line (see Figure 7.5). There were eighteen trials. In reality, only one person was a true naive participant, and he answered second to last. The others were experimental confederates instructed to give incorrect responses on twelve focal trials: on six trials, they picked a line that was too long, and on six a line that was too short. There was a control condition in which participants performed the task privately with no group influence; as less than 1 per cent of the control participants' responses were errors, it can be assumed that the task was unambiguous.

The results of the experiment were intriguing. There were large individual differences, with about 25 per cent of participants remaining steadfastly independent throughout, about 50 per cent conforming to the erroneous majority on six or more focal trials, and 5 per cent conforming on all twelve focal trials. The average conformity rate was 33 per cent, computed as the total number of instances of conformity across the experiment, divided by the product of the number of participants in the experiment and the number of focal trials in the sequence.

After the experiment, Asch asked his **participants** why they conformed. They all said they had initially experienced uncertainty and self-doubt because of the disagreement between themselves and the group, and that this gradually evolved into self-consciousness, fear of disapproval and feelings of anxiety and even loneliness. Different reasons were given for yielding. Most participants knew they saw things differently from the group but felt that their perceptions may have been inaccurate and that the group was actually correct. Others did not believe that the group was correct but simply went along with the group in order not

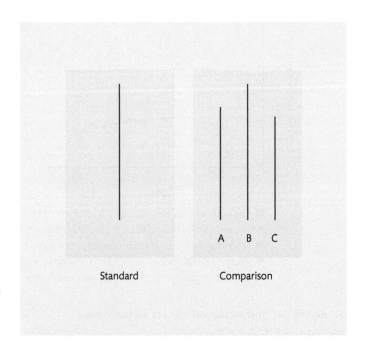

Figure 7.5 Sample lines used in conformity experiment

Participants in Asch's conformity studies had simply to say which one of the three comparison lines was the same length as the standard line.

Source: Based on Asch (1951).

to stand out. (Consider how this might apply to Tom's self-doubts in the second 'What do *you* think?' question.) A small minority reported that they actually saw the lines as the group did. Independents were either entirely confident in the accuracy of their own judgements or were emotionally affected but guided by a belief in individualism or in doing the task as directed (i.e. being accurate and correct).

These subjective accounts should be treated cautiously – perhaps the participants were merely trying to verbally justify their behaviour and engage in self-presentation. For instance, an fMRI study by Berns and associates found that those who conformed may actually have experienced changed perception, and that those who did not conform showed brain activity in the amygdala associated with elevated emotions – a cost of nonconformity may be accentuated emotions and anxiety (Berns, Chappelow, Zink, Pagnoni, Martin-Skurski, & Richard, 2005).

Nevertheless, the subjective accounts suggest, perhaps in line with the fMRI evidence, that one reason why people conform, even when the stimulus is completely unambiguous, may be to avoid censure, ridicule and social disapproval. This is a real fear. In another version of his experiment, Asch (1951) had sixteen naive participants confronting one confederate who gave incorrect answers. The participants found the confederate's behaviour ludicrous and openly ridiculed and laughed at him. Even the experimenter found the situation so bizarre that he could not contain his mirth and also ended up laughing at the poor confederate!

Perhaps, then, if participants were not worried about social disapproval, there would be no felt pressure to conform? To test this idea, Asch conducted another variation of the experiment, in which the incorrect majority called out their judgements publicly but the single naive participant wrote his down privately. Conformity dropped to 12.5 per cent.

Morton Deutsch and Harold Gerard (1955) extended this modification. They wondered whether they could entirely eradicate pressure to conform if: (a) the task was unambiguous, (b) the participant was anonymous and responded privately; or (c) the participant was not under any sort of surveillance by the group. Why should you conform to an erroneous majority when there is an obvious, unambiguous and objectively correct answer, and the group has no way of knowing what you are doing?

To test this idea, Deutsch and Gerard confronted a naive participant face-to-face with three confederates who made unanimously incorrect judgements of lines on focal trials, exactly as in Asch's original experiment. In another condition, the naive participant was anonymous, isolated in a cubicle and allowed to respond privately – no group pressure existed. There was a third condition in which participants responded face-to-face, but with an explicit group goal to be as accurate as possible – group pressure was maximised. Deutsch and Gerard also manipulated subjective uncertainty by having half the participants respond while the stimuli were present (the procedure used by Asch) and half respond after the stimuli had been removed (there would be scope for feeling uncertain).

As predicted, the results showed that decreasing uncertainty and decreasing group pressure (i.e. the motivation and ability of the group to censure lack of conformity) reduced conformity (Figure 7.6). Perhaps the most interesting finding was that people still conformed at a rate of about 23 per cent even when uncertainty was low (stimulus present) and responses were private and anonymous.

The discovery that participants still conformed when isolated in cubicles had a serendipitous methodological consequence – it was now possible to research conformity in a much more streamlined and resource-intense way. Richard Crutchfield (1955) devised an apparatus where participants in cubicles believed they were communicating with one another by pressing buttons on a console that illuminated responses, when in reality the cubicles were not interconnected and the experimenter was the source of all communication. In this way, several individuals could participate simultaneously and yet all would believe they were being exposed to a unanimous group. The time-consuming, costly and risky practice of using confederates was no longer necessary, and data could now be collected much more

Figure 7.6 Conformity as a function of uncertainty and perceived group pressure

- The length of lines was estimated either (a) when they were present (low uncertainty) or (b) after they had been removed (high uncertainty).
- Participants were confronted with the judgements of an incorrect and unanimous majority.
- Influence (percentage of errors) was stronger in the high uncertainty condition.
- Influence was weaker when accuracy was stressed as an important group goal.
- Influence was further weakened when judgements were private and anonymous.

Source: Based on data from Deutsch and Gerard (1955).

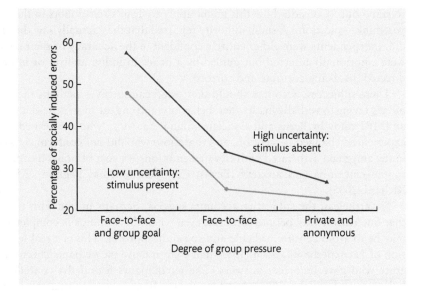

quickly under more controlled and varied experimental conditions (Allen, 1965, 1975). Nowadays, one can, of course, use a much more efficient computerised variant of Crutchfield's methodology.

Who conforms? Individual and group characteristics

The existence of significant individual differences in conformity led to a search for personality attributes that predispose some people to conform more than others. Those who conform tend to have low self-esteem, a high need for social support or approval, a need for self-control, low IQ, high anxiety, feelings of self-blame and insecurity in the group, feelings of inferiority, feelings of relatively low status in the group and a generally authoritarian personality (Costanzo, 1970; Crutchfield, 1955; Elms & Milgram, 1966; Raven & French, 1958; Stang, 1972). However, contradictory findings, and evidence that people who conform in one situation do not conform in another, suggest that situational factors may be more important than personality in conformity (Barocas & Gorlow, 1967; Barron, 1953; McGuire, 1968; Vaughan, 1964).

Alice Eagly drew a similar conclusion about gender differences in conformity. Women have been shown to conform slightly more than men in some conformity studies. This can be explained in terms of the tasks used in some of these studies – tasks with which women had less familiarity and expertise. Women were therefore more uncertain and thus more influenced than men (Eagly, 1978, 1983; Eagly & Carli, 1981; see **Chapters 6 and 9**).

A study by Frank Sistrunk and John McDavid (1971), in which males and females were exposed to group pressure in identifying various stimuli, illustrated this phenomenon. For some participants, the stimuli were traditionally masculine items (e.g. identifying a special type of wrench), for some, traditionally feminine items (e.g. identifying types of needlework) and for others the stimuli were neutral (e.g. identifying rock stars). As expected, women conformed more on masculine items, men more on feminine items, and both groups equally on neutral (non–sex-stereotypical) items – see Figure 7.7. (Is Sarah really a conformist female? See the third 'What do *you* think?' question.)

Women do, however, tend to conform a little more than men in public interactive settings like that involved in the Asch paradigm. One explanation is that it reflects women's greater concern with maintaining group harmony (Eagly, 1978). However, a later study put the emphasis on men's behaviour; women conformed equally in public and private contexts,

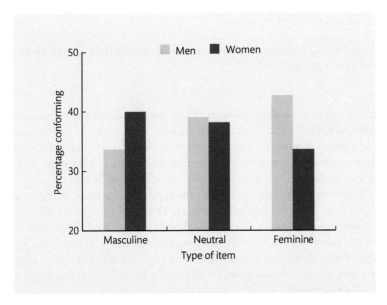

Figure 7.7 Conformity as a function of sex of participant and sex-stereotypicality of task

When a task is male-stereotypical, more women conform. When the task is female-stereotypical, more men conform.

Source: Based on data from Sistrunk and McDavid (1971).

whereas it was men who were particularly resistant to influence in public settings (Eagly, Wood, & Fishbaugh, 1981).

Bert Hodges and his colleagues have provided a different perspective on why people sometimes do not conform, even to a unanimous and expert majority (Hodges, Meagher, Norton, McBain, & Sroubek, 2014). They describe a *speaking-from-ignorance* effect, in which a layperson is invited by a group of experts to offer an opinion. Asch had set up what he thought was a moral dilemma, but some participants may have interpreted it as a context in which they needed to be guided by the norm of 'telling the truth' as they see it and the belief that the experts would give weight to their opinion.

Cultural norms

Do cultural norms affect conformity? Smith, Bond and Kağitçibaşi (2006) surveyed conformity studies that used Asch's paradigm or a variant thereof. They found significant intercultural variation. The level of conformity (i.e. percentage of incorrect responses) ranged from a low of 14 per cent among Belgian students (Doms, 1983) to a high of 58 per cent among Indian teachers in Fiji (Chandra, 1973), with an overall average of 31.2 per cent. Conformity was lower among participants from individualist cultures in North America and north-western Europe (25.3 per cent) than among participants from collectivist or interdependent cultures in Africa, Asia, Oceania and South America (37.1 per cent).

A meta-analysis of studies using the Asch paradigm in seventeen countries (R. Bond & Smith, 1996) confirmed that people who score high on Hofstede's (1980) collectivism scale conform more than people who score low (see also Figure 16.1, which shows summary data for non-Western versus various Western samples). For example, Norwegians, who have a reputation for social unity and responsibility, were more conformist than the French, who value critical judgement, diverse opinions and dissent (Milgram, 1961); and the Bantu of Zimbabwe, who have strong sanctions against nonconformity, were highly conformist (Whittaker & Meade, 1967).

Conformity in collectivist or interdependent cultures tends to be greater because conformity is viewed favourably, as a form of social glue (Markus & Kitayama, 1991). What is perhaps more surprising is that although conformity is lower in individualist Western societies, it is still remarkably high; even when conformity has negative overtones, people find it difficult to resist conforming to a group norm.

Situational factors in conformity

The two situational factors in conformity that have been most extensively researched are group size and group unanimity (Allen, 1965, 1975).

Group size

Asch (1952) found that as the unanimous group increased from one person to two, to three, and on up to fifteen, conformity increased and then decreased slightly: 3, 13, up to 35 and down to 31 per cent. Although some research reports a linear relationship between size and conformity (e.g. Mann, 1977), the most robust finding is that conformity reaches its full strength with a three- to five-person majority, and additional members have little effect (e.g. Stang, 1976).

Group size may have a different effect depending on the type of judgement being made and the motivation of the individual (Campbell & Fairey, 1989). With matters of taste, where there is no objectively correct answer (e.g. musical preferences), and where you are concerned about 'fitting in', group size has a relatively linear effect: the larger the majority, the more you are swayed. When there is a correct response and you are concerned about being correct, then the views of one or two others will usually be sufficient: the views of additional others are largely redundant.

Finally, David Wilder (1977) observed that size may refer not to the actual number of physically separate people in the group, but to the number of seemingly *independent* sources of influence in the group. For instance, a majority of three individuals who are perceived to be independent will be more influential than a majority of, say, five who are perceived to be in collusion and thus represent a single information source. In fact, people may actually find it difficult to represent more than four or five different pieces of information. Instead, they assimilate additional group members into one or other of these initial sources of information – hence the relative lack of effect of group size above three to five members.

Group unanimity

In Asch's original experiment, the erroneous majority was unanimous and the conformity rate was 33 per cent. Subsequent experiments have shown that conformity is significantly

Group size and conformity
Could an individual in this throng resist joining in?

reduced if the majority is not unanimous (Allen, 1975). Asch himself found that a correct supporter (i.e. a member of the majority who always gave the correct answer, and thus agreed with and supported the true participant) reduced conformity from 33 to 5.5 per cent.

It appears that support for remaining independent is not the crucial factor in reducing conformity. Rather, any sort of lack of unanimity among the majority seems to be effective. For example, Asch found that a dissenter who was even more wildly incorrect than the majority was equally effective. Vernon Allen and John Levine (1971) conducted an experiment where participants, who were asked to make visual judgements, were provided with a supporter who had normal vision or a supporter who wore such thick glasses as to raise serious doubts about his ability to see anything at all, let alone judge lines accurately. In the absence of any support, participants conformed 97 per cent of the time. The 'competent' supporter reduced conformity to 36 per cent, but most surprising was the fact that the 'incompetent' supporter reduced conformity as well, to 64 per cent (see Figure 7.8).

Supporters, dissenters and deviates may be effective in reducing conformity because they shatter the unanimity of the majority and thus make us feel less confident about our perceptions and attitudes (Koriat, Adiv, & Schwarz, 2016), and raise or legitimise the possibility of alternative ways of responding or behaving. For example, Nemeth and Chiles (1988) confronted participants with four confederates who either all correctly identified blue slides as blue, or among whom one consistently called the blue slide 'green'. Participants were then exposed to another group that unanimously called red slides 'orange'. The participants who had previously been exposed to the consistent dissenter were more likely to correctly call the red slides 'red'.

Processes of conformity

Social psychologists have proposed three main processes of social influence to account specifically for conformity (Nail, 1986): informational influence, normative influence and referent informational influence.

Informational and normative influence

The most enduring distinction is between informational influence and normative influence (Deutsch & Gerard, 1955; Kelley, 1952). **Informational influence** is a process where people accept information from another as *evidence* about reality. We need to feel confident that

Informational influence
An influence to accept information from another as evidence about reality.

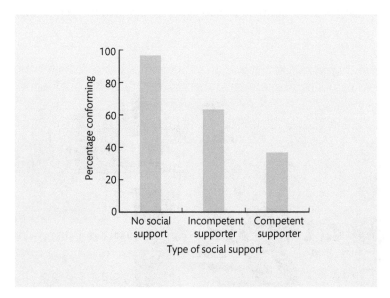

Figure 7.8 Conformity as a function of presence or absence of support, and of competence of supporter

Social support on a line judgement task reduced conformity, even when the supporter was patently unable to make accurate judgements because he was visually impaired.

Source: Based on data from Allen and Levine (1971).

our perceptions, beliefs and feelings are correct. Informational influence comes into play when we are uncertain, either because stimuli are intrinsically ambiguous or because there is social disagreement. When this happens, we initially make objective tests against reality; otherwise, we make social comparisons, as Festinger and others have pointed out (Festinger, 1950, 1954; Suls & Wheeler, 2000). Effective informational influence causes true cognitive change.

Informational influence was probably partially responsible for the convergence effects in Sherif's (1936) study that we have already discussed. Reality was ambiguous, and participants used other people's estimates as information to remove the ambiguity and resolve subjective uncertainty. In that kind of experimental setting, when participants were told that the apparent movement was in fact an illusion, they did not conform (e.g. Alexander, Zucker, & Brody, 1970); presumably, since reality itself was uncertain, their own subjective uncertainty was interpreted as a correct and valid representation of reality, and thus informational influence did not operate. On the other hand, Asch's (1952) stimuli were designed to be unambiguous in order to exclude informational influence. However, Asch did note that conformity increased as the comparison lines were made more similar to one another and the judgement task became more difficult. The moral? Informational influence rules in moments of doubt, not times of certainty.

Normative influence, in contrast, is a process where people conform to the positive expectations of others. People have a need for social approval and acceptance, which causes them to 'go along with' the group for instrumental reasons – to cultivate approval and acceptance, to avoid censure or disapproval or to achieve specific goals. Normative influence comes into play when we believe the group has the power and ability to reward or punish us according to what we do. For this to be effective, we need to believe that the group knows what we are doing – that we are under surveillance by the group. Effective normative influence creates surface compliance in public settings rather than true enduring cognitive change. There is considerable evidence that people often conform to a majority in public but do not necessarily internalise this as it does not carry over to private settings or endure over time (Nail, 1986).

There is little doubt that normative influence was the principal cause of conformity in the Asch paradigm – the lines being judged were unambiguous (informational influence would not be operating), but participants' behaviour was under direct surveillance by the group. We have also seen that privacy, anonymity and lack of surveillance reduce conformity in the Asch paradigm, presumably because normative influence was weakened.

One puzzling feature of Deutsch and Gerard's (1955) study is that even under conditions in which neither informational nor normative influence would be expected to operate, they

Normative influence
An influence to conform to the positive expectation of others, to gain social approval or to avoid social disapproval.

Normative influence
A peer group exerts a powerful pressure to conform, even when an activity is dangerous.

found residual conformity at a remarkably high rate of about 23 per cent. Perhaps social influence in groups needs to be explained in a different way.

Referent informational influence

The distinction between informational and normative influence is only one among many different terminologies that have been used in social psychology to distinguish between two types of social influence. It represents what Turner and his colleagues call a dual-process dependency model of social influence (Abrams & Hogg, 1990a; Hogg & Turner, 1987a; Turner, 1991). People are influenced by others because they are dependent on them either for information that removes ambiguity and thus establishes subjective validity, or for reasons of social approval and acceptance.

This dual-process perspective has been challenged on the grounds that as an explanation of conformity, it underemphasises the role of group belongingness. After all, an important feature of conformity is that we are influenced because we feel we belong, psychologically, to the group, and therefore the norms of the group are relevant standards for our own behaviour. The dual-process model has drifted away from group norms and group belongingness and focused on *interpersonal* dependency, which could just as well occur between individuals as among group members.

This challenge has come from **social identity theory** (Tajfel & Turner, 1986; also Abrams & Hogg, 2010; Hogg, 2006; see **Chapter 11**). This theory proposes a separate social influence process responsible for conformity to group norms, called **referent informational influence** (Hogg & Turner, 1987a; Turner, 1981b; also Gaffney & Hogg, 2016).

When we feel we identify strongly with a group that we are part of, several things happen. We feel a sense of belonging, and we define ourselves in terms of the group. We also recruit from memory and use information available in the immediate situation to determine the relevant attributes that capture our group's norms. We can glean information from the way that outgroup members or even unrelated individuals behave. But the most immediate source is the behaviour of fellow ingroup members, particularly those we consider to be generally reliable sources of the information we need. The ingroup norm that fits the context captures and accentuates both perceived similarities among ingroup members and perceived differences between our group and the relevant outgroup – it obeys the **meta-contrast principle**.

The process of *self-categorization* associated with social identity processes, group belongingness and group behaviour (Turner, Hogg, Oakes, Reicher, & Wetherell, 1987; see **Chapter 11**) brings us to see ourselves through the lens of our group. We assimilate our thoughts, feelings and behaviour to the group norm and act accordingly. To the extent that members of the group construct a similar group norm, self-categorization produces convergence within the group on that norm and increases uniformity – the typical conformity effect.

Referent informational influence differs from normative and informational influence in a number of important ways. People conform because they are group members, not to validate physical reality or to avoid social disapproval. People do not conform to other people but to a norm: other people act as a source of information about the appropriate ingroup norm. Because the norm is an internalised representation, people can conform to it without the surveillance of group members or, for that matter, anybody else.

Referent informational influence has direct support from a series of four conformity experiments by Hogg and Turner (1987a). For example, under conditions of private responding (i.e. no normative influence), participants conformed to a non-unanimous majority containing a correct supporter (i.e. no informational influence) only if it was the participant's explicit or implicit ingroup (see also Abrams, Wetherell, Cochrane, Hogg, & Turner, 1990). Other support for referent informational influence comes from research into group polarisation (e.g. Turner, Wetherell, & Hogg, 1989; see **Chapter 9**), crowd behaviour (e.g. Reicher, 1984; see **Chapter 11**) and social identity and stereotyping (e.g. Oakes, Haslam, & Turner, 1994; see **Chapter 11**).

Social identity theory
Theory of group membership and intergroup relations based on self-categorization, social comparison and the construction of a shared self-definition in terms of ingroup-defining properties.

Referent informational influence
Pressure to conform to a group norm that defines oneself as a group member.

Meta-contrast principle
The prototype of a group is that position within the group that has the largest ratio of 'differences to ingroup positions' to 'differences to outgroup positions'.

Minority influence and social change

Our discussion of social influence, particularly conformity, has focused on individuals yielding to direct or indirect social influence, most often from a numerical majority. Dissenters, deviates or independents have mainly been of interest indirectly, either as a vehicle for investigating the effects of different types of majority or in the role of conformist personality attributes. But we are all familiar with a very different, and very common, type of influence that can occur in a group: an individual or a numerical minority can sometimes change the views of the majority. Often such influence is based (in the case of individuals) on leadership or (in the case of subgroups) legitimate power (leadership is discussed in **Chapter 9**).

Minorities are typically at an influence disadvantage relative to majorities. Often, they are less numerous, and in the eyes of the majority, they have less legitimate power and are less worthy of serious consideration. Asch (1952), as we saw above, found that a single deviate (who was a confederate) from a correct majority (true participants) was ridiculed and laughed at. Sometimes, however, a minority that has little or no legitimate power can be influential and ultimately sway the majority to its own viewpoint. For example, in a variant of the single deviate study, Asch (1952) found a quite different response. When a correct majority of eleven true participants was confronted by a deviant/incorrect minority of nine confederates, the majority remained independent (i.e. continued responding correctly) but took the minority's responses far more seriously – no one laughed. Clearly, the minority had some influence over the majority, albeit not enough in this experiment to produce manifest conformity.

History illustrates the power of minorities. Think of it this way: if the only form of social influence was majority influence, then social homogeneity would have been reached tens of thousands of years ago, individuals and groups always being swayed to adopt the views and practices of the growing numerical majority. Minorities, particularly those that are active and organised, introduce innovations that ultimately produce social change, which can be for good or for ill: without **minority influence**, social change would be very difficult to explain. (See Box 7.4 for a recent example of a mass protest group with little no legitimate power challenging the authority of the US president.)

For example, American anti-war rallies during the 1960s had an effect on majority attitudes that hastened withdrawal from Vietnam. Similarly, the suffragettes of the 1920s gradually changed public opinion so that women were granted the vote, the Campaign for Nuclear

Minority influence
Social influence processes whereby numerical or power minorities change the attitudes of the majority.

Box 7.4 Our world
Massed protest

On January 21, 2017, perhaps the largest global massed one-day protest in human history occurred – the women's protest against the new Trump presidency in the United States. Trump had been inaugurated just the previous day. According to data-based estimates gathered by two political scientists in the United States, Jeremy Pressman and Erica Chenworth, over 4.5 million men, women and children, possibly as many as 5.6 million, participated in entirely peaceful protest marches around the world. While 100,000 protested in London, of course the largest marches were in the United States (4.1 million to 5.3 million), with possibly as many as one million in Washington and 750,000 and 500,000 respectively in America's two largest cities of Los Angeles and New York.

To what extent can this be considered a social change-oriented strategy of minority influence (see this chapter) and what is the underlying psychology of social mobilisation that translated discontent into action on such a massive scale, in the cold of mid-winter (see Chapter 11)? There were many reasons for the protest. One was a sense that Trump's presidency was not legitimate because it was based on an unjust procedure (see Chapter 11). Trump's main rival, Hilary Clinton, had secured 48.2% of the presidential votes while Trump only received 46.1% – Trump received almost 3 million fewer votes than Clinton. Another reason was that many Americans, largely minorities based on ethnicity, religion, race and disability, but also women, felt disrespected by their new president (see discussion of leadership in Chapter 9).

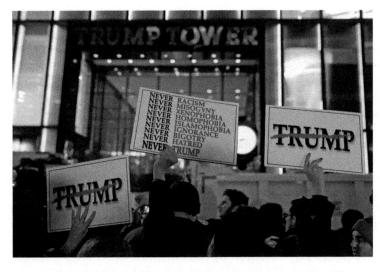

An active minority with style
Young activists protest against the inauguration of Donald Trump as US President.

Disarmament rallies in Western Europe in the early 1980s shifted public opinion away from the 'benefits' of nuclear proliferation, and the huge demonstrations in Leipzig in October 1989 lead to the collapse of the East German government and the fall of the Berlin Wall shortly after on November 9, 1989.

The consequences of social change are not always beneficial. The 2011 popular uprisings across North Africa and the Middle East, dubbed the Arab Spring, changed majority attitudes to some degree regarding governance in those countries, but they also left a power and governance vacuum that has been exploited by rebel militia and terrorist groups. On a more positive note, an excellent example of an active minority is Greenpeace: the group is numerically small (in terms of 'activist' members) but has important influence on public opinion through the high profile of some of its members and the wide publicity of its views.

The sorts of questions that are important here are whether minorities and majorities gain influence via different social practices, and, more fundamentally, whether the underlying psychology is different. There have been several recent overviews of minority influence research and theory (Hogg, 2010; Martin & Hewstone, 2003, 2008, 2010; Martin, Hewstone, Martin, & Gardikiotis, 2008), and for an earlier meta-analysis of research findings, see Wood, Lundgren, Ouellette, Busceme and Blackstone (1994).

Beyond conformity

Social influence research has generally adopted a perspective in which people conform to majorities because they are dependent on them for normative and informational reasons. Moscovici and his colleagues mounted a systematic critique of this perspective (Moscovici, 1976; Moscovici & Faucheux, 1972). They argued that there had been a **conformity bias** underpinned by a functionalist assumption in the literature on social influence. Nearly all research focused on how individuals or minorities yield to majority influence and conform to the majority, and assumed that social influence satisfies an adaptive requirement of human life: to align with the status quo and thus produce uniformity, perpetuate stability and sustain the status quo. In this sense, social influence *is* conformity. Clearly, conformity is an important need for individuals, groups and society. However, innovation and normative *change* are sometimes required to adapt to altered circumstances. Such change is difficult to understand from a conformity perspective, because it requires an understanding of the dynamics of active minorities.

Moscovici and Faucheux (1972) also famously 'turned Asch on his head'. They cleverly suggested that Asch's studies had actually been studies of minority influence, not majority influence. The Asch paradigm appears to pit a lone individual (true participant) against an

Conformity bias
Tendency for social psychology to treat group influence as a one-way process in which individuals or minorities always conform to majorities.

erroneous majority (confederates) on an unambiguous physical perception task. Clearly a case of majority influence in the absence of subjective uncertainty? Perhaps not.

The certainty with which we hold views lies in the amount of agreement we encounter for those views (Koriat, Adiv, & Schwarz, 2016): ambiguity and uncertainty are not properties of objects 'out there' but of other people's disagreement with us. This point is just as valid for matters of taste (if everyone disagrees with your taste in music, your taste is likely to change) as for matters of physical perception (if everyone disagrees with your perception of length, your perception is likely to change) (Moscovici, 1976, 1985a; Tajfel, 1969; Turner, 1985).

This sense of uncertainty would be particularly acute when an obviously correct perception is challenged. Asch's lines were *not* 'unambiguous'; there was disagreement between confederates and participants over the length of the lines. In reality, Asch's lone participant was a member of a large majority (those people outside the experiment who would call the lines 'correctly': that is, the rest of humanity) confronted by a small minority (the confederates who called the lines 'incorrectly'). Asch's participants were influenced by a minority: participants who remained 'independent' can be considered to be the conformists! 'Independence' in this sense is nicely described by the American writer Henry Thoreau (1854/1997) in his famous quote from *Walden*: 'If a man does not keep pace with his companions, perhaps it is because he hears a different drummer.'

In contrast to traditional conformity research, Moscovici (1976, 1985a) believed that there is disagreement and conflict within groups, and that there are three *social influence modalities* that define how people respond to such social conflict:

1 *Conformity* – majority influence in which the majority persuades the minority or deviates to adopt the majority viewpoint.

2 *Normalisation* – mutual compromise leading to convergence.

3 *Innovation* – a minority creates and accentuates conflict in order to persuade the majority to adopt the minority viewpoint.

Behavioural style and the genetic model

Building on this critique, Moscovici (1976) proposed a genetic model of social influence. He called it a 'genetic' model because it focused on how the dynamics of social conflict can generate (are genetic of) social change. He believed that in order to create change, active minorities actually go out of their way to create, draw attention to and accentuate conflict. The core premise was that all attempts at influence create conflict based on disagreement between the source and the target of influence. Because people generally do not like conflict, they try to avoid or resolve it. In the case of disagreement with a minority, an easy and common resolution is to simply dismiss, discredit or even pathologise the minority (Papastamou, 1986).

However, it is difficult to dismiss a minority if it 'stands up to' the majority and adopts a behavioural style that conveys uncompromising certainty about and commitment to its position, and a genuine belief that the majority ought to change to adopt the minority's position. Under these circumstances, the majority takes the minority seriously, reconsidering its own beliefs and considering the minority's position as a viable alternative.

The most effective behavioural style a minority can adopt to prevail over the majority is one in which, among other things, the minority promulgates a message that is consistent across time and context, shows *investment* in its position by making significant personal and material sacrifices, and evinces *autonomy* by acting out of principle rather than from ulterior or instrumental motives (Mugny, 1982). Consistency is the most important behavioural style for effective minority influence, as it speaks directly to the existence of an alternative norm and identity rather than merely an alternative opinion. Specifically, it:

• disrupts the majority norm and produces uncertainty and doubt;

• draws attention to the minority as an entity (e.g. Hamilton & Sherman, 1996);

- conveys the clear impression that there is an alternative coherent point of view;
- demonstrates certainty and an unshakeable commitment to this point of view;
- shows that (and how) the only solution to the conflict is espousal of the minority's viewpoint.

From an attribution theory perspective such as Kelley's (1967; see **Chapter 3**), this form of consistent and distinctive behaviour cannot be discounted – it demands to be explained. Furthermore, the behaviour is likely to be internally attributed by an observer to invariant and perhaps essentialist (e.g. Haslam, Rothschild, & Ernst, 1998) properties of the minority rather than to transient or situational factors.

All of this makes the minority even more of a force to be reckoned with and a focus of deliberation by the majority. Overall, a minority that is consistent raises uncertainty. It begs the question: if this minority espouses its viewpoint time and time again, is it the obvious and most viable resolution? (Considering these points, might Aleksei and Ivan have a chance against the system in the fourth 'What do *you* think?' question?)

Moscovici and his colleagues demonstrated the role of consistency in a series of ingenious experiments, referred to as the 'blue–green' studies (Maass & Clark, 1984). In a modified version of the Asch paradigm, Moscovici, Lage and Naffrechoux (1969) had four participants confront two confederates in a colour perception task involving blue slides that varied only in intensity. The confederates were either consistent, always calling the slides 'green', or inconsistent, calling the slides 'green' two-thirds of the time and 'blue' one-third of the time. There was also a control condition with no confederates, just six true participants. Figure 7.9 shows that the consistent minority were more influential than the inconsistent minority (9 per cent versus 2 per cent). We might feel that the reported rate of 9 per cent for the consistent minority is not that high when compared with a consistent majority (recall that Asch reported an average conformity rate of 33 per cent). Nevertheless, this simple experiment highlighted the fact that a minority of two could influence a majority of four.

There are two other notable results from an extension of this experiment, in which participants' real colour thresholds were tested privately after the social influence stage: (1) both experimental groups showed a lower threshold for 'green' than the control group – that is, they erred towards seeing ambiguous green–blue slides as 'green'; and (2) this effect was greater among experimental participants who were resistant to the minority – that is, participants who did not publicly call the blue slides 'green'.

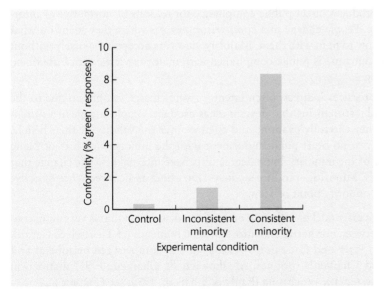

Figure 7.9 Conformity to a minority as a function of minority consistency

Although not as effective as a consistent majority, a consistent two-person minority in a six-person group was more influential than an inconsistent minority; that four people were influenced by two is quite remarkable.

Source: Based on data from Moscovici, Lage and Naffrechoux (1969).

Moscovici and Lage (1976) used the same colour perception task to compare consistent and inconsistent minorities with consistent and inconsistent majorities. There was also a control condition. As before, the only minority to produce conformity was the consistent minority (10 per cent conformity). Although this does not compare well with the rate of conformity to the consistent majority (40 per cent), it is comparable with the rate of conformity to the inconsistent majority (12 per cent). However, the most important finding was that the *only* participants in the entire experiment who actually changed their blue–green thresholds were those in the consistent minority condition. Other studies have shown that the most important aspects of consistency are synchronic consistency (i.e. consensus) among members of the minority (Nemeth, Wachtler, & Endicott, 1977) and perceived consistency, not merely objective repetition (Nemeth, Swedlund, & Kanki, 1974).

Moscovici's (1976) focus on the importance of behavioural style was extended by Gabriel Mugny (1982), who focused on the strategic use of behavioural styles by real, active minorities struggling to change societal practices. Because minorities are typically powerless, they must negotiate with the majority rather than unilaterally adopt a behavioural style. Mugny distinguished between rigid and flexible negotiating styles, arguing that a rigid minority that refuses to compromise on any issues risks being rejected as dogmatic, and a minority that is too flexible, shifting its ground and compromising, risks being rejected as inconsistent (the classic case of 'flip-flopping'). There is a fine line to tread, but some flexibility is more effective than total rigidity. A minority should continue to be consistent with regard to its core position but should adopt a relatively open-minded and reasonable negotiating style on less core issues (e.g. Mugny & Papastamou, 1981).

Conversion theory

In 1980 Moscovici supplemented his earlier account of social influence based on behavioural style with his conversion theory (Moscovici, 1980, 1985a), and this remains the dominant explanation of minority influence. His earlier approach focused largely on how a minority's behavioural style (in particular, attributions based on the minority's consistent behaviour) could enhance its influence over a majority. Conversion theory is a more cognitive account of how a member of the majority processes the minority's message (see Box 7.5).

Moscovici argued that majorities and minorities exert influence through different processes:

1 Majority influence produces direct public compliance for reasons of normative or informational dependence. People engage in a *comparison process* where they focus on what others say to know how to fit in with them. Majority views are accepted passively without much thought. The outcome is public compliance with majority views with little or no private attitude change.

2 Minority influence produces indirect, often latent, private change in opinion due to the cognitive conflict and restructuring that deviant ideas produce. People engage in a *validation process* where they carefully examine and cogitate over the validity of their beliefs. The outcome is little or no overt public agreement with the minority, for fear of being viewed as a member of the minority, but a degree of private internal attitude change that may only surface later. Minorities produce a **conversion effect** as a consequence of active consideration of the minority point of view.

Conversion effect
When minority influence brings about a sudden and dramatic internal and private change in the attitudes of a majority.

Moscovici's dual-process model of influence embodies a distinction that is very similar to that discussed earlier between normative and informational influence (cf. Deutsch & Gerard, 1955), and is related to Petty and Cacioppo's (1986a) distinction between peripheral and central processing, and Chaiken's (Bohner, Moskowitz, & Chaiken, 1995) distinction between heuristic and systematic processing (Eagly & Chaiken, 1993; see **Chapter 6**).

Conversion
If you and your friends repeatedly and consistently told Peter that this was recently re-named The Shard, might he eventually believe you?

Box 7.5 Our world
Conversion on the Internet?

About 3.2 billion people (half the world's population) use the Internet, and they use it to communicate, obtain information, and persuade others. How can active minorities create social change through conversion, as discussed in this chapter, in a world dominated by the Internet? One argument is that it makes things easier as a minority can easily bombard the majority with its consistent alternative message.

However, the alternative argument may carry more weight. The Internet allows people almost unfettered freedom to choose what information they expose themselves to, and people overwhelmingly chose web sites that confirm their existing beliefs and ultimately their identity and self-concept. In this way people largely live in informational 'bubbles' that insulate them from alternative world views. Such bubbles are further reinforced by web sites and search engines, such as Facebook and Google, which operate algorithms to selectively guess what information a specific user might prefer to see. Paradoxically, people may be protected by the Internet from alternative (majority or minority) viewpoints. If people are not exposed to alternative viewpoints, they are unlikely to experience deep cognitive change that ultimately translates into conversion.

Empirical evidence for conversion theory can be organised around three testable hypotheses (Martin & Hewstone, 2003): direction-of-attention, content-of-thinking and differential-influence. There is support for the *direction-of-attention hypothesis* – majority influence causes people to focus on their relationship to the majority (interpersonal focus), whereas minority influence causes people to focus on the minority message itself (message focus) (e.g. Campbell, Tesser, & Fairey, 1986). There is also support for the *content-of-thinking hypothesis* – majority influence leads to superficial examination of arguments, whereas minority influence leads to detailed evaluation of arguments (e.g. Maass & Clark, 1983; Martin, 1996; Mucchi-Faina, Maass, & Volpato, 1991).

The *differential-influence hypothesis*, that majority influence produces more public/direct influence than private/indirect influence whereas minority influence produces the opposite, has received most research attention and support (see Wood, Lundgren, Ouellette, Busceme, & Blackstone, 1994). For example, the studies described above by Moscovici, Lage and Naffrechoux (1969) and Moscovici and Lage (1976) found, as would be expected from conversion theory, that conversion through minority influence took longer to reveal itself than compliance through majority influence; there was evidence for private change in colour thresholds (i.e. conversion) among participants exposed to a consistent minority, although they did not behave (or had not yet behaved) publicly in line with this change.

Another series of studies, by Anne Maass and Russell Clark (1983, 1986), report three experiments investigating people's public and private reactions to majority and minority influence regarding the issue of gay rights. In one of these experiments, Maass and Clark (1983) found that publicly expressed attitudes conformed to the expressed views of the majority (i.e. if the majority was pro-gay, then so were the participants), while privately expressed attitudes shifted towards the position espoused by the minority (see Figure 7.10).

Perhaps the most intriguing support for the *differential-influence hypothesis* comes from a series of fascinating experiments by Moscovici and Personnaz (1980, 1986), who employed the blue–green paradigm described earlier. Individual participants, judging the colour of obviously blue slides that varied only in intensity, were exposed to a single confederate who always called the blue slides 'green'. They were led to believe that most people (82 per cent) would respond as the confederate did, or that only very few people (18 per cent) would. In this way, the confederate was a source of majority or minority influence. Participants publicly called out the colour of the slide, and then (and this is the ingenious twist introduced by Moscovici and Personnaz) the slide was removed and participants wrote down privately the colour of the after-image. Unknown to most people, including the participants, the after-image is always the complementary colour. So, for blue slides the after-image would be yellow, and for green slides it would be purple.

There were three phases to the experiment: an influence phase, where participants were exposed to the confederate, preceded and followed by phases where the confederate was absent and there was thus no influence. The results were remarkable (see Figure 7.11). Majority influence hardly affected the chromatic after-image: it remained yellow, indicating that participants had seen a blue slide. Minority influence, however, shifted the after-image

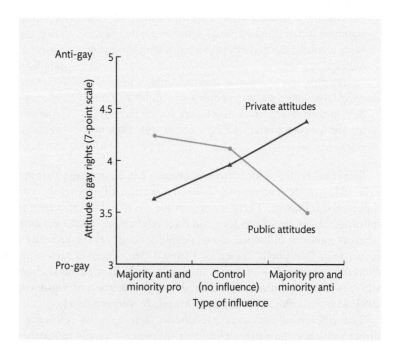

Figure 7.10 Public and private attitude change in response to majority and minority influence

Relative to a no-influence control condition, heterosexual public attitudes towards gay rights closely reflected the pro- or anti-gay attitudes of the majority. However, private attitudes reflected the pro- or anti-gay attitudes of the minority.

Source: Based on data from Maass and Clark (1983).

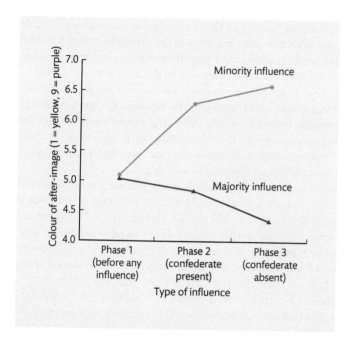

Figure 7.11 Reported colour of chromatic after-image as a result of majority and minority influence

Participants exposed to a majority member who wrongly identified blue slides as green did not change their perception; their after-images did not alter. However, participants exposed to a minority member who called the blue slides green did change their perception; their after-images changed and continued to change even after influence had ceased.

Source: Based on data from Moscovici and Personnaz (1980).

towards purple, indicating that participants had actually 'seen' a green slide! The effect persisted even when the minority confederate was absent.

This controversial finding clearly supports the idea that minority influence produces indirect, latent internal change, while majority influence produces direct, immediate behavioural compliance. Moscovici and Personnaz have been able to replicate it, but others have been less successful. For example, in a direct replication, Doms and Van Avermaet (1980) found after-image changes after both minority and majority influence, and Sorrentino, King and Leo (1980) found no after-image shift after minority influence, except among participants who were suspicious of the experiment.

To try to resolve the contradictory findings, Robin Martin conducted a series of five careful replications of Moscovici and Personnaz's paradigm (Martin, 1998). His pattern of findings revealed that participants tended to show a degree of after-image shift only if they paid close attention to the blue slides – this occurred among participants who were either suspicious of the experiment or who were exposed to many, rather than a few, slides.

The key point is that circumstances that made people attend more closely to the blue slides caused them actually to see more green in the slides and thus to report an after-image that was shifted towards the after-image of green. These findings suggest that Moscovici and his colleagues' intriguing after-image findings may not reflect distinct minority/majority influence processes but may be a methodological artefact. This does not mean that conversion theory is wrong, but it does question the status of the blue–green studies as evidence for conversion theory. Martin (1998) comes to the relatively cautious conclusion that the findings may at least partially be an artefact of the amount of attention participants were paying to the slides: the greater the attention, the greater the after-image shift.

Convergent–divergent theory

Charlan Nemeth (1986, 1995) offered a slightly different account of majority/minority differences in influence. Because people expect to share attitudes with the majority, the discovery through majority influence that their attitudes are in fact in disagreement with those of the majority is surprising and stressful. It leads to a self-protective narrowing of focus of attention. This produces convergent thinking that inhibits consideration of alternative views. In contrast, because people do not expect to share attitudes with a minority, the discovery of disagreement associated with minority influence is unsurprising and not stressful and does not narrow focus of attention. It allows divergent thinking that involves consideration of a range of alternative views, even ones not proposed by the minority.

In this way, Nemeth believes that exposure to minority views can stimulate innovation and creativity, generate more and better ideas, and lead to superior decision-making in groups. The key difference between Nemeth's (1986) convergent–divergent theory and Moscovici's (1980) conversion theory hinges on the relationship between 'stress' and message processing: for Nemeth, majority-induced stress restricts message processing; for Moscovici, minority-induced stress elaborates message processing.

Convergent–divergent theory is supported by research using relatively straightforward cognitive tasks. Minority influence improves performance relative to majority influence on tasks that benefit from divergent thinking (e.g. Martin & Hewstone, 1999; Nemeth & Wachtler, 1983); majority influence improves performance relative to minority influence on tasks that benefit from convergent thinking (e.g. Peterson & Nemeth, 1996); and minority influence leads to the generation of more creative and novel judgements than does majority influence (e.g. Mucchi-Faina, Maass, & Volpato, 1991; Nemeth & Wachtler, 1983).

For example, the Nemeth studies (Nemeth, 1986; Nemeth & Wachtler, 1983) used Asch-type and blue–green paradigms in which participants exposed to majority or minority influence converged, with little thought, on majority responses; but minorities stimulated divergent, novel, creative thinking, and more active information processing, which increased the probability of correct answers. Mucchi-Faina, Maass and Volpato (1991) used a different paradigm with students at the University of Perugia. They found that the students generated more original and creative ideas for promoting the international image of the city of Perugia when they had been exposed to a conventional majority and a creative minority than vice versa, or where the majority and the minority were both original or both conventional.

Research on convergent–divergent theory also shows that minority influence leads people to explore different strategies for problem-solving whereas majority influence restricts people to the majority-endorsed strategy (e.g. Butera, Mugny, Legrenzi, & Pérez, 1996; Peterson & Nemeth, 1996) and that minority influence encourages issue-relevant thinking whereas majority influence encourages message-relevant thinking (e.g. De Dreu, De Vries, Gordijn, & Schuurman, 1999).

Social identity and self-categorization

We have noted above in this chapter that referent informational influence theory (e.g. Abrams & Hogg, 1990a; Hogg & Turner, 1987a; Turner & Oakes, 1989), views prototypical ingroup members as the most reliable source of information about what is normative for the group – the attitudes and behaviours that define and characterise the group. Through the process of self-categorization, group members perceive themselves and behave in line with the norm.

From this perspective, minorities should be extremely ineffective sources of influence. Groups in society that promulgate minority viewpoints are generally widely stigmatised by the majority as social outgroups, or are 'psychologised' as deviant individuals. Their views are rejected as irrelevant and are ridiculed and trivialised in an attempt to discredit the minority (e.g. the treatment of gays, environmentalists, intellectuals; see **Chapter 10** for a discussion of discrimination against outgroups). All this resistance on the part of the majority makes it very difficult for minorities to be influential.

So, from a social identity perspective, how can a minority within one's group be influential? According to David and Turner (2001), the problem for ingroup minorities is that the majority group makes intragroup social comparisons that highlight and accentuate the minority's otherness, essentially concretising a majority-versus-minority intergroup contrast within the group.

The key to effective minority influence is for the minority to somehow make the majority shift its level of social comparison to focus on intergroup comparisons with a genuine shared outgroup. This process automatically transcends intragroup divisions and focuses attention on the minority's ingroup credentials. The minority is now viewed as part of the ingroup, and there is indirect attitude change that may not be manifested overtly. For example, a radical faction within Islam will have more influence within Islam if Muslims make intergroup comparisons between Islam and the West than if they dwell on intra-Islam comparisons between majority and minority factions.

Research confirms that minorities do indeed exert more influence if they are perceived by the majority as an ingroup (Maass, Clark, & Haberkorn, 1982; Martin, 1988; Mugny & Papastamou, 1982). For example, a recent study of the American Tea Party movement (an ultra-right-wing faction of the Republican Party) found that that Republicans primed to feel uncertain about themselves polarised their political attitudes more towards those of the Tea Party when they were also primed to focus on a genuine intergroup comparison between Republicans and Democrats (Gaffney, Rast, Hackett, & Hogg, 2014).

Studies by David and Turner (1996, 1999) show that ingroup minorities produced more indirect attitude change (i.e. conversion) than did outgroup minorities, and majorities produced surface compliance. However, other research has found that an outgroup minority has just as much indirect influence as an ingroup minority (see review by Pérez & Mugny, 1998) and, according to Martin and Hewstone (2003), more research is needed to confirm that conversion is generated by the process of self-categorization.

Vested interest and the leniency contract

Overall, minorities are more influential if they can avoid being categorized by the majority as a despised outgroup and can be considered by the majority as part of the ingroup. The challenge for a minority is to be able to achieve this at the same time as promulgating an unwaveringly consistent alternative viewpoint that differs from the majority position. How can minorities successfully have it both ways – be thought of as an ingroup *and* hold an unwavering outgroup position?

The trick psychologically is to establish one's legitimate ingroup credentials before drawing undue critical attention to one's distinct minority viewpoint. Crano's context-comparison model of minority influence describes how this may happen (e.g. Crano, 2001; Crano & Alvaro, 1998; Crano & Chen, 1998; Crano & Seyranian, 2009). When a minority's message involves weak or unvested attitudes (i.e. attitudes that are relatively flexible, not fixed or absolute), an ingroup minority can be quite persuasive – the message is distinctive and attracts attention and elaboration, and, by virtue of the message being unvested and the minority a clear ingroup, there is little threat that might invite derogation or rejection of the minority. An outgroup minority is likely to be derogated and not influential.

When the message involves strong or vested (i.e. fixed, inflexible and absolute) attitudes, it is more difficult for the minority to prevail. The message is not only highly distinctive but speaks to core group attributes. The inclination is to reject the message and the minority outright. However, the fact that the minority is actually part of the ingroup makes members reluctant to do so – to derogate people who are, after all, ingroup members. One way out of this dilemma is to establish with the minority what Crano calls a leniency contract.

Essentially, the majority assumes that because the minority is an ingroup minority, it is unlikely to want to destroy the majority's core attributes, and so the majority is lenient towards the minority and its views. This enables the majority to elaborate open-mindedly on the ingroup minority's message, without defensiveness or hostility and without derogating the minority. This leniency towards an ingroup minority leads to indirect attitude change. An outgroup minority does not invite leniency and is therefore likely to be strongly derogated as a threat to core group attitudes.

The logic behind this analysis is that disagreement between people who define themselves as members of the same group is both unexpected and unnerving – it raises subjective uncertainty about themselves and their attributes, and motivates uncertainty reduction (Hogg, 2007b, 2012). Where common ingroup membership is important and 'inescapable', there will be a degree of redefinition of group attributes in line with the minority: that is, the minority has been effective. Where common ingroup membership is unimportant and easily denied, there will be no redefinition of ingroup attributes in line with the minority: that is, the minority will be ineffective.

Attribution and social impact

Attribution
The process of assigning a cause to our own behaviour, and that of others.

Many aspects of minority influence suggest an underlying **attribution** process (Hewstone, 1989; Kelley, 1967; see **Chapter 3**). Effective minorities are consistent and consensual, distinct from the majority, unmotivated by self-interest or external pressures and flexible in style. This combination of factors encourages a perception that the minority has chosen its position freely. It is therefore difficult to explain away its position in terms of idiosyncrasies of individuals (although this is, as we saw earlier, a strategy that is attempted), or in terms of external inducements or threats. Perhaps, then, there is actually some intrinsic merit to its position. This encourages people to take the minority seriously (although again, social forces work against this) and at least consider its position; such cognitive work is an important precondition for subsequent attitude change.

Although majorities and minorities can be defined in terms of power, they also of course refer to numbers of people. Although 'minorities' are often both less powerful and less numerous (e.g. West Indians in Britain), they can be less powerful but more numerous (e.g. Tibetans versus Chinese in Tibet). Perhaps not surprisingly, an attempt has been made to explain minority influence purely in terms of social influence consequences of relative numerosity.

Social impact
The effect that other people have on our attitudes and behaviour, usually as a consequence of factors such as group size, and temporal and physical immediacy.

Bibb Latané drew on **social impact** theory to argue that as a source of influence increases in size (number), it has more influence (Latané, 1981; Latané & Wolf, 1981). However, as the cumulative source of influence gets larger, the impact of each additional source is reduced – a single source has enormous impact, the addition of a second source increases impact but not by as much as the first, a third even less, and so on. A good analogy is switching on a single light in a dark room – the impact is huge. A second light improves things, but only a little. If you have ten lights on, the impact of an eleventh is negligible. Evidence does support this idea: the more numerous the source of influence, the more impact it has, with incremental changes due to additional sources decreasing with increasing size (e.g. Mullen, 1983; Tanford & Penrod, 1984).

But how does this account for the fact that minorities can actually have influence? One explanation is that the effect of a large majority on an individual majority member has reached a plateau: additional members or 'bits' of majority influence have relatively little impact. Although a minority viewpoint has relatively little impact, it has not yet plateaued: additional members or 'bits' of minority influence have a relatively large impact. In this way, exposure to minority positions can, paradoxically, have greater impact than exposure to majority viewpoints.

Two processes or one?

Although the social impact perspective can account for some quantitative differences between majority and minority influence at the level of overt public behaviour, even Latané and Wolf (1981) concede that it cannot explain the qualitative differences that exist, particularly at the private level of covert cognitive changes. However, these qualitative differences, and particularly the process differences proposed by Moscovici's (1980) conversion theory, remain the focus of some debate.

For instance, there is some concern that the postulation of separate processes to explain minority and majority influence has revived the opposition of informational and normative influence (Abrams & Hogg, 1990a; David & Turner, 2001; Turner, 1991). As we saw earlier in this chapter, this opposition has problems in explaining other social influence phenomena. Instead, whether minorities or majorities are influential or not may be a matter of social identity dynamics that determine whether people are able to define themselves as members of the minority (majority) group or not (e.g. Crano & Seyranian, 2009; David & Turner, 2001).

In addition, theoretical analyses by Kruglanski and Mackie (1990) and a meta-analysis by Wood and colleagues (Wood, Lundgren, Ouellette, Busceme, & Blackstone, 1994) together suggest that people who are confronted with a minority position, particularly face-to-face with real social minorities and majorities, tend not only to resist an overt appearance of alignment with the minority, but also privately and cognitively to avoid alignment with the minority. This conflicts with Moscovici's dual-process conversion theory.

Summary

- Social influence can produce surface behavioural compliance with requests, obedience of commands, internalised conformity to group norms and deep-seated attitude change.

- People tend to be more readily influenced by reference groups, because they are psychologically significant for our attitudes and behaviour, than by membership groups, as they are simply groups to which we belong by some external criterion.

- Given the right circumstances, we all have the potential to obey commands blindly, even if the consequences of such obedience include harm to others.

- Obedience is affected by the proximity and legitimacy of authority, by the proximity of the victim and by the degree of social support for obedience or disobedience.

- Group norms are enormously powerful sources of conformity: we all tend to yield to the majority.

- Conformity can be reduced if the task is unambiguous and we are not under surveillance, although even under these circumstances there is often residual conformity. Lack of unanimity among the majority is particularly effective in reducing conformity.

- People may conform in order to feel sure about the objective validity of their perceptions and opinions, to obtain social approval and avoid social disapproval, or to express or validate their social identity as members of a specific group.

- Active minorities can sometimes influence majorities: this may be the very essence of social change.

- To be effective, minorities should be consistent but not rigid, should be seen to be making personal sacrifices and acting out of principle, and should be perceived as being part of the ingroup.

- Minorities may be effective because, unlike majority influence which is based on 'mindless' compliance, minority influence causes latent cognitive change as a consequence of thought produced by the cognitive challenge posed by the novel minority position.

- Minorities can be more effective if they are treated by the majority group as ingroup minorities rather than outgroup minorities.

Key terms

Agentic state
Attribution
Autokinesis
Compliance
Conformity
Conformity bias
Conversion effect

Dual-process dependency model
Frame of reference
Informational influence
Membership group
Meta-contrast principle
Minority influence
Normative influence

Norms
Power
Reference group
Referent informational influence
Social identity theory
Social impact
Social influence

Literature, film and TV

American Beauty and Revolutionary Road

Two powerful films by Sam Mendes that explore conformity and independence. Set in American suburbia, the 1999 film *American Beauty*, starring Kevin Spacey, is a true classic about suffocating conformity to social roles, and what can happen when people desperately try to break free. *Revolutionary Road* is a 2008 film, starring Leonardo DiCaprio and Kate Winslet, which explores the same theme with a focus on the drudgery and routine of adult life and the lost dreams of youth, and again on the challenge and consequences of change.

Little Miss Sunshine

Hilarious 2006 film, directed by Jonathan Dayton and Valerie Faris. A breathtakingly dysfunctional family sets out in their decrepit VW van to drive from Arizona to Los Angeles for their daughter Olive (Abigail Breslin) to appear in an absolutely grotesque children's beauty pageant. Featuring Toni Collette, Steve Carell, Greg Kinnear and

Alan Arkin, this is a film about interpersonal relations and families (**relevant to Chapter 14**) but also about non-conformity and violation of social conventions.

Eichmann in Jerusalem: A Report on the Banality of Evil

Highly influential 1963 book by H. Arendt on the Nuremberg war trials of the Nazis. It shows how these "monsters" came across as very ordinary people who were only following orders.

Made in Dagenham

This feel-good and light-hearted 2010 film directed by Nigel Cole and starring Sally Hawkins dramatises a strike (and surrounding events) by Ford sewing machinists in Dagenham in Britain in 1968. The strike was aimed at securing equal pay for women – and it was successful. The film shows social influence through protest and persuasion rather than violence and revolution.

Guided questions

1   Is it true that women conform more than men to group pressure?

2   Why did Stanley Milgram undertake his controversial studies of *obedience to authority*?

3   How does the social context impact on people when they need to state their opinions in public?

4   What are the three major social influence processes associated with conformity?

5   Can a *minority group* really bring about social change by confronting a majority?

Learn more

Baron, R. S., & Kerr, N. (2003). *Group process, group decision, group action* (2nd ed.). Buckingham, UK: Open University Press. A general overview of some major topics in the study of group processes, including social influence phenomena.

Brown, R. J. (2000). *Group processes* (2nd ed.). Oxford, UK: Blackwell. A very readable introduction to group processes, which also places an emphasis on social influence processes within groups, especially conformity, norms and minority influence.

Cialdini, R. B., & Trost, M. R. (1998). Social influence: Social norms, conformity, and compliance. In D. T. Gilbert, S. T. Fiske, & G. Lindzey (Eds.), *The handbook of social psychology* (4th ed., Vol. 2, pp. 151–192). New York: McGraw-Hill. A thorough overview of social influence research with a particular emphasis on norms and persuasion.

Fiske, S. T. (2010). Interpersonal stratification: Status, power, and subordination. In S. T. Fiske, D. T. Gilbert, & G. Lindzey (Eds.), *Handbook of social psychology* (5th ed., Vol. 2, pp. 941–982). New York: Wiley. Detailed and up-to-date overview of research on the psychology of status, which also covers research on power.

Fiske, S. T., & Berdahl, J. (2007). Social power. In A. W. Kruglanski, & E. T. Higgins (Eds.), *Social psychology: Handbook of basic principles* (2nd ed., pp. 678–692). New York: Guilford Press. A detailed overview of the social psychology of power.

Hogg, M. A. (2010). Influence and leadership. In S. T. Fiske, D. T. Gilbert, & G. Lindzey (Eds.), *Handbook of social psychology* (5th ed., Vol. 2, pp. 1166–1207). New York: Wiley. Up-to-date and detailed coverage of research on social influence processes, with a major section on minority influence.

Martin, R., & Hewstone, M. (2007). Social influence processes of control and change: Conformity, obedience to authority, and innovation. In M. A. Hogg & J. Cooper (Eds.), *The SAGE handbook of social psychology: Concise student edition* (pp. 312–332). London: SAGE. A comprehensive review of social influence research, including conformity, obedience and minority influence.

Martin, R., & Hewstone, M. (Eds.) (2010). *Minority influence and innovation: Antecedents, processes and consequences*. Hove, UK: Psychology Press. An edited book that has contributions on minority influence by most of the leaders in the field of minority influence research.

Moscovici, S., Mugny, G., & Van Avermaet, E. (2008). *Perspectives on minority influence*. Cambridge, UK: Cambridge University Press. An overview of research on minority influence by leading scholars of this notably European topic.

Turner, J. C. (1991). *Social influence*. Buckingham, UK: Open University Press. Scholarly discussion of social influence which takes a critical stance from a European perspective and places particular emphasis on social identity, minority influence and the role of group membership and group norms.

Chapter 8
People in groups

Chapter contents

What do *you* think?

1 Alone in his room, James can reliably play a tricky guitar riff really well – precise and fluent. When his friends ask him to play it for them, it all goes horribly wrong. Why do you think this happens?

2 You want to make sure that new members of the small organisation you run are totally committed to it and its goals. You could make the experience of joining smooth, easy and pleasant; or you could make it quite daunting with a bewildering array of initiation rites and embarrassing hurdles to clear. Which would be more effective, when and why?

3 Would you offer to reward a close family member with money after enjoying a meal at their house? Why not?

4 Andrea writes very quickly and neatly and is good at taking notes. She works for a large corporation and is very ambitious to rise to the top. She finds it flattering that her boss assigns her the role of taking notes in important executive meetings. She is keen to please and so always agrees – leaving her sitting at the back scribbling away on her notepad while others talk and make decisions. Is she wise to agree? Why, or why not?

What is a group?

Group
Two or more people who share a common definition and evaluation of themselves and behave in accordance with such a definition.

Groups occupy much of our daily life. We live, work, relax, socialise and play in groups. Groups also largely determine the people we are and the sorts of lives we live. Selection panels, juries, committees and government bodies influence what we do, where we live and how we live. The groups to which we belong determine what language we speak, what accent we have, what attitudes we hold, what cultural practices we adopt, what education we receive, what level of prosperity we enjoy and ultimately who we are. Even those groups to which we do not belong, either by choice or by exclusion, have a profound impact on our lives. In this tight matrix of group influences, the domain of the autonomous, independent, unique self may indeed be limited.

Groups differ in many different ways (Deaux, Reid, Mizrahi, & Ethier, 1995). Some have a large number of members (e.g. a nation, a gender), and others are small (a committee, a family); some are relatively short-lived (a group of friends, a jury), and some endure for thousands of years (an ethnic group, a religion); some are concentrated (a flight crew, a selection committee), others dispersed (academics, Facebook 'friends'); some are highly structured and organised (an army, an ambulance team), and others are more informally organised (a supporters' club, a community action group); some have highly specific purposes (an assembly line, an environmental protest group), and others are more general (a tribal group, a teenage 'gang'); some are relatively autocratic (an army, a police force), others relatively democratic (a university department, a commune); and so on.

Any social group can therefore be described by an array of features that highlight similarities to, and differences from, other groups. These can be very general features, such as membership size (e.g. a religion versus a committee), but they can also be very specific features, such as group practices and beliefs (e.g. Catholics versus Muslims, liberals versus conservatives, Masai versus Kikuyu). This enormous variety of groups can be reduced by limiting the number of significant dimensions to produce a restricted taxonomy of groups. Social psychologists have tended to focus more on group size, group 'atmosphere', task structure and leadership structure than other dimensions.

Categories and group entitativity

Entitativity
The property of a group that makes it seem like a coherent, distinct and unitary entity.

Human groups are categories – some people share characteristics and are in the group, and people who do not share the characteristics are not in the group. As such, human groups should differ in ways that categories in general differ. One of the key ways in which categories differ is in terms of entitativity (Campbell, 1958). **Entitativity** is the property of a group that makes it appear to be a distinct, coherent and bounded entity. High-entitativity groups

Entitativity
A group comprises individuals but sometimes it may seem to be an indivisible entity. Do these Las Ramblas troubadours qualify?

have clear boundaries and are internally well-structured and relatively homogeneous; low-entitativity groups have fuzzy boundaries and structure and are relatively heterogeneous. The members of high-entitativity groups are more interdependent and have a more tightly shared fate than members of a low-entitativity group.

Groups certainly differ in terms of entitativity (Hamilton & Sherman, 1996; Lickel, Hamilton, Wieczorkowska, Lewis, & Sherman, 2000). Hamilton and Lickel and colleagues claim there are qualitative differences in the nature of groups as they decrease in entitativity, and that groups can be classified into four different general types with decreasing entitativity: intimacy groups, task groups, social categories and loose associations.

Common-bond and common-identity groups

One classic and important distinction in the social sciences between types of human groups was originally made in 1887 by the sociologist Ferdinand Tönnies (1887/1955) between *Gemeinschaft* (i.e. community) and *Gesellschaft* (i.e. association): that is, social organisation based on close interpersonal bonds and social organisation based on more formalised and impersonal associations. This distinction has resurfaced in contemporary social psychology in a slightly different form that focuses on a general distinction between similarity-based or categorical groups, and interaction-based or dynamic groups (Arrow, McGrath, & Berdahl, 2000; Wilder & Simon, 1998).

For example, Debbie Prentice and colleagues (Prentice, Miller, & Lightdale, 1994) distinguish between *common-bond* groups (groups based upon attachment among members) and *common-identity* groups (groups based on direct attachment to the group). Kai Sassenberg has found that members of common-bond groups operate according to an egocentric principle of maximising their rewards and minimising their costs with respect to their own contributions – in common-bond groups, personal goals are more salient than group goals. In contrast, members of common-identity groups operate according to an altruistic principle of maximising the group's rewards and minimising its costs through their own contributions – in common-identity groups, group goals are more salient than personal goals because the group provides an important source of identity (Sassenberg, 2002; Utz & Sassenberg, 2002).

Other research, by Elizabeth Seeley and her colleagues (Seeley, Gardner, Pennington, & Gabriel, 2003) found that men and women differ in their preferences for group type and that this may have consequences for the longevity of the group. Women were more attached to groups in which they felt close to the other members (common bonds were more important); men rated groups as important when they were attached to individual members and the group as a whole (common identity was more important). If the common bonds in a group disappear, the group may no longer be valuable for women, whereas the common identity of the group would allow men to remain attracted to it. Thus, some men's groups may last longer than women's groups because of the greater importance they place on group identity.

Groups and aggregates

Not all collections of people can be considered groups in a psychological sense. For example, people with green eyes, strangers in a dentist's waiting room, people on a beach, children waiting for a bus – are these groups? Perhaps not. More likely these are merely social aggregates, collections of unrelated individuals – not groups at all. The important social psychological question is what distinguishes groups from aggregates; it is by no means an easy question to answer. Social psychologists differ in their views on this issue. These differences are, to some extent, influenced by whether the researcher favours an individualistic or a collectivistic perspective on groups (Abrams & Hogg, 2004; Turner & Oakes, 1989).

Individualists believe that people in groups behave in much the same way as they do in pairs or by themselves, and that group processes are really nothing more than interpersonal processes between a number of people (e.g. Allport, 1924; Latané, 1981). *Collectivists* believe that the behaviour of people in groups is influenced by unique social processes and cognitive representations that can only occur in and emerge from groups (Hogg & Abrams, 1988; McDougall, 1920; Sherif, 1936; Tajfel & Turner, 1986).

Definitions

Although there are almost as many definitions of the social group as there are social psychologists who research social groups, David Johnson and Frank Johnson (1987) have identified seven major emphases. The group is:

1   a collection of individuals who are interacting with one another;
2   a social unit of two or more individuals who perceive themselves as belonging to a group;
3   a collection of individuals who are interdependent;
4   a collection of individuals who join together to achieve a goal;
5   a collection of individuals who are trying to satisfy a need through their joint association;
6   a collection of individuals whose interactions are structured by a set of roles and norms;
7   a collection of individuals who influence each other.

Their definition incorporates all these emphases:

> A group is two or more individuals in face-to-face interaction, each aware of his or her membership in the group, each aware of the others who belong to the group, and each aware of their positive interdependence as they strive to achieve mutual goals.
>
> Johnson and Johnson (1987, p. 8)

This definition, and many of the emphases in the previous paragraph, cannot encompass large groups and/or do not distinguish between interpersonal and group relationships. This is a relatively accurate portrayal of much of the classic social psychology of group processes, which is generally restricted, explicitly or implicitly, to small, face-to-face, short-lived, interactive, task-oriented groups. In addition, 'group processes' generally do not mean *group* processes, but interpersonal processes between more than two people. However, more recently the study of group processes has been increasingly influenced by perspectives that consider the roles of identity and relations between large-scale social categories (e.g. Brown, 2000; Hogg & Tindale, 2001; Stangor, 2016).

Group effects on individual performance

Mere presence and audience effects: social facilitation

Perhaps the most elementary *social* psychological question concerns the effect of the presence of other people on someone's behaviour (see Box 8.1). Gordon Allport (1954a) asked: 'What changes in an individual's normal solitary performance occur when other people are present?' (p. 46). You are playing a musical instrument, fixing the car, reciting a poem or exercising in the gym, and someone comes to watch; what happens to your performance? Does it improve or deteriorate?

This question intrigued Norman Triplett (1898), credited by some as having conducted the first social psychology experiment, although there has been controversy about this (see **Chapter 1**). From observing that people cycled faster when paced than when alone, and faster when in competition than when paced, Triplett hypothesised that competition between people energised and improved performance on motor tasks. To test this idea, he had young

Box 8.1 Your life
Public speaking can be scary

How nervous do *you* feel about standing up in front of an audience, say your class, to make a formal presentation? If so, you are in good company. Richard Branson, the founder of Virgin, writes on the Virgin web site:

> I loathe making speeches, and always have . . . I deliver a lot of them these days, but it's almost as true today as it was when I first spoke in public as a student some 50-odd years ago. Back then, my school was having a contest in which we had to memorize a short speech and present it to the other students. If we stumbled at any point, we were 'gonged,' which ended the speech. I remember being scared half to death when my turn came and I had to stand in front of my classmates; I still

break out in a cold sweat just thinking back to the excruciating experience.

People sometimes say a bit of anxiety is a good thing as it keeps you 'stoked' and focused – is this true? What about simply 'winging it' – is that a wise idea? How about thinking of the audience sitting there completely naked – would this work? What could you do to use an audience to your benefit – to make your public performance soar? Think about these questions while reading this section of Chapter 8 on audience effects and social facilitation. You too may become a fabulous orator like Winston Churchill or Barack Obama.

---

children reeling a continuous loop of line on a 'competition machine'. He confirmed his hypothesis: more children reeled the line more quickly when racing against each other in pairs than when performing alone (see **Chapter 1** for details).

Floyd Allport (1920) termed this phenomenon **social facilitation** but felt that Triplett confined it too narrowly to the context of competition, and that it could be widened to allow for a more general principle: that an improvement in performance could be due to the **mere presence** of conspecifics (i.e. members of the same species) as coactors (doing the same thing but not interacting) or as a passive audience (passively watching).

Until the late 1930s, there was an enormous amount of research on social facilitation, much of it conducted on an exotic array of animals. For example, we now know that cockroaches run faster, chickens, fish and rats eat more and pairs of rats copulate more when being 'watched' by conspecifics, or when conspecifics are also running, eating or copulating! However, research has also revealed that social presence can produce quite the opposite effect – social inhibition, or a decrease in task performance.

Contradictory findings such as these, in conjunction with imprecision in defining the degree of social presence (early research focused on coaction, whereas later research focused on passive **audience effects**), led to the near demise of social facilitation research by about 1940.

Drive theory

In 1965, Robert Zajonc published a classic theoretical statement, called **drive theory** (see Figure 8.1), which revived social facilitation research and kept it alive for many decades (see Geen, 1989; Guerin, 1986, 1993). Zajonc set himself the task of explaining what determines whether social presence (mainly in the form of a passive audience) facilitates or inhibits performance.

Drive theory argues that because people are relatively unpredictable (you can rarely know with any certainty exactly what they are going to do), there is a clear advantage to the species for people's presence to cause us to be alert and in readiness. Increased arousal or motivation is thus an instinctive reaction to social presence. Such arousal functions as a 'drive' that energises (i.e. causes us to enact) that behaviour which is our dominant response (i.e. best learnt, most habitual) in that situation. If the dominant response is correct (we feel the task is easy), then social presence produces an improved performance; if it is incorrect (we feel the task is difficult), then social presence produces an impaired performance.

Social facilitation
An improvement in the performance of well-learnt/easy tasks and a deterioration in the performance of poorly learnt/difficult tasks in the mere presence of members of the same species.

Mere presence
Refers to an entirely passive and unresponsive audience that is only physically present.

Audience effects
Impact of the presence of others on individual task performance.

Drive theory
Zajonc's theory that the physical presence of members of the same species instinctively causes arousal that motivates performance of habitual behaviour patterns.

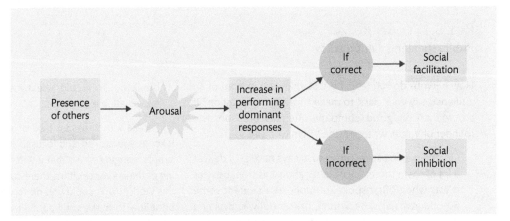

Figure 8.1 Zajonc's drive theory of social facilitation

• The presence of others automatically produces arousal, which 'drives' dominant responses.
• Performance is improved by a 'correct' dominant response, but is impaired by an 'incorrect' dominant response.

Source: Based on Zajonc (1965).

The audience effect
She has been practicing hard at home. What will determine whether she will soar or crash in front of an audience?

Let us illustrate this with an example. You are a novice violinist with a small repertoire of pieces to play. There is one piece that, when playing alone, you find extremely easy because it is very well learnt – you almost never make mistakes. If you were to play this piece in front of an audience (say, your friends), drive theory would predict that, because your dominant response is to make no mistakes, your performance would be greatly improved. In contrast, there is another piece that, when playing alone, you find extremely difficult because it is not very well learnt – you almost never get it right. It would be a rash decision indeed to play this in front of an audience – drive theory would predict that, because the dominant response contains all sorts of errors, your performance would be truly awful, much worse than when you play alone.

Evaluation apprehension

Although early research tends on the whole to support drive theory (Geen & Gange, 1977; Guerin & Innes, 1982), some social psychologists have questioned whether mere presence instinctively produces drive. Nickolas Cottrell (1972) proposed an **evaluation apprehension model**, in which he argues that we quickly learn that the social rewards and punishments (e.g. approval and disapproval) we receive are based on others' evaluations of us. Social presence thus produces an acquired arousal (drive) based on evaluation apprehension.

In support of this interpretation, Cottrell, Wack, Sekerak and Rittle (1968) found no social facilitation effect on three well-learnt tasks when the two-person audience was inattentive (i.e. blindfolded) and merely present (i.e. only incidentally present while ostensibly waiting to take part in a different experiment). This audience would be unlikely to produce much evaluation apprehension. However, a non-blindfolded audience that attended carefully to the participant's performance and had expressed an interest in watching would be expected to produce a great deal of evaluation apprehension. Indeed, this audience did produce a social facilitation effect.

Other research is less supportive. For example, Hazel Markus (1978) had male participants undress, dress in unfamiliar clothing (laboratory coat, special shoes), and then in their own clothing again. To minimise apprehension about evaluation by the experimenter, the task was presented as an incidental activity that the experimenter was not really interested in. The task was performed under one of three conditions: (1) alone; (2) in the presence of an incidental audience (low evaluation apprehension) – a confederate who faced away and was engrossed in some other task; (3) in the presence of an attentive audience (high evaluation apprehension) – a confederate who carefully and closely watched the participant dressing and undressing.

The results (see Figure 8.2) supported evaluation apprehension theory on the relatively easy task of dressing in familiar clothing; only an attentive audience decreased the time taken to perform this task. However, on the more difficult task of dressing in unfamiliar clothing, mere presence was sufficient to slow performance down and an attentive audience had no additional effect; this supports drive theory rather than evaluation apprehension.

Schmitt, Gilovich, Goore and Joseph (1986) conducted a similarly conceived experiment. Participants were given what they thought was an incidental task that involved typing their name into a computer (a simple task), and then entering a code name by typing their name

Evaluation apprehension model
The argument that the physical presence of members of the same species causes drive because people have learnt to be apprehensive about being evaluated.

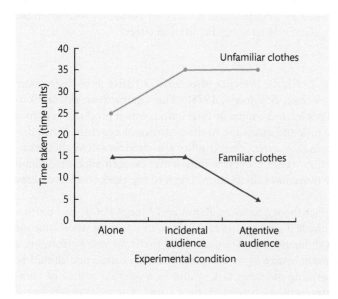

Figure 8.2 Time taken to dress in familiar and unfamiliar clothes as a function of social presence

- Participants dressed in their own clothing (easy task) or in unfamiliar clothing (difficult task).
- They dressed either alone, with an incidental audience present or with an attentive audience present.
- Evaluation apprehension occurred on the easy task: only the attentive audience reduced the time taken to dress up.
- There was a drive effect on the difficult task: both incidental and attentive audiences increased the time taken to dress.

Source: Based on data from Markus (1978).

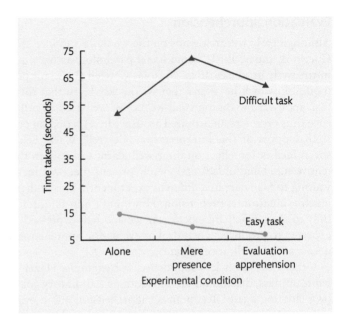

Figure 8.3 Time taken for an easy and a difficult typing task as a function of social presence

- Participants typed their name on a computer (easy task) or typed it backwards interspersed with digits (difficult task), alone, with an incidental audience present or with an attentive audience present.
- There was a drive effect on both the easy and the difficult task.
- The incidental audience improved performance on the easy task and impaired it on the difficult task. The attentive audience had no additional effect.

Source: Based on data from Schmitt, Gilovich, Goore and Joseph (1986).

backwards interspersed with ascending digits (a difficult task). These tasks were performed (1) *alone* after the experimenter had left the room; (2) in the *mere presence* of only a confederate who was blindfolded, wore a headset and was allegedly participating in a separate experiment on sensory deprivation; or (3) under the close *observation of the experimenter*, who remained in the room carefully scrutinising the participant's performance.

The results of the study (see Figure 8.3) show that mere presence accelerated performance of the easy task and slowed performance of the difficult task, and that evaluation apprehension had little additional impact. Mere presence appears to be a sufficient cause of, and evaluation apprehension not necessary for, social facilitation effects. (Can you reassure James about his guitar practice problem? See the first 'What do *you* think?' question.)

Bernard Guerin and Mike Innes (1982) have suggested that social facilitation effects may occur only when people are unable to monitor the audience and are therefore uncertain about the audience's evaluative reactions to their performance. In support of this idea, Guerin (1989) found a social facilitation effect on a simple letter-copying task only among participants who were being watched by a confederate whom they could *not* see. When the confederate could be clearly seen, there was no social facilitation effect.

Distraction–conflict theory

Distraction–conflict theory
The physical presence of members of the same species is distracting and produces conflict between attending to the task and attending to the audience.

According to Glen Sanders (1981, 1983), the presence of others can 'drive us to distraction' (see also Baron, 1986; Sanders, Baron, & Moore, 1978). The argument in **distraction–conflict theory** goes as follows. People are a source of distraction, which produces cognitive conflict between attending to the task and attending to the audience or coactors. While distraction alone impairs task performance, attentional conflict also produces drive that facilitates dominant responses. Together, these processes impair the performance of difficult tasks and, because drive usually overcomes distraction, improve the performance of easy tasks (see Figure 8.4).

In support of distraction–conflict theory, Sanders, Baron and Moore (1978) had participants perform an easy and a difficult digit-copying task, alone or coacting with someone performing either the same or a different task. They reasoned that someone performing a different task would not be a relevant source of social comparison, so distraction should be minimal, whereas someone performing the same task would be a relevant source of comparison and therefore highly distracting. As predicted, they found that participants in the

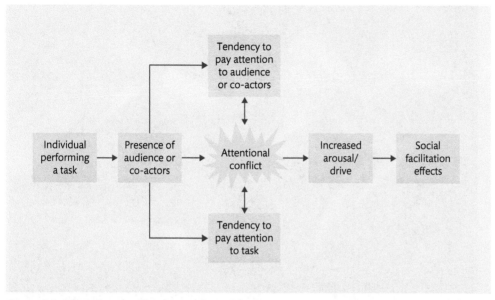

Figure 8.4 Distraction–conflict theory of social facilitation

The presence of an audience creates conflict between attending to the task and attending to the audience: Attentional conflict produces drive that has social facilitation effects.

Source: Based on Baron and Byrne (1987).

distraction condition made more mistakes on the difficult task, and copied more digits correctly on the simple task, than in the other conditions (again, see the first 'What do *you* think?' question).

Distraction–conflict theory has other strengths. Experiments show that any form of distraction (noise, movement, flashing lights), not only social presence, can produce social facilitation effects. In addition, unlike the evaluation apprehension model, it can accommodate results from studies of social facilitation in animals. It is difficult to accept that cockroaches eat more while other roaches are watching because they are anxious about evaluation; however, even the lowly roach can presumably be distracted.

Distraction–conflict theory also had the edge on evaluation apprehension in an experiment by Groff, Baron and Moore (1983). Whenever a tone sounded, participants had to rate the facial expressions of a person appearing on a TV monitor. At the same time, but as an ostensibly incidental activity, they had to squeeze as firmly as possible a bottle held in the hand (latency and strength of squeeze were measures of arousal/drive). Participants did the experiment (1) alone; (2) closely scrutinised by a confederate sitting to one side – this would be highly distracting, as the participant would need to look away from the screen to look at the observer; or (3) closely scrutinised by a confederate who was actually the person on the screen – no attentional conflict. As predicted by distraction–conflict theory, participants squeezed the bottle more strongly in the second condition.

Non-drive explanations of social facilitation

How do we know that 'drive' has a role in social facilitation? Drive is difficult to measure. Physiological measures of arousal such as sweating palms may monitor drive, but the absence of arousal is no guarantee that drive is not operating. Drive is actually a psychological concept and could even mean alertness in the context we are discussing. So, we should not be surprised that several non-drive explanations of social facilitation have been proposed.

One non-drive explanation of social facilitation is based on *self-awareness theory* (Carver & Scheier, 1981; Duval & Wicklund, 1972; Wicklund, 1975). When people focus their attention on themselves as an object, they make comparisons between their actual self (their

Distraction–conflict theory
Even an audience who cannot see what you are doing can be distracting and can impair your performance.

actual task performance) and their ideal self (how they would like to perform). Related to this line of reasoning is *self-discrepancy theory* (Higgins, 1987, 1998). (Both of these theories are described in Chapter 4.) The discrepancy between actual and ideal self increases motivation and effort to bring actual into line with ideal, so on easy tasks, performance improves. On difficult tasks, the discrepancy is too great, so people give up trying, and performance deteriorates. Self-awareness can be produced by a range of circumstances, such as looking at oneself in a mirror, but also by the presence of coactors or an audience.

Still focusing on the role of 'self' in social facilitation, Charles Bond (1982) believes that people are concerned with *self-presentation,* to make the best possible impression of themselves to others. As this is achievable on easy tasks, social presence produces an improved performance. On more difficult tasks, people make, or anticipate making, errors: this creates embarrassment, and embarrassment impairs task performance.

Yet another way to explain social facilitation, without invoking self or drive, is in terms of the purely *attentional consequences* of social presence. This analysis is based on the general idea that people narrow the focus of their attention when they experience attentional overload (Easterbrook, 1959). Robert Baron (1986) believes that people have a finite attention capacity, which can be overloaded by the presence of an audience. Attention overload makes people narrow their attention, give priority to attentional demands and focus on a small number of central cues. Difficult tasks are those that require attention to a large number of cues, so attentional narrowing is likely to divert attention from cues that we really ought to attend to: thus, social presence impairs performance. Simple tasks are ones that require attention to only a small number of cues, so attentional narrowing actually eliminates distraction caused by attending to extraneous cues and focuses attention on central cues: thus, social presence improves performance.

This general idea has been nicely supported in an experiment by Jean-Marc Monteil and Pascal Huguet (1999). The task was a Stroop task where participants have to name the colour of ink that different words are written in. Some words are neutral or consistent with the colour of ink (e.g. 'red' written in red ink) – this is an easy task with low response latencies (people respond quickly); whereas others clash (e.g. 'red' written in blue) – this is a difficult task with high latencies (people respond slowly). The participants performed the Stroop task alone or in the presence of another person. They found that latencies on the difficult task were significantly lower in the social presence condition. Social presence had narrowed attention on the colour of ink, so that semantic interference from the word itself was reduced.

Finally, Tony Manstead and Gün Semin (1980) have proposed a similar attention-based model, but with the emphasis placed on automatic versus controlled task performance. They argue that difficult tasks require a great deal of attention because they are highly controlled. An audience distracts vital attention from task performance, which thus suffers. Easy tasks require little attention because they are fairly automatic. An audience causes more attention to be paid to the task, which thus becomes more controlled and better performed.

Social facilitation revisited

Social psychologists have suggested and investigated many different explanations of what initially appeared to be a basic and straightforward social phenomenon. Some explanations fare better than others while some have not yet been properly tested, and after more than 100 years of research, a number of questions remain unanswered. Nevertheless, the study of audience effects remains an important topic for social psychology, as much of our behaviour occurs in the physical presence of others as an audience. A survey administered by Borden (1980) revealed that people feared speaking in front of an audience more than heights, darkness, loneliness and even death!

Also quite intriguingly and relevant to modern life, social facilitation effects can occur in the presence of virtual humans. Park and Catrambone (2012) had participants perform different tasks involving anagrams, mazes, and modular arithmetic that varied in difficulty. They did the tasks alone, in the company of another person, or in the company of a virtual human on a computer screen. Relative to the alone condition, the presence of a virtual human had exactly the same effect as the presence of a real human – performance of easy tasks improved and performance of difficult tasks deteriorated.

However, we should keep in perspective the actual magnitude of impact that mere presence has on behaviour. From an early **meta-analysis** of 241 social facilitation experiments involving 24,000 participants, Charles Bond and Linda Titus (1983) concluded that mere presence accounted for only a tiny 0.3 to 3.0 per cent of variation in behaviour.

Meta-analysis
Statistical procedure that combines data from different studies to measure the overall reliability and strength of specific effects.

Social presence may have greater impact if we focus on more than *mere* presence. For example, Ronay and Von Hippel (2010) found that the performance of male skateboarders was very significantly affected (improved performance but also many more crashes) by the presence of an attractive woman, and this was mediated by elevated testosterone. It is not just the presence of an audience but the relationship between performer and audience, and in this case hormones then played a role in risk-taking behaviour.

In a different example, a comprehensive review of the effects of social presence on how much people eat reveals that the nature of one's relationship to those who are socially present has an influence (Herman, Roth, & Polivy, 2003). When the others are friends or family and they are also eating, people tend to eat more simply because they spend more time at the table. In the presence of strangers who are eating, people follow the norm set by the others – if others eat more, they do also. In the presence of others who are not eating, people eat less because they are apprehensive about being evaluated negatively for eating too much.

In order to explain additional variation in the way that social facilitation operates, we now move from non-interactive contexts to more interactive contexts and true group processes.

Classification of group tasks

Social facilitation research distinguishes between easy and difficult tasks but restricts itself to tasks that do not require interaction, inter-individual coordination and division of labour. Many tasks fall into this category (e.g. getting dressed, washing the car, cycling) but many others do not (e.g. building a house, playing football, running a business). We could expect social presence to have a different effect on task performance, not only as a function of the degree of social presence (passive audience, coactor, interdependent interaction on a group task) but also as a function of the specific task being performed. What is needed is a taxonomy that classifies types of task based on a limited number of psychologically meaningful parameters.

In tackling the pragmatic question of whether groups perform better than individuals, Ivan Steiner (1972, 1976) developed a **task taxonomy** with three dimensions, based on answering three questions:

Task taxonomy
Group tasks can be classified according to whether a division of labour is possible; whether there is a predetermined standard to be met; and how an individual's inputs can contribute.

1 **Is the task divisible or unitary?**

- A *divisible* task is one that benefits from a division of labour, where different people perform different subtasks.
- A *unitary* task cannot sensibly be broken into subtasks. Building a house is a divisible task and pulling a rope a unitary task.

2 **Is it a maximising or an optimising task?**

- A *maximising* task is an open-ended task that stresses quantity: the objective is to do as much as possible.
- An *optimising* task is one that has a set standard: the objective is to meet the standard, neither to exceed nor fall short of it. Pulling on a rope would be a maximising task, but maintaining a specified fixed force on the rope would be an optimising task.

3 **How are individual inputs related to the group's product?**

- An *additive* task is one where the group's product is the sum of all the individual inputs (e.g. a group of people planting trees).
- A *compensatory* task is one where the group's product is the average of the individuals' inputs (e.g. a group of people estimating the number of bars in Amsterdam).
- A *disjunctive* task is one where the group selects as its adopted product one individual's input (e.g. a group of people proposing different things to do over the weekend will adopt one person's suggestion).
- A *conjunctive* task is one where the group's product is determined by the rate or level of performance of the slowest or least able member (e.g. a group working on an assembly line).
- A *discretionary* task is one where the relationship between individual inputs and the group's product is not directly dictated by task features or social conventions; instead, the group is free to decide on its preferred course of action (e.g. a group that *decides* to shovel snow together).

These parameters allow us to classify tasks. For example, a tug-of-war is unitary, maximising and additive; assembling a car is divisible, optimising and conjunctive; and many group decision-making tasks are divisible, optimising and disjunctive (or compensatory). As to whether groups are better than individuals, Steiner believed that in general, the actual group performance is always inferior to the group's potential (based on the potential of its human resources). This shortfall is due mainly to a **process loss** (e.g. losses due to the coordination of individual members' activities, disproportionate influence on the part of specific powerful group members and various social distractors). However, against this background, Steiner's taxonomy allows us to predict what sort of tasks favour group performance.

Process loss
Deterioration in group performance in comparison to individual performance due to the whole range of possible interferences among members.

For additive tasks, the group's performance is better than the best individual's performance. For compensatory tasks, the group's performance is better than that of most individuals, because the average is most likely to be correct. For disjunctive tasks, the group's performance is equal to or worse than the best individual – the group cannot do better than the best idea proposed. And for conjunctive tasks, the group's performance is equal to the worst individual's performance – unless the task is divisible, in which case a division of labour can redirect the weakest member to an easier task and so improve the group's performance.

Although Steiner emphasised the role of **coordination loss** in preventing a group performing optimally in terms of the potential of its members, he also raised the possibility of an entirely different, and more fundamentally psychological, type of loss – motivation loss.

Social loafing and social impact

Over 100 years ago, Maximilien Ringelmann (1913), a French professor of agricultural engineering, published a number of experiments investigating the efficiency of various numbers of people, animals and machines performing agricultural tasks (Kravitz & Martin, 1986). In one study, he had young men, alone or in groups of two, three or eight, pull horizontally on a rope attached to a dynamometer (an instrument that measures the amount of force exerted). He found that the force exerted per person decreased as a function of group size: the larger the group, the less hard each person pulled (see Figure 8.5). This is called the **Ringelmann effect**.

Our previous discussion suggests two possible explanations for this:

1 *Coordination loss* – owing to jostling, distraction and the tendency for people to pull slightly against one another, participants were prevented from attaining their full potential.

2 *Motivation loss* – participants were less motivated; they simply did not try so hard.

An ingenious study by Alan Ingham and his colleagues compared coordination and motivation losses in groups. In one condition, real groups of varying size pulled on a rope. The other condition had 'pseudo-groups' with only one true participant and a number of confederates. The confederates were instructed only to pretend to pull on the rope while making realistic grunts to indicate exertion. The true participant was in the first position and so did not know that the confederates behind him were not actually pulling. As Figure 8.6 shows, what transpired was that in pseudo-groups, participants reduced their effort. Because there was no coordination possible, no loss can be attributed to it; the decrease can be attributed only to a loss of *motivation*. In real groups, there was an additional reduction in individual effort that can be attributed to coordination loss (Ingham, Levinger, Graves, & Peckham, 1974).

Coordination loss
Deterioration in group performance compared with individual performance, due to problems in coordinating behaviour.

Ringelmann effect
Individual effort on a task diminishes as group size increases.

Figure 8.5 The Ringelmann effect: Force per person as a function of group size

As the number of people pulling horizontally on a rope increased, each person's exertion was reduced: people pulling in eight-person groups each exerted half the effort of a person pulling alone.

Source: Based on data from Ringelmann (1913).

Figure 8.6 Coordination and motivation losses in group rope-pulling

- As group size increased from 1 to 6, there was a decrease in each person's output.
- In pseudo-groups, this is due to reduced effort, i.e. motivation loss.
- In real groups, this is more marked as a result of coordination loss.

Source: Based on data from Ingham, Levinger, Graves and Peckham (1974).

Social loafing
A reduction in individual effort when working on a collective task (one in which our outputs are pooled with those of other group members) compared with working either alone or coactively (our outputs are not pooled).

This loss of motivation has been termed **social loafing** by Bibb Latané and his colleagues, who replicated the effect with shouting, cheering and clapping tasks. For instance, they had participants cheer and clap as loudly as possible alone or in groups of two, four or six. The amount of noise produced per person was reduced by 29 per cent in two-person groups, 49 per cent in four-person groups and 60 per cent in six-person groups. For the shouting task, participants shouted alone or in two- or six-person real groups or pseudo-groups (they wore blindfolds and headsets transmitting continuous 'white noise'). As in Ingham and colleagues' experiment, there was a clear reduction in effort for participants in pseudo-groups, with additional coordination loss for participants in real groups (Latané, Williams, & Harkins, 1979). See the results in Figure 8.7.

Social loafing, then, is a tendency for individuals to work less hard (i.e. loaf) on a task when they believe that others are also working on the task (see Box 8.2). More formally, it

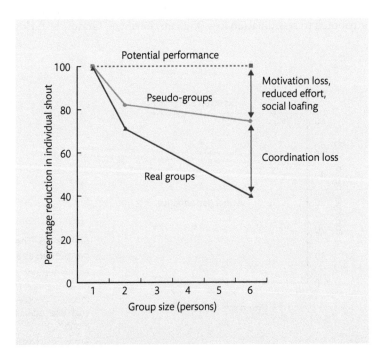

Figure 8.7 Reduction in volume of individual shouting in two-person and six-person real and pseudo-groups

- Social loafing: individual students shouted less loudly as group size increased.
- As in Figure 8.6, this demonstrates a loss of motivation in pseudo-groups and an additional loss due to a lack of coordination in real groups.

Source: Latané, Williams and Harkins (1979) Experiment 2.

Box 8.2 Your life
Don't you just love group projects?

In psychology classes (as in the wider world of work), you are often placed in small groups to work as a team on a collective project. How do you feel about this? Some of you may think, 'Oh, no, I'm going to end up doing all the work to compensate for all these other slackers.' Others may think, 'Great, I can sit back and loaf while someone else does all the work.' This is a very significant issue – imagine the consequences of loafing on the football pitch in a World Cup final, on the flight deck of a passenger plane, in a government crisis meeting or at NASA's Mission Control. The question of what determines whether people loaf or work hard to achieve group goals is very relevant to a very wide swath of social life. This section on social loafing provides some of the answers.

refers to 'a reduction in individual effort when working on a collective task (in which one's outputs are pooled with those of other group members) compared to when working either alone or coactively' (Williams, Karau, & Bourgeois, 1993, p. 131).

A notable feature of loafing is that as group size increases, the addition of new members to the group has a decreasingly significant incremental impact on effort: the reduction of effort conforms to a negatively accelerating power function (see Figure 8.8). So, for example, the reduction in individual effort as the consequence of a third person joining a two-person group is relatively large, while the impact of an additional member on a twenty-person group is minimal. The range within which group size seems to have a significant impact is about one to eight members.

Social loafing is related to the **free-rider effect** (Frohlich & Oppenheimer, 1970; Kerr, 1983) in research into social dilemmas and public goods (**Chapter 11**). A free rider is someone who takes advantage of a shared public resource without contributing to its maintenance. For example, a tax evader who uses the road system, visits national parks and benefits from public medical provision is a free rider. The main difference between loafing and free riding is that although loafers reduce effort on coactive tasks, they nevertheless do

Free-rider effect
Gaining the benefits of group membership by avoiding costly obligations of membership and by allowing other members to incur those costs.

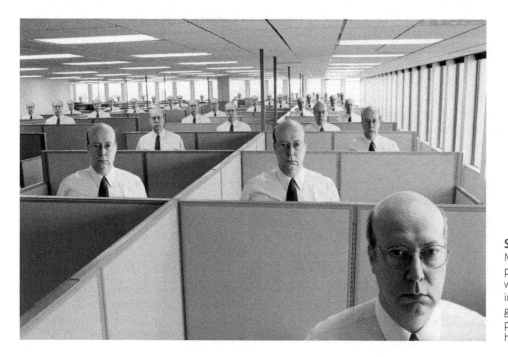

Social loafing
Modern offices can make people feel like clones working on mindless tasks in boring settings - not a great recipe for thrilling personal engagement in hard word.

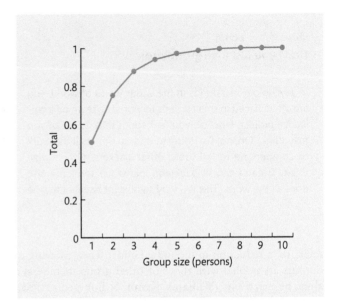

Figure 8.8 Total group output as a negatively accelerating power function of group size

As the group gets larger, each new member has less and less relative impact on group behaviour: the reduction in effort due to new members gets smaller.

contribute to the group product (there is a *loss* of motivation); in contrast, free riders exploit the group product while contributing nothing to it (there is a *different* motivation; see Williams, Karau, & Bourgeois, 1993).

Social loafing is a pervasive and robust phenomenon. A meta-analytic review by Karau and Williams (1993) of the seventy-eight social loafing studies conducted up to the early 1990s found loafing in 80 per cent of the individual–group comparisons that they made. This is an extraordinarily significant overall effect (see reviews by Harkins & Szymanski, 1987; Williams, Harkins, & Karau, 2003; Williams, Karau, & Bourgeois, 1993). The general loafing paradigm is one in which individual or coactive performance is compared either with groups performing some sort of additive task (e.g. brainstorming), or with the performance of pseudo-groups, in which people are led to *believe* that they are performing collectively with varying numbers of others, but in fact circumstances are arranged so that they are performing individually.

Loafing has been found in the laboratory as well as in the field, and in Western and Asian cultures. The effect has been recorded using physical tasks (e.g. clapping, rope pulling and swimming), cognitive tasks (e.g. generating ideas), evaluative tasks (e.g. quality ratings of poems) and perceptual tasks (e.g. maze performance). People even loaf when tipping in restaurants! In one study, 20 per cent of people gave tips when seated alone, but only 13 per cent tipped when seated in groups of five or six (Freeman, Walker, Bordon, & Latané, 1975).

A review of social motivation research concluded that there are three reasons why we loaf when we are in a group (Geen, 1991):

1 *Output equity* – we believe that others loaf; so, to maintain equity (Jackson & Harkins, 1985) and to avoid being a 'sucker' (Kerr & Bruun, 1983) we loaf.

2 *Evaluation apprehension* – we worry about being evaluated by others; but when we are anonymous and cannot be identified, we hang back and loaf, especially when a task is not engaging (Kerr & Bruun, 1981). However, when we can be identified and therefore evaluated, loafing is reduced (Harkins, 1987; Harkins & Szymanski, 1987).

3 *Matching to standard* – often, we do not have a clear sense of the group's standards or norms, so we hang back and loaf. However, the presence of a clear personal, social or group performance standard should reduce loafing (Goethals & Darley, 1987; Harkins & Szymanski, 1987; Szymanski & Harkins, 1987).

Group size may have the effect it does due to **social impact** (Latané, 1981). The experimenter's instructions to clap, shout, brainstorm or whatever (i.e. the social obligation to work as hard as possible) have a social impact on the participants. If there is one participant and one experimenter, the experimenter's instructions have maximal impact. If there are two participants, the impact on each participant is halved; if three it is one-third, and so on. There is a diffusion of individual responsibility that grows with group size. (See also how diffusion operates in the context of bystander apathy towards a victim in **Chapter 14**).

Loafing is not an inevitable consequence of group performance. Certain factors, apart from group size, influence the tendency to loaf (see Geen, 1991; Williams, Karau, & Bourgeois, 1993). For example, personal identifiability by the experimenter (Williams, Harkins, & Latané, 1981), personal involvement in the task (Brickner, Harkins, & Ostrom, 1986), partner effort (Jackson & Harkins, 1985), intergroup comparison (Harkins & Szymanski, 1989) and a highly meaningful task in association with expectation of poor performance by co-workers (Williams & Karau, 1991) have all been shown to reduce loafing.

In some circumstances, people may even work harder collectively than coactively, in order to compensate for anticipated loafing by others on important tasks or in important groups – there is a **social compensation** effect. In a study by Stephen Zaccaro (1984), participants each folded pieces of paper to make little tents in two- or four-person groups – the usual loafing effect emerged (see Figure 8.9). However, other participants who believed they were competing against an outgroup, and for whom the attractiveness and social relevance of the task were accentuated, behaved quite differently. The loafing effect was actually reversed: they constructed more tents in the larger group. This was an unusual finding. In contrast to the rather pessimistic view that groups inevitably inhibit individuals from attaining their true potential (Steiner, 1972), Zaccaro's study indicates that group life may, under certain circumstances, cause people to exceed their individual potential, i.e. there may be process gains in groups (Shaw, 1976).

There are other circumstances when people may work harder in groups than when alone (e.g. Guzzo & Dickson, 1996). One is when people place greater value on groups than on individuals. Collectivist Eastern cultures, in comparison to more individualist Western cultures, do this (Hofstede, 1980; Smith, Bond, & Kağitçibaşi, 2006; see **Chapter 16**). So it comes as no surprise, for example, to discover that people can work harder in groups than alone in China (Earley, 1989, 1994) and Japan (Matsui, Kakuyama, & Onglatco, 1987).

Social impact
The effect that other people have on our attitudes and behaviour, usually as a consequence of factors such as group size, and temporal and physical immediacy.

Social compensation
Increased effort on a collective task to compensate for other group members' actual, perceived or anticipated lack of effort or ability.

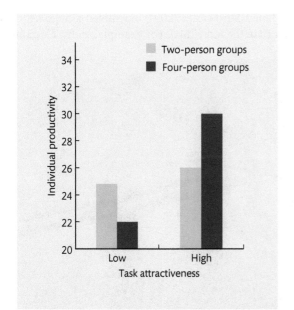

Figure 8.9 Individual effort as a function of task attractiveness and group size

- Social compensation. Participants performing a relatively unattractive paper-folding task loafed.
- Individual productivity was lower in four-person than two-person groups.
- For an attractive task, the loafing effect was reversed: individual productivity was higher in four- than two-person groups.

Source: Based on data from Zaccaro (1984).

Another circumstance where people work harder in groups is when groups and their members believe and expect that the group will be effective in achieving important goals (Guzzo, Jost, Campbell, & Shea, 1993; Sheppard, 1993).

There has been a revival of interest in the prospect of process gains in groups and the ability of groups to increase task motivation (Brown, 2000; Kerr & Park, 2001). From their meta-analysis of seventy-eight loafing studies, Karau and Williams (1993) identified task importance and the significance of the group to the individual as the two key factors that promote increased effort in groups. These factors may be related. People may be particularly motivated to work hard on tasks that are important precisely because they define membership of a group that is vital to their self-concept or social identity (Fielding & Hogg, 2000).

As an example, consider a study by Steve Worchel and his colleagues where participants made paper chains alone and then as a group (Worchel, Rothgerber, Day, Hart, & Butemeyer, 1998). In the group phase of the experiment, participants simply worked in their groups, or they were also in competition against an outgroup. In addition, they either had individual name tags and different-coloured coats, or everyone in the group had identical group name tags and wore identical-coloured coats. Worchel and his associates found clear evidence that people worked significantly harder in groups than alone when the group was highly *salient* – group name tags, identical-coloured coats and intergroup competition. The productivity increase was five paper chains. In the least salient condition, there was loafing (productivity dropped by four paper chains), and in the intermediate salience conditions, there was no significant departure from base rate (productivity of 11). Karau and Hart (1998) found a similar process gain in groups that were highly cohesive because they contained people who liked one another.

Generally, research on group performance has assumed that groups perform worse than individuals, and that process and motivation gains are more the exception than the rule. This premise that groups are generally worse than individuals also underpins much classic research on collective behaviours such as crowds (e.g. Zimbardo, 1970; see **Chapter 11**). However, other research emphasises that although people in groups may behave differently to people alone, there is a *change* rather than a deterioration of behaviour (Hogg & Abrams, 1988; Klein, Spears, & Reicher, 2007; Reicher, Spears, & Postmes, 1995), and that people, in organisational settings, actually like to work in groups and find them satisfying and motivating (Allen & Hecht, 2004). What we now know about social loafing can also be implemented in organisational and education settings, where group projects are so prevalent, to overcome loafing (Aggarwal & O'Brien, 2008).

In his book *The Wisdom of Crowds,* James Surowiecki (2004) assembled a huge list of instances where the group performs better than the individual. For example, in the TV game

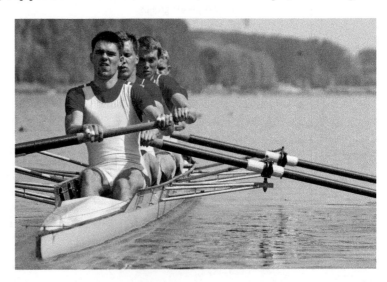

Group cohesiveness
Putting it all together, team spirit, total commitment, exhaustion-elation.

show *Who Wants to Be a Millionaire?* – where contestants can call an expert or poll the studio audience to decide which of four answers to the question is correct – Surowiecki found that the expert was correct 65 per cent of the time, but the audience (a collection of random people) yielded the right answer 91 per cent of the time.

Group cohesiveness

One of the most basic properties of a group is its **cohesiveness** (solidarity, *ésprit de corps*, team spirit, morale) – the way it 'hangs together' as a tightly knit, self-contained entity characterised by uniformity of conduct, attachment to the group, and mutual support between members. The strength of cohesiveness varies between groups, between contexts and across time. Groups with extremely low levels of cohesiveness appear to be hardly groups at all, so the term may also capture the very essence of being a group as opposed to not a group – the psychological process that transforms an aggregate of individuals into a group.

Cohesiveness is thus a descriptive term, used to define a property of the group as a whole. In this respect, it is quite closely related to the property of entitativity possessed by categories, which we discussed at the beginning of this chapter. But cohesiveness is also a term that describes the psychological process responsible for an individual's attachment to a group and its members and thus for the overall cohesiveness of the group. Herein lies a potential problem: it makes sense to say that a group is cohesive, but not that an individual is cohesive.

After almost a decade of informal usage, cohesiveness was formally defined by Festinger, Schachter and Back (1950) in a now-classic study. They believed that a field of forces, based on the attractiveness of the group and its members and the degree to which the group satisfies individual goals, acts upon the individual. The resultant valence of these forces of attraction produces cohesiveness, which is responsible for group membership continuity and adherence to group standards (see Figure 8.10).

Because concepts such as 'field of forces' are difficult to operationalise, and also because the theory was not precise about exactly how to define cohesiveness operationally (i.e. in

Cohesiveness
The property of a group that affectively binds people, as group members, to one another and to the group as a whole, giving the group a sense of solidarity and oneness.

Figure 8.10 Festinger, Schachter and Back's (1950) theory of group cohesiveness
Festinger, Schachter and Back (1950) believed that a field of forces, based on attraction and goal mediation, acts on individual group members to render the group more or less cohesive, and that cohesiveness influences membership continuity and adherence to group norms.
Source: Hogg (1992).

terms of specific measures or experimental manipulations), social psychologists almost immediately simplified their conception of cohesiveness. For instance, in their own research on the cohesiveness of student housing projects at the Massachusetts Institute of Technology, Festinger, Schachter and Back (1950) simply asked students: 'What three people . . . do you see most of socially?' (p. 37; see **Chapter 14** for further details of this study).

When we characterise cohesiveness in terms of interpersonal liking, we should not be surprised that factors that increase liking (e.g. similarity, cooperation, interpersonal acceptance, shared threat) generally raise cohesiveness. Further, elevated cohesiveness generates conformity to group standards, accentuated similarity, improved intragroup communication and enhanced liking (Cartwright, 1968; Dion, 2000; Hogg, 1992; Lott & Lott, 1965).

It has been suggested (Hogg, 1992, 1993; Turner, 1982, 1984) that this perspective on group cohesiveness represents a much wider *social cohesion* or *interpersonal interdependence* model of the social group (see Figure 8.11), where researchers differ only in which components of the model they emphasise. Because social psychologists have not really resolved the problem of knowing unambiguously how to operationalise cohesiveness (Evans & Jarvis, 1980; Mudrack, 1989), more recent research has tended to be in applied areas (Levine & Moreland, 1990). In sports psychology, in particular, some rigorous scales have been devised: for example, Widmeyer, Brawley and Carron's (1985) eighteen-item *group environment questionnaire* to measure the cohesiveness of sports teams.

A fundamental question that has been raised by social identity researchers (Hogg, 1992, 1993; Turner, 1984, 1985; see **Chapter 11**) asks to what extent an analysis of group cohesiveness in terms of aggregation (or some other arithmetic integration) of interpersonal attraction really captures a group process at all. To all intents and purposes, the group has disappeared entirely from the analysis and we are left simply with interpersonal attraction, about which we already know a great deal (Berscheid & Reis, 1998; see **Chapter 14**).

Personal attraction
Liking for someone based on idiosyncratic preferences and interpersonal relationships.

To resolve this issue, Hogg (1993) distinguished between **personal attraction** (true interpersonal attraction based on close relationships and idiosyncratic preferences) and

Figure 8.11 General framework of the social cohesion/interpersonal interdependence model

Source: Based on Hogg (1992).

social attraction (inter-individual liking based on perceptions of self and others in terms not of individuality but of group norms or prototypicality). Strictly speaking, personal attraction has nothing to do with groups, while social attraction is the 'liking' component of group membership. So, for example, you might like Jessica because you are close friends with a long conspiratorial history of intimacy (this is personal attraction) but also like her because you are both members of the same pub darts team (this is social attraction). Of course, the converse is that you might dislike Jessica because of a long history of interpersonal animosity (low personal attraction) or dislike her because she throws for a rival pub's darts team (low social attraction).

Social attraction, then, is the liking aspect of group membership. It is one of a constellation of effects (ethnocentrism, conformity, intergroup differentiation, stereotyping, ingroup solidarity) produced by the process of categorizing oneself and others as group members and of psychologically identifying with a group, as specified by self-categorization theory (Turner, Hogg, Oakes, Reicher, & Wetherell, 1987; see **Chapter 11**). It is an elegant irony, but also of course true, that you can like someone as a group member but not as an individual, and vice versa (Mullen & Copper, 1994).

This analysis has at least two major advantages over the traditional model:

1 It does not reduce group solidarity and cohesiveness to interpersonal attraction.
2 It is as applicable to small interactive groups (the only valid focus of traditional models) as to large-scale social categories, such as an ethnic group or a nation (people can feel attracted to one another on the basis of common ethnic or national group membership).

This perspective has empirical support. For example, Hogg and Turner (1985) aggregated people with others whom they ostensibly would like or dislike (the fact that the others were people they would like or dislike was irrelevant to the existence of the group), or explicitly categorized them as a group on the basis of the criterion that they would like, or dislike, one another. They found that interpersonal attraction was not automatically associated with greater solidarity (see Figure 8.12). Rather, where interpersonal liking was neither the implicit nor the explicit basis for the group (i.e. in the random categorization condition), group solidarity was unaffected by interpersonal attraction.

In another study, Hogg and Hardie (1991) gave a questionnaire to an Australian football team. Perceptions of team prototypicality and of norms were significantly related to

Social attraction
Liking for someone based on common group membership and determined by the person's prototypicality of the group.

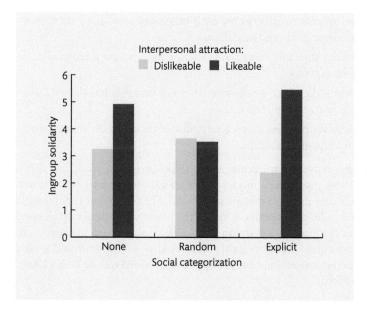

Figure 8.12 Ingroup solidarity as a function of interpersonal attraction and social categorization

Students who were explicitly categorized as a group on the basis of interpersonal liking or who were merely aggregated showed greater solidarity with likeable groups, while participants who were randomly categorized showed equal solidarity, irrespective of how likeable the group was.

Source: Hogg and Turner (1985).

measures of group-based social attraction but were not related to measures of interpersonal attraction. This differential effect was strongest among members who themselves identified most strongly with the team. Similar findings have been obtained from studies of women's netball teams playing in an amateur league (Hogg & Hains, 1996), and of organisational subgroups and quasi-naturalistic discussion groups (Hogg, Cooper-Shaw, & Holzworth, 1993).

This broader view of cohesion as linked to group solidarity and social identity may explain why loyalty is so important to group life. For example, in their social glue hypothesis, Mark Van Vugt and Claire Hart (2004) argue that group cooperation can be sustained only if members show ingroup loyalty and willingness to sacrifice self-gain or advantage for the good of the group; thus, disloyalty is reacted to very strongly (also see Levine & Moreland, 2002).

Group socialisation

An obvious feature of many of the groups with which we are familiar is that new members join, old members leave, members are socialised by the group, and the group in turn is imprinted with the contribution of individuals. Groups are dynamic structures that change continuously over time. However, this dynamic aspect of groups is often neglected in social psychology, where the analysis is rather static and excludes the passage of time. Many social psychologists feel that this considerably weakens the explanatory power of social psychological theories of group processes and intergroup behaviour (Condor, 1996, 2006; Levine & Moreland, 1994; Tuckman, 1965; Worchel, 1996).

The effects of time are taken more seriously in organisational psychology, where longitudinal analyses are relatively common and quite sophisticated (Wilpert, 1995). For example, Cordery, Mueller and Smith (1991) studied job satisfaction, absenteeism and employee turnover for a twenty-month period in two mineral-processing plants to discover that although autonomous work groups improved work attitudes, they also increased absenteeism and employee turnover.

Focusing on small interactive groups, Bruce Tuckman (1965) described a now famous five-stage developmental sequence that such groups go through:

1 *forming* – an orientation and familiarisation stage;
2 *storming* – a conflict stage, where members know each other well enough to start working through disagreements about goals and practices;
3 *norming* – having survived the storming stage, consensus, cohesion and a sense of common identity and purpose emerge;
4 *performing* – a period in which the group works smoothly as a unit that has shared norms and goals, and good morale and atmosphere;
5 *adjourning* – the group dissolves because it has accomplished its goals, or because members lose interest and motivation and move on.

Group socialisation
Dynamic relationship between the group and its members that describes the passage of members through a group in terms of commitment and of changing roles.

More recently, Dick Moreland and John Levine (1982, 1984; Levine & Moreland, 1994; Moreland, Levine, & Cini, 1993) presented a model of **group socialisation** to describe and explain the passage of individuals through groups over time. They focus on the dynamic interrelationship of group and individual members across the life span of the group. A novel feature of this analysis is that it focuses not only on how individuals change in order to fit into the group but also on how new members can, intentionally or unintentionally, be a potent source of innovation and change within the group (Levine, Moreland, & Choi, 2001). Three basic processes are involved:

1 **Evaluation:** Group members and potential members engage in an ongoing process of comparison of the past, present and future rewards of the group with the rewards of potential alternative relationships (Thibaut & Kelley, 1959; see discussion of social exchange theory in **Chapter 14**). Simultaneously, the group as a whole evaluates its individual members in terms of their contribution to the group. This bilateral evaluation process is motivated by the fact that people have goals and needs that create expectations. If such expectations are, or are likely to be, met, social approval is expressed; if they are not met, social disapproval is expressed, and actions may occur to modify behaviour or to reject individuals or the group.

2 **Commitment:** Evaluation affects the commitment of the individual to the group and the group to the individual in a relatively straightforward manner. Symmetrical positive commitment rests on both the group and the individual agreeing on goals and values, feeling positive ties, being willing to exert effort, and desiring to continue membership. However, at any given time, there may be commitment asymmetry, such that the individual is more committed to the group or the group to the individual. This creates instability because it endows the least committed party with greater power, and it therefore builds pressure towards a more equal level of commitment.

3 **Role transition:** Role transition refers to a sharp change in the type of role a member occupies in a group. Role transitions are superimposed on more continuous variation in commitment over time, and their occurrence is governed by groups' and individuals' criteria for the occurrence of a transition. There are three general types of role: (1) *non-member* – this includes prospective members who have not joined the group and ex-members who have left the group; (2) *quasi-member* – this includes new members who have not attained full member status, and marginal members who have lost that status; and (3) *full member* – people who are closely identified with the group and have all the privileges and responsibilities associated with actual membership.

Equipped with these processes, Moreland and Levine (1982, 1984) provide a detailed account of the passage of individual members through the group (see Figure 8.13). There are five distinct phases of group socialisation, involving reciprocal evaluation and influence by group and individual, each heralded and/or concluded by a clear role transition (see Box 8.3).

Moreland and his colleagues have conducted research on specific role transitions, particularly those associated with becoming a member (Brinthaupt, Moreland, &

Role transition
Graduation is a ritualised public ceremony that marks an important passage from one stage of life to another in a student's life.

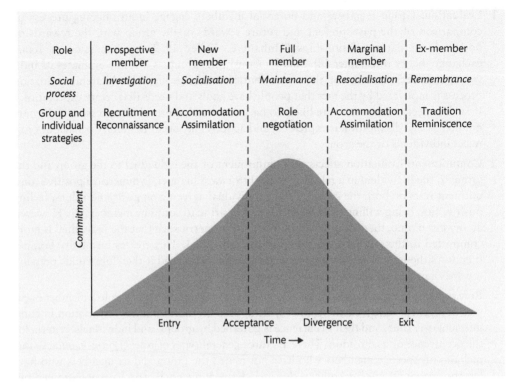

Figure 8.13 A model of the process of group socialisation

Group socialisation. The passage of an individual member through a group is accompanied by variation in commitment and is marked by role discontinuities.

Source: Moreland and Levine (1982).

Box 8.3   Research highlight
Phases of group socialisation

Moreland and Levine (1982, 1984; Moreland, Levine, & Cini, 1993) distinguished five phases of group socialisation (see Figure 8.13):

1   *Investigation*. The group recruits prospective members, who in turn reconnoitre the group. This can be more formal, involving interviews and questionnaires (e.g. joining an organisation), or less formal (e.g. associating yourself with a student political society). A successful outcome leads to a *role transition*: entry to the group.

2   *Socialisation*. The group assimilates new members, educating them in its ways. In turn, new members try to get the group to accommodate their views. Socialisation can be unstructured and informal, but also quite formal (e.g. an organisation's induction programme). Successful socialisation is marked by *acceptance*.

3   *Maintenance*. Role negotiation takes place between full members. Role dissatisfaction can lead to a role transition called *divergence*, which can be unexpected and unplanned. It can also be expected – a typical group feature (e.g. university students who diverge by graduating and leaving university).

4   *Resocialisation*. When divergence is expected, resocialisation is unlikely; when it is unexpected, the member is marginalised into a deviant role and tries to become resocialised. If successful, full membership is reinstated – if unsuccessful, the individual leaves. Exit can be marked by elaborate retirement ceremonies (e.g. the ritualistic stripping of insignia in a court martial).

5   *Remembrance*. After the individual leaves the group, both parties reminisce. This may be a fond recall of the 'remember when . . .' type or the more extreme exercise of a totalitarian regime in rewriting history.

Source: Moreland and Levine (1982).

Levine, 1991; Moreland, 1985; Moreland & Levine, 1989; Pavelchak, Moreland, & Levine, 1986). Role transitions are an important aspect of group life. They can be smooth and easy when individual and group are equally committed and share the same criteria about what a transition means and when it occurs, e.g. when a student commences postgraduate studies. Otherwise, conflict can occur over whether a role transition should or did occur, e.g. whether an employee's performance justifies a promotion rather than a bonus. For this reason, transition criteria often become formalised and public, and ritualised rites of passage or **initiation rites** become a central part of the life of the group. They can be pleasant events marked by celebration and the giving of gifts (e.g. graduation, a wedding), but more often than not they involve a degree of pain, suffering or humiliation (e.g. circumcision, a wake). These rites generally serve three important functions:

Initiation rites
Often painful or embarrassing public procedure to mark group members' movements from one role to another.

- *symbolic* – they allow consensual public recognition of a change in identity;
- *apprenticeship* – some rites help individuals become accustomed to new roles and normative standards;
- *loyalty elicitation* – pleasant initiations with gifts and special dispensations may elicit gratitude, which should enhance commitment to the group.

In the light of this last function, the prevalence and apparent effectiveness of disagreeable initiation rites is puzzling. Surely people would avoid joining groups with severe initiations, and if unfortunate enough not to be able to do this, then at the very least they should subsequently hate the group and feel no sense of commitment.

We can make sense of this anomaly in terms of **cognitive dissonance** (Festinger, 1957; discussed in **Chapter 6**). An aversive initiation creates dissonance between the two thoughts: 'I knowingly underwent a painful experience to join this group' and 'Some aspects of this group are not that great' (since group life is usually a mixture of positive and negative aspects). As an initiation is public and cannot be denied, I can reduce dissonance by revising my opinion of the group – downplaying negative aspects and focusing on positive aspects. The outcome for me is a more favourable evaluation of the group and thus greater commitment.

Cognitive dissonance
State of psychological tension produced by simultaneously having two opposing cognitions. People are motivated to reduce the tension, often by changing or rejecting one of the cognitions. Festinger proposed that we seek harmony in our attitudes, beliefs and behaviours and try to reduce tension from inconsistency among these elements.

This analysis predicts that the more unpleasant the initiation is, the more positive the subsequent evaluation of the group will be. The Aronson and Mills (1959) experiment (described in **Chapter 6**) is an investigation of this idea. You will recall that Aronson and Mills recruited female students to take part in a group discussion of the psychology of sex. Before joining the group, they listened to and rated a short extract of the discussion – an extremely tedious and stilted discussion of the secondary sexual characteristics of lower animals. It was quite rightly rated as such by control participants, and also by a second group of participants who had gone through a mild initiation where they read aloud five words with vague sexual connotations. However, a third group, who underwent an extreme initiation where they read out loud explicit and obscene passages, rated the discussion as very interesting.

Harold Gerard and Grover Mathewson (1966) were concerned that the effect may have arisen because the severe-initiation participants were either sexually aroused by the obscene passage and/or relieved at discovering that the discussion was not as extreme as the passage. To discount these alternative explanations, they replicated Aronson and Mills's study. Participants, who audited and rated a boring discussion they were about to join, were given mild or severe electric shocks either explicitly as an initiation or under some other pretext completely unrelated to the ensuing discussion. As cognitive dissonance theory predicted, the painful experience enhanced evaluation of the group only when it was perceived to be an initiation (see Figure 8.14). (Now answer the second 'What do *you* think?' question.)

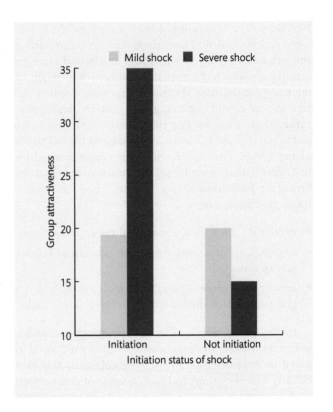

Figure 8.14 Group attractiveness as a function of severity of electric shock and initiation status of the shock

- Participants about to join a boring group discussion were given a mild or severe electric shock.
- When the shock was billed as an initiation, participants given the severe shock rated the group as more attractive than participants given the mild shock.

Source: Based on data from Gerard and Mathewson (1966).

Norms

Norms
Attitudinal and behavioural uniformities that define group membership and differentiate between groups.

Many years ago, the sociologist William Graham Sumner (1906) wrote about **norms** as 'folkways' – habitual customs displayed by a group because they had originally been adaptive in meeting basic needs. Later, Sherif (1936) described norms as 'customs, traditions, standards, rules, values, fashions, and all other criteria of conduct which are standardised as a consequence of the contact of individuals' (p. 3). Although norms can take the form of explicit rules that are enforced by legislation and sanctions (e.g. societal norms to do with private property, pollution and aggression), most social psychologists agree with Cialdini and Trost (1998) that norms are:

> rules and standards that are understood by members of a group and that guide and/or constrain social behaviour without the force of laws. These norms emerge out of interaction with others; they may or may not be stated explicitly, and any sanctions for deviating from them come from social networks, not the legal system. (p. 152)

Another sociologist, Harold Garfinkel (1967), focused on norms as the implicit, unobserved, taken-for-granted background to everyday life. People typically assume a practice is 'natural' or simply 'human nature' until the practice is disrupted by norm violation and people suddenly realise the practice is 'merely' normative. Indeed, Piaget's theory of cognitive development describes how children only slowly begin to realise that norms are not objective facts, and suggests that even adults find it difficult to come to this realisation (Piaget, 1928, 1955).

Ethnomethodology
Method devised by Garfinkel, involving the violation of hidden norms to reveal their presence.

Garfinkel devised a general methodology, called **ethnomethodology**, to detect these background norms. One specific method involved the violation of norms in order to attract people's attention to them. For example, Garfinkel had students act at home for fifteen minutes as if they were boarders: that is, they were polite, spoke formally and only when spoken to. Their families reacted with astonishment, bewilderment, shock, embarrassment and anger, backed up with charges of selfishness, nastiness, rudeness and lack of consideration! An implicit norm for familial interaction was revealed, and its violation provoked a strong reaction.

Social identity theorists place a particular emphasis on the group-defining dimension of norms (e.g. Abrams & Hogg, 1990a; Abrams, Wetherell, Cochrane, Hogg, & Turner, 1990; Hogg, 2010; Hogg & Smith, 2007; Turner, 1991). Norms are attitudinal and behavioural regularities that map the contours of social groups (small groups or large social categories) such that normative discontinuities mark group boundaries. Norms capture attributes that describe one group and distinguish it from other groups, and because groups define who we are, group norms are also prescriptive, telling us how we should behave as group members. Thus, the behaviour of students and lecturers at a university is governed by very different norms: knowing whether someone is a student or a lecturer establishes clear expectations of appropriate normative behaviour. (Reflect on the third 'What do *you* think?' question: what norms are in conflict?)

As Hogg and Reid (2006) have noted, this perspective on norms transcends the traditional distinction drawn in social psychology between descriptive norms ('is' norms) that describe behavioural regularities, and injunctive norms ('ought' norms) that convey approval or disapproval of the behaviour (e.g. Cialdini, Kallgren, & Reno, 1991). Instead, by tying norms to group membership, the descriptive and injunctive aspects of norms become integrated, and as we discuss later, group norms provide a moral compass for group members.

As an aside, norms and **stereotypes** are closely related – the terms 'normative behaviour' and 'stereotypical behaviour' mean virtually the same thing. However, research traditions have generally separated the two areas: norms referring to behaviour that is shared in a group, and stereotypes (see **Chapters 2, 10 and 11**) to shared generalisations made by individuals about members of other groups.

Stereotype
Widely shared and simplified evaluative image of a social group and its members.

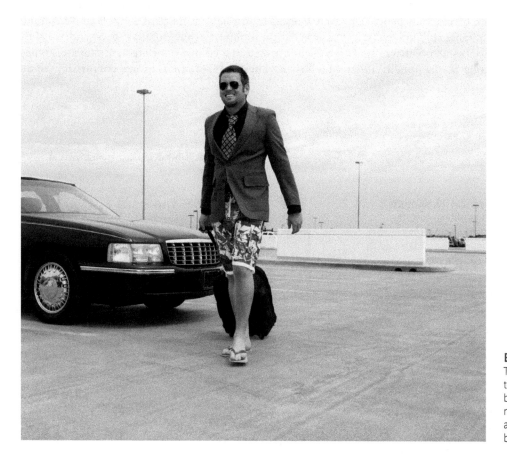

Ethnomethodology
The fact that this man seems to be headed to a serious business meeting dressed in rather splendid shorts draws attention to the existence of business dress norms.

Group norms can have a powerful effect on people. For example, Theodore Newcomb (1965) conducted a classic study of norms in the 1930s at a small American college called Bennington. The college had progressive and liberal norms but drew its students from conservative, upper-middle-class families. The 1936 American presidential election allowed Newcomb to conduct a confidential ballot. First-year students strongly favoured the conservative candidate, while third- and fourth-year students had shifted their voting preference towards the liberal and communist/socialist candidates (see Figure 8.15). Presumably, prolonged exposure to liberal norms had produced the change in political preference.

In a better-controlled study by Alberta Siegel and Sidney Siegel (1957), new students at a private American college were randomly assigned to different types of student accommodation – sororities and dormitories. At this particular college, sororities had a conservative ethos and the dormitories had more progressive liberal norms. Siegel and Siegel measured how conservative the students were at the beginning and end of the year. Figure 8.16 shows how exposure to liberal norms reduced conservatism.

Norms serve a function for the individual. They specify a limited range of behaviour that is acceptable in a certain context, and thus they reduce uncertainty and facilitate confident choice of the 'correct' course of action. Norms provide a **frame of reference** within which to locate our own behaviour. You will recall that this idea was explored by Sherif (1936) in his classic experiments dealing with norm formation (see Box 7.1 in **Chapter 7** for details). Sherif showed that when people made perceptual judgements alone, they relied on their own estimates as a frame of reference; however, when they were in a group, they used the group's range of judgements to converge quickly on the group mean.

Sherif believed that people were using other members' estimates as a social frame of reference to guide them: he felt that he had produced a primitive group norm experimentally. The norm was an emergent property of interaction between group members, but once created it acquired a life of its own. Members were later tested alone and still conformed to the norm. In one study people who were retested individually as much as a year later were, quite remarkably, still influenced by the group norm (Rohrer, Baron, Hoffman, & Swander, 1954).

This same point was strikingly demonstrated in a couple of related autokinetic studies (Jacobs & Campbell, 1961; MacNeil & Sherif, 1976). In a group comprising three

Frame of reference
Complete range of subjectively conceivable positions on some attitudinal or behavioural dimension, which relevant people can occupy in a particular context.

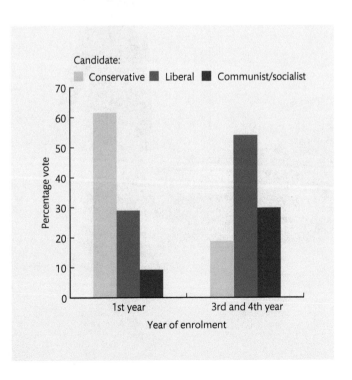

Figure 8.15 Newcomb's 1965 Bennington study: voting preference for 1936 presidential candidates as a function of exposure to liberal norms

First-year students at Bennington College in the USA showed a traditionally conservative voting pattern during the 1936 presidential election, while third- and fourth-year students, who had been exposed for longer to the college's liberal norms, showed a significantly more liberal voting pattern.

Source: Based on data from Newcomb (1965).

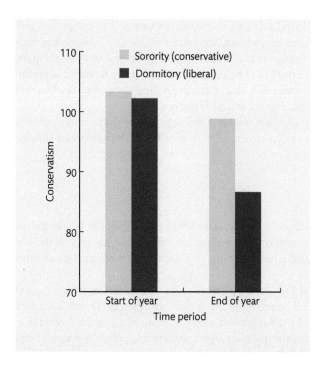

Figure 8.16 Effects of dormitory political norms on students' conservative or liberal voting preferences

Source: Based on data from Siegel and Siegel (1957).

confederates, who gave extreme estimates, and one true participant, a relatively extreme norm emerged. The group went through a number of 'generations', in which a confederate would leave and another true participant would join, until the membership of the group contained none of the original members. The original extreme norm still powerfully influenced the participants' estimates. This is an elegant demonstration that a norm is a true group phenomenon: it can emerge only from a group, yet it can influence the behaviour of the individual in the physical absence of the group (Turner, 1991). It is as if the group is carried in the head of the individual in the form of a norm.

Norms also serve functions for the group in so far as they coordinate the actions of members towards the fulfilment of group goals. In an early and classic study of factory production norms, Coch and French (1948) describe a group that set itself a standard of 50 units per hour as the minimum level to secure job tenure. New members quickly adopted this norm. Those who did not were strongly sanctioned by ostracism and in some cases had their work sabotaged. Generally speaking, there is good evidence from the study of goal setting in organisational work teams that, where group norms embody clear group goals for performance and production, group members work harder and are more satisfied (Guzzo & Dickson, 1996; Weldon & Weingart, 1993).

Norms are inherently resistant to change – after all, their function is to provide stability and predictability. However, norms initially arise to deal with specific circumstances. They endure as long as those circumstances prevail but ultimately change with changing circumstances. Norms vary in their 'latitude of acceptable behaviour': some are narrow and restrictive (e.g. military dress codes) and others wider and less restrictive (e.g. dress codes for university lecturers). In general, norms that relate to group loyalty and to central aspects of group life have a narrow latitude of acceptable behaviour, while norms relating to more peripheral features of the group are less restrictive. Finally, certain group members are allowed a latitude of acceptable behaviour that is greater than others: higher-status members (e.g. leaders) can get away with more than lower-status members and followers (this phenomenon is discussed in **Chapter 9** when we talk about leadership).

There is evidence for the patterning and structure of different types of norm from Sherif and Sherif's (1964) pioneering study of adolescent gangs in American cities. Participant observers infiltrated these gangs and studied them over several months. The gangs had given themselves names, had adopted various insignia and had strict codes about how gang members should dress. Dress codes were important, as it was largely through dress that the gangs differentiated themselves from one another. The gangs also had strict norms concerning sexual mores and how to deal with outsiders (e.g. parents, police); however, leaders were allowed some latitude in their adherence to these and other norms.

Norms are the yardstick of group conduct, and it is through norms that groups influence the behaviour of their members. The exact processes responsible are the subject of much of **Chapter 7**, which deals with social influence.

Morality

One key feature of norms, as foreshadowed earlier, is that they prescribe how we should and should not behave as members of a group that we feel we are part of and identify with. They convey a message of what is right and what is wrong and therefore what constitutes moral conduct.

Moral principles are fundamental organising principles for our behavior, which regulate behavioural activation (approach) and behavioural inhibition (avoidance) (Janoff-Bulman & Carnes, 2013; Higgins, 1998). Moral principles can also unite us, but they often divide us. Many of the most intractable and destructive conflicts in society are oriented around moral disagreement and conflict – conflict between good and evil.

Jonathan Haidt (2012) distinguishes between different moral principles, based on his 'moral foundations theory'. Disagreement between people with different political and religious orientations towards what is morally good rests on the fact that they prioritise different moral principles in their moral reasoning. This disagreement and conflict can be highly charged because moral principles and their expression and communication are associated with strong moral emotions such as guilt and shame (Giner-Sorolla, 2012). According to Joshua Greene (2013), although many moral judgements are automatic and emotional, they can also be highly controlled and rational. Greene views moral thinking as a more deliberate and controlled form of making moral judgements, and he argues that emotional responses to cultural and social differences explain value clashes and aggression between groups.

Perhaps most relevant to this chapter on groups is the view that morality and moral principles serve a social function for communities of people who live together in groups, and that shared ideas about what is the 'right' way to behave may vary, depending on the cultural, religious or political context in which this is defined (Ellemers, Pagliaro, & Barreto, 2013). The key point here is precisely that groups configure their normative attitudes and practices around what they consider to be right. Perhaps more provocatively, they build their moral principles on the groundwork of their normative practices. When groups compare themselves with other groups, they almost always seek to occupy the moral high ground, and in extreme cases of intergroup conflict they trade veiled or blatant accusations of moral bankruptcy.

Global moral principles that apply to all humanity, which is our largest normative community, are often the ultimate moral reference point for subgroups; such that the latter lay claim to embodying these principles in their normative attributes and to embodying them more exactly than competing outgroups – we are more human than they are (cf. Haslam, 2006; and our discussion of dehumanisation in **Chapter 10**).

Group structure

Cohesiveness, socialisation and norms refer mainly to uniformities in groups. In very few groups, however, are all members equal, performing identical activities or communicating freely. Within a group, members differ in what roles or subgroups they occupy, what status they have, who they can easily communicate with, how well they embody the group's norms, and the extent to which they are central or peripheral members. This is what is meant by **group structure**, and its features may not be readily visible to an outsider.

Roles

Roles are much like norms; they describe and prescribe behaviour. However, while norms apply to the group as a whole, roles apply to a subgroup of people within the group. Furthermore, while norms distinguish between groups, they are generally not intentionally derived to facilitate constructive interaction between groups in society. In contrast, roles are specifically designed to differentiate between people in the group for the greater good of the group as a whole.

Roles are not people but behavioural prescriptions that are assigned to people. They can be informal and implicit (e.g. in groups of friends) or formal and explicit (e.g. in aircraft flight crews). One quite general role differentiation in small groups is between task specialists (the 'ideas' people, who get things done) and socioemotional specialists (the people everyone likes because they address relationships in the group) (e.g. Slater, 1955). Roles may emerge in a group for a number of reasons:

- They represent a division of labour; only in the simplest groups is there no division of labour.
- They furnish clear-cut social expectations within the group and provide information about how members relate to one another.
- They furnish members with a self-definition and a place within the group.

Roles facilitate group functioning. However, inflexible role differentiation can sometimes be detrimental to the group. Take a real-life example. Rigid role differentiation (who does what) in pre-flight checks by the flight crew of a passenger airliner caused the crew to fail to engage a de-icing device, with the tragic consequence that the plane crashed shortly after takeoff (Gersick & Hackman, 1990). At the national and global levels, role differentiation between different security organisations (e.g. CIA, FBI, NSA, Interpol, national and regional police forces) can inhibit the free flow of information required to protect us against terrorism.

Roles can sometimes also be associated with larger category memberships (e.g. professional groups) outside the specific task-oriented groups. The task-oriented group can become a context for role conflict that is actually a manifestation of wider intergroup conflict. One example of this is conflict that can occur in a hospital between doctors and nurses (e.g. Oaker & Brown, 1986).

Although we often adopt a dramaturgical perspective when we speak of people 'acting' or 'assuming' roles, we are probably only partly correct. We may assume roles much like actors taking different parts, but many people see us only in particular roles and so infer that that is how we really are. Professional actors are easily typecast in exactly the same way – one reason why Paul Greengrass's 2006 film, *United 93*, about the 11 September 2001 terrorist attacks on the United States, is so incredibly powerful is that the actors are not high-profile individuals who have already been typecast. This tendency to attribute roles internally to dispositions of the role player is a likely example of **correspondence bias** (Gawronski, 2004; Gilbert & Malone, 1995; also see **Chapter 3**).

One practical implication of this is that you should avoid low-status roles in groups, or you may subsequently find it difficult to escape their legacy. Perhaps the most powerful and well-known social psychological illustration of the power of roles to modify behaviour is Zimbardo's (1971; Banuazizi & Movahedi, 1975) simulated prison experiment (see Box 8.4).

Ultimately, roles can influence who we are – our identity and concept of self (see Haslam & Reicher, 2005, 2012). Sociologists have elaborated this idea to explain how social

Group structure
Division of a group into different roles that often differ with respect to status and prestige.

Roles
Patterns of behaviour that distinguish between different activities within the group, and that interrelate to one another for the greater good of the group.

Correspondence bias
A general attribution bias in which people have an inflated tendency to see behaviour as reflecting (corresponding to) stable underlying personality attributes.

Box 8.4 Research classic
Guards versus prisoners: role behaviour in a simulated prison

Phillip Zimbardo was interested in how people adopt and internalise roles to guide behaviour. He was also interested in whether it is the prescription of the role rather than the personality of the role occupant that governs in-role behaviour. In a famous role-playing exercise, twenty-four psychologically stable male Stanford University student volunteers were randomly assigned the roles of prisoners or guards. The prisoners were arrested at their homes and initially processed by the police, then handed over to the guards in a simulated prison constructed in the basement of the psychology department at Stanford University.

Zimbardo had planned to observe the role-playing exercise over a period of two weeks. However, he had to stop the study after six days! Although the students were psychologically stable and those assigned to the guard or prisoner roles had no prior dispositional differences, things got completely out of hand. The guards continually harassed, humiliated and intimidated the prisoners, and they used psychological techniques to undermine solidarity and sow the seeds of distrust among them. Some guards increasingly behaved in a brutal and sadistic manner.

The prisoners initially revolted. However, they gradually became passive and docile as they showed symptoms of individual and group disintegration and an acute loss of contact with reality. Some prisoners had to be released from the study because they showed symptoms of severe emotional disturbance (disorganised thinking, uncontrollable crying and screaming), and in one case, a prisoner developed a psychosomatic rash all over his body.

Zimbardo's explanation of what happened in the simulated prison was that the students complied (too well!) with the roles that they thought were expected of them (see Haney, Banks, & Zimbardo, 1973). This has been challenged. Steve Reicher and Alex Haslam argue that the participants were confronted by a situation that raised their feelings of uncertainty about themselves, and that in order to reduce this uncertainty they internalised the identities available (prisoners or guards) and adopted the normatively appropriate behaviours to define themselves (Reicher & Haslam, 2006; Haslam & Reicher, 2012). The process was one of group identification and conformity to group norms motivated by uncertainty about their self-concept (see Hogg, 2012).

interaction and wider societal expectations about behaviour can create enduring and real identities for people – *role identity theory* (McCall & Simmons, 1978; Stryker & Statham, 1986; see Hogg, Terry, & White, 1995).

Status

Status
Consensual evaluation of the prestige of a role or role occupant in a group, or of the prestige of a group and its members as a whole.

All roles are not equal: some are more valued and respected and thus confer greater **status** on the role occupant. The highest-status role in most groups is the role of leader (see **Chapter 9**). In general, higher-status roles or their occupants have two properties:

1 consensual prestige;

2 a tendency to initiate ideas and activities that are adopted by the group.

For example, from his participant observation study of gangs in an Italian American immigrant community, the sociologist W. F. Whyte (1943) reported that even the relatively inarticulate 'Doc', who described his assumption of leadership of the thirteen-member Norton Gang in terms of who he had 'walloped', found that the consensual prestige that such wallopings earned him was insufficient alone to ensure his high-status position. He admitted that his status also rested on the fact that he was the one who always thought of things for the group to do.

Status hierarchies in groups are not fixed: they can vary over time, and from situation to situation. Take an orchestra: the lead violinist may have the highest-status role at a concert, while the union representative has the highest-status role in negotiations with management. One explanation of why status hierarchies emerge so readily in groups derives from social comparison theory (Festinger, 1954; Suls & Miller, 1977) – status hierarchies are the expression and reflection of intragroup social comparisons. Groups furnish a pool of relevant other people with whom we can make social comparisons to assess the validity of our opinions and abilities.

Certain roles in the group have more power and influence and, because they are therefore more attractive and desirable, have many more 'applicants' than can be accommodated. Fierce social comparisons on behavioural dimensions relevant to these roles inevitably mean that the majority of group members, who are unsuccessful in securing the role, must conclude that they are less able than those who are successful. There arises a shared view that those occupying the attractive role are superior to the rest – consensual prestige and high status. (Do you have any advice for Andrea? See the fourth 'What do *you* think?' question.)

Status hierarchies within groups often become institutionalised, so that members do not continually make social comparisons. Rather, they simply assume that particular roles or role occupants are of higher status than their own role or themselves. Research into the formation of status hierarchies in newly created groups supports this view. Strodtbeck, James and Hawkins (1957) assembled mock juries to consider and render a verdict on transcripts of actual trials. They found that the high-status role of jury foreman almost always went to people who had higher occupational status outside the context of the jury (e.g. teachers or psychologists rather than janitors or mechanics).

One explanation of this phenomenon is proposed by **expectation states theory** (Berger, Fisek, Norman, & Zelditch, 1977; Berger, Wagner, & Zelditch, 1985; see De Gilder & Wilke, 1994; Ridgeway, 2001). Status derives from two distinct sets of characteristics:

1 **Specific status characteristics** are attributes that relate directly to ability on the group task (e.g. being a good athlete in a sports team, a good musician in a band).
2 **Diffuse status characteristics** are attributes that do not relate directly to ability on the group task but are generally positively or negatively valued in society (e.g. being wealthy, having a white-collar occupation, being white).

Diffuse status characteristics generate favourable expectations that are generalised to all sorts of situations, even those that may not have any relevance to what the group does. Group members simply assume that someone who has high diffuse status (e.g. a medical doctor) will be better able than others to promote the group's goals (e.g. analysing trial transcripts in order to render a verdict) and therefore has higher specific status.

Typically, specific status and diffuse status each make their own additive contribution to a person's overall status in a newly formed group. So, if your town was assembling a cast for a musical in the local theatre, Brenda may well play a part because of her rich contralto voice (specific status) and Rudolf could be chosen because of his dreamy looks (diffuse status). But star billing will no doubt accrue to Sophie, the soprano – she has been a successful soprano in other productions (specific status); plus, she looks stunning in most costumes (diffuse status). Poor Rudolf can't sing to save his life, so he only has his diffuse status to contribute to his overall status in the group.

David Knottnerus and Theodore Greenstein (1981) investigated the different contributions of specific status and diffuse status in a newly formed group. Female participants worked with a female confederate on two supposedly related tasks. Specific status was manipulated by informing participants that they had performed better or worse than the confederate on the first task – a perceptual task. Diffuse status was manipulated by leading participants to believe that they were either younger or older than the confederate. The second task, a word construction task, allowed measures of yielding to the confederate's suggestions to be used as an index of effective status. The results (see Figure 8.17) showed that participants yielded more if they believed that they were of lower specific or lower diffuse status than the confederate. Other factors shown to contribute to high status in a group include seniority, assertiveness, past task success and high group orientation.

Expectation states theory
Theory of the emergence of roles as a consequence of people's status-based expectations about others' performance.

Specific status characteristics
Information about those abilities of a person that are directly relevant to the group's task.

Diffuse status characteristics
Information about a person's abilities that are only obliquely relevant to the group's task, and derive mainly from large-scale category memberships outside the group.

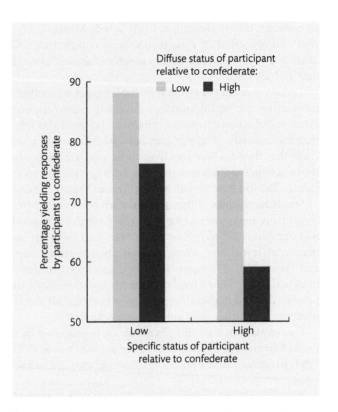

Figure 8.17 Yielding as a function of specific and diffuse status of participants relative to a confederate

Female participants yielded more often to a female confederate's suggestions in a word-construction task if the confederate had higher specific status (had performed well on a similar task) and had higher diffuse status (was older).

Source: Based on data from Knottnerus and Greenstein (1981).

Communication networks

People occupying different roles in a group need to coordinate their actions through communication, although not all roles need to communicate with one another. Thus, the structuring of a group with respect to roles entails an internal **communication network** that regulates who can communicate easily with whom. Although such networks can be informal, we are probably more familiar with the rigidly formalised ones in large organisations and bureaucracies (e.g. a university or government office). What are the effects on group functioning of different types of communication network, and what affects the sort of network that evolves?

Communication network
Set of rules governing the possibility or ease of communication between different roles in a group.

Alex Bavelas (1968) suggested that an important factor was the number of communication links to be crossed for one person to communicate with another. For example, if I can communicate with the dean of my faculty directly, there is one link; but if I have to go through the head of department, there are two. In Franz Kafka's (1925) classic novel *The Trial*, the central character 'K' was confronted by a bewildering and ever-increasing number of communication links in order to communicate with senior people in the organisation. Figure 8.18 shows some of the communication networks that have been researched experimentally; those on the left are more highly centralised than those on the right.

For relatively simple tasks, greater centralisation improves group performance (Leavitt, 1951): the hub person is able to receive, integrate and pass on information efficiently while allowing peripheral members to concentrate on their allotted roles. For more complex tasks, a less centralised structure is superior (Shaw, 1964), because the quantity and complexity of information communicated would overwhelm a hub person, who would be unable to integrate, assimilate and pass it on efficiently. Peripheral members would thus experience delays and miscommunication. For complex tasks, there are potentially serious coordination losses (Steiner, 1972; see earlier in this chapter) associated with overly centralised communication

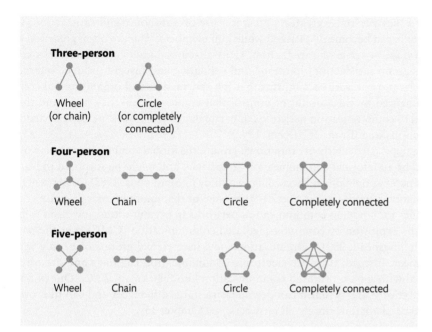

Figure 8.18 Communication networks that have been studied experimentally

The most studied communication networks are those involving three, four or five members (dots represent positions or roles or people, and lines represent communication channels). The networks on the left are highly centralised and become increasingly less centralised as you move to the right of the figure.

Communication networks
A multifaceted activity like making a film requires a division of labour and a centralised communication network focused on the team leader – something Star Wars Director J. J. Abrams knows well.

networks. However, centralisation for complex tasks may pay off in the long run once appropriate procedures have been well established and well learnt.

Another important consideration is the degree of autonomy felt by group members. Because they are dependent on the hub for regulation and flow of information, peripheral members have less power in the group, and they can feel restricted and dependent. According to the Dutch psychologist Mauk Mulder (1959), having more power – being more central and feeling like a 'key person' – creates a greater sense of autonomy and satisfaction; so peripheral members can become dissatisfied while hub members, who are often perceived to be group leaders, feel a sense of satisfaction. Centralised communication networks can therefore reduce group satisfaction, harmony and solidarity, and instead produce internal conflict. Research on organisations confirms that job satisfaction and organisational commitment are influenced by the amount of control that employees feel they have, and that control is related to communication networks, in particular to employees' perceived participation in decision-making (Evans & Fischer, 1992).

In almost all groups, particularly organisational groups, the formal communication network is complemented by an informal communication 'grapevine'. You might be surprised to learn that, contrary to popular opinion and according to a study by Simmonds (1985), 80 per cent of grapevine information is work-related, and 70–90 per cent of that information is accurate.

Finally, the rules for studying communication networks in organisations now need to be rewritten with the explosion of computer-mediated communication (CMC) over the past twenty years (Hollingshead, 2001). Organisations now have virtual groups of people who rarely need to meet. Instead, they use electronic communication channels and are often highly distributed without a centralised communication hub (Hackman, 2002). One potentially positive effect of CMC is that it can deemphasise status differences and can thus promote more equal participation among all members (see **Chapter 15**).

Subgroups and crosscutting categories

Almost all groups are structurally differentiated into subgroups. These subgroups can be nested within the larger group (e.g. different departments in a university, different divisions in a company). However, many subgroups represent larger categories that have members outside the larger group (e.g. social psychologists in a psychology department are also members of the larger group of social psychologists). In this case, the subgroups are not nested but are crosscutting categories (Crisp, Ensari, Hewstone, & Miller, 2003; Crisp & Hewstone, 2007).

Group processes are significantly affected by subgroup structure. The main problem is that subgroups often compete against one another, which can sometimes harm the larger group. For example, divisions in a company can take healthy competition one step too far and slip into outright conflict. Research shows that when one company takes over another company and therefore contains within it two subgroups, the original company and the new company, conflict between these two subgroups can be extreme (e.g. Cartwright & Schoenberg, 2006; Terry, Carey, & Callan, 2001). In these circumstances, it can be very difficult to provide effective leadership that bridges the deep division between subgroups – effective intergroup leadership is called for (Hogg, 2015; Hogg, Van Knippenberg, & Rast, 2012a; see **Chapter 9**).

Schism
Division of a group into subgroups that differ in their attitudes, values or ideology.

When groups contain subgroups that differ ideologically or in their core values and attitudes, a **schism** can occur (Sani, 2005) (see Box 8.5). If one subgroup feels that the larger group no longer represents its values and embodies its identity, it may feel uncertain about its social identity and seek greater autonomy and independence to define itself within the larger group (Wagoner & Hogg, 2016), or decide to split off entirely to become a separate group. In both cases, it may still try to convert the larger group. This can create extreme conflict that tears the larger group apart – this often happens in political and religious contexts (Sani & Reicher, 1998, 2000) but can also happen in artistic and scientific contexts. A key factor that transforms ideological disagreement into schism is lack of voice – the probability of schism is amplified if the smaller marginalised group feels its concerns about the majority's ideological and identity slippage is simply not being listened to or heard by the majority (Sani, 2005).

Box 8.5 Our world
Schisms in Europe and America: Brexit and Calexit

On 23 June 2016, the United Kingdom held a referendum in which 52 per cent of the votes cast were in favour of Britain leaving the European Union (EU) – Brexit, the UK withdrawal from the EU, prevailed. Britain joined the EU in 1973 as part of a post-World War II movement across Europe to build a globally competitive trading block and to establish a superordinate European identity that would transcend the nationalistic agenda that had contributed to the devastating wars of the twentieth century. At the time of the referendum, the EU had twenty-eight member states and a population of over 510 million people, with the triumvirate of Germany, Britain and France providing the economic foundation. What seemed to drive the UK 'leave' vote was a sense of loss of autonomy – specifically regarding immigration, trade and economics, and national identity and cultural practices.

Across the Atlantic a similar dynamic is emerging – a movement in California, sometimes called Calexit, to exit the United States and become an independent nation (see *Los Angeles Times*, 2017). The United States has 50 states and a population of 325 million. California,

which was acquired from Mexico in 1848, is by far the most populous US state, with 40 million people, and is currently ranked the sixth largest economy in the world. Californians have often toyed with secession. They feel they have a distinct identity and associated normative beliefs and practices that are more progressive than the rest of the nation, and they yearn for greater autonomy in areas such as immigration, governance, globalisation, environmental custodianship and so forth. The outcome of the 2016 US presidential election that placed Donald Trump in the White House energised Calexit. Californians voted 62 per cent to 32 per cent in favour of the Democratic contender Hillary Clinton over the Republican contender Trump. Californians felt they had been disenfranchised and had no voice in the nation and thus their own destiny – and so they sought autonomy through secession. Unlike Brexit, Calexit is very unlikely to succeed as it requires approval of most of the other states. The last time US states, eleven of them, seceded was in 1861 – what followed was the American Civil War!

The problem of subgroup conflict is often most evident, and indeed harmful, when larger groups contain socio-demographic subgroups that have destructive intergroup relations in society as a whole, such as Protestants and Catholics who work together in a Northern Irish business (Hewstone, Cairns, Voci, Paolini, McLernon, Crisp, et al., 2005). See **Chapter 11** for a full discussion of intergroup relations, including intergroup relations among crosscutting and nested subgroups.

Deviants and marginal members

Many, if not most, groups are also structured in terms of two kinds of member:

1 Those who best embody the group's attributes – core members who are highly prototypical of the group.
2 Those who do not – marginal or non-prototypical members.

Highly prototypical members often have significant influence over the group and may occupy leadership roles – we discuss them in **Chapter 9**. Marginal members are an entirely different story.

Research by José Marques and his colleagues shows that marginal members, in the sense of people who are on the fringe of the group because they have dislikeable characteristics (e.g. they are dishonest, narcissistic, bigoted), are disliked and can be treated as 'black sheep' (Marques & Páez, 1994) or deviants, and they can be evaluatively and materially excluded from the group. The research indicates that a person whose dislikeable attributes place them on the boundary between ingroup and outgroup are actually disliked more if they are classified as ingroup members than as outgroup members – they are treated as deviants or even traitors. The reason for this is that their undesirable attributes reflect poorly on the ingroup and thus poorly on social identity and members' self-concept – we would rather not have a bigot in our group but do not mind if they belong to an outgroup. The motivation is self-enhancement through positive social identity (Abrams & Hogg, 1988; Tajfel & Turner, 1986).

Marques and Abrams and their colleagues have elaborated this idea into a broader theory of **subjective group dynamics** (Marques, Abrams, Páez, & Taboada, 1998; Pinto, Marques, Levine, & Abrams, 2010), which focuses on marginal membership in the sense of not being a prototypical group member – a person who does not very closely embody the group's normative attributes. The motivation underlying evaluation of marginal members and prototype-based deviance is identity uncertainty reduction (cf. Hogg, 2012). So, it is unsurprising that marginal members have been shown to be more strongly rejected when the group is perceived to be highly entitative (Lewis & Sherman, 2010) – they pose a greater threat to the group's prototypical integrity.

Non-normative members of a group pose a threat to the integrity of the group's norms and thus identity; and this is particularly threatening if the non-normative member's divergence from the group norm is towards an outgroup (called an 'anti-norm deviant') than away from the outgroup (a 'pro-norm deviant'). Anti-norm deviants are evaluated more negatively than pro-norm deviants. Thus, 'black sheep', who are archetypal anti-norm deviants, are particularly harshly evaluated and treated (Marques, Abrams, Páez, & Hogg, 2001; Marques, Abrams, & Serodio, 2001). Paradoxically, marginal members can therefore serve an important function for groups – groups, particularly their leaders, can engage in a rhetoric of vilification and exclusion of marginal members in order to throw into stark relief what the group is and what it is not.

There are many ways to be marginal in a group. Marginal status in the guise of black sheep and anti-norm deviants can attract exclusion if it fails to benefit the group; however, marginal status may sometimes serve a more positive function for the group as a whole (Ellemers & Jetten, 2013). Pro-norm deviants may be one example. There is another, perhaps related way in which marginal members play an important group role – they can be agents of social change within the group. Under the right conditions, marginal members may be uniquely placed to act as critics of group norms, precisely because they are normatively marginal.

Research on intergroup criticism by Matthew Hornsey and his colleagues (Hornsey, 2005) shows that groups are more accepting of criticism from ingroup than outgroup members (Hornsey & Imani, 2004; Hornsey, Oppes, & Svensson, 2002) and from old-timers than newcomers (Hornsey, Grice, Jetten, Paulsen, & Callan, 2007). The rationale for this is that critics can have an uphill struggle to be heard if they are labelled and treated as deviants; and outgroup critics and newcomers can more readily be labelled in this way.

The challenge of gaining voice may be more easily overcome if a number of dissenters unite as a subgroup – we then effectively have a schism (see earlier), or an active minority within the group. Indeed, the analysis of how marginal members, deviants and dissenters may influence the larger group is, in many respects, the analysis of minority influence (which we discussed fully in **Chapter 7**).

However, small groups of individuals that feel they have been actively marginalised and excluded (or ostracised – see the next section) by multiple dominant or overarching groups can experience an acute sense of threat to belonging, identity, self-esteem, control and meaningful existence. This lethal concoction can lead to individual or group violence against the supposed source of exclusion and marginalisation (Betts & Hinsz, 2013). Examples abound – from school and campus shooters in the United States to global terrorism.

Subjective group dynamics
A process where normative deviants who deviate towards an outgroup (anti-norm deviants) are more harshly treated than those who deviate away from the outgroup (pro-norm deviants).

Why do people join groups?

This is not an easy question to answer. It depends on how we define a group, and of course, 'why' people join groups is not the same thing as 'how' people join groups. We also need to recognise that the groups to which we belong vary in the degree of free choice we had in joining. There is little choice in what sex, ethnic, national or social class groups we 'join': membership is largely designated externally. There is a degree of choice, although possibly less than we might think, in what occupational or political group we join; and there is a great deal of freedom in what clubs, societies and recreational groups we join. Even the most strongly externally designated social category memberships, such as sex and ethnicity, can permit a degree of choice in what the implications of membership in that group may be (e.g. the group's norms and practices), and this may reflect the same sorts of motives and goals for choosing freely to join less externally designated groups.

Reasons for joining groups

However, we can identify a range of circumstances, motives, goals and purposes that cause, in more or less immediate ways, people to join or form groups (e.g. aggregate, coordinate their actions, declare themselves members of a group). For example, physical proximity can promote group formation. We tend to get to like, or at least learn to put up with, people we are in close proximity with (Tyler & Sears, 1977). This promotes group formation: we form groups with those around us. Festinger, Schachter and Back's (1950) classic study of a student housing programme, which we discussed earlier (see also **Chapter 14**), concerned just this – the role of proximity in group formation, group cohesiveness and adherence to group standards. The recognition of similar interests, attitudes and beliefs can also cause people to become or join a group.

If people share goals that require behavioural interdependence for their achievement, this is another strong and reliable reason for joining groups. This idea lies at the heart of Sherif's (1966) realistic conflict theory of intergroup behaviour (discussed in **Chapter 11**). For example, if we are concerned about degradation of the environment, we are likely ultimately to join an environmental conservation group, because division of labour and interdependent action among like-minded people achieves a great deal more than the actions of a lone protester. People join groups to get things done that they cannot do on their own.

We can join groups for mutual positive support and the mere pleasure of affiliation: for example, to avoid loneliness (Peplau & Perlman, 1982). We can join groups for self-protection and personal safety: for example, adolescents join gangs (Ahlstrom & Havighurst, 1971) and mountaineers climb in groups for this reason. We can join groups for emotional support in times of stress: for example, support groups for AIDS sufferers and their relatives and friends fulfil this function.

Oscar Lewis's (1969) powerful account of a Catholic wake in Mexico, in his novel *A Death in the Sanchez Family*, describes the way in which people come together in stressful circumstances. Stanley Schachter (1959) has explored the same idea in controlled experimental circumstances. However, a word of qualification is needed. Extreme stress and deprivation (e.g. in concentration camps or after natural disasters) sometimes lead to social disintegration and individual isolation rather than group formation (Middlebrook, 1980). This is probably because the link between stress and affiliation is not mechanical: if affiliation is not the effective solution to the stress, then it may not occur. Thomas Keneally's (1982) account, in his powerful biographical novel *Schindler's Ark*, of atrocities committed by the Nazis against Jews in the Polish city of Kraków, supports this. Despite extreme stress, remarkably little affiliation occurred: affiliation was difficult to sustain and would probably only exacerbate the situation.

Box 8.6 Our world
Syria: A case study in uncertainty and existential terror

In 2011 Syria had a population of approximately 22 million. By the end of 2016, after almost six years of brutal civil war, 400,000 Syrians lay dead, 4.8 million had fled the country, 6.6 million were displaced internally, and 4 million children had had effectively no education. The cost of the devastation (we have all seen the post-apocalyptic images of Aleppo) was estimated at US$200 billion.

Human beings are incredibly resilient, but it is hard to imagine that the everyday confrontation with death and the overwhelming sense of unending economic, social and identity uncertainty will not have a profound impact. One prospect is that the Syrian experience may become (much like Iraq before it) fertile ground for extremism, with some people being attracted to all embracing ideologies that define extremist groups and identities. See how this possibility can be derived from terror management theory and uncertainty-identity theory – described in this chapter, but also see Chapters 4 and 11.

Motivations for affiliation and group formation

The question of why people join groups can be reframed in terms of what basic motivations cause people to affiliate (Hogg, Hohman, & Rivera, 2008; see also **Chapter 13**). According to Baumeister and Leary (1995), humans simply have a basic and overwhelming need to belong, and this causes them to affiliate and to join and be members of groups. Furthermore, the sense of belonging and being successfully connected to other human beings, interpersonally or in groups, produces a powerful and highly rewarding sense of self-esteem and self-worth (Leary, Tambor, Terdal, & Downs, 1995) – self-esteem acts as a sociometer that provides people with information about how well they are grounded and connected socially (Leary & Baumeister, 2000).

Terror management theory

The notion that the most fundamental human motivation is to reduce the terror of the inevitability of death. Self-esteem may be centrally implicated in effective terror management.

According to **terror management theory** (Greenberg, Pyszczynski, & Solomon, 1986; Greenberg, Solomon, & Pyszczynski, 1997; Pyszczynski, Greenberg, & Solomon, 2004; Solomon, Greenberg, & Pyszczynski, 1991; see **Chapter 4**), the most fundamental threat that people face is the inevitability of their own death, and therefore people live their lives in perpetual terror of death. Fear of death is the most powerful motivating factor in human existence. People affiliate and join groups to reduce fear of death. Affiliation and group formation are highly effective terror management strategies because they provide symbolic immortality through connection to normative systems that outlive individuals. Thus, affiliation and group formation raise self-esteem and make people feel good about themselves – people feel immortal, and positive and excited about life.

One final and important motive for joining a group is to obtain a social identity (Hogg, 2006; Hogg & Abrams, 1988; Tajfel & Turner, 1986). Groups provide us with a consensually recognised and validated definition and evaluation of who we are, how we should behave and how we will be treated by others. According to **uncertainty–identity theory** (Hogg, 2007b, 2012; see **Chapter 11**), one fundamental motivation for joining and identifying with groups is to reduce feelings of uncertainty about who we are, how we should behave and how others will perceive and interact with us.

Uncertainty–identity theory

To reduce uncertainty and to feel more comfortable about who they are, people choose to identify with groups that are distinctive, are clearly defined and have consensual norms.

Hogg and his colleagues have conducted a number of experiments to show that people who are randomly categorized as members of a group under abstract laboratory conditions (minimal group paradigm; see **Chapter 11**) or as members of more substantial 'real life' groups actually identify with the group, and identify more strongly if (1) they are in a state of self- or self-related uncertainty, and (2) the group has properties that optimise its capacity to reduce self-uncertainty (e.g. it is a highly entitative group). Reflecting back on terror

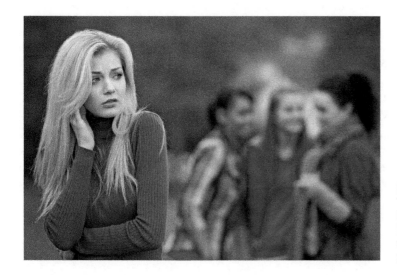

Social ostracism
This young girl feels the loneliness of exclusion- a loneliness that is amplified when the ostracism is patently obvious.

management theory, a number of scholars have suggested that the reason why making people focus on their own death (the mortality salience manipulation used by terror management theorists) is associated with group identification-related phenomena is not so much terror about the process of dying but uncertainty about what happens to oneself after death (Hohman & Hogg, 2011, 2015; Martin & Van den Bos, 2014; Van den Bos, 2009). Hohman and Hogg (2011) conducted two experiments that support this idea, that self-related existential uncertainty, not existential terror, plays the key role in group identification and people's defence of their cultural world views.

In addition to uncertainty considerations, we are motivated to join groups that are consensually positively evaluated (e.g. high status) and thus furnish a positive social identity. This is because we and others evaluate us in terms of the relative attractiveness, desirability and prestige of the groups to which we belong (Abrams & Hogg, 1988; Hogg & Abrams, 1990; Long & Spears, 1997; Tajfel & Turner, 1986; see also **Chapter 11**).

Why *not* join groups?

Perhaps the question 'Why do people join groups?' should be stood on its head: 'Why do people not join groups?' Not being a member of a group is a lonely existence, depriving us of social interaction, social and physical protection, the capacity to achieve complex goals, a stable sense of who we are, and confidence in how we should behave (see **Chapter 13**).

Being actively excluded from a group, **social ostracism**, can be particularly painful and have widespread effects (Williams, 2002, 2009). Kip Williams has devised an intriguing and powerful paradigm to study the consequences of being excluded from a group (Williams, Shore, & Grahe, 1998; Williams & Sommer, 1997). Three-person groups of students waiting for an experiment begin to throw a ball to one another across the room. After a while, two of the students (actually confederates) exclude the third student (true participant) by not throwing them the ball. It is very uncomfortable even to watch the video of this study. (Imagine how the participant felt!) True participants appear self-conscious and embarrassed, and many try to occupy themselves with other activities such as playing with keys, staring out of the window or meticulously scrutinising their wallets. This paradigm has been very successfully adapted as a web paradigm called cyber-ostracism (Williams, Cheung, & Choi, 2000).

Social ostracism
Exclusion from a group by common consent.

We now know a fair bit about the causes and consequences of ostracism. For example:

- Those who ostracise generally underestimate the degree of social pain that it causes (Nordgren, Banas, & MacDonald, 2011).

- Being ostracised can induce a lack of feeling of meaningful existence (Zadro, Williams, & Richardson, 2004) and can cause aggression (Wesselmann, Butler, Williams, & Pickett, 2010; Williams & Warburton, 2003).

- Feelings of ostracism can be easily induced – for example, by a computer (Zadro, Williams, & Richardson, 2004), or by a hated outgroup such as the Ku Klux Klan (Gonsalkorale & Williams, 2007). Feeling ostracised may occur even when being excluded actually pays (e.g. winning money) but being included does not pay (e.g. losing money; see Van Beest & Williams, 2006).

Summary

- Although there are many definitions of 'group', social psychologists generally agree that at very least, a group is a collection of people who define themselves as a group and whose attitudes and behaviour are governed by the norms of the group. Group membership often also entails shared goals, interdependence, mutual influence and face-to-face interaction.

- People perform easy, well-learnt tasks better, and difficult, poorly learnt tasks worse, in the presence of other people than on their own.

- We may be affected in this way for a number of reasons. Social presence may instinctively drive habitual behaviour, we may learn to worry about performance evaluation by others, we may be distracted by others, or others may make us self-conscious or concerned about self-presentation.

- Tasks differ not only in difficulty but also in their structure and objectives. Whether a task benefits from division of labour, and how individual task performances are interrelated, have important implications for the relationship between individual and group performance.

- People put less effort into task performance in groups than when alone, unless the task is involving and interesting, their individual contribution is clearly identifiable or the group is important to their self-definition, in which case they can sometimes exert more effort in a group than alone.

- Members of cohesive groups feel more favourably inclined towards one another as group members and are more likely to identify with the group and conform to its norms.

- Group membership is a dynamic process in which our sense of commitment varies, we occupy different roles at different times, we endure sharp transitions between roles and we are socialised by the group in many different ways.

- Groups develop norms in order to regulate the behaviour of members, to define the group and to distinguish the group from other groups. Group and societal norms can provide a moral compass for our behaviour.

- Groups are structured internally into different roles that regulate interaction and best serve the collective interest of the group. Roles prescribe behaviour. They also vary in their desirability and thus influence status within the group. Groups are also internally structured in terms of subgroups and central and marginal group members.

- People may join or form groups to get things done that cannot be done alone, to gain a sense of identity and reduce self-uncertainty, to obtain social support or simply for the pleasure of social interaction.

- Being excluded or ostracised by a group is aversive and can lead to extreme reactions.

Key terms

Audience effects
Cognitive dissonance
Cohesiveness
Communication network
Coordination loss
Correspondence bias
Diffuse status characteristics
Distraction–conflict theory
Drive theory
Entitativity
Ethnomethodology
Evaluation apprehension model
Expectation states theory
Frame of reference

Free-rider effect
Group
Group socialisation
Group structure
Initiation rites
Mere presence
Meta-analysis
Norms
Personal attraction
Process loss
Ringelmann effect
Roles
Schism
Social attraction

Social compensation
Social facilitation
Social impact
Social loafing
Social ostracism
Specific status characteristics
Status
Stereotype
Subjective group dynamics
Task taxonomy
Terror management theory
Uncertainty–identity theory

Literature, film and TV

The Damned United

This 2009 biographical sports drama directed by Tom Hooper and starring Michael Sheen, Timothy Spall and Colm Meaney explores the challenges involved in fashioning a cohesive and effective team. Set in the late 1960s and early 1970s, it focuses on the British football teams Derby County and Leeds United – showing how Brian Clough (played by Sheen) over a period of only a few years brings Derby County from near the bottom of the football league to the top of the first division. However, when Clough is appointed in 1974 as manager of Leeds United, he fails miserably in the challenge of uniting the team under his leadership. The film is also relevant to our discussion of leadership (**Chapter 9**) and our discussion of intergroup behaviour (**Chapter 11**). Another biographical sports drama that is relevant is the 2011 film *Moneyball*, starring Brad Pitt and Philip Seymour Hoffman. Set in the world of American baseball, it shows how Billy Beane (played by Pitt), as general manager, transformed the thoroughly dysfunctional Oakland Athletics into a highly competitive team.

Castaway

A 2000 film directed by Robert Zemeckis, starring Tom Hanks. The film is about the consequences of exclusion, and loneliness. Tom Hanks's character is abandoned on an island. He uses pictures, and decorates a volleyball to look like a person whom he calls 'Wilson' – Wilson allows him to remain socially connected.

Homeland

A phenomenally popular political thriller TV series which first aired in 2011 and is still going strong. It stars Claire Danes as Carrie Mathison, who is a brilliant, ruthless but dysfunctional CIA officer with bipolar disorder. *Homeland* pretty much covers all of social psychology, but with its focus on combatting terrorism (al-Qaeda, DAISH, Taliban) as a threat to the homeland, it locates individual and interpersonal behaviour in the wider context of group processes and intergroup relations. It explores themes of culture, identity, aggression, leadership, influence, persuasion and conformity.

Fresh Meat

A very successful British sitcom that first aired in 2011. Six students who are freshers at the fictional Manchester Medlock University live in a shared house off-campus – you can probably imagine the endless opportunity for group processes of all sorts. A related British sitcom from the 1980s is *The Young Ones*; a violent punk, a pseudo-intellectual would-be anarchist, a long-suffering hippie, and a smooth-operator all live in one chaotic house.

Guided questions

1   What makes a group a group?

2   How and why does the presence of other people affect an individual's performance?

3   Use your knowledge of *social loafing* to explain why workers are sometimes less productive than expected.

4   *Roles* have an important function in groups – but can role-play be dangerous?

5   Why do people join groups?

Learn more

Baron, R. S., & Kerr, N. (2003). *Group process, group decision, group action* (2nd ed.). Buckingham, UK: Open University Press. A general overview of topics in the study of group processes.

Brown, R. J. (2000). *Group processes* (2nd ed.). Oxford, UK: Blackwell. A very readable introduction to group processes which also places an emphasis on social influence processes within groups, especially conformity, norms and minority influence.

Cialdini, R. B., & Trost, M. R. (1998). Social influence: Social norms, conformity, and compliance. In D. T. Gilbert, S. T. Fiske, & G. Lindzey (Eds.), *The handbook of social psychology* (4th ed., Vol. 2, pp. 151–192). New York: McGraw-Hill. A thorough overview of social influence research, with an excellent section on norms.

Gruenfeld, D. H., & Tiedens, L. Z. (2010). Organizational preferences and their consequences. In S. T. Fiske, D. T. Gilbert, & G. Lindzey (Eds.), *Handbook of social psychology* (5th ed., Vol. 2, pp. 1252–1287). New York: Wiley. Up-to-date and detailed overview of social psychological theory and research on organisational processes, including group processes in organisations.

Hackman, J. R., & Katz, N. (2010). Group behavior and performance. In S. T. Fiske, D. T. Gilbert, & G. Lindzey (Eds.), *Handbook of social psychology* (5th ed., Vol. 2, pp. 1208–1251). New York: Wiley. Comprehensive, detailed and up-to-date date coverage of group behaviour.

Hogg, M. A., & Smith, J. R. (2007). Attitudes in social context: A social identity perspective. *European Review of Social Psychology, 18*, 89–131. A theory-oriented review article that hinges on a discussion of how norms are tied to groups, group membership and social identity.

Hogg, M. A., & Tindale, R. S. (Eds.) (2001). *Blackwell handbook of social psychology: Group processes*. Oxford, UK: Blackwell. A collection of twenty-six chapters from leading experts covering the entire field of group processes.

Leary, M. R. (2010). Affiliation, acceptance, and belonging: The pursuit of interpersonal connection. In S. T. Fiske, D. T. Gilbert, & G. Lindzey (Eds.), *Handbook of social psychology* (5th ed., Vol. 2, pp. 864–897). New York: Wiley. This chapter includes detailed discussion of why people might be motivated to affiliate with others and thus form groups.

Levine, J. M. (Ed.) (2013). *Group processes*. New York: Psychology Press. Absolutely up-to-date and comprehensive set of chapters by leading scholars on all aspects of group processes.

Levine, J. M., & Hogg, M. A. (Eds.) (2010). *Encyclopedia of group processes and intergroup relations*. Thousand Oaks, CA: SAGE. A comprehensive and readable compendium of entries on all aspects of the social psychology of groups, written by all the leading scholars in the field.

Levine, J., & Moreland, R. L. (1998). Small groups. In D. T. Gilbert, S. T. Fiske, & G. Lindzey (Eds.), *The handbook of social psychology* (4th ed., Vol. 2, pp. 415–469). New York: McGraw-Hill. A comprehensive overview of the field of small groups – the most recent fifth edition of the handbook does not have a chapter dedicated to small interactive groups.

Stangor, C. (2016). *Social groups in action and interaction* (2nd ed.). New York: Psychology Press. Completely up-to-date, comprehensive and accessible coverage of the social psychology of processes within and between groups.

Williams, K. D., Harkins, S. G., & Karau, S. J. (2007). Social performance. In M. A. Hogg & J. Cooper (Eds.), *The SAGE handbook of social psychology: Concise student edition* (pp. 291–311). London: SAGE. A comprehensive overview of theory and research focusing on how people's performance is affected by being in a group.

Chapter 9
Leadership and group decision-making

Chapter contents

What do *you* think?

1 Jane is a fearsome and energetic office manager who bustles around issuing orders. She expects and gets prompt action from her employees when she is around. How hard do you think her employees work when she is out of the office?

2 Your organisation is faced by a crisis that has united you all into a tight and cohesive unit. You need a new boss who is able to be innovative and to have the group's full support. Should you appoint Steve, who has all the leadership skills but comes from outside the organisation? Or should you appoint Martin, who has compliantly worked his way up through the organisation for over ten years?

3 The design group at Acme Aerospace meets to design a rocket for a Mars landing. There are eight of you. Because decisions have to be made quickly and smoothly, your charismatic and powerful group leader has selected members so that you are all very much of one mind. This is a very difficult task and there is a great deal of competitive pressure from other space agencies. Will this arrangement deliver a good design?

Leaders and group decisions

In **Chapter 8** we learned that groups vary in size, composition, longevity and purpose. They also vary in entitativity and cohesiveness, have different norms, and are structured into roles and subgroups in different ways. However, almost all groups have some form of unequal distribution of power and influence whereby some people lead and others follow. Even in the case of ostensibly egalitarian or leaderless groups, one rarely needs to scratch far beneath the surface to stumble upon a tacit leadership structure (e.g. Counselman, 1991). Although leadership can take a variety of forms (e.g. democratic, autocratic, informal, formal, laissez-faire), it is a fundamental aspect of almost all social groups.

We know (see end of **Chapter 8**) that people can assemble as a group for many different reasons and to perform many different tasks. One of the most common reasons is to make decisions through some form of group discussion. In fact, many of the most important decisions that affect our lives are made by groups, often groups of which we are not members. One could argue that most decisions that people make are actually group decisions – not only do we frequently make decisions as a group, but even those decisions that we seem to make on our own are made in reference to what groups of people may think or do.

This chapter continues the discussion of group processes. It focuses on two of the most significant group phenomena – leadership and group decision-making.

Leadership

In the many groups to which we belong – teams, committees, organisations, friendship cliques, clubs – we encounter leaders: people who have the 'good' ideas that everyone else agrees on; people whom everyone follows; people who have the ability to make things happen. Leaders enable groups to function as productive and coordinated wholes. Leadership is so integral to the human condition that it may even serve an evolutionary function for the survival of our species (Van Vugt, Hogan, & Kaiser, 2008).

Effective leadership has an enormous impact. For example, one US study showed that highly performing executives added US$25 million more than average performers to the value of their company (Barrick, Day, Lord, & Alexander, 1991), and another study showed that effective CEOs (chief executive officers) improved company performance by 14 per cent (Joyce, Nohria, & Roberson, 2003). For example, Steve Jobs, the founder and long-time CEO of Apple, played an absolutely pivotal role in that company's ascendance – exercising autocratic leadership and extraordinary vision to build Apple into a dominant force in the modern world of computing and electronic communication (Isaacson, 2011). In the sports context, Jacobs and Singell (1993) studied the performance of American baseball teams over a twenty-year period and found that successful teams had managers who exercised superior tactical skills or who were skilled in improving the performance of individual team members.

On a larger canvas, history and political news often comprise stories of the deeds of leaders and tales of leadership struggles – for an enthralling and beautifully written insight into the life of one of the twentieth century's greatest leaders, read Nelson Mandela's (1994) autobiography *The Long Walk to Freedom*. Margaret Thatcher's (1993) autobiography *The Downing Street Years* also makes fascinating reading. There are also (auto)biographies of Richard Branson, Steve Jobs, Bob Geldof, Bono and countless more that provide insight into effective leadership in the business and public spheres.

Biography is frequently about leadership, and most classic accounts of history are mainly accounts of the actions of leaders. Our day-to-day life is pervaded by the impact of leadership – for example, leadership in the political, governmental, corporate, work, educational, scientific and artistic spheres – and we all, to varying degrees, occupy leadership roles ourselves. Not surprisingly, people take a keen interest in leadership and we all have our own views on leaders and leadership.

Incompetent leadership and leadership in the service of evil, in particular, are of great concern to us all (e.g. Kellerman, 2004). Whereas good leaders have the attributes of integrity, decisiveness, competence and vision (Hogan & Kaiser, 2006), extremely bad or dangerous leaders devalue others and are indifferent to their suffering, are intolerant of criticism and suppress dissent, and have a grandiose sense of entitlement (Mayer, 1993). The four most prominent patterns of bad leadership are: failure to build an effective team, poor interpersonal skills to manage the team, insensitivity and lack of care about others, and inability to adjust to being promoted above one's skills or qualifications (Leslie & Van Velsor, 1996). Very bad leaders also have what is called the dark triad of personality variables – narcissism, Machiavellianism and psychopathy (Paulhus & Williams, 2002).

Dictatorial leaders are particularly harmful because they tend to surround themselves with a ruling elite that they cajole ideologically and through rewards and punishment. This allows them to control the masses by fear and the exercise of raw power rather than by providing leadership (Moghaddam, 2013). It is largely the ruling elites, not the masses, that play the key role in creating and toppling dictators. In a similar vein, Machiavellian and narcissistic leaders also employ power, which is ultimately a form of bullying and tyranny based on fear (e.g. Haslam & Reicher, 2005), rather than a show of leadership.

Machiavellian leaders are prepared to do pretty much anything to maintain their status and position of power in the group (they carefully plot and plan and play different individuals and groups off against each other in the group); and narcissistic leaders are consumed with grandiosity, self-importance, envy, arrogance, haughtiness and lack of empathy, as well as a sense of entitlement, feelings of special/unique/high status and fantasies of unlimited success (Baumeister, Smart, & Boden, 1996; Rosenthal & Pittinsky, 2006; also see **Chapter 4**).

To understand how leaders lead, what influences the person who is likely to be a leader in a particular context and what the social consequences of **leadership** may be, social psychology has embraced a variety of theoretical perspectives and emphases. However, after the end of the 1970s, social psychology paid diminishing attention to leadership. The 1985 third edition of the *Handbook of Social Psychology* dedicated a full chapter to leadership (Hollander, 1985), whereas the 1998 fourth edition had no chapter on leadership. In contrast, there has been a corresponding frenzy of research on leadership in organisational psychology (e.g. Northouse, 2009; Yukl, 2013) – it is here, in the management and organisational sciences, where most leadership research is to be found. However, leadership is quite definitely a topic that transcends disciplinary boundaries – although organisational leadership is important, so is political/public leadership and team leadership.

Recently, there has been a revival of interest in leadership among social psychologists – for instance, there are two chapters on leadership in Hogg and Tindale's (2001) *Blackwell Handbook of Social Psychology: Group Processes* (Chemers, 2001; Lord, Brown, & Harvey, 2001), one in Kruglanski and Higgins's (2007) second edition of *Social Psychology: A Handbook of Basic Principles* (Hogg, 2007a), one in the fifth edition of the *Handbook of Social Psychology* (Hogg, 2010) and one in Levine's (2013) edited volume on *Group Processes* (Hogg, 2013b). There is also an entire social psychology-oriented book on leadership by Haslam, Reicher and Platow (2011).

Leadership
Getting group members to achieve the group's goals.

Defining leadership

It is difficult to find a consensual definition of leadership – definitions depend on what aspect of leadership is being investigated, from what disciplinary or theoretical perspective, and for what practical purpose. From a social psychological perspective, Chemers (2001) nicely defined leadership as 'a process of social influence through which an individual enlists and mobilises the aid of others in the attainment of a collective goal' (p. 376). Leadership requires there to be an individual, or clique, who influences the behaviour of another individual or group of individuals – where there are leaders, there must be followers.

Another way to look at leadership is to ask: what is *not* leadership? If a friend cajoled you to spend the weekend cleaning her flat and you agreed, either because you liked her or because you were afraid of her, it would be influence but not leadership – a classic case of compliance (e.g. Cialdini & Trost, 1998; see **Chapter 6**). Related to this, the exercise of power is generally not considered to be leadership (e.g. Chemers, 2001; Lord, Brown, & Harvey, 2001; Raven, 1993), although power may be a consequence of effective leadership (Turner, D. D., 2005). If you agreed because you knew that there was a community norm to clean at the weekend, that would be conformity to a norm (e.g. Turner, J. C., 1991), not an example of leadership. If, on the other hand, your friend had first convinced you that a community-cleaning norm should be developed, and you subsequently adhered to that norm, then that most definitely would be leadership. Leaders play a critical role in defining collective goals. In this respect, leadership is more typically a group process than an interpersonal process. It is an influence process that plays out more noticeably in group contexts than in interpersonal contexts.

Another question about leadership is: what is 'good' leadership? This question is poorly put; it needs to be unpacked into two different questions relating to effective/ineffective leaders and good/bad leaders. An *effective* leader is someone who is successful in setting new goals and influencing others to achieve them. Here, the evaluation of leadership is largely an objective matter of fact – how much influence did the leader have in setting new goals, and were the goals achieved?

In contrast, evaluating whether the leader is good or bad is largely a subjective judgement based on one's preferences, perspectives and goals, and on whether the leader belongs to one's own group or another group. We evaluate leaders in terms of their character (e.g. nice, nasty, charismatic), the ethics and morality of the means they use to influence others and achieve goals (e.g. persuasion, coercion, oppression, democratic decision making) and the nature of the goals towards which they lead their followers (e.g. saving the environment, reducing starvation and disease, producing a commodity, combating oppression, engaging in genocide). Here *good* leaders are those who have attributes we applaud, use means we approve of, and set and achieve goals we value.

Thus, secular Westerners and supporters of al-Qaeda might disagree on whether Osama bin Laden was a *good* leader (they disagree on the value of his goals and the morality of his means) but may agree that he was a relatively *effective* leader (agreeing that he mobilised fundamentalist Muslims around his cause).

Personality traits and individual differences

Great, or notorious, leaders such as Churchill, Gandhi, Hitler, Mandela, Stalin and Thatcher seem to have special and distinctive capabilities that mark them off from the rest of us. Unsurprisingly, we tend to seek an explanation in terms of unique properties of these people (i.e. personality characteristics that predispose certain people to lead) rather than the context or process of leadership. For example, we tend to personify history in terms of the actions of great people: the French occupation of Moscow in 1812 was Napoleon's doing; the 1917 Russian Revolution was 'caused' by Lenin; and the 1980s in Britain were 'the Thatcher years'. Folk wisdom also tends to attribute great leaps forward in science – historian of science Thomas Kuhn (1962) calls them *paradigm shifts* – to the independent actions of great people such as Einstein, Freud, Darwin and Copernicus.

Great person theory
Perspective on leadership that attributes effective leadership to innate or acquired individual characteristics.

This preference for a **great person theory** that attributes leadership to personality may be explained in terms of how people construct an understanding of their world. Earlier (**Chapter 3**) we saw that people tend to attribute others' behaviour to stable underlying traits (e.g. Gawronski, 2004; Gilbert & Malone, 1995; Haslam, Rothschild, & Ernst, 1998) and that this is accentuated where the other person is the focus of our attention. Leaders certainly do stand out against the background of the group and are therefore the focus of our attention, which strengthens the perception of a correspondence between traits and behaviour (e.g. Fiske & Dépret, 1996; Meindl, 1995; Meindl, Ehrlich, & Dukerich, 1985).

Does greatness beckon
Barack Obama, the first black president of the United States, completed two terms of office. Historians debate the accolade of greatness, but agree that his presidency was historic.

Social psychologists are little different from people in everyday life. They too have tried to explain leadership in terms of personality traits that make some people more effective leaders than others. The great person theory of leadership has a long and illustrious pedigree, going back to Plato and ancient Greece. Although some scholars, for example Francis Galton (1892) in the nineteenth century, have maintained that leaders are born and not made, most scholars do not believe that effective leadership is an innate attribute. Instead, they believe leadership ability is a constellation of personality attributes acquired very early in life that imbues people with charisma and a predisposition to lead (e.g. Carlyle, 1841; House, 1977).

A prodigious quantity of research has been conducted to identify these correlates of effective leadership. For example, leaders apparently tend to be above average with respect to size, health, physical attractiveness, self-confidence, sociability, need for dominance and, most reliably, intelligence and talkativeness. Intelligence is important probably because leaders are expected to think and respond quickly and have more ready access to information than others, and talkativeness because it attracts attention and makes the person perceptually salient. But we can all identify effective 'leaders' who do not possess these attributes – for example, Gandhi and Napoleon certainly were not large, the Dalai Lama is not 'talkative', and we will let you generate your own examples of leaders who do not appear to be very intelligent!

Early on, Ralph Stogdill reviewed the leadership literature and concluded that leadership is not the 'mere possession of some combination of traits' (Stogdill, 1948, p. 66). More recently, others have exclaimed that the search for a leadership personality is simplistic and futile (e.g. Conger & Kanungo, 1998). In general, correlations among traits, and between traits and effective leadership, are low (Stogdill, 1974, reports an average correlation of 0.30).

Nevertheless, the belief that some people are better leaders than others because they have enduring traits that predispose them to effective leadership persists. This view has re-emerged in a different guise in modern theories of transformational leadership (see the 'Transformational leadership' section later in this chapter) that emphasise the role of charisma in leadership (e.g. Avolio & Yammarino, 2003; Bass, 1985; Conger & Kanungo, 1998). Rather than focusing on specific traits, this tradition focuses on what are called the **Big Five** personality dimensions: extraversion/surgency, agreeableness, conscientiousness, emotional stability and intellect/openness to experience. A definitive meta-analysis of data from seventy-three studies by Timothy Judge and his associates (Judge, Bono, Ilies, & Gerhardt,

Big Five
The five major personality dimensions of extraversion/surgency, agreeableness, conscientiousness, emotional stability and intellect/openness to experience.

2002) found that these attributes have an overall correlation of 0.58 with leadership. The best predictors of effective leadership were being extraverted, open to experience, and conscientious.

There are also constellations of attributes that are associated with genuinely "bad" leadership. In particular, there is a "dark triad" of personality variables (narcissism, Machiavellianism, psychopathy – see **Chapter 4**) that is associated with negativity or indifference towards others. Increased narcissism is characterised by exaggerated self-worth, Machiavellianism by callous manipulation of others for personal gains, and psychopathy by callous affect and impulsivity (Paulhus & Williams, 2002). I am sure we can all readily think of leaders like this!

Situational perspectives

In contrast to personality and individual differences approaches that attribute effective leadership to having particularly enduring trait constellations is the view that anyone can lead effectively if the situation is right. The most extreme form of this perspective is to deny any influence at all to the leader. For example, much of Leo Tolstoy's epic novel *War and Peace* is a vehicle for his critique of the great person account of history: 'To elicit the laws of history we must leave aside kings, ministers and generals, and select for study the homogeneous, infinitesimal elements which influence the masses' (Tolstoy, 1869, p. 977). Likewise, Karl Marx's theory of history places explanatory emphasis on the actions of groups, not individuals.

This perspective may be too extreme. For example, Dean Simonton (1980) analysed the outcome of 300 battles for which there were reliable archival data on the generals and their armies. Although situational factors, such as the size of the army and diversification of command structure, were correlated with casualties inflicted on the enemy, some personal attributes of the leader, to do with experience and previous battle record, were also associated with victory. In other words, although situational factors influenced outcome, so did the attributes of the leader.

From time to time, then, we may find ourselves in situations where we are leaders. An often-cited illustration of this is the case of Winston Churchill. Although many considered him to be argumentative, opinionated and eminently unsuited to government, these were precisely the characteristics needed in a great wartime leader. However, as soon as the Second World War was over, he was voted out of government, as these were not considered to be the qualities most needed in a peacetime leader.

Social psychologists have found the same thing under more controlled conditions. For example, in their classic studies of intergroup relations at boys' summer camps in the United States (see **Chapter 11** for details), Muzafer Sherif and his colleagues (Sherif, Harvey, White, Hood, & Sherif, 1961) divided the boys into groups. When the groups later met in competition, a boy in one group displaced the original leader because of his greater physical prowess and other qualities suggesting he was better equipped to lead the group successfully in a competitive confrontation. Carter and Nixon (1949) (not the former US presidents!) found the same effect when pairs of school pupils performed three different tasks – an intellectual task, a clerical task and a mechanical assembly task. Those who took the lead in the first two tasks rarely led in the mechanical assembly task.

Overall, leadership reflects task or situational demands and is not purely governed by individual personality, although personal qualities may play a role. Balancing the Churchill example above, leaders can sometimes change to accommodate changed circumstances. When Nelson Mandela was released in 1990 from twenty-six years of imprisonment, most of it in isolation on Robben Island off Cape Town, the political terrain had altered dramatically. Yet he was able to read the changes and go on to lead the African National Congress to political victory in South Africa in 1994. Effective leadership is a matter of the right combination of personal characteristics and situational requirements.

What leaders do

If effective leadership is an interaction between leader attributes and situational requirements, then we need to know about leader attributes. We have seen that personality is not as reliable a leadership attribute as one might think. Perhaps what leaders actually do, their actual behaviour, is more reliable? This idea spawned some of social psychology's classic leadership research.

For example, Ronald Lippitt and Ralph White (1943) used after-school activities clubs for young boys as an opportunity to study the effects of different styles of leadership on group atmosphere, morale and effectiveness. The leaders of the clubs were actually confederates of the researchers, and they were trained in each of three distinct leadership styles:

1 **Autocratic leaders** organised the club's activities, gave orders, were aloof and focused exclusively on the task at hand.

2 **Democratic leaders** called for suggestions, discussed plans and behaved like ordinary club members.

3 **Laissez-faire leaders** left the group to its own devices and generally intervened minimally.

Each club was assigned to a particular leadership style. One confederate was the leader for seven weeks and then the confederates were swapped around; this happened twice, so that each confederate adopted each leadership style, but each group was exposed to only one leadership style (although enacted by three different confederates). This clever control allowed Lippitt and White to distinguish leadership behaviour per se from the specific leader who was behaving in that way. In this way they could rule out personality explanations.

Lippitt and White's findings are described in Figure 9.1. Democratic leaders were liked significantly more than autocratic or laissez-faire leaders. They created a friendly, group-centred, task-oriented atmosphere that was associated with relatively high group productivity, which was unaffected by whether the leader was physically present or not. In contrast, autocratic leaders created an aggressive, dependent and self-oriented group atmosphere, which was associated with high productivity only when the leader was present. (How would you rate bustling Jane in the first 'What do *you* think?' question?) Laissez-faire leaders created a friendly, group-centred but play-oriented atmosphere that was associated with low productivity, which

Autocratic leaders
Leaders who use a style based on giving orders to followers.

Democratic leaders
Leaders who use a style based on consultation and obtaining agreement and consent from followers.

Laissez-faire leaders
Leaders who use a style based on disinterest in followers.

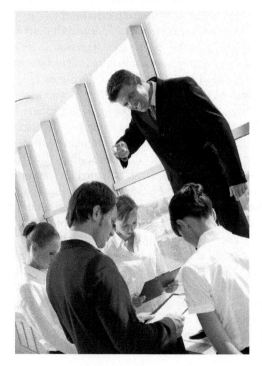

An autocratic leader
'I like to do all the talking myself. It saves time and prevents arguments' (Oscar Wilde).

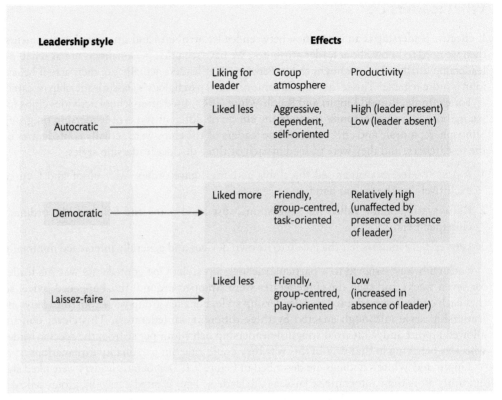

Figure 9.1 Leadership styles and their effects

Autocratic, democratic and laissez-faire leadership styles have different combinations of effects on group atmosphere and productivity, and on liking for the leader.

Source: Based on Lippitt and White (1943).

increased only if the leader was absent. Lippitt and White used these findings to promote their view that democratic leadership was more effective than other leadership behaviour.

Lippitt and White's distinction between autocratic and democratic leadership styles re-emerges in a slightly different guise in later work. From his studies of interaction styles in groups, Robert Bales, a pioneer in the study of small group communication, identified two key leadership roles – *task specialist* and *socioemotional specialist* (Bales, 1950; Slater, 1955). Task specialists concentrate on reaching solutions, often making suggestions and giving directions; socioemotional specialists are attentive to the feelings of other group members. A single person rarely occupies both roles – rather, the roles devolve onto separate individuals, and the person occupying the task-specialist role is more likely to be the dominant leader.

Casual observation of groups and organisations supports this dual-leadership idea. For example, one theme that punctuated election struggles between the Labour Party and the Conservative Party during the 1980s in Britain had to do with what sort of leader the country should have. The Labour leader at the time, Neil Kinnock, was, among other things, heralded as a friendly and approachable leader concerned with people's feelings, and the Conservative leader, Margaret Thatcher, as the hard-headed, task-oriented economic rationalist.

Leader behaviour description questionnaire (LBDQ)
Scale devised by the Ohio State leadership researchers to measure leadership behaviour and distinguish between 'initiating structure' and 'consideration' dimensions.

The Ohio State leadership studies constitute a third major leadership programme (e.g. Fleishman, 1973; Stogdill, 1974). In this research a scale for measuring leadership behaviour was devised, the **leader behaviour description questionnaire** (LBDQ) (Shartle, 1951), and a distinction was drawn between *initiating structure* and *consideration*. Leaders high on initiating structure define the group's objectives and organise members' work towards the attainment of these goals: they are task-oriented. Leaders high on consideration are concerned with the welfare of subordinates and seek to promote harmonious relationships in the group: they are relationship-oriented. Unlike Bales (1950), who believed that task-oriented and socioemotional attributes were inversely related, the Ohio State researchers believed their dimensions to be independent – a single person could be high on both initiating structure (task-oriented) and consideration (socioemotional), and such a person would be a particularly effective leader.

Research supports this latter view – the most effective leaders are precisely those who score above average on both initiating structure and consideration (Stogdill, 1974). For example, Richard Sorrentino and Nigel Field (1986) conducted detailed observations of twelve problem-solving groups over a five-week period. Those group members who were rated high on both the task and socioemotional dimensions of Bales's (1950) system were subsequently elected by groups to be their leaders.

The general distinction between a leadership style that pays more attention to the group task and getting things done, and one that pays attention to relationships among group members, is quite pervasive (see Box 9.1). For example, as we shall see, it appears in Fiedler's (1964) influential contingency theory of leadership, and in a slightly different guise in leader–member exchange (LMX) theory's emphasis upon the quality of the leader's relationship with his or her followers (e.g. Graen & Uhl-Bien, 1995).

Furthermore, it is a distinction that may hold across cultures, but with the caveat that what counts as task-oriented or socioemotional leadership behaviour may vary from culture to culture. For example, from their leadership research in Japan, Jyuji Misumi and Mark Peterson (1985) identify a similar distinction – in this case between task performance and group maintenance. They note that whether a behaviour counts as one or the other differs from culture to culture – for example, the leader eating lunch with his or her workmates is associated with high group maintenance in some cultures but not others.

The same conclusion was drawn by Peter Smith and his colleagues (Smith, Misumi, Tayeb, Peterson, & Bond, 1989) from research in the United States, Britain, Hong Kong and Japan. They found that performance and maintenance behaviour were universally valued in leaders, but that what counted as each type of behaviour varied from culture to culture. For example, leaders need to assess workers' task performance: in Britain and America, the considerate way to do this is by speaking directly with workers; whereas in East Asia, this is viewed as inconsiderate, and the considerate way is to speak with the individual's co-workers.

Having learnt something about what effective leaders do, we now need to turn our attention to what situational factors invite or benefit from which leadership behaviours. How do behaviour and situation interact to produce effective leadership?

Box 9.1 Your life
How should you lead?

You have been appointed to act as leader of a small student committee that advises the university administration on campus environmental and quality-of-life issues. This can be quite daunting if you have not done this before – what sort of a leader should you be? The more you think about it, the more the options and possibilities seem endless.

Should you lead from the front in a directive or 'autocratic' manner, or should you lead from behind in a more consultative and democratic manner? Should you focus the group primarily on the task at hand, or should you focus on relationships among members within the group?

Should you interact with all group members in the same way, or should you recognise diversity of contributions and interact more closely with some than others? Perhaps it depends on the size of the group, the nature of the group task, the difficulty of the task, the amount of prior experience members have, how important you and fellow members think the group and its task are, how tightly knit the group is, how well structured the group is in terms of task-related roles, how much you and others identify with the group and so forth. How do you decide about all this? This chapter should help – it discusses leadership styles and factors that influence which work best.

Contingency theories

Contingency theories
Theories of leadership that consider the leadership effectiveness of particular behaviours or behavioural styles to be contingent on the nature of the leadership situation.

Contingency theories of leadership recognise that the leadership effectiveness of leadership behaviours or styles is *contingent* on the leadership situation – some styles are better suited to some situations or tasks than are others. For example, different behavioural styles are suited to an aircrew in combat, an organisational decision-making group, a ballet company or a nation in economic crisis.

Fiedler's contingency theory

The first and best-known contingency theory in social psychology is that of Fred Fiedler (1964). Fiedler, like Bales (1950), distinguished between *task-oriented leaders* who are authoritarian, value group success and derive self-esteem from accomplishing a task rather than being liked by the group; and *relationship-oriented leaders* who are relaxed, friendly, non-directive and sociable, and gain self-esteem from happy and harmonious group relations.

Least-preferred co-worker (LPC) scale
Fiedler's scale for measuring leadership style in terms of favourability of attitude towards one's least-preferred co-worker.

Fiedler measured leadership style in a rather unusual way; with his **least preferred co-worker (LPC) scale** where respondents rated the person they least preferred as a co-worker on a number of dimensions (e.g. pleasant–unpleasant, boring–interesting, friendly–unfriendly). The resultant LPC scores were used to differentiate between two different leadership styles.

- A high LPC score indicated a *relationship-oriented* leadership style because the respondent felt favourably inclined towards a fellow member even if he or she was not performing well.
- A low LPC score indicated a *task-oriented* leadership style because the respondent was harsh on a poorly performing co-worker.

Fiedler classified situations in terms of three dimensions in descending order of importance:

- the quality of leader–member relations;
- the clarity of the structure of the task; and
- the intrinsic power and authority the leader had by virtue of his or her position as leader.

Good leader–member relations in conjunction with a clear task and substantial position power furnished maximal 'situational control' (making leadership easy), whereas poor leader–member relations, a fuzzy task and low position power furnished minimal

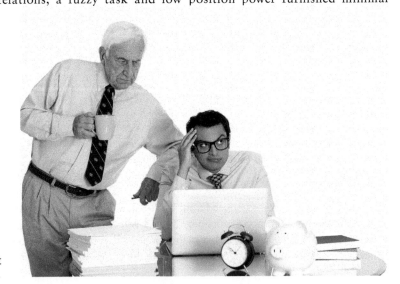

Least preferred co-worker
A first step in measuring your leadership style is to nominate the person with whom you find it most difficult to work.

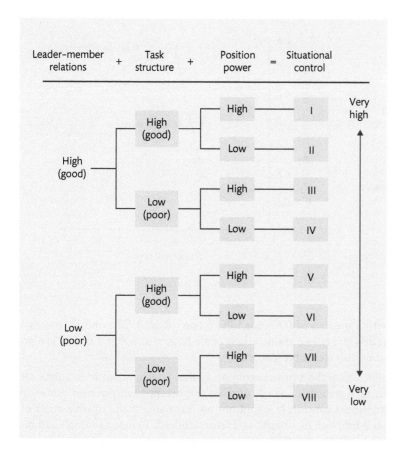

Figure 9.2 Fiedler's eight-category situational control scale as a function of leader–member relations, task structure and position power

- An eight-category scale of situational control (I, *very high*, to VIII, *very low*) can be constructed by classifying situations as having good/bad leader–member relations, good/bad task structure and high/low position power.

- The a priori assumption, that leader–member relations are more important than task structure, which is more important than position power, means that a situation is first classified by leader–member relations, then within that by task structure, and then within that by position power.

Source: Based on Fiedler (1965).

'situational control' (making leadership difficult). **Situational control** can be classified quite precisely from I ('very high') to VIII ('very low'), by dichotomising conditions under each of the three factors as good or bad (high or low) (see Figure 9.2).

Fiedler used the concept of situational control to make leadership effectiveness predictions:

- Task-oriented (low LPC) leaders would be most effective when situational control is low (the group needs a directive leader to focus on getting things done) *and* when it is high (the group is doing just fine, so there is little need to worry about morale and relationships within the group).

- Relationship-oriented (high LPC) leaders are more effective when situational control lies between these extremes.

These predictions are illustrated in Figure 9.3, which also shows a composite of LPC–performance correlations reported by Fiedler (1965) from published studies. The results match the prediction rather well.

Meta-analyses confirm this. Strube and Garcia (1981) conducted a meta-analysis of 178 empirical tests of the theory, and Schriesheim, Tepper and Tetrault (1994) conducted a further meta-analysis of a subset of these studies. Overall, Fiedler's predictions based on contingency theory have generally been supported. However, let's not be too hasty – there is both controversy and criticism (e.g. Peters, Hartke, & Pohlmann, 1985):

- Fiedler's view that leadership style is a characteristic of the individual that does not change across time and situations is inconsistent with: (1) contemporary perspectives on personality that views personality as able to vary in these very ways (e.g. Snyder & Cantor, 1998); (2) evidence of relatively low test–retest reliability (correlations ranging

Situational control
Fiedler's classification of task characteristics in terms of how much control effective task performance requires.

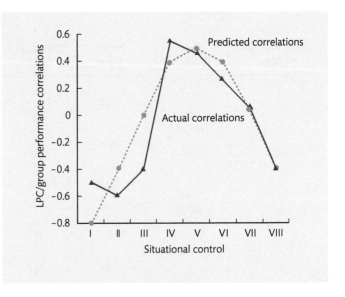

Figure 9.3 Predicted and obtained correlations between least preferred co-worker (LPC) scores and group performance as a function of situational control

- When situational control is very high or very low, contingency theory predicts a negative correlation between LPC scores and quality of group performance.
- A group performs poorly for a relationship-oriented leader (high LPC score), but well for a task-oriented leader (low LPC score).
- When control is intermediate, a positive correlation is predicted: relationship-oriented leaders are more effective. The obtained correlations came from a series of supportive studies.

Source: Based on data from Fiedler (1965).

from 0.01 to 0.93, with a median of 0.67) for LPC scores (Rice, 1978); and (3) the ease with which Lippitt and White (1943) trained their confederates to adopt different leadership styles in the classic study described earlier.

- Fiedler may be wrong to make the a priori assumption that leader–member relations are more important than task structure, which is more important than position power in the assessment of situational control. It would not be surprising if the relative order of importance were itself a function of situational factors. Indeed, Ramadhar Singh and his colleagues (Singh, Bohra, & Dalal, 1979) obtained a better fit between predictions and results when the favourability of the eight octants was based on subjective ratings by participants rather than Fiedler's a priori classification.

- Contingency theory distinguishes between the leadership effectiveness of high- and low-LPC leaders, classifying 'highs' as those with an LPC score greater than 64 and 'lows' as those with an LPC score of less than 57. So, how do people in the 57–64 range behave? This is a valid question, since about 20 per cent of people fall in this range. John Kennedy (1982) (once again not a former US president!) conducted a study to address this question. He found that high and low scorers behaved as predicted by contingency theory, but that middle scorers performed best of all and that situational favourability did not influence their effectiveness. This certainly limits contingency theory – it does not seem to be able to explain the leadership effectiveness of approximately 20 per cent of people or instances.

- Although contingency theory explores how the properties of the person and situation interact to influence leadership effectiveness, it neglects the group processes that are responsible for the rise and fall of leaders, and the situational complexion of leadership.

Normative decision theory

Normative decision theory (NDT)
A contingency theory of leadership that focuses on the effectiveness of different leadership styles in group decision-making contexts.

A second contingency theory, which is focused specifically on leadership in group decision-making contexts, is **normative decision theory** (NDT; e.g. Vroom & Jago, 1988). NDT identifies three decision-making strategies among which leaders can choose:

- *autocratic* (subordinate input is not sought);
- *consultative* (subordinate input is sought, but the leader retains the authority to make the final decision); and
- *group decision-making* (leader and subordinates are equal partners in a truly shared decision-making process).

The effectiveness of these strategies is contingent on the quality of leader–subordinate relations (which influences how committed and supportive subordinates are), and on task clarity and structure (which influences how much the leader needs subordinate input).

In decision-making contexts, autocratic leadership is fast and effective if subordinate commitment and support are high and the task is clear and well structured. When the task is less clear, greater subordinate involvement is needed, and therefore consultative leadership is best. When subordinates are not very committed or supportive, group decision-making is required to increase participation and commitment. Predictions from NDT are reasonably well supported empirically (e.g. Field & House, 1990) – leaders and managers report better decisions and better subordinate ratings when they follow the prescriptions of the theory. However, there is a tendency for subordinates to prefer fully participative group decision-making, even when it is not the most effective strategy.

Path-goal theory

A third contingency theory is **path-goal theory** (PGT; House, 1996), although it can also be classified as a transactional leadership theory (see the next section). PGT rests on the assumption that a leader's main function is to motivate followers by clarifying the paths (i.e. behaviours and actions) that will help them reach their goals. It distinguishes between the two classes of leader behaviour identified by the leader behaviour description questionnaire (LBDQ), described earlier: *structuring*, where the leader directs task-related activities, and *consideration*, where the leader addresses followers' personal and emotional needs. Structuring is most effective when followers are unclear about their goals and how to reach them – e.g. the task is new, difficult or ambiguous. When tasks are well understood, structuring is less effective. It can even backfire because it seems like meddling and micro-management. Consideration is most effective when the task is boring or uncomfortable, but not when followers are already engaged and motivated, because being considerate can seem distracting and unnecessary.

Empirical support for path–goal theory is mixed, with tests of the theory suffering from flawed methodology as well as being incomplete and simplistic (Schriesheim & Neider, 1996). The theory also has an interpersonal focus that underplays the ways in which a leader can motivate an entire work group rather than just individual followers.

Transactional leadership

Although popular, contingency theories are rather static. They do not capture the dance of leadership – leaders and followers provide support and gratification to one another, which allows leaders to lead and encourages followers to follow (Messick, 2005). This limitation is addressed by theories of **transactional leadership**.

The key assumption here is that leadership is a 'process of exchange that is analogous to contractual relations in economic life [and] contingent on the good faith of the participants' (Downton, 1973, p. 75). Leaders transact with followers to get things done – creating expectations and setting goals, and providing recognition and rewards for task completion (Burns, 1978). Mutual benefits are exchanged (transacted) between leaders and followers against a background of contingent rewards and punishments that shape up cooperation and trust (Bass, 1985). Leader–member transactions may also have an equity dimension (Walster, Walster, & Berscheid, 1978; also see **Chapter 14**). Because effective leaders play a greater role in steering groups to their goals than do followers, followers may reinstate equity by rewarding the leader with social approval, praise, prestige, status and power – in other words, with the trappings of effective leadership.

Idiosyncrasy credit

A well-known early approach to leadership that focused on leader–follower transactions is Edwin Hollander's (1958) analysis of **idiosyncrasy credit**. For leaders to be effective, they need their followers to allow them to be innovative in experimenting with new ideas and new

Path-goal theory (PGT)
A contingency theory of leadership that can also be classified as a transactional theory – it focuses on how 'structuring' and 'consideration' behaviours motivate followers.

Transactional leadership
Approach to leadership that focuses on the transaction of resources between leader and followers. Also a style of leadership.

Idiosyncrasy credit
Hollander's transactional theory, in which followers reward leaders for achieving group goals by allowing them to be relatively idiosyncratic.

directions – they need to be allowed to be idiosyncratic. Drawing on the equity argument presented earlier, Hollander wondered what circumstances would encourage such a transaction between leader and followers – one where followers would provide their leader with the resources to be able to be idiosyncratic.

He believed that certain behaviours build up idiosyncrasy credit with the group – a resource that the leader can ultimately 'cash in'. A good 'credit rating' can be established by:

- initially conforming closely to established group norms;
- ensuring that the group feels that it has democratically elected you as the leader;
- making sure that you are seen to have the competence to fulfil the group's objectives; and
- being seen to identify with the group, its ideals and its aspirations.

A good credit rating gives the leader legitimacy in the eyes of the followers to exert influence over the group and to deviate from existing norms – in other words, to be idiosyncratic, creative and innovative.

Research provides some support for this analysis. Merei (1949) introduced older children who had shown leadership potential into small groups of younger children in a Hungarian nursery. The most successful leaders were those who initially complied with existing group practices and who only gradually and later introduced minor variations. In another study, Hollander and Julian (1970) found that leaders of decision-making groups who were ostensibly democratically elected enjoyed more support from the group, felt more competent at the task and were more likely to suggest solutions that diverged from those of the group as a whole.

An alternative explanation, not grounded in notions of interpersonal equity and transaction, and idiosyncrasy credit, for why the conditions described earlier allow a leader to be innovative is based on the social identity theory of leadership (e.g. Hogg & Van Knippenberg, 2003; Hogg, Van Knippenberg, & Rast, 2012b; see the 'Social identity and leadership' section in this chapter). Here the term *innovation credit* is used instead (Abrams, Randsley de Moura, Marques, & Hutchison, 2008; Randsley de Moura, Abrams, Hutchison, & Marques, 2011).

Abrams and colleagues argue that it is actually innovation, not idiosyncrasy, that the group gives the leader leeway to indulge in. Whatever leaders do and however they acquire the mantle of leadership, the key factor that underpins their ability to get group members behind an innovative vision for the group rests on perceptions that the leader is 'one of us' – a *prototypical* and trustworthy group member who identifies with the group and thus will do it no harm (e.g. Platow & Van Knippenberg, 2001). If one identifies strongly with the group

Idiosyncrasy credit
You may take a few liberties, but only once you get to the top.

oneself, then one trusts such a leader (e.g. Yamagishi & Kiyonari, 2000) and is prepared to follow their lead largely irrespective of how innovative and counter-normative their behaviour may be – whatever the leader does is likely to be in the best interest of the group.

In supporting the notion of innovation credit, Daan van Knippenberg and his colleagues (Van Knippenberg, Van Knippenberg, & Bobbio, 2008) argued that in leading collective innovation and change, prototypical leaders would be more trusted to be 'agents of continuity', guardians of the group identity, than non-prototypical leaders, and thus more effective in motivating followers' willingness to contribute to the change. This is precisely what they found across two scenario experiments focusing on an organisational merger.

Leader–member exchange theory

Leader–member transactions play a central role in **leader–member exchange (LMX) theory** (e.g. Graen & Uhl-Bien, 1995; Sparrowe & Liden, 1997), which describes how the quality of exchange relationships (i.e. relationships where resources such as respect, trust and liking are exchanged) between leaders and followers can vary. Originally, LMX theory was called the **vertical dyad linkage (VDL) model** (Danserau, Graen, & Haga, 1975). According to VDL researchers, leaders develop dyadic exchange relationships with different specific subordinates. In these dyadic relationships, the subordinate can be treated either as a close and valued 'ingroup' member with the leader or in a more remote manner as an 'outgroup' member who is separate from the leader.

As the VDL model evolved into LMX theory, this dichotomous, ingroup versus outgroup, treatment of leader–member exchange relationships was replaced by a continuum of quality of exchange relationships. These relationships range from ones that are based on mutual trust, respect and obligation (high-quality LMX relationships), to ones that are rather mechanically based on the terms of the formal employment contract between leader and subordinate (low-quality LMX relationships).

In high-quality LMX relationships, subordinates are favoured by the leader and receive valued resources, which can include material (e.g. money, privileges) as well as psychological (e.g. trust, confidences) benefits. Leader–member exchanges go beyond the formal employment contract, with managers showing influence and support, and giving the subordinate greater autonomy and responsibility. High-quality LMX relationships should motivate subordinates to internalise the group's and the leader's goals. In low-quality LMX relationships, subordinates are disfavoured by the leader and receive fewer valued resources. Leader–member exchanges simply adhere to the terms of the employment contract, with little attempt by the leader to develop or motivate the subordinate. Subordinates will simply comply with the leader's goals, without necessarily internalising them as their own.

LMX theory predicts that effective leadership hinges on the development of high-quality LMX relationships. These relationships enhance subordinates' well-being and work performance, and bind them to the group more tightly through loyalty, gratitude and a sense of inclusion. Because leaders usually have to relate to a large number of subordinates, they cannot develop high-quality LMX relationships with everyone – it is more efficient to select some subordinates in whom to invest a great deal of interpersonal energy, and to treat the others in a less personalised way. The selection process takes time because it goes through a number of stages: *role taking* (the leader has expectations and tries out different roles on the subordinate), *role making* (mutual leader–member exchanges, e.g. of information or support, establish the subordinate's role), and *role routinisation* (the leader–member relationship has become stable, smooth-running and automatic).

Research confirms that differentiated LMX relationships do exist in most organisations. High-quality LMX relationships are more likely to develop when the leader and the subordinate have similar attitudes, like one another, belong to the same socio-demographic groups and both perform at a high level. High-quality LMX relationships are also associated with (most studies are correlational, not causal) better-performing and more satisfied workers who are more committed to the organisation and less likely to leave (Schriesheim, Castro, &

Leader-member exchange (LMX) theory
Theory of leadership in which effective leadership rests on the ability of the leader to develop good-quality personalised exchange relationships with individual members.

Vertical dyad linkage (VDL) model
An early form of leader-member exchange (LMX) theory in which a sharp distinction is drawn between dyadic leader-member relations: the subordinate is treated as either an ingroup member or an outgroup member.

Cogliser, 1999). The stages of LMX relationship development are consistent with more general models of group development (e.g. Levine & Moreland, 1994; Tuckman, 1965; see **Chapter 8**).

The main limitation of LMX theory is that it focuses on dyadic leader–member relations. There is a problem. As we have noted, leadership is a group process – even if a leader appears to be interacting with one individual, that interaction is framed by and located in the wider context of shared group membership. Followers interact with each other as group members and are influenced by their perceptions of the leader's relations with other group members (e.g. Hogg, Martin, & Weeden, 2004; Scandura, 1999).

Let us consider this from the perspective of the social identity theory of leadership (e.g. Hogg & Van Knippenberg, 2003; see the 'Social identity and leadership' section in this chapter). Members who identify strongly with a group might find that differentiated LMX relationships that favour some members over others are too personalised and fragment the group. They would not endorse such leaders. Instead, they might prefer a less personalised leadership style that treated all members relatively equally as group members and would endorse such leaders more strongly. This hypothesis has been tested and supported in two field surveys of leadership perceptions in organisations in Wales and in India (Hogg, Martin, Epitropaki, Mankad, Svensson, & Weeden, 2005).

Transformational leadership

Transformational leadership
Approach to leadership that focuses on the way that leaders transform group goals and actions – mainly through the exercise of charisma. Also a style of leadership based on charisma.

Transactional theories of leadership represent a particular focus on leadership. However, transactional leadership is itself a particular leadership *style* that can be contrasted to other leadership styles. In defining transactional leadership, political scientist James Burns (1978) contrasted it with **transformational leadership**: transactional leaders appeal to followers' self-interest, whereas transformational leaders inspire followers to adopt a vision that involves more than individual self-interest (Judge & Bono, 2000).

There are three key components of transformational leadership:

1 *individualised consideration* (attention to followers' needs, abilities and aspirations, in order to help raise aspirations, improve abilities and satisfy needs);

2 *intellectual stimulation* (challenging followers' basic thinking, assumptions and practices to help them develop newer and better mindsets and practices); and

3 *charismatic/inspiring leadership*, which provides the energy, reasoning and sense of urgency that transforms followers (Avolio & Bass, 1987; Bass, 1985).

Transformational leadership theorists were mortified that the charisma/inspiration component inadvertently admitted notorious dictators such as Hitler, Stalin and Pol Pot into the hallowed club of transformational leaders – all were effective leaders in so far as they mobilised groups around their goals. So, a distinction was drawn between good charismatic leaders with socialised charisma that they use in a 'morally uplifting' manner to improve society, and bad charismatic leaders who use personalised charisma to tear down groups and society – the former are transformational, the latter are not (e.g. O'Connor, Mumford, Clifton, Gessner, & Connelly, 1995; also see the earlier section of this chapter on defining leadership).

The distinction between transactional and transformational leadership has been joined by a third type of leadership – laissez-faire (non-interfering) leadership, which involves not making choices or taking decisions, and not rewarding others or shaping their behaviour. According to Avolio (1999), laissez-faire leaders provide a baseline anchor-point in his 'full-range leadership model', which has transformational leadership sitting at the apex (Antonakis & House, 2003).

Multifactor leadership questionnaire (MLQ)
The most popular and widely used scale for measuring transactional and transformational leadership.

First published by Bass and Avolio (1990), the **multifactor leadership questionnaire** (MLQ) was designed to measure transactional and transformational leadership. Now in its fifth version, it has been used in every conceivable organisation, at every conceivable level

Transformational leadership
A nation yearns for a leader who inspires, who exudes energy and a sense of urgency. How is Donald Trump doing?

and on almost every continent. It has become the de facto leadership questionnaire of choice of the organisational and management research communities – producing numerous large-scale meta-analyses of findings (e.g. Lowe, Kroeck, & Sivasubramaniam, 1996; also see Avolio & Yammarino, 2003).

A contemporary challenge for transformational leadership theory is to fill in the 'black box' of transformation – to specify exactly what happens in the head of individual followers to transform their thoughts and behaviour to conform to the leader's vision. Shamir, House and Arthur (1993) suggest that followers personally identify with the leader and in this way make the leader's vision their own. Dvir, Eden, Avolio and Shamir (2002) suggest that the behaviour of transformational leaders causes followers to identify more strongly with the organisation's core values.

Both these ideas resonate with the social identity theory of leadership (e.g. Hogg & Van Knippenberg, 2003; see the 'Social identity and leadership' subsection in this chapter). Where group members identify strongly with a group, leaders who are considered central/prototypical group members are able to be innovative in defining a group's goals and practices. Strong identification is associated with internalisation of group norms as one's own beliefs and actions. In this way, leaders can transform groups.

Charisma and charismatic leadership

The notion of charisma is so central to transformational leadership theory that, as we saw earlier, a distinction was drawn between good and bad charisma in order to distinguish between non-transformational villains (e.g. Hitler) and transformational heroes (e.g. Gandhi). This distinction is, of course, problematic – one person's transformational leader can be another's war criminal or vice versa (much as one person's freedom fighter is another's terrorist).

Was Osama bin Laden a transformational leader? What about Barack Obama? Your answer may rest more on your political persuasion and ideological leanings than on transformational leadership theory's notion of good versus bad charisma (see the earlier discussion in this chapter of effective/ineffective versus good/bad dimensions of leadership). How about Rupert Murdoch, founder and CEO of News Corp, and Steve Jobs, founder and CEO of Apple? Both are undoubtedly transformational and charismatic, but did they have 'bad charisma' because they appeared to fail to ensure organisational ethical conduct (in the case of Murdoch and the phone-hacking scandal which broke in the media in 2011) or acted narcissistically (in the case of Jobs – see Isaacson, 2011)?

Charismatic leadership
Leadership style based upon the leader's (perceived) possession of charisma.

There is a more general issue concerning the role of charisma in transformational leadership. Scholars talk of **charismatic leadership** as a product of (a) the leader's personal charisma and (b) followers' reactions to the leader's charisma in a particular situation – personal charisma alone may not guarantee charismatic leadership (e.g. Bryman, 1992). However, it is difficult to escape the inference that personal charisma is an enduring personality trait – in which case some of the limitations of past personality theories of leadership have been reintroduced (Haslam & Platow, 2001; Mowday & Sutton, 1993). Indeed, charismatic/transformational leadership has explicitly been linked to the Big Five personality dimensions of extraversion/surgency, agreeableness and intellect/openness to experience (e.g. Judge, Bono, Ilies, & Gerhardt, 2002). Charismatic leadership is also linked to the related construct of visionary leadership (e.g. Conger & Kanungo, 1998) and the view that people differ in terms of how visionary they are as leaders. Visionary leaders are special people who can identify desirable future goals and objectives for a group and mobilise followers to internalise these as their own.

There is no doubt that charisma makes it easier to be an effective leader, probably because charismatic people are emotionally expressive, enthusiastic, driven, eloquent, visionary, self-confident and responsive to others (e.g. House, Spangler, & Woycke, 1991; Riggio & Carney, 2003). These attributes allow a person to be influential and persuasive and therefore able to make others buy their vision for the group and sacrifice personal goals for collective goals. Meindl and Lerner (1983; Meindl, Ehrlich, & Dukerich, 1985) talk about visionary leaders heightening followers' sense of shared identity, and how this shared identity produces a collective 'heroic motive' that puts group goals ahead of personal goals.

An alternative perspective on the role of charisma in leadership is that a charismatic personality is constructed for the leader by followers; charisma is a consequence or correlate, not a cause, of effective leadership. For example, Meindl (1995; Meindl, Ehrlich, & Dukerich, 1985; also see Shamir, Pillai, Bligh, & Uhl-Bien, 2006) talks of the *romance of leadership*; people tend to attribute effective leadership to the leader's behaviour and to overlook the leader's shortcomings (e.g. Fiske & Dépret, 1996). The social identity theory of leadership (e.g., Hogg & Van Knippenberg, 2003; see the 'Social identity and leadership' subsection in this chapter) provides a similar analysis, but with an emphasis on the role of shared identity in charismatic leadership. Social identity processes in groups that members identify strongly with make group prototypical (central) leaders influential, attractive and trustworthy, and allow them to be innovative. Followers attribute these qualities internally to the leader's personality, thus constructing a charismatic leadership personality (Haslam & Platow, 2001; Platow & Van Knippenberg, 2001).

Leader perceptions and leadership schemas

Leader categorization theory

Leader categorization theory
We have a variety of schemas about how different types of leaders behave in different leadership situations. When a leader is categorized as a particular type of leader, the schema fills in details about how that leader will behave.

Social cognition (see **Chapter 2**) has framed an approach to leadership that focuses on the schemas we have of leaders and on the causes and consequences of categorizing someone as a leader. Called **leader categorization theory** (LCT) or implicit leadership theory (e.g. Lord, Brown, Harvey, & Hall, 2001; Lord & Brown, 2004; Lord & Hall, 2003), it is assumed that our perceptions of leadership play a key role in decisions we make about selecting and endorsing leaders. This influences leaders' power bases, and thus their ability to influence others and to lead effectively.

People have implicit theories of leadership that shape their perceptions of leaders. In assessing a specific leader, leadership schemas (called 'prototypes' by Lord and his colleagues) based on these implicit theories of leadership are activated, and characteristics of the specific leader are matched against the relevant schema of effective leadership. These schemas of leadership can describe general context-independent properties of effective leaders, or very specific properties of leadership in a very specific situation.

LCT predicts that the better the match is between the leader's characteristics and the perceiver's leadership schema, the more favourable are leadership perceptions. For example, if your leadership schema favours 'intelligent', 'organised' and 'dedicated' as core leadership attributes, you are more likely to endorse a leader the more you feel the leader actually to be intelligent, organised and dedicated.

LCT focuses on categories and associated schemas of leadership and leaders (e.g. military generals, prime ministers, CEOs), not on schemas of social groups as categories (e.g. a psychology department, a corporation, a sports team). LCT's leader categories are tied to specific tasks and functions that span a variety of different groups: for example, a CEO schema applies similarly to companies such as Apple, Dell, Virgin, Toyota, Starbucks and Google, whereas each company may have very different group norms and prototypes. LCT largely leaves unanswered the question of how schemas of group membership influence leadership, a question which is addressed by the social identity theory of leadership (e.g. Hogg & Van Knippenberg, 2003; described in the 'Social identity and leadership' section).

Expectation states and status characteristics

Another theory that focuses on leader categorization processes, but is more sociological and does not go into social cognitive details as extensively as leader categorization theory, is expectation states theory or **status characteristics theory** (e.g. Berger, Fisek, Norman, & Zelditch, 1977; Berger, Wagner, & Zelditch, 1985; Ridgeway, 2003). Influence (and thus leadership) within groups is attributed to possession of *specific status characteristics* (characteristics that match what the group actually does) and *diffuse status characteristics* (stereotypical characteristics of high-status groups in society). To be effective, leaders need to have characteristics that equip them for effective task performance (i.e. specific status characteristics) and characteristics that categorise them as members of high-status socio-demographic categories (i.e. diffuse status characteristics). Effective leadership is an additive function of perceived group task competence and perceived societal status.

Social identity and leadership

Leadership is a relationship where some members of a group (usually one member) are able to influence the rest of the group to embrace, as their own, new values, attitudes and goals, and to exert effort on behalf of and in pursuit of those values, attitudes and goals. An effective leader inspires others to adopt values, attitudes and goals that define group membership, and to behave in ways that serve the group as a collective. An effective leader can transform individual action into group action. Thus, leadership has an important identity function. People look to their leaders to express and epitomise their identity, to clarify and focus their identity, to forge and transform their identity and to consolidate, stabilise and anchor their identity.

This identity perspective on leadership (e.g. Haslam, Reicher, & Platow, 2011) has been placed centre-stage by the **social identity theory of leadership** (Hogg, 2001; Hogg & Van Knippenberg, 2003; Hogg, Van Knippenberg, & Rast, 2012b). As people identify more strongly with a group, they pay closer attention to the group prototype and to what and who is more prototypical of the group: this is because the prototype defines the group and one's identity as a group member. Under these circumstances, prototypical members tend to be more influential than less prototypical members and thus more effective as leaders; therefore, prototypical leaders tend to be more effective as leaders than non-prototypical leaders. Although leadership schemas, as described by leader categorization theory (see earlier in this chapter), generally do govern leader effectiveness, when a group becomes a salient and important basis for self-conception and identity, group prototypicality becomes important, perhaps more important than leader schemas.

This idea was first supported in a laboratory experiment by Hains, Hogg and Duck (1997), in which participants were explicitly categorized or merely aggregated as a group (group

Status characteristics theory
Theory of influence in groups that attributes greater influence to those who possess both task-relevant characteristics (specific status characteristics) and characteristics of a high-status group in society (diffuse status characteristics). Also called expectation states theory.

Social identity theory of leadership
Development of social identity theory to explain leadership as an identity process whereby in salient groups prototypical leaders are more effective than less prototypical leaders.

membership salience was therefore either high or low). Before taking part in an interactive group task, they rated the leadership effectiveness of a randomly appointed leader, who was described as being either a prototypical or non-prototypical group member and as possessing or not possessing characteristics that were consistent with general leadership schemas. As predicted, schema-consistent leaders were generally considered more effective than schema-inconsistent leaders; however, when group membership was salient, group prototypicality became an important influence on perceived leadership effectiveness (see Figure 9.4).

These findings were replicated in a longitudinal field study of Outward Bound groups (Fielding & Hogg, 1997), and in further experiments (e.g. Hogg, Hains, & Mason, 1998) and correlational studies (e.g. Platow & Van Knippenberg, 2001). Other studies show that in salient groups, ingroup leaders (i.e. more prototypical leaders) are more effective than outgroup leaders (i.e. less prototypical leaders) (Duck & Fielding, 1999; Van Vugt & De Cremer, 1999). This is a very robust and reliable effect – prototypical leaders are more strongly endorsed and considered more effective than less prototypical leaders, particularly by people who consider the group to be a central part of their social identity (Van Knippenberg, 2011).

A number of social identity-related processes (see Abrams & Hogg, 2010; Hogg, 2006, for overview) make prototypical leaders more influential in salient groups:

- Because prototypical members best embody the group's attributes, they are viewed as the source rather than the target of conformity processes – they are the ones with whom other members seem to align their behaviour (cf. Turner, J. C., 1991).

- Prototypical members are liked as group members (a process of depersonalised social attraction), and, because group members usually agree on the prototype, the group as a whole likes the leader – he or she is popular (Hogg, 1993). This process facilitates influence (we are more likely to comply with requests from people we like – Berscheid & Reis, 1998). It also accentuates the perceived evaluative (status) differential between leader and followers.

- Prototypical leaders find the group more central and important to self-definition, and therefore identify more strongly with it. They have significant investment in the group and are more likely to behave in group-serving ways. They closely embody group norms and are more likely to favour the ingroup over outgroups, to treat ingroup members fairly and to act in ways that promote the ingroup. These actions confirm their

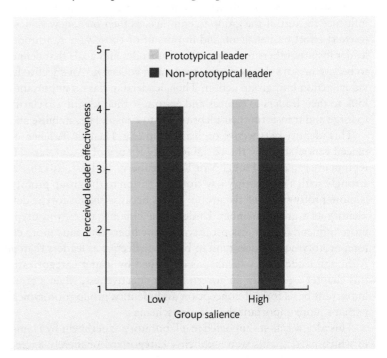

Figure 9.4 Leader effectiveness as a function of group prototypicality of the leader and salience of the group

- When group salience was high, features of the leader that were prototypical for the group became important in determining how effective the leader was perceived as being.
- When group salience was low, being prototypical did not have this impact.

Source: Based on data from Hains, Hogg and Duck (1997).

prototypicality and membership credentials and encourage group members to trust them to be acting in the best interest of the group even when it may not appear that they are – prototypical leaders are furnished with legitimacy (Tyler, 1997; Tyler & Lind, 1992; see Platow, Reid, & Andrew, 1998). A consequence is that prototypical leaders can be innovative and transformational. Paradoxically, they can diverge from group norms and conform less than leaders who are *not* prototypical (Abrams, Randsley de Moura, Marques, & Hutchison, 2008; Randsley de Moura, Abrams, Hutchison, & Marques, 2011).

- Because the prototype is central to group life, information related to the prototype attracts attention. A prototypical leader is the most direct source of prototype information, and so stands out against the background of the group. Members pay close attention to the leader and, as in other areas of social perception and inference, attribute his or her behaviour to invariant or essential properties of the leader's personality – they engage in the **correspondence bias** (Gawronski, 2004; Gilbert & Malone, 1995; **see Chapter 3**). This process can construct a charismatic personality for the leader (the behaviours being attributed include being the source of influence, being able to gain compliance from others, being popular, having higher status, being innovative and being trusted) which further strengthens his or her position of leadership (Haslam & Platow, 2001).

Correspondence bias
A general attribution bias in which people have an inflated tendency to see behaviour as reflecting (corresponding to) stable underlying personality attributes.

Prototypical leaders succeed in their position by acting as prototype managers – what Reicher and Hopkins have aptly called 'entrepreneurs of identity' (Reicher & Hopkins, 2001, 2003), and Seyranian calls social identity framing (Seyranian, 2012; Seyranian & Bligh, 2008). They communicate in ways that construct, reconstruct or change the group prototype; and this protects or promotes their central position in the group. This process is called *norm talk* (Hogg & Giles, 2012; Hogg & Tindale, 2005; also see Fiol, 2002; Gardner, Paulsen, Gallois, Callan, & Monaghan, 2001; Reid & Ng, 2000). A key attribute of an effective leader, therefore, is precisely this visionary and transformational activity that defines or changes: (a) what the group sees itself as being, and (b) the members' identity (Reicher, Haslam, & Hopkins, 2005). Leaders who feel they may not be prototypical often engage in group-oriented acts to strengthen their membership credentials (e.g. Platow & Van Knippenberg, 2001). There are many ways in which leaders can engage in norm talk and act as entrepreneurs of identity (see Box 9.2).

There is now substantial evidence that leaders actively construct identity in this way through their communications. Identity entrepreneurship and social identity framing have been shown in studies of Margaret Thatcher and Neil Kinnock's speeches concerning the British miner's strike in 1984–5 (Reicher & Hopkins, 1996b), the political mobilisation attempts of British Muslims concerning voting or abstaining from British elections (Hopkins, Reicher, & Kahani-Hopkins, 2003), anti-abortion speeches (Hopkins & Reicher, 1997; Reicher & Hopkins, 1996a), the preservation of hunting in the United Kingdom by focusing on the connection of nation and place (Wallwork & Dixon, 2004), Scottish politicians' speeches (Reicher & Hopkins, 2001); US presidents' speeches (Seyranian & Bligh, 2008), Patrice Lumumba's speeches during the Congolese decolonisation from Belgium (Klein & Licata, 2003) and attempts by prisoners to mobilise both prisoners and guards against management during the BBC prison study experiment (Reicher, Hopkins, Levine, & Rath, 2005).

The social identity theory of leadership has empirical support from laboratory experiments and more naturalistic studies and surveys, and it has re-energised leadership research in social and organisational psychology that focuses on the role of group membership and social identity (Ellemers, De Gilder, & Haslam, 2004; Haslam, Reicher, & Platow, 2011; Van Knippenberg & Hogg, 2003; Van Knippenberg, Van Knippenberg, De Cremer, & Hogg, 2004; also see Hogg, 2007a). Along with leader categorization theory (Lord & Brown, 2004; see earlier in this chapter), it also connects with a trend in leadership research to attend to the role of followers in leadership – for leaders to lead, followers must follow. One aspect of this trend focuses on what is rather awkwardly dubbed 'followership'; and there is now

Box 9.2 Your life
Norm talk and identity entrepreneurship

Have you considered standing for public office – after the 2016 presidential contest in the United States, perhaps not? Think about the most recent national leadership contest in your country. What strategies did the leadership contenders use to portray themselves as 'one of us' and thus win over the electorate? What strategies might you consider in competing for leadership?

Research suggests that there are five ways in which you as a leader can protect and enhance how group prototypically you are perceived by your followers:

1   Talk up your prototypicality and/or talk down aspects of your own behaviour that are non-prototypical.
2   Identify deviants or marginal members to highlight your own prototypicality or to construct a particular prototype for the group that enhances your prototypicality.

3   Secure your own leadership position by vilifying contenders for leadership and casting them as non-prototypical.
4   Identify as relevant comparison outgroups groups that cast the most favourable light on your own prototypicality.
5   Engage in a discourse that raises or lowers identity salience. If you are highly prototypical, then raising salience will provide you with the leadership benefits of high prototypicality; if you are not very prototypical, then lowering salience will protect you from the leadership pitfalls of not being very prototypical.

research that explores how followers can be empowered to create great and effective leaders (e.g. Kelley, 1992; Riggio, Chaleff, & Lipman-Blumen, 2008; Shamir, Pillai, Bligh, & Uhl-Bien, 2006).

Trust and leadership

Trust plays an important role in leadership (e.g. Dirks & Ferrin, 2002) – we all get very concerned about corporate corruption and unethical and untrustworthy business and government leaders (e.g. Brown, Treviño, & Harrison, 2005; Kellerman, 2004). If we are to follow our leaders, we need to be able to trust them to be acting in the best interest of us all as a group, rather than in their own self-interest.

We are therefore often suspicious and unwilling to trust or endorse our leaders if we feel that what they say or do does not reflect what they really think and who they really are – we believe they are inauthentic. Leaders earn trust, loyalty and support if they can ensure that their followers believe they are authentic (Avolio & Gardner, 2005; Rego, Vitória, Magalhães, Ribeiro, & e Cunha, 2013; Walumbwa, Avolio, Gardner, Wernsing, & Peterson, 2008). For example, during the 2016 US presidential election, the Republican Party tried to weaken electoral support for Hillary Clinton, the Democratic Party's presidential nominee, by orchestrating a concerted attack on her as being inauthentic and thus untrustworthy and dislikeable.

Trust facilitates leadership because people are more likely to smoothly bring their attitudes and behaviours into line with a leader they trust than one they distrust. Trust energises the pursuit of cognitive congruence, whereas distrust energises a negational mindset in which people to stop and think and generate cognitive opposition (Mayo, 2015).

Group value model
View that procedural justice within groups makes members feel valued, and thus leads to enhanced commitment to and identification with the group.

Justice and fairness

Leaders need their followers to trust them so that they are able to be innovative and transformational. An important basis for trusting one's leaders is the perception that they have acted in a fair and just manner. According to Tom Tyler's **group value model** (Lind & Tyler, 1988) and his **relational model of authority in groups** (Tyler, 1997; Tyler & Lind, 1992), perceptions of fairness and justice are critical to group life. Because leaders make decisions with important consequences for followers (e.g. promotions, performance appraisals, allocation of duties), followers are concerned about how fair the leader is in making these decisions. In judging fairness, followers evaluate a leader in terms of both **distributive justice** and **procedural justice**. Justice and fairness judgements influence reactions to decisions and to the authorities making these decisions, and thus influence leadership effectiveness (De Cremer, 2003; De Cremer & Tyler, 2005).

Procedural justice is particularly important in leadership contexts, probably because fair procedures convey respect for group members. This encourages followers to feel positive about the group, to identify with it and to be cooperative and compliant (Tyler, 2011). As members identify more strongly with the group, they care more that the leader is procedurally fair (e.g. Brockner, Chen, Mannix, Leung, & Skarlicki, 2000), and care less that the leader is distributively fair. This asymmetry arises because with increasing identification, concern about instrumental outcomes, i.e. incentives and sanctions (distributive justice), is outweighed by concern about relationships within the group (procedural justice) (e.g. Vermunt, Van Knippenberg, Van Knippenberg, & Blaauw, 2001).

Social dilemmas

The fact that justice, particularly procedural justice, facilitates effective leadership, because it builds trust and strengthens group identification, raises the possibility that leadership may be a way to resolve social dilemmas. **Social dilemmas** are essentially a crisis of trust – people behave selfishly because they do not trust others to sacrifice their immediate self-interest for the longer-term greater good of the collective (e.g. Dawes & Messick, 2000; Liebrand, Messick, & Wilke, 1992). (We discuss social dilemmas more fully in **Chapter 11**.)

Social dilemmas are notoriously difficult to resolve (Kerr & Park, 2001). However, they are not impossible to resolve if one can address the trust issue. One way to do this is to build mutual trust among people by causing them to identify strongly as a group – people tend to trust ingroup members (e.g. Brewer, 1981; Yamagishi & Kiyonari, 2000) and therefore are more likely to sacrifice self-interest for the greater good (e.g. Brewer & Schneider, 1990; De Cremer & Van Vugt, 1999). Leadership plays a critical role in this process because a leader can transform selfish individual goals into shared group goals by building a sense of common identity, shared fate, interindividual trust and custodianship of the collective good (e.g. De Cremer & Van Knippenberg, 2003; Van Vugt & De Cremer, 1999).

Gender gaps, glass ceilings and glass cliffs

Throughout most of the world, men and women both lead and exercise authority in different domains of life. However, in the worlds of work, politics and ideology, it is typically men who occupy top leadership positions. If one restricts oneself to liberal democracies like those in Western Europe, where more progressive gender attitudes have developed over the past forty or fifty years, it is still the case that although women are now relatively well represented in middle management, they are still underrepresented in senior management and 'elite' leadership positions – there is a **glass ceiling** (Eagly & Karau, 1991; Eagly, Karau, & Makhijani, 1995; Eagly, Makhijani, & Klonsky, 1992).

Are men really better suited than women to leadership? Research suggests not. Although women and men tend to have different leadership styles, which implies that different leadership contexts may suit different genders, women are usually rated as just as effective leaders as men – and in general they are perceived to be marginally more transformational and participative, and more praising of followers for good performance (Eagly, Johannesen-Schmidt, Van Engen, & Vinkenburg, 2002). If women and men are equally capable of being effective leaders, why is there a gender gap in leadership?

Relational model of authority in groups
Tyler's account of how effective authority in groups rests upon fairness- and justice-based relations between leader and followers.

Distributive justice
The fairness of the outcome of a decision.

Procedural justice
The fairness of the procedures used to make a decision.

Social dilemmas
Situations in which short-term personal gain is at odds with the long-term good of the group.

Glass ceiling
An invisible barrier that prevents women, and minorities in general, from attaining top leadership positions.

Glass ceiling
Women make it to the top - Facebook's chief operating officer Sheryl Sandberg is a case in point. But they can still encounter more obstacles than men do (watch www.makers.com/sheryl-sanberg.

Role congruity theory
Mainly applied to the gender gap in leadership – because social stereotypes of women are inconsistent with people's schemas of effective leadership, women are evaluated as poor leaders.

One explanation proposed by Alice Eagly is in terms of **role congruity theory** (Eagly, 2003; Eagly & Karau, 2002; Heilman, 1983). Because there is greater overlap between general leader schemas and agentic male stereotypes (men are assertive, controlling and dominant) than between leader schemas and communal female stereotypes (women are affectionate, gentle and nurturant), people have more favourable perceptions of male leaders than of female leaders. These leadership perceptions facilitate or impede effective leadership. They place women in a tricky situation: if they are communal, they may not fit the schema of being a leader so well; if they are agentic. they run the risk, like Margaret Thatcher, of being dubbed the 'Iron Lady', 'Her Malignancy' or 'Attila the Hen' (Genovese, 1993).

Research provides some support for role congruity theory (Martell, Parker, Emrich, & Crawford, 1998; Shore, 1992). One implication of the theory is that the evaluation of male and female leaders will change if the leadership schema changes or if people's gender stereotypes change. For example, research has shown that men leaders are evaluated more favourably than women leaders when the role is defined in more masculine terms, and vice versa when the role is defined in less masculine terms (Eagly, Karau, & Makhijani, 1995).

Another obstacle to gender equality in leadership can be understood in terms of the social identity theory of leadership (discussed earlier). In groups that are central to self-definition, male or female leaders are seen as and actually are effective if the group's norms are consistent with the members' gender stereotypes. So, people with traditional gender stereotypes will endorse a male rather than a female leader of a group with instrumental norms (e.g. a trucking company) and a female rather than a male leader of a group with more expressive norms (e.g. a childcare group); but people with less traditional gender stereotypes are less inclined to respond in this way, or even act in the reverse way (Hogg, Fielding, Johnson, Masser, Russell, & Svensson, 2006).

A third obstacle to gender equality in leadership is that women claim authority less effectively than men – men claim and hold many more leadership positions overall than women (Bowles & McGinn, 2005). However, once women or men claim authority, they are equally effective. Bowles and McGinn propose four main barriers to women claiming authority. The first is role incongruity, as discussed above. The second is lack of critical management experience. The third is family responsibility, which compromises a woman's ability to find the time commitment required of leadership positions.

A fourth obstacle is lack of motivation – women are not as 'hungry' for leadership as are men. They shy away from self-promotion and take on less visible background roles with informal titles like 'facilitator' or 'coordinator'. Although the link has not been made explicit, one underlying reason for women's alleged reticence to claim authority may be stereotype threat (Inzlicht & Schmader, 2011; Steele & Aronson, 1995; Steele, Spencer, & Aronson, 2002; see **Chapter 10**) – women fear that negative stereotypes about women and leadership will be confirmed, and so they feel less motivated to lead. In addition, a woman who promotes herself and claims leadership has to contend with popular stereotypes of women. She runs the risk of being seen as 'pushy', attracting negative reactions from both men and women (Rudman, 1998; Rudman & Glick, 2001). (We return to the topic of stereotype threat in **Chapter 10**.)

Michelle Ryan and her colleagues have suggested that women in leadership not only confront a glass ceiling but also a **glass cliff** (Ryan & Haslam, 2007; Ryan, Haslam, Morgenroth, Rink, Stoker, & Peters, 2016). Women are more likely than men to be appointed to leadership positions associated with increased risk of failure and criticism because these positions involve the management of groups that are in crisis. As a result, women often confront a glass cliff in which their position as leader is precarious and probably doomed to failure.

Haslam and Ryan (2008) conducted three experiments in which management graduates, high-school students or business leaders selected a leader for a hypothetical organisation whose performance was either improving or declining (i.e. failing). As predicted, a woman was more likely to be selected ahead of an equally qualified man when the organisation's performance was declining rather than improving. Further, participants who made these 'glass cliff appointments' also believed that such positions (a) suited the distinctive leadership abilities that women possess and (b) were good leadership opportunities for women. There is a sting in the tail: the participants also believed that a position in a failing organisation would be particularly stressful for women – because of the 'emotional labour' involved! It would appear that women may be favored in times of poor performance, not because they are expected to improve the situation, but because they are seen to be good people managers and can take the blame for organisational failure (Ryan, Haslam, Hersby, & Bongiorno, 2011).

Ryan and colleagues report other supportive studies that focus on political leadership (Ryan, Haslam, & Kulich, 2010). An archival study of the 2005 UK General Election revealed that, in the Conservative Party, women contested harder-to-win seats than did men. Another study experimentally investigated the selection of a candidate by undergraduates in a British political science class to contest a by-election in a seat that was either safe (held by own party with a large margin) or risky (held by an opposition party with a large margin). Their findings showed that a male candidate was more likely than a woman to be selected to contest a safe seat, but a woman was strongly preferred when the seat was hard to win.

Intergroup leadership

An under-explored aspect of leadership is its intergroup context – leaders not only lead the members of their group, but in different ways they lead their group *against* other groups. The political and military leaders who are often invoked in discussions of leadership are leaders in a truly intergroup context – they lead their political parties, their nations or their armies *against* other political parties, nations or armies.

Leadership rhetoric is often about *us* versus *them*, about defining the ingroup in contrast to specific outgroups or deviant ingroup factions (Reicher, Haslam, & Hopkins, 2005; Seyranian, 2012). The nature of intergroup relations can also influence leadership by changing group goals or altering intragroup relations. Earlier, we described how a leadership change in one of Sherif's groups of boys at a summer camp was produced by intergroup competition (Sherif, Harvey, White, Hood, & Sherif, 1961). In another study, of simulated bargaining between union and management, relatively insecure leaders (who were likely to be deposed by their group) actively sought to bargain by competing in order to secure their leadership (Rabbie & Bekkers, 1978). Perhaps this captures the familiar tactic where political leaders pursue an aggressive foreign policy (where they believe they can win) in order to combat unpopularity experienced at home. For example, the 1982 Falklands War between

Stereotype threat
Feeling that we will be judged and treated in terms of negative stereotypes of our group, and that we will inadvertently confirm these stereotypes through our behaviour.

Glass cliff
A tendency for women rather than men to be appointed to precarious leadership positions associated with a high probability of failure and criticism.

Argentina and Britain, which arose in the context of political unpopularity at home for both governments, certainly boosted Margaret Thatcher's leadership; and the two Gulf Wars of 1991 and 2003 may initially have consolidated leadership for US presidents Bush senior and Bush junior, respectively.

But there is another side to intergroup leadership – the building of a unified group identity, vision and purpose across deep subgroup divisions within the group. Although social identity theory is a theory of intergroup relations (e.g. Tajfel & Turner, 1986), the social identity theory of leadership actually has an intragroup focus – on within-group prototypicality, shared group membership and ingroup trust. The great challenge of effective leadership, however, often is not merely to transcend *differences among individuals*, but to bridge profound *divisions between groups* to build an integrative vision and identity. For example: effective leadership of Iraq must bridge historic differences between Sunnis, Shi'ites and Kurds; effective leadership of the United States must bridge a profound gulf between Democrats and Republicans; effective leadership of the European Union must bridge vast differences among its 28 member states. 'Leadership', as the term is often used in common parlance, is often better characterised as intergroup leadership (Hogg, 2009; Pittinsky, 2009; Pittinsky & Simon, 2007). (Reflect on 'What do *you* think?' question 2: should Steve or Martin take the role of new boss?)

Hogg and his colleagues have recently proposed a model of intergroup leadership (Hogg, 2015; Hogg, Van Knippenberg, & Rast, 2012a). Effective intergroup leadership faces the daunting task of building social harmony and a common purpose and identity out of conflict among groups. One problem is that intergroup leaders are often viewed as representing one group more than the other; they are outgroup leaders to one subgroup and therefore suffer compromised effectiveness (Duck & Fielding, 1999, 2003). This problem has been well researched in the context of organisational mergers and acquisitions. Acquisitions often fail precisely because the leader of the acquiring organisation is viewed with suspicion as a member of the former outgroup organisation (e.g., Terry, Carey, & Callan, 2001).

These problems can be accentuated by ingroup projection – a phenomenon where groups nested within a larger superordinate group overestimate how well their own characteristics are represented in the superordinate group (Wenzel, Mummendey, & Waldzus, 2007). In this case, a leader of the superordinate group who belongs to one subgroup will be viewed by the other subgroup as not at all prototypical of the superordinate group.

One interesting wrinkle to this is that lower/minority status subgroups often do not engage in ingroup projection; both subgroups agree that the dominant subgroup's attributes are best represented in the superordinate group (Sindic & Reicher, 2008). In this situation, the minority subgroup *will* view a superordinate leader who comes from the majority subgroup as prototypical. However, such a leader will not gain an advantage from this because the minority group feels underrepresented and therefore is unlikely to identify sufficiently strongly with the superordinate group (Hohman, Hogg, & Bligh, 2010).

Hogg and colleagues suggest that effective intergroup leadership rests on the leader's ability to construct an *intergroup relational identity* (Hogg, 2015; Hogg, Van Knippenberg, & Rast, 2012a). Intergroup leaders strive to build a common ingroup identity (Gaertner & Dovidio, 2000; Gaertner, Dovidio, Anastasio, Bachman, & Rust, 1993; see **Chapter** 11). However, this needs to be carried out carefully; it can easily backfire when it threatens the subgroup identity of subgroups.

In contrast, an intergroup relational identity is a self-definition in terms of one's subgroup membership that incorporates the subgroup's relationship with another subgroup as part of the overarching group's identity. This is an identity that recognises the integrity and valued contribution of subgroup identities and the way that they and the superordinate group are actually defined in terms of collaborative subgroup relations. There are a number of actions that leaders can take to build an intergroup relational identity and thus sponsor effective intergroup performance. These include (a) rhetoric championing the intergroup collaboration as a valued aspect of group identity, (b) intergroup boundary spanning to exemplify the intergroup relationship, and (c) the formation of a boundary-spanning leadership coalition.

In concluding this section, the great challenge of leadership is often not merely to transcend individual differences, but to bridge profound group divisions and build an integrative vision and identity. Most theories and studies of leadership focus on leading individuals within a single group, whereas many if not most leadership contexts involve intergroup relations (Pittinsky & Simon, 2007).

Group decision-making

Groups perform many tasks, of which making decisions is one of the most important. The course of our lives is largely determined by decisions made by groups: for example, selection committees, juries, parliaments, committees of examiners and groups of friends. In addition, many of us spend a significant portion of our working lives making decisions in groups.

Social psychologists have long been interested in the social processes involved in group decision-making, and in whether groups make better or different decisions than do individuals.

We might think that humans come together to make decisions because groups would make better decisions than individuals – two heads are better than one. However, as we learnt in **Chapter 8**, groups can impair and distort performance in many ways. Another dimension of group decision-making comes into play when members of the decision-making group are formally acting as *representatives* of different groups. This is more properly called intergroup decision-making and is dealt with later in the text (see **Chapter 11**).

Rules governing group decisions

A variety of models have been developed to relate the distribution of initial opinions in a decision-making group to the group's final decision (Stasser & Dietz-Uhler, 2001; Stasser, Kerr, & Davis, 1989). Some of these are complex computer-simulation models (Hastie, Penrod, & Pennington, 1983; Penrod & Hastie, 1980; Stasser, 1988; Stasser & Davis, 1981), while others, although expressed in a formalised mathematical style, are more immediately related to real groups.

One of the best-known models, described by James Davis, identifies a small number of explicit or implicit decision-making rules, called **social decisions schemes**, that groups can adopt (Davis, 1973; Stasser, Kerr, & Davis, 1989). Knowledge of the initial distribution of individual opinions in the group, and what rule the group is operating under, allows prediction, with a high degree of certainty, of the final group decision. We can apply these rules to institutionalised groups, such as a parliament, but also to informal groups, such as a group of friends deciding which film to watch (see Box 9.3).

Social decisions schemes Explicit or implicit decision-making rules that relate individual opinions to a final group decision.

The particular rule that a group adopts can be influenced by the nature of the decision-making task. For *intellective tasks* (there is a demonstrably correct solution, such as a mathematical puzzle) groups tend to adopt the truth-wins rule; for *judgemental tasks* (there is no demonstrably correct solution, such as what colour to paint the living room) the majority-wins rule (Laughlin, 1980; Laughlin & Ellis, 1986).

Decision rules also differ in terms of strictness and the distribution of power among group members:

- *Strictness* refers to the amount of agreement required by the rule – unanimity is extremely strict and majority-wins less strict.

- *Distribution of power* among members refers to how authoritarian the rule is – authoritarian rules concentrate power in one member, while egalitarian rules spread power among all members (Hastie, Penrod, & Pennington, 1983).

Box 9.3 Our world
Social decisions schemes: Ways that a group can reach a decision

James Davis distinguished between several explicit or implicit decision-making rules that decision-making groups can adopt:

- *Unanimity* – Discussion is aimed at pressurising deviants to conform.
- *Majority wins* – Discussion confirms the majority position, which is then adopted as the group position.

- *Truth wins* – Discussion reveals the position that can be demonstrated to be correct.
- *Two-thirds majority* – Unless there is a two-thirds majority, the group is unable to reach a decision.
- *First shift* – The group ultimately adopts a decision in line with the direction of the first shift in opinion shown by any member of the group.

Source: Based on Davis (1973); Stasser, Kerr and Davis (1989).

In general, stricter rules have lower power concentration and are thus more egalitarian, with decision-making power more evenly distributed across the group – unanimity is very strict but very low in power concentration, while two-thirds majority is less strict but has greater power concentration (Hastie, Penrod, & Pennington, 1983). The rule adopted can have an effect, largely as a function of its strictness, not only on the group's decision itself but also on members' preferences, their satisfaction with the group decision, the perception and nature of group discussion, and members' feelings for one another (Miller, 1989). For example, stricter decision rules can make final agreement in the group slower, more exhaustive and difficult to attain, but it can enhance liking for fellow members and satisfaction with the quality of the decision.

Social transition scheme
Method for charting incremental changes in member opinions as a group moves towards a final decision.

Norbert Kerr's **social transition scheme** model focuses attention on the actual pattern of member positions moved through by a group operating under a particular decision, en route to its final decision (Kerr, 1981; Stasser, Kerr, & Davis, 1989). In order to do this, members' opinions are monitored during the process of discussion (Kerr & MacCoun, 1985), either by periodically asking the participants or by having them note any and every change in their opinion. These procedures can be intrusive, so an issue is how much they affect the natural ongoing process of discussion.

One other line of research on group decision-making focuses on hidden profiles (Stasser & Titus, 2003). A hidden profile is a situation in which group members have shared information favouring an inferior choice or decision, and unshared private information favouring a superior choice or decision. In this situation, groups typically choose an inferior alternative and make an inferior decision. A recent meta-analysis of sixty-five hidden profiles studies (Lu, Yuan, & McLeod, 2012) concluded that groups mentioned more pieces of common information than unique information, and hidden profile groups were eight times less likely to find the correct solution or come to an optimal decision than were groups with full information.

Brainstorming

Brainstorming
Uninhibited generation of as many ideas as possible in a group, in order to enhance group creativity.

Some decision-making tasks require groups to come up with creative and novel solutions. A common technique is **brainstorming** (Osborn, 1957). Group members try to generate lots of ideas very quickly and forget their inhibitions or concerns about quality – they simply say whatever comes to mind, are non-critical, and build on others' ideas when possible. Brainstorming is supposed to facilitate creative thinking and thus make the group more creative. Popular opinion is so convinced that brainstorming works that it is widely used in business and advertising agencies.

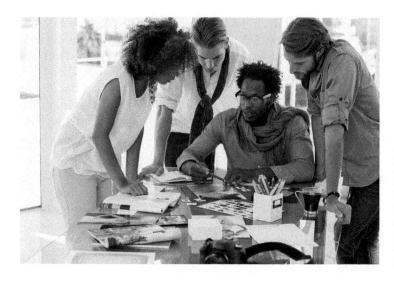

Brainstorming
Encouraging an uninhibited outpouring of ideas is a strategy sometimes used to enhance a groups creativity, and how it can be fun – but how well does this strategy work?

However, research tells us otherwise. Although brainstorming groups do generate *more* ideas than non-brainstorming groups, the individuals in the group are no more creative than if they had worked alone. Wolfgang Stroebe and Michael Diehl (1994) reviewed the literature and concluded that *nominal* groups (i.e. brainstorming groups in which individuals create ideas on their own and do not interact) are twice as creative as groups that actually interact (see also Diehl & Stroebe, 1987; Mullen, Johnson, & Salas, 1991).

The inferior performance of brainstorming groups can be attributed to at least four factors (Paulus, Dzindolet, Poletes, & Camacho, 1993):

1 *Evaluation apprehension* – despite explicit instructions to encourage the uninhibited generation of as many ideas as possible, members may still be concerned about making a good impression. This introduces self-censorship and a consequent reduction in productivity.

2 *Social loafing and free riding* – there is motivation loss because of the collective nature of the task (see **Chapter 8**).

3 *Production matching* – because brainstorming is novel, members use average group performance to construct a performance norm to guide their own generation of ideas. This produces regression to the mean.

4 **Production blocking** – individual creativity and productivity are reduced owing to interference effects from contending with others who are generating ideas at the same time as one is trying to generate one's own ideas.

Production blocking
Reduction in individual creativity and productivity in brainstorming groups due to interruptions and turn taking.

Stroebe and Diehl (1994) reviewed evidence for these processes and concluded that production blocking is probably the main obstacle to unlocking the creative potential of brainstorming groups. They discuss a number of remedies, of which two have particular promise.

1 *Electronic brainstorming* reduces the extent to which the production of new ideas is blocked by such things as listening to others or waiting for a turn to speak (Hollingshead & McGrath, 1995): groups that brainstorm electronically via computer can produce more ideas than non-electronic groups and more ideas than nominal electronic groups (Dennis & Valacich, 1993; Gallupe, Cooper, Grise, & Bastianutti, 1994).

2 *Heterogeneous groups* in which members have diverse types of knowledge about the brainstorming topic may create a particularly stimulating environment that alleviates the effects of production blocking; if production blocking is also reduced by other means, heterogeneous brainstorming groups might outperform heterogeneous nominal groups.

Illusion of group effectivity
Experience-based belief that we produce more and better ideas in groups than alone.

Given convincing evidence that face-to-face brainstorming does not actually improve individual creativity, why do people so firmly believe that it does and continue to use it to generate new ideas in groups? This paradox may stem from an **illusion of group effectivity** (Diehl & Stroebe, 1991; Stroebe, Diehl, & Abakoumkin, 1992; also see Paulus, Dzindolet, Poletes, & Camacho, 1993). We all take part in group discussions from time to time, and so we all have some personal experience with generating ideas in groups. The illusion of group effectivity is an experience-based belief that we actually produce more and better ideas in groups than when alone.

This illusion may be generated in at least three ways:

1 Although groups have fewer non-redundant original ideas than the sum of individuals working alone, they produce more ideas than any single member would produce alone. People in groups are exposed to more ideas than when alone. They find it difficult to remember whether the ideas produced were their own or those of other people and so exaggerate their own contribution. They feel that they have been individually more productive and were facilitated by the group when in fact they were less productive. Stroebe, Diehl and Abakoumkin (1992) had participants brainstorm in four-person nominal or real groups and asked them to estimate the percentage of ideas: (1) that they had suggested; (2) that others had suggested but they had also thought of; (3) that others had suggested but they had not thought of. The results show that participants in real groups overestimate the percentage of ideas that they thought they had but did not suggest, relative to participants in nominal groups (see Figure 9.5).

2 Brainstorming is generally great fun. People enjoy brainstorming in groups more than alone and so feel more satisfied with their performance.

3 People in groups know they call out only some of the ideas they have, because others have already suggested their remaining ideas. Although all members are in the same position, the individual is not privy to others' undisclosed ideas – and so attribute the relatively low public productivity of others to their own relatively high latent productivity. The group is seen to have enhanced or confirmed their own high level of performance.

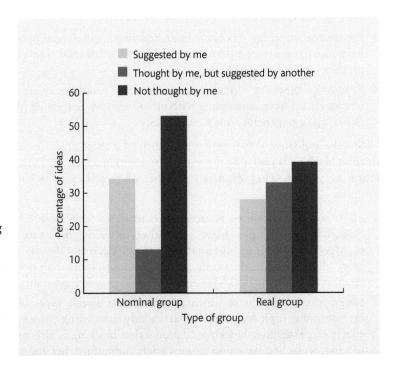

Figure 9.5 Percentage of ideas assigned to self and to others in nominal and real brainstorming groups

Relative to participants in nominal brainstorming groups, participants in real brainstorming groups underestimated the number of ideas they had not thought of and overestimated the number of ideas they had thought of but actually had been suggested by others.

Source: Based on data from Stroebe, Diehl and Abakoumkin (1992).

Group memory

Another important aspect of group decision-making is the ability to recall information. For instance, juries need to recall testimony to arrive at a verdict, and personnel selection panels need to recall data that differentiate candidates to make an appointment. Group remembering can even be the principal reason for certain groups to come together: for example, groups of old friends often meet mainly to reminisce. On a larger scale, organisations need to acquire, distribute, interpret and store enormous amounts of information. This task of *organisational learning* is enormously complex (Argote, 2013).

Group remembering

Do groups remember more material and remember material more accurately than individuals? Different people recall different information; so when they come together as a group to share this information the group has effectively remembered more than any one individual (Clark & Stephenson, 1989, 1995). Groups recall more than individuals because members communicate unshared information and because the group recognises true information when it hears it (Lorge & Solomon, 1955). However, the superiority of groups over individuals varies depending on the memory task. On simple and artificial tasks (e.g. nonsense words), group superiority is more marked than on complex and realistic tasks (e.g. a story). One explanation is 'process loss' (Steiner, 1976; see **Chapter 8**). In trying to recall complex information, groups fail to adopt appropriate recall and decision strategies, and so underuse all of the group's human resources.

However, group remembering is more than a collective regurgitation of facts. It is a constructive process by which an agreed joint account is worked out. Some individuals' memories will contribute to the developing consensus, while others' memories will not. In this way, the group shapes its own version of the truth. This version then guides individual members about what to store as a true memory and what to discard as an incorrect memory. The process of reaching consensus is subject to the range of social influence processes discussed earlier (see **Chapter 7**), and to the group decision-making biases discussed in this chapter. Most research into group remembering focuses on how much is remembered by individuals and by groups. However, there are other approaches: Clark and Stephenson and their associates have looked at the content and structure of what is remembered (see Box 9.4 and Figure 9.6), and Middleton and Edwards (1990) have adopted a discourse analysis approach (discussed in **Chapter 15**).

Transactive memory

A different perspective on group remembering is that different members remember different things (memory specialisation is distributed), but everyone also needs to remember 'who remembers what' – who to go to for information. Dan Wegner calls this **transactive memory**, a term suggesting that group members have transacted an agreement (Wegner, 1987, 1995; also see Moreland, Argote, & Krishnan, 1996). This idea refers to how individuals in couples and groups can share memory load so that each individual is responsible for remembering only part of what the group needs to know, but all members know who is responsible for each memory domain. Transactive memory is a shared system for encoding, storing and retrieving information. It allows a group to remember significantly more information than if no transactive memory system was present (Hollingshead, 1996).

For example, the psychology departments in our universities need to remember an enormous amount of practical information to do with research, postgraduate supervision, undergraduate teaching, equipment and administrative matters. There is far too much for a single individual to remember. Instead, certain individuals are formally responsible for particular domains (e.g. research), but all of us have a transactive memory that allows us to remember who is responsible for each domain. Transactive memory is also very common in close relationships such as marriage: for example, both partners know that one of them remembers financial matters and the other remembers directions.

Transactive memory
Group members have a shared memory for who within the group remembers what and is the expert on what.

Box 9.4 Research highlight
Can two heads remember better than one?

There are differences between individual and group remembering.

Noel Clark, Geoffrey Stephenson and their associates conducted a series of experiments on group remembering (e.g. Clark, Stephenson, & Rutter, 1986; Stephenson, Abrams, Wagner, & Wade, 1986; Stephenson, Clark, & Wade, 1986). Clark and Stephenson (1989, 1995) give an overview of this research. Generally, students or police officers individually or collectively (in four-person groups) recalled information from a five-minute police interrogation of a woman who had allegedly been raped. The interrogation was real, or it was staged and presented as an audio recording or a visual transcript. The participants had to recall freely the interrogation and answer specific factual questions (cued recall). The way in which they recalled the information was analysed for content to investigate:

- the amount of correct information recalled;
- the number of reconstructive errors made – that is, inclusion of material that was consistent with but did not appear in the original stimulus;
- the number of confusional errors made – that is, inclusion of material that was inconsistent with the original stimulus;
- the number of metastatements made – that is, inclusion of information that attributed motives to characters or went beyond the original stimulus in other ways.

Figure 9.6 (adapted from Clark & Stephenson, 1989) shows that groups recalled significantly more correct information and made fewer metastatements than individuals, but they did not differ in the number of reconstructions or confusional errors.

Source: Based on Clark and Stephenson (1989).

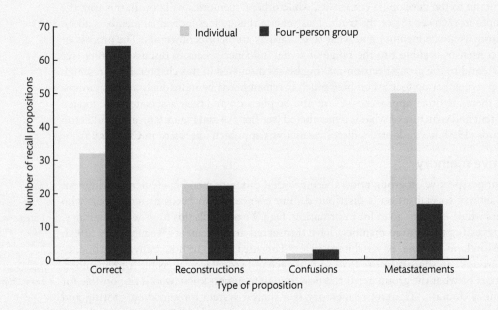

Figure 9.6 Differences between individual and collective remembering

There are qualitative and quantitative differences between individual and collective remembering. Isolated individuals or four-person groups recalled police testimony from the interrogation of an alleged rape victim. In comparison to individuals, groups recalled more information that was correct and made fewer metastatements (statements making motivational inferences and going beyond the information in other related ways).

Source: Based on data from Clark and Stephenson (1989).

Transactive memory is a group-level representation: although it is represented in the mind of the individual, it can emerge only through psychological involvement in a group and otherwise has no value or use. For example, who else beyond her teammates cares if it is Mary's turn to bring orange juice to the sports team's practice this month? There can be no such thing as individual transactive memory. In this respect, the concept of transactive memory is related to William McDougall's (1920) notion of a **group mind** (**Chapters 1 and 11**) – a state of mind and mode of cognition found in groups that is qualitatively different from that found in individuals.

Wegner, Erber and Raymond (1991) describe the development of transactive memory. When groups or couples first form, the basis of transactive memory is usually social categorization. People stereotypically assign memory domains to individuals on the basis of their category memberships. For example, members of heterosexual couples might initially develop a transactive memory in which memory is allocated on the basis of sex-role stereotypes – both partners assume that the go-to person for cooking and social arrangements is the woman and the go-to person for car and plumbing repairs is the man. Category-based transactive memory is the default mode. In most cases, however, groups go on to develop more sophisticated memory-assignment systems:

- *Groups can negotiate responsibility for different memory domains* – for instance, couples can decide through discussion who will be responsible for bills, who for groceries, who for cars and so forth.

- *Groups can assign memory domains on the basis of relative expertise* – for instance, a conference-organising committee might assign responsibility for the social programme to someone who has successfully discharged that duty before.

- *Groups can assign memory domains on the basis of access to information* – for instance, the conference-organising committee might assign responsibility for publicity to someone who has a good graphics package and a list of potential registrants, and who has close contacts with advertising people.

There is a potential pitfall to transactive memory. The uneven distribution of memory within a couple or a group means that when an individual leaves, there is a temporary loss or reduction in group memory (see Box 9.5). This can be very disruptive: for example, if the person in my department responsible for remembering undergraduate teaching matters should suddenly leave, a dire crisis would arise. Groups often recover quickly, as there may be other people (often already with some expertise and access to information) who can immediately shoulder the responsibility. In couples, however, partners are usually irreplaceable. Once one person leaves the couple, perhaps through death or separation, a whole section of group memory vanishes. It is possible that the depression associated with bereavement is, at least in part, due to the loss of memory. Happy memories are lost, our sense of who we are is undermined by lack of information, and we have to take responsibility for remembering a variety of things we did not have to remember before.

Group mind
McDougall's idea that people adopt a qualitatively different mode of thinking when in a group.

Group culture

Group memory can be viewed more broadly through the lens of socially shared cognition and group culture (Tindale, Meisenhelder, Dykema-Engblade, & Hogg, 2001). We tend to think of culture as something that exists at the societal level – the customs (routines, rituals, symbols and jargon) that describe large-scale social categories such as ethnic or national groups (see **Chapter 16**). However, there is no reason to restrict culture to such groups. Moreland, Argote and Krishnan (1996) argue that culture is an instance of group memory and therefore can exist in smaller groups such as organisations, sports teams, work groups and even families. The analysis of group culture is most developed in the study of work groups (Levine & Moreland, 1991): such groups develop detailed knowledge about norms,

Box 9.5 Our world
The group that learns together stays together

Transactive memory: combating its loss and facilitating its development

Transactive memory means that when an individual leaves a group, there is a temporary loss of, or reduction in, group memory, which can be very disruptive for group functioning. Linda Argote and her colleagues performed an experiment in which laboratory groups met over a number of consecutive weeks to produce complex origami objects (Argote, Insko, Yovetich, & Romero, 1995). Member turnover did indeed disrupt group learning and performance, and its impact grew worse over time, presumably because more established groups had more established transactive memories. Attempts to reduce the problem by providing newcomers with individual origami training were unsuccessful.

The productivity implications for work groups and organisations are very serious, given that staff turnover is a fact of organisational life and that new members are almost always trained individually. Moreland, Argote and Krishnan (1996) argue that transactive memory systems develop more rapidly and operate more efficiently if group members learn together rather than individually. Thus, new members of organisations or work groups should be trained together rather than apart. Moreland and associates report a series of laboratory experiments in which group training is indeed superior to individual training for the development and operation of transactive memory.

A natural example of a pitfall of transactive memory comes from the 2000 Davis Cup tennis tournament. The British doubles team comprised Tim Henman and Greg Rusedski, who had trained together as a smoothly operating team for which Britain had very high hopes. Immediately before the doubles match against the Ecuadorian team, Rusedski had to drop out and was replaced by Arvind Parmar. Henman and Parmar had not teamed up before and so had not developed a transactive memory system. They went down to a wholly unexpected straight-sets defeat by Ecuador.

allies and enemies, cliques, working conditions, motivation to work, performance and performance appraisal, who fits in and who is good at what.

Groupthink

Groups sometimes follow deficient decision-making procedures that produce poor decisions. The consequences of such decisions can be disastrous. Irving Janis (1972) used an archival method, relying on retrospective accounts and content analysis, to compare a number of American foreign policy decisions that had unfavourable outcomes (e.g. the 1961 Bay of Pigs fiasco, the 1941 defence of Pearl Harbor) with others that had favourable outcomes (e.g. the 1962 Cuban missile crisis). Janis coined the term **groupthink** to describe the group decision-making process that produced the poor decisions. Groupthink was defined as a mode of thinking in which the desire to reach unanimous agreement overrides the motivation to adopt proper rational decision-making procedures (Janis, 1982; Janis & Mann, 1977).

The antecedents, symptoms and consequences of groupthink are displayed in Figure 9.7. The principal cause of groupthink is excessive group cohesiveness (see **Chapter 8** for discussion of cohesiveness), but there are other antecedents that relate to basic structural faults in the group and to the immediate decision-making context. Together, these factors generate symptoms that are associated with defective decision-making procedures: for example, there is inadequate and biased discussion and consideration of objectives and alternative solutions, and a failure to seek the advice of experts outside the group (see the third and fourth 'What do *you* think?' questions).

Descriptive studies of groupthink (e.g. Hart, 1990; Hensley & Griffin, 1986; Tetlock, 1979) largely support the general model (but see Tetlock, Peterson, McGuire, Chang, & Feld, 1992), whereas experimental studies tend to find mixed or little support for the role of

Groupthink
A mode of thinking in highly cohesive groups in which the desire to reach unanimous agreement overrides the motivation to adopt proper rational decision-making procedures.

Antecedents
- Excessive group **cohesiveness**
- **Insulation** of group from external information and influence
- **Lack of impartial leadership and of norms** encouraging proper procedures
- **Ideological homogeneity** of membership
- High **stress** from external threat and task complexity

Symptoms
- Feelings of **invulnerability** and unanimity
- Unquestioning belief that the group must be **right**
- Tendency to ignore or **discredit information** contrary to group's position
- Direct **pressure** exerted on dissidents to bring them into line
- **Stereotyping** of outgroup members

Poor decision-making procedures (ones with low chance of success or favourable outcomes)

Figure 9.7 Antecedents, symptoms and consequences of groupthink
Source: Janis and Mann (1977).

Group think
Choosing a new Pope is a high-pressure decision with enormous global consequences - there are 1.3 billion Catholics, almost one fifth of the world's population. The 2013 papal conclave was a meeting of 115 like-minded individuals sequested away for two days in complete isolation in the Sistine Chapel.

cohesiveness. Experiments establish background conditions for groupthink in four-person laboratory or quasi-naturalistic groups, and then manipulate cohesiveness (usually as friends versus strangers) and either a leadership variable (directiveness or need-for-power) or procedural directions for effective decision-making.

Some have found no relationship between cohesiveness and groupthink (Flowers, 1977; Fodor & Smith, 1982), some have found a positive relationship only under certain conditions (Callaway & Esser, 1984; Courtright, 1978; Turner, Pratkanis, Probasco, & Leve, 1992), and some a negative relationship (Leana, 1985).

These problems have led people to suggest other ways to approach the explanation of groupthink (Aldag & Fuller, 1993; Hogg, 1993). For example, group cohesiveness may need to be more precisely defined before its relationship to groupthink can be specified (Longley & Pruitt, 1980; McCauley, 1989); at present, it ranges from close friendship to group-based liking. Hogg and Hains (1998) conducted a laboratory study of four-person discussion groups involving 472 participants to find that symptoms of groupthink were associated with cohesiveness, but only where cohesion represented group-based liking, not friendship or interpersonal attraction.

It has also been suggested that groupthink is merely a specific instance of 'risky shift': a group that already tends towards making a risky decision polarises through discussion to an even more risky decision (Myers & Lamm, 1975; see the next section, 'Group polarisation'). Others have suggested that groupthink may not really be a group process at all but just an aggregation of coping responses adopted by individuals to combat excessive stress (Callaway, Marriott, & Esser, 1985). Group members are under decision-making stress and thus adopt defensive coping strategies that involve suboptimal decision-making procedures, which are symptomatic of groupthink. This behaviour is mutually reinforced by members of the group and thus produces defective group decisions.

Group polarisation

Folk wisdom has it that groups, committees and organisations are inherently more conservative in their decisions than individuals. Individuals are likely to take risks, while group decision-making is a tedious averaging process that errs towards caution. This is consistent with much of what we know about conformity and social influence processes in groups (see **Chapter 7**). Sherif's (1936) autokinetic studies (discussed in **Chapters 7 and 8**) illustrate this averaging process very well.

Imagine, then, the excitement with which social psychologists greeted the results of James Stoner's (1961) unpublished master's thesis (also see Stoner, 1968). Stoner's participants played the role of counsellor/adviser to imaginary people facing choice dilemmas (Kogan & Wallach, 1964), where a desirable but risky course of action contrasted with a less desirable but more cautious course of action (see Box 9.6). Participants made their own private recommendations and then met in small groups to discuss each dilemma and reach a unanimous group recommendation. Stoner found that groups tended to recommend the risky alternative more than did individuals. Stoner's (1961) finding was quickly replicated by Wallach, Kogan and Bem (1962). This phenomenon has been called **risky shift**, but later research documented group recommendations that were more cautious than those of individuals, causing risky shift to be treated as part of a wider phenomenon of **group polarisation** (Moscovici & Zavalloni, 1969).

Group polarisation (Isenberg, 1986; Myers & Lamm, 1976; Wetherell, 1987) is defined as a tendency for groups to make decisions that are more extreme than the mean of individual members' initial positions, in the direction already favoured by that mean. So, for example, group discussion among a collection of people who already slightly favour capital punishment is likely to produce a group decision that strongly favours capital punishment. Although half a century of research has produced many different theories to explain polarisation, they can be simplified to three major perspectives: persuasive arguments, social comparison/cultural values and social identity theory.

Persuasive arguments

Persuasive arguments theory focuses on the persuasiveness of novel arguments in changing people's opinions (Burnstein & Vinokur, 1977; Vinokur & Burnstein, 1974). People tend to rest their opinions on supportive arguments that they express publicly in a group. So people in

Risky shift
Tendency for group discussion to produce group decisions that are more risky than the mean of members' pre-discussion opinions, but only if the pre-discussion mean already favoured risk.

Group polarisation
Tendency for group discussion to produce more extreme group decisions than the mean of members' pre-discussion opinions, in the direction favoured by the mean.

Persuasive arguments theory
View that people in groups are persuaded by novel information that supports their initial position, and thus become more extreme in their endorsement of their initial position.

Box 9.6 Research classic
Giving advice on risk-taking

An example of a choice dilemma

Suppose that the participant's task was to advise someone else on a course of action that could vary between two extremes – risky and cautious. The following is an example of such a choice dilemma (Kogan & Wallach, 1964).

> Mr L, a married 30-year-old research physicist, has been given a five-year appointment by a major university laboratory. As he contemplates the next five years, he realises that he might work on a difficult long-term problem which, if a solution can be found, would resolve basic scientific issues in the field and bring him scientific honours. If no solution were found, however, Mr L would have little to show for his five years in the laboratory and this would make it hard for him to get a

good job afterwards. On the other hand, he could, as most of his professional associates are doing, work on a series of short-term problems where solutions would be easier to find but where the problems are of lesser scientific importance.

Imagine that you (the participant) are advising Mr L. Listed below are several probabilities or odds that a solution would be found to the difficult, long-term problem that Mr L has in mind. Please put a cross beside the *lowest* probability that you would consider acceptable to make it worthwhile for Mr L to work on the more difficult, long-term problem.

The participant then responds on a ten-point scale, indicating the odds that Mr L would solve the long-term problem.

Source: Based on Kogan and Wallach (1964).

---

a group that leans in a particular direction will hear not only familiar arguments they have heard before, but also novel ones not heard before but that support their own position (Gigone & Hastie, 1993; Larson, Foster-Fishman, & Keys, 1994). As a result, their opinions will become more entrenched and extreme, and the view of the group as a whole will become polarised.

For example, someone who already favours capital punishment is likely, through discussion with like-minded others, to hear new arguments in favour of capital punishment and come to favour its introduction more strongly. The process of thinking about an issue strengthens our opinions (Tesser, Martin, & Mendolia, 1995), as does the public repetition of our own and others' arguments (Brauer, Judd, & Gliner, 1995).

Social comparison/cultural values

According to this view, referred to as either **social comparison theory** or **cultural values theory** (Jellison & Arkin, 1977; Sanders & Baron, 1977), people seek social approval and try to avoid social censure. Group discussion reveals which views are socially desirable or culturally valued, so group members shift in the direction of the group in order to gain approval and avoid disapproval. For example, favouring capital punishment and finding yourself surrounded by others with similar views might lead you to assume that this is a socially valued attitude – even if it is not. In this example, seeking social approval could lead you to become more extreme in supporting capital punishment. There are two variants of the social comparison perspective:

- *The bandwagon effect* – on learning which attitude pole (i.e. extreme position) is socially desirable, people in an interactive discussion may compete to appear to be stronger advocates of that pole. Jean-Paul Codol (1975) called this the *primus inter pares* (first among equals) effect.

- *Pluralistic ignorance* – because people sometimes behave publicly in ways that do not reflect what they actually think, they can be ignorant of what everyone really thinks (Miller & McFarland, 1987; Prentice & Miller, 1993 – also see **Chapters 5 and 6**).

Social comparison (theory)
Comparing our behaviours and opinions with those of others in order to establish the correct or socially approved way of thinking and behaving.

Cultural values theory
The view that people in groups use members' opinions about the position valued in the wider culture, and then adjust their views in that direction for social approval reasons.

One thing that group discussion can do is to dispel pluralistic ignorance. Where people have relatively extreme attitudes but believe that others are mostly moderate, group discussion can reveal how extreme others' attitudes really are. This liberates people to be true to their underlying beliefs. Polarisation is not so much a shift in attitude as an expression of true attitudes.

Social identity theory

The persuasive arguments and social comparison approaches are supported by some studies but not others (Mackie, 1986; Turner, J. C., 1991; Wetherell, 1987). For example, polarisation has been obtained where arguments and persuasion are unlikely to play a role (e.g. perceptual tasks; Baron & Roper, 1976) and where lack of surveillance by the group should minimise the role of social desirability (Goethals & Zanna, 1979; Teger & Pruitt, 1967). In general, it is not possible to argue that one perspective has a clear empirical advantage over the other. Isenberg (1986) has suggested that both are correct (they explain polarisation under different circumstances) and that we should specify the range of applicability of each.

There is a third perspective, promoted by John Turner and his colleagues (Turner, 1985; Turner, Hogg, Oakes, Reicher, & Wetherell, 1987; also see **Chapter 11**). Unlike persuasive arguments and social comparison/cultural values theories, **social identity theory**, specifically its focus on the social categorization process (**self-categorization theory**), treats polarisation as a regular conformity phenomenon (Turner & Oakes, 1989). People in discussion groups construct a representation of the group norm from the positions held by group members and in contrast to those positions assumed or known to be held by people not in the group or in a specific outgroup.

Because such norms not only minimise variability within the group (i.e. among ingroup members) but also differentiate the ingroup from outgroups, they are not necessarily the mean ingroup position: they can be polarised away from an explicit or implicit outgroup (see Figure 9.8). Self-categorization, the process responsible for identification with a group, produces conformity to the ingroup norm – and thus, if the norm is polarised, group polarisation. If the norm is not polarised, self-categorization produces convergence on the mean group position.

Research supports this perspective in (1) confirming how a norm can be polarised (Hogg, Turner, & Davidson, 1990); (2) showing that people are more persuaded by ingroup members than outgroup members or individuals; and (3) showing that group polarisation occurs only if an initial group tendency is perceived to represent a norm rather than an aggregate of individual opinions (Mackie, 1986; Mackie & Cooper, 1984; Turner, Wetherell, & Hogg, 1989).

This perspective on polarisation has recently been used in the context of the split within the US Republican Party between moderates and the extreme right-wing Tea Party faction (Gaffney, Rast, Hackett, & Hogg, 2014). Moderate Republicans shifted their views to the left (away from the Tea Party) when a direct comparison between themselves and the Tea Party was primed, and to the right (towards the Tea Party) when a comparison with the common outgroup (the Democratic Party) was primed. The polarisation effect was enhanced among participants who were primed to feel uncertain about their identity.

A recent experiment by Zlatan Krizan and Robert Baron (2007) suggests some boundary conditions that need to be met for self-categorization to explain group polarisation. Specifically, (a) the ingroup should be an important source of social identity, (b) the intergroup distinction should be chronically salient and (c) the group discussion topic should be self-relevant or otherwise engaging. It is when these conditions are met that group members are most affected by the contextual salience of social categories and by their desire to maximise similarity with the ingroup while distancing themselves from the outgroup.

Social identity theory
Theory of group membership and intergroup relations based on self-categorization, social comparison and the construction of a shared self-definition in terms of ingroup-defining properties.

Self-categorization theory
Turner and associates' theory of how the process of categorizing oneself as a group member produces social identity and group and intergroup behaviours.

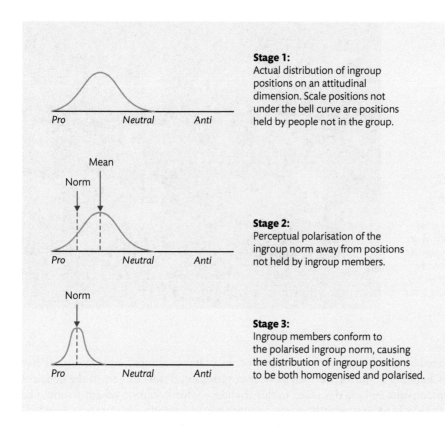

Stage 1:
Actual distribution of ingroup positions on an attitudinal dimension. Scale positions not under the bell curve are positions held by people not in the group.

Stage 2:
Perceptual polarisation of the ingroup norm away from positions not held by ingroup members.

Stage 3:
Ingroup members conform to the polarised ingroup norm, causing the distribution of ingroup positions to be both homogenised and polarised.

Figure 9.8 Group polarisation as self-categorization-induced conformity to a polarised group

Group polarisation can occur because people categorise themselves in terms of, and conform to, an ingroup defined by a norm that is polarised away from positions not held by ingroup members.

Jury verdicts

People are fascinated by juries. Not surprisingly, they are the focus of countless novels and movies – John Grisham's novel *The Runaway Jury* and the 2003 movie adaptation dramatically highlight many of the important social psychological points made below about jury decision-making. Returning to reality, the 1995 murder trial of the American sports star O. J. Simpson and the 2004 child 'abuse' trial of Michael Jackson virtually brought the United States to a standstill because people could not miss the exciting televised instalments. Across the Atlantic in South Africa, the many iterations of the trial of Oscar Pistorius, accused of murdering his girlfriend Reeva Steenkamp, riveted the nation for three years from 2014 to 2016.

Juries represent one of the most significant decision-making groups, not only because they are brandished as a symbol of all that is democratic, fair and just in a society, but also because of the consequences of their decisions for defendants, victims and the community. A jury consists of laypeople and, in criminal law, is charged with making a crucial decision involving someone's innocence or guilt. In this respect, juries are an alternative to judges and are fundamental to the legal system of various countries around the world. They are most often associated with British law, but other countries (e.g. Argentina, Japan, Russia, Spain and Venezuela) have made changes to include input from lay citizens (Hans, 2008). In some cultures a group of laypeople symbolises a just society – and when this group is a jury, its decision must be seen as fair treatment of all involved.

Jury verdicts can have wide-ranging and dramatic consequences outside the trial. A case in point is the 1992 Los Angeles riots, which were sparked by an unexpected 'not guilty'

Jury decision-making

Like all groups, juries may err in reaching an optimal conclusion. An old movie cliché of an emotional appeal may influence the jury, if not the judge.

verdict delivered by an all-white jury in the case of the police beating of a black suspect (see Box 11.1 in **Chapter 11**). Juries are also, of course, groups and thus subject to the deficiencies of group decision-making discussed in this chapter – which decision schemes should be used, who should lead and why, how are groupthink and group polarisation avoided? (Hastie, 1993; Hastie, Penrod, & Pennington, 1983; Kerr, Niedermeier, & Kaplan, 1999; Tindale, Nadler, Krebel, & Davis, 2001).

Characteristics of the defendant and the victim can also affect the jury's deliberations. Physically attractive defendants are more likely to be acquitted (Michelini & Snodgrass, 1980) or to receive a lighter sentence (Stewart, 1980), although biases can be reduced by furnishing sufficient factual evidence (Baumeister & Darley, 1982), by presenting the jury with written rather than spoken, face-to-face testimony (Kaplan, 1977; Kaplan & Miller, 1978), or by explicitly directing the jury to consider the evidence alone (Weiten, 1980). Race can also affect the jury. In the United States, for example, blacks are more likely to receive prison sentences (Stewart, 1980). Furthermore, people who murder a white have been more than twice as likely than those who murder a black to receive the death penalty, a sentence determined by the jury in the United States (Henderson & Taylor, 1985).

Brutal crimes often stir up a call for draconian measures. However, the introduction of harsh laws with stiff penalties (e.g. the death penalty) can backfire – it discourages jurors from convicting (Kerr, 1978). Consider the anguish of a jury deliberating on a case in which the defendant has vandalised a car, and where a conviction would carry a mandatory death penalty. Research in the United States has shown that whether jurors do or do not support the death penalty has a reliable but small impact on the verdict – one to three verdicts out of one hundred would be affected (Allen, Mabry, & McKelton, 1998).

Juries often have to remember and understand enormous amounts of information. Research suggests that there is a **recency** effect, in which information delivered later in the trial is more heavily weighted in decision-making (Horowitz & Bordens, 1990). In addition, inadmissible evidence (evidence that is given by witnesses or interjected by counsel but is subsequently ruled to be inadmissible for procedural reasons by the judge) still has an effect on jury deliberation (Thompson & Fuqua, 1998). Juries also deal with complex evidence,

Recency
An order of presentation effect in which later presented information has a disproportionate influence on social cognition.

enormous amounts of evidence, and complex laws and legal jargon – all three of which make the jury deliberation process extremely demanding and prey to suboptimal decision-making (Heuer & Penrod, 1994).

The jury 'foreman' is important in guiding the jury to its verdict, as that person occupies the role of leader (see earlier in this chapter). Research suggests that the foreman is most likely to be someone of higher socio-economic status, someone who has had previous experience as a juror or someone who simply occupies the seat at the head of the table at the first sitting of the jury (Strodtbeck & Lipinski, 1985). This is of some concern, as diffuse status characteristics (Berger, Fisek, Norman, & Zelditch, 1977; Ridgeway, 2001, discussed in **Chapter 8**), are influencing the jury process.

Jurors who are older, less well educated or of lower socio-economic status are more likely to vote to convict. However, men and women do not differ, except that women are more likely to convict defendants in rape trials (Nemeth, 1981). Jurors who score high on authoritarianism favour conviction when the victim is an authority figure (e.g. a police officer), while jurors who are more egalitarian have the opposite bias of favouring conviction when the defendant is an authority figure (Mitchell, 1979).

With respect to decision schemes, if two-thirds or more of the jurors initially favour one alternative, then that is likely to be the jury's final verdict (Stasser, Kerr, & Bray, 1982). Without such a majority, a hung jury is the likely outcome. The two-thirds majority rule is modified by a tendency for jurors to favour acquittal, particularly where evidence is not highly incriminating; under these circumstances, a minority favouring acquittal may prevail (Tindale, Davis, Vollrath, Nagao, & Hinsz, 1990).

Jury size itself can matter, according to a meta-analysis by Michael Saks and Mollie Marti (1997). Larger juries, say of twelve rather than six members, are more likely to empanel representatives of minority groups. If a particular minority is 10 per cent of the jury pool, random selection means that a minority member will be included in each twelve-person jury but in only 50 per cent of six-person juries. Furthermore, if minority or dissident viewpoints matter, they have greater impact in larger than in smaller juries. If one-sixth of a jury favours acquittal, then in a six-person jury the 'deviate' has no social support, whereas in a twelve-person jury he or she does. Research on conformity and independence, and on minority influence (see **Chapter 7**), suggests that the dissident viewpoint is more likely to prevail in the twelve- than in the six-person jury.

Summary

- Leadership is a process of influence that does not require coercion – coercion may undermine true leadership and produce mere compliance and obedience.

- Although some broad personality attributes are associated with effective leadership (e.g. extraversion/surgency, intellect/openness to experience, and conscientiousness), personality alone is rarely sufficient.

- Leadership is a group process in which one person transforms other members of the group so that they adopt a vision and are galvanised into pursuing the vision on behalf of the group – leadership is not simply managing a group's activities. Transformational leadership is facilitated by charisma, consideration and inspiring followers.

- Leadership involves transactions between leader and followers – leaders do something for the group, and the group in return does something for the leader to allow the leader to lead effectively.

- Leadership has an identity dimension – followers look to their leaders to mould, transform and express who they are, their identity. Being perceived to be 'one of us' can facilitate leadership.

- Trust plays an important role in leadership – leaders have greater scope to be innovative if the group trusts them.

- Effective and good leadership are not the same thing – effective leaders successfully influence the group to adopt and achieve (new) goals, whereas good leaders pursue goals that we value, use means that we approve of, and have qualities that we applaud.

- There is a general distinction between task-focused (structuring) and person/relationship-focused (consideration) leadership style – their relative effectiveness and the effectiveness of other leadership styles depends on context (e.g. the nature of the group, the nature of the task).

- Leadership effectiveness can be improved if the leaders' attributes and behaviour are perceived to fit general or task-specific schemas that we have of effective leadership, or the norms/prototype of a group membership/identity that we share with the leader.

- Group decisions can sometimes be predicted accurately from the pre-discussion distribution of opinions in the group, and from the decision-making rule that prevails in the group at that time.

- People believe that group brainstorming enhances individual creativity, despite evidence that groups do not do better than non-interactive individuals and that individuals do not perform better in groups than alone. This illusion of group effectivity may be due to distorted perceptions during group brainstorming and the enjoyment that people derive from group brainstorming.

- Groups, particularly established groups that have a transactive memory structure, are often more effective than individuals at remembering information.

- Highly cohesive groups with directive leaders are prone to groupthink – poor decision-making based on an overzealous desire to reach consensus.

- Groups that already tend towards an extreme position on a decision-making dimension often make even more extreme decisions than the average of the members' initial positions would suggest.

- Juries are not free from the usual range of group decision-making biases and errors.

Key terms

Autocratic leaders	Group value model	Path–goal theory
Big Five	Groupthink	Persuasive arguments theory
Brainstorming	Idiosyncrasy credit	Procedural justice
Charismatic leadership	Illusion of group effectivity	Production blocking
Contingency theories	Laissez-faire leaders	Recency
Correspondence bias	Leader behaviour description questionnaire	Relational model of authority in groups
Cultural values theory	tionnaire	Risky shift
Democratic leaders	Leader categorization theory	Risky shift
Distributive justice	Leader–member exchange (LMX)	Role congruity theory
Glass ceiling	theory	Self-categorization theory
Glass cliff	Leadership	Situational control
Great person theory	Least-preferred co-worker (LPC) scale	Social comparison (theory)
Group mind	Multifactor leadership questionnaire	Social decisions schemes
Group polarisation	Normative decision theory	Social dilemmas

Social identity theory
Social identity theory of leadership
Social transition scheme

Status characteristics theory
Stereotype threat
Transactional leadership

Transactive memory
Transformational leadership
Vertical dyad linkage (VDL) model

Literature, film and TV

Triumph of the Will and *Downfall*

A pair of films portraying one of the most evil leaders of the twentieth century in two different ways. *Triumph of the Will* is Leni Reifenstahl's classic 1934 film about Adolf Hitler – a film that largely idolises him as a great leader come to resurrect Germany. The film 'stars' the likes of Hitler, Hermann Goering and others. **This film is also relevant to Chapter 6 (persuasion).** *Downfall* is a controversial 2004 film by Oliver Hirschbiegel based on a book by the historian Joachim Fest. It portrays Hitler's last days in his bunker beneath Berlin up to his suicide on 30 April 1945. The film is controversial because it portrays Hitler largely as a sad dysfunctional human being rather than a grotesque monster responsible for immeasurable human suffering.

Twelve Angry Men and *The Runaway Jury*

Two films based on books that highlight jury decision-making. *Twelve Angry Men* is a classic 1957 film directed by Sidney Lumet and starring Henry Fonda. Set entirely in the jury room, it is an incredibly powerful portrayal of social influence and decision-making processes within a jury. *The Runaway Jury* is a 2003 film by Gary Fleder, with John Cusack, Dustin Hoffman and Gene Hackman, that dramatises the way that juries can be unscrupulously manipulated.

Thirteen Days

A 2000 film by Roger Donaldson. It is about the Cuban missile crisis which lasted for two weeks in October 1962 and was about as close as we got to all-out nuclear war between the West and the Soviet Union. The focus is on Kennedy's decision-making group. Is there groupthink or not? Wonderful dramatisation of presidential/high-level decision making under crisis. **Also relevant to Chapter 11 (intergroup behaviour).**

The Last King of Scotland

This 2006 film by Kevin MacDonald, based on the eponymous novel by Giles Foden, is a complex portrayal of the 1970s Ugandan dictator Idi Amin (played by Forest Whitaker) – an all-powerful and charismatic leader who can be charming interpersonally but will go to any lengths to protect himself from his paranoia about forces trying to undermine him. Amin was responsible for great brutality – 500,000 deaths and the expulsion of all Asians from the country.

Guided questions

1 What is the *great person* theory of leadership, and how effective a theory is it?

2 How is a transformational leader different from a transactional leader?

3 Is it possible for a highly cohesive group to become oblivious to the views and expectations of the wider community?

4 What factors inhibit the productivity of group brainstorming?

5 Sometimes a group makes a decision that is even more extreme than any of its individual members might have made. How so?

Learn more

Baron, R. S., & Kerr, N. (2003). *Group process, group decision, group action* (2nd ed.). Buckingham, UK: Open University Press. A general overview of topics in the study of group processes, with excellent coverage of group decision-making.

Brown, R. J. (2000). *Group processes* (2nd ed.). Oxford, UK: Blackwell. A very readable introduction to group processes, which takes a European perspective and also covers intergroup relations. It has a section on leadership.

Gilovich, T. D., & Gryphon, D. W. (2010). Judgment and decision making. In S. T. Fiske, D. T. Gilbert, & G. Lindzey (Eds.), *Handbook of social psychology* (5th ed., Vol. 1, pp. 542–588). New York: Wiley. Although primarily about individual decision-making, this detailed and up-to-date chapter is also relevant to group decision-making.

Goethals, G. R., & Sorenson, G. (Eds.) (2004). *Encyclopedia of leadership*. Thousand Oaks, CA: Sage. This is a true monster resource – four volumes, around 2,000 pages, 1.2 million words, and 373 short essay-style entries written by 311 scholars including virtually everyone who is anyone in leadership research. All you ever wanted to know about leadership is somewhere in this book.

Gruenfeld, D. H., & Tiedens, L. Z. (2010). Organizational preferences and their consequences. In S. T. Fiske, D. T. Gilbert, & G. Lindzey (Eds.), *Handbook of social psychology* (5th ed., Vol. 2, pp. 1252–1287). New York: Wiley. Up-to-date and detailed overview of social psychological theory and research on organisational processes, including decision-making and leadership in organisations.

Hackman, J. R., & Katz, N. (2010). Group behavior and performance. In S. T. Fiske, D. T. Gilbert, & G. Lindzey (Eds.), *Handbook of social psychology* (5th ed., Vol. 2, pp. 1208–1251). New York: Wiley. Comprehensive, detailed and up-to-date coverage of group behaviour.

Hogg, M. A. (2010). Influence & leadership. In S. T. Fiske, D. T. Gilbert, & G. Lindzey (Eds.), *Handbook of social psychology* (5th ed., Vol. 2, pp. 1166–1207). New York: Wiley. Detailed and up-to-date overview of leadership theory and research, which treats leadership as a process of social influence in groups.

Hogg, M. A. (2013b). Leadership. In J. M. Levine (Ed.), *Group processes* (pp. 241–66). New York: Psychology Press. An up-to-date and comprehensive overview of leadership research, from the perspective of social psychology rather than organisational and management science, although the latter are also covered.

Hollander, E. P. (1985). Leadership and power. In G. Lindzey & E. Aronson (Eds.), *Handbook of social psychology* (3rd ed., Vol. 2, pp. 485–537). New York: Random House. A classic review of leadership research in social psychology.

Levine, J. M. (Ed.) (2013). *Group processes*. New York: Psychology Press. Absolutely up-to-date and comprehensive set of chapters by leading scholars on all aspects of group processes.

Levine, J. M., & Hogg, M. A. (Eds.) (2010). *Encyclopedia of group processes and intergroup relations*. Thousand Oaks, CA: SAGE. A comprehensive and readable compendium of entries on all aspects of the social psychology of groups, written by all the leading scholars in the field.

Levine, J., & Moreland, R. L. (1998). Small groups. In D. T. Gilbert, S. T. Fiske, & G. Lindzey (Eds.), *The handbook of social psychology* (4th ed., Vol. 2, pp. 415–469). New York: McGraw-Hill. A comprehensive overview of the field of small groups in which most group decision-making research is done – the most recent 2010 fifth edition of the handbook does not have a chapter dedicated to small interactive groups.

Stangor, C. (2016). *Social groups in action and interaction* (2nd ed.) New York: Psychology Press. Completely up-to-date, comprehensive and accessible coverage of the social psychology of processes within and between groups.

Tindale, R. S., Kameda, T., & Hinsz, V. B. (2003). Group decision making. In M. A. Hogg & J. Cooper (Eds.), *The SAGE handbook of social psychology* (pp. 381–403). London: SAGE. Comprehensive coverage of research on group decision-making, with a particular emphasis on the shared nature of group decisions.

Yukl, G. (2013). *Leadership in organizations* (8th ed.). Upper Saddle River, NJ: Pearson. Straightforward, comprehensive, completely up-to-date and very readable coverage of leadership from the perspective of organisations, where most leadership research tends to be done.

Chapter 10
Prejudice and discrimination

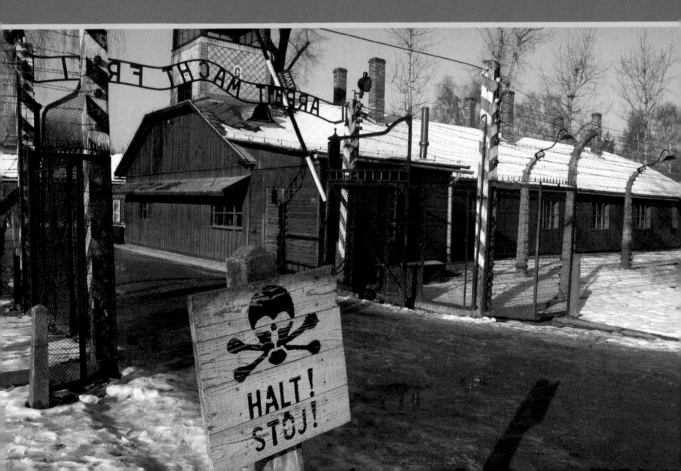

Chapter contents

What do *you* think?

1 Tom is convinced that he is not homophobic – he just does not much enjoy being around
   gay people or talking about homosexuality. As proof of his 'goodwill' he donates five pounds
   each year to AIDS charity collectors. Are you convinced that Tom is not prejudiced?

2 How would you feel if someone less qualified than you was given a job in preference to you
   because that person belonged to a historically disadvantaged social group?

3 A neighbourhood group in Britain proposes to send the children of new immigrants to a special
   school, where first they can learn to speak English and later continue the rest of their education.
   The group says that this is for the good of the children. Would you have any concerns about
   this?

4 Armand is a native of Israel now living in Sweden, and is very traditional in his politics and
   religion. He does not like local immigrants from Palestine, as he believes the Palestinians occupy
   land belonging to Israel. But actually, he does not like any immigrants. How might you explain
   his views?

Nature and dimensions of prejudice

Prejudice
Unfavourable attitude towards a social group and its members.

Prejudice and discrimination are two of the greatest problems faced by humanity. When one group of people hates another group of people so profoundly that they can torture and murder innocent non-combatants, we have a serious problem on our hands. Because prejudice and discrimination stand squarely in the path of enlightenment, an understanding of the causes and consequences of prejudice is one of humanity's great challenges. We can put people on the moon, we can genetically modify living organisms, we can replace dysfunctional organs, we can whizz around the world at an altitude of 10,000 metres and we can communicate with almost anyone anywhere via the Internet. But, in recent history, we have seemed helpless in preventing events such as Palestinians and Israelis from fighting over Jerusalem or Catholics and Protestants from tearing Northern Ireland apart. All groups, large and small, in society can be prejudiced, and prejudice has always been with us; it is part of the human condition. For example, by the sixteenth century, commerce between Europe and China was sufficiently well-developed for Chinese to be regularly encountering Europeans. LaPiere and Farnsworth (1949) quote a letter from a Confucian scholar to his son that eloquently captures derogatory sixteenth-century Chinese attitudes towards Europeans:

> These 'Ocean Men' are tall beasts with deep sunken eyes and beak-like noses . . . Although undoubtedly men, they seem to possess none of the mental faculties of men. The most bestial of peasants is far more human . . . It is quite possible that they are susceptible to training, and could with patience be taught the modes of conduct proper to a human being.
>
> Cited by LaPiere and Farnsworth (1949, p. 228)

Dehumanisation
Stripping people of their dignity and humanity.

Prejudice becomes a particularly serious problem when it is associated with **dehumanisation** of an outgroup – if people can be viewed as less than human, then atrocities against them become essentially no different from squishing an insect. It is also a serious problem when those who are prejudiced are in a position of power that furnishes them with the ability and resources to discriminate against an outgroup. Discrimination is associated with much of the pain and human suffering in the world, ranging from restricted opportunities and narrowed horizons to physical violence and **genocide**.

Genocide
The ultimate expression of prejudice by exterminating an entire social group.

Most people in liberal democratic societies consider prejudice a particularly unpalatable aspect of human behaviour, with terms such as 'racist' and 'bigot' being reserved as profound insults. Yet almost all of us experience prejudice in one form or another, ranging from relatively minor assumptions that people make about us to crude and offensive bigotry, or violence. People make and behave in accordance with assumptions about our abilities and aspirations on the basis of, for example, our age, ethnicity, race or sex, and we often find ourselves automatically making the same sorts of assumption about others.

Herein lies a paradox: prejudice is socially undesirable, yet it pervades social life. Even in societies where prejudice is institutionalised, sophisticated justifications are used to deny that prejudice is actually being practised. The system of apartheid in South Africa was a classic case of institutionalised prejudice, yet it was packaged publicly as recognition of and respect for cultural differences (see Nelson Mandela's fascinating autobiography, 1994). Indeed, the content of our stereotypes about a particular group can often serve the function of justifying prejudice and discrimination against that group – stereotypes explain not only what a group is, but why the group is that way, and why groups are treated the way they are (Crandall, Bahns, Warner, & Schaller, 2011).

Prejudice is a topic of research in its own right, but it is also a topic that draws on a range of other aspects of social psychology. In this chapter, we discuss the nature of prejudice, what forms it takes and what its consequences are, and we also discuss some theories of prejudice. Then (in **Chapter 11**), we continue our treatment but focus more widely on intergroup relations – prejudice and discrimination are intergroup phenomena, and thus (**Chapters 10 and 11**) go together. However, prejudice rests on negative stereotypes of groups (see **Chapter 2**), it often translates into aggression towards an outgroup (see **Chapter 12**) and it pivots on the sort of people we think we are (see **Chapter 4**) and the sorts of people we think others are (see **Chapters 2 and 3**). The relationship between prejudice and discrimination can also be viewed as the attitude–behaviour relationship in the context of attitudes towards a group (see **Chapters 5 and 6**).

In many respects, social psychology is uniquely placed to rise to the challenge of understanding prejudice. Prejudice is a social psychological phenomenon. In fact, prejudice is doubly social – it involves people's feelings about and actions towards other people, and it is guided and given a context by the groups to which we belong and the historical circumstances of specific intergroup relations in which these groups find themselves.

Prejudiced attitudes and discriminatory behaviour

As the term 'prejudice' literally means 'prejudgement' (from the Latin *prae* and *judicium*), it is usual to consider prejudice as an attitude (see **Chapter 5**) where the attitude object is a social group (e.g. Americans, West Indians, politicians, students). A traditional view (e.g. Allport, 1954b) of prejudice, which is consistent with the wider **three-component attitude model** (see **Chapter 5**), is that it has three components:

1 *cognitive* – beliefs about a group;

2 *affective* – strong feelings (usually negative) about a group and the qualities it is believed to possess;

3 *conative* – intentions to behave in certain ways towards a group (the conative component is an *intention* to act in certain ways, not the action itself).

However, not all attitude theorists are comfortable with the tripartite model (**see Chapter 5**), and there are other definitions of prejudice that do include discriminatory behaviour. For example, Rupert Brown defines prejudice as:

> the holding of derogatory social attitudes or cognitive beliefs, the expression of negative affect, or the display of hostile or discriminatory behaviour towards members of a group on account of their membership of that group.
>
> Brown (1995, p. 8)

Box 10.1 provides a fanciful account of how prejudice may arise and become the basis for discrimination. Although a fictional example, it does capture many of the main features of prejudice that need to be explained. The first issue, which is essentially the attitude–behaviour relationship (see **Chapter 5**), is the relationship between prejudiced beliefs and the practice of discrimination. You will recall (from **Chapter 5**) that Richard LaPiere (1934), a social scientist, spent two years travelling around the United States with a young Chinese American couple. They visited 250 hotels, caravan parks, tourist homes and restaurants, and were refused service in only one (i.e. 0.4 per cent); there was little anti-Chinese prejudice. After returning home, LaPiere contacted 128 of these establishments with the question, 'Will you accept members of the Chinese race as guests in your establishment?' The responses included 92 per cent 'No', 7 per cent 'Uncertain, depends on circumstances' and 1 per cent 'Yes'. There was overwhelming prejudice!

Three-component attitude model
An attitude consists of cognitive, affective and behavioural components. This threefold division has an ancient heritage, stressing thought, feeling and action as basic to human experience.

Box 10.1 Our world
Prejudice and discrimination on campus

The emergence of a fictional 'stigmatised group'

A study by Joe Forgas (1983) has shown that students have clear beliefs about different campus groups. One such target group was 'engineering students', who were described in terms of their drinking habits (beer, and lots of it), their cultural preferences (sports and little else) and their style of dress (practical and conservative). This is a prejudgement, in so far as it is assumed that all engineering students are like this. If these beliefs (the *cognitive* component) are not associated with any strong feelings (*affect*) or any particular intention to act (*conation*), then no real problem exists and we would probably not call this a prejudice – simply a harmless generalisation (see **Chapter 5** for a discussion of the tripartite model of attitude).

However, if these beliefs were associated with strong negative feelings about engineering students and their characteristics, then a pattern of conations would almost inevitably arise. If you hated and despised engineering students and their characteristics, and you felt that they were less than human, you would probably intend to avoid them, perhaps humiliate them whenever possible, and even dream of a brave new world without them.

This is now quite clearly prejudice, but it may still not be much of a social problem. Strong social and legislative pressures would inhibit public expression of such extreme views or the realisation of conation in action, so people would probably be unaware that others shared their views. However, if people became aware that their prejudices were widely shared, they would discuss with one another and form organisations to represent their views. Under these circumstances, more extreme conations might arise, such as suggestions to isolate engineering students in one part of the campus and deny them access to certain resources on campus (e.g. the bar, or the student union building). Individuals or small groups might now feel empowered to discriminate against individual engineering students, although wider social pressures would probably prevent widespread discrimination.

However, if the students gained legitimate overall power in the university, they would be free to put their plans into action. They could indulge in systematic discrimination against engineering students: deny them their human rights, degrade and humiliate them, herd them into ghettos behind barbed wire, and systematically exterminate them. Prejudice would have become enshrined in, and legitimated by, the norms and practices of the community.

An implication of LaPiere's real-world study is that prejudice can be difficult to detect. A controlled experiment that nicely illustrates this was conducted later by Sam Gaertner and Jack Dovidio (1977). White female undergraduates waiting to take part in an experiment overheard a supposed 'emergency' in an adjoining room in which several chairs seemed to fall on a female confederate, who was either white or black. The participants were led to believe that they were alone with the confederate or that there were two other potential helpers. Ordinarily, we would expect the usual bystander effect (see **Chapter 13** for details), in which participants would be less willing to go to the aid of the 'victim' when other potential helpers were available.

Figure 10.1 shows that there was only a weak bystander effect when the victim was white, but that the effect was greatly amplified when the victim was black (compare columns 3 and 4). The white participants discriminated overtly against the black victim only when other potential helpers were present.

There is an important lesson here: under certain circumstances, prejudice may go undetected. If the 'two potential helpers' condition had not been included, this experiment would have revealed that white women were more willing to aid a black victim than a white victim. It was only with the inclusion of the 'two potential helpers' condition that underlying prejudice was revealed. The absence of overt discrimination should always be treated with caution, as prejudice can be expressed in many indirect and subtle ways (see the subsection 'Maintenance of sex stereotypes and roles' in this chapter).

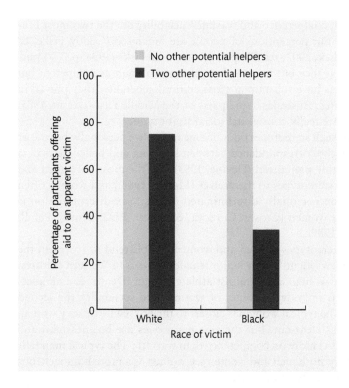

Figure 10.1 Bystander apathy as a function of race of victim

When there were no other potential helpers available, white females offered assistance to a black or a white confederate who had suffered an emergency. However, when other helpers were available, they were significantly less inclined to assist the black confederate than the white confederate: weak bystander apathy in the presence of a white victim was amplified many times over when the victim was black.

Source: Based on data from Gaertner and Dovidio (1977).

Targets of prejudice and discrimination

Prejudice knows no cultural or historical boundaries – it is certainly not the exclusive province of people who are middle-aged, white, heterosexual or male. Human beings are remarkably versatile in being able to make almost any social group a target of prejudice. However, certain groups are the enduring victims of prejudice because they are formed by social categorizations that are vivid, omnipresent and socially functional, and the target groups themselves occupy low power positions in society. These groups are those based on race, ethnicity, sex, age, sexual orientation and physical and mental health. Research shows that of these, sex, race and age are the most prevalent bases for stereotyping (Mackie, Hamilton, Susskind, & Rosselli, 1996). Not surprisingly, most research on prejudice has focused on these three dimensions, particularly on sex and race/ethnicity.

Sexism

Almost all research on **sexism** focuses on prejudice and discrimination against women (Deaux & LaFrance, 1998); mainly by men but also by women. This is because women have historically suffered most as the victims of sexism – primarily because of their lower power position relative to men in business, government and employment. However, sex roles may have persisted because, although they provide men with agency-based structural power, they have provided women with communal-based dyadic or interpersonal power (e.g. Jost & Banaji, 1994). Of course, if men occupy low power positons in occupations and in society, they can be disadvantaged because of their gender and become the targets of sexism (Croft, Schmader, & Block, 2015).

Sexism
Prejudice and discrimination against people based on their gender.

Sex stereotypes

Research on sex stereotypes has revealed that both men and women believe that men are competent and independent, and women are warm and expressive (Broverman, Vogel, Broverman, Clarkson, & Rosenkrantz, 1972; Spence, Helmreich, & Stapp, 1974) – according to the stereotype content model, competence and warmth/sociability are the two most fundamental dimensions on which our perceptions of people are organised (Cuddy, Fiske, & Glick, 2008; Fiske, Cuddy, & Glick, 2007; see **Chapter 2**). As Susan Fiske (1998, p. 377) puts it: 'The typical woman is seen as nice but incompetent, the typical man as competent but maybe not so nice.' These beliefs have substantial cross-cultural generality: they prevail in Europe, North and South America, Australasia and parts of the Middle East (Deaux, 1985; Williams & Best, 1982). These are really consensual social **stereotypes**.

Stereotype
Widely shared and simplified evaluative image of a social group and its members.

Just because we know about such stereotypes does not mean that we personally believe or subscribe to them. In fact, a tight correspondence between knowing and believing occurs only among people who are highly prejudiced (Devine, 1989). For the most part, men and women do not apply strong sex stereotypes to themselves (Martin, 1987), and women often deny feeling that they have been personally discriminated against: sex discrimination is something experienced by *other* women (Crosby, Cordova, & Jaskar, 1993; Crosby, Pufall, Snyder, O'Connell, & Whalen, 1989).

Although there are generic stereotypes of men and women, people tend to represent the sexes in terms of subtypes. Reviews identify four major female subtypes in Western cultures: housewife, sexy woman, career woman and feminist/athlete/lesbian (Deaux & LaFrance, 1998; Fiske, 1998). The first two embody attributes of warmth and sociability, the second two attributes of competence. The typical woman is closest to the housewife or sexy woman subtype. Male subtypes are less clear-cut, but the two main ones are businessman and 'macho man'. Here the emphasis is more on competence than warmth. The typical man falls between the two poles. Generally, both men and women see women as a more homogeneous group than men (Lorenzi-Cioldi, Eagly, & Stewart, 1995).

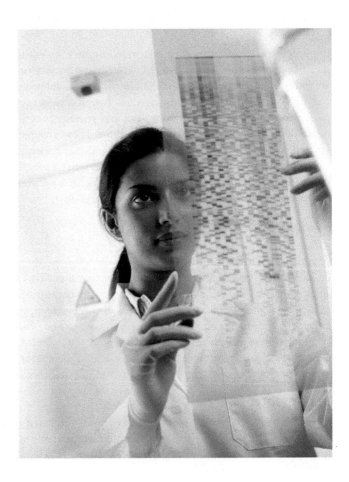

Sex stereotypes can be challenged
This young scientist refined a method of DNA matching that helps in solving crime.

Presumably, competence, independence, warmth and expressiveness are all highly desirable and valued human attributes – at least in Western cultures. If this were true, there would be no differential evaluative connotation of the stereotype. However, earlier research suggested that female-stereotypical traits are significantly less valued than male-stereotypical traits. Inge Broverman and her colleagues asked seventy-nine practising mental health clinicians (clinical psychologists, psychiatrists, social workers) to describe a healthy, mature, socially competent individual, who was either (1) 'a male', (2) 'a female' or (3) 'a person'. Both male and female clinicians described a healthy adult man and a healthy adult person in almost exactly the same terms (reflecting competence). The healthy adult woman was considered significantly more submissive, excitable and appearance-oriented – characteristics not attached to either the healthy adult or the healthy man (Broverman, Broverman, Clarkson, Rosencrantz, & Vogel, 1970). It is ominous that women were not considered to be normal, healthy adult people!

Behaviour and sex roles

Might sex stereotypes accurately reflect sex differences in personality and behaviour? Perhaps men and women really do have different personalities? David Bakan (1966), for example, has argued that men are more agentic (i.e. action-oriented) than women, and women are more communal than men (see also Williams, 1984). This is a complicated issue. Traditionally, the **sex role** occupied by men has differed from that occupied by women in society (men pursue full-time out-of-home jobs, while females are 'homemakers'), and as we saw in **Chapter 8**, roles constrain behaviour in line with role requirements.

Sex differences, if they do exist, may simply reflect the fact that men and women occupy different roles in groups and society, and role assignment may be determined and perpetuated by the social group that has more power (typically men) (Eagly & Steffen, 1984; Koenig & Eagly, 2014). According to **role congruity theory**, when people behave in ways that are inconsistent with role expectations observers react negatively — this research generally focuses on women attracting negative reactions and a possible backlash when they occupy leadership roles (Eagly & Karau, 2002; see below, and **Chapter 9**).

An alternative argument might be that there are intrinsic personality differences between men and women that suit the sexes to different roles: that is, there is a biological imperative behind role assignments. This is a debate that can be, and is, highly politicised.

Social psychological research indicates that there are a small number of systematic differences between the sexes, but they are not very diagnostic: in other words, knowing someone's position on one of these dimensions is not a reliable predictor of that person's sex (Parsons, Adler, & Meece, 1984). For example, research on male and female military cadets (Rice, Instone, & Adams, 1984) and male and female managers (Steinberg & Shapiro, 1982) found that perceived stereotypical differences were an exaggeration of minor differences. In general, sex stereotypes are more myth than a reflection of reality (Eagly & Carli, 1981; Swim, 1994).

One reason why sex stereotypes persist is that role assignment according to **gender** persists. In general, women make up the majority of restaurant servers, telephone operators, secretaries, nurses, babysitters, dental hygienists, librarians and elementary/kindergarten teachers, while most lawyers, dentists, truck drivers, accountants, top executives and engineers are male (Greenglass, 1982). Certain occupations become labelled as 'women's work' and are accordingly valued less.

To investigate this idea, Alice Eagly and Valerie Steffen (1984) asked male and female students to rate, on sex-stereotypical dimensions, an imaginary man or woman who was described as being either a 'homemaker' or employed full-time outside the home. In a third condition, no employment information was given. Figure 10.2 shows that, irrespective of sex, homemakers were perceived to be significantly more feminine (in their traits) than full-time employees. This suggests that certain roles may be sex-typed, and that as women

Sex role
Behaviour deemed sex-stereotypically appropriate.

Role congruity theory
Mainly applied to the gender gap in leadership – because social stereotypes of women are inconsistent with people's schemas of effective leadership, women are evaluated as poor leaders.

Gender
Sex-stereotypical attributes of a person.

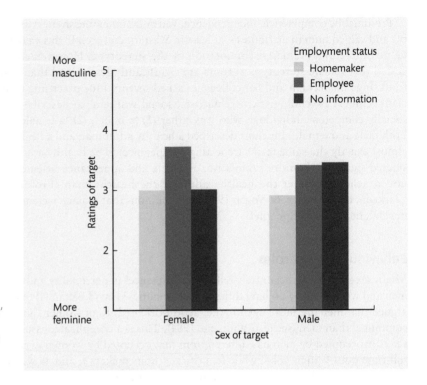

Figure 10.2 Trait ratings as a function of sex and employment status of target

Male and female students rated a 'homemaker' as significantly more feminine than someone described as a full-time employee, irrespective of the target's sex.

Source: Based on data from Eagly and Steffen (1984).

increasingly take on masculine roles, there could be substantial change in sex stereotypes. However, the converse may also occur: as women take up a traditional male role, that role may become less valued.

Any analysis of intergroup relations between the sexes should not lose sight of the fact that in general, men still have more sociopolitical power than women to define the relative status of different roles in society. Not surprisingly, women can find it difficult to gain access to higher-status masculine roles/occupations. Older research found that in some American universities, women applicants for postdoctoral positions could be discouraged by condescending reactions from male peers and academic staff (e.g. 'You're so cute, I can't see you as a professor of anything'; Harris, 1970), and that there was a bias against hiring women for academic positions (e.g. Fidell, 1970; Lewin & Duchan, 1971). Things have changed enormously in the last forty years, so it would be most alarming to find this form of blatant discrimination in modern Western universities.

However, these changes have been slower and less extensive outside the more progressive environment of universities. Women can still find it difficult to attain top leadership positions in large organisations, a phenomenon called the **glass ceiling** (e.g. Eagly, 2003; Eagly, Karau, & Makhijani, 1995), or they find themselves precariously perched on a **glass cliff** because they have been placed in a crisis-leadership role that will attract criticism and is ultimately doomed to failure (Haslam & Ryan, 2008; Ryan & Haslam, 2007; Ryan, Haslam, Morgenroth, Rink, Stoker, & Peters, 2016) – see **Chapter 9**.

Women are well represented in middle management, but on the way up, and just within sight of the top, they hit an invisible ceiling, a glass ceiling. One explanation is that male prejudice against women with power generates a *backlash* that constructs the glass ceiling (e.g. Rudman & Glick, 1999, 2001; see Box 10.2). Again, either sex can hit a glass ceiling if gender stereotypes are inconsistent with the organisation's norms. For example, Young and James (2001) found that male flight attendants hit a glass ceiling because, to put it simply, stereotypes about men prevent people from expecting men to make 'good' flight attendants – male stereotypes block promotion.

Glass ceiling
An invisible barrier that prevents women, and minorities, from attaining top leadership positions.

Glass cliff
A tendency for women rather than men to be appointed to precarious leadership positions associated with a high probability of failure and criticism.

Maintenance of sex stereotypes and roles

One of the most powerful forces in the transmission and maintenance of traditional sex stereotypes is the media. We are all familiar with the unsubtle forms that this may take: semi-clad women draped over boats, cars, motorcycles and other consumer products; the decorative role of women in some TV game shows; the way that women can be extraneous to the central plot of a drama and are presented only as sexual/romantic entertainment; the way that women in some reality TV shows are selected to occupy grotesque female stereo-typical roles. Although the cumulative power of these images should not be underestimated, there are more subtle forms that may be equally or even more powerful, as they are more difficult to detect and thus combat.

For example, Dane Archer and his colleagues coined the term **face-ism** to describe how depictions of men often give greater prominence to the head, while depictions of women give greater prominence to the body (Archer, Iritani, Kimes, & Barrios, 1983). Archer and col-leagues analysed 1,750 visual images of men and women (newspaper and magazine pictures, as well as drawings made by students) and discovered that in almost all instances this was the case (also see Copeland, 1989). Next time you watch a TV interview or documentary, for example, note how the camera tends to focus on the face of men but on the face and upper body of women. Face-ism conveys the view that, relative to men, women are more important for their physical appearance than for their intellectual capacity: facial prominence in photos has been shown to signify ambition and intelligence (Schwartz & Kurz, 1989).

Face-ism
Media depiction that gives greater prominence to the head and less prominence to the body for men, but vice versa for women.

Box 10.2 Research highlight
Backlash: self-promoting women can be socially rejected

Violation of gender stereotypes can result in social and economic reprisal – called *backlash*. According to Laurie Rudman and Peter Glick, women who are perceived to be assertive or highly competent violate stereotypical expec-tations that women possess *communal* traits and ought therefore to be social- and service-oriented (e.g. kind, sympathetic and concerned about others). It is a man's job to be *agentic* (e.g. forceful, decisive and independent) (Rudman, 1998; Rudman & Glick, 1999, 2001). As a conse-quence, competent women can be disliked and viewed as interpersonally unskilled, and therefore less likely to be hired than identically qualified men. Penalising agentic women is especially pronounced if a job inherently requires being more communal. Men do not suffer com-parable consequences (i.e. a decrease in perceived com-petence) when they are seen as highly communal (Croft, Schmader, & Block, 2015). According to Rudman and Glick, this asymmetry rests on the fact that gender stereo-types are more prescriptive of how women should behave than of how men should behave – gender stereotypes place women in a tighter straightjacket than men.

Research provides evidence for this analysis of back-lash. For example, Madeleine Heilman and her colleagues (Heilman, Wallen, Fuchs, & Tamkins, 2004) had students take part in a personnel decision-making task. They were given information about a male-stereotypical job (Assistant Vice President for Sales in an aircraft company) and about fictitious employees who were holding the job. These employees were described as either male or female, and as having a record of either clear previous success or ambiguous previous success. Participants rated the employees on competence-related measures and on interpersonal liking and hostility. There were two findings:

- If previous success was clear, male and female employ-ees were rated as equally competent; but if previous success was ambiguous, the male employee was rated as significantly more competent than the female.
- If previous success was clear, male employees were liked significantly more than female employees; but if previous success was ambiguous, males and females were equally liked.

These findings indicate that in ambiguous situations, women are denied competence in a male-stereotypical arena (e.g. a 'male' job market), and in situations where their competence cannot be doubted, they are less liked and personally derogated. (For a review of how gender stereotypes affect women in the workplace, see Heilman and Parks-Stamm, 2007.)

Sex stereotypes are maintained
Do you think the British girl group, Little Mix, perpetuate a female stereotype? Or do you think they are concentrating on progressing their careers in the industry?

Sik Hung Ng has noted another subtle form of sexism in the use of the generic masculine (Ng, 1990; see also Wetherell, 1986) – people's use of the masculine pronouns (he, him, his, etc.) and terms such as 'mankind' when they are talking about people in general. This practice can convey the impression that women are an aberration from the basic masculine mould of humanity. The sex-typing of occupations and roles can be maintained by use of terms such as 'housewife' and 'chairman'. Because it is largely through language that we represent our world (see **Chapter 15**), changes in sex stereotypes may require changes in the words, phrases and expressions that we habitually use in our written and verbal discourse. For example, language codes such as the publication manual for the American Psychological Association (adhered to by psychologists around the world) have clear guidelines for non-sexist use of language.

There is now substantial evidence that success or failure is explained in different ways depending on the sex of the actor (see intergroup attribution in **Chapter 3**). In general, a successful performance by a man tends to be attributed to ability, while an identical performance by a woman is attributed to luck or the ease of the task (see Figure 10.3). For example, Kay Deaux and Tim Emswiller (1974) had students watch fellow students perform well on perceptual tasks that were male-stereotypical (e.g. identifying a wheel jack) or female-stereotypical (e.g. identifying types of needlework). On the masculine tasks, male success was

Figure 10.3 Attribution of successful performance of an identical task performed by a man or a woman

Different attributions are made for a successful performance by a man (ability, effort) or a woman (luck, easy task), and this leads to different assessments of deservingness and recognition.

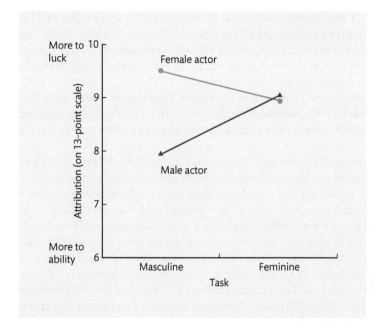

Figure 10.4 Ability versus luck attribution for male or female success on masculine and feminine tasks

Students who watched fellow students perform well on male-stereotypical or female-stereotypical perceptual tasks over-attributed male success on male tasks to ability relative to luck.

Source: Based on data from Deaux and Emswiller (1974).

attributed to ability more than was female success (see Figure 10.4). On feminine tasks, there was no differential **attribution**.

There are some circumstances when this bias may be overturned. For example, sex-stereotypical attributions disappear when the attention of the person who is evaluating the behaviour is directed on to the behaviour and away from the actor (Izraeli, Izraeli, & Eden, 1985). There is also evidence that women who succeed in traditionally masculine activities (e.g. becoming a top manager) are seen as more deserving than a similarly successful man (Taynor & Deaux, 1973).

In general, however, sex-stereotypical attributions (made by both men and women) tend to create different evaluations of our own worth as a man or a woman. That is, for the same level of achievement, women may consider themselves less deserving than men. Indeed, Brenda Major and Ellen Konar (1984) found this among male and female management students in the early 1980s. The women's estimates of their realistic starting salaries were approximately 14 per cent lower than the men's estimates of their starting salaries, and 31 per cent lower with regard to estimated peak salaries.

Attribution
The process of assigning a cause to our own behaviour, and that of others.

Changes in sexism

While these forms of discrimination are difficult, and thus slow, to change, there is evidence that in Western democratic societies most forms of blatant sex discrimination are on the wane – however, sexual harassment in various forms persists (Willness, Steel, & Lee, 2007). Western nations vary considerably in when women were granted the right to vote. This occurred in Britain in 1928 and in New Zealand in 1893. Switzerland delayed until 1971, and in one Swiss canton (Appenzell Inner-Rhoden), women were excluded from the cantonal vote until as recently as 1990. And it was only in 2015 that women in Saudi Arabia were granted the right to vote.

Societies are also increasingly passing anti-discrimination legislation and (particularly in the United States) legislation for affirmative action. Affirmative action involves systematically appointing properly qualified minorities to positions in which they are historically underrepresented (e.g. senior management in organisations, senior government positions), with the aim of making such positions appear more attainable for minorities. One of the features of the 1997 British general election was an affirmative action push to increase the representation of women in Parliament – when the Blair government took office in May 1997, the number of women MPs almost doubled, from 62 to 120 out of 659 seats (9 per cent to 18 per cent). After the 2015 general election, 191 of 650 MPs were women (29 per cent).

Social psychological research has detected some effects of these changes. For example, in the early 1970s, Kathryn Bartol and Anthony Butterfield (1976) found that female leaders in organisations were valued less relative to male leaders. By the early 1980s, this effect had vanished (Izraeli & Izraeli, 1985), although Eagly (2003) cites a Gallup Poll conducted in 1995 that found that across twenty-two nations, both sexes still preferred to have a male boss.

In the mid-1960s, Goldberg (1968; see also Pheterson, Kiesler, & Goldberg, 1971) had women students evaluate identical pieces of written work attributed to a man (John T. McKay) or a woman (Joan T. McKay) and found that those pieces ostensibly authored by a woman were downgraded relative to those ostensibly authored by a man. A replication of this study in the late 1980s found no such effect, and a survey of 104 studies involving 20,000 people showed that the most common finding was no gender bias (Swim, Borgida, Maruyama, & Myers, 1989). Finally, no sex discrimination was found either in a study of performance evaluations of more than 600 male and female store managers (Peters, O'Connor, Weekley, Pooyan, Frank, & Erenkrantz, 1984), or in a study of the compensation worth of predominantly male or predominantly female occupations determined by experts in employment compensation (Schwab & Grams, 1985).

Discrimination on the basis of gender is now illegal in many nations, and sexism is socially unacceptable in many or most domains of life in Western society. This can sometimes make it difficult to detect traditional or old-fashioned sexism. Researchers have tried to measure sex stereotypes in more subtle and complex ways to reflect more modern forms of sexism (Glick & Fiske, 1996; Swim, Aikin, Hall, & Hunter, 1995).

For example, Peter Glick and Susan Fiske (1996, 1997, 2001) constructed an *ambivalent sexism inventory*, which differentiates between hostile and benevolent attitudes to women on dimensions relating to attractiveness, dependence and identity. Sexists have benevolent attitudes (heterosexual attraction, protection, gender role complementarity) towards traditional women (e.g. pink-collar job holders, 'sexy chicks', housewives) and hostile attitudes (heterosexual hostility, domination, competition) towards non-traditional women (e.g. career women, feminists, athletes, lesbians). The expression of benevolent sexism is typically evaluated less negatively than hostile sexism because it does not look so obviously like sexism (Barreto & Ellemers, 2005), so not surprisingly benevolent sexist behaviour is more evident in public settings and hostile sexist behaviour in private settings (Chisango, Mayekiso, & Thomae, 2015).

Men and women can react against sexist behaviour but for different reasons. For example, in 2009 Italians protested against the sexist behaviour of their prime minister Silvio Berlusconi. However, women did so out of anger and condemnation of Berlusconi's hostile and benevolent sexist behaviour, whereas men did so out of humiliation and condemnation of hostile sexism and in order to restore their gender's reputation (Paladino, Zaniboni, Fasoli, Vaes, & Volpato, 2014).

Glick and Fiske (1997) have extended their inventory to measure women's hostile and benevolent attitudes towards men, and twenty years of research have confirmed that hostile and benevolent sexism are closely associated – people who are hostile sexists are also benevolent sexists (Glick & Fiske, 2001, 2011) – and this relationship prevails across cultures (Glick, Fiske, Mladinic, Saiz, Abrams, Masser, & López López, 2000; Glick, Lameiras, Fiske, Eckes, Masser, Volpato, & Wells, 2004).

In their review of research into prejudice against women, Alice Eagly and Antonio Mladinic (1994) concluded that there is no longer any tendency to devalue women's work, that a positive stereotype of women relative to men is emerging, and that most people like women more than men. Although no doubt true, this conclusion should be tempered by the fact that most research is conducted in democratic Western societies; elsewhere, the plight of women is not so rosy. For example, under the rule of the Taliban in Afghanistan in the 1990s, women were denied the right to an education, in Nigeria women have been sentenced to death by stoning for infidelity, and in many cultures there are restrictions placed on women's choices about their bodies and reproduction. The list is long. One particularly sobering statistic comes from the economist Stephan Klasen (1994): at the time of his research, sex-selective abortions and infanticide had led to 76,000,000 (that's right, 76 *million*) 'missing women'.

Racism

Discrimination on the basis of race or ethnicity is responsible historically for some of the most appalling acts of mass inhumanity. While sexism is responsible for the continuing practice of selective infanticide, in which female babies (and foetuses) are killed, this is largely restricted to a handful of developing countries (Freed & Freed, 1989). Genocide is universal: in recent times it has been carried out in, for example, Germany, Iraq, Bosnia and Rwanda.

Most research on **racism** has focused on anti-black attitudes and behaviour in the United States. Historically, white people's stereotypes of blacks in the United States are negative and reflect a general perception of rural, enslaved, manual labourers (LeVine & Campbell, 1972; Mackie, Hamilton, Susskind, & Rosselli, 1996; Plous & Williams, 1995). In this respect, the stereotype is similar to that of Latino Americans but quite different from that of Asians and Jews.

Research into anti-black attitudes in the United States documents a dramatic reduction in unfavourable attitudes since the 1930s (e.g. Devine & Elliot, 1995; Dovidio, Brigham, Johnson, & Gaertner, 1996; Smedley & Bayton, 1978; see Figure 10.5). Much the same has occurred with ethnic minorities in Britain and Western Europe, although recent years have witnessed a revival of overt ethnic prejudice, tied to immigration, among some sectors of the population.

Racism
Prejudice and discrimination against people based on their ethnicity or race.

New racism

From this, should we conclude that racial prejudice has disappeared in Western industrial nations? Possibly not. Figure 10.5 shows a decline over sixty years since the 1930s in the characterisation of African Americans as superstitious, lazy and ignorant. What the figure does

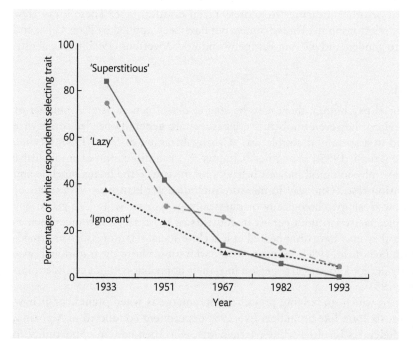

Figure 10.5 Decline over time of white derogation of African Americans

The percentage of white participants selecting the derogatory stereotypic traits 'superstitious', 'lazy' and 'ignorant' to describe African Americans has diminished dramatically since 1933.

Source: Based on data from Dovidio, Brigham, Johnson and Gaertner (1996).

not show are different data from a study by Patricia Devine and Andrew Elliot (1995), in which 45 per cent of respondents still felt that African Americans were lazy. In addition, Devine and Elliot found that more than 25 per cent of their respondents characterised African Americans as athletic, rhythmic, low in intelligence, criminal, hostile and loud. The stereotype has changed but not gone away. Furthermore, when a group of covert racists get together (in the pub, at a political rally, at a demonstration), wider social mores of respect and tolerance hold little sway and the public expression of racist attitudes is common.

Because explicit and blatant racism (derogatory stereotypes, name calling or ethnophaulisms, abuse, persecution, assault and discrimination) is illegal and thus socially censured, it is now more difficult to find. Most people in most contexts do not behave in this way. However, racism may not only or merely have gone 'underground'; it may actually have changed its form. This idea lies at the heart of a number of theories of new or modern racism. People may still be racist at heart, but in a different way – they may represent and express racism differently, perhaps more subtly (Crosby, Bromley, & Saxe, 1980).

This new form of racism has been called *aversive racism* (Gaertner & Dovidio, 1986), *modern racism* (McConahay, 1986), *symbolic racism* (Kinder & Sears, 1981; Sears, 1988), *regressive racism* (Rogers & Prentice-Dunn, 1981) and *ambivalent racism* (Hass, Katz, Rizzo, Bailey, & Eisenstadt, 1991). Although there are differences between these theories, they all share the view that people experience a conflict between, on the one hand, deep-seated emotional antipathy towards racial outgroups, and on the other, modern egalitarian values that exert pressure to behave in a non-prejudiced manner (Brewer & Miller, 1996; Brown, 1995; Hilton & Von Hippel, 1996). For example, according to Sam Gaertner and John Dovidio's (1986) notion of aversive racism, deep-seated racial antipathy expresses itself as overt racism when the situation is one in which egalitarian values are weak. According to David Sears's (1988) notion of symbolic racism, negative feelings about blacks (based on early learnt racial fears and stereotypes) blend with moral values embodied in the Protestant ethic to justify some anti-black attitudes and therefore legitimise their expression.

Generally, modern or subtle forms of racism reflect how people resolve an underlying antipathy based on race with their belief in equality between groups – in essence, it is a type of cognitive dissonance resolution process (Gawronski, Peters, Brochu, & Strack, 2008). The resolution is achieved by avoidance and denial of racism – separate lives, avoidance of the topic of race, denial of being prejudiced, denial of racial disadvantage and thus opposition to affirmative action or other measures to address racial disadvantage. These ideas grew from studies on race relations in the United States, but have been applied by Peter Glick and Susan Fiske (1996) to gender, and by Tom Pettigrew and Roel Meertens (1995) to racial attitudes in Europe.

Detecting racism

The challenge to social psychology, then, is to be able to *detect* new racism. A number of scales have been devised; however, unobtrusive measures are generally needed, otherwise people may respond in a socially desirable way (Crosby, Bromley, & Saxe, 1980; Devine, 1989; Greenwald & Banaji, 1995); see earlier (**Chapter 5**) for a discussion of unobtrusive measures of attitudes (physiological indices, behavioural measures, the bogus pipeline and the implicit association test). One way to measure prejudice unobtrusively is in terms of social distance – how close, psychologically or physically, people are willing to get to one another. For example, racist attitudes persist in contexts of close social distance (such as marriage), although they may have disappeared in less close social relations (such as attending the same school) (Schofield, 1986). In India, people who subscribe to the traditional caste system will typically accept a lower-caste person into their home but will not consider marrying one (Sharma, 1981).

Another context in which underlying prejudice can emerge is when prejudiced behaviour does not obviously look like prejudice. In a 1981 experiment conducted in Alabama, white or black confederates insulted white participants, who then had an opportunity to

New racism
Cultural practices often contrast in modern multicultural societies. Even those who are passionate egalitarians can find disconcerting.

administer a shock to the confederate. Angered whites gave larger shocks to the black confederate. In another condition where no insults were forthcoming, participants gave smaller shocks to the black confederate than to the white confederate (Rogers & Prentice-Dunn, 1981).

Prejudice can also surface inadvertently in people's relatively automatic cognition (see **Chapter 2**). For example, Duncan (1976) had white students in California observe on TV what they thought was a live conversation between a black man and a white man. The conversation degenerated into an argument in which one lightly shoved the other. When the white did the shoving, the behaviour was interpreted as playful: only 13 per cent of participants interpreted it as violent. When the black did the shoving, 73 per cent interpreted the action as violent.

Other evidence for well-concealed prejudice comes from an experiment by Sam Gaertner and John McLaughlin (1983). Participants were given pairings of the words white or black (clearly indicating the respective social categories) with various positive or negative descriptive adjectives. Their task was to decide whether the pairings were meaningful or not and then communicate their decision by pressing a button labelled 'yes' or 'no'. The speed of response is an index of how well the pairing represents an existing attitude in the mind of the participant – faster responses indicate an existing attitude. The results (see Figure 10.6) show no tendency among participants to pair negative words more strongly with black or white. However, participants were much quicker at deciding whether positive words were meaningfully paired with white than with black.

The principle underlying this procedure for detecting prejudice is automaticity (Bargh, 1989). Stereotypes can be automatically generated by categorization, and categorization can automatically arise from category primes (e.g. an accent, a face, a costume). If the primes or the categories are outside consciousness, then people can have little control over the stereotype.

In one of Devine's experiments (Devine, 1989), African American primes (e.g. lazy, slavery, blacks, Negroes, niggers, athletic) were presented too quickly for people to be aware of them. As a result, a neutral act by someone called 'Donald' was interpreted as consistent with

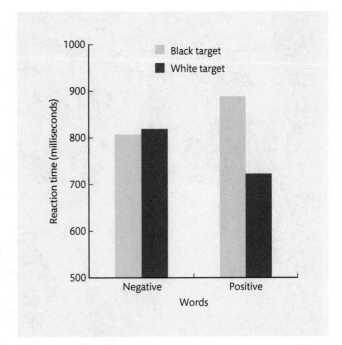

Figure 10.6 Reaction time for deciding whether positive or negative words are meaningfully paired with the social categories black or white

White participants did not differentially associate negative words with racial labels. However, positive words were more quickly associated with 'white' than 'black'.

Source: Based on data from Gaertner and McLaughlin (1983).

negative racial stereotypes. People clearly had deep-seated negative stereotypes of African Americans. High- and low-prejudice people did not differ in their susceptibility to preconscious priming, a provocative result that was conceptually replicated by Russell Fazio and his colleagues (Fazio, Jackson, Dunton, & Williams, 1995). However, other research shows that the automatic effect is more marked for people who score high on prejudice as measured by modern racism scales (Lepore & Brown, 1997; Wittenbrink, Judd, & Park, 1997).

The notion of automaticity is related to the idea that categories and their stereotypical attributes are implicitly linked in memory. Thus, concealed prejudice can be detected by unobtrusive methods that reveal underlying stereotypical associations. This idea is the basis of the **implicit association test** (IAT) which we discussed in detail in **Chapter 5** (Greenwald, McGhee, & Schwartz, 1998 – also see Ashburn-Nardo, Voils, & Monteith, 2001; Cunningham, Preacher, & Banaji, 2001; Greenwald, Banaji, Rudman, Farnham, Nosek, & Mellott, 2002).

There has been much debate over the extent to which implicit cognitive associations actually reflect real behaviour that has impact on people and on society. A recent overview of meta-analyses concludes that although implicit associations do not very strongly predict real prejudice, the effects are 'large enough to explain discriminatory impacts that are societally significant either because they can affect many people simultaneously or because they can repeatedly affect single persons' (Greenwald, Banaji, & Nosek, 2015, p. 553).

Racism can very subtly and unintentionally be imbedded in the words we use, the way we express ourselves and the way we communicate with and about racial outgroups (e.g. Potter & Wetherell, 1987; Van Dijk, 1993; Van Dijk & Wodak, 1988; see also **Chapter 15**). An example of the meticulous attention to detail to be found in some of this work is Teun Van Dijk's (1987) lengthy analysis of spontaneous everyday talk among whites in the Netherlands and in Southern California about other races (e.g. blacks, East Indians, North Africans, Hispanics, Asians). A total of 180 free-format interviews conducted between 1980 and 1985 were analysed qualitatively to show how racism is imbedded in and reproduced by everyday discourse. (See Wetherell, Taylor and Yates (2001) for an account of the methodology of discourse analysis.)

A more cognitive index of language-based prejudice is the linguistic intergroup bias effect (Franco & Maass, 1996; Maass, 1999; Maass, Salvi, Arcuri, & Semin, 1989; see **Chapter 5**).

Implicit association test
Reaction-time test to measure attitudes – particularly unpopular attitudes that people might conceal.

Anne Maass and her colleagues discovered that people use concrete language that simply describes events when talking about positive outgroup (and negative ingroup) characteristics; but they use more general and abstract terms that relate to enduring traits when talking about negative outgroup (and positive ingroup) characteristics. In this way, we can detect negative outgroup attitudes: people start to become abstract and general when talking about their prejudices.

Finally, although we often have some control over what we say, we have less control over non-verbal communication channels; these can be a rich indicator of underlying emotions and prejudices (Burgoon, Buller, & Woodall, 1989; DePaulo & Friedman, 1998; see also **Chapter 15**).

Racial and ethnic prejudices are extremely pervasive if, as is almost always the case, we have been brought up in societies in which such prejudices have prevailed. Most of us are aware of the relevant stereotypes, and the task at hand is consciously to resist automatic stereotypical reactions – it would seem that less prejudiced people are more adept at this (Devine, 1989). Tom Pettigrew noted:

> Many Southerners have confessed to me . . . that even though in their minds they no longer feel prejudice towards Blacks, they still feel squeamish when they shake hands with a Black. These feelings are left over from what they learnt in their families as children.
>
> Pettigrew (1987, p. 20)

In summary, overt racism and ethnic prejudice are both illegal and morally condemned, and most people think and act accordingly, but a long history of such prejudices cannot be shrugged off so easily. The germs of racism still exist, and racism can be detected in various subtle forms. Racial and cultural resentment and partiality lurk beneath the surface – relatively dormant but ready to be activated by a social environment (e.g. a political regime) that might legitimise the expression of prejudice. The violence in Bosnia that began in 1992, the horrors in Rwanda in 1994, and the persecution of Shi'a Muslims and Yazidis by DAISH in Syria and Iraq are chilling reminders of this. Also worrying is the increased media prominence over the past decade of the far right in many Western countries such as France, Germany and Britain. Even if not intended, the media partially provides a supportive and legitimising environment for the public expression of old-fashioned racist attitudes.

Finally, although research suggests that overt discrimination may be on the wane in many Western democracies, this does not mean that the social consequences of decades or even centuries of racism will change so quickly. Although attitudes towards blacks have improved dramatically over the past thirty years, the physical, material and spiritual plight of blacks in many Western countries has not. For example, in the United States, African Americans make up about 12 per cent of the population but 37 per cent of prison inmates, and they are incarcerated mainly for non-violent drug offences. This creates a vicious cycle. Hetey and Eberhardt (2014) showed that when an individual penal institution is perceived to have a higher rate of black inmates, people would use this as an argument to increase their support for more punitive policies.

Ageism

The existence of age-related, or generational, stereotypes is undeniable. We all have them, and they can generate expectancies and misunderstandings that are felt particularly strongly in work contexts. Susan Mitchell (2002) identified four distinct generational stereotypes that may be partly attributable to real changes in behaviour due to ageing, but are also influenced by value differences in your social environment during early adult development:

- *Traditionalists*, born between 1925 and 1945, are practical; patient, loyal and hardworking; respectful of authority; and rule followers.
- *Baby boomers*, born between 1946 and 1960, are optimistic; value teamwork and cooperation; are ambitious; and are workaholic.

- *Generation X*, born between 1961 and 1980, are sceptical, self-reliant risk-takers who balance work and personal life.
- *Millennials* (Generation Y), born between 1981 and 1999, are hopeful; they value meaningful work, diversity and change; and are technologically savvy.

Those born since the end of the 1990s have variously been called the Internet Generation, Generation Text, or the Always-On Generation – the main feature is easy and continuous access to information and other people due to Internet connectivity. This generation is largely expected to be nimble, quick-acting multi-taskers who count on the Internet as their external brain, who have a thirst for instant gratification and quick fixes and who have limited patience and a lack of deep-thinking ability.

Ageism
Prejudice and discrimination against people based on their age.

The main issue, however, of **ageism** is how the elderly are treated. In many cultures, particularly those in which the extended family thrives, older members of the community are revered – they are considered to be wise and knowledgeable teachers and leaders. In other societies, largely those in which the nuclear family has displaced the extended family, this is often not the case. Countries such as Britain, The Netherlands, Australia, New Zealand and the United States fall into this latter category. In these societies, the qualities of youth are highly valued, and elderly people (a group that is rapidly increasing in relative number) attract unfavourable stereotypes. However, there is a range of subtypes, including the John Wayne conservative (patriotic, religious, nostalgic), the small-town neighbour (frugal, quiet, conservative), the perfect grandparent (wise, kind, happy), the golden-ager (adventurous, sociable, successful), the despondent (depressed, neglected), the severely impaired (incompetent, feeble) and the shrew/curmudgeon (bitter, complaining, prejudiced) (Brewer, Dull, & Lui, 1981).

Elderly people are generally treated as relatively worthless and powerless members of the community. They are denied many basic human rights, and their special needs go untended. Being the target of ageist stereotypes and discrimination has also been shown to detrimentally impact the health of older people (Levy, 2009; Levy, Zonderman, Slade, & Ferrucci, 2009; Pascoe & Richman, 2009).

Young adults often consider people over 65 to be grouchy, unhealthy, unattractive, unhappy, miserly, inefficient, socially unskilled, overly self-disclosing, overly controlling, feeble, egocentric, incompetent, abrasive, frail and vulnerable (see Noels, Giles, & Le Poire, 2003). These are not merely descriptive stereotypes. They are very much prescriptive – they prescribe and therefore control how older people should behave (North & Fiske, 2013). Young people expect older people to conform to their stereotypes of the elderly, and when older people do, the young react positively. But when older people violate stereotypical expectations, the young can react negatively with resentment and anger.

Furthermore, the young generally have little to do with the elderly, so intergenerational encounters tend to activate intergroup rather than interpersonal perceptions, which reinforce negative stereotypes that lead to avoidance and minimisation of intergenerational contact. The cycle continues and the elderly remain socially isolated and societally marginalised. This can all be made worse by the existence of communication problems between different generations (e.g. Fox & Giles, 1993; Harwood, Giles, & Ryan, 1995; Hummert, 1990; Kite & Johnson, 1988; Williams, 1996; see **Chapter 15**).

A final, interesting, observation is that the extremely old seem to pass through the ageism lens and are once again accorded respect – however, perhaps more in the media than on the street. For example, witness the media coverage of the British Queen Mother's 100th birthday in 2000, and Queen Elizabeth II's diamond jubilee in 2012.

Discrimination against sexual minorities

Sexual minorities and the LGBTQ (lesbian, gay, bisexual, transgender and queer) community are a target of prejudice and discrimination around the world (Herek & McLemore, 2013). This was not always the case. Two millennia ago, the Romans were relatively tolerant of all forms of sexual orientation. It was with the advent of Christianity that social norms concerning sexual behaviour became more restrictive, homosexuality (focused mainly on same-sex intercourse between males) was considered deviant and immoral and the persecution of homosexuals became legitimate and acceptable.

For example, an older survey in the United States showed that the majority of people believed that homosexuality was 'sick' and should be outlawed (Levitt & Klassen, 1974), and more recently it was found that only 39 per cent of people 'would see a homosexual doctor' (Henry, 1994). It was only in 1973 that the American Psychiatric Association formally removed homosexuality from its list of mental disorders. And of course, to this day there are wide swathes of the globe, including some Islamic republics and African nations, where same-sex sexual relations are illegal and punishable by death (Bereket & Adam, 2008).

However, in the West there has been a progressive liberalisation of attitudes towards same-sex relations since the late 1960s. The AIDS epidemic of the 1980s set things back and whipped up negative attitudes in some sections of society (Altman, 1986; Herek & Glunt, 1988; see Box 10.3) – showing that deeply entrenched homophobic prejudices persist in certain sectors of the community. But now, huge gay and lesbian pride celebrations like San Francisco Pride, started in 1972, and the Sydney Gay and Lesbian Mardi Gras, started in 1978, attract virtually no negative reactions and are celebrated by all. And of course, same-sex marriage is now legal in the United States, Canada and most of Western Europe and South America. All these factors have helped build resilience in the lesbian, gay and bisexual community in the face of prejudice (Kwon, 2013).

However, in their review of sexual prejudice, Herek and McLemore (2013) warn that despite these advances, lesbian, gay and bisexual people remain widely stigmatised – as we saw earlier for racism and sexism, prejudices often linger unseen despite changed social norms and legislation. In the case of sexual prejudice, organised religion, particularly in its traditional or fundamentalist guise, remains a troublesome correlate of sexual prejudice (Batson, Schoenrade, & Ventis, 1993; Herek, 1987; Herman, 1997).

Discrimination on the basis of physical or mental handicap

Prejudice and discrimination against the physically handicapped has a long past, in which such people have been stigmatised and treated as repugnant and subhuman (Jodelet, 1991). For example, most circuses had a side-show alley in which various 'freaks' would be displayed (powerfully portrayed in Tod Browning's 1932 movie *Freaks*), and many dramas hinge on the curiosity value of the physically handicapped (e.g. David Lynch's 1980 movie *Elephant Man*, Fellini's 1969 movie *Satyricon* and Victor Hugo's 1831 novel *Notre-Dame de Paris*).

Overt discrimination against people on the basis of physical handicap is now illegal and socially unacceptable in most Western societies. Many countries go out of their way to be sensitive to the special requirements of people with physical disabilities: for example, the provision of ramps for people in wheelchairs, and audible signals at pedestrian crossings. The staging of the Paralympics every four years is another step in the normalisation of physical handicap.

People generally no longer derogate the physically handicapped, but they still stereotype them in line with the stereotype content model (Cuddy, Fiske, & Glick, 2008) as being warm but incompetent (Rohmer & Louvet, 2012). They are also often uneasy in their presence and uncertain about how to interact with them (Heinemann, 1990) – an instance of intergroup anxiety (e.g. Stephan, 2014; Stephan & Stephan, 1985, 2000; see **Chapter 11**). This can unintentionally produce patronising attitudes, speech and behaviour that serve to emphasise and perpetuate handicap (Fox & Giles, 1996a, 1996b; see also **Chapter 15**).

The improvement of attitudes over the past twenty-five years towards physical handicap has not extended to mental/psychological handicap. In medieval times, women with schizophrenia were labelled witches and burnt at the stake; Hitler's 'Final Solution' applied not

Box 10.3 Our world
AIDS and anti-gay prejudice

Fear surrounding AIDS has been used to justify discrimination against homosexuals

AIDS is a serious and deadly illness that develops in people infected with HIV. The virus is transmitted through exchange of certain bodily fluids: for example, through blood transfusions, by needle sharing among intravenous drug users and by some sexual practices among gay men. Although AIDS is by no means a gay disease, the majority of people infected in Western countries have tended to be gay (63 per cent of AIDS cases in the United States up to 1988 were gay; Herek & Glunt, 1988), so people assume a link between AIDS and homosexuality.

Fear and ignorance of AIDS, in conjunction with knowledge of its association with gays, has activated latent prejudices against gays. In many ways, AIDS has provided moral justification (grounded in fear for self and society) for overt discrimination against gay people: homophobics have felt free to come out of the closet. The promotion of gay rights can be seen by such people as tantamount to the promotion of AIDS itself.

Gregory Herek and Eric Glunt's (1988, p. 888) discussion of public reaction in the United States to AIDS produced telling evidence for the way AIDS has been linked to homosexuality and used to justify anti-gay attitudes. The epidemic was virtually ignored by the US media in the early 1980s because it was merely a 'story of dead and dying homosexuals' and it was sometimes referred to as the 'gay plague'. Patrick Buchanan, a Republican columnist, wrote (1987, p. 23): 'There is one, only one, cause of the AIDS crisis – the wilful refusal of homosexuals to cease indulging in the immoral, unnatural, unsanitary, unhealthy, and suicidal practice of anal intercourse, which is the primary means by which the AIDS virus is being spread'. He felt (Buchanan, 1987: p. 23) that the 'Democratic Party should be dragged into the court of public opinion as an un-indicted co-conspirator in America's AIDS epidemic [for] seeking to amend state and federal civil rights laws to make sodomy a protected civil right, to put homosexual behaviour, the sexual practice by which AIDS is spread, on the same moral plane with being female or being black.'

The Catholic Church used the apparent link between AIDS and homosexuality to argue against civil rights protection for gay people. Others were more extreme: a mayoral candidate for the city of Houston was heard to joke publicly that his solution to the city's AIDS problem would be to 'shoot the queers' (quoted in Herek & Glunt, 1988, p. 888).

---

only to the Jews but also to the insane; and in Stalin's Soviet Union, dissidents were labelled 'insane' in order to justify their incarceration. Although the Hospital of St Mary of Bethlehem (popularly corrupted to Bedlam) in London has long been closed, similar conditions may prevail in asylums around the world: instances have been exposed more recently in, for example, Greece and Romania. These are extreme cases, but ignorance and fear fuel strong prejudices, and both institutionalised and face-to-face discrimination still prevail.

Mental illness is often treated as a stigma that brings shame on the family. So it is not surprising to learn that cultures of honour where a premium is placed on protecting the honour of the family (e.g. Rodriguez Mosquera, 2013) are particularly prone to hide family members who have mental health problems and prevent them from seeking help for the mental health services (Brown, Imura, & Mayeuz, 2014). This of course harms the family member and sustains the prejudice.

Overall, Western societies prefer to overlook mental illness and abdicate responsibility for the mentally ill. This is reflected in remarkably low funding for research into most mental illnesses and poor resourcing for the care and therapy of psychiatric patients. Since the early 1980s there has been a policy in, for example, Britain and the United States to 'deinstitutionalise' chronic psychiatric patients, which means they are released from hospital without provision of adequate community resources for their support.

Another facet of prejudice against the mentally ill is the use of the 'mad' label to dehumanise and justify discrimination against minority-status groups as a whole. 'Different' becomes 'mad' (Szasz, 1970). This is the serious side of what we regularly do in jest – 'You must be mad!' is something we might say on hearing someone outline a novel (read 'different') scheme. Research from the 1960s and 1970s indicates that the stereotypical behaviour of women did not conform to what people considered to be the behaviour of a typical, well-adjusted, adult human being (Broverman, Broverman, Clarkson, Rosencrantz, & Vogel, 1970) – in this sense, women were 'maladjusted' (Chesler, 1972; Eichler, 1980). A similar process, in which cultural difference is pathologised by the dominant white middle-class group, has occurred with respect to blacks and other racial/ethnic minorities (Nahem, 1980; Waxman, 1977).

There is a further twist to the story. Prejudice often creates brutal conditions of existence (poverty, poor health, low self-esteem, violence, etc.), which may produce certain types of psychiatric disorder in minority groups. In this way, fear and ignorance about psychiatric illness dovetails with and may amplify ethnic or racial prejudices.

Forms of discrimination

The preceding discussion deals with some general targets of prejudice, and in so doing it inevitably speaks about different forms that discrimination may take. One important point is that a great deal of prejudice is expressed in subtle and often hidden ways – crude overt discrimination is now less common. We have already described modern forms of prejudice. Here we say a bit more about three types of behaviour that do not look obviously like discrimination but nevertheless may conceal underlying prejudices: reluctance to help, tokenism and reverse discrimination.

Reluctance to help

Reluctance to help other groups to improve their position in society, by passively or actively failing to assist their efforts, is one way to make sure they remain disadvantaged. This strategy can be adopted by individuals (landlords may be reluctant to rent accommodation to ethnic minorities), organisations (organisations may be reluctant to provide appropriate facilities for employees in wheelchairs), or society as a whole (governments may be resistant to legislate in favour of adequate maternity leave provisions).

Reluctance to help can also be a hallmark of aversive racism (see earlier in this chapter) – the combination of racial anxiety and antipathy, coupled with a belief that the magnitude of disadvantage is overstated, encourages people not to offer help. Studies show that reluctance to help is manifested only in certain conditions: specifically, when such reluctance can be attributed to some factor other than prejudice. Gaertner and Dovidio's (1977) experiment, described earlier in this chapter, is an illustration of reluctance to help. White participants were more reluctant to help a black than a white confederate faced with an emergency, but only when they believed that other potential helpers were present.

Tokenism

Tokenism refers to a relatively small or trivial positive act, a token, towards members of a minority group. The action is then invoked to deflect accusations of prejudice and as a justification for declining to engage in larger and more meaningful positive acts or for subsequently engaging in discrimination ('Don't bother me, haven't I already done enough?'). For example, studies by Donald Dutton and Robert Lake (1973) and David Rosenfield and his colleagues (Rosenfield, Greenberg, Folger, & Borys, 1982) found that white participants who had performed a small favour for a black stranger were subsequently less willing to engage in more effortful forms of helping than were those who had not performed the small favour. This effect was accentuated when the token action (the small favour) activated negative stereotypes about blacks: for example, when the favour involved giving money to a black panhandler (beggar). (Do you think Tom has a problem? See the first 'What do *you* think?' question.)

Tokenism
The practice of publicly making small concessions to a minority group in order to deflect accusations of prejudice and discrimination.

Tokenism can be employed by organisations and society more broadly. In the United States, there has been criticism of the token employment of minorities (e.g. African Americans, Latinos) by organisations that then fail to take more fundamental and important steps towards equal opportunities. Such organisations may employ minorities as tokens to help deflect accusations of prejudice. Tokenism at this level can have damaging consequences for the self-esteem of those who are employed as token minorities (Chacko, 1982; see the next subsection, 'Reverse discrimination').

Tokenism can also be considered in a very straightforward numerical sense. For example, Rosabeth Kanter (1977) considered a minority to be a token when its numerical representation in a group was very small. Wright has built on this to focus on the nature of the barriers a minority may confront to enter a majority group, defining tokenism as 'any intergroup context in which the boundaries between the advantaged and disadvantaged groups are not entirely closed, but where there exists severe restrictions on access to advantaged positions on the basis of group membership' (Wright, 2001, p. 224).

Reverse discrimination

Reverse discrimination
The practice of publicly being prejudiced in favour of a minority group in order to deflect accusations of prejudice and discrimination against that group.

A more extreme form of tokenism is **reverse discrimination**. People with residual prejudiced attitudes may sometimes go out of their way to favour members of a group against which they are prejudiced more than members of other groups. For example, Thomas Chidester (1986) had white students engage in a 'get acquainted' conversation through audio equipment with another student, who was ostensibly either black or white. The white students systematically evaluated black strangers more favourably than white strangers. Similar findings emerged from the Dutton and Lake (1973) study cited earlier. (Relate these results to the first 'What do *you* think?' question.)

Because reverse discrimination favours a minority group member, it can have beneficial effects in the short term. In the long run, however, it may have harmful consequences for its recipients (Fajardo, 1985; see later in this chapter), and there is no evidence that reverse discrimination reduces the deep-seated prejudices of the discriminator. However, from both a cognitive dissonance point of view (Festinger, 1957; see **Chapter 6**) and a self-perception theory point of view (Bem, 1972; see **Chapter 4**) someone who engages in reverse

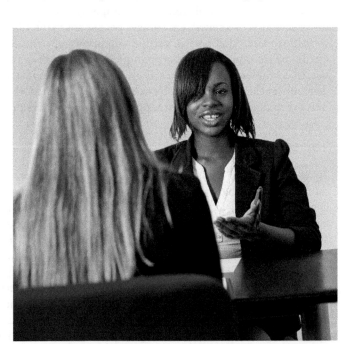

Tokenism
Although smiling, she is already concerned. Has she been hired only to satisfy a government diversity initiative?

discrimination without any apparent external pressure to do so might be expected to change their attitudes and self-concept in line with their behaviour. Overall, reverse discrimination is an effective way to conceal prejudices, but it can also reflect ambivalence, the desire to appear egalitarian or genuine feelings of admiration and respect (Carver, Glass, & Katz, 1977; Gaertner & Dovidio, 1986).

For the researcher, the challenge is to know when behaviour that goes out of its way to favour a minority is reverse discrimination or is actually a genuine attempt to rectify disadvantage (e.g. affirmative action – see the second 'What do *you* think?' question).

Stigma and other effects of prejudice

The effects of prejudice on the victims of prejudice are diverse, ranging from relatively minor inconvenience to enormous suffering. In general, prejudice is harmful because it stigmatises groups and the people who belong to those groups (Crocker, Major, & Steele, 1998; Goffman, 1963; Swim & Stangor, 1998). From a meta-analysis of 134 studies, Elizabeth Pascoe and Laura Richman (2009) conclude that perceived discrimination has a significant negative effect on both mental and physical health; it also significantly elevates stress and is associated with unhealthy behaviours. Gordon Allport (1954b) identified more than fifteen possible consequences of being a victim of prejudice. Let us examine some of these.

Stigma

Jennifer Crocker and her colleagues define **stigma** as follows: 'Stigmatised individuals possess (or are believed to possess) some attribute, or characteristic, that conveys a social identity that is devalued in a particular social context' (Crocker, Major, & Steele, 1998, p. 505). The targets of prejudice and discrimination are members of stigmatised groups; thus they are stigmatised individuals. The subjective experience of stigma hinges on two factors: visibility/concealability and controllability.

Visible stigmas, such as race, gender, obesity and age mean that people cannot easily avoid being the target of stereotypes and discrimination – being a member of a visibly stigmatised group makes the experience of prejudice inescapable (Steele & Aronson, 1995). Visibly stigmatised people cannot conceal the stigma to cope with the stereotypes, prejudice and harassment that the stigma may trigger.

Concealable stigmas, such as homosexuality, some illnesses and some ideologies and religious affiliations, allow people to avoid the experience of prejudice. Gregory Herek (2007) refers to this kind of concealment as an *internalised stigma*. However, the cost of concealment can be high (Goffman, 1963). People have to be untrue to themselves and super-vigilant to ensure their stigma does not surface inadvertently. Although a concealable stigmatised identity can be expressed freely at home (a private context), the same may not apply in public contexts such as work if it attracts negative outcomes, and this may cause people to feel they have a 'divided self' (Sedlovskaya, Purdie-Vaughs, Eibach, LaFrance, Romero-Canyas, & Camp, 2013).

Controllable stigmas are those that people believe, rightly or wrongly, are chosen rather than assigned: for example, obesity, smoking and homosexuality are thought to be controllable – people are believed to be responsible for having chosen to be these things. Uncontrollable stigmas are those that people believe others have little choice in possessing: for example, race, sex and some illnesses. Controllable stigmas invite much harsher reactions and more extreme discrimination than uncontrollable stigmas. For example, Chris Crandall (1994) has shown that the reason why 'fat' people attract such negative reactions in contemporary Western cultures is not only that obesity is highly stigmatised but also that people believe it is controllable (also see Crandall, D'Anello, Sakalli, Lazarus, Nejtardt, & Feather, 2001; Crandall, Nierman, & Hebl, 2009).

Stigma
Group attributes that mediate a negative social evaluation of people belonging to the group.

People who believe they have a controllable stigma try hard to escape the stigma. As with concealability, this can have a high cost. Many stigmas that people believe are controllable are actually not controllable or are extremely difficult to control (in some cases, obesity falls into this category). Attempts to control the stigma are largely futile, and people can experience profound feelings of failure and inadequacy in addition to the negativity of the stigma itself. However, some people do focus their energy on re-evaluating the stigma and on fighting prejudice and discrimination against their group (Crocker & Major, 1994).

Stigma persists for a number of obvious reasons (see Crocker, Major, & Steele, 1998). Individuals and groups gain a relatively positive sense of self and social identity if they compare themselves or their group with other individuals or groups that are stigmatised – there is a self-evaluative advantage in having stigmatised outgroups as downward comparison targets (Hogg, 2000b; Hogg & Gaffney, 2014). Stigma can legitimise inequalities of status and resource distribution that favour a dominant group; such groups will certainly ensure that the stigma remains in place, because it serves a system justification function – it justifies the status quo (Jost & Banaji, 1994; Jost & Kramer, 2002; Jost & Van der Toorn, 2012). People may need to stigmatise groups that have different world views from their own, because if they did not degrade and discredit outgroups in this way, then the frail sense of certainty in, and controllability over, life that they gain from their own world view would be shattered (Solomon, Greenberg, & Pyszczynski, 1991).

Finally, Robert Kurzban and Mark Leary (2001) give an evolutionary account of stigma. Stigmatisation is the outcome of an adaptive cognitive process that helps us avoid poor social exchange partners who may threaten our access to resource or who, by virtue of being different, may carry communicable pathogens.

Self-worth, self-esteem and psychological well-being

Stigmatised groups are, by definition, devalued. They have relatively low status and little power in society, and find it difficult to avoid society's negative image of them. For example, African Americans over the age of fourteen are aware that others have negative images of them (Rosenberg, 1979), as are Mexican Americans (Casas, Ponterotto, & Sweeney, 1987), homosexuals (D'Emilio, 1983) and many women (Crosby, 1982). Members of stigmatised groups tend to internalise these evaluations to form an unfavourable self-image that can depress **self-esteem** in relevant contexts (see **Chapter 4**). For example, research reveals that women generally share men's negative stereotypes of women, often evaluate themselves in terms of such stereotypes and, under circumstances where sex is the salient basis of self-perception, actually report a reduction in self-esteem (e.g. Hogg, 1985; Hogg & Turner, 1987b; Smith, 1985).

Self-esteem
Feelings about and evaluations of oneself.

However, groups and their members are ingenious in finding ways to combat low status and consensual low regard, so depressed self-esteem is by no means an inevitable consequence of prejudice (e.g. Dion & Earn, 1975; Dion, Earn, & Yee, 1978; Tajfel & Turner, 1986; see also **Chapter 11**). Although some stigmatised individuals are vulnerable to low self-esteem, diminished life satisfaction and in some cases depression, most members of stigmatised groups are able to weather the assaults and are resilient in sustaining a positive self-image (Crocker & Major, 1989, 1994; Crocker, Major, & Steele, 1998; Kwon, 2013).

On a day-to-day basis, self-esteem can be assailed by prejudice, ranging from crude racial epithets and blatant physical attack to slights such as being ignored by a salesperson in a store or being served last in a bar. The journalist Ellis Cose (1993) describes how an African American partner in a law firm was denied access to his office because a young white lawyer who did not know him assumed that because he was black, he was engaged in criminal activity.

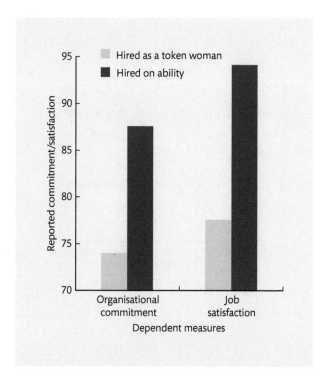

Figure 10.7 Organisational commitment and job satisfaction as a function of perceived basis of being hired

A pitfall of tokenism. Women managers who felt they had been hired as a token woman reported less organisational commitment and less job satisfaction than women who felt they had been hired because of their ability.

Source: Based on data from Chacko (1982).

More subtle forms of prejudice can also damage self-esteem. For example, Thomas Chacko (1982) asked women managers to rate the extent to which a number of factors (their ability, experience, education or sex) had influenced their being hired for the job. They also indicated their commitment to the organisation and their satisfaction with various aspects of the job. Those who felt that they had been hired merely as token women reported less organisational commitment and job satisfaction than those who felt that they had been hired because of their ability (see Figure 10.7). This is one way in which tokenism can have negative consequences.

Reverse discrimination can also affect self-esteem. Daniel Fajardo (1985) conducted a study in which white teachers graded four essays that were reliable examples (drawn from college entrance records) of poor, average or excellent quality. The teachers understood that the essays were written by either black or white high-school students applying to enter university. Results showed that the teachers evaluated identical essays more favourably when they were attributed to black students than to white students (see Figure 10.8), particularly when the essays were of average quality.

In the short run, reverse discrimination may boost minority students' self-confidence. In the long run, however, some students will develop unrealistic opinions of their abilities and future prospects, resulting in damage to self-esteem when such hopes collide with reality. Reverse discrimination may also prevent students from seeking the help they sometimes need early in their schooling, and this can lead to educational disadvantage.

Relatedly, the policy of affirmative action, which is designed to rectify historical under-representation of certain groups in high-status occupations and positions in society, can have the unintended effect of provoking negative reaction from members of traditionally advantaged groups. They may experience a sense of injustice and relative deprivation (see **Chapter 11**), which provokes behaviour designed to re-establish equity (see **Chapter 12**) or reassert the superior status of their group. This can impact minorities in ways that eventually affect their self-esteem.

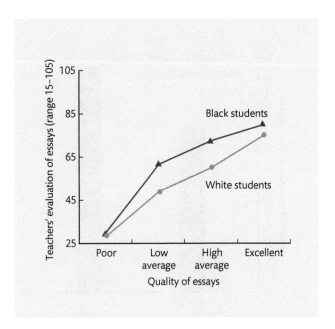

Figure 10.8 White teachers' evaluations of student essays of varying quality as a function of student race

White teachers evaluated black students' essays more favourably than white students' essays, particularly where the essays were of average, rather than poor or excellent, quality. An unintended consequence of reverse discrimination such as this is that black students would be less likely to seek or be given guidance to improve their actually very average performance.

Source: Based on data from Fajardo (1985).

Stereotype threat

Stereotype threat
Feeling that we will be judged and treated in terms of negative stereotypes of our group, and that we will inadvertently confirm these stereotypes through our behaviour.

Because stigmatised groups know the negative stereotypes that others have of them, they experience what Claude Steele and Joshua Aronson (1995; Steele, Spencer, & Aronson, 2002) call **stereotype threat** (also see Inzlicht & Schmader, 2011; Maass & Cadinu, 2003; Schmader, Johns, & Forbes, 2008; Shapiro & Neuberg, 2007). People who are stigmatised are aware that others may judge and treat them stereotypically. So, on tasks that really matter to them, and particularly when they feel the context is dominated by a cultural world view that differs from that of their own group, they worry that through their behaviour they may confirm the stereotypes – that their behaviour will become a self-fulfilling prophecy (see the 'Self-fulfilling prophecies' section later in this chapter). These concerns increase anxiety and negative thoughts (Cadinu, Maass, Rosabianca, & Kiesner, 2005), and limit working memory (Van Loo & Rydell, 2013). They can also impair task performance. For example, an academically ambitious West Indian Briton, aware of stereotypes of intellectual inferiority, may be extremely anxious when answering a question in class. She would worry that the slightest mistake would be interpreted stereotypically. This anxiety would distract her and quite probably impair her answer to the question.

To test the stereotype threat hypothesis, Steele and Aronson had black and white students anticipate taking a 'very difficult' test (items from the verbal Graduate Record Exam) that was defined as being 'diagnostic of intellectual ability' or as 'just a laboratory exercise'. They then completed a number of measures designed to assess awareness of racial stereotypes: for example, they completed ambiguous sentence fragments such as _____CE or _____ERIOR. As predicted, black students who were anticipating the very difficult test of intellectual ability were more likely than other participants to complete the fragments with race-related words (e.g. race, inferior). Steele and Aronson also found that black students actually performed worse on these tests than white students of equivalent scholastic aptitude.

Stereotype threat has been found in many different contexts (see Wright & Taylor, 2003): for example, women and mathematics, low socio-economic status and intelligence, the elderly and memory, women and negotiation skills, and black and white men and athletic performance. It has even been found among men who find themselves in female-dominated communal roles and are aware of the stereotype that men are poor communicators who find it difficult to express emotion and relate to others (Croft, Schmader, & Block, 2015). One intriguing study by Phillip Goff and his colleagues found that stereotype threat even caused people in inter-racial encounters to position themselves further apart from one another (Goff, Steele, & Davies, 2008; also see social distance in **Chapter 15, Table 15.3**). There is also evidence for the opposite of stereotype threat, called *stereotype lift*, among members of groups that attract favourable societal stereotypes (Walton & Cohen, 2003).

Research has identified ways to combat the negative impact of stereotype threat (Maass & Cadinu, 2003; Shapiro & Neuberg, 2007):

- know about stereotype threat (Schmader & Martens, 2005);
- reduce the degree to which one's identity is tied to a performance that may attract negative feedback (Major & Schmader, 1998);
- reduce the extent to which one's self-esteem is tied to such a performance (Pronin, Steele, & Ross, 2004);
- identify strongly with one's stigmatised group (e.g., Schmader, 2002);
- have extensive favourable intergroup contact with the anxiety-provoking outgroup (Crisp & Abrams, 2008).

Feeling powerful can also combat stereotype threat. Women performing a maths test who were primed to feel powerful experienced less stereotype threat and constraints on working memory and performed better on the test (Van Loo & Rydell, 2013).

Failure and disadvantage

Victims of prejudice belong to groups that have restricted access to many resources that society makes available for people to thrive and succeed, such as good education, health, housing and employment. Discrimination therefore creates visible evidence of real disadvantage and of manifest failure to achieve society's high standards. This sense of failure can be internalised by victims of prejudice so that they become chronically apathetic and un-motivated: they simply give up trying because of the obvious impossibility of succeeding.

There is some evidence that in certain circumstances, women tend to anticipate failure more than men and thus lose motivation (e.g. Smith, 1985). As we saw earlier, when they do succeed, they may attribute their success externally to factors such as luck or the ease of the task.

Later (in **Chapter 11**), we discuss deprivation and disadvantage more fully. One observation to make here is that although stigmatised groups are clearly disadvantaged, members of those groups often deny any personal experience of discrimination. For example, Faye Crosby and her colleagues found that employed women who were discriminated against with respect to pay rarely indicated that they had personally experienced any sex discrimination (Crosby, 1982). Further, the denial of personal discrimination was remarkably high (Crosby, 1984; Crosby, Cordova & Jaskar, 1993; Crosby, Pufall, Snyder, O'Connell, & Whalen, 1989) and has been found among members of other stigmatised groups (Guimond & Dubé-Simard, 1983; Major, 1994; Taylor, Wright, & Porter, 1994).

Attributional ambiguity

Attribution processes can impact stigmatised people in a rather unusual way, via attributional ambiguity. People who are stigmatised can be very sensitive to the causes of others' treatment of them (Crocker & Major, 1989). Did she fail to serve me at the bar because I am black, or simply because someone else shouted louder? Did she serve me ahead of all others because I am black and she is trying to conceal her racism? Was I promoted quickly to comply with an affirmative action policy or because of my intrinsic ability? Attributional ambiguity can quite obviously lead to suspicion and mistrust in social interactions.

Attributional ambiguity also does no favours to stigmatised individuals' self-esteem. Stigmatised people often fail to take personal credit for positive outcomes – they attribute them to affirmative action, tokenism or reverse discrimination. They may also under-attribute negative reactions from others to prejudice. For example, Karen Ruggiero and Don Taylor (1995) had women receive negative evaluations from a male evaluator. The likelihood that the evaluator was prejudiced was varied experimentally. The women attributed the negative evaluation to prejudice only when the evaluator was almost 100 per cent likely to be prejudiced. Otherwise, they attributed all of the more ambiguous evaluations to the inadequacy of their own work.

Self-fulfilling prophecies

Self-fulfilling prophecy
Expectations and assumptions about a person that influence our interaction with that person and eventually change their behaviour in line with our expectations.

Prejudiced attitudes lead to overt or covert discriminatory behaviour, and in time this can create disadvantage. In this way, a stereotypical belief can create a material reality that confirms the belief: it is a **self-fulfilling prophecy** (see reviews by Jussim, Eccles, & Madon, 1996; Jussim & Fleming, 1996). For example, Dov Eden (1990) primed platoon leaders in the Israeli Defence Force to have high expectations for the performance of members of their platoon. Behold – after an eleven-week training programme, platoons with high-expectation leaders outperformed platoons with 'no-expectation' leaders. Perhaps the most famous study of self-fulfilling prophecy was conducted by Rosenthal and Jacobson (1968) – see Box 10.4.

Another classic study of self-fulfilling prophecy was conducted by Carl Word and his colleagues. In a first experiment, white participants, acting as job interviewers, interviewed black and white applicants. They were found to treat the black and white applicants very differently – more speech errors (e.g. poor grammar, imprecision, disrupted fluency), shorter interviews and less non-verbal engagement with the blacks than with the whites. In a second experiment, another set of white participants was trained to use either the black or the white interview style obtained in the first experiment to interview a white job applicant. Interviewers who used the black interview style subsequently considered that the white applicant had performed less well and was more nervous than did those interviewers who used the white interview style (Word, Zanna, & Cooper, 1974).

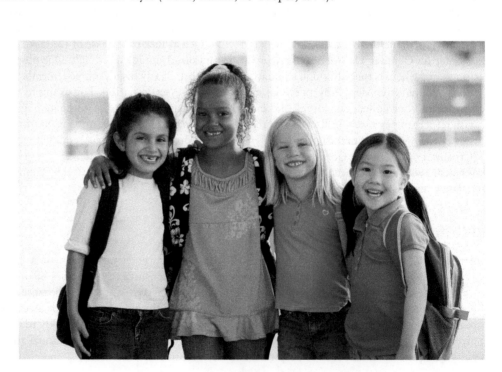

Self-fulfilling prophecy
These children differ in personality and race – factors that can create scholastic expectations that may become reality.

Box 10.4 Research classic
Pygmalion in the classroom

Dov Eden (1990) referred to the Pygmalion effect as 'a special case of the self-fulfilling prophecy'. *Pygmalion* is, of course, the name of a play by George Bernard Shaw, brought to the stage and screen in *My Fair Lady*, in which a simple Cockney girl is transformed into a society lady with an upper-class accent. Robert Rosenthal and Lenore Jacobson brought this myth to life in their famous work, *Pygmalion in the Classroom* (1968). Their book's cover said: 'Simply put, when teachers expect students to do well and show intellectual growth, they do; when teachers do not . . . [students] may in fact be discouraged in a number of ways.'

Rosenthal and Jacobson administered an IQ test to elementary schoolchildren and told their teachers that the results of the test would be a reliable predictor of which children would 'bloom' (show rapid intellectual development in the near future). The teachers were given the names of the twenty 'bloomers'; in fact, the twenty names were chosen randomly by the researchers, and there were no IQ differences between bloomers and non-bloomers. Very quickly, the teachers rated the non-bloomers as being less curious, less interested and less happy than the bloomers: that is, the teachers developed stereotypical expectations about the two groups. Grades for work were consistent with these expectations.

Rosenthal and Jacobson measured the children's IQ at the end of the first year and at the start and end of the second year. They found that in both years, the bloomers showed a significantly greater IQ gain than the non-bloomers (see Figure 10.9). Sceptics simply did not believe this, so Rosenthal and Rubin (1978) conducted a meta-analysis of 345 follow-up studies to prove that the phenomenon really exists. Rosenthal did not limit the positive potential of the effect to education. He saw how it could be applied in business and in medicine: the expectations of managers could have consequences for their employees, and those of clinicians for the mental and physical health of their patients.

Figure 10.9 IQ gain among elementary schoolchildren as a function of teachers' stereotypical expectations

Pygmalion in the classroom. Elementary schoolchildren showed IQ gains over their first and second years at school; however, the gains were much greater for the 'bloomers' – a randomly selected group that the teacher was led to believe had greater IQ potential.

Source: Based on data from Rosenthal and Jacobson (1968).

The process whereby beliefs create reality has been researched systematically by Mark Snyder and his colleagues (Snyder, 1981, 1984). One paradigm involves creating an expectation in the observer that someone they are going to meet ('the actor') has an extravert personality. The consequences for both the observer's and the actor's beliefs and behaviour are carefully tracked through the entire interaction process to an end point, where the actor's behaviour and self-perception conform to the initial expectation (see Figure 10.10).

Meta-analysis
Statistical procedure that combines data from different studies to measure the overall reliability and strength of specific effects.

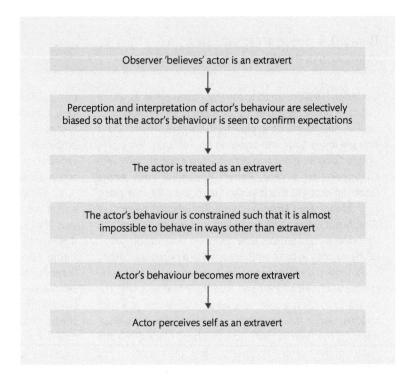

Figure 10.10 A sequence of steps through which beliefs may ultimately create reality

Source: Based on data in Snyder (1981, 1984).

There is good evidence for the creation of behavioural confirmation of stereotypical expectations based on gender, limited evidence in the case of race and ethnicity, and no evidence for socioeconomic status (Jussim & Fleming, 1996).

Social psychological research on self-fulfilling prophecy has focused almost exclusively on dyadic influence. Under these circumstances, expectations do create reality, but the overall effect is small: only about 4 per cent of someone's behaviour is affected by another's expectations. Lee Jussim and his colleagues concluded that, although 4 per cent may appear small, it is quite significant if you consider self-fulfilling prophecy effects in the real world of intergroup relations (Jussim, Eccles, & Madon, 1996; Jussim & Fleming, 1996). In natural dyadic interactions, people may be more inclined to perceive others in terms of personality rather than social stereotypes. In intergroup contexts, however, stereotypes and group perceptions come into play. The stereotypes match reality to some degree (stereotypes are not entirely arbitrary), and the actor encounters stereotypical expectations over and over again from many different outgroup members in a variety of social contexts. The 4 per cent will be greatly magnified.

Stereotype threat (Steele, Spencer, & Aronson, 2002; see the previous subsection, 'Stereotype threat') may also contribute to a self-fulfilling prophecy. Indeed, research into race-related academic underachievement in the United States invokes stereotype threat as a contributing factor. Black students are continually anxious about stereotypical interpretation of their academic failures. Cumulatively, this produces enormous anxiety and can encourage black students to reduce their efforts, to have lower academic ambitions and ultimately to drop out of school altogether. A similar stereotype threat analysis has been used in the United States for women's underachievement and underrepresentation in mathematics and science.

Dehumanisation, violence and genocide

Much of the emphasis of this chapter has been on indirect or subtle forms of prejudice and their effects. This reflects relatively accurately the state of affairs in most Western democracies, where anti-discrimination legislation is in place; and campaigns to purge language of racist and sexist terminology have been relatively effective.

However, we should not lose sight of the extremes of prejudice. Prejudiced attitudes tend to have common themes: the targets of prejudice are, for example, considered to be dirty, stupid, insensitive, repulsive, aggressive and psychologically unstable (Brigham, 1971; Katz & Braly, 1933). Such terms evaluate others as relatively worthless human beings who do not need or deserve to be treated with consideration, courtesy and respect. Together with fear and hatred, this is a potent mix. It dehumanises other people (Haslam, 2006), and given certain social circumstances, it can permit individual violence, mass aggression or systematic extermination.

Dehumanisation was first explored scientifically by Herbert Kelman (1976). It is a process through which people are denied membership in a community of interconnected individuals and are cast outside the 'moral circle', to a place where the rights and considerations attached to being human no longer apply (Opotow, 1990). Paradoxically, dehumanisation and its effects can be exacerbated when people feel socially connected – more precisely, being satisfactorily socially connected to some people (one's ingroup) can allow one to safely dehumanise outgroup members. Adam Waytz and Nicholas Epley (2012) report four experiments to support this: participants who were led to feel socially connected were less likely to attribute humanlike mental states to members of various social groups, particularly distant others compared to close others, and were also more likely to recommend harsh treatment for others who are dehumanised.

Dehumanisation denies people human uniqueness and human nature (Haslam, 2006; Haslam & Loughnan, 2014; Haslam, Loughnan, & Kashima, 2008; also see Bain, Vaes, & Leyens, 2014; Vaes, Leyens, Paladino, & Miranda, 2012). *Human uniqueness* refers to attributes that distinguish humans from other animals, such as refinement, civility, morality and higher cognition. When people are denied human uniqueness (a process of animalistic dehumanisation), they are likened to animals and seen as childlike, immature, coarse, irrational or backward. *Human nature* refers to attributes that are shared and fundamental features of humanity, such as emotionality, agency, warmth and cognitive flexibility. When people are denied human nature attributes (a process of mechanistic dehumanisation), they are explicitly or implicitly likened to objects or machines and seen as cold, rigid, inert and lacking emotion and agency.

Dehumanisation may have a unique brain activity signature that differentiates it from the normal perception of people as human beings. Lasana Harris and Susan Fiske (2009) characterise dehumanised perception as a response to people and groups that are considered low on both key traits of warmth and competence and thus elicit disgust, which is a key emotion in dehumanisation (Frank, Matsumoto, & Hwang, 2015). They review fMRI studies to conclude that dehumanised perception is associated with reduced activity in those parts of the brain, specifically the medial prefrontal cortex, associated with person perception, feelings of empathy, and theory of mind processes in which we infer people's motives and understand their thoughts and mental states.

Overall dehumanisation is associated with infra-humanisation (Vaes, Leyens, Paladino, & Miranda, 2012) – the internal attribution of sophisticated, uniquely human, secondary and higher emotions more to ingroup members than outgroup members, and thus a view of outgroups as less human and more infra-human (animal-like) than ingroups (e.g. Cortes, Demoulin, Rodriguez, Rodriguez, & Leyens, 2005; Leyens, Demoulin, Vaes, Gaunt, & Paladino, 2007; Leyens, Rodriguez-Perez, Rodriguez-Torres, Gaunt, Paladino, Vaes, et al., 2001). This attribution process is subject to **essentialism** – the attributed qualities are viewed as reflecting invariant, possibly innate, attributes of the group (Haslam, Rothschild, & Ernst, 1998; Medin & Ortony, 1989; see **Chapter 3**). For example, Nazi propaganda of the 1930s and 1940s portrayed Jews as rats, and during the Rwandan genocide of 1994, the Hutu portrayed the Tutsi they were exterminating as cockroaches.

Curiously, we can sometimes dehumanise ourselves (Bastian, Jetten, Chen, Radke, Harding, & Fasoli, 2013). This happens when we feel we have behaved in a way that we consider immoral because it has emotionally or physically hurt others – for example, when we

Essentialism
Pervasive tendency to consider behaviour to reflect underlying and immutable, often innate, properties of people or the groups they belong to.

have ostracised someone. By viewing ourselves in the context of this behavior as acting like a machine or animal, we effectively distance ourselves from the behavior and thus protect the integrity of our larger conception of self.

However, in the absence of explicit institutional or legislative support, dehumanisation usually sponsors individual acts of violence against an outgroup. For example, in several cities in Britain in 2011 there were attacks on Asian immigrants, in the United States the Ku Klux Klan was notorious for its lynchings of blacks (see the powerful 1988 movie *Mississippi Burning*), in Germany there have been Nazi-style attacks on Turkish immigrants, and in India female infanticide is still practised – albeit covertly (Freed & Freed, 1989). The Abu Ghraib prisoner abuse scandal which broke in 2004 is a good example of dehumanisation – some American guards at Abu Ghraib prison just outside Baghdad engaged in appalling acts of degradation of Iraqi prisoners of war, all caught on video.

When prejudice is morally accepted and legally endorsed in a society, then systematic acts of mass discrimination can occur. This can take the form of systems of apartheid, in which target groups are isolated from the rest of the community. South Africa from 1948 to 1994 is probably the best-known recent example of this, but a similar system of segregation was practised in educational contexts in the United States until the mid-1950s. The existence of reservations for native peoples in 'new world' countries, such as Australia and the United States, may also attest to a form of segregation. Apartheid and segregation often come equipped with a formidable array of social justifications in terms of benefits for the segregated group (see the third 'What do *you* think?' question).

The most extreme form of legitimised prejudice is genocide (Staub, 1989), where the target group is systematically exterminated. The dehumanisation process makes it relatively easy for people to perpetrate the most appalling acts of degradation and violence on others (see Thomas Keneally's biographical novel *Schindler's Ark* (1982), or the 1984 movie *The Killing Fields*). For example, Stalin targeted anyone he felt was plotting against him and, until his death in 1953, exiled 40 million people to brutal labour camps in Siberia (the Gulags); 15 million people died. The most chilling and best-documented instance of highly targeted genocide is the Holocaust of the early 1940s, in which 6 million Jews were systematically exterminated by the Nazis in death camps in central Europe. At the massive Auschwitz–Birkenau complex in Poland, 2 million Jews were gassed between January 1942 and the summer of 1944 (a rate of 2,220 men, women and children each day).

There are more recent examples of genocide: Pol Pot's 'killing fields' in Cambodia in the 1970s; Saddam Hussein's extermination of Kurds in northern Iraq and Shi'ites in southern Iraq; the Bosnian Serbs' 1992–5 campaign of 'ethnic cleansing' in Bosnia; the 100-day genocide of close to a million Tutsi by the Hutu in Rwanda in 1994; and the 2003–10 systematic slaughter of hundreds of thousands of non-Arabs in the western Sudanese region of Darfur.

Genocide can also be practised more indirectly, by creating conditions of massive material disadvantage where a group effectively exterminates itself through disease, and through suicide and murder based on alcoholism, drug abuse and acute despair. The plight of the Australian Aborigines, Canadian 'Eskimos' and Brazilian Indians falls squarely into this camp. Another form of genocide (although 'ethnic death' is a more appropriate term to distinguish it from the brutality of the Holocaust) is cultural assimilation, in which entire cultural groups may disappear as discrete entities through widespread intermarriage and systematic suppression of their culture and language (e.g. Taft, 1973; see **Chapter 15**). This may be particularly prevalent in societies that do not properly promote cultural pluralism (e.g. England's past treatment of the Welsh and the Scottish, China's treatment of Uyghurs and Tibetans and Japan's treatment of Filipinos living in Japan). Another form of ethnic death occurs when a group is excluded from the official history of a nation. The journalist John Pilger (1989) notes that this was the case for Australian Aborigines.

Explanations of prejudice and discrimination

Why are people prejudiced? Not surprisingly, theories of prejudice have focused on more extreme forms of prejudice, in particular the aggression and violence discussed earlier. At the beginning of the twentieth century, it was popular to consider prejudice to be an innate and instinctive reaction to certain categories of person (e.g. certain races), much as animals would react in instinctive ways to one another (Klineberg, 1940). This sort of approach is no longer popular, as it does not stand up well to scientific scrutiny.

However, there may be an innate *component* to prejudice. There is some evidence that higher animals, including humans, have an inherent fear of the unfamiliar and unusual (Hebb & Thompson, 1968), which might set the mould for negative attitudes towards groups that are considered different in certain ways. There is also evidence for a **mere exposure effect** (Zajonc, 1968) – people's attitudes towards various stimuli (e.g. other people) improve through repeated exposure or familiarity with the stimulus, provided that initial reactions to the stimuli are not negative (Perlman & Oskamp, 1971).

Mere exposure effect
Repeated exposure to an object results in greater attraction to that object.

Another perspective is that prejudices are learnt. Gordon Allport, and later Henri Tajfel (1981b) argued that hatred and suspicion of certain groups is learnt early in life, before the child even knows anything about the target group, and that this provides an emotional framework that colours all subsequent information about, and experience with, the group (see Brown, 1995; Durkin, 1995; Milner, 1996). For example, Martyn Barrett and Janis Short (1992) found that 5- to 10-year-old English children had little factual knowledge about other European countries, yet they expressed clear preferences; French and Spanish were liked most, followed by Italians, and Germans were liked least. Ethnic biases are very marked among 4- to 5-year-olds because at that age, the sociocognitive system is reliant on obvious perceptual features that are unambiguous bases for categorization and social comparison (Aboud, 1988). However, Adam Rutland (1999) found that national and ethnic stereotypes did not crystallise until a little later, after the age of 10. These emotional preferences provide a potent framework for acquisition of parental attitudes and behaviour (Goodman, 1964; Katz, 1976; see **Chapter 5**).

The transmission of parental prejudices can occur through parental modelling (e.g. the child witnesses parental expressions of racial hatred), instrumental/operant conditioning (e.g. parental approval for racist behaviour and disapproval for non-racist behaviour) and classical conditioning (e.g. a white child receives a severe parental scolding for playing with an Asian child).

In this section we discuss some major theories of prejudice – including a consideration of what role individual differences may play (Hodson & Dhont, 2015). These approaches focus largely on prejudice as the mass expression of aggression against certain groups. In Chapter 11, we continue with the theme of prejudice, but in a different guise – one that views prejudice as a form of intergroup behaviour associated with social categorization and identity processes.

Frustration–aggression

The rise of anti-Semitism in Europe, particularly Germany, during the 1930s placed the explanation of prejudice high on social psychology's agenda. In 1939, John Dollard and his colleagues published their **frustration–aggression hypothesis**, in which they argued that 'the occurrence of aggressive behaviour always presupposes the existence of frustration, and contrariwise, the existence of frustration always leads to some form of aggression' (Dollard, Doob, Miller, Mowrer, & Sears, 1939, p. 1). The theory was grounded in the psychodynamic assumption that a fixed amount of psychic energy is available for the human mind to perform psychological activities, and that the completion of a psychological activity is *cathartic*: that is, it dissipates aroused energy and returns the system to psychological equilibrium.

Frustration–aggression hypothesis
Theory that all frustration leads to aggression, and all aggression comes from frustration. Used to explain prejudice and intergroup aggression.

Dollard and colleagues argued that personal goals entail arousal of psychic energy for their achievement, and that goal achievement is cathartic. However, if goal achievement is impeded (i.e. frustrated), psychic energy remains activated, and the system remains in a state of psychological disequilibrium that can be corrected only by aggression. In other words, frustration produces an 'instigation to aggress', and the only way to achieve catharsis is through aggression.

The target of aggression is usually the perceived agent of frustration, but in many cases the agent of frustration is amorphous (e.g. a bureaucracy), indeterminate (the economy), too powerful (someone very big and strong wielding a weapon), unavailable (a specific individual bureaucrat) or someone you love (a parent). These, and other circumstances, prevent or inhibit aggression against the perceived source of frustration and cause the entire amount of frustration-induced aggression to be *displaced* on to an alternative target (a person or an inanimate object) that can be legitimately aggressed against without fear. In other words, a scapegoat is found.

Scapegoat
Individual or group that becomes the target for anger and frustration caused by a different individual or group or some other set of circumstances.

Although this theory has been applied extensively, and relatively successfully, to the study of interpersonal aggression (see **Chapter 12**), Dollard and colleagues' principal aim was to explain intergroup aggression – specifically, the violence and aggression associated with prejudice. If a large number of people (a group) is frustrated in its goals by another group that is too powerful or too remote to be aggressed against, the aggression is displaced on to a weaker group, which functions as a scapegoat. Figure 10.11 shows how the frustration–aggression hypothesis could be used to explain the rise of anti-Semitism in Germany in the 1920s and 1930s.

Figure 10.11 The frustration–aggression hypothesis account of the rise of anti-Semitism in Germany in the 1920s and 1930s

The sequence of principles in the frustration–aggression hypothesis is mirrored in the way events unfolded in Germany before and after the First World War, ultimately leading to state-sanctioned overt anti-Semitism.

Theoretical principles	Historical events
Personal goals	Political and economic hegemony of Germany (early twentieth century)
Psychic energy activated to achieve goals. State of psychological readiness	Each and every German in a state of arousal (First World War, 1914–18)
Frustration of goal achievement	Defeat by Western Allies, followed by punitive conditions of Treaty of Versailles (1919)
Frustration-induced undissipated arousal. Instigation to aggress. Source of frustration (allies) too powerful	Economic and political crisis (postwar to early 1920s)
Location of scapegoat, catharsis achieved by displacement of aggression	Anti-Semitism of 1920s and 1930s

An archival study by Carl Hovland and Robert Sears (1940) provides some support for this analysis. They correlated an economic index of frustrated ambitions (the price of cotton) with an index of racial aggression (number of lynchings of blacks) in the southern United States over a fifty-year period. The two indices were negatively correlated: as the price of cotton fell (frustration), the number of lynchings increased (displaced aggression).

Research on intergroup aggression has focused on **displacement**, which lies at the heart of Dollard and associates' account of scapegoating and thus prejudice and intergroup aggression. In one study (Miller & Bugelski, 1948), young men at a summer camp eagerly anticipated a night on the town but had their goals frustrated by the camp authorities, which announced that they would have to stay behind to perform some boring and difficult tests. Relative to a control group that was not frustrated in this way, the young men's stereotypical attitudes towards two minority groups deteriorated as a consequence of the frustration.

Other research is inconclusive (see Baumeister, Dale, & Sommer, 1998). For example, the frustration of doing badly on a test or experimental task has been shown to increase racial prejudice (Cowen, Landes, & Schaet, 1958), reduce prejudice (Burnstein & McRae, 1962) or leave prejudice unaffected (Stagner & Congdon, 1955), and there is no systematic evidence for an inverse correlation between international and intranational aggression (i.e. aggression displaced on to another nation is not available to be vented intranationally) (Tanter, 1966, 1969).

In some of this research, it is difficult to know whether aggression is displaced (i.e. the entire quantity of aggression is vented on a specific scapegoat) or generalised (i.e. anger towards the agent of frustration spills over on to irrelevant other stimuli). For example, in the Miller and Bugelski (1948) study, the participants also felt angry towards the camp authorities. If both displacement and generalisation are operating, it becomes difficult to predict the target of aggression.

To address this problem, Neal Miller (1948) suggested that displacement and generalisation might work against one another. Thus, scapegoats would not be too similar to the real source of frustration (displacement is based on inhibition of aggression against the real source of frustration, and such inhibition will be stronger for targets that are more similar to the real source), but not too dissimilar, either (generalisation implies that aggression will decrease as the potential target is less and less similar to the real source). Although it is often possible with the advantage of hindsight to use this principle to account for the scapegoat, it is difficult to predict it with any certainty (e.g. Horowitz, 1973).

The frustration–aggression hypothesis confronts another, major, obstacle from research showing that frustration is neither necessary nor sufficient for aggression. Aggression can occur in the absence of frustration, and frustration does not necessarily result in aggression (Bandura, 1973; Berkowitz, 1962). The consequence is that the frustration–aggression hypothesis can explain only a limited subset of intergroup aggression. Other constructs are needed to explain either other forms of intergroup aggression or prejudice and intergroup aggression as a whole.

In an attempt to rescue the hypothesis, Leonard Berkowitz (1962) proposed three changes:

1 The probability of frustration-induced aggression actually being vented is increased by the presence of situational cues to aggression, including past or present associations of a specific group (scapegoat) with conflict or dislike.

2 It is not objective frustration that instigates aggression but the subjective (cognitive) feeling of being frustrated.

3 Frustration is only one of a large number of aversive events (e.g. pain, extreme temperatures and other noxious stimuli) that can instigate aggression.

This revamped frustration–aggression theory has support for the role of environmental cues and cognitive mediators in controlling the amount and direction of aggression (Berkowitz, 1974; Konečni, 1979). Miller and his colleagues concluded that eight decades of research on the frustration–aggression link show that frustration: (a) can but need not lead to aggression, (b) that the powerful can show frustration-induced aggression in an overt way

Displacement
Psychodynamic concept referring to the transfer of negative feelings on to an individual or group other than that which originally caused the negative feelings.

but the powerless can also show aggression more indirectly, (c) that a series of minor frustrations can build up to increase the probability of aggression (Miller, Pederson, Earlywine, & Pollock, 2003). However, the main application of the revamped frustration–aggression theory has been in the explanation of **collective behaviour** (riots) and **relative deprivation** (both discussed in **Chapter 11**).

Despite these modifications, the frustration–aggression hypothesis has other limitations as an explanation of mass intergroup aggression and prejudice. The phenomenon to be explained involves the attitudes and behaviour of a large number of people being regulated and directed so that there is a substantial uniformity as well as a clear logic to it. Critics have argued that the frustration–aggression hypothesis does not adequately explain this core feature of prejudice, and that the reason for this is that it is a reductionist approach that arrives at group behaviour by aggregating individual psychological/emotional states in a communication vacuum (Billig, 1976; Brown, 2000; Hogg & Abrams, 1988).

For instance, the group members in this model do not speak to one another and are not exposed to mass communication or history. They are passive victims of individual frustration and anger, rather than active participants in a social process involving construction, internalisation and the enacting of group norms (see **Chapter 7**). Aggression is only widespread and directed at the same target because a large number of people individually express aggression simultaneously, and coincidentally select the same target.

The authoritarian personality

In their work *The Authoritarian Personality* published in 1950, Theodor Adorno and Else Frenkel-Brunswik (along with Levinson and Sanford) described a personality syndrome they believed predisposed certain people to be authoritarian. The historical context for the

Collective behaviour
The behaviour of people en masse – such as in a crowd, protest or riot.

Relative deprivation
A sense of having less than we feel entitled to.

Power and authority
Respect for authority figures, deference to authority, and obsession with rank and status.

authoritarian personality theory was the role of fascism, an extreme form of right-wing ideology, in the Holocaust – Adorno and Frenkel-Brunswik, who were both Jewish, had fled Hitler's regime in Germany and Austria respectively.

The theory proposed that autocratic and punitive child-rearing practices were responsible for the emergence in adulthood of various clusters of beliefs. These included: ethnocentrism; an intolerance of Jews, African Americans and other ethnic and religious minorities; a pessimistic and cynical view of human nature; conservative political and economic attitudes; and a suspicion of democracy. (Apply these ideas to the case of Armand in the fourth 'What do *you* think?' question.) Associated with the theory was a now-legendary scale known as the California F-scale – originally intended to measure tendencies towards fascism, it was treated as a more general measure of authoritarianism.

The results of early research were encouraging, although Roger Brown (1965) raised several methodological criticisms. Among the most damning were the following:

- The various scales used were scored in such a way that people's tendency to agree with items (acquiescent response set) would artificially inflate the correlation between the scales.

- Because the interviewers knew both the hypotheses and the authoritarianism scores of the interviewees, there was a danger of confirmatory bias (Rosenthal, 1966).

The authoritarian personality has, over almost seventy years, attracted an enormous amount of interest (e.g. Bray & Noble, 1978; Christie & Jahoda, 1954; Titus & Hollander, 1957; for an overview, see Duckitt, 2000). However, there are some limitations to a personality explanation of prejudice (Billig, 1976; Brown, 1995, 2000; Hogg & Abrams, 1988; Reynolds, Turner, Haslam, & Ryan, 2001). Powerful situational and sociocultural factors are underemphasised.

Tom Pettigrew (1958) tested the authoritarian personality theory in a cross-cultural comparison between South Africa and the southern and northern United States. He found that although whites from South Africa and the southern United States were significantly more racist than those from the northern United States, they did not differ in how authoritarian their personalities were. Pettigrew concluded from this and other findings that, while personality may predispose some people to be prejudiced in some contexts, a culture of prejudice that embodies societal norms legitimising prejudice is both necessary and sufficient.

This conclusion is supported by other findings. For example, Ralph Minard (1952) found that the majority (60 per cent) of white miners in a West Virginia coal-mining community readily shifted from racist to non-racist attitudes and behaviour in response to situational norms encouraging or inhibiting prejudice, and Walter Stephan and David Rosenfield (1978) found that inter-racial contact was a more important determinant of change in racial attitudes among children than parental background.

Adorno's team believed that prejudice is developed in childhood as an enduring personality style. This perspective is particularly troublesome in the light of evidence for sudden and dramatic changes in people's attitudes and behaviour regarding social groups. For example, the extreme anti-Semitism in Germany between the wars arose in a short period of only ten years – far too short a time for a whole generation of German families to adopt new child-rearing practices giving rise to authoritarian and prejudiced children.

Even more dramatic are sudden changes in attitudes and behaviour in response to single events. There are many examples: the Japanese bombing of Pearl Harbor in 1941, the Argentinian occupation of the Falkland Islands in 1982, and of course the 9/11 terrorist attacks in New York and Washington in 2001. Personalities did not have time to change, yet attitudes and behaviour did.

In reality, prejudice is like most other forms of human behaviour – an interaction between large-scale social forces, evolution-based behavioural and cognitive parameters, and individual human beings' unique biographies of experiences and relationships (Snyder & Cantor, 1998). Against the background of large scale societal, intergroup and social identity

Authoritarian personality
Personality syndrome originating in childhood that predisposes individuals to be prejudiced.

Ethnocentrism
Evaluative preference for all aspects of our own group relative to other groups.

Acquiescent response set
Tendency to agree with items in an attitude questionnaire. This leads to an ambiguity in interpretation if a high score on an attitude questionnaire can be obtained only by agreeing with all or most items.

determinants of prejudice, there will be individual differences in if, when and how prejudice is experienced and expressed, and these differences will largely rest on people's past and current unique experiences in life (Hodson & Dhont, 2015).

Dogmatism and closed-mindedness

Dogmatism
Cognitive style that is rigid and intolerant and predisposes people to be prejudiced.

Milton Rokeach (1948, 1960) proposed another approach to prejudice that is closely related to the authoritarian personality theory. Since authoritarianism is not restricted to people who are politically and economically right wing (e.g. Tetlock, 1984), Rokeach focused on cognitive style, specifically a generalised syndrome of intolerance called **dogmatism** or closed-mindedness (Box 10.5). Dogmatism is characterised by isolation of contradictory belief systems from one another, resistance to belief change in the light of new information and appeals to authority to justify the correctness of existing beliefs. Scales devised by Rokeach (1960) to measure these personality styles have good reliability, correlate well with measures of authoritarianism and have been used extensively.

However, dogmatism as an explanation of prejudice has the same limitations as the authoritarian personality theory. This concept reduces a group phenomenon to an aggregation of individual personality predispositions and largely overlooks the wider sociocultural context of prejudice and the role of group norms (Billig, 1976; Billig & Cochrane, 1979).

Right-wing authoritarianism

Recently, the idea of authoritarianism has been revived but without the psychodynamic and personality aspects. Bob Altemeyer (1981, 1988, 1994, 1998; see also Duckitt, 1989; Duckitt, Wagner, du Plessis, & Birum, 2002) approached authoritarianism as a collection of attitudes, with three components:

1 *conventionalism* – adherence to societal conventions that are endorsed by established authorities;

2 *authoritarian aggression* – support for aggression towards social deviants; and

3 *authoritarian submission* – submission to society's established authorities.

A Right-Wing Authoritarianism (RWA) scale was developed to measure this constellation of attitudinal factors. From this perspective, authoritarianism is an ideology that

---

Box 10.5 Your life
Close encounters with dogmatic and closed-minded authoritarians

We all run into people from time to time who we feel are dogmatic and closed-minded, and possibly authoritarian. In your experience, are they also reliably prejudiced? What about how stable these attributes are across different situations – is someone who is authoritarian in one situation (e.g. work) authoritarian in another (e.g. family)? For example – if a team leader in stressful circumstances, such as military conflict or an emergency on the flight deck of an aircraft, is autocratic, can you also assume they are also bigots? What about the police? It is fashionable to assume that because police are trained to give orders and thus appear autocratic, they are also racists. Is this assumption justified? Also, is it plausible to assume that because someone sticks to their guns and appears dogmatic, they are prejudiced as well? For example, climate change scientists do this, but are rarely prejudiced; whereas climate change deniers, who are also dogmatic, tend to be socially conservative and, some research suggests, more inclined towards prejudice (e.g. Unsworth & Fielding, 2014). What do you think? In this chapter we discuss the relationship between on the one hand authoritarianism, dogmatism and closed-mindedness, and on the other prejudice.

varies from person to person. It suggests that positions of power within a social hierarchy come from correct and moral behaviour (i.e. following social conventions). Questioning authority and tradition is a transgression that invites the wrath of legitimate authorities. Authoritarianism thus legitimises and maintains the status quo. One question that has been raised about RWA is whether it may be less tied to individual differences and more affected by context – the same person may vary in his or her RWA in different contexts (e.g. Stenner, 2009).

Social dominance theory

The role of ideology in prejudice is also central to work by Jim Sidanius and Felicia Pratto, who describe a sophisticated, but nonetheless mainly 'individual differences', analysis of exploitative power-based intergroup relations – called **social dominance theory** (e.g. Pratto, 1999; Pratto, Sidanius, Stallworth, & Malle, 1994; Sidanius & Pratto, 1999).

Social dominance theory explains the extent to which people accept or reject societal ideologies or myths that legitimise hierarchy and discrimination or that legitimise equality and fairness. People who desire their own group to be dominant and superior to outgroups have a high social dominance orientation, which encourages them to reject egalitarian ideologies and to accept myths that legitimise hierarchy and discrimination. These kinds of people are more inclined to be prejudiced than people with a low social dominance orientation.

Social dominance theory originally focused on the desire for ingroup domination over outgroups. The effect can sometimes be paradoxical. For example, high social dominance orientation members of dominant groups can support affirmative action, which would at first sight seem to erode hierarchy, in order to strategically appease subordinate groups and ultimately protect and enhance the hierarchy (Chow, Lowery, & Hogan, 2013). Some research has also suggested that social dominance orientation may have a wider impact. Milfont and colleagues report four studies showing that people with a high social dominance orientation have low environmental concern and are more willing to dominate and exploit the natural environment, and this is independent of other correlates such as authoritarianism and political ideology (Milfont, Richter, Sibley, & Fischer, 2013).

Social dominance theory has developed to describe a more general desire for unequal relations between groups, irrespective of whether one's own group is at the top or the bottom of the status hierarchy (e.g. Sidanius, Levin, Federico, & Pratto, 2001; Duckitt, 2006). This development makes social dominance theory look more like **system justification theory** (e.g. Jost & Hunyadi, 2002; Jost & Van der Toorn, 2012; see **Chapter 11** for details). System justification theory argues that certain social conditions cause people to resist social change and instead justify and protect the existing social system, even if it maintains one's own group's position of disadvantage.

Social dominance theory has been criticised on the grounds that social dominance orientation is actually highly responsive to situational and more enduring features of the intergroup context (e.g. Turner & Reynolds, 2003). In support of this view, Schmitt, Branscombe and Kappen (2003) report five studies showing that attitudes towards inequality are dependent on where one's group falls in the hierarchy and how salient one's group is relative to other groups. It is a person's group identity that primarily drives their orientation towards inequality, and their social dominance orientation plays a secondary role. Wilson and Liu (2003) take issue with social dominance theory's evolution-based view that men endorse hierarchy more than women. They report evidence that the link between gender and social dominance orientation virtually disappears when strength of gender identification is factored in. Women who identified highly with their gender had a higher social dominance orientation than men.

Social dominance theory
Theory that attributes prejudice to an individual's acceptance of an ideology that legitimises ingroup-serving hierarchy and domination, and rejects egalitarian ideologies.

System justification theory
Theory that attributes social stasis to people's adherence to an ideology that justifies and protects the status quo.

Belief congruence

Belief congruence theory
The theory that similar beliefs promote liking and social harmony among people while dissimilar beliefs produce dislike and prejudice.

At the same time as he developed his personality theory of prejudice (see above), Rokeach (1960) proposed a separate **belief congruence theory**. Belief systems are important anchoring points for individuals, and interindividual similarity or congruence of belief systems confirms the validity of our own beliefs. Congruence is therefore rewarding and produces attraction and positive attitudes (Byrne, 1971; Festinger, 1954). The converse is that incongruence produces negative attitudes. For Rokeach (1960), 'belief is more important than ethnic or racial membership as a determinant of social discrimination' (p. 135) – prejudice is not an attitude based on group memberships but an individual's reaction to a perceived lack of belief congruence.

Research has used a paradigm where participants report their attitudes towards others (presented photographically or as verbal descriptions) who are either of the same or a different race, and have either similar or different beliefs to the participant. The findings show that belief does seem to be a more important determinant of attitude than race (e.g. Byrne & Wong, 1962; Hendrick, Bixenstine, & Hawkins, 1971; Rokeach & Mezei, 1966). However, when it comes to more intimate behaviour such as friendship, race is more important than belief (e.g. Insko, Nacoste, & Moe, 1983; Triandis & Davis, 1965).

There are at least two problems with belief congruence as an explanation of prejudice. The first is that Rokeach (1960) hedges his theory with an important qualification. Under circumstances where prejudice is institutionalised or socially sanctioned, belief congruence plays no part – prejudice is a matter of ethnic group membership (see Figure 10.12). This is a restrictive exemption clause that excludes what we would consider to be the most obvious and distressing manifestations of prejudice: for example, ethnic prejudice in Rwanda and religious prejudice in Northern Ireland would be excluded.

A second problem arises with the relatively small amount of prejudice that Rokeach has left himself to explain. His explanation of how belief congruence may influence prejudice in these circumstances may actually be an explanation of how belief similarity produces interpersonal attraction (Brown, 2000; Brown & Turner, 1981). The research paradigm used to test belief congruence theory has people rate their attitude towards a number of stimulus individuals presented one after the other (a repeated measures design). Some

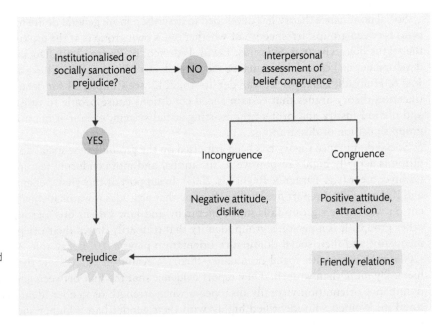

Figure 10.12 Belief congruence theory

In the absence of socially sanctioned prejudice, prejudice is a matter of interpersonal assessment of belief congruence.

Source: Based on Rokeach (1960).

Belief congruence
Similar clothes, similar beliefs and similar behaviour make a potent recipe for liking and social harmony.

stimuli are of the same race and others of a different race (the race variable), and they all have different beliefs from one another (the belief variable). The absence of clear belief homogeneity within each group and belief discontinuity between groups may muddy intergroup boundaries and focus attention on differences between stimulus individuals rather than on their racial or ethnic group memberships. The research paradigm may inadvertently have diminished the contextual salience of race or ethnicity, such that participants react to the stimulus individuals as individuals, not as members of racial or ethnic groups.

This interpretation has some support from experiments where group membership is clearly differentiated from belief similarity. For example, in one of Tajfel's studies, children gave rewards to anonymous other children, who either were defined as having similar attitudes to them (on the basis of a picture-preference task) or for whom no information on similarity was provided. The children were either explicitly categorized as being members of the same group (simply labelled X group) or were not categorized (Billig & Tajfel, 1973). This research adopted the **minimal group paradigm**, which is described in **Chapter 11**. The focal outcome measure was **discrimination** in favour of some target children over others.

Figure 10.13 shows that, although belief similarity increased favouritism (as would be predicted from belief congruence theory), the effect of categorization on favouritism was much stronger, and it was only in the two categorization conditions that the amount of discrimination was statistically significant (i.e. discrimination scores were significantly greater than zero). Belief congruence theory would not predict these last two effects; similar findings emerged from an experiment by Vernon Allen and David Wilder (1975). Perhaps most conclusively, Michael Diehl (1988) found that, although attitudinally similar individuals were liked more than dissimilar individuals (although there was little difference in discrimination), attitudinally similar outgroups were liked less than (and discriminated against more than) dissimilar outgroups.

Minimal group paradigm
Experimental methodology to investigate the effect of social categorization alone on behaviour.

Discrimination
The behavioural expression of prejudice.

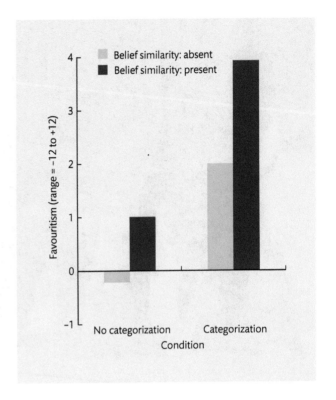

Figure 10.13 Favouritism as a function of belief similarity and common group membership

Although participants in a minimal group study favoured similar others over those for whom no similarity information was provided, there was much stronger favouritism for others who were simply explicitly categorized as being ingroup members: in fact, statistically significant favouritism was expressed only towards ingroup members.

Source: Based on data from Billig and Tajfel (1973).

Other explanations

There are two other major perspectives on the explanation of prejudice. The first concerns how people construct and use stereotypes. This is dealt with mainly in **Chapter 2** as part of our discussion of social cognition and social thinking, but it also surfaces in **Chapter 11**. The second approaches prejudice and discrimination as an aspect of intergroup behaviour as a whole. This is dealt with in **Chapter 11**.

Because it can be treated as an extension and continuation of this chapter, we have reserved our discussion of prejudice reduction for the end of **Chapter 11**. The main practical reason for studying the social psychology of prejudice is to gain sufficient understanding of the phenomenon to try to reduce its incidence and to alleviate conflict. Arguments about ways in which prejudice may be reduced rest on the particular perspectives on, and theories of, prejudice to which one subscribes. The intergroup perspectives and theories (dealt with in **Chapter 11**) suggest strategies that are different from those suggested by the person-centred explanations in this chapter.

Summary

- Prejudice can be considered to be an attitude about a social group, which may or may not be expressed in behaviour as overt discrimination.

- The most pervasive prejudices are based on sex, race, ethnicity, age, sexual orientation and physical and mental handicap. In most Western nations, legislation and social attitudes have significantly reduced these prejudices in recent years (with the exception perhaps of the last two), but there is still a long way to go.

- Legislation and social disapproval have inhibited more extreme expressions of prejudice. Prejudice is more difficult to detect when it is expressed covertly or in restricted contexts, and it may go almost unnoticed as it is embedded in ordinary everyday assumptions, language and discourse.

- The victims of prejudice can suffer material and psychological disadvantage, low self-esteem, stigma, depressed aspirations and physical and verbal abuse. In its most extreme form, prejudice can express itself as dehumanisation and genocide.

- Prejudice may be a relatively ordinary reaction to frustrated goals, in which people vent their aggression on weaker groups, which serve as scapegoats for the original source of frustration. By no means can all prejudices be explained in this way.

- Prejudice may be abnormal behaviour expressed by people who have developed generally prejudiced personalities, perhaps as a consequence of being raised in harsh and restrictive families. This may explain why some individuals are prejudiced, but the presence of a social environment that encourages prejudice seems to be a stronger and more diagnostic determinant.

- These sorts of explanation of prejudice do not deal well with the widespread collective nature of the phenomenon. They overlook the fact that people communicate with one another and are influenced by propaganda and mass communication.

Key terms

Acquiescent response set
Ageism
Attribution
Authoritarian personality
Belief congruence theory
Collective behaviour
Dehumanisation
Discrimination
Displacement
Dogmatism
Essentialism
Ethnocentrism
Face-ism

Frustration–aggression hypothesis
Gender
Genocide
Glass ceiling
Glass cliff
Implicit association test
Mere exposure effect
Meta-analysis
Minimal group paradigm
Prejudice
Racism
Relative deprivation
Reverse discrimination

Role congruity theory
Scapegoat
Self-esteem
Self-fulfilling prophecy
Sex role
Sexism
Social dominance theory
Stereotype
Stereotype threat
Stigma
System justification theory
Three-component attitude model
Tokenism

Literature, film and TV

Hotel Rwanda

A chilling 2004 biographical and historical drama directed by Terry George, starring Don Cheadle and also with Nick Nolte. Set against the backdrop of the Rwandan genocide – a period of 100 days in 1994 when Hutus massacred between 500,000 and 1 million Tutsis – Paul Rusesabagina (Cheadle), a Hutu hotel manager, tries to shelter Tutsi refugees in his Belgian-owned luxury hotel in Kigali. This film is also relevant to the discussion of pro-social and altruistic behaviour (**see Chapter 14**).

The Help

A 2011 film directed by Tate Taylor and starring Emma Stone, Viola Davis and Octavia Spencer. Set in Jackson, Mississippi, in the early 1960s, the film is a powerful portrayal of race relations played out in the intimate context of white Southern women and their black servants and nannies (the 'help'). Stone plays a local journalist (Eugenia 'Skeeter' Phelan) with modern progressive attitudes that reflect the civil rights movement of the time. She interviews 'the help' to write a book telling their stories about being black in the Deep South – complex stories that interweave feelings of stigma, disadvantage and dehumanisation with closeness to the white families they have often lived with for decades, and love for the white children they look after.

Conspiracy

A 2001 film with Kenneth Branagh and Colin Firth. A chilling dramatisation of the top-secret two-hour Nazi meeting in which fifteen men debated and ultimately agreed upon Hitler's 'Final Solution', the extermination of the entire Jewish population of Europe. Based on the lone surviving transcript of the meeting's minutes and shot in real time, the film recreates one of the most infamous gatherings in world history. This is relevant not only to topics of dehumanisation and genocide but also group decision-making in general.

The Boy in the Striped Pyjamas

A 2006 John Boyne novel that was made into a 2008 film by Mark Herman. A young boy, Bruno, befriends another boy, Shmuel, who wears strange striped pyjamas and lives behind an electrified fence. Bruno discovers that he is not permitted to be friends with Shmuel. Bruno is German and his father runs a World War II prison camp for Jews awaiting extermination; and Shmuel, who is Jewish, is awaiting extermination. A very powerful film that engages with issues of intergroup contact and friendship across group boundaries.

Guided questions

1 Which groups are the most common targets of prejudice? Give an account of why any one group has traditionally been such a target.

2 Blatant racism may be publicly censured yet still lurk in the background. How might you detect it?

3 What does the frustration–aggression hypothesis really tell us about prejudice?

4 What is the background to the study of the *authoritarian personality*?

5 Is it possible for a teacher's expectations of a pupil's educational capacity – for better or for worse – to influence the intellectual development of that pupil?

Learn more

Brewer, M. B. (2003). *Intergroup relations* (2nd ed.). Philadelphia, PA: Open University Press. A readable overview of research on intergroup relations, which includes coverage of issues directly relating to prejudice.

Brewer, M. B. (2007). The social psychology of intergroup relations: Social categorization, ingroup bias, and outgroup prejudice. In A. W. Kruglanski, & E. T. Higgins (Eds.), *Social psychology: Handbook of basic principles* (2nd ed., pp. 785–804). New York: Guilford Press. Comprehensive coverage of research on prejudice, discrimination and intergroup behaviour.

Brown, R. J. (1995). *Prejudice: Its social psychology*. Oxford, UK: Blackwell. Styled as the sequel to Allport's classic 1954 book, *The Nature of Prejudice*, this is an accessible, detailed and comprehensive coverage of what social psychology has learnt about prejudice.

Crocker, J., Major, B., & Steele, C. (1998). Social stigma. In D. T. Gilbert, S. T. Fiske, & G. Lindzey (Eds.), *The handbook of social psychology* (4th ed., Vol. 2, pp. 504–553). New York: McGraw-Hill. A thorough overview of research on the experience of being the target of prejudice and a member of a stigmatised group.

Dovidio, J. F., & Gaertner, S. L. (2010). Intergroup bias. In S. T. Fiske, D. T. Gilbert, & G. Lindzey (Eds.), *Handbook of social psychology* (5th ed., Vol. 2, pp. 1084–121). New York: Wiley. Up-to-date and detailed coverage of research on intergroup discrimination.

Dovidio, J., Glick. P., Hewstone, M., & Esses, V. (Eds.) (2010). *Handbook of prejudice, stereotyping and discrimination*. London: SAGE. A collection of chapters by leading researchers on stereotyping, prejudice and intergroup behaviour.

Dovidio, J. F., Glick, P. G., & Rudman, L. (Eds.) (2005). *On the nature of prejudice: Fifty years after Allport*. Malden, MA: Blackwell. Collection of chapters on prejudice by leading scholars to mark the 50th anniversary of Allport's classic, *The Nature of Prejudice*.

Duckitt, J. (1992). *The social psychology of prejudice*. New York: Praeger. A comprehensive review of the literature on the nature and causes of prejudice and ethnocentrism.

Jones, J. M. (1996). *The psychology of racism and prejudice*. New York: McGraw-Hill. An authoritative discussion of the causes and consequences of stereotyping and prejudice.

Levine, J. M., & Hogg, M. A. (Eds.) (2010). *Encyclopedia of group processes and intergroup relations*. Thousand Oaks, CA: SAGE. A comprehensive and readable compendium of entries on all aspects of the social psychology of groups, including intergroup relations and prejudice, written by all the leading scholars in the field.

Stangor, C. (Ed.) (2000). *Stereotypes and prejudice: Essential readings*. Philadelphia, PA: Psychology Press. Annotated collection of key publications on stereotyping and prejudice. There is an introductory overview chapter and commentary chapters introducing each reading.

Wright, S. C., & Taylor, D. M. (2007). The social psychology of cultural diversity: Social stereotyping, prejudice, and discrimination. In M. A. Hogg, & J. Cooper (Eds.), *The SAGE handbook of social psychology: Concise student edition* (pp. 361–387). London: SAGE. A comprehensive overview of research on prejudice and discrimination, which deals with stereotyping and also tackles issues to do with social diversity.

Yzerbyt, V., & Demoulin, S. (2010). Intergroup relations. In S. T. Fiske, D. T. Gilbert, & G. Lindzey (Eds.), *Handbook of social psychology* (5th ed., Vol. 2, pp. 1024–1083). New York: Wiley. A thorough overview of the field of intergroup relations, which includes discussion of prejudice and discrimination. This most recent edition of the classic handbook is a primary source for theory and research.

Chapter 11
Intergroup behaviour

Chapter contents

What do *you* think?

1   Richard, an old-fashioned conservative, agrees with the newspaper editorial: 'Nurses should stop complaining about their pay. After all, the hospital orderlies, with even lower pay, keep their mouths shut and just get on with their job.' What can you say?

2   Jean and Alison are close school friends. When they go to university, they are assigned to different halls of residence that are right next door to one another but that have very different cultures and are in fierce competition with each other. What will happen to their friendship?

3   'There is no other way. The rainforest has to go. We need the timber now – and if we don't take it, they will.' The news bulletin gets you thinking about the way people abuse scarce resources. Is there a way forward?

4   Have you watched a crowd demonstrating in a TV news item and wondered how it actually started? Is it possible that a fundamental aspect of their belief system has somehow been transformed?

5   When football supporters get together in a crowd, they seem to regress into some sort of super-beast – emotional, fickle, antisocial and dangerous. You've probably heard this kind of description before, but is it psychologically accurate?

What is intergroup behaviour?

Conflicts between nations, political confrontations, revolutions, inter-ethnic relations, nego-tiations between corporations, and competitive team sports are all examples of **intergroup behaviour**. An initial definition of intergroup behaviour might therefore be 'any behaviour that involves interaction between one or more representatives of two or more separate social groups'. This definition fairly accurately characterises much of the intergroup behaviour that social psychologists study; however, by focusing on face-to-face *interaction*, it might be a little restrictive.

A broader, and more accurate, definition would be that any perception, cognition or behaviour that is influenced by people's recognition that they and others are members of distinct social groups is intergroup behaviour. This definition has an interesting implication: it acknowledges that the real or perceived relations between social groups (e.g. between eth-nic groups, between nations) can have far-reaching and pervasive effects on the behaviour of members of those groups – effects that go well beyond situations of face-to-face encounters. This type of definition stems from a particular perspective in social psychology: an inter-group perspective which views much social behaviour as being influenced by the social cate-gories to which we belong, and the power and status relations between those categories. A broad perspective such as this on the appropriate type of theory to develop is called a **metatheory** (see **Chapter 1**).

In many ways, this chapter on intergroup behaviour brings together under one umbrella the preceding discussions of social influence (**Chapter 7**), group processes (**Chapters 8 and 9**), and prejudice and discrimination (**Chapter 10**). Social influence and group processes are gen-erally treated as occurring within groups, but wherever there is a group to which people belong (i.e. an ingroup), there are other groups to which those people do not belong (out-groups). There is almost always an intergroup, or ingroup–outgroup, context for whatever happens in groups. It is unlikely that processes in groups will be unaffected by relations between groups. As we saw earlier (**Chapter 10**), prejudice and discrimination are forms of intergroup behaviour (e.g. between different races, between different age groups, between the sexes). One of the recurring themes of this discussion (see **Chapter 10**) is that personality or interpersonal explanations of prejudice and discrimination (e.g. authoritarian personality, dogmatism, frustration–aggression) may have limitations because they do not adequately consider the intergroup aspect of the phenomena.

The study of intergroup behaviour confronts important questions about the difference between individuals (and interpersonal behaviour) and groups (and intergroup behaviour), and how harmonious intergroup relations can be transformed into conflict, and vice versa. Social psychological theories of intergroup behaviour ought therefore to have direct rele-vance to applied contexts: for example, in the explanation of intergroup relations in employ-ment contexts (Hartley & Stephenson, 1992).

Intergroup behaviour
Behaviour among individuals that is regulated by those individuals' awareness of and identification with different social groups.

Metatheory
Set of interrelated concepts and principles concerning which theories or types of theory are appropriate.

Relative deprivation and social unrest

Our earlier discussion (in **Chapter 10**) of the frustration–aggression hypothesis (Dollard, Doob, Miller, Mowrer, & Sears, 1939) as an explanation of intergroup prejudice, discrimi-nation and aggression concluded with Leonard Berkowitz's (1962) modification of the origi-nal theory. Berkowitz argued that subjective (not objective) frustration is one of an array of aversive events (e.g. heat, cold) that produce an instigation to aggress, and that the actual expression of aggression is strengthened by aggressive associations (e.g. situational cues, past associations).

Berkowitz (1972a) used this analysis to explain collective intergroup aggression – specifically riots. At the time, the United States had recently experienced a number of riots that had

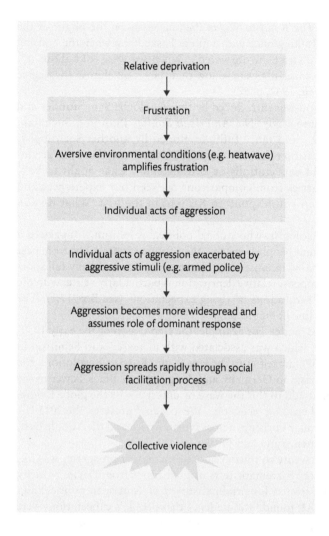

Figure 11.1 A 'long, hot summer' explanation of collective violence

Frustration caused by relative deprivation is expressed as individual aggression due to the presence of aversive and aggressive environmental stimuli, and this becomes collective aggression through a process of social facilitation.

Source: Based on Berkowitz (1972a).

occurred during long periods of hot weather: for example, the Watts riots in Los Angeles in August 1965 and the Detroit riots in August 1967 (see Figure 11.1). Heat can be an 'aversive event' that facilitates individual and collective aggression (e.g. Anderson & Anderson, 1984; Baron & Ransberger, 1978; Carlsmith & Anderson, 1979; see also **Chapter 12**).

Berkowitz argued that under conditions of perceived relative deprivation (e.g. blacks in the United States in the late 1960s), people feel frustrated. The heat of a long, hot summer amplifies the frustration (especially in poor, overcrowded urban neighbourhoods with little air conditioning or cooling vegetation) and increases the prevalence of individual acts of aggression, which are in turn exacerbated by the presence of aggressive stimuli (e.g. armed police). Individual aggression becomes widespread and is transformed into true collective violence by a process of social facilitation (Zajonc, 1965; see **Chapter 8**), whereby the physical presence of other people facilitates dominant behaviour patterns (in this case, aggression).

Relative deprivation

An important precondition for intergroup aggression is **relative deprivation** (Walker & Smith, 2002). Deprivation is not an absolute condition. It is always relative to other conditions: one person's new-found prosperity may be someone else's terrible deprivation. George

Relative deprivation
A sense of having less than we feel entitled to.

Orwell captures this beautifully in *The Road to Wigan Pier*, his essay on the plight of the British working class in the 1930s: 'Talking once with a miner I asked him when the housing shortage first became acute in his district; he answered, "When we were told about it", meaning that "'til recently people's standards were so low that they took almost any degree of overcrowding for granted"' (Orwell, 1962, p. 57).

The concept of relative deprivation was introduced by the sociologist Sam Stouffer and his colleagues in their huge wartime study *The American Soldier* (Stouffer, Suchman, DeVinney, Star, & Williams, 1949), and more fully developed by another sociologist, James Davis (1959). Relative deprivation refers to a perceived discrepancy between attainments or actualities ('what is') and expectations or entitlements ('what ought to be'). Most simply, relative deprivation arises from comparisons between our experiences and our expectations (Gurr, 1970). (Can you respond to Richard in the first 'What do *you* think?' question?)

J-curve
A graphical figure that captures the way in which relative deprivation arises when attainments suddenly fall short of rising expectations.

James Davies (1969), another sociologist, who studied political revolutions, suggested a **J-curve** model to represent the way that people construct their future expectations from past and current attainments. Under certain circumstances, attainments may suddenly fall short of rising expectations. When this happens, relative deprivation is particularly acute, with the consequence of collective unrest – revolutions of rising expectations (see Box 11.1). The J-curve gets its name from the solid line in Figure 11.2.

Historical events do fit the J-curve model. For example, the Depression of the early 1930s caused a sudden fall in farm prices, which was associated with increased anti-Semitism in Poland (Keneally, 1982). Davies (1969) himself cites the French and Russian Revolutions, the American Civil War, the rise of Nazism in Germany and the growth of Black Power in the United States in the 1960s. We might add to this the wave of unrest across the globe following the 2008 stock market crash and ensuing recession – the 'occupy' protests, the 2011 UK riots, and the 2011 'Arab Spring' popular uprisings across North Africa and the Middle East, including Tunisia, Egypt, Libya, Yemen, Syria and Jordan.

In all these cases, a long period (twenty to thirty years) of increasing prosperity was followed by a steep and sudden recession. Systematic tests of predictions from Davies's theory are less encouraging. For example, from a longitudinal survey of American political and social attitudes, Marylee Taylor (1982) found little evidence that people's expectations were constructed from their immediate past experience, or that satisfaction was based on the degree of match between actualities and these expectations.

The British sociologist Gary Runciman (1966) made an important distinction between two forms of relative deprivation:

Egoistic relative deprivation
A feeling of personally having less than we feel we are entitled to, relative to our aspirations or to other individuals.

1 **egoistic relative deprivation**, which derives from the individual's sense of deprivation relative to other similar individuals; and

2 **fraternalistic relative deprivation**, which derives from comparisons with dissimilar others, or members of other groups.

Fraternalistic relative deprivation
Sense that our group has less than it is entitled to, relative to its aspirations or to other groups.

Studies that measure both types of relative deprivation suggest they are independent (e.g. Crosby, 1982), and that it is fraternalistic, specifically intergroup, relative deprivation, not egoistic (i.e. interpersonal) relative deprivation, that is associated with social unrest. For example, Ronald Abeles (1976) found that black militancy in the United States was more closely associated with measures of fraternalistic than egoistic relative deprivation. Serge Guimond and Lise Dubé-Simard (1983) found that militant francophones in Montreal felt more acute dissatisfaction and frustration when making intergroup salary comparisons between francophones and anglophones, rather than egoistic comparisons.

In India, where there had been a rapid decline in the status of Muslims relative to Hindus, Rama Tripathi and Rashmi Srivasta (1981) found that those Muslims who felt most fraternalistically deprived (e.g. in terms of job opportunities, political freedom) expressed the greatest hostility towards Hindus. And in a study of unemployed Australian workers, Iain

Box 11.1 Our world
Rising expectations and collective protest

The 1992 Los Angeles riots provided a riveting, real-life example of relative deprivation perceived by a large group of people

The Los Angeles riots that erupted on 29 April 1992 resulted in more than 50 dead and 2,300 injured. The proximal cause was the acquittal by an all-white suburban jury of four Los Angeles police officers accused of beating a black motorist, Rodney King. The assault with which the police officers were charged had been captured on video and played on national TV. Against a background of rising unemployment and deepening disadvantage, this acquittal was seen by blacks as a particularly poignant symbol of the low value placed by white America on American blacks.

The flashpoint for the riot was the intersection of Florence and Normandie Avenues in South Central Los Angeles. Initially, there was some stealing of liquor from a local off-licence, breaking of car windows and pelting of police. The police moved in en masse but then withdrew to try to de-escalate the tension. This left the intersection largely in the hands of the rioters, who attacked whites and Hispanics. Reginald Denny, a white truck driver who happened to be driving through, was dragged from his cab and brutally beaten; the incident was watched live on TV by millions and has largely come to symbolise the riots.

South Central Los Angeles was relatively typical of black ghettos in the United States at that time. However, the junction of Florence and Normandie was not in the worst part of the ghetto by any means. It was a relatively well-off black neighbourhood in which the poverty rate dropped during the 1980s from 33 to only 21 per cent. That the initial outbreak of rioting would occur here, rather than in a more impoverished neighbourhood, is consistent with relative deprivation theories of social unrest.

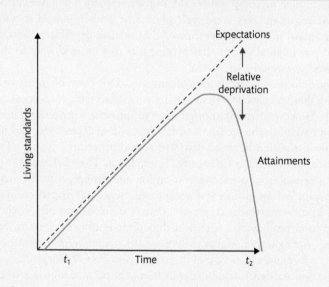

Figure 11.2 The J-curve hypothesis of relative deprivation

Relative deprivation is particularly acute when attainments suffer a sudden setback in the context of expectations that continue to rise.

Source: Based on Davies (1969).

Walker and Leon Mann (1987) found that it was principally those who reported most fraternalistic deprivation who were prepared to contemplate militant protest, such as demonstrations, lawbreaking and destruction of private property. Those who felt egoistically deprived reported symptoms of personal stress (e.g. headaches, indigestion, sleeplessness). This study is particularly revealing in showing how egoistic and fraternalistic deprivation produce different outcomes, and that it is the latter that is associated with social unrest as intergroup or collective protest (see the subsection 'Social protest and collective action') or aggression.

The subjective nature of deprivation is nicely captured in a study by Reeve Vanneman and Tom Pettigrew (1972). Urban whites in United States who expressed the most negative attitudes towards blacks were those who felt most strongly that whites as a group were poorly off relative to blacks as a group. The deprivation is clearly fraternalistic; and, as whites were in reality *better off* than blacks, it is clearly subjective. This points to the competitive nature of claiming to be deprived. There is sometimes quite a fierce dynamic of competitive victimhood in which both advantaged and disadvantaged groups declare themselves the real victims in order to lay claim to the moral high ground (Noor, Shnabel, Halabi, & Nadler, 2012; see Young & Sullivan, 2016).

Fraternalistic relative deprivation does not automatically translate into competitive intergroup behaviour or social protest. At least four other factors are involved. First, people need to identify strongly with their ingroup for the relative deprivation to actually matter. A longitudinal study of women activists by Caroline Kelly and Sara Breinlinger (1996) found that relative deprivation predicted involvement in women's group activities only among women who identified strongly with women as a group. Dominic Abrams (1990) found that Scottish teenagers supported the Scottish National Party more strongly if they felt a sense of fraternalistic relative deprivation relative to the English and if they identified strongly with being Scottish.

Second, groups that feel relatively deprived are unlikely to engage in collective action unless such action is considered a practical and feasible way of bringing about social change (see the next subsection 'Social protest and collective action'). A role-playing study by Joanne Martin and her colleagues illustrates this rather nicely (Martin, Brickman, & Murray, 1984). They had women workers imagine they were managers who were slightly to greatly underpaid relative to men of comparable rank in the company. They were also given information that the women managers were well placed or poorly placed to mobilise resources to change their situation. The results showed that relative deprivation was closely tied to the magnitude of pay inequality, but that protest was tied more closely to the perceived probability that protest would be successful.

Third, relative deprivation rests on perceptions of injustice. One form of injustice is distributive injustice – feeling that you have less than you are entitled to relative to expectations, other groups and so forth. However, there is another form of injustice – procedural injustice, in which you feel that you have been the victim of unfair procedures. Tom Tyler and his colleagues have explored this distinction between distributive and procedural justice (Tyler & Lind, 1992; Tyler & Smith, 1998; see De Cremer & Tyler, 2005). They believe that procedural injustice may be a particularly potent motivation for intergroup protest. Procedural justice is especially important within groups – if people experience unfair procedures, they tend to dis-identify and lose commitment to group goals (see discussion of leadership in **Chapter 9**). In intergroup contexts, however, it may be difficult to untangle unjust procedures from unjust distributions: for example, status differences (distributive injustice) between groups may rest on unfair procedures (procedural injustice) (Brockner & Wiesenfeld, 1996).

Finally, as fraternalistic relative deprivation depends on the particular ingroup–outgroup comparison that is made, it is important to be able to predict with whom we compare ourselves (Martin & Murray, 1983; Walker & Pettigrew, 1984). From social comparison theory (Festinger, 1954; see Križan & Gibbons, 2014; Suls & Wheeler, 2000), we would expect comparisons to be made with similar others. Some of the research cited above certainly supports this (e.g. Abeles, 1976; Runciman, 1966). For instance, Faye Crosby's (1982) 'paradox of the contented female worker' may arise because women workers compare their salaries and working conditions with other women, which avoids much larger gender-based inequalities in pay and conditions (Major, 1994). However, many intergroup comparisons, particularly those that lead to the most pronounced conflict, are made between markedly different groups (e.g. black and white South Africans). One way to approach this issue is to consider the extent to which groups are involved in real conflict over scarce resources (see the next section, 'Realistic conflict').

Social protest and collective action

People's response to relative deprivation often involves sustained social protest to achieve social change. The study of protest is complex. It requires articulation of constructs from social psychology, sociology and political science (Becker & Tausch, 2015; Klandermans, 1997, 2003; Reicher, 1996; Stürmer & Simon, 2004; Van Zomeren, Postmes, & Spears, 2008). As the study of how individual discontents or grievances are transformed into collective action, the study of protest has as one of its key questions: how and why do sympathisers become mobilised as activists or participants?

Bert Klandermans (1997) argues that this involves the relationship between individual attitudes and behaviour (see **Chapter 5**). Sympathisers hold sympathetic attitudes towards an issue, yet these attitudes do not automatically translate into behaviour. There was some latent ethnocentrism even in the absence of intergroup competition (see the subsection 'Cooperation, competition and social dilemmas' later in this chapter). It is tempting to 'free ride' (see **Chapter 8**) – to remain a sympathiser rather than become a participant. Klandermans also believes that protest is intergroup behaviour that occurs in what he calls 'multiorganisational fields': that is, protest movements involve the clash of ideas and ideologies between groups, and politicised and strategic positioning with other more or less sympathetic organisations. He describes four steps in social movement participation (for an overview, see Stürmer & Simon, 2004):

1 Becoming part of the mobilisation potential. First, you must be a sympathiser. The most important determinants of mobilisation potential are fraternalistic relative deprivation (feeling relatively deprived as a group), an us-versus-them orientation that targets an outgroup as responsible for your plight, and a belief that social change through collective action is possible.

2 Becoming a target of mobilisation attempts. Being a sympathiser is not enough – you must also be informed about what you can do and what is being done (e.g. occupations, demonstrations, lobbying). Media access and informal communication networks are critical here.

3 Developing motivation to participate. Being a sympathiser and knowing what is going on is not sufficient – you must also be motivated to participate. Motivation arises from the value that you place on the outcome of protest and the extent to which you believe that the protest will actually deliver the goods (an expectancy–value analysis; Ajzen & Fishbein, 1980). Motivation is strongest if the collective benefit of the outcome of protest is highly valued (collective motive), if important others value your participation (normative motive) and if valued personal outcomes are anticipated (reward motive). The normative and reward motives are important to prevent sympathisers from free-riding on others' participation. This analysis of motivation is strikingly similar to Ajzen and Fishbein's (1980) theory of reasoned action account of the attitude–behaviour relationship (see **Chapter 5**).

4 Overcoming barriers to participation. Finally, even strong motivation may not translate into action if there are insurmountable obstacles, such as no transport to the demonstration, or ill health. However, these obstacles are more likely to be overcome if motivation is very high.

Klandermans is talking about collective protest, where the background assumption is that protest is aimed at achieving a social good. However, some aspects of his model, particularly how people are targeted and become motivated, has more than passing relevance to the process of radicalization that we associate with individual or collective acts of terrorism (Horgan, 2014). Becker and Tausch (2015) invoke a distinction made by Wright and his colleagues (Wright, Taylor, & Moghaddam, 1990) between normative collective action (in line with the morality of the status quo – for example, peaceful protest) and non-normative collective action (in violation of the morality of the status quo – for example, violence and terrorism), and they introduce an emotion component. Normative protest is associated with sustained anger, which is ultimately an action-focused constructive emotion, whereas non-normative protest is associated with contempt, which dehumanises a group and essentialises its reprehensible conduct as unchangeable (Bell, 2013; Fischer & Roseman, 2007).

Returning to Klandermans, Bernd Simon (2003; Stürmer & Simon, 2004) feels that the cost–benefit aspect of Klanderman's model places too much emphasis on individual decision-making. Simon proposes a social identity analysis (also see Haslam & Reicher, 2012; Van Zomeren, Leach, & Spears, 2012; Van Zomeren, Postmes, & Spears, 2008). He argues that when people identify very strongly with a group, they have a tightly shared perception of collective injustice, needs and goals. They also share attitudes and behavioural intentions, trust and like one another and are collectively influenced by group norms and legitimate group leaders. Furthermore, group motivation eclipses personal motivation – it overcomes the dilemma of social action (Klandermans, 2002). Provided that members believe that protest is an effective way forward, these processes increase the probability of participation in collective protest (Bluic, McGarty, Reynolds, & Muntele, 2007).

Realistic conflict

Ethnocentrism
Evaluative preference for all aspects of our own group relative to other groups.

A key feature of intergroup behaviour is **ethnocentrism** (Brewer & Campbell, 1976; LeVine & Campbell, 1972), described by William Sumner as:

> a view of things in which one's own group is the centre of everything, and all others are scaled and rated with reference to it . . . Each group nourishes its own pride and vanity, boasts itself superior, exalts its own divinities, and looks with contempt on outsiders. Each group thinks its own folkways the only right one . . . Ethnocentrism leads a people to exaggerate and intensify everything in their own folkways which is peculiar and which differentiates them from others.
>
> Sumner (1906, p. 13)

In contrast to other perspectives on prejudice, discrimination and intergroup behaviour that explain the origins of ethnocentrism in terms of individual or interpersonal processes (e.g. frustration – aggression, relative deprivation, authoritarianism, dogmatism), Muzafer Sherif (1962) believed that 'we cannot extrapolate from the properties of individuals to the characteristics of group situations' (p. 8) and that the origins of ethnocentrism lie in the nature of intergroup relations. For Sherif:

> *Intergroup relations* refer to relations between two or more groups and their respective members. Whenever individuals belonging to one group interact, collectively or individually, with another group or its *members in terms of their group identifications* we have an instance of intergroup behaviour.
>
> Sherif (1962, p. 5)

Sherif believed that where groups compete over scarce resources, intergroup relations become conflictual and ethnocentric. He tested this idea in a series of famous field experiments conducted in 1949, 1953 and 1954 at summer camps for young boys in the United States (Sherif, 1966). The procedure involved three phases:

1 *Phase 1:* The boys arrived at the camp, which, unknown to them, was run by the experimenters. They engaged in various camp-wide activities, through which they formed friendships.

2 *Phase 2:* The camp was then divided into two groups that split up friendships. The groups were isolated, with separate living quarters and daily activities, and they developed their own norms and status differences. The groups made little reference to each other apart from some embryonic ethnocentrism.

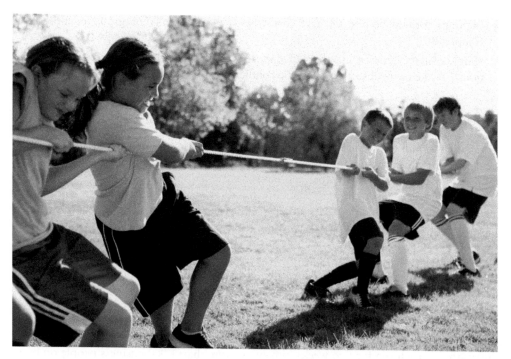

Realistic conflict
Sherif showed that intergroup competition led to conflict and then discrimination. This is heightened when groups compete for a goal that only one group can achieve.

3 *Phase 3:* The groups were brought together to engage in organised intergroup competitions embracing sports contests and other activities. This generated fierce competition and intergroup hostility, which rapidly generalised to situations outside the organised competitions. Ethnocentric attitudes and behaviour were amplified and coupled with intergroup aggression and ingroup solidarity. Almost all intergroup encounters degenerated into intergroup hostility: for example, when the two groups ate together, the meal became an opportunity for the groups to throw food at each other. Intergroup relations deteriorated so dramatically that two of the experiments were hastily concluded at this stage.

In one experiment, however, it was possible to proceed to a fourth stage:

4 *Phase 4:* The two groups were provided with **superordinate goals**, goals they both desired but were unable to achieve on their own. The groups had to work together in cooperation.

Superordinate goals
Goals that both groups desire but that can be achieved only by both groups cooperating.

As an example of a superordinate goal (also dealt with later in this chapter), the groups were told that the truck delivering a movie that both groups wanted to watch had become bogged down and would need to be pulled out, but that everyone would be needed to help as the truck was very heavy. Sherif had a wonderful sense of symbolism – the rope used cooperatively by the boys to pull the truck was the same rope that had previously been used in an aggressive tug-of-war between the warring groups. Sherif and colleagues found a gradual improvement in intergroup relations as a consequence of the groups engaging in cooperative intergroup interactions to achieve superordinate goals.

There are some notable points about these experiments:

• There was some latent ethnocentrism even in the absence of intergroup competition (see the next subsection 'Realistic conflict theory').

• Prejudice, discrimination and ethnocentrism arose as a consequence of real intergroup conflict.

• The boys did not have authoritarian or dogmatic personalities.

• The less frustrated group (the winners) was usually the one that expressed the greater intergroup aggression.

- Ingroups formed despite the fact that friends were actually outgroup members (see **Chapter 8**).
- Simple contact between members of opposing groups did not improve intergroup relations (see the next subsection 'Realistic conflict theory').

Realistic conflict theory

Realistic conflict theory
Sherif's theory of intergroup conflict that explains intergroup behaviour in terms of the nature of goal relations between groups.

To explain his findings, Sherif (1966) proposed a **realistic conflict theory** of intergroup behaviour, in which the nature of the goal relations among individuals and groups determines the nature of interindividual and intergroup relations (see Figure 11.3). Individuals who share goals requiring interdependence for their achievement cooperate and form a group, while individuals who have mutually exclusive goals (i.e. a scarce resource that only one can obtain, such as winning a chess game) engage in interindividual competition, which prevents group formation or contributes to the collapse of an existing group. At the intergroup level, mutually exclusive goals produce intergroup conflict and ethnocentrism, while shared goals requiring intergroup interdependence for their achievement (i.e. superordinate goals) reduce conflict and encourage intergroup harmony. For a summary of Sherif's range of contributions to social psychology, see Vaughan (2010b).

Sherif's model is generally supported by other naturalistic experiments (Fisher, 1990). For example, Robert Blake and Jane Mouton (1961) employed similar procedures in a series of thirty studies, each run for two weeks, involving more than 1,000 business people on management training programmes in the United States. Phillip Zimbardo's simulated prison experiment (Haney, Banks, & Zimbardo, 1973; see **Chapter 8**) also illustrates how mutually exclusive intergroup goals produce conflict and hostile intergroup relations. Sherif's studies have been successfully replicated in Lebanon (Diab, 1970) and the former Soviet Union

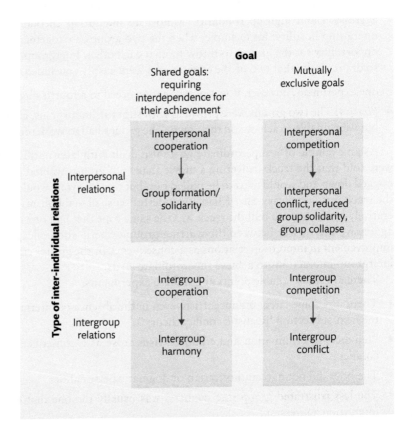

Figure 11.3 Realistic group conflict theory

Goal relations between individuals and groups determine cooperative or competitive interdependence, and thus the nature of interpersonal and intergroup behaviour.

Source: Based on Sherif (1966).

(Andreeva, 1984), but in Britain, Andrew Tyerman and Christopher Spencer (1983) were not so successful. Tyerman and Spencer used an established Scout group as participants and found that the different 'patrols' did not express anywhere near as much hostility as expected. Furthermore, it was easy to increase inter-patrol cooperation even in the absence of a superordinate goal. Tyerman and Spencer attribute this to the fact that a well-established superordinate group already existed.

Realistic conflict theory makes good sense and is useful for understanding intergroup conflict, particularly in applied settings. For example, Marilynn Brewer and Donald Campbell (1976) surveyed thirty tribal groups in Africa and found greater derogation of tribal outgroups that lived close by and were therefore likely to be direct competitors for scarce resources, such as water and land. (See the third 'What do *you* think?' question: Jean and Alison have a problem since their 'tribes' live so close to each other.) Ronald Fisher (1990, 2005) went a bit further to outline how establishing superordinate goals can be used to help resolve conflict between communities, and even between nations.

Realistic conflict theory suffers from a problem. Because so many variables are operating together in the various studies, how can we know that it is the nature of goal relations that ultimately determines intergroup behaviour? Might the cause actually be the cooperative or competitive nature of interaction, or perhaps merely the existence of two separate groups (e.g. Dion, 1979; Turner, 1981b)? These causal agents are confounded – an observation that we pursue later in this chapter.

Cooperation, competition and social dilemmas

Realistic conflict theory focuses on the relationship between people's goals, the competitive or cooperative nature of their behaviour and the conflicting or harmonious nature of their relations. We can study these relationships in abstract settings by designing 'games' with different goal relations for two or more people to play. The mathematician John Von Neumann and economist Oskar Morgenstern (1944) introduced a model for analysing situations where people are in conflict over some non-trivial outcome (e.g. money, power). Variously called *decision theory*, *game theory* or *utility theory*, this initiated a prodigious amount of research in the 1960s and 1970s.

The highly abstract nature of the research raised questions about its relevance (generalisability) to real-world conflict, which contributed to its decline in the 1980s (Apfelbaum & Lubek, 1976; Nemeth, 1970). Much of this research is concerned with interpersonal conflict (see **Chapter 14**). However, in its broader context of the study of social dilemmas as crises of human trust that undermine cooperation (e.g. Van Lange, Balliet, Parks, & Van Vugt, 2014), it has important implications for intergroup conflict: for example, the prisoner's dilemma, the trucking game and the commons dilemma (e.g. Liebrand, Messick, & Wilke, 1992).

The prisoner's dilemma

Introduced by R. D. Luce and Howard Raïffa (1957; Rapoport, 1976), the **prisoner's dilemma** is the most widely researched game. It is based on an anecdote. Detectives question two obviously guilty suspects separately, with only enough evidence to convict them of a lesser offence. The suspects are separately offered a chance to confess, knowing that if one confesses but the other does not, the confessor will be granted immunity and the confession will be used to convict the other of the more serious offence. If both confess, each will receive a moderate sentence. If neither confesses, each will receive a very light sentence. The dilemma faced by the prisoners can be summarised by a *pay-off matrix* (see Figure 11.4).

Although mutual non-confession produces the best joint outcome, mutual suspicion and lack of trust almost always encourage both to confess. This finding has been replicated in hundreds of prisoner's dilemma experiments, using a variety of experimental conditions and pay-off matrices (Dawes, 1991). The prisoner's dilemma is described as a 'two-person,

Prisoner's dilemma
Two-person game in which both parties are torn between competition and cooperation and, depending on mutual choices, both can win or both can lose.

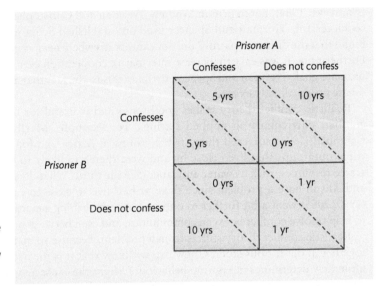

Figure 11.4 The prisoner's dilemma

Each quadrant displays the prison sentence that Prisoner A receives (above the diagonal) and Prisoner B receives (below in diagonal) if both, one or neither confesses.

mixed motive, non-zero-sum game'. This is quite a mouthful; but it means that two people are involved, they each experience a conflict between being motivated to cooperate and motivated to compete, and the outcome can be that both parties gain or both lose. In contrast, a zero-sum game is one in which one party's gain is always the other's loss – think of a pie: the larger the portion I take, the smaller the portion left for you.

The trucking game

In this game, there are two trucking companies, Acme and Bolt, which transport goods from one place to another (Deutsch & Krauss, 1960). Each company has its own private route, but there is a much faster shared route, which has a major drawback – a one-lane section (see Figure 11.5). Clearly, the mutually beneficial solution is for the two companies to take it in turns to use the one-lane section. Instead, research reveals again and again that participants fight over use of the one-lane section. Typically, both enter and meet head-on in the middle and then waste time arguing until one backs up. Again, mutual mistrust has produced a suboptimal joint outcome.

These games highlight detrimental consequences of lack of trust that have obvious real-world analogues. For example, mutual distrust between Iran and Iraq fuelled their terrible conflict in the 1980s over which of them rightfully owned the Shatt-al-Arab waterway. When they laid down their arms in 1988 after horrific atrocities, over a million civilian and military casualties and the devastation of their economies, the borders remained precisely where they were when the war began eight years earlier.

Game theory rests on a rationalistic characterisation of humankind as *homo œconomicus* – a model of human psychology that derives from Western thinking about work and industry (Cartwright, 2011; Stroebe & Frey, 1982; see also discussion of normative models and behavioural decision theory in **Chapter 2**). Possibly due to this perspective, a problem with research based on game theory is that it is relatively asocial. For example, it often overlooks the role of direct and indirect communication. Direct communication in two- and *n*-person prisoner's dilemma games very reliably reduces conflict and increases cooperation (Liebrand, 1984; Meleady, Hopthrow, & Crisp, 2013). Interactants' responses also fulfil an indirect communicative function in which flexible and responsive behaviour increases cooperation (Apfelbaum, 1974).

Similarly, people's perceptions of the game are often overlooked. For example, the allocation or exchange of goods or resources always raises questions of perceived fairness and

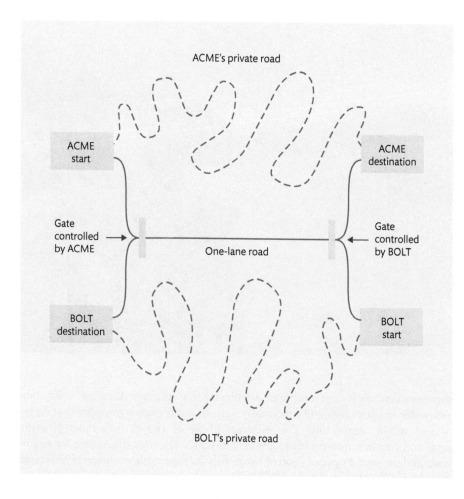

Figure 11.5 The trucking game

Two participants play a game where they work for separate trucking companies that transport goods from one place to another. They can use their own private roads, but there is also a much shorter shared route that has the drawback of having a one-lane section.

Source: Deutsch and Krauss (1960).

justice. Typically, people construe experimental games as competitive contexts. However, if the game is introduced in different terms – for example, as an investigation of human interaction or international conflict resolution – people behave in a more cooperative manner (Abric & Vacherot, 1976; Eiser & Bhavnani, 1974). Furthermore, interactants are more confident of fair solutions, behave more cooperatively and are more satisfied with outcomes if rules of fairness are explicitly invoked (McClintock & Van Avermaet, 1982; Mikula, 1980).

The commons dilemma

Many other social dilemmas involve a number of individuals or groups exploiting a limited resource (Foddy, Smithson, Schneider, & Hogg, 1999; Kerr & Park, 2001). These are essentially *n*-person prisoner's dilemmas – if everyone cooperates, an optimal solution for all is reached, but if everyone competes, then everyone loses. The **commons dilemma**, or 'tragedy of the commons' (Hardin, 1968), gets its name from the common pasture that English villages used to have. People could graze their cattle on this land, and if all used it in moderation, it would replenish itself and continue to benefit them all. However, imagine 100 farmers surrounding a common that could support only 100 cows. If each grazed one cow, the common would be maximally utilised and minimally taxed. However, one farmer might reason that if they grazed an additional cow, their output would be doubled, minus a very small cost due to overgrazing – a cost borne equally by all 100 farmers. So, this farmer adds a second cow. If all 100 farmers reasoned in this way, they would rapidly destroy the common, thus producing the tragedy of the commons.

Commons dilemma
Social dilemma in which cooperation by all benefits all, but competition by all harms all.

Commons dilemma
A climatic tragedy in which a failure to cooperate leads to harm for all.

The commons dilemma is an example of a replenishable resource dilemma – the commons is a renewable resource that will continually support many people provided that everyone shows restraint in 'harvesting' the resource. Many of the world's most pressing environmental and conservation problems are replenishable resource dilemmas: for example, rainforests and the world's population of ocean fish are renewable resources if harvested appropriately (Clover, 2004) (see the third 'What do *you* think?' question).

Another type of social dilemma is called a *public goods dilemma*. Public goods are provided for everyone: for example, public health, national parks, the national road network, public radio and TV. Because public goods are available to all, people are tempted to use them without contributing to their maintenance. There is a **free-rider effect** (Kerr, 1983; Kerr & Bruun, 1983; see **Chapter 8**), in which people self-interestedly exploit a resource without caring for it.

Free-rider effect
Gaining the benefits of group membership by avoiding costly obligations of membership and by allowing other members to incur those costs.

For example, if you alone avoid paying your taxes, it only minimally impacts the provision of a police force, an ambulance service or a functioning road system; but if everyone reasoned similarly, there would be no emergency services to race to your rescue on the now effectively non-existent road system. Likewise, if you alone download music and movies without paying, the impact is small; but if millions of people do so, then the detrimental impact on these creative industries is lethal. If I fail to fix my car exhaust or plant trees in my garden, it contributes minimally to noise, atmospheric and visual pollution; if everyone living in my neighbourhood did likewise, then it would become a horrible place to live.

Reflecting on the tragedy of the commons, Garrett Hardin observed:

> Ruin is the destination to which all men rush, each pursuing his own best interest in a society that believes in the freedom of the commons. Freedom in a commons brings ruin to all.
>
> Hardin (1968, p. 162)

Research on social dilemmas finds that when self-interest is pitted against the collective good, the usual outcome is competition and resource destruction (Edney, 1979; Sato, 1987). However, some studies also find high levels of voluntary social cooperation (Caporael, Dawes, Orbell, & Van de Kragt, 1989). A series of studies by Brewer and her colleagues (Brewer & Kramer, 1986; Brewer & Schneider, 1990; Kramer & Brewer, 1984, 1986) identifies one condition under which this can occur. When people identify with the common good – in other words, they derive their social identity (see the section 'Social identity' later in this chapter) from the entire group that has access to the resource – self-interest is subordinate to the common good. However, the same research finds that when different *groups*, rather than individuals, have access to a public good, the ensuing intergroup competition ensures ethnocentric actions that are far more destructive than mere self-interest. International competition over limited resources such as rainforests, fish and wetlands tragically accelerates their disappearance.

Resolving social dilemmas

Generally, people find it difficult to escape the trap of a social dilemma. They are crises of trust, where people fail to trust one another (Van Lange, Balliet, Parks, & Van Vugt, 2014) and human greed and greedy individuals prevail (Seuntjens, Zeelenberg, Van de Ven, & Breugelmans, 2015). Even appeals to altruistic norms are surprisingly ineffective (Kerr, 1995) – if you know that others are free riding, you certainly do not want to be taken for a sucker (Kerr & Bruun, 1983). Because selfish behaviour prevails in social dilemmas, structural solutions are often imposed to cause the dilemma to disappear (Kerr, 1995). Structural solutions include measures such as limiting the number of people accessing the resource (e.g. via permits), limiting the amount of the resource that people can take (e.g. via quotas), handing over management of the resource to an individual (a leader) or a single group, facilitating free communication among those accessing the resource, and shifting the pay-off to favour cooperation over competition.

The problem with structural solutions is that they require an enlightened and powerful authority to implement measures, manage the bureaucracy and police violations. This can be hard to bring about. A case in point is the inability, in the face of global catastrophe, for the world's nations to put a structural solution in place to limit carbon emissions to avert climate change. We have had global summits and accords aplenty, hosted by pretty much every major nation on the planet. Yet, some countries still will not sacrifice personal gain for the greater good of humanity – leading, in complete frustration and desperation, to an alliance in 2007 between Richard Branson and Al Gore to provide a 25-million-dollar carrot for design initiatives to remove carbon dioxide from the atmosphere. We now have the 2015 Paris Agreement that emerged from the 195-nation 21st United Nations Framework Convention on Climate Change (UNFCCC). By mid-2016 almost all 195 countries had signed the agreement but only 22 had ratified it, which is too few for it to enter into force.

One structural solution is the appointment of a leader to manage the resource (e.g. De Cremer & Van Vugt, 2002; Rutte & Wilke, 1984; Van Vugt & De Cremer, 1999). Leaders are very effective at resolving social dilemmas under certain circumstances. People with a prosocial orientation are relatively open to leadership when their group is faced with a social dilemma, particularly if they identify strongly with the group (De Cremer, 2000; De Cremer & Van Vugt, 1999). Leader charisma is not critical, but it is important that the leader can be viewed as 'one of us', as a representative member of the group (De Cremer, 2002). People with a pro-self-orientation are less open to leadership, unless they identify strongly with the group and can view the leader as group serving and representative of the group. Charismatic leaders are particularly good at helping pro-self members behave in prosocial and group-serving ways.

If structural solutions are so difficult, what other options do we have? One factor that is particularly effective in resolving social dilemmas is group identification (Foddy, Smithson, Schneider & Hogg, 1999; Van Vugt & De Cremer, 1999). Where people identify very strongly with a group that accesses a shared resource, those people act in ways that benefit the group as a whole rather than themselves as separate from the group (e.g. Brewer & Kramer, 1986; Brewer & Schneider, 1990; De Cremer, Van Knippenberg, Van Dijk, & Van Leeuwen, 2008). It is as if a large number of individuals competing for access have been transformed into a single person who carefully tends the resource. This is a good analogy. Identification with a group actually does transform people psychologically in this way.

Identification facilitates constructive communication that builds trust (Meleady, Hopthrow, & Crisp, 2013); it facilitates communication that develops conserving norms (e.g. Bouas & Komorita, 1996; Meleady, Hopthrow, & Crisp, 2013); it encourages adherence to those norms (e.g. Sattler & Kerr, 1991); it inspires perceptions of distributive and procedural justice (Tyler & Smith, 1998); and it makes people feel that their conserving actions really do have an effect (Kerr, 1995). Indeed, privatisation of a public good can increase selfish non-conserving behaviour precisely because it inhibits these social identity processes (Van Vugt, 1997).

Social identity

Minimal groups

Realistic conflict theory (Sherif, 1966) traces intergroup behaviour to goal interdependence but potentially confounds a number of possible causal agents. Research also suggests that ethnocentric attitudes and competitive intergroup relations are easy to trigger and difficult to suppress. For example, embryonic ethnocentrism was found in phase 2 of Sherif's summer camp studies, when groups had just formed but there was no realistic conflict between them (see also Blake & Mouton, 1961; Kahn & Ryen, 1972). Other researchers have found that competitive intergroup behaviour spontaneously emerges:

- even when goal relations between groups are not interdependent (Rabbie & Horwitz, 1969);
- under conditions of explicitly non-competitive intergroup relations (Ferguson & Kelley, 1964; Rabbie & Wilkens, 1971);
- under conditions of explicitly cooperative intergroup relations (Rabbie & DeBrey, 1971).

What, then, are the minimal conditions for intergroup behaviour: that is, conditions that are both necessary and sufficient for a collection of individuals to be ethnocentric and to engage in intergroup competition? (Jean and Alison's problem can be approached in the context of the minimal intergroup paradigm. See the second 'What do *you* think?' question.)

Minimal group paradigm
Experimental methodology to investigate the effect of social categorization alone on behaviour.

Tajfel and his colleagues devised an intriguing research methodology to answer this question – the **minimal group paradigm** (Tajfel, Billig, Bundy, & Flament, 1971). British schoolboys, participating in what they believed was a study of decision-making, were assigned to one of two groups completely randomly, but allegedly on the basis of their expressed preference for paintings by the artists Vassily Kandinsky or Paul Klee. The children knew only which group they themselves were in (Kandinsky group or Klee group), with the identity of outgroup and fellow ingroup members concealed by the use of code numbers. The children then individually distributed money between pairs of recipients identified only by code number and group membership.

This pencil-and-paper task was repeated for a number of different pairs of ingroup and outgroup members, excluding self, on a series of distribution matrices carefully designed to tease out the strategies that were being used. The results showed that against a background of fairness, the children strongly favoured their own group: they adopted the ingroup favouritism strategy (FAV) described in Box 11.2. This is a rather startling finding, as the groups were indeed minimal. They were created on the basis of a flimsy criterion, had no past history or possible future, the children did not even know the identity of other members of each group, and no self-interest was involved in the money distribution task as self was not a recipient.

Subsequent experiments were even more minimal. For example, Billig and Tajfel (1973) explicitly randomly categorized their participants as X- or Y-group members, thereby

Box 11.2 Research classic
The minimal group paradigm

Distribution strategies and sample distribution matrices (participants circled pairs of numbers to indicate how they wished to distribute the points)

A. *Two sample distribution matrices.* Within each matrix, participants circle the column of numbers that represents how they would like to distribute the points (representing real money) in the matrix between ingroup and outgroup members.

1	Ingroup member:	7	8	9	10	11	12	13	14	15	16	17	18	19
	Outgroup member:	1	3	5	7	9	11	13	15	17	19	21	23	25
2	Ingroup member:	18	17	16	15	14	13	12	11	10	9	8	7	6
	Outgroup member:	5	6	7	8	9	10	11	12	13	14	15	16	17

B. *Distribution strategies.* From an analysis of responses on a large number of matrices, it is possible to determine the extent to which the participants' distribution of points is influenced by each of the following strategies.

• Fairness	F	Equal distribution of points between groups
• Maximum joint profit	MJP	Maximise total number of points obtained by both recipients together, irrespective of which group receives most
• Maximum ingroup profit	MIP	Maximise number of points for the ingroup
• Maximum difference	MD	Maximise the difference in favour of the ingroup in the number of points awarded
• Favouritism	FAV	Composite employment of MIP and MD

Source: Tajfel (1970); based on Hogg and Abrams (1988).

eliminating any possibility that they might infer that people in the same group were interpersonally similar to one another because they ostensibly preferred the same artist. Turner (1978) abolished the link between points and money. The task was simply to distribute points. Other studies have included, in addition to the points distribution task, measures of attitudinal, affective and conative aspects of ethnocentrism. Another study used actual coins as rewards (Vaughan, Tajfel, & Williams, 1981). Seven- and 12-year-old children simply distributed coins to unidentified ingroup and outgroup members. Marked ingroup bias emerged in both age groups.

The robust finding from hundreds of minimal group experiments conducted with a wide range of participants is that merely being categorized as a group member produces ethnocentrism and competitive intergroup behaviour (Bourhis, Sachdev, & Gagnon, 1994; Diehl, 1990; Tajfel, 1982). Other studies have shown that minimal categorization can generate ingroup bias at the implicit level and is thus an effect over which people may have no conscious control (Otten & Wentura, 1999), and that social categorization can have a very wide range of automatic effects. For example, Jay Van Bavel and William Cunningham (2011) report the intriguing finding that self-categorized Americans living in New York erroneously estimated Mexico (a feared and threatening outgroup) to be geographically closer than Canada (a non-threatening outgroup) – an elegant confirmation of the saying that you should keep your friends close, and your enemies closer!

Social categorization is necessary but may not be sufficient for intergroup behaviour. For example, Hogg and his colleagues conducted a number of minimal group experiments to show that if participants are made more certain and confident about how to use the complex and unusual minimal group matrices, categorization does not produce group identification

Social categorization
Classification of people as members of different social groups.

and intergroup discrimination (e.g. Grieve & Hogg, 1999; see Hogg, 2000c, 2007b, 2012). One reason why people identify with groups, even minimal groups, may be to reduce feelings of uncertainty (see the subsection 'Uncertainty reduction'). Thus, categorization produces identification and discrimination only if people identify with the category, and they identify with the category only if the categorization is likely to reduce feelings of uncertainty in the situation.

The minimal group paradigm did not go unchallenged. For example, there was a lively debate over the measures, procedures and statistics used (Aschenbrenner & Schaefer, 1980; Bornstein, Crum, Wittenbraker, Harring, Insko, & Thibaut, 1983; Branthwaite, Doyle, & Lightbown, 1979; Turner, 1980, 1983), and over the extent to which favouritism reflects rational economic self-interest rather than social identity-based intergroup differentiation (Rabbie, Schot, & Visser, 1989; Turner & Bourhis, 1996).

Another objection was that the conditions of the experiments create a demand characteristic where participants conform to the transparent expectations of the experimenters or simply to general norms of intergroup competitiveness (Gerard & Hoyt, 1974). This interpretation seems unlikely in the light of evidence that discrimination is not associated with awareness of being under surveillance (Grieve & Hogg, 1999) and that discrimination can be reduced when adherence to and awareness of discriminatory norms is increased (Billig, 1973; Tajfel & Billig, 1974). In fact, participants who are not actually categorized but only have the experiment described to them predict significantly less discrimination (i.e. there is no norm of discrimination) than is actually displayed by participants who are categorized (St Claire & Turner, 1982). Also, it can be almost impossible to encourage participants to follow an explicitly cooperative norm in a minimal intergroup situation (Hogg, Turner, Nascimento-Schulze, & Spriggs, 1986).

Although it is not a criticism of the minimal group paradigm, Amélie Mummendey and her colleagues have identified a positive–negative asymmetry in the minimal group effect (Mummendey & Otten, 1998; Otten, Mummendey, & Blanz, 1996; see also Peeters & Czapinski, 1990). In the usual paradigm, participants give positively valued resources (points); the effect is much weaker or can disappear when they give negatively valued resources (e.g. punishment), or when instead of giving resources they subtract resources.

Finally, the minimal group effect really does reflect what happens in maximal or real-life groups. Groups really do strive to favour themselves over relevant outgroups. For example, Rupert Brown (1978), capitalising on competitive wage negotiations in Britain in the 1970s, found that shop stewards from one department in an aircraft engineering factory sacrificed as much as £2 a week in absolute terms in order to increase their relative advantage over a competing outgroup to £1. Furthermore, studies of nurses revealed that although nurses are supposed to be caring and self-sacrificing, ingroup identification was associated with just as much ingroup favouritism as among other less self-sacrificing groups (Oaker & Brown, 1986; Skevington, 1981; Van Knippenberg & Van Oers, 1984).

Social identity theory

Social identity theory
Theory of group membership and intergroup relations based on self-categorization, social comparison and the construction of a shared self-definition in terms of ingroup-defining properties.

Self-categorization theory
Turner and associates' theory of how the process of categorizing oneself as a group member produces social identity and group and intergroup behaviours.

The fundamental role of social categorization in intergroup behaviour, as demonstrated by minimal group studies, led to the introduction by Tajfel and Turner of the concept of social identity (Tajfel, 1974; Tajfel & Turner, 1986). This simple idea has evolved over the past forty years to become perhaps the pre-eminent social psychological analysis of group processes, intergroup relations and the collective self – **social identity theory**. Social identity theory has a number of theoretically compatible and integrated subtheories and emphases. For example, Tajfel and Turner's (1986) original analysis focused on intergroup relations and is called the *social identity theory of intergroup relations*. Turner and colleagues' later focus on self-categorization and group processes as a whole, **self-categorization theory**

(Turner, Hogg, Oakes, Reicher, & Wetherell, 1987), is called the *social identity theory of the group* (see Abrams & Hogg, 2001, 2010; Hogg, 2006; Hogg & Abrams, 1988, 2007; Turner, 1999; see also **Chapter 4**). For a summary of Tajfel's range of contributions to social psychology, see Vaughan (2010c).

Social identity and group membership

Two core premises of social identity theory are: (a) society is structured into distinct social groups that stand in power and status relations to one another (e.g. blacks and whites in the United States, Catholics and Protestants in Northern Ireland, Sunnis and Shi'ites in Iraq), and (b) social categories (large groups such as a nation or church, but also intermediate groups such as an organisation, or small groups such as a club) provide members with a social identity – a definition and evaluation of who one is and a description and evaluation of what this entails. Social identities not only *describe* attributes but also *prescribe* what one should think and how one should behave as a member. For example, being a member of the social category 'student' means not only defining and evaluating yourself and being defined and evaluated by others as a student, but also thinking and behaving in characteristically student ways.

Social identity is that part of the self-concept that comes from group membership. It is associated with group and intergroup behaviours, which have some general characteristics: ethnocentrism, **ingroup favouritism** and **intergroup differentiation**; conformity to ingroup norms; ingroup solidarity and cohesion; and perception of self, outgroupers and fellow ingroupers in terms of relevant group **stereotypes**.

Social identity is quite separate from personal identity, which is that part of the self-concept that derives from personality traits and the idiosyncratic personal relationships we have with other people (Turner, 1982). Personal identity is associated not with group and intergroup behaviours, but with interpersonal and individual behaviour. People have a repertoire of as many social and personal identities as they have groups they identify with, or close relationships and idiosyncratic attributes in terms of which they define themselves. However, although we have many discrete social and personal identities, we subjectively experience the self as an integrated whole person with a continuous and unbroken biography – the subjective experience of self as fragmented discontinuous selves would be problematic and associated with various psychopathologies.

Social identity theory distinguishes social from personal identity as a deliberate attempt to avoid explaining group and intergroup processes in terms of personality attributes or interpersonal relations. Social identity theorists believe that many social psychological theories of group processes and intergroup relations are limited because they explain the phenomena by aggregating effects of personality predispositions or interpersonal relations.

The **authoritarian personality** theory and the **frustration–aggression hypothesis** are examples of this latter type of explanation of prejudice and discrimination (Billig, 1976; see **Chapter 10**). To illustrate: if a social psychologist asks why people stick their arms out of car windows to indicate a turn, the question would remain unanswered by an explanation in terms of the biochemistry of muscle action. An explanation in terms of adherence to social norms would be more appropriate (although inappropriate to a biochemist asking the same question). It is the problem of **reductionism** (see **Chapter 1** for details) that prompts social identity theorists to distinguish between social and personal identity (Doise, 1986; Israel & Tajfel, 1972; Moscovici, 1972; Taylor & Brown, 1979; Turner & Oakes, 1986).

Social categorization, prototypes and depersonalisation

Self-categorization theory (Turner, Hogg, Oakes, Reicher, & Wetherell, 1987), the social identity theory of the group, specifies how categorization operates as the social cognitive underpinning of social identity phenomena. People cognitively represent social categories/groups

Social identity
That part of the self-concept that derives from our membership in social groups.

Ingroup favouritism
Behaviour that favours one's own group over other groups.

Intergroup differentiation
Behaviour that emphasises differences between our own group and other groups.

Stereotype
Widely shared and simplified evaluative image of a social group and its members.

Authoritarian personality
Personality syndrome originating in childhood that predisposes individuals to be prejudiced.

Frustration–aggression hypothesis
Theory that all frustration leads to aggression, and all aggression comes from frustration. Used to explain prejudice and intergroup aggression.

Reductionism
Explanation of a phenomenon in terms of the language and concepts of a lower level of analysis, usually with a loss of explanatory power.

Prototype
Cognitive representation of the typical/ideal defining features of a category.

Meta-contrast principle
The prototype of a group is that position within the group that has the largest ratio of 'differences to ingroup positions' to 'differences to outgroup positions'.

Entitativity
The property of a group that makes it seem like a coherent, distinct and unitary entity.

as prototypes. A **prototype** is a fuzzy set of attributes (perceptions, beliefs, attitudes, feelings, behaviours) that describes one group and distinguishes it from relevant other groups. Prototypes obey the **meta-contrast principle** – they maximise the ratio of intergroup differences to intragroup differences, and in so doing they accentuate group entitativity. **Entitativity** (Campbell, 1958; Hamilton & Sherman, 1996) is the property of a group that makes it seem like a coherent, distinct and unitary entity (see **Chapter 8**).

Meta-contrast ensures that group prototypes are not simply the average of ingroup attributes, and that the most prototypical person in a group is therefore not the average group member. Because prototypes also capture intergroup distinctiveness, they are typically displaced from the group average in a direction away from the relevant comparison outgroup. Prototypes are ideal rather than average types, and it is conceivable that a group prototype may be so ideal that not a single member actually embodies it.

Prototypes are cognitive representations of groups. As such they are closely related to stereotypes (see **Chapter 2**). However, from a social identity perspective a prototype is a stereotype only if it is *shared* by group members (Tajfel, 1981a). Finally, prototypes are context dependent. What this means is that the properties of a specific prototype change as a function of the comparison outgroup, the ingroup members present and the goals of the comparison or interaction. This context dependence can be quite extreme in newly forming groups (a task group) but is less extreme in better-established groups (e.g. ethnic groups) that are more firmly anchored in enduring intergroup stereotypes.

Context effects on prototypes can be found in, for example, perceptions between national groups (e.g. Rutland & Cinnirella, 2000) and between political factions (Gaffney, Rast, Hackett, & Hogg, 2014). For example, Nick Hopkins and Christopher Moore (2001) found that Scots perceived themselves to be different from the English, but that this difference diminished when they made comparisons between Scots and Germans. Even though the Scots might not like it, they saw their prototype moving a little closer to the English prototype!

Although identities and their associated attributes are influenced by context, they are not *determined* by context. Van Bavel and Cunningham (2010) propose an *iterative reprocessing model* – they cite neuroscience research showing how identity-defining attributes stored in memory are activated and modified by contextual cues to meet specific contextual demands, but are not necessarily fundamentally changed in an enduring sense unless a specific context becomes pervasive in one's life.

Depersonalisation
The perception and treatment of self and others not as unique individual persons but as prototypical embodiments of a social group.

The process of categorizing someone leads to **depersonalisation**. When we categorise others, we see them through the lens of the relevant ingroup or outgroup prototype – we view them as members of a group, not as unique idiosyncratic individuals. We perceptually accentuate their similarity to (i.e. assimilate them to) the relevant prototype, thus perceiving them stereotypically and ethnocentrically. When we categorise ourselves, exactly the same happens – we define, perceive and evaluate ourselves in terms of our ingroup prototype, and behave in line with that prototype. Self-categorization produces ingroup normative behaviour (conformity to group norms; see **Chapter 7**) and self-stereotyping (see **Chapter 2**) and is therefore the process that causes us to behave like group members. Depersonalisation is not the same thing as dehumanisation – although it can produce dehumanisation (see **Chapter 10**) if the outgroup is deeply hated and is stereotyped in ways that deny its members respect or human dignity.

Depersonalisation is the categorization-based cognitive process that transforms self-attributes to embody to greater or lesser degree the group prototype. Others have interpreted this cognitive mechanism slightly differently. Bill Swann and his colleagues use the term *identity fusion* to describe a process in which social categorization fuses the individual/personal self to the group with the consequence that self and group become indistinguishable (Swann, Gómez, Seyle, Morales, & Huici, 2009; Swann, Jetten, Gomez, Whitehouse, & Bastian, 2012). Complete fusion lays the groundwork for group extremism. Van Veelen and colleagues also talk about how the personal self becomes indistinguishable from the group

(Van Veelen, Otten, Cadinu, & Hansen, 2016). They argue that this can occur by assignment of group attributes to personal self (depersonalisation) or by projection of personal attributes onto the group (projection).

Psychological salience

What determines the point at which one social identity or another becomes the psychologically salient basis for social categorization of self and others? Without an answer to this question, social identity researchers would have a serious scientific problem – they would be unable to predict or manipulate social identity-contingent behaviours.

Penny Oakes and her colleagues have drawn on work by Campbell (1958) and Bruner (1958) to answer this question (Oakes, 1987; Oakes, Haslam, & Turner, 1994; Oakes & Turner, 1990; see **Chapter 2**). Social categories that are (a) chronically accessible to us (e.g. readily available in our memory) and/or (b) accessible in the situation (e.g. there are clear situational cues to the category) come into operation as the basis of self-categorization if they make good sense of the situation by (a) accounting for similarities and differences between people (i.e. they fit the way the situation is structured) and (b) accounting for why people behave as they do (i.e. they fit the norms that people seem to adhere to). This can be put technically: salience is an interactive function of *chronic accessibility* and *situational accessibility* on the one hand, and *structural fit* and *normative fit* on the other. Van Bavel and Cunningham's (2010) iterative reprocessing model (see above) suggests that this is an iterative process in which attributes in memory are called on and temporarily modified to meet contextual demands and goals.

Positive distinctiveness and self-enhancement

Social identity is motivated by two underlying processes: self-enhancement and uncertainty reduction. A key premise of social identity theory is that groups stand in status and prestige relations to one another – some groups simply have more prestige and higher status than others, and people in a given context are aware of this. Unsurprisingly, groups compete with one another over social status and prestige (Tajfel & Turner, 1986; also see Hogg & Abrams, 1988). They compete to be different from one another in favourable ways because positive intergroup distinctiveness provides group members with a favourable (positive) social identity. Unlike interpersonal comparisons, which generally strive for similarity (e.g. Festinger, 1954; Suls & Wheeler, 2000), intergroup comparisons strive to establish differences that evaluatively favour the ingroup.

The pursuit of positive distinctiveness and positive social identity underpins a range of phenomena (Ellemers, Spears, & Doosje, 1999); for example, delinquency. Nick Emler and his colleagues suggest that delinquency, particularly among boys, is strategic behaviour designed to manage a favourable reputation in the eyes of relevant peers (Emler & Hopkins, 1990; Emler & Reicher, 1995). Delinquent behaviour is therefore usually a group activity that occurs in public, because this satisfies its identity-confirming function (Emler, Ohana, & Moscovici, 1987). Furthermore, delinquent behaviour is particularly appealing to children who come from backgrounds that are unlikely to facilitate good academic performance at school: delinquency offers an alternative source of positive identity (it is so attractive that most children toy with it to some extent at one time or another). Reicher and Emler (1985) have suggested that one reason that boys are much more likely than girls to become delinquent is that there is greater pressure on boys to perform well at school, and therefore underachievement is more poignantly felt: the motivation to establish an alternative positive social identity is so much stronger.

Positive distinctiveness as a group-level process maps onto a very basic human motivation for self-esteem through self-enhancement (Sedikides & Strube, 1997; see **Chapter 4**). Drawing on this, social identity researchers have suggested that self-esteem is a key motive in social identity contexts. Research (Abrams & Hogg, 1988; Crocker & Luhtanen, 1990;

Crocker & Major, 1989; Hogg & Abrams, 1990; Long & Spears, 1997; Rubin & Hewstone, 1998) on self-esteem motivation has shown that:

- intergroup differentiation elevates self-esteem;
- depressed self-esteem does not motivate intergroup differentiation;
- it is collective self-esteem, not personal self-esteem, that is related to group processes;
- people in groups are highly creative and competent at protecting themselves from the low self-esteem consequences of low status group membership.

Uncertainty reduction

Social identity processes are, according to *uncertainty–identity theory,* also motivated by uncertainty reduction (Hogg, 2000c, 2007b, 2012). People are fundamentally motivated to know who they are and how they relate to other people – they need to feel relatively certain about what to think, feel and do, and about what others will think, feel and do. We need to know what to expect from other people in order to make life predictable and allow us to plan effective action.

Group identification very effectively reduces uncertainty. Identification with a group, through relevant prototypes, immediately and automatically defines our relationships with ingroup and outgroup others and sets out how we and others will act. Experimental research, largely using variants of the minimal group paradigm, has shown that people identify with groups and identify more strongly with groups when they are uncertain (e.g. Grieve & Hogg, 1999).

However, when we feel uncertain about ourselves, we prefer to identify with highly entitative groups as they provide a better structured and clearer sense of self (Castano, Yzerbyt, & Bourgignon, 2003; Hogg, Sherman, Dierselhuis, Maitner, & Moffitt, 2007; Hogg, Meehan, & Farquharson, 2010; Yzerbyt, Castano, Leyens, & Paolino, 2000). In addition, we can perceptually accentuate the entitativity of existing groups we belong to (Sherman, Hogg, & Maitner, 2009). This preference for high-entitativity groups has an important implication.

When uncertainty is acute, enduring and highly self-relevant, people may strive to identify with groups that are not merely entitative but extreme (Hogg, 2014). Such groups can be described as group centric (Kruglanski, Pierro, Mannetti, & De Grada, 2006). They are normatively homogenous, inward looking, intolerant of dissent, highly ethnocentric, and governed by a powerful, all-embracing, orthodox ideological system. In addition, they have strong, even autocratic leadership. A study of Australian university students found that self-related uncertainty increased support for an extremist campus protest group (Hogg, Meehan, & Farquharson, 2010), and a study of members of organisations in Britain found that self-related uncertainty was associated with greater support for an autocratic organisational leader (Rast, Hogg, & Giessner, 2013).

This may explain why extremism, orthodoxy and group intolerance often arise in times of societal uncertainty associated with war, revolution, economic collapse or natural disaster. It also explains the enduring attraction of religious identities (they provide a distinctive sense of self, a repertoire of customs and rituals, a well-established ideology and a powerful moral compass, and they even deal with existential uncertainty), and the tendency for religiosity to drift into religious zealotry (Hogg, Adelman, & Blagg, 2010).

Social identity and intergroup relations

Social identity theory was originally developed to explain intergroup conflict and social change – this was Tajfel's original social identity theory (Tajfel, 1974; Tajfel & Turner, 1986).

To pursue positive social identity, groups and individuals can adopt different behavioural strategies, the choice of which is determined by people's beliefs about the nature of relations between their own and other groups (Ellemers, 1993; Hogg & Abrams, 1988; Tajfel & Turner, 1986; Taylor & McKirnan, 1984) – see Figure 11.6. These beliefs, which may or may not accord with the reality of intergroup relations (they are ideological constructs), hinge first on whether it is possible, as an individual, to 'pass' from a lower-status group and gain acceptance into a higher-status group. A **social mobility belief system** inhibits group action on the part of subordinate groups. Instead, it encourages people to dissociate themselves from the group and pursue acceptance for themselves and their immediate family in the dominant group. The belief in social mobility is enshrined in Western democratic political systems.

Where people believe that intergroup boundaries are impermeable to 'passing', a **social change belief system** exists. Positive social identity can be achieved only by group action, and the action taken is influenced by whether the status quo (the existing status and power hierarchy) is perceived to be secure or insecure. Take the case of an insecure system. The traditional Hindu caste system in India has long been secure (Sharma, 1981), but this is now challenged on the Indian sub-continent by young people when choosing their mates (Ghimire, Axinn, Yabiku, & Thornton, 2006). On the other hand, if the status quo is considered stable, legitimate and thus secure, it is difficult to conceive of an alternative social structure (i.e. no **cognitive alternatives** exist), let alone a path to real social change. Groups may then adopt **social creativity** strategies:

- They can make intergroup comparisons on novel or unorthodox dimensions that favour the subordinate group. For example, Gerard Lemaine (1966, 1974) had children engage in an intergroup competition to build the best hut, and he found that groups that were provided with poor building materials, and so had no possibility of winning, emphasised how good a garden they had made.

Social mobility belief system
Belief that intergroup boundaries are permeable. Thus, it is possible for someone to pass from a lower-status into a higher-status group to improve social identity.

Social change belief system
Belief that intergroup boundaries are impermeable. Therefore, a lower-status individual can improve social identity only by challenging the legitimacy of the higher-status group's position.

Cognitive alternatives
Belief that the status quo is unstable and illegitimate, and that social competition with the dominant group is the appropriate strategy to improve social identity.

Social creativity
Group-based behavioural strategies that improve social identity but do not directly attack the dominant group's position.

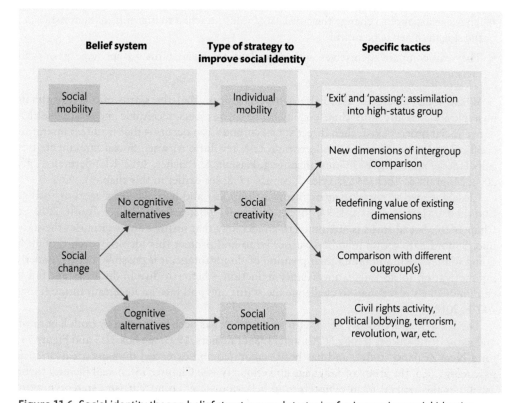

Figure 11.6 Social identity theory: belief structures and strategies for improving social identity
Beliefs about the nature of intergroup relations influence the general strategies and specific tactics that group members can adopt to try to maintain or achieve positive social identity.

Social action
Even a peaceful
demonstration can
challenge the status quo
and a state's power base.

- They can attempt to change the consensual value attached to ingroup characteristics (e.g. the slogan 'Black is beautiful').
- They can compare themselves with other low- or lower-status groups (e.g. 'poor white racism').

Social competition
Group-based behavioural
strategies that improve
social identity by directly
confronting the dominant
group's position in society.

Where social change is associated with recognition that the status quo is illegitimate, unstable and insecure, and where cognitive alternatives (i.e. conceivable and attainable alternative social orders) exist, then direct **social competition** occurs – that is, direct intergroup conflict (e.g. political action, collective protest, revolutions, war). Social movements typically emerge under these circumstances (e.g. Haslam & Reicher, 2012; Klandermans, 1997, 2003; Milgram & Toch, 1969; Tyler & Smith, 1998; see earlier in this chapter).

System justification theory
Theory that attributes social
stasis to people's adherence
to an ideology that justifies
and protects the status quo.

Closely related to social identity theory is John Jost and his colleagues' **system justification theory** (Jost & Banaji, 1994; Jost & Hunyadi, 2002; Jost & Van der Toorn, 2012; see **Chapter 10**). Social stasis is attributed to an ideology that justifies and legitimises the status quo. Subordinate group members subscribe to and protect this ideology even though by doing so they are maintaining their position of disadvantage. It is possible that the underlying motivation to do this is uncertainty reduction – better to live in disadvantage but be certain of one's place than to challenge the status quo and face an uncertain future (Hogg, 2007b, 2012).

The social identity theory of intergroup relations has been supported by both laboratory and naturalistic studies (Hogg & Abrams, 1988; Ellemers, 1993; see Box 11.3 and Figure 11.7 for a New Zealand study), and has been elaborated and extended in many areas of social psychology (e.g. the study of language and ethnicity; see **Chapter 15**). Social identity theory attributes the general form of intergroup behaviour (e.g. ethnocentrism, stereotyping) to social categorization-related processes, and the specific manifestation (e.g. conflict, harmony) to people's beliefs about the nature of intergroup relations.

Box 11.3 Our world
Social change: Growth of pride in an indigenous people

Maori people are New Zealand's indigenous people and currently make up about 15 per cent of the population. The remainder of the population is predominantly Pakeha (i.e. European). Graham Vaughan collected data on ingroup (ethnic) preferences of younger (6–8 years) and older (10–12 years) Maori and Pakeha children from urban and rural backgrounds (Vaughan, 1978a, 1978b). The data were collected at various times during the 1960s, which was a period of considerable social change in New Zealand; these data are displayed in Figure 11.7. The arrows represent an age trend from younger to older children within each ethnic group at each time and at each location. Choices above 50 per cent represent ingroup preference and those below 50 per cent outgroup preference.

Against an overall reduction in ethnocentrism for older children (presumably a developmental trend), the data show that urban Pakeha preferred their own group but were less ethnocentric than rural Pakeha, and rural Maori showed more marked outgroup preference than urban Maori. The most interesting finding was that, between 1961 and 1971, urban Maori actually changed from making outgroup to making ingroup preferences – a change that reflected the rise in the late 1960s and early 1970s of an assertive Brown (Maori) Power movement modelled on the American Black Power movement of the late 1960s.

Intergroup perceptions may be less ethnocentric in the city for a number of reasons, including perhaps inter-ethnic contact. Maori who moved to the city were often cut off from the traditional Polynesian extended family (and from other aspects of Maori culture) and found that they had to compete with Pakeha for work. There was a gradual realignment of ethnic power relations and greater possibility of less-unequal status inter-ethnic contact. Perhaps this contributed to some extent to reduced prejudice on the part of Pakeha and elevated ethnic pride on the part of Maori.

Figure 11.7 Ingroup bias among Maori and Pakeha children as a function of social change (time, nature of intergroup contact)

The direction of the arrows depicts an age trend from younger to older children in each group. By 1971, older urban Maori were exhibiting more ingroup bias than older urban Pakeha. Between 1961 and 1971, there was a systematic decrease in Pakeha ingroup bias and Maori outgroup bias, which was more pronounced for older than younger children.

Source: Vaughan (1978b); in Tajfel (1978).

Alex Haslam and his colleagues capture this in a study of subtle changes in Australians' stereotypes of Americans after the first Gulf War in 1991 (Haslam, Turner, Oakes, McGarty, & Hayes, 1992). Australians who were making comparisons between Australia, Britain and the United States had a relatively unfavourable stereotype of Americans that deteriorated further during the course of the Gulf conflict, particularly on dimensions reflecting arrogance, argumentativeness and traditionalism. The reason why attitudes

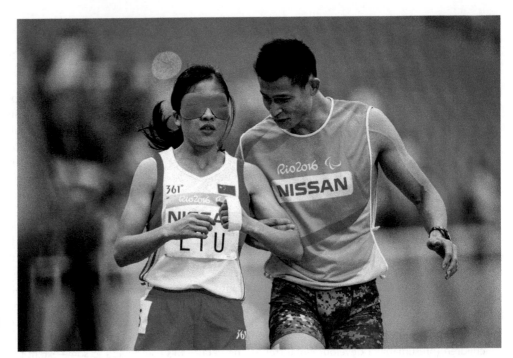

Social change
These Rio Paralympics athletes promote a positive image of disabled people. In this case, a blind athlete just needs a helping hand along the way.

deteriorated on these particular dimensions rather than others was that these dimensions related directly to the perceived actions of Americans in relation to other nations during the war.

Other aspects

Social identity theory has many other important components, extensions and applications, most of which are discussed elsewhere in this text. These include:

- *Referent informational influence* theory (Abrams & Hogg, 1990a; Turner, 1991; Turner & Oakes, 1989), which deals with conformity (**Chapter 7**) and group polarisation (**Chapter 9**).
- The *social attraction hypothesis*, which deals with cohesion and attraction phenomena in groups (Hogg, 1993, **Chapter 8**).
- The theory of *subjective group dynamics*, which deals with deviance processes in groups (Marques, Abrams, Páez, & Taboada, 1998; Pinto, Marques, Levine, & Abrams, 2010; **Chapter 8**).
- The social identity theory of *leadership* (Hogg & Van Knippenberg, 2003; Hogg, Van Knippenberg, & Rast, 2012b; **Chapter 9**).
- The social identity theory of *attitude–behaviour relations* (Terry & Hogg, 1996; Hogg & Smith, 2007; **Chapter 5**).
- The social identity theory of *deindividuation* phenomena (Klein, Spears, & Reicher, 2007; Reicher, Spears, & Postmes, 1995; see the subsection 'Deindividuation and self-awareness' later in this chapter).
- Social identity analysis of *creativity* (Haslam, Adarves-Yorno, Postmes, & Jans, 2013)
- *Collective guilt* – where you feel guilty, as a group member, about past transgressions committed by your group (Doosje, Branscombe, Spears, & Manstead, 2006; Goldenberg, Halperin, Van Zomeren, & Gross, 2016).

Social cognition

Although self-categorization theory has a social cognitive emphasis on group and intergroup behaviour (Farr, 1996), it explicitly articulates with a more broadly social analysis (Doise, 1986; see **Chapter 1**). This is because, as we have seen, it is part of the broader social identity theory. Social cognition (see **Chapter 2** for full coverage), however, provides a number of other more purely cognitive explanations, which focus on cognitive and perceptual effects that have important implications for intergroup behaviour.

Categorization and relative homogeneity

The most obvious effect is stereotyping. The categorization of people (or objects) causes an **accentuation effect** (Tajfel, 1959). Categorization perceptually accentuates similarities among people in a category and differences between people from different categories on dimensions believed to be associated with the categorization: that is, stereotypical dimensions (Doise, 1978; Eiser & Stroebe, 1972; Tajfel & Wilkes, 1963). Accentuation may be asymmetrical – people perceptually homogenise outgroup members more than ingroup members: '*they* all look alike, but *we* are diverse' (Brigham & Malpass, 1985; Quattrone, 1986).

> **Accentuation effect**
> Overestimation of similarities among people within a category and dissimilarities between people from different categories.

John Brigham and Paul Barkowitz (1978) had black and white college students indicate for seventy-two photographs of black and white faces how certain they were that they had seen each photograph in a previously presented series of twenty-four photographs (twelve of blacks and twelve of whites). Figure 11.8 shows that participants found it more difficult to recognise outgroup than ingroup faces. This effect is robust. It has emerged in other studies comparing 'Anglos' with blacks (Bothwell, Brigham, & Malpass, 1989), with Hispanics (Platz & Hosch, 1988) and with Japanese (Chance, 1985), and from studies of student eating clubs (Jones, Wood, & Quattrone, 1981), college sororities (Park & Rothbart, 1982) and artificial laboratory groups (Wilder, 1984).

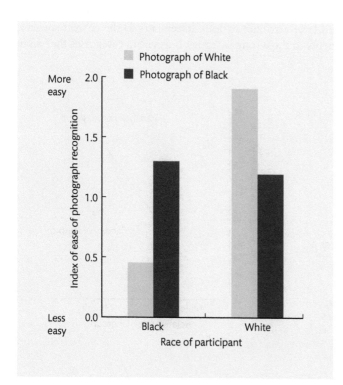

Figure 11.8 Ease of recognition of faces as a function of race of participant and race of person in photograph

Black and white participants had more difficulty identifying faces they had seen before if the faces were of racial outgroup rather than racial ingroup members.

Source: Based on data from Brigham and Barkowitz (1978).

Relative homogeneity effect

Tendency to see outgroup members as all the same, and ingroup members as more differentiated.

The **relative homogeneity effect** is enhanced on dimensions that define a group (Lee & Ottati, 1993) and when groups are in competition (Judd & Park, 1988; see Ostrom & Sedikides, 1992). The principal explanation is that we are more familiar with and have more detailed knowledge about ingroup than outgroup members, and therefore can better differentiate them (Linville, Fischer, & Salovey, 1989; Wilder, 1986). Although sensible, this may not be the complete story. For example, the outgroup homogeneity effect occurs when participants report no greater familiarity with the ingroup than with the outgroup (Jones, Wood, & Quattrone, 1981) and when there is equally minimal information about both groups (Wilder, 1984). Walter Stephan (1977) found that children in both segregated and integrated schools (i.e. with lower or higher intergroup familiarity) rated their own group as more homogeneous than two outgroups. If outgroup homogeneity is not inevitable, what factors influence the relative homogeneity effect?

One clue is that most research has used majority ingroups, but Stephan's (1977) groups were minority groups (Chicanos and blacks). The relative outgroup homogeneity effect is stronger when the outgroup is perceived to be relatively small – a minority (Bartsch & Judd, 1993; Mullen & Hu, 1989). To test the idea that relative homogeneity is influenced by the majority–minority status of the ingroup, Bernd Simon and Rupert Brown (1987) conducted a minimal group study. Relative group size was varied, and participants rated the variability of both ingroup and outgroup and indicated how much they identified with the ingroup. Figure 11.9 shows that majorities rated the outgroup as less variable than the ingroup (the usual outgroup homogeneity effect), but minorities did the opposite. Moreover, this latter ingroup homogeneity effect was accompanied by greater group identification. This is consistent with social identity theory: minorities categorise themselves more strongly as a group and are thus more strongly depersonalised (see earlier in this chapter) in their perceptions, attitudes and behaviour.

Memory

Social categorization is associated with category-based memory for people (Fiske & Taylor, 1991). Shelley Taylor and her colleagues had participants listen to taped mixed-sex or mixed-race discussion groups and later attribute various statements to the correct speaker. They rarely attributed the statements to the wrong category, but within categories they were

Figure 11.9 Perceived intragroup variability of ingroup and outgroup as a function of relative majority or minority status of ingroup

Majorities rated the outgroup as less variable than the ingroup (the usual relative homogeneity effect). However, minorities did the opposite – they rated the outgroup as more variable than the ingroup.

Source: Based on data from Simon and Brown (1987).

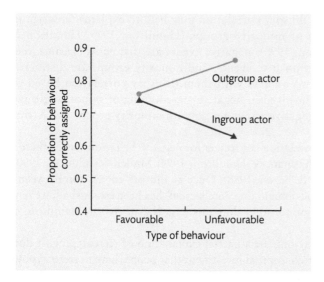

Figure 11.10 Assignment of behaviours to actors as a function of item favourability and ingroup/outgroup status of actor

Participants were equally good at recalling whether it was an ingroup or outgroup member who performed favourable behaviours, but they were better at recalling outgroup than ingroup actors who performed unfavourable behaviours.

Source: Based on Howard and Rothbart (1980).

not good at identifying the correct speaker: that is, they made few between-category errors but many within-category errors (Taylor, Fiske, Etcoff, & Ruderman, 1978).

The category-based memory effect can be selective. John Howard and Myron Rothbart (1980) had participants read statements describing the behaviour of ingroup or outgroup members – some behaviour reflected favourably and some unfavourably on the actor. Later, for each behaviour, participants had to recall whether it was an ingroup or an outgroup member who performed the behaviour. Participants were equally accurate at recalling whether it was an ingroup or outgroup member who performed favourable behaviour, but they were more accurate at recalling outgroup than ingroup actors who performed unfavourable behaviour (see Figure 11.10).

These experiments show how information about people can be represented cognitively and organised as category attributes that minimise differences between people in the same category. Furthermore, evaluative biases may influence what information is associated with a particular category.

Distinctive stimuli and illusory correlation

A particularly important influence on what information is associated with which categories is how distinctive the information is. Anything that is out of the ordinary (objects, events and people who are statistically infrequent, rare, unusual, relatively vivid or conspicuous) attracts our attention and we become more cognitively active (Taylor & Fiske, 1978). So, for example, we attend more to a single man in a group of women, a single black in a group of whites, or to a person we understand to be a genius, a terrorist or a movie star. Distinctive individuals can also disproportionately influence the overall images we construct of groups. We generalise from distinctive individuals to the group as a whole, particularly when we have few prior expectations and/or are unfamiliar with the category (Quattrone & Jones, 1980). For instance, on the basis of meeting one extremely stupid (i.e. distinctive individual) Martian (i.e. unfamiliar group), we are apt to stereotype the group as stupid.

Another effect of distinctiveness is that people tend to perceive an **illusory correlation**, based on *paired distinctiveness* or *associative meaning*, between distinctive events that occur at the same time (Chapman, 1967; illusory correlation is discussed fully in

Illusory correlation
Cognitive exaggeration of the degree of co-occurrence of two stimuli or events, or the perception of a co-occurrence where none exists.

Chapter 2). Distinctiveness-based illusory correlation may help to explain stereotyping, particularly negative stereotypes of minority groups (Hamilton, 1979; Hamilton & Sherman, 1989; Mullen & Johnson, 1990): negative events are distinctive because they are subjectively less frequent than positive events; and minority groups are distinctive because people have relatively few contacts with them. Illusory correlation based on associative meaning may also be involved in negative stereotyping of minority groups: people have preconceptions that negative attributes go with minority groups (McArthur & Friedman, 1980).

Distinctiveness-based illusory correlation is stronger for negative behaviour, when there is high memory load (McConnell, Sherman, & Hamilton, 1994; Mullen & Johnson, 1990), and when people are aroused (Kim & Baron, 1988). Once an illusory correlation between a group and a negative attribute in one domain (e.g. intellectual) has been established, we tend to generalise the negative impression to other domains (e.g. social; Acorn, Hamilton, & Sherman, 1988).

However, illusory correlation may only be a partial explanation of stereotyping. It does not consider the emotional and self-conceptual investment that people have in stereotyping, or the real power and status differentials between groups that stereotype one another. As we have seen in this chapter and in **Chapter 10**, how we construct and use stereotypes is framed by intergroup relations and governed by cognitive, affective and rhetorical motives (Leyens, Yzerbyt, & Schadron, 1994; McGarty, Haslam, Turner, & Oakes, 1993; Oakes, Haslam, & Turner, 1994).

Optimal distinctiveness

Optimal distinctiveness
People strive to achieve a balance between conflicting motives for inclusiveness and separateness, expressed in groups as a balance between intragroup differentiation and intragroup homogenisation.

Distinctiveness enters into intergroup behaviour in rather a different way in Marilynn Brewer's (1991) theory of **optimal distinctiveness** (see Leonardelli, Pickett, & Brewer, 2010). Building on her dual-process model of information processing (Brewer, 1988, 1994; see **Chapter 2**), Brewer argues that the default mode for processing information about others is in terms of their category membership (satisfying a need to recognise similarities among people). However, if one is ego-involved in the task, or related to or interdependent with the stimulus person, then information processing is based on very specific and personalised information about the person (this satisfies a need to recognise differences between people). In most contexts, people strive to achieve a satisfactory level of distinctiveness for others and for themselves in order to resolve the tension between the needs for similarity and difference. In intergroup behaviour, this manifests as a degree of differentiation between group members, including self, against a background of homogenisation. A related phenomenon, called the *primus inter pares* effect, was earlier identified by Jean-Paul Codol (1975) to describe how people in groups differentiate themselves from one another in competition to be the most representative or best group member.

From Brewer's perspective, people are driven by conflicting motives for inclusion/sameness (satisfied by group membership) and for distinctiveness/uniqueness (satisfied by individuality), so they try to strike a balance between these two motives to achieve optimal distinctiveness. Smaller groups over-satisfy the need for distinctiveness, so people strive for greater inclusiveness, while large groups over-satisfy the need for inclusiveness, so people strive for distinctiveness.

One implication of this idea is that people should be more satisfied with membership of mid-size groups than groups that are very large or very small (Hornsey & Jetten, 2004). This idea is usually tested in the laboratory with a restricted range of relative group sizes. To investigate groups that varied enormously in relative size, Dominic Abrams (1994) analysed survey data on political identity from over 4,000 18- to 21-year-olds in England and Scotland. He found that small parties (Green, Social Democrat, Scottish Nationalist) did indeed provide members with a more solid and distinct identity than did the large parties (Labour, Conservative).

Intergroup emotions

People in groups that are important to them feel strong emotions about outgroups and fellow members of their own groups, and about events and behaviours that relate to group membership – strength of emotion and type of emotion are key features of intergroup relations. Research addressing this aspect of intergroup relations has been sparse. However, the past twenty years has witnessed an upsurge in research on intergroup emotions (Goldenberg, Halperin, Van Zomeren, & Gross, 2016; Iyer & Leach, 2008).

Diane Mackie and Eliot Smith proposed an **intergroup emotions theory** (IET) to address emotions in group contexts (Mackie, Devos, & Smith, 2000; Mackie & Smith, 2002a; also see Mackie, Maitner, & Smith, 2009; Mackie & Smith, 2002b). It builds on social identity theory, and on appraisal theories of emotion that view individual emotions as arising from appraisals of whether a situation is going to harm or benefit oneself personally (e.g. Lazarus, 1991; Parkinson & Manstead, 1992; see **Chapter 2**). In group contexts, the self is a collective self, and so appraisals operate at the level of whether a situation is going to harm or benefit 'us', not necessarily oneself as an individual.

When people identify with a group, associated intergroup emotions come into play, and the more strongly someone identifies with their group, the stronger the emotions are (e.g. Wohl & Branscombe, 2008). Harm to the ingroup, which often emanates from the actions of outgroups, is appraised as self-harming. This generates negative emotions about the outgroup. Behaviour that promotes the ingroup, often emanating from fellow ingroup members, generates positive emotions about the ingroup and its members. Emotions have an action tendency. Outgroup emotions may translate into discrimination or prejudice-related behaviours, and ingroup emotions into solidarity and cohesion-related behaviours. From IET it can also be predicted that emotions felt by fellow ingroup members will quickly be felt by self – owing to the common identity bond that exists.

People have some control over the generation of their emotions and regulate them to advance specific goals (Gross, 2015). In the intergroup context, the regulation goals are not personal but are group-based (Goldenberg, Halperin, Van Zomeren, & Gross, 2016; Maitner, Mackie, & Smith, 2006). Tamir (2016) distinguishes between two types of goals: hedonic goals to increase pleasant (e.g. pride, respect, hope) and decrease unpleasant (e.g. guilt) group-based emotions; and instrumental goals that are usually associated with short-term negative emotional experiences such as fear, anger and frustration that have instrumental value to the group.

Intergroup emotions may also be affected by people's regulatory focus (Higgins, 1998; see **Chapter 4**); specifically, whether group members have a promotion or prevention intergroup focus (Jonas, Sassenberg, & Scheepers, 2010). In intergroup contexts, a *promotion focus* strengthens people's positive emotion-related bias and behavioural tendencies towards the ingroup; a *prevention focus* strengthens their negative emotion-related bias and behavioural tendencies against the outgroup (Shah, Brazy, & Higgins, 2004).

Other research on intergroup and collective emotions has focused on specific group-based emotions. There have been studies of collective guilt and shame and how these emotions affect people's intentions to perform acts of reparation and reconciliation, specifically public apologies and political action intentions (e.g. Branscombe & Doosje, 2004; Brown, Gonzalez, Zagefka, Manzi, & Cehajic, 2008; Doosje, Branscombe, Spears, & Manstead, 1998, 2006; Iyer, Schmader, & Lickel, 2007; Nadler & Shnabel, 2015).

Collective guilt arises if people feel that their group's blameworthy actions are or were under their control and that they are therefore to some extent responsible. Collective shame arises if people feel that their group's actions reflect poorly on the image of the group but that the actions were not under their control and that they largely had no responsibility for the actions. It is collective guilt, not shame, that therefore sponsors intergroup behaviours aimed at righting the wrong – such as apologising or making reparation. Collective shame is likely to motivate people to avoid or escape the shame-evoking event or even the ingroup itself if it is seen as the source of the shameful outcome.

Intergroup emotions theory
Theory that, in group contexts, appraisals of personal harm or benefit in a situation operate at the level of social identity and thus produce mainly positive ingroup and negative outgroup emotions.

Collective behaviour and the crowd

Collective behaviour
The behaviour of people en masse – such as in a crowd, protest or riot.

Collective behaviour usually refers to large numbers of people who are in the same place at the same time, behaving in a uniform manner that is volatile, highly emotional and in violation of social norms (Graumann & Moscovici, 1986; Milgram & Toch, 1969; Moscovici, 1985b). This can include rumours (see **Chapter 3**), fads and fashions, social movements and cults, and contagions of expression, enthusiasm, anxiety, fear and hostility.

Contagions include some of the most bizarre behaviour imaginable (Klapp, 1972). In the 1630s, tulip mania swept north-western Europe, with people trading small fortunes for a single, ultimately worthless, bulb; in the fifteenth century, there was an epidemic in Europe in which nuns bit each other; in the eighteenth century, there was an epidemic of nuns meowing like cats; between the tenth and the fourteenth centuries in Europe, there were frequent episodes of dancing mania, with people continually dancing from town to town until they dropped and even died; and in the mid- and late 1980s, there were epidemics in China of men complaining hysterically about shrinkage of the penis and an overwhelming fear of impending death!

Usually, however, the study of collective behaviour is a more sober business. It is the study of crowd behaviour. The crowd is a vivid event, both for those who are involved and for those who witness the events first-hand or through literature and the media (see Box 11.4). Consider the Nazi rallies of the 1930s, civil rights and anti-Vietnam War rallies in Washington in the 1960s and early 1970s, celebrations at the fall of the Berlin Wall in 1990, political demonstrations in the streets of Tehran in 2009 and the anti-Trump marches across the United States and the rest of the world in early 2017; and think of rock festivals since the late 1960s, the 2011 protests in Tahrir Square in Cairo, huge crowds at Queen Elizabeth II's diamond jubilee in London in 2012 and the massive pro-democracy rallies in Istanbul and other Turkish cities in 2016. There is also the impossibility of navigating the crowds in Oxford Street in London during the run-up to Christmas every year. But everything is dwarfed by some of the Hindu pilgrimages in India – on one single day in 2013, 30 million pilgrims were present at the Hindu festival of Maha Kumbh Mela in Allahabad. Crowd events are nothing if not varied.

People can also quite like being in crowds – it can be energising and uplifting. Tewari and colleagues report longitudinal data from pilgrims at the Maha Kumbh Mela that shows how participation in the collective event significantly improved well-being (Tewari, Khan, Hopkins, Srinivasan, & Reicher, 2012).

Box 11.4 Your life
In a crowd

Most of us have been involved in a crowd event – a demonstration or rally, a music concert or festival, a street celebration. In the context of our discussion of crowd behaviour in this chapter, reflect on your own experiences in a crowd.

- Did you feel strong emotions (e.g., elation, anger, sadness), and did these feelings seem to be influenced by the shifting emotions expressed by those around you?
- Did you feel lost in the crowd – personally unidentifiable and unaccountable and thus liberated to behave in possibly socially unacceptable ways that you would not normally behave?
- Did you feel a strong bond of camaraderie and shared identity with others in the crowd?
- Did you sometimes feel unsure about how you as a member of this crowd should behave – what you should do to accurately express your crowd's identity and your membership credentials?
- When unsure about how to behave, how did you find out – who did you look to for guidance?

Crowd behaviour can be difficult to research in the laboratory. However, attempts have been made. For example, John French (1944) locked his participants in a room and then wafted smoke under the door while sounding the fire alarm. Research ethics aside, the study was not successful as an attempt to create panic in the laboratory. One group kicked open the door and knocked over the smoke generator, and members of another group calmly discussed the possibility that their reactions were being observed by the experimenters!

Early theories

One of the earliest theories of collective behaviour was proposed by Gustave LeBon (1896/1908), who lived through a period of great social turmoil in France. He observed and read accounts of the great revolutionary crowds of the revolution of 1848 and the Paris Commune of 1871 – accounts such as those to be found in Zola's novels *Germinal* and *La Débacle* and Hugo's *Les Misérables*. He was appalled by the 'primitive, base and ghastly' behaviour of the crowd, and how people's civilised conscious personality seemed to vanish and be replaced by savage animal instincts. LeBon believed that:

> by the mere fact that he forms part of an organised crowd, a man descends several rungs in the ladder of civilisation. Isolated, he may be a cultivated individual; in a crowd he is a barbarian – that is, a creature acting by instinct.
>
> LeBon (1896/1908, p. 12)

LeBon believed that crowds produce primitive and homogeneous behaviour because (see Figure 11.11):

- members are anonymous and thus lose personal responsibility for their actions;
- ideas and sentiments spread rapidly and unpredictably through a process of contagion;
- unconscious antisocial motives ('ancestral savagery') are released through suggestion (a process akin to hypnosis).

LeBon is still important (see Apfelbaum & McGuire, 1986; Hogg & Abrams, 1988; Reicher, 1987, 1996, 2001), mainly because his view that crowd behaviour is pathological/ abnormal has influenced later theories of collective behaviour (e.g. Freud, 1921; McDougall, 1920; Zimbardo, 1970). Freud, for example, believed that the crowd 'unlocks' the

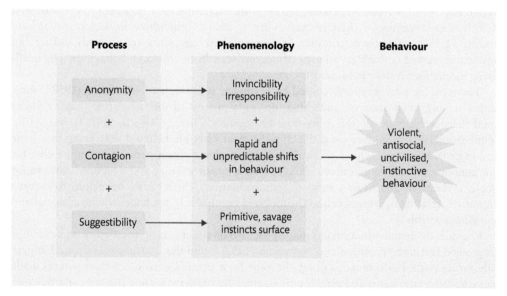

Figure 11.11 LeBon's model of the crowd

Anonymity, contagion and suggestibility operate together to produce antisocial, violent crowd behaviour.

Source: Based on Hogg (1992).

unconscious. Society's moral standards maintain civilised behaviour because they are installed in the human psyche as the super-ego. In crowds, the super-ego is supplanted by the leader of the crowd, who now acts as the hypnotist controlling unconscious and uncivilised id impulses. Crowd leaders have this effect because of a deep and primitive instinct in all of us to regress, in crowds, to the 'primal horde' – the original brutal human group at the dawn of existence. Civilisation is able to evolve and thrive only if the leader of the primal horde, the 'primal father', is overthrown. This analysis has been used to explain how the 'Reverend' Jim Jones had such enormous power over his cult followers that more than 900 of them collectively committed suicide at Jonestown in Guyana in 1978 (Ulman & Abse, 1983). (Reflect on the fourth 'What do *you* think?' question at the beginning of this chapter).

Another influential early theorist is William McDougall, who characterised the crowd as:

> excessively emotional, impulsive, violent, fickle, inconsistent, irresolute and extreme in action, displaying only the coarser emotions and the less refined sentiments; extremely suggestible, careless in deliberation, hasty in judgment, incapable of any but the simpler and imperfect forms of reasoning, easily swayed and led, lacking in self-consciousness, devoid of self-respect and of a sense of responsibility, and apt to be carried away by the consciousness of its own force, so that it tends to produce all the manifestations we have learnt to expect of any irresponsible and absolute power.
>
> McDougall (1920, p. 45)

McDougall believed that the most widespread instinctive emotions are the simple primitive ones (e.g. fear, anger). These would therefore be the most common and widely shared emotions in any human aggregate. More complex emotions would be rare and less widely shared. Stimuli eliciting the primitive simple emotions would therefore cause a strong shared reaction, while those eliciting more complex emotions would not. Primary emotions spread and strengthen rapidly in a crowd, as each member's expression of the emotion acts as a further stimulus to others – a snowball effect dubbed 'primitive sympathy'. This effect is not easily dampened, as members feel depersonalised and have a lowered sense of personal responsibility.

Deindividuation and self-awareness

More recent explanations of collective behaviour discard some of the specifics of earlier approaches (e.g. the emphasis on instinctive emotions, the psychodynamic framework) but retain the overall perspective. People refrain from exercising their impulsive, aggressive and selfish nature because of their identifiability as unique individuals in societies that have norms against 'uncivilised' conduct. In crowds, these restraints are relaxed, and we can revert to type and embark on an orgy of aggressive, selfish, antisocial behaviour. The mediating mechanism is **deindividuation**.

Deindividuation
Process whereby people lose their sense of socialised individual identity and engage in unsocialised, often antisocial, behaviours.

The term 'deindividuation', coined by Festinger, Pepitone and Newcomb (1952), originates in Jung's definition of 'individuation' as 'a process of differentiation, having for its goal the development of the individual personality' (Jung, 1946, p. 561). It was Philip Zimbardo (1970) who developed the concept most fully. He believed that being in a large group provides people with a cloak of anonymity that diffuses personal responsibility for the consequences of their actions. This leads to a loss of identity and a reduced concern for social evaluation: that is, to a state of deindividuation, which causes behaviour to become impulsive, irrational, regressive and disinhibited because it is not under the usual social and personal controls.

Research on deindividuation has mainly focused on the effects of anonymity on behaviour in groups. Festinger, Pepitone and Newcomb (1952) found that participants dressed in grey laboratory coats and seated in a poorly lit room for a group discussion of their parents made more negative comments about their parents than did participants in a control condition (see

Deindividuation
People in uniforms, and in
large groups, have a cloak
of anonymity.

also Cannavale, Scarr, & Pepitone, 1970). Similarly, participants dressed in laboratory coats used more obscene language when discussing erotic literature than did more easily identifiable individuals (Singer, Brush, & Lublin, 1965).

Zimbardo (1970) conducted a series of experiments where participants were deindividuated by wearing cloaks and hoods (reminiscent of the Ku Klux Klan). In one experiment, deindividuated female students gave electric shocks to a female confederate in a paired-associate learning task that were twice the duration of those given by conventionally dressed participants. In another classic study, Zimbardo constructed a simulated prison in the basement of the Psychology Department of Stanford University, and found that students who were deindividuated by being dressed as guards were extremely brutal to other students who were deindividuated as prisoners (Zimbardo, Haney, Banks, & Jaffe, 1982; see **Chapter 8**). There is also evidence that people are more willing to lynch someone (Mullen, 1986) or bait a disturbed person to jump from a building if it is dark and they are in a larger group (Mann, 1981; see **Chapter 12**).

Finally, Ed Diener and his colleagues conducted a clever study that took advantage of Halloween – when the streets were filled with children, disguised and thus anonymous, who were trick-or-treating (Diener, Fraser, Beaman, & Kelem, 1976). The researchers observed the behaviour of more than 1,300 children, alone or in groups, who approached twenty-seven focal homes in Seattle where they were warmly invited in and told to 'take *one* of the candies' on a table. Half the children were first asked their names and where they lived, to reduce deindividuation. Groups and deindividuated children were more than twice as likely to take extra candy. The transgression rate varied from 8 per cent of individuated individuals to 80 per cent of deindividuated groups.

Although anonymity often seems to increase aggressive antisocial behaviour (Dipboye, 1977), there are problematic findings. Zimbardo (1970) used his deindividuation paradigm with Belgian soldiers and found that they gave electric shocks of shorter duration when dressed in cloaks and hoods. Zimbardo suggests that this might be because the soldiers were an intact group (i.e. already deindividuated), and the 'cloak and hood' procedure had the paradoxical effect of reducing deindividuation.

Figure 11.12 Administration of electric shocks as a function of deindividuation and type of uniform

- In a paired-associate learning task, women participants dressed in either of two uniforms believed that they gave shocks of various levels to a confederate learner.

- Those dressed as Ku Klux Klan members gave increased levels of shock to the learner, whereas those dressed as nurses gave reduced levels.

- Further, deindividuated participants (i.e. those not wearing large personal name badges) were not more aggressive, and in fact those deindividuated as nurses were the least aggressive of all.

Source: Based on data from Johnson and Downing (1979).

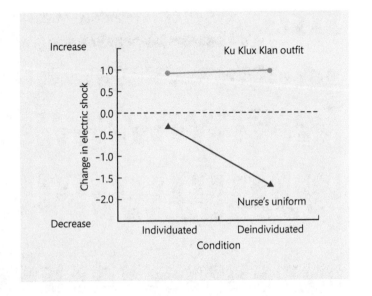

However, other studies reported reduced aggression when a person is anonymous or when a member of a group (Diener, 1976). In one study by Robert Johnson and Leslie Downing (1979), female participants administered shocks to confederate 'learners' in a paired-associate learning task. The women were deindividuated when clothed to resemble either a Ku Klux Klan member or a nurse. The experimenter highlighted the impact of the clothing by explicitly commenting on the resemblance. Half of each group also wore a large badge displaying their name in order to individuate them (i.e. deindividuation was reduced). Deindividuation failed to increase aggression, even among those dressed as Ku Klux Klan members (see Figure 11.12). However, those dressed as nurses were significantly less aggressive than those dressed as Ku Klux Klan members, and deindividuated nurses were the least aggressive of all.

These studies tell us two important things, First, anonymity does not automatically lead people to be more aggressive and antisocial. Second, normative expectations surrounding situations of deindividuation may influence behaviour. In the Johnson and Downing study, when women were dressed like a nurse, they became more caring. There is also a striking similarity between Zimbardo's method of deindividuation (i.e. hood and robe) and the wearing of the *chador* (full-length veil) by women in some Islamic countries (Jahoda, 1982). Far from setting free antisocial impulses, the *chador* very precisely specifies one's social obligations.

Diener has more fully explored the role of self-awareness in deindividuation, by invoking Duval and Wicklund's (1972) notion of objective self-awareness (awareness of oneself as an object of attention):

> A deindividuated person is prevented by situational factors present in a group from becoming self-aware. Deindividuated persons are blocked from awareness of themselves as separate individuals and from monitoring their own behaviour.
>
> Diener (1980, p. 210)

The crowd reduces self-awareness to create a psychological state of deindividuation that has specific consequences for behaviour (see Figure 11.13). Although these consequences do not inevitably include aggression, they do facilitate the emergence of antisocial behaviour. In support of Diener's model, Steven Prentice-Dunn and Ronald Rogers (1982) found that participants who were prevented from becoming self-aware, by being blasted with loud rock music in a darkened room while working on a collective task, subsequently gave more intense electric

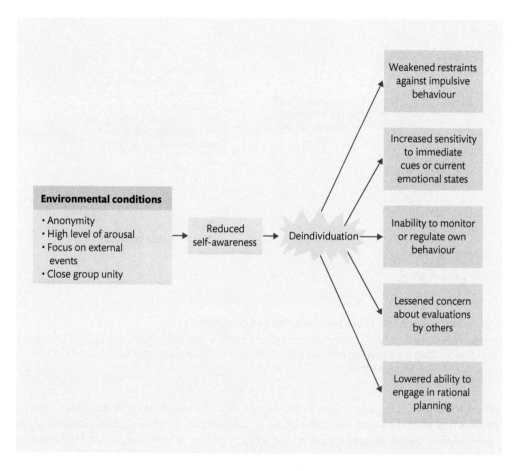

Figure 11.13 Self-awareness and deindividuation

Environmental factors present in crowd situations reduce self-awareness and create a state of deindividuation that produces typical crowd behaviours.

Source: Based on Diener (1980).

shocks to a 'learner' than did participants who had been working individually in a quiet, well-illuminated room under instructions to concentrate on their own thoughts and feelings.

Another perspective on deindividuation distinguishes between public and private self-awareness (Carver & Scheier, 1981; Scheier & Carver, 1981). Reduced attention to one's private self (feelings, thoughts, attitudes and other private aspects of self) is equated with deindividuation, but it does not necessarily produce antisocial behaviour unless the appropriate norms are in place (see Figure 11.14). It is reduced attention to one's public self (how one wishes others to view one's conduct) that causes behaviour to be independent of social norms and thus to become antisocial.

All models of deindividuation, including those focused on self-awareness, dwell on *loss* – loss of individuality, loss of identity, loss of awareness and 'loss' of desirable behaviour. Critics have suggested that all this talk about 'loss' may at best restrict the range of collective behaviour we can talk about and may at worst provide an inadequate understanding altogether. Instead, we should be focusing on *change* – change of identity, change of awareness and change of behaviour (e.g. Klein, Spears, & Reicher, 2007; Postmes & Spears, 1998; Reicher, Spears, & Postmes, 1995; also see Haslam & Reicher, 2005, 2012) (see the fifth 'What do *you* think?' question).

Emergent norm theory

Emergent norm theory takes a very different approach to explaining collective behaviour (Turner, 1974; Turner & Killian, 1957). Rather than treating it as pathological or instinctual behaviour, it focuses on collective behaviour as norm-governed behaviour, much like any other

Emergent norm theory
Collective behaviour is regulated by norms based on distinctive behaviour that arises in the initially normless crowd.

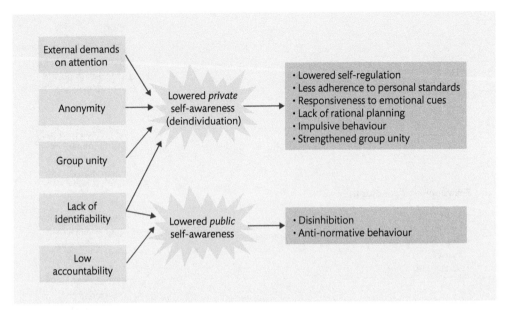

Figure 11.14 Private and public self-awareness and deindividuation

Environmental factors present in crowd situations reduce public and/or private self-awareness, but it is the reduction of public self-awareness that is associated with disinhibited and anti-normative crowd behaviours.
Source: Based on Hogg and Abrams (1988).

group behaviour. The sociologist R. H. Turner (not the social psychologist John Turner) believes that what is distinct about the crowd is that it has no formal organisation or tradition of established norms to regulate behaviour, so the problem of explaining crowd behaviour is to explain how a norm emerges from within the crowd (hence, 'emergent norm theory'; see Figure 11.15). People in a crowd find themselves together under circumstances where there are no clear norms to guide behaviour. Their attention is attracted by distinctive behaviour (or the behaviour of distinctive individuals). This behaviour implies a norm, and consequently there is pressure against non-conformity. Inaction on the part of the majority is interpreted as tacit confirmation of the norm, which consequently amplifies pressures against non-conformity.

By focusing on norms, emergent norm theory acknowledges that members of a crowd may communicate with one another in the elaboration of appropriate norms of action. However, the general nature of crowd behaviour is influenced by the role of distinctive behaviour, which is presumably behaviour that is relatively rare in most people's daily lives: for instance, anti-social behaviour. Two other critical observations have been made. Diener (1980) observes that a norm-regulated crowd would have to be a self-aware crowd (there is no need for people to comply with norms unless they are identifiable and thus individuated and self-aware), yet evidence indicates that self-awareness is very low in crowds. An experiment by Leon Mann and his colleagues (Mann, Newton, & Innes, 1982) supports Diener's view: irrespective of whether a norm of leniency or aggressiveness had been established by a confederate, participants were more aggressive when anonymous than when identifiable. However, anonymous participants were also more aggressive when the aggressive norm was in place.

The second critical observation comes from Steven Reicher (1982, 1987), who reminds us that crowds rarely come together in a normative vacuum. More often than not, members of a crowd congregate for a specific purpose and thus bring with them a clear set of shared norms to regulate their behaviour as members of a specific group (e.g. a crowd of people welcoming the Queen, watching the Olympics, demonstrating outside Parliament, protesting on campus, or shopping on Oxford Street). The lack of tradition of established norms that Turner refers to may be more myth than reality. There is a logic to the crowd, Reicher argues, that is not adequately captured by emergent norm theory.

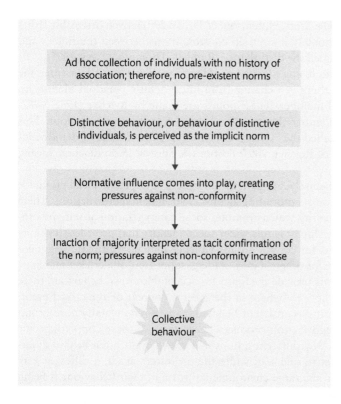

Ad hoc collection of individuals with no history of association; therefore, no pre-existent norms

↓

Distinctive behaviour, or behaviour of distinctive individuals, is perceived as the implicit norm

↓

Normative influence comes into play, creating pressures against non-conformity

↓

Inaction of majority interpreted as tacit confirmation of the norm; pressures against non-conformity increase

↓

Collective behaviour

Figure 11.15 Emergent norm theory

In initially normless crowds, distinctive behaviours are the basis for a relevant norm to emerge to regulate behaviour.

Source: Based on Turner and Killian (1957).

Social identity theory

An important aspect of crowd behaviour that is usually ignored is that it is actually an *intergroup* phenomenon (Reicher & Potter, 1985). Many crowd events involve direct confrontation between, for instance, police and rioters or rival gangs or team supporters. Even where there is no direct confrontation, there is symbolic confrontation in that the crowd event symbolises a confrontation between, for instance, the crowd (or the wider group it represents) and the state. For example, Cliff Stott and his colleagues' analysis of riots at football matches shows clearly how these events are intergroup confrontations between supporters and police, and that how the rioting supporters behave is significantly impacted by how the police behave,

Emergent norm theory

Is urban disorder a response to primitive aggressive instincts – or is it an example of normatively regulated goal-oriented action?

and vice versa (Stott & Adang, 2004; Stott, Hutchison, & Drury, 2001). Even ostensibly issue-less student campus riots are ultimately intergroup confrontations between the rioters and the authorities who are called to quell the disturbance (Ruddell, Thomas, & Way, 2005).

A second point is that, far from losing identity, people in the crowd actually assume the identity provided by the crowd: there is a change from idiosyncratic personal identity to shared social identity as a crowd member. These points are made by Reicher (1982, 1987, 1996, 2001), who applies social identity theory (this chapter) to collective behaviour. This analysis has been extended and called the SIDE model (social identity model of deindividu-ation phenomena; Klein, Spears, & Reicher, 2007; Postmes & Spears, 1998; Reicher, Spears, & Postmes, 1995).

People come together, or find themselves together, as members of a specific social group for a specific purpose (e.g. conservationists protesting against environmental destruction). There is a high degree of shared social identity, which promotes social categorization of self and oth-ers in terms of that group membership. It is this wider social identity that provides the limits for crowd behaviour. For example, for certain groups violence may be legitimate (e.g. neo-Nazi groups across Europe), while for others it may not (e.g. supporters at a cricket match).

While these general group norms provide the limits for acceptable crowd behaviour, there are often few norms to indicate how to behave in the specific context of the crowd event. Crowd members look to the identity-consistent behaviour of others, usually core group members, for guidance. Self-categorization produces conformity to these context-specific norms of conduct. This explains why different groups in a crowd event often behave differ-ently. For example, the police act in one way, while the protesters act in a different way because, despite being exposed to the same environmental stimuli, their behaviour is being controlled by different group memberships.

This analysis seems to be consistent with what actually goes on in a crowd. For example, Robert Fogelson's (1970) analysis of American race riots of the 1960s showed one notewor-thy feature: that the violence was not arbitrary and without direction; and Milgram and Toch (1969) report accounts from participants in the Watts riot in which a sense of positive social identity is strongly emphasised. Reicher (1984; Reicher & Potter, 1985) uses his analy-sis to account for a specific riot, which occurred in the spring of 1980 in the St Paul's district of Bristol (this was a forerunner of subsequent widespread rioting in other cities in Britain during the early 1980s). Three important points that emerged from this analysis were:

1 The violence, burning and looting were not unconstrained: the crowd was 'orderly' and the rioters were selective. Aggression was directed only at symbols of the state – the banks, the police and entrepreneurial merchants in the community.

2 The crowd remained within the bounds of its own community – St Paul's.

3 During and as a consequence of the riot, rioters felt a strong sense of positive social iden-tity as members of the St Paul's community.

All this makes sense when it is recognised that the riot was an anti-government protest on the part of the St Paul's community, an economically disadvantaged area of Bristol with very high unemployment during a time of severe national unemployment. Reicher's general anal-ysis of riots has also been used successfully to explain the spate of urban riots that swept Britain in 2011 (Reicher & Stott, 2011), and the riot that occurred at the 1999 Woodstock music festival marking the thirtieth anniversary of the original festival (Vider, 2004).

Improving intergroup relations

Different theories of prejudice and intergroup behaviour suggest different ways to improve intergroup relations by reducing prejudice and intergroup conflict. From the perspective of personality theories (e.g. authoritarian personality, dogmatism; **Chapter 10**), prejudice reduction requires changing the personality of the prejudiced person. It would involve inhibiting those parental strategies of child-rearing that create bigoted people. From the perspective of frustration–aggression theory (**Chapter 10**) or relative deprivation theory (this chapter), prejudice and intergroup conflict can be minimised by preventing frustration, lowering people's expectations, distracting people from realising that they are frustrated, providing people with harmless (non-social) activities through which to vent their frustration, or ensuring that aggressive associations are minimised among frustrated people.

Minimisation of aggressive cues and increasing non-aggressive cues is important. Substantial research shows that if weapons are made less available, aggression is reduced. When Jamaica implemented strict gun control and censorship of gun scenes on TV and in films in 1974, robbery and shooting rates dropped dramatically (Diener & Crandall, 1979), and when Washington, DC, introduced handgun control laws, there was a similar reduction in violent crime (Loftin, McDowall, Wiersema, & Cottey, 1991). The mere sight of a gun, either real or an image, can induce a **weapons effect** (see **Chapter 12**). In contrast, non-aggressive cues such as infants and laughter can reduce aggression (Berkowitz, 1984; see also an account in **Chapter 12** of how media depiction of violence can increase the incidence of later antisocial acts).

Weapons effect
The mere presence of a weapon increases the probability that it will be used aggressively.

For realistic conflict theory (this chapter), the existence of superordinate goals and cooperation for their achievement gradually reduces intergroup hostility and conflict. Avoidance of mutually exclusive goals would also help. Finally, from a social identity perspective (this chapter), prejudice and overt conflict will wane to the extent that intergroup stereotypes become less derogatory and polarised, and mutually legitimised non-violent forms of intergroup competition exist.

Propaganda and education

Propaganda messages, such as official exhortations that people should not be prejudiced, are usually predicated on an absolute standard of morality (e.g. humanism). This may be effective for people who subscribe to the standard of morality that is being invoked. It may also suppress more extreme forms of discrimination because it communicates social disapproval of discrimination.

Since prejudice is at least partly based in ignorance (Stephan & Stephan, 1984), education – particularly the formal education of children – that promotes tolerance of diversity may reduce bigotry (Stephan, 2014; Stephan & Stephan, 2001). This can involve teaching children about the moral implications of discrimination or teaching them facts about different groups. One problem with this strategy is that formal education has only a marginal impact if children are systematically exposed to prejudice outside the classroom (e.g. bigoted parents, chauvinistic advertising and the material consequences of discrimination).

Another educational strategy that may be more effective is to allow children to experience being a victim of prejudice. In 1970 Jane Elliot, an Iowa schoolteacher, made a short movie called *The Eye of the Storm* of a classroom demonstration where she divided her class of very young children into those with blue and those with brown eyes. For one day the 'brown eyes', and then for one day the 'blue eyes', were assigned inferior status: they were ridiculed, denied privileges, accused of being dull, lazy and sloppy, and made to wear a special collar. It was hoped that the experience of being stigmatised would be unpleasant enough to make the children think twice about being prejudiced against others.

One problem about prejudice is that it is *mindless*, a knee-jerk reaction to others as stereotypes. Recall from earlier in this chapter that even minimal intergroup categorization can automatically produce ingroup favouritism (Otten & Wentura, 1999). What would happen if children were taught to be mindful of others, to think about others not as stereotypes but as complex, whole individuals? Would stereotypical reactions be reduced? Langer, Bashner and Chanowitz (1985) explored this idea in the context of how young children think and feel about

Traditional sex roles
Stereotypes are difficult to change and perhaps more so in the face of subtle advertising.

the handicapped. Children who were trained to be *mindful* of others showed more positive attitudes and behaviour towards other children who were handicapped. Generally, the development of an ability to empathise with others significantly reduces one's capacity to harm those others physically, verbally or indirectly via decisions and institutions (Miller & Eisenberg, 1988). Empathy is one strand in the development of acting prosocially (see **Chapter 13**).

Intergroup contact

Unfavourable outgroup attitudes lie at the heart of prejudice and conflict. Such attitudes are enshrined in widespread social ideologies and are maintained by failure or inability to access information that disconfirms or improves negative attitudes. In most cases, such isolation is reinforced by real social and physical isolation of different groups from one another – the Protestant–Catholic situation in Northern Ireland is a case in point (Hewstone, Cairns, Voci, Paolini, McLernon, Crisp, et al., 2005). There is simply a chronic lack of intergroup contact, and little opportunity to meet real members of the outgroup. The groups are kept apart by educational, occupational, cultural and material differences, as well as by anxiety about negative consequences of contact for oneself (Stephan, 2014; Stephan & Stephan, 1985).

Intergroup anxiety

People are often anxious about interacting with members of a stigmatised group. They worry about doing or saying the wrong thing, about what the other person thinks of them and, ultimately, that the interaction will be bumpy, stressful and uncomfortable. Better to simply avoid interacting with stigmatised groups. Stephan and Stephan (2000), in their integrated threat model, identify four sources of anxiety that people can experience about and in anticipation of intergroup contact:

1 *realistic threat* – a sense of threat to the very existence of one's group, well-being, political power and so forth;

2 *symbolic threat* – a threat posed by the outgroup to one's values, beliefs, morals and norms;

3 *intergroup anxiety* – a threat to self (e.g. embarrassment, fear of rejection) which is experienced during intergroup interactions; and

4 *negative stereotypes* – fear of intergroup anxiety (not actually experienced intergroup anxiety but imagined or anticipated) based on negative stereotypes of an outgroup.

Focusing on intergroup anxiety, Stephan (2014) proposes that it has three components: *affective* (aversive feelings of apprehension, distress and unease), *cognitive* (people expect to be embarrassed, disliked, rejected, discriminated against and disapproved of by their own group) and *physiological* (increased cortisol, elevated blood pressure and other forms of physiological arousal). These 'symptoms' are caused by four types of factors: *personality traits and personal characteristics* (e.g. low empathy, high aggressiveness, intolerance of ambiguity and complexity – Stephan also cites strong ingroup identification as a personal characteristic), *negative attitudes and cognitions* (e.g. prior prejudices towards and unfavourable stereotypes of the outgroup), *personal experience* (e.g. little prior contact with the outgroup), and *situational factors* (e.g. unclear situation and roles, competitive orientation, unfriendly and hostile interaction, disrespectful treatment).

Intergroup anxiety has many consequences. Stephan (2014) groups them as *cognitive* (depleted cognitive resources, impaired executive functioning and a feeling that one's negative attitudes towards the outgroup have been confirmed), *affective and emotional* (affectively consistent evaluations of the outgroup are instantiated – on a more positive note, guilt may arise if the encounter was less awkward than anticipated), and *behavioural* (overt, verbal and non-verbal behaviours that reflect one's feelings of anxiety, awkwardness and annoyance).

Overall, intergroup anxiety can cause people to avoid face-to-face intergroup contact and prefer some form of segregated existence. In some cases, a more extreme response to perceived intergroup threat may be *collective narcissism* (Golec de Zavala, Cichocka, Eidelson, & Jayawickreme, 2009) – in which a group develops a strong sense of ethnocentrism, entitlement, superiority, omnipotence, egocentrism, need for recognition and acknowledgement, coupled with high but unstable self-esteem and a fragile sense of self.

How effective is contact?

One situation where contact or anticipated contact always whips up a storm of discontent is immigration. We have all seen coverage of the reaction of many European countries to the massive influx of migrants and refugees from Africa, the Middle East and Afghanistan – in 2015, about one million people travelled by boat to European shores, and then headed overland mainly to Germany, Britain and Scandinavia. Immigration raises all sorts of fears, ranging from competition for employment to erosion of cultural values.

Although the ideas outlined in Box 11.5 make good sense, more than half a century of research on the contact hypothesis yields a complex picture (e.g. Amir, 1976; Cook, 1985; Fox & Giles, 1993; Schofield, 1991), at least partly due to the predominance of uncontrolled field studies and partly because Allport's list of conditions has been extended to become overly specific. Nevertheless, Tom Pettigrew and Linda Tropp (2006) report an authoritative meta-analysis of 515 contact studies conducted between 1949 and 2000, with 713 samples across thirty-eight participating nations that reveals a robust effect – there is good evidence for Allport's core contention that cooperation, shared goals, equal status and the support of local authorities and norms are the most important and beneficial preconditions for intergroup contact to produce positive intergroup attitude change. Certain forms of contact can, paradoxically, reduce stereotype threat – the tendency for people to worry that their behaviour will confirm others' negative stereotypes of their group (Crisp & Abrams, 2008; see **Chapter 10**).

There are, however, some critical issues concerning precisely how contact may have effects (see overviews by Brewer & Miller, 1996; Brown, 1995, 1996; Hewstone, 1994, 1996; Pettigrew, 1998). These issues include the role of similarity and the process of generalisation

Box 11.5 Our world
Can intergroup contact improve intergroup relations?

One interesting line of research suggests that host nations construe the threat posed by immigration in different ways and thus respond to immigration differently depending on whether they define their national cultural identity in terms of heritage, history, blood ties and ties to the land (e.g. Germany, Italy, France and New Zealand), or in terms of common identity, shared civic values, and the social contract (e.g. Australia, Canada and the United States) (e.g. Citrin, Green, Muste, & Wong, 1997; Esses, Dovidio, Semenya, & Jackson, 2005; Esses, Jackson, Dovidio, & Hodson, 2005). The former is largely an ethnic national identity that prioritises community and common bonds (*Gemeinschaft*) – immigration is viewed as a cultural threat; the latter is largely a civic national identity that prioritises instrumental association and common identity (*Gesellschaft*) – immigration is viewed as a threat to civil society and access to employment. This distinction closely maps on to Prentice, Miller and Lightdale's (1994) distinction between common bond and common identity groups (discussed in **Chapter 8**).

Under the right circumstances, however, contact can reduce anxiety and improve intergroup relations (Brown & Hewstone, 2005; Pettigrew, 1998; Pettigrew & Tropp, 2006).

This is the **contact hypothesis** and was first proposed scientifically by Gordon Allport (1954b) in the year that the US Supreme Court paved the way for racial desegregation of the American education system. Here are Allport's conditions for contact:

- It should be prolonged and involve cooperative activity rather than casual and purposeless interaction. It was precisely this sort of contact that improved relations in Sherif's (1966) summer camp studies.
- It should occur within the framework of official and institutional support for integration. Although legislation against discrimination, or for equal opportunities, will not in itself abolish prejudice, it provides a social climate that is conducive to the emergence of more tolerant social practices.
- It should bring together people or groups of equal social status. Unequal status contact is more likely to confirm stereotypes and thus entrench prejudices.

For the role that the Internet can play in intergroup contact, together with a review of the contact hypothesis, see Amichai-Hamburger and McKenna (2006).

Contact hypothesis
The view that bringing members of opposing social groups together will improve intergroup relations and reduce prejudice and discrimination.

of favourable interindividual attitudes to favourable intergroup attitudes. It is also important to bear in mind that intergroup contact that is unpleasant simply confirms one's worst fears and can strengthen one's prior prejudices and inhibit future contact (Stephan, 2014). Indeed, Barlow and colleagues conclude from a pair of studies conducted in Australia and the United States that negative contact worsened intergroup attitudes than positive contact improved intergroup attitudes Barlow, Paolini, Pedersen, Hornsey, Radke, Harwood, et al., 2012).

Similarity

Prejudice is often grounded in ignorance and the perception of irreconcilable intergroup differences (Pettigrew, 1971; Stephan & Stephan, 1984). Contact causes people to recognise that they are in fact a great deal more similar than they had thought, and hence they get to like one another (Byrne, 1971; also see **Chapter 13**). There are some problems with this perspective:

- Because groups are often very different, contact can unearth more profound or more widespread differences and hence reduce liking further and worsen intergroup attitudes (e.g. Barlow, Paolini, Pedersen, Hornsey, Radke, Harwood, et al., 2012).
- As groups are actually so different, it may be misleading to promulgate the view that they are similar; this will establish false positive expectations that are disconfirmed by contact.
- Research indicates that intergroup attitudes are not merely a matter of ignorance or unfamiliarity; rather, they reflect real conflict of interest between groups and are often maintained by the very existence of social categories. New knowledge made available by contact is unlikely to change attitudes.

The contact hypothesis
Ethnically mixed social occasions, like this street scene, are now common in many countries. When does such close contact between cultures improve intergroup relations?

Generalisation

Contact between representatives of different groups is supposed to improve attitudes towards the group as a whole – not just the specific outgroup members involved in the encounter. Weber and Crocker (1983) suggested three models of how this might happen:

1 *Bookkeeping* – the accumulation of favourable information about an outgroup gradually improves the stereotype. If outgroup information is stored in terms of exemplars, dramatic attitude changes can occur as new exemplars are added or retrieved (Smith & Zárate, 1992).

2 *Conversion* – dramatically counter-stereotypical information about an outgroup causes a sudden change in attitudes.

3 *Subtyping* – stereotype-inconsistent information produces a subtype, so the outgroup stereotype becomes more complex but the superordinate category remains unchanged.

Overall, contact can improve attitudes towards the participants but is less likely to generalise to the group as a whole (Amir, 1976; Cook, 1978). One reason for this is that most intergroup contact is actually *interpersonal* contact: that is, contact between individuals as individuals, not group members. There is no good reason why an attitude towards one person should generalise to other people who are not categorically related to that person. For example, if you like Miguel as a friend, and the fact that he happens to be Spanish is irrelevant, then your liking for Miguel will not generalise to anyone else who just happens to be Spanish, or to the category 'Spanish' as a whole.

This raises an interesting paradox: perhaps intergroup contact is more likely to generalise if people's group affiliations are made *more*, not less, salient during contact – the *mutual differentiation model* (Hewstone & Brown, 1986; Johnston & Hewstone, 1990). There is some support for this idea. David Wilder (1984) had participants from rival colleges come into contact over a cooperative task where the outgroup person, who was either highly typical or highly atypical of that college, behaved in a pleasant or unpleasant manner. Figure 11.16 shows that, relative to a no-contact control, only where contact was both pleasant and with a typical outgroup member was there generalised improvement of attitude (see also Rothbart & John, 1985; Weber & Crocker, 1983).

Norman Miller and Marilynn Brewer (1984; Miller, Brewer, & Edwards, 1985) have a different perspective. They argue that contact that draws attention to people's group affiliations will rapidly degenerate into conflict and thus a worsening of generalised attitudes. Instead, they recommend interpersonal encounters that stress socioemotional aspects and avoid group- or task-related aspects of the encounter: that is, 'decategorization' or

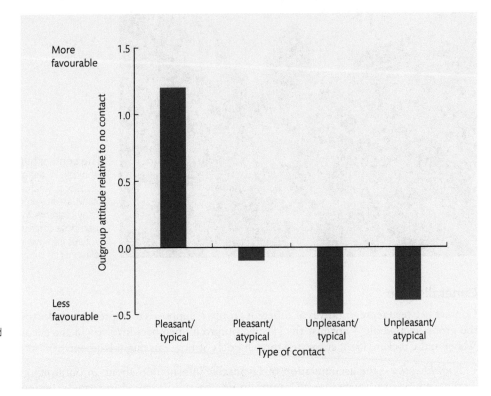

Figure 11.16 Outgroup attitude as a function of pleasantness of contact and outgroup typicality of target

Relative to no contact, attitudes towards a rival college improved only when contact was both pleasant and with a typical member of the other college.

Source: Based on data from Wilder (1984).

personalisation. This seems to work (Hamburger, 1994), but as yet the idea has been tested only in abstract experimental settings, where intergroup relations lack the powerful emotions and personal investments associated with 'real' intergroup relations. Where real intergroup conflict exists (e.g. between Israelis and Palestinians), it may be almost impossible to distract people from their group affiliations.

Stephen Wright and his colleagues propose two promising variants of the interpersonal contact idea, called **extended contact** and vicarious contact (Wright, Aron, McLaughlin-Volpe, & Ropp, 1997; also see Dovidio, Eller, & Hewstone, 2011). The two variants are very similar, but strictly speaking, extended contact refers to *knowing* that an ingroup member is friends with an outgroup member, and vicarious contact refers to *observing* an ingroup member interacting with an outgroup member (Vezzali, Hewstone, Capozza, Giovannini, & Wölfer, 2014).

Intergroup attitudes can improve if people witness or have knowledge of rewarding cross-group interpersonal friendships between others – if my friend John has close outgroup friends, then maybe the outgroup is not quite as bad as I thought. This inference is possible because members of the same group have a common identity that links them and allows them, in the words of Wright, Aron and Tropp (2002), to *include the other in the self* –to develop a degree of intersubjectivity that allows them to experience others as themselves.

A substantial body of evidence now exists to confirm that cross-group friendships in the guise of extended and vicarious contact can indeed improve intergroup attitudes (Davies, Tropp, Aron, Pettigrew, & Wright, 2011; Vezzali, Hewstone, Capozza, Giovannini, & Wölfer, 2014). Indirect contact has some advantages over direct contact: it can occur where there is profound intergroup segregation, it evokes less intergroup anxiety, generalisation is more likely because group membership is salient, and one does not need to actually know any outgroup members personally. Indirect contact is also easy to implement, through reading stories, watching videos, and even monitoring Facebook.

Extended contact
Knowing about an ingroup member who shares a close relationship with an outgroup member can improve one's own attitudes towards the outgroup.

Building on the idea of extended contact, Richard Crisp has also suggested that *imagined contact* may help improve intergroup attitudes (Crisp & Turner, 2012). For example, Sofia Stathi and her colleagues report three experiments: participants who imagined a pleasant encounter with a single outgroup member subsequently felt more confident about future interactions with the outgroup in general. They also found that imagining contact was most effective at promoting generalisation when group as opposed to individuating information was salient, and when the imagined interaction involved an outgrouper who was typical as opposed to atypical (Stathi, Crisp, & Hogg, 2011).

A meta-analysis of over 70 studies of imagined contact concluded that it significantly improves intergroup attitudes, emotions, intentions and behaviour, and the effect is stronger if people cognitively elaborate on the context within which they imagined contact (Miles & Crisp, 2014). The effect is also stronger among children than adults, supporting the possibility that imagined contact can be a key component of educational strategies aiming to promote social harmony. Given that prejudice can be sustained by intergroup isolation and therefore many groups simply have limited contact with one another, imagined contact may have significant potential as a tool for improving intergroup attitudes.

Related to extended, vicarious and imagined contact, is the notion that perspective taking plays a role in improving intergroup attitudes. If we are able to take the perspective of another person and experience the world as they do, we are less likely to harbour negative attitudes about that person and perhaps more likely to behave prosocially towards them (see **Chapter 14**). There is now evidence that perspective taking can improve intergroup attitudes (Galinsky, 2002; Galinsky & Moskowitz, 2000; Vescio, Sechrist, & Paolucci, 2003).

Another process that does not involve drawing attention to the original intergroup context is 'recategorization'. Sam Gaertner's *common ingroup identity model* (Gaertner & Dovidio, 2000; Gaertner, Dovidio, Anastasio, Bachman, & Rust, 1993; Gaertner, Mann, Murrell, & Dovidio, 1989; Gaertner, Rust, Dovidio, Bachman, & Anastasio, 1996) suggests that if members of opposing groups can be encouraged to recategorise themselves as members of the same group, intergroup attitudes will, by definition, not only improve but actually disappear (see later in this chapter for some limitations of this process).

Contact policy in multicultural contexts

Initially, it might seem that the most non-discriminatory and unprejudiced way to approach inter-ethnic relations is to be 'colour-blind': that is, to ignore group differences completely (Berry, 1984; Schofield, 1986). This is a 'melting-pot' policy, where all groups are ostensibly treated as equal (see also the concept of *assimilation* discussed in **Chapter 16**). There are at least three limitations of this approach:

1 It ignores the evidence that discrimination has disadvantaged certain groups (e.g. regarding education or health), and that unless positive steps are taken to rectify the problem, the disadvantage will simply persist.

2 It ignores the reality of ethnic/cultural differences (e.g. the Muslim dress code for women).

3 The melting pot is not really a melting pot at all, but rather a 'dissolving' pot, where ethnic minorities are dissolved and assimilated by the dominant social group: minority groups are stripped of their cultural heritage and cease to exist.

The extensive riots in France in November 2005 and the spate of terrorist attacks in France in 2015 and 2016 have been attributed to that country's adoption of cultural monism and ethnic assimilation – an approach that does not formally recognise cultural/ethnic differences within France despite the presence of huge numbers of North African Muslims. This assimilationist policy of being blind to cultural/ethnic/racial differences has, ironically, created ghettos of cultural disadvantage and associated discrimination and prejudice. A quite remarkable side effect of this denial of culture difference is that there are virtually no statistics on cultural/ethnic issues in France.

The alternative to assimilationism is pluralism or multiculturalism (Verkuyten, 2006) – an approach that recognises the reality of cultural diversity in an attempt to improve negative attitudes and redress disadvantage, at the same time as it preserves the cultural integrity of different groups (see **Chapter 16**). This approach champions a multicultural society in which intergroup relations between the constituent groups are harmonious. Empirical research suggests that intergroup arrangements that resemble multiculturalism may be effective in reducing intergroup conflict (Hornsey & Hogg, 2000a; see the subsection 'Pluralism and diversity'). However, recent events indicate that pluralism needs to be implemented carefully in order for it not to sustain hidden conflicts and nourish separatism. Cases in point are Britain and Australia. Although both countries in different ways provide strong political support for pluralism, it was disaffiliated Muslim youths who bombed public transport in London in July 2005, and in Australia there were large anti-Lebanese riots in Sydney in December 2005.

Superordinate goals

In his summer camp studies, Sherif (1966) managed to improve intergroup relations between warring factions by having them cooperate to achieve superordinate goals (shared goals that were unachievable by either group alone). The effectiveness of superordinate goals has been confirmed by other studies (Brown & Abrams, 1986; Ryen & Kahn, 1975; Turner, 1981b; Worchel, 1979). The European Union provides a wonderful natural laboratory to study the effect of a superordinate identity (European) on inter-subgroup relations (between nations within Europe) (e.g. Chryssochoou, 2000; Cinnirella, 1997; Huici, Ros, Cano, Hopkins, Emler, & Carmona, 1997). One particularly effective superordinate goal is resistance to a shared threat from a common enemy (Dion, 1979; Wilder & Shapiro, 1984). This is the basis of alliances that can temporarily improve relations between erstwhile opponents (e.g. the existence of the former Soviet Union provided a common foe to unite Western nations for almost forty-five years).

There is an important qualification. Superordinate goals do not reduce intergroup conflict if the groups fail to achieve the goal. Steve Worchel and his colleagues created competitive, cooperative or independent relations between two groups and then provided a superordinate goal that the groups either achieved or failed to achieve. The superordinate goal improved intergroup relations in all cases except where previously competitive groups failed to achieve the goal. In this condition, relations actually deteriorated (Worchel, Andreoli, & Folger, 1977). However, unsuccessful intergroup cooperation to achieve a superordinate worsens intergroup relations only when the failure can be attributed, rightly or wrongly, to the actions of the outgroup (Worchel & Novell, 1980).

Where there is sufficient external justification, and the outgroup is not blamed, there is the more usual improvement in intergroup relations. For example, the 1982 Falklands conflict between Britain and Argentina provided a superordinate goal to reduce factional conflict within Argentina. The cooperative exercise within Argentina failed (Argentina lost the war), and, because the actions of the junta could easily be blamed, there was renewed factional conflict, which led almost immediately to the junta being overthrown (Latin American Bureau, 1982).

Pluralism and diversity

One of the main problems of intergroup relations is that, in most contexts, groups are actually subgroups wholly nested within larger groups or cross-cut with them (Crisp, Ensari, Hewstone, & Miller, 2003; see **Chapter 8**). For example, Catalans are primarily a subgroup within Spain, whereas Basques are a crosscutting category that spans the border between Spain and France. In both cases, it is rare for subgroups to be equally represented in the defining features of the overarching identity – more often than not, one group is much better represented, with the consequence that other groups feel subordinate (Mummendey & Wenzel, 1999; Wenzel, Mummendey, & Waldzus, 2007). Catalans and Basques feel their attributes are poorly represented in the overarching Spanish identity. A similar problem arises when one organisation merges with or acquires another organisation – the post-merger entity contains within it both pre-merger entities and usually one pre-merger entity has lower status and poorer representation in the post-merger entity (e.g. Terry, Carey, & Callan, 2001).

Even where relations among subgroups are reasonably good, another problem, associated with superordinate goals, emerges. Intense or prolonged cooperation to achieve a shared goal can gradually blur intergroup boundaries (Gaertner & Dovidio, 2000; see the discussion earlier in this chapter of the common ingroup identity model). Although this may seem an ideal solution to intergroup conflict, it can backfire. Even though the groups may have superordinate goals, they may also want to maintain their individual identities and so resist the perceived threat of becoming a single entity. New conflicts can thus arise to maintain intergroup distinctiveness. This effect has been observed in a chemical plant (Blake, Shepard, & Mouton, 1964), an engineering factory (Brown, 1978) and the laboratory (Brown & Wade, 1987; Deschamps & Brown, 1983). The building clamour for autonomy among some nations in the European Union, culminating in Britain's 2016 vote to exit the EU, is often attributed to excessive pressure from Brussels for cultural homogenisation that has eroded national distinctiveness.

Hornsey and Hogg (2000a, 2000b, 2000c) have conducted a programme of research suggesting that a careful balancing of superordinate identity and positive subgroup distinctiveness may provide a promising blueprint for social harmony. This mimics the sociopolitical strategy of multiculturalism or cultural pluralism that is pursued explicitly by countries such as Australia and Canada, implicitly by Britain and, through the promotion of diversity, by the United States. This arrangement works because by retaining distinct cultural identities, there is no threat that would provoke intergroup hostility. At the same time, the existence of a superordinate identity allows subgroups to see themselves as distinct groups, with complementary roles, all working on the same team towards integrative goals. More broadly, this idea suggests that the answer to intergroup conflict may be to build groups that not only are based on tolerance for diversity but actually celebrate diversity as a defining feature of their social identity (Hogg, 2015; also see Hogg & Hornsey, 2006; Niedenthal & Beike, 1997; Roccas & Brewer, 2002; Wright, Aron, & Tropp, 2002).

A final point about goal relations and social harmony picks up on our earlier discussion of zero-sum and non-zero-sum goals. Where two groups see their goal relations as *zero-sum*, they are characterising their relationship as competitive – if they get a lot, we get a little. There is a fixed pie to divide up, and therefore their actions are frustrating our goals. Where two groups see their goal relations as *non-zero-sum*, they are characterising their relationship as cooperative – if they get a lot, we get a lot. The pie can get bigger if we work together, and therefore their actions are helping us to achieve our goals. Goal relations do not have to be accurate perceptions – they are subject to ideology and rhetoric. Take the immigration debates in Britain, France, Germany and virtually any country around the world. One side argues that immigration is bad because immigrants come along and take people's jobs and soak up public money – a zero-sum rhetoric that is associated with xenophobia, prejudice and intolerance towards immigrants. The other side argues that immigration is good because immigrants bring skills, energy and enthusiasm, which creates new jobs and additional wealth – a non-zero-sum rhetoric that is associated with internationalism and positive attitudes towards immigrants and immigration.

Communication and negotiation

Groups in conflict can try to improve intergroup relations by communicating directly about the conflict and negotiating to resolve it. This involves bargaining, mediation or arbitration. These are very complex procedures that are prey to all sorts of psychological barriers to dispute resolution (e.g. self-esteem, emotion, misattribution; Ross & Ward, 1995; Thompson, 2015; Thompson & Loewenstein, 2003; Thompson, Medvec, Seiden, & Kopelman, 2001). One real problem is that it can be difficult for negotiators to take the perspective of the other – a failure that is amplified by the intergroup nature of the negotiation and which makes compromise almost impossible (Carroll, Bazerman, & Maury, 1988; Galinsky & Mussweiler, 2001). In addition, many negotiations are between cultures, and thus a host of cross-cultural communication issues can arise to complicate things (e.g. Carnevale & Leung, 2001; Kimmel, 1994; see also R. Bond & Smith, 1996; Smith & M. H. Bond, 1998).

Bargaining

Intergroup negotiations are generally between representatives of opposing groups: for example, trade union and management may try to resolve disputes by direct negotiation between representatives. One of the most significant intergroup negotiations of the twentieth century was the February 1945 meeting in Yalta in the Crimea between Stalin, Churchill and Roosevelt, as representatives of the soon-to-be victorious Allies of the Second World War: the Soviet Union, Britain and the United States. The negotiation of international differences at that meeting has determined the nature of the world to the present day. Social psychological research indicates that when people are **bargaining** on behalf of social groups to which they belong, they tend to bargain much more fiercely and less compromisingly than if they were simply bargaining for themselves (Benton & Druckman, 1974; Breaugh & Klimoski, 1981). The effect is enhanced when negotiators are aware that they are being observed by their constituents, either directly or through the media (Carnevale, Pruitt, & Britton, 1979).

This 'bullish' strategy of relative intransigence is less likely to secure a satisfactory compromise than a more interpersonal orientation where both parties make reciprocal concessions (Esser & Komorita, 1975). Direct negotiation between group representatives is therefore quite likely to reach an impasse where neither group feels it can compromise without losing face.

A case in point is George H. W. Bush and Saddam Hussein's media-orchestrated bargaining over the plight of Kuwait in 1990, which seemed mainly to involve Bush threatening to 'kick Saddam's ass' and Hussein threatening to make 'infidel' Americans 'swim in their own blood' – not a good start. More recently, in 2006, the Iranian president Mahmoud Ahmadinejad and the US president George W. Bush traded insults in which Ahmadinejad accused Bush of being an infidel, and the latter accused the former of being a member of the 'axis of evil' – again, not a promising start. Research shows that the expression of anger in negotiations backfires and makes things much worse when the negotiation is associated with a conflict of values (as is true in the cases mentioned here), not just a conflict of interest (Harinck & Van Kleef, 2012)

Ian Morley has explored the interplay of intergroup and interpersonal factors in bargaining, to show that bargaining often follows a sequence of stages (Morley & Stephenson, 1977). The first stage is an intergroup one where representatives act in terms of group memberships and assess each group's power and the strength of each group's case. The second stage is more interpersonal, with individuals trying to establish harmonious interpersonal relations with one another in order to solve problems more easily. The final stage is again more intergroup, with negotiators making sure that the final decision is consistent with the historical aims of their own group. Close interpersonal relations, which are encouraged by more informal bargaining procedures and contexts, can facilitate negotiation. However, close interpersonal relations also have a drawback – the group as a whole can become fearful of a 'sell-out' and can resort or return to more confrontational intergroup behaviour, which hinders the negotiation process.

Intergroup bargaining is often studied as a way to achieve wider social change. However, more often than not, it is actually a way to maintain the status quo (Morley, Webb, & Stephenson, 1988). Groups in conflict isolate a specific aspect of disagreement to resolve. The resolution of the specific disagreement then allows broader intergroup issues to remain unchanged.

Mediation

To break negotiation deadlock, a third party can be brought in for **mediation** between the groups (Pruitt, 1981). To be effective, mediators should have power and must be seen by both groups to be impartial (Lim & Carnevale, 1990), and the groups should already be fairly close in their positions (Rubin, 1980). Biased mediators are ineffective because they are not

Bargaining
Process of intergroup conflict resolution where representatives reach agreement through direct negotiation.

Mediation
Process of intergroup conflict resolution where a neutral third party intervenes in the negotiation process to facilitate a settlement.

Mediation
An effective mediator needs to have power and to be seen as impartial. In this respect, a football World Cup context is no different from a legal setting.

trusted, and weak mediators are ineffective because they exert little pressure on intransigent groups to be reasonable.

Although mediators have no power to impose a settlement, they can help in several important ways:

1 They are able to *reduce the emotional heat* associated with deadlock (Tetlock, 1988).

2 They can help to *reduce misperceptions*, encourage understanding and establish trust.

3 They can propose *novel compromises* that allow both groups to appear to win: that is, to change a zero-sum conflict (one in which one group's gains are precisely the other group's losses; the more one gains, the more the other loses) into a non-zero-sum conflict (where both groups can gain).

4 They can help both parties make a *graceful retreat*, without losing face, from untenable positions.

5 They can *inhibit unreasonable claims* and behaviour by threatening to expose the group publicly as being unreasonable.

6 They can *reduce intragroup conflict* and thus help a group to clarify its consensual position.

History provides instances of effective mediation. For example, Henry Kissinger's shuttle diplomacy of the mid-1970s, which involved meeting each side separately over a period of two years after the 1973 Arab–Israeli conflict, produced a number of significant agreements between Israel and its Arab neighbours (Pruitt, 1981). In the late 1970s, using a slightly different strategy, Jimmy Carter secluded Egypt's president Anwar Sadat and Israel's prime minister Menachem Begin at Camp David near Washington in the United States. After thirteen days, an agreement was reached that ended a state of war that had existed between Israel and Egypt since 1948.

Arbitration

Many intergroup conflicts are so intractable, the underlying interests so divergent, that mediation is ineffective. The last resort is **arbitration**, in which the mediator or some other third party is invited to impose a mutually binding settlement. Research shows that arbitration really is the last resort for conflict resolution (McGillicuddy, Welton, & Pruitt, 1987). The prospect of arbitration can backfire, because both groups adopt outrageous final positions in the hope that arbitration will produce a more favourable compromise (Pruitt & Rubin, 1986). A way to combat this is through *final-offer arbitration*, where the third party chooses one of the final offers. This tends to encourage more reasonable final positions.

Arbitration
Process of intergroup conflict resolution in which a neutral third party is invited to impose a mutually binding settlement.

Conciliation

Although direct communication may help to improve intergroup relations, tensions and suspicions often run so high that direct communication is impossible. Instead, conflicting groups threaten, coerce or retaliate against one another, and if this behaviour is reciprocated, there is an escalation of the conflict. For example, during the Second World War, Germany believed it could move Britain to surrender by bombing its cities, and the Allies believed that they could break Germany's will by bombing *its* cities. Similarly, Japan believed it could dissuade the United States from interfering in its imperial expansion in Asia by bombing Pearl Harbor, and the United States believed it could bring North Vietnam to the negotiating table by sustained bombing of cities and villages.

There are uncountable examples of the terrible consequences of threat, coercion and retaliation. Can this cycle be broken by one side adopting an unconditionally cooperative strategy in the hope that the other side will reciprocate? Laboratory research suggests that this does not work: unilateral unconditional cooperation simply invites retaliation and exploitation (Shure, Meeker, & Hansford, 1965).

Charles Osgood (1962) suggested a more effective alternative that involves **conciliation** (i.e. not retaliation), but with enough strength to discourage exploitation. Called 'graduated and reciprocated initiatives in tension reduction' (with the acronym GRIT), it invokes social psychological principles relating to the norm of reciprocity and the attribution of motives. GRIT involves at least two stages:

Conciliation
Process whereby groups make cooperative gestures to one another in the hope of avoiding an escalation of conflict.

1 One party announces its conciliatory intent (allowing a clear attribution of non-devious motive), clearly specifies a small concession it is about to make (activates reciprocity norm) and invites its opponent to do likewise.

2 The initiator makes the concession exactly as announced and in a publicly verifiable manner. There is now strong pressure on the other group to reciprocate.

Laboratory research provides evidence for the effectiveness of this procedure. For example, a *tit-for-tat* strategy that begins with one cooperative act and proceeds by matching the other party's last response is both conciliatory and strong, and can improve interparty relations (Axelrod & Dion, 1988; Komorita, Parks, & Hulbert, 1992). Direct laboratory tests of GRIT by Linskold and his colleagues (e.g. Linskold, 1978; Linskold & Han, 1988) confirm that the announcement of cooperative intent boosts cooperation, repeated conciliatory acts breed trust, and maintenance of power equality protects against exploitation. GRIT-type strategies have been used effectively in international relations: for example, between the Soviet Union and the United States during the Berlin crisis of the early 1960s, and between Israel and Egypt on a number of occasions.

Summary

- Intergroup behaviour is any behaviour that is influenced by group members' perceptions of an outgroup.

- Group members may engage in collective protest to the extent that subjectively they feel deprived as a group relative to their aspirations or relative to other groups.

- Competition for scarce resources tends to produce intergroup conflict. Cooperation to achieve a shared goal reduces conflict.

- Social categorization may be the only necessary precondition for being a group and engaging in intergroup behaviour, provided that people identify with the category.

- Self-categorization is the process responsible for psychologically identifying with a group and behaving as a group member (e.g. conformity, stereotyping, ethnocentrism, ingroup solidarity).

- Social identity processes and phenomena are motivated by the need to reduce self-related uncertainty and to enhance the prestige of groups one identifies with.

- Social comparison and the need for self-esteem motivate groups to compete in different ways (depending on the nature of intergroup relations) for relatively positive social identity.

- Crowd behaviour may not represent a loss of identity and regression to primitive antisocial instincts. Instead, it may be group behaviour that is governed by local contextual norms that are framed by a wider social identity.

- Prejudice, discrimination and intergroup conflict are difficult to reduce. Together, education, propaganda and shared goals may help, and simply bringing groups physically or psychologically into contact with one another can be effective provided a number of conditions are met. Other strategies include bargaining, mediation, arbitration and conciliation.

Key terms

Accentuation effect	Fraternalistic relative deprivation	Realistic conflict theory
Arbitration	Free-rider effect	Reductionism
Authoritarian personality	Frustration–aggression hypothesis	Relative deprivation
Bargaining	Illusory correlation	Relative homogeneity effect
Cognitive alternatives	Ingroup favouritism	Self-categorization theory
Collective behaviour	Intergroup behaviour	Social categorization
Commons dilemma	Intergroup differentiation	Social change belief system
Conciliation	Intergroup emotions theory	Social competition
Contact hypothesis	J-curve	Social creativity
Deindividuation	Mediation	Social identity
Depersonalisation	Meta-contrast principle	Social identity theory
Egoistic relative deprivation	Metatheory	Social mobility belief system
Emergent norm theory	Minimal group paradigm	Stereotype
Entitativity	Optimal distinctiveness	Superordinate goals
Ethnocentrism	Prisoner's dilemma	System justification theory
Extended contact	Prototype	Weapons effect

Literature, film and TV

Germinal

Emile Zola's 1885 novel drawing attention to the misery experienced by poor French people during France's Second Empire. The descriptions of crowd behaviour are incredibly powerful and were drawn upon by later social scientists, such as Gustave Le Bon, to develop their theories of collective behaviour.

The Road to Wigan Pier

George Orwell's 1937 novel capturing the plight of the English working class. A powerful, and strikingly contemporary, portrayal of relative deprivation.

Gran Torino

Clint Eastwood's 2008 film in which he also stars. Set in contemporary Detroit, Eastwood's character, Walt Kowalski, is a proud and grizzled Korean War veteran whose floridly bigoted attitudes are out of step with changing times. Walt refuses to abandon the neighbourhood he has lived in all his life, despite its changing demographics. The film is about his developing friendship with a Hmong teenage boy and his immigrant family – a poignant, and subtly uplifting, commentary on intergroup friendship and the development of intergroup tolerance and respect.

The Battle for Spain

Antony Beevor's 2006 history of the 1936–1939 Spanish Civil War – supremely scholarly, a bestseller and a real page-turner. A perfect case study for everything discussed in this chapter, it is a powerful account of the multilevel and contradictory complexities of intergroup relations in a global context. There is the ebb and flow of battle between the right-wing Nationalist and the left-wing Republican forces. But this war was also an endless conflict among nations and political factions struggling for power and influence in the early ascendance of Communism and the ominous run-up to the Second World War – Nazis, Fascists, Anarchists, Stalinists and Trotskyites all play a part, as do the nations of Germany, Italy, France, Britain, Mexico and the Soviet Union.

Star Wars

With apologies to Trekkies, no book is complete without a reference to *Star Wars*! The original trilogy came out in the late 1970s and early 1980s, the prequel trilogy in the early 2000s, and the sequel trilogy in the late 2010s (with the final film currently scheduled for release in 2019). George Lucas's *Star Wars* is a space epic that can, among many other things, be considered a study of group processes and intergroup relations on a galactic scale – a cosmic struggle between good and evil to control the galactic empire and rule the universe. This struggle is associated with 'the force' – the Jedi are custodians of 'the force' which they use for good to build a benign galactic government, whereas the Sith use the 'dark side' of the force for evil in order to destroy the Jedi and build a brutal totalitarian regime to rule the universe. *Star Wars* is fabulous entertainment, but it is also replete with social psychological themes relevant to the present chapter but also more broadly across the spectrum of the discipline.

Guided questions

1 How does the experience of relative deprivation impact the tendency to aggress?
2 According to Sherif, prejudice arises when intergroup goals are incompatible. What does this mean? Did he offer a solution?
3 What is social identity? Can a person have multiple social identities?
4 How are minority group members' beliefs about intergroup relations important in planning for social change?
5 Trying to reduce prejudice by simply providing intergroup contact between people from different groups may not work very well. Why?

Learn more

Abrams, D., & Hogg, M. A. (2010). Social identity and self-categorization. In J. F. Dovidio, M. Hewstone, P. Glick, & V. M. Esses (Eds.), *The SAGE handbook of prejudice, stereotyping and discrimination* (pp. 179–193). London: SAGE. Up-to-date, detailed and comprehensive coverage of social identity research and theory.

Brewer, M. B. (2003). *Intergroup relations* (2nd ed.). Philadelphia, PA: Open University Press. A very readable and complete overview of research on intergroup relations.

Brewer, M. B. (2007). The social psychology of intergroup relations: Social categorization, ingroup bias, and outgroup prejudice. In A. W. Kruglanski & E. T. Higgins (Eds.), *Social psychology: Handbook of basic principles* (2nd ed., pp. 785–804). New York: Guilford Press. Comprehensive coverage of research on intergroup behaviour, and prejudice and discrimination.

Brown, R. J., & Gaertner, S. (Eds.) (2001). *Blackwell handbook of social psychology: Intergroup processes*. Oxford, UK: Blackwell. A collection of twenty-five chapters from leading social psychologists, covering the entire field of intergroup processes.

De Dreu, C. K. W. (2010). Social conflict: The emergence and consequences of struggle and negotiation. In S. T. Fiske, D. T. Gilbert, & G. Lindzey (Eds.), *Handbook of social psychology* (5th ed., Vol. 2, pp. 983–1023). New York: Wiley. Up-to-date and comprehensive discussion of intergroup conflict and the role of negotiation in resolving such conflicts.

Dovidio, J. F., & Gaertner, S. L. (2010). Intergroup bias. In S. T. Fiske, D. T. Gilbert, & G. Lindzey (Eds.), *Handbook of social psychology* (5th ed., Vol. 2, pp. 1084–1121). New York: Wiley. Up-to-date and detailed coverage of research on intergroup bias as a feature of intergroup behaviour.

Dovidio, J., Glick. P., Hewstone, M., & Esses, V. (Eds.) (2010). *Handbook of prejudice, stereotyping and discrimination*. London: SAGE. A collection of chapters by leading researchers on intergroup behaviour in the context of stereotyping and prejudice.

Fiske, S. T. (2010). Interpersonal stratification: Status, power, and subordination. In S. T. Fiske, D. T. Gilbert, & G. Lindzey (Eds.), *Handbook of social psychology* (5th ed., Vol. 2, pp. 941–982). New York: Wiley. Up-to-date and detailed overview of research on the power and status aspects of intergroup relations.

Hogg, M. A. (2006). Social identity theory. In P. J. Burke (Ed.), *Contemporary social psychological theories* (pp. 111–136). Palo Alto, CA: Stanford University Press. Easily readable and still up-to-date overview of contemporary social identity theory.

Hogg, M. A. (2013a). Intergroup relations. In J. Delamater, & A. Ward (Eds.), *Handbook of social psychology* (2nd ed., pp. 533–562). New York: Springer. Very accessible overview and review of social psychology research on intergroup relations, prejudice and discrimination.

Hogg, M. A., & Abrams, D. (Eds.) (2001). *Intergroup relations: Essential readings*. Philadelphia, PA: Psychology Press. Annotated collection of key publications on intergroup relations. There is an introductory overview chapter and commentary chapters introducing each reading.

Hogg, M. A., & Abrams, D. (2007). Intergroup behavior and social identity. In M. A. Hogg & J. Cooper (Eds.), *The SAGE handbook of social psychology* (pp. 407–431). London: SAGE. A comprehensive overview of research on intergroup relations and social identity processes.

Levine, J. M. (Ed.) (2013). *Group processes*. New York: Psychology Press. Absolutely up-to-date and comprehensive set of chapters by leading scholars on all aspects of group and intergroup processes.

Levine, J. M., & Hogg, M. A. (Eds.) (2010). *Encyclopedia of group processes and intergroup relations*. Thousand Oaks, CA: SAGE. A comprehensive and readable compendium of entries on all aspects of the social psychology of groups, written by all the leading scholars in the field.

Stangor, C. (2016). *Social groups in action and interaction* (2nd ed.). New York: Psychology Press. Completely up-to-date, comprehensive and accessible coverage of the social psychology of processes within and between groups.

Thompson, L. L. (2015). *The mind and heart of the negotiator* (6th ed.). New York: Pearson. The most recent edition of this classic book on the psychology of negotiation.

Tropp, L. R. (Ed.) (2012). *The Oxford handbook of intergroup conflict*. New York: Oxford University Press. Twenty-one chapters by leading scholars focus on intergroup conflict, reduction of prejudice and conflict, and the challenge of building peace.

Van Lange, P. A. M., Balliet, D., Parks, C. D., & Van Vugt, M. (2014). *Social dilemmas: Understanding human cooperation*. New York: Oxford University Press. Up-to-date and comprehensive discussion of social dilemmas and the dynamics of human cooperation.

Yzerbyt, V., & Demoulin, S. (2010). Intergroup relations. In S. T. Fiske, D. T. Gilbert, & G. Lindzey (Eds.), *Handbook of social psychology* (5th ed., Vol. 2, pp. 1024–183). New York: Wiley. A thorough overview of the field of intergroup relations, in the most recent edition of the classic handbook – a primary source for theory and research.

Chapter 12
Aggression

Chapter contents

What do *you* think?

1   Do you think the world is becoming a safer, less violent place to live? Psychologist Steven Pinker thinks so, when judged over a very lengthy time span.

2   Mary is sarcastic to her boyfriend, Tony, and circulates nasty rumours about him, but she never pushes or shoves him. Tony is never sarcastic to Mary and never circulates rumours about her, but he does push and shove her. Who is more 'aggressive'?

3   We've all seen those nature movies – a nasty-looking pack of African hunting dogs viciously tearing some poor little creature to bits and snarling aggressively at each other. Are humans like this? How far does animal behaviour inform our understanding of human aggression?

4   According to your neighbour, watching violent movies and playing gory computer games is a good way to let off steam. Can you counter this view?

5   Tom has quite a collection of favourite porn sites. His girlfriend knows this and asks him to give up his habit. Tom says: 'It doesn't hurt anyone. I'm not turning into a rapist, you know!' As a budding social psychologist, how would you advise him?

Aggression in our community

What catches your attention about aggression? Is it vivid media reports of casualties of war, innocent victims of terrorism or children slaughtered in a mass shooting? What about a burglary in your neighbourhood, or news of serious injuries to a child by a close relative? How about a newspaper story of a rape in a nearby town? Some of these – perhaps not all – are criminal acts against persons or property and may be shockingly violent. Would unkind words between two people count as aggression? As we shall see, all of these are important issues in our daily lives and qualify to varying degrees as acts of aggression, some fairly trivial and others monstrous.

Let's talk about murder. In 2008, the number of murders per 100,000 people was five in the United States, fourteen in Russia, forty in Colombia and a staggering sixty in Jamaica (see the map in Figure 12.1). How does your country measure up? Assuming national statistics are equally reliable, murder rates may vary for many reasons; for example, access to lethal weapons, conditions of poverty or war and cultural and subcultural support for violence. We explore these influences in this chapter. We will also revisit correlates of murder in the section 'Societal influences'.

Many of us occasionally witness aggression, and most of us regularly witness evidence and symbols of aggressive acts or aggressive people: graffiti, vandalism, violent arguments, misogynistic music and, of course, weapons. Victims of aggression often have less power or are disadvantaged: the very young, the old, the sick and people from different ethnic backgrounds. In a survey of 11- and 12-year-old children, half had been punched, kicked, beaten or hit by other children, and two-thirds had been threatened with physical abuse or had been emotionally abused by their peers (Lind & Maxwell, 1996).

Most of us have probably 'played' aggressive games (fighting, video games, contact sports), but have felt constrained by the potential for harm to occur. A survey of 10,000 women reported that 20 per cent felt 'very unsafe' when walking out at night, even though less than 1 per cent reported actually having been attacked in the last year – better 'safe than sorry' (Jones, Gray, Kavanagh, Moran, Norton, & Seldon, 1994). There is some evidence that the

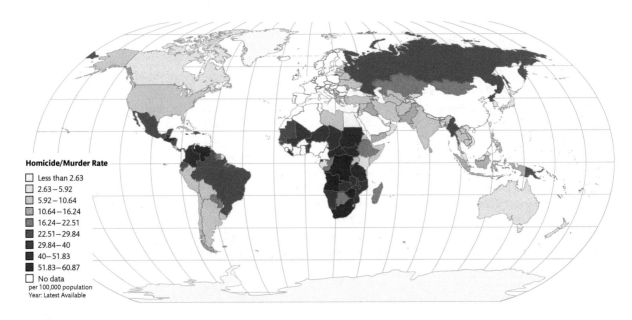

Figure 12.1 International homicide rates per 100,000

Note: This map, and several related maps, were last updated in 2011.

Source: UNODC: Global Study on Homicide .

modern world may indeed have become a more violent place – terrorism is perhaps at the top of the list here (the 2015 Paris attacks that killed 130, and the 2016 Nice attack that killed 86), but mass shootings have also become more prevalent in Western countries, particularly of course the United States (the 2016 Orlando nightclub shooting killed 50 and injured 53).

Several factors have been implicated: violence against children in homes (Straus, 2001), exposure to violent media among children (Bushman & Huesmann, 2001), ready availability of guns in some countries (O'Donnell, 1995) and even global warming (Anderson, Bushman, & Groom, 1997). However, in his book *The Better Angels of Our Nature: The Decline of Violence in History and Its Causes*, Steven Pinker (2011) has suggested and provided supportive evidence that, on the contrary, the world has actually become a less aggressive place than it used to be.

We would add to a list of potential causes of aggression and violence the pervasive effects of relative deprivation, involving the widening gap perceived by very poor people when they compare themselves with those who are better off. The notion of the '99 per cent' promoted by the occupy movements that started in 2011 underscores a post-recession awareness of and dissatisfaction with growing economic inequality – although it should be noted that most of the demonstrations were not violent.

It is also notable that vivid pictorial and video portrayals of violence and aggression are now inescapable. In the late 1960s and early 1970s, the world was shocked by TV and magazine images of the Vietnam War, but now images of aggression and violence are the daily diet of news and current affairs channels on TV and simply a click away on YouTube and a host of other web resources and social media. Aggression is simply more accessible now than it used to be.

If aggression is omnipresent, is it an inescapable part of human nature? Some scholars (e.g. Ardrey, 1961) claim that aggression is a basic human instinct, an innate fixed action pattern that we share with other species. If aggression has a genetic foundation, then presumably its expression is inevitable. Other scholars paint a less gloomy picture, arguing that even if aggressive tendencies are a part of our behavioural repertoire, it may be possible to control and possibly prevent the expression of the tendency as actual behaviour. The immediate challenges for psychologists are to identify the reasons why people aggress against others and to find ways of reducing the harmful effects on the victims, the aggressor and society. But first, consider some of the attempts that have been made to define 'aggression'.

Definitions and measurement

Defining aggression

Researchers have found it difficult to agree about how to describe aggression, explain it or isolate its components. One person may define aggression physically as pushing, shoving and striking, while another may add features such as threatening speech, verbal insults and facial expressions. Simply ignoring or ostracising someone can also count as aggression – it certainly can produce aggressive reactions (DeWall, Twenge, Bushman, Im, & Williams, 2010; Warburton, Williams, & Cairns, 2006; Wesselmann, Butler, Williams, & Pickett, 2010; Williams & Warburton, 2003). What is 'aggressive' is partly shaped by societal and cultural norms. Among the Amish of Pennsylvania, the bar is very low – shunning or ostracism is considered an extremely harsh treatment – whereas in most gang subcultures, the bar is much higher – physical mutilation and murder can be commonplace. The part played by culture in the norms controlling aggression is discussed in **Chapter 16**.

Social psychology has defined aggression in many different ways:

- behaviour resulting in personal injury or destruction of property (Bandura, 1973);
- behaviour intended to harm another of the same species (Scherer, Abeles, & Fischer, 1975);

- behaviour directed towards the goal of harming or injuring another living being who is motivated to avoid such treatment (Baron, 1977);
- intentional infliction of some form of harm on others (Baron & Byrne, 2000);
- behaviour directed towards another individual carried out with the proximate (immediate) intent to cause harm (Anderson & Huesmann, 2003).

What, then, should qualify as the key components of aggression (see Box 12.1)? Michael Carlson and his colleagues have suggested that more common ground is found, across findings and contexts, by defining aggression broadly as 'the intent to harm' (Carlson, Marcus-Newhall, & Miller, 1989).

Measuring aggression

Values
A higher-order concept thought to provide a structure for organising attitudes.

In practice, scientists are like most of us – they use definitions that correspond to their **values**. As a result, the behaviour studied may differ from one researcher to another, and across different cultures, and yet be called 'aggression'. For example, are bodily cues of anger directed towards someone else the same as actually fighting? Are protests by indigenous peoples about their traditional lands comparable to acts of international terrorism? Or is spanking a child in the same category as the grisly deeds of a serial killer?

Operational definition
Defines a theoretical term in a way that allows it to be manipulated or measured.

Although the problem of definition is not resolved, researchers have developed **operational definitions** (see **Chapter 1**) so that they can manipulate and measure aggression in empirical research. However, different researchers have used different operationalisations, which include:

1 *Analogues of behaviour:*
- punching an inflated plastic doll (Bandura, Ross, & Ross, 1963);
- pressing a button supposed to deliver an electric shock to someone else (Buss, 1961).

2 *Signal of intention:*
- verbal expression of willingness to use violence in an experimental laboratory setting (Geen, 1978).

Box 12.1 Your life
Components of definitions of aggression

How much should a satisfactory definition of aggression include? Is motive important? What about the nature of the target? Are some situations too complex to reach a clear decision? Consider things you have done or behaviour you have witnessed, and consider which of the following would qualify as aggression:

- actual harm, but not an unsuccessful act of violence;
- physical injury, but not psychological harm (such as verbal abuse);
- harm to people, but not to animals or property;
- harm to people in war;
- harm in a rule-governed context (such as a boxing match);

- intentional harm, but not negligent harm;
- belief by a victim that harm has occurred;
- injury in a victim's alleged 'best interests' (such as smacking a child);
- self-injury, such as self-mutilation or suicide;
- social ostracism.

This list is not exhaustive. You may think of other elements of behaviour that may or may not render it aggressive, according to your perspective. Discuss some of these issues with a friend. Is it difficult to agree on a definition?

3 *Ratings by self or others:*
- written self-report by institutionalised teenage boys about their prior aggressive behaviour (Leyens, Camino, Parke, & Berkowitz, 1975);
- pencil-and-paper ratings by teachers and classmates of a child's level of aggressiveness (Eron, 1982).

4 *Indirect aggression:*
- relational aggression – e.g. damaging a person's peer relationships (Crick & Grotpeter, 1995) or spreading rumours (Lansford, Skinner, Sorbring, Di Giunta, Deater-Deckard, Dodge, et al., 2012; Warren, Richardson, & McQuillin, 2011).

The first of these measures are **analogues** (i.e. substitutes for physical aggression), which have been developed to enable researchers to conduct ethical research on aggression (see **Chapter 1**) – it is difficult to justify an actual physical assault against a person in an experimental setting.

A key question is whether we can generalise findings from analogue measures of aggression to a larger population in real-life settings. For example, what is the **external validity** of the aggression (electric shock) machine developed by Arnold Buss (1961), which is similar to the apparatus used by Stanley Milgram (1963) in his studies of obedience (**Chapter 7**)? In a test of this device, prisoners with histories of violence administered higher levels of shock to a confederate (Cherek, Schnapp, Moeller, & Dougherty, 1996; also see Anderson & Bushman, 1997). Similarly, there is a parallel between the laboratory and real life regarding effects on aggression of alcohol, high temperatures, direct provocation and violence in the media.

What counts as aggression is very diverse, and no single definition is able to capture this diversity. (Are Mary and Tony each aggressive? Check the first 'What do *you* think?' question.)

Analogue
Device or measure intended to faithfully mimic the 'real thing'.

External validity
Similarity between circumstances surrounding an experiment and circumstances encountered in everyday life.

Theoretical perspectives

How we measure aggression is linked to how we define it, and both are determined by our theoretical position. Given aggression's impact on our lives, it should be no surprise to find that theories of aggression are plentiful.

Trying to understand why humans aggress against their own kind, and the factors that make them behave with viciousness and brutality towards one another in ways and degrees unparalleled in other animals, has led to much speculation since ancient times (Geen & Donnerstein, 1983). Explanations of aggression fall into two broad classes, the biological and the social, although this distinction is not entirely rigid. A debate over which of the two explanations is superior is an example of the **nature–nurture controversy**: is human action determined by our biological inheritance or by our social environment? (A related instance of this debate involves the origins of prosocial behaviour; see **Chapter 13**.)

Because our interest is social psychological, it favours a focus on social factors and therefore theories that incorporate a social learning component. However, a biological contribution to aggression cannot be ignored. After all, violence is a reaction of our bodily system. One issue is that some biological explanations are so biological that they might seem to be a threat to any form of theory that is social.

Nature–nurture controversy
Classic debate about whether genetic or environmental factors determine human behaviour. Scientists generally accept that it is an interaction of both.

Biological explanations

The starting point for these explanations is that aggression is an innate action tendency. Although modification of the consequent behaviour is possible, the wellspring is not. Aggression is an instinct: that is, a pattern of responses that is genetically predetermined. If

Instinct
Innate drive or impulse, genetically transmitted.

so, it should show the characteristics of an instinct. According to primate biologist Arthur Riopelle (1987), an **instinct** is:

- *goal-directed* and terminates in a specific consequence (e.g. an attack);
- *beneficial* to the individual and to the species;
- *adapted* to a normal environment (although not to an abnormal one);
- *shared* by most members of the species (although its manifestation can vary from individual to individual);
- *developed* in a clear way as the individual matures;
- *unlearned* on the basis of individual experience (although it can become manifest in relation to learnt aspects within a context).

Three approaches have shared most, if not all, of these biological attributes in their explanation of human aggression. All argue that aggressive behaviour is an inherent part of human nature, that we are programmed at birth to act in that way. The oldest is the psychodynamic approach, dating back to the early part of the twentieth century. This was followed a little later by ethological approaches, based on the study of animal behaviour. The third approach, which is more recent, comes mainly from evolutionary social psychology.

Psychodynamic theory

Neo-Freudians
Psychoanalytic theorists who modified the original theories of Freud.

In *Beyond the Pleasure Principle*, Freud (1920/1990) proposed that human aggression stems from an innate 'Death Instinct', *Thanatos*, which is in opposition to a 'Life Instinct', *Eros*. Thanatos is initially directed at self-destruction, but later in development it becomes redirected outwards towards other people. Freud's background as a physician influenced his notion of the death instinct, which was also partly a response to the large-scale destruction of the First World War. Like the sexual urge, which stems from Eros, an aggressive urge stemming from Thanatos builds up naturally from bodily tensions and needs to be expressed. Freud's ideas were revised by later theorists, known as **neo-Freudians**, who viewed aggression as a more rational, but nonetheless innate, process whereby people sought a healthy release for primitive survival instincts that are basic to all animal species (Hartmann, Kris, & Loewenstein, 1949).

Ethology

Ethology
Approach that argues that animal behaviour should be studied in the species' natural physical and social environment. Behaviour is genetically determined and is controlled by natural selection.

Releasers
Specific stimuli in the environment thought by ethologists to trigger aggressive responses.

In the 1960s, three highly influential books were published, making the case for the instinctual basis of human aggression on the grounds of a comparison with animal behaviour: Konrad Lorenz's *On Aggression* (1966), Robert Ardrey's *The Territorial Imperative* (1966) and Desmond Morris's *The Naked Ape* (1967). The general perspective that underpins this explanation of aggression is referred to as **ethology**, a branch of biology devoted to the study of instincts, or fixed action patterns, among all members of a species when living in their natural environment.

Like the neo-Freudians, ethologists stressed the functional aspects of aggression; but they also recognised that, while the potential or instinct for aggression may be innate, actual aggressive behaviour is elicited by specific stimuli in the environment, known as **releasers**. Lorenz invoked evolutionary principles to propose that aggression has survival value. An animal is considerably more aggressive towards other members of its species, which functions to distribute the individuals and/or family units in such a way as to make the most efficient use of available resources, such as sexual selection and mating, food and territory. Most of the time, intraspecies aggression may not even result in actual violence, as one animal will display instinctual threat gestures that are recognised by the other animal, which can then depart the scene – 'the Rottweiler growls so the Chihuahua runs'.

Even if fighting does break out, it is unlikely to result in death, since the losing animal can display instinctual appeasement gestures that divert the victor from actually killing: for

Threat displays
'Nice little puppy!'
Aggression in animals is
often limited by
appeasement gestures. Do
you think appeasement will
work with Mad Max?

example, some animals will lie on the ground belly up in an act of subordination. Over time, in animals such as monkeys that live in colonies, appeasement gestures can help to establish dominance hierarchies or pecking orders. Thus, there is an innate urge to aggress, but its expression is conditional on appropriate stimulation by environmental releasers.

Lorenz (1966) extended the argument to humans, who he believed also inherited a **fighting instinct**. However, its survival value for humans is less clear than is the case for other animals. This is largely because humans lack well-developed killing appendages, such as large teeth or claws, so that clearly recognisable appeasement gestures seem not to have evolved (or may have disappeared over the course of evolution).

There are two implications from this approach: (1) once we start being violent, we do not seem to know when to stop; and (2) in order to kill, we generally need to resort to weapons. The advanced technology of our times has produced frightful devices that can slaughter people in large numbers. Furthermore, this can be accomplished at a great distance, so that even the visual and auditory feedback cues of the victim's anguish are not available to persuade the victor to desist. The battle of the Somme clocked up nearly 1.7 million killed and injured over a four-month period in 1916.

This insanity culminated in the hydrogen bomb. In October 1961, the Soviet Union detonated Tsar Bomba, a 57-megaton device, in a remote archipelago in the Arctic Ocean. The largest, most powerful nuclear weapon ever detonated, it was three thousand times the force of the 1945 Hiroshima atom bomb that killed 200,000 people. At the height of the Cold War, there was a stockpile of 65,000 nuclear bombs ('down' to about 15,375 in 2016). In short, humans have the ability to harm others easily, and with very little effort. And we have not even mentioned biological or chemical weapons.

Fighting instinct
Innate impulse to aggress
which ethologists claim is
shared by humans with
other animals.

Evolutionary social psychology

Evolutionary social psychology developed out of evolutionary theory and sociobiology (see **Chapter 1**) but has been presented as a revised perspective on the entire discipline of social psychology. Evolutionary social psychology is an ambitious approach that not only assumes an innate basis for aggression but also claims a biological basis for all social behaviour (Caporael, 2007; Kenrick, Maner, & Li, 2005; Neuberg, Kenrick, & Schaller, 2010; Schaller,

**Evolutionary social
psychology**
An extension of
evolutionary psychology
that views complex social
behaviour as adaptive,
helping the individual, kin
and the species as a whole
to survive.

Simpson, & Kenrick, 2006). Evolutionary perspectives on altruism and interpersonal attraction are discussed in **Chapters 13 and 14.**

Derived from Darwinian theory, the evolutionary argument is provocative: specific behaviour has evolved because it promotes the survival of genes that allow the individual to live long enough to pass the same genes on to the next generation. Aggression is adaptive because it must be linked to living long enough to procreate. As such, it is helpful to the individual and to the species. Consider the situation where danger threatens the offspring of a species. Most animals, and usually the mother, will react with a high level of aggression, often higher than they would normally exhibit in other situations. A mother bird, for example, may take life-threatening risks to protect her young – and heaven help you if you are hiking in the woods and happen to get between a bear and her cubs.

In territorial species, the defence of space is linked to aggression, and being aggressive can also increase access to resources (Vaughan, 2010d). For humans, the goals for which aggressive behaviour is adaptive include social and economic advantage, either to defend the resources that we already have or to acquire new ones.

Limitations of biological arguments

Biological explanations of aggression have considerable appeal because they resonate with the popular assumption that violence is part of human nature, and with our common experience that some emotions, anger in this case, are associated with strong bodily reactions. The seventeenth-century philosopher Thomas Hobbes famously remarked that people's lives are 'nasty, brutish and short'. Broadly speaking, however, behavioural scientists (Goldstein, 1987; Rose & Rose, 2000; Ryan, 1985) question the sufficiency of the explanation of aggression when it is based entirely on the cornerstone of instinct, on the grounds that the concept of instinct: (a) depends on energy that is unknown, unknowable and immeasurable; (b) is supported by only limited and biased empirical observation of actual human behaviour; (c) has little utility in the prevention or control of aggression and (d) relies on circular logic, proposing causal connections for which there is no evidence.

In summary, the view among most social psychologists who research human aggression is that evolutionary social psychology's overall contribution to an understanding of the incidence and maintenance of aggression (as distinct from its expression) is limited (Geen, 1998). (See the second 'What do *you* think?' question.) However, some evolutionary stalwarts have argued:

> to say that an individual has a trait is not to say that his or her overt behavior is insensitive to the environment . . . Rather, the behavioral manifestation of a given genotype depends critically on inputs from, and reactions to, the environment.
>
> Kenrick, Li and Butner (2003, p. 12)

In other words, there is an interaction between what is inherited and the kinds of behaviour that a context permits. For example, if Igor is by nature an irritable person, it might be in his best interests not to be his usual confrontational self (a behavioural trait) when a gang of powerful bullies visits the neighbourhood bar. This is an interactionist argument and the view is in effect a biosocial approach.

Social and biosocial explanations

Biosocial theories
In the context of aggression, theories that emphasise an innate component, though not the existence of a full-blown instinct.

Generally, social psychologists have not favoured theories of aggression defined in terms of instinct – they prefer approaches that emphasise the role of learning and of the social context. Some of these nevertheless incorporate a biological element, and we refer to them as **biosocial theories**. The two outlined in this section propose that a drive (or state of arousal) is a precondition for aggression, although they differ in how internal and external factors are thought to interact to promote aggressive reactions.

Frustration and aggression

In its original form, the **frustration–aggression hypothesis** linked aggression to an antecedent condition of frustration. It derived from the work of a group of psychologists at Yale University in the 1930s, and it has been used to explain prejudice (as described in **Chapter 10**). The anthropologist John Dollard and his psychologist colleagues proposed that aggression was always caused by some kind of frustrating event or situation; conversely, frustration invariably led to aggression (Dollard, Doob, Miller, Mowrer, & Sears, 1939). This reasoning has been applied to the effects of job loss on violence (Catalano, Novaco, & McConnell, 1997) and the role of social and economic deprivation in 'ethnic cleansing' of the Kurds in Iraq and of non-Serbs in Bosnia (Dutton, Boyanowsky, & Bond, 2005; Staub, 1996, 2000). We might also speculate that terrorism is at least partly fuelled by chronic and acute frustration over the ineffectiveness of other mechanisms to achieve socio-economic and cultural goals – people are unlikely to become suicide bombers unless all other channels of goal achievement have proved ineffective.

Frustration–aggression theory had considerable appeal, inasmuch as it was decidedly different from the Freudian approach. According to J. H. Goldstein (1980, pp. 262–263), 'it was a theory with no psychoanalytic mumbo jumbo. No need to bother about such phantoms as ids, egos, superegos, and ego defence mechanisms.' Later research revealed that the basic hypothesis was simplistic and far from a complete explanation for aggressive behaviour (see Berkowitz, 1993; Miller, Pederson, Earlywine, & Pollock, 2003). One major flaw is the theory's loose definition of 'frustration' and the difficulty in predicting which kinds of frustrating circumstance may lead to aggression.

Frustration–aggression hypothesis
Theory that all frustration leads to aggression, and all aggression comes from frustration. Used to explain prejudice and intergroup aggression.

Excitation transfer

A later approach, that invoked the concept of drive, is Dolf Zillmann's (1979, 1988) **excitation-transfer model**. The expression of aggression (or any other emotion) is a function of: (a) a learnt aggressive behaviour, (b) arousal or excitation from another source and (c) the person's interpretation of the arousal state, such that an aggressive response seems appropriate.

Zillmann suggests that this residual arousal transfers from one situation to another in a way that promotes the likelihood of an aggressive response, especially if aggressive

Excitation-transfer model
The expression of aggression is a function of learnt behaviour, some excitation from another source, and the person's interpretation of the arousal state.

Road rage
Sitting in traffic is a daily frustration for many people that occasionally spills over into aggression.

Figure 12.2 Applying the excitation-transfer model of aggression

Source: Based on Zillman (1979).

behaviour is well established in someone's behavioural repertoire. According to Zillmann, any experience that increases the level of overall excitation can lead to unintended consequences.

Look at the example in Figure 12.2. A student has been exercising at the gym and is still physically aroused when driving to the local supermarket. Here, another customer's car sneaks forward into the parking space that the student is trying to reverse into. Although the event might ordinarily be mildly annoying, this time the residual excitation from the gym session (now forgotten) triggers verbal abuse from the student (not you, of course).

Heightened arousal can often lead us to be more aggressive than we are normally: for example, exclaiming with annoyance at our partner when we are already upset about dropping some crockery in the kitchen, severely scolding a child who accidentally gets lost or making gestures while driving in stressful traffic conditions. If you drive a red car, you might want to watch out. In a French study, a car was arranged to block other drivers waiting at a traffic light. When the car was red rather than blue, green, black or white, frustrated drivers were quicker to honk their horns or flash their headlights (Guéguen, Jacob, Lourel, & Pascua, 2012)! The extreme level of excitement that often occurs at football matches can erupt into violence between rival groups of fans (Kerr, 2005).

All of these instances make some sense in terms of Zillmann's theory, which can be applied to the experience of sexual arousal as well (see the section on erotica later in this chapter), or to any kind of former stimulation whose effects linger over time. The general concept of arousal is retained in Anderson and Bushman's (2002a) general aggression model, to which we return in a later section.

Hate crimes

Biological and social models of aggression can provide a convincing analysis of why people aggress against others. Sometimes, violence is linked to prejudice, as noted in our discussion of the frustration–aggression hypothesis earlier in this chapter (also see **Chapter 10**). **Hate crimes** are an instance. However, some old targets of prejudice have been replaced: the lynchings of African Americans in the South during the 1930s have given way to different forms of persecution, and the persecution of other minorities (Green, Glaser, & Rich, 1998). In some countries, hate crimes now are a class of criminal offence (Vaughan, 2010a). See Box 12.2 for an example of how a gay man was persecuted.

Hate crimes
A class of violence against members of a stereotyped minority group.

Aggression can be learnt

The gradual control of aggressive impulses in an infant clearly depends upon an extensive learning process (Miles & Carey, 1997). **Social learning theory** is a wide-ranging behavioural approach in psychology, and it features the processes responsible for (a) the *acquisition*

Social learning theory
The view championed by Bandura that human social behaviour is not innate but learnt from appropriate models.

Box 12.2 Our world
Hate crimes, gays and the case of Matthew Shepard

A group whose members have been the victims of frequent and extreme hate crimes is the gay community. Aggression is frequently perpetrated against homosexuals by people who have no direct dealings with their victims other than being motivated by strong negative feelings towards homosexuality. Many homosexual people report being the victims of such hate crimes, and one study found that 94 per cent of its homosexual participants had been victimised for reasons associated with their sexuality (National Gay and Lesbian Task Force, 1990). Franklin (2000) surveyed 489 racially and economically diverse students at a community college in North Carolina in the United States: 10 per cent reported that they had physically assaulted or threatened to assault a person whom they knew or assumed to be homosexual; 24 per cent reported that they had verbally abused people they thought were homosexual.

Matthew Shepard was a 21-year-old gay college student in Wyoming who was the victim of a hate crime against gay people. He was murdered in 1998 by two 22-year-old men. Matthew was taken from a bar five days earlier to a remote prairie, where he was tied to a fence and whipped in the face with a gun until he lost consciousness. He was then left to die in the freezing weather. His killers admitted to laughing while they attacked Matthew. Each assailant received two life sentences. Attempts by the prosecution to secure the death penalty were thwarted by Matthew's mother, who appealed for clemency for the men. Both of the men's girlfriends were also charged with being an accessory to the crime.

This hate crime, although not uncommon, sparked worldwide outrage in gay and lesbian communities, and Matthew became something of a symbol for the persecution that many minority group members experience. (see the Westborough Baptist anti-gay home page, some of whose members picketed his funeral, at **http://www. godhatesfags.com/**.)

---

of a behaviour or a behavioural sequence, (b) the *instigation* of overt acts and (c) the *maintenance* of the behaviour.

Social learning theory's best-known proponent is Albert Bandura (Bandura, 1977; Bandura & Walters, 1963), who applied it specifically to aggression (Bandura, 1973). Of course, if antisocial behaviour can be learnt, so can prosocial behaviour (see **Chapter 13**). Although Bandura acknowledged the role of biological factors in aggression, the theory's emphasis is on the role of experience, which can be direct or vicarious. Through socialisation, children learn to aggress because either they are directly rewarded or someone else appears to be rewarded for aggression.

The idea of **learning by direct experience** is based on B. F. Skinner's operant reinforcement principles: a behaviour is maintained by rewards and punishments actually experienced by the child. For example, if Jonathan takes Margaret's biscuit from her, and no one intervenes, then he is reinforced by now having the biscuit. The idea of **learning by vicarious experience** maintains that learning occurs through the processes of modelling and imitation of other people.

The concept of imitation is not new. The French sociologist Gabriel Tarde (1890), for example, devoted a whole book, *Les lois de l'imitation*, to the subject and boldly asserted that 'Society *is* imitation'. What is unique in social learning theory is the proposition that the behaviour to be imitated must be seen to be rewarding in some way, and that some models, such as parents, siblings and peers, are more appropriate for the child than others. The learning sequence of aggression can be extended beyond direct interactions between people to include media images, such as on television. It can also explain how adults learn in later life.

According to Bandura, whether a person is aggressive in a particular situation depends on:

- a person's previous experiences of others' aggressive behaviour;
- how successful aggressive behaviour has been in the past;

Learning by direct experience
Acquiring a behaviour because we were rewarded for it.

Learning by vicarious experience
Acquiring a behaviour after observing that another person was rewarded for it.

Vicarious learning
Children can learn to be aggressive by playing video games in which heroic characters are reinforced for aggression.

- the current likelihood that an aggressive person will be either rewarded or punished;
- the complex array of cognitive, social and environmental factors in the situation.

Bandura's studies used a variety of experimental settings to show that children quite readily mimic the aggressive acts of others. Adults in particular make potent models, no doubt because children perceive their elders as responsible and authoritative figures (also see **Chapters 5 and 14**). Early findings pointed to a clear **modelling** effect when the adult was seen acting aggressively in a live setting. Even more disturbingly, this capacity to behave aggressively was also found when children saw the adult model acting violently on television (see Box 12.3 and Figure 12.3).

An interesting theoretical development is a blending of social learning theory with the learning of a particular kind of cognitive schema – the **script** (see **Chapter 2**). Children learn rules of conduct from those around them, so that aggression becomes internalised. A situation is recognised as frustrating or threatening: for example, a human target is identified, and a learnt routine of aggressive behaviour is enacted (Perry, Perry, & Boldizar, 1990). Once established in childhood, an aggressive sequence is persistent (Anderson & Huesmann, 2003; Huesmann, 1988). Research on age trends for murder and manslaughter in the United States shows that this form of aggression quickly peaks among 15- to 25-year-olds and then declines systematically (US Department of Justice, 2001).

The social learning approach has had a significant impact on research on aggression. It has also touched a chord in our community and has directly increased research into the effects of violence in the visual media on both children and adults. If violence is learnt, exposure to aggressive and successful models leads people to imitate them. Being aggressive can become an established pattern of behaving, even a way of life, which is likely to repeat itself by imitation across generations (Huesmann, Eron, Lefkowitz, & Walder, 1984). This does not necessarily mean that change is impossible. If aggression can be learnt, presumably it can also be modified and remedied. This is the basis of behaviour modification programmes, such as anger management, used by clinical and community psychologists to help people find less aggressive ways of expressing themselves and dealing with others.

Finally, what effects does spanking have on the social development of children? From social learning theory, you might predict that children will learn that striking another is not punished, at least if the aggressor is more powerful! In a two-year longitudinal study of children and their parents, Murray Straus and his colleagues recorded how often a child was spanked (none to three or more times) each week. Across a two-year period, they found an almost linear relationship over time between the rate of spanking and the level of antisocial

Modelling
Tendency for a person to reproduce the actions, attitudes and emotional responses exhibited by a real-life or symbolic model. Also called *observational learning*.

Script
A schema about an event.

Box 12.3 Research classic
Sock it to the Bobo doll!

Can the mere observation of an act be sufficient to learn how to perform it? Albert Bandura and his colleagues addressed this question in a series of experiments at Stanford University. This work had a considerable impact on the acceptance of social factors within the narrower field of experimental research on learning, but it also had a long-term effect on wider thinking about the origins of aggression. According to the social learning theory of observational learning, observing a behaviour produces a cognitive representation in the observer, who then experiences vicarious reinforcement. This kind of reinforcement refers to a process whereby the outcome for the model, whether rewarding or punishing, becomes a remote reinforcement for the observer. If this is so, then aggression is likely to be one of many forms of behaviour that can be learnt.

Bandura, Ross and Ross (1963) tested this idea in one study of four- and five-year-old children who watched a male or female adult play with a commercially popular inflated Bobo doll. There were four conditions:

1 *Live*. The adult model came into the room where the child was playing. After playing with some Tinker Toys, the adult then began to act aggressively towards the Bobo doll. The acts included sitting on the doll, hitting its nose, banging it on the head with a mallet and kicking it around the room. The words used were 'sock him in the nose', 'pow', 'kick him', 'hit him down' and the like. After this, the child was left to play with the Bobo doll.

2 *Videotape*. This was the same as the live sequence but had been filmed on videotape for the child to view.

3 *Cartoon*. The model acted in the same way but was dressed in a cat uniform, and the room was decorated as if it were in a cartoon.

4 *Control*. The child skipped all of these conditions and went directly to play with the Bobo doll.

The results in Figure 12.3 show that the children who watched an adult behave aggressively in any condition behaved more aggressively later. The most effective condition for modelling aggressive behaviour was the live sequence. However, the finding that the cartoon and videotaped conditions also increased imitative aggression in children provided fuel for critics who argued that graphic presentations of violence in films and television could have serious consequences for children's later behaviour.

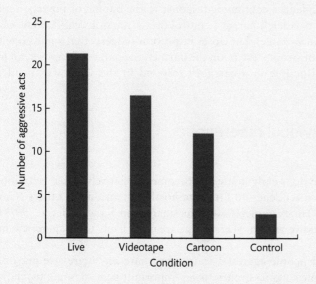

Figure 12.3 How children learn aggression through mere observation

Source: Based on data from Bandura and Walters (1963).

behaviour. What is more, children who were not spanked at all showed less antisocial behaviour after two years (Straus, Sugarman, & Giles-Sims, 1997).

Another study, by Brian Boutwell and his colleagues, was able to disentangle environmental and genetic factors (Boutwell, Franklin, Barnes, & Beaver, 2011). Boutwell and colleagues' data were drawn from a large-scale US longitudinal study of children born in 2001 that included twins (about 1,300 fraternal and 250 identical), which allows one to estimate a genetic impact on behaviour. The results pointed to a genetic susceptibility to long-term antisocial behaviour that was more marked in children who were spanked. This effect was negligible in girls.

Personal and situational variations

None of the foregoing theories provides a full explanation for the diversity of aggression, and even when a precipitating event is apparent, there are other, less obvious contributing factors. Consider how cultural values (see **Chapter 16**) and social pressures may contribute to a pub brawl involving unemployed immigrants, even though intoxication may seem to be the cause. Other examples are the underlying effects of poverty, chronic frustration and social disadvantage, which cumulatively often lead to acts of both public and domestic violence.

Another way to try to understand aggression is to focus on personal and situational variables. Although it is possible to distinguish conceptually between the person and the situation, common sense suggests that an interaction of the two determines how people behave (see Ross & Nisbett, 1991). Like an echo of Kurt Lewin's early field theory notion of a tension between the person and the environment (see **Chapter 1**), people bring to any situation their unique characteristics and their individual way of construing the situation. Although separation of person variables from situation variables in situations of aggression may be an oversimplification and a matter of conceptual convenience, it does reflect the way in which most research has been conducted.

Consider some contexts in which aggression occurs: reacting to being teased, a carry-over from a near-miss traffic accident, a continuing response to the burden of poverty, a method for dealing with a nagging partner, a parent's control over a fractious child. Some of these appear to involve situational variables, but closer inspection suggests that some go with the person, or with a category of people (the poor, the partner, the parent). However, an important caveat is that not all people in a category respond in the same way in identical situations.

Personality and individual differences

Personality

The tendency to aggress develops early in life and becomes a relatively stable behaviour pattern that can be linked to a tendency to attribute hostile intentions to others (Graham, Hudley, & Williams, 1992). For example, Rowell Huesmann and Nancy Guerra (1997) found that children who are aggressive at eight years of age are more likely to be aggressive in later years.

This might suggest that people aggress because they have an 'aggressive personality'. Indeed, evaluation of people's aggressiveness is an important part of some psychological tests and clinical assessments (Sundberg, 1977): for example, in determining the likelihood of reoffending among violent offenders (Mullen, 1984). Can you rate your friends according to how much or how little they typically tend towards aggressive behaviour?

It is unlikely that some people are 'naturally' more aggressive than others; however, it is true that some of us can be more aggressive than others because of our age, gender, culture and life experiences. Violent offenders tend to have low self-esteem and poor frustration tolerance. However, narcissistic people who have inflated self-esteem and a sense of entitlement seem to be particularly prone to aggression (Bushman & Baumeister, 1998). Social workers often recognise children who have been exposed to above-average levels of violence, particularly in their homes, as being 'high risk' and in need of primary intervention.

A meta-analysis of 27 studies and 2,646 participants reveals that criminality is associated with having an insecure **attachment style** (Ogilvie, Newman, Todd, & Peck, 2014). Offenders were much more likely than non-offenders to have a childhood history of insecure attachment, and that this applied to all types of criminality (i.e. sexual offending, violent offending, non-violent offending and domestic violence even in the absence of psychopathology). See **Chapter 14** for details of attachment theory; and Table 14.1 for the main attachment styles, including secure (versus insecure) attachment.

Attachment styles
Descriptions of the nature of people's close relationships, thought to be established in childhood.

Type A personality

Research has identified a behaviour pattern called **Type A personality** (Matthews, 1982). Type A people are overactive and excessively competitive in their encounters with others, and may be more aggressive towards those perceived to be competing with them on an important task (Carver & Glass, 1978). They are also prone to coronary heart disease. Type A people prefer to work alone rather than with others when they are under stress, probably to avoid exposure to incompetence in others and to feel in control of the situation (Dembroski & MacDougall, 1978).

Type A personality
The 'coronary-prone' personality – a behavioural correlate of heart disease characterised by striving to achieve, time urgency, competitiveness and hostility.

Type A behaviour can be socially destructive in a number of ways. For example, Type A personalities have been reported to be more prone to abuse children (Strube, Turner, Cerro, Stevens, & Hinchey, 1984) and, in managerial roles in organisations, have been found to experience more conflict with peers and subordinates, but not their own supervisors (Baron, 1989). They apparently knew when to draw the line!

Hormones

Is it a popular fallacy that hormonal activity could be related to aggression? Perhaps not – there may be a real link. Brian Gladue (1991) reported higher levels of overt aggression in males than in females. Moreover, this sex difference applied equally to heterosexual and homosexual males when compared with females – biology (male/female) rather than gender orientation was the main contributing variable. In a second study, Gladue and his colleagues measured testosterone levels through saliva tests in their male participants and also assessed whether they were Type A or Type B personalities (Berman, Gladue, & Taylor, 1993). The levels of shock administered to an opponent in an experimental setting were higher when the male was either higher in testosterone or a Type A personality, or both. Overall, there is a small correlation of 0.14 between elevated testosterone (in both males and females) and aggression (Book, Starzyk, & Quinsey, 2001) – if it was causal, testosterone would explain 2 per cent of variation in aggression.

However, a correlation between levels of testosterone and aggression does not establish causality. Causality could operate in the opposite direction: for example, playing and winning at chess or tennis can cause a temporary elevation of testosterone level (Gladue, Boechler, & McCall, 1989; Mazur, Booth, & Dabbs, 1992). A more convincing link between the two was pinpointed by two studies in The Netherlands (Cohen-Kettenis & Van Goozen, 1997; Van Goozen, Cohen-Kettenis, Gooren, Frijda, & Van der Poll, 1995). Transsexuals who were treated with sex hormones as part of their gender reassignment showed increased or decreased proneness to aggression according to whether the direction of change was female to male or male to female.

Although reviews of both animal and human studies confirm a link between testosterone and aggression, they also implicate other hormones – norepinephrine (noradrenaline), dopamine and serotonin (Anholt & Mackay, 2012; Chichinadze, Chichinadze, &

Lazarashvili, 2011). The larger picture concerning the role of hormones is complex for several reasons: (a) studies vary in focusing on aggression induced by fear, stress and anger, as well as on instrumental aggression; (b) the hormones involved may be correlates of rather than causes of aggression; and (c) an environmental trigger is usually required to activate both a hormonal response and the expression of aggressive behaviour.

Gender and socialisation

Sociocultural theory
Psychological gender differences are determined by individuals' adaptations to restrictions based on their gender in their society. Also called *social role theory*.

Sexual selection theory
Sex differences in behaviour are determined by evolutionary history rather than society.

Both social and developmental psychology have traditionally emphasised the differential socialisation of gendered characteristics – e.g. homemaker versus worker. This is an explanation based on **sociocultural theory**, and not on **sexual selection theory** based in evolutionary social psychology (Archer, 2004).

A wealth of research has confirmed that men tend to be more aggressive than women across cultures and socioeconomic groups. However, the size of the difference varies according to the kind and context of aggression. Men are more likely than women to be physically violent, whereas women are as likely as men to use verbal attack in similar contexts, although the degree to which they aggress may be less (Eagly & Steffen, 1986; Harris, 1992). A meta-analysis of gender differences in aggression among children across nine countries revealed two trends (Lansford, Skinner, Sorbring, Di Giunta, Deater-Deckard, Dodge, et al., 2012):

1 Boys, like men, consistently show more *physical* aggression than girls.

2 Gender and nationality interact in the case of *relational* aggression – e.g. it occurs more frequently among Italian girls than Italian boys, but less frequently among Chinese girls than Chinese boys.

Catharsis

Catharsis
A dramatic release of pent-up feelings: the idea that aggressive motivation is 'drained' by acting against a frustrating object (or substitute), or by a vicarious experience.

Cathartic hypothesis
The notion that acting aggressively, or even just viewing aggressive material, reduces feelings of anger and aggression.

An instrumental reason for aggression is **catharsis**. We aggress as an outlet or release for pent-up emotion – the **cathartic hypothesis**. Although associated with Freud, the idea can be traced back to Aristotle and ancient Greek tragedy: by acting out their emotions, people can purify their feelings (Scherer, Abeles, & Fischer, 1975). The idea has popular appeal. Perhaps 'letting off steam' from frustration can restore equanimity. The author of a popular book gave this advice:

> Punch a pillow or a punching bag. Punch with all the frenzy you can. If you are angry at a particular person, imagine his or her face on the pillow or punching bag, and vent your rage physically and verbally. You will be doing violence to a pillow or punching bag so that you can stop doing violence to yourself by holding in poisonous anger.
>
> Lee (1993, p. 96)

In Japan, some companies have already followed this principle, providing a special room with a toy replica of the boss upon which employees can relieve their tensions by 'bashing the boss!' (Middlebrook, 1980).

However, questions about the efficacy of the catharsis hypothesis have been around for many years (Geen & Quanty, 1977; Konečni & Ebbesen, 1976), and more recent experimental research has gone further to outright reject the argument that cathartic behaviour can reduce subsequent aggression (see Bushman, 2002; Krahé, 2014). Bushman, Baumeister and Stack (1999) found that those who hit a punching bag, believing that it reduced stress, were more likely later to punish someone who had transgressed against them (see Box 12.4).

Craig Anderson and his colleagues reported five experiments that demonstrated the effects of songs with violent lyrics on both aggressive feelings and thoughts (Anderson, Carnagey, & Eubanks, 2003). Students listened to rock songs that were either violent or non-violent, and then rated pairs of words for their semantic similarity. The word meanings were either clearly aggressive (e.g. *blood, butcher, choke, gun*) or ambiguously aggressive (e.g. *alley, bottle, rock, stick*). The word pairs were aggressive–ambiguous, aggressive–aggressive, or ambiguous–ambiguous (the latter two pairings being controls). As shown in Figure 12.4,

Catharsis
This is an anger management centre where you can drop by to let it all hang out - in this case beating someone up.

Box 12.4 Research highlight
Letting it 'all hang out' may be worse than useless

Have you ever felt really angry and then 'let it all out' by screaming, punching a pillow or breaking a plate? Did you feel better afterwards? There is a common perception that such 'designer outbursts' of aggression are an effective way of reducing anxiety and aggression. Wann and colleagues (Wann, Carlson, Holland, Jacob, Owens, & Wells, 1999) found that many participants in their experiments believed that catharsis, achieved in particular by viewing violent sports, can lower the likelihood of subsequent aggression. However, the cathartic hypothesis has little support; research suggests that the opposite is true: cathartic aggression actually increases aggression in general. If so, then the common belief that catharsis is an effective remedy for pent-up anger and aggression is a dangerous misconception.

A study by Bushman, Baumeister and Stack (1999) tested the cathartic hypothesis by asking students to read one of three fake newspaper articles: (1) a pro-catharsis article in which a prominent university researcher claimed that cathartic behaviour relieved the tendency to aggress; (2) an anti-catharsis article quoting a research finding of no link between catharsis and a reduction in later aggression; and (3) a 'control' article completely unrelated to aggression or catharsis.

The students were then asked to write an essay that was critiqued by another student (in fact, by the experimenter) while they waited. The essays were returned with very negative written comments designed to induce anger, such as 'this is one of the worst essays I have ever read!' Angered students who had read the pro-catharsis article were more inclined to choose a punching bag exercise as an optional task than those who had read either the anti-catharsis or the control article. Those who had not been angered by the critique of their essays were still more likely to choose to punch a bag if they had read the pro-catharsis article than those who had not. The results of this study highlight how the media or popular belief can influence people to choose cathartic stress relief, and how this choice is affected by the amount of anger people are feeling.

The initial study was extended to a situation where an essay writer could later interact with the essay critic. After reading one of the three articles, some students were asked to spend two minutes punching a punching bag.

Next, they completed a competitive reaction time task in which they selected a degree of punishment (noise volume) to deliver to the competitor (supposedly in another room) when the competitor was slower. As a final twist, just before this encounter, a group of students were led to believe that this competitor was the person who had negatively critiqued their essay.

Those who expected to interact with their critic were more willing to engage in punching the bag before their 'meeting'. Also, those who had read the pro-catharsis article were more aggressive in the task (delivering louder noises) even after punching the bag – which, according to popular belief, should be a cathartic exercise and reduce aggression. This study suggests that catharsis does not relieve stress and is actually 'worse than useless'!

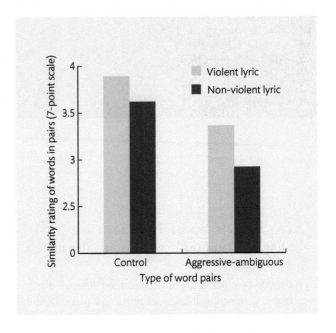

Figure 12.4 Ratings of how similar aggressive or ambiguous word pairs are after hearing violent or non-violent lyrics

- Participants listened to songs with lyrics that were either violent or non-violent.
- Violent lyrics triggered aggressive associations in words previously ambiguous in meaning.
- This contradicts the cathartic hypothesis, since listening to violent lyrics should lessen rather than increase aggressive thinking.

Source: Based on data from Anderson, Carnagey and Eubanks (2003).

there was a priming effect (greater semantic similarity) from hearing violent lyrics, which occurred for aggressive–ambiguous pairs (e.g. *blood/stick*) more than for control pairs (*butcher/gun* or *alley/rock*). This increase in aggressive thinking goes against the cathartic hypothesis.

Bushman delivered this parting shot to the cathartic hypothesis after one of his studies:

Does venting anger extinguish or feed the flame? The results from the present research show that venting to reduce anger is like using gasoline to put out a fire – it only feeds the flame.

Bushman (2002, p. 729)

Alcohol

When the wine goes in, strange things come out.

Johann von Schiller, *The Piccolomini*, 1799; cited in Giancola, Josephs, Parrott and Duke (2010)

It is often assumed that alcohol befuddles the brain and 'liberates' us to behave in antisocial, illegal or embarrassing ways. How many people sing karaoke only after a few drinks? This is a particular form of the *disinhibition hypothesis* (see later in this chapter): that is, alcohol compromises cortical control and increases activity in more primitive brain areas. The causal link between alcohol and aggressive behaviour seems firmly established (Bartholow, Pearson,

Gratton, & Fabiani, 2003; Bushman & Cooper, 1990; Giancola, 2003). Additionally, people who drink more are more aggressive (Bailey & Taylor, 1991). Even people who do not often consume alcohol can become aggressive when they do (LaPlace, Chermack, & Taylor, 1994).

In an experimental study of the effects of alcohol on aggression, male students were assigned to either an alcohol or placebo condition (Taylor & Sears, 1988). They were placed in a competition involving reaction time with another participant. In each pair, the person who responded more slowly on a given trial would receive an electric shock from the opponent. The level of shock to be delivered could be set at various intensity levels and was selected by each person before that trial commenced. The opponent's shock settings were actually determined by the experimenter. The shocks were always low intensity and the win/loss frequency was 50 per cent. The results in Figure 12.5 show the proportions of high-intensity shocks given by participants who were in either an alcohol or a placebo condition.

There were four sequential stages (none → mild → strong → none) of social pressure in which a confederate, who was watching the proceedings, sometimes encouraged the participant to give a shock. The results show an interaction between taking alcohol and being pressured to aggress: participants who had imbibed were more susceptible to influence and continued to give high-intensity shocks even after the pressure was later withdrawn. In an extension by Gustafson (1992), intoxicated males were more aggressive than those who were sober, and they delivered a more intense shock when they were provoked.

The analogy to real life is the *context* of social drinking, such as at a party or in a bar, where others may goad the drinker to be aggressive. Statistics on the connection between alcohol and aggression are suggestive, not clear-cut. To investigate this, Flowe and her colleagues recruited male drinkers from several 'pubs' and measured their blood alcohol level and its effects on hypothetical sexual aggression assessed (Flowe, Stewart, Sleath, & Palmer, 2011). The men were questioned about scenarios to see how far they would go in their advances with four women, who were dressed either modestly or more provocatively. Possible actions within the scenarios ranged from kissing to increasingly intimate sexual contact; and further to acts of sexual aggression, and ultimately to rape. The results showed that higher levels of blood alcohol were linked to the likelihood of sexual aggression, including rape. These effects were more marked if a hypothetical woman was dressed provocatively.

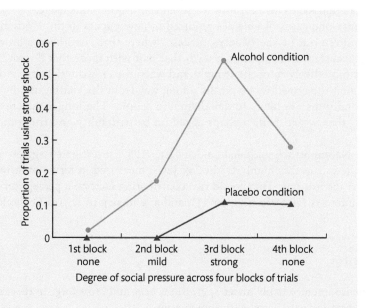

Figure 12.5 Alcohol, social pressure and males' willingness to shock a passive opponent

Source: Based on Taylor and Sears (1988).

Alcohol impairs various higher-order cognitive operations, such as attention, encoding information and retrieving information from memory. These alcohol-induced impairments have been shown to put people at risk in interpersonal encounters by (Bartholow, Pearson, Gratton, & Fabiani, 2003). Specifically, they may prevent changes to positive impressions when negative behaviours indicate that doing so would be adaptive, and may promote changes in negative impressions such that potentially threatening people are deemed less dangerous. These effects are a likely precursor to disinhibited and socially inappropriate behaviour, regardless of the consequences. The impairment brought about by drinking beyond moderation has been described as *alcohol myopia*, which narrows our attention to provocative cues rather than inhibitory ones – hence the connection between alcohol and aggression (Giancola, Josephs, Parrott, & Duke, 2010).

Alcohol can also have indirect effects on aggression. There can be a *placebo effect*. If we expect alcohol to make us more aggressive, it very well might. Laurent Bègue and his colleagues showed, in a controlled naturalistic field experiment, that when male students drank a cocktail placebo that they *believed* contained alcohol, they behaved more aggressively (Bègue, Subra, Arvers, Muller, Bricout, & Zorman, 2009). There can also be a *priming effect*. A laboratory experiment by William Pedersen and his colleagues showed that merely *priming* thoughts of alcohol also increases the incidence of aggressive behaviour (Pedersen, Vasquez, Bartholow, Grosvenor, & Truong, 2014).

Disinhibition, deindividuation and dehumanisation

Sometimes people act 'out of character'. **Disinhibition** refers to a reduction in the usual social forces that operate to restrain us from acting antisocially, illegally or immorally. There are several ways in which people lose their normal inhibitions against aggression. In Box 12.5, we consider the case where the *aggressor* experiences a state of **deindividuation**. This process (discussed in more detail in **Chapter 11**) involves changes in situational factors affecting an aggressor, such as the presence of others or lack of identifiability. As well, we include factors that focus on how the victim is perceived, such as being less than human – **dehumanisation**.

Leon Mann (1981) explored deindividuation in a particular context relating to **collective aggression**, the 'baiting crowd'. The typical situation involves a person threatening to jump from a high building, a crowd gathers below, and some begin to chant 'jump, jump'. In one dramatic case in New York in 1938, thousands of people waited at ground level, some for eleven hours, until a man jumped to his death from a seventeenth-floor hotel ledge.

Mann analysed twenty-one cases of suicides reported in newspapers in the 1960s and 1970s. He found that in ten out of the twenty-one cases where there had been a crowd watching, baiting had occurred. In comparing crowds that bait with those that do not, he found that baiting was more likely to occur at night and when the crowd was large (more than 300 people), and that the crowd was typically a long way from the victim, usually at ground level. These conditions are likely to deindividuate people. The longer the crowd waited, the more likely they would bait, perhaps egged on by irritability and frustration (see Figure 12.6).

In a study in Israel, Naomi Struch and Shalom Schwartz (1989) investigated aggression among non-Orthodox Jews towards highly Orthodox Jews, measured in terms of strong opposition to Orthodox institutions. They found two contributing factors: a perception of intergroup conflict of interests (also see **Chapter 11**), and a tendency to regard Orthodox Jews as 'inhuman'.

Situational variables

Two aspects of our environment reliably affect aggression, *heat* and *crowding*. In this section, we also discuss aggression associated with sports events.

Disinhibition
A breakdown in the learnt controls (social mores) against behaving impulsively or, in this context, aggressively. For some people, alcohol has a disinhibiting effect.

Deindividuation
Process whereby people lose their sense of socialised individual identity and engage in unsocialised, often antisocial, behaviours.

Dehumanisation
Stripping people of their dignity and humanity.

Collective aggression
Unified aggression by a group of individuals, who may not even know one another, against another individual or group.

Box 12.5 Our world
Deindividuation and dehumanisation

Being deindividuated

Deindividuation reduces the perceived likelihood that one will be punished for acting aggressively.

A dramatic example of how a real, or perceived, reduction in the likelihood of punishment can enhance aggression and violence was seen in the 1968 My Lai incident, during the Vietnam War, where American soldiers slaughtered an entire village of innocent civilians. In the official inquiry, it was revealed that the same unit had previously killed and tortured civilians without any disciplinary action; that the area was a designated 'free-fire' zone, so that it was considered legitimate to shoot at anything that moved; and indeed, that the whole ethos of the war was one of glorified violence (Hersh, 1970).

In addition, there was a sense of anonymity, or *deindividuation*, that came from being part of a large group, and this further enhanced the soldiers' perception that they would not be punished as individuals. (See the effects of deindividuation in **Chapter 11.**) This sense of anonymity is thought to contribute to the translation of aggressive emotion into actual violence: it may occur through being part of a large group or gathering, as in the crowd that baits a suicide to jump (Mann, 1981) or a pack rape at a gang convention; or it may happen through something that protects anonymity in another way, such as the white hoods worn by Ku Klux Klan members (Middlebrook, 1980), the stocking worn over the face of an armed robber or terrorist or the Hallowe'en masks that prompt children to steal sweets and money (Diener, Fraser, Beaman, & Kelem, 1976). Malamuth (1981) found that almost one-third of male students questioned at an American university admitted there was a likelihood that they would rape if they were certain of not getting caught!

Dehumanising the victim

A variation of deindividuation in the aggressor can occur when the victim, rather than the aggressor, is anonymous or dehumanised in some way (Haslam, 2006; Haslam & Loughnan, 2014; Haslam, Loughnan, & Kashima, 2008; see **Chapter 10**), so that the aggressor cannot easily see the personal pain and injury suffered by the victim. This can weaken any control that may be applied through feelings of shame and guilt.

Terrible examples of this phenomenon have been documented, such as the violent treatment of psychiatric patients and prisoners who were either kept naked or dressed identically so that they were indistinguishable as individuals (Steir, 1978). Again, having faceless and deindividuated victims in violent films and television programmes can disinhibit some viewers, encouraging them to play down the injury and thus be more likely to imitate the violent acts (Bandura, 1986).

Extreme and inhumane instances of disinhibition come from war: for example, the extermination of tens of thousands of people by a single atomic blast in Hiroshima and again in Nagasaki in 1945. Carol Cohn (1987) presented a revealing analysis of the ways in which military personnel 'sanitise', and thereby justify, the use of nuclear weaponry by semantics that dehumanise the likely or actual victims, referring to them as 'targets', 'the aggressed' or even 'collateral damage'.

The same semantic strategies were used by the American military in the Vietnam War to refer to Vietnamese civilians as 'gooks' to rationalise and justify killing them (Sabini & Silver, 1982); by Hutu reference to Tutsi as 'cockroaches' during the Rwanda genocide to facilitate exterminating them; and Nazi reference to Jews as 'rats' and 'vermin' to lay the seeds of the Holocaust. In 1993 Bosnian Serbs, in what was once part of Yugoslavia, referred to acts of genocide against the Muslim population as 'ethnic cleansing'. The media can also unwittingly lessen the impact of the horror of large-scale killing. A phrase often used on television during the Allied bombing campaigns in Iraq in 1991 was 'theatre of war', inviting the audience to sit back and be entertained.

Brock Bastian and his colleagues have used the term cyber-dehumanisation in the context of violent video game play (also see Box 12.6). For example, participants playing the game *Mortal Kombat* felt that both they themselves and their opponents were diminished as humans (Bastian, Jetten, & Radke, 2012).

See Chapter 10 for other examples of dehumanisation.

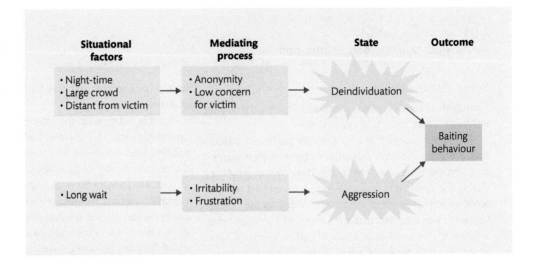

Figure 12.6 The baiting crowd: an exercise in deindividuation and frustration

Source: Based on Mann (1981).

Heat

You would not be surprised to hear that aggression is linked to ambient temperature, given that our language links aggression to *body temperature*. We can be 'hot under the collar' or 'simmering with rage', or tell someone else to 'cool down'. As the ambient temperature rises, there are increases in domestic violence (Cohn, 1993), violent suicide (Maes, De Meyer, Thompson, Peeters, & Cosyns, 1994) and collective violence (Carlsmith & Anderson, 1979).

Keith Harries and Stephen Stadler (1983) examined the incidence of aggravated assault in Dallas over the twelve months of 1980. Assaults were more prevalent when it was hotter and more humid than normal, but not when it was excessively hot and humid. Another study, of the incidence of murders and rapes over a two-year period, found a positive relationship with fluctuations in the daily average temperature (Anderson & Anderson, 1984). Douglas Kenrick and Steven MacFarlane (1986) gauged motorists' responses to a car blocking the road at a green light by recording the amount of horn honking. As the heat went up, so did the honking. The relationship between heat and aggression was even recorded in Ancient Rome (Anderson, Bushman, & Groom, 1997). Perhaps surprisingly, even in normally very hot climates such as in India, people report more negative moods on the hottest days (Ruback & Pandey, 1992).

The relationship between heat and aggression follows an inverted U (Halpern, 1995): as the temperature rises, so does aggression, at least to a certain level. When it gets very hot, aggression levels out and then declines, a trend suggesting that extreme heat saps our energy. We should note here that the critical variable is likely to be the *ambient temperature*. Ellen Cohn and James Rotton (1997) tracked rates of physical assault according to temperature throughout each day over a two-year period in Minneapolis (1987–8). Their data reflect an inverted U-curve (see Figure 12.7).

Cohn and Rotton also found that assaults were more frequent later in the evening than at other times. Most people in Minneapolis work in temperature-controlled environments during the day; as a result, the effects of ambient temperature did not show up until people left work. Further analysis revealed that it is temperature per se that accounts for the curvilinear trend, and not simply time of day (Cohn & Rotton, 2005). Cohn and Rotton (1997) also reported a link between heat and *alcohol consumption*. When people drink more alcohol in the evening to quench their thirst, alcohol becomes a mediating variable leading to aggression.

Crowding

Crowding that leads to fighting has long been recognised in a variety of animal species (e.g. Calhoun, 1962). For humans, crowding is a subjective state and is characterised by feeling that one's personal space has been encroached (see **Chapter 15**). There is a distinction

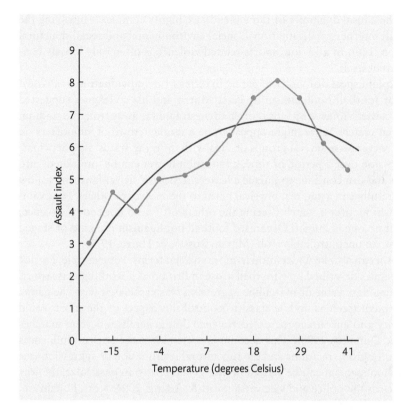

Figure 12.7 Relationship between rate of assaults and outdoor temperature

A curve has been fitted to the data. The effect appears as an inverted U-curve.

Source: Based on data from Cohn and Rotton (1997).

between invasion of personal space and a high level of population density, but in practical terms there is also an overlap. Urbanisation requires more people to share a limited amount of space, with elevated stress and potentially antisocial consequences.

In a study conducted in Toronto, Wendy Regoeczi (2003) noted that population density as a gross measure can contribute to the overall level of crime in an area. However, variables crucial to a state of crowding are more finely grained – household density (persons per house) and neighbourhood density (detached housing versus high-rise housing). Her results showed that density on both measures correlated positively with self-reported feelings of aggression and also of withdrawal from interacting with strangers.

In a prison context, Claire Lawrence and Kathryn Andrew (2004) confirmed a consistent finding in studies of the penal environment. Feeling crowded made it more likely that events in a UK prison were perceived as aggressive and the protagonists as more hostile and malevolent. In an acute psychiatric unit in New Zealand, Bradley Ng and his colleagues found that 'crowding' (inferred from higher ward occupancy rates) was associated with a higher number of violent incidents and increased verbal aggression (Ng, Kumar, Ranclaud, & Robinson, 2001).

Sports events

Sports events can be associated with spectator violence. Since the early 1970s, European, but particularly English, football has become strongly associated with hooliganism – to such an extent, for example, that the violence of some English fans in Belgium associated with Euro 2000 undoubtedly contributed to England's failure to be chosen to host the World Cup in 2006. England was made to wait a little longer! Popular hysteria has characterised 'soccer hooliganism' in terms of the stereotyped images of football fans on the rampage (Murphy, Williams, & Dunning, 1990).

However, spectator and fan violence are not just a feature of European football events. Sports riots have been recorded across six continents and in a variety of different sports

(Russell, 2004), and the causal dynamics of fan violence are highly complex – involving the interplay of individual, interpersonal, situational, social environmental and social structural factors (Spaaij, 2014, p. 146). In addition, sports-related violence is often only loosely connected to the sports event itself.

It is tempting to explain spectator violence purely in terms of deindividuation in a crowd setting, but a study of football hooliganism by Peter Marsh and his colleagues suggested another contributing cause. Violence by fans is often orchestrated far away from the stadium and long before a given match. What might appear to be a motley crowd of supporters on match day can actually comprise several groups of fans with differing status. By participating in ritualised aggression over a period of time, a faithful follower can be 'promoted' into a higher-status group and can continue to pursue a 'career structure'. Rival fans who follow their group's rules carefully can avoid real physical harm to themselves or others. For example, chasing the opposition after a match ('seeing the others off') need not end in violence; the agreed code is that no one is caught! Organised football hooliganism is a kind of staged production rather than an uncontrollable mob (Marsh, Russer, & Harré, 1978).

Football hooliganism can also be understood in more societal terms. For example, Patrick Murphy and his colleagues described how football arose in Britain as a working-class sport. By the 1950s, a working-class value of masculine aggression was associated with the game. Attempts by a government (seen as middle class) to control this aspect of the sport would enhance class solidarity and encourage increased violence that generalises beyond matches (Murphy, Williams, & Dunning, 1990). This account is societal (see the Societal influences section) and involves intergroup relations and the subcultural legitimation of aggression (see **Chapter 10**). Finally, hooliganism can be viewed in intergroup terms: in particular, the way hooligans behave towards the police and vice versa (Stott & Adang, 2004; Stott, Hutchison, & Drury, 2001; **also see Chapter 11**).

General aggression model

General aggression model
Anderson's model that includes both personal and situational factors, and cognitive and affective processes in accounting for different kinds of aggression.

Let us reflect on the variety of theories and of factors that have been researched in the study of aggression. Are all of these theories useful, and do all factors predict aggressive behaviour? On balance, the answer is yes, but in isolation their usefulness is limited. To try to join up the dots, so to speak, Anderson and Bushman (2002a) have developed a **general aggression model** (GAM) (see Figure 12.8). The key tenet of the model is that the interplay of the personal and situational variables that we have discussed activates three kinds of internal state (affect, cognition and arousal), and that a person's appraisal of the situation is predominantly either thoughtful or impulsive, and the consequence is the social encounter.

Figure 12.8 A general model of aggression
Aggression is a social encounter that follows several steps. It starts with a person with specific characteristics in a particular context. The person and the situation are inputs that influence appraisals (thoughtful or impulsive) via affective, cognitive and arousal routes. The person's actions then rest on whether the appraisal is thoughtful or impulsive.
Source: Anderson and Bushman (2002a).

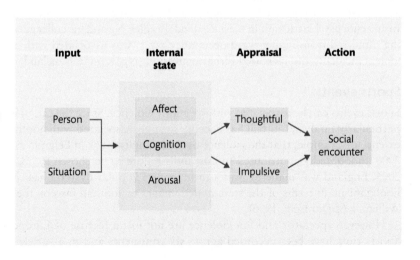

The GAM has helped frame subsequent research on aggression. For example, Julia Hosie and her colleagues investigated the role of personality factors among Australian male offenders in a real-life setting – a community forensic mental health service for psychiatric and psychological evaluation before being sentenced (Hosie, Gilbert, Simpson, & Daffern, 2014). The personality measures, which included **Big Five** personality traits, are an example of 'Person' inputs depicted in Figure 12.7. Take a second example. Nicola Bowes and Mary McMurran (2013) conducted a meta-analysis to test for a relationship between aggression-related thought processes and violent behaviour. They found that beliefs that bolster violence are correlated with actual violence, and they were able to show how cognition can mediate between input and action (see Figure 12.7).

Big Five
The five major personality dimensions of extraversion/ surgency, agreeableness, conscientiousness, emotional stability and intellect/openness to experience.

Societal influences

Disadvantaged groups

Social disadvantage can be an underlying cause of aggression, although of course such groups are also the victims of violence. A review of youth violence in the United States found the rates of homicide and non-lethal violence to be higher among young, urban-poor, minority males, largely due to a mix of social and ecological factors (Tolan & Gorman-Smith, 2002).

At-risk youth show signs of antisocial behaviour as children, but in inner-city areas they are likely to have dysfunctional families, rented accommodation, concentrated poverty and below-average neighbourhood facilities, and to be isolated from norms that define and promote acceptable social behaviour. The presence of prosocial moral norms is an important bulwark against aggression, particularly among young people. Their absence has been repeatedly and reliably shown to create moral disengagement (Bandura, 2002) that can lead young people to be aggressive and specifically to bully their peers (Gini, Pozzoli, & Hymel, 2014).

Earlier (see **Chapter 11**), we explored the relationship between disadvantage and intergroup behaviour. One key factor in the relationship between disadvantage and aggression specifically is the extent to which a disadvantaged group has a sense of **relative deprivation**, particularly a sense that it is deprived relative to other groups (called fraternalistic relative deprivation: Runciman, 1966), or that against a background of rising expectations the group has suddenly experienced a dramatic setback (Davies, 1969).

Relative deprivation
A sense of having less than we feel entitled to.

Relative deprivation is a sense of discontent associated with feeling that the chance of improving one's condition is minimal. If improvement cannot be achieved legitimately, a deprived individual might commit vandalism, assault or burglary; at an intergroup level, this could extend to collective aggression, such as violent protest or rioting. The Los Angeles race riots of 1992 were ostensibly triggered by a jury verdict that acquitted white police officers of beating a black motorist. Although this was the immediate cause, there was also an enduring undercurrent of relative deprivation among African Americans in the neighbourhoods of Los Angeles where the rioting occurred (see Box 11.1 in **Chapter 11**). The dynamics underlying the spate of similar protests and riots in 2015 in Baltimore and 2016 in Milwaukee are almost identical, with the important difference that they occurred within the framework of a wider struggle against injustice and disadvantage – the *Black Lives Matter* movement.

There is reasonable support for the validity of the concept of relative deprivation, from both experiments and historical analyses (Walker & Smith, 2002). Relative deprivation provides a plausible, partial explanation for events such as increased violence against immigrants – for example, Middle Eastern and North African migrants and refugees entering Europe in 2015 and 2016 – when unemployment is at a very high level.

Criminality and demographics

We feature two individual demographics that have attracted the attention of researchers, gender and race, and include data that focus specifically on homicide.

Gender
Sex-stereotypical attributes of a person.

Stereotypes based on **gender** most often depict men as being more aggressive than women. It is possible that as gender roles in Western societies are re-orientated, women's inhibitions against violence will diminish – emancipation may be criminogenic. The redefinition of male and female roles (also see Chapter 14) in most Western societies in recent decades is correlated with a rise in alcohol and drug abuse among women. The return of women to the workforce has coincided with widespread unemployment, a further trigger for increased offences against persons (and property). Although criminal violence is still more prevalent among men than women, the rate of violent offending, in particular murder, has increased more rapidly among women. We include race (or ethnicity) because of accumulating relevant data (see Figure 12.9 for an American study by Cooper and Smith (2011), who included both offenders and victims in their analyses).

Cultural norms
Norms whose origin is part of the tradition of a culture.

Throughout history, there have always been differences in **cultural norms** and values that have shaped some societies as more, and some as less, aggressive than others.

Attitudes towards aggression and violence vary over time and between cultures, and also between groups within cultures and nations. Western nations view democracy, human rights

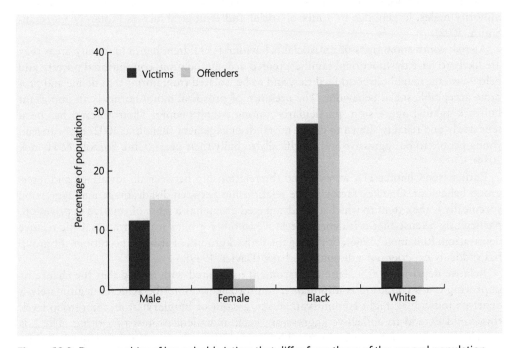

Figure 12.9 Demographics of household victims that differ from those of the general population

- The original data set consists of homicide rates in 2009 and 2010 per 100,000 for offenders and victims.
- The offenders and victims were divided into one of four categories: male white, female white, male black or female black.
- The homicide rates have been converted to percentages based on the numbers of offenders and victims in each of the four categories.
- The key findings were that:
  - when compared with females, males were at least three times as likely to be victims, and nearly nine times more likely to be offenders;
  - when compared with whites, blacks were more than six times as likely to be victims, and nearly eight times more likely to be offenders.

Source: Based on data from Cooper and Smith (2011).

and non-violence as core cultural values – but this was not necessarily always the case. The reasons are usually evident. A history of repeated invasions, a geography that made some settlements more competitive or more vulnerable, and a bio-evolutionary factor of physique that permitted successful raids by some groups, have all in part shaped the social philosophies of particular societies.

Examples of philosophical underpinnings that can subtly affect whole nations are evident in comparisons between the Eastern and Western cultures (Bell & Chaibong, 2003). These broad differences can spill over into how intergroup aggression is expressed (Forbes, Collinsworth, Zhao, Kohlman, & LeClaire, 2011). However, these philosophies are also dynamic and can change rapidly according to context. Examples of this in recent decades are the development of both aggressive Zionism and radical Islam.

Some societies or groups in society subscribe to a **culture of honour** that places a unique emphasis on upholding and defending the reputation and person of oneself and one's family; in particular, it is of utmost importance for men to maintain reputations for being competent providers and strong protectors (Nisbett & Cohen, 1996; Nowak, Gelfand, Borkowski, Cohen, & Hernandez, 2016; also see **Chapter 16**). In such cultures men are particularly prone to detecting personal slights, insults and threats and to reacting aggressively to them (Cohen, Nisbett, Bowdle, & Schwarz, 1996). Osterman and Brown (2011) even found that violence towards self, in the form of suicide, was elevated, particularly among rural whites, in US states characterised by a culture of honour.

Joseph Vandello, Dov Cohen and their colleagues have extensively studied the impact of a culture of honour on domestic violence (Vandello & Cohen, 2003; Vandello, Cohen, Grandon, & Franiuk, 2009). Regions that place a value on violence to restore honour include some Mediterranean countries, the Middle East and Arab countries, Central and South America, and the southern United States. This research, comparing Brazilian and US honour culture participants with northern US participants, and comparing peoples in the Americas generally, reached three conclusions:

1 Female infidelity damages a man's reputation, particularly in honour cultures.

2 A man's reputation can be partly restored by exacting retribution.

3 Cultural values of female loyalty and sacrifice on one hand, and male honour on the other, validate abuse in a relationship. The same values reward a woman who 'soldiers on' in the face of violence.

Attitudes towards *honour killings* of women who had 'dishonoured' their family in Amman, Jordan, were the focus of a large-scale study by criminologists Manuel Eisner and Lana Ghuneim (2013). They found that adolescents whose world views were collectivist and patriarchal were more accepting of honour killings. Among both males and females, approval of honour killings was stronger among adolescents from poorer and less-educated families with a traditional background, and who showed moral disengagement that inured them to violence. In addition, approval was strongest among males who had a history of harsh paternal discipline and placed a premium on a norm of female chastity.

Eisner and Ghuneim (2013) were disappointed that: 'Within a country that is considered to be modern by Middle Eastern standards this represents a high proportion of young people who have at least some supportive attitudes to honor killing' (p. 413). Outside honour cultures, aggression against women is generally not a matter to display publicly. In patriarchal cultures, men and boys are proud of male-directed violence but ashamed of female-directed aggression (Hilton, Harris, & Rice, 2000).

Interpersonal violence occurs in most societies, but some societies actively practise a lifestyle of non-aggression. There may be as many as twenty-five societies with a world view based on cooperation rather than competition (Bonta, 1997). Among these are the Hutterite and Amish communities in the United States, the Inuit of the Arctic region, the Kung of southern and central Africa, the Bushmen of Southern Africa and the Ladakhis of Tibet. Such communities are

Culture of honour
A culture that endorses male violence as a way of addressing threats to social reputation or economic position.

Subculture of violence
Within modern urban cultures, there are subgroups of young people who adhere to a norm that violence is the most effective way to settle a dispute.

small, sometimes scattered and relatively isolated, which suggests that these may be necessary preconditions for peaceful existence. The anthropologist Gorer (1968) argued that evidence of peaceful societies disproves the notion that humans have a 'killer' instinct.

Despite evidence of cross-cultural and cross-national variations in aggression, we need to retain a focus:

it is individuals who hit, curse, challenge, ignore, fail to warn, testify against, gossip about, retaliate for being hurt by, and form alliances against others, either singly or as part of a group.
Bond (2004, p. 74)

Subculture of violence

Subculture of violence
A subgroup of society in which a higher level of violence is accepted as the norm.

Many societies include minority subgroups in which violence is legitimised as a lifestyle – they represent a **subculture of violence** (Toch, 1969). The norms of such groups reflect an approval of aggression, and there are both rewards for violence and sanctions for non-compliance. In urban settings, these groups are often labelled and self-styled as gangs, and the importance of violence is reflected in their appearance and behaviour (Alleyne & Wood, 2010).

In his book *Political Violence: The Behavioral Process,* Harold Nieburg (1969) painted a graphic picture of the traditional initiation rite for the Sicilian Mafia. After a long lead-up period of observation, the new Mafia member would attend a candlelit meeting of other members and be led to a table showing the image of a saint, an emblem of high religious significance. Blood taken from his right hand would be sprinkled on the saint, and he would swear an oath of allegiance binding him to the brotherhood. In a short time, he would then prove himself worthy by executing a suitable person selected by the Mafia.

Machismo
A code in which challenges, abuse and even differences of opinion must be met with fists or other weapons.

Machismo plays a key role in encouraging a subculture of violence among boys and young men. This is evident in Latin American families (Ingoldsby, 1991). It is also evident in another Latin culture, Italy, where aggression is encouraged in adolescent boys from traditional villages in the belief that it shows sexual prowess and shapes a dominant male in the household (Tomada & Schneider, 1997). One consequence of this is that there is more male bullying in Italian schools than in England, Spain, Norway or Japan (Genta, Menesini, Fonzi, Costabile, & Smith, 1996).

Anthony Volk and his colleagues put a somewhat predictable evolutionary spin on cross-national bullying. Since adolescent male bullying occurs across cultures and time, e.g. ancient Greece, medieval China and renaissance Europe, it is in essence adaptive, not maladaptive – it gives bullies an advantage by signalling *reproductive fitness* in boys (Volk, Camilleri, Dane, & Marini, 2012; also see **Chapter 14**).

Mass media

Violence is one of the most fun things to watch.

Quentin Tarentino, cited in Weaver and Kobach (2012)

The impact of *mass media* on aggression has long been a popular and controversial preoccupation. There are many examples of people emulating violent acts such as assault, rape and murder in almost identical fashion to portrayals in films or television programmes; and likewise of the disinhibitory effects of watching an excessive amount of sanitised violence, mostly on television. Findings from laboratory research on **desensitisation** can sometimes be difficult to generalise to everyday life because participants are exposed only to mild forms of television violence for relatively short periods of time (Freedman, 1984; Geen & Donnerstein, 1983).

Violence can be presented, particularly on film and television, in such a way that it sanitises the aggressive acts and the injury sustained by victims, and portrays aggressors as the good guys who go unpunished (Bandura, 1973, 1986). This can have a particularly powerful effect on children, who, according to social learning theory, will readily mimic the behaviour of a model who is reinforced for aggressing, or at least escapes punishment (Bandura, 1973). There has been considerable debate about whether violent video games can also have harmful effects on children (see Box 12.6 and then consider how you would deal with the third 'What do *you* think?' question).

Desensitisation
A serious reduction in a person's responsiveness to material that usually evokes a strong emotional reaction, such as violence or sexuality.

Box 12.6 Our world
Do gory video games make young people more aggressive?

There is frequent and often heated debate about the effects of violence in video games. Some believe these games increase levels of aggression in children, whereas others argue that such games actually reduce aggression. The former claim that contact between characters in the games is often graphically violent, and that children will copy this in their everyday interactions with others; *social learning theory* is sympathetic to this view. We noted in Box 12.2, for example, that some young children may imitate cartoon characters. Opponents of this view believe that children may experience the benefits of *catharsis* from playing the games, by venting some energy and by relaxing. Again, we have already called into question the efficacy of catharsis in this connection (see Box 12.3).

Will children become desensitised to the consequences of acting aggressively in real-life situations by playing out violent scenes? Certainly, the content of the games themselves is of some concern. Tracy Dietz (1998) examined thirty-three popular video games, and found that nearly 80 per cent contained aggression as part of either the immediate object or the long-term strategy.

Mark Griffiths's (1997) review of research concluded that aggression levels increase in younger children but not in teenage children. However, he cautioned, on methodological grounds, that most of the relevant research is restricted to observations of children's free play activity following game-playing.

Emil Van Schie and Oene Wiegman (1997) conducted a large-scale study of game-playing among more than 300 children in The Netherlands. They found:

- There was no significant relationship between time spent gaming and subsequent levels of aggression.
- Video gaming did not replace children's other leisure activities.
- The amount of time spent gaming was positively correlated with the child's measured level of intelligence.

On the other hand, they also found that children who spent more time playing video games were less likely to behave prosocially (see **Chapter 13** for discussion of factors associated with prosocial behaviour in children).

Bushman, Anderson and colleagues have empirically tested the link between violent videos and aggression among college students. Students who had played a violent video game later described the main character as being more aggressive and angry (Bushman & Anderson, 2002), and showed a lowered GSR and heart rate, a desensitisation effect, as they later viewed a videotape of real-life violence (Carnagey, Anderson, & Bushman (2007).

In another study, students were selected in two groups – those with either very high or very low previous exposure to violent video games. EEGs were collected while they viewed several games of extreme violence for 25 minutes. The low-exposure students showed a drop in the brain's response to violence – a desensitisation effect. The high-exposure students did not, perhaps because they were chronically desensitised. Despite this, students from both groups administered high levels of punishing noise to an opponent in a computer game when compared with control participants (Engelhardt, Bartholow, Kerr, & Bushman, 2011).

Michele Ybarra and her colleagues conducted a large-scale longitudinal survey in the United States. They gathered data from nearly 1,500 young people who played at least some violent video, computer or Internet games during a one-year period. Of these, 1.4 per cent% reported that they carried a weapon to school 'in the past month'. The weapons included a knife, a gun, a bat, a pipe or other weapon (Ybarra, Huesmann, Korchmaros, & Reisner, 2014).

Barbara Krahé (2014a) reviewed her own extensive experimental research in Germany and concluded that:

> It provides experimental evidence in support of mediating variables, such as hostile attributional style, increased normative acceptance of aggression, and emotional desensitisation, which might explain the pathways from media violence use to aggression. (p. 71)

Finally, a telling meta-analytic review by Tobias Greitmeyer and Dirk Mügge (2014) of ninety-eight studies of both violent and prosocial video games with 36,965 participants concluded: 'Whereas violent video games increase aggression and aggression-related variables and decrease prosocial outcomes, prosocial video games have the opposite effects' (p. 578).

An early (1979–81) study, conducted by Peter Sheehan (1983), of boys and girls at Australian primary schools reported correlations between television viewing habits and aggression. Violent programme viewing and peer-rated aggression were significantly associated ($r = 0.25$) among older children (8–10 years), and the association was stronger among boys than girls. Other studies have supported this finding – there is an association between mass media violence and both intrapersonal and interpersonal aggression (see Phillips, 1986), and between the overall amount of violent television watched and aggressive behaviour (Huesmann & Miller, 1994). It is not merely that people imitate violence modelled on the screen or read about in newspapers and magazines, or that they are desensitised and disinhibited; rather, there is evidence that seeing and reading about violence in general actually promotes greater aggression in some people.

Stephen Black and Susan Bevan (1992) investigated aggression among filmgoers who watched either a very violent or a non-violent film. Participants completed an aggression questionnaire either before entering or after leaving the cinema. Those who chose to watch the violent film had higher pre-viewing aggression scores, and aggression scores were even higher after watching the film. Gender differences were minimal (see Figure 12.10). A meta-analysis by Anderson and Bushman (2002b) concludes that regardless of how one studies the media violence/aggression link, the outcomes are the same – significant, a substantial positive relationship exists (and this is despite some methodological concerns with research in this area; see Ferguson & Savage, 2012).

According to a report from the Media Violence Commission of the International Society for Research on Aggression, 'research clearly shows that media violence consumption increases the relative risk of aggression, defined as intentional harm to another person that could be verbal, relational, or physical' (Krahé, Berkowitz, Brockmeyer, Bushman, Coyne, Dill, et al., 2012, p. 336). On balance, the issue is not whether but *why* violent media increase aggression.

Neo-associationist analysis
A view of aggression according to which mass media may provide images of violence to an audience that later translate into antisocial acts.

A cognitive analysis

Research suggests that media can trigger violence as an automatic reaction to aggressive scenes or descriptions (Berkowitz, 1984; Eron, 1994; Huesmann, 1988). Leonard Berkowitz (1984) has adopted a **neo-associationist analysis**, which includes the idea that merely thinking

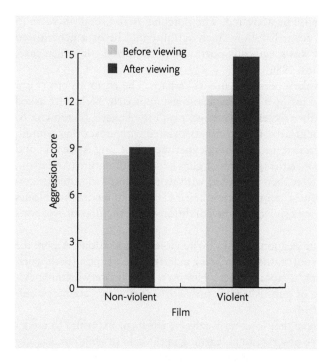

Figure 12.10 Filmgoers' aggression scores before and after watching a non-violent or a violent film

● People who attend screenings of violent films may be generally more disposed to aggression, according to their scores on an aggression questionnaire.

● Viewing a violent film has an additional effect, because their aggression scores rise afterwards.

Source: Based on data from Black and Bevan (1992).

about an act can facilitate its performance (**see Chapter 1**). According to neo-associationism, real or fictional images of violence that are presented to an audience can translate later into antisocial acts. Conversely, exposure to images of people helping others can lead later to prosocial acts (see Figure 12.11).

Berkowitz argued that memory can be viewed as a collection of networks, each consisting of nodes. A node can include substantive elements of thoughts and feelings, connected through associative pathways. When a thought comes into focus, its activation radiates out from that particular node via the associative pathways to other nodes, which in turn can lead to a **priming** effect (also see **Chapter 2**). Consequently, if you have been watching a movie depicting a violent gang 'rumble', other semantically related thoughts can be primed, such as *punching, kicking* and *shooting a gun*. This process can be mostly automatic, without much conscious thinking involved. Similarly, feelings associated with aggression, such as some components of the emotion of anger, or of other related emotions (e.g. of fear or

Priming
Activation of accessible categories or schemas in memory that influence how we process new information.

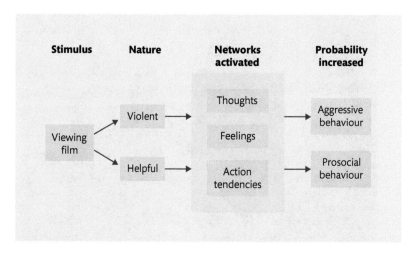

Figure 12.11 'Unconscious' effects of the media: a neo-associationist analysis
Source: Based on Berkowitz (1984).

disgust; Berkowitz, 2012) may likewise be activated. The outcome is an overall increase in the probability that an aggressive act will follow. Such action could be of a generalised nature, or it may be similar to what was specifically portrayed in the media – in which case, it could be a 'copy-cat crime' (Phillips, 1986).

Weapons effect
The mere presence of a weapon increases the probability that it will be used aggressively.

Can the mere sight of a gun provoke a person to use it? Perhaps. The **weapons effect** is a phenomenon that can be accounted for by a neo-associationist approach. Berkowitz asked the question, 'Does the finger pull the trigger or the trigger pull the finger?' (Berkowitz & LePage, 1967). If weapons suggest aggressive images not associated with most other stimuli, a person's range of attention is curtailed. In a priming experiment by Craig Anderson and his colleagues, participants first viewed either pictures of guns or scenes of nature (Anderson, Anderson, & Deuser, 1996). They were then presented with words printed in different colours that had either aggressive or neutral connotations. Their task was to report the colours of the words. Their response speed was slowest in the condition where pictures of weapons preceded aggressive words.

We should not infer from this that weapons always invite violent associations. A gun, for example, might be associated with sport rather than being a destructive weapon (Berkowitz, 1993) – hence the more specific term 'weapons effect'. However, there is overwhelming evidence that availability or ownership of guns is significantly correlated with a country's suicide and homicide rates (Stroebe, 2014).

Huesmann and his colleagues argue that long-term adverse effects of exposure to media violence are likely based on extensive observational learning in the case of children, accompanied by the acquisition of aggressive *scripts*, whereas short-term effects among adults and children are more likely based on *priming* (Huesmann, Mois-Titus, Podolski, & Eron, 2003). For example, Sarah Coyne and her colleagues used a priming technique to study female college students' responses to three kinds of content in video scenes: physical aggression, relational aggression or no aggression. The content of both physical aggression and relational aggression primed later aggressive thoughts, making them more accessible in memory (Coyne, Linder, Nelson, & Gentile, 2012).

Rape myths, erotica and aggression

If exposure to erotica in magazines and videos can lead to sexual arousal, might it also be linked to aggression? A meta-analysis of forty-six studies by Elizabeth Oddone-Paolucci and her colleagues suggests so. They found that exposure of men to *pornography* was connected to sexual deviancy, sexual assault and attitudes to intimate relationships and rape myths (Oddone-Paolucci, Genuis, & Violato, 2000).

The weapons effect
Guns evoke images associated with few other stimuli. They shoot, they kill. Even a toy firearm is unlikely to have neutral connotations.

Rape myths

What do we know about rape myths? Philipp Sussenbach and his colleagues give examples of beliefs that typify rape myth acceptance (RMA): 'A lot of women lead a man on and then they cry rape' and 'Many women secretly desire to be raped'. Here are some of their findings based on an RMA scale:

- In a correlational study of German residents (Sussenbach & Bohner, 2011), those who scored high on RMA also scored high on Right Wing Authoritarianism (see **Chapter 10**).

- In an experimental study of eye movement responses to a supposed police photograph of a rape scene (Sussenbach, Bohner, & Eyssel, 2012), participants who scored high on RMA more quickly attended to rape-consistent cues, i.e. two wine glasses and a bottle.

- In an experimental study using a mock jury, high RMA scorers were more lenient in sentencing when irrelevant rape myth-consistent information to the case was presented. This suggested that rape myth acceptance is a cognitive **schema** that acts as a bias towards blaming the victim, even when there is lack of certainty about the facts (Eyssel & Bohner, 2011).

Schema
Cognitive structure that represents knowledge about a concept or type of stimulus, including its attributes and the relations among those attributes.

Erotica and aggression

Research indicates that any effect of erotica on aggression depends on the kind of erotica viewed. For example, viewing pictures of attractive nudes (mild erotica) has a distracting effect (such pictures reduce aggression when compared with neutral pictures) (Baron, 1979; Ramirez, Bryant, & Zillmann, 1983), whereas viewing images of explicit lovemaking (highly erotic) can increase aggression (Baron & Bell, 1977; Zillmann, 1984, 1996). Sexually arousing non-violent erotica could lead to aggression because of excitation-transfer (see Figure 12.2 earlier in this chapter). However, excitation-transfer includes the experience of a later frustrating event, which acts as a trigger to aggress. In short, there has not been a convincing demonstration of a direct link between erotica per se and aggression.

In a more dramatic demonstration, Zillmann and Bryant (1984) exposed participants to a massive amount of violent pornography and then had them actively irritated by a confederate. Participants became more callous about what they had seen: they viewed rape more tolerantly and became more lenient about prison sentences that they would recommend (see Figure 12.12). However, the experimental design involves a later provoking event, so this outcome could be an instance of excitation transfer.

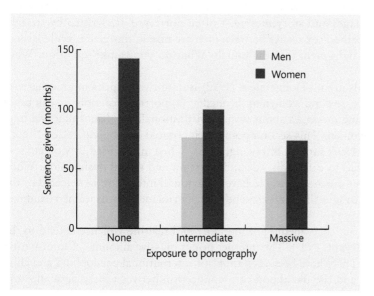

Figure 12.12 Effect of number of pornographic films viewed on lenience in sentencing
Source: Based on data from Zillmann and Bryant (1984).

In the context of pornography, correlational rather than experimental studies based on larger population samples point to a different possibility. In examining the association between pornography and sexual offending, Michael Seto and his colleagues suggest that people who are already predisposed to sexually offend are the most likely to be affected by pornography exposure as well as to show the strongest consequences (Seto, Maric, & Barbaree, 2001).

When violence is mixed with sex in films, there is, at the very least, evidence of male desensitisation to aggression against women – callous and demeaning attitudes (Donnerstein & Linz, 1994; Mullin & Linz, 1995). A meta-analysis by Paik and Comstock (1994) found that sexually violent TV programmes were linked to later aggression, and this was most clearly evident in male aggression against women (Donnerstein & Malamuth, 1997).

Daniel Linz and his colleagues reported that when women were depicted enjoying violent pornography, men were later more willing to aggress against women – although, interestingly, not against men (Linz, Donnerstein, & Penrod, 1988). Perhaps just as telling are other consequences of such material: it can perpetuate the myth that women actually enjoy sexual violence. It has been demonstrated that portrayals of women apparently enjoying such acts reinforce rape myths and weaken social and cognitive restraints against violence towards women (Malamuth & Donnerstein, 1982). Zillmann and Bryant (1984) pointed out that the cumulative effect of exposure to violent pornography trivialises rape by portraying women as 'hyperpromiscuous and socially irresponsible'.

There has been a growth of resistance to violent pornographic material by women's movements in recent years. A *feminist perspective* emphasises two concerns about continual exposure of men to media depicting violence and/or sexually explicit material involving women:

1 Exposure to violence will cause men to become callous or desensitised to violence against female victims.

2 Exposure to pornography will contribute to the development of negative attitudes towards women.

Some feminist writers (see Gubar & Hoff, 1989) maintain that pornography degrades and dehumanises women when it depicts women as subordinate to men and existing solely to satisfy men's sexual needs. In Russell Geen's (1998) review, an attitude of callousness – perhaps a value – develops by using pornography over a long period. A woman is reduced to being a sexual reward for the conquering male (Mosher & Anderson, 1986). In her analysis of widely available pornography (videos, DVDs and Internet sites), Marilyn Corsianos (2007) found that the images and storylines most often portrayed are written by straight men for straight men. Further, sex scenes between men are rare in this genre, while lesbian acts are fantasies for straight men. (See the fourth 'What do *you* think?' question. What might you now tell Tom?)

In summary, Linz, Wilson and Donnerstein (1992) isolate two culprits in an otherwise confusing mix of violence, sex and women in the media: (a) portrayal of violence can beget violence, and (b) degrading messages about women institutionalise a demeaning and one-dimensional image of women. This second point is elaborated by **objectification theory** (Fredrickson & Roberts, 1997; Moradi & Huang, 2008). When internalised by women, sexual objectification can lead to eating disorders, depression and sexual dysfunction. When men objectify women, they are more likely to have behavioural intentions (as detected by the **implicit association test**) to sexually harass and be sexually violent towards women (Rudman & Mescher, 2012).

Links between media violence, media pornography and real-life violence extend to the Internet (see Durkin & Bryant, 1995). The Internet brings massive amounts of information directly into our homes. There have been revelations of international paedophilia and child pornography networks, and the likelihood of a connection between these networks and

Objectification theory
Women's life experiences and gender socialisation routinely include experiences of sexual objectification.

Implicit association test
Reaction-time test to measure attitudes – particularly unpopular attitudes that people might conceal.

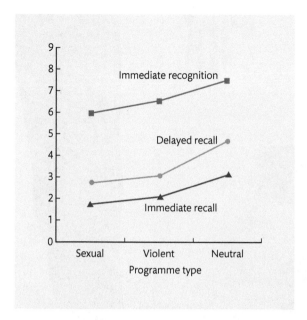

Figure 12.13 Sex, violence and memory for television advertisements

- People watched TV programmes that were sexually explicit, violent or neutral.
- They then both recalled and identified nine brand advertisements contained in the programmes.
- More brands were remembered in the neutral programme.
- The moral: sex (and violence) does not always sell!

Source: Bushman and Bonacci (2002).

child sexual abuse. However, even if these variables are correlated, care must be exercised in drawing a causal inference.

Before we close this section, let us return to the issue of how sexual content is used in a particular medium – advertising. Exploiting sex (and violence) in advertising can sometimes backfire if it is intended that a product be more memorable and therefore a commercial success. Brad Bushman and Angelica Bonacci (2002) studied more than 300 young to middle-aged people who watched one of three television programmes, each containing nine brand advertisements. The programme themes were sexually explicit, violent or neutral. Later, the participants tried to recall the brands and to identify them from photographs. The lesson is salutary – see Figure 12.13.

Domestic and intimate partner violence

Domestic violence against women, children and elders is a major social and public health issue with important psychological aspects (Tolan, Gorman-Smith, & Henry, 2006). However, intimate partner violence has attracted most research attention (Esquivel-Santoveña & Dixon, 2012; Shorey, Tirone, & Stuart, 2014), and there is now a substantial amount of data available.

An early American survey of more than 2,000 families revealed that an assault with intent to injure had occurred in three out of ten married couples, and in one out of six within the past year (Straus, Gelles, & Steinmetz, 1980). The acts were pushing, hitting with the fist, slapping, kicking, throwing something and beating up, and a few were threatened with a gun or knife.

It may be surprising to learn that women are slightly more likely than men to use physical aggression against their partners in heterosexual relationships (Archer, 2000). This sex difference in intimate partner violence arises for a number of reasons (Cross & Campbell, 2011):

- *Evolutionary perspective* (Archer, 2013) – human fear is an adaptive human emotional response to threat that reduces exposure to physical danger. For females, there is a higher level of fear in the face of direct aggression.

Domestic violence
When the act is physical, there is usually a gender asymmetry. The male has the advantage of physical strength used as a means of controlling the relationship.

- *Biological perspective* – oxytocin is a hormone that regulates several reproductive and maternal behaviours, including childbirth. When released in responding to danger, it mediates the reduction of stress associated with fear.

- *Intimate partner violence* – the release of oxytocin is more pronounced in the presence of an intimate partner. If threat is involved, the higher level of oxytocin associated with the partner reduces the stress experienced and increases the likelihood of female aggression.

- *Cultural norms* – women in Western cultures often equal or exceed men in their level of aggression. Norms that govern the expression of aggression vary across cultures and provide another causal path for sex differences in aggression to emerge.

In general, however, violent females do less harm than violent males; and because male violence is usually more severe, the terms 'battered woman' (Walker, 1993) or, more generally, 'gendered violence' (DeKeseredy, 2011) are often used by researchers.

Here is a sobering statistic, based on North American research: about one-quarter of those homicides where the killer knows the victim are spousal. According to Todd Shackelford (2001), American women in cohabiting relationships incur about nine times the risk of being murdered as women in marital relationships, a trend that is similar in Canada. The breakup rate is also higher for cohabiting partners. There are other correlates of cohabiting: being poorer, younger and having stepchildren. A meta-analysis carried out by John Archer (2006) revealed a cultural impact on female domestic violence – much higher rates are found in societies that are modern, secular and liberal, and where women are emancipated in both the local economy and the family. The suggestion is that this reflects a change in women's traditional roles in society.

Very different interpretations can be made of violence between partners (Archer, 2000). Family conflict researchers have emphasised mutual combat between the partners, whereas feminist writers portray violent encounters between male perpetrators and female victims. Walter DeKeseredy (2011) found that conservative fathers' rights groups in the United States sometimes distribute anti-feminist literature; furthermore, there may be a patriarchy that undermines women's health and safety. David Buss and Joshua Duntley (2011; also see Archer, 2013) have offered a contrary view of domestic violence that is based on evolutionary social psychology. If we expect a general state of harmony in intimate relationships, we ignore a reality in sexual conflict: men are primarily in conflict with other men and women with other women. Sexual conflict is actually an outcome of the incompatible evolutionary interests of men and women.

Gender asymmetry?

Studies of same-sex relationships show that lesbians, bisexuals and gay men are also victims of acts of violence in the home (Klinger & Stein, 1996; Letellier, 1994) – the rate of intimate partner violence is similar across heterosexual males, heterosexual females and homosexual males (Nowinski & Bowen, 2012).

The image of a man being battered by a woman may be difficult to envisage. Richard Harris and Cynthia Cook (1994) investigated students' responses to three scenarios: a husband battering his wife, a wife battering her husband and a gay man battering his male partner, each in response to verbal provocation. The first scenario, a husband battering his wife, was rated as more violent than the other two scenarios. Further, 'victim blaming' – an example of **belief in a just world** (see **Chapter 3**) – was attributed most often to a gay victim, who was also judged most likely to leave the relationship. It seems that the one act takes on a different meaning according to the gender of the aggressor and the victim.

DeKeseredy (2006) and Claire Renzetti (2006) are agreed in deciding that both gender and ethnic asymmetries underlie partner abuse:

- Most sexual assaults in heterosexual relationships are committed by men.
- Much of women's use of violence is in self-defence against their partner's assault (see Cross & Campbell, 2011).
- Men and women in different ethnic groups 'do gender' differently, including variations in perceptions of when it is appropriate to use violence.

In general, there are obstacles to drawing reliable conclusions across the studies quoted in this section. These obstacles arise from variations in sample size, methodology and even national differences in gender equality and empowerment (Cross & Campbell, 2011; Esquivel-Santoveña & Dixon, 2012; Nowinski & Bowen, 2012).

Belief in a just world
Belief that the world is a just and predictable place where good things happen to 'good people' and bad things to 'bad people'.

Hurting the one we 'love'

Why do people hurt those closest to them? There are no simple answers, but there are some factors that play a role:

- *learnt patterns of aggression*, imitated from parents and significant others, together with low competence in responding non-aggressively; there is a generational cycle of child abuse (Straus, Gelles, & Steinmetz, 1980), and the chronic repetition of violence in some families has been identified as an **abuse syndrome**;
- the *proximity* of family members, which makes them more likely to be sources of annoyance or frustration, and targets when these feelings are generated externally;
- *stresses*, especially financial difficulties, unemployment and illnesses (including postnatal depression; see Searle, 1987); this partly accounts for domestic violence being much more common in poorer families;
- the division of *power* in traditional nuclear families, favouring the man, which makes it easier for less democratic styles of interaction to predominate (Claes & Rosenthal, 1990);
- high *alcohol* consumption, which is a common correlate of male abuse of a spouse (Stith & Farley, 1993).

Abuse syndrome
Factors of proximity, stress and power that are associated with the cycle of abuse in some families.

An interaction of these factors, heightened by the normal stresses of day-to-day living that we all encounter, means that those we live closest to are, ironically, the likely targets of our aggression.

Institutionalised aggression

Role of society

Not all societies or groups in society define aggression as an altogether bad thing. In Western industrial societies, the contemporary value placed on non-violence is an outcome of historical and sociocultural factors. It is an ethic that derives from a combination of politics, religion, philosophy and events in recent history, including the atrocities of the First and Second World Wars, the threat of nuclear annihilation associated with the Cold War, and the anti-war focus of protests against the Vietnam War and nuclear escalation. An emphasis on non-violence is a sociocultural value judgement about the significance and purpose of aggression. However, since the end of the Second World War, the West has been continuously involved in wars around the world, and retaliated swiftly and violently in 2001 to al-Qaeda's terrorist atrocities in the United States by invading Afghanistan.

We have noted that biological theories argue that aggression has useful properties. Apart from personal self-defence, are there examples of human aggression that seem reasonable? Issues of definition resurface: there are ways in which some kinds of aggression are used to bring about positive outcomes. Where these involve groups or a whole society, they preserve the **social order** (Kelvin, 1970) or can be vehicles for positive social change or the struggle against oppression – Mao Zedong famously maintained that 'War is the continuation of politics . . . by other means' and that 'Political power grows out of the barrel of a gun'.

Social order
The balance and control of a social system, regulated by norms, values, rules and law.

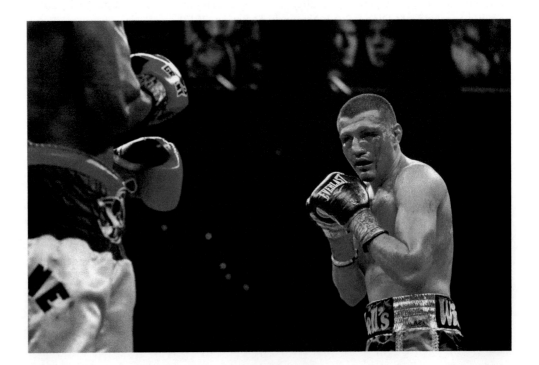

Institutionalised aggression
Many sports involve aggression, but aggression that is carefully governed by rules and regulations.

Human societies depend for their continuity on social norms; those that are well established become deeply embedded as core values that are widely shared in a community, such as caring for our fellows. Ultimately, law provides protection for a social system. Occasionally, the mechanisms of social order even sanction the use of violence. While the functions of some kinds of **institutionalised aggression** can be legitimate, there can also be both socially desirable and undesirable effects. The need for law and order can lead to arrests (desirable) but also to prisoner abuse (undesirable). Parental discipline can lead to verbal criticism (desirable?) but also to severe physical punishment (undesirable).

Terrorism is an instance of extreme violence that comes vividly to mind. Since the 11 September 2001 attacks on New York and Washington, we have witnessed a never-ending, almost daily onslaught of reports of grotesque acts of terrorism around the globe. Although the vast majority of these atrocities occur in Afghanistan, the Middle East and Africa, virtually no corner of the globe has escaped these cowardly assaults and bombings of crowded places where ordinary people are merely going about their daily lives. For example, in Europe alone there was the Madrid train bombing in 2004, the train and bus bombings in London in 2005, the Paris bombings in 2015 and, in 2016, we have had the Istanbul airport, the Brussels airport, and the Nice waterfront.

Various groups argue that their powerless position leaves no alternative – only deadly acts of terror will ensure that their fight for justice is taken seriously. Significant moral and political issues underlie judgements about aggression, as they do about suicide, abortion and euthanasia. All of these can be made to fit a definition of aggression.

> **Institutionalised aggression**
> Aggression that is given formal or informal recognition and social legitimacy by being incorporated into rules and norms.

War

Tragically, large-scale aggression and war, which can be linked to the topics of prejudice, discrimination and intergroup behaviour (discussed in **Chapters 10 and 11**), are part of the human condition. Two million years of human evolution, industrialisation, the communications revolution, philosophy, art and poetry have had no effect whatsoever – collective violence continues unabated. Recent years have witnessed monstrous violence in Syria, Somalia, Bosnia, Croatia, Kosovo, Rwanda, Chechnya, Afghanistan and Iraq. While we might like to think that we have evolved gracefully from the Renaissance period, the last century was by far the bloodiest in systematic human slaughter (Dutton, Boyanowski, & Bond, 2005).

A way of glimpsing the continuing tragedy is to consider the incidence and severity of wars. Most of us will think of two world wars as the most obvious examples of widespread violence, but there are many others. The estimates in Figure 12.14 are drawn from a number of sources, and are limited to the twentieth century. The data include interstate wars, civil wars, wars of independence, genocide, massacres and atrocities. They remain selective by excluding other instances of mass death that numbered fewer than *1 million* people!

A neglected consequence of war is its long-term effects. Societies with more war have more warlike sports, beliefs in malevolent magic, and severe punishment for crime – and, perhaps surprisingly, have higher rates of homicide and assault (Ember & Ember, 1994).

Role of the state

The worst acts of inhumanity are committed against humanity itself. Warfare is not possible without a supporting psychological structure involving the beliefs and emotions of a people. If such a structure is lacking, leaders will use propaganda to create one (see **Chapter 6**). In times of war, both the soldiers who are fighting and the people at home need to maintain good morale. Genocide is a kind of legitimised prejudice translated into behaviour (see **Chapter 11**). Some political regimes have fostered beliefs in genetic differences between

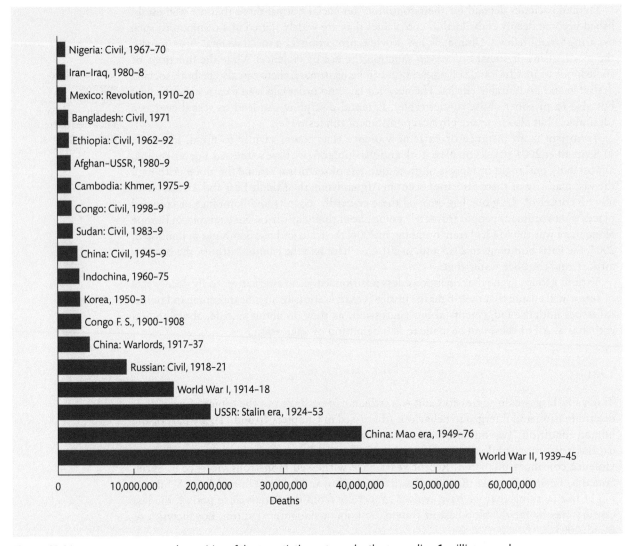

Figure 12.14 Wars, massacres and atrocities of the twentieth century: deaths exceeding 1 million people
Source: Based on data from White (2004).

groups of people to justify oppression and slaughter. Ideologies of racial, moral and social inferiority were the cornerstones of the Nazi programmes directed against gypsies, political non-conformists, homosexuals, the mentally handicapped, ill people and, of course, Jews. Antagonism expressed by Hitler led German citizens to avoid Jews, even those who were neighbours and friends. This created a climate for enacting the Nuremberg laws of discrimination. It was a small step towards burning synagogues, arresting huge numbers of people and attacking Jews on the street. The last link in the chain was the industrial-style slaughter of millions of people.

There is an irony in the term 'war'. Bond (2004) noted that not all complex societies are democratic – indeed, Moghaddam (2013) has argued that the normal default state of human governance is probably dictatorship – and that totalitarian regimes employ widespread violence as a form of control and domination.

War is not the most deadly form of violence. Indeed, while 36 million people have been killed in battle in all foreign and domestic wars in our [twentieth] century, at least 119 million more have been killed by government genocide, massacres, and other mass killing. And about 115 million of these were killed by totalitarian governments (as many as 95 million by communist ones).

Rummel (1988); cited in Bond (2004, p. 68)

The role of the state suggests to its citizens that aggression is reasonable in certain circumstances – and thus normative. And, as we have seen in a number of earlier chapters, people confirm to norms or obey orders, and some people may have an authoritarian streak that particularly inclines them to obey (**Chapter 10**). Indeed, a powerful autocracy constrains its citizens to obey without question.

Role of the person

In this context, Stanley Milgram's (1974) research on blind destructive obedience (see **Chapter 7**) is very relevant. Milgram showed how ordinary people could do terrible things (give apparently lethal electric shocks to a stranger who simply made mistakes on a learning task in a laboratory) when conditions encouraged blind obedience to authority. Just think about it – Milgram's participants were prepared to electrocute someone who had poorly learned which words went with which, simply because someone in a white coat told them to do so! Milgram gave the lie to the idea that terrible things are done by a few unusually psychopathic people: on the contrary, his results suggested that many of us would have responded in the same way (Blass, 2004).

Although his work was criticised for its supposed artificiality, as well as for his deception of participants to commit an 'immoral act', Milgram defended himself on the grounds that he contributed to the understanding of ordinary people's willingness to aggress when obeying a legitimate authority. A few years after the original experiment (Milgram, 1963) came news of the massacre by American forces of men, women and children in Vietnam in 1969, at a village called My Lai (see details in Dutton, Boyanowski, & Bond, 2005). This war scarred the American psyche, and this incident has acquired a unique reputation by exploding the Western myth that it is the 'enemy' that commits atrocities.

Milgram generalised to everyday life. Citizens are taught from childhood to obey both the laws of the state and the orders of those who represent its authority. In so doing, citizens enter an **agentic state** of thinking and distance themselves from personal responsibility for their actions.

Agentic state
A frame of mind thought by Milgram to characterise unquestioning obedience, in which people as agents transfer personal responsibility to the person giving orders.

Levels of explanation

We noted earlier that different levels of explanation are adopted to explain aggression and a wide variety of social behaviours (see **Chapter 1**). In the context of war, explanations vary from being person-centred to being group-centred. Research on authoritarianism has argued that prejudice, discrimination, violence and wartime atrocities reside in extreme or deviant personalities. Milgram moved away from this by suggesting that ordinary people can feel they are agents of the state and will carry out orders that can harm others when the voice of authority seems legitimate. Sherif (Sherif & Sherif, 1953) moved further away from an individual level of explanation by relating large-scale conflict to the nature of intergroup relations, suggesting that discriminatory acts against an outgroup will flourish only when the objective interests of one's own group are threatened. Recently, Bond (2004) has emphasised the necessity to have both individual and societal levels of analysis of aggression and, very clearly, of war.

Tajfel (1974) outlined a group-centred approach to aggression and war by suggesting that the very existence of ingroups lays the foundation for prejudice, discrimination and conflict.

Outgroups provide a reference and must be kept at bay (see **Chapter 11**). Tajfel contrasted an account of aggression based on the person with one based on the group. The first account is an individualist perspective offered by Berkowitz (1962). The second is by Tajfel, who took Berkowitz's own words and made crucial substitutions of terms that implicate society as the 'cause' (see Box 12.7). Tajfel's perspective underpins social identity theory (Tajfel & Turner, 1986; see **Chapter 11**) which provides an analysis of the interplay of cognitive processes and beliefs about social structure that produce a variety of more or less extreme forms of intergroup behaviour.

Collective group-based aggression has also recently been viewed as an aspect of extremism that may be a correlate or consequence of uncertainty (Hogg & Blaylock, 2012; Hogg, Kruglanski, & Van den Bos, 2013). Resting on substantial historical evidence that violent extremism is often associated with societal uncertainty (Staub, 1989, 2010), one argument is that uncertainty about one's social identity as a member of a subjectively important group can lead people to go to violent extremes to protect and promote their group's ideology, way of life and ultimately identity in society (Hogg, 2007b, 2012, 2014). Others have used the term *group-centrism* to describe a constellation of uncertainty-provoked actions (Kruglanski, Pierro, Mannetti, & De Grada, 2006), and have focused on the way that uncertainty can lead people to behave extremely to protect their cultural world views (Martin & Van den Bos, 2014; Van den Bos, 2009).

Box 12.7 Research highlight
Two different levels of explanation of aggression and war

Adorno, Frenkel-Brunswik, Levinson and Sanford (1950) explained prejudice and discrimination in terms of a personality characteristic called the authoritarian personality (see **Chapter 10**). A similar individual level of explanation emerges in Berkowitz's (1962, p. 167) account of the causes of aggression:

> Granting all this, the present writer is still inclined to emphasise the importance of individualistic considerations in the field of group relations. Dealings between groups ultimately become problems of the psychology of the individual. Individuals decide to go to war; battles are fought by individuals; and peace is established by individuals. It is the individual who adopts the beliefs prevailing in his society, even though the extent to which these opinions are shared by many people is a factor governing his readiness to adopt them, and he transmits these views to other individuals. Ultimately, it is the single person who attacks the feared and disliked ethnic minority group, even though many people around him share his feelings and are very important in determining his willingness to aggress against this minority.

Tajfel, working at Bristol University in the early 1970s, regarded this view as typical of the restricted level of explanation offered by personality and individual differences levels of explanation. In an unpublished paper written in 1974, he deliberately rewrote Berkowitz's words as follows, using words in italics to emphasise where an individual focus is replaced by a societal one:

> Granting all this, the present writer is still inclined to emphasise the importance of considering the field of group relations in terms of social *structure*. Dealings between groups cannot be accounted for by the psychology of the individual. *Governments* decide to go to war; battles are fought by *armies*; and peace is established by *governments*. The social conditions in which groups live largely determine their beliefs and the extent to which they are shared. Ultimately, a single person's attack on an ethnic minority group that he dislikes or fears would remain a trivial occurrence had it not been for the fact that he acts in unison with others who share his feelings and are very important in determining his willingness to aggress against this minority.

Source: Tajfel (1974); cited in Vaughan (1988).

Reducing aggression

How one reduces aggression depends on the level of explanation of aggression that is adopted. At an individual level – where the person is the focus as the aggressor – effective interventions involve political decisions, a budget and a community will. There are now effective techniques grounded in behavioural and counselling psychology that require the cooperation of regional agencies, schools and families for their implementation.

School bullying is a particular problem that has become a focus of research. Hong and Espelage (2012) reviewed studies and meta-analyses of research on school bullying and peer victimisation, to conclude that the impact of anti-bullying programs has been low, and that punitive tactics (e.g. corporal punishment and suspension) have proved ineffective (cf. A. P. Goldstein, 1999). They suggest that a more effective approach would be multipronged. This would involve modifying the behaviour of both bullies and their victims and of non-involved bystanders, addressing classroom and school climate, and reaching out to the family, community, and wider society.

Regarding attitudes towards women that promote aggression, there are direct educational opportunities that can be used. For example, media studies courses can help develop critical skills that evaluate whether and how women are demeaned, and in what way we might undermine rape myths (Linz, Wilson, & Donnerstein, 1992).

Laws can also play a role in reducing aggression or its effects. Take gun ownership laws in the United States as an example. You now know something of the weapons effect. Consider this irony: guns and ammunition may be kept in the home to confer protection. The same guns are overwhelmingly used to kill a family member or an intimate acquaintance, particularly in homes with a history of drug use and physical violence (Kellerman, Rivara, Rushforth, Banton, Reay, Francisco, et al., 1993). Related to the legal system, the underlying causes of aggression need to be addressed – specifically the life conditions of those groups plagued by cyclical violence and most likely to be involved in individual or collective violence. A significant underlying factor is poverty (Belsky, 1993) and relative (intergroup) deprivation.

Mass violence such as genocide and war is a different matter. There is room for the introduction of **peace studies** into the formal education system. Peace education is more than an anti-war campaign: it has broadened to cover all aspects of peaceful relationships and

Peace studies
Multidisciplinary movement dedicated to the study and promotion of peace.

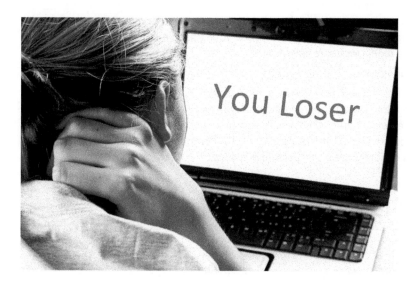

Cyber bullying
According to one slogan, 'cyber bullying leaves bruises – inside'.

coexistence. By teaching young children how to build and maintain self-esteem without being aggressive (the culture of self-esteem may nourish aggression – see **Chapter 4**), it is hoped that there will be a long-term impact that will expand into all areas of people's lives (see Shorey, Tirone, & Stuart, 2014).

We cannot wave a magic wand and banish violence. At both individual and societal levels, there is room for social psychologists and others to work towards harmony in a world of increasing stress and dwindling resources. Let us now turn to the kinder face of humanity (**Chapter 13**).

Summary

- Aggression is defined differently depending on the researcher's underlying theoretical perspective. One simple definition is 'the intentional infliction of some type of harm on others'.

- There are two major classes of theory about the origins of aggression; one emphasising its biological origins and the other its social origins.

- Biological explanations can be traced to Darwinian evolutionary theory. They include Freud's psychodynamic approach, ethological theory and, more recently, evolutionary social psychology. These approaches emphasise genetically determined behaviour patterns shared by a species.

- Social explanations emphasise the role of societal influences and/or learning processes. Some incorporate a biological component, such as the frustration–aggression hypothesis and excitation-transfer theory. Social learning theory is a developmental approach that emphasises reinforcement principles and the influence that models have on the young child.

- Some research into causes has concentrated on characteristics of the person, such as personality and gender. Other research has focused on transitory states, such as frustration, catharsis, provocation and alcohol, brain injury or mental illness, and disinhibition.

- Other research has focused on the situation; including stressors in the physical environment, such as heat and crowding. A significant societal variable is relative deprivation – the perceived disadvantage that some groups have in relation to those holding power.

- A social approach to aggression allows for the possibility of change over time and cultural context. For example, there is evidence for increased aggression in women over recent time, and for cultural differences in rates of physical aggression, reflecting long-standing differences in norms and values.

- The role played by the mass media, particularly television, in aggression has been controversial. The continued portrayal of violence may desensitise young people to the consequences of violence and provide a model for future behaviour.

- Reports of domestic violence, particularly against a partner, have a high profile in our community. Whether domestic violence is actually more common is unclear.

- War and terrorism are a shocking, massive stain on humanity. Arguments about their causes and prevention that are defined purely in political terms miss many crucial points: the role of intergroup relations themselves, the fact that people actually hurt other people, and the perpetuation across generations of outgroup stereotypes and prejudice.

Key terms

Abuse syndrome	Analogue	Belief in a just world
Agentic state	Attachment styles	Big Five

Biosocial theories
Catharsis
Cathartic hypothesis
Collective aggression
Cultural norms
Culture of honour
Dehumanisation
Deindividuation
Desensitisation
Disinhibition
Ethology
Evolutionary social psychology
Excitation-transfer model
External validity
Fighting instinct

Frustration–aggression hypothesis
General aggression model
Gender
Hate crimes
Implicit association test
Instinct
Institutionalised aggression
Learning by direct experience
Learning by vicarious experience
Machismo
Modelling
Nature–nurture controversy
Neo-associationist analysis
Neo-Freudians
Objectification theory

Operational definition
Peace studies
Priming
Relative deprivation
Releasers
Schema
Script
Sexual selection theory
Social learning theory
Social order
Sociocultural theory
Subculture of violence
Type A personality
Values
Weapons effect

Literature, film and TV

Syriana and *The Killing Fields*

Two films showing different sides of state-sponsored aggression. *Syriana* is a 2005 geopolitical thriller directed by Stephen Gaghan and starring George Clooney and Matt Damon. Focused on the complexity and intrigue of petroleum politics and the Middle East, this film is a powerful commentary on strategic state-sponsored aggression, individual suicide terrorism and the personal cost of violence. Other films in the same genre include *Rendition* and *The Kingdom* (both released in 2007). *The Killing Fields* is a 1984 film directed by Roland Joffé, starring Sam Waterston, John Malkovich and Haing S. Ngor. It is a chilling and disturbing portrayal of the 1970s genocide in Cambodia. The Khmer Rouge, led by Pol Pot, exterminated between 2 million and 3 million Cambodians (the actual figure may never be known) during the second half of the 1970s.

City of God

A 2002 film by Fernando Meirelles portraying gang violence in the slums of Rio de Janeiro. We see how easily aggression and violence become a way of life when there is no protection on the streets and a gun can give you safety, power and popularity. This is most poignantly demonstrated by the story of 11-year-old Li'l Dice, who murders everyone in a brothel and goes on to become a powerful gang leader and drug dealer within a couple of years, thriving on the power afforded by his brutality.

Pulp Fiction

Quentin Tarantino's 1994 classic, starring John Travolta, Samuel T. Jackson and Uma Thurman. The violent lives of mobsters and small-time criminals in Los Angeles are graphically dramatised; but the film is also memorable for its clever and humorous dialogue and its focus on the characters' perspectives on life and on their essential humanness.

In Bruges

A 2008 black comedy directed by Martin McDonagh, starring Colin Farrell, Brendan Gleeson and Ralph Fiennes and set in – surprise, surprise – Bruges. Farrell and Gleeson play two hitmen exiled to Bruges to lie low because Farrell accidentally shot a child in a church. Unbeknownst to Farrell, their mobster boss (played by Fiennes) has sent them to Bruges for Gleeson to kill him. An atmospheric and humorous film that is full of memorable lines and scenes. Although about mobsters and small-time criminals, this film contrasts nicely with *Pulp Fiction* in that the violence is understated and even 'polite', but it does invite thought about the role of aggression and violence in people's lives.

We Need to Talk about Kevin

A 2011 British-American drama by Lynne Ramsay, starring Tilda Swinton as the mother of a highly disturbed and psychopathic adolescent who murders his father and sister and then commits a cold-blooded massacre at his school – using a bow and arrows. This is a harrowing and disturbing movie, and of course relevant to the seemingly endless litany of school and university campus massacres in the USA – for example the 2012 Sandy Hook elementary school massacre in the US of 20 six-year-olds and 6 adults, and the 2007 Virginia Tech University massacre of 32 people. The film addresses the interplay of inherited behaviour, mental health and family relationships in the emergence of cold-blooded aggression expressed through school killings most often by adolescents and young adults.

Guided questions

1   What is the *frustration–aggression hypothesis*? Does it help explain the origins of aggression?
2   Can children really learn quite quickly how to be aggressive?
3   Does the incidence of aggression vary in relation to gender or culture?
4   Does viewing television violence make people more aggressive?
5   In what ways can the tendency to aggress be reduced?

Learn more

Anderson, C. A., & Huesmann, L. R. (2007). Human aggression: A social-cognitive view. In M. A. Hogg & J. Cooper (Eds.), *The SAGE handbook of social psychology: Concise student edition* (pp. 259–287). London: SAGE. Comprehensive and accessible overview of research on human aggression, by two of the world's leading aggression researchers.

Baron, R. A., & Richardson, D. R. (1994). *Human aggression* (2nd ed.). New York: Plenum. A heavily cited source for research on human aggression.

Berkowitz, L. (1993). *Aggression: Its causes, consequences and control*. Philadelphia, PA: Temple University Press. Another work by an authority in the field with a good coverage of the topic.

Buford, B. (1993). *Among the thugs*. New York: Vintage. An insider's perspective on the world of English football 'hooligans' in British and other European settings. The work is compelling – one reviewer described it as '*A Clockwork Orange* comes to life'.

Bushman, B. J., & Huesmann, L. R. (2010). Aggression. In S. T. Fiske, D. T. Gilbert, & G. Lindzey (Eds.), *Handbook of social psychology* (5th ed., Vol. 2, pp. 833–863). New York: Wiley. Currently the most up-to-date, detailed and comprehensive coverage of theory and research on all aspects of and perspectives on human aggression.

Campbell, A. (1993). *Men, women, and aggression*. New York: HarperCollins. A discussion of sex, gender and aggression.

Glick, R. A., & Roose, S. P. (Eds.) (1993). *Rage, power, and aggression*. New Haven, CT: Yale University Press. A collection of chapters reviewing research, theory and clinical perspectives on the origins, nature and development of aggression.

Goldstein, A. P. (1994). *The ecology of aggression*. New York: Plenum. As the title suggests, the focus is on how aggression can be influenced by ecological factors, which can be both physical and social.

Krahé, B. (2013). *The social psychology of aggression* (2nd ed.). New York: Psychology Press. Up-to-date and authoritative text on the social psychology of aggression by one of the world's leading aggression researchers.

Rose, H., & Rose, S. (Eds.) (2000). *Alas, poor Darwin: Arguments against evolutionary psychology.* London: Vintage. A group of scholars from a variety of biological, philosophical and social science backgrounds raise concerns about the adequacy of genetic accounts of social behaviour, including aggression.

Staub, E. (2010). *The panorama of mass violence: Origins, prevention, healing and reconciliation.* New York: Oxford University Press. Analysis of mass violence including genocide, with some thoughts on prevention and healing. Staub is one of the world's leading experts on group aggression.

Chapter 13
Prosocial behaviour

Chapter contents

What do *you* think?

1   Arthur spots this headline in his local newspaper: 'Altruistic dolphin saves surfer!' Interesting, he thinks, but that's not altruism . . . or is it?

2   Alex is fit and healthy, his whole life ahead of him. His twin brother's future is uncertain. He now needs dialysis more than once a week. After months of thinking, some of it agonising, Alex's mind is made up – he will donate a kidney to his brother. Would you want to help your really close kin? Is there an evolutionary aspect to this?

3   Lily is 13 years old and tall for her age. One afternoon, she confronts a suspicious-looking stranger loitering near a young girl playing in the local park. The stranger takes to his heels when Lily challenges him. It is the talk of the neighbourhood, and there is mention of a medal for bravery. Hearing this, your social psychology classmate points out: 'It's just as well that Lily's usual playmates were not around, or that little girl might not have received any help.' What could your classmate mean?

4   You turn the corner of a city street to see a man sprawled across the footpath in front of you. What do you do? What might you want to know more about before deciding what to do?

Now for something completely different

In Chapter 10, we saw how people can dislike or hate others simply because they are not members of their group. In Chapter 11, we saw how groups discriminate and compete destructively against each other, and in Chapter 12, we saw how aggressive human beings can be. One would be forgiven for gloomily concluding that people are basically full of hatred and aggression. It was the philosopher Thomas Hobbes who famously proclaimed in *Leviathan,* his 1651 treatise on the human condition, that life is 'solitary, poor, nasty, brutish and short'.

This chapter stands in contrast as we turn to the positive and altruistic aspect of human nature. We now ask why, when and how people decide to help others even if they in turn pay the ultimate sacrifice. We try to explain phenomena such as soldiers throwing themselves on live grenades to save their comrades, firefighters losing their own lives while rescuing people from the collapsing World Trade Center towers in New York on 11 September 2001, and people such as Oscar Schindler and Miep Gies taking huge personal risks to save Jews in Nazi Europe.

This focus on the good in people shares much with a perspective across psychology generally, called *positive psychology* (e.g. Csikszentmihalyi & Nakamura, 2011; Seligman & Csikszentmihalyi, 2000; Sheldon, Kashdan, & Steger, 2011; Snyder & Lopez, 2009). Positive psychology has its origins in work by Martin Seligman (1991) and is sometimes rather inaccurately characterised as the study of happiness. It is actually a much broader perspective that has its natural home in developmental psychology and the organisational sciences and includes a very applied and action-research focus (e.g. Donaldson, Csikszentmihalyi, & Nakamura, 2011). It is a movement within the behavioural sciences aimed at enhancing human strengths that make life worth living; such as creativity, joy, flow, responsibility, and optimal performance and achievement. It focuses on how people and communities can fulfil their emotional, creative and behavioural potential and experience positive emotions and personalities within positive institutions. Although we do not discuss positive psychology directly in this chapter, much of the social psychology of prosocial behaviour can be considered as contributing to a positive view of humankind.

Prosocial behaviour, helping behaviour and altruism

Researchers refer to acts that benefit another person as prosocial behaviour, helping behaviour or altruistic behaviour. These terms are often used interchangeably. However, there are some distinctions, and differences in the way they are used in the social psychological literature (Schroeder, Penner, Dovidio, & Piliavin, 1995).

Prosocial behaviour
Acts that are positively valued by society.

Prosocial behaviour broadly encompasses acts that are valued positively by society – contrast it with antisocial behaviour. Lauren Wispé (1972) defined prosocial behaviour as behaviour that has positive social consequences and contributes to the physical or psychological well-being of another person. It is voluntary and is intended to benefit others (Eisenberg, Fabes, Karbon, Murphy, Wosinski, Polazzi, et al., 1996). Being prosocial includes both being helpful and altruistic. It also includes acts of charity, cooperation, friendship, rescue, sacrifice, sharing, sympathy and trust. What is considered prosocial is defined by society's norms.

Helping behaviour
Acts that intentionally benefit someone else.

Helping behaviour is a subcategory of prosocial behaviour. Helping is intentional, and it benefits another living being or group. If you accidentally drop a ten-pound note and someone finds it and spends it, you have not performed a helping behaviour. But if you gave ten pounds to Connie who really needed it, you have helped her. On the other hand, making a large public donation to a charity because you wanted to appear generous is not helping behaviour. Some corporate donations to a good cause may be driven by product promotion; e.g. in pursuit of a long-term increase in profit. Helping can even be antisocial; e.g. overhelping, when giving help is designed to make others look inferior (Gilbert & Silvera, 1996).

Altruism is another subcategory of prosocial behaviour. It refers to an act that is meant to benefit another person rather than oneself. True altruism should be selfless, but it can be difficult to prove true selflessness (Batson, 1991). For example, can we ever really know that an act does not stem from a long-term ulterior motive, such as ingratiation? Ervin Staub (1977) noted that there are sometimes 'private' rewards associated with acting prosocially, such as feeling good or being virtuous. There is a considerable debate over how magnanimous human nature really is (Maner, Luce, Neuberg, Cialdini, Brown, & Sagarin, 2002).

Altruism
A special form of helping behaviour, sometimes costly, that shows concern for fellow human beings and is performed without expectation of personal gain.

The Kitty Genovese murder

Social psychological research into helping behaviour began in the late 1950s. Over a thousand articles dealing with altruism and helpfulness were published in the following twenty-five years (Dovidio, 1984). We now know a great deal more about why we sometimes turn our backs on people requiring assistance, but also why we often go out of our way to help those in need. A single event is credited with providing the main impetus to this research – the murder of a young woman called Kitty Genovese in New York in 1964. The report of her murder appalled New York residents (see Box 13.1).

The Kitty Genovese murder strongly influenced social psychology's research agenda for studying prosocial and helping behaviour, particularly in the early days. According to Rachel Manning and her colleagues, this now-iconic event focused research attention on the psychology of *not* helping and on how groups act as impediments to helping (Manning, Levine, & Collins, 2007). The positive role played by groups in collective intervention in emergencies was underplayed, though this bias has been redressed in recent years (Levine & Crowther, 2008). To substantiate their critique, Manning and colleagues examined archival material to make the provocative claim that there is actually no evidence for the presence of 38 witnesses to the murder, or that witnesses observed the murder, or that witnesses remained inactive.

Box 13.1 Research classic
The Kitty Genovese murder: A trigger for research on helping behaviour

A sad night in New York City

Late one night in March 1964, Kitty Genovese was on her way home from work when she was attacked by a knife-wielding maniac.

The scene was Kew Gardens in the borough of Queens in New York, a respectable neighbourhood. Her screams and struggles drove off the attacker at first but, seeing no one come to the woman's aid, the man attacked again. Once more she escaped, shouting and crying for help. Yet her screams were to no avail and she was soon cornered again. She was stabbed eight more times and then sexually molested. In the half-hour or so that it took for the man to kill Kitty, not one of her neighbours helped her.

About half an hour after the attack began, the local police received a call from an anonymous witness. He reported the attack but would not give his name because he did not want to 'get involved'. The next day, when the police interviewed the area's residents, thirty-eight people openly admitted to hearing the screaming. They had all had time to do something but failed to act. It is perhaps understandable that some had not rushed out into the street for fear of also being attacked, but why did they not at least call the police?

This particularly tragic and horrific event received national media attention in America, all asking why none of the neighbours had helped. Not surprisingly, this resulted in heightened interest from social psychologists, including Latané and Darley (1976, p. 309):

This story became the journalistic sensation of the decade. 'Apathy,' cried the newspapers. 'Indifference,' said the columnists and commentators. 'Moral callousness', 'dehumanisation', 'loss of concern for our fellow man', added preachers, professors and other sermonisers. Movies, television specials, plays and books explored this incident and many like it. Americans became concerned about their lack of concern.

Prosocial behaviour is difficult to explain with traditional theories of human behaviour. The reason for this is that psychologists, and philosophers before them, have generally assumed that human behaviour is egoistic. Everything we do is ultimately done to benefit ourselves – self-interest reigns supreme. Prosocial behaviour is unusual because it seems to be independent of reinforcement, and it reflects an optimistic and positive view of human beings. How can effort and sacrifice for another person be reinforcing in the usual sense?

Why and when people help

Nature–nurture controversy
Classic debate about whether genetic or environmental factors determine human behaviour. Scientists generally accept that it is an interaction of both.

A recurring theme in psychology is the **nature–nurture controversy** – a debate over the extent to which behaviour is determined by biology or social learning. In **Chapter 12**, we saw how this plays out in relation to aggression. It surfaces again here. There are two quite different perspectives on why and when people help others – one grounded in biology and evolutionary theory, and the other in social learning theory. Other perspectives give a more biosocial account, reflecting the role of empathy, cognition and characteristics of the situation in which help is either given or not.

Biology and evolution

The biological position is that, just as humans have innate tendencies to eat and drink, so they have innate tendencies to help others. If true, it could be a reason why human beings have been so successful in an evolutionary sense. The question whether altruism is a trait that has evolutionary survival value has been asked by social psychologists (e.g. Campbell, 1975), sociobiologists (e.g. Wilson, 1975), and **evolutionary social psychologists** (e.g. Buss & Kenrick, 1998). (See Tomasello and Vaish (2013) for a review of the origins of human cooperation and morality.)

Evolutionary social psychology
An extension of evolutionary psychology that views complex social behaviour as adaptive, helping the individual, kin and the species as a whole to survive.

Consider this scenario. A small child, Margaret, and her friend, Red, were seated in the back seat of Margaret's parents' car. Suddenly the car burst into flames. Red jumped from the car but realised that Margaret was still inside. He jumped back into the burning car, grabbed Margaret by the jacket and pulled her to safety (Batson, 1983). Should we view these actions as reflecting an altruistic impulse inherited from our ancestors? The answer is still being debated, but the fact that Red was an Irish setter – yes, a dog! – adds some weight to the argument that there is a genetic aspect to altruism and prosocial behaviour. It also begs the question: can other animals be altruistic? (Think back to Arthur's quandary in the first 'What do *you* think?' question.)

> Vampire bats regurgitate blood to others despite the possibility of dying if three days elapse without consuming blood. Ground squirrels give alarm calls even though they alert predators to their own presence. Cleaner fish enter the mouths of their hosts to remove parasites even at risk of being eaten. Florida scrub jays often stay at home with their parents, forgoing the benefits of personal reproduction to help rear their younger siblings. These cases of cooperation have generated a substantial amount of theoretical and empirical interest over the past several decades, primarily focusing on adaptive accounts of cooperative behaviors.
>
> Stevens, Cushman and Hauser (2005, p. 499)

Evolutionary biologists have grappled with these and other instances of cooperation in the animal world. Jeffrey Stevens and his colleagues (Stevens, Cushman, & Hauser, 2005) have distinguished two reliable explanations of cooperative behaviour in animals and humans:

- Mutualism – cooperative behaviour benefits the cooperator as well as others; a defector will do worse than a cooperator.

- Kin selection – those who cooperate are biased towards blood relatives because it helps propagate their own genes; the lack of direct benefit to the cooperator indicates *altruism*.

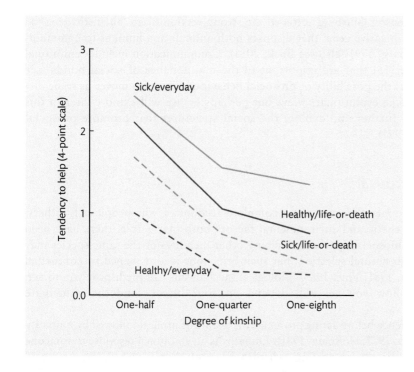

Figure 13.1 Helping kin who are either healthy or sick: life-or-death versus everyday situations

- There is an interaction between health, kinship and willingness to help.

- Participants chose between people who varied in kinship in two conditions: healthy versus sick individuals, and giving help in a situation that was life-or-death versus merely 'everyday'.

- They were generally more willing to help closer kin than more distant kin.

- They also preferred to help people who were sick rather than healthy in an everyday situation, but who were healthy rather than sick in a perilous situation.

Source: Burnstein, Crandall and Kitayama (1994).

Kin selection is the obvious candidate as an evolutionary account of human altruism. Is there any such evidence? Eugene Burnstein and his colleagues (Burnstein, Crandall, & Kitayama, 1994) studied 'decision rules' for being altruistic that might reflect genetic overlap between persons. Participants, who rated how likely they would be to help others in several situations (see Figure 13.1), favoured the sick over the healthy in everyday situations but favoured the healthy over the sick in life-or-death situations. They took more account of kinship in everyday situations and the healthy in life-or-death situations. Finally, people were more likely to assist the very young or the very old in everyday situations, but under famine conditions, people prefer to help 10-year-olds or 18-year-olds rather than infants or older people. These data are consistent with the idea that close kin will get crucial help when 'the chips are down'. (Consider Alex's decision in the second 'What do *you* think?' question.)

The idea that we are 'wired' to help others, as well as kin, has generated substantial debate: for example, between psychologists and sociobiologists (Vine, 1983). Few social psychologists accept an exclusively evolutionary explanation of human prosocial behaviour, and they accept evolutionary explanations only to a limited extent. The philosopher Derek Turner asked the question, 'Is altruism an anomaly?' We can ask psychological questions about people's motives for helping others and philosophical questions also about moral obligations to do so. We can also ask biological questions about what we have inherited, but one concept is a sticking point – *fitness altruism*: 'How could natural selection ever smile upon organisms that sacrifice their own reproductive fitness for another's benefit?' (Turner, 2005, p. 317). If I adopt a child who is not kin, is that a strong case for fitness altruism? If so, what are its genetic mechanisms and how did they evolve?

A problem with evolutionary theory as a sole explanation of altruism is the lack of convincing human evidence. For example, a case such as the failure to help Kitty Genovese is difficult to explain at a biological level. Another criticism is the scant attention afforded by evolutionary theorists to the work of social learning theorists, in particular to the role of modelling (see the subsection 'Learning to be helpful').

Ross Buck and Benson Ginsburg softened the strong version of an 'altruistic gene' by proposing a 'communicative gene' that disposes both animals and humans to communicate (Buck & Ginsburg, 1991; also see Buck, 2011). Communication includes emotional signals (see **Chapter 15**) that are important in the maintenance of social bonds (see **Chapter 14**) and thus the possibility of prosocial behaviour. This idea moves us some distance from an extreme evolutionary view, but perhaps, as we will explore later in this chapter, we can go further and explore the social structures that promote prosocial behaviour (Darley, 1991).

Empathy and arousal

On its own, evolutionary theory is not a complete account of why people help others. However, because genetic and environmental factors both play a role, there have been attempts to forge a biosocial approach. Helping other members of the same species may have evolved through natural selection, but such behaviour is also shaped by contextual influences (Hoffman, 1981; Vine, 1983). Biological mechanisms can predispose you to act; but if, when and how you act will depend on your history and the immediate circumstances.

Empathy
Ability to feel another person's experiences; identifying with and experiencing another person's emotions, thoughts and attitudes.

A common experience before acting prosocially is a state of arousal followed by **empathy** (Gaertner & Dovidio, 1977; Hoffman, 1981). Empathy is an emotional response to someone else's distress, a reaction to witnessing a disturbing event. Adults and children respond empathically to signs that a person is troubled, which implies that watching someone suffer is unpleasant. Have you ever looked away when a film shows someone being tortured? Censors forewarn us if a film depicts scenes of violence, and most of us have been in an audience when a few tears are not far away. Even infants one or two days old can respond to the distress of another infant (Sagi & Hoffman, 1976; Simner, 1971). In real life, people often fail to act prosocially because they are actively engaged in *avoiding* empathy (Shaw, Batson, & Todd, 1994). However, when we really do help, are we merely trying to reduce our own discomfort?

The extra ingredient is empathy, an ability to identify with someone else's experiences, particularly their feelings (Krebs, 1975). Empathy is related to perspective taking, being able to see the world through others' eyes, but it is not the same thing. Generally speaking, empathy is affect- and feeling-based (I feel your pain), whereas perspective taking is cognition-based (I see your pain) (e.g. Batson, Early, & Salvarani, 1997; Maner, Luce, Neuberg, Cialdini, Brown, & Sagarin, 2002; see 'Labelling the arousal' in Box 13.2).

Bystander-calculus model
In attending to an emergency, the bystander calculates the perceived costs and benefits of providing help compared with those associated with not helping.

Empathy costs of not helping
Piliavin's view that failing to help can cause distress to a bystander who empathises with a victim's plight.

Personal costs of not helping
Piliavin's view that not helping a victim in distress can be costly to a bystander (e.g. experiencing blame).

Calculating whether to help

The **bystander-calculus model** of helping involves body and mind, a mixture of physiological processes and cognitive processes. According to sociologist Jane Piliavin, when we think someone is in trouble, we work our way through three stages or sets of calculations before we respond (Piliavin, Piliavin, Dovidio, Gaertner, & Clark, 1981). First, we are physiologically aroused by another's distress. Second, we label this arousal as an emotion. Third, we evaluate the consequences of helping. See Box 13.2.

Interestingly, *not* helping can also involve costs. Piliavin distinguished between **empathy costs of not helping** and **personal costs of not helping**. A critical factor is the relationship between the bystander and the victim. We have already seen that empathic concern is one motive for helping a distressed person; conversely, not helping when you feel empathic concern results in empathy costs (e.g. anxiety) in response to the other's plight. Thus, the clarity of the emergency, its severity and the closeness of the bystander to the victim will increase

Box 13.2 Research highlight
Steps in the bystander-calculus model

There are three steps in Jane Piliavin's bystander-calculus model of helping:

1 Physiological arousal

Our first reaction to someone in distress is physiological, an empathic response. The greater the arousal, the greater the chance that we will help. How quickly we react is related to the level of our body's response: e.g. the quicker our heartbeat, the quicker we respond (Gaertner & Dovidio, 1977). There is also a cognitive aspect. As the victim's plight becomes clearer and more severe, our physiological arousal increases.

2 Labelling the arousal

Being aroused is one thing, but feeling a specific emotion (fear, anger, love) is another. Generally, arousal does not automatically produce specific emotions; people's cognitions or thoughts about the arousal play a critical role in determining the nature of the emotions they feel (e.g. Parkinson & Manstead, 1992). Sometimes our response is also to feel distressed. Dan Batson suggested that situational cues often trigger another set of responses, *empathic concern* (Batson & Coke, 1981), and that when bystanders believe they are similar to a victim, they are more likely to experience empathic concern.

3 Evaluating the consequences

Finally, bystanders evaluate the consequences of acting before they help a victim, choosing an action that will reduce their personal distress at the lowest cost (a cost-benefit analysis is also used in a social exchange approach to close relationships; see **Chapter 10**). The main costs of helping are time and effort: the greater these costs, the less likely that a bystander will help (Darley & Batson, 1973).

---

the costs of not helping. Anything that increases the impact of the victim's state on the bystander will increase empathy costs if one does not give help.

Personal costs of not helping are many and varied, such as public censure or self-blame. Certain characteristics of the person in distress also affect the costs of not helping: for instance, the greater the victim's need for help, the greater the costs of not helping (Piliavin, Piliavin, Dovidio, Gaertner, & Clark, 1981). If you believe that a victim might die if you do not help, the personal costs are likely to be high. If a tramp in the street asked you for money to buy alcohol, the personal costs of refusing might not be high; but if the request was for money for food or medicine, the costs might be quite high.

Other things being equal, the more similar the victim is to the bystander, the more likely the bystander is to help (Krebs, 1975). Similarity causes greater physiological arousal in bystanders and thus greater empathy costs of not helping. Similar victims may also be friends, for whom the costs of not helping would be high. Recall the evolutionary view that preservation of our genes is the basis of protecting our kin. The Piliavin model would simply note the high level of similarity between bystander and victim, thereby increasing the cost of not helping to an excruciating level. Think of the agony if you did not try to enter a blazing house to rescue your own child.

Returning to the Genovese case, the bystander-calculus model suggests that, although the onlookers would have been aroused and felt personal distress and empathic concern, the empathy costs and personal costs were not sufficient. Personal costs, in particular, may have deterred people from intervening. What if they got killed themselves? The costs of not helping could be either high or low, depending on how people interpreted the situation: for example, was it merely a heated marital spat? Situational influences are significantly involved when adults decide whether to help in an emergency – a point that has been confirmed by Latané and Darley's step-by-step decision approach, which we discuss later in this chapter.

Empathy and altruism

According to the bystander-calculus model, people intervene in an emergency because they find it unpleasantly arousing and they seek relief (see reviews by Batson & Oleson, 1991; Dovidio, Piliavin, Gaertner, Schroeder, & Clark, 1991). This suggests that 'altruism' is a misnomer because it is really motivated by self-interest, or egoism. Piliavin and Charng (1990, p. 27) are more optimistic:

> There appears to be a 'paradigm' shift away from [an] earlier position that behaviour that appears to be altruistic must, under close scrutiny, be revealed as reflecting egoistic motives. Rather, theory and data now being advanced are more compatible with the view that true altruism – acting with the goal of benefiting another – does exist and is part of human nature.

Batson and his colleagues (Batson, Duncan, Ackerman, Buckley, & Birch, 1981) suggest that an act is truly altruistic only if people seek to help even when they will no longer be troubled by observing the suffering of another person (e.g. turning back to help after passing a stranded motorist). This invites a different perspective on the Genovese case. The bystanders felt disturbed, but not enough to act: perhaps they could not identify with the victim. Hans-Werner Bierhoff and Elke Rohmann (2004) concur that true altruism is most likely to emerge in situations where the potential helper can easily not help – just quietly escape or slip away.

Perspective taking

According to Patricia Oswald (1996) empathy requires *perspective taking* – we need to be able to experience the world from someone else's perspective. Furthermore, perspective taking, increased empathy and increased helping all seem to go together (Maner, Luce, Neuberg, Cialdini, Brown, & Sagarin, 2002). According to Jean Decety and Klaus Lamm (2006), the capacity to take the perspective of and empathise with another has evolutionary

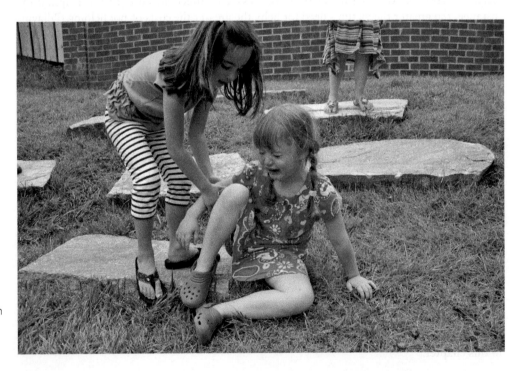

An alarm bell
An infant will respond with empathetic concern to another's distress signals, especially to those of another infant.

significance. Some non-human primates respond to the feelings of others, but humans can both feel and act intentionally on behalf of others. It is this capacity that may account for the importance of **empathic concern** in altruism.

Batson and his colleagues (Batson, Early, & Salvarini, 1997; Batson, Van Lange, Ahmad, & Lishner, 2003) make an important distinction concerning perspective taking: between appreciating how another person feels and actually feeling the other person's feelings as your own. Different kinds of empathy lead to different kinds of motivation to help. Actively imagining how *another* feels produces empathy, which leads to altruistic motivation. However, actively imagining how *you* would feel produces empathy, but it also produces self-oriented distress, and involves a mix of altruism and egoism. Perhaps people who have experienced something stressful will empathise more with a person who is in a similar situation. For example, people who have been homeless or extremely ill may empathise more with a person in the same condition.

Are women more empathic than men? The answer seems generally to be yes (Klein & Hodges, 2001). In one study, for example, participants read a same-sex adolescent's description of a stressful life event, such as being the object of ridicule and teasing because of acne, or being betrayed and rejected (Batson, Sympson, Hindman, Decruz, Todd, Weeks, et al., 1996). Women reported more empathy with a same-sex teenager when they had had similar experiences during their adolescence, an effect not found with men (see Figure 13.2). Batson accounted for this sex difference in terms of socialisation: women value interdependence and are more other-oriented, while men value independence and are more self-oriented. In another study by Batson (Batson, Charng, Orr, & Rowland, 2002), students were induced to feel empathy towards a convicted drug addict and then to generalise their reaction by voting for allocating university funds (not their own money, of course!) to help other drug addicts. In this instance, empathy for a person from a stigmatised group led to action and also to attitude change (attitude change is also discussed in **Chapter 6**).

Empathy is a vital ingredient in altruism – it is empathy that 'directs' us to respond to the needs of another. From a review of the literature, De Waal (2008) writes: 'Evidence is

Empathic concern
An element in Batson's theory of helping behaviour. In contrast to personal distress (which may lead us to flee from the situation), it includes feelings of warmth, being soft-hearted and having compassion for a person in need.

Figure 13.2 Difference between women and men in empathising with a distressed teenager

● We might expect that people with prior experience of a stressful situation would empathise more with a same-sex teenager undergoing that same experience.

● In this study, only women with prior experience showed an increase in empathy.

Source: Based on Batson et al. (1996).

accumulating that this mechanism is phylogenetically ancient, probably as old as mammals and birds' (p. 279). Lower forms, then, can recognise an emotional display in a conspecific. However, in higher animals, this capacity to share an emotional state has evolved into actual concern for a conspecific and ultimately into perspective-taking.

Empathy, emotions and motivation

Empathic concern invokes various emotions: sympathy, tenderness, perhaps feelings of sadness or distress for another – and *compassion* (Batson, Eklund, Chermok, Hoyt, & Ortis, 2007). Goetz and her colleagues distinguish empathy from compassion, defining the latter as 'the feeling that arises in witnessing another's suffering and that motivates a subsequent desire to help' (Goetz, Keltner, & Simon-Thomas, 2010, p. 351). Generally speaking, compassion can be defined as a distinct emotion (Keltner & Lerner, 2010) – an emotion that can be linked to *compassionate love* that some feel for close others and even for humanity (Berscheid, 2010; Sprecher & Fehr, 2005; also see discussion of close relationships in **Chapter 14**). In contrast, empathy is a vicarious emotion triggered by the plight of others.

Learning to be helpful

A different explanation of helping is that prosocial behaviour is intricately bound with becoming socialised: it is learned, not innate. The processes of classical conditioning, instrumental conditioning and observational learning all contribute to being prosocial. This learning theory perspective on prosocial behaviour has recently been pursued particularly strongly within developmental and educational psychology – for example, there is research showing how prosocial behaviour is acquired in childhood (Eisenberg, Guthrie, Murphy, Shepard, Cumberland, & Carlo, 1999).

Childhood is a critical period for learning. Carolyn Zahn-Waxler has studied the development of emotions in children, concluding that how we respond to distress in others is connected to the way we learn to share, help and provide comfort, and that these patterns emerge between the ages of 1 and 2 (Zahn-Waxler, Radke-Yarrow, Wagner, & Chapman, 1992). There are several ways in which these responses can be learnt:

- *Giving instructions.* In her studies of parenting, Joan Grusec found that simply telling children to be helpful to others actually works (Grusec, Kuczynski, Rushton, & Simutis, 1978). Telling a child what is appropriate establishes an expectation and a later guide for action. However, preaching about being good is of doubtful value unless a fairly strong form is used (Rice & Grusec, 1975). Furthermore, telling children to be generous if the 'preacher' behaves inconsistently is pointless: 'do as I say, not as I do' does not work. Grusec reported that when an adult acted selfishly but urged children to be generous, the children were actually less generous.

- *Using reinforcement.* Behaviour that is rewarded is more likely to be repeated. When young children are rewarded for offering to help, they are more likely to offer help again later. Similarly, if they are not rewarded, they are less likely to offer help again (Grusec, 1991). (See Figure 13.3 for work by Rushton on reinforcement and helping.)

- *Exposure to models.* In his review of factors that influence children to give help, J. Philippe Rushton (1976) concluded that reinforcement is effective in shaping behaviour, but **modelling** is even more effective. Watching someone else helping another is a powerful form of learning. Take the case of young Johnny who first helps his mummy to carry some shopping into the house and then wants to help in putting it away, and then cleans up his bedroom. Well, maybe not the last bit!

Modelling
Tendency for a person to reproduce the actions, attitudes and emotional responses exhibited by a real-life or symbolic model. Also called *observational learning.*

Learning to be helpful through observation is a particular case of a wider process of observational learning that also accounts for how people learn attitudes (**Chapter 5**) and how people learn to act aggressively (**Chapter 12**). In older studies of the effects of viewing

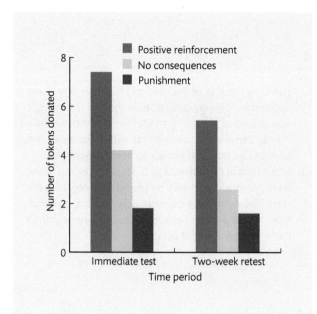

Figure 13.3 The effects of reward and punishment on children's willingness to behave generously

- Boys aged 8–11 years watched an adult who played a game to win tokens.

- Then the adult generously donated some by putting them in a bowl to be given later to a child pictured in a poster, a boy who was 'poor little Bobby, who had no Mummy or Daddy to look after him'.

- Next, the child played the game. In one condition, the adult used verbal reinforcers as rewards or punishments for behaving generously (e.g. either 'good for you', or 'that's kind of silly . . . now you will have fewer tokens for yourself').

- Both tactics had strong effects on how the boys behaved, immediately and after a two-week interval.

- While this study employed reinforcement principles, it clearly also featured the effects of watching a model.

Source: Based on Rushton and Teachman (1978).

Learning to be prosocial
Young children soon learn the value of sharing and helping one another.

prosocial behaviour on television, the general finding has been that children's *attitudes* towards prosocial behaviour are improved (Coates, Pusser, & Goodman, 1976; Rushton, 1979). However, the effect on prosocial behaviour was weak and even weaker as time passed.

Children who behave prosocially are also able to tolerate a delay in gratification (Long & Lerner, 1974) and are more popular with their peers (Dekovic & Janssens, 1992). There are also close developmental links between prosocial skills, coping and social competence (Eisenberg, Fabes, Karbon, Murphy, Wosinski, Polazzi, et al., 1996), which suggests an overall socialisation process into adulthood. We can take some comfort that it is never too late – adults can also be influenced by a helpful model. Check the example in Box 13.3.

Box 13.3 Research highlight
The case of the helpful motorist: The role of modelling

A model showing us how to perform a helpful act reminds us that helping is appropriate, increases our confidence in being able to help and gives us information about the consequences of helping others (Rushton, 1980).

In a study of the *modelling effect*, James Bryan and Mary Test (1967) investigated whether a model would influence the number of people who might stop to help a woman change a car tyre. There were two conditions:

1 In the experimental condition, motorists first passed a woman whose car had a flat tyre; another car had pulled to the side of the road and the male driver was apparently helping her to change the tyre. This condition provided a helping model for participants who shortly came upon another car with a flat tyre. This time, the woman was alone and needed assistance.

2 In the control condition, only the second car and driver were present; there was no model. The results were clear. The motorists who were exposed to a prosocial model were over 50 per cent more likely to help than those in the no-model condition.

Social learning theory
The view championed by Bandura that human social behaviour is not innate but learnt from appropriate models.

When a person observes a model and behaves in kind, is this just a matter of mechanical imitation? Research by Albert Bandura (1973) suggests otherwise (also see **Chapter 12**). According to social learning theory, it is the knowledge of what happens to the model that determines whether or not the observer will help. As with direct learning, a positive outcome increases a model's effectiveness in influencing the observer to help, while a negative outcome decreases the model's effectiveness. Harvey Hornstein (1970) conducted an experiment where people observed a model returning a lost wallet. The model either appeared pleased to be able to help, appeared displeased at the bother of having to help or showed no strong reaction. Later, the participant came across another 'lost' wallet. Those who had observed the pleasant consequences helped the most; those who observed the unpleasant consequences helped the least. Observing the outcomes for another person is called learning by vicarious experience (also see **Chapter 12**); it can increase the prevalence of both selfish and selfless behaviour (Midlarsky & Bryan, 1972).

Learning by vicarious experience
Acquiring a behaviour after observing that another person was rewarded for it.

Game playing and the media

Obvious as it may seem, children can profit from a simple education in moral reasoning. Lawrence Rosenkoetter (1999) found that children who watched television comedies that included a moral lesson engaged more frequently in prosocial behaviour than children who did not, provided they understood the principle involved. Gentile and his colleagues investigated the effects of playing video games featuring prosocial acts on prosocial behaviour measured by questionnaires (Gentile, Anderson, Yukawa, Ihori, Saleem, et al., 2009). In a series of three developmental studies, three age groups of Singaporeans, Americans and Japanese played a variety of both prosocial and violent video games. A central finding was that when the video content was prosocial, the participants acted in more helpful ways, but when it was violent, they acted in more hurtful ways. These effects were consistent across cultures and age groups.

The effects of the media can be broadened to include music. For example, Tobias Greitmeyer (2009) found that both German and British participants who listened to prosocial songs were more willing to offer help to other people, without request. Greitmeyer and Osswald (2010) have reported that viewing prosocial videos increased the rate of helping behaviour; and further, these videos made prosocial cognitions more accessible. Consequently, they argued that the General Aggression Model (GAM) could be developed into a General Learning Model (GLM), as proposed by Katherine Buckley and Craig Anderson (2006). (See how the GAM works in **Chapter 12, Figure 12.8.**)

The impact of attribution

People make causal attributions for helping. To continue being helpful on more than one occasion requires a person to internalise the idea of 'being helpful' (see self-perception theory, **Chapter 4**). Helpfulness can then be a guide in the future when helping is an option. A self-attribution can be even more powerful than reinforcement for learning helping behaviour: young children who were told they were 'helpful people' donated more tokens to a needy child than those who were reinforced with verbal praise, and this effect persisted over time (Grusec & Redler, 1980). Indeed, Perry and his colleagues found that children may feel bad and experience self-criticism when they fail to live up to the standards implied by their own attributions (Perry, Perry, Bussey, English, & Arnold, 1980).

If we are wondering whether to offer help to someone in need, we usually try to figure out who or what this person might be. Sometimes we may even blame an innocent victim for their plight. One reason why we might do this is to make the world seem like a just place where bad things happen to bad people and good things to good people – the **just-world hypothesis** (Furnham, 2003; Lerner & Miller, 1978; see **Chapter 3**). People are responsible for their own plight and get what they deserve, and since we tend to assume that we are good people, we can then breathe a sigh of relief that nothing bad will happen to us.

So, someone who has an accident may have deserved it (Bulman & Wortman, 1977). Therefore, if some victims deserve their fate, we can think 'Good, they had that coming to them!' and not help them. Some witnesses in the Kitty Genovese case may have believed that it was her fault for being out so late – a familiar response to many crimes. Take another rather disturbing example: perhaps a rape victim 'deserved' what happened because her clothing was too tight or revealing? Accepting that the world must necessarily be a just place begins in childhood and is a learnt attribution.

Fortunately, most of us respond to evidence that suffering is undeserved. Accepting this undermines the power of belief in a just world and allows justice to be done. A necessary precondition of actually helping is to believe that the help will be effective. Miller (1977) isolated two factors that can convince a would-be helper: (1) the victim is a special case rather than one of many, and (2) the need is temporary rather than persisting. Each of these allows us to decide that giving aid 'right now' will be effective.

Invoking this line of reasoning, Peter Warren and Iain Walker (1991) showed that if the needs of a person in distress can be specified, others can use this information to determine if giving help is justified. In a field study of more than 2,500 recipients, a letter mail-out solicited donations for a refugee family from Sudan. Cover letters with slightly different wording were used. More donations were recorded when the letter highlighted that: (1) the donation was restricted to this particular family rather than being extended to other people in Sudan; and (2) the family's need was only short term. In short, the case was just and action would be effective.

Just-world hypothesis
According to Lerner and Miller, people need to believe that the world is a just place where they get what they deserve. As evidence of undeserved suffering undermines this belief, people may conclude that victims deserve their fate.

The bystander effect

We noted earlier that social psychologists were curious and concerned about the lack of involvement of witnesses and bystanders during the Kitty Genovese murder. The initial frenzy of research that followed was aimed at discovering when people would help in an emergency. Subsequently, the question broadened beyond emergencies to include prosocial contexts more generally: when will people help in non-emergencies by performing such deeds as giving money, donating blood or contributing their time or effort? The emphasis is on situational factors that affect **bystander intervention** in real-life situations in the real world, rather than on the origins or learning of helping behaviour.

Perhaps the most influential and thoroughly studied factor that affects prosocial behaviour is whether the potential helper is alone or in the company of others. What we now

Bystander intervention
This occurs when an individual breaks out of the role of a bystander and helps another person in an emergency.

Bystander effect
People are less likely to help in an emergency when they are with others than when alone. The greater the number, the less likely it is that anyone will help.

know is that a lone bystander is more likely to help than any of several bystanders, a phenomenon known as the **bystander effect**. (Apply this to account for Lily's bravery in the third 'What do *you* think?' question.) Unlike Piliavin's account of helping based on empathy discussed earlier, the model suggested by Latané and Darley (1970) features a decision-making process based on how other people respond.

Latané and Darley's cognitive model

Stemming directly from the wide public discussion and concern about the Genovese case, Bibb Latané and John Darley began a programme of research (Darley & Latané, 1968), now considered a classic in social psychology. Surely, these researchers asked, empathy for another's suffering, or at the very least a sense of civic responsibility, should lead to an intervention in a situation of danger? Furthermore, where several bystanders are present, there should be a correspondingly greater probability that someone will help. Consider first the elements of an **emergency situation**:

Emergency situation
Often involves an unusual event, can vary in nature, is unplanned and requires a quick response.

- It can involve danger, for person or property.
- It is an unusual event, rarely encountered by the ordinary person.
- It can differ widely in nature, from a bank on fire to a pedestrian being mugged.
- It is not foreseen, so that prior planning of how to cope is improbable.
- It requires instant action, so that leisurely consideration of options is not feasible.

At this juncture, note a similarity between the nature of an emergency and the autokinetic paradigm used by Sherif (e.g. Sherif, 1935) to study the development of social norms (see **Chapters 7 and 8**). Both involve uncertainty, ambiguity and a lack of structure; both require us to make a judgement or decision; and in both cases, we are likely to look to others for guidance on how to think and act. So, a core prediction about an emergency is that people will react quite differently depending on whether others are present or absent, and on how those others act.

Latané and Darley noted that it would be easy simply to label the failure to help a victim in an emergency as apathy – an uncaring response to the problems of others. However, they reasoned that the apparent lack of concern shown by the witnesses in the Genovese case could conceal other processes. An early finding was that failure to help occurred more often when the size of the group of witnesses increased. Latané and Darley's cognitive model of bystander intervention proposes that whether a person helps depends on the outcomes of a series of decisions. At any point along this path, a decision could be made that would terminate helping behaviour. The steps in this model are described in Box 13.4, and the decision process is illustrated in Figure 13.4. (Reflect now on your likely thought processes in the fourth 'What do *you* think?' question.) A series of experiments is outlined in this section to illustrate how this model works.

'Where there's smoke there's fire'

Latané and Darley (1970) invited male students to an interview room to discuss some of the problems involved in life at a large university. While the students were completing a preliminary questionnaire, smoke began to pour in from a wall vent. This continued for six minutes until the room was full of smoke. Participants were either alone, with two other participants they did not know, or with two confederates who completely ignored the smoke. What would the participants do, and how long would they take to do it? The researchers wondered if people in such situations look to others as a guide. This is exactly what happened. Participants who were alone were more likely to report the smoke than were those with other strangers. While 75 per cent of the participants who were alone took positive action, only 38 per cent of the two-stranger groups intervened. Participants in the presence of two

Box 13.4 Research classic
Steps in Latané and Darley's cognitive model

Deciding whether to help

1 Do we even notice an event where helping may be required, such as an accident?

2 How do we interpret the event? We are most likely to define a situation as an emergency, and most likely to help, when we believe that the victim's condition is serious and is about to deteriorate rapidly. Lance Shotland and Ted Huston (1979) found that people were more likely to help in emergencies (e.g. someone needs an insulin shot for diabetes) than in non-emergencies (e.g. needing some allergy medicine). Verbal distress cues (e.g. screaming) are particularly effective and increase the likelihood of bystander intervention: the act of screaming can lead to receiving help 75 per cent or more of the time. Bystander apathy is markedly

reduced once people interpret a situation as an emergency (Clark & Word, 1974; Gaertner & Dovidio, 1977).

3 Do we accept personal responsibility for helping? Sometimes a person witnessing an emergency knows that there are other onlookers but cannot see their reactions. This was clearly the case in the Genovese incident. Sometimes the decision to assume responsibility is determined by how competent the bystander feels in the particular situation. For both steps 2 and 3, the influence of other people is clearly a determining factor.

4 What do we decide to do?

5 Is help given? If we doubt whether the situation is an emergency, or if we do not know what to do if it is, the way others behave can influence how we respond.

Source: Based on Darley and Latané (1968).

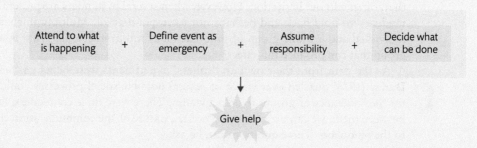

Figure 13.4 Deciding whether or not to help, according to Latané and Darley's cognitive model
Source: Based on data from Latané and Darley (1970).

passive confederates were even less likely to report the situation, taking action only 10 per cent of the time!

Latané and Darley suggested that the presence of others can inhibit people from responding to an emergency: the more people, the slower the response. Even worse, many of the people who did not respond were persuaded that if others were passive, there was no emergency. Some later reported that there was no danger from the smoke. In a real emergency, this could easily have proved fatal.

'A lady in distress'

Latané and Rodin (1969) replicated these results, extending the analysis to situations where others might be in danger. Male participants were alone or in pairs filling out a questionnaire and heard a woman in another room struggle to open a filing cabinet. They then heard a loud crash, followed by a cry of pain, and moans and groans. Helping occurred 70 per cent of the time among participants who were alone but only 40 per cent of the time among those in pairs. The presence of a passive confederate suggested that the situation was not critical, and helping plunged to 7 per cent. A refinement was added. Pairs of friends helped more often – 70 per cent of the time.

'He's having a fit'

Must bystanders be physically present to lessen the chance of helping? Darley and Latané (1968) devised an experiment where students could communicate with each other only via microphones while in separate cubicles. The students believed that the group consisted of two people (self and a victim), four people or six people. The 'victim' told the others over the intercom system that he was epileptic. Later he was heard to choke and gasp, apparently having a seizure, and then became quiet. Would the number of presumed bystanders who might help increase the time it took a participant to help?

The results showed that the more 'bystanders' an individual thought were present, the less likely they were to help. Before the end of the fit, the percentage of participants who helped was: 85 when alone, 62 when they thought that were two others present and 31 when they thought there were four others present. Things improved with time – after six minutes had elapsed, the respective percentages were 100, 81 and 62.

Processes contributing to bystander apathy

Let us take stock. To respond to an emergency, people must stop whatever they are doing and engage in some unusual, unexpected behaviour. Lone bystanders will usually do just that, often without hesitation. However, when several bystanders are present, there is a clear tendency to hold back and perhaps not to respond at all. Multiply this effect across each individual and a whole group of onlookers may fail to intervene. What is it, then, about a group that can produce this effect?

As the data from their own and others' experiments were being gathered, Latané and Darley (1976) puzzled over which of several possible social processes could be responsible for the reluctance of groups to help a victim. There were three contenders. In distinguishing between them, we can use the analogy of the nature of the communication channel available to the onlookers. Three questions can be asked:

1 Is the individual aware that others are present?
2 Can the individual actually see or hear the others and be aware of how they are reacting?
3 Can these others monitor the behaviour of the individual?

Each of the following processes is distinctive in terms of how these questions are answered:

Diffusion of responsibility
Tendency of an individual to assume that others will take responsibility (as a result, no one does). This is a hypothesised cause of the bystander effect.

Fear of social blunders
The dread of acting inappropriately or of making a foolish mistake witnessed by others. The desire to avoid ridicule inhibits effective responses to an emergency by members of a group.

- **Diffusion of responsibility.** Think back to social loafing (discussed in **Chapter 8**), where a person who is part of a group often offloads responsibility for action to others. In the case of an emergency, the presence of other onlookers provides the opportunity to transfer responsibility for acting, or not acting, to them. The communication channel does not imply that the individual can be seen by the others or can see them. It is necessary only that they be available, somewhere, for action. People who are alone are most likely to help a victim because they believe they carry the entire responsibility for action. If they do not act, nobody else will. Ironically, the presence of just one other witness allows diffusion of responsibility to operate among all present.

- *Audience inhibition.* Other onlookers can make people self-conscious about taking action; people do not want to appear foolish by overreacting. In the context of prosocial behaviour, this process is sometimes referred to as a **fear of social blunders**. Have you felt a dread of being laughed at for misunderstanding little crises involving others? What if it is not as it seems? What if someone is playing a joke? Am I being set-up for a *YouTube*

Diffusion of responsibility
A heart-wrenching scene – a homeless woman stands in flood waters in Venice, begging, unsuccessfully, from a crowd of pedestrians hurrying by.

spoof? The communication channel implies that the others can see or hear the individual, but it is not necessary that they can be seen.

- *Social influence*. Other onlookers provide a model for action. If they are passive and unworried, the situation may seem less serious. The communication channel implies that the individual can see the others, but not vice versa.

The three-in-one experiment

We are now ready to consider the most complicated of Latané and Darley's experiments, designed specifically to detect the operation of each of the three processes just outlined. By the use of TV monitors and cameras, participants were induced to believe that they were in one of four conditions with respect to other onlookers. They could (1) see and be seen; (2) see, but not be seen; (3) not see, but be seen; or (4) neither see nor be seen. This complexity was necessary to allow for the consequences of sequentially adding social influence and audience inhibition effects to that of diffusion of responsibility.

We should note here that diffusion of responsibility must always be involved if a bystander is, or is thought to be, present at the moment of the emergency. However, the additive effect of another process can be assessed and then compared with the effect of diffusion acting on its own. You will get a good idea of how this was done by studying Box 13.5.

Limits to the bystander effect

The presence of bystanders generally reduces the chance of an individual offering help in an emergency. However, variations in the composition of the bystanders can diminish failure to respond.

Bystanders who are strangers to each other inhibit helping even more because communication between them is slower. When bystanders are known to each other, there is much less inhibition of prosocial behaviour than in a group of strangers (Latané & Rodin, 1969; Rutkowski, Gruder, & Romer, 1983). However, Jody Gottlieb and Charles Carver (1980) showed that even among strangers, inhibition is reduced if they know that there will be an opportunity to interact later and possibly explain their actions. Overall, the bystander effect is strongest when the bystanders are anonymous strangers who do not expect to meet one another again, which was most likely the situation in the Genovese case. Catherine Christy and Harrison Voigt (1994) found that bystander apathy is reduced if the victim is an acquaintance, friend or relative, or is a child being abused in a public place.

The studies above have this much in common: bystanders who are strangers and who are present by chance at an emergency generally do not constitute a group – friends do. Mark

Levine and his colleagues have amplified this point in several experiments. Even when bystanders are strangers, they may still help provided they share a self-relevant social category membership and associated social identity (Levine & Manning, 2013). For example, if the victim is female and the bystanders are male, gender becomes a salient category, males are now a group, and the sex-role stereotype of the chivalrous male can 'spring into action' (Levine & Crowther, 2008). The key point is that normative expectations about how to respond in a particular situation come into play if a social identity is primed by the context. In the absence of a salient identity to guide appropriate action, people are very much on their own to figure out what to do (also see the discussion of collective behaviour in **Chapter 11**).

Box 13.5 Research classic
The three-in-one experiment: A shocking experience

Students who had agreed to take part in a study of 'repression' found that their task was to rate whether the way in which a target person responded to verbal stimuli indicated whether they had received an electric shock or not. When certain words were presented, the target person would receive a shock from the experimenter. The participant would watch this on closed-circuit television in another room and judge when shocks had been delivered by studying the target person's overall behaviour. The experiment was carried out at night in a deserted building at Princeton University. Participants were to work in pairs (except in the Alone condition), although in fact the second rater in each case was a confederate of the experimenter.

Each pair of participants was initially taken to a control room, where there was an antiquated shock generator. Commenting on it, the experimenter said that the parts were from army surplus and were not reliable. In front of the generator was a chair, with a TV camera pointing at it. The experimenter then noted that the target person was late and that time could be saved by filling in a background questionnaire. The participants were ushered to their individual cubicles, each of which contained two TV monitors and a camera. Monitor 1 was operating and showed the control room they had just left, with the shock generator in clear view. The experimenter apologised for the presence of monitor 2 and the camera, saying they belonged to another, absent, staff member and could not be touched. Both items were operating. This extra, supposedly superfluous, equipment provided the basis for several experimental conditions. Monitor 2 could show the neighbour in the next cubicle, and the camera could show the participant to the neighbour. There were five conditions:

1 *Alone.* This is a baseline condition where no other person is present with the real participant. The camera in the real participant's room is pointing at the ceiling,

and monitor 2 shows a shot of the ceiling of the second cubicle but no sign of anybody else.

2 *Diffusion of responsibility.* As in the remaining conditions, there are two people, but no communication. Monitor 2 shows only the ceiling of the other cubicle (where its camera is pointing). The camera in the real participant's room is pointing at the ceiling. It is different from the 'alone' condition, however, as the participant knows that a bystander is present.

3 *Diffusion plus social influence.* The participant sees the other's response, but not vice versa. One camera is trained on someone, in this case the bystander. The confederate can be seen working on a questionnaire on monitor 2.

4 *Diffusion plus audience inhibition.* The other sees the participant's response, but not vice versa. One camera is trained on someone, in this case the participant. Although the bystander cannot be seen, presumably the participant can.

5 *Diffusion plus social influence plus audience inhibition.* The two people see each other. Both cameras are trained on them, and they can be seen on the respective monitors.

The emergency was created when the experimenter left the participant in the cubicle and returned to the control room to adjust the shock generator, visible on monitor 1. On the screen, the experimenter could be seen to pick up some wires. They must not have been the right wires, because the experimenter screamed, jumped in the air, threw himself against the wall, and fell to the floor out of camera range with his feet sticking up. About fifteen seconds later he began to moan softly, and he continued until help was received or for about six minutes (Latané & Darley, 1976, p. 327).

What will the real participant do in each condition? See the results in Figure 13.5.

Figure 13.5 The effects of three processes on willingness to help a victim

- The graph shows the cumulative number of participants (vertical axis) who helped the prostrate experimenter as time went by, measured in seconds (horizontal axis).
- There were four experimental conditions, distinguishing between the Alone condition and three sets of Bystander conditions.
- The results were combined for two of these conditions (diffusion of responsibility plus either audience inhibition or social influence); their effects did not differ and both involved one-way communication.
- As the degree of communication increased, helping decreased: (a) simple diffusion of responsibility (no communication) reduced helping; (b) this declined further when either social influence or audience inhibition was added (one-way communication); (c) when all three processes operated (two-way communication), the least help was given.

Source: Based on data from Latané and Darley (1976).

The person in the equation

With so many situational factors affecting prosocial behaviour, we might wonder if aspects of the person have much impact. Let us re-establish some balance by observing the psychological maxim that 'behaviour is a product of the person and the environment'.

Are there personal characteristics that are relatively independent of the situation? Research has concentrated on two areas: transitory psychological states and personality characteristics. The former includes passing moods and feelings, which all of us may experience; the latter implies relatively permanent attributes.

Mood states

We have all experienced days where things seem to go perfectly and others when things go totally wrong, and we know that this can affect how we interact with other people. Prosocial research has shown that people who feel good are much more likely to help someone in need than are people who feel bad.

Good moods

A typical experimental paradigm has participants believe they have succeeded or failed at a task they are asked to perform. It then transpires that those who believe they have been successful are more helpful than those who believe they have failed or those who have received no feedback. Alice Isen (1970) found that teachers who were more successful on a task were more likely to contribute later to a school fundraising drive. Those who had done well in fact donated seven times as much as the others! So, such momentary feelings as success on a relatively innocuous task can dramatically affect prosocial behaviour.

Isen suggested that doing well creates a 'warm glow of success', which makes people more likely to help. (You can compare this effect with the *reinforcement–affect model* of interpersonal liking in **Chapter 14**.) When people feel good, they are less preoccupied with themselves and are more sensitive to the needs and problems of others. Being in a good mood means that people are more likely to focus on positive things (Isen, Clark, & Schwartz, 1976), to have a more optimistic outlook on life and to see the world in pleasant ways (Isen & Stalker, 1982).

People who hear good news on the radio express greater attraction towards strangers and greater willingness to help than people who hear bad news (Holloway, Tucker, & Hornstein, 1977), and people are in better moods and are more helpful on sunny, temperate days than on overcast, cold days (Cunningham, 1979). Even experiences such as reading aloud statements expressing elation, or recalling pleasant events from our childhood, can increase the rate of helping. The evidence consistently demonstrates that good moods produce helpful behaviour under a variety of circumstances.

Bad moods

In contrast to people who are in good moods, people who feel bad, sad or depressed are internally focused. They concentrate on themselves, their problems and worries (Berkowitz, 1970), are less concerned with the welfare of others and help others less (Weyant, 1978). Berkowitz (1972b) showed that self-concern lowered the rate and amount of helping among students awaiting the outcome of an important exam. Likewise, Darley and Batson (1973) led seminary students, who were due to give a speech, to think they were quite late, just in time or early. They then had the opportunity to help a man who had apparently collapsed in an alley. The percentages that helped were: quite late, 10 per cent; just in time, 45 per cent; and early, 63 per cent.

Self-focus does not always reduce helping. Isen and her colleagues found that some kinds of self-concern may cause people to be more helpful (Isen, Horn, & Rosenhan, 1973). Guilt is one such feeling (see Box 13.6). In addition, not all bad moods reduce helping. A review of research on the behavioural consequences of anger, which is definitely a bad mood, shows that there can be prosocial behavioral consequences that revolve around combating injustice and promoting moral principles and cooperative conduct (Van Doorn, Zeelenberg, & Breugelmans, 2014).

Overall, the research on mood and similar psychological states is complex (see **Chapter 2**) and indicates that experiencing success and feeling good generally lead to prosocial helping behaviour, but that bad moods may or may not lead to helping, depending on whether they are moderated by self-concern. Nevertheless, a common consequence of providing help is that the helper ends up *feeling good* (Williamson & Clark, 1989) and has, at least for a while, a more positive self-evaluation. For example, William Klein (2003) reports a study where student participants were given comparative feedback on a verbal task performance. When the feedback was positive (i.e. that they had performed better than a second student) the participant reported feeling pleased (suggesting a more positive self-evaluation) and was more willing to give helpful hints to a third student about to undertake a similar task. This study is another example of the feeling-good factor triggering prosocial behaviour.

Box 13.6 Your life
The case of the guilty helper

'Oh dear! You've smashed my camera'

We are all familiar with that urge to help someone when we have accidentally broken something or hurt someone – an urge that often translates into actual helping behaviour. Research has shown that people who have accidentally broken something or injured someone really do show an increase in helping behaviour. When participants believed they had ruined an experiment, cheated on a test, broken expensive equipment or inflicted pain on another, they were much more likely to help the person against whom they had transgressed.

Dennis Regan and his colleagues led a group of female participants to believe they had broken an expensive camera. Later, when they had the chance to help another woman who had dropped some groceries, 50 per cent of the 'guilty' participants intervened to help, whereas only 15 per cent of a control group did so (Regan, Williams, & Sparling, 1972).

One explanation for this guilty helper effect is the image-reparation hypothesis: people want to make amends. If you have hurt someone, you can restore self-esteem by making it up. However, the complication is that the guilty party will actually help anyone in need, not just the person towards whom they feel guilty. It is difficult to see how their self-esteem can be threatened in this way.

According to Bob Cialdini's negative relief state model (e.g. Cialdini & Kenrick, 1976), hurting another person, or even seeing this happen, causes a bystander to experience a negative affect state. This motivates them to do something to relieve this feeling. We come to learn that helping can alleviate negative moods. Consequently, people are motivated to feel good rather than to look good. If so, this process is better described as hedonism than altruism, as it is motivated by self-interest.

This view gains support from the finding that people who have inflicted, or who have witnessed, harm or pain, and then receive an unexpected monetary reward or social approval immediately afterwards, are less helpful than participants who are left in a bad mood (Cialdini, Darby, & Vincent, 1973; McMillen, 1971).

Attributes of the person

Special interpersonal relationships can make bystanders feel particularly personally responsible in an emergency. This is more likely, for example, if there is a special bond with or commitment to the victim (Geer & Jarmecky, 1973; Moriarty, 1975; Tilker, 1970), or if the victim is especially dependent on the bystander (Berkowitz, 1978).

Individual differences

Are there other individual factors that can make people more helpful, even temporarily? Are there individual differences or personality predispositions to be helpful? Latané and Darley (1970) believe not – helping behaviour could not be predicted from *personality measures* including authoritarianism, alienation, trustworthiness, Machiavellianism (the tendency to manipulate others) and need for approval.

However, some people do seem to be consistently more helpful than others. Famous figures such as Florence Nightingale, Albert Schweitzer and Mother Teresa come to mind. Evidence for a 'Good Samaritan' syndrome of attributes is generally weak (Schwartz, 1977). Helping behaviour is associated with the belief that our fate lies within our control, mature moral judgement, and the tendency to take responsibility for others' welfare (Eisenberg-Berg, 1979; Staub, 1974). However, even this evidence is not strong enough (i.e. the correlations are small) to clearly distinguish Good Samaritans from the rest of humanity, and some doubt that the attempt is meaningful (Bar-Tal, 1976; Schwartz, 1977).

But there is some evidence that personality attributes can predict prosocial behaviour. For example, a study of 340 young adults found that people who scored high on the attributes of agreeableness, self-transcendence values, and empathic self-efficacy were more likely to engage in prosocial behaviour (Caprara, Alessandri, & Eisenberg, 2012). In addition, people who are consistently helpful in emergencies tend to be taller, heavier, physically stronger and better trained to cope with crimes and emergencies (see Huston, Ruggiero, Conner, & Geis, 1981). (How might any of these points throw additional light on Lily's bravery in 'What do *you* think?' question 3?).

The ability to forgive also seems to play a significant role in prosocial behaviour – *forgiveness* is valued in many cultures and can help close relationships survive (see **Chapter 14**). Karremans, Van Lange and Holland (2005) have studied the 'spill-over' effects of forgiveness. They found that people who are willing to forgive a significant other person (e.g. a partner) for offending them can later be more prosocial in general – such as volunteering to work for or donate money to a charity (revisit the second 'What do *you* think?' question). Forgiving and apologis-ing have also been studied in intergroup contexts – where a group that has been harmed by an outgroup forgives the outgroup for its actions, or a group apologises for doing harm to an outgroup and it feels responsible for doing the harm (Iyer & Leach, 2008; see **Chapter 11**).

Keltner and his colleagues have studied a connection between embarrassment and proso-cial behaviour. Like compassion, which we discussed earlier, embarrassment is a distinct emotion and is linked to appeasement displays in non-human primates (Keltner & Buswell, 1997; Keltner & Lerner, 2010). Appeasement signals both submission and acceptance of a transgression; embarrassment acknowledges that the social order has been breached. In a series of studies, Feinberg, Willer and Keltner (2012) provided evidence that differences in our capacity to feel embarrassed are a guide to how helpful we might be to others.

Attachment styles
Descriptions of the nature of people's close relationships, thought to be established in childhood.

Research by Mikulincer and his colleagues focusing on **attachment styles** (see **Chapter 14**) found that people who are securely attached are more likely to be compassionate and altruis-tic (Mikulincer & Shaver, 2005). This link to early childhood (attachment styles are devel-oped in childhood) is echoed in a longitudinal study spanning the period from four years of age to early adulthood. There were stable individual differences – the child who shares, helps and offers emotional comfort to others continues to do so in adulthood (Eisenberg, Guthrie, Murphy, Shepard, Cumberland, & Carlo, 1999). Of course, stability could be attributed to environmental constancies, such as secure attachment.

Overall, researchers are careful to avoid using the word 'personality' as a complete expla-nation. The common view shared by researchers is that there is no stand-alone, altruistic or prosocial personality (Bierhoff & Rohmann, 2004). Whether a person acts prosocially might, at best, be determined by their personality acting in unison with attributes of the situation and of the person requiring help (Gergen, Gergen, & Meter, 1972; Snyder & Cantor, 1998).

But how about religion? Although organised religion is often associated with bigotry and extremism (Batson, Schoenrade, & Ventis, 1993; Berger, 1999; Haidt, 2012; Hogg, Adelman, & Blagg, 2010) it is also the case that almost all religions promote empathy and helping other human beings as a core ideological principle. Presumably when people, particularly those who subscribe to a religious ideology, are religiously primed, they should be more inclined to help others and behave prosocially (Galen, 2012; Norenzayan & Shariff, 2008). A meta-analysis of twenty-five well-controlled studies found that religious priming did indeed significantly predict various measures of prosocial behaviour primarily directed towards religious ingroup members, and the effect was stronger among believers (Shariff, Willard, Andersen, & Norenzayan, 2016). Shariff and colleagues are careful to note that religious priming can also predict other behaviours that include racism and other non-prosocial atti-tudes and behaviors directed at outgroups and non-believers.

Living in big cities

Latané and Darley (1970) found that obvious demographic variables, such as number of siblings and parents' occupation, were not correlated with helping behaviour. However, size of one's hometown was. People from small-town backgrounds were more likely to help than those from larger cities, a finding replicated by Gelfand, Hartmann, Walder and Page (1973).

Paul Amato (1983) conducted a systematic study of the effect of population size on helping. He investigated people's willingness to help in fifty-five Australian cities and towns, focusing on behaviours such as picking up fallen envelopes, giving a donation to charity, giving a favourite colour for a student project, correcting inaccurate directions that were overheard and helping a stranger who had hurt a leg and collapsed on the footpath. With the exception of picking up the fallen envelope, the results showed that as population size rose (i.e. in the larger towns and cities), helping decreased. The results for four of the helping measures are shown in Figure 13.6. Best-fit regression lines for each set of data points are shown. You can see that there is a consistent trend downwards for helping a stranger as the size of the population rises.

Larger populations are usually in urban settings whereas smaller populations are in rural settings. Maybe this, rather than population per se, is the reason for differences in helping? Perhaps rural people care more because they feel less crowded, less rushed and less overwhelmed by noise; and generally feel less 'urban overload' and environmental stress than their fellows in a big and bustling city (Bonnes & Secchiaroli, 1995; Halpern, 1995).

The 'Scrooge effect'

Might people become more caring for others as they face their own mortality? Research on mortality salience and terror management suggests that prosocial behaviour can be a collateral benefit of being reminded that our lives end in death – a case of 'Repent! Do good!'

> At Christmas time, one of the most cherished and frequently told stories in Western culture is Charles Dickens's *A Christmas Carol*. In this story, the ghost of Christmas past and the ghost of Christmas present show Ebenezer Scrooge how his cruelty and selfishness has adversely affected his own life and the lives of others. However, it is not until the ghost of Christmas future shows Scrooge a glimpse of his own future, inscribed on the head of a tombstone, that his stinginess and greed give way to benevolence and compassion for others. Dickens is telling us that one should value kindness and concern for others over selfishness and material riches or else die an insignificant and lonely death.
>
> Jonas, Schimel, Greenberg and Pyszczynski (2002, p. 1342)

Jonas and colleagues put **terror management theory** (e.g. Greenberg, Solomon and Pyszczynski, 1997; see **Chapter 2**) to the test by interviewing pedestrians who were walking towards a funeral parlour marked with a large sign that read 'Howe's Mortuary'. Some interviews were carried out three blocks away while others took place right in front of the home and in full view of the sign. After the interview, the pedestrians rated several charities in terms of the benefits they provided people. A charity was rated more favourably when the pedestrians were in front of the funeral parlour. Like Scrooge, they saw *Christmas future*.

Terror management theory
The notion that the most fundamental human motivation is to reduce the terror of the inevitability of death. Self-esteem may be centrally implicated in effective terror management.

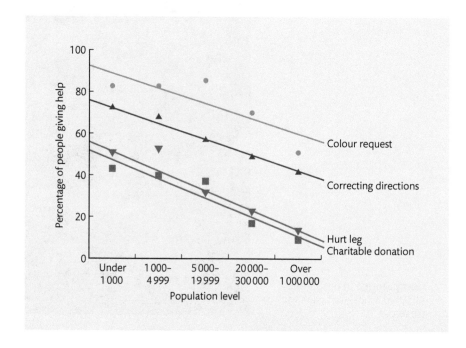

Figure 13.6 Effect of population level on willingness to help a stranger

- Regression lines have been fitted to the original data points for each helping measure.
- In cities with large populations, strangers can expect less help from the inhabitants.

Source: Based on data from Amato (1983).

Strictly speaking, a terror management theory explanation of this effect is that when people confront the inevitability of their own death, and a funeral parlour would certainly do this, they strive for symbolic immortality by defending their cultural world views – in this case, the value placed by society on doing good through the institution of charities.

Competence: 'have skills, will help'

Feeling competent to deal with an emergency makes it more likely that help will be given; there is the awareness that 'I know what I'm doing' (Korte, 1971). Specific kinds of competence have increased helping in these contexts:

- People who were told they had a high tolerance for electric shock were more willing to help others move electrically charged objects (Midlarsky & Midlarsky, 1976).

- People who were told they were good at handling rats were more likely to help to recapture a 'dangerous' laboratory rat (Schwartz & David, 1976).

- The competence effect may even generalise. Kazdin and Bryan (1971) found that people who thought they had done well on a health examination or even on a creativity task were later more willing to donate blood.

Certain 'packages' of skills are perceived as being relevant to some emergencies. In reacting to a stranger who was bleeding, people with first-aid training intervened more often than those who were untrained (Shotland & Heinold, 1985).

Pantin and Carver (1982) made student participants feel more competent by showing them a series of films on first aid and emergencies. Three weeks later, they had the chance to help a confederate who was apparently choking. The bystander effect was weakened by having previously seen the films. Pantin and Carver also reported that the increase in helping persisted over time. This area of skill development is at the core of Red Cross first-aid training courses for ordinary people in many countries.

The impact of skill level was tested experimentally by comparing professional help with novice help (Cramer, McMaster, Bartell, & Dragna, 1988). Participants were two groups of students, one highly competent (registered nurses) and the other less competent (general

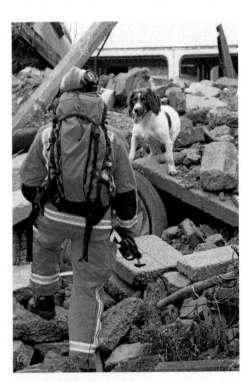

Competence in emergency
All skilled hands – and paws – to
the rescue.

students). In a contrived context, each participant waited in the company of a non-helping confederate. The nurses were more likely than the general students to help a workman, seen earlier, who had apparently fallen off a ladder in an adjoining corridor (a rigged accident, with pre-recorded moans). In responding to a post-experimental questionnaire, the nurses specified that they felt they had the skills to help.

Overall, situations highlighting the fact that a person possesses relevant skills implies that these skills should be used. The self-perception is: 'I know what to do, so I have the responsibility to act.' Competence may be situation-specific, but there is the possibility that it may endure over time and also generalise to non-related situations.

Leaders and followers

A variation on the theme of competence is the case of acting as a leader. We might think that a leader is, by definition, more generally competent than followers and more likely to initiate all kinds of action, including helping in an emergency. The skills component of leadership could probably be used to account for some helping outcomes. Even so, a study by Baumeister and his colleagues (Baumeister, Chesner, Senders, & Tice, 1988) specified an additional feature of the leadership role (also see **Chapter 9**) that goes beyond the 'have skills, will help' explanation: being a leader acts as a cue to generalised responsibility. In an emergency situation, the leader does not experience the same degree of diffusion of responsibility as ordinary group members. Box 13.7 describes how Baumeister and colleagues tested this idea.

Gender differences

Are men destined to be 'knights in shining armour'? The literature of romance but also of science indicates that men are more likely to help women than vice versa. Examples of research contexts include helping a motorist in distress (flat tyre, stalled car), or offering a ride to a hitchhiker (Latané & Dabbs, 1975). When the person in need of such help is female,

---

Box 13.7 Research highlight
Acting like a leader counteracts diffusion of responsibility: 'Who's in charge around here?'

A key requirement of effective leadership is to guide decision-making for a group (see **Chapter 9**) and, in an emergency, to provide control and direction for action. In an experiment by Roy Baumeister and his colleagues (Baumeister, Chesner, Senders, & Tice, 1988) thirty-two male and female students were led to believe they had been allocated to four-person groups, in which one member was allegedly randomly assigned to act as leader. The students were told that their task was to decide which survivors of a nuclear war should be allowed to join the group in its bomb shelter. The assistants could make recommendations, but their designated leader would make the final decision.

Participants were actually tested individually, half as leaders and half as followers, and group discussion was simulated using tape recordings over an intercom system. At a critical point, each participant was exposed to a simulated emergency when the recorded voice of a male group member faltered and said, 'Somebody come help me, I'm choking!' He then had a fit of coughing and went silent.

The experimenter met those who came out of the test room to help, telling them there was no problem. All were later debriefed.

Those designated as leaders were much more likely to help: as high as 80 per cent (twelve of fifteen) leaders helped, but only 35 per cent (six of seventeen) followers did so.

Now, the leaders in this study were randomly allocated to their role, so the outcome cannot be explained in terms of their actually having a set of personal skills. In Baumeister's view, acting as a leader brings with it a generalised responsibility, which:

- goes beyond the immediate requirement of the group task to involve other external events;
- provides a buffer against the usual process of diffusion of responsibility to which ordinary members are prone, and which can mediate the seeming indifference to helping a victim.

Sociocultural theory
Psychological gender differences are determined by individuals' adaptations to restrictions based on their gender in their society. Also called *social role theory*.

passing cars are much more likely to stop than for a man or for a male–female pair (Pomazal & Clore, 1973; West, Whitney, & Schnedler, 1975). Those who stop are typically young men driving alone. A meta-analysis by Alice Eagly and Maureen Crowley (1986) showed that the strongest combination was that of males being more helpful to women, despite a baseline difference of women showing more empathy generally than men. Read about an interesting study that explored a connection between sexual arousal and the likelihood of helping someone of either sex who is in trouble (see Box 13.8 and Figure 13.7.)

Box 13.8 Your life
Prosocial behaviour and male-female interactions

Do you suspect that male barmen serve women waiting at the bar more quickly than men waiting at the bar? If true, perhaps chivalry really does exist – where men altruistically go out of their way to help women who need help rather than men who need help? Or maybe the motivation is less pure – might men simply be motivated by sexual attraction to help women in trouble? The more you think about this, the more complicated it becomes.

But sexual attraction probably does pay a role according to Benson, who found that more physically attractive women received more help (Benson, Karabenick, & Lerner, 1976). Przybyla (1985) clarified the effect of sexual arousal more directly. Male and female students watched either an erotic or non-erotic video, or no video at all. When leaving the laboratory, they passed either a male or a female confederate who 'accidentally' knocked over a stack of papers and cried out 'Oh no!' Will the passer-by help to clean up the mess? The results are shown in Figure 13.7. Almost all

the males who had seen an erotic tape were motivated to help a female. They also spent a relaxed six minutes helping her, but a man in need got short shrift – thirty seconds!

Przybyla noted that both men and women reported degrees of arousal when viewing the erotic tape. The more aroused the man felt, the longer he spent helping a woman, an effect not extended to another man. In contrast, the more aroused women spent less time helping anyone. It is possible that male altruism towards women is confounded with a desire to be romantic. However, women are less likely to initiate interactions with strangers (especially men), due perhaps to socialisation experiences. This is consistent with **sociocultural theory** in accounting for cross-gender helping and has been supported in a more recent study by Karakashian, Walter, Christopher and Lucas (2006).

Figure 13.7 Helping an opposite-sex stranger as a function of sexual arousal
- Male and female students watched either an erotic or non-erotic video, or none at all.
- The use of erotic material was to induce sexual arousal and explore its consequences on helping others.
- They then saw either a male or a female confederate who needed some help.
- There was one huge sex difference: males, but not females, were very ready to help an opposite-sex stranger.

Source: Based on data from Przybyla (1985).

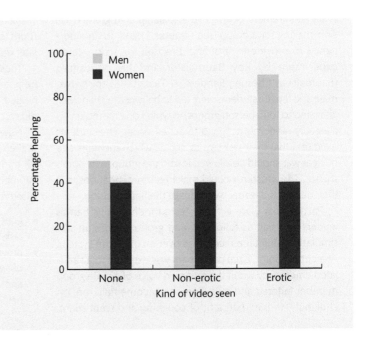

A later review by Eagly (2009) concluded that men and women are alike in the *degree* to which they behave prosocially, but differ in the *kinds* of actions that they perform. She proposes a role for both biology (not to be ignored) and society:

> The specialty of women is prosocial behaviors that are more communal and relational, and that of men is behaviors that are more agentic and collectively oriented as well as strength intensive. These sex differences, which appear in research in various settings, match widely shared gender role beliefs. The origins of these beliefs lie in the division of labor, which reflects a biosocial interaction between male and female physical attributes and the social structure. The effects of gender roles on behavior are mediated by hormonal processes, social expectations, and individual dispositions.
>
> Eagly (2009, p. 644)

Helping to prevent crime

Most of us would agree that crime is not prosocial behaviour but that prevention of crime is. Research has focused on the causes and prevention of petty and non-violent crime, such as property theft and shoplifting, and of misdemeanours, such as classroom cheating. Preventing crime can itself involve prosocial behaviour; for example, the development of neighbourhood watch schemes and accompanying media campaigns. People are most likely to engage in non-violent crime if the benefits are high and the costs are low. Fraud and tax evasion are often perceived as having high benefits and low costs (Hassett, 1981; Lockard, Kirkevold, & Kalk, 1980).

A riskier crime is property theft, which is statistically more common among younger men. As individuals mature, their assessment of the costs and benefits changes. Older people are more likely to deceive a customer or lie about a product or service than actually to steal something. However, research into property theft illustrates two important factors related to prosocial behaviour: responsibility and commitment.

People are most likely to help others if they have a feeling of *responsibility* for providing assistance. For example, we saw earlier that people feel responsible if they are the only witness to a crime or accident, or if they have been trained to deal with emergencies. Feeling responsible for providing aid increases the likelihood of prosocial behaviour. **Prior commitment** is a specific form of responsibility that can induce a prosocial act.

In a series of real-life encounters, Moriarty (1975) identified people who were sitting alone on a crowded beach and then went and sat next to them with a radio and blanket. Shortly afterwards, he talked to them and either simply asked for a match (smoking was prevalent in those days!), or asked them to watch his things while he went for a short walk. All participants agreed to the second request, thereby committing themselves to be *responsible bystanders*. Then a confederate came along, picked up the radio and walked away. Of participants who were only asked for a match, just 20 per cent complied, compared with 95 per cent for those specifically asked to be responsible. These participants even ran after and grabbed the confederate until the experimenter returned!

The powerful effects of such prior commitments have been demonstrated in other ways: for example, watching a stranger's suitcase in a laundrette (Moriarty, 1975), watching another student's books in a library (Shaffer, Rogel, & Hendrick, 1975) and watching a stranger's books in a classroom (Austin, 1979). The results were similar, with a high likelihood of prosocial interventions following explicit prior commitment.

Cheating, stealing, lying and other unethical acts are of enormous social relevance (e.g. Kirkwood, 2012; McCabe, Butterfield, & Trevino, 2012) and have also been the focus of social psychology. Massive American surveys (Gallup, 1978; Hassett, 1981) revealed that about two-thirds of the population had cheated in school at least once. In a study of over 24,000 people, Hassett found that surprisingly high numbers of people had broken various rules of ethical conduct. About 25 per cent had cheated on an expense account, 40 per cent had driven while

Prior commitment
An individual's agreement in advance to be responsible if trouble occurs: for example, committing oneself to protect the property of another person against theft.

drunk, and 65 per cent had stolen office supplies from their employers. Understanding the types of situation that can induce such behaviour or the types of people most likely to commit such acts could give clues to reduce their occurrence and even to replace them with prosocial alternatives. Cheating in athletics is also, of course, a huge issue. It captured public attention through the doping scandal surrounding the cyclist Lance Armstrong (in 2012 he was found guilty by the US Anti-Doping Agency of using performance-enhancing drugs). Cheating in athletics was also a messy backdrop to the 2016 Rio de Janeiro Olympic Games.

Shoplifting

Stealing goods from shops is a crime that has been of interest to psychologists investigating prosocial behaviour (Gelfand, Hartmann, Walder, & Page, 1973). Bickman and Rosenbaum (1977) found that most people would report a thief to the management, if reminded by an experimental confederate. But posters or other mass media messages are not very effective in reducing shoplifting. It is possible that impersonal reminders such as these influence attitudes about shoplifting and about reporting thieves but do not change the behaviour itself (Bickman & Green, 1977).

Programmes have been developed to reduce shoplifting by informing people about its nature and its costs, in both financial and human terms. But the most effective method for increasing prosocial interventions in shoplifting has been found to be a lecture stressing how and why to report this crime and the reasons why bystanders are sometimes inhibited from taking action (Klentz & Beaman, 1981).

Exam cheating

Are there personality correlates? In a very early study, MacKinnon (1933) distinguished between cheaters and non-cheaters. He reported that cheaters more often expressed anger towards the task and were more destructive or aggressive in the exam room (kicking the

Cheating
Drug cheating in sport has received considerable media attention, heightened by the rewards available in an international arena.

table leg or pounding their fists on the table); non-cheaters more often blamed themselves for not solving the problems, tended to verbalise the problems and develop other strategies to help to solve them, and behaved more nervously and fidgeted more. Weeks later, the students were asked if they had cheated. Those who had not cheated readily said so; those who had cheated either denied it or admitted it but said they felt no guilt about it. Further, such feelings of guilt appeared to be a critical variable in determining whether a person cheated or not: 84 per cent of the non-cheaters said they would feel guilty if they were to cheat. Those who did not cheat reported the most guilt at the thought of cheating; those who had cheated reported the least guilt. MacKinnon assumed that cheating was dispositional – a personality characteristic that was inherent in a 'cheater'.

Later studies also pursued links between cheating and personality. Students who cheat tend to be low in ability to delay gratification (Yates & Mischel, 1979), high in sociopathic tendencies (Lueger, 1980), high in need for approval (Milham, 1974), low in interpersonal trust (Rotter, 1980), high in chronic self-destructive tendencies (Kelley, Byrne, Przybyla, Eberly, Eberly, Greenlinger, Wan, et al., 1985), low in adherence to the work ethic and in the desire to perform tasks industriously (Eisenberger & Shank, 1985) and high in the belief that transgressions are not automatically punished (Karniol, 1982). Despite these findings, correlations for the general population are typically modest, suggesting that situational factors play a significant role, which may be just as well if remedial measures are to be found.

One short-term situational effect is *arousal* – a feeling of excitement or a thrill from taking a chance. Why not cheat, at least when there is little chance of being caught (Scitovsky, 1980)? Lueger (1980) approached arousal differently: it is distracting and makes us less able to regulate our behaviour. In his study, participants saw either an arousing film or a relaxing one and then had the chance to cheat while taking a test. In the relaxed condition, 43 per cent cheated, but in the aroused condition, 70 per cent cheated. Warning students about to sit an exam of the penalties for being caught cheating paradoxically may increase cheating (Heisler, 1974), perhaps because they are also more aroused. Much of this research has pursued ways of *discouraging cheating*. A conventional strategy has been to increase the severity of punishments available. However, one estimate is that only about one in five self-reported cheaters are ever caught (Gallup, 1978).

Consider again MacKinnon's (1933) study: perhaps something that increases feelings of guilt may lead to a decrease in cheating? People usually agree that cheating is wrong, and those who do cheat disapprove as strongly as those who do not (Hughes, 1981). Some institutions have introduced programmes to raise the ethical awareness of their pupils and to promote prosocial behaviour in various ways (see Britell, 1981; Dienstbier, Kahle, Willis, & Tunnell, 1980). Dienstbier and colleagues' study reported some success from focusing less on students' assumed lack of morality and more on how to make ethical standards salient. Similarly, reducing student cheating by priming socially approved norms of academic honesty continues to show promise as an intervention in more recent experimental work (Lonsbary, 2007).

In summary, many people readily confess all kinds of occasional, unethical or illegal behaviour. Non-violent crimes such as fraud, tax evasion, insurance scams, shoplifting, exam cheating and particularly intellectual property theft (illegal downloads), which may have serious consequences for others, are prevalent in our society. Research not only tries to understand the causes of these behaviours but also explores solutions, such as advertising campaigns, community interventions and deterrents based on surveillance techniques.

Health support networks

The use of the term 'victim' so often in this chapter connects with a health-related facet of prosocial behaviour – **social support networks**. A victimising event such as cancer has profound effects on how significant others (family, friends, workmates, medical staff)

Social support network
People who know and care about us and who can provide back-up during a time of stress.

**A social support
network**
Surrounding yourself
with others who care
can help you cope with
life's trials and
tribulations.

might interact with a patient: an initial reaction of aversion can give way to a façade projecting good cheer. Not surprisingly, the victim can feel stigmatised and unwanted. Dakof and Taylor (1990) argued that the reactions of members of a support network are moderated by the nature of the relationship that people have with the victim and, in a wider sense, by the cultural constraints imposed on social interactions. In most nuclear families, those close to a cancer victim are more likely to be overprotective than withdrawing. Their study concentrated on how a victim views the nature of help and how this interacts with its source.

Their participants were fifty-five cancer patients, mostly whites, in Los Angeles. Patients valued as helpful those acts by intimate providers (family, friends) that related to the victim's self-esteem and emotional support, such as concern, empathy and affection. In contrast, the acts of medical staff and other cancer patients that patients viewed as helpful were informational and tangible support, such as prognosis and technical or medical care. When either group stepped out of the appropriate role, the act became misguided and unhelpful. In the case of nursing staff, acts considered helpful tended to be those that were closer to the acts appreciated among people intimate to the victim.

Receiving help

This chapter has focused on the psychology of the 'helper': when will we help, why do we hesitate, and how can we increase helping in our community? There is another angle that we should consider. Does the recipient always want help? We have discussed how there can be psychological costs in helping (Piliavin, Piliavin, Dovidio, Gaertner, & Clark, 1981), which raises the question of whether this also applies to the person who is thought to need help. Nadler (1986, 1991) believes that it does.

Western society encourages people to be self-reliant and to achieve as individuals. To ask for help, then, confronts people with a dilemma: the benefits of being helped are tempered by the costs of appearing dependent on others. In a study in Israel, Nadler (1986) compared the help-seeking tendencies of *kibbutz* dwellers with those of city dwellers. People in *kibbutzim*, who are socialised to cherish collectivism, sought help on a difficult task only when they thought the performance of their group as a whole was to be compared with other groups. However, Israeli city people, who are typically more Western and individualistic, sought help only when they thought their individual performance was to be compared with other individuals. (For details of this research, see **Chapter 16**, particularly Figure 16.4 and Box 16.4.)

People can also resist or react negatively to help when they feel that being helped confirms a negative stereotype that they are dependent and powerless in society. For example, women are often (benevolently) stereotyped as being dependent, in particular dependent on men, for help (see **Chapter 10**). Wakefield and colleagues conducted an experiment where female students were made aware that women may be stereotyped by men as dependent, and were then placed in a situation where they needed help (Wakefield, Hopkins, & Greenwood, 2012). Those made aware of the dependency stereotype (compared to controls who were not) were less willing to seek help, and those who did seek help felt worse the more help they sought.

Most acts of help in our day-to-day lives do not involve strangers. Rather, they take place in ongoing relationships between friends, partners and close relatives. The recipient will make attributions about the helper's motives and interpret the help given in terms of what it means to the relationship: for example: 'My partner is wonderful!' or 'You can always count on Mum!' In a series of studies, Ames and his colleagues concluded that when we receive help, we attend 'to help from the heart (*affect*), from the head (*cost–benefit*), or by the book (*roles*)' (Ames, Flynn, & Weber, 2004, p. 472). In all of these cases, prosocial acts nourish a relationship and help to define the identities of those involved.

Norms, motives and self-sacrifice

Norms for helping

Often we help others simply because 'something tells us' we should. We ought to help that little old lady cross the street, return a wallet we found, help a crying child. Group and societal **norms** play a key role in developing and sustaining prosocial behaviour – they provide a background influence on human behaviour (see **Chapter 7**) and are of course learnt rather than innate. A norm is a standard of action that describes and prescribes what is expected, 'normal' or proper.

Almost every society or culture has a norm that concern for others is good and that selfishness is bad. An unwritten rule is that when the cost is not very great and another person is in need, we should help. If a norm of social responsibility is universal, it indicates that it is functional and that it facilitates social life. One way to account for why we help others is, therefore, to say that it is *normative*. There are social rewards for behaving in accordance with the norm and sanctions for violating the norm. Sanctions may range from mild disapproval to incarceration or worse, depending on the threat posed to the existing social order.

Two general norms play a key role in prosocial and helping behaviour:

1 *The reciprocity norm* – we should help those who help us. This norm, also referred to as the **reciprocity principle**, is as universal as the incest taboo (Gouldner, 1960). However,

Norms
Attitudinal and behavioural uniformities that define group membership and differentiate between groups.

Reciprocity principle
This is sometimes called the reciprocity norm, or 'the law of doing unto others what they do to you'. It can refer to an attempt to gain compliance by first doing someone a favour, or to mutual aggression, or to mutual attraction.

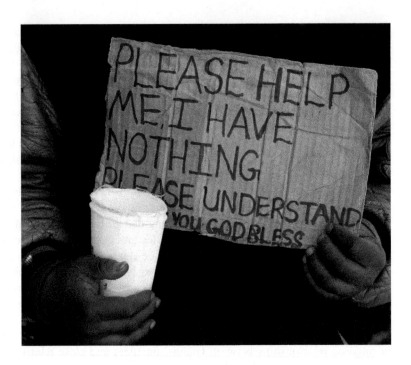

Social responsibility norm
Helping someone in need is a matter of compassion, not simply an act that reduces one's own sense of distress.

Social responsibility norm
The idea that we should help people who are dependent and in need. It is contradicted by another norm that discourages interfering in other people's lives.

the extent to which we should reciprocate varies. We feel deeply indebted when someone freely makes a big sacrifice for us, but much less so if what they do is smaller and expected (Tesser, Gatewood, & Driver, 1968). Further, people might give help only in return for help given in the past or anticipated in the future (see the discussion of social exchange in **Chapter 14**). People driven by egoism are more likely to act prosocially when they believe their reputations are at stake (Simpson & Willer, 2008).

2 The **social responsibility norm**. We should give help freely to those in need without regard to future exchanges. Members of a community are often willing to help the needy, even when they remain anonymous donors and do not expect or anticipate any social reward (Berkowitz, 1972b). In practice, people usually apply this norm selectively, e.g. to those in need through no fault of their own, but not to callers at the front door. The extent to which people internalise beliefs about the future of our planet as a norm has been linked to environmental activism (Fielding, McDonald, & Louis, 2008; Stern, Dietz, & Guagnano, 1995).

Of course, neither norm can plausibly explain prosocial behaviour in animals (Stevens, Cushman, & Hauser, 2005). Reciprocity and social responsibility, as norms that guide behaviour, seem to be distinctive to humans. Even so, although the overarching norm that we should help others is endorsed verbally, it may not be very compelling – it is an ideal that does not readily translate into actual behaviour (Teger, 1970). As an ideal, the prosocial ethic may be an expression of people paying lip service to being responsible citizens. When and why do people actually adhere to these norms? Situational variables covered earlier in this chapter play a role.

Motives and goals

Batson (1994; Batson, Ahmad, & Tsang, 2002) has argued that what prompts us to help others is a matter of motivation, and motivation involves goals. Is the action an *instrumental goal*, an intermediate step on the path to a person's ultimate self-interest? Or is it an

Box 13.9 Research highlight
Four motives for helping others

His research over many years has led Batson to conclude that four motives control prosocial behaviour. How often we help, and the various ways that we might help, depend on one of the following:

1   **Egoism:** Prosocial acts benefit one's self. We may help others to secure material, social and self-reward; and to escape punishment.

2   **Altruism:** Prosocial acts contribute to the welfare of others. Acting altruistically does not imply that someone should reciprocate. This kind of prosocial motivation is esteemed in many cultures.

3   **Collectivism:** Prosocial acts contribute to the welfare of a social group, e.g. one's family, ethnic group or country. Of course, actions that benefit one's ingroup may harm an outgroup (see **Chapter 11**).

4   **Principlism:** Prosocial acts follow a moral principle, such as 'the greatest good for the greatest number'. Although the link between moral reasoning and prosocial behaviour is not strong, the two processes are at least related (Underwood & Moore, 1982).

Source: Based on Batson (1994); Batson, Ahmad and Tsang (2002).

---

ultimate goal in its own right, with any self-benefit an unintended side effect? We summarise Batson's ideas in Box 13.9. If instrumental goals only serve self-interest, then instrumental goal-oriented helping is not altruistic. However, if the 'self' in self-interest is a collective self – a 'we' – then instrumental goal-oriented behaviour that benefits the group or community and thus ourselves as part of the collective is closer to altruism. Take for example the **commons dilemma**, which can be combatted if people are prepared to sacrifice short-term personal gain for the long-term collective good (see **Chapter 11**).

Commons dilemma
Social dilemma in which cooperation by all benefits all, but competition by all harms all.

Volunteers and martyrs

Prosocial and helping behaviours almost always involve some kind of cost to the actor. The cost can be relatively small (a commitment of time or money) or enormous (one's life). One form of spontaneous helping is volunteering; an activity that is critical to the maintenance of society and of communities embedded in society, particularly in times of economic and social hardship (Wilson, 2000). For a community to benefit from a high level of volunteering, it must clearly identify situations and opportunities and enhance a sense of personal control among the volunteers (Clary & Snyder, 1991, 1999).

Volunteers commonly offer to others a sense of community, or civic participation (Omoto & Snyder, 2002). This can reveal itself through acting as a companion for the elderly, counselling troubled people, tutoring the illiterate, making home visits to the terminally ill through the hospice movement or supporting people with AIDS. In the United States in 1998, more than 1 million people gave 3.5 hours per week acting in these and similar ways. There is also a political dimension. In the United States, those on the political Right may promote the activities of voluntary organisations to save government funding, while those on the Left favour a grassroots approach to achieve social change (Omoto, Snyder, & Hackett, 2010).

Mark Davis and his colleagues have shown that voluntary activities that entail exposure to distress, which is an example of a response invoking empathy, require well-designed training programmes to prepare the volunteer (Davis, Hall, & Meyer, 2003). Volunteering involves some degree of self-sacrifice (time, money, health, family), so people who are driven to volunteer cater their commitment to their resources. The rich and famous often have resources, so it is not surprising that those who do volunteer are given a high media profile. This is not a bad thing, as they can act as powerful prosocial role models. All of us are familiar with the global charity work of Melinda and Bill Gates (founder of Microsoft), the philanthropy of the business magnate Warren Buffett, the fierce advocacy for Haiti that the actor Sean Penn has pursued, and the humanitarian gestures of actors and musicians and such as Bob Geldof, the founder of Live Aid, and of Bono, Oprah Winfrey, George Clooney, Angelina Jolie and many others.

Although volunteering, philanthropy and humanitarian acts such as these are in many respects the pinnacle of prosocial behaviour, the sceptics among us sometimes wonder to what extent the underlying motive is influenced by more self-oriented goals. Batson allows that community involvement can be driven by an egoistic motive (Batson, Ahmad, & Tsang, 2002), but argues that it is just one of four (egoism, altruism, collectivism, principlism), and that all four have both strengths and weaknesses. In recruiting volunteers, an effective strategy is to guide potential volunteers in ways that help them supplement egoism with additional reasons to volunteer based on altruism, principlism, or both.

Evert van der Vliert and colleagues have conducted research into wider contextual factors that influence the role played by egoism and altruism in volunteering (Van der Vliert, Huang, & Levine, 2004). In a cross-cultural comparison of volunteers in thirty-three countries, they found the two motives can be separated in some countries but not in others. The picture they paint is complex. Put simply, the weight given to each motive depends on a country's ecology (the climate) and its overall wealth.

This brings us to martyrs – people who endure suffering and can sacrifice their lives for a cause. There are countless examples, ranging from hunger strikers in Northern Ireland in 1981, to Joan of Arc's burning at the stake in Rouen in 1431, to demonstrations in the face of heavily armed security forces around the world (e.g. the Sharpeville massacre in South Africa in 1960). Nelson Mandela puts it well:

> I have cherished the ideal of a democratic and free society in which all persons will live together in harmony and with equal opportunities. It is an ideal for which I hope to live for and to see realized. But, My Lord, if it needs be, it is an ideal for which I am prepared to die (Nelson Mandela).
>
> Cited in Bélanger, Caouette, Sharvit and Dugas (2014, p. 494).

When we think of martyrs, we tend to think of self-sacrifice for a noble cause – as in Mandela's case. However, people can also sacrifice themselves for an evil cause. All that matters is that the sacrifice is for a cause that someone believes in. So, does that mean that suicide terrorists are altruists? Is it altruistic to walk into a crowded market and then blow oneself up, or open fire in a crowded disco or airport in the certain knowledge of being killed?

The language of altruism does not really help us here. Suicide terrorism is better characterised as intergroup behaviour (see **Chapters 10 and 11**) – it is a behaviour designed to promote one's own group over a competing group. It can also be personally instrumental in the sense that terrorist organisations lure disadvantaged people into suicide attacks with the promise of substantial financial support for their family.

We have treated *altruism* as characteristically prosocial in this chapter. *Martyrdom*, however, centres on the willingness to sacrifice one's life for others. The Canadian social psychologist Jocelyn Bélanger argues that across history, martyrdom has typically been driven by religious and political ideologies: Christianity, Judaism, early Islam; the death of the philosopher Socrates; the Japanese Kamikaze pilots in World War II; and the Tamil Tigers of Sri Lanka. Ideologies are also at the heart of organised *suicide terrorism*; a situation where a particular ideology encompasses inflicting harm on others as well as self-sacrifice (Bélanger, Caouette, Sharvit, & Dugas, 2014; Kruglanski, Chen, Dechesne, & Fishman, 2009). Since ideology is not psychopathology, when martyrs and suicide terrorists are willing to die for a cause, they are neither altruists nor psychopaths.

Summary

- Prosocial behaviour refers to acts positively valued by society, including helping and altruistic behaviour. Helping behaviour refers to intentional acts designed to benefit another person. Altruistic behaviour refers to behaviour motivated by the desire to benefit another with no expectation of personal gain or reward. It is difficult to identify purely altruistic behaviour because motives or rewards may not be observable.

- The Kitty Genovese murder stimulated and launched a frenzy of research on prosocial behaviour generally and bystander intervention specifically.

- Two major perspectives on the origin and nature of prosocial behaviour in humans stand in contrast. One is biological and is derived from evolutionary theory. The other is social and is based on reinforcement principles, with an added feature of modelling. Most social psychologists are wary of too heavy an emphasis on the biology.

- A third account is more integrative, featuring arousal, empathy and a cost–benefit analysis.

- Where there is an emergency, the bystander effect comes into play. Aid is more likely when just a solitary bystander is present. Situational factors are also important determinants of helping in an emergency.

- Evidence for individual differences and personality attributes that encourage helping is mixed. Personality correlates of helping are weak, but people's mood, attachment style and competence can have considerable influence in some contexts.

- Other prosocial behaviour research focuses on gender roles, preventing or reporting theft or shoplifting, and examination and other forms of cheating.

- Recipients of prosocial acts can sometimes feel their sense of autonomy has been compromised. However, most help is actually given to people we know, and our actions contribute to how the relationship is defined.

- Prosocial behaviour is often prescribed by societal and cultural norms – we behave prosocially because it is the right thing to do. For this reason, many people volunteer to help others in the community or society more broadly. High-profile philanthropists and humanitarians may act as powerful prosocial role models.

- Martyrs sacrifice themselves for a cause or an ideology. Ideologies that promoted hatred of outgroups often legitimise violence against outgroups – this can underpin suicide terrorism which is better understood as ingroup-serving or even self-serving behaviour than altruism.

Key terms

Altruism	Empathy costs of not helping	Prior commitment
Attachment styles	Evolutionary social psychology	Prosocial behaviour
Bystander effect	Fear of social blunders	Reciprocity principle
Bystander intervention	Helping behaviour	Social learning theory
Bystander-calculus model	Just-world hypothesis	Social responsibility norm
Commons dilemma	Learning by vicarious experience	Social support network
Diffusion of responsibility	Modelling	Sociocultural theory
Emergency situation	Nature–nurture controversy	Terror management theory
Empathic concern	Norms	
Empathy	Personal costs of not helping	

Literature, film and TV

Schindler's Ark

Thomas Keneally's 1982 novel about how Otto Schindler, a German industrialist (and member of the Nazi Party) living in Krakow during the Second World War, took enormous risks to save 1,200 Jews from the gas chambers of Auschwitz. The book was made into a 1993 film called *Schindler's List*, directed by Stephen Spielberg and starring Liam Neeson and Ben Kingsley.

Amélie

A 2001 French romantic comedy by Jean-Pierre Jeunet and starring Audrey Tautou. The film is a wonderfully whimsical and idealised depiction of contemporary Parisian life, set in Montmartre. Amélie is a young waitress whose life is directionless until she finds an old box of childhood memorabilia that she is determined to return to its owner, now a grown man. She makes a deal with herself in the process: if she finds him and it makes him glad, she will devote her life to goodness and doing good.

Becoming Warren Buffett

What kind of people are philanthropists – what motivates them to give away most of their wealth? This 2017 documentary about the famously frugal, quirky and slightly 'geekish' billionaire business magnate and investor Warren Buffett (chairman of the investment company Berkshire Hathaway since 1970) gives fascinating insight about one such person. Buffet's wealth in 2017 was estimated at a colossal 78.7 billion dollars, yet he lives in the same modest home he has always owned (in Omaha, Nebraska) and drives himself to work each day. He has pledged to donate 99% of his wealth to philanthropic causes, most through the Bill and Melinda Gates foundation. In 2010, Buffett formed a pact with Gates (Microsoft) and Mark Zuckerberg (Facebook) to donate at least half their wealth to charity and inspire other super-wealthy individuals to do likewise.

Dallas Buyers Club

A highly acclaimed 2013 biographical drama starring Matthew McConaughey, Jennifer Garner and Jared Leto. Set during the AIDS crisis of the 1980s McConaughey's character, Ron Woodroof, contracts HIV and goes to great lengths in the face of homophobic prejudice and hysterical popular fear of AIDS to illegally smuggle anti-AIDS pharmaceutical drugs into Texas to treat not only himself, but a huge number of fellow AIDS sufferers. He cleverly sets up a buyers' club through which to distribute the drugs and thus circumvent legislation policed by the American Food and Drug Administration. Woodroof is a complex character and his undeniably prosocial behaviour is certainly not altruistic as it is also self-serving.

The Wolf of Wall Street and other films

Martin Scorsese's 2013 film *The Wolf of Wall Street*, starring Leonardo DiCaprio, is part of a genre of films about corruption and fraud in the US banking industry. This genre has its origins in Tom Wolfe's 1987 novel *The Bonfire of the Vanities* which, set in the New York financial world of the 1980s, is a powerful commentary on greed, selfishness and unfettered personal ambition – the antithesis of prosocial or altruistic behaviour. Also in 1987, the film *Wall Street* came out – written and directed by Oliver Stone, and starring Michael Douglas, this film brought us 'master of the universe' Gordon Gekko and his credo 'Greed is good' – a credo that was an anthem of the 1980s. A number of more recent films remind us that greed still thrives in the early twenty-first century. In addition to *The Wolf of Wall Street*, there is the 2011 TV movie *Too Big to Fail*, starring William Hurt, Edward Asner and Paul Giamatti, and the 2015 film *The Big Short*, starring Steve Carrell, Ryan Gosling and Christian Bale. Together these films are a chilling dramatisation of the US housing bubble and the ensuing financial meltdown of 2007–8 that raised the very real possibility of another great depression. Scary films about the consequences of too much greed, selfishness and power, but also fabulous explorations of group processes and decision making and of leadership (**Chapters 8** and **9**).

Guided questions

1   How has evolutionary theory influenced social psychology's approach to understanding the origins of altruism?

2   What is *empathy* and how is it related to helping others who are in need?

3 Is there evidence that children can learn to be helpful?

4 What factors in the situation, or what kinds of individual differences between potential helpers, would increase the chances of help being given to a child who is being bullied?

5 What advice could a social psychologist give to a school board to help reduce exam cheating?

Learn more

Batson, C. D. (1998). Altruism and prosocial behaviour. In D. T. Gilbert, S. T. Fiske, & G. Lindzey (Eds.), *The handbook of social psychology* (4th ed., Vol. 2, pp. 282–316). New York: McGraw-Hill. Authoritative overview of the topic of prosocial behaviour. The most recent fifth edition of the handbook, published in 2010, does not have a chapter on prosocial behaviour.

Batson, C. D., Van Lange, P. A. M., Ahmad, N., & Lishner, D. A. (2007). Altruism and helping behavior. In M. A. Hogg & J. Cooper (Eds.), *The SAGE handbook of social psychology: Concise student edition* (pp. 241–258). London: SAGE. Comprehensive, up-to-date and easily accessible overview of research on altruism and prosocial behaviour.

Clark, M. S. (Ed.) (1991). *Prosocial behavior*. Thousand Oaks, CA: SAGE. A collection of chapters by leading scholars who have played a significant role in developing the social psychology of helping behaviour.

Rose, H., & Rose, S. (Eds.) (2000). *Alas, poor Darwin: Arguments against evolutionary psychology*. London: Vintage. Scholars from a variety of biological, philosophical and social science backgrounds raise concerns about the adequacy of genetic and evolutionary accounts of social behaviour, including altruism.

Schroeder, D. A., Penner, L. A., Dovidio, J. F., & Piliavin, J. A. (1995). *The psychology of helping and altruism*. New York: McGraw-Hill. A good general overview of research on prosocial behaviour.

Snyder, M., & Omoto, A. M. (2007). Social action. In A. W. Kruglanski, & E. T. Higgins (Eds.), *Social psychology: Handbook of basic principles* (2nd ed., pp. 940–61). New York: Guilford Press. A comprehensive, up-to-date and detailed discussion of collective prosocial behaviour – how people can come together to do good.

Spacapan, S., & Oskamp, S. (Eds.) (1992). *Helping and being helped*. Newbury Park, CA: SAGE. Contributors deal with a wide range of real-life helping behaviour; including kidney donation, spousal support of stroke patients, and family support for people with Alzheimer's disease.

Chapter 14
Attraction and close relationships

Chapter contents

What do *you* think?

1 Carol finds David more attractive than Paul, but bumps into him less often. Who do you think Carol is most likely to get to like and perhaps have a relationship with?

2 Erik and Charles have been chatting over a few drinks when Erik remarks that he is 'profiting' from his latest romantic relationship. Charles does not know what to say but thinks this a callous comment. Can you offer a more benign interpretation?

3 Even when they were dating, Kamesh felt that Aishani was mostly uncomfortable when they were with other people. She also avoided having other members of their families visit them. Now, Aishani does not seem very interested in their new baby. Are these events somehow connected?

4 Can we study love scientifically — or should we pack the statistics away and leave it to the poets?

Liking, loving and affiliating

Collectively, our species is *Homo sapiens* – wise, knowing and judicious humans. However, as we have seen throughout this book, the *sapiens* bit is arguable – people are strongly influenced by feelings, emotions and self-interest, all tied to our fundamentally social nature. Not only are our judgements sub-optimal, but we love and help, hate and fight. This chapter deals with the liking and the loving part, and more fundamentally with why we want to be with others. Perhaps there is a term missing from our dictionary: *Homo socius* – humans who can be allies, friends and partners. We start with the process of attraction, then take a step back to explore the reasons why we affiliate with (i.e. choose the company of) and become attached to others, and ask the time-honoured question, 'What is love?' We conclude with how our most intimate relationships can be maintained and what happens when they break down.

The scientific study of close relationships is, according to Steve Duck (2008), a relatively recent extension of earlier research in social psychology on interpersonal attraction. However, it is now well established and even has two dedicated journals – *Journal of Social and Personal Relationships* and *Personal Relationships*. In this chapter, we focus mainly on close relationships rather than *friendship*; however, there are many points of contact between the two, including the contributory role of evolution (see review by Seyfarth & Cheney, 2012). But first, what is interpersonal attraction?

Attractive people

We just *know* when we are attracted to someone. We are allured, perhaps charmed, captivated, even enthralled. We want to know and spend time with that person. At one level, attraction is necessary for friendships of any kind to begin, though many first meetings are by chance. At another level, attraction can be the precursor to an intimate relationship. Do you believe in love at first sight?

Perhaps you subscribe to other popular sayings such as: *never judge a book by its cover, beauty is only skin deep* and *beauty is in the eye of the beholder*. Unfortunately for some of us, there is evidence that the primary cue in initially determining our evaluation of others is how they look. A **meta-analysis** of more than one hundred studies by Judith Langlois and her colleagues (Langlois, Kalakanis, Rubenstein, Larson, Hallam, & Smoot, 2000) found that these sayings are myths rather than maxims. As a cautionary note, the overall impact of the findings is reduced because some studies focus on just two categories – the attractive and the unattractive. Bearing this in mind, Langlois and colleagues concluded that attractive people are different from those who are unattractive in how they are judged, how they are treated and how they behave.

Meta-analysis
Statistical procedure that combines data from different studies to measure the overall reliability and strength of specific effects.

Two key empirical findings were: (a) attractive children received higher grades from their teachers, showed higher levels of intellectual competence and were more popular and better adjusted than their unattractive counterparts; and (b) attractive adults were more successful in their jobs, liked more, more physically healthy and more sexually experienced than unattractive adults – they also had had more dates, held more traditional attitudes, had more self-confidence and self-esteem and had slightly higher intelligence and mental health.

There are other things we know about the advantages of having good looks:

- If you are female, babies will gaze longer (Slater, Von der Schulenburg, Brown, Badenoch, Butterworth, Parsons, & Samuels, 1998)!
- In computer-simulation studies, attractiveness is associated with some feminisation of facial features, even for male faces (Rhodes, Hickford, & Jeffrey, 2000), and with having a slimmer figure (Gardner & Tockerman, 1994).

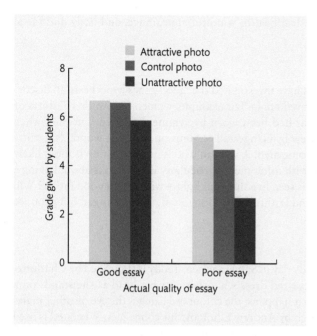

Figure 14.1 Being attractive can lead to better essay grades

Source: Based on data from Landy and Sigall (1974).

- An attractive person is a youthful person (Buss & Kenrick, 1998), is judged as more honest (Yarmouk, 2000) and, if a female defendant, gets an easier time from jurors (Sigall & Ostrove, 1975).

We noted that attractive children receive higher grades than unattractive children. David Landy and Harry Sigall (1974) studied this effect experimentally among university students, asking the question, 'Does beauty signal talent?' Male students graded one or other of two essays of different quality, attached to which was a photograph of the supposed writer, a female student. The same essays were also rated by control participants, but without any photograph. The 'good' and 'poor' essays were paired in turn with either an attractive photograph or a relatively unattractive photograph. The answer to the researchers' question was 'yes' – sad to relate, better grades were given to the attractive female student (see Figure 14.1).

With attractiveness being such an asset, those who spend big on cosmetics and fashion could be making a real investment in their future! Short of this, just a smile can also work wonders Joe Forgas and his colleagues found that students who smile are punished less after a misdemeanour than those who do not (Forgas, O'Connor, & Morris, 1983).

Evolution and attraction

Evolutionary theory, which identifies biological factors that trigger aggression, altruism and the emotions (see **Chapters 2, 12, 13 and 15**), also helps us understand some aspects of why we are attracted to some people, and how we might go about choosing a long-term partner. In an extreme form, David Buss (2003) applied **evolutionary social psychology** to argue that close relationships can be understood only in terms of evolutionary theory. Let us consider what modern research has told us about our natural endowment.

Evolutionary social psychology
An extension of evolutionary psychology that views complex social behaviour as adaptive, helping the individual, kin and the species as a whole to survive.

The role of our genes

The meta-analysis by Langlois and colleagues cited earlier suggested that the development of interpersonal attraction was partly related to how we select a mate. According to the evolutionary concept of *reproductive fitness*, people guess whether a prospective mate has good genes, using cues such as physical health, youthful appearance, and body and facial symmetry.

Fertility

Steven Gangestad and his colleagues have investigated the 'good genes hypothesis' in discovering what traits women find attractive in men. For example, women who sniffed T-shirts of unknown origin preferred those that had been worn by symmetrical men, but only when they were about to ovulate! (See review by Gangestad & Simpson, 2000.) A woman's fertility status can affect how she relates to some men. A woman who is near ovulation is more likely to prefer a man who is competitive with other men, particularly if she thinks about having a short-term mate. A long-term mate is seen in a different light – will he be a good father? Will he be financially successful, warm and faithful? (See Gangestad, Garver-Apgar, Simpson, & Cousins, 2007.)

Seeing red

Men have their foibles, too. One windy day in San Francisco, Teddy is transfixed by Charlotte, an incredibly beautiful woman, whose red dress whooshes over her head as she stands on a grate (*The Woman in Red,* 1984). As it happens, the colour red catches the eye of other males as well as Teddy, according to research by Andrew Elliot and his colleagues. When red is used as a background colour in photos of a woman, it enhances her sexual attractiveness, though not her perceived intelligence. The red-sex link may simply reflect cultural traditions (e.g. red lipstick) or gender stereotypes. But maybe there is more to it – something more visceral. The colour red has been found to be a signal of readiness for mating in a range of animal species (Elliot & Niesta, 2008). The effect of red clothing was studied directly in comparing the evaluations of a woman dressed in either a red shirt or a white shirt. For men, the woman in red was sexually receptive, and in turn this mediated their perception of her as both attractive and sexually desirable (Pazda, Elliot, & Greitemeyer, 2012).

The hourglass figure

There is little doubt that men have a strong interest in women's bodies and, consciously or not, respond to the female waist-to-hip ratio (WHR). Typically, men prefer the classic hourglass figure (a ratio of 0.70); the good genes hypothesis suggests this signifies youthfulness, good health and fertility. However, there are cultural and ecological influences: in foraging societies, being thin may mean being ill and so men prefer their women to be heavier (i.e. larger WHRs). In Western societies, where heaviness may indicate ill health, men prefer slimmer women (i.e. smaller WHRs) (Marlowe & Wetsman, 2001). These effects point to the role of social and contextual factors that go beyond genes.

Attractive faces

As well as acknowledging the role of biological explanation, Langlois and colleagues (Langlois, Kalakanis, Rubenstein, Larson, Hallam, & Smoot, 2000) also tested the validity of three well-known maxims: *beauty is in the eye of the beholder, never judge a book by its cover* and *beauty is only skin-deep.* These question the assumption that physical beauty is ultimately important in real-life decisions, implying that social factors must play some part in how relationships are formed. For example, socialisation theory emphasises the effects on judgements of beauty of social and cultural norms and of experience; and social expectancy theory argues that social stereotypes (see **Chapter 2**) create their own reality.

How would evolutionary theory deal with the maxim *beauty is in the eye of the beholder*? Is physical attractiveness a matter of personal preference or fashion dictates, or is it something else – in our genes? Research by Gill Rhodes (2006) on face perception speaks to this question. Rhodes has investigated the social information that our faces convey, including the cues that make a face attractive. One interesting finding is the 'pulling power' of the **averageness effect** (see Box 14.1 and Figure 14.2).

In closing this section, we should note that there are similarities and differences between the sexes in how important physical attraction is in mate preferences. Norman Li and his colleagues have noted that men more often choose mates who are physically attractive, whereas women choose mates more often who have social status (Li, Yong, Tov, Sng, Fletcher, Valentine, et al., 2013). We explore the role of social status below.

Averageness effect
Humans have evolved to prefer average faces to those with unusual or distinctive features.

The search for ideals

Other characteristics of being attractive may derive *in part* from our genes. Garth Fletcher (Fletcher, Tither, O'Loughlin, Friesen, & Overall, 2004; also see Buss, 2003) studied the ideals (or standards) that college students look for in a partner. In long-term

---

Box 14.1 Your life
Physical appeal – evolutionary or cultural?

What kind of faces do you find most attractive? Is it a matter of personal preference? Is it a matter of culture or subcultural norms? Or, does evolution play a role? Perhaps it's a little bit of each.

The preferences of very young children and the existence of substantial cross-cultural consistency challenge the notion that standards of beauty are entirely dictated by culture. For example, body and facial symmetry (of right and left halves) in both men and women contributes to standards that most people use in judging beauty. Perhaps surprisingly, facial averageness is another plus.

Gill Rhodes (2006) has researched how we process information about the human face, asking whether facial beauty depends more on common physical qualities than on striking features. Participants judged caricatures of faces, each of which was systematically varied from average to distinctive. She found that averageness, rather than distinctiveness, was correlated with facial attractiveness

(also see Rhodes, Sumich, & Byatt, 1999). The averageness effect has also been found in other studies (e.g. Langlois, Roggman, & Musselman, 1994).

Rhodes (Rhodes & Tremewan, 1996) suggested an evolutionary basis for this effect: average faces draw the attention of infants to those objects in their environment that most resemble the human face – an average face is like a prototype. Face preferences may be adaptations that guide mate choice. Why would facial averageness (and also facial symmetry) make a person more attractive? One possibility is that these cues make a face seem more familiar and less strange. Another possibility is that both averageness and symmetry are signals of good health and therefore of 'good genes' – cues that we latch on to in searching for a potential mate.

See Figure 14.2 for examples of how averageness has been created by combining sets of real faces into composite faces.

Figure 14.2 What makes a face attractive?
- Anchor points were used to align features across individual photographs.
- Face composites were created by averaging the features of twenty-four real faces.
- These four faces are composites and are usually rated as more attractive than a real individual face.

Source: Rhodes (2006).

relationships, three 'ideal partner' dimensions guide the preferences of both men and women:

- warmth–trustworthiness – showing care and intimacy;
- vitality–attractiveness – signs of health and reproductive fitness;
- status–resources – being socially prominent and financially sound.

A fair conclusion is that because humans are biological and physical entities, biological and physical characteristics are an important cue to initial attraction, and there is an evolutionary and universal basis for some of this. Let us turn now to a number of social and contextual factors also related to what we find attractive.

What increases liking?

Suppose that someone has passed your initial 'attraction' test. What other factors encourage you to take the next step? This question has been well researched, to identify several important factors that determine how we come to like people even more:

- Proximity – do they live or work close by?
- Familiarity – do we feel that we know them?
- Similarity – are they people who are like us?

Proximity

Proximity
The factor of living close by is known to play an important role in the early stages of forming a friendship.

There is a good chance that you will get to like people who are in reasonable **proximity** to where you live or work – think of this as the neighbourhood factor. In a famous study of a student housing complex, Leon Festinger and his colleagues found that people were more likely to choose as friends those living in the same building and even on the same floor (Festinger, Schachter, & Back, 1950). Subtle architectural features that influence social contact, such as the location of a staircase, can also affect the process of making acquaintances and establishing friendships.

Look at the apartment block in Figure 14.3. Of the lower-floor residents, those in apartments 1 and 5 interacted most often with people living on the upper floor. Note that the

Proximity
Chatting with neighbours in the street is an important form of social interaction. It increases mutual liking and also promotes cooperation.

Figure 14.3 Friendship choice, physical proximity and housing design

Source: Based on Festinger, Schachter and Back (1950).

residents in apartments 1 and 5 are close to the staircases used by upper-floor residents and are therefore more likely to encounter them. Friendships occurred more often between 1 and 6 than between 2 and 7; and likewise between 5 and 10 than between 4 and 9. Although the physical distance between residents within each pair is the same, the interaction rate varied: becoming acquainted depended on the traffic flow.

People who live close by are *accessible*, so that interacting with them requires little effort and the rewards of interaction have little cost. Consider your immediate neighbours: you expect to continue interacting with them, and it is better that you are at ease when you do rather than feeling stressed. If at the outset you think that you are more likely to interact with John rather than Brian, it is probable that you will anticipate (perhaps hope!) that you will like John more (Berscheid, Graziano, Monson, & Dermer, 1976). In the first 'What do *you* think?' question, who will Carol like more, David or Paul?

Proximity became a more nuanced psychological concept during the twentieth century. The potentially negative impact of having a 'long-distance lover' is lessened by a phone call, an email, Facebook posting or, better still, by real-time audio-video contact using, for example, Skype or FaceTime (see review by Bargh & McKenna, 2004). Can we actually pursue a relationship on the net? (See Box 14.2.)

Familiarity

Proximity generally leads to greater familiarity – a friend is rather like your favourite pair of shoes, something that you feel comfortable with. **Familiarity** can account for why we gradually come to like the faces of strangers if we encounter them more often (Moreland & Beach, 1992). In contrast, when something familiar seems different, people feel uncomfortable. For example, people do not usually like mirror reversals of photos of their own or others' faces (Mita, Dermer, & Knight, 1977).

Familiarity enhances liking in much the same way as repeated presentation of a stimulus enhances liking for it – the **mere exposure effect** (Zajonc, 1968) as used by advertisers to make us feel familiar with new products (see the effect of repetitive advertising in **Chapter 6**). In a classroom setting, Dick Moreland and Scott Beach (1992) found that students rated another new 'student' (actually, collaborating with the investigators) as more attractive the more often they saw her (see Figure 14.4). If you want to be liked, be around!

Familiarity certainly leads to attraction (Reis, Maniaci, Caprariello, Eastwick, & Finkel, 2011), but perhaps not always. Michael Norton and his colleagues note that that the more we learn about another person, the more we uncover things that make that person *dissimilar* from ourselves, and that this can lead to dislike: the 'less is more' effect (Norton, Frost, & Ariely, 2007). For example, there are data showing that workers like their bosses less the longer they have worked for them; and celebrities become less liked as people learn more about their politics, faith and attitudes (Norton, Frost, & Ariely, 2013). The bottom line here is probably that all things being equal, familiarity does create a positive perception and thus increases attraction, but if along the way we stumble upon dissimilarities and learn undesirable things about

Familiarity
As we become more familiar with a stimulus (even another person), we feel more comfortable with it and we like it more.

Mere exposure effect
Repeated exposure to an object results in greater attraction to that object.

Box 14.2 Your life
Meeting on the net

Consider your cyber-relationships. How many do you have, how deep do they go, how do they map onto your "real" relationships? There is enormous individual variability, but it is rare to find a person who does not have at least a handful of cyber-relationships, and some proudly boast of having thousands of such relationships.

Access to the Internet allows people to meet, form friendships, fall in love, live together or get married. A cyberspace relationship does not necessarily remain suspended in cyberspace; some online 'friends' actually meet and form 'real' relationships.

In cyberspace, some sources of information about another person are absent – you can't touch them, and depending on the medium, you might not be able to hear them or see them. Even so, cyber-relationships can progress rapidly from knowing little about the other person to being intimate; equally, they can be ended very quickly, literally with the 'click of a button'.

From the outset, text-based Internet-mediated relationships differ markedly from offline relationships. A first meeting via the Internet does not give access to the usual range of physical and spoken linguistic cues that help to

form an impression – however, the now-prevalent social media posting of photos and videos, and the possibility of using real-time interactive audio-visual media such as FaceTime or Skype, may move online relationship development closer to the offline world.

David Jacobson (1999) investigated impression formation in comparing online expectation with offline experiences: that is, when people who had met online actually met in person. He found significant discrepancies – people had often formed erroneous impressions about characteristics such as talkativeness ('they seemed so quiet in person') and expansiveness ('they seemed so terse online but were very expressive offline'). People online often constructed images based on stereotypes, such as the vocation of the unseen person. One participant reported:

> I had no idea what to expect with Katya. From her descriptions I got the impression she would be overweight, kinda hackerish, but when we met, I found her very attractive. Normal sized, nice hair, not at all the stereotypical programmer.

> Jacobson (1999, p. 13)

Figure 14.4 Mere exposure and attraction

- This study tested the 'mere exposure' effect in a university class setting.
- Four new women 'students' took part in the class on 0, 5, 10 or 15 occasions.
- At the end of term, students in the class rated slides of the women for several characteristics.
- There was a weak effect for familiarity but a strong and increasing effect across visits for attractiveness.

Source: Based on Moreland and Beach (1992).

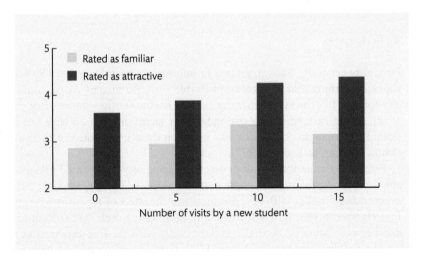

the other person, then that initially favourable impression may change (see the discussion of first impression formation in **Chapter 2**) and attraction may wane.

Attitude similarity

Familiarity that unearths differences may undermine attraction. The implication is that familiarity or otherwise that is associated with recognition of similarity, specifically attitude similarity, is an important basis for liking. In an early study by Theodore Newcomb (1961), students received rent-free housing in return for filling in questionnaires about their attitudes and values before they arrived. Changes in interpersonal attraction were measured over the course of a semester. Initially, attraction went hand-in-hand with proximity – students liked those who lived close by. Then another factor came into play: having compatible attitudes. As the semester progressed, the focus shifted to **similarity of attitudes**. Students with similar pre-acquaintance attitudes became more attracted to one another. This makes good sense. In real life, it takes time to discover whether or not a housemate thinks and feels the same way as you do about a variety of social issues.

Research by Don Byrne and Gerald Clore on the connection between sharing attitudes with another person and liking them has shown that interpersonal similarity in attitudes is an important ingredient in maintaining a relationship (e.g. Byrne, 1971; Clore & Byrne, 1974). The results were so reliable and consistent that Clore (1976) formulated a 'law of attraction' – attraction towards a person bears a linear relationship to the actual proportion of similar attitudes shared with that person. This law was thought to be applicable to more than just attitudes. Anything that other people do that agrees with your perception of things is rewarding, i.e. reinforcing. The more other people agree, the more they act as reinforcers for you and the more you like them. For example, if you suddenly discover that someone you are going out with likes the same obscure rock band as you, your liking for that person will increase.

Conversely, differences in attitudes and interests can lead to avoidance and dislike (Singh & Ho, 2000). The notion that we should be consistent in our thinking, as described by cognitive dissonance theory and other theories of cognitive consistency (see **Chapter 4**), may explain this. An inconsistency, such as recognising that we like something but that someone else does not, is cause for worry. An easy way to resolve this is to not like that person – this re-establishes consistency. Thus, we usually choose or preserve the company of similar others – it makes us feel comfortable.

Natasha Tidwell and her colleagues investigated the link between similarity and initial attraction in a contemporary setting: speed dating (Tidwell, Eastwick, & Finkel, 2013). They also differentiated between *perceived* and *actual* similarity. The former is an assumption that a person might make about another, whereas the latter is an independent (or objective) assessment of what two people have in common (cf. Becker, 2013). The nature of speed dating is such that we make quick assumptions based on fleeting evidence about how generally similar or dissimilar someone is to ourselves. In this research, perceived similarity was the more important predictor. In a brief encounter, actual similarity may be a weak determinant of romantic attraction.

Social matching

Matchmaking has long been important in society. But in the modern world it has become a hugely profitable commercial enterprise, which involves pairing people up on the basis of their having compatible attitudes, but also sharing demographic characteristics. Even a seemingly trivial similarity such as one's name can increase attraction. See the **archival research** by Jones, Pelham, Carvallo and Mirenberg (2004) in Box 14.3, and see Figure 14.5.

Assortative mating

Life is not a lucky dip. People seeking a partner do not usually choose one at random, but try to *match* each other on several features. Peruse the personal columns in your local newspaper, or relevant social media, to see how people describe themselves and what they look for in a potential partner. We bring previously held beliefs to the situation – beliefs about appropriateness such as gender, physique, socioeconomic class and religion. Matching is a form of **assortative mating**. Susan Sprecher (1998) found that in addition to proximity and

Similarity of attitudes
One of the most important positive, psychological determinants of attraction.

Archival research
Non-experimental method involving the assembly of data, or reports of data, collected by others.

Assortative mating
A non-random coupling of individuals based on their resemblance to each other on one or more characteristics.

Box 14.3 Our world
What's in a name? A search in the marriage archives

Jones and colleagues (Jones, Pelham, Carvallo, & Mirenberg, 2004) downloaded marriage records that included the names of brides and grooms from the website *Ancestry.com*, dating back to the nineteenth century. Several common names were focused on: Smith, Johnson, Williams, Jones and Brown. The researchers predicted that people would seek out others who simply resemble them, and found that people disproportionately married someone whose first or last name resembles their own. It seems that we are egotists at heart. Someone who is similar enough to activate mental associations with 'me' must be a fairly good choice!

In some initial experimental work, the researchers found that people were more attracted to someone with: (a) a random experimental code number (such as a PIN)

resembling their own birth date, (b) a surname containing letters from their own surname and (c) a number on a sports jersey that had been paired subliminally, on a computer screen, with their own name.

These findings prompted them to carry out an *archival study* of marriage among people with matching surnames. They found the most frequent choices of a marriage partner had the same last name. More than 60 per cent of the Smiths married another Smith, more than 50 per cent of the Joneses married another Jones, and more than 40 per cent of the Williamses married another Williams. All of these choices were well beyond chance.

We can note with passing interest that the senior researcher is named John Jones!

Source: Based on Jones, Pelham, Carvallo and Mirenberg (2004, Study 2).

Figure 14.5 'Alias Smith and Jones': name matching and marriage

- A database of surnames was constructed based on early American archival marriage records.
- Commonly occurring names provided large enough samples to find those that were identical prior to marriage.
- Matched surnames – the Smiths, the Joneses and even the Williamses – were well beyond chance.

Source: Based on data from Jones, Pelham, Carvallo and Mirenberg (2004), Study 2.

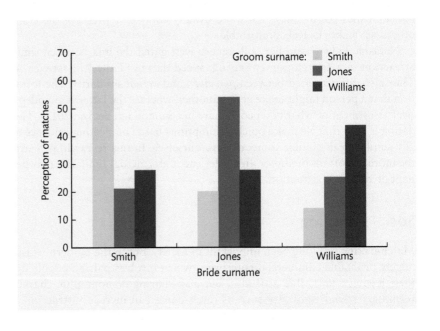

familiarity, people who are evenly matched in their physical appearance, social background and personality, sociability and interests and leisure activities are more likely to be attracted to one another. There is perhaps some truth in the saying *birds of a feather flock together*.

People certainly rely on the kinds of cues we have discussed to assess potential mates (Kavanagh, Robins, & Ellis, 2010). However, people also calibrate a level of aspiration by using their personal mating 'sociometer'. A sociometer is a measure of self-esteem based on feeling socially included or excluded by other people. (We discuss this in relation to the self in **Chapter 4**.) Kavanagh and colleagues' study suggests that people use a form of matching

Assortative mating
Similarity of age, ethnicity and culture are among factors that increase interpersonal liking, dating and mating.

by choosing a mate at a similar level of aspiration to themselves, one that is neither too accepting nor rejecting.

Do cohort studies, conducted across time, support this? Gruber-Baldini and her colleagues carried out such a longitudinal study of married couples over 21 years old (Gruber-Baldini, Schaie, & Willis, 1995). At the time of first testing, they found similarities in age, education, intellectual aptitude and flexibility of attitudes. An additional finding was that some spouses became even more alike over time in attitude flexibility and word fluency. Thus, initial similarity in the phase of assortative mating was enhanced by their experiences together. There is also a strong element of reality testing when it comes to looks, since people usually settle on a romantic partner who is similar to their own level of physical attractiveness (Feingold, 1988).

Studies of dating across ethnic or cultural groups reveal a complex interplay of factors involving *similarity of culture* that influences attraction. A study of heterosexual dating preferences among four ethnic groups in the United States (Asian, African, Latino and Euro/white Americans) showed that participants generally preferred partners from their own ethnic group (Liu, Campbell, & Condie, 1995). Gaining approval from one's social network was the most powerful predictor of partner preferences, followed by similarity of culture and physical attractiveness. While similarity of culture and ethnicity are important determinants of partner choice, inter-racial studies point to other factors, particularly changes in sociocultural sexual attitudes and cultural differences in dating practices and how intimate relationships develop, along with the more obvious factors of proximity and similarity.

Ethnicity and Internet dating

In the context of assortative mating, two large-scale Internet dating site studies examined ethnic preferences when choosing a dating partner. George Yancey (2007) compared the ethnic choices of white, black, Hispanic and Asian contributors to *Yahoo Personals*. Willingness to meet with partners of different race varied: women were less likely than men to date inter-racially, while Asians were more likely than whites or Hispanics to date blacks. Perhaps unsurprisingly, willingness to date inter-racially was lower among those who were politically conservative or aligned with the religious right. Several demographic factors (age, city size, level of education) had little influence on ethnic dating preferences.

Glenn Tsunokai and his colleagues analysed the ethnic choices of heterosexual and gay Asian male contributors to *Match.com* (Tsunokai, McGrath, & Kavanagh, 2014), to discover that heterosexual Asian females and gay Asian males were more inclined to 'cross the colour line' by dating whites, when compared with earlier inter-racial research on attractiveness and partner choice.

A more indirect form of Internet dating is a by-product of *social networking sites* (SNSs), the most popular of which is Facebook – a site with, at the end of 2014, about 1.4 billion active users. Jesse Fox and her associates studied stages of developing relationships (as outlined by Knapp, 1978) among university students who used Facebook in their quest (Fox, Warber, & Makstaller, 2013). They concluded that Facebook was actually a 'double-edged sword' because it allowed the user to learn about, but also to spy on, potential and current partners. The information gleaned can be worrisome, both about oneself and about a partner. Consider these excerpts from the focus group participants:

> Terrence: Facebook makes starting a relationship more accessible and easier.
> Perry: It's good in the beginning, just getting to know people. But if the relationship actually takes off, then Facebook can't do any good.
> Tamara: I kind of wish Facebook didn't exist.
> Leah (*nods*): It's ruining the world.

> (Fox, Warber, & Makstaller, 2013, pp. 785–786)

Personal characteristics

Personality

Although similarity is an important predictor of attraction, people also find other things attractive in a friend or partner. In a study of three kinds of relationship (romantic, and same-gender and opposite-gender friendship), Sprecher (1998) confirmed that having similar interests, leisure activities, attitudes, values and social skills were determinants of attraction. However, these factors were less important than other personal characteristics: for example, having a 'desirable personality', warmth and kindness, and reciprocal liking. Proximity and familiarity were also important; in contrast, intelligence, earning potential and competence were relatively unimportant. Catherine Cottrell and her colleagues added another attribute that topped the list in the profile of an ideal mate – trustworthiness (Cottrell, Neuberg, & Li, 2007). Their findings generalise to other interdependent relationships, such as are found in work and athletic teams. We discuss the importance of *trust* later in this chapter but can note for now that it takes us beyond attraction when considering how close relationships develop and how they are maintained.

Self-disclosure and trust

Self-disclosure
The sharing of intimate information and feelings with another person.

A willingness to reveal some aspects of oneself in conversation (i.e. **self-disclosure**) is an important determinant of long-term intimacy in a relationship. According to the *social penetration* model (Altman & Taylor, 1973), people share more intimate topics with a close friend than a casual acquaintance or stranger, and reveal more to people they like and trust. The converse is also true. People prefer other people who reveal more about their feelings and thoughts (Collins & Miller, 1994). Disclosing personal information and being sensitive and responsive to our partner's disclosures are important, both in developing relationships (Laurenceau, Barrett, & Pietromonaco, 1998) and in maintaining them (Cross, Bacon, & Morris, 2000).

In a study by Jeffrey Vittengl and Craig Holt (2000), students who did not know one another took part in brief conversations, before and after which they rated their positive and negative affect as well as their willingness to self-disclose. Greater self-disclosure led to increased positive affect. Despite this, self-disclosure is not universal; the amount and depth of information shared with another vary according to culture and gender. For example, a meta-analysis of 205 studies of self-disclosure showed that women reveal more about themselves than men (Dindia & Allen, 1992).

With respect to culture, Kurt Lewin (1936) long ago observed differences between Americans and Germans. Americans disclosed more than Germans in initial encounters but did not become as intimate as Germans as their relationships progressed. More recent research focusing on the more profound distinction between individualist and collectivist cultures (America and Germany are both individualistic cultures) finds that people from individualist cultures self-disclose more information than people from collectivist cultures (see **Chapter 16**). When information is shared, individualists give more personal information whereas collectivists share information about group membership (Gudykunst, Matsumoto, Ting-Toomey, Nishida, Kim, & Heyman, 1996; for a review of cultural differences in disclosure, see Goodwin, 1999).

Another reason why self-disclosure is important in relationships may be that trust sustains relationships. In life, people try to reduce risk, but they also need and seek out relationships. The problem is that relationships are a risky business in which people make themselves vulnerable to others. People need to build interpersonal trust to manage relationship-based risk (Cvetkovich & Löfstedt, 1999). Self-disclosure plays an important role in reducing risk and building trust – the more that your friend or partner self-discloses, the safer you feel in the relationship and the more you trust him or her. Trust and good relationships go hand-in-hand (Holmes, 2002; Rempel, Ross, & Holmes, 2001).

The central role of trust in relationships may cause problems for the development of new relationships and maintenance of established relationships online (Green & Carpenter, 2011). Existing relationships typically benefit from the addition of an online dimension – allowing more ready and frequent communication in an atmosphere of already established mutual trust. However, a rapidly growing number of people use social networking and dating sites as a context in which to meet new people and develop new relationships. It is here the spectres of deception and lowered moral standards loom large. How do you know whether to trust someone, and how much to self-disclose? The paradox is that the relative anonymity and sense of privacy afforded by online communication also encourages honesty and self-disclosure, both of which are important for trust and relationship development (Caspi & Gorsky, 2006; Christopherson, 2007).

Cultural stereotypes

When collectivist societies are compared with individualistic societies, the former are found to nurture a self that is interdependent rather than independent, and to encourage interpersonal relationships that are harmonious rather than competitive (see **Chapters 4** and **16**). However, some have wondered whether there really is such a big cultural difference in how potential friends and partners are evaluated. For example, Linda Albright and colleagues compared participants from the United States and China, using the same method of data collection in each country (Albright, Malloy, Dong, Kenny, Fang, Winquist, et al., 1997). Within-culture data were based on face-to-face interactions, and across-culture data were based on photographs. They found that the **Big Five** personality dimensions (which contain a variety of more specific traits) were used consistently in both countries and both within and across cultures. An attractive person was perceived positively regardless of the ethnicity of the judge or of the target.

Other research by Ladd Wheeler and Youngmee Kim (1997) that compared Koreans and North Americans largely supported Albright and colleagues' findings. However, Wheeler and Kim also found some cultural differences (see Figure 14.6). Stereotypes associated with attractiveness include several that are common to both cultures ('universal') and overlap with the Big Five dimensions, but the two cultures did differ to some extent regarding what they considered to represent being physically attractive:

- For North Americans, positive stereotypes include being assertive, dominant and strong – characteristics associated with *individualism*.

- For Koreans, positive stereotypes include being empathic, generous, sensitive, honest and trustworthy – characteristics associated with *collectivism*.

Big Five
The five major personality dimensions of extraversion/surgency, agreeableness, conscientiousness, emotional stability and intellect/openness to experience.

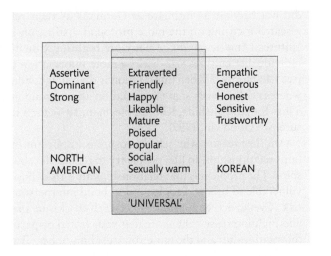

Figure 14.6 Cultural variation and attraction

- Korean participants rated traits for their association with photographs of people who varied in physical beauty.
- Their ratings were compared with previously published American and Canadian data.
- Some traits were 'universal', associated with the three national groups.
- Other traits were specific either to individualistic cultures (North American) or to a collectivist culture (Korean).

Source: Based on Wheeler and Kim (1997).

Attraction and rewards

Rarely in psychology does one theory account for a phenomenon in its totality. More often, several theories contribute perspectives that focus on different facets or underlying processes. Theories of attraction are no exception. At the broadest level, theories of attraction can be divided into those that view human nature as striving to maintain cognitive consistency, and those that view human nature as the pursuit of pleasure and the avoidance of pain – behaviourist or reinforcement approaches. Consistency theories, such as balance theory (**Chapter 5**) and cognitive dissonance theory (**Chapter 6**), allow a simple proposition. People normally like others who are similar to them – agreement is an affirming experience that generates positive affect. However, if people who like one another disagree, they experience tension and then try to modify their attitudes to make them more similar. If relative strangers who do not share a particularly strong bond of attraction disagree, there is less sense of imbalance or dissonance, and they are unlikely to pursue contact.

We now turn to two approaches based directly on reinforcement, and two other approaches based on a social exchange model of people's behaviour, but also derived from reinforcement principles.

A reinforcement approach

The general idea is simple. People who reward us directly become associated with pleasure and we learn to like them; people who punish us directly become associated with pain and we dislike them. These ideas have a long history in philosophy, literature and general psychology, and they have also been applied in social psychology to help explain interpersonal attraction (Walster, Walster, & Berscheid, 1978).

In a variation related to classical or Pavlovian conditioning (also see **Chapter 5**), Byrne and Clore (1970) proposed a **reinforcement-affect model** – just as Pavlov's dog learns to associate the sound of a bell with the positive reinforcement of food, so humans can associate another person with other positive or negative aspects of the immediate environment. They proposed that any *background* (and neutral) stimulus that may even be associated accidentally with reward becomes positively valued. However, if it is associated with punishment, it becomes negatively valued.

An example of this was an early environmental experiment by Griffitt and Veitch (1971) that showed how simple background features, such as feeling hot or crowded, can diminish our attraction to a stranger (see Box 14.4 and Figure 14.7).

Reinforcement-affect model
Model of attraction which postulates that we like people who are around when we experience a positive feeling (which itself is reinforcing).

Box 14.4 Research classic
Evaluating a stranger when we feel hot and crowded

Imagine that after completing a twenty-four-item attitude scale measuring opinions on a variety of social issues, you were later invited to participate, by completing a further series of questionnaires, along with other students in an investigation of 'judgemental processes under altered environmental conditions'. You were not to know that you were in one of eight different experimental groups. Dressed lightly in cotton shorts and a cotton shirt, you and your group enter an 'environmental chamber', 3 metres long and 2.2 metres wide.

By having eight groups, William Griffitt and Russell Veitch (1971) were able to test three independent variables: (a) *heat*, the ambient temperature, which was either normal at 23°C or hot at 34°C; (b) *population density* which consisted of having either 3–5 group members or 12–16 group members in the chamber at one time; (c) *attitude similarity*. Note that some participants would really have experienced a degree of environmental stress by working on their questionnaires in an environment that was either hot or crowded. As a measure of attitude similarity, each participant also rated an anonymous stranger after they had first inspected the stranger's responses to the twenty-four-item attitude scale – the same scale that the

participants had completed earlier. What they saw was fictitious. The stranger had made similar responses to a proportion of the items – to either 0.25 (low similarity) or 0.75 (high similarity) of them – as those made by that participant.

Finally, the stranger was also rated in order to calculate a measure of attraction based on two questions: how much the stranger would probably be liked, and how desirable would the stranger be as a work partner.

The result for attitude similarity was striking. Not surprisingly, the stranger who was more similar to a participant was considerably more attractive than one who was less similar, confirming the importance of attitude similarity in determining initial attraction, discussed in an earlier section.

The other results show that feeling hot or feeling crowded also affected how attractive a stranger was judged. In the context of classical conditioning, this means that the mere association of a negatively valued background stimulus, in this case two different environmental stressors, can make another person seem less attractive.

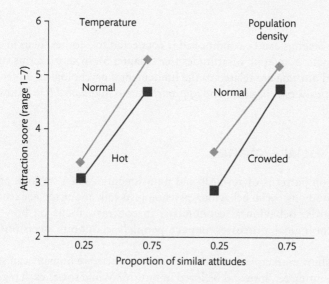

Figure 14.7 Attraction and the reinforcing effects of background features

- Students rated a fictitious stranger as more attractive when they shared a higher proportion of similar attitudes.
- Stressful background factors, such as feeling hot or feeling crowded, reduced the attractiveness of the stranger.

Source: Based on Griffitt and Veitch (1971).

Social exchange
Marriage is not entered into lightly. In long-term relationships, partners carefully weigh up the respective costs and benefits of the relationship.

Automatic activation
According to Fazio, attitudes that have a strong evaluative link to situational cues are more likely to automatically come to mind from memory.

The study of how our feelings can be conditioned is connected to another focus in social psychology, on the **automatic activation** of attitudes (see **Chapter 5**). In short, terms such as *affect*, *stimulus value* and *attitude* are related to the fundamental psychological dimensions of *good* versus *bad*, *positive* versus *negative* and *approach* versus *avoidance* (De Houwer & Hermans, 2001).

Relationships as a social exchange

Social exchange
People often use a form of everyday economics when they weigh up costs and rewards before deciding what to do.

Behaviourism
An emphasis on explaining observable behaviour in terms of reinforcement schedules.

Reinforcement is based on patterns of rewards and punishments. When we look at how economics is applied to studying social behaviour, psychologists talk about **social exchange**: payoffs, costs and rewards. Behavioural economists, in contrast, focus on how well-established social psychological processes impact people's economic decisions (see Cartwright, 2014).

So, is there a relationships marketplace out there – a place where we humans can satisfy our needs to interact, be intimate, 'love and be loved in return'? While social exchange theory is one of a family of theories based on **behaviourism**, it is also an approach to studying interpersonal relationships that incorporates *interaction*. Further, it deals directly with close relationships.

Costs and benefits

If two people are to progress in a relationship, it will be because they gain from the way that they exchange benefits (i.e. rewards). Social exchange is a model of behaviour introduced by the sociologist George Homans (1961): it accounts for our interpersonal relationships using economic concepts and is wedded to behaviourism. Whether we like someone is determined by the **cost-reward ratio**: 'What will it cost me to get a positive reward from that person?' Social exchange theory also argues that each participant's outcomes are determined by their *joint* actions.

A relationship is an ongoing everyday activity. We try to obtain, preserve or exchange things of value with other human beings. We bargain. What are we prepared to give in exchange for what they will give us? Some exchanges are brief and shallow, while others are long-term and extremely complex and important. In all cases, we experience outcomes or payoffs that depend on what others do. Over time, we try to fashion a way of interacting that is rational and mutually beneficial.

Social exchange is a give-and-take relationship between people, and relationships are examples of business transactions. So, is this a dry approach to the study of important relationships? If so, its proponents argue, it is nevertheless valid. Indeed, social exchange is a core feature of one of the most significant approaches to leadership – transactional theories of leadership that trace effective leadership to mutually beneficial leader-follower exchanges (e.g. Graen & Uhl-Bien, 1995; Hollander, 1958; see **Chapter 9**).

Broadly speaking, resources exchanged include: goods, information, love, money, services and status (Foa & Foa, 1975). Each can be particular, so that its value depends on who gives the reward. So, a hug (a specific case of 'love') will be more valued if it comes from a special person. Each reward can also be concrete, as money clearly is. There are also costs in a relationship, such as the time it takes to pursue it or the way one's friends may frown on it. Because resources are traded with a partner, we try to use a **minimax strategy** – minimise costs and maximise rewards. Of course, we may not be conscious of doing so and would probably object to the idea that we do!

John Thibaut and Hal Kelley's (1959) *The Social Psychology of Groups* was a highly influential book that underpinned much subsequent research. It argued that we must understand the *structure* of a relationship in order to deal with the behaviour that takes place, as it is this structure that defines the rewards and punishments available. According to the minimax strategy, what follows is that a relationship is unsatisfactory when the costs exceed the rewards. In practice, people exchange resources with one another in the hope that they will earn a **profit**: that is, one in which the rewards exceed the costs. This is a novel way of defining a 'good relationship'. How might you interpret what Erik meant in the second 'What do *you* think?' question?

Comparison levels

A final important component of social exchange theory is the part played by each person's **comparison level** or CL – a standard against which all of one's relationships are judged. People's comparison levels are the product of their past experiences with other people in similar exchanges. If the result in a present exchange is positive (i.e. a person's profit exceeds their CL), the relationship will be considered satisfying and the other person will seem attractive. However, dissatisfaction follows if the final result is negative (i.e. the profit falls below the CL). There is a blessing in this model because it is possible for both people in a relationship to be making a profit and therefore to gain satisfaction. The CL concept is helpful in accounting for why some relationships might be acceptable at some times but not at others (see Box 14.5).

Cost-reward ratio
Tenet of social exchange theory, according to which liking for another is determined by calculating what it will cost to be reinforced by that person.

Minimax strategy
In relating to others, we try to minimise the costs and maximise the rewards that accrue.

Profit
This flows from a relationship when the rewards that accrue from continued interaction exceed the costs.

Comparison level
A standard that develops over time, allowing us to judge whether a new relationship is profitable or not.

Box 14.5   Your life
What do you get from a relationship? An exercise in social exchange

Just how calculating are you in developing a new relationship or sustaining an existing relationship? What might you weigh up and what motives might influence your calculus? You may, according to social psychology research, be more calculating than you think; and your deliberations may be influenced by your comparison level.

A person's comparison level or CL is idiosyncratic, as each person has had unique experiences. Your CL is the average value of all outcomes of relationships with others in your past, and also of outcomes for others that you may have heard about. It can vary across different kinds of relationship, so your CL for your doctor will be different from that for a lover.

Your entry point into a new relationship is seen against a backdrop of the other people you have known (or known about) in that context, together with the profits and losses you have encountered in relating to them. This running average constitutes a baseline for your relationships in that particular sphere. A new encounter could be judged as satisfactory only if it exceeded this baseline.

Take as an example a date that you have had with another person. The outcome is defined as the rewards (having a nice time, developing a potential relationship) minus the costs (how much money it cost you, how difficult or risky it was to arrange, whether you feel you blew your chance to make a good impression). The actual outcome will be determined by how it compares with other dates you have had in similar circumstances in the past or at present, and perhaps by how successful other people's dates have seemed to you.

To complicate matters a little, your CL can change over time. Although age may not make you any wiser, as you get older you are likely to expect more of some future commitment to another person than when you were younger.

There is an additional concept – the *comparison level for alternatives*. Suppose that you are in an already satisfying relationship but then meet someone new, an enticing stranger. As the saying goes, 'the grass always looks greener on the other side of the fence'. In social exchange language, there is the prospect here of an increase in rewards over costs.

Does all this sound too calculating to you? Be honest, now! Whatever the outcome, the situation has become unstable. Decisions, decisions . . .

Social exchange, equity and justice

Does exchange theory have a future? In sum, the answer is yes. A strong feature of exchange theory is that it accommodates variations in relationships, including:

- differences between people in how they perceive rewards and costs (you might think that free advice from your partner is rewarding, others might not);
- differences within the person based on varying CLs, both over time and across different contexts (I like companionship, but I prefer to shop for clothes alone).

The theory is frequently used. For example, Caryl Rusbult has shown how *investment* includes the way that rewards, costs and CLs are related to both satisfaction and commitment in a relationship (Rusbult, Martz, & Agnew, 1998). It is also a significant perspective in how we understand social justice (explored further in this section) and leadership (see **Chapter 9**), and in understanding how the breakdown of a relationship often follows a lack of commitment (Le & Agnew, 2003; discussed later). Indeed, Western society may actually be founded on a system of social exchange within which we strive for *equity*, or balance, in our relationships with others (Walster, Walster, & Berscheid, 1978).

Most people believe that outcomes in an exchange should be fair and just, enshrined in a society's laws and norms: we should comply with the 'rules'. What is thought to be just and fair is a feature of group life (see the role of leadership in **Chapter 9**) and of intergroup relations (**Chapter 11**). Equity and equality are not identical concepts. In a work setting, *equality* requires that all people are paid the same, whereas *equity* requires that those who work hardest or do the most important jobs are paid more.

People are happiest in relationships when they believe that the give and take is approximately equal. **Equity theory** was developed in the context of workplace motivation and popularised in social psychology by J. Stacey Adams (1965). It covers two main situations:

1 a mutual exchange of resources (as in marriage);

2 an exchange where limited resources must be distributed (such as a judge awarding compensation for injury).

In both, equity theory predicts that people expect resources to be given out *fairly*, in proportion to their contribution. (See how a norm of equity has been applied to help understand prosocial behaviour in **Chapter 13**.) If we help others, it is fair to expect them to help us. Equity exists between Jack and Jill when:

$$\frac{\text{Jack's outcomes}}{\text{Jack's inputs}} = \frac{\text{Jill's outcomes}}{\text{Jill's inputs}}$$

Jack estimates the ratio of what he has got out of his relationship with Jill to what he has put into the relationship, and then compares this ratio with the ratio applying to Jill (see Figure 14.8). If these ratios are equal, Jack will feel that each of them is being treated fairly or equitably. Jill, of course, will have her own ideas about what is fair. Perhaps Jack is living in a dream world!

When a relationship is equitable, the participants' outcomes (rewards minus costs) are proportional to their inputs or contributions to the relationship. The underlying concept is **distributive justice** (Homans, 1961). It is an aspect of social justice and refers more generally to practising a norm of fairness in the sharing of goods that each member of a group receives. Equity theory can be applied to many areas of social life, such as exploitative relationships, helping relationships and intimate relationships (Walster, Walster, & Berscheid, 1978). The more inequitably people are treated, the more distress they feel. When we experience continuing inequity, the relationship is likely to end (Adams, 1965).

Distributive justice (fair allocation of resources) should be distinguished from **procedural justice** (fair procedures – that may or may not result in an equal allocation of resources). Procedural justice is particularly important within groups where members' attachment to the group rests more on being treated fairly (procedural justice) than on equal allocation of resources within the group (De Cremer & Tyler, 2005; Tyler & Smith, 1998; **Chapter 11**).

Equity theory
A special case of social exchange theory that defines a relationship as equitable when the ratio of inputs to outcomes are seen to be the same by both partners.

Distributive justice
The fairness of the outcome of a decision.

Procedural justice
The fairness of the procedures used to make a decision.

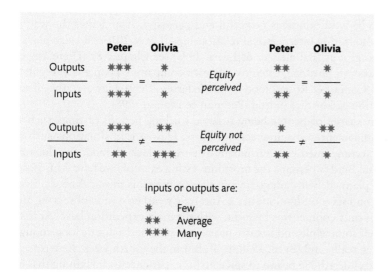

Figure 14.8 Equity theory applied to two equitable and two inequitable relationships
Source: Based on Baron and Byrne (1987).

The role of norms

Although Adams (1965) thought that people *always* prefer an equity norm when allocating resources, this may not always be the case (Deutsch, 1975). When resources are shared out according to inputs, we may evaluate our friend's inputs differently from a stranger's. Strangers tend to allocate resources on the basis of *ability*, whereas friends allocate on the basis of both *ability* and *effort* (Lamm & Kayser, 1978). A norm of mutual obligation, rather than equity, to contribute to a common cause may be triggered when a friendship is involved: we expect our friends more so than strangers to pull their weight – perhaps to help us paint our new house!

There is also a sex difference here: women prefer an equality norm and men an equity norm (Major & Adams, 1983). This difference may be based on gender-stereotyped roles in which women strive for harmony and peace in interactions by treating people equally. And we have also seen that in a group context, intragroup procedural justice may be more important than distributive justice or equality (see **Chapter 11**).

In anticipation of a later section entitled 'Relationships that work – and those that don't', we add a rider: not everyone studying close relationships is that enamoured of social exchange and equity theory models. For example, Andrew Ledbetter and his colleagues argue that relationship partners who focus too narrowly on equity for themselves make hard work of sustaining their relationship (Ledbetter, Stassen-Ferrara, & Dowd, 2013). They offer a variant on traditional exchange and equity models — *self-expansion theory*. A working close relationship is better served when the partners expand themselves to include the other. This happens when partners share some of their thoughts, using relational language (e.g. bringing plural pronouns into play) and by acting communally.

Attachment

Research on attachment initially focused on the bonding that occurs between infant and caregiver, but it has now expanded to include the different ways that adults make connections with those who are close to them. First, we explore a phenomenon that underpins this topic – affiliation.

Social isolation and the need to affiliate

Need to affiliate
The urge to form connections and make contact with other people.

The **need to affiliate**, to be with others, is powerful and pervasive. It underlies the way in which we form positive and lasting interpersonal relationships (Leary, 2010) and also plays a key role in attachment to groups (Baumeister & Leary, 1995; see **Chapter 8**). There are, of course, times when we wish to be alone, to enjoy our own company – people also regulate their need for privacy (O'Connor & Rosenblood, 1996; Pedersen, 1999). However, the effects of too much social isolation can be dire indeed (Perlman & Peplau, 1998).

There have been many stories of people being isolated for long periods of time, such as prisoners in solitary confinement and shipwreck survivors. However, in situations such as these, isolation is often accompanied by punishment or perhaps lack of food. For this reason, the record of Admiral Byrd is perhaps the most interesting example we have – his isolation was voluntary and planned, with adequate supplies to meet his physical needs. Byrd volunteered in 1934 to spend six months alone at an Antarctic weather station observing and recording conditions. His only contact was by radio with the main expedition base. At first, he wanted to 'be by myself for a while and to taste peace and quiet and solitude long enough to find out how good they really are' (Byrd, 1938, p. 4). But in the fourth week, he wrote of feeling lonely, lost and bewildered. He began to spice up his experience by imagining that he was among familiar people. After nine weeks, Byrd became preoccupied with religious questions and, like Monty Python, dwelt on the 'meaning of life'. His thoughts turned to ways of believing that he was not actually by himself: 'The human race, then, is not alone in the universe. Though I am cut off from human beings, I am not alone' (p. 185). After three months, he became severely depressed, apathetic and assailed by hallucinations and bizarre ideas.

The social psychologist William McDougall (1908) suggested that humans are innately motivated to gather together and to be part of a group, as some animals do that live in herds or colonies. This was a straightforward **instinct** theory. It was roundly criticised by the behaviourist John Watson (1913), who argued that accounting for herding behaviour by calling it a herding instinct was a very weak position. Later biological explanations of social behaviour were much more sophisticated. Affiliation has been extensively researched, so we have been selective in choosing just two topics. Do people want company when they become anxious? How serious are the consequences of inadequate caregiving for infants?

Instinct
Innate drive or impulse, genetically transmitted.

Isolation and anxiety

In his classic work *The Psychology of Affiliation*, Stanley Schachter (1959) described a connection between being isolated and feeling anxious. Being alone can make people want to be with others, even with strangers for a short period. Having company serves to reduce anxiety, and this can happen for two reasons. Other people might serve as a distraction from a worrying situation, or else as a yardstick for the process of **social comparison**. Schachter's research confirmed the latter explanation. James Kulik and his colleagues have shown how this process can be used to speed up recovery from surgery, specifically for heart patients (Kulik, Mahler, & Moore, 1996; see Box 14.6).

Social comparison (theory)
Comparing our behaviours and opinions with those of others in order to establish the correct or socially approved way of thinking and behaving.

The need to affiliate can be affected by temporary states such as fear, and it is not just any person that we want to be with, but someone specific. Schachter's original assertion can be amended to read: 'Misery loves the company of those in the same miserable situation' (Gump & Kulik, 1997). Reduction of anxiety is only one need that invokes the process of social comparison. In a broader context, we make these comparisons whenever we look to the views of a special group, our friends. How people come to be part of this special group is discussed later in this chapter.

One situation in which isolation can be particularly painful is when it is intentionally imposed on you by another individual or by an entire group – when you are shunned or ostracised (Williams, 2002, 2009). Earlier, in **Chapter 8**, we discussed ostracism as something that happens in the context of a group – but of course, individuals can ostracise one another in interpersonal relationships with equally dramatic effect. Feeling ostracised, which can even be elicited by something as seemingly trivial as someone averting their gaze, can make one feel one's relationship has been devalued (Wirth, Sacco, Hugenberg, & Williams, 2010), cause self-esteem to plummet and even make people feel that they have no meaningful existence (e.g. Zadro, Williams, & Richardson, 2004).

Effects of social deprivation

Lack of social affiliation, in the form of social deprivation, in infancy has particularly devastating effects. The British psychiatrist John Bowlby (1988) documents the impact of the release of two movies on researchers studying children in the 1950s, one by René Spitz, *Grief: A Peril in Infancy* (1947), and the other by James Robertson, *A Two-Year-Old Goes to Hospital* (1952). Survival, it transpired, depends on physical needs but also on a quite independent need for care and intimate interaction.

The psychoanalyst René Spitz (1945) reported on babies who had been in an overcrowded institution for two years, left there by mothers unable to look after them. The babies were

Attachment
Early studies by Harlow and Bowlby showed that babies need nurturing as well as food. Lots of cuddling, warmth and softness works wonders.

Box 14.6 Research highlight
Heart to heart: Effects of sharing a room before surgery

Kulik, Mahler and Moore (1996) recorded the verbal interactions of heart patients, studying the effects of pre-operative room-mate assignments on patterns of affiliation, including how anxious they were before the operation and their speed of recovery afterwards. If social comparison were to play a part in this context, then it should reveal itself if the other person is also a cardiac patient. The results confirmed that social comparison was at work:

- Patients were significantly more likely to clarify their thoughts, by talking about the surgery and the prospects of recovery afterwards, when their room-mate was a cardiac rather than a non-cardiac patient.

- This effect was strongest when the room-mate had already undergone the operation. When patient A was pre-operative and patient B was post-operative, patient A would be less anxious, as measured by the number of anxiety-reducing drugs and sedatives requested by patients the night before surgery.

- Patients were also more likely to be discharged sooner if assigned to a room-mate who was cardiac rather than non-cardiac, measured by the length of stay following the procedure.

Hospitalism
A state of apathy and depression noted among institutionalised infants deprived of close contact with a caregiver.

fed but rarely handled, and were mostly confined to their cots. Compared with other institutionalised children who had been given adequate care, they were less mentally and socially advanced, and their mortality rate was extremely high. Spitz coined the term **hospitalism** to describe the psychological condition in which he found these children. Hospitalism came to life vividly with heart-wrenching television footage of little children abandoned in Romanian orphanages in the early 1990s. Robertson was a psychiatric social worker and psychoanalyst working at the Tavistock Clinic and Institute in London, and was acknowledged by Bowlby as an inspiration. His remarkable film dealt with the emotional deterioration of a young girl separated from her mother for eight days while in hospital for minor surgery.

Other research of that time, by Harry Harlow and his colleagues at the University of Wisconsin, focused on the devastating effects of social isolation on newborn rhesus monkeys (Harlow, 1958; Harlow & Harlow, 1965). This included deprivation of contact with their mothers. A monkey mother provides more than contact, food, rocking and warmth: she is the first link in the chain of the baby's experience of socialisation. Harlow's research was extended to babies that were totally isolated from contact with any living being for up to 12 months. Such long periods of solitary confinement had drastic consequences. The infant monkeys would sometimes huddle in a corner, rock back and forth repetitively, and bite themselves. When later exposed to normal peers, they did not enter into the rough-and-tumble play of the others, and they failed to defend themselves from attack. As adults, they were sexually incompetent. In addition, Harlow's early studies pointed to the importance of warmth in contact between a mother and infant, laying the groundwork for attachment (Williams & Bargh, 2008).

Attachment styles

Clearly, long-term social deprivation in infants is psychologically traumatic – in particular separation from a long-term caregiver, typically the mother. Bowlby (1969) and his colleagues at the Tavistock Institute in England focused on the **attachment behaviour** of infants to their mothers, noting that young children keep close to their mothers. Young children send signals to their caregiver by crying and smiling, and maintained proximity by clinging or following, all of which Bowlby attributed to an innate affiliative drive. Compared with affiliation, attachment involves that extra step of a close relationship at a particular point in time with just a few, perhaps one, other person.

For Bowlby and many other social psychologists, attachment behaviour is not limited to the mother–infant experience but can be observed throughout the life cycle. In Bowlby's words, it accompanies people 'from the cradle to the grave'. Stable adult relationships 'come from somewhere' (Berscheid, 1994), and research suggests that they originate in childhood attachment dynamics that leave us with particular **attachment styles** that influence us for the rest of our lives. In explaining the way that we as adults experience both love and loneliness, Cindy Hazan and Phillip Shaver (1987) defined three attachment styles – *secure*, *avoidant* and *anxious* – that are also found in children (see Table 14.1).

Judy Feeney and Pat Noller (1990) found that attachment styles developed in childhood carry on to influence the way heterosexual romantic relationships are formed in later life. They assessed attachment levels, communication patterns and relationship satisfaction among married couples, and found that securely attached individuals (comfortable with closeness and having low anxiety about relationships) were more often paired with similarly secure spouses.

Other research has shown that people with an avoidant style often report aversive sexual feelings and experiences and are less satisfied and more stressed from parenting when a baby

Attachment behaviour
The tendency of an infant to maintain close physical proximity with the mother or primary caregiver.

Attachment styles
Descriptions of the nature of people's close relationships, thought to be established in childhood.

Table 14.1 Characteristics of three attachment styles

Attachment style	Characteristics
Secure	Trust in others; not worried about being abandoned; belief that one is worthy and liked; find it easy to be close to others; comfortable being dependent on others, and vice versa.
Avoidant	Suppression of attachment needs; past attempts to be intimate have been rebuffed; uncomfortable when close to others; find it difficult to trust others or to depend on them; feel nervous when anyone gets close.
Anxious	Concern that others will not reciprocate one's desire for intimacy; feel that a close partner does not really offer love, or may leave; want to merge with someone and this can scare people away.

Source: Based on Hazan and Shaver (1987).

arrives (Birnbaum, Reis, Mikulincer, Gillath, & Orpaz, 2006; Rholes, Simpson, & Friedman, 2006), and less close to their children as they grow older (Rholes, Simpson, & Blakely, 1995). A narrative review of more than sixty relevant studies of self-reported attachment styles and parenting concludes that secure attachment is robustly and reliably associated with more positive parenting behaviour, emotions, cognitions and outcomes, whereas insecure attachment is associated with more negative parenting behaviour, emotions, cognitions and outcomes (Jones, Cassidy, & Shaver, 2015). Now consider the third 'What do *you* think?' question. What might have happened in Aishani's life before she met Kamesh that could account for her current predicament?

Studies of romantic relationships suggest that Bowlby was right – attachment is a process that operates throughout life rather than just a feature of infancy, and attachment styles adopted early in life prevail in later relationships. We now know a great deal about attachment styles and romantic relationships:

- *Securely attached* adults find it easier to get close to others and to enjoy affectionate and long-lasting relationships (Brennan & Shaver, 1995); they also bolster a feeling of energy and a willingness to explore their social and physical environment (Luke, Sedikides, & Carnelley, 2012).

- *Avoidantly attached* adults are less comfortable being close with others, more hampered by jealousy and less likely to disclose (Brennan & Shaver, 1995); they are more likely to be unfaithful (DeWall, Lambert, Slotter, Pond, Deckman, et al., 2011); they are faster than secure adults to generate fight-flight schema when threatened (Ein-Dor, Mikulincer, & Shaver, 2011); and less likely to be empathically accurate when interpreting the thoughts and feelings of strangers (Izhaki-Costi & Schul, 2011).

- *Anxiously attached* adults fall in love more easily, they experience more emotional highs and lows in their relationships and are more often unhappy (Brennan & Shaver, 1995); they are also more vigilant to possible threat (Ein-Dor, Mikulincer, & Shaver, 2011); they show hurt feelings that transforms threats into guilt in their partner (Overall, Girme, Lemay, & Hammond, 2014); yet they do not succeed in forming a satisfying relationship (McClure & Lydon, 2014).

Research by Claudia Brumbaugh and Chris Fraley (2006) shows that an attachment style in one romantic relationship is very likely to carry over to another relationship. However, people's styles are not set in concrete. Lee Kirkpatrick and Cindy Hazan (1994) conducted a study over a four-year period to show that an insecure partner may become less so if a current partner is secure and the relationship engenders trust. More recently, Nathan Hudson and his colleagues studied *partner regulation* in 172 couples across five time periods. They found that attachment security was coordinated – changes in one partner's level of security directly affected the other partner's level of security (Hudson, Fraley, Brumbaugh, & Vicary, 2014).

Another study, a large-scale meta-analysis, found that the negative association between anxious and avoidant attachment on the one hand and relationship satisfaction and commitment on the other became even more negative in more enduring relationships (Hadden, Smith, & Webster, 2014). This research is correlational, so the question of whether relationship deterioration is a cause or effect cannot be answered. Perhaps the negative impact of anxious and avoidant attachment on the relationship builds up over time; conversely, over time the initial rosy glow fades and the relationship deteriorates and impacts attachment concerns.

Enter Facebook

Imagine the following scenario: A woman is worried that her boyfriend does not love her as much as she loves him and fears that he will leave her for someone else. Driven by anxiety and suspicion, she logs onto Facebook to see if she can find any evidence of his extra-dyadic

Secure attachment style
Children benefit from contact with compassionate caregivers. They are more likely to be both self-sufficient and trusting of others.

transgressions. On his Facebook page, she sees that he has recently added three attractive women to his list of friends, he has been tagged in a photo with his arm around an unknown pretty girl, and his relationship status is still listed as 'single' rather than 'in a relationship.' Seeing his Facebook page has only made her feel worse – jealous, insecure, and scared of rejection. Nevertheless, she checks his Facebook page a few hours later to see if she can find any new information.

Marshall, Bejanyan, Di Castro and Lee (2013, p. 1)

The initial appeal of social networking web sites was not only the chance to keep in touch with others but also to sustain romantic relationships. With the arrival of Facebook came the capacity for surveillance, even of those who are very close to us. Marshall and colleagues studied the correlation between attachment styles and Facebook surveillance and Facebook jealousy (Marshall, Bejanyan, Di Castro, & Lee, 2013). Their participants included samples of those who had either responded to an online survey and of partners in a heterosexual relationship. They found that people who were anxiously attached were less trusting, they were more likely to check their partner's Facebook page and were more jealous of what they unearthed there. Amy Muise and her colleagues explored a gender difference, finding that women responded to feelings of jealousy more often than men by monitoring their partner on Facebook (Muise, Christofides, & Desmarais, 2014).

Longitudinal research

Most research on attachment styles has not examined children and therefore is not genuinely developmental. The studies to which we have referred typically measure the attachment style of adults and have no independent estimate of children's attachment style. Even cross-sectional studies of different age groups tested at the one time are not, strictly speaking, developmental.

In contrast, Eva Klohnen conducted a genuinely longitudinal programme of research across more than thirty years. Women who had been avoidant or secure in their attachment styles in their 20s were still so in their 40s and 50s. Differences in how they related were also maintained across the years. Compared with secure women, avoidant women were more distant from others, less confident and more distrustful, but more self-reliant (Klohnen & Bera, 1998).

This intra-individual stability across time begs another question – across history, have predominant attachment styles changed? Konrath and colleagues conducted a meta-analysis of 94 samples, comprising 25,243 American college students, over the period 1988 to 2011 (Konrath, Chopik, Hsing, & O'Brien, 2014). They discovered that over this period, the percentage of securely attached students had dropped from 49.0 per cent to 41.6 per cent, whereas the percentage of insecure attachment styles had increased from 51.0 per cent to 58.4 per cent. Konrath and colleagues suggest this is because over this period, students had reported a decline in positive models of other people and greater comfort in being without close emotional relationship. One might speculate about what role computer-mediated relationships (e.g. social media, and Facebook 'friends') might play in this.

Attachment theory has attracted growing attention since the 1980s and has also become fashionable in the popular literature devoted to love, our next topic.

Close relationships

What does a close relationship conjure up for you? Perhaps warm fuzzies, perhaps passion and maybe love. But when you search your memory banks, there can be other worrisome thoughts too – try jealousy, for one.

Emotion-in-relationships model
Close relationships provide a context that elicits strong emotions due to the increased probability of behaviour interrupting interpersonal expectations.

Close relationships are a crucible for a host of strong emotions (Fitness, Fletcher, & Overall, 2007). According to the **emotion-in-relationships model**, relationships pivot on strong, well-established and wide-ranging expectations about a partner's behaviour (Berscheid & Ammazzalorso, 2001). People who can express their emotions are generally valued in close relationships, particularly by others with a secure attachment style (Feeney, 1999). There is, however, a caveat. The elevated tendency to feel *all* emotions in close relationships makes it important for us to manage their expression, particularly negative emotions (Fitness, 2001). If I engage in an orgy of uninhibited expression of all I feel for my partner, the relationship may not be long for this world. The way that I show my feelings for my partner needs to be carefully, even strategically, managed.

What is love?

We have discussed the processes of interpersonal attraction. We have explored the way we choose acquaintances and friends, the powerful need to affiliate with a range of people, and how we become attached to particular individuals. So now we come to that all-absorbing human interest – love. Can we extend these principles to understand relationships with the very special people whom we love; and are liking and loving different? Once a neglected topic of empirical study, **love** is now a popular focus of research (Dion & Dion, 1996).

Love
A combination of emotions, thoughts and actions which are often powerful, and usually associated with intimate relationships.

People commonly talk about passion, romance, companionship, infatuation and sexual attraction but would have difficulty defining these terms. Couple this with the way that love is regarded as magical and mysterious – the stuff of poetry and song rather than science – and the difficulty of taking love into the laboratory becomes compounded. Despite this, our knowledge is growing (see the fourth 'What do *you* think?' question); but not surprisingly, it is difficult to conduct experiments on love, so most research is survey- and interview-based.

Zick Rubin (1973) distinguished between *liking* and *loving* and developed scales to measure each separately. Take a few examples of Rubin's items. Julie thinks Artie is 'unusually well adjusted', 'is one of the most likeable people' she knows and 'would highly recommend him for a responsible job'. When it comes to Frankie, Julie 'finds it easy to ignore his faults', 'if she could never be with him she would feel miserable' and 'feels very possessive towards him'. Which one does Julie like, and which one does she love? Other researchers have added that *liking* involves the desire to interact with a person, *loving* adds the element of trust, and *being in love* implies sexual desire and excitement (Regan & Berscheid, 1999).

Love
Romantic love involves intense and occasionally confused emotions. Compassionate love develops slowly from the continuous sharing of intimacy.

Kinds of love

In a study of what kinds of love there might be, Beverley Fehr (1994) asked this question: do ordinary people and love researchers *think* of love in the same way? She answered this by analysing the factors underlying several love scales commonly used in psychological research, and also by having ordinary people generate ideas about the kinds of love that they thought best described various close relationships in a number of scenarios. Fehr found both a simple answer and a more complex one:

* There was reasonable agreement across her data sets that there are at least two broad categories of love: (a) companionate love and (b) passionate or romantic love. This finding substantiated earlier work by Hatfield and Walster (1981).

* The scales devised by love researchers made relatively clear distinctions between types and subtypes of love, whereas ordinary people's views were fuzzy.

Passionate love is an intensely emotional state and a confusion of feelings: tenderness, sexuality, elation and pain, anxiety and relief, altruism and jealousy. **Companionate love**, in contrast, is less intense, combining feelings of friendly affection and deep attachment (Hatfield, 1987). A distinction between passionate and companionate love makes good sense. There are many people we enjoy being with, and yet with whom we are not 'in love'. More recently, Ellen Berscheid (2010) has focused attention on *compassionate love*, suggesting synonyms such as selfless, unconditional, caring, altruistic (see **Chapter 13**) – even communal – love. Others have also maintained that acting with compassion is a form of love (Collins, Kane, Metz, Cleveland, Khan, et al., 2014; Fehr, Harasymchuk, & Sprecher, 2014; Rauer, Sabey, & Jensen, 2014; Reis, Maniaci, & Rogge, 2014).

In general, love can trigger emotions such as sadness, anger, fear and happiness (Shaver, Morgan, & Wu, 1996; see **Chapter 15** for a discussion of 'primary' emotions). Hendrick and Hendrick (1995) also reported gender differences in the meaning that people give to love: men are more inclined to treat love as a game; whereas women are more friendship-oriented and pragmatic but also more possessive.

Passionate (or romantic) love
State of intense absorption in another person involving physiological arousal.

Companionate love
The caring and affection for another person that usually arises from sharing time together.

Love and romance

In 1932, the American songwriters Rodgers and Hart asked the question 'Isn't it romantic?' and also tried to tell us what love is. Social psychologists have been more prosaic, sticking to descriptions of acts and thoughts that point to being 'in love'. Romantic love and friendship share a common root of becoming acquainted, and are generally triggered by the same factors – proximity, similarity, reciprocal liking and desirable personal characteristics. Our lover is very likely to be a friend, albeit a special one!

However, there is more to love. People who are in love report that they think of their lover constantly; they want to spend as much time as possible with, and are often unrealistic about, their lover (Murstein, 1980). Not surprisingly, the lover becomes the focus of the person's life, to the exclusion of other friends (Milardo, Johnson, & Huston, 1983). It is a very intense emotion and almost beyond control.

Have you ever fallen in love? We speak of 'falling in love' as though it is an accident, something that happens to us rather than a process in which we actively participate. What happens when we fall in this way? Arthur Aron and his colleagues addressed this in a short-term longitudinal study of undergraduate students who completed questionnaires about their love experiences and their concept of self every two weeks for ten weeks (Aron, Paris, & Aron, 1995). Those who reported that they fell in love during this period reported positive experiences that were centred on their self-concept. Since somebody now loved them, their self-esteem increased. Further, their self-concept had 'expanded' by incorporating aspects of the other person; and they also reported an increase in self-efficacy, e.g. not only making plans but making the plans work.

A widely accepted claim about falling in love is that it is culture-bound: for people to experience it, a community needs to believe in love and offer it as an option, through fiction and real-life examples. If it is an accident, then at least some people from all cultures should fall in love – but is this the case? Attachment theory has argued that love is both a biological and a social process and cannot be reduced to a historical or cultural invention (Hazan & Shaver, 1987). Indeed, there is evidence of romantic love, not necessarily linked to marriage which is simply a social contract, in the major literate civilisations of early historic times – Rome, Greece, Egypt and China (Mellen, 1981). For example, although romance was not an essential ingredient in choosing a spouse in ancient Rome, love between a husband and wife could develop.

Biology and evolution may also play a role in sex differences in heterosexual love. Ackerman and his colleagues blended an evolutionary perspective and a cost–benefit analysis to argue that confessing one's love for the first time is more likely to come from men than from women. Romantic love underpins mate search, but mate retention and kin care require *commitment*: 'Let's get serious'. Sexual access may be a benefit of romantic love, but as a partnership it also brings sexual obligation. For a woman, the costs of love can be relatively immediate with prospects of gestation and lactation. Traditionally, the costs for a man are less pressing: a promise of resources down the track – prestige and power ('getting the dream job'); and security which equates to kin care (Ackerman, Griskevicius, & Li, 2011).

Labels and illusions

Love as a label

Three-factor theory of love
Hatfield and Walster distinguished three components of what we label 'love': a cultural concept of love, an appropriate person to love and emotional arousal.

In Elaine Hatfield and William Walster's (1981) **three-factor theory of love**, romantic love is a product of three interacting variables:

1 a cultural determinant that acknowledges love as a state;

2 the presence of an appropriate love object – in most cultures, the norm is a member of the opposite sex and of similar age;

3 emotional arousal, self-labelled 'love', that is felt when interacting with, or even thinking about, an appropriate love object.

Label or not, those of us who have been smitten report powerful feelings. Although the idea of labelling arousal may not seem intuitively appealing, it has a basis in research. Our physiological reactions are not always well differentiated across the emotions, such as when we describe ourselves as angry, fearful, joyful or sexually aroused (Fehr & Stern, 1970).

Recall Schachter and Singer's (1962) argument that arousal prompts us to make a causal attribution (see **Chapter 3**) and appraisal theories of emotion that argue that felt emotions are based on our appraisals largely of harm and benefit (e.g. Blascovich, 2008; Lazarus, 1991; see **Chapter 2**). Some cues (e.g. heightened heart rate) suggest that the cause is internal, and we then label the experience as an emotion. If we feel aroused following an insult,

Box 14.7 Research classic
Excitement and attraction on a suspension bridge

Donald Dutton and Arthur Aron (1974) conducted a famous experiment on a suspension bridge spanning Capilano Canyon in British Columbia. They described the setting in this way:

> The 'experimental' bridge was the Capilano Canyon Suspension Bridge, a five-foot-wide, 450-foot-long, bridge constructed of wooden boards attached to wire cables that ran from one side to the other of the Capilano Canyon. The bridge has many arousal-inducing features such as a tendency to tilt, sway, and wobble, creating the impression that one is about to fall over the side; (b) very low handrails of wire cable which contribute to this impression; and (c) a 230-foot drop to rocks and shallow rapids below the bridge.

> Dutton and Aron (1974, pp. 510–511)

The participants were young men who crossed rather gingerly over a high and swaying suspension bridge, one at a time. An attractive young woman approached each one on the pretext of conducting research, asking if they would complete a questionnaire for her. Next, she gave them her name and her phone number in case they wanted to ask more questions later. Many called her. However, very few made the phone call if the interviewer was a man or if the setting was a lower and safer 'control' bridge. Arousal in a perilous situation, it seems, enhances romance!

The phenomenon of accidental arousal enhancing the attractiveness of an already attractive person described is reliable, according to a meta-analysis of thirty-three experimental studies (Foster, Witcher, Campbell, & Green, 1998).

we are likely to label the feeling as anger. However, if we are interacting with an attractive member of appropriate gender depending on our sexual orientation, we will possibly label the arousal as sexual attraction, liking and even a precursor to love. See Box 14.7 on how even danger, or at least excitement, can act as a precursor to romance!

The three-factor theory stresses that love depends on past learning of the concept of love, the presence of someone to love, and arousal. Even if these components are necessary, they are not sufficient for love to occur. If they were, love could easily be taken into the laboratory. The ingredients would require that John's culture includes a concept of love and that Janet provides arousal by being attractive, or by chasing John around the room, or by paying him a compliment – and hey, presto! 'Love'!

We know that sexual arousal itself does not define love, and that lust and love can be distinguished. Think of the anecdote in which a person is called to account for an extramarital affair by a spouse and makes the classic response 'But, dear, it didn't *mean* anything!'

Love and illusions

People bring various ideals or images into a love relationship that can impact on the way it might develop. A person can fall out of love quickly if the partner is not what (or who) they were first thought to be. The initial love was not for the partner but for some *ideal image* that the person had formed of this partner, such as 'the knight in shining armour'. Possible sources for these images are previous lovers, characters from fiction and childhood love objects such as parents. A physical characteristic similar to one possessed by the image can start a chain reaction where other characteristics of the image are transferred to the partner.

It is the images we hold about an ideal partner that seem best to differentiate love from liking. Some of these images may be based on illusions. One of these is the belief in romantic destiny – '*We were meant for each other*'. This illusion can be helpful, both in feeling initially satisfied and in maintaining a relationship longer (Knee, 1998). Romance in general is entwined with fantasy and positive illusions (Martz, Verette, Arriaga, Slovic, Cox, & Rusbult, 1998; Murray & Holmes, 1997). A positive illusion about one's partner and the relationship as a whole may not be a bad thing – it helps one make allowances that sustain the relationship through inevitable ups and downs (Murray, Holmes, & Griffin, 2003). When a partner falls short of one's ideals, we can highlight virtues and minimise faults.

No greater love

Robert Sternberg (1988)'s research identifies commitment and intimacy as being as crucial as passion to some experiences of love. *Passion* is roughly equivalent to sexual attraction; *intimacy* refers to feelings of warmth, closeness and sharing; *commitment* is our resolve to maintain the relationship, even in moments of crisis. These same three dimensions have been confirmed in other research as statistically independent factors (Aron & Westbay, 1996). While sexual desire and romantic love are linked in experience, Diamond has pointed out that they may have evolved as different biological systems with different goals:

> Desire is governed by the *sexual mating* system, the goal of which is sexual union for the purpose of reproduction. Romantic love, however, is governed by the *attachment* or *pair-bonding* system.
>
> Diamond (2003, p. 174)

It follows that attachment or pair-bonding can be directed towards both other-gender and same-gender partners. Where same-sex sexual attraction fits in, this model is not entirely clear.

Consummate love
Sternberg argues that this is the ultimate form of love, involving passion, intimacy and commitment.

In Sternberg's model, romance is exceeded by one other experience, **consummate love**, which includes all three factors. By systematically creating combinations of the presence or absence of each factor, we can distinguish eight cases, ranging in degree of bonding from no love at all to consummate love. From this some interesting relationships emerge. Fatuous love is characterised by passion and commitment but no intimacy (e.g. the 'whirlwind Hollywood romance'). The differentiation between varieties of love by Sternberg appears to be robust (Diamond, 2003). Have you experienced some of the relationships in Figure 14.9?

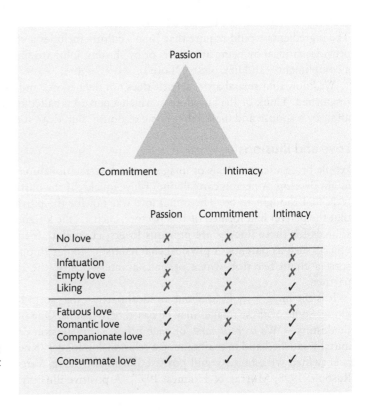

	Passion	Commitment	Intimacy
No love	X	X	X
Infatuation	✓	X	X
Empty love	X	✓	X
Liking	X	X	✓
Fatuous love	✓	✓	X
Romantic love	✓	X	✓
Companionate love	X	✓	✓
Consummate love	✓	✓	✓

Figure 14.9 Sternberg's (1988) triangle of love

- Three factors (passion, commitment and intimacy) are crucial in characterising different experiences of love. When all three are present, we can speak of consummate love.

- When only one or two are present, we love in a different way. Two commonly experienced kinds include romantic love and companionate love.

Source: Sternberg (1988).

From a review of the empirical literature research, Berscheid concluded that research on love, in particular studies based on psychometric testing, generally does not address the process of change in close relationship love:

> Relationships are temporal in nature. Like rivers, they flow through time and space and change as the properties of the environment in which they are embedded change. The significance of this fact for love and other relationship phenomena is, to paraphrase ancient sage Heraclitus: 'One never steps in the same river twice.'
>
> Berscheid (2010, p. 11)

In the following sections, we include a variety of studies that deal with change, either by tracking a relationship over time or by researching partners who have been together for several years prior to the investigation. This will invite us naturally to ask how a close relationship is maintained and what factors might indicate its impending failure. But first we ask the question: do we marry for love?

Marriage

Love and marriage

Love and romance being the essence of deciding to get married has long been a popular theme in literature. And yet, in Western culture there has been a change in attitude over time, even across a single generation. Simpson and his colleagues compared three time samples (1967, 1976 and 1984) of people who answered this question: 'If a man (woman) had all the qualities you desired, would you marry this person if you were not in love with him (her)?' The answer 'No' was much higher in 1984, but in 1967 women were much more likely to say 'Yes' (Simpson, Campbell, & Berscheid, 1986). A later study documented a trend in Western cultures towards long-term relationships outside marriage (Hill & Peplau, 1998). Even so, American data suggest that love is still an accurate predictor of getting married, but is not enough to guarantee a happy and stable relationship.

There is also a widespread assumption, backed by cultural institutions, that humans are sexually monogamous and that monogamy is beneficial and has positive outcomes. At least that is what is promoted by society. In reality, sexual monogamy is an historically recent phenomenon; but it certainly is accepted and promoted by the dominant culture as a foundation of society and as the only appropriate way to have a romantic relationship. This raises the question of whether it is indeed better for our relationships and our psychological well-being to be monogamous. A review of relevant evidence suggests no – there is no evidence that monogamy provides greater sexual, relational or family benefits than does non-monogamy (Conley, Ziegler, Moors, Matsick, & Valentine, 2012). However, because monogamy is socially valued, it does provide a sense of moral superiority to those who are monogamous.

Most research on marriage focuses on the Western concept of marriage and may thus seem culturally myopic. In one sense, it is – because 'marriage', as a social and legal contract, takes different forms in different cultures and groups, and has changed over time. However, almost all love relationships in all cultures and groups have some kind of public contract to identify the relationship.

Arranged marriages

Most cultures have long preferred the careful arrangement of 'suitable' partners for their children. Arranged marriages can be very successful, particularly if we judge them by their duration and social function: having children, caring for aged parents, reinforcing the extended family and building a stronger community. They can, and often do, also act as treaties between communities and tribal groups. Historically, this function has been absolutely central (Evans-Pritchard, 1951; Fox, 1967) – it became weaker in post-industrial societies, particularly Western ones, that are organised around nuclear families that have to move around to respond to the job market.

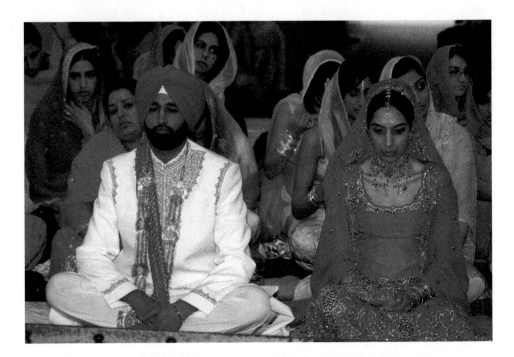

Arranged marriages
Marriage serves such an important function for the community that young people may not be able to chose their partners freely.

There have been several studies of arranged marriages in India. In one, mutual love was rated lower by arranged couples than by 'love' couples – at first (Gupta & Singh, 1982). Over time, this trend reversed. In a second study, female students preferred the idea of an arranged marriage, provided they consented to it; but they endorsed the 'love marriage' provided their parents consented (Umadevi, Venkataramaiah, & Srinivasulu, 1992). In a third study, students who preferred love marriages were liberal in terms of their mate's sociocultural background, whereas those who preferred arranged marriages would seek a partner from within their own kin group (Saroja & Surendra, 1991).

Has the dichotomy of arranged and love marriages been oversimplified? The anthropologist Victor De Munck (1996) investigated love and marriage in a Sri Lankan Muslim community. Arranged marriages were the cultural preference. However, romantic love also contributed to the final decision, even when parents officially selected the partner.

These studies highlight the importance and respect that some cultures afford their elders as legitimate matchmakers. Many Westerners believe that they would never consider an arranged marriage. However, dating and international marriage-match agencies are growing rapidly in popularity in Western culture, perhaps reflecting diminished opportunities for people to meet, particularly those with busy lives.

Same-sex romantic relationships

Gay and lesbian relationships have been under-represented in research on close relationships. With increasing social acceptance and legal recognition of same-sex relationships that has gathered real momentum in the West since probably the early 1980s, this has changed. There is greater recognition that theories of relationships simply cannot assume that close relationships are heterosexual (Peplau & Fingerhut, 2007; also see Herek, 2007, 2011). There is also recognition that the basic social psychology of same-sex relationships will mirror that of heterosexual relationships in most respects, but that there may be some differences – such as increased stress arising from frequent experiences of societal stigmatism and discrimination (Totenhagen, Butler, & Ridley, 2012). From an international perspective, there is still a long way to go – homosexual acts remain a criminal, sometimes capital, offence in many African, Islamic and Middle Eastern nations (e.g. Bereket & Adam, 2008).

Even in Western nations, same-sex marriages, civil unions, gay adoption and lesbian, gay, bisexual, transgender and queer (LGBTQ) sexuality have been matters of fierce public debate (Herek, 2011; Herek & McLemore, 2013). As mentioned earlier (**Chapter 10**), the situation has improved in recent years, with same-sex marriage now legal in the United States, Canada and most of Western Europe and South America, However, not that long ago, California, the most socially progressive state in the United States, had legalised same-sex marriage only to have it overturned in 2008 – 52 per cent of Californians voted 'yes' on a ballot proposition actively denying same-sex couples the same legal rights as heterosexuals. The vote, which correlated strongly and predictably with religiosity and sociopolitical ideology, was subsequently overturned in 2012 by the main appeal court in California on the grounds, according to their ruling which was published in the media, that the ballet proposition 'serves no purpose, and has no effect, other than to lessen the status and human dignity of gays and lesbians in California and to officially reclassify their relationships and families as inferior to those of opposite-sex couples'.

Relationships that work (and those that don't)

Maintaining relationships

Research on relationship maintenance deals mostly with marriage – partly an historical artefact, but also because of the central role played by traditional heterosexual marriage in child-rearing. However, in view of what we have discussed in this chapter, marriage is only one of a number of love relationships, and in this section, we do not draw a distinction between de facto marriage relationships and other long-term intimate relationships.

External influences, such as pressure from in-laws, are other factors beyond love that can perpetuate a marriage relationship; alternatively, a progressive weakening of external obstacles to separation can be linked to an escalating divorce rate (Attridge & Berscheid, 1994). Benjamin Karney and Thomas Bradbury (1995) studied some 200 variables in a longitudinal study of marital satisfaction and stability. Positive outcomes were predicted by groups of positively valued variables (e.g. education, employment and desirable behaviour), whereas negative outcomes were predicted by groups of negatively valued variables (e.g. neuroticism, an unhappy childhood and negative behaviour). However, no factor in isolation was a reliable predictor of satisfaction.

Social support networks play an important role in sustaining close relationships. This is because: "Romantic relationships do not exist in a vacuum; they are embedded in social networks of family members, friends, and acquaintances" (Sprecher, 2011, p. 630). Marital satisfaction is greater where there is an overlap between both spouses' support networks. For example, wives reported more marital satisfaction when their networks included relatives or friends of their husband; or when members in a wife's network were related to members in the husband's network. Similarly, marital satisfaction was higher among husbands when their networks overlapped with those of their wives (Cotton, Cunningham, & Antill, 1993).

Social support network
People who know and care about us and who can provide back-up during a time of stress.

Social support of this form does not only increase marital satisfaction but it more widely builds relationship satisfaction, and close and caring relationships have been shown to significantly benefit health and well-being and cause people to thrive (Feeney & Collins, 2015). In particular, such relationships help people deal with life's adversity and actively pursue life's opportunities.

Margaret Clark and Nancy Grote (1998) have adopted equity theory's focus on benefits and costs to identify actions that help or hinder a relationship:

- *Benefits* help. They can be intentional (e.g. 'My husband complimented me on my choice of clothing'), or unintentional (e.g. 'I like being in public with my wife because she is attractive').

- *Costs* hinder. They can be intentional (e.g. 'My wife corrected my grammar in front of other people'), or unintentional (e.g. 'My husband kept me awake at night by snoring').

Box 14.8 Our world
Mutual support works in intimate relationships

Kieran Sullivan and her colleagues have studied the longitudinal effects of mutual support among newlyweds, focusing on causes of and solutions for *relationship distress*. They recruited 172 couples, aged 18–35 years, who had been married less than six months and observed them in conversations as they solved marital problems they had experienced and discussed ways in which they had given each other personal support. The researchers contacted the participants ten times over a 10-year period, the first three

times in an observational setting and the remaining times by having each person complete a marital satisfaction questionnaire. During this time, 37 couples divorced – a divorce rate of 22 per cent.

Relationship distress occurs when a partner discloses important thoughts or feelings that are not validated or understood by the other; or when either partner acts to invalidate the other. The consequences suggest that one's partner has no understanding, care or compassion.

Source: Sullivan, Pasch, Johnson and Bradbury (2010).

- *Communal behaviour* helps. Sometimes it can be a benefit to one partner but a cost to the other (e.g. 'I listened carefully to something my wife wanted to talk about even though I had no interest in the issue').

Romance novels suggest that 'love endures', whereas TV soap operas and reality shows often focus on relationship breakups. A longitudinal study spanning ten years of American newlyweds found a steady decline in marital satisfaction among both husbands and wives (Kurdeck, 1999). This decline included two accelerated downturns, one after the first year, 'the honeymoon is over', and the other in the eighth year, 'the seven year itch'! Causes and solutions for distress in longitudinal relationships have been explored by Kieran Sullivan and her colleagues (Sullivan, Pasch, Johnson, & Bradbury, 2010; see Box 14.8).

A relationship that survives is one where partners adapt, and where they modify their expectations of one another. Companionate love can preserve a relationship because it involves deep friendship and caring, which is grounded in myriad shared experiences over time. But relationships also thrive and endure when people feel a sense of self-determination associated with feelings of autonomy, competence and relatedness, and where partners are together for integrated and intrinsic reasons (Knee, Hadden, Porter, & Rodriguez, 2013). These conditions sponsor open, authentic, non-defensive behaviours and stances that are particularly valuable in weathering ego-threatening conflict. In these respects, both the Western 'love' marriage and the Eastern arranged marriage can result in a similar powerful bonding between partners.

Many of the themes summarised in this section tally with Ted Huston's (2009) description of the 'behavioural ecology' of marriages that work. His longitudinal studies show that spouses who get on:

- are *domestic partners* – with either traditional or workable and customised gender role patterns;
- are *lovers* – since sex is a core element of most marriages;
- are *companions and friends* – mostly in genial relationships with shared activities;
- are supported by a *social support network* – consisting of friends and relatives with whom they visit and socialise.

For better or for worse

When do partners live up to the maxim 'For better or for worse'? Jeff Adams and Warren Jones (1997) pinpointed three factors that contribute to an ongoing relationship:

1 *personal dedication* – positive attraction to a particular partner and relationship;

2 *moral commitment* – a sense of obligation, religious duty or social responsibility, controlled by a person's values and moral principles;

3 *constraint commitment* – factors that make it costly to leave a relationship, such as lack of attractive alternatives, and various social, financial or legal investments in the relationship.

Commitment

We have referred to commitment several times in this chapter. Commitment increases the chance that partners will stay together, and even entertaining the idea of becoming committed is important (Berscheid & Reis, 1998). Wieselquist and her colleagues found a link between commitment and marital satisfaction, acts that promote a relationship, and trust (Wieselquist, Rusbult, Foster, & Agnew, 1999).

There is a series of risk factors that predict a relationship breakup, such as negative modes of communication and lack of a social support network. Longitudinal research finds that healthy relationships that are protected from these risks are characterised by (1) strong psychological attachment, (2) a long-term orientation and (3) an intention to persist (Arriaga & Agnew, 2001). These components feed into commitment; and highly committed partners have a greater chance of staying together (Adams & Jones, 1997). The very idea of subjectively committing oneself to a relationship can be more important than the conditions that led to commitment (Berscheid & Reis, 1998). Subjective commitment may be related to our self-construal, the way we think about ourselves (see **Chapter 4**). In a study by Cross, Bacon and Morris (2000), people who construed themselves as being the sort of people who are interdependent with others were more committed to important relationships than individuals who did not construe themselves in this way.

Jennifer Wieselquist and her colleagues found that commitment has been linked to marital satisfaction (Wieselquist, Rusbult, Foster, & Agnew, 1999), to behaviour that promotes a relationship and to trust. Promoting a relationship includes 'inspiring' acts, such as being accommodating to one's partner's needs and being willing to make some sacrifices. Wieselquist's model is *cyclical*: inspiring acts bring forth a partner's trust and reciprocal commitment, and subsequent interdependence for both in the relationship. In a similar vein, Dominik Schoebi and his colleagues distinguish between commitment and marital satisfaction as concepts, and although they are empirically related, mutual commitment can add an extra benefit. In an eleven-year longitudinal study of married couples, they found that when commitment includes an intention to maintain the relationship, separation or divorce is less likely. On the other hand, it takes just one partner to demonstrate a lower level of commitment than the other – a 'weak link' partner – for a slide down the path to probable dissolution to begin (Schoebi, Karney, & Bradbury, 2012).

Trust and forgiveness

Being able to trust someone and their motives is absolutely key to the development and maintenance of relationships. Trust can preserve a relationship in the face of adversity (Miller & Rempel, 2004). Lack of trust is associated with an insecure attachment style (Mikulincer, 1998) – however, this feeling of rejection when coping with a threatening interpersonal situation can be offset when both partners are highly committed (Tran & Simpson, 2009).

Forgiveness also plays a key role in relationship preservation. *To err is human, to forgive divine*: sometimes it pays to turn the other cheek – forgive a partner who has transgressed. It is a benefit with high value (McCullough, Worthington, & Rachal, 1997), as is its counterpart, apologising for giving offence (Azar, 1997). Frank Fincham (2000) has characterised forgiveness as an interpersonal construct: *you* forgive *me*. It is a process and not an act, and resonates in histories, religions and values of many cultures. Forgiveness is a solution to estrangement, and a positive alternative to relationship breakdown. In a meta-analysis of 175 studies, Ryan Fehr and his colleagues found that interpersonal forgiveness occurred more frequently in a relationship that was close, committed and satisfying (Fehr, Gelfand, & Nag, 2010). Forgiving a partner is also an act that can extend to later prosocial acts (see Karremans, Van Lange, & Holland, 2005; **Chapter 13**).

Commitment
The desire or intention to continue an interpersonal relationship.

An ideal partner

Men and women differ in their mating partner preferences – essentially, women place greater emphasis than men on partner properties that make their partner a parent who can protect and provide for the family unit. These differences derive from evolutionary pressures that have built mental and behavioural processes designed to resolve recurring challenges faced by our ancestors – e.g. food scarcity, harsh environment, dangerous wild animals (Buss & Schmitt, 1993).

There is, however, an alternative view; that mating preferences reflect people's current, not evolutionary, environment (Zentner & Eagly, 2015). Depending on environmental conditions, men and women may or may not display sex-stereotypic mating preferences – this is because mating partner preference will be proximally influenced by both men and women's evaluation of the benefits and costs of a particular partner in helping them achieve their own anticipated life outcomes. So, for example, one's ethnic and cultural background, socio-economic circumstances, personal aspirations and gender and sociopolitical values will impact mating preferences. Zentner and Eagly (2015) show how these proximal factors significantly impact people's mating preferences.

At a more micro level, does your partner meet your ideals? How well do you match the expectations of your partner? Are these considerations important to your relationship? These are questions that Garth Fletcher and his colleagues have explored (Fletcher, Simpson, Thomas, & Giles, 1999). Our ideal image of a partner has developed over time and usually predates a relationship in the present.

In a study of romantic relationships by Campbell, Simpson, Kashy and Fletcher (2001), people rated their ideal romantic partners on three dimensions: warmth–trustworthiness, vitality–attractiveness and status–resources, the same dimensions proposed by Fletcher as important when selecting a mate (discussed earlier). The results were in accord with the *ideal standards model*: people who think that their current partner closely matches their image of an ideal partner are more satisfied with their relationship.

This model has been extended to include how people maintain and perhaps improve a relationship by trying to regulate or control a partner's behaviour. So, for example, one can influence one's partner's self-concept so that, as reflected in their behaviour, it becomes more similar to one's own ideal self – this is called the Michelangelo effect (see **Chapter 4**; Drigotas, Rusbult, Wieselquist, & Whitton, 1999; Rusbult, Finkel, & Kumashiro, 2009). See how Nickola Overall and her colleagues have tackled this general idea in Box 14.9.

Relationship breakdown

George Levinger (1980) points to four factors that herald the end of a relationship, including those of same-sex partners (Schullo & Alperson, 1984):

1   A new life seems to be the only solution.
2   Alternative partners are available (also see Arriaga & Agnew, 2001).
3   There is an expectation that the relationship will fail.
4   There is a lack of commitment to a continuing relationship.

Rusbult and Zembrodt (1983) believe that once deterioration has been identified, it can be responded to in any of four ways. A partner can take a passive stance and show:

- *loyalty*, by waiting for an improvement to occur; or
- *neglect*, by allowing the deterioration to continue.

Alternatively, a partner can take an active stance and show:

- *voice behaviour*, by working at improving the relationship; or
- *exit behaviour*, by choosing to end the relationship.

Box 14.9 Research highlight
Strategies for sustaining a long-term relationship

According to Nickola Overall and her colleagues, people use a variety of cognitive tactics to maintain their relationships when they judge their partner to be less than ideal. They may weather little storms along the way by:

- enhancing a partner's virtues and downplaying the faults (Murray & Holmes, 1999);
- lowering their expectations to fit more closely with what their partner offers (Fletcher, Simpson, & Thomas, 2000);
- adjusting their perceptions so that their partner bears resemblance to their ideal (Murray, Holmes, & Griffin, 1996).

Another approach is to work more directly on the partner. You will recall that people use **self-regulation** when they try to rationalise perceived self-concept discrepancies between how they are and how they want to be (see **Chapter 4**). Overall, Fletcher and Simpson (2006) have used a similar, but more complex, idea based on the ideal standards model, with its pivotal dimensions of warmth–trustworthiness, vitality–attractiveness and status–resources. This model casts new light on how we can try to improve and sustain a long-term relationship – **partner regulation**. Begin by comparing what we perceive with what we want relating to our partner — test the perception

against our ideal standards. Regulation kicks in when the reality begins to fall short. Overall and colleagues give this example: Mary places considerable importance on one of the three dimensions, status–resources; but her partner John has limited potential to be financially secure. Mary encourages John to retrain or look for another job, perhaps a major challenge. But there are brownie points on offer – John's status and resources could come much closer to Mary's ideal and lift the quality of their relationship.

In a longitudinal study extending over one year, Overall, Fletcher, Simpson and Sibley (2009) asked how successful different communication strategies might be in bringing about desired change in a partner. They found that partner regulation is a two-edged sword.

Direct and negative regulation attempts to alter traits or behaviour, e.g. by demanding or nagging, can fail and cause stress in the short term but actually work in the long term – if a partner is obliging. Subtle and positive regulation attempts, such as being humorous and validating towards a partner, can work in the short term but fail to produce significant relationship change in the long term. 'Sometimes, even in loving, intimate relationships, it may pay to be cruel, or at least candid and honest, in order to be kind' (Overall et al., 2009, p. 638).

It is not clear whether the passive or the active approach leads to more pain at the final breakup. Other factors are involved, such as previous levels of attraction, the amount of time and effort invested and the availability of new partners. It can also depend on the person's available social contact, such as support from family and friends. It is often loneliness that adds to the pain and makes life seem unbearable; if this is minimised, recovery from the ending of a relationship can be faster.

Consequences of failure

A break-up is a process, not a single event. Steve Duck (1982, 2007) has offered a detailed **relationship dissolution model** of four phases that partners pass through (see Box 14.10 and Figure 14.10). Each phase culminates in a threshold at which a typical form of action follows. Not surprisingly, Christopher Fagundes (2012) found that university students experienced considerable emotional turmoil during a two-month period following a romantic breakup. Distress was more evident among students who: (a) were more anxiously attached (see **Table 14.1**), (b) did not act as 'terminators' of the relationship and (c) continued to reflect longer about the negative emotions they had experienced after the breakup.

You may well think, 'This is pretty grim stuff.' It is. Most often, the breakup of long-term relationships, and of marriages, is extremely distressing. Partners who were close have tried hard over a long period to make it work – they have mutually reinforced each other and have had good times along with the bad. In the breakup of marriage, at least one partner has reneged on a contract (Simpson, 1987). And of course, the breakup can impact third parties. Consider the consequences of a family breakup for children. Archival research of a

Self-regulation
Strategies that we use to match our behaviour to an ideal or 'ought' standard.

Partner regulation
Strategy that encourages a partner to match an ideal standard of behaviour.

Relationship dissolution model
Duck's proposal of the sequence through which most long-term relationships proceed if they finally break down.

Box 14.10 Your life
Phases in the breakup of a relationship

Think about your last romantic relationship breakup – this is never a pleasant exercise. Did the breakup progress through a number of phases, each phase relentlessly setting up the next step? Social psychologists believe that relationship breakups do indeed follow a predictable series of general steps.

1 The *intrapsychic phase* starts as a period of brooding with little outward show, perhaps in the hope of putting things right. This can give way to needling the partner and seeking out a third party to be able to express one's concerns.

2 The *dyadic* (i.e. two-person) *phase* leads to deciding that some action should be taken, short of leaving the partner, which is usually easier said than done. Arguments point to differences in attributing responsibility for what is going wrong. With luck, they may talk their problems through.

3 The *social phase* involves a new element: in saying that the relationship is near an end, the partners may negotiate with friends, both for support for an uncertain future and for reassurance of being right. The social network will probably take sides, pronounce on guilt and blame and, like a court, sanction the dissolution.

4 The final *grave-dressing phase* can involve more than leaving a partner. It may include the division of property, access to children, and working to assure one's reputation. Each partner wants to emerge with a self-image of reliability for a future relationship. The metaphor for the relationship is death: there is its funeral, it is buried and marked by erecting a tablet. This 'grave-dressing' activity seeks a socially acceptable version of the life and death of the relationship.

Source: Based on Duck (1982, 2007).

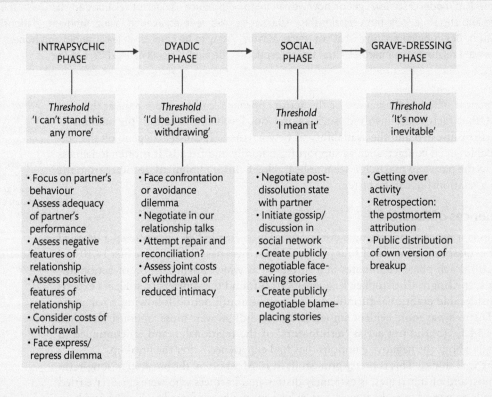

Figure 14.10 When things go wrong: phases in dissolving an intimate relationship
Source: Based on Duck (1982).

Relationship breakdown
'Should I stay or should I go?' According to Duck's model, with an end in sight they will seek support from their respective social networks.

longitudinal study of more than 1,200 people over the period 1921–91 showed that men and women whose parents had divorced were more likely also to experience divorce themselves (Tucker, Friedman, Schwartz, Criqui, Tomlinson-Keasey, Wingard, et al., 1997).

Serious domestic conflict also undermines parent–child relationships. Heidi Riggio (2004) studied young adults from families affected by divorce or chronic and high levels of conflict, finding that they more often felt lacking in social support and more anxious in their own relationships. Add divorce to the mix and the quality of the relationship with the father, although not with the mother, was also diminished, perhaps because interaction with mothers was expected to continue.

In short, most of us probably live in the hope that a long-term intimate relationship will involve loyalty, trust and commitment – forever. There is truth in the adage *Look before you leap*.

Summary

- Attraction is necessary for friendships to form and is a precursor to an intimate relationship.

- Evolution and human genetic inheritance play a role in accounting for what attracts people to each other.

- Variables that play a significant role in determining why people are attracted towards each other include physical attributes, whether they live or work close by, how familiar they are and how similar they are, especially in terms of attitudes and values.

- Explanations of attraction include: reinforcement (a person who engenders positive feelings is liked more); social exchange (an interaction is valued if it increases benefits and reduces costs); and the experience of equitable outcomes for both parties in a relationship.

- Affiliation with others is a powerful human motivation. Long-term separation from others can have disturbing intellectual and social outcomes, and may lead to irreversible psychological damage in young children.

- Life-cycle studies of affiliation led to research into attachment and attachment styles. The ways that children connect psychologically to their caregiver can have long-term consequences for how they establish relationships in adulthood.

- Love is distinguished from mere liking. It also takes different forms, such as romantic love and companionate love.
- Maintaining a long-term relationship involves partner regulation, using strategies that bring a partner closer to one's expectations or standards.
- The breakup of a long-term relationship can be traced through a series of stages. The relationship dissolution model notes four phases: intrapsychic, dyadic (two-person), social and grave-dressing.

Key terms

Archival research	Emotion-in-relationships model	Profit
Assortative mating	Equity theory	Proximity
Attachment behaviour	Evolutionary social psychology	Reinforcement–affect model
Attachment styles	Familiarity	Relationship dissolution model
Automatic activation	Hospitalism	Self-disclosure
Averageness effect	Instinct	Self-regulation
Behaviourism	Love	Similarity of attitudes
Big Five	Mere exposure effect	Social comparison (theory)
Commitment	Meta-analysis	Social exchange
Comparison level	Minimax strategy	Social support network
Consummate love	Need to affiliate	Three-factor theory of love
Cost–reward ratio	Partner regulation	
Distributive justice	Procedural justice	

Literature, film and TV

Sex and the City, Friends and Gavin and Stacey

These are classic TV series of a genre that explores, both seriously and with wit and humour, the complexity of friendships and sexual and love relationships. Although these series have finished, they did such an excellent job that we will be seeing re-runs for a very long time.

Casablanca

Many film critics feel that *Casablanca* is the greatest film ever – a 1942 all-time classic directed by Michael Curtiz, starring Humphrey Bogart (as Rick) and Ingrid Bergman (as Ilsa), and also with Sydney Greenstreet and Peter Lorré. A love affair between Rick and Ilsa is disrupted by the Nazi occupation of Paris – some years later, Ilsa shows up in Rick's Café in Casablanca. The film is about love, friendship and close relationships, as well as hatred and jealousy, against the background of war, chaos and other impossible obstacles. Another absolute classic in the same vein is David Lean's 1965 film *Dr Zhivago*, based on the novel by Boris Pasternak and starring Omar Sharif and Julie Christie.

The Kids Are All Right

A highly acclaimed 2010 film directed by Lisa Cholodenko, starring Annette Bening and Julianne Moore as a lesbian couple with two teenage kids. Mark Ruffalo plays the sperm donor who is tracked down by the younger teenager. This is a fabulous, very entertaining and often funny, but deadly serious, portrayal of the normality of non-heterosexual relationships and non-traditional marriage in modern-day society.

Love Actually

An absolutely classic 2003 British feel-good movie about . . . love. The cast includes Hugh Grant, Liam Neeson, Colin Firth, Laura Linney, Emma Thompson, Alan Rickman, Kiera Knightley, Bill Nighy and Rowan Atkinson. Billy Bob Thornton does a fabulous cameo as the assertive US president visiting the new British prime minister, played by Grant and transparently modelled on Tony Blair. The movie is all about the ups, downs and obstacles to love and has too many fabulously memorable scenes to count.

Guided questions

1 What does evolutionary social psychology have to say about how humans select a mate?

2 How can a *cost–benefit analysis* be applied to predict the future of an intimate relationship?

3 How does a person's attachment *style* develop, and can it continue later in life?

4 Is romantic love universal, and is it the only kind of love?

5 What has social psychology told us about why some relationships work?

Learn more

Berscheid, E. (2010). Love in the fourth dimension. *Annual Review of Psychology, 61,* 1– 25. An insightful overview of social psychology's sometimes stumbling approach to the nature of love. As its title suggests, this review also discusses change in the nature of love across time.

Bradbury, T. N., & Karney, B. R. (2010). *Intimate relationships.* New York: Norton. A leading and up-to-date text specifically focused on the social psychology of intimate relationships.

Clark, M. S., & Lemay, E. P., Jr (2010). Close relationships. In S. T. Fiske, D. T. Gilbert, & G. Lindzey (Eds.), *Handbook of social psychology* (5th ed., Vol. 2, pp. 898–940). New York: Wiley. Currently the most up-to-date, detailed and comprehensive coverage of the social psychology of close relationships.

Duck, S. (2007). *Human relationships* (4th ed.). London: SAGE. Duck is a leading relationship researcher who focuses in this book on people's interactions, acquaintances, friendships and relationships. Students can use the resources provided to apply the concepts in their personal lives.

Fitness, J., Fletcher, G. J. O., & Overall, N. (2007). Interpersonal attraction and intimate relationships. In M. A. Hogg & J. Cooper (Eds.), *The SAGE handbook of social psychology: Concise student edition* (pp. 219–240). London: SAGE. Detailed but accessible overview of research on close relationships, which includes emotion in relationships and evolutionary dimensions of relationships.

Fletcher, G. J. O., Simpson, J., Campbell, L., & Overall, N. (2013). *The science of intimate relationships.* New York: Wiley-Blackwell. Up-to-date and definitive text on the science of intimate relationships.

Goodwin, R. (1999). *Personal relationships across cultures.* London: Routledge. Covers research from around the world to explore how differences in cultural values influence how people form and maintain various kinds of relationship.

Leary, M. R. (2010). Affiliation, acceptance, and belonging: The pursuit of interpersonal connection. In S. T. Fiske, D. T. Gilbert, & G. Lindzey (Eds.), *Handbook of social psychology* (5th ed., Vol. 2, pp. 864–897). New York: Wiley. This chapter includes detailed discussion of why people might be motivated to affiliate with others and thus form relationships and groups.

Mikulincer, M., & Goodman, G. S. (Eds.) (2006). *Dynamics of romantic love: Attachment, caregiving, and sex.* New York: Guilford. Topics such as intimacy, jealousy, self-disclosure, forgiveness and partner violence are examined from the perspective of attachment, caregiving and sex.

Rholes, W. S., & Simpson, J. A. (2004). *Adult attachment: Theory, research, and clinical implications.* New York: Guilford Press. Attachment theory is considered from physiological, emotional, cognitive and behavioural perspectives.

Rose, H., & Rose, S. (Eds.) (2000). *Alas, poor Darwin: Arguments against evolutionary psychology.* London: Vintage. Scholars from a variety of biological, philosophical and social science backgrounds raise concerns about the adequacy of genetic and evolutionary accounts of social behaviour, including partner selection.

Shaver, P. R., & Mikulincer, M. (2007). Attachment theory and research: Core concepts, basic principles, conceptual bridges. In A. W. Kruglanski & E. T. Higgins (Eds.), *Social psychology: Handbook of basic principles* (2nd ed., pp. 650–677). New York: Guilford Press. A comprehensive coverage of research and theory on human attachment and affiliation.

Chapter 15
Language and communication

Chapter contents

What do *you* think?

1　Kamalini lived most of her early life in Sri Lanka. When she shops for rice in a shop near you, she checks for colour, smell and whether it is free from grit, and she can put names to at least seven varieties. Are her senses more acute than yours? Is her vocabulary richer than yours?

2　En Li worked as a shop assistant in Shanghai after leaving school at 14 years of age, and arrived in London at 18 with just a smattering of English. What support factors might help her master English?

3　Pablo, his wife Diana and young son Paulo have recently moved from Colombia to the United States. They think it is important for their son to speak both Spanish and English. Will it be useful for Paulo to be bilingual?

4　Santoso has recently arrived in The Hague after emigrating from Jakarta. At his first job interview, he did not make much eye contact with the human resources manager. Why might he have not done so, and will it hurt his prospects?

Communication

Communication
Transfer of meaningful information from one person to another.

Gestures
Meaningful body movements and postures.

Communication lies at the heart of social interaction: when we interact, we communicate. Try to think of any social interaction that is free of communication. We constantly transmit information about what we sense, think and feel – even about who we are – and some of our 'messages' are unintentional. We communicate through words, facial expressions, signs, **gestures** and touch; and we do this face-to-face or by phone, writing, texting, emails or video.

Communication is social in many ways: it involves our relationships with others, it is built upon a shared understanding of meaning and is how people influence one another. It requires a sender, a message, a receiver and a channel of communication. However, any communicative event is enormously complex: a sender is also a receiver and vice versa, and there may be multiple, sometimes contradictory, messages travelling together via an array of different verbal and non-verbal channels.

The study of communication is an enormous undertaking that can draw on a wide range of disciplines, such as psychology, social psychology, sociology, linguistics, sociolinguistics, philosophy and literary criticism. Social psychology's contribution is potentially enormous – a potential that has perhaps not been fully realised due to social psychology's emphasis on social cognition and more recently brain processes and structures (see **Chapter 2**) rather than on human interaction. The study of communication, particularly through language and speech, is under-researched, despite the fact that communication plays an important role in structuring cognition (Markus & Zajonc, 1985; Zajonc, 1989).

This disappointment aside, social psychological research tends to distinguish between the study of language and the study of non-verbal communication. But there is also a focus on conversation and the nature of discourse. The structure of this chapter reflects the existence of these three overlapping areas of research. Scholars find that a full understanding of communication needs to incorporate both verbal and non-verbal communication (Ambady & Weisbuch, 2010; Gasiorek, Giles, Holtgraves, & Robbins, 2012; Holtgraves, 2010; Semin, 2007). We also touch on computer-mediated communication, which is rapidly becoming the dominant channel of communication for many people (Birchmeier, Dietz-Uhler, & Stasser, 2011; Hollingshead, 2001).

Language

Language
A system of sounds that convey meaning because of shared grammatical and semantic rules.

Utterance
Sounds made by one person to another.

Locution
Words placed in sequence.

Illocution
Words placed in sequence and the context in which this is done.

Spoken languages are based on rule-governed structuring of meaningless sounds (phonemes) into basic units of meaning (morphemes), which are further structured by morphological rules into words and by syntactic rules into sentences. The meanings of words, sentences and entire utterances are determined by semantic rules. Together, these rules represent grammar. It is because shared knowledge of morphological, syntactic and semantic rules permits the generation and comprehension of almost limitless meaningful utterances that **language** is such a powerful communication medium.

Meaning can be communicated by language at a number of levels. These range from a simple **utterance** (a sound made by one person to another) to a **locution** (words placed in sequence, e.g. 'It's hot in this room'), to an **illocution** (the locution and the context in which it is made: 'It's hot in this room' may be a statement, or a criticism of the institution for not providing cooled rooms, or a request to turn on the air conditioner or a plea to move to another room) (Austin, 1962; Hall, 2000).

Mastery of language also requires us to know the cultural rules for what it is appropriate to say – and when, where, how and to whom to say it. The study of language in this wider social context is where social psychology can make a significant contribution, but so can sociology in the guise of sociolinguistics (Fishman, 1989; Meyerhoff, 2011), and where the study of discourse can become the focus of analysis (Edwards & Potter, 1992; McKinlay & McVittie, 2008; Potter & Wetherell, 1987). Finally, the philosopher John Searle (1979) identifies five sorts of meaning that people can intentionally use language to communicate; they can use language to:

1 say how something is signified;

2 get someone to do something;

3 express feelings and attitudes;

4 make a commitment; and

5 accomplish something directly.

Language is a distinctly human form of communication (see Box 15.5, 'The gestural origins of language'). Although young apes have been taught to combine basic signs to communicate meaningfully (Gardner & Gardner, 1971; Patterson, 1978), even the most precocious ape cannot match the complexity of hierarchical language structure used by a normal 3-year-old child (Limber, 1977). This species specificity of language suggests that it may have an innate component. Noam Chomsky (1957) argued that the most basic universal rules of grammar are innate (called a 'language acquisition device') and are activated by social interaction to 'crack the code' of language. Others argue that the basic rules of language do not have to be innate. They can easily be learnt through prelinguistic interaction between a child and its parents (Lock, 1978, 1980), and the meanings of utterances are so dependent on social context that they are unlikely to be innate (Bloom, 1970; Rommetveit, 1974; see Durkin, 1995).

Language, thought and cognition

Language is social in all sorts of ways: as a system of symbols, it lies at the heart of social life (Mead, 1934). It may be even more important than this. Perhaps thought itself is determined by language. We tend to perceive and think about the world in terms of linguistic categories, and thinking often involves a silent internal conversation with ourselves. Lev Vygotsky (1962) believed that inner speech was the medium of thought, and that it was interdependent with external speech (the medium of social communication). This interdependence suggests that cultural differences in language and speech are reflected in cultural differences in thought.

The linguists Edward Sapir and Benjamin Whorf proposed a more extreme version of this idea in their theory of **linguistic relativity** (Whorf, 1956). Brown writes:

> Linguistic relativity is the reverse of the view that human cognition constrains the form of language. Relativity is the view that the cognitive processes of a human being – perception, memory, inference, deduction – vary with the structural characteristics – lexicon, morphology, syntax – of the language [we speak].

Brown (1986, p. 482)

Linguistic relativity
View that language determines thought and therefore people who speak different languages see the world in very different ways.

The strong version of the Sapir–Whorf hypothesis is that language entirely determines thought, so people who speak different languages actually see the world in entirely different ways and effectively live in entirely different cognitive-perceptual universes. Inuit (Eskimos) have a much more textured vocabulary for snow than other people; does this mean that they actually see more differences than we do? In English, we differentiate between living and non-living flying things, while the Hopi of North America do not; does this mean that they actually see no difference between a bee and an aeroplane? Japanese personal pronouns differentiate between interpersonal relationships more subtly than do English personal pronouns; does this mean that English speakers cannot tell the difference between different relationships? (To what would you attribute Kamalini's skills in the first 'What do *you* think?' question?)

The strong form of the Sapir–Whorf hypothesis is now generally considered too extreme (but see Box 15.1), and a weak form seems to accord better with the facts (Hoffman, Lau, & Johnson, 1986). Language does not determine thought. Rather, it permits us to communicate more easily about those aspects of the physical or social environment that are important for the community (e.g. Krauss & Chiu, 1998). If it is important to be able to communicate about snow, it is likely that a rich vocabulary concerning snow will develop. If you want or need to discuss wine in any detail and with any ease, it is useful to be able to master the arcane vocabulary of the wine connoisseur.

Although language may not determine thought, it certainly can constrain thought so that it is more or less easy to think about some things than others. If there is no simple word for something, it is more difficult to think about it. For this reason, there is a great deal of borrowing of words from one language by another: for example, English has borrowed *Zeitgeist* from German, *raison d'être* from French, *aficionado* from Spanish and *verandah* from Hindi. This idea is powerfully illustrated in George Orwell's novel *1984*, which describes a fictional totalitarian regime based on Stalin's Soviet Union. The regime develops its own highly restricted language, called Newspeak, designed specifically to inhibit people from even thinking non-orthodox or heretical thoughts, because the relevant words do not exist.

Further evidence for how language constrains thought comes from research by Andrea Carnaghi and her colleagues (Carnaghi, Maas, Gresta, Bianchi, Cardinu, & Arcuri, 2008). In German, Italian and some other Indo-European languages (including English), nouns and adjectives can have different effects on how we perceive people. Compare 'Mark is *homosexual*' (using an adjective) with 'Mark is *a homosexual*' (using a noun). When describing a person, use of an adjective suggests an attribute of an individual; but use of a noun implies a social group and membership of that group. The latter is more likely to invoke further stereotypic inferences (see **Chapters 2** and **10**) and an associated process of **essentialism** (e.g. Haslam, Rothschild, & Ernst, 1998) that maps attributes onto invariant, often bio-genetic properties of the category.

Essentialism
Pervasive tendency to consider behaviour to reflect underlying and immutable, often innate, properties of people or the groups they belong to.

Another way to view the relationship between cognition and thinking on the one hand and language on the other is that 'thinking is for doing' (Fiske, 1992) and language, through its role in social interaction and communication, allows thought to have effects in the real world outside one's own head. Thought as an intended action or effect is translated into reality via language.

According to the linguistic category model (Semin, 2000; Semin & Fiedler, 1991; see Rubini, Menegatti, & Moscatelli, 2014) words can be placed in one of four linguistic categories that vary from very concrete to very abstract – the more abstract the word, the more

---

Box 15.1 Our world
Groups in space: The spatial agency bias

Anne Maass and her colleagues have reported an intriguing study showing that whether our culture writes from left to right or vice versa influences how we place people in pictures (Maass, Suitner, Favaretto, & Cignacchi, 2009). There is a *spatial agency bias* in which people, from their visual perspective, tend to place/depict more agentic groups to the left of less agentic groups (e.g. pictures of men and women have the man on the left of the woman). However, this only happens for people whose language is written left-right (e.g. English); for those whose language is written right-left (e.g. Arabic) the spatial agency bias leads to more agentic groups being depicted to the right of less agentic groups. The way we scan the world as a

consequence of the way our language is written affects the way we portray the world – what we scan first is given priority and is assumed to be more agentic and of higher status.

An intriguing implication of this is that in British culture, men being positioned to the left of women, say in mixed-gender news reports or panel discussions, reinforces the assumption that men are more agentic and of higher status. Perhaps if this was switched so that the woman was on the left, the perception would be challenged and the woman would be seen to have greater authority.

This research identifies an intriguing real-world impact of language on cognition and perception.

ambiguous its intent is. Abstract words are more open to alternative interpretations than are concrete words. People's goals in society then influence their use of language. For example, research on language usage in politics shows that politicians use abstract language to reinforce support from the party faithful but concrete language to persuade the undecided (Rubini, Menegatti, & Moscatelli, 2014). Other research finds that people who use abstract language are viewed as having greater power – the reason being that abstract language use appears to reflect both a willingness to judge and a general style of abstract thinking (Wakslak, Smith, & Han, 2014).

Paralanguage and speech style

Language communicates not only by *what* is said but also by *how* it is said. **Paralanguage** refers to all the non-linguistic accompaniments of speech – volume, stress, pitch, speed, tone of voice, pauses, throat clearing, grunts and sighs (Knapp, 1978; Trager, 1958). Timing, pitch and loudness (the *prosodic* features of language; e.g. Argyle, 1975) are particularly important, as they can dramatically change the meaning of utterances: a rising intonation at the end of a statement transforms it into a question or communicates uncertainty, doubt or need for approval (Lakoff, 1973). Prosodic features are important cues to underlying emotions: low pitch can communicate sadness or boredom, while high pitch can communicate anger, fear or surprise (Frick, 1985). Fast speech often communicates power and control (Ng & Bradac, 1993).

Klaus Scherer (1974) systematically varied, by means of a synthesiser, a range of paralinguistic features of short neutral utterances and then had people identify the emotion that was being communicated. Table 15.1 shows how different paralinguistic features communicate information about the speaker's feelings.

Paralanguage
The non-linguistic accompaniments of speech (e.g. stress, pitch, speed, tone, pauses).

Table 15.1 Emotions displayed through paralinguistic speech cues

Speech style	Perceived as
Moderate **variation in loudness**: Extreme **variation in loudness**:	pleasantness, activity, *happiness* *fear*
Moderate **variation in pitch**: Extreme **variation in pitch**:	*anger*, boredom, disgust, *fear* pleasantness, activity, *happiness, surprise*
Lowering **pitch**: Rising **pitch**:	pleasantness, boredom, *sadness* potency, *anger, fear, surprise*
Low **pitch**: High **pitch**:	pleasantness, boredom, *sadness* activity, potency, *anger, fear, surprise*
Slow **speed**: Fast **speed**:	boredom, disgust, *sadness* pleasantness, activity, potency, *anger, fear, happiness, surprise*
Laconic **speech**: Crisp **speech**:	potency, boredom, *disgust, fear, sadness* pleasantness, activity, *happiness, surprise*
High **accentuation and emphasis**: Moderate **accentuation and emphasis**: Low **accentuation and emphasis**:	pleasantness, *happiness*, boredom, *sadness* potency, activity *anger, disgust, fear, surprise*
Minor **tone**: Major **tone**:	*anger* pleasantness, *happiness*
Flat **speech**: Rhythmic **speech**:	boredom activity, *fear, surprise*

Based on: Scherer (1974)
Note: Universal facial expressions of emotions were first identified by Darwin (1872). Six basic emotions (shown in italics above) and blends between them, were distinguished in later work by Ekman (1982, 2003).

Speech style
The way in which something is said (e.g. accent, language), rather than the content of what is said.

In addition to these paralinguistic cues, something can be said in different accents, different language varieties and different languages altogether. These are important **speech style** differences that have been extensively researched in social psychology (Holtgraves, 2014). The social psychology of language tends to focus more on how something is said than on what is said, with speech style rather than speech content; whereas discourse analytic approaches (see later in this chapter) also place importance on what is said, speech content.

Social markers in speech

Interpersonal differences in speech style are relatively minor (Giles & Street, 1985). We have a repertoire of styles, and we automatically or deliberately tailor the way we speak to the context of the communicative event. For instance, we speak slowly and use short words and simple grammatical constructions when we speak to foreigners and children (Clyne, 1981; Elliot, 1981). We use longer and more complex constructions, or more formalised language varieties or standard accents, when we are in a formal context such as an interview.

Penelope Brown and Colin Fraser (1979) charted the different components of a communicative situation that may influence speech style, and they distinguish between two broad features: (1) the scene (e.g. its purpose, time of day, whether there are bystanders); (2) the participants (e.g. their personality, ethnicity, whether they like each other). Since this is an objective classification of situations, we should remember that different people might not define the same objective situation in the same way. What is a formal context to one may seem quite informal to another. It is how the situation is subjectively perceived that influences speech style.

Adrian Furnham (1986) goes one step further in pointing out that not only do we cater speech style to what we think the situation calls for, but we can also seek out situations that are appropriate to a preferred speech style. If you want to have an informal chat, you are likely to choose a pleasant café rather than a seminar room as the venue.

Social markers
Features of speech style that convey information about mood, context, status and group membership.

Contextual variation in speech style means that speech style itself can tell us something about the context: in other words, speech contains clues to who is speaking to whom, in what context and about what. Speech contains **social markers** (Scherer & Giles, 1979). Some of the most researched markers are of group memberships such as social class, ethnicity, sex and age. Social markers are often clearly identifiable and act as very reliable clues to group membership. For instance, most Britons can quite easily identify Americans, Australians and South Africans from speech style alone, and (see Watson, 2009) are probably even better at identifying people who come from Exeter, Birmingham, Liverpool, Leeds and Essex! Speech style can activate a listener's attitudes towards the group that the speaker represents. Recall the lengths to which Eliza Doolittle went in the film *My Fair Lady* to acquire a standard English accent in order to conceal her Cockney origins.

Matched-guise technique
Research methodology to measure people's attitudes towards a speaker based solely on speech style.

This idea is the basis of one of the most widely used research paradigms in the social psychology of language – the **matched-guise technique** – devised to investigate language attitudes based on speech alone (Lambert, Hodgson, Gardner, & Fillenbaum, 1960). The method involves people rating short extracts of speech that are identical in all paralinguistic, prosodic and content respects, differing only in speech style (accent, dialect, language). All the speech extracts are spoken by the same person – someone who is fluently bilingual. The speaker is rated on a number of evaluative dimensions, which often fall into two distinct clusters that reflect competence and warmth as the two most basic dimensions of social perception (Cuddy, Fiske, & Glick, 2008; Fiske, Cuddy, & Glick, 2007; see **Chapter 2**):

1 *status* variables (e.g. intelligent, competent, powerful);
2 *solidarity* variables (e.g. close, friendly, warm).

The matched-guise technique has been used extensively in a wide range of cultural contexts to investigate how speakers of standard and non-standard language varieties are evaluated.

The standard language variety is the one that is associated with high economic status, power and media usage. In Britain, for example, it is what has been called **received pronunciation** (RP) English. Non-standard varieties include regional accents (e.g. Yorkshire), non-standard urban accents (e.g. Birmingham) and minority ethnic languages (e.g. Hindi in Britain).

Research reveals that standard varieties are more favourably evaluated on status and competence dimensions (such as intelligence, confidence, ambition) than non-standard varieties (e.g. Giles & Powesland, 1975). Non-standard speakers are more favourably evaluated on solidarity dimensions. For example, Cindy Gallois and her colleagues found that both white Australians and Australian Aborigines upgraded Aboriginal-accented English on solidarity dimensions (Gallois, Callan, & Johnstone, 1984). In another study, Hogg, Joyce and Abrams (1984) found that Swiss Germans upgraded speakers of non-standard Swiss German relative to speakers of High German on solidarity dimensions.

Language, identity and ethnicity

Matched-guise and other studies suggest that how we speak (our accent or even language) can affect how others evaluate us. This is unlikely to be because certain speech styles are intrinsically more pleasing than others, but rather because speech styles are associated with particular social groups that are consensually evaluated more or less positively in society. Use of a speech style that is associated with a lower-status group may cause people to regard you in terms of their evaluation of that group – with implications for how you may perceive yourself, your group and other groups, and how you may act in society. This suggests that processes associated with intergroup relations and group membership can affect language behaviour.

Howard Giles and Richard Bourhis and their colleagues applied principles from **social identity theory** (see **Chapter 11**) to develop an intergroup perspective on the social psychology of language (Giles, Bourhis, & Taylor, 1977; Giles & Johnson, 1981, 1987). Because the original analysis focused mainly on ethnic groups that differ in speech style, the theory is called **ethnolinguistic identity theory**; however, the wider intergroup analysis of language and communication casts a much wider net to embrace all manner of intergroup contexts (e.g. Giles, 2012; Giles & Maass, 2016; Giles, Reid, & Harwood, 2010).

Speech style and ethnicity

Ethnic groups can differ in appearance, dress, cultural practices, and religious beliefs. However, language or speech style is often one of the most distinct and clear markers of *ethnic identity* (see **Chapter 4**) – social identity as a member of an **ethnolinguistic group** (an ethnic group defined by language or speech style). For instance, the Welsh and the English in the United Kingdom are most distinctive in terms of accent and language. Speech style is an important and often central stereotypical or normative property of group membership: one of the most powerful ways to display your Welshness is to speak English with a marked Welsh accent – or, even better, to speak Welsh itself.

Language or speech style cues ethnic identity. Therefore, whether people accentuate or de-emphasise their ethnic language will be influenced by the extent to which they consider their ethnic identity as a source of self-respect and pride. This perception will in turn be influenced by the real nature of the power and status relations between ethnic groups in society. Research in England, on regional accents rather than ethnic groups, illustrates this rather beautifully (e.g. Watson, 2009). Some accents are strengthening and spreading and others retreating or fading, but overall, despite mobility, mass culture and the smallness of England, the accent landscape is remarkably unchanged. Northern accents in particular such as Scouse and Geordie have thrived due to low immigration and marked regional pride, Brummie is spreading into the Welsh Marches due to population spread, and Cockney-influenced Estuary English threatens to saturate East Anglia and South East England due to its relatively new 'trendy' image.

Received pronunciation (RP)
Standard, high-status, spoken variety of English.

Social identity theory
Theory of group membership and intergroup relations based on self-categorization, social comparison and the construction of a shared self-definition in terms of ingroup-defining properties.

Ethnolinguistic identity theory
Application and extension of social identity theory to deal with language behaviour of ethnolinguistic groups.

Ethnolinguistic group
Social group defined principally in terms of its language.

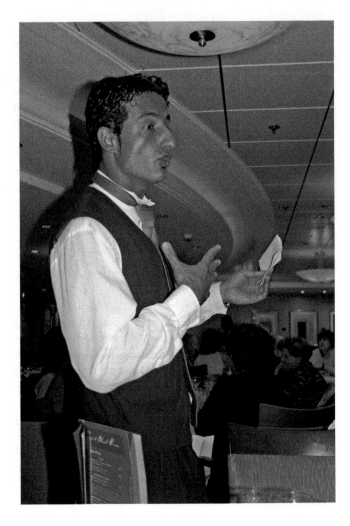

Communication
We communicate with both a spoken and a written language. We also use a rich mix of expressions, gestures and emblems — all contextualised by ethnicity and nationality.

Focusing back on ethnic groups, almost all societies are multicultural, containing a single dominant high-status group whose language is the lingua franca of the nation, and a number of other ethnic groups whose languages are subordinate. However, it is in new world immigrant countries such as the United States, Canada and Australia that the biggest variety of large ethnic minorities occurs. Not surprisingly, much of the research into ethnicity and language comes from these countries, particularly Australia and Canada. For example, in Australia, English is the lingua franca, but there are also large ethnic Chinese, Italian, Greek and Vietnamese Australian communities — language research has been conducted in all these communities (e.g. Gallois, Barker, Jones, & Callan, 1992; Gallois & Callan, 1986; Giles, Rosenthal, & Young, 1985; Hogg, D'Agata, & Abrams, 1989; McNamara, 1987; Smolicz, 1983; see **Box 16.5** in **Chapter 16**).

Language and vitality

Ethnolinguistic vitality
Concept describing objective features of an inter-ethnic context that influence language, and ultimately the cultural survival or disappearance of an ethnolinguistic group.

Giles, Bourhis and Taylor (1977) introduced the term **ethnolinguistic vitality** to describe those objective features of an inter-ethnic context that influence language behaviour (see Figure 15.1). Ethnic groups that are high on status, and demographic and institutional support variables, have high ethnolinguistic vitality. This encourages continued use of the language and thus ensures its survival and the survival of the ethnolinguistic group itself as a distinct entity in society. Low vitality is associated with declining use of the ethnic language, its gradual disappearance and often the disappearance of the ethnolinguistic group itself as a distinct entity: that is, there is language death or language suicide.

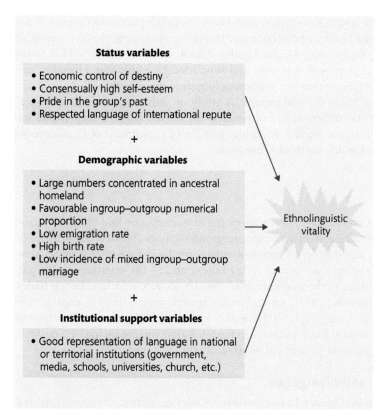

Status variables

- Economic control of destiny
- Consensually high self-esteem
- Pride in the group's past
- Respected language of international repute

+

Demographic variables

- Large numbers concentrated in ancestral homeland
- Favourable ingroup–outgroup numerical proportion
- Low emigration rate
- High birth rate
- Low incidence of mixed ingroup–outgroup marriage

+

Institutional support variables

- Good representation of language in national or territorial institutions (government, media, schools, universities, church, etc.)

Ethnolinguistic vitality

Figure 15.1 When is a language vital?
Ethnolinguistic vitality is influenced by status, demographic and institutional support variables.
Source: Giles, Bourhis and Taylor (1977); based on Hogg and Abrams (1988).

Objective ethnolinguistic vitality configurations can be calculated for different groups (Giles, 1978; Saint-Blancat, 1985), but it is **subjective vitality** – that is, people's *own* perception of the vitality of their group – that more directly influences language usage (Bourhis, Giles, & Rosenthal, 1981; Harwood, Giles, & Bourhis, 1994; Sachdev & Bourhis, 1993). In general, there is a correspondence between objective and subjective vitality, but the two need not be identical.

Ethnic minorities may consider their language to have more or less vitality than objective indices indicate. Under some circumstances, a dominant group may actively encourage a minority to underestimate the vitality of its language in order to inhibit ethnolinguistic revival movements that may threaten the status quo. Inter-ethnic relations, and subjective perceptions of these relations, may thus influence language behaviour.

In Canada, the 1960s marked the beginning of a strong and enduring French-language revival in the province of Quebec, which can be understood in terms of changes in subjective vitality (Bourhis, 1984; Sachdev & Bourhis, 2005). Other revivals include Hebrew, considered a dead language half a century ago, in Israel; Flemish in Belgium; Welsh in the United Kingdom; Hindi in India; and again, Welsh in both Wales and beyond (see Coupland, Bishop, Evans, & Garrett, 2006; Fishman, 1989). These studies converge on the finding that ethnolinguistic vitality is strongest among speakers who are competent in the language.

A language can also die. There are many instances of loss of ethnolinguistic identity: in Canada, Italian and Scottish Canadians generally consider themselves Anglo-Canadian; third-generation Japanese in Brazil have entirely lost their Japanese culture; in Australia, linguistic vitality has declined from first- to second-generation Greek, Italian and Vietnamese Australians (see Edwards & Chisholm, 1987; Hogg, D'Agata, & Abrams, 1989; Kanazawa & Loveday, 1988).

Rodrigue Allard and Réal Landry (1994) have extended the subjective vitality notion to place greater emphasis on interpersonal communicative environments. They argue that what

Subjective vitality
Individual group members' representation of the objective ethnolinguistic vitality of their group.

really counts for an ethnic language to thrive, such as among francophones in Canada, is not subjective beliefs about the vitality of the language but rather the interpersonal network of linguistic contacts that people have (also see Landry, Allard, & Deveau, 2007). This makes good sense: a language can thrive if it is used and supported by legislation. However, perceived vitality may still be important – it influences linguistic opportunities, linguistic and identity motivations and linguistic evaluations. A study of Italian Australians (Hogg & Rigoli, 1996) found that Italian-language competence was related not to interpersonal linguistic contacts but to subjective vitality. (Consider how En Li's command of English could improve in the second 'What do *you* think?' question.)

Speech accommodation

Social categories such as ethnic groups may develop and maintain or lose their distinctive languages or speech styles as a consequence of intergroup relations. However, categories do not speak. People speak, and they speak to one another, usually in face-to-face interaction. When people speak, they adapt their speech style to the context – the situation, and in particular the listener. This idea is the foundation of **speech accommodation theory** (Giles, 1984; Giles, Taylor, & Bourhis, 1973), which invokes specific motivations to explain how people accommodate their speech style to those who are present. The motives that may be involved include a desire to help the listener to understand what you are saying or a desire to promote a specific impression of yourself in order to obtain social approval.

Speech accommodation theory
Modification of speech style to the context (e.g. listener, situation) of a face-to-face interindividual conversation.

Speech convergence and divergence

Based on the assumption that most talk involves people who are potentially of unequal status, speech accommodation theory describes the type of accommodation that might occur as a function of the social orientation that the speakers may have towards one another (see Table 15.2). Where a simple interpersonal orientation exists (e.g. between two friends), bilateral **speech convergence** occurs. Higher-status speakers shift their accent or speech style 'downwards' towards that of lower-status speakers, who in turn shift 'upwards'. In this context, convergence satisfies a need for approval or liking. Convergence increases interpersonal speech style similarity and thus enhances interpersonal approval and liking (Bourhis, Giles, & Lambert, 1975), particularly if the convergence behaviour is clearly intentional (Simard, Taylor, & Giles, 1976). This process is based on the well-supported idea that similarity typically leads to attraction (e.g. Byrne, 1971; see **Chapter 14**).

Speech convergence
Accent or speech style shift towards that of the other person.

Now consider the case where an intergroup orientation exists. If the lower-status group has low subjective vitality coupled with a belief in social mobility (i.e. that one can pass, linguistically, into the higher-status group), there is unilateral upward convergence on the part of the lower-status speaker and unilateral **speech divergence** on the part of the higher-status speaker. In intergroup contexts, divergence establishes psycholinguistic distinctiveness: it differentiates the speaker's ingroup on linguistic grounds from the outgroup. Where an intergroup orientation exists and the lower-status group has high subjective vitality

Speech divergence
Accent or speech style shift away from that of the other person.

Table 15.2 Speech accommodation as a function of status, social orientation and subjective vitality

	Social orientation and vitality of lower-status group		
	Interpersonal		Intergroup
Speaker status		Low vitality *(Social mobility)*	High vitality *(Social change)*
Higher	Downward convergence	Upward divergence	Upward divergence
Lower	Upward convergence	Upward convergence	Downward divergence

coupled with a belief in social change (i.e. that one cannot pass into the higher-status group), bilateral divergence occurs. Both speakers pursue *psycholinguistic distinctiveness*.

Speech accommodation theory has been well supported empirically (Gallois, Ogay, & Giles, 2005; Giles, 2016). For example, Bourhis and Giles (1977) found that Welsh adults accentuated their Welsh accent in the presence of RP English speakers (i.e. the standard non-regional variety of English). Bourhis, Giles, Leyens and Tajfel (1979) found a similar effect in Belgium, with Flemish speakers in the presence of French speakers. In both cases, a language revival was under way at the time, and thus an intergroup orientation with high vitality was salient. In a low-vitality social mobility context, Hogg (1985) found that female students in Britain shifted their speech style 'upwards' towards that of their male partners.

Accommodation in intergroup contexts reflects an intergroup or social identity dynamic where speech style is governed by the speakers' motivations to adopt ingroup or outgroup speech patterns. These motivations are in turn informed by perceptions of the relative status and prestige of the speech varieties and their associated groups, and the vitality of their own ethnolinguistic group.

Stereotyped speech

What may actually govern changes in speech style is conformity to stereotypical perceptions of the appropriate speech norm (see Chapter 7). Thakerar, Giles and Cheshire (1982) recognised this in distinguishing between objective and subjective accommodation. People converge on or diverge from what they perceive to be the relevant speech style. Objective accommodation may reflect this, but in some circumstances, it may not: for instance, subjective *con*vergence may look like objective *di*vergence if the speech style **stereotype** is different from the actual speech behaviour of the other speaker.

Stereotype
Widely shared and simplified evaluative image of a social group and its members.

Even the 'Queen's English' is susceptible to some accommodation towards a more popular stereotype (Harrington, 2006). A phonetic analysis of Queen Elizabeth II's speech contained in her Christmas broadcasts to the Commonwealth since 1952 point to a gradual change in the Royal vowels, moving from 'upper-class' RP to a more 'standard' and less aristocratic RP. Possibly this reflects a softening of the once-strong demarcation between the social classes – social change can sometimes be a catalyst for speech change. Where once she might have said 'thet men in the bleck het', she would now say 'that man in the black hat'.

Recently, speech accommodation theory has been extended to incorporate non-verbal communication (non-verbal behaviour is discussed later in this chapter). Now more accurately called **communication accommodation theory** (Gallois, Ogay, & Giles, 2005; Giles, Mulac, Bradac, & Johnson, 1987; Giles & Noels, 2002; see Giles, 2016), it acknowledges that convergence and divergence can occur non-verbally as well as verbally. For instance, Anthony Mulac and his colleagues found that women in mixed-sex dyads converged towards the amount of eye contact (now called 'gaze' – see later in this chapter) made by their partner (Mulac, Studley, Wiemann, & Bradac, 1987). While accommodation is often synchronised between verbal and non-verbal channels, this is not necessarily the case. Frances Bilous and Robert Krauss (1988) found that women in mixed-sex dyads converged towards men on some dimensions (e.g. total words uttered and interruptions) but diverged on others (e.g. laughter).

Communication accommodation theory
Modification of verbal and non-verbal communication styles to the context (e.g. listener, situation) of a face-to-face interaction – an extension of speech accommodation theory to incorporate non-verbal communication.

Bilingualism and second-language acquisition

Most countries are bilingual or multilingual, meaning that people need to be able to speak two or more languages with some proficiency in order to communicate effectively and get things done in different contexts. Bilingualism is relatively common, but in some instances people need to be trilingual (see Box 15.2). Such countries contain a variety of ethnolinguistic groups, with a single dominant group whose language is the lingua franca. Very few countries (e.g. Japan and Portugal) are effectively monolingual.

Box 15.2 Our world
Being trilingual in Montreal

Since the 1970s, Montreal's population has become bilingual. In earlier decades, its residents were more likely to be bilingual francophones than bilingual anglophones (Lamarre & Paredes, 2003); an asymmetry that reflected the relative status of the two language groups – English was very clearly the dominant group. Social change, specifically in the use of French, was enacted in law as part of Quebec's language policy – its 1977 *Charte de la langue française* gave French official status in schools alongside English. The perceived status of French improved significantly over the years.

This change in relative French–English status has had significant consequences for the children of new immigrants: they are now mostly *trilingual*. At one time they would have preferred to learn English as their second language, on the grounds that anglophones were the dominant group, but now they choose to speak three languages – a degree of their ancestral or native language at home and the two local languages in public.

Bilingualism through second-language acquisition is for most people not simply a recreational activity – it is a vital necessity for survival. For example, Indians (by far the largest foreign-born group in the United Kingdom – in 2015 almost 800,000 of the UK population of 56 million were foreign-born Indians) can speak Hindi, Marathi, Gujarati and so forth in some or even many contexts, but do have to learn English in order to be formally educated and to be able to participate fully in employment, culture and day-to-day life in Britain.

Acquisition of a second language is not merely a matter of acquiring basic classroom proficiency, as one might in order to be able to 'get by' on holiday – it is the wholesale acquisition of a language embedded in its cultural context (Gardner, 1979). Second-language acquisition requires native-like mastery (being able to speak like a native speaker), and this hinges more on the motivations of the second-language learner than on linguistic aptitude or pedagogical factors. Failure to acquire native-like mastery can undermine self-confidence and cause physical and social isolation, leading to material hardship and psychological suffering. For example, Noels, Pon and Clément (1996) found low self-esteem and marked symptoms of stress among Chinese Canadians with poor English skills.

Bilingualism
So, you can't read Welsh? If you plan to live in Wales it might be helpful to know a little Welsh.

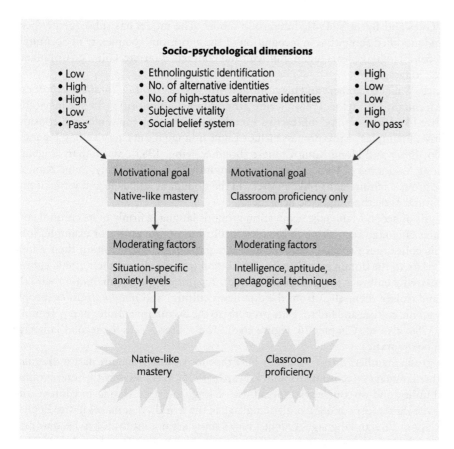

Figure 15.2 Intergroup model of second-language acquisition

Learning a second language is influenced by motivational goals formed by the wider context of social identity and intergroup relations.

Source: Giles and Byrne (1982).

Building on earlier models (Gardner, 1979; Clément, 1980), Giles and Byrne (1982) proposed an intergroup model of second-language acquisition. There are five *socio-psychological dimensions* that influence a subordinate group member's motivational goals in learning the language of a dominant group (see Figure 15.2):

1 strength of ethnolinguistic identification;

2 number of alternative identities available;

3 number of high-status alternative identities available;

4 subjective vitality perceptions;

5 social beliefs regarding the possibility of passing linguistically into the dominant group.

Low identification with one's ethnic ingroup, low subjective vitality and a belief that one can 'pass' linguistically, coupled with a large number of other potential identities of which many are high-status, are conditions that motivate someone to acquire native-like mastery in the second language. Proficiency in the second language is considered economically and culturally useful; it is *additive* to our identity. Realisation of this motivation is facilitated or inhibited by how confident or anxious we feel about using the second language in specific contexts. The converse set of socio-psychological conditions (see Figure 15.2) motivates people to acquire only classroom proficiency. Through fear of assimilation, the second language is considered *subtractive* in that it may attract ingroup hostility and accusations of ethnic betrayal. Intelligence and aptitude may also affect proficiency.

Language, culture and migration

The intergroup model in Figure 15.2 found broad support in a study by Bradford Hall and William Gudykunst (1986) in Arizona. The English-language ability of over 200 international students from a wide range of cultural and linguistic backgrounds could be explained in terms of Giles and Byrne's (1982) intergroup model. The model has subsequently been developed and modified somewhat in recognition of the enormous complexity of accurately modelling second-language learning in multicultural contexts (Garrett, Giles, & Coupland, 1989; Giles & Maass, 2016).

For instance, Wallace Lambert and his colleagues proposed a *multiculturalism hypothesis* (Lambert, Mermigis, & Taylor, 1986). Secure ethnolinguistic minorities do not inevitably consider native-like mastery to be subtractive – on the contrary, they can sometimes consider it to be additive. Examples of this process include English-language mastery among Japanese (San Antonio, 1987) and Hong Kong Chinese (Bond & King, 1985), and Italian language mastery among Valdotans (a French-speaking community in northern Italy; Saint-Blancat, 1985). These groups acquire native-like mastery in the dominant language and yet maintain their own cultural and ethnolinguistic heritage.

This analysis of second-language acquisition grounds language firmly in its cultural context and relates language acquisition to broader acculturation processes. For example, John Berry and his colleagues distinguished between *integration* (people maintain their ethnic culture and relate to the dominant culture), *assimilation* (people give up their ethnic culture and wholeheartedly embrace the dominant culture), *separation* (people maintain their ethnic culture and isolate themselves from the dominant culture) and *marginalisation* (people give up their ethnic culture and fail to relate properly to the dominant culture (Berry, Trimble, & Olmedo, 1986; also see **Chapter 16, Figure 16.5**). The consequences for second-language learning can be dramatic.

Majority-group members do not generally have the motivation to acquire native-like mastery of another language. According to John Edwards (1994), it is precisely the international prestige and utility, and of course widespread use of English (after Mandarin Chinese and Spanish, it is the third most common native language in the world), that makes native English speakers such poor foreign-language students: they simply are not motivated to become proficient. Itesh Sachdev and Audrey Wright (1996) pursued this point. They found that White English children were more motivated to learn European languages than Asian languages: the former were considered more useful and of higher status, even though the children in their sample had significantly more day-to-day contact with Asian than with European languages and people. (Reflect now on the third 'What do *you* think?' question: would it be a good idea for Paulo to be bilingual?)

Intergroup language and communication

The identity-defining function of language in intergroup contexts was first, and has largely been, explored in the context of national, ethnic and regional language and speech style groups – the discussion in the previous section has described this research. However, this intergroup analysis is, and has successfully been, applied to a wider range of social identity and intergroup communicative contexts (Giles, 2012; Giles & Maass, 2016; Giles, Reid, & Harwood, 2010). In most cases, the focus is not just on language and speech but also more broadly on communication.

Here we focus on gender and age, but there is also research on social categories defined by sexual orientation (e.g. Hajek & Giles, 2005), disability (e.g. Ryan, Bajorek, Beaman, & Anas, 2005), religion (e.g. Klocek, Novoa, & Moghaddam, 2010) and police and community (e.g. Giles, Choi, & Dixon, 2010); and on intergroup communication in families (e.g. Soliz, 2010) and in education (e.g. Edwards, 2010), health care (e.g. Watson, Gallois, Hewitt, & Jones, 2012) and organisational (e.g. Peters, Morton, & Haslam, 2010) contexts.

Gender

Gender is one of the most fundamental and far-reaching bases for one's identity, perceptions, and interactions with other people (Brewer & Lui, 1989). So, it is not surprising to discover that there is substantial research on how gender impacts language, speech and communication (Palomares, 2012).

Speech style differences between men and women have been studied most extensively in Western countries (Aries, 1996; Smith, 1985) where there are clear stereotypes about sex differences in speech (Haas, 1979; see **Chapter 10**). For example, women are often assumed to be more talkative, polite, emotional, positive, supportive and tentative, less assertive and more likely to talk about home and family. Real speech differences are much smaller than stereotypes lead one to believe (Aries, 1997), and such differences are influenced by context. Even paralinguistic differences that are grounded in physiology (women's voices have a higher pitch, softer volume, greater variability and more relaxed and mellifluous tone) are influenced by context and show marked within-sex variability (Montepare & Vega, 1988). Overall, however, sex differences in language, speech and communication are very real – a meta-analysis by Campbell Leaper and Melanie Ayres (2007) confirmed that women's language usage and speech and communication styles are indeed more affiliative and less assertive than those of males.

Because speech style is stereotypically sex-typed (Weatherall, 1998), it is not surprising to discover that both men and women can adopt more or less masculine or feminine speech styles depending on whether they have a more or less traditional sex-role orientation (Smith, 1985), or are more or less gender-schematic in the way they view themselves (Palomares, 2004). Non-traditional men tend to eschew more masculine speech styles, and non-traditional women eschew more feminine speech styles. In line with speech accommodation theory, speech style can also vary according to the immediate communicative context. In the case of gender differences, the way that men and women speak, particularly to each other, is sometimes linked to power (see Box 15.3).

When children are socialised in relatively sex-segregated groups, boys and girls acquire different kinds of interaction and communication styles that carry over into adulthood. Girls emphasise cooperation and equality and attend sensitively to relationships and situations. Boys emphasise competition and hierarchical relations and assert their individual identity. Much like interactions between cultural groups with different language communication norms, men and women interact with different assumptions and goals in a conversation. Since some of the

Box 15.3 Your life
Speech style, gender and power

Have you noticed how some people seem to make statements as though they are questions? 'Let's go to the pub?' rather than 'Let's go to the pub.' Why is this; how does it make you feel about the person; what effect does it have on your interaction and relationship?

Social psychologists have studied this as part of a wider phenomenon of 'powerless speech'. There is evidence that women can adopt a 'powerless' form of speech when addressing men or in the company of men (O'Barr & Atkins, 1980; Wiemann & Giles, 1988). Women tend to adopt a more masculine (more powerful) speech style when speaking to male strangers or acquaintances (Hall & Braunwald, 1981; Hogg, 1985) but a more feminine (less powerful) style when speaking to intimate male friends (Montepare & Vega, 1988).

The linguist Robin Lakoff's *Language and Woman's Place* (2004) outlined the nature of powerless speech: it involves greater use of *intensifiers* (e.g. 'very', 'really', 'so'), *hedges* (e.g. 'kind of', 'sort of', 'you know'), *tag questions* (e.g. '. . . didn't they?'), *empty adjectives* ('gorgeous', 'adorable',

'divine'), rising intonation, which transforms a declarative statement into a question, and *polite forms of address*.

Power can also be associated with the ability to interrupt and take control of the floor (Ng, Bell, & Brooke, 1993; Ng & Bradac, 1993; Reid & Ng, 1999). In mixed-sex conversations, women have been shown to interrupt less often than men: Zimmerman and West (1975) reported that 98 per cent of interruptions were by men. However, other research suggests that women can interrupt more often than men (Dindia, 1987).

Powerless speech is not confined to women; it simply reflects status differences in interactions and has been shown to characterise low-status speakers in general (Lind & O'Barr, 1979). A study of stereotypical beliefs about speech styles by Popp and her colleagues found that women – and, even more so, blacks – have a less direct and more emotional style than that of white men (Popp, Donovan, Crawford, Marsh, & Peele, 2003). In this sense, the speech of women is now better described as a powerless rather than a female linguistic style (Blankenship & Holtgraves, 2005).

same forms can carry different meanings and serve different functions for men and women, inter-sex miscommunication is almost inevitable (e.g. Mulac, Bradac, & Gibbons, 2001).

One should not, however, overreach in generalising from research on gender differences in language and communication: contextual factors are underplayed, and it is culturally constrained largely to men and women who are white, middle-class and Western (e.g. Crawford, 1995; Eckert & McConnell-Ginet, 1999).

Age groups and generations

Through life we all pass through a sequence of age groups (infant, child, teenager, youth, young adult, adult, middle-aged, old) and are born into generational cohorts. Society has distinct stereotypical beliefs and expectations about the attitudes and behaviour associated with how old people are, their age groups (Hummert, 2012); but also associated with when they were born, their generation (e.g. baby boomers, Generation X, millennials – Myers & Davis, 2012). Age, along with gender, is one of the most fundamental bases of one's identity, and one's perceptions of and interactions with other people (Brewer & Lui, 1989).

Ageism
Prejudice and discrimination against people based on their age.

In Western society **ageism** is common – old people are generally considered to be frail, incompetent, of low status and largely worthless (Hummert, 2012; Noels, Giles, & Le Poire, 2003; see **Chapter 10**). In a perverse form of speech accommodation strategy, younger people often adopt a sort of 'baby talk' to communicate with both institutionalised and non-institutionalised elderly people (Caporael, Lukaszewski, & Cuthbertson, 1983; Giles & Gasiorek, 2011; Ryan, Giles, Bartolucci, & Henwood, 1986). This can be accompanied by 'elderspeak' – the use of simple and short sentences (Kemper, 1994). While some elderly find this nurturant, many believe it is patronising (Nelson, 2005).

At the same time, young people feel that the elderly fail to modify their speech, and they find this irritating (Fox & Giles, 1993; Williams, 1996). Intergenerational encounters between the young and the elderly are thus likely to reinforce stereotypes rather than disconfirm them (see discussion of intergroup contact in **Chapter 11**). These intergenerational effects are widespread, and research by Giles and his associates has found, quite surprisingly, that they are more pronounced in East Asian settings (Giles, Noels, Ota, Ng, Gallois, Ryan, et al., 2001).

Because age categories are so pervasive, we all know what is expected of us once we reach a particular age. Indeed, along with race and gender, age is one of the primitive, well-learnt and automatic forms of social categorization (Mackie, Hamilton, Susskind, & Rosselli, 1996; Nelson, 2005). Almost every official form you complete asks for your age and sex. As these experiences accumulate, it makes it difficult for elderly people not to 'act their age'. The social costs of not acting our age can be extreme – as was entertainingly illustrated in an old 1980s movie, *Cocoon*. Research confirms this – Alex Schoemann and Nyla Branscombe (2011) found that middle-aged women who tried to dress and act younger than their years were evaluated by college students as being less likeable and more deceitful than those who acted their age. Overall, younger people in particular seem to find it irritating when older people do not 'act their age' (North & Fiske, 2013).

Perhaps, then, elderly people talk a great deal about their age, make painful disclosures about their health and exhibit other symptoms of elderly speech, not so much because of their age but because they are constrained to conform to social expectations (Coupland, Coupland, Giles, & Henwood, 1988). Intergenerational communication can certainly be problematic and can even have effects on psychological and physical well-being (Williams & Nussbaum, 2001). However, intra-generational communication can be facilitated and rendered rewarding and efficient by the fact that generational cohorts have shared experiences of life and thus a shared world view to frame their language use and communication and speech style (see Myers & Davis, 2012).

Intergenerational communication is, however, adversely affected by intergenerational competition, mainly between adolescents and young adults on the one hand and full adults on the other, over scarce resource – primarily jobs (e.g. Garstka, Hummert, & Branscombe, 2005; see Hummert, 2012). Associated with this intergroup context is a bilateral rhetoric of generational victimhood – the young feel victims of the old not freeing up jobs by retiring, and the old feel victims of organisations preferring to hire cheaper, younger labour. The old and the young can compete over who is the greater victim – a dynamic of competitive victim-hood arises (Noor, Shnabel, Halabi, & Nadler, 2012).

Communicating without words

Speech rarely occurs in isolation from non-verbal cues. Even on the phone, people tend auto-matically to use gestures that cannot possibly be 'seen' by the person at the other end of the line. Similarly, phone and computer-mediated communication (CMC) conversations can often be difficult precisely because many non-verbal cues are not accessible. However, non-verbal channels do not necessarily work in concert with speech to facilitate understanding. Sometimes the non-verbal message starkly contradicts the verbal message (e.g. threats, sarcasm and other negative messages accompanied by a smile; Bugental, Love, & Gianetto, 1971; Noller, 1984).

Speech
Vocal production of language.

Functions of non-verbal communication

Did you know that people can produce about 20,000 different facial expressions and about 1,000 different cues based on paralanguage? There are also about 700,000 different physical gestures, facial expressions and movements (see Birdwhistell, 1970; Hewes, 1957; Pei, 1965). And, people acquire, without any formal training, consummate mastery of this rich reper-toire of non-verbal behaviour very early in life.

How on earth do we cope? Even the briefest interaction can involve the fleeting and simul-taneous use of a large number of these devices, making it very difficult even to code behav-iour, let alone analyse the causes and consequences of particular **non-verbal communications**. The importance of non-verbal behaviour is well-recognised in social psychology (Ambady & Weisbuch, 2010; Burgoon, Buller, & Woodall, 1989; DePaulo & Friedman, 1998; Matsumoto, Frank, & Hwang, 2012).

Non-verbal behaviour can serve many purposes (Patterson, 1983). We can use it to:

Non-verbal communication
Transfer of meaningful information from one person to another by means other than written or spoken language (e.g. gaze, facial expression, posture, touch).

- glean information about feelings and intentions of others (e.g. non-verbal cues are often reliable indicators of whether someone likes you);
- regulate interactions (e.g. non-verbal cues can signal the approaching end of an utterance, or that someone else wishes to speak);
- express intimacy (e.g. touching and mutual eye contact);
- establish dominance or control (e.g. non-verbal threats);
- facilitate goal attainment (e.g. pointing).

Variations in non-verbal behaviour

These functions of non-verbal communication will become evident in our discussion of gaze, facial expressions, body language, touch and interpersonal distance. Perhaps because we acquire non-verbal behaviour unawares, we tend not to be conscious that we are using non-verbal cues or that we are being influenced by others' use of such cues: non-verbal com-munication goes largely unnoticed, yet it has enormous impact.

This is not to say that non-verbal behaviour is completely uncontrolled. On the contrary, social norms have a strong influence. For example, even if delighted at the demise of an arro-gant narcissist or foe, we are unlikely to smile at their funeral – *Schadenfreude* is not a noble emotion to express, except perhaps to those who are also boundlessly gleeful! Individual and group differences also have an influence on, or are associated with, non-verbal behaviour – some people are simply better than others at noticing and using non-verbal cues. Robert Rosenthal and his colleagues (Rosenthal, Hall, DiMatteo, Rogers, & Archer, 1979) devised a *profile of non-verbal sensitivity* (PONS) as a way to map some of these individual and group differences. All things being equal, non-verbal competence improves with age, is more advanced among suc-cessful people and is compromised among people with a range of psychopathologies.

Gender differences

Women are generally better than men at decoding both visual cues and auditory cues, such as voice tone and pitch (E. T. Hall, 1979; J. A. Hall, 1978, 1984). The most likely explanation is a social rather than evolutionary one (Manstead, 1992), including child-rearing strategies that encourage girls more than boys to be emotionally expressive and attentive. One question is whether women's greater competence is due to greater knowledge about non-verbal cues. The answer, according to Janelle Rosip and Judith Hall (2004), is yes – women have a slight advantage, based on results from their *test of non-verbal cue knowledge* (TONCK). A meta-analysis by William Ickes has shown that when motivated to do so, women can become even more accurate: for example, when they think they are being evaluated for their empathy or when gender-role expectations of empathy are brought to the fore (Ickes, Gesn, & Graham, 2000).

We can all improve our non-verbal skills, and there is evidence that we can to some extent be trained to do this (e.g. Matsumoto & Hwang, 2011). Non-verbal skills can be useful for improving interpersonal communication, detecting deception, presenting a good impression and hiding our feelings. Not surprisingly, there are scores of practical books and courses on communications skills. Why not try yourself out on the TONCK?

Relationships and attachment

Attachment styles
Descriptions of the nature of people's close relationships, thought to be established in childhood.

People have different **attachment styles** that influence their relationships (see **Chapter 14**) and their non-verbal behaviour. In the case of an intimate relationship, we might expect partners to enhance each other's emotional security by accurately decoding non-verbal cues and responding appropriately (Schachner, Shaver, & Mikulincer, 2005). Although there are studies of non-verbal behaviour in parent–child interactions and how this relates to the development of attachment styles in children (Bugental, 2005), there is less research on how adult attachment styles are reflected non-verbally in close relationships. For example, if Harry is vigilant to threat in his relationship with Sally, he may take her (ambiguous) silence as rejection.

Using the face to express emotions

You may already suspect that emotions play a major part in communicating our feelings, through our body and especially our facial expressions, and that there is a time and a place when we should do so (Keltner & Lerner, 2010). Keeping a 'stiff upper lip' is not always the smartest move – but neither is having an emotional meltdown. Along with our body posture and paralanguage, our facial expression can tell others something about our personality and even our likely social actions, such as whether we might be cooperative or prosocial (Niedenthal & Brauer, 2012).

The scientific study of facial expression has largely focused on the way in which different expressions communicate emotions. Darwin (1872) believed that there are a small number of universal emotions and that associated with these emotions are universal facial expressions. Subsequent research generally identified six basic emotions (happiness, surprise, sadness, fear, disgust and anger), from which more complex or blended emotions are derived (Ekman, 1982, 2003; Scherer, 1986; but also see Ortony & Turner, 1990). There are studies that distinguished between displays of contempt, embarrassment, pride, shame, desire and awe (Keltner & Lerner, 2010), and the facial display for anxiety can be recognised as distinct from fear (Perkins, Inchley-Mort, Pickering, Corr, & Burgess, 2012). There are also studies showing cross-cultural gender differences in how often both basic and complex emotions are experienced (Fischer, Mosquera, Van Vienan, & Manstead, 2004). Women more often report feeling 'powerless' emotions (e.g. fear, sadness, shame, guilt), while men more often report feeling powerful emotions (e.g. anger, hostility).

A basic emotion has a distinctive pattern of facial muscle activity: for instance, surprise is associated with raised eyebrows, dropped jaw, horizontal wrinkles across the forehead, raised upper eyelids and lowered lower eyelids (Ekman & Friesen, 1975). A computer program has even been developed that can simultaneously vary different facial components (e.g. roundness of eyes, thickness of lips, curve of eyebrows, distance between mouth and eyes) to reproduce recognisable emotional expressions on a computer screen (Katsikitis, Pilowsky, & Innes, 1990).

Human facial expressions associated with basic emotions are relatively universal. Paul Ekman and his colleagues showed people a series of photographs of faces expressing the six basic emotions and had them report the emotions being expressed (Ekman, 1971; Ekman & Friesen, 1971; Ekman, Friesen, O'Sullivan, Chan, Diacoyanni-Tarlatzis, Heider, et al., 1987). People from a variety of Western and Latin cultures (Argentina, Brazil, Chile, Germany, Greece, Italy, Scotland, the United States), Asian cultures (Hong Kong, Japan, Sumatra, Turkey) and tribal cultures (Borneo, New Guinea) were remarkably accurate in identifying the six emotions from facial expression by people from both the same and different cultures.

Ekman's method depended on participants rating photographs of posed rather than natural (candid) emotional expressions. Robert Krauss and his colleagues adopted a more naturalistic technique in which people identified emotions as they occurred on videotapes of Japanese and American soap operas (Krauss, Curran, & Ferleger, 1983). Like Ekman's findings, there was remarkable cross-cultural agreement.

Ekman's argument that the primary emotions are universal has not gone unchallenged (e.g. Russell, Bachorowski, & Fernandez-Dols, 2003), but his work has generated a large number of studies and continues to do so. Undeterred, Ekman has developed a Facial Action Coding System (FACS), a standardised method to measure facial movement based on small units of muscles that reflect a variety of underlying emotional states (Ekman, Friesen, & Hager, 2002). This technique has even been adapted to measure facial responses in chimpanzees (Vick, Waller, Parr, Pasqualini, & Bard, 2007). The aim of such work is to make cross-species comparisons of 'emotions' with humans, in an evolutionary quest for characteristics that are uniquely human and those that may be shared with other primates.

The apparent universality of facial expressions of emotion may either reflect universals of *ontogeny* (cross-cultural commonalities in early socialisation) or *phylogeny* (an innate link between emotions and facial muscle activity). The contribution of phylogeny has some support from research with people born deaf, blind and without hands. Although these people have limited access to the conventional cues that we would use to learn which facial expressions go with which emotions, they express basic emotions in much the same manner as

Unlearned facial displays
Crying and smiling - innate expressions of emotion. Later in life we learn when to display different feelings.

Six basic emotions
Anger, happiness, surprise, fear, sadness and disgust. But, which is which?

people who are not handicapped in these ways (Eibl-Eibesfeldt, 1972). The same has been found from research on sighted and non-sighted people. For example, David Matsumoto and Bob Willingham (2009) compared the expressions of athletes at the 2004 Paralympic Games (both congenitally and non-congenitally blind) with the expressions of sighted athletes in the 2004 Olympic Games.

Hillary Elfenbein and Noah Eisenkraft (2010) have added a word of caution about the methods used when researching the facial expression of an emotion. The meaning attached to an expression can vary depending on whether the expression has been posed or is spontaneous – occurring 'in the wild'. They call for more naturalistic research, noting that in a real-life context the observer is more likely to use situational cues in decoding an emotion.

Facial display rules

Having made an argument for universals in the facial expression of the emotions, we must now introduce an important qualification. There are marked cultural and situational rules, called **display rules**, governing the expression of emotions (see Figure 15.3, also Box 15.4).

Display rules
Cultural and situational rules that dictate how appropriate it is to express emotions in a given context.

These rules exist because we also use our facial expressions to communicate with someone else (Gallois, 1993). There are shades of surprise: when we 'choose' one of these, we might accompany our facial display by vocalising with something like 'oh my god' or 'whew'. In a fine-grained analysis of conversations, Sue Wilkinson and Celia Kitzinger (2006) have demonstrated that we are equipped to respond with surprise several turns in

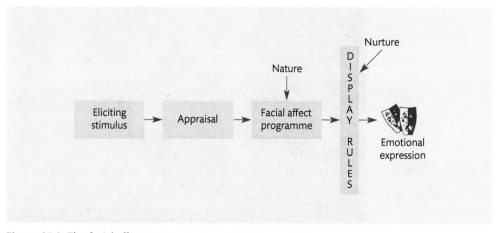

Figure 15.3 The facial affect programme: expressing an emotion

- Rapid facial signals accompany many affective states.
- These signals are the facial affect programme, or facial 'blueprints'.
- They distinguish primary emotions from their blends.
- There is an interplay between nature and nurture:
  - Signals have a genetic base, whereas
  - Display rules arise from experience and provide a little control over what we show others.

Source: Based on Ekman (1971).

advance. Perhaps you can remember talking with a friend and can guess what is about to be announced – your face begins to move . . . OMG, the suspense!

There are cultural, gender and situational variations in display rules. The expression of emotion is encouraged for women and in Mediterranean cultures but is discouraged for men and in northern European and East Asian cultures (e.g. Argyle, 1975). In Japan, people are taught to control facial expressions of negative emotion and to use laughter or smiling to conceal anger or grief. In Western cultures, it is impolite to display happiness at beating an

---

Box 15.4 Your life
Misunderstanding the locals

Think of the last time you went on holiday somewhere foreign, very foreign. One problem you will have encountered is the obvious one, that the locals speak a language you do not speak or understand – you are Dutch and they are Chinese, you are British and they are Thai and so forth. But another common problem is that their non-verbals and display rules, discussed in this chapter, confuse you. For example, they may look away from you when they speak whereas you look at them when you are speaking – this disrupts conversational flow and can lead to feelings that they are indifferent and you are aggressive. Another example – they appear impassive and unemotional, whereas you are animated in expressing your feelings. These cultural misinterpretations based on non-verbals and display rules can be amplified by other cultural differences. For example, people from individualistic cultures typically assert their views come what may (this can be interpreted as pushiness), whereas people from collectivist cultures tend to defer to those with higher social status (can be interpreted as lack of knowledge). Another example – in some cultures people do not like to disappoint, so if asked how to get somewhere, they will give directions even if they have no idea where your destination is.

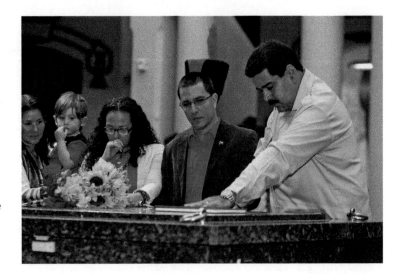

Nature–nurture controversy
How grief stricken were these people at the passing of the former Venezuelan president Hugo Chavez?

Nature–nurture controversy
Classic debate about whether genetic or environmental factors determine human behaviour. Scientists generally accept that it is an interaction of both.

opponent in tennis by laughing, yet happy laughter is acceptable at a party. Similarly, it is fine to cry at a funeral but not on hearing disappointing news in a business setting. Ekman's theory has been described as 'one of the first theories to explain how a psychological process could be both universal and culture-specific' (Matsumoto, 2004, p. 49).

We are of course dealing here with the **nature–nurture controversy**, a point that is nicely illustrated by James Russell's (1994) investigation of the varying success that people from different parts of the world have in decoding (or labelling) the six primary emotions (shown in the photo). His results are shown in Figure 15.4.

A meta-analysis has confirmed that both universal and cultural components are involved in recognising the emotions (Elfenbein & Ambady, 2002), and also how we experience them (Kitayama, Mesquita, & Karasawa, 2006). One interesting finding is that people are more accurate at facial recognition and decoding emotions expressed by people from the same ethnic or regional group as themselves. Just as there are language dialects, there may be emotional dialects, shaped by geographic, national and social boundaries.

Figure 15.4 Cross-cultural success at decoding facial expressions of primary emotions

- People from three educational/cultural groups were compared: literate and from the West (20 studies) or elsewhere (11 studies), and non-literate from elsewhere (three studies).
- Recognition of happiness was high in all cultures.
- Agreement about other emotions fell away, depending on: (a) what was thought to be a culturally appropriate expression, and (b) exposure to a literature that provided models of how to express an emotion.

Source: Based on data from Russell (1994).

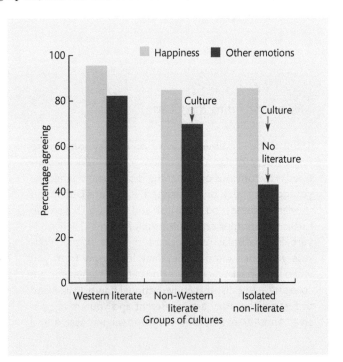

We use our face to *express* our emotions; however, we use display rules to *communicate* with others. This distinction underpinned a series of naturalistic studies of smiling, by Robert Kraut and Robert Johnston (1979). They studied the frequency of smiling in a range of settings, including bowling alleys, ice hockey arenas and public footpaths. People were more likely to smile when talking to others than when alone, and this was significantly more pronounced among women than men (LaFrance, Hecht, & Levy-Paluck, 2003). Whether they were really happy or not seemed to have little influence on whether people smiled or not: smiling was a more important way to communicate happiness than using words to express happiness. Figure 15.5 shows the percentage of bowlers in competition who smiled either when facing their teammates (social interaction) or facing the pins (no social interaction), as an outcome of bowling well or poorly. These findings were replicated in a study of football fans as well as bowlers (Ruiz-Belda, Fernández-Dols, Carrera, & Barchard, 2003): our smiles usually, but not always, require an audience.

Focusing on cross-cultural differences in emotional displays, Ekman (1973) monitored facial expressions of American students in America and Japanese students in Japan watching a very stressful film in private and talking about it to the experimenter afterwards. In private, both groups displayed negative emotions, but in public only the Americans gave facial expressions indicating negative emotions. In public, the Japanese students' facial expressions were indicative of positive emotions. A meta-analysis of 162 studies by Marianne LaFrance and her colleagues showed that Western women were encouraged to smile more often than their Asian counterparts (LaFrance, Hecht, & Levy-Paluck, 2003). There are quite clearly different cultural (and gender) display rules.

Finally, facial movements are more than cues to our emotions; they are also used deliberately to support or even to replace spoken language. We raise our eyebrows to emphasise a question, or furrow our brows and squint our eyes to reflect doubt or scorn. A relatively new development – American Sign Language (ASL) – is linked to Ekman's work on the facial expression of basic emotions. ASL is a convention that uses a set of sign language facial expressions, which have emotional meaning and are dynamic, i.e. they occur in real time (Grossman & Kegl, 2007).

Figure 15.5 People smile more when they are interacting with others rather than when they perform well

- Players at a bowling alley smiled much more when facing their teammates than when facing the pins.
- Smiling was much less strongly related to whether they were performing well or not.

Source: Based on data from Kraut and Johnston (1979).

Gaze and eye contact

There are often voice and words in a silent look.

Ovid; cited in Kleinke (1986, p. 78)

Gaze
Looking at someone's eyes.

We spend a great deal of time gazing at each other's eyes. In two-person settings, people spend 61 per cent of the time gazing, and a **gaze** lasts about three seconds (Argyle & Ingham, 1972). Eye contact refers more precisely to mutual gaze. People in pairs spend about 30 per cent of their time engaging in mutual gaze, and a mutual gaze lasts less than a second.

Gaze is perhaps the most information-rich non-verbal communication channel (Kleinke, 1986). It allows us to make inferences about people's feelings, credibility, honesty, competence and attentiveness. This information is so important that we still gaze, despite the fact that under certain circumstances (e.g. passing a stranger in the street), eye contact itself is uncomfortable and even embarrassing. Absence of eye behaviour can be equally unnerving. Consider how disconcerting it can be to interact with someone whose eyes you cannot see (e.g. someone wearing dark glasses) or someone who continually avoids eye contact. If someone averts their gaze from you, even unintentionally, you can feel that you or your relationship with that person is devalued, or even that you are being rejected and ostracised (Wirth, Sacco, Hugenberg, & Williams, 2010).

Conversely, obscuring from others where your own eyes are looking can increase your own sense of security and privacy: for example, female tourists visiting notably chauvinistic societies are often encouraged to wear dark glasses and to avoid eye contact with male strangers. In many societies, women secure privacy in public places by wearing a veil, or staring intently at their mobile device.

We look more at people we like than at those we dislike. Greater gaze signals intimacy, particularly if the gaze is mutual. This appears to be such common knowledge that even false information that someone has looked at you quite often increases your liking for that person (Kleinke, 1986).

Visual dominance

A meta-analysis by Judith Hall and her colleagues confirms that gaze plays an important role in communicating status and exercising control – other important factors are increased facial expressiveness, postural expansion (looking bigger), decreased interpersonal distance, and louder voice (Hall, Coats, & Smith-LeBeau, 2005). People gaze more when they are trying to be persuasive or trying to ingratiate themselves (Kleinke, 1986). A stern stare can also express disapproval, dominance or threat. It can stop someone talking or even cause flight. For instance, Ellsworth, Carlsmith and Henson (1972) found that drivers waiting at an intersection departed much more speedily when stared at than when not stared at by a person standing on the corner.

Visual dominance behaviour
Tendency to gaze fixedly at a lower-status speaker.

Higher-status people can adopt a specific pattern of gaze behaviour in order to exert control. They gaze more than lower-status people at a partner (Dovidio & Ellyson, 1985; Exline, 1971). This is **visual dominance behaviour**, a tendency to gaze fixedly at a lower-status speaker. Leaders who adopt this visual dominance pattern tend to be given higher leadership ratings than leaders who do not (Exline, Ellyson, & Long, 1975). Overall, the powerless tend to pay more attention to the powerful than vice versa, because people without power are highly motivated to learn about those who have power over them (Fiske & Dépret, 1996; also see Fiske, 2010; Fiske & Berdahl, 2007).

Status and gender

Women generally engage in more eye contact than men, which in some contexts likely reflects a traditional lower-status power position (Duncan, 1969; Henley, 1977; Henley & Harmon, 1985). Jack Dovidio and his colleagues studied the role of power in gender-related differences in gaze by having mixed-sex pairs discuss three topics of conversation – one where the man had more expertise, one where the woman had more expertise and one where

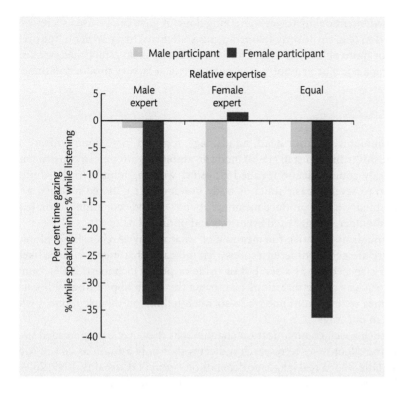

Figure 15.6 Gaze, gender expertise and dominance

- A dominant gaze pattern occurs when people gaze more when speaking than listening. See the vertical axis to check how this was calculated.

- In this graph, the less negative the bars, the more they indicate a dominant gaze pattern.

- Both men and women in male–female dyads assumed the dominant gaze pattern when they were in the high-status, expert role.

- When status was not specified, men simply assumed the dominant gaze pattern.

Source: Based on data from Dovidio et al. (1988).

the partners had equal expertise (Dovidio, Ellyson, Keating, Heltman, & Brown, 1988). The percentage of speaking time, and separately of listening time, spent gazing was recorded.

The results in Figure 15.6 show that when the man or the woman was an expert (high status), they dominated – gazing almost as much or more while speaking as listening. When the man or the woman was not an expert (low status), they showed the low-status pattern – gazing more while listening than speaking. The interesting finding in this study is that when the man and the woman were equally expert, the man would dominate whereas the woman showed the low-status pattern.

Status and ethnicity

Gaze regulates interaction. Mutual gaze, making eye contact, is an important means of initiating conversation (Argyle, 1971; Cary, 1978), and we avoid eye contact if we do not wish to be drawn into conversation. Once a conversation is underway, gaze plays an important role in regulating the course of the conversation. White adults spend on average 75 per cent of the time gazing when listening and 41 per cent of the time gazing when speaking (Argyle & Ingham, 1972). A listener can decrease gaze to signal an intention to gain the floor, while a speaker can increase gaze to signal an intention to stop speaking.

LaFrance and Mayo (1976) have shown that this pattern is reversed among African Americans, who gaze more when speaking than when listening. This complicates communication in inter-racial interactions. For example, a white speaker may interpret a black listener's *low* rate of gaze as lack of interest, rudeness or an attempt to butt in and take the floor, while a black speaker may interpret a white listener's *high* rate of gaze in the same way. From the perspective of the listener, a white may interpret a black speaker's high rate of gaze as arrogance and/or an invitation to take the floor, while a black may interpret a white speaker's low rate of gaze in the same way. There is less eye contact during the course of an interview in Japan than in the West. Unlike Western listeners, who are socialised to look at a speaker's eyes, Japanese listeners find it less stressful to focus on the speaker's knees (Bond & Komai, 1976), a practice that might be unnerving to some! (What do you now think about Santoso's plight? See the fourth 'What do *you* think?' question.)

Gaze can also be used intentionally to get something done. A gaze can be used secretly to communicate information (e.g. surprise at an outrageous statement) to a partner in the presence of a third party, or more publicly to signal a routine activity in an established working relationship (e.g. sailing a boat) or in a noisy environment (e.g. a factory production line).

Postures and gestures

Kinesics
Linguistics of body communication.

Your eyes and face communicate. Your head, hands, legs, feet and torso communicate as well. The anthropologist Ray Birdwhistell (1970) made an ambitious attempt to construct an entire linguistics of body communication, called **kinesics**. Working mainly in the United States, he identified up to seventy basic units of body movement (e.g. flared nostrils) and described rules of combination that produce meaningful units of body communication (e.g. the combination of a shoulder shrug, raised eyebrows and upturned palms).

We use our hands and arms to enrich the meaning of what we say (Archer, 1997; Ekman & Friesen, 1972). There are gender differences: research indicates that men are more likely than women to raise a clenched fist as a symbol of pride or power (Schubert, 2004). Some gestures are universal, such as giving directions by moving the arm and pointing with a finger or thumb. Sometimes we even continue to do so when talking on the telephone – why should technology get in our way?

Hand gestures are such a rich communication channel that they may have preceded spoken language in humans. Neuroscience research indicates that only a brain as complex as yours and mine can handle what a real language depends on – syntax (Corballis, 1999, 2004). See Box 15.5 for a short evolutionary history of how language came about.

Kerri Johnson and her colleagues confirm a common observation, that we use both body shape and body motion as cues to someone's gender: e.g. some men swagger and some women sway when they walk (Johnson, Gill, Reichman, & Tassinary, 2007). We also draw inferences about a person's sexual orientation. Gender-typical combinations of cues, such as a tubular body with shoulder swagger or an hourglass body with hip sway, are interpreted to imply a heterosexual orientation. Gender atypical combinations are interpreted to imply a homosexual orientation (lesbian or gay).

Emblems
Gestures that replace or stand in for spoken language.

Emblems, on the other hand, are special kinds of gesture that replace or stand in for spoken language, such as the wave of the hand in greeting; or less friendly hand signals that we are all familiar with! Some emblems are widely understood across cultures, but many are culture-specific. The same thing can be indicated by different gestures in different cultures, and the same gesture can mean different things in different cultures.

Phone language
Facial expressions and hand gestures are superfluous when we talk on the phone.

Box 15.5 Research highlight
The gestural origins of language

The hands have it

Can chimps talk? Not as we know it. Animal vocalisation in general is stimulus-bound – a relatively small number of utterances connected to specific cues, such as a food source or a predator. Our own cries that sometimes accompany the primary emotions (see 'Using the face to express emotions' earlier in this chapter) may be the vestiges of the utterances of our primate ancestors.

Corballis has argued that language evolved something like this:

1. Hominids diverged from the other great apes (6–7 million years ago).
2. Bipedal hominids, such as *Australopithecus*, used hand gestures (5 million years ago).
3. Syntax was added to gestures, and then vocalisation (2 million years ago).
4. Speech now dominated gesture in *Homo sapiens* (100,000 years ago).

Chimpanzees and the early hominids could undoubtedly vocalise well before the arrival of *Homo sapiens*, but vocal control was largely involuntary. Anatomical and cortical changes necessary for voluntary control of vocalisation were probably not complete until the emergence of *Homo sapiens*. Vocal language freed the hands for manufacture, allowing the development of pedagogy through combined speech and manual action, and permitted communication at night. These developments may explain the so-called 'human revolution' within the past 100,000 years, characterised by increasing technological innovation and the demise of all other hominids.

A limited use of gesture to communicate may extend back more than 25 million years to the common ancestors of humans, apes and monkeys. However, when hominids (our human line) stood up and walked, their hands were no longer instruments of locomotion and could serve extensively as tools for gestural communication. Like speech, gestural language depends on the left side of the brain.

Today, examples of gestural language include:

- sign languages used by the deaf;
- communicating with someone who speaks a different language;
- hand gestures that accompany speech, often superfluously, as when talking on the phone;
- religious communities bound by a vow of silence;
- sophisticated manual hand signs among Australian Aborigines and American Plains Indians.

Source: Based on Corballis (1999, 2004).

For instance, we in the West refer to 'self' by pointing at our chest, while in Japan they put a finger to the nose (DeVos & Hippler, 1969). A sideways nod of the head means 'no' in Britain but 'yes' in India, and in Turkey 'no' is indicated by moving the head backwards and rolling the eyes upwards (Rubin, 1976). In Britain, we invite people to approach by beckoning with an upturned finger, while Indians use all four downturned fingers. In Britain, if you were to draw your finger across your throat it would mean that someone was in big trouble. The same gesture in Swaziland means 'I love you' – in Japan, it means 'I've lost my job'. Cross-cultural differences in the meaning of gestures can have serious consequences. Be careful when and where you gesture with a forefinger and thumb forming a circle. You would probably think it meant 'it's okay' or 'great'; in Brazil, it means 'screw you!' (Burgoon, Buller, & Woodall, 1989).

Status differences

Body language can do more than just illustrate or replace spoken language. It can also convey, or intentionally be used to communicate, the relative status of people who are interacting (Hall, Coats, & Smith-LeBeau, 2005; Mehrabian, 1972). In a study of people interacting in dyads, Larissa Tiedens and Alison Fragale (2003) found that higher-status or dominant individuals took up more space by adopting an expansive posture: relaxed, open, with arms and legs akimbo and a backward lean to the body. Those who were lower-status or submissive made responses that were complementary: they took up less space and adopted a constricted posture, with arms and legs in, and a curved torso.

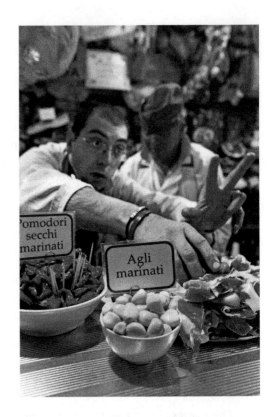

Hand Gestures
Two coming right up,
Signora!

These status differences in posture can often be seen in interactions between men and women; men adopt an expansive posture and women a submissive posture (Henley, 1977). However, posture does not only convey status; it also conveys liking. People who like one another tend to lean forward, maintain a relaxed posture and face one another (Mehrabian, 1972). And, in real life, non-verbal cues to status usually operate in combination (Hall, Coats, & Smith-LeBeau, 2005), so it can be difficult to make reliable status inferences from posture alone taken out of context. For example: a sense of *immediacy* involves eye contact, body relaxation, direct orientation, smiling, vocal expressiveness, close physical distance and hand gesturing (Prisbell, 1985), while an impression of *dominance* involves touching, pointing, invading space and standing over another person (Henley & Harmon, 1985).

Touch

Social touch is perhaps the earliest form of communication we learn. Do you have flashbacks to your childhood, or have you watched very young children? Long before we learn language, and even before we are adept at using body illustrators or gestures, we give and receive information by touch. There are many different types of touch (e.g. brief, enduring, firm, gentle) to different parts of the body (e.g. hand, shoulder, chest). The meaning of a touch varies as a function of the type of touch, the context within which the touch occurs, who touches whom, and what the relationship is between the interactants (e.g. husband and wife, doctor and patient, strangers). As Thayer (1986) notes, our language reflects facets of the varied meanings of touch – e.g. 'a soft touch', 'a gripping experience', 'deeply touched'.

From an analysis of 1,500 bodily contacts between people, Jones and Yarbrough (1985) identified five discrete categories of touch:

- *Positive affect* – to communicate appreciation, affection, reassurance, nurturance or sexual interest.
- *Playful* – to communicate humour and playfulness.

- *Control* – to draw attention or induce compliance.
- *Ritualistic* – to satisfy ritualised requirements (e.g. greetings and departures).
- *Task-related* – to accomplish tasks (e.g. a nurse taking one's pulse, or a violin teacher positioning a student's hand).

To these can be added *negative affect* (gently pushing an annoying hand away) and *aggressive touches* (slaps, kicks, shoves, punches) (Burgoon, Buller and Woodall, 1989).

Even the most incidental and fleeting touches can have significant effects. Male and female customers in a restaurant gave larger tips after their female server touched them casually on the hand (Crusco & Wetzel, 1984). In another study, university library clerks briefly touched the hand of students checking out books. Women who had been touched expressed greater liking for the clerk, and even for the library, than those who had not been touched (Fisher, Rytting, & Heslin, 1976). Male students were stolidly unaffected by touch. When a romantic song was playing in a nightclub, young women were more likely to comply with a request from a young man to dance when lightly touched on the forearm (Guéguen, 2007).

Sheryle Whitcher and Jeffrey Fisher (1979) also reported a gender difference, this time in a health setting. They arranged for patients to be touched or not touched by a female nurse during a pre-operative teaching interaction. Although the touches were brief and 'professional', they had significant effects on post-operative physiological and questionnaire measures. Female patients who had been touched reported less fear and anxiety, and had lower blood pressure, than those who had not been touched. Unfortunately, male patients who had been touched were more anxious and had higher blood pressure! Let us explore gender differences a little further.

Gender differences

In general, men touch women more often than women touch men, and people are more likely to touch members of the opposite than the same sex (Henley, 1973). Women derive greater pleasure from being touched than men (Major, 1981), but the circumstances of the touch are important. Richard Heslin (1978) asked men and women how much they would enjoy having various parts of the body 'squeezed and patted' by strangers or close friends of the same or the opposite sex. Figure 15.7 shows that both sexes agreed that being touched by someone of the same sex was relatively unpleasant, and that being touched by an opposite-sex close friend was relatively pleasant, but they disagreed about the pleasantness of being touched by an opposite-sex stranger. Women did not enjoy being touched by strange men, but men enjoyed being touched by strange women! Heslin (1978) also found that men were much more likely than women to read sexual connotations into touch, with all sorts of obvious implications for miscommunication and misinterpretation (Heslin & Alper, 1983). It should, however, be noted that this research is old so does not report whether or not these effects are moderated by sexual orientation.

Gender differences in touch may reflect more general status differences in touch: people who initiate touch are perceived to be of higher status than those who receive a touch (Major & Heslin, 1982). Major (1981) has argued that the usual gender differences in touch (women react more positively than men) occur only when status differences between interactants are ambiguous or negligible: under these circumstances, wider societal assumptions about sex-linked status differences come into play. When the toucher is clearly higher in status than the recipient, both men and women react positively to being touched.

Cultural differences

Finally, there is substantial cross-cultural variation in the amount of actual use made of touch. People from Latin American, Mediterranean and Arab countries touch a great deal, while people from northern Europe, North America, Australia and Asia do not (Argyle, 1975). From a study of the touching behaviour of couples in cafés in different countries, Sidney Jourard (1966) observed, in a one-hour period, no touching in London, 2 touches in

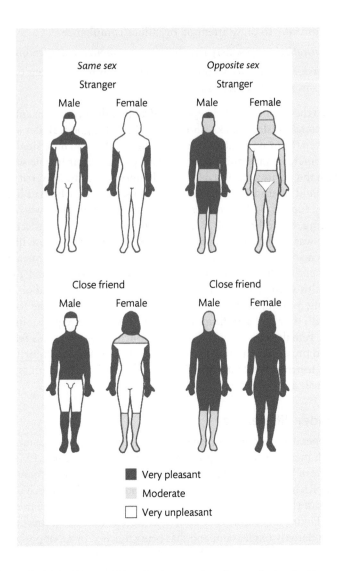

Figure 15.7 How pleasant is it to be touched?

- Men and women differ in how pleasant they find being touched on different parts of the body.

- The degree of pleasantness varies according to whether people are touched by same-sex or opposite-sex strangers or friends.

- The figures at the top left are men and women being touched by a same-sex stranger.

- The figures at the top right are men and women being touched by an opposite-sex stranger, etc.

- There was no breakdown in these results by sexual orientation.

Source: Responses to Touch as an Index of Sex Role Norms and Attitudes by Richard Heslin, Washington, DC: American Psychological Association (1978), reprinted with permission.

Florida, 110 touches in Paris and 180 in Puerto Rico. Perhaps a Londoner dating in Puerto Rico or a Parisian dating in Florida might feel uncomfortable!

Up close and personal

Proxemics
Study of interpersonal distance.

We have seen how parts of our bodies can send messages. The distance between our bodies does this as well – the study of interpersonal distance is called **proxemics**. Over and above the fact that physical closeness increases the number of non-verbal cues that can be detected and 'talking' becomes richer, people use interpersonal distance to regulate privacy and intimacy: the greater the distance, the more private you can be. The anthropologist Edward Hall's (1966) work *The Hidden Dimension* identified four *interpersonal distance zones* found mainly in the United States – ranging from high to low intimacy, each a little more removed from our bodies (see Table 15.3).

Personal space
Physical space around people's bodies which they treat as a part of themselves.

If you feel intimate with someone you will move closer, but if you feel a difference in status you will keep physically further away – see reviews by Hayduk (1983) and Hall, Coats and Smith-LeBeau (2005). Being physically near a person can occasionally be 'too close for comfort'. **Personal space**, a now-popular term also introduced by Hall (1966), reflects the importance that people place on their body buffer zone. Here are two research examples, one experimental and the other observational, relating to liking and status.

Table 15.3 Four zones of space in social interaction: How close is comfortable?

Zone	Distance	Description
Intimate distance	Up to 0.5 m	Physical contact can take place. Much is exposed about a person. Cues come from sight, sound, smell, body temperature and depth and pace of breathing.
Personal distance	0.5–1.25 m	This transitional area between intimate contact and formal behaviour is the norm in Western countries for everyday interactions with friends and acquaintances. Touching is still possible. Although many cues are still available, the effects of body temperature, smell and breathing are greatly reduced.
Social distance	1.25–4 m	This is typical for both casual and business interactions. Many cues are lost, but verbal contact is easily maintained. Furniture arrangement helps to achieve this. In an office, the desk is about 75 cm deep, and allowing for chair space, people interacting across the desk are just over one metre apart. A bigger desk can signal rank.
Public distance	4–8 m	Communication cues now lose some impact. It is a common distance for public speakers, celebrities and lecturers. In a lecture hall, lecterns are usually placed about 3.5 m back from the first row of seats. Courtrooms use this intervening space to prevent easy exchanges with the judge. The message? Interaction is not wanted.

Source: Hall (1966).

Interpersonal distance
Her personal space is being invaded - or is it?

- *Liking* – female students talked with a female confederate (i.e. a collaborator of the experimenter), with the goal of either appearing friendly or of avoiding the appearance of friendliness. The friendly students placed their chairs on average 1.5 metres from the confederate, while those who did not want to appear friendly placed their chairs 2.25 metres away (Rosenfeld, 1965).
- *Status* – Navy personnel maintained greater interpersonal distance when interacting with someone of a different rank than with someone of the same rank, and the effect was stronger as the difference in rank increased (Dean, Willis, & Hewitt, 1975).

Protecting personal space

Interpersonal distance is such a potent cue to intimacy that if it seems inappropriate, we can feel very uncomfortable. Michael Argyle and Janet Dean (1965) proposed an intimacy–equilibrium theory, which predicts that when intimacy signals are increased in one modality, they are decreased in other modalities (e.g. eye contact). For instance, on approaching a stranger who is still some distance away, you might gaze discreetly; as soon as the approaching stranger enters your social zone (about 3.5 metres), you avert your gaze and look away; or on your own turf, you might show a ritualised recognition (a smile or mumbled greeting).

Have you had that crowded feeling in a lift? According to intimacy–equilibrium theory, we can reduce intimacy cues by assiduously staring at the floor numbers flashing by (Zuckerman, Miserandino, & Bernieri, 1983). It is much easier nowadays. We can all stare fixedly at our portable communication devices, with the added advantage of making us seem terribly important and 'in demand'. Close seating arrangements can similarly make one feel crowded (Sommer, 1969). Look at how people try to create space between themselves and other passengers in an airport terminal, or become increasingly engrossed in reading, staring at their handheld device or listening to their iPods as numbers build up.

People are often stressed when their personal space is invaded. Dennis Middlemist and his colleagues conducted a memorable study where a male confederate loitered outside a men's urinal until someone entered. The confederate followed the man into the urinal and stood in another cubicle that varied in distance from him. The closer they were, the longer the man took to begin urinating and the faster the act was completed (Middlemist, Knowles, & Mutter, 1976)! (Sadly, we doubt that this wonderfully vivid study would get past a university research ethics committee today.)

Individual differences in perceived personal space, which vary dramatically across age, gender and cultures, frequently lead to violations. For instance, John Aiello and Stanley Jones (1971) found that African American and working-class children in the United States tend to stand closer to people than do white or non-working-class children. Likewise, people in Southern Europe, the Middle East and Latin America also stand closer, while in some tribal communities in Africa and Indonesia, people will often touch while talking (Argyle & Dean, 1965).

Impression management and deception

Non-verbal communication can be subliminal and automatic. We are often unaware that we or other people are using it. However, we do have some control and awareness, and we can use non-verbal cues strategically to create an impression of ourselves or to influence other people's beliefs, attitudes and behaviour (DePaulo, 1992). We can also sometimes detect others' strategic use of non-verbal cues.

This raises the possibility that people may try to hide their true feelings or communicate false feelings or information by controlled use of appropriate non-verbal cues. In general, such attempts at deception are not completely successful, as there is information leakage via non-verbal channels. As Freud (1905) so eloquently remarked: 'He that has eyes to see and ears to hear may convince himself that no mortal can keep a secret. If his lips are silent, he chatters with his fingertips; betrayal oozes out of him at every pore.'

Research indicates that people are relatively good at controlling the verbal content of a message to conceal deception – but that people are not very good at discriminating between truth and lies (Bond & DePaulo, 2006; Hauch, Blandón-Gitlin, Masip, & Sporer, 2015). Liars try to avoid saying things that might give them away, so they tend to make fewer factual statements, they are prone to making vague, sweeping statements and they leave gaps in the conversation (Knapp, Hart, & Dennis, 1974). There is also a tendency for attempts at deception to be accompanied by a slightly raised vocal pitch (Ekman, Friesen, & Scherer, 1976).

Facial expressions are generally not very 'leaky': people tend to make a special and concerted effort to control facial cues to deception. However, with so much attention diverted to facial cues, other channels of non-verbal communication are left unguarded. For example, deceivers tend to touch their face more often (Ekman & Friesen, 1974) or to fiddle with their hands, their glasses or other external objects (Knapp, Hart, & Dennis, 1974).

A meta-analysis revealed that people are more accurate at judging audible than visible deception (Bond & DePaulo, 2006). A more recent meta-analysis that focused on verbal behaviour alone concluded that those who intend to deceive experience greater cognitive load, use more negative emotion words (especially those that convey anger) and terms of denial, and distance themselves more from events (Hauch, Blandón-Gitlin, Masip, & Sporer, 2015). Despite all this, there are some effective professional lie-catchers out there! In an American study (Ekman, O'Sullivan, & Frank, 1999), federal police officers and sheriffs were more accurate in detecting lies than judges; and clinical psychologists with an interest in deception techniques were more accurate than academic and regular clinical psychologists.

Some people are better than others at concealing deception. For instance, people who habitually monitor their own behaviour carefully tend to be better liars (Siegman & Reynolds, 1983; see **Chapter 4** for more on self-monitoring). People who are highly motivated to deceive because, for instance, they believe it to be necessary for career advancement, tend to be adept at controlling verbal channels (DePaulo, Lanier, & Davis, 1983) but, ironically, poor at controlling other channels. This is often their downfall.

However, people are generally rather poor at detecting deception (Bond & DePaulo, 2006; DePaulo, 1994). Even those whose jobs are, in essence, the detection of deception (e.g. in the customs, police, legal and intelligence professions) are often not significantly better than the general population (Kraut & Poe, 1980). People who do detect deception tend to feel only generally suspicious and are not sure exactly what false information is being communicated (DePaulo & Rosenthal, 1979; DePaulo & DePaulo, 1989). Interestingly, although women are better than men at reading other people's non-verbal cues (Hall, 1978), they are no better than men at detecting deception (DePaulo & Rosenthal, 1979).

What about using computers to detect deception? Many computer programs have been devised to do just this – but they primarily focus on verbal cues. The first program was tried out way back in 1974, by Knapp, Hart and Dennis (1974) – it mainly analysed word frequencies. Not until about 2000 was there a more systematic attempt to use computers to detect deception (see Tausczik & Pennebaker, 2010). Hauch and colleagues conducted a meta-analysis of forty-four relevant studies to assess the effectiveness of computers as lie detectors (Hauch, Blandón-Gitlin, Masip, & Sporer, 2015). They concluded with scepticism that computers are better than people – computers are better at counting cues, but humans are better at making Gestalt judgements that incorporate non-verbal and contextual information.

Does this discussion of deception lead to the conclusion that we are more likely to get away with a lie than be detected? Zuckerman, DePaulo and Rosenthal (1981) reviewed research on deception and concluded that overall, receivers have the edge: they are slightly better at detecting deception than senders are at concealing it.

Impression management and deception have another consequence, which we have already discussed (see **Chapters 4, 5 and 10**). Social psychology often tries to assess people's underlying attitudes and feelings by administering questionnaires or conducting surveys or interviews. Our discussion of impression management and deception suggests that this enterprise is fraught with difficulties. Social psychologists are continually seeking non-reactive unobtrusive

Bogus pipeline technique
A measurement technique
that leads people to believe
that a 'lie detector' can
monitor their emotional
responses, thus measuring
their true attitudes.

measures. For example, there is the **bogus pipeline technique** (Jones & Sigall, 1971), where research participants are led to believe that the researchers have unambiguous physiological measures against which to check the validity of their attitudinal responses (see **Chapter 5**).

Another example: Maass and her associates take advantage of the linguistic intergroup bias effect (Franco & Maass, 1996; Maass, 1999; Maass & Arcuri, 1996; Maass, Salvi, Arcuri, & Semin, 1989) to detect underlying prejudices through speech style. Prejudiced people talk about the negative attributes of outgroups in broad and general terms that nevertheless make the attributes appear to be enduring and immutable, whereas they talk about the positive attributes of outgroups in very concrete, specific terms that are transitorily tied to the specific context.

Conversation and discourse

Although language and non-verbal communication are considered separately in this chapter, they usually occur together in communication (Cappella & Palmer, 1993). Non-verbal and paralinguistic behaviour can influence the meaning of what is said and can also serve important functions in regulating the flow of conversation. Analyses of communication are increasingly integrating verbal and non-verbal dimensions (e.g. Giles, 2012) – for example, as we saw earlier, speech accommodation theory has morphed into communication accommodation theory (Gallois, Ogay, & Giles, 2005; Giles, 2016).

Conversation

A context in which spoken language and non-verbal cues work together is conversation. Conversations have distinct phases (e.g. opening and closing) and an array of complex cultural rules that govern every phase of the interaction (Clark, 1985). For instance, there are ritualistic openings (e.g. 'Hello') and closings (e.g. 'Well, I must go'). We can signal the end of a face-to-face conversation non-verbally by moving apart and looking away (looking at your watch or portable device is a common but unsubtle, perhaps rude, way of doing this) and end a phone conversation by lengthening pauses before responding.

During a conversation, it is important to have rules about turn taking, otherwise there would be conversational chaos. Many years ago, Argyle (1975) described a number of concrete signals that people use to indicate that they are ending their turn and giving the listener an opportunity to take the floor:

- coming to the end of a sentence;
- raising or lowering the intonation of the last word;
- drawing out the last syllable;
- leaving a sentence unfinished to invite a continuation (e.g. 'I was going to go to the beach, but, uh …');
- body motions such as ceasing hand gestures, opening the eyes wide or lifting the head with the last note of a question, sitting back, or looking directly at the listener.

Attempts to butt in before the speaker is ready to yield the floor invite *attempt-suppressing* signals. The voice maintains the same pitch, the head remains straight, the eyes remain unchanged, the hands maintain the same gesture and the speaker may speak louder or faster and may keep a hand in mid-gesture at the end of sentences. At the same time, listeners may regularly signal that they are still listening and not seeking to interrupt. We do this by using **back-channel communication**: the listener nods or says 'mm-hmm' or 'okay' or 'right'. Depending on context, an interruption may be considered rude, may signify greater influence and power, and can also signify involvement, interest and support (Dindia, 1987; Ng, 1996; Ng, Bell, & Brooke, 1993; Ng & Bradac, 1993; Reid & Ng, 1999). See Box 15.6 for an example between persons of unequal power.

**Back-channel
communication**
Verbal and non-verbal ways
in which listeners let
speakers know they are still
listening.

Box 15.6 Our world
Speaking with your doctor

Power imbalance in doctor–patient communication

Effective communication is of paramount importance in the doctor–patient consultation. In order to make a correct diagnosis and provide proper treatment, the communicative context should allow the doctor to obtain as much relevant information as possible. To do this, the doctor should develop rapport with the patient, appear empathic, encourage the patient to speak frankly and openly and, generally, do a substantial amount of listening. Is this your experience of visiting a doctor?

Research in the United States revealed a marked conversational imbalance, with the doctor controlling the conversation (Fisher & Todd, 1983; West, 1984). The doctor did most of the talking, initiated 99 per cent of utterances, left only 9 per cent of questions to be asked by the patient, asked further questions before the patient finished answering the last one, interrupted the patient more, determined agenda and topic shifts, and controlled the termination of the consultation.

This communication pattern reflects a power and status imbalance between doctor and patient that resides in social status differences, unshared expertise and knowledge, and uncertainty and to some extent anxiety on the part of the patient. This is all accentuated by the context of the consultation – the doctor's surgery. Far from encouraging communicative openness, this conversational imbalance may inhibit it, and communication may in many instances be counterproductive as far as diagnosis and treatment are concerned.

The course of conversation differs depending on how well the interactants know one another. Close friends are more interpersonally responsive and tend to raise more topics and disclose more about themselves (Hornstein, 1985). Under these circumstances, women are more likely than men to talk about and self-disclose relational and personal topics (Davidson & Duberman, 1982; Jourard, 1971), but both sexes adhere to a reciprocity norm governing the intimacy of self-disclosure (Cozby, 1973). The reciprocity norm is relaxed in longer-term relationships (Morton, 1978).

Effective communication, largely through conversation, is central to enduring intimate relationships (see **Chapter 14**). Where such a relationship is a heterosexual marriage, there is a genuine potential, as we saw earlier, for miscommunication between the man and the woman (e.g. Mulac, Bradac, & Gibbons, 2001). Effective communication is one of the strongest correlates of marital satisfaction (Snyder, 1979), and marital therapists identify communication problems as one of the major features of marital distress (Craddock, 1980).

Pat Noller (1984) has analysed communication between heterosexual married partners in detail by asking people to imagine situations where they have to communicate something to their partners and to verbalise the communication (i.e. encode what they intend to communicate). The partner then has to decode the communication to discover what was intended; several choices are given, and only one can be selected.

Using this paradigm, Noller discovered that couples who scored high on a scale of marital adjustment were much more accurate at encoding their own and decoding their partner's communications than were couples who scored low. In general, women were better than men at encoding messages, particularly positive ones. Maritally dissatisfied couples tended to spend more time arguing, nagging, criticising and being coercive, and were poor and unresponsive listeners. On balance, it seems that poor marital communication may be a symptom of a distressed relationship rather than something brought to the relationship by partners (Noller, 1984; Noller & Fitzpatrick, 1990). People who have problems encoding and decoding messages within the marriage may have no such problems in their relationships with others.

The way we have just explored the analysis of everyday conversation, or talk-in-interaction, focuses on what is communicated and how. However, it does not generally focus on the semantic and motivational subtleties of what is said, why, and to what ends. This latter somewhat wider analysis is called 'conversation analysis'; typically referred to simply as CA

(Sidnell, 2010; Sidnell & Stivers, 2012; Wetherell, 1998). It is an approach that focuses on what people actually say during interaction. CA has its origins in Harold Garfinkel's (1967) *eth-nomethodology*, and for most of us it seems more closely associated with sociology, gender studies and discursive psychology than social psychology as presented in this text. Conversation analysis does not generally delve into the subtext of the interaction, whereas discourse analysis and discursive psychology, to which we now turn, do (Wilkinson & Kitzinger, 2006; Wooffitt, 2005).

Discourse

The social psychology of language and communication tends to analyse speech styles and non-verbal communication rather than the actual text of the communication. It also tends to break the communicative act down into component parts and then reconstructs more complex communications from the interaction of different channels. This approach may have some limitations.

For example, a great deal of language research has rested on the use of the matched-guise technique (Lambert, Hodgson, Gardner, & Fillenbaum, 1960; see earlier in this chapter). This technique isolates the text of a speech from the speech style (i.e. non-text), in order to see how the speaker is evaluated on the basis of the group that is marked by the speech style. However, the text of a speech is rarely truly neutral: it rarely carries no information on group membership (e.g. older and younger people talk about different things and use some language differently). Furthermore, the meaning of the text can itself be changed by speech style. Thus, text and non-text features of utterances are inextricable, together conveying meaning, which influences attitude (Giles, Coupland, Henwood, Harriman, & Coupland, 1990). This suggests that we might need to look to the entire **discourse** (what is said, in what way, by whom and for what purpose) in order to understand the contextualised attitudes that emerge (e.g. Billig, 1987; Edwards & Potter, 1992; McKinlay & McVittie, 2008; Potter & Wetherell, 1987).

> **Discourse**
> Entire communicative event or episode located in a situational and sociohistorical context.

This idea has been taken up by a number of researchers in the study of racism and sexism as they are imbedded in and created by discourse (Condor, 1988; Potter & Wetherell, 1987; Van Dijk, 1987, 1993; also see **Chapter 10**). It has also been employed in the study of youth language (Widdicombe & Wooffitt, 1990, 1994), intergenerational talk (Giles & Gasiorek, 2011; Harwood, Giles, & Ryan, 1995), homophobia and prejudice against people with HIV (Pittam & Gallois, 1996), political rhetoric (Billig, 1987, 1991, 1996), and collective action and protest (Reicher, 1996, 2001). The entire discourse is considered the unit of analysis, and it is through discourse that people construct categories of meaning. For instance, 'the economy' does not really exist for most of us. It is something that we bring into existence through talk (see the discussion of **social representations** in **Chapters 3** and **5**).

> **Social representations**
> Collectively elaborated explanations of unfamiliar and complex phenomena that transform them into a familiar and simple form.

A concrete example of **discourse analysis** is Mark Rapley's (1998) analysis of Pauline Hanson's maiden speech to the Australian Federal Parliament in September 1996. Hanson suddenly rose to prominence in Australia in 1996 when she was unexpectedly elected to the federal parliament. She immediately formed, and was leader of, the eponymous political party 'Pauline Hanson's One Nation Party'. One Nation's platform was nationalism, monoculturalism, opposition to affirmative action, anti-immigration, anti-intellectualism, anti-arts, economic isolationism and promotion of the right to own and bear arms – an ultra-conservative platform that was mirrored in the party's organisational structure, which was highly authoritarian. Rapley conducted a careful analysis of Hanson's speeches to identify One Nation's true agenda. Rapley believed, and was able to show, that a relatively thin veneer of modern prejudice (see **Chapter 10**) concealed an underlying current of old-fashioned prejudice.

> **Discourse analysis**
> A set of methods used to analyse text – in particular, naturally occurring language – in order to understand its meaning and significance.

The analysis of discourse is clearly a very useful tool for revealing hidden agendas and laying bare concealed prejudices (Wetherell, Taylor, & Yates, 2001). However, the discourse analysis approach in social psychology often goes one step further by arguing that many social psychological concepts such as attitude, motivation, cognition and identity may likewise be constituted through discourse, and therefore any discussion of them as real causal processes or structures is misguided. If accepted in its extreme form, this idea necessarily rejects much of social psychology and invites a new social psychology that focuses on talk, not people, groups or cognition, as the basic social psychological unit (also see **Chapter 1**).

This is an interesting and provocative idea, which forms the core of the *discourse analysis* approach to social psychology (e.g. Edwards, 1997; McKinlay & McVittie, 2008; Potter, 1996; Potter & Wetherell, 1987; Potter, Wetherell, Gill, & Edwards, 1990; Wooffitt, 2005). It has its origins in poststructuralism (Foucault, 1972), ethnomethodology (Garfinkel, 1967), ethogenics (Harré, 1979) and dramaturgical perspectives (Goffman, 1959). Critics, however, worry that it is too extreme in its rejection of cognitive processes and structures (Abrams & Hogg, 1990b; Zajonc, 1989), and that it may be more profitable to retain cognition and theorise how it articulates with language (see Gasiorek, Giles, Holtgraves, & Robbins, 2012; Holtgraves, 2010).

Computer-mediated communication

No chapter on communication would be complete without recognition that people in the developed world increasingly communicate electronically with one another via phone, email, and a huge variety of Internet formats. The biggest development is the explosion of *computer-mediated communication* (CMC) over the past thirty years, and then, much more recently, the communicative role of social media in people's lives since the launch of Facebook in 2004 (by the end of 2014, Facebook had almost 1.4 billion users). Not surprisingly, research on social psychological aspects of CMC and social media is gathering steam (Birchmeier, Dietz-Uhler, & Stasser, 2011; Hollingshead, 2001; McGrath & Hollingshead, 1994). There are at least six general findings:

1 CMC, in the absence of video, restricts paralanguage and non-verbal communication channels. As we saw earlier (**Chapter 14**), there is a paradox. This can compromise perceptions of trust that are important in establishing new relationships, but less important in existing relationships where trust already exists (Green & Carpenter, 2011); but the relative anonymity and sense of privacy of online communication also encourages honesty and self-disclosure which are important for trust and relationship development (Caspi & Gorsky, 2006; Christopherson, 2007). However, non-verbal and paralanguage cues can be introduced into CMC by emphasis – for example, 'YES!!!' – or by means of emoticons and emojis – for example, the sideways 'smiley' :-) or actual smiley face. Video chat clearly brings the communication channels much closer to real life.

Gender-specific texting
'I don't know who it is but only a guy would text like that'

2 CMC can suppress the amount of information that is exchanged, such as non-verbal vocal and physical cues. Generally, procedural aspects of group discussion that improve information exchange and group decisions in face-to-face settings may not have the same effect in computer-mediated settings (Hollingshead, 1996; Straus & McGrath, 1994). However, this is not an inevitable outcome, because people can still infuse a message with contextual and stylistic cues about gender (see number point 6 in this list), individual attributes, attitudes and their emotional state (Walther, Loh, & Granka, 2005; Walther & Parks, 2002).

3 CMC has a 'participation-equalisation effect', which evens out many of the status effects that occur in face-to-face communicative contexts. People may feel less inhibited because they are less personally identifiable (see **deindividuation** in **Chapter 11**). The effect depends on how effectively identity and status markers are concealed by the electronic medium (Spears & Lea, 1994). For example, emails usually have a signature that clearly indicates the identity and status of the communicator. According to the social identity analysis of deindividuation phenomena (Klein, Spears, & Reicher, 2007; Reicher, Spears, & Postmes, 1995) personal anonymity in the presence of a highly salient social identity will make people conform strongly to identity-congruent norms and be easily influenced by group leaders and normative group members. CMC research has confirmed this (Postmes, Spears, & Lea, 1998; Postmes, Spears, Sakhel, & de Groot, 2001; Sassenberg & Boos, 2003; Spears, Lea, Postmes, & Wolbert, 2011).

4 Although, on balance, CMC hinders interaction and group performance initially, over time people adapt quite successfully to their mode of communication (Arrow, Berdahl, Bouas, Craig, Cummings, Lebie, et al., 1996; Walther, 1996). In many ways people gradually respond to CMC as if it was not computer-mediated. For example, Williams and his associates found that when people are ignored in email interactions or chat rooms, they can interpret it as ostracism (called cyber-ostracism) and can react much as they would in face-to-face settings (Williams, Cheung, & Choi, 2000; Zadro, Williams, & Richardson, 2004; see **Chapter 8** for more on social ostracism).

5 Using the Internet to 'surf' does not impact negatively on users. They do not inevitably become lonely or depressed, or withdraw from interacting socially with others in real-life settings. Internet users in general have no less contact with friends and family than non-users; it seems that users do, however, spend less time watching television and reading newspapers (see review by Bargh & McKenna, 2004).

6 Personality attributes are related to how much people use social media (Correa, Hinsley, & de Zúñiga, 2010), and to what kind of social media they prefer (e.g. Facebook versus Twitter) (Hughes, Rowe, Batey, & Lee, 2012). For example, research on personality and social media usage among Americans found that heavy users tend to score high on extraversion and openness to experience but low on emotional stability (Correa, Hinsley, & de Zúñiga, 2010). This is, however, moderated by gender and age. Extraverted men and women both used social media more frequently, but social instability only predicted greater use among men. Extraversion was a particularly strong predictor of use among younger people, and openness to experience was a particularly strong predictor among older people.

We have already noted that men and women differ in how they communicate non-verbally when interacting with each other. A laboratory study by Rob Thomson and Tamar Murachver (2001) found gender differences in language used in students' email messages, even when the sex of the recipient was unknown to the sender. Females used more intensive adverbs (e.g. 'it was *really* good'), hedges (e.g. 'it was sort of interesting') and emotive references (e.g. 'I was *upset*'), and they provided more personal information (e.g. where they worked). Males were more insulting (e.g. 'you were *stupid* to take that course') and offered more opinions (e.g. 'the protest was worthwhile'). Gender effects are clearest when the topic of discussion is gender-stereotypic (Thomson, 2006). Perhaps from your own knowledge of gender-stereotypical behaviour you are not surprised at these findings!

Deindividuation
Process whereby people lose their sense of socialised individual identity and engage in unsocialised, often antisocial, behaviours.

Summary

- Language is a shared, rule-governed and meaningfully structured system of elementary sounds. Speech is the articulation of language.

- Language does not determine thought, but it eases how we communicate with others about what is important.

- The way we speak informs others about our feelings, motives and our membership of social groups, such as gender, status, nationality and ethnicity.

- Ethnic groups may actively promote their own language, or gradually abandon it, depending on the degree of vitality they consider their ethnolinguistic group to possess in a multi-ethnic context.

- People tailor their speech style to the context in which they communicate. Minority ethnic groups tend to converge on higher-status speech styles unless they believe the status hierarchy illegitimate and the vitality of their own group to be high.

- For a minority ethnolinguistic group, motivation is crucial if its members wish to master the dominant group's language as a second language.

- Non-verbal channels of communication (e.g. gaze, facial expression, posture, gesture, touch, interpersonal distance) carry important information about our attitudes, emotions and relative status.

- People communicate non-verbally, with gender, status and cultural differences, through their postures, gestures and touch. Interpersonal distance is a cue to the nature of an interpersonal relationship.

- We are less aware of and have less control over non-verbal communication than spoken language. Non-verbal cues in a face-to-face setting can often give away attempts to conceal information.

- Non-verbal cues play an important role in regulating turn taking and other features of conversation.

- Much can be learnt from analysing discourse, by focusing on complete communicative events.

- Studies of computer-mediated communication and social media usage reveal consistencies with other ways of conversing and transmitting information (e.g. ostracising others in a chat room, unknowingly providing cues to one's gender), and they reveal personality correlates of social media usage.

Key terms

Ageism	Ethnolinguistic identity theory	Proxemics
Attachment styles	Ethnolinguistic vitality	Received pronunciation
Back-channel communication	Gaze	Social identity theory
Bogus pipeline technique	Gestures	Social markers
Communication	Illocution	Social representations
Communication accommodation theory	Kinesics	Speech
	Language	Speech accommodation theory
Deindividuation	Linguistic relativity	Speech convergence
Discourse	Locution	Speech divergence
Discourse analysis	Matched-guise technique	Speech style
Display rules	Nature–nurture controversy	Stereotype
Emblems	Non-verbal communication	Subjective vitality
Essentialism	Paralanguage	Utterance
Ethnolinguistic group	Personal space	Visual dominance behaviour

Literature, film and TV

Blue Valentine and The Martian

Two films that capture very different aspects of communication. *Blue Valentine* is a 2010 romantic drama starring Ryan Gosling and Michelle Williams, who play a married couple whose marriage is collapsing. The film highlights miscommunication and the hurtful use of language in a dysfunctional relationship. Not a cheery movie. Much more exciting is Ridley Scott's 2015 film *The Martian*, starring Matt Damon, Jessica Chastain, Chiwetel Ejiofor, Sean Bean, Jeff Daniels and Kristen Wiig. Matt Damon's character is stranded on Mars and has to survive until a rescue mission can reach him – it takes six months to travel from Earth to Mars. The key to survival is being able to communicate with Earth, a mere 225 million kilometres away – and his communication system is damaged and Earth thinks he is dead.

The Thick of It, In the Loop, and Veep

The Thick of It is a British comedy TV that satirises the workings of the British Government – first broadcast in 2005 and concluded in 2012. A key theme and feature of the series is the use of language to control people, create illusion and spin, and construct and deconstruct reality – one memorable neologism that has entered into everyday discourse to refer to government failing is 'omnishambles'. This series inspired a hilarious 2009 film, *In the Loop*, directed by Armando Iannucci and starring Pater Capaldi, James Gandolfini and Tom Hollander. Because this film focuses on interactions between the British and American governments, it is also relevant to our discussion of culture (**in Chapter 16**). *Veep* is a highly acclaimed 2012 US TV comedy series, first aired in 2012, that also builds on *The Thick of it*, but here the context is the US Government and the main protagonist is the vice president (hence, Veep) – the language aspect is less evident.

Babel

A 2006 film by Alejandro González Inárritu, with Brad Pitt, Cate Blanchett and Gael Garcia Bernal. It is a powerful, atmospheric multi-narrative drama exploring the theme that cross-cultural assumptions prevent people from understanding and communicating with one another. Each subplot features people out of their familiar cultural context: American children lost in the US-Mexican borderlands, a deaf Japanese girl mourning and alone in a hearing world, and two Americans stranded in the Moroccan desert.

Lost in Translation

A 2003 film written and directed by Sofia Coppola, starring Bill Murray and Scarlet Johansson. The film (which is also relevant to **Chapter 16**) illustrates how you can feel like a fish out of water in a foreign culture where you do not speak the language and do not really understand the culture. This is also a film about life crises – two Americans at very different stages in their lives but with similar relationship problems are marooned in a large Japanese mega-city and are drawn to each other.

Guided questions

1   How does language shape a person's identity?

2   What motivates a person to learn a second language? How can the challenge of adapting to a host culture for an immigrant group be eased?

3   How do non-verbal cues help to inform us about another person?

4   How accurate are people in recognising basic emotions?

5   What is personal space? How and why do we use it?

Learn more

Ambady, N., & Weisbuch. M. (2010). Nonverbal behavior. In S. T. Fiske, D. T. Gilbert, & G. Lindzey (Eds.), *Handbook of social psychology* (5th ed., Vol. 1, pp. 464–497). New York: Wiley. Up-to-date comprehensive and detailed coverage of theory and research on non-verbal communication.

Bayley, B., & Schechter, S. R. (Eds.) (2003). *Language socialization in bilingual and multilingual societies*. Clevedon, UK: Multilingual Matters. Sociolinguists, educationalists and other social scientists take an international perspective on language socialisation and bilingualism from early childhood to adulthood. Contexts include home, schools, communities and the workplace.

Birchmeier, Z., Dietz-Uhler, B., & Stasser, G. (Eds.) (2011). *Strategic uses of social technology: An interactive perspective of social psychology*. Cambridge, UK: Cambridge University Press. A collection of chapters that gives a good indication of where social psychology is in terms of understanding computer-mediated communication.

Comrie, B., Matthews, S., & Polinsky, M. (Eds.) (2003). *The atlas of languages* (Rev. ed.). New York: Facts on File. A richly illustrated treatment of the origin and development of languages throughout the world.

Giles, H. (Ed.) (2012). *The handbook of intergroup communication*. New York: Routledge. Up-to-date and comprehensive collection of concise and tightly focused chapter on all aspects of intergroup communication – a must-read for those interested in intergroup communication.

Giles, H., & Maass, A. (Eds.) (2016). *Advances in intergroup communication*. New York: Peter Lang. Even more recent and definitive collection of chapters on what we know about intergroup communication.

Giles, H., & Robinson, W. P. (Eds.) (1993). *Handbook of language and social psychology*. Oxford, UK: Pergamon Press. A classic early collection of critical and review chapters, covering interpersonal communication from a language and social psychology perspective.

Grasser, A. C., Millis, K. K., & Swan, R. A. (1997). Discourse comprehension. *Annual Review of Psychology, 48*, 163–189. A dispassionate overview of the technical contributions of discourse analysis to psychology in general.

Holtgraves, T. (2010). Social psychology and language: Words, utterances and conversations. In S. T. Fiske, D. T. Gilbert, & G. Lindzey (Eds.), *Handbook of social psychology* (5th ed., Vol. 2, pp. 1386–1422). New York: Wiley. Comprehensive and detailed coverage of social psychological theory and research on the role of language in communication.

Holtgraves, T. (Ed.) (2014). *The Oxford handbook of language and social psychology*. New York: Oxford University Press. Definitive collection of chapters that cover all aspects of the social psychology of language.

Keltner, D., & Lerner, J. S. (2010). Emotion. In S. T. Fiske, D. T. Gilbert, & G. Lindzey (Eds.), *Handbook of social psychology* (5th ed., Vol. 1, pp. 317–352). New York: Wiley. Although this chapter is about emotion, its coverage of the communication of emotion is excellent.

Matsumoto, D., Frank, M. G., & Hwang, H. S. (Eds.) (2012). *Nonverbal communication: Science and applications*. Thousand Oaks, CA: Sage. Up-to-date and comprehensive collection of chapters on what we know about non-verbal communication.

Noels, K. A., Giles, H., & Le Poire, B. (2003). Language and communication processes. In M. A. Hogg & J. Cooper (Eds.), *The SAGE handbook of social psychology* (pp. 232–257). London: SAGE. A very accessible review, from a social psychological perspective, of research on language and communication – includes both verbal and non-verbal communication.

Russell, J. A., & Fernandez-Dols, J. M. (Eds.) (1997). *The psychology of facial expression: Studies in emotion and social interaction*. Cambridge, UK: Cambridge University Press. A critical overview of theoretical perspectives on facial expression. These include ethological, neurobehavioural and developmental views.

Semin, G. (2007). Grounding communication: Synchrony. In A. W. Kruglanski, & E. T. Higgins (Eds.), *Social psychology: Handbook of basic principles* (2nd ed., pp. 630–649). New York: Guilford Press. A conceptually ambitious chapter – it sets an agenda for integrating levels of explanation to provide a full framework for understanding human communication.

Chapter 16
Culture

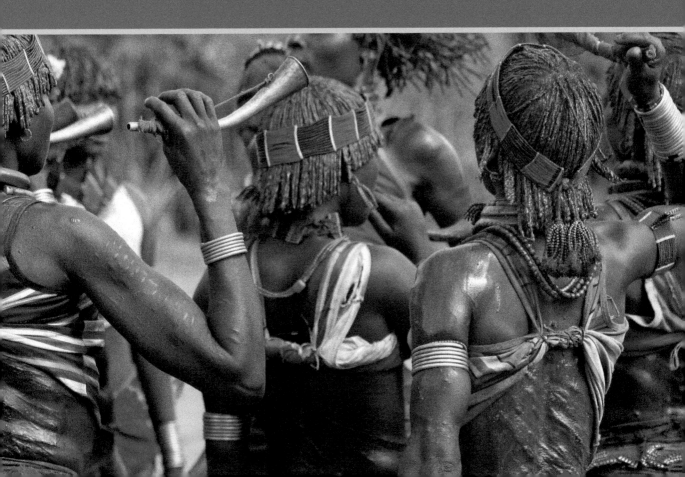

Chapter contents

What do *you* think?

1 Daan is Dutch and has been brought up to defend openly what he believes to be true. After living in South Korea for a few months, he has noticed that the locals are more concerned about maintaining harmony in their social relationships than in deciding who is right and who is wrong. Why, he wonders, can they not just speak their minds?

2 Bernice and Joeli are indigenous Fijians who have studied social psychology at the University of the South Pacific in Suva. They are concerned that what they have studied is based on Western theory, with limited relevance to the traditional group-centred values of their community. Do they have a point?

3 Horacio is a researcher from Brazil. He argues that negotiating with a shy business executive in Hong Kong may be no more challenging than communicating with a Brazilian teenager, since to an adult a teenager might just as well be from another culture. What point is he making?

4 Keiko and her new husband are Japanese. After a traditional wedding in Hokkaido, they emigrated to Oslo. Then a dilemma arose – should they maintain the customs of their homeland, or should they become entirely Norwegian? Do they have any other options?

5 Jessica is a social psychology student who lives in London and is proud of her Cornish heritage. She has read about the paths that migrants might choose in adapting to a host culture. Then an idea occurs to her – to apply the concept of being a migrant to being Cornish. They are a minority group in a predominantly English culture. So what is the status of Cornish culture: integrated, assimilated, separated or marginalised?

The cultural context

Culture is a pervasive but slippery construct. It has been 'examined, poked at, pushed, rolled over, killed, revived and reified ad infinitum' (Lonner, 1984, p. 108). There is a great deal of popular obsession and talk about culture, cultural differences, cultural sensitivity, cultural change, culture shock, subcultures and culture contact. But what precisely is culture? How much and through what processes does it affect people, and how in turn is it affected by people? In his presidential address to the American Association for the Advancement of Science in 1932, the sociologist Franz Boas made a plea for his own discipline to pay much greater attention to cultural variation in behaviour:

> It seems a vain effort to search for sociological laws disregarding what should be called social psychology, namely, the reaction of the individual to culture. They can be no more than empty formulas that can be imbued with life only by taking account of individual behaviour in cultural settings.
>
> Cited in Kluckhohn (1954, p. 921)

Boas believed culture to be central to social science, and that the study of culture's influence on people is the definition of the discipline of social psychology. This is not an isolated view. Wundt (1897, 1916), the founder of psychology as an experimental science, believed that social psychology was all about collective phenomena such as culture – a view shared by Durkheim (1898), one of the founders of sociology (see Farr, 1996; Hogg & Williams, 2000; also see **Chapter 1**).

Throughout this text, we have drawn attention to the impact of culture on behaviour: for example, earlier (in **Chapter 3**) we discussed how culture intrudes upon intergroup attributions (see **Figure 3.7**). In this chapter, we assemble and integrate these observations but go further to ask fundamental questions about the universality of social psychological processes and about the relevance of social psychological principles to cultures in which the principles were not developed.

Cross-cultural psychologists, and some social psychologists, have provided evidence for cultural variation in a range of quite basic human behaviours and social psychological processes. Most of this research identifies a general difference between Eastern and Western cultures – indeed, the main debate in social psychology about 'culture' has been largely restricted to this contrast, or more accurately, the contrast between on the one hand (Eastern) collectivism and tight-knit societies, and on the other (Western) individualism and loose-knit societies.

The big question, then, is 'how deep do these differences go?' Are they merely differences in normative practices, or do they go much deeper – reflecting fundamental perceptual and cognitive processes, or possibly even brain activity? Maybe normative practices and cognitive activity mutually influence one another:

> Individual thoughts and actions influence cultural norms and practices as they evolve over time, and these cultural norms and practices influence the thoughts and actions of individuals.
>
> Lehman, Chiu and Schaller (2004, p. 689)

In this chapter, we also explore the role of language barriers to effective communication, the nature of acculturation, and what role social and cross-cultural psychologists can play in helping to improve intercultural relations. The issues discussed in this final chapter build upon and reflect on many of the themes and ideas explored earlier in the text – we hope that this chapter provides a cultural context and a cultural challenge to earlier chapters.

Locating culture in social psychology

Has social psychology neglected culture?

How far have you travelled recently? With cheap airfares, the world is increasingly at your doorstep. Most Europeans have travelled extensively within Europe; Americans have explored Mexico, and Australians and New Zealanders check out Indonesia and Thailand. Russians live in London, Japanese chill out in Hawaii, and the Dutch head for Tuscany. In addition, almost all of us, particularly if we live in huge cities like London, Paris, Amsterdam and Istanbul, rub shoulders daily with a rich cultural mix of people from all over the world in our daily life. Then there is the Internet, which can deliver cultural variation to us any-where and everywhere.

One of the first things that strikes you in a foreign land is the different language or accent, along with the appearance and dress of the local people, followed closely by cuisine. Other dif-ferences may be more subtle and slower to emerge – they reflect underlying values, attitudes, and representational and explanatory systems. Culture infuses behaviour and is the lifeblood of ethnic and national groups. Because cultural practices are shared within a culture and differ between cultures, the study of culture is closely related to the study of groups. However, the social psychology of group processes and intergroup relations has historically talked about norms and normative regularities and differences rather than culture (see **Chapters 8, 9** and **11**).

It is also the case, historically, that psychological theory and research in social psychology have been dominated by one cultural perspective – that of middle-class, largely white, America (Farr, 1996). This is, of course, not surprising as so many psychologists have been middle-class white Americans – English is the global language of science, and the United States is not only wealthy enough to promote basic scientific research but is also by far the largest English-speaking nation. A leading cross-cultural psychologist noted a few decades back that:

> One of the key facts about psychology is that most of the psychologists who have ever lived and who are now living can be found in the United States . . . The rest of the world has only about 20 per cent of the psychologists that are now or have ever been alive.
>
> Triandis (1980, p. ix)

There is a natural tendency for people to fail to recognise that their life is only one of many possible lives – that what may appear natural may merely be normative (Garfinkel, 1967). The problem for social psychology is that this cultural perspective has been dominant – social psychology is **culture-bound** and also, to a notable extent, **culture-blind**. For exam-ple, most major introductory social psychology texts are American. They are highly schol-arly and authoritative and are beautifully produced, but they are written primarily by Americans for Americans. However, they are used across the globe, and the cultural refer-ents and scientific priorities can seem a little alien to someone brought up and living outside the United States. One reason we wrote this text was to balance this by providing a text with a more global perspective (see the **Preface** and **Chapter 1**).

Culture-bound
Theory and data conditioned by a specific cultural background.

Culture-blind
Theory and data untested outside the host culture.

Things have certainly changed over the past couple of decades. There has been a rebal-ancing that has placed culture firmly on the social psychological agenda (see the publications listed in the 'Learn more' section at the end of this chapter). The hegemony of White American social psychology that characterised the discipline in the 1950s through into the early 1980s has weakened, primarily due to the ascendance of European social psychology, but also due to the growing number of social psychologists who, although mostly trained in North America, have an East Asian ethnic background. Nevertheless, mainstream social psychology is still primarily conducted from the cultural perspective of North America, North West Europe and Australasia.

Another reason why social psychologists have underemphasised culture may be the exper-imental method (Vaughan & Guerin, 1997). As explained earlier (**Chapter 1**), social psy-chologists generally, and with good cause, consider laboratory experiments to be the most rigorous way to test causal theories – a love affair with laboratory experimentation that dates back to the early twentieth century. Laboratory experiments focus on the manipulation of focal variables in isolation from other variables, such as participants' biographical and cultural backgrounds. However, people *do* bring their autobiographical and cultural baggage into the laboratory – as Henri Tajfel (1972) so eloquently put it, you simply cannot do experiments in a social vacuum.

This is not a trivial issue. Because experiments largely regard culture as the unproblematic backdrop to research, this method may prevent researchers from realising that culture may itself be a variable that influences the processes being studied. If psychological variables are manipulated in only one cultural context, how can we be sure that the effect of the manipulations will be the same in another culture – culture may moderate the effect of the manipulations on the dependent variables. This suggests that culture itself can and perhaps should be an independent variable, and that experimentation could be a powerful way to investigate culture. Heine writes:

> If culture is the social situation writ large, then it perhaps follows that the experimental methods applied by social psychologists would be most appropriate for studying many questions regarding how culture affects people's thoughts and behaviors.
>
> Heine (2010, p. 1427)

Defining culture

There is no single agreed-on definition of culture. Decades of fiery debate among anthropologists, sociologists and psychologists have produced a plethora of definitions. Boas (1930, p. 30) defined culture as 'the social habits of a community', and Peter Smith and Michael Bond (1998, p. 69) as 'systems of shared meanings'. These elements, shared activity and shared meaning, should both be included in a definition of culture and do seem to capture Heine's (2016) focus on culture as a group of individuals who acquire shared ideas, beliefs, technology, habits or practices through learning from others. In discussing variations in definition, Brislin noted:

> Kroeber and Kluckhohn [1952] concluded that many definitions contained 'patterns . . . of behaviour transmitted by symbols, constituting the distinctive achievements of human groups . . . [and] ideas and their attached values'. Herskovits proposed the equally influential generalization that culture is 'the man-made part of the human environment'. Triandis made a distinction between physical [e.g. houses and tools] and subjective culture [e.g. people's values, roles, and attitudes].
>
> Brislin (1987, p. 275)

Although definitions vary, they share the view that culture is an enduring product of and influence on human interaction. In line with this broad perspective, we view culture as the set of cognitions and practices that characterise a specific social group and distinguish it from others. In the same vein, Geert Hofstede (2001, p. 9) referred to culture as 'the collective programming of the mind that distinguishes the members of one group or category of people from another'. In essence, culture is the expression of *group norms* at the national, racial and ethnic levels (see **Chapter 8** on norms, **Chapter 4** on self and identity, and **Chapter 11** on intergroup behaviour).

This view is consistent with that of Moreland and colleagues (Levine & Moreland, 1991; Moreland, Argote, & Krishnan, 1996; also see **Chapter 9**), who argue that culture is an instance of group memory and so culture can apply to social collectives of all sizes – including families, work groups and organisations (Smith, Bond, & Kağıtçıbaşi, 2006). This perspective sets the agenda for an analysis of culture and cultural phenomena that uses the language and concepts of the social psychology of social influence, group processes, intergroup relations, and self and identity.

Culture, history and social psychology

The early origins of social psychology in nineteenth-century Germany were marked by a concern to describe collective phenomena (see **Chapter 1**). The work of these folk psychologists, their *Völkerpsychologie*, recognised that groups differ in their beliefs and practices and that describing and explaining these differences should be a focus of social psychology (e.g. Wundt, 1916). However, as it gathered momentum, social psychology very quickly focused on the individual rather than the group.

A notable exception was a focus among developmental psychologists in the former Soviet Union, the *Russian cultural-historical school*, on how people interact with their environment through the medium of human thought that is constructed, learnt and sustained collectively (e.g. Luria, 1928; Vygotsky, 1978). This general perspective has contemporary relevance to more recent research related to the linguistic category model (discussed in **Chapter 15**) of how thought and language are related (Semin, 2000; Semin & Fiedler, 1991; also Fiske, 1992; Rubini, Menegatti, & Moscatelli, 2014). The ideas of 'the Russians', specifically, have been developed and extended more recently (Cole, 1996; Rogoff, 2003) and have had an influence on contemporary cultural psychology.

In contrast to social psychology, by the beginning of the twentieth century anthropologists were increasingly studying group phenomena and differences, and investigating the concept of culture and the process of cultural transmission.

Völkerpsychologie
Early precursor of social psychology, as the study of the collective mind, in Germany in the mid- to late-nineteenth century.

Origins in cultural anthropology

During and after the sixteenth century, a confluence of factors contributed to new ways of construing the self, the individual and the social group (see **Chapter 4**):

- *Secularisation* – a new focus on the here and now rather than the afterlife.
- *Industrialisation* – people were required to be mobile in order to seek work, and therefore they needed to have a portable personal identity rather than one imbedded in a social structure based on the geographically fixed extended family.
- *Enlightenment* – a philosophy that endowed individuals with rationality and the ability and intellect to manage their social lives and to construct and maintain complex systems of normative social behaviour: culture (also see Allport, 1954a; Fromm, 1941; Weber, 1930).

By the late nineteenth and early twentieth centuries, cross-cultural research had formed the basis of modern cultural anthropology. Some of the key works that shaped cultural anthropology were, in the United Kingdom, James Frazer's (1890) *The Golden Bough* and Malinowski's (1927) *Sex and Repression in Savage Society* and, in the United States, Boas's (1911) *The Mind of Primitive Man*. In terms of what was to follow, the most influential of these early figures was Franz Boas at Columbia University, who single-mindedly championed the proposition that personality is formed by culture. This was not an easy sell in an intellectual milieu where social behaviour was thought to be biologically determined: for example, by Freud and fellow psychodynamic theorists (see **Chapter 12**).

Boas's ideas were promoted by two of his students, Margaret Mead (1928/1961) and Ruth Benedict (1934). On the basis of detailed **ethnographic research**, they provided rich and graphic descriptions of cultures that differed enormously in terms of the behavioural practices that were sanctioned or proscribed by social norms. Mead, who was also trained in psychology, made a concerted effort to divert anthropology from studying the universal biological bases of behaviour to a study of how culture impacts psychological development (Price-Williams, 1976). As a consequence, by the 1950s, cross-cultural research had made a significant contribution to theories of child development and socialisation (Child, 1954).

There have been other isolated but influential instances of early psychological studies that drew from cultural anthropology. At Cambridge University, Bartlett conducted a series of

Ethnographic research
Descriptive study of a specific society, based on fieldwork, and requiring immersion of the researcher in the everyday life of its people.

experiments (e.g. Bartlett, 1923, 1932) on social and cultural factors affecting memory. In one, he borrowed a folk tale, *The War of the Ghosts*, from Boas. His participants read the tale and later reconstructed it as precisely as possible from memory. In a variation using serial reproduction, each participant in a group passed a recalled version on to the next participant, in an analogue of spreading a rumour (see **Chapter 3**). In both cases, the original story was systematically reconstructed to bring it into line with what they would remember easily. The consequence was a 'cultural' transformation of the tale.

This early research is remarkably consistent with Serge Moscovici's (e.g. 1988) more recent notion of social representations (see Lorenzi-Cioldi & Clémence, 2001), which is discussed in **Chapters 3** and **5**. You will recall that social representations are shared frameworks for rendering the world meaningful, and that they are developed and maintained by social interaction.

In 1940 Otto Klineberg published an influential text, *Social Psychology*, in which he introduced findings from ethnology (the 'science of races') and comparative sociology. This was an innovation well ahead of its time – for much of the twentieth century, social psychologists often distanced themselves from cross-cultural research. There were two reasons: they were unwilling to be seen as 'tender-minded', particularly since anthropologists were often wedded to psychoanalytic theory and methods (Segall, 1965); they were also increasingly committed to using experimental methods and felt that cross-cultural research was merely descriptive (Vaughan & Guerin, 1997; see above and **Chapter 1**).

Rise of cross-cultural psychology

The public coming-out of cross-cultural psychology was marked by publication of the *International Journal of Psychology* in Paris in 1966 and the *Journal of Cross-Cultural Psychology* in the United States in 1970. In the opening article of the inaugural issue of this latter journal, two eminent social psychologists, Lois and Gardner Murphy (Murphy & Murphy, 1970) discussed the promise of cross-cultural psychology.

The arrival of cross-cultural psychology has also been marked by publication of authoritative handbooks (e.g., Berry, Dasen, & Saraswathi, 1997; Berry, Poortinga, & Pandey, 1997; Triandis, Lambert, Berry, Lonner, Heron, Brislin, & Draguns, 1980). However, according to Steven Heine (2012), the modern era of cultural psychology is very clearly marked by the publication of three seminal works in quick succession by Harry Triandis (1989), Jerome Bruner (1990), and Hazel Markus and Shinobu Kitayama (1991) – the last of these is by far the most heavily cited and influential single paper in cultural psychology.

Cross-cultural psychologists sought answers to three questions:

1 Are Western psychological theories valid in other cultures?

2 Are there psychological constructs that are culture-specific?

3 How can we evolve a psychology with universal relevance?

Cultural anthropologists have long been interested in the second and third of these questions (Kluckhohn, 1954). With the arrival of the new subdiscipline came new terminology and a new distinction: the **etic–emic distinction**, drawn by analogy with the linguistic distinction between phonetics and phonemics (see **Chapter 15**). Smith and Bond (1998, p. 57) describe the etic-emic distinction very clearly:

Etic-emic distinction
Contrast between psychological constructs that are relatively culture-universal and those that are relatively culture-specific.

> Berry . . . argues that 'etic' analyses of behaviour are those that focus on universals, principally those that . . . are either simple or variform. For example, we all eat, we almost all have intimate relations with certain others, and we all have ways of attacking enemies. An 'emic' analysis of these behaviours, on the other hand, would focus on the different, varied ways in which each of these activities was carried out in any specific cultural setting. Successful emic analyses could be expected to establish generalisations that were only valid locally.
>
> Smith and Bond (1998, p. 57)

Power distance, for example, is an etic construct because it can be observed in most cultures, while *amae,* or passive love, is an emic construct that is probably limited to Japanese culture. (Power distance and *amae* are discussed later in this chapter.) Emic constructs may 'grow' into etic ones if they are appropriately investigated and established across cultures.

The formal recognition of the subdiscipline is complete; it has its own journals, books, conferences, societies and university courses. But, is it *cross-cultural psychology* or *cultural psychology* – the two terms seem to be used interchangeably? Cross-cultural psychology has tended to use traditional social psychological methods (questionnaires, interviews) and statistical procedures to compare and contrast ethnic and national groups (see Smith, Bond, & Kağıtçıbaşı, 2006); whereas cultural psychology has tended to use more qualitative and discourse analytic methods to study people's fundamental grounding in their culture (e.g. Shweder, 1991). However, a distinction based on methodology may not be helpful in fully understanding culture. The term cultural psychology is probably now most common, and it transcends methodology and meta-theory to refer to the overall social psychological study of culture (Heine, 2010, 2016).

Much of what follows in this chapter focuses on cross-cultural, and sometimes cross-national, comparisons. But if our data are cross-cultural, can we do justice to the complexities inherent in an individual culture? The cross-cultural psychologist Michael Bond has suggested that the cultural challenge may be beyond us: 'Cross-cultural psychologists will never get it culturally right, only cross-culturally right' (Bond, 2003, p. 281). We return to this challenge later in the chapter.

Culture, thought and behaviour

Culture, cognition and attribution

Earlier (in **Chapter 3**), we saw how cultural knowledge allows us to make contextually appropriate causal attributions of behaviour – failure to attend to culture would have 'interesting' consequences for the unfortunate attributor. We also saw that there are cultural variations in *attributional style*, such as differences in ethnocentric bias between Malay and Chinese people in Singapore (Hewstone & Ward, 1985) – a case of the **ultimate attribution error** (see **Chapter 3, Figure 3.7**).

In another example, Hindu Indians were much less likely than North Americans to make dispositional rather than situational attributions (Miller, 1984; see **Chapter 3, Figure 3.8**) – a case of the **fundamental attribution error**, or more accurately, the **correspondence bias** (Gawronski, 2004). There is now a large body of research confirming that the correspondence bias may be grounded in a Western, cultural world view of the person as independent and, thus, as internally motivated. Many studies have shown that in non-Western cultures, where an alternative, more socio-centric, collectivistic or more interdependent view predominates, the bias is much weaker (Kitayama & Uskul, 2011). Recent research has gone further, showing that this cultural difference occurs even in early automatic stages of information processing (Na & Kitayama, 2011).

A review by Darrin Lehman highlights a subtle but consistent difference in *thought processes* between East Asians and Americans (Lehman, Chiu, & Schaller, 2004). The intellectual tradition of East Asians (and other collectivist cultures) is generally more holistic and relationship-oriented, whereas Americans (and other individualistic cultures) are usually more analytic and linear in their thinking. In Box 16.1 we describe findings suggesting that East Asians differ in subtle ways of thinking and of attributing causes when they are compared with North Americans. We shall see later that this broad East–West difference is reflected in different conceptions of the self and in the way that values are expressed. Nisbett has referred rather nicely to the 'geography of thought' to suggest that people from East Asia and the West have had different systems of thinking for thousands of years.

Ultimate attribution error
Tendency to attribute bad outgroup and good ingroup behaviour internally, and to attribute good outgroup and bad ingroup behaviour externally.

Fundamental attribution error
Bias in attributing another's behaviour more to internal than to situational causes.

Correspondence bias
A general attribution bias in which people have an inflated tendency to see behaviour as reflecting (corresponding to) stable underlying personality attributes.

Box 16.1 Our world
East Asian and American differences in thinking and in explaining behaviour

Is it possible that thought processes among East Asian peoples differ from those in the West? Studies by Nisbett, Peng and Choi suggest they do in subtle ways. East Asians more often:

- have a better memory for objects in their context (e.g. the *wolf* is in the *dark forest*);
- are prone to perceptual error when a stimulus object needs to be judged against a distracting background (e.g. judging if a fixed rod remains perpendicular as a frame behind it starts to rotate);
- are sensitive to people's social backgrounds when judging them;
- accept deductions when the premises are believable;
- take notice of typical examples when solving tasks based on categories;
- accept apparent contradictions about themselves (e.g. agreeing *that equality is more important than ambition* at one moment in time but then disagreeing with this later);
- are less surprised by unexpected behaviour;
- look at arguments from both sides, and compromise when there is conflict;
- expect trends in behaviour in the future to be variable rather than consistent.

Source: Based on Choi and Nisbett (2000); Masuda and Nisbett (2001); Peng and Nisbett (1999).

This general social–explanatory dynamic may play a role in face-saving. One notable difference between (Western) individualistic cultures and (Eastern) collectivist cultures is the value placed on and behaviour associated with face-saving. What may underlie this is a cultural difference in how people respond to shame (Sheikh, 2014; Tangney & Dearing, 2002), which is consistent with the broader view that cultural differences in the subjective and psychological experience of emotion are few but there are large differences in how people express and respond to emotions (Van Osch, Zeelenberg, & Breugelmans, 2016; see **Chapter 2**). In individualistic societies, feelings of shame are blamed on others as the cause and are externalised as anger, resentment, hostility and aggression; whereas in collectivistic cultures, shame sponsors restorative and reparative behaviours designed to repair harm and sustain relationships (e.g. Brown, Gonzalez, Zagefka, Manzi, & Cehajic, 2008).

The last finding in Box 16.1 has an interesting implication. Westerners often have difficulty with the notion of regression to the mean because they assume permanence, that what happens at time one will happen at time two or that an existing trend will continue (Nisbett, Krantz, Jepson, & Kunda, 1983; see **Chapter 1**). This is because Westerners play down the role of situational influences on events and behaviours. However, East Asians focus more on the situation and do not assume permanence – so instead of expecting what happens at time one to be the same as what happens at time two, they realise that as the situation changes, so will the behaviour. They expect behaviour to vary across time and that trends are not linear – they have a better intuitive understanding of regression to the mean.

Another interesting cultural difference is in the stereotype rebound effect – the tendency for people who are instructed to suppress their stereotypes to subsequently show evidence of stronger stereotype expression. Shen Zhang and Jennifer Hunt (2008) had US and Chinese participants write about a gay man, under instructions to suppress their stereotypes or with no instruction – both instructed groups successfully suppressed their stereotypes. After a filler task they were asked, without instruction, to write another essay about a gay man. The predicted stereotype rebound effect emerged, but only for the US participants; the Chinese still managed to suppress their anti-gay stereotypes. The explanation is that collectivist/interdependent cultures help people learn to suppress (the expression of) their feelings and attitudes in order to maintain social harmony – thus Asians who suppress stereotypes do not experience a rebound. Spencer-Rodgers and her colleagues found that Chinese were more likely than Americans to use stereotypes when group membership is a salient cue. We can think of this as group-level rather than individual-level stereotyping, i.e. the group in question is high in **entitativity** (Spencer-Rodgers, Williams, Hamilton, Peng, & Wang, 2007).

Finally, Kitayama and his colleagues have reported differences between Japanese and American participants in their experience of cognitive dissonance (Kitayama, Snibbe, Markus, & Suzuki, 2004; see **Chapter 6**). Japanese feel dissonance only when social cues are active, such as becoming aware of their peers' opinions when making a decision.

Entitativity
The property of a group that makes it seem like a coherent, distinct and unitary entity.

Culture, conformity and obedience

Solomon Asch's (1951) study of conformity to group pressure (see **Chapter 7**) is one of the most widely replicated social psychology experiments of all time. Smith and Bond (1998) report a **meta-analysis** of Asch-type studies carried out in the United States and sixteen other countries, which reveals considerable variation in the degree of conformity across different cultures. Conformity was generally stronger outside Western Europe and North America (see Figure 16.1). The reason why conformity in the Asch paradigm is greater in non-Western cultures is probably that participants did not wish to cause embarrassment by disagreeing with the majority's erroneous responses – conforming to the majority was a way to allow the majority to 'save face'.

Meta-analysis
Statistical procedure that combines data from different studies to measure the overall reliability and strength of specific effects.

Conformity in subsistence cultures

The way in which people function interpersonally and in groups can be profoundly affected by where they work and live. For example, people from both Western and Eastern cultures experience physical and psychological stress when they live for extended periods in polar regions (Taylor, 1987). Furthermore, our geographical location can interact with kinship and family structure, child development and group norms regarding economic practices (e.g. Price-Williams, 1976; Smith & Bond, 1998).

An early study of two subsistence cultures compared their behaviour in an Asch-type conformity setting. One was a food-accumulating culture, the Temne from Sierra Leone, and the other a hunter–gatherer society, the Canadian Eskimos (Inuit) (Berry, 1967; see Box 16.2).

Obedience to authority

In considering some of the major findings of social psychology, Smith and Bond (1998) concluded that perhaps the only finding that reliably replicates across cultures is obedience to authority (see **Chapter 7**). This would hardly be surprising, given that authority is a

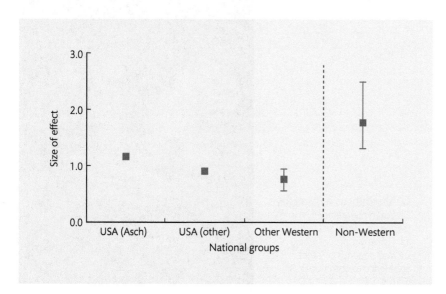

Figure 16.1 Variations in size of conformity effect across cultures

- This analysis of 'effect size' shows that conformity rates were lower in American and other Western samples than in samples from other parts of the world.
- The rates among Americans have also dropped since Asch conducted his studies.

Source: Based on Smith and Bond (1998).

The Temne of Sierra Leone provide an intriguing example of how culture can influence conformity

Using a variant of Asch's conformity paradigm, John Berry (1967) hypothesised that a people's hunting and food-gathering practices should affect the extent that individuals conform to their group. To study this, he compared the Temne people of Sierra Leone with the Inuit (Eskimos) of Canada and found much greater conformity among the Temne.

The Temne subsist on a single crop, which they harvest in one concerted effort once a year. As this requires enormous cooperation and coordination of effort, consensus and agreement are strongly valued and represented in Temne culture. Berry quotes one participant as saying, 'When Temne people choose a thing, we must all agree with the decision – this is what we call cooperation' (Berry, 1967, p. 417).

In contrast, the Inuit economy involves continual hunting and gathering on a relatively individual basis. An Inuit looks after himself and his immediate family; thus, consensus is less strongly emphasised in Inuit culture.

cornerstone of any social system. Later, we touch on some more substantial differences, and several interesting variations by culture.

Culture and socialisation

By the 1930s, anthropologists at Columbia University (Boas, Benedict, Mead) had established that child development was inextricably bound up with cultural norms. According to Margaret Mead, Samoan norms dictate that young people 'should keep quiet, wake up early, obey, and work hard and cheerfully' (Mead, 1928/1961, p. 130), whereas among the Manus in New Guinea there was a culturally induced disposition towards being 'the aggressive, violent, overbearing type' (Mead, 1930/1962, p. 233).

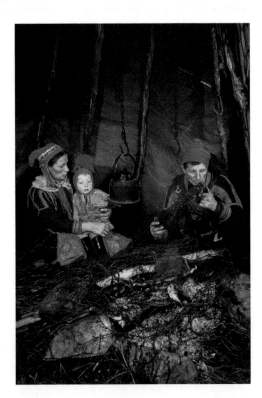

Conformity as a necessity
Dining in their reindeer skin teepee, this Sami family lives in a harsh environment where survival depends on strict adherence to communal norms.

Research on socialisation has been extended by Ciğdem Kağitçibaşi to include explorations of family structure and values, and what kind of value is placed upon children in different cultures – and how these interact with a society's economy (see Smith, Bond, & Kağitçibaşi, 2006). These issues, centred on the family, affect how a person relates to others and how the self develops: will an individual become more independent or interdependent?

Families and aggression

'It is a fundamental aspect of human nature; people live in a dog-eat-dog world; people need to compete to survive and prosper' (Bonta, 1997, p. 299). Bonta was quoting another author and noted twenty-five striking exceptions to this so-called rule. In contrast to comparisons of socialised aggression often featured in cross-cultural commentaries, there are societies that emphasise the importance of cooperation; they devalue achievement because they believe it leads to violence. They are usually non-Western communities and are mostly small and isolated (see **Chapter 12**).

Norms that support a **subculture of violence** are also channelled through the family, which is why rates of violence have traditionally been higher in the American South than in other parts of the United States – the trends are confined to situations involving oneself, one's family or one's possessions (see Box 16.3 and Table 16.1). Studies use the concept of **culture of honour** (Nisbett & Cohen, 1996) to give meaning to a regional pattern of behaviour (see **Chapter 12**). In this instance, it is linked to a tradition of aggression, particularly among men (Cohen, Nisbett, Bowdle, & Schwarz, 1996) in dealing with threat. It is prevalent in some Mediterranean countries, the Middle East and Arab countries, and the Southern United States, and is clearly related to **machismo** in Latin American families. It can also be linked to acts of beneficence, however: a person can be honour-bound to help as well as to hurt. The Arabic term *izzat* has the same sense.

Cultures of honour can have terrible social consequences – they are often violent and misogynistic (beatings, acid attacks and honour killings). They arise in harsh environments

Subculture of violence
A subgroup of society in which a higher level of violence is accepted as the norm.

Culture of honour
A culture that endorses male violence as a way of addressing threats to social reputation or economic position.

Machismo
A code in which challenges, abuse and even differences of opinion must be met with fists or other weapons.

Box 16.3 Our world
Southern honour

Historically, the Southern United States has had higher homicide rates than the rest of the country. Nisbett and his colleagues link greater violence in the South to the herding economy that developed in its early settlements. In other parts of the world, herders have typically resorted to force more readily when they needed to protect their property, especially in contexts where their animals can roam widely.

When self-protection can be so important, a culture of honour may develop. An individual must let an adversary know that intrusion will not be tolerated. In old Louisiana, a wife and her lover were surrendered by law to the husband, who might punish as he saw fit, including killing them. Even today, laws in the South relating to violent actions are more tolerant of violence than those in the North – for example, relating to gun ownership, spouse

abuse, corporal punishment and capital punishment. According to David Fischer (1989), Southern violence is not indiscriminate. For example, rates for robbery in the South are no higher than those in the North. The culture of honour would apply to self-protection, protection of the family or when affronted.

The persistence of higher levels of violence so long after the pioneering days may follow from the use of more violent child-rearing in the South (see the discussion of learnt patterns of aggression and the abuse syndrome in **Chapter 12**). Boys are told to stand up for themselves and to use force in so doing, while spanking is regarded as the normal solution for misbehaviour. Table 16.1 shows comparative responses, from the South and elsewhere, of appropriate ways of using violence for self-protection.

Source: Cohen and Nisbett (1997); Nisbett and Cohen (1996); Vandello and Cohen (2003).

Table 16.1 Males using violence in self-defence: differences in the United States between Southern and non-Southern attitudes

Question and region	Percentage agreeing	Percentage agreeing strongly
A man has a right to kill:		
(a) *in self-defence*		
South	92	70
Non-South	88	57
(b) *to defend his family*		
South	97	80
Non-South	92	67
(c) *to defend his house*		
South	69	56
Non-South	52	18

Source: Based on Blumenthal, Kahn, Andrews and Head (1972); cited in Taylor, Peplau, and Sears (2000).

where cooperation and loyalty are necessary for survival, and they are sustained by the absence of reliable institutions and effective authorities (Nowak, Gelfand, Borkowski, Cohen, & Hernandez, 2016). However, when institutions are reliable and authorities effective, cultures of honour, even in harsh environments, have less survival value and so become weaker or gradually disappear over time.

Two psyches: East meets West

Fiske, Kitayama, Markus and Nisbett (1998) refer to two very different culturally patterned social systems, or psyches: the European American (called loosely, Western) and East Asian (called loosely, Eastern). (See Bell & Chaibong, 2003; Forbes, Collinsworth, Zhao, Kohlman, & LeClaire, 2011.) This distinction is convenient and does reflect the bulk of cultural comparisons reported in the literature. However, it may be insufficiently textured to capture more subtle cultural differences between subgroups.

Another, closely related, description of the two regions is that people in Western cultures have an *independent* self-construal (self-concept) and people in Eastern cultures have an *interdependent* self-construal (Markus & Kitayama, 1991, 2003; Schimmack, Oishi, & Diener, 2005). Much of the focus of contemporary cultural psychology is on this general distinction between the interdependent self of collectivist societies and the independent self of individualistic societies (Nisbett, 2003).

The general distinctions, East–West and independent–interdependent, are useful. For example, Latin American cultures, such as that found in Mexico, are both collectivist and strongly based on interdependence among individuals (Diaz-Guerrero, 1987). However, the terms 'collectivism' and 'individualism' have not always been used consistently (Oyserman, Coon, & Kemmelmeier, 2002), and other terminology such as independence–interdependence and private self-collective have been used as if isomorphic with collectivism–individualism (also see Brewer & Chen, 2007).

Cultural-level distinctions in terms of collectivism–individualism or tightness-looseness (see the subsection 'Individualism and collectivism' later in this chapter) may be reflected in differences in how people construe themselves and their social relationships. Both the self and the basis on which social relations are conducted are relatively independent in historically newer and market-oriented, person-centred societies. However, they are interdependent in historically older and traditional, group-centred societies. In **Chapter 4** we discussed self and identity; exploring the nature of self and asking whether or when the self is best described as independent, interdependent, collective, relational, autonomous and so on. However, it is worth revisiting several points here in the context of culture.

Two kinds of self

Hazel Markus and Shinobu Kitayama (1991) introduced the concepts of **independent self** and **interdependent self** to distinguish between the different kinds of self found in different cultures (see Table 16.2). People in individualistic (Western) cultures generally have an independent self, whereas people in collectivist (Eastern) cultures have an interdependent self.

The independent self is an autonomous entity with clear boundaries between self and others. Internal attributes, such as thoughts, feelings and abilities, are stable and largely unaffected by social context. The behaviour of the independent self is governed and constituted primarily according to one's inner and dispositional characteristics. In contrast, the interdependent self has flexible and diffuse boundaries between self and others. It is tied into relationships and is highly responsive to social context. Others are seen as a part of the self, and the self is seen as a part of other people. There is no self without the collective. One's behaviour is governed and organised primarily according to perception of other people's thoughts, feelings and actions. This distinction between two kinds of self has important implications for how people relate to significant others in their cultures. Think back now to Daan's concern about 'speaking out' in South Korea (the first 'What do *you* think?' question).

Brewer and Gardner (1996) make a similar distinction between the individual self, which is defined by personal traits that differentiate the self from all others, and the relational self, which is defined in relation to specific other people with whom one interacts in a group context. However, Kağitçibaşi (2005) makes a somewhat different distinction based on the observation that Markus and Kitayama's juxtaposition of autonomy with independence and relatedness with interdependence fails to capture the fact that being connected does not imply a lack of autonomy. Kağitçibaşi has proposed an alternative two-dimensional model in which variation in autonomy and in relatedness form four types of self-conception. Individualistic societies recognise the importance of the need for autonomy while ignoring the equally important need for relatedness, whereas collectivistic societies have done the reverse.

Whatever dimensions differentiate self-conception, cultural differences in how the self is construed are probably implicit – we operate the way we do with little conscious awareness (Kitayama, Snibbe, Markus, & Suzuki, 2004). A review by Vivian Vignoles and his colleagues concluded that despite cultural differences in self-conception, the need to have a

Independent self
A self that is relatively separate, internal and unique.

Interdependent self
A self that is relatively dependent on social relations and has more fuzzy boundaries.

Table 16.2 Western and Eastern cultural models of the person

The independent self	The interdependent self
is bounded, stable, autonomous	is connected, fluid, flexible
has personal attributes that guide action	participates in social relationships that guide action
is achievement-oriented	is oriented to the collective
formulates personal goals	meets obligations and conforms to norms
defines life by successful goal achievement	defines life by contributing to the collective
is responsible for own behaviour	is responsible with others for joint behaviour
is competitive	is cooperative
strives to feel good about the self	subsumes self in the collective

Source: Based on Fiske, Kitayama, Markus and Nisbett (1998).

Figure 16.2 Representations of the self: independent versus interdependent

Source: Based on Markus and Kitayama (1991).

distinctive and integrated sense of self may be universal (Vignoles, Chryssochoou, & Breakwell, 2000). Likewise, the pursuit of self-esteem may be universal (Wagner, Gerstorf, Hoppmann, & Luszcz, 2013), but how it is pursued differs culturally (Falk & Heine, 2015) – in Western cultures it is pursued through overt self-enhancement, in Eastern cultures through emphasising interconnectedness (Kitayama, Markus, Matsumoto, & Norasakkunkit, 1997) – see **Chapter 4**.

So, self-distinctiveness and self-esteem mean something different in individualist and collectivist cultures. In one it is the isolated and bounded self that gains meaning and value from separateness, whereas in the other it is the relational self that gains meaning from its relations with others. Susan Cross and her colleagues suggest that the interdependent self is based on different relations in individualistic and collectivist cultures. In the former it is based on close interpersonal relationships, whereas in the latter it is based on a relationship with the group as a whole (Cross, Bacon, & Morris, 2000). Consider a different context: in organisational settings, Chinese employees are selected according to their ties to current employees rather than traditional selection tools, such as tests and interviews (Markus, 2004).

People from individualist cultures consistently generate primarily independent descriptions of themselves when answering the question 'Who am I?' whereas those from collectivist cultures generate interdependent descriptions (Hannover & Kühnen, 2004). Furthermore, when people from East Asia are compared with those from the West, there are other differences in how they make moral judgements, attribute causes, process information and seek happiness (Choi & Choi, 2002).

Dimensions for comparing cultures

Remaining within a broad East–West cultural dichotomy, there are many dimensions on which we can compare cultures. We can compare them in terms of their values, their degree of individualism and collectivism, their orientation towards social norms and their enforcement, the way in which they make social comparisons to ground their social identity, how prosocial they are, and the nature and role played by relationships.

Values

The study of **values** has a long history in the social and behavioural sciences, with psychology adopting a different **level of explanation** to sociology. Psychology explores values at the level of the individual (see **Chapter 5**), whereas sociology adopts a societal perspective. Within both disciplines, however, values are viewed as broad constructs used by individuals and societies to orient people's specific attitudes and behaviour in an integrated and meaningful way. Values are tied to groups, social categories and cultures, and are therefore socially constructed and socially maintained. Not surprisingly, the study of values is central to the analysis of culture (Fiske, Kitayama, Markus, & Nisbett, 1998). In this section, we consider the research of Hofstede and Schwartz.

Hofstede (1980) set out to identify a limited number of dimensions that could differentiate between different cultures. He conducted a now-classic study in which he distributed a questionnaire to 117,000 managers of a large multinational company in forty different countries. Using factor analysis, he isolated four dimensions on which these countries could be compared (in 1991, on the basis of an expanded sample of fifty countries, he added a fifth dimension – time perspective):

1 *Power distance* – the degree to which unequal power in institutions and practices is accepted, or, alternatively, egalitarianism is endorsed (e.g. can employees freely express disagreement with their manager?).

2 *Uncertainty avoidance* – planning for stability in dealing with life's uncertainties (e.g. believing that company rules should never be broken).

3 *Masculinity–femininity* – valuing attributes that are either typically masculine (e.g. achieving, gaining material success) or typically feminine (e.g. promoting interpersonal harmony, caring).

Values
A higher-order concept thought to provide a structure for organising attitudes.

Level of explanation
The types of concepts, mechanisms and language used to explain a phenomenon.

Collective decision making
In making group decisions people can be concerned not to damage their relationships with fellow group members.

Individualism
Societal structure and world view in which people prioritise standing out as an individual over fitting in as a group member.

Collectivism
Societal structure and world view in which people prioritise group loyalty, commitment and conformity, and belonging and fitting into groups, over standing out as an isolated individual.

4 Individualism–collectivism – whether one's identity is determined by personal choices or by the collective (e.g. having the freedom to adapt your approach to the job).

These four dimensions are the basis of the data shown in Table 16.3. The top and bottom quartiles among the forty countries have been ranked by an index on each dimension. Take the following examples:

- Denmark is low on power distance (0.18), uncertainty avoidance (0.23) and masculinity (0.16) but high on individualism (0.74) – Danes do not easily accept hierarchical relationships, they tolerate uncertain outcomes, are caring and egalitarian, but individualistic.

- Japan is high on uncertainty avoidance (0.92) and masculinity (0.95) – Japanese seek clear-cut outcomes, want to reduce life's uncertainties and want to achieve and gain material success.

- Singapore is high on power distance (0.74) but low on individualism (0.20) – Singaporeans tend to accept hierarchical relationships and are collectivist.

An interesting aspect of this analysis is that Eastern and Western countries do not always conform to an East–West dichotomy. Of these dimensions, by far the most popular for the work that was to follow was individualism–collectivism (Fiske, Kitayama, Markus, & Nisbett, 1998; Smith & Bond, 1998). It was the one deemed to capture the essence of the East–West dichotomy discussed above.

Table 16.3 Cross-cultural differences in work-related values

	Power distance		Uncertainty avoidance		Individualism		Masculinity	
Lowest	Austria	0.11	Singapore	0.08	Venezuela	0.12	Sweden	0.05
quartile	Israel	0.13	Denmark	0.23	Colombia	0.13	Norway	0.08
	Denmark	0.18	Hong Kong	0.29	Pakistan	0.14	Netherlands	0.14
	New Zealand	0.22	Sweden	0.29	Peru	0.16	Denmark	0.16
	Ireland	0.28	Great Britain	0.35	Taiwan	0.17	Yugoslavia	0.21
	Norway	0.31	Ireland	0.35	Singapore	0.20	Finland	0.26
	Sweden	0.31	India	0.40	Thailand	0.20	Chile	0.28
	Finland	0.33	Philippines	0.44	Chile	0.23	Portugal	0.31
	Switzerland	0.34	USA	0.46	Hong Kong	0.25	Thailand	0.34
	Great Britain	0.35	Canada	0.48	Portugal	0.27	Spain	0.42
	Turkey	0.66	Turkey	0.85	France	0.71	Colombia	0.64
	Colombia	0.67	Argentina	0.86	Sweden	0.71	Philippines	0.64
	France	0.68	Chile	0.86	Denmark	0.74	Germany (FR)	0.66
	Hong Kong	0.68	France	0.86	Belgium	0.75	Great Britain	0.66
	Brazil	0.69	Spain	0.86	Italy	0.76	Ireland	0.68
	Singapore	0.74	Peru	0.87	New Zealand	0.79	Mexico	0.69
	Yugoslavia	0.76	Yugoslavia	0.88	Canada	0.80	Italy	0.70
	India	0.77	Japan	0.92	Netherlands	0.80	Switzerland	0.70
	Mexico	0.81	Belgium	0.94	Great Britain	0.89	Austria	0.70
Highest	Venezuela	0.81	Portugal	1.04	Australia	0.90	Venezuela	0.73
quartile	Philippines	0.94	Greece	1.12	USA	0.91	Japan	0.95

Source: Based on Hofstede (1980).

Shalom Schwartz, in a 1992 study and a subsequent Polish study (Schwartz & Bardi, 1997), pursued an alternative approach, based on a tradition dating back to Rokeach's classic early work on values (Rokeach, 1973; see **Chapter 5**). Schwartz started with fifty-six values thought to exist in different cultures. He then had more than 40,000 teachers and students from fifty-six nations rate these values for their relevance to themselves. Using a multidimensional scaling technique, he identified two distinct and meaningful dimensions:

1 *openness to change versus conservatism*, e.g. ranging from autonomy to security and tradition;

2 *self-enhancement versus self-transcendence*, e.g. ranging from mastery and power to egalitarianism and harmony with nature.

There are similarities between Schwartz's first dimension and Hofstede's individualism–collectivism, and between Schwartz's second dimension and Hofstede's power distance. An advantage of Schwartz's approach is that he carried out separate analyses, one at the level of individuals and another at the level of cultures.

Fiske, Kitayama, Markus and Nisbett (1998) concluded that cross-cultural work on values, together with other research (e.g. Smith, Dugan, & Trompenaars, 1996), pointed to three groupings of nations in terms of their value orientations:

1 Western European nations are individualistic and egalitarian;

2 Eastern European nations are individualistic and hierarchical;

3 Asian nations are collectivist and hierarchical.

Other research on value differences between cultures has identified further similarities among different approaches. For example, Smith and Bond (1998) suggested a similarity between the concepts of power distance in Hofstede's theory, and authority ranking (where relationships are defined by power and status) in Fiske's relationship models theory that we discuss later in this chapter. Bond (1996) suggested that there is a fundamental Chinese value not captured by Western research: Confucian work dynamism, which highlights role obligations towards the family. (See the second 'What do *you* think?' question.)

Individualism and collectivism

The study of cultural values focuses on value constellations that differentiate between societies. The most influential distinction is Hofstede's distinction between individualistic and collectivist societies. Eastern and more traditional agrarian societies tend to be collectivist, and indeed the default mode of human social organisation is probably collectivism – individualism is very likely a product of the mode of production of the modern industrial world and the associated fragmentation of extended families into nuclear families (see **Chapter 4** for Baumeister's 1987 account of the history of self).

A plausible assumption is that people in collectivist and individualistic societies generally subscribe to the relevant values: that is, the values are internalised by individuals as part of their personal value system. Triandis and his colleagues (Triandis, 1994b; Triandis, Leung, Villareal, & Clack, 1985) explicitly addressed this assumption. They introduced the concepts of *allocentrism* and *idiocentrism* to describe collectivism and individualism, respectively, at the individual level of analysis. Allocentric people tend towards cooperation, social support, equality and honesty, whereas idiocentric people tend towards need for achievement, anomie, alienation, loneliness and values such as a comfortable life, pleasure and social recognition.

Triandis and his associates found that people could be more or less allocentric or more or less idiocentric in different situations. The reason why cultures as a whole differ is that they differ in the prevalence of situations that call for either allocentrism or idiocentrism. Collectivist cultures have a higher proportion of situations requiring allocentrism than idiocentrism, whereas the opposite is true for individualistic cultures.

Tightness–looseness

Another way in which cultures can be distinguished is in terms of cultural tightness and looseness, which refers to the strength of social norms and the extent to which norm violation is sanctioned and normative deviants are not tolerated (Gelfand, Nishi, & Raver, 2006). Tight cultures have clearly defined and restrictive norms whose violation is strictly sanctioned; loose societies have more loosely defined norms whose violation is more tolerated. A study of tightness–looseness across thirty-three nations placed East Asian nations (e.g. Singapore) at the tight extreme and Western nations (e.g. The Netherlands) at the loose extreme (Gelfand, Raver, Nishii, Leslie, Lun, et al., 2011). Another study comparing the fifty US states placed, as one would expect, Deep Southern states (Mississippi, Alabama, Arkansas) at the tight extreme, and West Coast states (California, Oregon, Washington) at the loose extreme (Harington & Gelfand, 2014).

Cooperation, competition and social identity

One dimension along which a social situation can be structured is cooperation–competition; a situation may favour cooperative or competitive interactions involving individuals or groups. In gaming research, this was encapsulated by the **prisoner's dilemma** (see **Chapter 11**).

Steve Hinkle and Rupert Brown (1990) pursued this idea and suggested an interesting qualification to **social identity theory** (see **Chapter 11**). They argue that groups can indeed vary in terms of their social orientation from *collectivist* to *individualist*, but they can also vary in their orientation towards defining themselves through comparisons or not – they can vary from a *comparative ideology* to a *non-comparative ideology*. For example, some groups, such as sports teams, are intrinsically comparative – they often require a comparison group to estimate their worth. Other groups are non-comparative, such as a family whose members are close and would think it unnecessary to compare their group's qualities with, say, those of their neighbours (see Figure 16.3).

The implication of this analysis is that not all intergroup contexts generate discrimination – groups vary in the extent to which they engage in intergroup discrimination. Those located in the top left-hand quadrant of Figure 16.3 show most (or any) discrimination.

Prisoner's dilemma
Two-person game in which both parties are torn between competition and cooperation and, depending on mutual choices, both can win or both can lose.

Social identity theory
Theory of group membership and intergroup relations based on self-categorization, social comparison and the construction of a shared self-definition in terms of ingroup-defining properties.

Ideology
A systematically interrelated set of beliefs whose primary function is explanation. It circumscribes thinking, making it difficult for the holder to escape from its mould.

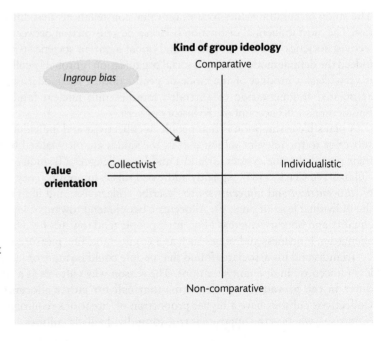

Figure 16.3 People's values interact with their group's orientation towards making intergroup comparisons

- Groups may have a comparative or non-comparative **ideology**, depending on whether intergroup comparisons are important in sustaining identity or not.
- Ingroup bias occurs when a person has a collectivist value orientation and is a member of a group with a comparative ideology.
- This combination occurs in the figure's upper-left quadrant.

Source: Based on Hinkle and Brown (1990, p. 48).

Brown and his colleagues (Brown, Hinkle, Ely, Fox-Cardamone, Maras, & Taylor, 1992) confirmed this idea in a study where they measured individualistic and collectivist values among British participants who were members of groups that were either relatively comparative or non-comparative. They found that outgroup discrimination was highest when a person's orientation was collectivist and the ingroup was comparative. (We should note here that conformity rates are also higher in non-Western, collectivist cultures – refer back to Figure 16.1 – which might be expected if collectivism implies greater ingroup identification.)

The relationship between cultural orientation and social identity has been taken further in three studies designed to show that the more strongly people identify with a (cultural) group, the more strongly they will endorse and conform to the norms of individualism or collectivism that define the relevant (cultural) group. In the first study (Jetten, Postmes, & McAuliffe, 2002), North Americans (individualist culture) were more individualistic when they highly identified with their culture than when they did not; Indonesians (collectivist culture) were less individualistic when they identified more strongly with their culture.

In the second and third studies (McAuliffe, Jetten, Hornsey, & Hogg, 2003) participants were categorized as members of an ad hoc group described as having either an individualist or a collectivist group culture. They then evaluated a group member based on a series of statements, manipulated to reflect individualism or collectivism, ostensibly made by the group member. Participants evaluated collectivist behaviour more positively than individualist behaviour when the group norm prescribed collectivism, but this preference was attenuated when group norms prescribed individualism. Furthermore, consistent with the idea that evaluations were driven by conformity to *salient norms*, attenuation occurred only for high identifiers, not low identifiers.

In two further studies (Hornsey, Jetten, McAuliffe, & Hogg, 2006), dissenting group members were better tolerated and less likely to be rejected when the group had an individualistic norm and participants identified strongly with the group (also see Hornsey, 2005). This research lends support to Gelfand's tightness–looseness distinction discussed above (e.g. Gelfand, Nishi, & Raver, 2006) and has potentially far-reaching implications – suggesting, for example, that creativity, innovation and normative change might be better served in groups or societies that are more individualistic.

A fundamental feature of many people's overall social identity is whether or not they are religious and identify with an organised religion. Of course, different regions of the world have historically been crucibles for different religions – and most research suggests that despite secularisation, or perhaps because of it and the uncertainty associated with social change (Hogg, Adelman, & Blagg, 2010), religion is growing in importance across much of the planet (Berger, 1999) – although in Western societies it is declining. The question is not so much whether there are cultural differences in religiosity, but whether there are cultural differences in associated moral principles (e.g., Haidt, 2012).

Richard Shweder and his colleagues argue that there are three distinct codes of ethics that guide people's moral judgement: autonomy, community and divinity (Shweder, Much, Mahapatra, & Park, 1997). Heine (2012) notes that the distribution of these codes of ethics varies around the world: *autonomy*, which stresses the protection of individual rights, prevails among high socio-economic Westerners; *community*, which stresses interpersonal relational duties and obligations, prevails in cultures where interdependence is privileged; and *divinity*, which stresses the perceived natural and divinely ordained order of things, prevails among lower socio-economic Westerners and those who subscribe to orthodox and fundamentalist religions.

Collectivism and prosocial behaviour

We noted earlier (in **Chapter 13**) that **prosocial behaviour** is more prevalent in rural areas than in cities. Given that city living may seem to encourage more individualistic behaviour, it is tempting to ask whether collectivists are generally more likely to offer and receive help from others than are individualists.

Prosocial behaviour
Acts that are positively valued by society.

Arie Nadler (1986; also see Nadler, 1991), believing that self-reliance and individual achievement are fostered by Western lifestyles, compared the help-seeking tendencies of Israeli high school students living in *kibbutzim* with those dwelling in cities. In Israel, social-isation in a *kibbutz* stresses collectivist values, a lifestyle where communal and egalitarian outlook is important, and being cooperative with peers is crucial (Bettleheim, 1969). *Kibbutz* dwellers rely on being comrades – they depend heavily on group resources, and they treat group goals as paramount. In contrast, the Israeli city context is typically Western, with an emphasis on individualist values including personal independence and individual achievement.

Seeking help has a strong sociocultural component. Nadler found that the two groups treated a request for aid in dramatically different ways. If it was clear that the situation affected the outcome for the group as a whole, *kibbutz* dwellers were much more likely than city dwellers to seek help, and vice versa if the benefit was defined in individual terms. There were no differences between men and women in these trends. See how Nadler tested this idea, as described in Box 16.4, and check the results in Figure 16.4.

Relationships

Relational theory
An analysis based on structures of meaningful social relationships that recur across cultures.

Schema
Cognitive structure that represents knowledge about a concept or type of stimulus, including its attributes and the relations among those attributes.

As we saw earlier, in **Chapter 14**, relationships play a central role in human life. It would not, then, be surprising to learn that there might be a limited number of naive models of rela-tionships that people have and apply in different situations, and different relationship mod-els may prevail in different cultures. In pursuing this idea, Alan Fiske developed a **relational theory** based on the concept of **schema** (Fiske, 1992; Fiske & Haslam, 1996; Haslam, 1994; see **Chapter 2** for discussion of schemas).

Fiske proposed four models of relationships:

1 *Communal sharing (CS)* – the group transcends the individual. People in a CS rela-tionship experience solidarity and a collective identity. Examples are lovers, teams and families.

Box 16.4 Research highlight
Sociocultural values and the tendency to seek help

'For my comrade's sake, will you help me?'

The participants were high-school students in Israel. Half grew up and lived with their families on various *kibbutzim* and attended a high school catering to the needs of *kib-butz* dwellers. The city dwellers grew up and lived with their families in two middle-sized towns in northern Israel, and attended their local high school. The study was con-ducted in the students' classrooms.

The students tried to solve twenty anagrams, and the task's importance was made salient by suggesting that per-formance could predict success in other domains in life. They were told that: (1) some anagrams had never been solved; (2) if they could not solve one, they could seek help from the investigator. The percentage of occasions on which help was requested was recorded (e.g. if help was

sought on five out of ten unsolved anagrams, the help-seeking score was 50 per cent).

In a two-by-two experimental design, half the *kibbutz* group and half the city group had first received a *group-oriented task* instruction – their scores would be compared with the average of other classes. The other half had an *individual-oriented task* instruction – their scores would be compared with other individuals.

Would help be sought according to the nature of the group and of the instruction? Perhaps *kibbutz* dwellers would seek help more often if they were group-oriented, while city dwellers would look for help if they were individual-oriented.

See the results in Figure 16.4.

Source: Based on Nadler (1986).

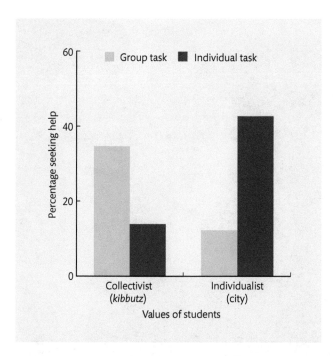

Figure 16.4 Collectivist values, individualist values and when to seek help

Source: Based on data from Nadler (1986).

2 *Authority ranking (AR)* – the AR relationship is defined by precedence and a linear hierarchy. Examples are how a subordinate individual relates to an army officer and, in Chinese society, the tradition of filial piety.

3 *Equality matching (EM)* – based on attending to balance in a social exchange. Examples of an EM relationship are reciprocating in a tit-for-tat manner, taking biblical vengeance, being egalitarian and car-pooling.

4 *Market pricing (MP)* – based on a sense of proportional outcomes. Examples of MP are prices, rents, salaries and taxes. In an MP interpersonal relationship, the partners calculate their relative costs and benefits (see discussion of the cost–reward ratio in **Chapter 14**).

Across the course of a day one can cycle through all these models as one's interaction partners and contexts change. An example of how the four relationship models work is given in Box 16.5.

Box 16.5 Your life
Four relationship models for a mother and son

Consider your relationship with your mother. She is primarily your mother, but the specifics of that relationship can change over a lifetime – but also even in the course of a day. These changes can be described by Fiske's relationship model.

In practice, people may use any of Fiske's four relationship models in accordance with the multiple roles that people play at different moments in time. Sally is John's mother. In the course of a normal day, they adopt different ways of relating to each other without being very conscious of the changes that take place. At home in the morning, Sally prepares breakfast with John. She makes the drinks, while he checks the food and places utensils on the table – neither one minding who puts in more effort (CS). Later that morning Sally goes to work, where she is a company manager. John, a sales representative in the same company, is told by his mother that his sales figures are improving (AR). After dinner that night, they play a game of chess, which the better player will win (EM). Before going to bed, John asks Sally for a loan to buy a car. She thinks carefully and they discuss his proposition. Finally she agrees, provided that he paints the house and makes a good job of it (MP). Together, they feel that their overall relationship is complex and that life is rich.

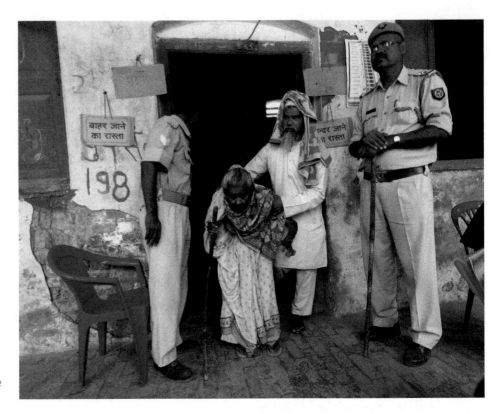

Authority ranking
This 105 year old lady in northern India has just cast her vote. Respect for elders is a cornerstone of collective stories.

However, the prevalence of different models may vary from culture to culture as some models are better suited to some activities and sociocultural practices than others. Fiske and colleagues (Fiske, Kitayama, Markus, & Nisbett, 1998) provide an illustration with respect to land: it can be an investment (MP), a kingdom (AR), a mark of equal status if all citizens can own it or not own it (EM), and a motherland, or even a commons, defining a collective identity (CS). Perhaps not surprisingly, at the cultural level MP is more common in individualistic cultures and CS in collectivist cultures; AR occurs more frequently in East Asian cultures, as it once did in feudal Europe; and EM prevails in interdependent cultures, in some Asian countries and in Melanesia.

There is clearly some convergence between the two principal ways of comparing cultures we have discussed in this chapter. There are common features in characterising cultures, whether we use *values* or *relational models*.

Culture through the lens of norms and identity

Different cultures can be viewed in terms of their material structures, their means of production, their legal and political systems, their language, food and dress and so forth (Cohen, 2001). But, from a social psychological point of view, what stands out, and is captured in our working definition of culture, is that cultures are social categories (they may be concentrated in an ancestral homeland or spread around the world) that provide people with an identity that governs almost every aspect of their lives in such a profound way that it appears the natural order of things. In this short section, we simply reiterate and draw out this logic.

Our culture provides us with an identity and a set of attributes that define that identity. Culture influences what we think, how we feel, how we dress, what and how we eat, how we speak, what values and moral principles we hold, how we interact with one another and how we understand the world around us. It can even justify the use of force through 'codes of legitimation' and 'ideologies of antagonism' towards some outgroups (Bond, 2004). Culture pervades almost all aspects of our existence. Perhaps because of this, culture is often the taken-for-granted background to everyday life (e.g. Garfinkel, 1967), and we may only really become aware of features of our culture when we encounter other cultures or when our own culture is threatened. Culture, like other entrenched normative systems, may only be revealed to us by intercultural exposure, or by intercultural conflict.

A key feature of cultural attributes is that they are tightly integrated in a logical way that makes our lives and the world we live in meaningful. In this sense, culture has some of the attributes of social attributions (see Hewstone, 1989), social representations (see Lorenzi-Cioldi & Clémence, 2001) and ideologies (Thompson, 1990) (see **Chapters 3** and **5**). At the cognitive level, our own culture might be represented schematically as a well-organised and compact prototype (see **Chapter 2**).

Because culture makes the world meaningful, we might expect cultural revivals to occur under conditions of societal uncertainty (e.g. Hogg, 2007b, 2012): for example, prolonged economic crises. Because culture defines identity, we would also expect cultural revivals when the prestige or distinctiveness of our culture is threatened by other cultural groups. In these respects, culture would obey the principles of intergroup behaviour described by social identity theory (see **Chapter 11**). Indeed, research on language revivals, where language is central to culture, shows precisely this (e.g. Giles & Johnson, 1987; see **Chapter 15**).

Another key feature of cultural attributes is that they are shared among members of the culture, and they differentiate between cultures – they are normative and thus obey the general principles of norms (**Chapter 8**). For example, cultural leaders may be allowed greater latitude for cultural divergence than are other members of the culture (e.g. Sherif and Sherif, 1964; see **Chapter 8**). Cultural forms may emerge and be sustained or modified through human interaction, as described by Moscovici's (e.g. 1988) theory of social representations (see **Chapter 3**), and through talk, as described by discourse perspectives on social psychology (e.g. McKinlay & McVittie, 2008; Potter, 1996; see **Chapter 15**).

The dynamics of large-scale cultures may be very similar to the dynamics of small-scale cultures in organisations and small groups. In such cases the processes of group socialisation (e.g. Levine & Moreland, 1994; see **Chapter 8**) and group memory (e.g. Moreland, Argote, & Krishnan, 1996; see **Chapter 9**) may operate at the societal level.

The main message of this, necessarily brief, section is that while culture can be studied as an independent topic in its own right, there is a real sense in which it is actually an integral part of social psychology as a whole.

Contact between cultures

Cultural groups do not live in isolation – they come into contact with one another, increasingly so with each passing decade. You do not need to be a tourist to taste another culture. New York is probably the best example of a total cultural mélange, although the same can be seen in other Western gateway cities such as London, Paris, Istanbul, Los Angeles and Amsterdam. Intercultural contact can be an enriching experience, a force for good and for beneficial change, but it can also be a pressure cooker, in which perceived threats and ancient animosities boil over into conflict (see Prentice & Miller, 1999).

Most intercultural contact does not last long enough to cause a permanent change in behaviour or in people's attitudes towards another cultural group. Recall the complexities of the **contact hypothesis** – it can be difficult to create conditions of contact that will produce enduring improvement in intergroup attitudes and feelings (see **Chapter 11**). Even a brief face-to-face encounter between people from different cultures is actually more likely to produce or strengthen stereotypes and prejudices (see **Chapters 2, 10** and **11**). A variety of

Contact hypothesis
The view that bringing members of opposing social groups together will improve intergroup relations and reduce prejudice and discrimination.

factors are likely to lead to negative outcomes: for example, language differences, pre-existing prejudice, ethnocentrism, intergroup anxiety or a history of intergroup conflict.

Communication, language and speech style

As discussed in **Chapter 15**, multilingual, and thus multicultural, societies usually have a high-status dominant group whose language is the lingua franca and whose cultural practices dominate. Consequently, language difference can be a significant obstacle to smooth and harmonious intercultural encounters (see Giles, 2012; Giles & Maass, 2016). If you are in France and cannot speak French very well, you have a major hurdle in communicating with the locals. Phrase books and sign language can take you only so far.

Even accent and speech style present a problem – native speakers may be less attentive to people with a foreign accent. For example, in an Australian study, Gallois and Callan (1986) found that native speakers of Australian English tended to be less engaged in listening to speakers with an Italian accent – an effect probably compounded by negative stereotypes of immigrants from southern Europe. In another Australian study, Gallois, Barker, Jones and Callan (1992) found that the communication style of overseas Chinese students might reinforce unfavourable stereotypes of that group (see Box 16.6).

The magnitude of perceived cultural difference can influence *intercultural contact*. The extent to which a culture is perceived to be dissimilar to our own can affect intercultural interaction. An early social distance study by Vaughan (1962) showed that the more dissimilar a culture is perceived to be, the more people wish to distance themselves from members of that cultural group – the underlying reason may be old-fashioned intergroup dislike and hostility, but it could also be anxiety about interacting with an outgroup that is very different from one's s own group (Stephan, 2014). In any event, the likelihood of developing intercultural contacts is reduced.

The setting of contact between groups is also important (see **Chapter 11**). For example, cooperation, shared goals and equal status, all of which are more likely to be present in intercultural contact within the same society, can make contact a more positive experience. However, there are other features of such contact that can act as a barrier. For example,

The global village
Multinationals and cheap air travel are two factors that may contribute to the dilution of cultural distance.

Box 16.6 Our world
Ethnic differences in communication style can affect a student's perceived academic ability

Chinese students have become easily the largest single ethnic group of overseas students enrolled in universities in Western, particularly English-speaking, nations. For example, in the period 2010–15, the proportion of Chinese students rose from 0.8 per cent to 1.5 per cent in the United States, and from 2.8 per cent to 4 per cent in the United Kingdom. Australia has always hosted the largest proportion of Chinese students, which has diminished only a little over the 2010–15 period, from 7.8 per cent to 6.5 per cent.

Owing to cultural differences in communication styles, these students have sometimes found it difficult to adjust to local communication norms, which encourage students to speak out in class and in interaction with academic staff.

Cindy Gallois and her colleagues (Gallois, Barker, Jones, & Callan, 1992) studied this phenomenon in the context of Australian universities. They prepared twenty-four carefully scripted videotapes of communications between a student and a lecturer, in which the student adopted a submissive, assertive or aggressive communication style to ask for help with an assignment or to complain about a

grade. The student was either a male or a female Anglo-Australian or an ethnic Chinese (the lecturer was always Anglo-Australian and the same sex as the student).

Gallois and colleagues had Australian students, ethnic Chinese students (i.e. from Hong Kong, Singapore or Malaysia) and lecturers view the videotaped vignettes and rate the students on a number of behavioural dimensions and on the effectiveness of their communication style. All participants agreed that the aggressive style was inappropriate, ineffective and atypical of students of any ethnic background. Consistent with stereotypes, submissiveness was considered more typical of Chinese than Australian students, and assertiveness more typical of Australian than Chinese students. Chinese students felt that the submissive style was more effective than the assertive style. However, lecturers and Australian students interpreted the submissive style as being less effective and indicating less need for assistance.

Clearly, this assumption that a submissive style indicates lack of need and interest could nourish a view that Chinese students are less talented than their Australian counterparts.

Kochman (1987) has shown that African Americans use an intonation and expressive intensity in their speech that distinguishes them from the white majority. This can be an intentional sociolinguistic marker; serving to draw an intergroup line and acting to protect their ethnic identity (see **Chapters 11** and **15**).

International contact can add further barriers – we are now dealing with different nations, territories and political institutions, and the norms that relate to these (Smith, Bond, & Kağitçibaşi, 2006). International contact is also often shorter-term, less frequent and more variable in intimacy, relative status and power. In the remainder of this section, we deal with intercultural communication that is cross-national.

A quite marked East–West difference is that East Asians are more likely to use 'code' – messages with implicit meanings for each communicator (Burgoon, Buller, & Woodall, 1989). This is recognised in Chinese society, for example, as *hanxu* (Gao, Ting-Toomey, & Gudykunst, 1996). Consequently, an East–West interaction can sometimes generate misunderstandings (Gallois & Callan, 1997). In a conversation between an American and a Japanese, for example, the American might seem blunt and the Asian evasive.

There are also marked cultural differences in non-verbal behaviour (see **Chapter 15**). Culturally relevant facial **display rules** are used to communicate our emotions, and body posture (**kinesics**) can point to our cultural background, as do variations in touching and interpersonal distance. There are some differences between Eastern and Western cultures in the rate of mutual gaze in certain social contexts. For example, Bond and Komai (1976) found that young Japanese males made less eye contact than Western samples with an interviewer during the course of an interview.

Display rules
Cultural and situational rules that dictate how appropriate it is to express emotions in a given context.

Kinesics
Linguistics of body communication.

As another example, suppose that someone gestured to you with a forefinger and thumb forming a circle: you would probably think they meant 'it's okay' or 'great'. However, there are cultures where this is the symbol for 'money', 'worthless' or even 'screw you!' (Burgoon, Buller & Woodall, 1989; Morris, Collett, Marsh, & O'Shaughnessy, 1979).

Sometimes an action that is quite normal in one culture violates a moral standard in another. Western women, for example, should avoid wearing revealing clothing in many Islamic countries. Unfortunately, breaches of a cultural norm are often committed in ignorance, such as sitting or standing on a table in an area where food is served, which offends Maori custom in New Zealand. Intergroup and therefore intercultural contact can be severely curtailed if it leads to anxiety and uncertainty (Hogg, 2012; Stephan, 2014; see **Chapter 11**).

Language and understanding

Language itself poses a problem. The direct translation of words from one language to another does not necessarily preserve meaning. Edmund Glenn (1976) provided examples of differences in word meanings when changing from English to French or Russian. The use of the personal pronoun 'I', for example, usually has a subjective connotation in English but extends to objective connotations in French or Russian. In English, 'as long as I understand that' could be rendered in French as '*s'il s'agit de*', an idiom meaning 'if what is being dealt with is'. In English there is a single word for 'here', whereas in Spanish there is a distinction between right here (*aquí*) and hereabouts (*acá*).

In addition to direct translation problems, a language can pose a larger problem when words, or word usage, are entwined with culturally specific concepts. For example, Yoshi Kashima and Emiko Kashima (1998) show that, for certain statements, the first-person personal pronoun 'I' is dropped in Japanese but not in English. What is intriguing is that this may reflect the self-conceptual difference between the independent self and the interdependent self, discussed earlier (see Table 16.2 and Figure 16.2). Individualistic English speakers use 'I' to represent the self as separate from all others, whereas collectivist Japanese speakers drop 'I' to incorporate significant others into the self. Another example, again from Japanese: the Japanese have a word, *amae*, to identify an emotional state with communicative implications that are fundamental to traditional Japanese culture. According to Doi:

> *Amaeru* [*amae* is its noun form] can be translated as 'to depend and presume upon another's love' . . . [It] has a distinct feeling of sweetness, and is generally used to express a child's attitude toward an adult, especially his parents. I can think of no English word equivalent to *amaeru* except for 'spoil', which, however, is a transitive verb and definitely has a bad connotation . . . I think most Japanese adults have a dear memory of the taste of sweet dependency as a child and, consciously or unconsciously, carry a lifelong nostalgia for it.
>
> Doi (1976, p. 188)

In this quotation, the context is that of adult and child, but *amae* also applies to students and professors, and to work teams and their supervisors. By custom, Japanese people have a powerful need to experience *amae*, and knowledge of this state provides an emotional basis for interpersonal communication. A person who experiences *amae* during conversation will provide non-verbal cues (e.g. silences, pensive looks and even unnatural smiles) to 'soften the atmosphere' for the other person. It follows that these cues are not likely to be interpreted appropriately by someone unfamiliar with both the language and the culture. (Reflect on the irony in the third 'What do *you* think?' question.)

At a political level, intercultural communication can sometimes involve subtle word games in negotiating outcomes that minimise public humiliation (see Box 16.7).

Box 16.7 Our world
When is being 'sorry' an apology?

An international event in April 2001 highlighted how language differences can reflect conceptual differences. An American surveillance aircraft was damaged in an accident with a Chinese plane off the coast of China and was forced to land in Chinese territory. The Chinese pilot was lost at sea. The Chinese government insisted that the American government make a formal apology before they would return the American crew. Such an apology (*dao qian*) is an admission of responsibility and an expression of remorse.

At first, the American expression was one of 'regret' (*yihan*), which carries no acknowledgement of guilt. The American president next expressed 'sincere regret' (*shen biao qian yi*) for the missing pilot and said he was 'very sorry' (*zhen cheng yihan*) for the unauthorised landing. Both expressions are ambiguous with respect to implying blame.

The American crew was finally released and both governments may have felt that face was saved.

Acculturation and culture change

When people migrate, they find it almost impossible to avoid close contact with members of the host culture and with other immigrant cultural groups. Enduring close contact inevitably produces changes in behaviour and thinking among new migrants. The process of internalising the rules of behaviour characteristic of another culture is **acculturation**, and when it applies to a whole group, we have large-scale culture change. However, immigrant groups have some choice about the form that these changes take – the starkest choice is between assimilating and remaining separate.

Acculturation
The process whereby individuals learn about the rules of behaviour characteristic of another culture.

The logic of acculturation applies not only to an immigrant group (e.g. Indians moving to the United Kingdom), but also to the host group, particularly if immigration is relatively large relative to the host population. For example, in 2009 New Zealand, with a tiny highly concentrated population of only 4.4 million, had a larger number of Chinese immigrants than the United Kingdom with a population of 56 million. And the massive influx of close to one million migrants and refugees into Europe in 2015 fuelled a powerful cultural backlash and empowered xenophobic attitudes across the continent that probably played a role in the UK's 2016 referendum-based vote to leave the European Union. Acculturation also affects indigenous populations that are overwhelmed by mass migration into their traditional lands – for example, the plight of just over 5 million Tibetans and 8 million Uyghurs in the face of 1,240 million Han Chinese.

Culture change can lead to acculturative stress. For example, look again at how ethnic minorities can suffer depression when their culture is eroded by an ethnic majority (see Box 4.4 in **Chapter 4**).

An acculturating individual can have *dual identities*: for example, a feeling that one is both a Mexican American and an Anglo-American (Buriel, 1987), a Greek and an Australian (Rosenthal, 1987). A similar concept, *bicultural identity*, is used in research into ethnic socialisation in children (see Phinney & Rotheram, 1987). When the self is derived from multiple cultural backgrounds, people can have multicultural minds that provide them with access to more than one self-concept (see Heine, 2010). They can, on occasion, draw on a blend of these self-concepts; or they can frame-switch by alternating between different self-concepts as a function of situational factors that prime different self-conceptions (also see Hong, Morris, Chiu, & Benet-Martínez, 2000).

Immigrants who arrive in a new country face a dilemma: will they maintain their social identity as defined by their home culture, or will they change their social identity so that it is now defined by the host culture? How can this be resolved? The cross-cultural psychologist Berry (e.g. Berry, Trimble, & Olmedo, 1986) identified four different paths to acculturation (also see **Chapter 15** – these paths influence the process of second-language acquisition). In weighing up home culture and dominant culture, immigrants can choose between:

1   *integration* – maintaining home culture but also relating to dominant culture;

2   *assimilation* – giving up home culture and embracing dominant culture;

3   *separation* – maintaining home culture and being isolated from dominant culture;

4   *marginalisation* – giving up home culture and failing to relate properly to dominant culture.

These choices are shown in Figure 16.5. (Reflect on the dilemma faced by Keiko and her husband in the fourth 'What do *you* think?' question at the beginning of this chapter. Then consider how you might respond to Jessica's poser in the fifth 'What do *you* think?' question.)

Leaving aside issues of learning a second language (see **Chapter 15**), the most popular path for immigrants is integration, and is the one associated with the least stress in acculturating (Berry, Kim, Minde, & Mok, 1987). A key factor in stress reduction is the availability of a **social support network**, just as it is in dealing with the breakdown of a close relationship (see **Chapter 14**). Choosing to integrate makes sense based on theories of intergroup relations that discuss maximising harmony and stability (e.g. Hogg, 2015; Hornsey & Hogg, 2000a; Moghaddam, 2008; Verkuyten, 2006; Vescio, Hewstone, Crisp, & Rubin, 1999; see **Chapter 11**). Groups tend to get on better together when their cherished identities and practices are respected and allowed to flourish within a superordinate culture – one that also allows groups to feel that their relations to one another are not competitive but are more akin to different teams that 'pull together'.

However, successful integration is a process that takes considerable time and, in many instances, competes with a host culture's expectation of assimilation. For second-generation immigrants (the children of the original settlers), conflict with their elders is minimised if all actually integrate. If integration is a 'good' solution for the individual immigrant, is it also good for whole groups of immigrants, and indeed for the host culture? Before we return to

Social support network
People who know and care about us and who can provide back-up during a time of stress.

Acculturation stress
These newly naturalised German citizens may face further hurdles. As well as aiming for language fluency they must also address subtleties in the social mores of their new country.

Figure 16.5 Four paths to acculturation

- Berry et al. described four ways in which immigrants can reconcile their ancestral culture with the new host culture.
- The positive valence (+) indicates that, to an extent, an immigrant adopts the host culture or retains the ancestral culture – or both.
- The negative valence (–) indicates that, to an extent, an immigrant fails to adopt the host culture or to retain elements of the ancestral culture – or both.
- The optimal outcome for an immigrant is integration.

Source: Based on Berry, Trimble and Olmedo (1986).

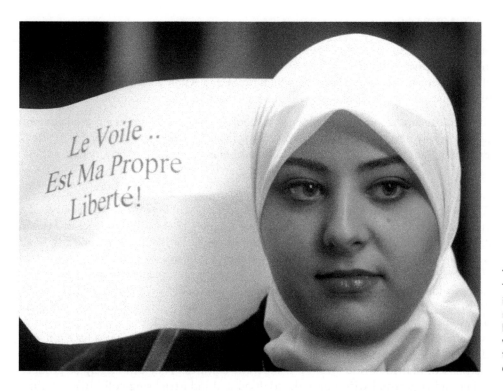

The path of separation? This French girl solved an immigrants dilemma by refusing to remove her headdress - she was not willing to assimilate entirely to a new culture. Or has she chosen to integrate?

the challenge posed by cultural pluralism or multiculturalism, we explore how well social psychology has addressed culture and cross-cultural issues in its research, its theories, and its wider meta-theory.

Testing social psychology cross-culturally

The publication of Michael Bond's (1988) *The Cross-Cultural Challenge to Social Psychology* was, in many respects, a call to arms – much like Franz Boas's 1932 plea to his discipline of sociology (see the start of this chapter). When would social psychologists pay heed to the possible limitations of untested universal assumptions in developing their theories? The challenges are multiple, occurring across cultures as nations, and within a culture when addressing status-defined majority–minority group relations.

The cross-cultural challenge

Although the cross-cultural challenge is typically targeted at social psychology, it actually cuts both ways. Cross-cultural and cultural psychologists can and should draw on principles from social psychology and use them beyond the culture in which they were developed (Moghaddam, 1998; Smith, Bond, & Kağitçibaşi, 2006). Take the instance of improving intercultural relations. Social psychologists would argue that intercultural relations are a special case of intergroup relations, in which case an understanding of what drives intercultural conflict, discrimination and stereotyping is informed by the social psychology of intergroup behaviour (**Chapter 11**), of the self-concept (**Chapter 4**), of prejudice and discrimination (**Chapter 10**), of language and communication (**Chapter 15**) and of stereotyping (**Chapters 2** and **10**). What are the challenges, in the reverse direction, to social psychologists?

Indigenous social psychologies

Indigenous psychology
A psychology created by and for a specific cultural group – based on the claim that culture can be understood only from within its own perspective.

Should we promulgate an **indigenous psychology**? Put differently, should each culture have its own social psychology that reflects its unique perspective in the topics it studies and the explanatory constructs it develops? Middle Eastern and Asian countries in particular can have legitimate concerns about a pervasive and encroaching Western-centric world view:

> the ideology and techniques of modern psychology [in general] are being overlaid upon already highly developed systems of psychological belief, derived from Hinduism, Islam, Buddhism, Taoism, Confucianism, Shintoism and Marxism-Leninism, or varying combinations of these.
>
> Turtle (1994, pp. 9–10)

The most successful example of an indigenous *social* psychology is the development of a relatively distinct European social psychology (see **Chapter 1**). As a consequence of fascism and the Second World War, social psychology in Europe in the 1940s, 1950s and early 1960s was largely an outpost of American social psychology. In this context, Serge Moscovici (1972) worried that American social psychology was culturally alien for Europeans because it did not address European priorities and interests, and it adopted an interpretative framework or **metatheory** that clashed with European metatheory. He advocated a European social psychology grounded specifically in the cultural context of Europe.

Metatheory
Set of interrelated concepts and principles concerning which theories or types of theory are appropriate.

Although Europe (particularly north-west Europe) and the United States have different traditions, histories and world views, as cultures they are remarkably similar – both are industrialised, individualistic Western democratic cultures. They can largely be grouped together and contrasted with non-industrialised and industrialising collectivist cultures around the world. Thus, even if we make a distinction between European and American social psychology, the difference is not really that great, and due to globalisation, travel and the Internet, is shrinking with each passing year.

Roy Malpass (1988), an American, reminds us that scientific psychology is a Euro-American enterprise (see the historical origins of social psychology in **Chapter 1**). As such, people from Western cultures are both the scientists and the objects of study. Thus, we should not be surprised at a call for indigenous psychologies from the Asian region – for Filipinos by Enriquez (1993), for Chinese by Yang (Yang & Bond, 1990) and for Indians by Sinha (1997). The formation of both the Asian Association of Social Psychology and the *Asian Journal of Social Psychology* in 1995 has, in the ensuing years, nurtured social psychology in East Asia, stimulating research using indigenous themes and raising issues about the nature of indigenous psychologies (Kashima, 2005; Kim, 2000; Ng & Liu, 2000; Yang, 2000).

A starting point for an indigenous social psychology is to develop theories and apply them within the same culture. This issue is particularly relevant for developing nations that have serious social problems to solve – the well-meaning application of theories that are developed, say, in Europe or the United States may have limited effectiveness. For example, Moghaddam (1998) describes how the application of the Western idea that modernisation can be achieved by motivating people to act like entrepreneurs has backfired – it brought about a collapse of traditional communities (e.g. among Pygmies in central Africa) and ecologies (e.g. in parts of Brazil). Indeed, one of the fundamental problems of globalisation is precisely the assumption that people in developing nations have the same social psychological resources as people in the West (Stiglitz, 2002).

Another problem is the tendency for social psychological theory, and social action, to focus on static social relations rather than on dynamic processes that may change those relations (Moghaddam, 1990). There have been some notable exceptions, such as social identity theory (e.g. Tajfel & Turner, 1986; Hogg & Abrams, 1988; see **Chapter 11**) and theories of minority influence (e.g. Martin & Hewstone, 2010; Moscovici, 1976; see **Chapter 7**). These theoretical orientations, from Europe, were part of a deliberate strategy to address a European scientific and social agenda and to differentiate European from American social psychology (see **Chapter 1**; also Israel & Tajfel, 1972).

Whether independent indigenous psychologies are actually necessary to solve problems in each and every culture is a moot point. Neglected in the current debate is an older question of linking theory to practice, culture notwithstanding. The question arises as to whether an **action research** approach (see **Chapter 6**), which is oriented towards practical outcomes, is more useful. In a similar vein, Fathali Moghaddam (1990, 1998) has advocated a **generative psychology** – he cites examples of the success of such an approach in the 1990s in Latin America and Turkey.

Action research
The simultaneous activities of undertaking social science research, involving participants in the process and addressing a social problem.

Generative psychology
A psychology intended to generate positive social change through direct intervention.

The search for universals

The tabulation of human attributes and classes of behaviour with universal application was a characteristic of early cultural anthropology. This is still the case today in social psychology – most social psychologists are generally committed to the search that concerned Boas, a quest for universal laws of social behaviour and the specification of universal psychological processes.

A call for multiple indigenous psychologies that apply to a host of specific cultural groups raises issues that touch on the relationship between science, on the one hand, and ideology and political agenda on the other; issues of epistemology and the constitution of valid knowledge; and the role of abstract scientific inquiry in society. For every new indigenous psychology, there may be a different set of laws and principles. Do we run the risk of scientific Balkanisation? In addition, associated with the drive for locally relevant theory is usually the poststructuralist assumption of cultural relativism – the view that all cultural belief systems and practices are equally acceptable, and that there are no universal psychological truths. There are no easy answers to or resolutions of these issues.

A realistic target is to encourage social psychologists to broaden their discipline to articulate fundamental social cognition and perception, such as social categorization (**Chapter 2**), with emergent social properties, such as group norms and social representations (**Chapters 5, 7 and 9**). It is in this way that we can gain an insight into human behaviour in its general form and in its context-specific cultural and historical expression. The *universal* and the *cultural* are the two interdependent moments of the dialectic of a mature social psychology. (See Heine and Buchtel (2009) for a discussion of universality versus variability of personality traits across cultures.)

The challenge of cross-cultural research and cultural psychology for social psychologists is not that it can be difficult to do cross-cultural research. Although cross-cultural research presents its challenges, so too does, for example, social cognition research (Devine, Hamilton, & Ostrom, 1994; see **Chapter 2**) and research into small interactive task-oriented groups (e.g. Moreland, Hogg, & Hains, 1994; see **Chapters 2 and 8**).

The real challenge is to try to overcome our own cultural myopia – to try to see things from different cultural perspectives as well as to be aware of the cultural limitations of our own thinking (see Smith, Bond, & Kağitçibaşi, 2006). Social psychologists, like all people, are blinkered by their own cultural parameters, adopting perspectives and addressing questions that are culturally relevant. They incline us towards culture-specific psychologies rather than a universal science. A collateral problem of this is that the psychology of the dominant scientific culture can oust all other psychologies and hinder the development of true universalism.

A social psychology that is relevant to all peoples would have a laudable sociopolitical role to play on the global stage, perhaps guiding humanitarians dedicated to solving widespread and pressing problems in the developing world. As well, social psychology could help to explain how basic social psychological processes interact with socioculturally specific processes. Activities like these may help us to understand destructive blind obedience, intergroup conflict, family violence, social dilemmas and social change. They may also tell us why noble attitudes rarely translate into noble acts.

The multicultural challenge

There is also a wider challenge to the many societies of the world – can multiple cultures coexist? In a society of diverse cultures, should all cultural forms be permitted to flourish (even if they engage in such practices as infanticide, genital mutilation and honour killing), or should cultures change with changing global values? For example, as an extreme case, consider the campaign in Afghanistan against al-Qaeda and the Taliban, or in Syria and Iraq against DAISH. Is this a struggle against universal evil, or is it the forceful imposition of one cultural world view over another? This is, of course, a highly politicised question, which is beyond the scope of a scientific text. It confronts issues of cultural relativism and what has been called the *postmodern paradox* (Dunn, 1998) – the tendency for people to embrace fundamentalist belief systems in order to find a distinct and prescriptive identity that resolves the sense of anomie and moral vacuum in modern industrialised society.

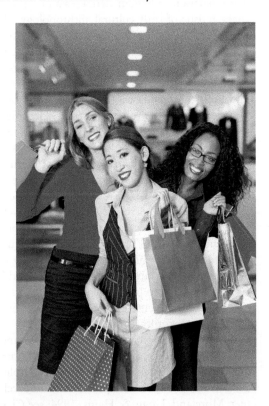

Cultural diversity
These young women have different ethnic origins and clearly enjoy each other's company.

Managing cultural diversity

A 'lesser' problem is the 'simple' question of how to manage cultural diversity in pluralistic societies (Guimond, de la Sablonnière, & Nugier, 2014). This is the cultural application of resolving intergroup conflict that we discussed previously (**Chapter 11**) and touched on earlier in this chapter. At the intergroup level, you will recall, there is increasing support for the idea that groups live more harmoniously together if their cherished identities and practices are respected. Groups will flourish within a superordinate culture that also allows them to feel that their relations to one another are cooperative rather than competitive.

At the cultural and national levels, the debate is largely over the relative merits of assimilationism and multiculturalism (see Prentice & Miller, 1999). For example, Moghaddam (1998, 2008) has contrasted assimilationist policies with those that manage cultural diversity by promoting multiculturalism (see Figure 16.6). Assimilation can be of two kinds, total and 'melting-pot'. The former implies the obliteration of a culture, whereas the latter is less extreme and allows a new form of the dominant culture to emerge.

Multiculturalism is a more positive and embracing view of both dominant and minority cultures. In its laissez-faire form, cultural diversity can continue without help from the host culture. Ethnic enclaves, such as the many Chinatowns that can be found in various cities of the world, Little India in Singapore and expatriate European communities in some Asian cities are examples of laissez-faire multiculturalism. In its active form, a nation's policy sustains cultural diversity. For example, there is government support in Canada and Australia for a variety of activities designed to sustain, to some degree, the cultural integrity of various immigrant groups. At the psychological level, active multiculturalism sustains cultural units that can be either individualistic or collectivist. Belanger and Pinard (1991) have suggested that there is a worldwide trend to sustain collectivist cultures.

There is, of course, another face to cultural diversity. Not everyone experiences or views it as a blessing. Host cultures can view it as a cultural and economic threat that needs to be combated by restrictive and exclusionary policies – out of anger, some people can resort to hate speech and hate crimes. Immigrant groups can feel economically and culturally disadvantaged, and isolated in what are effectively cultural 'ghettos' – out of anger, they are prey to radicalization. Furthermore, assimilationism and multiculturalism along with

Figure 16.6 Types of assimilation and types of cultural pluralism

- Cultural diversity is a challenge to society.
- Immigrant or indigenous minorities may assimilate fully or may leave some mark on the host culture in the process.
- Alternatively, cultural pluralism may flourish, either by accident or design.

Source: Based on Allport (1954b) and Moghaddam (1998).

colourblindness are sophisticated and enduring ideologies that underpin the political process and associated debates over national identity (Guimond, de la Sablonnière, & Nugier, 2014). They are socially divisive and can act as organising principles for highly charged social conflict.

In Western European cities such as London, Paris and Rome, high levels of immigration and large immigrant populations have coincided with a growth of intergroup confrontation and, in some cases, acts of individual or collective terror. The finger of blame has been pointed at many groups, for example North Africans, Muslims and Eastern Europeans. However, the root problem is unlikely to be solely cultural difference – unemployment, economic disadvantage, inadequate education and housing and so forth, all play a very significant role. Where resources are scarce, a zero-sum mentality can prevail, or be whipped up by parties with a vested interest in conflict; and this can often harden intergroup boundaries and sponsor conflict and sustain prejudices (e.g. Sherif, 1966; **Chapter 11**).

Multiculturalism is not only evident but is increasing in many parts of the world. Take three instances: more business is being transacted between China and the West; the expansion of the European community has had large numbers of people relocate from Eastern to Western Europe; and Southern California's largest ethnic group is Hispanics, primarily from Mexico just across the border. In addition, Internet access has made business, governmental, academic and personal communication very easy. In short, globalisation has accelerated. More than ever, these changes require psychologists to have more accurate definitions of culture, and of how it can influence how people think, feel and behave (Hong & Mallorie, 2004). Furthermore, cultures are not set in stone. Cultures in contact, especially living side by side, are probably cultures that will change. A vibrant social psychology is one that can track change both within and between cultures and contribute to cooperative development.

Where to from here?

In making cross-cultural comparisons, we have referred most frequently to those between Western and East Asian cultures. One might say that these cultures provide the most extreme psychological contrasts, but at a more prosaic level, the reason is simple: there has been an upsurge of research by social psychologists in China, Japan and Korea or who work in or were trained in the West but are ethnically East Asian. This does, however, raise the question of where African and South Asian cultures, and to some extent Middle Eastern and Latin American cultures, fit in the mix. Let us close with this observation:

> For many social-personality psychologists who do not engage in cross-cultural research it has been difficult enough to be convinced that those who grow up participating in East Asian cultures can be so different from those who grow up participating in European North American cultures. The notion that one may have to go through this learning process again and again with still different cultures can be unsettling.
>
> Lehman, Chiu and Schaller (2004, p. 689)

Summary

- The roots of social psychology are Western, and the discipline had until recently underemphasised the role of culture. If social psychological processes are really universal, they should stand up to cross-cultural scrutiny.

- People, including psychologists, often use their own cultural standards to interpret the behaviour of people from different cultural backgrounds.

- Anthropologists rather than psychologists conducted almost all research dealing with culture and behaviour in the early twentieth century.
- Cultures vary considerably in social behaviour, including cognitive processes and attributional style. Norms that govern conformity and aggression also differ across cultures.
- People in the East have a different way of viewing themselves and relating to each other from people in the West. Eastern people are collectivist and nurture interdependence, whereas Western people are individualistic and nurture independence.
- Modern systems that characterise cultures include crucial differences in values, in particular, and a different distribution of individualism and collectivism.
- Intercultural communication can sometimes lead to misunderstandings in meaning and intentions.
- Acculturating groups such as migrants face different acculturative choices, varying from retaining their ethnic identity to merging with the dominant culture. Acculturative stress is a common problem.
- Some social psychological principles may be applied across cultures and some may not. There is a tension between fostering principles that may apply only to an indigenous people and the pursuit of principles that are universal.
- The world's societies are increasingly multicultural. To both foster cultural diversity and maintain intergroup harmony is a challenge.

Key terms

Acculturation
Action research
Collectivism
Contact hypothesis
Correspondence bias
Culture of honour
Culture-blind
Culture-bound
Display rules
Entitativity
Ethnographic research
Etic–emic distinction

Fundamental attribution error
Generative psychology
Ideology
Independent self
Indigenous psychology
Individualism
Interdependent self
Kinesics
Level of explanation
Machismo
Meta-analysis
Metatheory

Prisoner's dilemma
Prosocial behaviour
Relational theory
Schema
Social identity theory
Social support network
Subculture of violence
Ultimate attribution error
Values
Völkerpsychologie

Literature, film and TV

Bend It Like Beckham and East Is East

A 2002 film directed by Gurinder Chadha, starring Parminder Nagra as the Indian girl 'Jess'. *Bend it Like Beckham* is a light-hearted film about the clashing of different cultures in the United Kingdom, and about how culture creates expectations and ways of doing things that seem normal – Jess is at the intersection of different role expectations based on culture and gender. In a very similar vein, *East Is East* is a 1999 culture-clash comedy set in Salford in the 1970s – George Kahn is a Pakistani immigrant who runs a fish-and-chip shop and tries to bring up his sons in traditional Pakistani ways. He gradually comes to realise that his sons see themselves as British and will never conform to his strict rules on marriage, food, dress and religion.

Rachel Getting Married

A 2008 film by Jonathan Demme, starring Anne Hathaway. This superbly powerful commentary on, among other things, culture as commodity has as its setting a wealthy wedding party at a country mansion in the Eastern United States. The wedding hosts and guests are liberal, educated and politically correct – but they are cringingly pretentious and inauthentic as they cycle through different cultural practices and symbols as mere decoration and entertainment. The only authentic and genuinely human character at the wedding is the younger daughter Kym, played by Hathaway, who is just out of rehab.

Persepolis

A 2007 French film that explores cultural anomie. The young Marji Statrapi celebrates the removal of the Shah in the 1979 Iranian revolution, but she quickly finds herself an outsider as Iran lurches towards Islamic fundamentalism and a new form of tyranny. For her own protection, her family sends her to Vienna to study and build a new life, but Marji finds it an abrasive and difficult culture that is hard to fit into. When she returns to Iran, things have changed so much that she feels like a stranger in her own culture – she must decide where she belongs.

Crash

An incredibly powerful and sophisticated 2004 Paul Haggis film about cultural diversity, starring Don Cheadle, Sandra Bullock, Matt Dillon and Jennifer Esposito. Set in the cultural melting pot of Los Angeles, a sprawling city of 17 million, it shows how different cultures are often suspicious of one another and how all cultures have stereotypes of one another that can turn ugly when people are anxious and stressed. A sobering film that moves away from the old-fashioned 'white male redneck' caricature of prejudice and raises challenging questions about how and if cultures really can live in harmony in the global village.

Guided questions

1   Can culture constrain the way we think?

2   What do you understand by the *independent* and *interdependent self*, and how is this related to culture?

3   How are *individualism* and *collectivism* connected to the world's cultures?

4   What is *acculturative stress*, and what are the main contributory factors?

5   Should the development of indigenous social psychologies be pursued?

Learn more

Adamopoulos, J., & Kashima, Y. (Eds.) (1999). *Social psychology and cultural context*. London: SAGE. Social and cross-cultural psychologists from around the world discuss the cultural context of social psychology and how social psychological phenomena are influenced by culture.

Berry, J. W., Segall, M. H., and Kağitçibaşi, Ç. (Eds.) (1997). *Handbook of cross-cultural psychology* (2nd ed.). Boston, MA: Allyn and Bacon. A three-volume review of all major areas of cross-cultural psychology.

Chiu, C.-Y., & Hong, Y.-Y. (2007). Cultural processes: Basic principles. In A. W. Kruglanski & E. T. Higgins (Eds.), *Social psychology: Handbook of basic principles* (2nd ed., pp. 785– 804). New York: Guilford Press. Comprehensive and detailed coverage of the social psychology of culture.

Chryssochoou, X. (2004). *Cultural diversity: Its social psychology*. Oxford, UK: Blackwell. An accessible and well-illustrated social psychological discussion of processes, for example migration, in multi-cultural societies.

Fiske, A. P., Kitayama, S., Markus, H. R., & Nisbett, R. E. (1998). The cultural matrix of social psychology. In D. T. Gilbert, S. T. Fiske, & G. Lindzey (Eds.), *The handbook of social psychology* (4th ed., Vol. 2, pp. 915–981). New York: McGraw-Hill. A detailed review of theories and processes underlying the connection between social psychology and culture.

Heine, S. J. (2010). Cultural psychology. In S. T. Fiske, D. T. Gilbert, & G. Lindzey (Eds.), *Handbook of social psychology* (5th ed., Vol. 2, pp. 1423–1464). New York: Wiley. Comprehensive and detailed coverage of the social psychology of culture and the cultural context of social psychology. It includes an excellent treatment of theoretical and methodological issues.

Heine, S. J. (2016). *Cultural psychology* (3rd ed.). New York: Norton. Comprehensive, up-to-date and scholarly coverage of the social psychological study of culture and the impact of culture on behaviour.

Moghaddam, F. M. (1998). *Social psychology: Exploring universals across cultures*. New York: Freeman. A general text that explicitly builds cultural constructs and analysis into the treatment of traditional social psychological topics.

Moghaddam, F. M. (2008). *Multiculturalism and intergroup relations: Psychological implications for democracy in global context*. Washington, DC: American Psychological Association. A thoughtful and detailed social psychological examination of contemporary multicultural society – dangers, opportunities and potential benefits.

Schaller, M., & Crandall, C. S. (Eds.) (2004). *The psychological foundations of culture*. Mahwah, NJ: Erlbaum. Questions about the origins, evolution and nature of culture are examined in relation to cognition, motivation and social interaction.

Smith, P. B., Bond, M. H., & Kağitçibaşi, Ç. (2006). *Understanding social psychology across cultures*. London: SAGE. A substantially revised version of an earlier book (Smith & Bond, 1998), organised around three sections: an overall framework, core issues and global change.

Triandis, H. (1994). *Culture and social behaviour*. New York: McGraw-Hill. An old classic, but still an excellent source of material on cross-cultural differences in behaviour.

Glossary

Abuse syndrome Factors of proximity, stress and power that are associated with the cycle of abuse in some families.

Accentuation effect Overestimation of similarities among people within a category and dissimilarities between people from different categories.

Accentuation principle Categorization accentuates perceived similarities within and differences between groups on dimensions that people believe are correlated with the categorization. The effect is amplified where the categorization and/or dimension has subjective importance, relevance or value.

Accessibility Ease of recall of categories or schemas that we already have in mind.

Acculturation The process whereby individuals learn about the rules of behaviour characteristic of another culture.

Acquiescent response set Tendency to agree with items in an attitude questionnaire. This leads to an ambiguity in interpretation if a high score on an attitude questionnaire can be obtained only by agreeing with all or most items.

Action research The simultaneous activities of undertaking social science research, involving participants in the process and addressing a social problem.

Actor–observer effect Tendency to attribute our own behaviours externally and others' behaviours internally.

Affect–infusion model Cognition is infused with affect such that social judgements reflect current mood.

Ageism Prejudice and discrimination against people based on their age.

Agentic state A frame of mind thought by Milgram to characterise unquestioning obedience, in which people as agents transfer personal responsibility to the person giving orders.

Altruism A special form of helping behaviour, sometimes costly, that shows concern for fellow human beings and is performed without expectation of personal gain.

Analogue Device or measure intended to faithfully mimic the 'real thing'.

Anchoring and adjustment A cognitive short cut in which inferences are tied to initial standards or schemas.

Arbitration Process of intergroup conflict resolution in which a neutral third party is invited to impose a mutually binding settlement.

Archival research Non-experimental method involving the assembly of data, or reports of data, collected by others.

Associative meaning Illusory correlation in which items are seen as belonging together because they 'ought' to, on the basis of prior expectations.

Associative network Model of memory in which nodes or ideas are connected by associative links along which cognitive activation can spread.

Assortative mating A non-random coupling of individuals based on their resemblance to each other on one or more characteristics.

Attachment behaviour The tendency of an infant to maintain close physical proximity with the mother or primary caregiver.

Attachment styles Descriptions of the nature of people's close relationships, thought to be established in childhood.

Attitude (a) A relatively enduring organisation of beliefs, feelings and behavioural tendencies towards socially significant objects, groups, events or symbols. (b) A general feeling or evaluation – positive or negative – about some person, object or issue.

Attitude change Any significant modification of an individual's attitude. In the persuasion process this involves the communicator, the communication, the medium used and the characteristics of the audience. Attitude change can also occur by inducing someone to perform an act that runs counter to an existing attitude.

Attitude formation The process of forming our attitudes, mainly from our own experiences, the influences of others and our emotional reactions.

Attribution The process of assigning a cause to our own behaviour, and that of others.

Attributional style An individual (personality) predisposition to make a certain type of causal attribution for behaviour.

Audience Intended target of a persuasive communication.

Audience effects Impact of the presence of others on individual task performance.

Authoritarian personality Personality syndrome originating in childhood that predisposes individuals to be prejudiced.

Autocratic leaders Leaders who use a style based on giving orders to followers.

Autokinesis Optical illusion in which a pinpoint of light shining in complete darkness appears to move about.

Automatic activation According to Fazio, attitudes that have a strong evaluative link to situational cues are more likely to automatically come to mind from memory.

Availability heuristic A cognitive short-cut in which the frequency or likelihood of an event is based on how quickly instances or associations come to mind.

Averageness effect Humans have evolved to prefer average and symmetrical faces to those with unusual or distinctive features.

Averaging A method of forming positive or negative impressions by averaging the valence of all the constituent attributes.

Back-channel communication Verbal and non-verbal ways in which listeners let speakers know they are still listening.

Balance theory According to Heider, people prefer attitudes that are consistent with each other over those that are inconsistent. A person (P) tries to maintain consistency in attitudes to, and relationships with, other people (O) and elements of the environment (X).

Bargaining Process of intergroup conflict resolution where representatives reach agreement through direct negotiation.

Base-rate information Pallid, factual, statistical information about an entire class of events.

Behaviour What people actually do that can be objectively measured.

Behavioural decision theory Set of normative models (ideal processes) for making accurate social inferences.

Behaviourism An emphasis on explaining observable behaviour in terms of reinforcement schedules.

Belief congruence theory The theory that similar beliefs promote liking and social harmony among people while dissimilar beliefs produce dislike and prejudice.

Belief in a just world Belief that the world is a just and predictable place where good things happen to 'good people' and bad things to 'bad people'.

Big Five The five major personality dimensions of extraversion/surgency, agreeableness, conscientiousness, emotional stability and intellect/openness to experience.

Biosocial theories In the context of aggression, theories that emphasise an innate component, though not the existence of a full-blown instinct.

BIRGing Basking in Reflected Glory; that is, name-dropping to link yourself with desirable people or groups and thus improve other people's impression of you.

Bogus pipeline technique A measurement technique that leads people to believe that a 'lie detector' can monitor their emotional responses, thus measuring their true attitudes.

Bookkeeping Gradual schema change through the accumulation of bits of schema-inconsistent information.

Brainstorming Uninhibited generation of as many ideas as possible in a group, in order to enhance group creativity.

Bystander-calculus model In attending to an emergency, the bystander calculates the perceived costs and benefits of providing help compared with those associated with not helping.

Bystander effect People are less likely to help in an emergency when they are with others than when alone. The greater the number, the less likely it is that anyone will help.

Bystander intervention This occurs when an individual breaks out of the role of a bystander and helps another person in an emergency.

Case study In-depth analysis of a single case (or individual).

Catharsis A dramatic release of pent-up feelings: the idea that aggressive motivation is 'drained' by acting against a frustrating object (or substitute), or by a vicarious experience.

Cathartic hypothesis The notion that acting aggressively, or even just viewing aggressive material, reduces feelings of anger and aggression.

Causal schemata Experience-based beliefs about how certain types of causes interact to produce an effect.

Central traits Traits that have a disproportionate influence on the configuration of final impressions, in Asch's configural model of impression formation.

Charismatic leadership Leadership style based upon the leader's (perceived) possession of charisma.

Cognition The knowledge, beliefs, thoughts and ideas that people have about themselves and their environment. May also refer to mental processes through which knowledge is acquired, including perception, memory and thinking.

Cognitive algebra Approach to the study of impression formation that focuses on how people combine attributes that have valence into an overall positive or negative impression.

Cognitive alternatives Belief that the status quo is unstable and illegitimate, and that social competition with the dominant group is the appropriate strategy to improve social identity.

Cognitive consistency A model of social cognition in which people try to reduce inconsistency among their cognitions, because they find inconsistency unpleasant.

Cognitive consistency theories A group of attitude theories stressing that people try to maintain internal consistency, order and agreement among their various cognitions.

Cognitive dissonance State of psychological tension produced by simultaneously having two opposing cognitions. People are motivated to reduce the tension, often by changing or rejecting one of the cognitions. Festinger proposed that we seek harmony in our attitudes, beliefs and behaviours and try to reduce tension from inconsistency among these elements.

Cognitive miser A model of social cognition that characterises people as using the least complex and demanding cognitions that are able to produce generally adaptive behaviours.

Cognitive theories Explanations of behaviour in terms of the way people actively interpret and represent their experiences and then plan action.

Cohesiveness The property of a group that affectively binds people, as group members, to one another and to the group as a whole, giving the group a sense of solidarity and oneness.

Collective aggression Unified aggression by a group of individuals, who may not even know one another, against another individual or group.

Collective behaviour The behaviour of people en masse – such as in a crowd, protest or riot.

Collectivism Societal structure and world view in which people prioritise group loyalty, commitment and conformity, and belonging and fitting in to groups, over standing out as an isolated individual.

Commitment The desire or intention to continue an interpersonal relationship.

Commons dilemma Social dilemma in which cooperation by all benefits all, but competition by all harms all.

Communication Transfer of meaningful information from one person to another.

Communication accommodation theory Modification of verbal and non-verbal communication styles to the context (e.g. listener, situation) of a face-to-face interaction – an extension of speech accommodation theory to incorporate non-verbal communication.

Communication network Set of rules governing the possibility or ease of communication between different roles in a group.

Companionate love The caring and affection for another person that usually arises from sharing time together.

Comparison level A standard that develops over time, allowing us to judge whether a new relationship is profitable or not.

Compliance Superficial, public and transitory change in behaviour and expressed attitudes in response to requests, coercion or group pressure.

Conciliation Process whereby groups make cooperative gestures to one another in the hope of avoiding an escalation of conflict.

Configural model Asch's *Gestalt*-based model of impression formation, in which central traits play a disproportionate role in configuring the final impression.

Confirmation bias The tendency to seek, interpret and create information that verifies existing explanations for the cause of an event.

Conformity Deep-seated, private and enduring change in behaviour and attitudes due to group pressure.

Conformity bias Tendency for social psychology to treat group influence as a one-way process in which individuals or minorities always conform to majorities.

Confounding Where two or more independent variables covary in such a way that it is impossible to know which has caused the effect.

Consensus information Information about the extent to which other people react in the same way to a stimulus X.

Consistency information Information about the extent to which a behaviour Y always co-occurs with a stimulus X.

Conspiracy theory Explanation of widespread, complex and worrying events in terms of the premeditated actions of small groups of highly organised conspirators.

Constructs Abstract or theoretical concepts or variables that are not observable and are used to explain or clarify a phenomenon.

Consummate love Sternberg argues that this is the ultimate form of love, involving passion, intimacy and commitment.

Contact hypothesis The view that bringing members of opposing social groups together will improve intergroup relations and reduce prejudice and discrimination.

Contingency theories Theories of leadership that consider the leadership effectiveness of particular behaviours or behavioural styles to be contingent on the nature of the leadership situation.

Conversion Sudden schema change as a consequence of gradual accumulation of schema-inconsistent information.

Conversion effect When minority influence brings about a sudden and dramatic internal and private change in the attitudes of a majority.

Coordination loss Deterioration in group performance compared with individual performance, due to problems in coordinating behaviour.

Correlation Where changes in one variable reliably map onto changes in another variable, but it cannot be determined which of the two variables *caused* the change.

Correspondence bias A general attribution bias in which people have an inflated tendency to see behaviour as reflecting (corresponding to) stable underlying personality attributes.

Correspondent inference Causal attribution of behaviour to underlying dispositions.

Cost-reward ratio Tenet of social exchange theory, according to which liking for another is determined by calculating what it will cost to be reinforced by that person.

Covariation model Kelley's theory of causal attribution – people assign the cause of behaviour to the factor that covaries most closely with the behaviour.

Cultural norms Norms whose origin is part of the tradition of a culture.

Cultural values theory The view that people in groups use members' opinions about the position valued in the wider culture, and then adjust their views in that direction for social approval reasons.

Culture of honour A culture that endorses male violence as a way of addressing threats to social reputation or economic position.

Culture-blind Theory and data untested outside the host culture.

Culture-bound Theory and data conditioned by a specific cultural background.

Data Publicly verifiable observations.

Dehumanisation Stripping people of their dignity and humanity.

Deindividuation Process whereby people lose their sense of socialised individual identity and engage in unsocialised, often antisocial, behaviours.

Demand characteristics Features of an experiment that seem to 'demand' a certain response.

Democratic leaders Leaders who use a style based on consultation and obtaining agreement and consent from followers.

Dependent variables Variables that change as a consequence of changes in the independent variable.

Depersonalisation The perception and treatment of self and others not as unique individual persons but as prototypical embodiments of a social group.

Desensitisation A serious reduction in a person's responsiveness to material that usually evokes a strong emotional reaction, such as violence or sexuality.

Diffuse status characteristics Information about a person's abilities that are only obliquely relevant to the group's task, and derive mainly from large-scale category memberships outside the group.

Diffusion of responsibility Tendency of an individual to assume that others will take responsibility (as a result, no one does). This is a hypothesised cause of the bystander effect.

Disconfirmation bias The tendency to notice, refute and regard as weak, arguments that contradict our prior beliefs.

Discount If there is no consistent relationship between a specific cause and a specific behaviour, that cause is discounted in favour of some other cause.

Discourse Entire communicative event or episode located in a situational and sociohistorical context.

Discourse analysis A set of methods used to analyse text – in particular, naturally occurring language – in order to understand its meaning and significance.

Discrimination The behavioural expression of prejudice.

Disinhibition A breakdown in the learnt controls (social mores) against behaving impulsively or, in this context, aggressively. For some people, alcohol has a disinhibiting effect.

Displacement Psychodynamic concept referring to the transfer of negative feelings on to an individual or group other than that which originally caused the negative feelings.

Display rules Cultural and situational rules that dictate how appropriate it is to express emotions in a given context.

Distinctiveness information Information about whether a person's reaction occurs only with one stimulus, or is a common reaction to many stimuli.

Distraction–conflict theory The physical presence of members of the same species is distracting and produces conflict between attending to the task and attending to the audience.

Distributive justice The fairness of the outcome of a decision.

Dogmatism Cognitive style that is rigid and intolerant and predisposes people to be prejudiced.

Door-in-the-face tactic Multiple-request technique to gain compliance, in which the focal request is preceded by a larger request that is bound to be refused.

Double-blind Procedure to reduce experimenter effects, in which the experimenter is unaware of the experimental conditions.

Drive theory Zajonc's theory that the physical presence of members of the same species instinctively causes arousal that motivates performance of habitual behaviour patterns.

Dual-process dependency model General model of social influence in which two separate processes operate – dependency on others for social approval and for information about reality.

Effort justification A special case of cognitive dissonance: inconsistency is experienced when a person makes a considerable effort to achieve a modest goal.

Egoistic relative deprivation A feeling of personally having less than we feel we are entitled to, relative to our aspirations or to other individuals.

Elaboration–likelihood model Petty and Cacioppo's model of attitude change: when people attend to a message carefully, they use a central route to process it; otherwise they use a peripheral route. This model competes with the heuristic–systematic model.

Emblems Gestures that replace or stand in for spoken language.

Emergency situation Often involves an unusual event, can vary in nature, is unplanned and requires a quick response.

Emergent norm theory Collective behaviour is regulated by norms based on distinctive behaviour that arises in the initially normless crowd.

Emotion-in-relationships model Close relationships provide a context that elicits strong emotions due to the increased probability of behaviour interrupting interpersonal expectations.

Empathic concern An element in Batson's theory of helping behaviour. In contrast to personal distress (which may lead us to flee from the situation), it includes feelings of warmth, being soft-hearted and having compassion for a person in need.

Empathy Ability to feel another person's experiences; identifying with and experiencing another person's emotions, thoughts and attitudes.

Empathy costs of not helping Piliavin's view that failing to help can cause distress to a bystander who empathises with a victim's plight.

Entitativity The property of a group that makes it seem like a coherent, distinct and unitary entity.

Equity theory A special case of social exchange theory that defines a relationship as equitable when the ratio of inputs to outcomes are seen to be the same by both partners.

Essentialism Pervasive tendency to consider behaviour to reflect underlying and immutable, often innate, properties of people or the groups they belong to.

Ethnocentrism Evaluative preference for all aspects of our own group relative to other groups.

Ethnographic research Descriptive study of a specific society, based on fieldwork, and requiring immersion of the researcher in the everyday life of its people.

Ethnolinguistic group Social group defined principally in terms of its language.

Ethnolinguistic identity theory Application and extension of social identity theory to deal with language behaviour of ethnolinguistic groups.

Ethnolinguistic vitality Concept describing objective features of an inter-ethnic context that influence language, and ultimately the cultural survival or disappearance of an ethnolinguistic group.

Ethnomethodology Method devised by Garfinkel, involving the violation of hidden norms to reveal their presence.

Ethology Approach that argues that animal behaviour should be studied in the species' natural physical and social environment. Behaviour is genetically determined and is controlled by natural selection.

Etic–emic distinction Contrast between psychological constructs that are relatively culture-universal and those that are relatively culture-specific.

Evaluation apprehension model The argument that the physical presence of members of the same species causes drive because people have learnt to be apprehensive about being evaluated.

Evaluative conditioning A stimulus will become more liked or less liked when it is consistently paired with stimuli that are either positive or negative.

Evolutionary psychology A theoretical approach that explains 'useful' psychological traits, such as memory, perception or language, as adaptations through natural selection.

Evolutionary social psychology An extension of evolutionary psychology that views complex social behaviour as adaptive, helping the individual, kin and the species as a whole to survive.

Excitation-transfer model The expression of aggression is a function of learnt behaviour, some excitation from another source, and the person's interpretation of the arousal state.

Exemplars Specific instances of a member of a category.

Expectancy–value model Direct experience with an attitude object informs a person how much that object should be liked or disliked in the future.

Expectation states theory Theory of the emergence of roles as a consequence of people's status-based expectations about others' performance.

Experimental method Intentional manipulation of independent variables in order to investigate effects on one or more dependent variables.

Experimental realism Psychological impact of the manipulations in an experiment.

Experimenter effects Effects produced or influenced by clues to the hypotheses under examination, inadvertently communicated by the experimenter.

Extended contact Knowing about an ingroup member who shares a close relationship with an outgroup member can improve one's own attitudes towards the outgroup.

External (or situational) attribution Assigning the cause of our own or others' behaviour to external or environmental factors.

External validity Similarity between circumstances surrounding an experiment and circumstances encountered in everyday life.

Face-ism Media depiction that gives greater prominence to the head and less prominence to the body for men, but vice versa for women.

False consensus effect Seeing our own behaviour as being more typical than it really is.

Familiarity As we become more familiar with a stimulus (even another person), we feel more comfortable with it and we like it more.

Family resemblance Defining property of category membership.

Fear of social blunders The dread of acting inappropriately or of making a foolish mistake witnessed by others. The desire to avoid ridicule inhibits effective responses to an emergency by members of a group.

Fighting instinct Innate impulse to aggress which ethologists claim is shared by humans with other animals.

fMRI (functional magnetic resonance imaging) A method used in social neuroscience to measure where electrochemical activity in the brain is occurring.

Foot-in-the-door tactic Multiple-request technique to gain compliance, in which the focal request is preceded by a smaller request that is bound to be accepted.

Forewarning Advance knowledge that one is to be the target of a persuasion attempt. Forewarning often produces resistance to persuasion.

Frame of reference Complete range of subjectively conceivable positions on some attitudinal or behavioural dimension, which relevant people can occupy in a particular context.

Fraternalistic relative deprivation Sense that our group has less than it is entitled to, relative to its aspirations or to other groups.

Free-rider effect Gaining the benefits of group membership by avoiding costly obligations of membership and by allowing other members to incur those costs.

Frustration–aggression hypothesis Theory that all frustration leads to aggression, and all aggression comes from frustration. Used to explain prejudice and intergroup aggression.

Fundamental attribution error Bias in attributing another's behaviour more to internal than to situational causes.

Fuzzy sets Categories are considered to be fuzzy sets of features organised around a prototype.

Gaze Looking at someone's eyes.

Gender Sex-stereotypical attributes of a person.

General aggression model Anderson's model that includes both personal and situational factors, and cognitive and affective processes in accounting for different kinds of aggression.

Generative psychology A psychology intended to generate positive social change through direct intervention.

Genocide The ultimate expression of prejudice by exterminating an entire social group.

Gestalt psychology Perspective in which the whole influences constituent parts rather than vice versa.

Gestures Meaningful body movements and postures.

Glass ceiling An invisible barrier that prevents women, and minorities in general, from attaining top leadership positions.

Glass cliff A tendency for women rather than men to be appointed to precarious leadership positions associated with a high probability of failure and criticism.

Great person theory Perspective on leadership that attributes effective leadership to innate or acquired individual characteristics.

Group Two or more people who share a common definition and evaluation of themselves and behave in accordance with such a definition.

Group mind McDougall's idea that people adopt a qualitatively different mode of thinking when in a group.

Group polarisation Tendency for group discussion to produce more extreme group decisions than the mean of members' pre-discussion opinions, in the direction favoured by the mean.

Group socialisation Dynamic relationship between the group and its members that describes the passage of members through a group in terms of commitment and of changing roles.

Group structure Division of a group into different roles that often differ with respect to status and prestige.

Group value model View that procedural justice within groups makes members feel valued, and thus leads to enhanced commitment to and identification with the group.

Groupthink A mode of thinking in highly cohesive groups in which the desire to reach unanimous agreement overrides the motivation to adopt proper rational decision-making procedures.

Guttman scale A scale that contains either favourable or unfavourable statements arranged hierarchically. Agreement with a strong statement implies agreement with weaker ones; disagreement with a weak one implies disagreement with stronger ones.

Hate crimes A class of violence against members of a stereotyped minority group.

Hedonic relevance Refers to behaviour that has important direct consequences for self.

Helping behaviour Acts that intentionally benefit someone else.

Heuristics Cognitive short-cuts that provide adequately accurate inferences for most of us most of the time.

Heuristic–systematic model Chaiken's model of attitude change: when people attend to a message carefully, they use systematic processing; otherwise they process information by using heuristics, or 'mental short-cuts'. This model competes with the elaboration–likelihood model.

Hospitalism A state of apathy and depression noted among institutionalised infants deprived of close contact with a caregiver.

Hypotheses Empirically testable predictions about what co-occurs with what, or what causes what.

Ideology A systematically interrelated set of beliefs whose primary function is explanation. It circumscribes thinking, making it difficult for the holder to escape from its mould.

Idiosyncrasy credit Hollander's transactional theory, in which followers reward leaders for achieving group goals by allowing them to be relatively idiosyncratic.

Illocution Words placed in sequence and the context in which this is done.

Illusion of control Belief that we have more control over our world than we really do.

Illusion of group effectivity Experience-based belief that we produce more and better ideas in groups than alone.

Illusory correlation Cognitive exaggeration of the degree of co-occurrence of two stimuli or events, or the perception of a co-occurrence where none exists.

Implicit association test Reaction-time test to measure attitudes – particularly unpopular attitudes that people might conceal.

Implicit personality theories Idiosyncratic and personal ways of characterising other people and explaining their behaviour.

Impression management People's use of various strategies to get other people to view them in a positive light.

Independent self A self that is relatively separate, internal and unique.

Independent variables Features of a situation that change of their own accord or can be manipulated by an experimenter to have effects on a dependent variable.

Indigenous psychology A psychology created by and for a specific cultural group – based on the claim that culture can be understood only from within its own perspective.

Individualism Societal structure and world view in which people prioritise standing out as an individual over fitting in as a group member.

Induced compliance A special case of cognitive dissonance: inconsistency is experienced when a person is persuaded to behave in a way that is contrary to an attitude.

Information integration theory The idea that a person's attitude can be estimated by averaging across the positive and negative ratings of the object.

Information processing The evaluation of information; in relation to attitudes, the means by which people acquire knowledge and form and change attitudes.

Informational influence An influence to accept information from another as evidence about reality.

Ingratiation Strategic attempt to get someone to like you in order to obtain compliance with a request.

Ingroup favouritism Behaviour that favours one's own group over other groups.

Initiation rites Often painful or embarrassing public procedure to mark group members' movements from one role to another.

Inoculation A way of making people resistant to persuasion. By providing them with a diluted counter-argument, they can build up effective refutations to a later, stronger argument.

Instinct Innate drive or impulse, genetically transmitted.

Institutionalised aggression Aggression that is given formal or informal recognition and social legitimacy by being incorporated into rules and norms.

Interdependent self A self that is relatively dependent on social relations and has more fuzzy boundaries.

Intergroup attribution Process of assigning the cause of one's own or others' behaviour to group membership.

Intergroup behaviour Behaviour among individuals that is regulated by those individuals' awareness of and identification with different social groups.

Intergroup differentiation Behaviour that emphasises differences between our own group and other groups.

Intergroup emotions theory (IET) Theory that, in group contexts, appraisals of personal harm or benefit in a situation operate at the level of social identity and thus produce mainly positive ingroup and negative outgroup emotions.

Internal (or dispositional) attribution Process of assigning the cause of our own or others' behaviour to internal or dispositional factors.

Internal validity Psychological impact of the manipulations in an experiment.

J-curve A graphical figure that captures the way in which relative deprivation arises when attainments suddenly fall short of rising expectations.

Just-world hypothesis According to Lerner and Miller, people need to believe that the world is a just place where they get what they deserve. As evidence of undeserved suffering undermines this belief, people may conclude that victims deserve their fate.

Kinesics Linguistics of body communication.

Laboratory A place, usually a room, in which data are collected, usually by experimental methods.

Laissez-faire leaders Leaders who use a style based on disinterest in followers.

Language A system of sounds that convey meaning because of shared grammatical and semantic rules.

Leader behaviour description questionnaire (LBDQ) Scale devised by the Ohio State leadership researchers to measure leadership behaviour and distinguish between 'initiating structure' and 'consideration' dimensions.

Leader categorization theory We have a variety of schemas about how different types of leaders behave in different leadership situations. When a leader is categorized as a particular type of leader, the schema fills in details about how that leader will behave.

Leader–member exchange (LMX) theory Theory of leadership in which effective leadership rests on the ability of the leader to develop good-quality personalised exchange relationships with individual members.

Leadership Getting group members to achieve the group's goals.

Learning by direct experience Acquiring a behaviour because we were rewarded for it.

Learning by vicarious experience Acquiring a behaviour after observing that another person was rewarded for it.

Least-preferred co-worker (LPC) scale Fiedler's scale for measuring leadership style in terms of favourability of attitude towards one's least-preferred co-worker.

Level of explanation The types of concepts, mechanisms and language used to explain a phenomenon.

Likert scale Scale that evaluates how strongly people agree/disagree with favourable/unfavourable statements about an attitude object.

Linguistic relativity View that language determines thought and therefore people who speak different languages see the world in very different ways.

Locution Words placed in sequence.

Looking-glass self The self derived from seeing ourselves as others see us.

Love A combination of emotions, thoughts and actions which are often powerful, and usually associated with intimate relationships.

Low-ball tactic Technique for inducing compliance in which a person who agrees to a request still feels committed after finding that there are hidden costs.

Machismo A code in which challenges, abuse and even differences of opinion must be met with fists or other weapons.

Matched-guise technique Research methodology to measure people's attitudes towards a speaker based solely on speech style.

Mediation Process of intergroup conflict resolution where a neutral third party intervenes in the negotiation process to facilitate a settlement.

Membership group Kelley's term for a group to which we belong by some objective external criterion.

Mere exposure effect Repeated exposure to an object results in greater attraction to that object.

Mere presence Refers to an entirely passive and unresponsive audience that is only physically present.

Message Communication from a source directed to an audience.

Meta-analysis Statistical procedure that combines data from different studies to measure the overall reliability and strength of specific effects.

Meta-contrast principle The prototype of a group is that position within the group that has the largest ratio of 'differences to ingroup positions' to 'differences to outgroup positions'.

Metatheory Set of interrelated concepts and principles concerning which theories or types of theory are appropriate.

Mindlessness The act of agreeing to a request without giving it a thought. A small request is likely to be agreed to, even if a spurious reason is provided.

Minimal group paradigm Experimental methodology to investigate the effect of social categorization alone on behaviour.

Minimax strategy In relating to others, we try to minimise the costs and maximise the rewards that accrue.

Minority influence Social influence processes whereby numerical or power minorities change the attitudes of the majority.

Modelling Tendency for a person to reproduce the actions, attitudes and emotional responses exhibited by a real-life or symbolic model. Also called *observational learning*.

Moderator variable A variable that qualifies an otherwise simple hypothesis with a view to improving its predictive power (e.g. A causes B, but only when C (the moderator) is present).

Motivated tactician A model of social cognition that characterises people as having multiple cognitive strategies available, which they choose among on the basis of personal goals, motives and needs.

Multifactor leadership questionnaire (MLQ) The most popular and widely used scale to measure transactional and transformational leadership.

Multiple-act criterion Term for a general behavioural index based on an average or combination of several specific behaviours.

Multiple requests Tactics for gaining compliance using a two-step procedure: the first request functions as a set-up for the second, real request.

Mundane realism Similarity between circumstances surrounding an experiment and circumstances encountered in everyday life.

Naive psychologist (or scientist) Model of social cognition that characterises people as using rational, scientific-like, cause–effect analyses to understand their world.

Narcissism A personality trait that is volatile, comprising self-love and an inflated or grandiose view of oneself.

Nature–nurture controversy Classic debate about whether genetic or environmental factors determine human behaviour. Scientists generally accept that it is an interaction of both.

Need to affiliate The urge to form connections and make contact with other people.

Neo-associationist analysis A view of aggression according to which mass media may provide images of violence to an audience that later translate into antisocial acts.

Neo-behaviourist One who attempts to explain observable behaviour in terms of contextual factors and unobservable intervening constructs such as beliefs, feelings and motives.

Neo-Freudians Psychoanalytic theorists who modified the original theories of Freud.

Non-common effects Effects of behaviour that are relatively exclusive to that behaviour rather than other behaviours.

Non-verbal communication Transfer of meaningful information from one person to another by means other than written or spoken language (e.g. gaze, facial expression, posture, touch).

Normative decision theory (NDT) A contingency theory of leadership that focuses on the effectiveness of different leadership styles in group decision-making contexts.

Normative influence An influence to conform to the positive expectation of others, to gain social approval or to avoid social disapproval.

Normative models Ideal processes for making accurate social inferences.

Norms Attitudinal and behavioural uniformities that define group membership and differentiate between groups.

Objectification theory Women's life experiences and gender socialisation routinely include experiences of sexual objectification.

One-component attitude model An attitude consists of affect towards or evaluation of the object.

Operational definition Defines a theoretical term in a way that allows it to be to manipulated or measured.

Optimal distinctiveness People strive to achieve a balance between conflicting motives for inclusiveness and separateness, expressed in groups as a balance between intragroup differentiation and intragroup homogenisation.

Outcome bias Belief that the outcomes of a behaviour were intended by the person who chose the behaviour.

Overjustification effect In the absence of obvious external determinants of our behaviour, we assume that we freely choose the behaviour because we enjoy it.

Paired distinctiveness Illusory correlation in which items are seen as belonging together because they share some unusual feature.

Paralanguage The non-linguistic accompaniments of speech (e.g. stress, pitch, speed, tone, pauses).

Partner regulation Strategy that encourages a partner to match an ideal standard of behaviour.

Passionate (or romantic) love State of intense absorption in another person involving physiological arousal.

Path–goal theory (PGT) A contingency theory of leadership that can also be classified as a transactional theory – it focuses on how 'structuring' and 'consideration' behaviours motivate followers.

Peace studies Multidisciplinary movement dedicated to the study and promotion of peace.

Peripheral traits Traits that have an insignificant influence on the configuration of final impressions, in Asch's configural model of impression formation.

Personal attraction Liking for someone based on idiosyncratic preferences and interpersonal relationships.

Personal constructs Idiosyncratic and personal ways of characterising other people.

Personal costs of not helping Piliavin's view that not helping a victim in distress can be costly to a bystander (e.g. experiencing blame).

Personal identity The self defined in terms of unique personal attributes or unique interpersonal relationships.

Personal space Physical space around people's bodies which they treat as a part of themselves.

Personalism Behaviour that appears to be directly intended to benefit or harm oneself rather than others.

Persuasive arguments theory View that people in groups are persuaded by novel information that supports their initial position, and thus become more extreme in their endorsement of their initial position.

Persuasive communication Message intended to change an attitude and related behaviours of an audience.

Positivism Non-critical acceptance of science as the only way to arrive at true knowledge: science as religion.

Post-decisional conflict The dissonance associated with behaving in a counter-attitudinal way. Dissonance can be reduced by bringing the attitude into line with the behaviour.

Power Capacity to influence others while resisting their attempts to influence.

Prejudice Unfavourable attitude towards a social group and its members.

Primacy An order of presentation effect in which earlier presented information has a disproportionate influence on social cognition.

Priming Activation of accessible categories or schemas in memory that influence how we process new information.

Prior commitment An individual's agreement in advance to be responsible if trouble occurs: for example, committing oneself to protect the property of another person against theft.

Prisoner's dilemma Two-person game in which both parties are torn between competition and cooperation and, depending on mutual choices, both can win or both can lose.

Procedural justice The fairness of the procedures used to make a decision.

Process loss Deterioration in group performance in comparison to individual performance due to the whole range of possible interferences among members.

Production blocking Reduction in individual creativity and productivity in brainstorming groups due to interruptions and turn-taking.

Profit This flows from a relationship when the rewards that accrue from continued interaction exceed the costs.

Prosocial behaviour Acts that are positively valued by society.

Protection motivation theory Adopting a healthy behaviour requires cognitive balancing between the perceived threat of illness and one's capacity to cope with the health regimen.

Prototype Cognitive representation of the typical/ideal defining features of a category.

Proxemics Study of interpersonal distance.

Proximity The factor of living close by is known to play an important role in the early stages of forming a friendship.

Racism Prejudice and discrimination against people based on their ethnicity or race.

Radical behaviourist One who explains observable behaviour in terms of reinforcement schedules, without recourse to any intervening unobservable (e.g. cognitive) constructs.

Reactance Brehm's theory that people try to protect their freedom to act. When they perceive that this freedom has been curtailed, they will act to regain it.

Realistic conflict theory Sherif's theory of intergroup conflict that explains intergroup behaviour in terms of the nature of goal relations between groups.

Received pronunciation (RP) Standard, high-status, spoken variety of English.

Recency An order of presentation effect in which later presented information has a disproportionate influence on social cognition.

Reciprocity principle This is sometimes called the reciprocity norm, or 'the law of doing unto others what they do to you'. It can refer to an attempt to gain compliance by first doing someone a favour, or to mutual aggression, or to mutual attraction.

Reductionism Explanation of a phenomenon in terms of the language and concepts of a lower level of analysis, usually with a loss of explanatory power.

Reference group Kelley's term for a group that is psychologically significant for our behaviour and attitudes.

Referent informational influence Pressure to conform to a group norm that defines oneself as a group member.

Regression Tendency for initial observations of instances from a category to be more extreme than subsequent observations.

Regulatory focus theory A promotion focus causes people to be approach-oriented in constructing a sense of self; a prevention focus causes people to be more cautious and avoidant in constructing a sense of self.

Reinforcement–affect model Model of attraction which postulates that we like people who are around when we experience a positive feeling (which itself is reinforcing).

Relational model of authority in groups Tyler's account of how effective authority in groups rests upon fairness- and justice-based relations between leader and followers.

Relational theory An analysis based on structures of meaningful social relationships that recur across cultures.

Relationship dissolution model Duck's proposal of the sequence through which most long-term relationships proceed if they finally break down.

Relative deprivation A sense of having less than we feel entitled to.

Relative homogeneity effect Tendency to see outgroup members as all the same, and ingroup members as more differentiated.

Releasers Specific stimuli in the environment thought by ethologists to trigger aggressive responses.

Representativeness heuristic A cognitive short-cut in which instances are assigned to categories or types on the basis of overall similarity or resemblance to the category.

Reverse discrimination The practice of publicly being prejudiced in favour of a minority group in order to deflect accusations of prejudice and discrimination against that group.

Ringelmann effect Individual effort on a task diminishes as group size increases.

Risky shift Tendency for group discussion to produce group decisions that are more risky than the mean of members' pre-discussion opinions, but only if the pre-discussion mean already favoured risk.

Role congruity theory Mainly applied to the gender gap in leadership – because social stereotypes of women are inconsistent with people's schemas of effective leadership, women are evaluated as poor leaders.

Roles Patterns of behaviour that distinguish between different activities within the group, and that interrelate to one another for the greater good of the group.

Salience Property of a stimulus that makes it stand out in relation to other stimuli and attract attention.

Scapegoat Individual or group that becomes the target for anger and frustration caused by a different individual or group or some other set of circumstances.

Schema Cognitive structure that represents knowledge about a concept or type of stimulus, including its attributes and the relations among those attributes.

Schism Division of a group into subgroups that differ in their attitudes, values or ideology.

Science Method for studying nature that involves the collecting of data to test hypotheses.

Script A schema about an event.

Selective exposure hypothesis People tend to avoid potentially dissonant information.

Self-affirmation theory The theory that people reduce the impact of threat to their self-concept by focusing on and affirming their competence in some other area.

Self-assessment The motivation to seek out new information about ourselves in order to find out what sort of person we really are.

Self-categorization theory Turner and associates' theory of how the process of categorizing oneself as a group member produces social identity and group and intergroup behaviours.

Self-disclosure The sharing of intimate information and feelings with another person.

Self-discrepancy theory Higgins's theory about the consequences of making actual – ideal and actual – 'ought' self-comparisons that reveal self-discrepancies.

Self-efficacy Expectations that we have about our capacity to succeed in particular tasks.

Self-enhancement The motivation to develop and promote a favourable image of self.

Self-esteem Feelings about and evaluations of oneself.

Self-evaluation maintenance model People who are constrained to make esteem-damaging upward comparisons can underplay or deny similarity to the target, or they can withdraw from their relationship with the target.

Self-fulfilling prophecy Expectations and assumptions about a person that influence our interaction with that person and eventually change their behaviour in line with our expectations.

Self-handicapping Publicly making advance external attributions for our anticipated failure or poor performance in a forthcoming event.

Self-monitoring Carefully controlling how we present ourselves. There are situational differences and individual differences in self-monitoring.

Self-perception theory Bem's idea that we gain knowledge of ourselves only by making self-attributions; for example, we infer our own attitudes from our own behaviour.

Self-presentation A deliberate effort to act in ways that create a particular impression, usually favourable, of ourselves.

Self-regulation Strategies that we use to match our behaviour to an ideal or 'ought' standard.

Self-serving biases Attributional distortions that protect or enhance self-esteem or the self-concept.

Self-verification Seeking out information that verifies and confirms what we already know about ourselves.

Semantic differential An attitude measure that asks for a rating on a scale composed of bipolar (opposite) adjectives. (Also a technique for measuring the connotative meaning of words or concepts.)

Sex role Behaviour deemed sex-stereotypically appropriate.

Sexism Prejudice and discrimination against people based on their gender.

Sexual selection theory Sex differences in behaviour are determined by evolutionary history rather than society.

Similarity of attitudes One of the most important positive, psychological determinants of attraction.

Situational control Fiedler's classification of task characteristics in terms of how much control effective task performance requires.

Sleeper effect The impact of a persuasive message can increase over time when a discounting cue, such as an invalid source, can no longer be recalled.

Social attraction Liking for someone based on common group membership and determined by the person's prototypicality of the group.

Social categorization Classification of people as members of different social groups.

Social change belief system Belief that intergroup boundaries are impermeable. Therefore, a lower-status individual can improve social identity only by challenging the legitimacy of the higher-status group's position.

Social cognition Cognitive processes and structures that influence and are influenced by social behaviour.

Social comparison (theory) Comparing our behaviours and opinions with those of others in order to establish the correct or socially approved way of thinking and behaving.

Social compensation Increased effort on a collective task to compensate for other group members' actual, perceived or anticipated lack of effort or ability.

Social competition Group-based behavioural strategies that improve social identity by directly confronting the dominant group's position in society.

Social creativity Group-based behavioural strategies that improve social identity but do not directly attack the dominant group's position.

Social decisions schemes Explicit or implicit decision-making rules that relate individual opinions to a final group decision.

Social dilemmas Situations in which short term personal gain is at odds with the long-term good of the group.

Social dominance theory Theory that attributes prejudice to an individual's acceptance of an ideology that legitimises ingroup-serving hierarchy and domination, and rejects egalitarian ideologies.

Social exchange People often use a form of everyday economics when they weigh up costs and rewards before deciding what to do.

Social facilitation An improvement in the performance of well-learnt/easy tasks and a deterioration in the performance of poorly learnt/difficult tasks in the mere presence of members of the same species.

Social identity That part of the self-concept that derives from our membership in social groups.

Social identity theory Theory of group membership and intergroup relations based on self-categorization, social comparison and the construction of a shared self-definition in terms of ingroup-defining properties.

Social identity theory of leadership Development of social identity theory to explain leadership as an identity process whereby in salient groups prototypical leaders are more effective than less prototypical leaders.

Social impact The effect that other people have on our attitudes and behaviour, usually as a consequence of factors such as group size, and temporal and physical immediacy.

Social influence Process whereby attitudes and behaviour are influenced by the real or implied presence of other people.

Social judgeability Perception of whether it is socially acceptable to judge a specific target.

Social learning theory The view championed by Bandura that human social behaviour is not innate but learnt from appropriate models.

Social loafing A reduction in individual effort when working on a collective task (one in which our outputs are pooled with those of other group members) compared with working either alone or coactively (our outputs are not pooled).

Social markers Features of speech style that convey information about mood, context, status and group membership.

Social mobility belief system Belief that intergroup boundaries are permeable. Thus, it is possible for someone to pass from a lower-status into a higher-status group to improve social identity.

Social neuroscience Exploration of brain activity associated with social cognition and social psychological processes and phenomena.

Social order The balance and control of a social system, regulated by norms, values, rules and law.

Social ostracism Exclusion from a group by common consent.

Social psychology Scientific investigation of how people's thoughts, feelings and behaviour are influenced by the actual, imagined or implied presence of others.

Social representations Collectively elaborated explanations of unfamiliar and complex phenomena that transform them into a familiar and simple form.

Social responsibility norm The idea that we should help people who are dependent and in need. It is contradicted by another norm that discourages interfering in other people's lives.

Social support network People who know and care about us and who can provide back-up during a time of stress.

Social transition scheme Method for charting incremental changes in member opinions as a group moves towards a final decision.

Sociocognitive model Attitude theory highlighting an evaluative component. Knowledge of an object is represented in memory along with a summary of how to appraise it.

Sociocultural theory Psychological gender differences are determined by individuals' adaptations to restrictions based on their gender in their society. Also called *social role theory*.

Source The point of origin of a persuasive communication.

Specific status characteristics Information about those abilities of a person that are directly relevant to the group's task.

Speech Vocal production of language.

Speech accommodation theory Modification of speech style to the context (e.g. listener, situation) of a face-to-face interindividual conversation.

Speech convergence Accent or speech style shift towards that of the other person.

Speech divergence Accent or speech style shift away from that of the other person.

Speech style The way in which something is said (e.g. accent, language), rather than the content of what is said.

Spreading attitude effect A liked or disliked person (or attitude object) may affect not only the evaluation of a second person directly associated but also others merely associated with the second person.

Statistical significance An effect is statistically significant if statistics reveal that it, or a larger effect, is unlikely to occur by chance more often than 1 in 20 times.

Statistics Formalised numerical procedures performed on data to investigate the magnitude and/or significance of effects.

Status Consensual evaluation of the prestige of a role or role occupant in a group, or of the prestige of a group and its members as a whole.

Status characteristics theory Theory of influence in groups that attributes greater influence to those who possess both task-relevant characteristics (specific status characteristics) and characteristics of a high-status group in society (diffuse status characteristics). Also called expectation states theory.

Stereotype Widely shared and simplified evaluative image of a social group and its members.

Stereotype threat Feeling that we will be judged and treated in terms of negative stereotypes of our group, and that we will inadvertently confirm these stereotypes through our behaviour.

Stigma Group attributes that mediate a negative social evaluation of people belonging to the group.

Subculture of violence A subgroup of society in which a higher level of violence is accepted as the norm.

Subject effects Effects that are not spontaneous, owing to demand characteristics and/or participants wishing to please the experimenter.

Subjective group dynamics A process where normative deviants who deviate towards an outgroup (anti-norm deviants) are more harshly treated than those who deviate away from the outgroup (pro-norm deviants).

Subjective vitality Individual group members' representation of the objective ethnolinguistic vitality of their group.

Subtyping Schema change as a consequence of schema-inconsistent information, causing the formation of subcategories.

Summation A method of forming positive or negative impressions by summing the valence of all the constituent person attributes.

Superordinate goals Goals that both groups desire but that can be achieved only by both groups cooperating.

Symbolic interactionism Theory of how the self emerges from human interaction that involves people trading symbols (through language and gesture) that are usually consensual and represent abstract properties rather than concrete objects.

System justification theory Theory that attributes social stasis to people's adherence to an ideology that justifies and protects the status quo.

t test Procedure to test the statistical significance of an effect in which the mean for one condition is greater than the mean for another.

Task taxonomy Group tasks can be classified according to whether a division of labour is possible; whether there is a predetermined standard to be met; and how an individual's inputs can contribute.

Terror management theory The notion that the most fundamental human motivation is to reduce the terror of the inevitability of death. Self-esteem may be centrally implicated in effective terror management.

Theory Set of interrelated concepts and principles that explain a phenomenon.

Theory of planned behaviour Modification by Ajzen of the theory of reasoned action. It suggests that predicting a behaviour from an attitude measure is improved if people believe they have control over that behaviour.

Theory of reasoned action Fishbein and Ajzen's theory of the relationship between attitudes and behaviour. A specific attitude that has normative support predicts an intention to act, which then predicts actual behaviour.

Third-person effect Most people think that they are less influenced than others by advertisements.

Three-component attitude model An attitude consists of cognitive, affective and behavioural components. This threefold division has an ancient heritage, stressing thought, feeling and action as basic to human experience.

Three-factor theory of love Hatfield and Walster distinguished three components of what we label 'love': a cultural concept of love, an appropriate person to love and emotional arousal.

Thurstone scale An 11-point scale with 22 items, 2 for each point. Each item has a value ranging from very unfavourable to very favourable. Respondents check the items with which they agree. Their attitude is the average scale value of these items.

Tokenism The practice of publicly making small concessions to a minority group in order to deflect accusations of prejudice and discrimination.

Transactional leadership Approach to leadership that focuses on the transaction of resources between leader and followers. Also a style of leadership.

Transactive memory Group members have a shared memory for who within the group remembers what and is the expert on what.

Transformational leadership Approach to leadership that focuses on the way that leaders transform group goals and actions – mainly through the exercise of charisma. Also a style of leadership based on charisma.

Two-component attitude model An attitude consists of a mental readiness to act. It also guides evaluative (judgemental) responses.

Type A personality The 'coronary-prone' personality – a behavioural correlate of heart disease characterised by striving to achieve, time urgency, competitiveness and hostility.

Ultimate attribution error Tendency to attribute bad outgroup and good ingroup behaviour internally, and to attribute good outgroup and bad ingroup behaviour externally.

Uncertainty–identity theory To reduce uncertainty and to feel more comfortable about who they are, people choose to identify with groups that are distinctive, are clearly defined and have consensual norms.

Unidimensionality A Guttman scale consists of a single (low to high) dimension. It is also cumulative; that is, agreement with the highest-scoring item implies agreement with all lower-scoring items.

Unobtrusive measures Observational approaches that neither intrude on the processes being studied nor cause people to behave unnaturally.

Utterance Sounds made by one person to another.

Values A higher-order concept thought to provide a structure for organising attitudes.

Vertical dyad linkage (VDL) model An early form of leader–member exchange (LMX) theory in which a sharp distinction is drawn between dyadic leader–member relations: the subordinate is treated as either an ingroup member or an outgroup member.

Visual dominance behaviour Tendency to gaze fixedly at a lower-status speaker.

Vividness An intrinsic property of a stimulus on its own that makes it stand out and attract attention.

Völkerpsychologie Early precursor of social psychology, as the study of the collective mind, in Germany in the mid- to late nineteenth century.

Weapons effect The mere presence of a weapon increases the probability that it will be used aggressively.

Weighted averaging Method of forming positive or negative impressions by first weighting and then averaging the valence of all the constituent person attributes.

References

Abeles, R. P. (1976). Relative deprivation, rising expectations, and black militancy. *Journal of Social Issues, 32,* 119–137.

Abelson, R. P. (1968). Computers, polls and public opinion – some puzzles and paradoxes. *Transaction, 5,* 20–27.

Abelson, R. P. (1972). Are attitudes necessary? In B. T. King (Ed.), *Attitudes, conflict and social change* (pp. 19–32). New York: Academic Press.

Abelson, R. P. (1981). The psychological status of the script concept. *American Psychologist, 36,* 715–729.

Abelson, R. P., Aronson, E., McGuire, W. J., Newcomb, T. M., Rosenberg, M. J., & Tannenbaum, P. H. (Eds.) (1968). *Theories of cognitive consistency: A sourcebook.* Chicago: Rand McNally.

Aboud, F. (1988). *Children and prejudice.* Oxford, UK: Blackwell.

Aboud, F. E. (1987). The development of ethnic self-identification and attitudes. In J. S. Phinney & M. J. Rotheram (Eds.), *Children's ethnic socialization: Pluralism and development* (pp. 32–55). Beverly Hills, CA: SAGE.

Abrams, D. (1990). Political identity: Relative deprivation, social identity and the case of Scottish Nationalism. *ESRC 16–19 Initiative Occasional Papers.* London: Economic and Social Research Council.

Abrams, D. (1994). Social self-regulation. *Personality and Social Psychology Bulletin, 20,* 473–483.

Abrams, D., & Hogg, M. A. (1988). Comments on the motivational status of self-esteem in social identity and intergroup discrimination. *European Journal of Social Psychology, 18,* 317–334.

Abrams, D., & Hogg, M. A. (1990a). Social identification, self-categorisation, and social influence. *European Review of Social Psychology, 1,* 195–228.

Abrams, D., & Hogg, M. A. (1990b). The social context of discourse: Let's not throw out the baby with the bath water. *Philosophical Psychology, 3,* 219–225.

Abrams, D., & Hogg, M. A. (2001). Collective identity: Group membership and self-conception. In M. A. Hogg & R. S. Tindale (Eds.), *Blackwell handbook of social psychology: Group processes* (pp. 425–460). Oxford, UK: Blackwell.

Abrams, D., & Hogg, M. A. (2004). Metatheory: Lessons from social identity research. *Personality and Social Psychology Review, 8,* 98–106.

Abrams, D., & Hogg, M. A. (Eds.) (1999). *Social identity and social cognition.* Oxford, UK: Blackwell.

Abrams, D., & Hogg, M. A. (2010). Social identity and self-categorization. In J. F. Dovidio, M. Hewstone, P. Glick, & V. M. Esses (Eds.), *The SAGE handbook of prejudice, stereotyping and discrimination* (pp. 179–193). London: SAGE.

Abrams, D., Randsley de Moura, G., Marques, J. M., & Hutchison, P. (2008). Innovation credit: When can leaders oppose their group's norms? *Journal of Personality and Social Psychology, 95,* 662–678.

Abrams, D., Wetherell, M. S., Cochrane, S., Hogg, M. A., & Turner, J. C. (1990). Knowing what to think by knowing who you are: Self-categorization and the nature of norm formation, conformity, and group polarization. *British Journal of Social Psychology, 29,* 97–119.

Abramson, L. Y., Seligman, M. E. P., & Teasdale, J. D. (1978). Learned helplessness in humans: Critique and reformulation. *Journal of Abnormal and Social Psychology, 87,* 49–74.

Abric, J. C., & Vacherot, C. (1976). The effects of representations of behaviour in experimental games. *European Journal of Social Psychology, 6,* 129–144.

Ackerman, J. A., Griskevicius, V., & Li, N. P. (2011). Let's get serious: Communicating commitment in romantic relationships. *Journal of Personality and Social Psychology, 100,* 1079–1094.

Acorn, D. A., Hamilton, D. L., & Sherman, S. J. (1988). Generalization of biased perceptions of groups based on illusory correlations. *Social Cognition, 6,* 345–372.

Adair, J., Dushenko, T. W., & Lindsay, R. C. L. (1985). Ethical regulations and their impact on research practice. *American Psychologist, 40,* 59–72.

Adamopoulos, J., & Kashima, Y. (Eds.) (1999). *Social psychology and cultural context.* London: SAGE.

Adams, J. M., & Jones, W. H. (1997). The conceptualization of marital commitment: An integrative analysis. *Journal of Personality and Social Psychology, 11,* 1177–1196.

Adams, J. S. (1965). Inequity in social exchange. *Advances in Experimental Social Psychology, 2,* 267–299.

Adorno, T. W., Frenkel-Brunswik, E., Levinson, D. J., & Sanford, R. M. (1950). *The authoritarian personality.* New York: Harper.

Aggarwal, P., & O'Brien, C. L. (2008). Social loafing on group projects: Structural antecedents and effect on student satisfaction. *Journal of Marketing Education, 30,* 255–264.

Ahlstrom, W., & Havighurst, R. (1971). *Four hundred losers: Delinquent boys in high school.* San Francisco, CA: Jossey-Bass.

Aiello, J. R., & Jones, S. E. (1971). Field study of the proxemic behavior of young children in three subcultural groups. *Journal of Personality and Social Psychology, 19,* 351–356.

Ajzen, I. (1989). Attitude structure and behavior. In A. R. Pratkanis, S. J. Breckler, & A. G. Greenwald (Eds.), *Attitude structure and function* (pp. 241–274). Hillsdale, NJ: Erlbaum.

Ajzen, I. (1998). Models of human social behavior and their application to health psychology. *Psychology and Health, 13,* 735–739.

Ajzen, I. (2001). Nature and operation of attitudes. *Annual Review of Psychology, 52,* 27–58.

Ajzen, I. (2002). Residual effects of past on later behavior: Habituation and reasoned action perspectives. *Personality and Social Psychology Review, 6,* 107–122.

Ajzen, I., & Fishbein, M. (1980). *Understanding attitudes and predicting social behavior.* Englewood Cliffs, NJ: Prentice Hall.

Ajzen, I., & Fishbein, M. (2005). The influence of attitudes on behavior. In D. Albarracín, B. T. Johnson, & M. P. Zanna (Eds.), *The handbook of attitudes* (pp. 173–221). Mahwah, NJ: Erlbaum.

Ajzen, I., & Madden, T. J. (1986). Prediction of goal-directed behavior: Attitudes, intentions and perceived behavioral control. *Journal of Experimental Social Psychology, 22,* 453–474.

Albarracín, D., Cohen, J. B., & Kumkale, G. T. (2003). When communications collide with recipients' actions: Effects of post-message behavior on intentions to follow the message recommendation. *Personality and Social Psychology Bulletin, 29,* 834–845.

Albarracín, D., & Vargas, P. (2010). Attitudes and persuasion: From biology to social responses to persuasive intent. In S. T. Fiske, D. T. Gilbert, & G. Lindzey (Eds.), *Handbook of social psychology* (5th ed., Vol. 1, pp. 394–427). New York: Wiley.

Albion, M. S., & Faris, P. W. (1979). *Appraising research on advertising's economic impacts* (Report no. 79–115). Cambridge, MA: Marketing Science Institute.

Albright, L., Malloy, T. E., Dong, Q., Kenny, D. A., Fang, X., Winquist, L., et al. (1997). Cross-cultural consensus in personality judgments. *Journal of Personality and Social Psychology, 72,* 558–569.

Aldag, R. J., & Fuller, S. R. (1993). Beyond fiasco: A reappraisal of the groupthink phenomenon and a new model of group decision processes. *Psychological Bulletin, 113,* 533–552.

Alexander, C. N., Zucker, L. G., & Brody, C. L. (1970). Experimental expectations and autokinetic experiences: Consistency theories and judgmental convergence. *Sociometry, 33,* 108–122.

Alicke, M. D., & Sedikides, C. (2009). Self-enhancement and self-protection: What they are and what they do. *European Review of Social Psychology, 20,* 1–48.

Allard, R., & Landry, R. (1994). Subjective ethnolinguistic vitality: A comparison of two measures. *International Journal of the Sociology of Language, 108,* 117–144.

Allen, M., Mabry, E., & McKelton, D. (1998). Impact of juror attitudes about the death penalty on juror evaluations of guilt and punishment. *Law and Human Behavior, 23,* 715–732.

Allen, N. J., & Hecht, T. D. (2004). The 'romance of teams': Towards an understanding of its psychological underpinnings and implications. *Journal of Occupational and Organizational Psychology, 77,* 439–461.

Allen, V. L. (1965). Situational factors in conformity. *Advances in Experimental Social Psychology, 2,* 133–175.

Allen, V. L. (1975). Social support for non-conformity. *Advances in Experimental Social Psychology, 8,* 1–43.

Allen, V. L., & Levine, J. M. (1971). Social support and conformity: The role of independent assessment of reality. *Journal of Experimental Social Psychology, 7,* 48–58.

Allen, V. L., & Wilder, D. A. (1975). Categorization, belief similarity, and group similarity. *Journal of Personality of Social Psychology, 32,* 971–977.

Alleyne, E., & Wood, J. L. (2010). Gang involvement: Psychological and behavioral characteristics of gang members, peripheral youth, and non-gang youth. *Aggressive Behavior, 36,* 423–436.

Allison, S. T., Mackie, D. M., & Messick, D. M. (1996). Outcome biases in social perception: Implications for dispositional inference, attitude change, stereotyping, and social behavior. *Advances in Experimental Social Psychology, 28,* 53–93.

Alloy, L. B., & Tabachnik, N. (1984). Assessment of covariation by humans and animals: The joint influence of prior expectations and current situational information. *Psychological Review, 91,* 112–149.

Allport, F. H. (1920). The influence of the group upon association and thought. *Journal of Experimental Psychology, 3,* 159–182.

Allport, F. H. (1924). *Social psychology.* Boston, MA: Houghton-Mifflin.

Allport, G. W. (1935). Attitudes. In C. M. Murchison (Ed.), *Handbook of social psychology* (pp. 789–844). Worcester, MA: Clark University Press.

Allport, G. W. (1954a). The historical background of modern social psychology. In G. Lindzey (Ed.), *Handbook of social psychology* (Vol. 1, pp. 3–56). Reading, MA: Addison-Wesley.

Allport, G. W. (1954b). *The nature of prejudice.* Reading, MA: Addison-Wesley.

Allport, G. W., & Postman, L. J. (1945). Psychology of rumor. *Transactions of the New York Academy of Sciences, 8,* 61–81.

Allport, G. W., & Postman, L. J. (1947). *The psychology of rumor.* New York: Holt, Rinehart & Winston.

Allport, G. W., & Vernon, P. E. (1931). *A study of values.* Boston, MA: Houghton-Mifflin.

Allyn, J., & Festinger, L. (1961). The effectiveness of unanticipated persuasive communications. *Journal of Abnormal and Social Psychology, 62,* 35–40.

Altemeyer, B. (1981). *Right-wing authoritarianism.* Winnipeg, Canada: University of Manitoba Press.

Altemeyer, B. (1988). *Enemies of freedom: Understanding right-wing authoritarianism.* San Francisco, CA: Jossey-Bass.

Altemeyer, B. (1994). Reducing prejudice in right-wing authoritarians. In M. P. Zanna & J. M. Olsen (Eds.), *The psychology of prejudice: The Ontario symposium* (pp. 131–148). Hillsdale, NJ: Erlbaum.

Altemeyer, B. (1998). The other 'authoritarian personality'. *Advances in Experimental Social Psychology, 30,* 47–92.

Altman, D. (1986). *AIDS and the new puritanism.* London and Sydney: Pluto Press.

Altman, I., & Taylor, D. A. (1973). *Social penetration: The development of interpersonal relationships.* New York: Holt, Rinehart & Winston.

Amato, P. R. (1983). Helping behavior in urban and rural environments: Field studies based on a taxonomic organisation of helping episodes. *Journal of Personality and Social Psychology, 45,* 571–586.

Ambady, N., & Weisbuch. M. (2010). Nonverbal behavior. In S. T. Fiske, D. T. Gilbert, & G. Lindzey (Eds.), *Handbook of social psychology* (5th ed., Vol. 1, pp. 464–497). New York: Wiley.

American Psychological Association (2002). Ethical principles of psychologists and code of conduct. *American Psychologist, 57*(12).

Ames, D. R., Flynn, F. J., & Weber, E. U. (2004). It's the thought that counts: On perceiving how helpers decide to lend a hand. *Personality and Social Psychology Bulletin, 30,* 461–474.

Amichai-Hamburger, Y., & McKenna, K. Y. A. (2006). The contact hypothesis reconsidered: Interacting via the Internet. *Journal of Computer-Mediated Communication, 11,* 825–843.

Amir, Y. (1976). The role of intergroup contact in change of prejudice and ethnic relations. In P. A. Katz (Ed.), *Towards the elimination of racism* (pp. 245–308). Elmsford, NY: Pergamon Press.

Anderson, C. A., & Anderson, D. C. (1984). Ambient temperature and violent crime: Tests of the linear and curvilinear hypothesis. *Journal of Personality and Social Psychology, 46,* 91–97.

Anderson, C. A., Anderson, K. B., & Deuser, W. E. (1996) Examining an affective framework: Weapon and temperature effects on aggressive thoughts, affect, and attitudes. *Personality and Social Psychology Bulletin, 22,* 366–376.

Anderson, C. A., & Bushman, B. J. (1997). External validity of trivial experiments: The case of laboratory aggression. *Review of General Psychology, 1,* 19–41.

Anderson, C. A., & Bushman, B. J. (2002a). Human aggression. *Annual Review of Psychology, 53,* 27–51.

Anderson, C. A., & Bushman, B. J. (2002b). The effects of media violence on society. *Science, 295,* 2377–2378.

Anderson, C. A., Bushman, B. J., & Groom, R. W. (1997). Hot years and serious and deadly assault: Empirical tests of the heat hypothesis. *Journal of Personality and Social Psychology, 73,* 1213–1223.

Anderson, C. A., Carnagey, N. L., & Eubanks, J. (2003). Exposure to violent media: The effects of songs with violent lyrics on aggressive thoughts and feelings. *Journal of Personality and Social Psychology, 84,* 960–971.

Anderson, C. A., & Godfrey, S. S. (1987). Thoughts about actions: The effects of specificity and availability of imagined behavioral scripts on expectations about oneself and others. *Social Cognition, 5,* 238–258.

Anderson, C. A., & Huesmann, L. R. (2003). Human aggression: A social-cognitive view. In M. A. Hogg & J. Cooper (Eds.), *The SAGE handbook of social psychology* (pp. 296–323). London: SAGE.

Anderson, C. A., & Huesmann, L. R. (2007). Human aggression: A social-cognitive view. In M. A. Hogg & J. Cooper (Eds.), *The SAGE handbook of social psychology: Concise student edition* (pp. 259–287). London: SAGE.

Anderson, C. A., & Slusher, M. P. (1986). Relocating motivational effects: A synthesis of cognitive and motivational effects on attributions for success and failure. *Social Cognition, 4,* 250–292.

Anderson, J., & McGuire, W. J. (1965). Prior reassurance of group consensus as a factor in producing resistance to persuasion. *Sociometry, 28,* 44–56.

Anderson, J. R. (1990). *Cognitive psychology and its implications* (3rd ed.). New York: Freeman.

Anderson, N. H. (1965). Adding versus averaging as a stimulus combination rule in impression formation. *Journal of Experimental Psychology, 70,* 394–400.

Anderson, N. H. (1971). Integration theory and attitude change. *Psychological Review, 78,* 171–206.

Anderson, N. H. (1978). Cognitive algebra: Integration theory applied to social attribution. In L. Berkowitz (Ed.), *Cognitive theories in social psychology* (pp. 1–126). New York: Academic Press.

Anderson, N. H. (1981). *Foundations of information integration theory.* New York: Academic Press.

Andreeva, G. (1984). Cognitive processes in developing groups. In L. H. Strickland (Ed.), *Directions in Soviet social psychology* (pp. 67–82). New York: Springer.

Anholt, R. R. H., & Mackay, T. F. C. (2012). Genetics of aggression. *Annual Review of Genetics, 46*, 145–164.

Antonakis, J., & House, R. J. (2003). An analysis of the full-range leadership theory: The way forward. In B. J. Avolio & F. J. Yammarino (Eds.), *Transformational and charismatic leadership: The road ahead* (pp. 3–33). New York: Elsevier.

Apfelbaum, E. (1974). On conflicts and bargaining. *Advances in Experimental Social Psychology, 7*, 103–156.

Apfelbaum, E., & Lubek, I. (1976). Resolution vs. revolution? The theory of conflicts in question. In L. Strickland, F. Aboud, & K. J. Gergen (Eds.), *Social psychology in transition* (pp. 71–94). New York: Plenum.

Apfelbaum, E., & McGuire, G. R. (1986). Models of suggestive influence and the disqualification of the social crowd. In C. F. Graumann & S. Moscovici (Eds.), *Changing conceptions of crowd mind and behavior* (pp. 27–50). New York: Springer.

Archer, D. (1997). Unspoken diversity: Cultural differences in gestures. *Qualitative Sociology, 20*, 79–105.

Archer, D., Iritani, B., Kimes, D. D., & Barrios, M. (1983). Face-ism: Five studies of sex differences in facial prominence. *Journal of Personality and Social Psychology, 45*, 725–735.

Archer, J. (2000). Sex differences in aggression between heterosexual partners: A meta-analytic review. *Psychological Bulletin, 126*, 697–702.

Archer, J. (2004). Sex differences in aggression in real-world settings: A meta-analytic review. *Review of General Psychology, 8*, 291–322.

Archer, J. (2006). Cross-cultural differences in physical aggression between partners: A social-role analysis. *Personality and Social Psychology Review, 10*, 133–153.

Archer, J. (2013). Can evolutionary principles explain patterns of family violence? *Psychological Bulletin, 139*, 403–440.

Ardrey, R. (1961). *African genesis*. New York: Delta Books.

Ardrey, R. (1966). *The territorial imperative*. New York: Atheneum.

Arendt, H. (1963). *Eichmann in Jerusalem: A report on the banality of evil*. New York: Viking.

Argote, L. (2013). *Organizational learning: Creating, retaining and transferring knowledge*. New York: Springer.

Argote, L., Insko, C. A., Yovetich, N., & Romero, A. A. (1995). Group learning curves: The effects of turnover and task complexity on group performance. *Journal of Applied Social Psychology, 25*, 512–529.

Argyle, M. (1971). *The psychology of interpersonal behaviour*. Harmondsworth, UK: Penguin.

Argyle, M. (1975). *Bodily communication*. London: Methuen.

Argyle, M. (1980). The development of applied social psychology. In R. Gilmour & S. Duck (Eds.), *The development of social psychology*. New York: Academic Press.

Argyle, M., & Dean, J. (1965). Eye-contact, distance and affiliation. *Sociometry, 28*, 289–304.

Argyle, M., & Ingham, R. (1972). Gaze, mutual gaze, and proximity. *Semiotica, 6*, 32–49.

Aries, E. (1996). *Men and women in interaction: Considering the differences*. New York: Oxford University Press.

Aries, E. (1997). Women and men talking: Are they worlds apart? In W. R. Walsh (Ed.), *Women, men and gender: Ongoing debates* (pp. 79–100). New Haven, CT: Yale University Press.

Arkes, H. R., Boehm, L. E., & Xu, G. (1991). Determinants of judged validity. *Journal of Experimental Social Psychology, 27*, 576–605.

Armitage, C. J., & Conner, M., (2001). Efficacy of the theory of planned behavior: A meta-analytic review. *British Journal of Social Psychology, 40*, 471–499.

Aron, A., Paris, M., & Aron, E. N. (1995). Falling in love: Prospective studies of self-concept change. *Journal of Personality and Social Psychology, 69*, 1102–1112.

Aron, A., & Westbay, L. (1996). Dimensions of the prototype of love. *Journal of Personality and Social Psychology, 70*, 535–551.

Aronson, E. (1984). *The social animal* (4th ed.). New York: Freeman.

Aronson, E. (1999). Dissonance, hypocrisy, and the self-concept. In E. Harmon-Jones & J. Mills (Eds.), *Cognitive dissonance: Progress on a pivotal theory in social psychology* (pp. 103–126). Washington, DC: American Psychological Association.

Aronson, E., Ellsworth, P. C., Carlsmith, J. M., & Gonzales, M. H. (1990). *Methods of research in social psychology* (2nd ed.). New York: McGraw-Hill.

Aronson, E., & Mills, J. (1959). The effects of severity of initiation on liking for a group. *Journal of Abnormal and Social Psychology, 59*, 177–181.

Arriaga, X. B., & Agnew, C. R. (2001). Being committed: Affective, cognitive, and conative components of relationship commitment. *Personality and Social Psychology Bulletin, 27*, 1190–1203.

Arrow, H., Berdahl, J. L., Bouas, K. S., Craig, K. M., Cummings, A., Lebie, L., McGrath, J. E., O'Connor, K. M., Rhoades, J. A., & Schlosser, A. (1996). Time, technology, and groups: An integration. *Computer Supported Cooperative Work, 4*, 253–261.

Arrow, H., McGrath, J. E., & Berdahl, J. L. (2000). *Small groups as complex systems: Formation, coordination, development, and adaptation*. Thousand Oaks, CA: SAGE.

Asch, S. E. (1946). Forming impressions of personality. *Journal of Abnormal and Social Psychology, 41*, 258–290.

Asch, S. E. (1951). Effects of group pressure upon the modification and distortion of judgements. In H. Guetzkow (Ed.), *Groups, leadership and men* (pp. 177–190). Pittsburgh, PA: Carnegie Press.

Asch, S. E. (1952). *Social psychology*. Englewood Cliffs, NJ: Prentice Hall.

Asch, S. E. (1956). Studies of independence and conformity: A minority of one against a unanimous majority. *Psychological Monographs: General and Applied, 70*, 1–70 (whole no. 416).

Aschenbrenner, K. M., & Schaefer, R. E. (1980). Minimal group situations: Comments on a mathematical model and on the research paradigm. *European Journal of Social Psychology, 10*, 389–398.

Ashburn-Nardo, L., Voils, C. I., & Monteith, M. J. (2001). Implicit associations as the seeds of intergroup bias: How easily do they take root? *Journal of Personality and Social Psychology, 81*, 789–799.

Ashmore, R. D. (1981). Sex stereotypes and implicit personality theory. In D. L. Hamilton (Ed.), *Cognitive processes in stereotyping and intergroup behavior* (pp. 37–81). Hillsdale, NJ: Erlbaum.

Ashmore, R. D., & Jussim, L. (1997). Towards a second century of the scientific analysis of self and identity. In R. Ashmore & L. Jussim (Eds.), *Self and identity: Fundamental issues* (pp. 3–19). New York: Oxford University Press.

Assael, H. (1981). *Consumer behavior and marketing action*. Boston, MA: Kent.

Atkin, C. K. (1977). Effects of campaign advertising and newscasts on children. *Journalism Quarterly, 54*, 503–558.

Atkin, C. K. (1980). *Effects of the mass media*. New York: McGraw-Hill.

Attridge, M., & Berscheid, E. (1994). Entitlement in romantic relationships in the United States: A social exchange perspective. In M. J. Lerner and G. Mikula (Eds.), *Entitlement and the affectional bond: Justice in close relationships* (pp. 117–148). New York: Plenum.

Augoustinos, M., & Innes, J. M. (1990). Towards an integration of social representations and social schema theory. *British Journal of Social Psychology, 29*, 213–231.

Augoustinos, M., & Tileaga, C. (2012). Twenty-five years of discursive psychology. *British Journal of Social Psychology, 51*, 405–412.

Austin, J. L. (1962). *How to do things with words*. Oxford, UK: Clarendon Press.

Austin, W. (1979). Sex differences in bystander intervention in a theft. *Journal of Personality and Social Psychology, 37*, 2110–2120.

Avolio, B. J. (1999). *Full leadership development: Building the vital forces in organizations*. Thousand Oaks, CA: SAGE.

Avolio, B. J., & Bass, B. M. (1987). Transformational leadership, charisma and beyond. In J. G. Hunt, B. R. Balaga, H. P. Dachler, & C. A. Schriesheim (Eds.), *Emerging leadership vistas* (pp. 29–50). Elmsford, NY: Pergamon Press.

Avolio, B. J., & Gardner, W. L. (2005). Authentic leadership development: Getting to the root of positive forms of leadership. *The Leadership Quarterly, 16*, 315–338.

Avolio, B. J., & Yammarino, F. J. (Eds.) (2003). *Transformational and charismatic leadership: The road ahead*. New York: Elsevier.

Axelrod, R., & Dion, D. (1988). The further evolution of cooperation. *Science, 242*, 1385–1390.

Azar, B. (1997). Forgiveness helps keep relationships steadfast. *APA Monitor*, 14 November.

Back, D., Küfner, A. C. P., Dufner, M., Gerlach, T. M., Rauthmann, J. F., & Denissen, J. J. (2013). Narcissistic admiration and rivalry: Disentangling the bright and dark sides of narcissism. *Journal of Personality and Social Psychology, 105*, 1013–1037.

Baddeley, A. D., Eysenck, M., & Anderson, M. C. (2009). *Memory*. Hove, England: Psychology Press.

Bailey, D. S., & Taylor, S. P. (1991). Effects of alcohol and aggressive disposition on human physical aggression. *Journal of Research in Personality, 25*, 334–342.

Bain, P. G., Kashima, Y., & Haslam, N. (2006) Conceptual beliefs about human values and their implications: Human nature beliefs predict value importance, value trade-offs, and responses to value-laden rhetoric. *Journal of Personality and Social Psychology, 91*, 351–367.

Bain, P. G., Vaes, J., & Leyens, J.-P. (2014). *Humanness and dehumanization*. New York: Psychology Press.

Bains, G. (1983). Explanations and the need for control. In M. Hewstone (Ed.), *Attribution theory: Social and functional extensions* (pp. 126–143). Oxford, UK: Blackwell.

Bakan, D. (1966). *The duality of human existence*. Chicago: Rand McNally.

Baldwin, J. M. (1897/1901). *Social and ethical interpretations in mental development*. New York: Macmillan.

Bales, R. F. (1950). *Interaction process analysis: A method for the study of small groups*. Reading, MA: Addison-Wesley.

Banaji, M. R., & Heiphetz, L. (2010). Attitudes. In S. T. Fiske, D. T. Gilbert, & G. Lindzey (Eds.), *Handbook of social psychology* (5th ed., Vol. 1, pp. 353–393). New York: Wiley.

Bandura, A. (1973). *Aggression: A social learning analysis*. Englewood Cliffs, NJ: Prentice Hall.

Bandura, A. (1977). *Social learning theory*. Englewood Cliffs, NJ: Prentice Hall.

Bandura, A. (1986). *Social foundations of thought and action: A social cognitive theory*. Englewood Cliffs, NJ: Prentice Hall.

Bandura, A. (1992). Exercise of personal agency through the self-efficacy mechanism. In R. Schwarzer (Ed.), *Self-efficacy: Thought control of action* (pp. 3–38). Washington: Hemisphere Press.

Bandura, A. (2002). Selective moral disengagement in the exercise of moral agency. *Journal of Moral Education, 312*, 101–119.

Bandura, A., Ross, D., & Ross, S. A. (1963). Imitation of film-mediated aggressive models. *Journal of Abnormal and Social Psychology, 66*, 3–11.

Bandura, A., & Walters, R. H. (1963). *Social learning and personality development*. New York: Holt, Rinehart & Winston.

Banks, W. C. (1976). White preference in Blacks: A paradigm in search of a phenomenon. *Psychological Bulletin, 83*, 1179–1186.

Banuazizi, A., & Movahedi, S. (1975). Interpersonal dynamics in a simulated prison: A methodological analysis. *American Psychologist, 30*, 152–160.

Bardi, A., & Schwartz, S. H. (2003). Values and behavior: Strength and structure of relations. *Personality and Social Psychology Bulletin, 29*, 1207–1220.

Bargh, J. A. (1984). Automatic and conscious processing of social information. In R. S. Wyer, Jr, & T. K. Srull (Eds.), *Handbook of social cognition* (Vol. 3, pp. 1–44). Hillsdale, NJ: Erlbaum.

Bargh, J. A. (1989). Conditional automaticity: Varieties of automatic influence in social perception and cognition. In J. S. Uleman & J. A. Bargh (Eds.), *Unintended thought* (pp. 3–51). New York: Guilford Press.

Bargh, J. A., Chaiken, S., Govender, R., & Pratto, F. (1992). The generality of the automatic attitude activation effect. *Journal of Personality and Social Psychology, 62*, 893–912.

Bargh, J. A., Lombardi, W. J., & Higgins, E. T. (1988). Automaticity of chronically accessible constructs in person X situation effects on person perception: It's just a matter of time. *Journal of Personality and Social Psychology, 55*, 599–605.

Bargh, J. A., & McKenna, K. Y. A. (2004). The internet and social life. *Annual Review of Psychology, 55*, 573–590.

Bargh, J. A., & Pratto, F. (1986). Individual construct accessibility and perceptual selection. *Journal of Experimental Social Psychology, 22*, 293–311.

Bargh, J. A., & Tota, M. E. (1988). Context-dependent automatic processing in depression: Accessibility of negative constructs with regard to self but not others. *Journal of Personality and Social Psychology, 54*, 925–939.

Bar-Hillel, M. (1980). The base-rate fallacy in probability judgements. *Acta Psychologica, 44*, 211–233.

Barjonet, P. E. (1980). L'influence sociale et des représentations des causes de l'accident de la route. *Le Travail Humain, 43*, 243–253.

Barlow, F. K., Paolini, S., Pedersen, A., Hornsey, M. J., Radke, H. R. M., Harwood, J., Rubin, M., & Sibley, C. G. (2012). The contact caveat: Negative contact predicts increased prejudice more than positive contact predicts reduced prejudice. *Personality and Social Psychology Bulletin, 38*, 1629–1643.

Barocas, R., & Gorlow, L. (1967). Self-report personality measurement and conformity behaviour. *Journal of Social Psychology, 71*, 227–234.

Baron, R. A. (1977). *Human aggression*. New York: Plenum.

Baron, R. A. (1979). Aggression, empathy, and race: Effects of victim's pain cues, victim's race, and level of instigation on physical aggression. *Journal of Applied Social Psychology, 9*, 103–114.

Baron, R. A. (1989). Personality and organisational conflict: The type A behavior pattern and self-monitoring. *Organisational Behavior and Human Decision Processes, 44*, 281–297.

Baron, R. A., & Bell, P. (1977). Sexual arousal and aggression by males: Effects of types of erotic stimuli and prior provocation. *Journal of Personality and Social Psychology, 35*, 79–87.

Baron, R. A., & Byrne, D. (1987). *Social psychology: Understanding human interaction* (5th ed.). Boston, MA: Allyn & Bacon.

Baron, R. A., & Byrne, D. (2000). *Social psychology: Under standing human interaction* (9th ed.). Boston, MA: Allyn & Bacon.

Baron, R. A., & Ransberger, V. M. (1978). Ambient temperature and the occurrence of collective violence: The 'long hot summer' revisited. *Journal of Personality and Social Psychology, 36*, 351–360.

Baron, R. A., & Richardson, D. R. (1994). *Human aggression* (2nd ed.). New York: Plenum.

Baron, R. S. (1986). Distraction–conflict theory: Progress and problems. *Advances in Experimental Social Psychology, 20*, 1–40.

Baron, R. S., & Kerr, N. (2003). *Group process, group decision, group action* (2nd ed.). Buckingham, UK: Open University Press.

Baron, R. S., & Roper, G. (1976). Reaffirmation of social comparison views of choice shifts: Averaging and extremity effects in an autokinetic situation. *Journal of Personality and Social Psychology, 33*, 521–530.

Barreto, M., & Ellemers, N. (2005). The burden of benevolent sexism: How it contributes to the maintenance of gender inequalities. *European Journal of Social Psychology, 35*, 633–642.

Barrett, L. F. (2006). Are emotions natural kinds? *Perspectives on Psychological Science, 1*, 28–58.

Barrett, M., & Short, J. (1992). Images of European people in a group of 5–10-year-old English school children. *British Journal of Developmental Psychology, 10*, 339–363.

Barrick, M. R., Day, D. V., Lord, R. G., & Alexander, R. A. (1991). Assessing the utility of executive leadership. *The Leadership Quarterly, 2*, 9–22.

Barron, F. (1953). Some personality correlates of independence of judgment. *Journal of Personality, 21*, 287–297.

Bar-Tal, D. (1976). *Prosocial behavior: Theory and research*. Washington, DC: Hemisphere Press.

Bartholow, B. D., Pearson, M. A., Gratton, G., & Fabiani, M. (2003). Effects of alcohol on person perception: A social cognitive neuroscience approach. *Journal of Personality and Social Psychology, 85*, 627–638.

Bartlett, F. C. (1923). *Psychology and primitive culture*. Cambridge, UK: Cambridge University Press.

Bartlett, F. C. (1932). *Remembering: A study in experiential and social psychology*. Cambridge, UK: Cambridge University Press.

Bartol, K. M., & Butterfield, D. A. (1976). Sex effects in evaluating leaders. *Journal of Applied Psychology, 61*, 446–454.

Bartsch, R. A., & Judd, C. M. (1993). Majority–minority status and perceived ingroup variability revisited. *European Journal of Social Psychology, 23*, 471–483.

Bass, B. M. (1985). *Leadership and performance beyond expectations*. New York: Free Press.

Bass, B. M., & Avolio, B. J. (1990). *Transformational leadership development: Manual for the Multifactor Leadership Questionnaire*. Palo Alto, CA: Consulting Psychologists Press.

Bastian, B., Jetten, J., Chen, H., Radke, H. R. M., Harding, J. F., & Fasoli, F. (2013). Losing our humanity: The self-dehumanizing consequences of social ostracism. *Personality and Social Psychology Bulletin, 39*, 156–169.

Bastian, B., Jetten, J., & Radke, H. R. M. (2012). Cyber-dehumanization: Violent video game play diminishes our humanity. *Journal of Experimental Social Psychology, 48*, 486–491.

Batson, C. D. (1983). Sociobiology and the role of religion in promoting prosocial behavior: An alternative view. *Journal of Personality and Social Psychology, 45*, 1380–1385.

Batson, C. D. (1991). *The altruism question: Toward a social-psychological answer*. Hillsdale, NJ: Lawrence Erlbaum.

Batson, C. D. (1994). Why act for the public good? Four answers. *Personality and Social Psychology Bulletin, 20*, 603–610.

Batson, C. D. (1998). Altruism and prosocial behaviour. In D. T. Gilbert, S. T. Fiske, & G. Lindzey (Eds.), *The handbook of social psychology* (4th ed., Vol. 2, pp. 282–316). New York: McGraw-Hill.

Batson, C. D., Ahmad, N., & Tsang, J. A. (2002). Four motives for community involvement. *Journal of Social Issues, 58*, 429–445.

Batson, C. D., Charng, J., Orr, R., & Rowland, J. (2002). Empathy, attitudes, and action: Can feeling for a member of a stigmatized group motivate one to help the group? *Personality and Social Psychology Bulletin, 28*, 1656–1666.

Batson, C. D., & Coke, J. S. (1981). Empathy: A source of altruistic motivation for helping? In J. P. Rushton & R. M. Sorrentino (Eds.), *Altruism and helping behavior: Social, personality, and developmental perspectives* (pp. 167–183). Hillsdale, NJ: Erlbaum.

Batson, C. D., Duncan, B., Ackerman, P., Buckley, T., & Birch, K. (1981). Is empathic emotion a source of altruistic motivation? *Journal of Personality and Social Psychology, 40*, 290–302.

Batson, C. D., Early, S., & Salvarani, G. (1997). Perspective taking: Imagining how another feels versus imagining how you would feel. *Personality and Social Psychology Bulletin, 23*, 751–758.

Batson, C. D., Eklund, J. H., Chermok, V. L., Hoyt, J. L., & Ortiz, B. G. (2007). An additional antecedent of empathic concern: Valuing the welfare of the person in need. *Journal of Personality and Social Psychology, 93*, 65–74.

Batson, C. D., & Oleson, K. C. (1991). Current status of the empathy–altruism hypothesis. In M. S. Clark (Ed.), *Prosocial behaviour* (pp. 62–85). Newbury Park, CA: SAGE.

Batson, C. D., Schoenrade, P., & Ventis, W. L. (1993). *Religion and the individual: A social-psychological perspective*. New York: Oxford University Press.

Batson, C. D., Sympson, S. C., Hindman, J. L., Decruz, P., Todd, R. M., Weeks, J. L., Jennings, G., & Burris, C. T. (1996). 'I've been there, too': Effect on empathy of prior experience with a need. *Personality and Social Psychology Bulletin, 22*, 474–482.

Batson, C. D., Van Lange, P. A. M., Ahmad, N., & Lishner, D. A. (2007). Altruism and helping behavior. In M. A. Hogg & J. Cooper (Eds.), *The SAGE handbook of social psychology: Concise student edition* (pp. 241–258). London: SAGE.

Battisch, V. A., Assor, A., Messé, L. A., & Aronoff, J. (1985). Personality and person perception. In P. Shaver (Ed.), *Review of personality and social psychology* (Vol. 6, pp. 185–208). Beverly Hills, CA: SAGE.

Baumeister, R. F. (1987). How the self became a problem: A psychological review of historical research. *Journal of Personality and Social Psychology, 52*, 163–176.

Baumeister, R. F. (1989). The optimal margin of illusion. *Journal of Social and Clinical Psychology, 8*, 176–189.

Baumeister, R. F. (1991). *Escaping the self: Alcoholism, spirituality, masochism, and other flights from the burden of selfhood*. New York: Basic Books.

Baumeister, R. F. (1998). The self. In D. T. Gilbert, S. T. Fiske, & G. Lindzey (Eds.), *Handbook of social psychology* (4th ed., Vol. 1, pp. 680–740). New York: McGraw-Hill.

Baumeister, R. F. (Ed.) (1993). *Self-esteem: The puzzle of low self-regard*. New York: Plenum.

Baumeister, R. F. (Ed.) (1999). *The self in social psychology*. Philadelphia, PA: Psychology Press.

Baumeister, R. F., Chesner, S. P., Senders, P. S., & Tice, D. M. (1988). Who's in charge here? Group leaders do lend help in emergencies. *Personality and Social Psychology Bulletin, 14*, 17–22.

Baumeister, R. F., & Covington, M. V. (1985). Self-esteem, persuasion, and retrospective distortion of initial attitudes. *Electronic Social Psychology, 1*, 1–22.

Baumeister, R. F., Dale, K., & Sommer, K. L. (1998). Freudian defense mechanisms and empirical findings in modern social psychology: Reaction formation, projection, displacement, undoing, isolation, sublimation, and denial. *Journal of Personality, 66*, 1081–1124.

Baumeister, R. F., & Darley, J. M. (1982). Reducing the biasing effect of perpetrator attractiveness in jury simulation. *Personality and Social Psychology Bulletin, 8*, 286–292.

Baumeister, R. F., & Leary, M. R. (1995). The need to belong: Desire for interpersonal attachments as a fundamental human motivation. *Psychological Bulletin, 117*, 497–529.

Baumeister, R. F., Smart, L., & Boden, J. M. (1996). Relation of threatened egotism to violence and aggression: The dark side of high self-esteem. *Psychological Review, 103*, 5–33.

Baumeister, R. F., & Sommer, K. L. (1997). What do men want? Gender differences and two spheres of belongingness: Comment on Cross and Madson. *Psychological Bulletin, 122*, 38–44.

Baumeister, R. F., Tice, D. M., & Hutton, D. G. (1989). Self-presentational motivations and personality differences in self-esteem. *Journal of Personality, 57*, 547–579.

Baumeister, R. F., & Vohs, K. D. (Eds.) (2007). *Encyclopedia of social psychology*. Thousand Oaks, CA: SAGE.

Baumeister, R. F., Zhang, L., & Vohs, K. D. (2004). Gossip as cultural learning. *Review of General Psychology, 8*, 111–121.

Baumgarten-Tramer, F. (1948). German psychologists and recent events. *Journal of Abnormal and Social Psychology, 43*, 452–465.

Baumrind, D. (1964). Some thoughts on ethics of research: After reading Milgram's 'Behavioral study of obedience'. *American Psychologist, 19*, 421–443.

Baumrind, D. (1985). Research using intentional deception: Ethical issues revisited. *American Psychologist, 40*, 165–174.

Bavelas, A. (1968). Communications patterns in task-oriented groups. In D. Cartwright & A. Zander (Eds.), *Group dynamics: Research and theory* (3rd ed., pp. 503–511). London: Tavistock.

Baxter, M. G., & Murray, E. A. (2002). The amygdala and reward. *Nature Reviews Neuroscience, 3*, 563–674.

Baxter, T. L., & Goldberg, L. R. (1988). Perceived behavioral consistency underlying trait attributions to oneself and another: An extension of the actor–observer effect. *Personality and Social Psychology Bulletin, 13*, 437–447.

Bayley, B., & Schechter, S. R. (Eds.) (2003). *Language socialization in bilingual and multilingual societies*. Clevedon, UK: Multilingual Matters.

Beattie, A. E., & Mitchell, A. A. (1985). The relationship between advertising recall and persuasion: An experimental investigation. In L. F. Alwitt & A. A. Mitchell (Eds.), *Psychological processes and advertising effects: Theory, research and applications*. Hillsdale, NJ: Erlbaum.

Beauvois, J. L., & Dubois, N. (1988). The norm of internality in the explanation of psychological events. *European Journal of Social Psychology, 18*, 299–316.

Beauvois, J. L., & Joule, R. V. (1996). *A radical dissonance theory*. London: Taylor & Francis.

Beck, L., & Ajzen, I. (1991). Predicting dishonest actions using the theory of planned behavior. *Journal of Research in Personality, 25*, 285–301.

Becker, J. C., & Tausch, N. (2015). A dynamic model of engagement in normative and non-normative collective action: Psychological antecedents, consequences, and barriers. *European Review of Social Psychology, 26*, 43–92.

Becker, O. A. (2013). Effects of similarity of life goals, values, and personality on relationship satisfaction and stability: Findings from a two-wave panel study. *Personal Relationships, 20*, 443–461.

Bègue, L., Subra, B., Arvers, P., Muller, D., Bricout, V., & Zorman, M. (2009). A message in a bottle: Extrapharmacological effects of alcohol on aggression. *Journal of Experimental Social Psychology, 45*, 137–142.

Bélanger, J. J., Caouette, J., Sharvit, K., & Dugas, M. (2014). The psychology of martyrdom: Making the ultimate sacrifice in the name of a cause. *Journal of Personality and Social Psychology, 107*, 494–515.

Belanger, S., & Pinard, M. (1991). Ethnic movements and the competition model: Some missing links. *American Sociological Review, 56*, 446–457.

Belch, G. E., & Belch, M. A. (2012). *Advertising and promotion: An integrated marketing communications perspective* (9th ed.). New York: McGraw-Hill.

Bell, D. A., & Chaibong, H. (2003). Introduction: The contemporary relevance of Confucianism. In D. A. Bell & H. Chaibong (Eds.), *Confucianism for the modern world* (pp. 1–28). New York: Cambridge University Press.

Bell, L. G., Wicklund, R. A., Manko, G., & Larkin, C. (1976). When unexpected behavior is attributed to the environment. *Journal of Research in Personality, 10*, 316–327.

Bell, M. (2013). *Hard feelings: The moral psychology of contempt.* New York: Oxford University Press.

Belsky, J. (1993). Etiology of child maltreatment: A developmental–ecological analysis. *Psychological Bulletin, 114*, 413–434.

Bem, D. J. (1967). Self perception: An alternative interpretation of cognitive dissonance. *Psychological Review, 74*, 183–200.

Bem, D. J. (1972). Self-perception theory. *Advances in Experimental Social Psychology, 6*, 1–62.

Bem, D. J., & Allen, A. A. (1974). On predicting some of the people some of the time: The search for cross-situational consistencies in behavior. *Psychological Review, 81*, 506–520.

Bem, D. J., & McConnell, H. K. (1970). Testing the self-perception explanation of dissonance phenomena: On the salience of premanipulation attitudes. *Journal of Personality and Social Psychology, 14*, 23–31.

Bem, S. L. (1981). Gender schema theory: A cognitive account of sex typing. *Psychological Review, 88*, 354–364.

Benedict, R. (1934). *Patterns of culture.* Boston, MA: Houghton Mifflin.

Bennett, E. B. (1955). Discussion, decision, commitment and consensus in group decision. *Human Relations, 8*, 25–73.

Bennett, M., & Sani, F. (Eds.) (2004). *The development of the social self.* New York: Psychology Press.

Benson, P. L., Karabenick, S. A., & Lerner, R. M. (1976). Pretty pleases: The effects of physical attractiveness, race, and sex on receiving help. *Journal of Experimental Social Psychology, 12*, 409–415.

Benton, A. A., & Druckman, D. (1974). Constituent's bargaining orientation and intergroup negotiations. *Journal of Applied Social Psychology, 4*, 141–150.

Bereket, T., & Adam, B. D. (2008). Navigating Islam and same-sex liaisons among men in Turkey. *Journal of Homosexuality, 55*, 204–222.

Berger, J., Fisek, M. H., Norman, R. Z., & Zelditch, M., Jr. (1977). *Status characteristics and social interaction.* New York: Elsevier.

Berger, J., Wagner, D., & Zelditch, M., Jr. (1985). Expectation states theory: Review and assessment. In J. Berger & M. Zelditch Jr (Eds.), *Status, rewards and influence* (pp. 1–72). San Francisco, CA: Jossey-Bass.

Berger, P. L. (1999). *The desecularization of the world: Resurgent religion and world politics.* Grand Rapids, MI: Eerdmans.

Berglas, S. (1987). The self-handicapping model of alcohol abuse. In H. T. Blane and K. E. Leonard (Eds.), *Psychological theories of drinking and alcoholism* (pp. 305–345). New York: Guilford Press.

Berglas, S., & Jones, E. E. (1978). Drug choice as a self- handicapping strategy in response to noncontingent success. *Journal of Personality and Social Psychology, 36*, 405–417.

Berkowitz, L. (1962). *Aggression: A social psychological analysis.* New York: McGraw-Hill.

Berkowitz, L. (1970). The self, selfishness and altruism. In J. Macaulay & L. Berkowitz (Eds.), *Altruism and helping behaviour.* New York: Academic Press.

Berkowitz, L. (1972a). Frustrations, comparisons, and other sources of emotion arousal as contributors to social unrest. *Journal of Social Issues, 28*, 77–91.

Berkowitz, L. (1972b). Social norms, feelings, and other factors affecting helping and altruism. *Advances in Experimental Social Psychology, 6*, 63–108.

Berkowitz, L. (1974). Some determinants of impulsive aggression: Role of mediated associations with reinforcements for aggression. *Psychological Review, 81*, 165–176.

Berkowitz, L. (1978). Decreased helpfulness with increased group size through lessening the effects of the needy individual's dependency. *Journal of Personality, 46*, 299–310.

Berkowitz, L. (1984). Some effects of thoughts on anti- and pro-social influences of media events: A cognitive-neo-association analysis. *Psychological Bulletin, 95*, 410–427.

Berkowitz, L. (1993). *Aggression: Its causes, consequences and control.* Philadelphia, PA: Temple University Press.

Berkowitz, L. (2012). A different view of anger: The cognitive-neoassociation conception of the relation of anger to aggression. *Aggressive Behavior, 38*, 322–333.

Berkowitz, L., & LePage, A. (1967). Weapons as aggression-eliciting stimuli. *Journal of Personality and Social Psychology, 7*, 202–207.

Berman, M., Gladue, B., & Taylor, S. (1993). The effects of hormones, type A behavior pattern, and provocation on aggression in men. *Motivation and Emotion, 17*, 125–138.

Bernard, M. M., Maio, G. R., & Olson, J. M. (2003). The vulnerability of values to attack: Inoculation of values and value-relevant attitudes. *Personality and Social Psychology Bulletin, 29*, 63–75.

Bernbach, W. (2002). *Bill Bernbach said.* New York: DDB Needham Worldwide.

Berns, G. S., Chappelow, J., Zink, C. F., Pagnoni, G., Martin-Skurski, M. E., & Richard, J. (2005). Neurobiological correlates of social conformity and independence during mental rotation. *Biological Psychiatry, 58*, 245–253.

Berry, J. W. (1967). Independence and conformity in subsistence level societies. *Journal of Personality and Social Psychology, 7*, 415–418.

Berry, J. W. (1984). Multicultural policy in Canada: A social psychological analysis. *Canadian Journal of Behavioural Science, 16*, 353–370.

Berry, J. W., Dasen, P. R., & Saraswathi, T. S. (Eds.) (1997). *Handbook of cross-cultural psychology, Vol. 2: Basic processes and human development* (2nd ed.). Needham Heights, MA: Allyn & Bacon.

Berry, J. W., Kim, U., Minde, T., & Mok, D. (1987). Comparative studies of acculturative stress. *International Migration Review, 21*, 491–511.

Berry, J. W., Poortinga, Y. P., & Pandey, J. (Eds.) (1997). *Handbook of cross-cultural psychology, Vol. 1: Theory and method* (2nd ed.). Needham Heights, MA: Allyn & Bacon.

Berry, J. W., Segall, M. H., and Kağıtçıbaşı, Ç. (Eds.) (1997). *Handbook of cross- cultural psychology* (2nd ed.). Boston, MA: Allyn and Bacon.

Berry, J. W., Trimble, J. E., & Olmedo, E. L. (1986). Assessment of acculturation. In W. J. Lonner & J. W. Berry (Eds.), *Field methods in cross-cultural research* (pp. 290–327). Beverly Hills, CA: SAGE.

Berscheid, E. (1994). Interpersonal relationships. *Annual Review of Psychology, 45*, 79–129.

Berscheid, E. (2010). Love in the fourth dimension. *Annual Review of Psychology, 61*, 1–25.

Berscheid, E., & Ammazzalorso, H. (2001). Emotional experience in close relationships. In G. J. O. Fletcher & M. Clark (Eds.), *Blackwell handbook of social psychology: Interpersonal processes* (pp. 253–278). Oxford, UK: Blackwell Publishers.

Berscheid, E., Graziano, W., Monson, T., & Dermer, M. (1976). Outcome dependency: Attention, attribution, and attraction. *Journal of Personality and Social Psychology, 34*, 978–989.

Berscheid, E., & Reis, H. T. (1998). Attraction and close relationships. In D. T. Gilbert, S. T. Fiske, & G. Lindzey (Eds.), *The handbook of social psychology* (4th ed., Vol. 2, pp. 193–281). New York: McGraw-Hill.

Bettleheim, B. (1969). *The children of the dream.* London: Thames and Hudson.

Betts, K. R., & Hinsz, V. B. (2013). Group marginalization: Extending research on interpersonal rejection to small groups. *Personality and Social Psychology Review, 17*, 355–370.

Bickman, L., & Green, S. K. (1977). Situational cues and crime reporting: Do signs make a difference? *Journal of Applied Social Psychology, 7*, 1–8.

Bickman, L., & Rosenbaum, D. P. (1977). Crime reporting as a function of bystander encouragement, surveillance, and credibility. *Journal of Personality and Social Psychology, 35*, 577–586.

Biener, L., & Abrams, D. (1991). The contemplation ladder: Validation of a measure of readiness to consider smoking cessation. *Health Psychology, 10*, 360–365.

Bierhoff, H.-W., & Rohmann, E. (2004). Altruistic personality in the context of the empathy–altruism hypothesis. *European Journal of Personality, 18*, 351–365.

Billig, M. (1973). Normative communication in a minimal inter-group situation. *European Journal of Social Psychology, 3*, 339–343.

Billig, M. (1976). *Social psychology and intergroup relations*. London: Academic Press.

Billig, M. (1978). *Fascists: A social psychological view of the National Front*. London: Harcourt Brace Jovanovich.

Billig, M. (1987). *Arguing and thinking: A rhetorical approach to social psychology*. Cambridge, UK: Cambridge University Press.

Billig, M. (1991). *Ideology and opinions: Studies in rhetorical psychology*. London: SAGE.

Billig, M. (1996). *Arguing and thinking: A rhetorical approach to social psychology*. Cambridge, UK: Cambridge University Press.

Billig, M. (2008). *The hidden roots of critical psychology*. London: Sage.

Billig, M., & Cochrane, R. (1979). Values of political extremists and potential extremists: A discriminant analysis. *European Journal of Social Psychology, 9*, 205–222.

Billig, M., & Tajfel, H. (1973). Social categorisation and similarity in intergroup behaviour. *European Journal of Social Psychology, 3*, 27–52.

Bilous, F. R., & Krauss, R. M. (1988). Dominance and accommodation in the conversational behaviours of same- and mixed-gender dyads. *Language and Communication, 8*, 183–194.

Birchmeier, Z., Dietz-Uhler, B., & Stasser, G. (Eds.) (2011). *Strategic uses of social technology: An interactionist perspective of social psychology*. Cambridge, UK: Cambridge University Press.

Birdwhistell, R. (1970). *Kinesics and context: Essays on body movement communication*. Philadelphia, PA: University of Pennsylvania Press.

Birnbaum, G. E., Reis, H. T., Mikulincer, M., Gillath, O., & Orpaz, A. (2006). When sex is more than just sex: Attach ment orientations, sexual experience, and relationship quality. *Journal of Personality and Social Psychology, 91*, 929–943.

Black, S. L., & Bevan, S. (1992). At the movies with Buss and Durkee: A natural experiment on film violence. *Aggressive Behavior, 18*, 37–45.

Blake, R. R., & Mouton, J. S. (1961). Reactions to intergroup competition under win/lose conditions. *Management Science, 7*, 420–435.

Blake, R. R., Shepard, H. A., & Mouton, J. S. (1964). *Managing intergroup conflict in industry*. Texas: Gulf Publishing.

Blankenship, K. L., & Holtgraves, T. (2005). The role of different markers of linguistic powerlessness in persuasion. *Journal of Language and Social Psychology, 24*, 3–24.

Blascovich, J. (2008). Challenge and threat. In A. J. Elliot (Ed.), *Handbook of approach and avoidance motivation* (pp. 431–446). New York: Erlbaum.

Blascovich, J., & Mendes, W. B. (2010). Social psychophysiology and embodiment. In S. T. Fiske, D. T. Gilbert, & G. Lindzey (Eds.), *Handbook of social psychology* (5th ed., Vol. 1, pp. 194–227). New York: Wiley.

Blascovich, J., & Seery, M. D. (2007). Visceral and somatic indexes of social psychological constructs. In A. W. Kruglanski & E. T. Higgins (Eds.), *Social psychology: Handbook of basic principles* (2nd ed., pp. 19–38). New York: Guilford Press.

Blascovich, J., & Tomaka, J. (1996). The biopsychosocial model of arousal regulation. *Advances in Experimental Social Psychology, 28*, 1–51.

Blass, T. (2004). *The man who shocked the world: The life and legacy of Stanley Milgram*. New York: Basic Books.

Bloom, L. (1970). *Language development: Form and function in emerging grammars*. Cambridge, MA: MIT Press.

Bluic, A. M., McGarty, C., Reynolds, K., & Muntele, D. (2007). Opinion-based group membership as a predictor of commitment to political action. *European Journal of Social Psychology, 37*, 19–32.

Blumenthal, M. D., Kahn, R. L., Andrews, F. M., & Head, K. B. (1972). *Justifying violence: Attitudes of American men*. Ann Arbor, MI: Institute for Social Research.

Blumer, H. (1969). *Symbolic interactionism: Perspective and method*. Englewood Cliffs, NJ: Prentice Hall.

Boas, F. (1911). *The mind of primitive man*. New York: Macmillan.

Boas, F. (1930). Anthropology. *Encyclopedia of the Social Sciences, 2*, 73–110.

Bochner, S., & Insko, C. A. (1966). Communicator discrepancy, source credibility, and opinion change. *Journal of Personality and Social Psychology, 4*, 614–621.

Bodenhausen, G. V., & Lichtenstein, M. (1987). Social stereotypes and information-processing strategies: The impact of task complexity. *Journal of Personality and Social Psychology, 52*, 871–880.

Bogardus, E. S. (1925). Measuring social distances. *Journal of Applied Sociology, 9*, 299–308.

Bohner, G., Bless, H., Schwarz, N., & Strack, F. (1988). What triggers causal attributions? The impact of valence and subjective probability. *European Journal of Social Psychology, 18*, 335–345.

Bohner, G., Chaiken, S., & Hunyadi, P. (1994). The role of mood and message ambiguity in the interplay of heuristic and systematic processing. Special issue: Affect in social judgments and cognition. *European Journal of Social Psychology, 24*, 207–221.

Bohner, G., Moskowitz, G. B., & Chaiken, S. (1995). The interplay of heuristic and systematic processing of social information. *European Review of Social Psychology, 6*, 33–68.

Bond, C. F., Jr. (1982). Social facilitation: A self-presentational view. *Journal of Personality and Social Psychology, 42*, 1042–1050.

Bond, C. F., Jr, & DePaulo, B. M. (2006). Accuracy of deception judgments. *Personality and Social Psychology Review, 10*, 214–234.

Bond, C. F., Jr, & Titus, L. J. (1983). Social facilitation: A meta-analysis of 241 studies. *Psychological Bulletin, 94*, 265–292.

Bond, M. H. (1996). Chinese values. In M. H. Bond (Ed.), *The handbook of Chinese psychology* (pp. 208–227). Hong Kong: Oxford University Press.

Bond, M. H. (2003). Marrying the dragon to the phoenix: Twenty-eight years of doing a psychology of the Chinese people. *Journal of Psychology in Chinese Societies, 4*, 269–283.

Bond, M. H. (2004). Culture and aggression: From context to coercion. *Personality and Social Psychology Review, 8*, 62–78.

Bond, M. H. (Ed.) (1988). *The cross-cultural challenge to social psychology*. Newbury Park, CA: SAGE.

Bond, M. H., & King, A. Y. C. (1985). Coping with the threat of Westernisation in Hong Kong. *International Journal of Intercultural Relations, 9*, 351–364.

Bond, M. H., & Komai, H. (1976). Targets of gazing and eye contact during interviews: Effects on Japanese nonverbal behaviour. *Journal of Personality and Social Psychology, 34*, 1276–1284.

Bond, R., & Smith, P. B. (1996). Culture and conformity: A meta-analysis of the Asch line judgment task. *Psychological Bulletin, 119*, 111–137.

Bonnes, M., & Secchiaroli, G. (1995). *Environmental psychology: A psycho-social introduction*. London: Sage.

Bonta, B. D. (1997). Cooperation and competition in peaceful societies. *Psychological Bulletin, 121*, 299–320.

Book, A. S., Starzyk, K. B., & Quinsey, V. L. (2001). The relationship between testosterone and aggression: A meta-analysis. *Aggression and Violent Behavior, 6*, 579–599.

Borden, R. J. (1980). Audience influence. In P. B. Paulus (Ed.), *Psychology of group influence* (pp. 99–131). Hillsdale, NJ: Erlbaum.

Bornstein, G., Crum, L., Wittenbraker, J., Harring, K., Insko, C. A., & Thibaut, J. (1983). On the measurement of social orientations in the minimal group paradigm. *European Journal of Social Psychology, 13*, 321–350.

Bornstein, R. F. (1989). Exposure and affect: Overview and meta-analysis of research, 1968–1987. *Psychological Bulletin, 106*, 265–289.

Bosveld, W., Koomen, W., & Vogelaar, R. (1997). Construing a social issue: Effects on attitudes and the false consensus effect. *British Journal of Social Psychology, 36*, 263–272.

Bothwell, R. K., Brigham, J. C., & Malpass, R. S. (1989). Cross-racial identification. *Personality and Social Psychology Bulletin, 15*, 19–25.

Bouas, K. S., & Komorita, S. S. (1996). Group discussion and cooperation in social dilemmas. *Personality and Social Psychology Bulletin, 22*, 1144–1150.

Bourhis, R. Y. (1984). *Conflict and language planning in Quebec*. Clevedon, UK: Multilingual Matters.

Bourhis, R. Y., & Giles, H. (1977). The language of intergroup distinctiveness. In H. Giles (Ed.), *Language, ethnicity and intergroup relations* (pp. 119–135). London: Academic Press.

Bourhis, R. Y., Giles, H., & Lambert, W. E. (1975). Social consequences of accommodating one's style of speech: A cross-national investigation. *International Journal of the Sociology of Language*, 6, 55–72.

Bourhis, R. Y., Giles, H., Leyens, J. P., & Tajfel, H. (1979). Psycholinguistic distinctiveness: Language divergence in Belgium. In H. Giles & R. St Clair (Eds.), *Language and social psychology* (pp. 158–185). Oxford, UK: Blackwell.

Bourhis, R. Y., Giles, H., & Rosenthal, D. (1981). Notes on the construction of a 'subjective vitality questionnaire' for ethnolinguistic groups. *Journal of Multilingual and Multicultural Development*, 2, 144–155.

Bourhis, R. Y., Sachdev, I., & Gagnon, A. (1994). Intergroup research with the Tajfel matrices: Methodological notes. In M. Zanna & J. Olson (Eds.), *The psychology of prejudice: The Ontario symposium* (Vol. 7, pp. 209–232). Hillsdale, NJ: Erlbaum.

Boutwell, B. B., Franklin, C. A., Barnes, J. C., & Beaver, K. M. (2011). Physical punishment and childhood aggression: The role of gender and gene–environment interplay. *Aggressive Behavior*, 37, 559–568.

Bowes, N., & McMurran, M. (2013). Cognitions supportive of violence and violent behavior. *Aggression and Violent Behavior*, 18, 660–665.

Bowlby, J. (1969). *Attachment and loss*: (Vol. 1) *Attachment*. London: Hogarth Press.

Bowlby, J. (1988). *A secure base: Parent–child attachment and healthy human development*. New York: Basic Books.

Bowles, H. R., & McGinn, K. L. (2005). Claiming authority: Negotiating challenges for women leaders. In D. M. Messick & R. M. Kramer (Eds.), *The psychology of leadership: New perspectives and research* (pp. 191–208). Mahwah, NJ: Erlbaum.

Bowman, C. H., & Fishbein, M. (1978). Understanding public reaction to energy proposals: An application of the Fishbein model. *Journal of Applied Social Psychology*, 8, 319–340.

Bradbury, T. N., & Karney, B. R. (2010). *Intimate relationships*. New York: Norton.

Branscombe, N. R., & Doosje, B. (Eds.) (2004). *Collective guilt: International perspectives*. Cambridge, UK: Cambridge University Press.

Branthwaite, A., Doyle, S., & Lightbown, N. (1979). The balance between fairness and discrimination. *European Journal of Social Psychology*, 9, 149–163.

Brauer, M., Judd, C. M., & Gliner, M. D. (1995). The effects of reoperated expressions on attitude polarization during group discussion. *Journal of Personality and Social Psychology*, 68, 1014–1029.

Bray, R. M., & Noble, A. M. (1978). Authoritarianism and decisions of mock juries: Evidence of jury bias and group polarization. *Journal of Personality and Social Psychology*, 36, 1424–1430.

Breakwell, G. M., & Canter, D. V. (1993). *Empirical approaches to social representations*. Oxford, UK: Clarendon Press.

Breaugh, J. A., & Klimoski, R. J. (1981). Social forces in negotiation simulations. *Personality and Social Psychology Bulletin*, 7, 290–295.

Breckler, S. J. (1984). Empirical validation of affect, behavior, and cognition as distinct components of attitude. *Journal of Personality and Social Psychology*, 47, 1191–1205.

Breckler, S. J., & Wiggins, E. C. (1989a). On defining attitude and attitude theory: Once more with feeling. In A. R. Pratkanis, S. J. Breckler, & A. G. Greenwald (Eds.), *Attitude structure and function* (pp. 407–427). Hillsdale, NJ: Erlbaum.

Breckler, S. J., & Wiggins, E. C. (1989b). Affect versus evaluation in the structure of attitudes. *Journal of Experimental Social Psychology*, 25, 253–271.

Breckler, S. J., Pratkanis, A. R., & McCann, C. D. (1991). The representation of self in multidimensional cognitive space. *British Journal of Social Psychology*, 30, 97–112.

Brehm, J. W. (1966). *A theory of psychological reactance*. New York: Academic Press.

Brennan, K. A., & Shaver, P. R. (1995). Dimensions of adult attachment, affect regulation, and romantic relationship functioning. *Personality and Social Psychology Bulletin*, 21, 267–283.

Brewer, M. B. (1981). Ethnocentrism and its role in interpersonal trust. In M. B. Brewer & B. Collins (Eds.), *Scientific inquiry and the social sciences* (pp. 345–360). San Francisco, CA: Jossey-Bass.

Brewer, M. B. (1988). A dual process model of impression formation. In T. K. Srull & R. S. Wyer (Eds.), *Advances in social cognition: A dual process model of impression formation* (Vol. 1, pp. 1–36). Hillsdale, NJ: Erlbaum.

Brewer, M. B. (1991). The social self: On being the same and different at the same time. *Personality and Social Psychology Bulletin*, 17, 475–482.

Brewer, M. B. (1994). Associated systems theory: If you buy two representational systems, why not many more? In R. Wyer & T. Srull (Eds.), *Advances in social cognition* (Vol. 7, pp. 141–147). Hillsdale, NJ: Erlbaum.

Brewer, M. B. (2001). The many faces of social identity: Implications for political psychology. *Political Psychology*, 22, 115–125.

Brewer, M. B. (2003). *Intergroup relations* (2nd ed.). Philadelphia, PA: Open University Press.

Brewer, M. B. (2007). The social psychology of intergroup relations: Social categorization, ingroup bias, and outgroup prejudice. In A. W. Kruglanski & E. T. Higgins (Eds.), *Social psychology: Handbook of basic principles* (2nd ed., pp. 785–804). New York: Guilford Press.

Brewer, M. B., & Campbell, D. T. (1976). *Ethnocentrism and intergroup attitudes: East African evidence*. New York: Halsted-Press (Sage).

Brewer, M. B., & Chen, Y-R. (2007). Where (who) are collectives in collectivism? Toward conceptual clarification of individualism and collectivism. *Psychological Review*, 114, 133–151.

Brewer, M. B., Dull, V., & Lui, L. (1981). Perceptions of the elderly: Stereotypes as prototypes. *Journal of Personality and Social Psychology*, 41, 656–670.

Brewer, M. B., & Gardner, W. (1996). Who is this 'We'? Levels of collective identity and self representation. *Journal of Personality and Social Psychology*, 71, 83–93.

Brewer, M. B., & Kramer, R. M. (1986). Choice behavior in social dilemmas: Effects of social identity, group size, and decision framing. *Journal of Personality and Social Psychology*, 50, 543–549.

Brewer, M. B., & Lui, L. L. (1989). The primacy of age and sex in the structure of person categories. *Social Cognition*, 7, 262–274.

Brewer, M. B., & Miller, N. (1996). *Intergroup relations*. Buckingham, UK: Open University Press.

Brewer, M. B., & Pierce, K. P. (2005). Social identity complexity and outgroup tolerance. *Personality and Social Psychology Bulletin*, 31, 428–437.

Brewer, M. B., & Schneider, S. (1990). Social identity and social dilemmas: A double-edged sword. In D. Abrams & M. A. Hogg (Eds.), *Social identity theory: Constructive and critical advances* (pp. 169–184). London: Harvester Wheatsheaf.

Brickner, M. A., Harkins, S. G., & Ostrom, T. M. (1986). Effects of personal involvement: Thought provoking implications of social loafing. *Journal of Personality and Social Psychology*, 51, 763–770.

Brief, A. P., Dukerich, J. M., & Doran, L. I. (1991). Resolving ethical dilemmas in management: Experimental investigation of values, accountability, and choice. *Journal of Applied Social Psychology*, 21, 380–396.

Brigham, J. C. (1971). Ethnic stereotypes. *Psychological Bulletin*, 76, 15–38.

Brigham, J. C., & Barkowitz, P. B. (1978). Do 'they all look alike'? The effect of race, sex, experience and attitudes on the ability to recognise face. *Journal of Applied Social Psychology*, 8, 306–318.

Brigham, J. C., & Malpass, R. S. (1985). The role of experience and contact in the recognition of faces of own- and other-race persons. *Journal of Social Issues*, 41, 139–156.

Brinthaupt, T. M., Moreland, R. L., & Levine, J. M. (1991). Sources of optimism among prospective group members. *Personality and Social Psychology Bulletin*, 17, 36–43.

Brislin, R. W. (1987). Cross-cultural psychology. In R. J. Corsini (Ed.), *Concise encyclopedia of psychology* (pp. 274–287). New York: Wiley.

Britell, J. K. (1981). Ethics courses are making slow inroads. *New York Times, Education Section*, 26 April, p. 44.

Broadbent, D. E. (1985). *Perception and communication*. London: Pergamon Press.

Brockner, J., Chen, Y.-R., Mannix, E. A., Leung, K., & Skarlicki, D. P. (2000). Culture and procedural fairness: When the effects of what you do depend on how you do it. *Administrative Science Quarterly*, 45, 138–159.

Brockner, J., & Wiesenfeld, B. M. (1996). The interactive impact of procedural and outcome fairness on reactions to a decision: The effects of what you do depend on how you do it. *Psychological Bulletin, 120,* 189–208.

Broverman, I. K., Broverman, D. M., Clarkson, F., Rosencrantz, P. S., & Vogel, S. (1970). Sex-role stereotypes and clinical judgments of mental health. *Journal of Consulting and Clinical Psychology, 34,* 1–7.

Broverman, I. K., Vogel, S. R., Broverman, D. M., Clarkson, F. E., & Rosenkrantz, P. S. (1972). Sex-role stereotypes and clinical judgments of mental health: A current appraisal. *Journal of Social Issues, 28,* 59–78.

Brown, J. D. (2012). Understanding the better than average effect: Motives (still) matter. *Personality and Social Psychology Bulletin, 38,* 209–219.

Brown, M. E., Treviño, L. K., & Harrison, D. A. (2005). Ethical leadership: A social Learning perspective for construct development and testing. *Organizational Behavior and Human Decision Processes, 97,* 1127–1134.

Brown, P., & Fraser, C. (1979). Speech as a marker of situation. In K. R. Scherer & H. Giles (Eds.), *Social markers in speech* (pp. 33–108). Cambridge, UK: Cambridge University Press.

Brown, R. (1965). *Social psychology.* New York: Free Press.

Brown, R. (1986). *Social psychology* (2nd ed.). New York: Free Press.

Brown, R., & Fish, D. (1983). The psychological causality implicit in language. *Cognition, 14,* 237–273.

Brown, R., Gonzalez, R., Zagefka, H., Manzi, J., & Cehajic, S. (2008). Nuestra Culpa: Collective guilt and shame as predictors of reparation for historical wrongdoing. *Journal of Personality and Social Psychology, 94,* 75–90.

Brown, R. J. (1978). Divided we fall: An analysis of relations between sections of a factory workforce. In H. Tajfel (Ed.), *Differentiation between social groups: Studies in the social psychology of intergroup relations* (pp. 395–429). London: Academic Press.

Brown, R. J. (1995). *Prejudice: Its social psychology.* Oxford, UK: Blackwell.

Brown, R. J. (1996). Tajfel's contribution to the reduction of intergroup conflict. In W. P. Robinson (Ed.), *Social groups and identities: Developing the legacy of Henri Tajfel* (pp. 169–189). Oxford, UK: Butterworth-Heinemann.

Brown, R. J. (2000). *Group processes* (2nd ed.). Oxford, UK: Blackwell.

Brown, R. J., & Abrams, D. (1986). The effects of intergroup similarity and goal interdependence on intergroup attitudes and task performance. *Journal of Experimental Social Psychology, 22,* 78–92.

Brown, R. J., & Gaertner, S. (Eds.) (2001). *Blackwell handbook of social psychology: Intergroup processes.* Oxford, UK: Blackwell.

Brown, R. J., & Hewstone, M. (2005). An integrative theory of intergroup contact. *Advances in Experimental Social Psychology, 37,* 255–343.

Brown, R. J., Hinkle, S., Ely, P. C., Fox-Cardamone, L., Maras, P., & Taylor, L. A. (1992). Recognising group diversity: Individualist–collectivist and autonomous–relational social orientations and their implications for intergroup processes. *British Journal of Social Psychology, 31,* 327–342.

Brown, R. J., & Turner, J. C. (1981). Interpersonal and intergroup behaviour. In J. C. Turner & H. Giles (Eds.), *Intergroup behaviour* (pp. 33–65). Oxford, UK: Blackwell.

Brown, R. J., & Wade, G. S. (1987). Superordinate goals and intergroup behavior: The effects of role ambiguity and status on intergroup attitudes and task performance. *European Journal of Social Psychology, 17,* 131–142.

Brown, R. P., Imura, M., & Mayeux, L. (2014). Honor and the stigma of mental healthcare. *Personality and Social Psychology Bulletin, 40,* 1119–1131.

Brumbaugh, C. C., & Fraley, R. C. (2006). Transference and attachment: How do attachment patterns get carried forward from one relationship to the next? *Personality and Social Psychology Bulletin, 32,* 552–560.

Bruner, J. (1990) *Acts of meaning.* Cambridge, MA: Harvard University Press.

Bruner, J. S. (1957). On perceptual readiness. *Psychological Review, 64,* 123–152.

Bruner, J. S. (1958). Social psychology and perception. In E. E. Maccoby, T. M. Newcomb, & E. L. Hartley (Eds.), *Readings in social psychology* (3rd ed., pp. 85–94). New York: Henry Holt & Co.

Bruner, J. S., & Goodman, C. C. (1947). Value and need as organising factors in perception. *Journal of Abnormal and Social Psychology, 42,* 33–44.

Bruner, J. S., & Tagiuri, R. (1954). The perception of people. In G. Lindzey (Ed.), *Handbook of social psychology* (Vol. 2, pp. 634–654). Reading, MA: Addison-Wesley.

Brunswik, E. (1956). *Perception and the representative design of psychological experiments* (2nd ed.). Berkeley, CA: University of California Press.

Bryan, J. H., & Test, M. A. (1967). Models and helping: Naturalistic studies in aiding behavior. *Journal of Personality and Social Psychology, 6,* 400–407.

Bryman, A. (1992). *Charisma and leadership in organizations.* London: SAGE.

Buchanan, G. M., & Seligman, M. E. P. (1995). *Explanatory style.* Hillsdale, NJ: Erlbaum.

Buchanan, P. J. (1987). AIDS and moral bankruptcy. *New York Post,* 2 December, p. 23.

Buck, R. (2011). Communicative genes in the evolution of empathy and altruism. *Behavior Genetics, 41,* 876–888.

Buck, R., & Ginsburg, B. (1991). Spontaneous communication and altruism: The communicative gene hypothesis. In M. S. Clark (Ed.), *Prosocial behaviour* (pp. 149–175). Newbury Park, CA: SAGE.

Buckley, K. E., & Anderson, C. A. (2006). A theoretical model of the effects and consequences of playing video games. In P. Vorderer & J. Bryant (Eds.), *Playing video games: Motives, responses, and consequences* (pp. 363–378). Mahwah, NJ: Erlbaum.

Buckner, H. T. (1965). A theory of rumour transmission. *Public Opinion Quarterly, 29,* 54–70.

Budd, R. J., North, D., & Spencer, C. (1984). Understanding seat-belt use: A test of Bentler and Speckart's extension of the 'theory of reasoned action'. *European Journal of Social Psychology, 14,* 69–78.

Buford, B. (1993). *Among the thugs.* New York: Vintage.

Bugental, D. B. (2005). Interdisciplinary insights on nonverbal responses within attachment relationships *Journal of Nonverbal Behavior, 29,* 177–186.

Bugental, D. E., Love, L. R., & Gianetto, R. M. (1971). Perfidious feminine faces. *Journal of Personality and Social Psychology, 17,* 314–318.

Buhrmester, M., Kwang, T., & Gosling, S.D. (2011). Amazon's mechanical turk: A new source of inexpensive, yet high-quality data? *Perspectives on Psychological Science, 5,* 3–5.

Bulman, R. J., & Wortman, C. B. (1977). Attributions of blame and coping in the 'real world': Severe accident victims react to their lot. *Journal of Personality and Social Psychology, 35,* 351–363.

Bunge, C. (1903). *Principes de psychologie individuelle et sociale.* Paris: Alcan.

Burger, J. M. (1981). Motivational biases in the attribution of responsibility for an accident: A meta-analysis of the defensive attribution hypothesis. *Psychological Bulletin, 90,* 496–513.

Burger, J. M. (2009). Replicating Milgram: Would people still obey today? *American Psychologist, 64,* 1–11.

Burgoon, J. K., Buller, D. B., & Woodall, W. G. (1989). *Nonverbal communication: The unspoken dialogue.* New York: Harper and Row.

Burgoon, M., Pfau, M., & Birk, T. S. (1995). An inoculation theory explanation for the effects of corporate issue/advocacy advertising campaigns. *Communication Research, 22,* 485–505.

Buriel, R. (1987). Ethnic labelling and identity among Mexican Americans. In J. S. Phinney & M. J. Rotheram (Eds.), *Children's ethnic socialization: Pluralism and development* (pp. 134–152). Newbury Park, CA: SAGE.

Burnham, W. H. (1910). The group as a stimulus to mental activity. *Science, 31,* 761–767.

Burns, J. M. (1978). *Leadership.* New York: Harper & Row.

Burnstein, E., Crandall, C., & Kitayama, S. (1994). Some neo-Darwinian decision rules for altruism: Weighing cues for inclusive fitness as a function of the biological importance of the decision. *Journal of Personality and Social Psychology, 67,* 773–789.

Burnstein, E., & McRae, A. (1962). Some effects of shared threat and prejudice in racially mixed groups. *Journal of Abnormal and Social Psychology, 64,* 257–263.

Burnstein, E., & Vinokur, A. (1977). Persuasive argumentation and social comparison as determinants of attitude polarization. *Journal of Experimental Social Psychology, 13,* 315–332.

Bushman, B. J. (1984). Perceived symbols of authority and their influence on compliance. *Journal of Applied Social Psychology, 14,* 501–508.

Bushman, B. J. (1988). The effects of apparel on compliance: A field experiment with a female authority figure. *Personality and Social Psychology Bulletin, 14,* 459–467.

Bushman, B. J. (2002). Does venting anger feed or extinguish the flame? Catharsis, rumination, distraction, anger, and aggressive responding. *Personality and Social Psychology Bulletin, 28,* 724–731.

Bushman, B. J., & Anderson, C. A. (2002). Violent video games and hostile expectations: A test of the general aggression model. *Personality and Social Psychology Bulletin, 28,* 1679–1686.

Bushman, B. J., & Baumeister, R. F. (1998). Threatened egotism, narcissism, self-esteem, and direct and displaced aggression: Does self-love or self-hate lead to violence? *Journal of Personality and Social Psychology, 75,* 219–229.

Bushman, B. J., Baumeister, R. F., & Stack, A. D. (1999). Catharsis, aggression, and persuasive influence: Self-fulfilling or self-defeating prophecies? *Journal of Personality and Social Psychology, 76,* 367–376.

Bushman, B. J., & Bonacci, A. M. (2002). Violence and sex impair memory for television ads. *Journal of Applied Psychology, 87,* 557–564.

Bushman, B. J., & Cooper, H. M. (1990). Effects of alcohol on human aggression: An integrative research review. *Psychological Bulletin, 107,* 341–354.

Bushman, B. J., & Huesmann, L. R. (2001). Effects of televised violence on aggression. In D. Singer (Ed.), *Handbook of children and the media* (pp. 223–254). Thousand Oaks, CA: SAGE.

Bushman, B. J., & Huesmann, L. R. (2010). Aggression. In S. T. Fiske, D. T. Gilbert, & G. Lindzey (Eds.), *Handbook of social psychology* (5th ed., Vol. 2, pp. 833–863). New York: Wiley.

Bushman, B. J., & Stack, A. D. (1996). Forbidden fruit versus tainted fruit: Effects of warning labels on attraction to television violence. *Journal of Experimental Psychology: Applied, 2,* 207–226.

Buss, A. H. (1961). *The psychology of aggression.* New York: Wiley.

Buss, D. M. (2003). *The evolution of desire: Strategies of human mating* (rev. ed.). New York: Free Press.

Buss, D. M., & Duntley, J. D. (2011). The evolution of intimate partner violence. *Aggression and Violent Behavior, 16,* 411–419.

Buss, D. M., & Kenrick, D. T. (1998). Evolutionary social psychology. In D. T. Gilbert, S. T. Fiske, & G. Lindzey (Eds.), *The handbook of social psychology* (4th ed., Vol. 2, pp. 982–1026). New York: McGraw-Hill.

Buss, D. M., & Reeve, H. K. (2003). Evolutionary psychology and developmental dynamics: Comment on Lickliter and Honeycutt (2003). *Psychological Bulletin, 129,* 848–853.

Buss, D. M., & Schmitt, D. P. (1993). Sexual strategies theory: An evolutionary perspective on human mating. *Psychological Review, 100,* 204–232.

Butera, F., Mugny, G., Legrenzi, P., & Pérez, J. A. (1996). Majority and minority influence, task representation and inductive reasoning. *British Journal of Social Psychology, 35,* 123–136.

Byrd, R. E. (1938). *Alone.* New York: Putnam.

Byrne, D. (1971). *The attraction paradigm.* New York: Academic Press.

Byrne, D., & Clore, G. L. (1970). A reinforcement model of evaluative responses. *Personality: An International Journal, 1,* 103–128.

Byrne, D., & Wong, T. J. (1962). Racial prejudice, interpersonal attraction, and assumed dissimilarity of attitudes. *Journal of Abnormal and Social Psychology, 65,* 246–252.

Cacioppo, J. T., & Petty, R. E. (1979). Attitudes and cognitive response: An electrophysiological approach. *Journal of Personality and Social Psychology, 37,* 2181–2199.

Cacioppo, J. T., & Petty, R. E. (1981). Electromyograms as measures of extent and affectivity of information processing. *American Psychologist, 36,* 441–456.

Cacioppo, J. T., & Petty, R. E. (1982). The need for cognition. *Journal of Personality and Social Psychology, 42,* 116–131.

Cacioppo, J. T., & Tassinary, L. G. (1990). Inferring psychological significance from physiological signals. *American Psychologist, 45,* 16–28.

Cadinu, M., Maass, A., Rosabianca, A., & Kiesner, J. (2005). Why do women underperform under stereotype threat? Evidence for the role of negative thinking. *Psychological Science, 16,* 572–578.

Calder, B. J., & Ross, M. (1973). *Attitudes and behavior.* Morristown, NJ: General Learning Press.

Calhoun, J. B. (1962). Population density and social pathology. *Scientific American, 206,* 139–148.

Callaway, M. R., & Esser, J. K. (1984). Groupthink: Effects of cohesiveness and problem-solving procedures on group decision making. *Social Behavior and Personality, 12,* 157–164.

Callaway, M. R., Marriott, R. G., & Esser, J. K. (1985). Effects of dominance on group decision making: Towards a stress-reduction explanation of groupthink. *Journal of Personality and Social Psychology, 49,* 949–952.

Campbell, A. (1993). *Men, women, and aggression.* New York: HarperCollins.

Campbell, D. T. (1957). Factors relevant to the validity of experiments in social settings. *Psychological Bulletin, 54,* 297–312.

Campbell, D. T. (1958). Common fate, similarity, and other indices of the status of aggregates of persons as social entities. *Behavioral Science, 3,* 14–25.

Campbell, D. T. (1975). On the conflict between biological and social evolution and between psychology and moral tradition. *American Psychologist, 30,* 1103–1126.

Campbell, J. D. (1986). Similarity and uniqueness: The effects of attribute type, relevance, and individual differences in self-esteem and depression. *Journal of Personality and Social Psychology, 50,* 281–294.

Campbell, J. D. (1990). Self-esteem and clarity of the self-concept. *Journal of Personality and Social Psychology, 59,* 538–549.

Campbell, J. D., & Fairey, P. J. (1985). Effects of self-esteem, hypothetical explanations, and verbalisations of expectancies on future performance. *Journal of Personality and Social Psychology, 48,* 1097–1111.

Campbell, J. D., & Fairey, P. J. (1989). Informational and normative routes to conformity: The effect of faction size as a function of norm extremity and attention to the stimulus. *Journal of Personality and Social Psychology, 57,* 457–468.

Campbell, J. D., Tesser, A., & Fairey, P. J. (1986). Conformity and attention to the stimulus: Some temporal and contextual dynamics. *Journal of Personality and Social Psychology, 51,* 315–324.

Campbell, L., Simpson, J. A., Kashy, D. A., & Fletcher, G. J. O. (2001). Ideal standards, the self, and flexibility of ideals in close relationships. *Personality and Social Psychology Bulletin, 27,* 447–462.

Campbell, M. C., & Keller, K. L. (2003). Brand familiarity and advertising repetition effects. *Journal of Consumer Research, 30,* 292–304.

Cannavale, F. J., Scarr, H. A., & Pepitone, A. (1970). Deindividuation in the small group: Further evidence. *Journal of Personality and Social Psychology, 16,* 141–147.

Cantor, N., & Kihlstrom, J. F. (1987). *Personality and social intelligence.* Englewood Cliffs, NJ: Prentice Hall.

Cantor, N., & Mischel, W. (1977). Traits as prototypes: Effects on recognition memory. *Journal of Personality and Social Psychology, 35,* 38–48.

Cantor, N., & Mischel, W. (1979). Prototypes in person perception. *Advances in Experimental Social Psychology, 12,* 3–52.

Caplow, T. (1947). Rumours in war. *Social Forces, 25,* 298–302.

Caporael, L. R. (2007). Evolutionary theory for social and cultural psychology. In A. W. Kruglanski & E. T. Higgins (Eds.), *Social psychology: Handbook of basic principles* (2nd ed., pp. 3–18). New York: Guilford Press.

Caporael, L. R., Dawes, R., Orbell, J., & Van de Kragt, A. (1989). Selfishness examined: Cooperation in the absence of egoistic incentives. *Behavioral and Brain Sciences, 12,* 683–699.

Caporael, L. R., Lukaszewski, M. P., & Cuthbertson, G. H. (1983). Secondary baby talk: Judgments by institutionalized elderly and their caregivers. *Journal of Personality and Social Psychology, 44,* 746–754.

Cappella, J. N., & Palmer, M. (1993). The structure and organisation of verbal and non-verbal behavior: Data for models of production. In H. Giles & W. P. Robinson (Eds.), *Handbook of language and social psychology* (pp. 141–161). Oxford, UK: Pergamon Press.

Caprara, G. V., Alessandri, G., & Eisenberg, N. (2012). Prosociality: The contribution of traits, values, and self-efficacy beliefs. *Journal of Personality and Social Psychology, 102,* 1289–1303.

Carli, L. L. (1990). Gender, language, and influence. *Journal of Personality and Social Psychology, 59,* 941–951.

Carlsmith, J. M., & Anderson, C. A. (1979). Ambient temperature and the occurrence of collective violence: A new analysis. *Journal of Personality and Social Psychology, 37,* 337–344.

Carlsmith, J. M., & Gross, A. E. (1969). Some effects of guilt on compliance. *Journal of Personality and Social Psychology, 11,* 232–239.

Carlson, M., Marcus-Newhall, A., & Miller, N. (1989). Evidence for a general construct of aggression. *Personality and Social Psychology Bulletin, 15,* 377–389.

Carlyle, T. (1841). *On heroes, hero-worship, and the heroic.* London: Fraser.

Carnagey, N. L., Anderson, C. A., & Bushman, B. J. (2007). The effect of video game violence on physiological desensitization to real-life violence. *Journal of Experimental Social Psychology, 43,* 489–496.

Carnaghi, A., Maas, A., Gresta, S., Bianchi, M., Cardinu, M., & Arcuri, L. (2008). *Nomina sunt omina:* On the inductive potential of nouns and adjectives in person perception. *Journal of Personality and Social Psychology, 94,* 839–859.

Carnevale, P. J., & Leung, K. (2001). Cultural dimensions of negotiation. In M. A. Hogg & R. S. Tindale (Eds.), *Blackwell handbook of social psychology: Group processes* (pp. 482–496). Oxford, UK: Blackwell.

Carnevale, P. J. D., Pruitt, D. G., & Britton, S. D. (1979). Looking tough: The negotiator under constituent surveillance. *Personality and Social Psychology Bulletin, 5,* 118–121.

Carrithers, M., Collins, S., & Lukes, S. (Eds.) (1986). *The category of the person.* Cambridge, UK: Cambridge University Press.

Carroll, J. S., Bazerman, M. H., & Maury, R. (1988). Negotiator cognitions: A descriptive approach to negotiators' understanding of their opponents. *Organizational Behavior and Human Decision Processes, 41,* 352–370.

Carter, L. F., & Nixon, M. (1949). An investigation of the relationship between four criteria of leadership ability for three different tasks. *The Journal of Psychology, 27,* 245–261.

Cartwright, D. (1968). The nature of group cohesiveness. In D. Cartwright & A. Zander (Eds.), *Group dynamics: Research and theory* (3rd ed., pp. 91–109). London: Tavistock.

Cartwright, D., & Harary, F. (1956). Structural balance: A generalisation of Heider's theory. *Psychological Review, 63,* 277–293.

Cartwright, E. (2011). *Behavioral economics.* New York: Routledge.

Cartwright, E. (2014). *Behavioral economics* (2nd ed.). New York: Routledge.

Cartwright, S., & Schoenberg, R. (2006). Thirty years of mergers and acquisitions research: Recent advances and future opportunities. *British Journal of Management, 17,* S1–S5.

Carver, C. S., & Glass, D. C. (1978). Coronary-prone behavior pattern and interpersonal aggression. *Journal of Personality and Social Psychology, 36,* 361–366.

Carver, C. S., Glass, D. C., & Katz, I. (1977). Favorable evaluations of Blacks and the disabled: Positive prejudice, unconscious denial, or social desirability. *Journal of Applied Social Psychology, 8,* 97–106.

Carver, C. S., & Scheier, M. F. (1981). *Attention and self-regulation: A control theory approach to human behavior.* New York: Springer.

Cary, M. S. (1978). The role of gaze in the initiation of conversation. *Social Psychology, 41,* 269–271.

Casas, J. M., Ponterotto, J. G., & Sweeney, M. (1987). Stereotyping the stereotyper: A Mexican American perspective. *Journal of Cross-cultural Psychology, 18,* 45–57.

Caspi, A., & Gorsky, P. (2006). Online deception: Prevalence, motivation, and emotion. *Cyber Psychology and Behavior, 9,* 54–59.

Castano, E., Yzerbyt, V., & Bourguignon, D. (2003). We are one and I like it: The impact of group entitativity on group identification. *European Journal of Social Psychology, 33,* 735–754.

Catalano, R., Novaco, R., & McConnell, W. (1997). A model of the net effect of job loss on violence. *Journal of Personality and Social Psychology, 72,* 1440–1447.

Chacko, T. I. (1982). Women and equal employment opportunity: Some unintended effects. *Journal of Applied Psychology, 67,* 119–123.

Chaffee, S. H., Jackson-Beeck, M., Durall, J., & Wilson, D. (1977). Mass communication in political communication. In S. A. Renshon (Ed.), *Handbook of political socialization: Theory and research* (pp. 223–258). New York: Free Press.

Chaiken, S. (1979). Communicator physical attractiveness and persuasion. *Journal of Personality and Social Psychology, 37,* 1387–1397.

Chaiken, S. (1983). Physical appearance variables and social influence. In C. P. Herman, E. T. Higgins, & M. P. Zanna (Eds.), *Physical appearance, stigma, and social behavior: Third Ontario symposium* (pp. 143–178). Hillsdale, NJ: Erlbaum.

Chaiken, S. (1987). The heuristic model of persuasion. In M. P. Zanna, J. M. Olsen, & C. P. Herman (Eds.), *Social influence: The Ontario symposium* (Vol. 5, pp. 3–39). Hillsdale, NJ: Erlbaum.

Chaiken, S., & Eagly, A. H. (1983). Communication modality as a determinant of persuasion: The role of communicator salience. *Journal of Personality and Social Psychology, 45,* 241–256.

Chaiken, S., Liberman, A., & Eagly, A. H. (1989). Heuristic and systematic processing within and beyond the persuasion context. In J. S. Uleman & J. A. Bargh (Eds.), *Unintended thought* (pp. 215–252). New York: Guilford Press.

Chaiken, S., & Maheswaran, D. (1994). Heuristic processing can bias systematic processing: Effects of source credibility, argument ambiguity, and task importance on attitude judgement. *Journal of Personality and Social Psychology, 66,* 460–473.

Chance, J. E. (1985). *Faces, folklore, and research hypotheses.* Presidential address to the Midwestern Psychological Association convention, Chicago.

Chandra, S. (1973). The effects of group pressure in perception: A cross-cultural conformity study. *International Journal of Psychology, 8,* 37–39.

Chaplin, W. F., John, O. P., & Goldberg, L. R. (1988). Conceptions of states and traits: Dimensional attributes with ideals as prototypes. *Journal of Personality and Social Psychology, 54,* 541–557.

Chapman, L. J. (1967). Illusory correlation in observational report. *Journal of Verbal Learning and Verbal Behavior, 6,* 151–155.

Charng, H.-W., Piliavin, J. A., & Callero, P. L. (1988). Role identity and reasoned action in the prediction of repeated behavior. *Social Psychology Quarterly, 51,* 303–317.

Chemers, M. M. (2001). Leadership effectiveness: An integrative review. In M. A. Hogg & R. S. Tindale (Eds.), *Blackwell handbook of social psychology: Group processes* (pp. 376–399). Oxford, UK: Blackwell.

Chen, H., Yates, B. T., & McGinnies, E. (1988). Effects of involvement on observers' estimates of consensus, distinctiveness, and consistency. *Personality and Social Psychology Bulletin, 14,* 468–478.

Chen, S., Boucher, H. C., & Tapias, M. P. (2006). The relational self revealed: Integrative conceptualization and implications for interpersonal life. *Psychological Bulletin, 132,* 151–179.

Chen, S., Chen, K. Y., & Shaw, L. (2004). Self-verification motives at the collective level of self-definition. *Journal of Personality and Social Psychology, 86,* 77–94.

Cherek, D. R., Schnapp, W., Moeller, F., & Dougherty, D. M. (1996). Laboratory measures of aggressive responding in male parolees with violent and nonviolent histories. *Aggressive Behaviour, 22,* 27–36.

Chesler, P. (1972). *Women and madness.* Garden City, NY: Doubleday.

Chichinadze, K., Chichinadze, N., & Lazarashvili, A. (2011). Hormonal and neurochemical mechanisms of aggression and a new classification of aggressive behavior. *Aggression and Violent Behavior, 16,* 461–471.

Chidester, T. R. (1986). Problems in the study of inter-racial interaction: Pseudo-interracial dyad paradigm. *Journal of Personality and Social Psychology, 50,* 74–79.

Child, I. L. (1954). Socialization. In G. Lindzey (Ed.), *The handbook of social psychology* (Vol. 2, pp. 655–692). Cambridge, MA: Addison-Wesley.

Chisango, T., Mayekiso, T., & Thomae, M. (2015). The social nature of benevolent sexism and the antisocial nature of hostile sexism: Is benevolent sexism more likely to manifest in public contexts and hostile sexism in private contexts? *International Journal of Psychology, 50,* 363–371.

Chiu, C.-Y., & Hong, Y.-Y. (2007). Cultural processes: Basic principles. In A. W. Kruglanski & E. T. Higgins (Eds.), *Social psychology: Handbook of basic principles* (2nd ed., pp. 785–804). New York: Guilford Press.

Choi, I., & Choi, Y. (2002). Culture and self-concept flexibility. *Personality and Social Psychology Bulletin, 28*, 1508–1517.

Choi, I., & Nisbett, R. E. (2000). Cultural psychology of surprise: Holistic theories and recognition of contradiction. *Journal of Personality and Social Psychology, 79*, 890–905.

Chomsky, N. (1957). *Syntactic structures*. The Hague: Mouton.

Chomsky, N. (1959). Verbal behavior [review of Skinner's book]. *Language, 35*, 26–58.

Chow, R. M., Lowery, B. S., & Hogan, C. M. (2013). Appeasement: Whites' strategic support for affirmative action. *Personality and Social Psychology Bulletin, 39*, 332–345.

Christensen, L. (1988). Deception in psychological research: When is its use justified? *Personality and Social Psychology Bulletin, 14*, 664–675.

Christie, R., & Jahoda, M. (Eds.) (1954). *Studies in the scope and method of 'the authoritarian personality'*. New York: Free Press.

Christopherson, K. M. (2007). The positive and negative implications of anonymity in internet social interactions: "On the internet, nobody knows you're a dog." *Computers in Human Behavior, 23*, 3038–3056.

Christy, C. A., & Voigt, H. (1994). Bystander responses to public episodes of child abuse. *Journal of Applied Social Psychology, 24*, 824–847.

Chryssochoou, X. (2000). The representation(s) of a new superordinate category: Studying the stereotype of the European in the context of European integration. *European Psychologist, 5*, 269–277.

Chryssochoou, X. (2004). *Cultural diversity: Its social psychology*. Oxford, UK: Blackwell.

Cialdini, R. B., Borden, R. J., Thorne, A., Walker, M. R., Freeman, S., & Sloan, L. R. (1976). Basking in reflected glory: Three (football) field studies. *Journal of Personality and Social Psychology, 34*, 366–375.

Cialdini, R. B., Cacioppo, J. T., Bassett, R., & Miller, J. A. (1978). Low-balling procedure for producing compliance: Commitment then cost. *Journal of Personality and Social Psychology, 36*, 463–476.

Cialdini, R. B., Darby, B. L., & Vincent, J. E. (1973). Transgression and altruism: A case for hedonism. *Journal of Personality and Social Psychology, 9*, 502–516.

Cialdini, R. B., & Goldstein, N. J. (2004). Social influence: Compliance and conformity. *Annual Review of Psychology, 55*, 591–621.

Cialdini, R. B., Kallgren, C. A., & Reno, R. R. (1991). A focus theory of normative conduct: Theoretical refinement and reevaluation of the role of norms in human behavior. *Advances in Experimental Social Psychology, 21*, 201–234.

Cialdini, R. B., & Kenrick, D. T. (1976). Altruism as hedonism: A social development perspective on the relationship of negative mood state and helping. *Journal of Personality and Social Psychology, 34*, 907–914.

Cialdini, R. B., & Petty, R. E. (1979). Anticipatory opinion effects. In R. Petty, T. Ostrom, & T. Brock (Eds.), *Cognitive responses in persuasion*. Hillsdale, NJ: Erlbaum.

Cialdini, R. B., & Trost, M. R. (1998). Social influence: Social norms, conformity, and compliance. In D. T. Gilbert, S. T. Fiske, & G. Lindzey (Eds.), *The handbook of social psychology* (4th ed., Vol. 2, pp. 151–192). New York: McGraw-Hill.

Cialdini, R. B., Trost, M. R., & Newsom, J. T. (1995). Preference for consistency: The development of a valid measure and the discovery of surprising behavioral implications. *Journal of Personality and Social Psychology, 69*, 318–328.

Cialdini, R. B., Vincent, J. E., Lewis, S. K., Catalan, J., Wheeler, D., & Darby, B. L. (1975). Reciprocal concessions procedure for inducing compliance: The door-in-the-face technique. *Journal of Personality and Social Psychology, 31*, 206–215.

Cinnirella, M. (1997). Towards a European identity? Interactions between the national and European social identities manifested by university students in Britain and Italy. *British Journal of Social Psychology, 36*, 19–31.

Citrin, J., Green, D. P., Muste, C., & Wong, C. (1997). Public opinion toward immigration reform: The role of economic motivations. *The Journal of Politics, 59*, 858–881.

Citrin, J., Wong, C., & Duff, B. (2001). The meaning of American national identity: Patterns of ethnic conflict and consensus. In R. D. Ashmore, L. Jussim & D. Wilder (Eds.), *Social identity, intergroup conflict, and conflict reduction* (Vol. 3, pp. 71–100). New York: Oxford University Press.

Claes, J. A., & Rosenthal, D. M. (1990). Men who batter women: A study in power. *Journal of Family Violence, 5*, 215–224.

Clark, H. H. (1985). Language use and language users. In G. Lindzey & E. Aronson (Eds.), *Handbook of social psychology* (3rd ed., Vol. 2, pp. 179–232). New York: Random House.

Clark, K. B., & Clark, M. P. (1939a). The development of consciousness of self and the emergence of racial identification in Negro preschool children. *Journal of Social Psychology, 10*, 591–599.

Clark, K. B., & Clark, M. P. (1939b). Segregation as a factor in the racial identification of Negro preschool children. *Journal of Experimental Education, 8*, 161–163.

Clark, K. B., & Clark, M. P. (1940). Skin color as a factor in racial identification and preference in Negro children. *Journal of Negro Education, 19*, 341–358.

Clark, M. S. (Ed.) (1991). *Prosocial behavior*. Thousand Oaks, CA: SAGE.

Clark, M. S., & Grote, N. K. (1998). Why aren't indices of relationship costs always negatively related to indices of relationship quality? *Personality and Social Psychology Review, 2*, 2–17.

Clark, M. S., & Lemay, E. P., Jr. (2010). Close relationships. In S. T. Fiske, D. T. Gilbert, & G. Lindzey (Eds.), *Handbook of social psychology* (5th ed., Vol. 2, pp. 898–940). New York: Wiley.

Clark, N. K., & Stephenson, G. M. (1989). Group remembering. In P. B. Paulus (Ed.), *Psychology of group influence* (2nd ed., pp. 357–391). Hillsdale, NJ: Erlbaum.

Clark, N. K., & Stephenson, G. M. (1995). Social remembering: Individual and collaborative memory for social information. *European Review of Social Psychology, 6*, 127–160.

Clark, N. K., Stephenson, G. M., & Rutter, D. R. (1986). Memory for a complex social discourse: The analysis and prediction of individual and group remembering. *Journal of Memory and Language, 25*, 295–313.

Clark, R. D., III, & Word, I. E. (1974). Where is the apathetic bystander? Situational characteristics of the emergency. *Journal of Personality and Social Psychology, 29*, 279–287.

Clark, T. N. (1969). *Gabriel Tarde: On communication and social influence*. Chicago: University of Chicago Press.

Clary, E. G., & Snyder, M. (1991). A functional analysis of altruism and prosocial behaviour: The case of volunteerism. In M. S. Clarke (Ed.), *Prosocial behaviour* (pp. 119–147). Newbury Park, CA: SAGE.

Clary, E. G., & Snyder, M. (1999). Considerations of community: The context and process of volunteerism. *Current Directions in Psychological Science, 8*, 156–159.

Clément, R. (1980). Ethnicity, contact and communication competence in a second language. In H. Giles, W. P. Robinson, & P. M. Smith (Eds.), *Language: Social psychological perspectives* (pp. 147–154). Oxford, UK: Pergamon Press.

Clore, G. L. (1976). Interpersonal attraction: An overview. In J. W. Thibaut, J. T. Spence, & R. C. Carson (Eds.), *Contemporary topics in social psychology* (pp. 135–175). Morristown, NJ: General Learning Press.

Clore, G. L., & Byrne, D. (1974). A reinforcement–affect model of attraction. In T. L. Huston (Ed.), *Foundations of interpersonal attraction* (pp. 143–165). New York: Academic Press.

Clover, C. (2004). *The end of the line: How over-fishing is changing the world and what we eat*. London: Ebury Press.

Clyne, M. G. (1981). 'Second generation' foreigner talk in Australia. *International Journal of the Sociology of Language, 28*, 69–80.

Coates, B., Pusser, H. E., & Goodman, I. (1976). The influence of 'Sesame Street' and 'Mister Rogers' Neighbourhood' on children's prosocial behavior in preschool. *Child Development, 47*, 138–144.

Coch, L., & French, J. R. P., Jr (1948). Overcoming resistance to change. *Human Relations, 1*, 512–532.

Codol, J.-P. (1975). On the so-called 'superior conformity of the self' behaviour: Twenty experimental investigations. *European Journal of Social Psychology, 5*, 457–501.

Cohen, D. (2001). Cultural variation: Considerations and implications. *Psychological Bulletin, 127*, 451–471.

Cohen, D., & Nisbett, R. E. (1997). Field experiments examining the culture of honor: The role of institutions in perpetuating norms about violence. *Personality and Social Psychology Bulletin, 23*, 1188–1199.

Cohen, D., Nisbett, R. E., Bowdle, B. F., & Schwarz, N. (1996). Insult, aggression, and the southern culture of honor: An "experimental ethnography". *Journal of Personality and Social Psychology, 70*, 945–960.

Cohen-Kettenis, P. T., & Van Goozen, S. H. M. (1997). Sex reassignment of adolescent transsexuals: A follow-up study. *Journal of the American Academy of Child and Adolescent Psychiatry, 36*, 263–271.

Cohn, C. (1987). Nuclear language. *Bulletin of the Atomic Scientists*, June, 17–24.

Cohn, E. G. (1993). The prediction of police calls for service: The influence of weather and temporal variables on rape and domestic violence. *Journal of Environmental Psychology, 13*, 71–83.

Cohn, E. G., & Rotton, J. (1997). Assault as a function of time and temperature: A moderator-variable time-series analysis. *Journal of Personality and Social Psychology, 72*, 1322–1334.

Cohn, E. G., & Rotton, J. (2005). The curve is still out there: A reply to Bushman, Wang, and Anderson's (2005) 'is the curve relating temperature to aggression linear or curvilinear?' *Journal of Personality and Social Psychology, 89*, 67–70.

Cohn, N. (1966). *Warrant for genocide: The myth of the Jewish world conspiracy and the Protocol of the Elders of Zion*. New York: Harper & Row.

Cohn, N. (1975). *Europe's inner demons: An enquiry inspired by the great witch hunt*. London: Chatto.

Cole, M. (1996). *Cultural psychology: A once and future discipline*. Cambridge, MA: Belknap Press.

Collins, B. E. (1974). Four separate components of the Rotter I–E sale: Belief in a difficult world, a just world, a predictable world, and a politically responsive world. *Journal of Personality and Social Psychology, 29*, 381–391.

Collins, B. E., & Raven, B. H. (1969). Group structure: Attraction, coalitions, communication, and power. In G. Lindzey & E. Aronson (Eds.), *Handbook of social psychology* (Vol. 4, pp. 102–204). Reading, MA: Addison-Wesley.

Collins, N. L., Kane, H. S., Metz, M. A., Cleveland, C., Khan, C., et al. (2014). Psychological, physiological, and behavioral responses to a partner in need: The role of compassionate love. *Journal of Social and Personal Relationships, 31*, 601–629.

Collins, N. L., & Miller, L. C. (1994). Self-disclosure and liking: A meta-analytic review. *Psychological Bulletin, 116*, 457–475.

Colvin, C. R., & Block, J. (1994). Do positive illusions foster mental health? An examination of the Taylor and Brown formulation. *Psychological Bulletin, 116*, 3–20.

Colvin, C. R., Block, J., & Funder, D. C. (1995). Overly positive evaluations and personality: Negative implications for mental health. *Journal of Personality and Social Psychology, 68*, 1152–1162.

Comrie, B., Matthews, S., & Polinsky, M. (Eds.) (2003). *The atlas of languages* (Rev. ed.). New York: Facts on File.

Condor, S. (1988). Race stereotypes and racist discourse. *Text, 8*, 69–90.

Condor, S. (1996). Social identity and time. In W. P. Robinson (Ed.), *Social groups and identities: Developing the legacy of Henri Tajfel* (pp. 285–315). Oxford, UK: Butterworth-Heinemann.

Condor, S. (2006). Temporality and collectivity: Diversity, history and rhetorical construction of national entitativity. *British Journal of Social Psychology, 45*, 657–682.

Condry, J. (1977). Enemies of exploration: Self-initiated versus other-initiated learning. *Journal of Personality and Social Psychology, 35*, 459–477.

Conger, J. A., & Kanungo, R. N. (1998). *Charismatic leadership in organizations*. Thousand Oaks, CA: SAGE.

Conley, T. D., Collins, B. E., & Garcia, D. (2000). Perceptions of women condom proposers among Chinese Americans, Japanese Americans, and European Americans, *Journal of Applied Social Psychology, 30*, 389–406.

Conley, T. D., Ziegler, A., Moors, A. C., Matsick, J. L., & Valentine, B. (2012). A critical examination of popular assumptions about the benefits and outcomes of monogamous relationships. *Personality and Social Psychology Review, 17*, 124–141.

Connell, R. W. (1972). Political socialization in the American family: The evidence reexamined. *Public Opinion Quarterly, 36*, 323–333.

Conner, M., Lawton, R., Parker, D., Chorlton, K., Manstead, A. S. R., & Stradling, S. (2007). Application of the theory of planned behavior to the prediction of objectively assessed breaking of posted speed limits. *British Journal of Psychology, 98*, 429–453.

Conner, M., Norman, P., & Bell, R. (2002). The theory of planned behavior and healthy eating. *Health Psychology, 21*, 194–201.

Conner, M., Warren, R., Close, S., & Sparks, P. (1999). Alcohol consumption and the theory of planned behaviour: An examination of the cognitive mediation of past behaviour. *Journal of Applied Social Psychology, 28*, 1676–1704.

Cook, S. W. (1978). Interpersonal and attitudinal outcomes in cooperating interracial groups. *Journal of Research and Development in Education, 12*, 97–113.

Cook, S. W. (1985). Experimenting on social issues: The case of school desegregation. *American Psychologist, 40*, 452–460.

Cooke, R., & Sheeran, P. (2004). Moderation of cognition–intention and cognition–behaviour relations: A meta-analysis of properties of variables from the theory of planned behaviour. *British Journal of Social Psychology, 43*, 159–186.

Cooper, A., & Smith, E. S. (2011). *Homicide trends in the United States, 1980–2008*. Washington, DC: US Department of Justice. Retrieved 15 May 2017 from https://www.bjs.gov/content/pub/pdf/htus8008.pdf.

Cooper, H. M. (1979). Statistically combining independent studies: Meta-analysis of sex differences in conformity. *Journal of Personality and Social Psychology, 37*, 131–146.

Cooper, J. (1999). Unwanted consequences and the self: In search of the motivation for dissonance reduction. In E. Harmon-Jones & J. Mills (Eds.), *Cognitive dissonance: Progress on a pivotal theory in social psychology* (pp. 149–174). Washington, DC: American Psychological Association.

Cooper, J. (2007). *Cognitive dissonance: 50 years of a classic theory*. London: SAGE.

Cooper, J., & Axsom, D. (1982). Effort justification in psychotherapy. In G. Weary & H. Mirels (Eds.), *Integrations of Clinical and Social Psychology*. London: Oxford University Press.

Cooper, J., & Croyle, R. T. (1984). Attitudes and attitude change. *Annual Review of Psychology, 35*, 395–426.

Cooper, J., & Fazio, R. H. (1984). A new look at dissonance theory. *Advances in Experimental Social Psychology, 17*, 229–265.

Cooper, J., & Hogg, M. A. (2007). Feeling the anguish of others: A theory of vicarious dissonance. *Advances in Experimental Social Psychology, 39*, 359–403.

Copeland, G. A. (1989): Face-ism and primetime television. *Journal of Broadcasting & Electronic Media, 33*, 209–214.

Corballis, M. C. (1999). The gestural origins of language. *American Scientist, 87*, 138–145.

Corballis, M. C. (2004). The origins of modernity: Was autonomous speech the critical factor? *Psychological Review, 111*, 543–552.

Cordery, J. L., Mueller, W. S., & Smith, L. M. (1991). Attitudinal and behavioral effects of autonomous group working: A longitudinal field study. *Academy of Management Journal, 34*, 464–476.

Corneille, O., Klein, O., Lambert, S., & Judd, C. M. (2002). On the role of familiarity with units of measurement in categorical accentuation: Tajfel and Wilkes (1963) revisited and replicated. *Psychological Science, 13*(4), 380–383.

Correa, T., Hinsley, A. W., & de Zúñiga, H. G. (2010). Who interacts on the Web? The intersection of users' personality and social media use. *Computers in Human Behavior, 26*, 247–253.

Corsianos, M. (2007). Mainstream pornography and "women": Questioning sexual agency. *Critical Sociology, 33*, 863–885.

Cortes, B. P., Demoulin, S., Rodriguez, R. T., Rodriguez, A. P., & Leyens, J.-P. (2005). Infrahumanization or familiarity? Attribution of uniquely human emotions to the self, the ingroup, and the outgroup. *Personality and Social Psychology Bulletin, 31*, 253–263.

Cose, E. (1993). *Rage of a privileged class*. New York: HarperCollins.

Costanzo, P. R. (1970). Conformity development as a function of self-blame. *Journal of Personality and Social Psychology, 14*, 366–374.

Cotton, S., Cunningham, J. D., & Antill, J. (1993). Network structure, network support and the marital satisfaction of husbands and wives. *Australian Journal of Psychology, 45*, 176–181.

Cottrell, C. A., Neuberg, S. L., & Li, N. P. (2007). What do people desire in others? A sociofunctional perspective on the importance of different valued characteristics. *Journal of Personality and Social Psychology, 92,* 208–231.

Cottrell, N. B. (1972). Social facilitation. In C. McClintock (Ed.), *Experimental social psychology* (pp. 185–236). New York: Holt, Rinehart & Winston.

Cottrell, N. B., Wack, D. L., Sekerak, G. J., & Rittle, R. H. (1968). Social facilitation of dominant responses by the presence of others. *Journal of Personality and Social Psychology, 9,* 245–250.

Counselman, E. (1991). Leadership in a long-term leaderless women's group. *Small Group Research, 22,* 240–257.

Coupland, N., Bishop, H., Evans, B., & Garrett, P. (2006). Imagining Wales and the Welsh language: Ethnolinguistic subjectivities and demographic flow. *Journal of Language and Social Psychology, 25,* 351–376.

Coupland, N., Coupland, J., Giles, H., & Henwood, K. (1988). Accommodating the elderly: Invoking and extending a theory. *Language in Society, 17,* 1–41.

Courtright, J. A. (1978). A laboratory investigation of groupthink. *Communication Monographs, 45,* 229–246.

Covell, K., Dion, K. L., & Dion, K. K. (1994). Gender differences in evaluations of tobacco and alcohol advertisements. *Canadian Journal of Behavioural Science, 26,* 404–420.

Cowen, W. L., Landes, J., & Schaet, D. E. (1958). The effects of mild frustration on the expression of prejudiced attitudes. *Journal of Abnormal and Social Psychology, 58,* 33–38.

Coyne, S. M., Linder, J. R., Nelson, D. A., & Gentile, D. A. (2012). "Frenemies, fraitors, and mean-em-aitors": Priming effects of viewing physical and relational aggression in the media on women. *Aggressive behavior, 38,* 141–149.

Cozby, P. C. (1973). Self-disclosure: A literature review. *Psychological Bulletin, 79,* 73–91.

Craddock, A. (1980). The impact of social change on Australian families. *Australian Journal of Sex, Marriage and the Family, 1,* 4–14.

Cramer, R. E., McMaster, M. R., Bartell, P. A., & Dragna, M. (1988). Subject competence and minimization of the bystander effect. *Journal of Applied Social Psychology, 18,* 1133–1148.

Crandall, C. S. (1994). Prejudice against fat people: Ideology and self-interest. *Journal of Personality and Social Psychology, 66,* 882–894.

Crandall, C. S., Bahns, A. J., Warner, R., & Schaller, M. (2011). Stereotypes as justifications of prejudice. *Personality and Social Psychology Bulletin, 37,* 1488–1498.

Crandall, C. S., D'Anello, S., Sakalli, N., Lazarus, E., Nejtardt, G. W., & Feather, N. T. (2001). An attribution-value model of prejudice: Anti-fat attitudes in six nations. *Personality and Social Psychology Bulletin, 27,* 30–37.

Crandall, C. S., Nierman, A., & Hebl, M. (2009). Anti-fat prejudice. In T. D. Nelson (Ed.), *Handbook of prejudice, stereotyping and discrimination* (pp 469–488). New York: Psychology Press.

Crano, W. D. (2001). Social influence, social identity, and ingroup leniency. In C. W. K. de Dreu & N. K. de Vries (Eds.), *Group consensus and minority influence: Implications for innovation* (pp. 122–143). Oxford, UK: Blackwell.

Crano, W. D., & Alvaro, E. M. (1998). The context/comparison model of social influence: Mechanisms, structure, and linkages that underlie indirect attitude change. *European Review of Social Psychology, 8,* 175–202.

Crano, W. D., & Brewer, M. B. (2015). *Principles and methods of social research* (3rd ed.). New York: Routledge.

Crano, W. D., & Chen, X. (1998). The leniency contract and persistence of majority and minority influence. *Journal of Personality and Social Psychology, 74,* 1437–1450.

Crano, W. D., & Prislin, R. (2006). Attitudes and persuasion. *Annual Review of Psychology, 57,* 345–374.

Crano, W. D., & Seyranian, V. (2009). How minorities prevail: The context/comparison-leniency contract model. *Journal of Social Issues, 65,* 335–363.

Crawford, M. (Ed.) (1995). *Talking difference: On gender and language.* London: SAGE.

Crick N., & Grotpeter J. 1995. Relational aggression, gender and social psychological adjustment. *Child Development, 66,* 710–722.

Crisp, R. J., & Abrams, D. (2008). Improving intergroup attitudes and reducing stereotype threat: An integrated contact model. *European Review of Social Psychology, 19,* 242–284.

Crisp, R. J., Ensari, N., Hewstone, M., & Miller, N. (2003). A dual-route model of crossed categorization effects. *European Review of Social Psychology, 13,* 35–74.

Crisp, R. J., & Hewstone, M. (2007). Multiple social categorization. *Advances in Experimental Social Psychology, 39,* 163–254.

Crisp, R. J., & Turner, R. N. (2012). The imagined contact hypothesis. *Advances in Experimental Social Psychology, 46,* 125–182.

Crocker, J. (1981). Judgement of covariation by social perceivers. *Psychological Bulletin, 90,* 272–292.

Crocker, J., Alloy, L. B., & Kayne, N. T. (1988). Attributional style, depression, and perceptions of consensus for events. *Journal of Personality and Social Psychology, 54,* 840–846.

Crocker, J., Fiske, S. T., & Taylor, S. E. (1984). Schematic bases of belief change. In J. R. Eiser (Ed.), *Attitudinal judgment* (pp. 197–226). New York: Springer.

Crocker, J., & Luhtanen, R. (1990). Collective self-esteem and ingroup bias. *Journal of Personality and Social Psychology, 58,* 60–67.

Crocker, J., & Major, B. (1989). Social stigma and self-esteem: The self-protective properties of stigma. *Psychological Review, 96,* 608–630.

Crocker, J., & Major, B. (1994). Reactions to stigma: The moderating role of justifications. In M. P. Zanna & J. M. Olson (Eds.), *The psychology of prejudice: The Ontario symposium* (Vol. 7, pp. 289–314). Hillsdale, NJ: Erlbaum.

Crocker, J., Major, B., & Steele, C. (1998). Social stigma. In D. T. Gilbert, S. T. Fiske, & G. Lindzey (Eds.), *The handbook of social psychology* (4th ed., Vol. 2, pp. 504–553). New York: McGraw-Hill.

Crockett, W. H. (1965). Cognitive complexity and impression formation. In B. A. Maher (Ed.), *Progress in experimental personality research* (Vol. 2, pp. 47–90). New York: Academic Press.

Croft, A., Schmader, T., & Block, K. (2015). An underexamined inequality: Cultural and psychological barriers to men's engagement with communal roles. *Personality and Social Psychology Review, 19,* 343–370.

Crosby, F. (1982). *Relative deprivation and working women.* New York: Oxford University Press.

Crosby, F. (1984). The denial of personal discrimination. *American Behavioral Scientist, 27,* 371–386.

Crosby, F., Bromley, S., & Saxe, L. (1980). Recent unobtrusive studies of black and white discrimination and prejudice: A literature review. *Psychological Bulletin, 87,* 546–563.

Crosby, F., Cordova, D., & Jaskar, K. (1993). On the failure to see oneself as disadvantaged: Cognitive and emotional components. In M. A. Hogg & D. Abrams (Eds.), *Group motivation: Social psychological perspectives* (pp. 87–104). London: Harvester Wheatsheaf.

Crosby, F., Pufall, A., Snyder, R. C., O'Connell, M., & Whalen, P. (1989). The denial of personal disadvantage among you, me, and all the other ostriches. In M. Crawford & M. Gentry (Eds.), *Gender and thought* (pp. 79–99). New York: Springer.

Cross, C. P., & Campbell, A. (2011). Women's aggression. *Aggression and Violent Behavior, 16,* 390–398.

Cross, K. P. (1977). Not can but will college teaching be improved? *New Directions for Higher Education, 17,* 1–15.

Cross, S. E., Bacon, P. L., & Morris, M. L. (2000). The relational–interdependent self-construal and relationships. *Journal of Personality and Social Psychology, 78,* 791–808.

Cross, S. E., & Madson, L. (1997). Models of the self: Self-construals and gender. *Psychological Bulletin, 122,* 5–37.

Cross, W. E. (1987). A two-factor theory of black identity: Implications for the study of identity development in minority children. In J. S. Phinney & M. J. Rotheram (Eds.), *Children's ethnic socialization: Pluralism and development* (pp. 117–133). Beverly Hills, CA: SAGE.

Crusco, A. H., & Wetzel, C. G. (1984). The Midas touch: The effects of interpersonal touch on restaurant tipping. *Personality and Social Psychology Bulletin, 10,* 512–517.

Crutchfield, R. A. (1955). Conformity and character. *American Psychologist, 10,* 191–198.

Csikszentmihalyi, M., & Nakamura, J. (2011). Positive psychology: Where did it come from, where is it going? In K. M. Sheldon, T. B. Kashdan, & M. F. Steger (Eds.), *Designing positive psychology* (pp. 2–9). New York: Oxford University Press.

Cuddy, A. J. C., Fiske, S., & Glick, P. (2008). Warmth and competence as universal dimensions of social perception: The stereotype content model and the BIAS map. *Advances in Experimental Social Psychology, 40*, 61–149.

Cunningham, M. R. (1979). Weather, mood, and helping behavior: Quasi-experiments with the sunshine samaritan. *Journal of Personality and Social Psychology, 37*, 1947–1956.

Cunningham, W. A., Preacher, K. J., & Banaji, M. R. (2001). Implicit attitude measures: Consistency, stability, and convergent validity. *Psychological Science, 12*, 163–170.

Cutrona, C. E., Russell, D., & Jones, R. D. (1985). Cross-situational consistency in causal attributions: Does attributional style exist? *Journal of Personality and Social Psychology, 47*, 1043–1058.

Cvetkovich, G., & Löfstedt, R. E. (Eds.) (1999). *Social trust and the management of risk.* London: Earthscan.

Czopp, A. M., & Monteith, M. J. (2006). Thinking well of African Americans: Measuring complimentary stereotypes and negative prejudice. *Basic and Applied Social Psychology, 28*, 233–250.

Dakof, G. A., & Taylor, S. E. (1990). Victims' perceptions of social support: What is helpful from whom? *Journal of Personality and Social Psychology, 58*, 80–89.

Danserau, F., Jr, Graen, G., & Haga, W. J. (1975). A vertical dyad linkage approach to leadership within formal organizations: A longitudinal investigation of the role-making process. *Organizational Behavior and Human Performance, 13*, 46–78.

Darley, J. M. (1991). Altruism and prosocial behavior: Reflections and prospects. In M. S. Clark (Ed.), *Prosocial behavior* (pp. 312–327). Newbury Park, CA: SAGE.

Darley, J. M., & Batson, C. D. (1973). From Jerusalem to Jericho: A study of situational and dispositional variables in helping behavior. *Journal of Personality and Social Psychology, 27*, 100–108.

Darley, J. M., & Latané, B. (1968). Bystander intervention in emergencies: Diffusion of responsibility. *Journal of Personality and Social Psychology, 8*, 377–383.

Darlington, R. B., & Macker, D. F. (1966). Displacement of guilt-produced altruistic behavior. *Journal of Personality and Social Psychology, 4*, 442–443.

Darwin, C. (1872). *The expression of emotions in man and animals.* Chicago: University of Chicago Press.

Das, E. H. H., de Wit, J. B. F., & Stroebe, W. (2003). Fear appeals motivate acceptance of action recommendations: Evidence for a positive bias in the processing of persuasive messages. *Personality and Social Psychology Bulletin, 29*, 650–664.

David, B., & Turner, J. C. (1996). Studies in self-categorization and minority conversion. Is being a member of the outgroup an advantage? *British Journal of Social Psychology, 35*, 179–199.

David, B., & Turner, J. C. (1999). Studies in self-categorization and minority conversion. The ingroup minority in intragroup and intergroup contexts. *British Journal of Social Psychology, 38*, 115–134.

David, B., & Turner, J. C. (2001). Majority and minority influence: A single process self-categorization analysis. In C. K. W. De Dreu & N. K. De Vries (Eds.), *Group consensus and innovation* (pp. 91–121). Oxford, UK: Blackwell.

Davidowicz, L. C. (1975). *The war against the Jews, 1933–1945.* New York: Holt, Rinehart & Winston.

Davidson, A. R., & Jacard, J. (1979). Variables that moderate the attitude–behavior relation: Results of a longitudinal survey. *Journal of Personality and Social Psychology, 37*, 1364–1376.

Davidson, L. R., & Duberman, L. (1982). Friendship: Communication and interactional patterns in same-sex dyads. *Sex Roles, 8*, 809–822.

Davies, J. C. (1969). The J-curve of rising and declining satisfaction as a cause of some great revolutions and a contained rebellion. In H. D. Graham & T. R. Gurr (Eds.), *The history of violence in America: Historical and comparative perspectives* (pp. 690–730). New York: Praeger.

Davies, K., Tropp, L. R., Aron, A., Pettigrew, T. F., & Wright, S. C. (2011). Cross-group friendships and intergroup attitudes: A meta-analytic review *Personality and Social Psychology Review, 15*, 332–351.

Davis, J. A. (1959). A formal interpretation of the theory of relative deprivation. *Sociometry, 22*, 280–96.

Davis, J. H. (1973). Group decision and social interaction: A theory of social decision schemes. *Psychological Review, 80*, 97–125.

Davis, M. H., Hall, J. A., & Meyer, M. (2003). The first year: Influences on the satisfaction, involvement, and persistence of new community volunteers. *Personality and Social Psychology Bulletin, 29*, 248–260.

Dawes, R. M. (1991). Social dilemmas, economic self-interest, and evolutionary self-interest. In D. R. Brown & J. E. Keith-Smith (Eds.), *Frontiers of mathematical psychology: Essays in honour of Clyde Coombs* (pp. 53–79). New York: Springer.

Dawes, R. M., Faust, D., & Meehl, P. E. (1989). Clinical versus actuarial judgment. *Science, 243*, 1668–1674.

Dawes, R. M., & Messick, D. M. (2000). Social dilemmas. *International Journal of Psychology, 35*, 111–116.

De Cremer, D. (2000). Leadership selection in social dilemmas – not all prefer it: The moderating effect of social value orientation. *Group Dynamics, 4*, 330–337.

De Cremer, D. (2002). Charismatic leadership and cooperation in social dilemmas: A matter of transforming motives? *Journal of Applied Social Psychology, 32*, 997–1016.

De Cremer, D. (2003). A relational perspective on leadership and cooperation: Why it matters to care and be fair. In D. Van Knippenberg & M. A. Hogg (Eds.), *Leadership and power: Identity processes in groups and organizations* (pp. 109–122). London: SAGE.

De Cremer, D., & Tyler, T. R. (2005). Managing group behavior: The interplay between procedural fairness, self, and cooperation. *Advances in Experimental Social Psychology, 37*, 151–218.

De Cremer, D., & Van Knippenberg, D. (2003). Cooperation with leaders in social dilemmas: On the effects of procedural fairness and outcome favorability in structural cooperation. *Organizational Behavior and Human Decision Processes, 91*, 1–11.

De Cremer, D., Van Knippenberg, D., Van Dijk, E., & Van Leeuwen, E. (2008). Cooperating if one's goals are collective-based: Social identification effects in social dilemmas as a function of goal transformation. *Journal of Applied Social Psychology, 38*, 1562–1579.

De Cremer, D., & Van Vugt, M. (1999). Social identification effects in social dilemmas: A transformation of motives. *European Journal of Social Psychology, 29*, 871–893.

De Cremer, D., & Van Vugt, M. (2002). Intergroup and intragroup aspects of leadership in social dilemmas: A relational model of cooperation. *Journal of Experimental Social Psychology, 38*, 126–136.

De Dreu, C. K. W. (2010). Social conflict: The emergence and consequences of struggle and negotiation. In S. T. Fiske, D. T. Gilbert, & G. Lindzey (Eds.), *Handbook of social psychology* (5th ed., Vol. 2, pp. 983–1023). New York: Wiley.

De Dreu, C. K. W., De Vries, N. K., Gordijn, E., & Schuurman, M. (1999). Convergent and divergent processing of majority and minority arguments: Effects on focal and related attitudes. *European Journal of Social Psychology, 29*, 329–348.

De Gilder, D., & Wilke, H. A. M. (1994). Expectation states theory and motivational determinants of social influence. *European Review of Social Psychology, 5*, 243–269.

De Houwer, J., & Hermans, D. (2001). Editorial: Auto matic affective processing. *Cognition and Emotion, 15*, 113–114.

De Houwer, J., Thomas, S., & Baeyens, F. (2001). Associative learning of likes and dislikes: A review of 25 years of research on human evaluative conditioning. *Psychological Bulletin, 127*, 853–869.

De Jong, P. F., Koomen, W., & Mellenbergh, G. J. (1988). Structure of causes for success and failure: A multi-dimensional scaling analysis of preference judgments. *Journal of Personality and Social Psychology, 55*, 1024–1037.

De Munck, V. C. (1996). Love and marriage in a Sri Lankan Muslim community: Toward an evaluation of Dravidian marriage practices. *American Ethnologist, 23*, 698–716.

De Waal, F. B. M. (2008). Putting the altruism back into altruism: The evolution of empathy. *Annual Review of Psychology, 59,* 279–300.

Dean, L. M., Willis, F. N., & Hewitt, J. (1975). Initial interaction distance among individuals equal and unequal in military rank. *Journal of Personality and Social Psychology, 32,* 294–299.

Deaux, K. (1976). *The behavior of women and men.* Monterey, CA: Brooks/Cole.

Deaux, K. (1985). Sex and gender. *Annual Review of Psychology, 36,* 49–81.

Deaux, K., & Emswiller, T. (1974). Explanations of successful performance on sex-linked tasks: What is skill for the male is luck for the female. *Journal of Personality and Social Psychology, 29,* 80–85.

Deaux, K., & LaFrance, M. (1998). Gender. In D. T. Gilbert, S. T. Fiske, & G. Lindzey (Eds.), *The handbook of social psychology* (4th ed., Vol. 1, pp. 788–827). New York: McGraw-Hill.

Deaux, K., & Philogene, G. (2001). *Representations of the social: Bridging theoretical traditions.* Oxford: Blackwell.

Deaux, K., Reid, A., Mizrahi, K., & Ethier, K. A. (1995). Parameters of social identity. *Journal of Personality and Social Psychology, 68,* 280–291.

Decety, J., & Lamm, C. (2006). Human empathy through the lens of social neuroscience. *The Scientific World Journal, 6,* 1146–1163.

Deci, E. L., & Ryan, R. M. (1985). *Intrinsic motivation and self-determination in human behavior.* New York: Plenum.

DeJong, W. (1979). An examination of self-perception mediation of the foot in the door effect. *Journal of Personality and Social Psychology, 37,* 2221–2239.

DeKeseredy, W. S. (2006). Future directions. *Violence against Women, 12,* 1078–1085.

DeKeseredy, W. S. (2011). Feminist contributions to understanding woman abuse: Myths, controversies, and realities *Aggression and Violent Behavior, 16,* 297–302.

Dekovic, M., & Janssens, J. M. (1992). Parents' child-rearing style and child's sociometric status. *Developmental Psychology, 28,* 925–932.

Delamater, J., & Ward, A. (Eds.) (2013). *Handbook of social psychology* (2nd ed.). New York: Springer.

Dembroski, T. M., & MacDougall, J. M. (1978). Stress effects on affiliation preferences among subjects possessing the Type A coronary-prone behavior pattern. *Journal of Personality and Social Psychology, 36,* 23–33.

D'Emilio, J. (1983). *Sexual politics, sexual communities: The making of a homosexual minority in the United States, 1940–1979.* Chicago: University of Chicago Press.

Dennis, A. R., & Valacich, J. S. (1993). Computer brainstorms: More heads are better than one. *Journal of Applied Psychology, 78,* 531–537.

Denzin, N. K., & Lincoln, Y. S. (Eds.) (2011). *The SAGE handbook of qualitative research* (4th ed.). Thousand Oaks, CA: SAGE.

DePaulo, B. (1992). Nonverbal behavior and self-presentation. *Psychological Bulletin, 111,* 203–243.

DePaulo, B. (1994). Spotting lies: Can humans learn to do better? *Current Directions in Psychological Science, 3,* 83–86.

DePaulo, B., & Friedman, H. S. (1998). Nonverbal communication. In D. T. Gilbert, S. T. Fiske, & G. Lindzey (Eds.), *The handbook of social psychology* (4th ed., Vol. 2, pp. 3–40). New York: McGraw-Hill.

DePaulo, B. M., Lanier, K., & Davis, T. (1983). Detecting the deceit of the motivated liar. *Journal of Personality and Social Psychology, 45,* 1096–1103.

DePaulo, B. M., & Rosenthal, R. (1979). Telling lies. *Journal of Personality and Social Psychology, 37,* 1713–1722.

DePaulo, P. J., & DePaulo, B. M. (1989). Can deception by salespersons and customers be detected through non-verbal behavioral cues? *Journal of Applied Social Psychology, 19,* 1552–1577.

Deschamps, J.-C. (1983). Social attribution. In J. Jaspars, F. D. Fincham, & M. Hewstone (Eds.), *Attribution theory and research: Conceptual, developmental and social dimensions* (pp. 223–240). London: Academic Press.

Deschamps, J.-C., & Brown, R. J. (1983). Superordinate goals and intergroup conflict. *British Journal of Social Psychology, 22,* 189–195.

Deutsch, M. (1975). Equity, equality and need: What determines which value will be used as a basis of distributive justice? *Journal of Social Issues, 31,* 137–149.

Deutsch, M., & Gerard, H. B. (1955). A study of normative and informational social influences upon individual judgment. *Journal of Abnormal and Social Psychology, 51,* 629–636.

Deutsch, M., & Krauss, R. M. (1960). The effect of threat upon interpersonal bargaining. *Journal of Abnormal and Social Psychology, 61,* 181–189.

Devine, P. G. (1989). Stereotypes and prejudice: Their automatic and controlled components. *Journal of Personality and Social Psychology, 56,* 5–18.

Devine, P. G., & Elliot, A. (1995). Are racial stereotypes really fading? The Princeton trilogy revisited. *Personality and Social Psychology Bulletin, 21,* 1139–1150.

Devine, P. G., Hamilton, D. L., & Ostrom, T. M. (Eds.) (1994). *Social cognition: Impact on social psychology.* San Diego, CA: Academic Press.

Devine, P. G., & Malpass, R. S. (1985). Orienting strategies in differential face recognition. *Personality and Social Psychology Bulletin, 11,* 33–40.

DeVos, G. A., & Hippler, A. E. (1969). Cultural psychology: Comparative studies of human behavior. In G. Lindzey & E. Aronson (Eds.), *Handbook of social psychology* (2nd ed., Vol. 4, pp. 322–417). Reading, MA: Addison-Wesley.

DeWall, C. N., Lambert, N. L., Slotter, E. B., Pond, R. S. Jr, Deckman, T., et al. (2011). So far away from one's partner, yet so close to romantic alternatives: Avoidant attachment, interest in alternatives, and infidelity. *Journal of Personality and Social Psychology, 101,* 1302–1316.

DeWall, C. N., Twenge, J. M., Bushman, B. J., Im, C., & Williams, K. D. (2010). A little acceptance goes a long way: Applying social impact theory to the rejection-aggression link. *Social Psychological and Personality Science, 1,* 168–174.

Diab, L. N. (1970). A study of intragroup and intergroup relations among experimentally produced small groups. *Genetic Psychology Monographs, 82,* 49–82.

Diamond, L. M. (2003). What does sexual orientation orient? A biobehavioral model distinguishing romantic love and sexual desire. *Psychological Review, 110,* 173–192.

Diaz-Guerrero, R. (1987). Historical sociocultural premises and ethnic socialization. In M. J. Rotheram (Ed.), *Children's ethnic socialization: Pluralism and development* (pp. 239–250). Newbury Park, CA: SAGE.

Dickens, C. (1854). *Hard times.* Harmondsworth, UK: Penguin.

Diehl, M. (1988). Social identity and minimal groups: The effects of interpersonal and intergroup attitudinal similarity on intergroup discrimination. *British Journal of Social Psychology, 27,* 289–300.

Diehl, M. (1990). The minimal group paradigm: Theoretical explanations and empirical findings. *European Review of Social Psychology, 1,* 263–292.

Diehl, M., & Stroebe, W. (1987). Productivity loss in brainstorming groups: Toward the solution of a riddle. *Journal of Personality and Social Psychology, 53,* 497–509.

Diehl, M., & Stroebe, W. (1991). Productivity loss in idea-generating groups: Tracking down the blocking effect. *Journal of Personality and Social Psychology, 61,* 392–403.

Diener, E. (1976). Effects of prior destructive behavior, anonymity, and group presence on deindividuation and aggression. *Journal of Personality and Social Psychology, 33,* 497–507.

Diener, E. (1980). Deindividuation: The absence of self-awareness and self-regulation in group members. In P. B. Paulus (Ed.), *Psychology of group influence* (pp. 209–242). Hillsdale, NJ: Erlbaum.

Diener, E., & Crandall, R. (1979). An evaluation of the Jamaican anticrime program. *Journal of Applied Social Psychology, 9,* 135–146.

Diener, E., Fraser, S. C., Beaman, A. L., & Kelem, R. T. (1976). Effects of deindividuation variables on stealing by Halloween trick-or-treaters. *Journal of Personality and Social Psychology, 33,* 178–183.

Diener, E., Kanazawa, S., Suh, E. M., & Oishi, S. (2015). Why people are in a generally good mood. *Personality and Social Psychology Review, 19,* 235–256.

Dienstbier, R. A., Kahle, L. R., Willis, K. A., & Tunnell, G. B. (1980). The impact of moral theories on cheating: Studies of emotion attribution and schema activation. *Motivation and Emotion, 4*, 193–216.

Dietz, T. L. (1998). An examination of violence and gender role portrayals in video games: Implications for gender socialization and aggressive behavior. *Sex Roles, 38*, 425–442.

DiFonzo, N., & Bordia, P. (2007). Rumor psychology: Social and organizational approaches. Washington, DC: American Psychological Association.

Dijksterhuis, A. (2010). Automaticity and the unconscious. In S. T. Fiske, D. T. Gilbert, & G. Lindzey (Eds.), *Handbook of social psychology* (5th ed., Vol. 1, pp. 228–267). New York: Wiley.

Dindia, K. (1987). The effects of sex of subject and sex of partner in interruptions. *Human Communication Research, 13*, 345–371.

Dindia, K., & Allen, M. (1992). Sex differences in self-disclosure: A meta-analysis. *Psychological Bulletin, 112*, 106–124.

Dion, K. K., Berscheid, E., & Walster, E. (1972). What is beautiful is good. *Journal of Personality and Social Psychology, 24*, 285–290.

Dion, K. K., & Dion, K. L. (1996). Toward understanding love. *Personal Relationships, 3*, 1–3.

Dion, K. L. (1979). Intergroup conflict and intragroup cohesiveness. In W. G. Austin & S. Worchel (Eds.), *The social psychology of intergroup relations* (pp. 211–224). Monterey, CA: Brooks/Cole.

Dion, K. L. (2000). Group cohesion: From 'field of forces' to multidimensional construct. *Group Dynamics, 4*, 7–26.

Dion, K. L., & Earn, B. M. (1975). The phenomenology of being a target of prejudice. *Journal of Personality and Social Psychology, 32*, 944–950.

Dion, K. L., Earn, B. M., & Yee, P. H. N. (1978). The experience of being a victim of prejudice: An experimental approach. *International Journal of Psychology, 13*, 197–214.

Dipboye, R. L. (1977). Alternative approaches to deindividuation. *Psychological Bulletin, 84*, 1057–1075.

Dirks, K. T., & Ferrin, D. L. (2002). Trust in leadership: Meta-analytic findings and implications for research and practice. *Journal of Applied Psychology, 87*, 611–628.

Doi, L. T. (1976). The Japanese patterns of communication and the concept of amae. In L. A. Samovar & R. E. Porter (Eds.), *Intercultural communication: A reader* (2nd ed., pp. 188–193). Belmont, CA: Wadsworth.

Doise, W. (1978). *Groups and individuals: Explanations in social psychology*. Cambridge, UK: Cambridge University Press.

Doise, W. (1982). Report on the European Association of Experimental Social Psychology. *European Journal of Social Psychology, 12*, 105–111.

Doise, W. (1986). *Levels of explanation in social psychology*. Cambridge, UK: Cambridge University Press.

Doise, W., Clémence, A., & Lorenzi-Cioldi, F. (1993). *The quantitative analysis of social representations*. London: Harvester Wheatsheaf.

Dolinski, D. (2000). On inferring one's beliefs from one's attempt and consequences for subsequent compliance. *Journal of Personality and Social Psychology, 78*, 260–272.

Doll, J., & Ajzen, I. (1992). Accessibility and stability of predictors in the theory of planned behaviour. *Journal of Personality and Social Psychology, 63*, 754–765.

Dollard, J., Doob, L. W., Miller, N. E., Mowrer, O. H., & Sears, R. R. (1939). *Frustration and aggression*. New Haven, CT: Yale University Press.

Doms, M. (1983). The minority influence effect: An alternative approach. In W. Doise & S. Moscovici (Eds.), *Current issues in European social psychology* (Vol. 1, pp. 1–32). Cambridge, UK: Cambridge University Press.

Doms, M., & Van Avermaet, E. (1980). Majority influence, minority influence, and conversion behavior: A replication. *Journal of Experimental Social Psychology, 16*, 283–292.

Donaldson, S. I., Csikszentmihalyi, M., & Nakamura, J. (Eds.) (2011). *Applied positive psychology: Improving everyday life, health, schools, work, and society*. London: Routledge.

Donnerstein, E., & Linz, D. (1994). Sexual violence in the mass media. In M. Costanzo & S. Oskamp (Eds.), *Violence and the law* (pp. 9–36). Thousand Oaks, CA: SAGE.

Donnerstein, E., & Malamuth, N. (1997). Pornography: Its consequences on the observer. In L. B. Schlesinger & E. Revitch (Eds.), *Sexual dynamics of anti-social behaviour* (2nd ed., pp. 30–49). Springfield, IL: Charles C. Thomas.

Doosje, B., Branscombe, N. R., Spears, R., & Manstead, A. S. R. (1998). Guilty by association: When one's group has a negative history. *Journal of Personality and Social Psychology, 75*, 872–886.

Doosje, B., Branscombe, N. R., Spears, R., & Manstead, A. S. R. (2006). Antecedents and consequences of group-based guilt: The effects of ingroup identification. *Group Processes and Intergroup Relations, 9*, 325–338.

Douglas, K. M., & Sutton, R. M. (2011). Does it take one to know one? Endorsement of conspiracy theories is influenced by personal willingness to conspire. *British Journal of Social Psychology, 50*, 544–555.

Dovidio, J. F. (1984). Helping behaviour and altruism: An empirical and conceptual overview. *Advances in Experimental Social Psychology, 17*, 361–427.

Dovidio, J. F., Brigham, J. C., Johnson, B. T., & Gaertner, S. L. (1996). Stereotyping, prejudice, and discrimination: Another look. In C. N. Macrae, C. Stangor, & M. Hewstone (Eds.), *Stereotypes and stereotyping* (pp. 276–319). New York: Guilford Press.

Dovidio, J. F., Eller, A., & Hewstone, M. (2011). Improving intergroup relations through direct, extended and other forms of indirect contact. *Group Processes and Intergroup Relations, 14*, 147–160.

Dovidio, J. F., & Ellyson, S. L. (1985). Patterns of visual dominance behavior in humans. In S. Ellyson & J. Dovidio (Eds.), *Power, dominance, and nonverbal behavior* (pp. 129–149). New York: Springer.

Dovidio, J. F., Ellyson, S. L., Keating, C. J., Heltman, K., & Brown, C. E. (1988). The relationship of social power to visual displays of dominance between men and women. *Journal of Personality and Social Psychology, 54*, 233–242.

Dovidio, J. F., & Gaertner, S. L. (2010). Intergroup bias. In S. T. Fiske, D. T. Gilbert, & G. Lindzey (Eds.), *Handbook of social psychology* (5th ed., Vol. 2, pp. 1084–1121). New York: Wiley.

Dovidio, J. F., Glick, P., Hewstone, M., & Esses, V. (Eds.) (2010). *Handbook of prejudice, stereotyping and discrimination*. London: SAGE.

Dovidio, J. F., Glick, P. G., & Rudman, L. (Eds.) (2005). *On the nature of prejudice: Fifty years after Allport*. Malden, MA: Blackwell.

Dovidio, J. F., Kawakami, K., & Beach, K. R. (2001). Implicit and explicit attitudes: Examination of the relationship between measures of intergroup bias. In R. Brown & S. Gaertner (Eds.), *Blackwell handbook of social psychology: Intergroup processes* (Vol. 4, pp. 175–197). Oxford, UK: Blackwell.

Dovidio, J. F., Pearson, A. R., & Orr, P. (2008). Social psychology and neuroscience: Strange bedfellows or a healthy marriage? *Group Processes and Intergroup Relations, 11*, 247–263.

Dovidio, J. F., Piliavin, J. A., Gaertner, S. L., Schroeder, D. A., & Clark, R. D., III. (1991). The arousal: Cost–reward model and the process of intervention: A review of the evidence. In M. S. Clark (Ed.), *Prosocial behaviour* (pp. 86–118). Newbury Park, CA: SAGE.

Downton, J. V. (1973). *Rebel leadership*. New York: Free Press.

Drigotas, S. M., Rusbult, C. E., Wieselquist, J., & Whitton, S. (1999). Close partner as sculptor of the ideal self: Behavioral affirmation and the Michelangelo phenomenon. *Journal of Personality and Social Psychology, 77*, 293–323.

Duck, J. M., & Fielding, K. S. (1999). Leaders and sub-groups: One of us or one of them? *Group Processes and Intergroup Relations, 2*, 203–230.

Duck, J. M., & Fielding, K. S. (2003). Leaders and their treatment of subgroups: Implications for evaluations of the leader and the superordinate group. *European Journal of Social Psychology, 33*, 387–401.

Duck, J. M., Hogg, M. A., & Terry, D. J. (1999). Social identity and perceptions of media persuasion: Are we always less influenced than others? *Journal of Applied Social Psychology, 29*, 1879–1899.

Duck, J. M., Hogg, M. A., & Terry, D. J. (2000). The perceived impact of persuasive messages on 'us' and 'them'. In D. J. Terry & M. A. Hogg (Eds.), *Attitudes, behavior, and social context: The role of norms and group membership* (pp. 265–291). Mahwah, NJ: Erlbaum.

Duck, S. (2007). *Human relationships* (4th ed.). Thousand Oaks, CA: SAGE.

Duck, S. (2008). A past and a future for relationship research. *Journal of Social and Personal Relationships, 25*, 189–200.

Duck, S. (Ed.) (1982). *Personal relationships, 4: Dissolving personal relationships*. London: Academic Press.

Duckitt, J. (1989). Authoritarianism and group identification: A new view of an old construct. *Political Psychology, 10*, 63–84.

Duckitt, J. (1992). *The social psychology of prejudice*. New York: Praeger.

Duckitt, J. (2000). Culture, personality and prejudice. In S. A. Renshon & J. Duckitt (Eds.), *Political psychology* (pp. 89–107). London: Macmillan.

Duckitt, J. (2006). Differential effects of right wing authoritarianism and social dominance orientation on outgroup attitudes and their mediation by threat from and competitiveness to outgroups. *Personality and Social Psychology Bulletin, 32*, 684–696.

Duckitt, J., Wagner, C., du Plessis, I., & Birum, I. (2002). The psychological bases of ideology and prejudice: Testing a dual process model. *Journal of Personality and Social Psychology, 83*, 75–93.

Duncan, S. (1969). Nonverbal communication. *Psychological Bulletin, 72*, 118–137.

Duncan, S. L. (1976). Differential social perception and attribution of intergroup violence: Testing the lower limits of stereotyping of blacks. *Journal of Personality and Social Psychology, 34*, 590–598.

Dunn, R. G. (1998). *Identity crises: A social critique of postmodernity*. Minneapolis, MN: University of Minnesota Press.

Dunning, D., Meyerowitz, J. A., & Holzberg, A. (1989). Ambiguity and self-evaluation: The role of idiosyncratic trait definitions in self-serving assessments of ability. *Journal of Personality and Social Psychology, 57*, 1082–1090.

Durkheim, E. (1898). Représentations individuelles et représentations collectives. *Revue de Metaphysique et de Morale, 6*, 273–302.

Durkin, K. (1995). *Developmental social psychology: From infancy to old age*. Oxford, UK: Blackwell.

Durkin, K. F., & Bryant, C. D. (1995). 'Log on to sex': Some notes on the carnal computer and erotic cyberspace as an emerging research frontier. *Deviant Behavior, 16*, 179–200.

Dutton, D. G., & Aron, A. P. (1974). Some evidence for heightened sexual attraction under conditions of high anxiety. *Journal of Personality and Social Psychology, 30*, 510–517.

Dutton, D. G., Boyanowsky, E. H., & Bond, M. H. (2005). Extreme mass homicide: From military massacre to genocide. *Aggression and Violent Behavior, 10*, 437–473.

Dutton, D. G., & Lake, R. (1973). Threat of own prejudice and reverse discrimination in interracial situations. *Journal of Personality and Social Psychology, 28*, 94–100.

Duval, S., & Wicklund, R. A. (1972). *A theory of objective self-awareness*. New York: Academic Press.

Dvir, T., Eden, D., Avolio, B. J., & Shamir, B. (2002). Impact of transformational leadership training on follower development and performance: A field experiment. *Academy of Management Journal, 45*, 735–744.

Eagly, A. H. (1978). Sex differences in influenceability. *Psychological Bulletin, 85*, 86–116.

Eagly, A. H. (1983). Gender and social influence: A social psychological analysis. *American Psychologist, 38*, 971–981.

Eagly, A. H. (1995). The science and politics of comparing women and men. *American Psychologist, 50*, 145–158.

Eagly, A. H. (2003). Few women at the top: How role incongruity produces prejudice and the glass ceiling. In D. Van Knippenberg & M. A. Hogg (Eds.), *Leadership and power: Identity processes in groups and organizations* (pp. 79–93). London: SAGE.

Eagly, A. H. (2009). The his and hers of prosocial behavior: An examination of the social psychology of gender. *American Psychologist, 64*, 644–658.

Eagly, A. H., Beall, A. E., & Sternberg, R. J. (Eds.) (2005). *The psychology of gender*. New York: Guilford Press.

Eagly, A. H., & Carli, L. (1981). Sex of researcher and sex-typed communications as determinants of sex differences in influenceability: A meta-analysis of social influence studies. *Psychological Bulletin, 90*, 1–20.

Eagly, A. H., & Chaiken, S. (1984). Cognitive theories of persuasion. *Advances in Experimental Social Psychology, 17*, 268–359.

Eagly, A. H., & Chaiken, S. (1993). *The psychology of attitudes*. Orlando, FL: Harcourt Brace Jovanovich.

Eagly, A. H., & Chaiken, S. (1998). Attitude structure and function. In D. T. Gilbert, S. T. Fiske, & G. Lindzey (Eds.), *The handbook of social psychology* (Vol. 1, pp. 269–322). Boston, MA: McGraw-Hill.

Eagly, A. H., & Chaiken, S. (2005). Attitude research in the 21st century: The current state of knowledge. In D. Albarracín, B. T. Johnson, & M. P. Zanna (Eds.), *The handbook of attitudes* (pp. 742–767). Mahwah, NJ: Erlbaum.

Eagly, A. H., & Crowley, M. (1986). Gender and helping behavior: A meta-analytic review of the social psychological literature. *Psychological Review, 100*, 283–308.

Eagly, A. H., Johannesen-Schmidt, M., Van Engen, M. L., & Vinkenburg, C. (2002). Transformational, transactional, and laissez-faire styles: A meta-analysis comparing men and women. *Psychological Bulletin, 129*, 569–591.

Eagly, A. H., & Karau, S. (1991). Gender and the emergence of leaders: A meta-analysis. *Journal of Personality and Social Psychology, 60*, 685–710.

Eagly, A. H., & Karau, S. J. (2002). Role congruity theory of prejudice toward female leaders. *Psychological Review, 109*, 573–598.

Eagly, A. H., Karau, S. J., & Makhijani, M. G. (1995). Gender and the effectiveness of leaders: A meta-analysis. *Psychological Bulletin, 117*, 125–145.

Eagly, A. H., Makhijani, M. G., & Klonsky, B. G. (1992). Gender and the evaluation of leaders: A meta-analysis. *Psychological Bulletin, 111*, 3–22.

Eagly, A. H., & Mladinic, A. (1994). Are people prejudiced against women? Some answers from research on attitudes, gender stereotypes, and judgments of competence. *European Review of Social Psychology, 5*, 1–35.

Eagly, A. H., & Steffen, V. J. (1984). Gender stereotypes stem from the distribution of women and men into social roles. *Journal of Personality and Social Psychology, 46*, 735–754.

Eagly, A. H., & Steffen, V. J. (1986). Gender and aggressive behavior: A meta-analytic review of the social psychological literature. *Psychological Bulletin, 100*, 309–330.

Eagly, A. H., Wood, W., & Fishbaugh, L. (1981). Sex differences in conformity: Surveillance by the group as a determinant of male nonconformity. *Journal of Personality and Social Psychology, 40*, 384–394.

Earley, P. C. (1989). Social loafing and collectivism: A comparison of the United States and the People's Republic of China. *Administrative Science Quarterly, 34*, 565–581.

Earley, P. C. (1994). Self or group: Cultural effects of training on self-efficacy and performance. *Administrative Science Quarterly, 39*, 89–117.

Easterbrook, J. A. (1959). The effect of emotion on cue utilization and organization of behavior. *Psychological Review, 66*, 183–201.

Ebbinghaus, H. (1885). *Memory: A contribution to experimental psychology*. H. A. Ruger & C. E. Bussenius (trans.). New York: Dover, 1964.

Eckert, P., & McConnell-Ginet, S. (1999). New generalizations and explanations in language and gender research. *Language in Society, 28*, 185–201.

Eden, D. (1990). Pygmalion without interpersonal contrast effects: Whole groups gain from raising manager expectations. *Journal of Applied Psychology, 75*, 394–398.

Edney, J. J. (1979). The nuts game: A concise commons dilemma analog. *Environmental Psychology and Nonverbal Behavior, 3*, 252–254.

Edwards, A. L. (1957). *Techniques of attitude scale construction*. New York: Appleton-Century-Crofts.

Edwards, D. (1997). *Discourse and cognition*. London: SAGE.

Edwards, D., & Potter, J. (Eds.) (1992). *Discursive psychology*. London: SAGE.

Edwards, J. (1994). *Multilingualism*. London: Routledge.

Edwards, J. (2010). *Language in the classroom*. Bristol, UK: Multilingual Matters.

Edwards, J., & Chisholm, J. (1987). Language, multi-culturalism and identity: A Canadian study. *Journal of Multilingual and Multicultural Development, 8*, 391–407.

Edwards, K. (1990). The interplay of affect and cognition in attitude formation and change. *Journal of Personality and Social Psychology, 59*, 202–216.

Edwards, K., & Smith, E. E. (1996). A disconfirmation bias in the evaluation of arguments. *Journal of Personality and Social Psychology, 71*, 5–24.

Ehrlich, H. J. (1973). *The social psychology of prejudice*. New York: Wiley.

Eibl-Eibesfeldt, I. (1972). Similarities and differences between cultures in expressive movements. In R. Hinde (Ed.), *Non-verbal communication* (pp. 297–314). Cambridge, UK: Cambridge University Press.

Eichler, M. (1980). *The double standard: A feminist critique of feminist social science*. London: Croom Helm.

Ein-Dor, T., Mikulincer, M., & Shaver, P. R. (2011). Attachment insecurities and the processing of threat-related information: Studying the schemas involved in insecure people's coping strategies. *Journal of Personality and Social Psychology, 101*, 78–93.

Einhorn, H. J., & Hogarth, R. M. (1981). Behavioral decision theory: Processes of judgment and choice. *Annual Review of Psychology, 32*, 53–88.

Eisen, S. V. (1979). Actor–observer differences in information inference and causal attribution. *Journal of Personality and Social Psychology, 37*, 261–272.

Eisenberg, N., Fabes, R. A., Karbon, M., Murphy, B. C., Wosinski, M., Polazzi, L., et al. (1996). The relationship of children's dispositional prosocial behaviour to emotionality, regulation, and social functioning. *Child Development, 67*, 974–992.

Eisenberg, N., Guthrie, I. K., Murphy, B. C., Shepard, S. A., Cumberland, A., & Carlo, G. (1999). Consistency and development of prosocial dispositions: A longitudinal study. *Child Development, 70*, 1360–1372.

Eisenberg-Berg, N. (1979). Relationship of prosocial moral reasoning to altruism, political liberalism and intelligence. *Developmental Psychology, 15*, 87–89.

Eisenberger, N. I., Lieberman, M. D., & Williams, K. D. (2003). Does rejection hurt? An fMRI study of social exclusion. *Science, 302*, 290–292.

Eisenberger, R., & Shank, D. M. (1985). Personal work ethic and effort training affect cheating. *Journal of Personality and Social Psychology, 49*, 520–528.

Eiser, J. R. (1986). *Social psychology: Attitudes, cognition and social behaviour*. Cambridge, UK: Cambridge University Press.

Eiser, J. R., & Bhavnani, K. K. (1974). The effects of situational meaning on the behaviour of subjects in the prisoner's dilemma game. *European Journal of Social Psychology, 4*, 93–97.

Eiser, J. R., & Stroebe, W. (1972). *Categorization and social judgement*. London: Academic Press.

Eisner, M., & Ghuneim, L. (2013). Honor killing attitudes amongst adolescents in Amman, Jordan. *Aggressive Behavior, 39*, 405–417.

Ekman, P. (1971). Universals and cultural differences in facial expressions of emotion. In J. K. Cole (Ed.), *Nebraska symposium on motivation* (Vol. 19, pp. 207–284). Lincoln, NE: University of Nebraska Press.

Ekman, P. (1973). Cross-cultural studies of facial expression. In P. Ekman (Ed.), *Darwin and facial expression* (pp. 169–222). New York: Academic Press.

Ekman, P. (1982). *Emotion in the human face*. New York: Cambridge University Press.

Ekman, P. (2003). *Emotions revealed*. New York: Times Books.

Ekman, P., & Friesen, W. V. (1971). Constants across cultures in the face and emotion. *Journal of Personality and Social Psychology, 17*, 124–129.

Ekman, P., & Friesen, W. V. (1972). Hand movements. *Journal of Communication, 22*, 353–374.

Ekman, P., & Friesen, W. V. (1974). Detecting deception from the body or face. *Journal of Personality and Social Psychology, 29*, 188–198.

Ekman, P., & Friesen, W. V. (1975). *Unmasking the face*. Englewood Cliffs, NJ: Prentice Hall.

Ekman, P., Friesen, W. V., & Hager, J. C. (2002). *Facial action coding system*. Salt Lake City, UT: Research Nexus.

Ekman, P., Friesen, W. V., O'Sullivan, M., Chan, A., Diacoyanni-Tarlatzis, I., Heider, K., Krause, R., Lecompte, W. A., Pitcairn, T., Riccibitti, P. E., Scherer, K., Tomita, M., & Tzavaras, A. (1987). Universals and cultural differences in the judgements of facial expressions of emotion. *Journal of Personality and Social Psychology, 53*, 712–717.

Ekman, P., Friesen, W. V., & Scherer, K. R. (1976). Body movement and voice pitch in deceptive interaction. *Semiotica, 16*, 23–27.

Ekman, P., O'Sullivan, M., & Frank, M. G. (1999). A few can catch a liar. *Psychological Science, 10*, 263–266.

Elfenbein, H. A., & Ambady, N. (2002). On the universality and cultural specificity of emotion recognition: A meta-analysis. *Psychological Bulletin, 128*, 203–235.

Elfenbein, H. A., & Eisenkraft, N. (2010). The relationship between displaying and perceiving nonverbal cues of affect: A meta-analysis to solve an old mystery. *Journal of Personality and Social Psychology, 98*, 301–318.

Ellemers, N. (1993). The influence of socio-structural variables on identity management strategies. *European Review of Social Psychology, 4*, 27–57.

Ellemers, N., De Gilder, D., & Haslam, S. A. (2004). Motivating individuals and groups at work: A social identity perspective on leadership and group performance. *Academy of Management Review, 29*, 459–478.

Ellemers, N., & Jetten, J. (2013). The many ways to be marginal in a group. *Personality and Social Psychology Review, 17*, 3–21.

Ellemers, N., Pagliaro, S., & Barreto, M. (2013). Morality and behavioral regulation in groups: A social identity approach. *European Review of Social Psychology, 24*, 160–193.

Ellemers, N., Spears, R., & Doosje, B. (Eds.) (1999). *Social identity*. Oxford, UK: Blackwell.

Elliot, A. J. (1981). *Child language*. Cambridge, UK: Cambridge University Press.

Elliot, A. J., & Niesta, D. (2008). Romantic red: Red enhances men's attraction to women. *Journal of Personality and Social Psychology, 95*, 1150–1164.

Ellis, R. J., Olson, J. M., & Zanna, M. P. (1983). Stereotypic personality inferences following objective versus subjective judgments of beauty. *Canadian Journal of Behavioral Science, 15*, 35–42.

Ellsworth, P. C., Carlsmith, J. M., & Henson, A. (1972). The stare as a stimulus to flight in human subjects: A series of field experiments. *Journal of Personality and Social Psychology, 21*, 302–311.

Ellsworth, P. C., & Gonzales, R. (2003). Questions and comparisons: Methods of research in social psychology. In M. A. Hogg & J. Cooper (Eds.), *The SAGE handbook of social psychology* (pp. 24–42). London: SAGE.

Elms, A. C. (1975). The crisis of confidence in social psychology. *American Psychologist, 30*, 967–976.

Elms, A. C. (1982). Keeping deception honest: Justifying conditions for social scientific research strategies. In T. L. Beauchamp & R. Faden (Eds.), *Ethical issues in social science research* (pp. 232–245). Baltimore, MD: Johns Hopkins University Press.

Elms, A. C., & Milgram, S. (1966). Personality characteristics associated with obedience and defiance toward authoritative command. *Journal of Experimental Research in Personality, 1*, 282–289.

Ember, C. R., & Ember, M. (1994). War, socialization, and interpersonal violence. *Journal of Conflict Resolution, 38*, 620–646.

Emler, N., & Hopkins, N. (1990). Reputation, social identity and the self. In D. Abrams & M. A. Hogg (Eds.), *Social identity theory: Constructive and critical advances* (pp. 113–130). London: Harvester Wheatsheaf.

Emler, N., Ohana, J., & Moscovici, S. (1987). Children's beliefs about institutional roles: A cross-national study of representations of the teacher's role. *British Journal of Educational Psychology, 57*, 26–37.

Emler, N., & Reicher, S. D. (1995). *Adolescence and delinquency: The collective management of reputation*. Oxford, UK: Blackwell.

Engelhardt, C. R., Bartholow, B. D., Kerr, G. T., & Bushman, B. J. (2011). This is your brain on violent video games: Neural desensitization to violence predicts increased aggression following violent video game exposure. *Journal of Experimental Social Psychology, 47*, 1033–1036.

Enriquez, V. G. (1993). Developing a Filipino psychology. In U. Kim & J. W. Berry (Eds.), *Indigenous psychologies: Research and experience in cultural context* (pp. 252–269). Newbury Park, CA: SAGE.

Erber, R. (1991). Affective and semantic priming: Effects of mood on category accessibility and inference. *Journal of Experimental Social Psychology, 27*, 480–498.

Erber, R., & Fiske, S. T. (1984). Outcome dependency and attention to inconsistent information. *Journal of Personality and Social Psychology, 47*, 709–726.

Eron, L. D. (1982). Parent–child interaction, television violence, and aggression of children. *American Psychologist, 37*, 197–211.

Eron, L. D. (1994). Theories of aggression: From drives to cognitions. In L. R. Huesmann (Ed.), *Aggressive behavior: Current perspectives* (pp. 3–11). New York: Plenum.

Esquivel-Santoveña, E. E., & Dixon, L. (2012). *Aggression and Violent Behavior, 17*, 208–219.

Esser, J. K., & Komorita, S. S. (1975). Reciprocity and concession making in bargaining. *Journal of Personality and Social Psychology, 31*, 864–872.

Esses, V. M., Dovidio, J. F., Semenya, A. H., & Jackson, L. M. (2005). Attitudes toward immigrants and immigration: The role of national and international identities. In D. Abrams, J. M. Marques, & M. A. Hogg (Eds.), *The social psychology of inclusion and exclusion* (pp. 317–337). Philadelphia, PA: Psychology Press.

Esses, V. M., Jackson, L. M., Dovidio, J. F., & Hodson, G. (2005). Instrumental relations among groups: Group competition, conflict, and prejudice. In J. F. Dovidio, P. Glick, & L. Rudman (Eds.), *Reflecting on the nature of prejudice* (pp. 227–243). Oxford, UK: Blackwell.

Evans, A. T., & Clark, J. K. (2012). Source characteristics and persuasion: The role of self-monitoring in self-validation. *Journal of Experimental Social Psychology, 48*, 383–386.

Evans, B. K., & Fischer, D. G. (1992). A hierarchical model of participatory decision-making, job autonomy, and perceived control. *Human Relations, 45*, 1169–1189.

Evans, N. J., & Jarvis, P. A. (1980). Group cohesion: A review and re-evaluation. *Small Group Behavior, 11*, 359–370.

Evans-Pritchard, E. E. (1937). *Witchcraft, oracles and magic among the Azande.* Oxford, UK: Oxford University Press.

Evans-Pritchard, E. E. (1951). *Kinship and marriage among the Nuer.* Oxford, UK: Clarendon Press.

Exline, R. V. (1971). Visual interaction: The glances of power and preference. In J. K. Cole (Ed.), *Nebraska symposium on motivation* (Vol. 19, pp. 163–206). Lincoln, NE: University of Nebraska Press.

Exline, R. V., Ellyson, S. L., & Long, B. (1975). Visual behavior as an aspect of power role relationships. In P. Pliner, L. Krames, & T. Alloway (Eds.), *Nonverbal communication of aggression* (Vol. 2, pp. 21–52). New York: Plenum.

Eyssel, F., & Bohner, G. (2011). Schema effects of rape myth acceptance on judgments of guilt and blame in rape cases: The role of perceived entitlement to judge. *Journal of Interpersonal Violence, 26*, 1579–1605.

Fagundes, C. P. (2012). Getting over you: Contributions of attachment theory for postbreakup emotional adjustment. *Personal Relationships, 19*, 37–50.

Fajardo, D. M. (1985). Author race, essay quality, and reverse discrimination. *Journal of Applied Social Psychology, 15*, 255–268.

Falk, C. F., & Heine, S. J. (2015). What is implicit self-esteem, and does it vary across cultures? *Personality and Social Psychology Review, 19*, 177–198.

Farr, R. M. (1996). *The roots of modern social psychology: 1872–1954.* Oxford, UK: Blackwell.

Farr, R. M., & Moscovici, S. (Eds.) (1984). *Social representations.* Cambridge, UK: Cambridge University Press.

Fast, N. J., Halevy, N., & Galinsky, A. D. (2012). The destructive nature of power without status. *Journal of Experimental Social Psychology, 48*, 391–394.

Fazio, R. H. (1986). How do attitudes guide behavior? In R. M. Sorrentino & E. T. Higgins (Eds.), *The handbook of motivation and cognition: Foundations of social behavior* (pp. 204–243). New York: Guilford Press.

Fazio, R. H. (1989). On the power and functionality of attitudes: The role of attitude accessibility. In A. R. Pratkanis, S. Breckler, & A. G.

Greenwald (Eds.), *Attitude structure and function* (pp. 153–179). Hillsdale, NJ: Erlbaum.

Fazio, R. H. (1995). Attitudes as object-evaluation associations: Determinants, consequences, and correlates of attitude accessibility. In R. E. Petty & J. A. Krosnick (Eds.), *Attitude strength: Antecedents and consequences* (pp. 247–282). Mahwah, NJ: Erlbaum.

Fazio, R. H., Blascovich, J., & Driscoll, D. M. (1992). On the functional value of attitudes: The influence of accessible attitudes upon the ease and quality of decision making. *Personality and Social Psychology Bulletin, 18*, 388–401.

Fazio, R. H., Effrein, E. A., & Falender, V. J. (1981). Self-perceptions following social interactions. *Journal of Personality and Social Psychology, 41*, 232–242.

Fazio, R. H., Jackson, J. R., Dunton, B. C., & Williams, C. J. (1995). Variability in automatic activation as an unobtrusive measure of racial attitudes: A bona fide pipeline. *Journal of Personality and Social Psychology, 69*, 1013–1027.

Fazio, R. H., Ledbetter, J. E., & Towles-Schwen, T. (2000). On the costs of accessible attitudes: Detecting that the attitude object has changed. *Journal of Personality and Social Psychology, 78*, 197–210.

Fazio, R. H., & Olson, M. A. (2003). Implicit measures in social cognition research: Their meaning and use. *Annual Review of Psychology, 54*, 297–327.

Fazio, R. H., & Olson, M. A. (2007). Attitudes: Foundations, functions, and consequences. In M. A. Hogg & J. Cooper (Eds.), *The SAGE handbook of social psychology: Concise student edition* (pp. 123–145). London: SAGE.

Fazio, R. H., & Powell, M. C. (1997). On the value of knowing one's likes and dislikes: Attitude accessibility, stress and health in college. *Psychological Science, 8*, 430–436.

Fazio, R. H., Sanbonmatsu, D. M., Powell, M. C., & Kardes, F. R. (1986). On the automatic activation of attitudes. *Journal of Personality and Social Psychology, 50*, 229–238.

Fazio, R. H., & Zanna, M. P. (1978). Attitudinal qualities relating to the strength of the attitude–behaviour relation. *Journal of Experimental Social Psychology, 14*, 398–408.

Fazio, R. H., Zanna, M. P., & Cooper, J. (1977). Dissonance and self-perception: An integrative view of each theory's proper domain of application. *Journal of Experimental Social Psychology, 13*, 464–479.

Feagin, J. (1972). Poverty: We still believe that God helps them who help themselves. *Psychology Today, 6*, 101–129.

Feather, N. T. (1974). Explanations of poverty in Australian and American samples: The person, society and fate. *Australian Journal of Psychology, 26*, 199–216.

Feather, N. T. (1985). Attitudes, values, and attributions: Explanations of unemployment. *Journal of Personality and Social Psychology, 48*, 876–889.

Feather, N. T. (1991). Human values, global self-esteem, and belief in a just world. *Journal of Personality, 59*, 83–106.

Feather, N. T. (1994). Attitudes toward high achievers and reactions to their fall: Theory and research toward tall poppies. *Advances in Experimental Social Psychology, 26*, 1–73.

Feather, N. T. (2002). Values and value dilemmas in relation to judgments concerning outcomes of an industrial conflict. *Personality and Social Psychology Bulletin, 28*, 446–459.

Feather, N. T., & Barber, J. G. (1983). Depressive reactions and unemployment. *Journal of Abnormal Psychology, 92*, 185–195.

Feather, N. T., & Davenport, P. R. (1981). Unemployment and depressive affect: A motivational and attributional analysis. *Journal of Personality and Social Psychology, 41*, 422–436.

Feather, N. T., & Simon, J. G. (1975). Reactions to male and female success and failure in sex-linked occupations: Impressions of personality, causal attributions, and perceived likelihood of different consequences. *Journal of Personality and Social Psychology, 31*, 20–31.

Feeney, B. C., & Collins, N. L. (2015). A new look at social support: A theoretical perspective on thriving through relationships. *Personality and Social Psychology Review, 19*, 113–147.

Feeney, J. A. (1999). Adult attachment, emotional control, and marital satisfaction. *Personal Relationships, 6*, 169–185.

Feeney, J. A., & Noller, P. (1990). Attachment style as a predictor of adult romantic relationships. *Journal of Personality and Social Psychology, 58,* 281–291.

Fehr, B. (1994). Prototype based assessment of laypeople's views of love. *Personal Relationships, 1,* 309–331.

Fehr, B., Harasymchuk, C., & Sprecher, S. (2014). Compassionate love in romantic relationships: A review and some new findings. *Journal of Social and Personal Relationships, 31,* 575–600.

Fehr, R. S., Gelfand, M. J., & Nag, M. (2010). The road to forgiveness: A meta-analytic synthesis of its situational and dispositional correlates. *Psychological Bulletin, 136,* 894–914.

Fehr, R. S., & Stern, J. A. (1970). Peripheral physiological variables and emotion: The James–Lange theory revisited. *Psychological Bulletin, 74,* 411–424.

Feinberg, M., Willer, R., & Keltner, D. (2012). Flustered and faithful: Embarrassment as a signal of prosociality. *Journal of Personality and Social Psychology, 102,* 81–97.

Feingold, A. (1988). Cognitive gender differences are disappearing. *American Psychologist, 43,* 95–103.

Fenigstein, A. (1984). Self-consciousness and the overperception of self as a target. *Journal of Personality and Social Psychology, 47,* 860–870.

Ferguson, C. J., & Savage, J. (2012). Have recent studies addressed methodological issues raised by five decades of television violence research? A critical review. *Aggression and Violent Behavior, 17,* 129–139.

Ferguson, C. K., & Kelley, H. H. (1964). Significant factors in overevaluation of own group's product. *Journal of Abnormal and Social Psychology, 69,* 223–228.

Festinger, L. (1950). Informal social communication. *Psychological Review, 57,* 271–282.

Festinger, L. (1954). A theory of social comparison processes. *Human Relations, 7,* 117–140.

Festinger, L. (1957). *A theory of cognitive dissonance.* Stanford, CA: Stanford University Press.

Festinger, L. (1964). *Conflict, decision and dissonance.* Stanford, CA: Stanford University Press.

Festinger, L. (1980). *Retrospections on social psychology.* New York: Oxford University Press.

Festinger, L., & Carlsmith, J. M. (1959). Cognitive consequences of forced compliance. *Journal of Abnormal and Social Psychology, 58,* 203–210.

Festinger, L., Pepitone, A., & Newcomb, T. M. (1952). Some consequences of deindividuation in a group. *Journal of Personality and Social Psychology, 47,* 382–389.

Festinger, L., Schachter, S., & Back, K. (1950). *Social pressures in informal groups: A study of human factors in housing.* New York: Harper.

Fidell, L. S. (1970). Empirical verification of sex discrimination in hiring practices in psychology. *American Psychologist, 25,* 1094–1098.

Fiedler, F. E. (1964). A contingency model of leadership effectiveness. *Advances in Experimental Social Psychology, 1,* 149–190.

Fiedler, F. E. (1965). The contingency model of leadership effectiveness. In H. Proshansky, B. Seidenberg (Eds.), *Basic studies in social psychology* (pp. 538–551). New York: Holt, Rinehart, and Winston.

Fiedler, K. (1982). Causal schemata: Review and criticism of research on a popular construct. *Journal of Personality and Social Psychology, 42,* 1001–1013.

Fiedler, K., Messner, C., & Bluemke, M. (2006). Unresolved problems with the I, the A, and the T: A logical and psychometric critique of the Implicit Association Test (IAT). *European Review of Psychology, 17,* 74–147.

Field, R. H. G., & House, R. J. (1990). A test of the Vroom–Yetton model using manager and subordinate reports. *Journal of Applied Psychology, 75,* 362–366.

Fielding, K. S., & Hogg, M. A. (1997). Social identity, self- categorisation and leadership: A field study of small interactive groups. *Group Dynamics, Theory, Research, and Practice, 1,* 39–51.

Fielding, K. S., & Hogg, M. A. (2000). Working hard to achieve self-defining group goals: A social identity analysis. *Zeitschrift für Sozialpsychologie, 31,* 191–203.

Fielding, K. S., McDonald R., & Louis, W. R. (2008). Theory of planned behaviour, identity and intentions to engage in environmental activism. *Journal of Environmental Psychology, 28,* 318–326.

Fincham, F. D. (1985). Attributions in close relationships. In J. H. Harvey & G. Weary (Eds.), *Attribution: Basic issues and applications* (pp. 203–234). Orlando, FL: Academic Press.

Fincham, F. D. (2000). The kiss of the porcupines: From attributing responsibility to forgiving. *Personal Relationships, 7,* 1–23.

Fincham, F. D., & Bradbury, T. N. (1987). Cognitive processes and conflict in close relationships: An attribution–efficacy model. *Journal of Personality and Social Psychology, 53,* 1106–1118.

Fincham, F. D., & Bradbury, T. N. (1993). Marital satisfaction, depression, and attributions: A longitudinal analysis. *Journal of Personality and Social Psychology, 64,* 442–452.

Fincham, F. D., & O'Leary, K. D. (1983). Causal inferences for spouse behavior in maritally distressed and non-distressed couples. *Journal of Social and Clinical Psychology, 1,* 42–57.

Fine, C. (2010). From scanner to soundbite: Issues in interpreting and reporting sex differences in the brain. *Current Directions in Psychological Science, 19,* 280–283.

Fiol, C. M. (2002). Capitalizing on paradox: The role of language in transforming organizational identities. *Organization Science, 13,* 653–666.

Fischer, A. H., Mosquera, P. M. R., Van Vienan, A. E. M., & Manstead, A. S. R. (2004). Gender and culture differences in emotion. *Emotion, 4,* 87–94.

Fischer, A. H., & Roseman, I. J. (2007). Beat them or ban them: The characteristics and social functions of anger and contempt. *Journal of Personality and Social Psychology, 93,* 103–115.

Fischer, D. (1989). *Albion's seed: Four British folkways in America.* New York: Oxford University Press.

Fishbein, M. (1967a). A behavior theory approach to the relation between beliefs about an object and the attitude toward the object. In M. Fishbein (Ed.), *Readings in attitude theory and measurement* (pp. 389–400). New York: Wiley.

Fishbein, M. (1967b). A consideration of beliefs and their role in attitude measurement. In M. Fishbein (Ed.), *Readings in attitude theory and measurement* (pp. 257–266). New York: Wiley.

Fishbein, M. (1971). Attitudes and the prediction of behaviour. In K. Thomas (Ed.), *Attitudes and behaviour* (pp. 52–83). London: Penguin.

Fishbein, M., & Ajzen, I. (1974). Attitudes toward objects as predictors of single and multiple behavior criteria. *Psychological Review, 81,* 59–74.

Fishbein, M., & Ajzen, I. (1975). *Belief, attitude, intention and behavior: An introduction to theory and research.* Reading, MA: Addison-Wesley.

Fishbein, M., Ajzen, I., & Hinkle, R. (1980). Predicting and understanding voting in American elections: Effects of external variables. In I. Ajzen & M. Fishbein (Eds.), *Understanding attitudes and predicting human behavior* (pp. 173–195). Englewood Cliffs, NJ: Prentice Hall.

Fishbein, M., Bowman, C. H., Thomas, K., Jacard, J. J., & Ajzen, I. (1980). Predicting and understanding voting in British elections and American referenda: Illustrations of the theory's generality. In I. Ajzen & M. Fishbein (Eds.), *Understanding attitudes and predicting human behavior* (pp. 196–216). Englewood Cliffs, NJ: Prentice Hall.

Fishbein, M., & Coombs, F. S. (1974). Basis for decision: An attitudinal analysis of voting behavior. *Journal of Applied Social Psychology, 4,* 95–124.

Fishbein, M., & Feldman, S. (1963). Social psychological studies in voting behavior: I. Theoretical and methodological considerations. *American Psychologist, 18,* 388.

Fisher, J. D., Rytting, M., & Heslin, R. (1976). Hands touching hands: Affective and evaluative effects of an interpersonal touch. *Sociometry, 39,* 416–421.

Fisher, R. J. (1990). *The social psychology of intergroup and international conflict resolution.* New York: Springer.

Fisher, R. J. (Ed.) (2005). *Paving the way: Contributions of interactive conflict resolution to peacemaking.* Rowman & Littlefield: Lanham, MD.

Fisher, S., & Todd, A. D. (1983). *The social organization of doctor–patient communication.* Washington, DC: Center for Applied Linguistics.

Fishman, J. A. (1989). *Language and ethnicity in minority sociolinguistic perspective.* Clevedon, UK: Multilingual Matters.

Fiske, A. P. (1992). The four elementary forms of sociality: Framework for a unified theory of social relations. *Psychological Review, 99,* 689–723.

Fiske, A. P., & Haslam, N. (1996). Social cognition is thinking about relationships. *Current Directions in Psychological Science, 5,* 143–148.

Fiske, A. P., Kitayama, S., Markus, H. R., & Nisbett, R. E. (1998). The cultural matrix of social psychology. In D. T. Gilbert, S. T. Fiske, & G. Lindzey (Eds.), *The handbook of social psychology* (4th ed., Vol. 2, pp. 915–981). New York: McGraw-Hill.

Fiske, S. T. (1980). Attention and weight on person perception. *Journal of Personality and Social Psychology, 38,* 889–906.

Fiske, S. T. (1992). Thinking is for doing: Portraits of social cognition from Daguerreotype to laser photo. *Journal of Personality and Social Psychology, 52,* 766–778.

Fiske, S. T. (1993a). Social cognition and social perception. *Annual Review of Psychology, 44,* 155–194.

Fiske, S. T. (1993b). Controlling other people: The impact of power on stereotyping. *American Psychologist, 48,* 621–628.

Fiske, S. T. (1998). Stereotyping, prejudice, and discrimination. In D. T. Gilbert, S. T. Fiske, & G. Lindzey (Eds.), *The handbook of social psychology* (4th ed., Vol. 2, pp. 357–414). New York: McGraw-Hill.

Fiske, S. T. (2010). Interpersonal stratification: Status, power, and subordination. In S. T. Fiske, D. T. Gilbert, & G. Lindzey (Eds.), *Handbook of social psychology* (5th ed., Vol. 2, pp. 941–982). New York: Wiley.

Fiske, S. T., & Berdahl, J. (2007) Social power. In A. W. Kruglanski & E. T. Higgins (Eds.), *Social psychology: Handbook of basic principles* (2nd ed., pp. 678–692). New York: Guilford.

Fiske, S. T., Cuddy, A., & Glick, P. (2007). Universal dimensions of social perception: Warmth and competence. *Trends in Cognitive Science, 11,* 77–83.

Fiske, S. T., Cuddy, A. J., Glick, P., & Xu, J. (2002). A model of (often mixed) stereotype content: Competence and warmth respectively follow from perceived status and competition. *Journal of Personality and Social Psychology, 82,* 878–902.

Fiske, S. T., & Dépret, E. (1996). Control, interdependence and power: Understanding social cognition in its social context. *European Review of Social Psychology, 7,* 31–61.

Fiske, S. T., Gilbert, D. T., & Lindzey, G. (Eds.) (2010). *Handbook of social psychology* (5th ed.). New York: Wiley.

Fiske, S. T., Lau, R. R., & Smith, R. A. (1990). On the varieties and utilities of political expertise. *Social Cognition, 8,* 31–48.

Fiske, S. T., & Neuberg, S. L. (1990). A continuum of impression formation, from category-based to individuating processes: Influences of information and motivation on attention and interpretation. *Advances in Experimental Social Psychology, 23,* 1–74.

Fiske, S. T., & Taylor, S. E. (1991). *Social cognition* (2nd ed.). New York: McGraw-Hill.

Fiske, S. T., & Taylor, S. E. (2013). *Social cognition: From brains to culture* (2nd ed.). Los Angeles: Sage.

Fiske, S. T., Xu., J., Cuddy, A., & Glick, P. (1999). (Dis)respecting versus (dis)liking: Status and interdependent predict ambivalent stereotypes of competence and warmth. *Journal of Social Issues, 55,* 473–489.

Fitness, J. (2001). Emotional intelligence in intimate relationships. In J. Ciarrochi, J. Forgas, & J. Mayer (Eds.), *Emotional intelligence in everyday life: A scientific enquiry* (pp. 98–112). Philadelphia, PA: Taylor & Francis.

Fitness, J., Fletcher, G., & Overall, N. (2007). Interpersonal attraction and intimate relationships. In M. A. Hogg & J. Cooper (Eds.), *The SAGE handbook of social psychology: Concise student edition* (pp. 219–240). London: SAGE.

Fleishman, E. A. (1973). Twenty years of consideration and structure. In E. A. Fleishman & J. F. Hunt (Eds.), *Current developments in the study of leadership.* Carbondale, IL: Southern Illinois University Press.

Fletcher, G. J. O., & Clark, M. S. (Eds.) (2001). *Blackwell handbook of social psychology: Interpersonal processes.* Oxford, UK: Blackwell.

Fletcher, G. J. O., Danilovics, P., Fernandez, G., Peterson, D., & Reeder, G. D. (1986). Attributional complexity: An individual differences measure. *Journal of Personality and Social Psychology, 51,* 875–884.

Fletcher, G. J. O., & Fincham, F. D. (Eds.) (1991). *Cognition in close relationships.* Hillsdale, NJ: Erlbaum.

Fletcher, G. J. O., Fincham, F. D., Cramer, L., & Heron, N. (1987). The role of attributions in the development of dating relationships. *Journal of Personality and Social Psychology, 53,* 481–489.

Fletcher, G. J. O., Simpson, J., Campbell, L., & Overall, N. (2013). *The science of intimate relationships.* New York: Wiley-Blackwell.

Fletcher, G. J. O., Simpson, J. A., & Thomas, G. (2000). Ideals, perceptions, and evaluations in early relationship development. *Journal of Personality and Social Psychology, 79,* 933–940.

Fletcher, G. J. O., Simpson, J. A., Thomas, G., & Giles, L. (1999). Ideals in intimate relationships. *Journal of Personality and Social Psychology, 76,* 72–89.

Fletcher, G. J. O., & Thomas, G. (2000). Behavior and on-line cognition in marital interaction. *Personal Relationships, 7,* 111–130.

Fletcher, G. J. O., Tither, J. M., O'Loughlin, C., Friesen, M., & Overall, N. (2004). Warm and homely or cold and beautiful? Sex differences in trading off traits in mate selection. *Personality and Social Psychology Bulletin, 30,* 659–672.

Fletcher, G. J. O., & Ward, C. (1988). Attribution theory and processes: A cross-cultural perspective. In M. H. Bond (Ed.), *The cross-cultural challenge to social psychology* (pp. 230–244). Newbury Park, CA: SAGE.

Flowe, H. D., Stewart, J., Sleath, E. R., & Palmer, F. T. (2011). Public house patrons' engagement in hypothetical sexual assault: A test of alcohol myopia theory in a field setting. *Aggressive Behavior, 37,* 547–558.

Flowers, M. L. (1977). A laboratory test of some implications of Janis's groupthink hypothesis. *Journal of Personality and Social Psychology, 35,* 888–896.

Floyd, D. L., Prentice-Dunn, S., & Rogers, R. W. (2000). A meta-analysis of research on protection motivation theory. *Journal of Applied Social Psychology, 30,* 407–429.

Foa, E. B., & Foa, U. G. (1975). *Resource theory of social exchange.* Morristown NJ: General Learning Press.

Focella, E. S., Stone, J., Fernandez, N. C., Cooper, J., & Hogg, M. A. (2016). Vicarious hypocrisy: Bolstering attitudes and taking action after exposure to a hypocritical ingroup member. *Journal of Experimental Social Psychology, 62,* 89–102.

Foddy, M., Smithson, M., Schneider, S., & Hogg, M. A. (Eds.) (1999). *Resolving social dilemmas: Dynamic, structural, and intergroup aspects.* Philadelphia, PA: Psychology Press.

Fodor, E. M., & Smith, T. (1982). The power motive as an influence on group decision making. *Journal of Personality and Social Psychology, 42,* 178–185.

Fogelson, R. M. (1970). Violence and grievances: Reflections on the 1960s riots. *Journal of Social Issues, 26,* 141–163.

Fong, G. T., Krantz, D. H., & Nisbett, R. E. (1986). The effects of statistical training on thinking about everyday problems. *Cognitive Psychology, 18,* 253–292.

Forbes, G. B., Collinsworth, L. L., Zhao, P., Kohlman, S., & LeClaire, J. (2011). Relationships among individualism—collectivism, gender, and ingroup/outgroup status, and responses to conflict: A study in China and the United States. *Aggressive Behavior, 37,* 302–314.

Forgas, J. P. (1983). The effects of prototypicality and cultural salience on perceptions of people. *Journal of Research in Personality, 17,* 153–173.

Forgas, J. P. (1994). The role of emotion in social judgments: An introductory review and an affect infusion model (AIM). *European Journal of Social Psychology, 24,* 1–24.

Forgas, J. P. (1995). Mood and judgment: The affect infusion model. *Psychological Bulletin, 117,* 39–66.

Forgas, J. P. (2002). Feeling and doing: Affective influences on interpersonal behavior. *Psychological Inquiry, 13,* 1–28.

Forgas, J. P. (Ed.) (2006). *Affect, cognition and social behavior.* New York: Psychology Press.

Forgas, J. P., & Fiedler, K. (1996). Us and them: Mood effects on intergroup discrimination. *Journal of Personality and Social Psychology, 70,* 36–52.

Forgas, J. P., Morris, S., & Furnham, A. (1982). Lay explanations of wealth: Attributions for economic success. *Journal of Applied Social Psychology, 12,* 381–397.

Forgas, J. P., O'Connor, K., & Morris, S. (1983). Smile and punishment: The effects of facial expression on responsibility attributions by groups and individuals. *Personality and Social Psychology Bulletin, 9,* 587–596.

Forgas, J. P., & Smith, C. A. (2007). Affect and emotion. In M. A. Hogg & J. Cooper (Eds.), *The SAGE handbook of social psychology: Concise student edition* (pp. 146–175). London: SAGE.

Forsterling, F. (1988). *Attribution theory in clinical psychology*. Chichester, UK: Wiley.

Foss, R. D., & Dempsey, C. B. (1979). Blood donation and the foot-in-the-door technique. *Journal of Personality and Social Psychology, 37*, 580–590.

Foster, C. A., Witcher, B. S., Campbell, W. K., & Green, J. D. (1998). Arousal and attraction: Evidence for automatic and controlled processes. *Journal of Personality and Social Psychology, 74*, 86–101.

Foster, E. K. (2004). Research on gossip: Taxonomy, methods, and future directions. *Review of General Psychology, 102*, 1015–1030.

Foucault, M. (1972). *The archaeology of knowledge*. London: Tavistock.

Fox, J., Warber, K. M., & Makstaller, D. C. (2013). The role of Facebook in romantic relationship development: An exploration of Knapp's relational stage model. *Journal of Social and Personal Relationships, 30*, 771–794.

Fox, R. (1967). *Kinship and marriage: An anthropological perspective*. New York: Cambridge University Press.

Fox, S. A., & Giles, H. (1993). Accommodating intergenerational contact: A critique and theoretical model. *Journal of Aging Studies, 7*, 423–451.

Fox, S. A., & Giles, H. (1996a). 'Let the wheelchair through!' An intergroup approach to interability communication. In W. P. Robinson (Ed.), *Social groups and identities: Developing the legacy of Henri Tajfel* (pp. 215–248). Oxford, UK: Butterworth-Heinemann.

Fox, S. A., & Giles, H. (1996b). Interability communication: Evaluating patronizing encounters. *Journal of Language and Social Psychology, 15*, 265–290.

Fox, S., & Hoffman, M. (2002). Escalation behavior as a specific case of goal-directed activity: A persistence paradigm. *Basic and Applied Social Psychology, 24*, 273–285.

Fox-Cardamone, L., Hinkle, S., & Hogue, M. (2000). The correlates of antinuclear activism: Attitudes, subjective norms, and efficacy. *Journal of Applied Social Psychology, 30*, 484–498.

Franco, F. M., & Maass, A. (1996). Implicit versus explicit strategies of outgroup discrimination: The role of intentional control in biased language use and reward allocation. *Journal of Language and Social Psychology, 15*, 335–359.

Frank, M. G., & Gilovich, T. (1989). Effect of memory perspective on retrospective causal attributions. *Journal of Personality and Social Psychology, 57*, 399–403.

Frank, M. G., Matsumoto, D., & Hwang, H. C. (2015). Intergroup emotions and political aggression: The ANCODI hypothesis. In J. P. Forgas, K. Fiedler, & W. D. Crano (Eds.), *Social psychology and politics* (pp. 183–189). New York: Psychology Press.

Franklin, K. (2000). Antigay behaviours among young adults: Prevalence, patterns, and motivators in a noncriminal population. *Journal of Interpersonal Violence, 15*, 339–362.

Frazer, J. G. (1890). *The golden bough*. London: Macmillan.

Fredericks, A. J., & Dossett, D. L. (1983). Attitude–behavior relations: A comparison of the Fishbein–Ajzen and the Bentler–Speckart models. *Journal of Personality and Social Psychology, 45*, 501–512.

Fredrickson, B. L., & Roberts, T. A. (1997). Objectification theory: Toward understanding women's lived experiences and mental health risks. *Psychology of Women Quarterly, 21*, 173–206.

Freed, R. S., & Freed, S. A. (1989). Beliefs and practices resulting in female deaths and fewer females than males in India. *Population and Environment, 10*, 144–161.

Freedman, J. L. (1984). Effect of television violence on aggressiveness. *Psychological Bulletin, 96*, 227–246.

Freedman, J. L., & Fraser, S. C. (1966). Compliance without pressure: The foot-in-the-door technique. *Journal of Personality and Social Psychology, 4*, 195–202.

Freedman, J. L., Wallington, S. A., & Bless, E. (1967). Compliance without pressure: The effect of guilt. *Journal of Personality and Social Psychology, 7*, 117–124.

Freeman, S., Walker, M. R., Bordon, R., & Latané, B. (1975). Diffusion of responsibility and restaurant tipping: Cheaper by the bunch. *Personality and Social Psychology Bulletin, 1*, 584–587.

Freides, D. (1974). Human information processing and sensory modality: Cross-modal functions, information complexity, memory, and deficit. *Psychological Bulletin, 81*, 284–310.

French, J. R. P. (1944). Organized and unorganized groups under fear and frustration. *University of Iowa Studies of Child Welfare, 20*, 231–308.

French, J. R. P., & Raven, B. H. (1959). The bases of social power. In D. Cartwright (Ed.), *Studies in social power* (pp. 118–149). Ann Arbor, MI: Institute for Social Research.

Freud, S. (1905). *Three contributions to the theory of sex*. New York: Dutton.

Freud, S. (1920/1990). *Beyond the pleasure principle*. New York: W. W. Norton.

Freud, S. (1921). Group psychology and the analysis of the ego. In J. Strachey (Ed.), *Standard edition of the complete psychological works* (Vol. 18, pp. 65–143). London: Hogarth Press.

Frey, D. (1986). Recent research on selective exposure to information. In L. Berkowitz (Ed.), *Advances in experimental psychology* (Vol. 19, pp. 41–80). New York: Academic Press.

Frey, D., & Rosch, M. (1984). Information seeking after decisions: The roles of novelty of information and decision reversibility. *Personality and Social Psychology Bulletin, 10*, 91–98.

Frick, R. W. (1985). Communication emotions: The role of prosodic features. *Psychological Bulletin, 97*, 412–429.

Frieze, I., & Weiner, B. (1971). Cue utilisation and attributional judgments for success and failure. *Journal of Personality, 39*, 591–605.

Frohlich, N., & Oppenheimer, J. (1970). I get by with a little help from my friends. *World Politics, 23*, 104–120.

Fromm, E. (1941). *Escape from freedom*. New York: Farrar & Rinehart.

Funder, D. C. (1982). On the accuracy of dispositional vs situational attributions. *Social Cognition, 1*, 205–222.

Funder, D. C. (1987). Errors and mistakes: Evaluating the accuracy of social judgment. *Psychological Bulletin, 101*, 75–90.

Funder, D. C., & Fast, L. A. (2010). Personality in social psychology. In S. T. Fiske, D. T. Gilbert, & G. Lindzey (Eds.), *Handbook of social psychology* (5th ed., Vol. 1, pp. 668–697). New York: Wiley.

Furnham, A. (1982). Explanations for unemployment in Britain. *European Journal of Social Psychology, 12*, 335–352.

Furnham, A. (1983). Attributions for affluence. *Personality and Individual Differences, 4*, 31–40.

Furnham, A. (1984). The Protestant work ethic: A review of the psychological literature. *European Journal of Social Psychology, 14*, 87–104.

Furnham, A. (1986). Some explanations for immigration to, and emigration from, Britain. *New Community, 13*, 65–78.

Furnham, A. (2003). Belief in a just world: Research progress over the past decade. *Personality and Individual Differences, 34*, 795–817.

Furnham, A., & Bond, M. H. (1986). Hong Kong Chinese explanations for wealth. *Journal of Economic Psychology, 7*, 447–460.

Gaertner, S. L., & Dovidio, J. F. (1977). The subtlety of white racism, arousal, and helping behavior. *Journal of Personality and Social Psychology, 35*, 691–707.

Gaertner, S. L., & Dovidio, J. F. (1986). The aversive form of racism. In J. F. Dovidio & S. L. Gaertner (Eds.), *Prejudice, discrimination, and racism* (pp. 61–89). New York: Academic Press.

Gaertner S. L., & Dovidio, J. F. (2000). *Reducing intergroup bias: The common ingroup identity model*. New York: Psychology Press.

Gaertner, S. L., Dovidio, J. F., Anastasio, P., Bachman, B., & Rust, M. (1993). The common ingroup identity model: Recategorization and the reduction of intergroup bias. *European Review of Social Psychology, 4*, 1–26.

Gaertner, S. L., Mann, J., Murrell, A., & Dovidio, J. F. (1989). Reducing intergroup bias: The benefits of recategorization. *Journal of Personality and Social Psychology, 57*, 239–249.

Gaertner, S. L., & McLaughlin, J. P. (1983). Racial stereotypes: Associations and ascriptions of positive and negative characteristics. *Social Psychology Quarterly, 46*, 23–40.

Gaertner, S. L., Rust, M. C., Dovidio, J. F., Bachman, B. A., & Anastasio, P. A. (1996). The contact hypothesis: The role of a common ingroup identity on reducing intergroup bias among majority and minority group members. In J. L. Nye & A. M. Bower (Eds.), *What's social about social cognition: Research on socially shared cognition in small groups* (pp. 230–260). Thousand Oaks, CA: SAGE.

Gaffney, A. M., & Hogg, M. A. (2016). Social identity and social influence. In S. Harkins, K. D. Williams, & J. Burger (Eds.), *The Oxford handbook of social influence* (pp. 1–39). New York: Oxford University Press.

Gaffney, A. M., Hogg, M. A., Cooper, J., & Stone, J. (2012). Witness to hypocrisy: Reacting to in-group hypocrites in the presence of others. *Social Influence, 7*, 98–112.

Gaffney, A. M., Rast, D. E., III, Hackett, J. D., & Hogg, M. A. (2014). Further to the right: Uncertainty, political polarization and the American 'Tea Party' movement. *Social Influence, 9*, 272–288.

Galen, L. W. (2012). Does religious belief promote prosociality? *Psychological Bulletin, 138*, 876–906.

Galinsky, A. D. (2002). Creating and reducing intergroup conflict: The role of perspective-taking in affecting out-group evaluations. In H. Sondak (Ed.), *Toward phenomenology of groups and group membership. Research on managing groups and teams* (Vol. 4, pp. 85–113). New York: Elsevier.

Galinsky, A. D., Gruenfeld, D. H., & Magee, J. C. (2003). From power to action. *Journal of Personality and Social Psychology, 85*, 453–466.

Galinsky, A. D., & Moskowitz, G. B. (2000). Perspective-taking: Decreasing stereotype expression, stereotype accessibility, and in-group favoritism. *Journal of Personality and Social Psychology, 78*, 708–724.

Galinsky, A. D., & Mussweiler, T. (2001). First offers as anchors: The role of perspective-taking and negotiator focus. *Journal of Personality and Social Psychology, 81*, 657–669.

Galizio, M., & Hendrick, C. (1972). Effect of musical accompaniment on attitude: The guitar as a prop for persuasion. *Journal of Applied Social Psychology, 2*, 350–359.

Gallois, C. (1993). The language and communication of emotion: Interpersonal, intergroup, or universal. *American Behavioral Scientist, 36*, 309–338.

Gallois, C., Barker, M., Jones, E., & Callan, V. J. (1992). Intercultural communication: Evaluations of lecturers and Australian and Chinese students. In S. Iwawaki, Y. Kashima, & K. Leung (Eds.), *Innovations in cross-cultural psychology* (pp. 86–102). Amsterdam: Swets & Zeitlinger.

Gallois, C., & Callan, V. J. (1986). Decoding emotional messages: Influence of ethnicity, sex, message type, and channel. *Journal of Personality and Social Psychology, 51*, 755–762.

Gallois, C., & Callan, V. J. (1997). *Communication and culture: A guide for practice*. Chichester, UK: Wiley.

Gallois, C., Callan, V. J., & Johnstone, M. (1984). Personality judgements of Australian Aborigine and white speakers: Ethnicity, sex and context. *Journal of Language and Social Psychology, 3*, 39–57.

Gallois, C., Ogay, T., & Giles, H. (2005). Communication accommodation theory: A look back and a look ahead. In W. Gudykunst (Ed.), *Theorizing about intercultural communication* (pp. 121–148). Thousand Oaks, CA: Sage.

Gallup, G. (1978). Gallup youth survey. *Indianapolis Star*, 18 October.

Gallupe, R. B., Cooper, W. H., Grise, M.-L., & Bastianutti, L. M. (1994). Blocking electronic brainstorms. *Journal of Applied Psychology, 79*, 77–86.

Galton, F. (1892). *Heredity genius: An inquiry into its laws and consequences*. London: Macmillan.

Gangestad, S. W., Garver-Apgar, C. E., Simpson, J. A., & Cousins, A. J. (2007). Changes in women's mate preferences across the ovulatory cycle. *Journal of Personality and Social Psychology, 92*, 151–163.

Gangestad, S. W., & Simpson, J. A. (2000). The evolution of human mating: Trade-offs and strategic pluralism. *Behavioral and Brain Sciences, 23*, 573–587.

Gao, G. (1996). Self and other: A Chinese perspective on interpersonal relationships. In W. B. Gudykunst, S. Ting-Toomey, & T. Nishida (Eds.), *Communication in personal relationships across cultures* (pp. 81–101). Thousand Oaks, CA: SAGE.

Gao, G., Ting-Toomey, S., & Gudykunst, W. B. (1996). Chinese communication processes. In M. H. Bond (Ed.), *Handbook of Chinese psychology* (pp. 280–293). Hong Kong: Oxford University Press.

Gardner, M. J., Paulsen, N., Gallois, C., Callan, V. J., & Monaghan, P. (2001). Communication in organizations: An intergroup perspective. In W. P. Robinson & H. Giles (Eds.), *The new handbook of language and social psychology* (pp. 561–584). Chichester, UK: Wiley.

Gardner, R. A., & Gardner, B. T. (1971). Teaching sign language to a chimpanzee. *Science, 165*, 664–672.

Gardner, R. C. (1979). Social psychological aspects of second language acquisition. In H. Giles & R. St Clair (Eds.), *Language and social psychology* (pp. 193–220). Oxford, UK: Blackwell.

Gardner, R. M., & Tockerman, Y. R. (1994). A computer–TV methodology for investigating the influence of somatotype on perceived personality traits. *Journal of Social Behavior and Personality, 9*, 555–563.

Gardner, W. L., Gabriel, S., & Diekman, A. B. (2000). Interpersonal approaches. In J. T. Cacioppo, L. G. Tassinary, & G. C. Berntson (Eds.), *Handbook of psychophysiology* (2nd ed., pp. 643–664). New York: Cambridge University Press.

Garfinkel, H. (1967). *Studies in ethnomethodology*. Englewood Cliffs, NJ: Prentice Hall.

Garrett, P., Giles, H., & Coupland, N. (1989). The contexts of language learning: Extending the intergroup model of second language acquisition. In S. Ting-Toomey & F. Korzenny (Eds.), *Language, communication, and culture* (pp. 201–221). Newbury Park, CA: SAGE.

Garstka, T. A., Hummert, M. L., & Branscombe, N. R. (2005). Perceiving age discrimination in response to intergenerational inequity. *Journal of Social Issues, 61*, 321–342.

Gasiorek, J., Giles, H., Holtgraves, T., & Robbins, S. (2012). Celebrating thirty years of the *JLSP*: Analyses and prospects. *Journal of Language and Social Psychology, 31*, 361–375.

Gaskell, G., & Smith, P. (1985). An investigation of youths' attributions for unemployment and their political attitudes. *Journal of Economic Psychology, 6*, 65–80.

Gawronski, B. (2003). Implicational schemata and the correspondence bias: On the diagnostic value of situationally constrained behavior. *Journal of Personality and Social Psychology, 84*, 1154–1171.

Gawronski, B. (2004). Theory-based bias correction in dispositional inference: The fundamental attribution error is dead, long live the correspondence bias. *European Review of Social Psychology, 15*, 183–217.

Gawronski, B., & Bodenhausen, G. V. (2011). The associative-propositional evaluation model: Theory, evidence and open questions. *Advances in Experimental Social Psychology, 44*, 59–127.

Gawronski, B., Peters, K. R., Brochu, P. M., & Strack, F. (2008). Understanding the relations between different forms of racial prejudice: A cognitive consistency perspective. *Personality and Social Psychology Bulletin, 34*, 648–665.

Gawronski, B., & Strack, F. (Eds.) (2012). *Cognitive consistency: A fundamental principle in social cognition*. New York: Guilford Press.

Gawronski, B., Walther, E., & Blank, H. (2005). Cognitive consistency and the formation of interpersonal attitudes: Cognitive balance affects the encoding of social information. *Journal of Experimental Social Psychology, 41*, 618–626.

Gazzaniga, M. S., Ivry, R, & Mangun, G. R. (2013). *Cognitive neuroscience: The biology of mind* (4th ed.). New York: Norton.

Geen, R. G. (1978). Some effects of observing violence on the behaviour of the observer. In B. A. Maher (Ed.), *Progress in experimental personality research* (Vol. 8, pp. 49–93). New York: Academic Press.

Geen, R. G. (1989). Alternative conceptions of social facilitation. In P. B. Paulus (Ed.), *Psychology of group influence* (2nd ed., pp. 15–51). Hillsdale, NJ: Erlbaum.

Geen, R. G. (1991). Social motivation. *Annual Review of Psychology, 42*, 377–399.

Geen, R. G. (1998). Aggression and antisocial behaviour. In D. T. Gilbert, S. T. Fiske, & G. Lindzey (Eds.), *The handbook of social psychology* (4th ed., Vol. 2, pp. 317–356). New York: McGraw-Hill.

Geen, R. G., & Donnerstein, E. (Eds.) (1983). *Aggression: Theoretical and empirical reviews*. New York: Academic Press.

Geen, R. G., & Gange, J. J. (1977). Drive theory of social facilitation: Twelve years of theory and research. *Psychological Bulletin, 84*, 1267–1288.

Geen, R. G., & Quanty, M. (1977). The catharsis of aggression: An evaluation of a hypothesis. *Advances in Experimental Social Psychology, 10*, 2–37.

Geer, J. H., & Jarmecky, L. (1973). The effect of being responsible for reducing another's pain on subject's response and arousal. *Journal of Personality and Social Psychology, 26*, 232–237.

Geertz, C. (1975). On the nature of anthropological understanding. *American Scientist, 63,* 47–53.

Gelfand, D. M., Hartmann, D. P., Walder, P., & Page, B. (1973). Who reports shoplifters? A field-experimental study. *Journal of Personality and Social Psychology, 25,* 276–285.

Gelfand, M. J., Nishii, L., & Raver, J. (2006). On the nature and importance of cultural tightness-looseness. *Journal of Applied Psychology, 91,* 1225–1244.

Gelfand, M. J., Raver, J. L., Nishii, L., Leslie, L. M., Lun, J., et al. (2011). Differences between tight and loose societies: A 33-nation study. *Science, 33,* 1100–1104.

Genovese, M. A. (1993). Women as national leaders: What do we know? In M. A. Genovese (Ed.), *Women as national leaders* (pp. 177–210). Newbury Park, CA: Sage.

Genta, M. L., Menesini, E., Fonzi, A., Costabile, A., & Smith, P. K. (1996). Bullies and victims in schools in central and south Italy. *European Journal of Psychology of Education, 11,* 97–110.

Gentile, D. A., Anderson, C. A., Yukawa, S., Ihori, N., Saleem, M., et al. (2009). The effects of prosocial video games on prosocial behaviors: international evidence from correlational, longitudinal, and experimental studies. *Personality and Social Psychology Bulletin, 35,* 752–763.

Gerard, H. B., & Hoyt, M. F. (1974). Distinctiveness of social categorisation and attitude toward ingroup members. *Journal of Personality and Social Psychology, 29,* 836–842.

Gerard, H. B., & Mathewson, G. C. (1966). The effects of severity of initiation on liking for a group: A replication. *Journal of Experimental Social Psychology, 2,* 278–287.

Gergen, K. J. (1971). *The concept of self.* New York: Holt, Rinehart & Winston.

Gergen, K. J. (1973). Social psychology as history. *Journal of Personality and Social Psychology, 26,* 309–320.

Gergen, K. J., Gergen, M. M., & Meter, K. (1972). Individual orientations to prosocial behavior. *Journal of Social Issues, 28,* 105–130.

Gersick, C. J., & Hackman, J. R. (1990). Habitual routines in task performing groups. *Organizational Behavior and Human Decision Processes, 47,* 65–97.

Ghimire, D. J., Axinn, W. G., Yabiku, S. T., & Thornton, A. (2006). Social change, premarital nonfamily experience, and spouse choice in an arranged marriage society. *American Journal of Sociology, 111,* 1181–1218.

Giancola, P. R. (2003). Individual difference and contextual factors contributing to the alcohol–aggression relation: diverse populations, diverse methodologies: An introduction to the special issue. *Aggressive Behavior, 29,* 285–287.

Giancola, P. R., Josephs, R. A., Parrott, D. J., & Duke, A. A. (2010). Alcohol myopia revisited: Clarifying aggression and other acts of disinhibition through a distorted lens. *Perspectives on Psychological Science, 5,* 265–278.

Gigone, D., & Hastie, R. (1993). The common knowledge effect: Information sharing and group judgment. *Journal of Personality and Social Psychology, 65,* 959–974.

Gilbert, D. T. (1995). Attribution and interpersonal per ception. In A. Tesser (Ed.), *Advanced social psychology* (pp. 99–147). New York: McGraw-Hill.

Gilbert, D. T. (1998). Ordinary personology. In D. T. Gilbert, S. T. Fiske, & G. Lindzey (Eds.), *The handbook of social psychology* (4th ed., Vol. 2, pp. 89–150). New York: McGraw-Hill.

Gilbert, D. T., Fiske, S. T., & Lindzey, G. (Eds.) (1998). *The handbook of social psychology* (4th ed.). New York: McGraw-Hill.

Gilbert, D. T., & Malone, P. S. (1995). The correspondence bias. *Psychological Bulletin, 117,* 21–38.

Gilbert, D. T., & Silvera, D. H. (1996). Overhelping. *Journal of Personality and Social Psychology, 70,* 678–690.

Giles, H. (1978). Linguistic differentiation in ethnic groups. In H. Tajfel (Ed.), *Differentiation between social groups: Studies in the social psychology of intergroup relations* (pp. 361–393). London: Academic Press.

Giles, H. (Ed.) (1984). The dynamics of speech accommodation theory. *International Journal of the Sociology of Language, 46,* whole issue.

Giles, H. (Ed.) (2012). *The handbook of intergroup communication.* New York: Routledge.

Giles, H. (Ed.) (2016). *Communication accommodation theory: Negotiating personal and social identities across contexts.* Cambridge, UK: Cambridge University Press.

Giles, H., Bourhis, R. Y., & Taylor, D. M. (1977). Towards a theory of language in ethnic group relations. In H. Giles (Ed.), *Language, ethnicity, and intergroup relations* (pp. 307–348). London: Academic Press.

Giles, H., & Byrne, J. L. (1982). The intergroup model of second language acquisition. *Journal of Multilingual and Multicultural Development, 3,* 17–40.

Giles, H., Choi, C. W., & Dixon, T. (2010). Police-civilian encounters. In H. Giles, S. A. Reid, & J. Harwood (Eds.), *Dynamics of intergroup communication* (pp. 65–76). New York: Peter Lang.

Giles, H., Coupland, N., Henwood, K., Harriman, J., & Coupland, J. (1990). The social meaning of RP: An intergenerational perspective. In S. Ramsaran (Ed.), *Studies in the pronunciation of English: A commemorative volume in honour of A. C. Gimson* (pp. 191–211). London: Routledge.

Giles, H., & Gasiorek, J. (2011). Intergenerational communication practices. In K. W. Schaie & S. L. Willis (Eds.), *Handbook of the psychology of aging* (7th ed., pp. 233–248) London: Academic Press.

Giles, H., & Johnson, P. (1981). The role of language in ethnic group relations. In J. C. Turner & H. Giles (Eds.), *Intergroup behaviour* (pp. 199–243). Oxford, UK: Blackwell.

Giles, H., & Johnson, P. (1987). Ethnolinguistic identity theory: A social psychological approach to language maintenance. *International Journal of the Sociology of Language, 68,* 66–99.

Giles, H., & Maass, A. (Eds.) (2016). *Advances in intergroup communication.* New York: Peter Lang.

Giles, H., Mulac, A., Bradac, J. J., & Johnson, P. (1987). Speech accommodation theory: The next decade and beyond. In M. McLaughlin (Ed.), *Communication yearbook* (Vol. 10, pp. 13–48). Newbury Park, CA: SAGE.

Giles, H., & Noels, K. A. (2002). Communication accommodation in intercultural encounters. In T. K. Nakayama & L. A. Flores (Eds.), *Readings in cultural contexts* (pp. 117–126). Boston, MA: McGraw-Hill.

Giles, H., Noels, K., Ota, H., Ng, S. H., Gallois, C., Ryan, E. B., et al. (2001). Age vitality in eleven nations. *Journal of Multilingual and Multicultural Development, 21,* 308–323.

Giles, H., & Powesland, P. F. (1975). *Speech style and social evaluation.* London: Academic Press.

Giles, H., Reid, S., & Harwood, J. (Eds.) (2010). *The dynamics of intergroup communication.* New York: Peter Lang.

Giles, H., & Robinson, W. P. (Eds.) (1993). *Handbook of language and social psychology.* Oxford, UK: Pergamon Press.

Giles, H., Rosenthal, D., & Young, L. (1985). Perceived ethno-linguistic vitality: The Anglo- and Greek-American setting. *Journal of Multilingual and Multicultural Development, 6,* 253–269.

Giles, H., & Street, R. (1985). Communicator characteristics and behaviour. In M. L. Knapp & G. R. Miller (Eds.), *Handbook of interpersonal communication* (pp. 205–261). Beverly Hills, CA: SAGE.

Giles, H., Taylor, D. M., & Bourhis, R. Y. (1973). Towards a theory of interpersonal accommodation through language: Some Canadian data. *Language in Society, 2,* 177–192.

Gillig, P. M., & Greenwald, A. G. (1974). Is it time to lay the sleeper effect to rest? *Journal of Personality and Social Psychology, 29,* 132–139.

Gilovich, T. D., & Gryphon, D. W. (2010). Judgment and decision making. In S. T. Fiske, D. T. Gilbert, & G. Lindzey (Eds.), *Handbook of social psychology* (5th ed., Vol. 1, pp. 542–588).

Giner-Sorolla, R. (2012). *Judging passions: Moral emotion in persons and groups.* Hove. UK: Psychology Press.

Gini, G., Pozzoli, T., & Hymel, S. (2014). Moral disengagement among children and youth: A meta-analytic review of links to aggressive behavior. *Aggressive Behavior, 40,* 56–68.

Gladue, B. A. (1991). Aggressive behavioural characteristics, hormones, and sexual orientation in men and women. *Aggressive Behavior, 17,* 313–326.

Gladue, B. A., Boechler, M., & McCall, K. D. (1989). Hormonal response to competition in human males. *Aggressive Behaviour, 15,* 409–422.

Glaser, J., & Banaji, M. R. (1999). When fair is foul and foul is fair: Reverse priming in automatic evaluation. *Journal of Personality and Social Psychology, 77,* 669–687.

Glassman, L. R., & Albarracín, D. (2006). Forming attitudes that predict future behavior: A meta-analysis of the attitude–behavior relation. *Psychological Bulletin, 132,* 788–822.

Glenn, E. S. (1976). Meaning and behaviour: Communication and culture. In L. A. Samovar & R. E. Porter (Eds.), *Intercultural communication: A reader* (2nd ed., pp. 170–193). Belmont, CA: Wadsworth.

Glick, P. (2002). Sacrificial lambs dressed in wolves' clothing: Envious prejudice, ideology, and the scapegoating of Jews. In L. S. Newman & R. Erber (Eds.), *Understanding genocide: The social psychology of the Holocaust* (pp. 113–142). London: Oxford.

Glick, P., & Fiske, S. T. (1996). The ambivalent sexism inventory: Differentiating hostile and benevolent sexism. *Journal of Personality and Social Psychology, 70,* 491–512.

Glick, P., & Fiske, S. T. (1997). Hostile and benevolent sexism: Measuring ambivalent sexist attitudes toward women. *Psychology of Women Quarterly, 21,* 119–135.

Glick, P., & Fiske, S. T. (2001). Ambivalent sexism. *Advances in Experimental Social Psychology, 33,* 115–188.

Glick, P., & Fiske, S. T. (2011). Ambivalent sexism revisited. *Psychology of Women Quarterly, 35,* 530–535.

Glick, P., Fiske, S. T., Mladinic, A., Saiz, J. L., Abrams, D., Masser B., & López, W. (2000). Beyond prejudice as simple antipathy: Hostile and benevolent sexism across cultures. *Journal of Personality and Social Psychology, 79,* 763–775.

Glick, P., Lameiras, M., Fiske, S. T., Eckes, T., Masser, B., Volpato, C., & Wells, R. (2004). Bad but bold: Ambivalent attitudes toward men predict gender inequality in 16 nations. *Journal of Personality and Social Psychology, 86,* 713–728.

Glick, R. A., & Roose, S. P. (Eds.) (1993). *Rage, power, and aggression.* New Haven, CT: Yale University Press.

Godin, G. R., Valois, P., Lepage, L., & Desharnais, R. (1992). Predictors of smoking behaviour: An application of Ajzen's theory of planned behaviour. *British Journal of Addiction, 87,* 1335–1343.

Goethals, G. R., & Darley, J. M. (1987). Social comparison theory: Self-evaluation and group life. In B. Mullen & G. Goethals (Eds.), *Theories of group behavior* (pp. 21–48). New York: Springer.

Goethals, G. R., & Nelson, R. E. (1973). Similarity in the influence process: The belief–value distinction. *Journal of Personality and Social Psychology, 25,* 117–122.

Goethals, G. R., & Sorenson, G. (Eds.) (2004), *Encyclopedia of leadership.* Thousand Oaks, CA: SAGE.

Goethals, G. R., & Zanna, M. P. (1979). The role of social comparison in choice shifts. *Journal of Personality and Social Psychology, 37,* 1469–1476.

Goetz, J. L., Keltner, D., & Simon-Thomas, E. (2010). Compassion: An evolutionary analysis and empirical review. *Psychological Bulletin, 136,* 351–374.

Goff, P. A., Steele, C. M., & Davies, P. G. (2008). The space between us: Stereotype threat and distance in interracial contexts. *Journal of Personality and Social Psychology, 94,* 91–107.

Goffman, E. (1959). *The presentation of self in everyday life.* New York: Doubleday/Anchor Books.

Goffman, E. (1963). *Stigma: Notes on the management of spoiled identity.* Englewood Cliffs, NJ: Prentice Hall.

Goldberg, M. E., & Gorn, G. J. (1974). Children's reactions to television advertising: An experimental approach. *Journal of Consumer Research, 1,* 69–75.

Goldberg, P. (1968). Are some women prejudiced against women? *Trans-Action, 5,* 28–30.

Goldenberg, A., Halperin, E., Van Zomeren, M., & Gross, J. J. (2016). The process model of group-based emotion: Integrating intergroup emotion and emotion regulation perspectives. *Personality and Social Psychology Review, 20,* 118–141.

Goldman, M., Creason, C. R., & McCall, C. G. (1981). Compliance employing a two-feet-in-the-door procedure. *Journal of Social Psychology, 114,* 259–265.

Goldstein, A. P. (1987). Aggression. In R. J. Corsini (Ed.), *Concise encyclopedia of psychology* (pp. 35–39). New York: Wiley.

Goldstein, A. P. (1994). *The ecology of aggression.* New York: Plenum.

Goldstein, A. P. (1999). Aggression reduction strategies: Effective and ineffective. *School Psychology Quarterly, 14,* 40–58.

Goldstein, J. H. (1980). *Social psychology.* New York: Academic Press.

Golec de Zavala, A., Cichocka, A., Eidelson, R., & Jayawickreme, N. (2009). Collective narcissism and its social consequences. *Journal of Personality and Social Psychology, 97,* 1074–1096.

Gollwitzer, P. M., & Bargh, J. A. (Eds.) (1996). *The psychology of action: Linking cognition and motivation to behavior.* New York: Guilford Press.

Gollwitzer, P. M., & Kinney, R. F. (1989). Effects of deliberative and implemental mind-sets on illusion of control. *Journal of Personality and Social Psychology, 56,* 531–542.

Gollwitzer, P. M., & Sheeran, P. (2006). Implementation intentions and goal achievement: A meta-analysis of effects and processes. *Advances in Experimental Social Psychology, 38,* 69–119.

Gonsalkorale, K., & Williams, K. D. (2007). The KKK won't let me play: Ostracism even by a despised outgroup hurts. *European Journal of Social Psychology, 37,* 1176–1185.

Goode, J. (2016). *I taste red: The science of wine tasting.* Oakland, CA: University of California Press.

Goodman, M. (1964). *Race awareness in young children* (2nd ed.). New York: Cromwell-Collier.

Goodman, M. E. (1946). Evidence concerning the genesis of interracial attitudes. *American Anthropologist, 38,* 624–630.

Goodman, M. E. (1952). *Race awareness in young children.* Cambridge, MA: Addison-Wesley.

Goodwin, R. (1999). *Personal relationships across cultures.* London: Routledge.

Goodwin, S. A., Gubin, A., Fiske, S. T., & Yzerbyt, V. Y. (2000). Power can bias impression processes: Stereotyping subordinates by default and by design. *Group Processes and Intergroup Relations, 3,* 227–256.

Gorassini, D. R., & Olson, J. M. (1995). Does self-perception change explain the foot-in-the-door effect? *Journal of Personality and Social Psychology, 69,* 91–105.

Gordon, R. A. (1996). Impact of ingratiation on judgments and evaluations: A meta-analytic investigation. *Journal of Personality and Social Psychology, 71,* 54–70.

Gorer, G. (1968). Man has no 'killer' instinct. In M. F. A. Montagu (Ed.), *Man and aggression* (pp. 27–36). New York: Oxford University Press.

Gorn, G. J. (1982). The effects of music in advertising on choice: A classical conditioning approach. *Journal of Marketing, 46,* 94–101.

Gorsuch, R. L., & Ortbergh, J. (1983). Moral obligation and attitudes: Their relation to behavioral intentions. *Journal of Personality and Social Psychology, 44,* 1025–1028.

Gottlieb, J., & Carver, C. S. (1980). Anticipation of future interaction and the bystander effect. *Journal of Experimental Social Psychology, 16,* 253–260.

Gouldner, A. W. (1960). The norm of reciprocity: A preliminary statement. *American Sociological Review, 25,* 161–178.

Graen, G. B., & Uhl-Bien, M. (1995). Relationship-based approach to leadership: Development of leader–member exchange (LMX) theory of leadership over 25 years: Applying a multi-level multi-domain approach. *The Leadership Quarterly, 6,* 219–247.

Graham, S., Hudley C., & Williams, E. (1992). An attributional approach to aggression in African-American children. *Developmental Psychology, 28,* 731–740.

Granberg, D. (1987). Candidate preference, membership group, and estimates of voting behavior. *Social Cognition, 5,* 323–335.

Grant, F., & Hogg, M. A. (2012). Self-uncertainty, social identity prominence and group identification. *Journal of Experimental Social Psychology, 48,* 538–542.

Grant, F., Hogg, M. A., & Crano, W. D. (2015). Yes, we can: Physical activity and group identification among healthy adults. *Journal of Applied Social Psychology, 45,* 383–390.

Grasser, A. C., Millis, K. K., & Swan, R. A. (1997). Discourse comprehension. *Annual Review of Psychology, 48,* 163–189.

Graumann, C. F., & Moscovici, S. (Eds.) (1986). *Changing conceptions of crowd mind and behavior*. New York: Springer.

Graumann, C. F., & Moscovici, S. (Eds.) (1987). *Changing conceptions of conspiracy*. New York: Springer.

Green, D. P., Glaser, J., & Rich, A. (1998). From lynching to gay bashing: The elusive connection between economic conditions and hate crime. *Journal of Personality and Social Psychology, 75*, 82–92.

Green, M. G., & Carpenter, J. M. (2011). Trust, deception, and identity on the internet. In Z. Birchmeier, B. Dietz-Uhler, & G. Stasser (Eds.), *Strategic uses of social technology: An interactionist perspective of social psychology* (pp. 40–62). Cambridge, UK: Cambridge University Press.

Greenberg, J., Pyszczynski, T., & Solomon, S. (1986). The causes and consequences of self-esteem: A terror management theory. In R. Baumeister (Ed.), *Public self and private self* (pp. 189–212). New York: Springer.

Greenberg, J., & Rosenfield, D. (1979). Whites' ethnocentrism and their attributions for the behavior of blacks: A motivational bias. *Journal of Personality, 47*, 643–657.

Greenberg, J., Solomon, S., & Pyszczynski, T. (1997). Terror management theory of self-esteem and cultural worldviews: Empirical assessments and conceptual refinements. *Advances in Experimental Social Psychology, 29*, 61–139.

Greenberg, J., Solomon, S., Pyszczynski, T., Rosenblatt, A., Burling, J., Lyon, D., Simon, L., & Pinel, E. (1992). Why do people need self-esteem? Converging evidence that self-esteem serves an anxiety-buffering function. *Journal of Personality and Social Psychology, 63*, 913–922.

Greenberg, J., Williams, K. D., & O'Brien, M. K. (1986). Considering the harshest verdict first: Biasing effects on mock juror verdict. *Personality and Social Psychology Bulletin, 12*, 41–50.

Greene, J. (2013). *Moral tribes: Emotion, reason, and the gap between us and them*. New York: Penguin Group.

Greenglass, E. R. (1982). *A world of difference: Gender roles in perspective*. Toronto: Wiley.

Greenwald, A. G. (1980). The totalitarian ego: Fabrication and revision of personal history. *American Psychologist, 35*, 603–618.

Greenwald, A. G., & Banaji, M. R. (1995). Implicit social cognition: Attitudes, self-esteem, and stereotypes. *Psychological Review, 102*, 4–27.

Greenwald, A. G., Banaji, M. R., & Nosek, B. A. (2015). Statistically small effects of the Implicit Association Test can have societally large effects. *Journal of Personality and Social Psychology, 108*, 553–561.

Greenwald, A. G., Banaji, M. R., Rudman, L. A., Farnham, S. D., Nosek, B. A., & Mellott, D. S. (2002). A unified theory of implicit attitudes, stereotypes, self-esteem, and self-concept. *Psychological Review, 109*, 3–25.

Greenwald, A. G., McGhee, D. E., & Schwartz, J. L. K. (1998). Measuring individual differences in implicit cognition: The implicit association test. *Journal of Personality and Social Psychology, 74*, 1464–1480.

Greenwald, A. G., Poehlman, T. A., Uhlmann, E. L., & Banaji, M. R. (2009). Understanding and using the Implicit Association Test: III. Meta-analysis of predictive validity. *Journal of Personality and Social Psychology, 97*, 17–41.

Greenwald, A. G., & Pratkanis, A. R. (1984). The self. In R. S. Wyer, Jr, & T. K. Srull (Eds.), *Handbook of social cognition* (Vol. 3, pp. 129–178). Hillsdale, NJ: Erlbaum.

Greenwald, A. G., & Pratkanis, A. R. (1988). On the use of 'theory' and the usefulness of theory. *Psychological Review, 95*, 575–579.

Gregg, A. P., Seibt, B., & Banaji, M. R. (2006). Easier done than undone: Asymmetry in the malleability of implicit preferences. *Journal of Personality and Social Psychology, 90*, 1–20.

Gregson, R. A. M., & Stacey, B. G. (1981). Attitudes and self-reported alcohol consumption in New Zealand. *New Zealand Psychologist, 10*, 15–23.

Greitmeyer, T. (2009). Effects of songs with prosocial lyrics on prosocial behavior: Further evidence and a mediating mechanism. *Personality and Social Psychology Bulletin, 35*, 1500–1511.

Greitmeyer, T., & Mügge, D. (2014). Video games do affect social outcomes: A meta-analytic review of the effects of violent and prosocial video game play. *Personality and Social Psychology Bulletin, 40*, 579–589.

Greitmeyer, T., & Osswald, S. (2010). Effects of prosocial video games on prosocial behavior. *Journal of Personality and Social Psychology, 98*, 211–221.

Grieve, P., & Hogg, M. A. (1999). Subjective uncertainty and intergroup discrimination in the minimal group situation. *Personality and Social Psychology Bulletin, 25*, 926–940.

Griffiths, M. (1997). Video games and aggression. *The Psychologist*, September, 397–401.

Griffitt, W. B., & Veitch, R. (1971). Hot and crowded: Influence of population density and temperature on interpersonal affective behavior. *Journal of Personality and Social Psychology, 17*, 92–98.

Groff, B. D., Baron, R. S., & Moore, D. L. (1983). Distraction, attentional conflict, and drivelike behavior. *Journal of Experimental Social Psychology, 19*, 359–380.

Gross, A. E., & Fleming, J. (1982). Twenty years of deception in social psychology. *Personality and Social Psychology Bulletin, 8*, 402–408.

Gross, J. J. (2015). Emotion regulation: Current status and future prospects. *Psychological Inquiry, 26*, 1–26.

Gross, J. J. (Ed.) (2014). *Handbook of emotion regulation* (2nd ed.). New York: Guilford Press.

Grossman, R. B., & Kegl, J. (2007). Moving faces: Categorization of dynamic facial expressions in American Sign Language by deaf and hearing participants. *Journal of Nonverbal Behavior, 31*, 23–38.

Gruber-Baldini, A. L., Schaie, K. W., & Willis, S. L. (1995). Similarity in married couples: A longitudinal study of mental abilities and rigidity–flexibility. *Journal of Personality and Social Psychology, 69*, 191–203.

Gruenfeld, D. H., & Tiedens, L. Z. (2010). Organizational preferences and their consequences. In S. T. Fiske, D. T. Gilbert, & G. Lindzey (Eds.), *Handbook of social psychology* (5th ed., Vol. 2, pp. 1252–1287). New York: Wiley.

Grusec, J. E. (1991). The socialisation of altruism. In M. S. Clark (Ed.), *Prosocial behaviour* (pp. 9–33). Newbury Park, CA: SAGE.

Grusec, J. E., Kuczynski, L., Rushton, J. P., & Simutis, Z. M. (1978). Modelling, direct instruction, and attributions: Effects on altruism. *Developmental Psychology, 14*, 51–57.

Grusec, J. E., & Redler, E. (1980). Attribution, reinforcement and altruism: A developmental analysis. *Developmental Psychology, 16*, 525–534.

Grzesiak-Feldman, M., & Suszek, H. (2008). Conspiracy stereotyping and perception of group entitativity of Jews, Germans, Arabs and homosexuals by Polish students. *Psychological Reports, 102*, 755–758.

Gubar, S., & Hoff, J. (Eds.) (1989). *For adult users only: The dilemma of violent pornography*. Bloomington, IN: Indiana University Press.

Gudykunst, W. B., Matsumoto, Y., Ting-Toomey, S., Nishida, T., Kim, K., & Heyman, S. (1996). The influence of cultural individualism–collectivism, self-construals, and individual values on communication styles across cultures. *Human Communication Research, 22*, 510–543.

Guéguen, N. (2007). Courtship compliance: The effect of touch on women's behavior. *Social Influence, 2*, 81–97.

Guéguen, N., Jacob, C., Lourel, M., & Pascua, A. (2012). When drivers see red: Car color frustrators and drivers' aggressiveness. *Aggressive Behavior, 38*, 166–169.

Guenther, C. L., & Alicke, M. D. (2010). Deconstructing the better-than-average effect. *Journal of Personality and Social Psychology, 99*, 755–770.

Guerin, B. (1986). Mere presence effects in humans: A review. *Journal of Experimental Social Psychology, 22*, 38–77.

Guerin, B. (1989). Reducing evaluation effects in mere presence. *Journal of Social Psychology, 129*, 183–190.

Guerin, B. (1993). *Social facilitation*. Cambridge, UK: Cambridge University Press.

Guerin, B., & Innes, J. M. (1982). Social facilitation and social monitoring: A new look at Zajonc's mere presence hypothesis. *British Journal of Social Psychology, 21*, 7–18.

Guimond, S., de la Sablonnière, R., & Nugier, A. (2014). Living in a multicultural world: Intergroup ideologies and the societal context of intergroup relations. *European Review of Social Psychology, 25*, 142–188.

Guimond, S., & Dubé-Simard, L. (1983). Relative deprivation theory and the Québec Nationalist Movement: The cognitive–emotion distinction and the personal–group deprivation issue. *Journal of Personality and Social Psychology, 44,* 526–535.

Gump, B. B., & Kulik, J. A. (1997). Stress, affiliation, and emotional contagion, *Journal of Personality and Social Psychology, 72,* 305–319.

Gupta, U., & Singh, P. (1982). An exploratory study of love and liking and types of marriages. *Indian Journal of Applied Psychology, 19,* 92–97.

Gurr, T. R. (1970). *Why men rebel.* Princeton, NJ: Princeton University Press.

Gustafson, R. (1992). Alcohol and aggression: A replication study controlling for potential confounding variables. *Aggressive Behavior, 18,* 21–28.

Guttman, L. A. (1944). A basis for scaling qualitative data. *American Sociological Review, 9,* 139–150.

Guzzo, R. A., & Dickson, M. W. (1996). Teams in organizations: Recent research on performance and effectiveness. *Annual Review of Psychology, 47,* 307–338.

Guzzo, R. A., Jost, P. R., Campbell, R. J., & Shea, G. P. (1993). Potency in groups: Articulating a construct. *British Journal of Social Psychology, 32,* 87–106.

Haas, A. (1979). Male and female spoken language differences: Stereotypes and evidence. *Psychological Bulletin, 86,* 616–626.

Hackman, J. R. (2002). *Leading teams: Setting the stage for great performances.* Boston, MA: Harvard Business School Press.

Hackman, J. R., & Katz, N. (2010). Group behavior and performance. In S. T. Fiske, D. T. Gilbert, & G. Lindzey (Eds.), *Handbook of social psychology* (5th ed., Vol. 2, pp. 1208–1251). New York: Wiley.

Hadden, B. W., Smith, C. V., & Webster, G. D. (2014). Relationship duration moderates association between attachment and relationship quality: Meta-analytic support for the temporal adult romantic attachment model. *Personality and Social Psychology Review, 18,* 42–58.

Haddock, G., Rothman, A. J., Reber, R., & Schwarz, N. (1999). Forming judgements of attitude certainty, intensity, and importance: The role of subjective experiences. *Personality and Social Psychology Bulletin, 25,* 231–232.

Haddock, G., & Zanna, M. P. (1999). Affect, cognition, and social attitudes. *European Review of Social Psychology, 10,* 75–100.

Hagger, M. S., & Chatzisarantis, N. L. D. (2006). Self-identity and the theory of planned behaviour: Between- and within-participants analyses. *British Journal of Social Psychology, 45,* 731–757.

Haidt, J. D. (2012). *The righteous mind: Why good people are divided by politics and religion.* New York: Random House.

Haines, H., & Vaughan, G. M. (1979). Was 1898 a great date in the history of social psychology? *Journal for the History of the Behavioural Sciences, 15,* 323–332.

Hains, S. C., Hogg, M. A., & Duck, J. M. (1997). Self- categorization and leadership: Effects of group proto typicality and leader stereotypicality. *Personality and Social Psychology Bulletin, 23,* 1087–1100.

Haire, M., & Grune, W. E. (1950). Perceptual defenses: Processes protecting an organized perception of another personality. *Human Relations, 3,* 403–412.

Hajek, C., & Giles, H. (2005). Intergroup communication schemas: Cognitive representations of talk with gay men. *Language and Communication, 25,* 161–181.

Halberstadt, J., Sherman, S. J., & Sherman, J. W. (2011). Why Barack Obama is Black: A cognitive account of hypodescent. *Psychological Science, 22,* 29–33.

Hall, B. J., & Gudykunst, W. B. (1986). The intergroup theory of second language ability. *Journal of Language and Social Psychology, 5,* 291–302.

Hall, E. T. (1966). *The hidden dimension.* New York: Doubleday.

Hall, E. T. (1979). Gender, gender roles, and nonverbal communication. In R. Rosenthal (Ed.), *Skill in nonverbal communication* (pp. 32–67). Cambridge, MA: Oelgeschlager, Gunn & Hain.

Hall, E. T., & Braunwald, K. G. (1981). Gender cues in conversations. *Journal of Personality and Social Psychology, 40,* 99–110.

Hall, J. A. (1978). Gender effects in decoding nonverbal cues. *Psychological Bulletin, 85,* 845–857.

Hall, J. A. (1984). *Nonverbal sex differences: Communication accuracy and expressive style.* Baltimore, MD: Johns Hopkins University Press.

Hall, J. A., Coats, E. J., & Smith-LeBeau, L. S. (2005). Nonverbal behavior and the vertical dimension of social relations: A meta-analysis. *Psychological Bulletin, 131,* 898–924.

Hall, K. (2000). Performativity. *Journal of Linguistic Anthropology, 9,* 184–187.

Halpern, D. (1995). *Mental health and the built environment: More than bricks and mortar?* London: Taylor & Francis.

Hamburger, Y. (1994). The contact hypothesis reconsidered: Effects of the atypical outgroup member on the outgroup stereotype. *Basic and Allied Social Psychology, 15,* 339–358.

Hamilton, D. L. (1979). A cognitive attributional analysis of stereotyping. *Advances in Experimental Social Psychology, 12,* 53–84.

Hamilton, D. L. (Ed.) (2004). *Social cognition: Essential readings.* New York: Psychology Press.

Hamilton, D. L., & Gifford, R. K. (1976). Illusory correlation in interpersonal personal perception: A cognitive basis of stereotypic judgments. *Journal of Experimental Social Psychology, 12,* 392–407.

Hamilton, D. L., & Sherman, J. W. (1989). Illusory correlations: Implications for stereotype theory and research. In D. Bar-Tal, C. F. Graumann, A. W. Kruglanski, & W. Stroebe (Eds.), *Stereotyping and prejudice: Changing conceptions* (pp. 59–82). New York: Springer.

Hamilton, D. L., & Sherman, J. W. (1994). Stereotypes. In R. S. Wyler Jr & T. K. Srull (Eds.), *Handbook of social cognition* (Vol. 2, pp. 1–68). Hillsdale, NJ: Erlbaum.

Hamilton, D. L., & Sherman, S. J. (1996). Perceiving persons and groups. *Psychological Review, 103,* 336–355.

Hamilton, D. L., Stroesser, S. J., & Driscoll, D. M. (1994). Social cognition and the study of stereotyping. In P. G. Devine, D. L. Hamilton, & T. M. Ostrom (Eds.), *Social cognition: Impact on social psychology* (pp. 291–321). San Diego, CA: Academic Press.

Hamilton, D. L., & Zanna, M. P. (1974). Context effects in impression formation: Changes in connotative meaning. *Journal of Personality and Social Psychology, 29,* 649–654.

Hampson, S. E., John, O. P., & Goldberg, L. R. (1986). Category breadth and hierarchical structure in personality: Studies in asymmetries in judgments of trait implications. *Journal of Personality and Social Psychology, 51,* 37–54.

Haney, C., Banks, C., & Zimbardo, P. (1973). A study of prisoners and guards in a simulated prison. *Naval Research Review, 9,* 1–17 [Reprinted in E. Aronson (Ed.), *Readings about the social animal* (3rd ed., pp. 52–67). San Francisco, CA: W. H. Freeman].

Hannover, B., & Kühnen, U. (2004). Culture, context, and cognition: The semantic procedural interface model of the self. *European Review of Social Psychology, 15,* 297–333.

Hans, V. P. (2008). Jury systems around the world. *Annual Review of Law and Social Science, 4,* 275–297.

Hardin, G. (1968). The tragedy of the commons. *Science, 162,* 1243–1248.

Harinck, F., & Van Kleef, G. A. (2012). Be hard on the interests and soft on the values: Conflict issue moderates the effects of anger in negotiations. *British Journal of Social Psychology, 51,* 741–752.

Harkins, S. G. (1987). Social loafing and social facilitation. *Journal of Experimental Social Psychology, 23,* 1–18.

Harkins, S. G., & Szymanski, K. (1987). Social loafing and social facilitation: New wine in old bottles. In C. Hendrick (Ed.), *Review of personality and social psychology: Group processes and intergroup relations* (Vol. 9, pp. 167–188). Newbury Park, CA: SAGE.

Harkins, S. G., & Szymanski, K. (1989). Social loafing and group evaluation. *Journal of Personality and Social Psychology, 56,* 934–941.

Harlow, H. F. (1958). The nature of love. *American Psychologist, 13,* 673–685.

Harlow, H. F., & Harlow, M. K. (1965). The affectional systems. In A. M. Schrier, H. F. Harlow, & F. Stollnitz (Eds.), *Behavior of non-human primates* (Vol. 2). New York: Academic Press.

Harmon-Jones, E. (2000). Cognitive dissonance and experienced negative affect: Evidence that dissonance increases experienced negative affect even in the absence of aversive consequences. *Personality and Social Psychology Bulletin, 27,* 889–898.

Harmon-Jones, E., & Winkielman, P. (Eds.) (2007). *Social neuroscience: Integrating biological and psychological explanations of social behavior*. New York: Guilford Press.

Harré, N., Foster, S., & O'Neill, M. (2005). Self-enhancement, crash-risk optimism and the impact of safety advertisements on young drivers. *British Journal of Psychology, 96*, 215–230.

Harré, R. (1979). *Social being: A theory for social psychology*. Oxford, UK: Blackwell.

Harries, K. D., & Stadler, S. J. (1983). Determinism revisited: Assault and heat stress in Dallas, 1980. *Environment and Behavior, 15*, 235–256.

Harrington, J. (2006). An acoustic analysis of 'happy-tensing' in the Queen's Christmas broadcasts. *Journal of Phonetics, 34*, 439–457.

Harrington, J. R., & Gelfand, M. J. (2014). Tightness–looseness across the 50 united states. *Proceedings of the National Academy of Sciences, 111*, 7990–7995.

Harris, E. E. (1970). *Hypothesis and perception*. London: Allen & Unwin.

Harris, L. T., & Fiske, S. T. (2006). Dehumanizing the lowest of the low: Neuro-imaging responses to extreme outgroups. *Psychological Science, 17*, 847–853.

Harris, L. T., & Fiske, S. T. (2009). Social neuroscience evidence for dehumanised perception. *European Review of Social Psychology, 20*, 192–231.

Harris, N. B. (1992). Sex, race, and experiences of aggression. *Aggressive Behavior, 18*, 201–217.

Harris, R. J., & Cook, C. A. (1994). Attributions about spouse abuse: It matters who the batterers and victims are. *Sex Roles, 30*, 553–564.

Hart, P. T. (1990). *Groupthink in government: A study of small groups and policy failure*. Amsterdam: Swets & Zeitlinger.

Hartley, J. F., & Stephenson, G. M. (Eds.) (1992). *Employment relations: The psychology of influence and control at work*. Oxford, UK: Blackwell.

Hartmann, H., Kris, E., & Loewenstein, R. M. (1949). Notes on a theory of aggression. *Psychoanalytic Study of the Child, 3–4*, 9–36.

Harvey, J. H. (1987). Attributions in close relationships: Research and theoretical developments. *Journal of Social and Clinical Psychology, 5*, 420–434.

Harwood, J., Giles, H., & Bourhis, R. Y. (1994). The genesis of vitality theory: Historical patterns and discoursal dimensions. *International Journal of the Sociology of Language, 108*, 167–206.

Harwood, J., Giles, H., & Ryan, E. B. (1995). Aging, communication, and intergroup theory: Social identity and intergenerational communication. In J. Nussbaum & J. Coupland (Eds.), *Handbook of communication and aging research* (pp. 133–159). Mahwah, NJ: Erlbaum.

Haslam, N. (1994). Categories of social relationship. *Cognition, 53*, 59–90.

Haslam, N. (2006). Dehumanization: An integrative review. *Personality and Social Psychology Review, 10*, 252–264

Haslam, N., Bastian, B., Bain, P., & Kashima, Y. (2006). Psychological essentialism, implicit theories, and intergroup relations. *Group Processes and Intergroup Relations, 9*, 63–76.

Haslam, N., Bastian, B., & Bissett, M. (2004). Essentialist beliefs about personality and their implications. *Personality and Social Psychology Bulletin, 30*, 1661–1673.

Haslam, N., & Loughnan, S. (2014). Dehumanization and infrahumanization. *Annual Review of Psychology, 65*, 399–423.

Haslam, N., Loughnan, S., & Kashima, Y. (2008). Attributing and denying humanness to others. *European Review of Social Psychology, 19*, 55–85.

Haslam, N., Rothschild, L., & Ernst, D. (1998). Essentialist beliefs about social categories. *British Journal of Social Psychology, 39*, 113–127.

Haslam, S. A. (2004). *Psychology in organisations: The social identity approach* (2nd ed.). London: SAGE.

Haslam, S. A., Adarves-Yorno, I., Postmes, T., & Jans, L. (2013). The collective origins of valued originality: A social identity approach to creativity. *Personality and Social Psychology review, 17*, 384–401.

Haslam, S. A., & Platow, M. J. (2001). Your wish is our command: The role of shared social identity in translating a leader's vision into followers' action. In M. A. Hogg & D. J. Terry (Eds.), *Social identity processes in organizational contexts* (pp. 213–228). Philadelphia, PA: Psychology Press.

Haslam, S. A., & Reicher, S. D. (2005). The psychology of tyranny. *Scientific American, 16*, 44–51.

Haslam, S. A., & Reicher, S. D. (2012). When prisoners take over the prison: A social psychology of resistance. *Personality and Social Psychology Review, 16*, 154–179.

Haslam, S. A., Reicher, S. D., & Platow, M. J. (2011). *The new psychology of leadership: Identity, influence and power*. New York: Psychology Press.

Haslam, S. A., & Ryan, M. K. (2008). The road to the glass cliff: Differences in the perceived suitability of men and women for leadership positions in succeeding and failing organizations. *The Leadership Quarterly, 19*, 530–546.

Haslam, S. A., Turner, J. C., Oakes, P. J., McGarty, C., & Hayes, B. K. (1992). Context-dependent variation in social stereotyping 1: The effects of intergroup relations as mediated by social change and frame of reference. *European Journal of Social Psychology, 22*, 3–20.

Hass, R. G., Katz, I., Rizzo, N., Bailey, J., & Eisenstadt, D. (1991). Cross-racial appraisal as related to attitude ambivalence and cognitive complexity. *Personality and Social Psychology Bulletin, 17*, 83–92.

Hassett, J. (1981). But that would be wrong … *Psychology Today*, November, 34–50.

Hastie, R. (1984). Causes and effects of causal attribution. *Journal of Personality and Social Psychology, 46*, 44–56.

Hastie, R. (1988). A computer simulation model of person memory. *Journal of Experimental Social Psychology, 24*, 423–447.

Hastie, R. (Ed.) (1993). *Inside the juror: The psychology of juror decision making*. Cambridge, UK: Cambridge University Press.

Hastie, R., & Park, B. (1986). The relationship between memory and judgment depends on whether the judgment task is memory-based or on-line. *Psychological Review, 93*, 258–268.

Hastie, R., Penrod, S. D., & Pennington, N. (1983). *Inside the jury*. Cambridge, MA: Harvard University Press.

Hatfield, E. (1987). Love. In R. J. Corsini (Ed.), *Concise encyclopedia of psychology* (pp. 676–677). New York: Wiley.

Hatfield, E., & Walster, G. W. (1981). *A new look at love*. Reading, MA: Addison-Wesley.

Hauch, V., Blandón-Gitlin, I., Masip, J., & Sporer, S. L. (2015). Are computers effective lie detectors? A meta-analysis of linguistic cues to deception. *Personality and Social Psychology Review, 19*, 307–342.

Haugtvedt, C. P., & Petty, R. E. (1992). Personality and persuasion: Need for cognition moderates the persistence and resistance of attitude changes. *Journal of Personality and Social Psychology, 63*, 308–319.

Hawking, S. W. (1988). *A brief history of time: From the Big Bang to black holes*. New York: Bantam.

Hawking, S. W., & Mlodinow, L. (2010). *The grand design*. New York: Bantam.

Hayduk, L. A. (1983). Personal space: Where we now stand. *Psychological Bulletin, 94*, 293–335.

Hazan, C., & Shaver, P. (1987). Romantic love conceptualized as an attachment process. *Journal of Personality and Social Psychology, 52*, 511–524.

Heaven, P. C. L. (1990). Human values and suggestions for reducing unemployment. *British Journal of Social Psychology, 29*, 257–264.

Hebb, D. O., & Thompson, W. R. (1968). The social significance of animal studies. In G. Lindzey & E. Aronson (Eds.), *Handbook of social psychology* (2nd ed., Vol. 2, pp. 729–774). Reading, MA: Addison-Wesley.

Heider, F. (1946). Attitudes and cognitive organisation. *Journal of Psychology, 21*, 107–112.

Heider, F. (1958). *The psychology of interpersonal relations*. New York: Wiley.

Heider, F., & Simmel, M. (1944). An experimental study of apparent behavior. *American Journal of Psychology, 57*, 243–259.

Heilman, M. E. (1983). Sex bias in work settings: The lack of fit model. *Research in Organizational Behavior, 5*, 269–298.

Heilman, M. E., & Parks-Stamm, E. J. (2007). Gender stereotypes in the workplace: Obstacles to women's career progress. *Advances in group Processes, 24*, 47–77.

Heilman, M. E., & Stopeck, M. H. (1985). Attractiveness and corporate success: Different causal attributions for males and females. *Journal of Applied Psychology, 70,* 379–388.

Heilman, M. E., Wallen, A. S., Fuchs, D., & Tamkins, M. M. (2004). Penalties for success: Reactions to women who succeed at male gender-typed tasks. *Journal of Applied Psychology, 89,* 416–427.

Heine, S. J. (2010). Cultural psychology. In S. T. Fiske, D. T. Gilbert, & G. Lindzey (Eds.), *Handbook of social psychology* (5th ed., Vol. 2, pp. 1423–1464). New York: Wiley.

Heine, S. J. (2016). *Cultural Psychology* (3rd ed.). New York: Norton.

Heine, S. J., & Buchtel, E. E. (2009). Personality: The universal and the culturally specific. *Annual Review of Psychology, 60,* 369–394.

Heinemann, W. (1990). Meeting the handicapped: A case of affective–cognitive inconsistency. *European Review of Social Psychology, 1,* 323–338.

Heisler, G. (1974). Ways to deter law violators: Effects of levels of threat and vicarious punishment on cheating. *Journal of Consulting and Clinical Psychology, 42,* 577–582.

Henderson, J., & Taylor, J. (1985). Study finds bias in death sentences: Killers of Whites risk execution. *Times Union,* 17 November, p. A19.

Hendrick, C., Bixenstine, V. E., & Hawkins, G. (1971). Race vs belief similarities as determinants of attraction: A search for a fair test. *Journal of Personality and Social Psychology, 17,* 250–258.

Hendrick, C., & Hendrick, S. S. (1995). Gender differences and similarities in sex and love. *Personal Relationships, 2,* 55–65.

Henley, N. M. (1973). The politics of touch. In P. Brown (Ed.), *Radical psychology* (pp. 421–433). New York: Harper & Row.

Henley, N. M. (1977). *Body politics: Power, sex, and nonverbal communication.* Englewood Cliffs, NJ: Prentice Hall.

Henley, N. M., & Harmon, S. (1985). The nonverbal semantics of power and gender: A perceptual study. In S. L. Ellyson & J. F. Dovidio (Eds.), *Power, dominance, and nonverbal behavior* (pp. 151–164). New York: Springer.

Henriques, J., Holloway, W., Urwin, C., Venn, C., & Walkerdine, V. (1984). *Changing the subject: Psychology, social regulation, and subjectivity.* London: Methuen.

Henry, W. A., III. (1994). Pride and prejudice. *Time,* 27 June, 54–59.

Hensley, T. R., & Griffin, G. W. (1986). Victims of groupthink: The Kent State University Board of Trustees and the 1977 gymnasium controversy. *Journal of Conflict Resolution, 30,* 497–531.

Herek, G. M. (1987). Religious orientation and prejudice: A comparison of racial and sexual attitudes. *Personality and Social Psychology Bulletin, 13,* 34–44.

Herek, G. M. (2007). Confronting sexual stigma and prejudice: Theory and practice. *Journal of Social Issues, 63,* 905–925.

Herek, G. M. (2011). Anti-equality marriage amendments and sexual stigma. *Journal of Social Issues, 67,* 413–426.

Herek, G. M., & Glunt, E. K. (1988). An epidemic of stigma: Public reaction to AIDS. *American Psychologist, 43,* 886–891.

Herek, G. M., & McLemore, K. A. (2013). Sexual prejudice. *Annual Review of Psychology, 64,* 309–333.

Herman, C. P., Roth, D. A., & Polivy, J. (2003). Effects of the presence of others on food intake: A normative interpretation. *Psychological Bulletin, 129,* 873–886.

Herman, D. (1997). *The antigay agenda: Orthodox vision and the Christian Right.* Chicago: University of Chicago Press.

Herr, P. M., Sherman, S. J., & Fazio, R. H. (1983). On the consequences of priming: Assimilation and contrast effects. *Journal of Experimental Social Psychology, 19,* 323–340.

Hersh, S. M. (1970). *My Lai: A report on the massacre and its aftermath.* New York: Vintage Books.

Heslin, R. (1978). Responses to touching as an index of sex-role norms and attitudes. Paper presented at the annual meeting of the American Psychological Association, Toronto, August.

Heslin, R., & Alper, T. (1983). Touch: A bonding gesture. In J. M. Wiemann & R. P. Harrison (Eds.), *Nonverbal interaction* (pp. 47–75). Beverly Hills, CA: SAGE.

Hess, E. H. (1965). The pupil responds to changes in attitude as well as to changes in illumination. *Scientific American, 212,* 46–54.

Hetey, R. C., & Eberhardt, J. I. (2014). Racial disparities in incarceration increase acceptance of punitive policies. *Psychological Science, 25,* 1949–1954.

Heuer, L., & Penrod, S. (1994). Trial complexity: A field investigation of its meaning and its effect. *Law and Human Behavior, 18,* 29–51.

Hewes, G. W. (1957). The anthropology of posture. *Scientific American, 196,* 123–132.

Hewstone, M. (1986). *Understanding attitudes to the European Community: A social-psychological study in four member states.* Cambridge, UK: Cambridge University Press.

Hewstone, M. (1989). *Causal attribution: From cognitive processes to collective beliefs.* Oxford, UK: Blackwell.

Hewstone, M. (1990). The 'ultimate attribution error': A review of the literature on intergroup causal attribution. *European Journal of Social Psychology, 20,* 311–335.

Hewstone, M. (1994). Revision and change of stereotypic beliefs: In search of the elusive subtyping model. *European Review of Social Psychology, 5,* 69–109.

Hewstone, M. (1996). Contact and categorization: Social psychological interventions to change intergroup relations. In C. N. Macrae, C. Stangor, & M. Hewstone (Eds.), *Stereotypes and stereotyping* (pp. 323–368). New York: Guilford Press.

Hewstone, M., & Antaki, C. (1988). Attribution theory and social explanations. In M. Hewstone, W. Stroebe, J.-P. Codol, & G. M. Stephenson (Eds.), *Introduction to social psychology: A European perspective* (pp. 111–141). Oxford, UK: Blackwell.

Hewstone, M., & Brown, R. J. (Eds.) (1986). *Contact and conflict in intergroup encounters.* Oxford, UK: Blackwell.

Hewstone, M., Cairns, E., Voci, A., Paolini, S., McLernon, F., Crisp, R. J., et al. (2005). Intergroup contact in a divided society: Challenging segregation in Northern Ireland. In D. Abrams, J. M. Marques, & M. A. Hogg (Eds.), *The social psychology of inclusion and exclusion* (pp. 265–292). New York: Psychology Press.

Hewstone, M., & Jaspars, J. M. F. (1982). Intergroup relations and attribution processes. In H. Tajfel (Ed.), *Social identity and intergroup relations* (pp. 99–133). Cambridge, UK: Cambridge University Press.

Hewstone, M., & Jaspars, J. M. F. (1984). Social dimensions of attribution. In H. Tajfel (Ed.), *The social dimension* (pp. 379–404). Cambridge, UK: Cambridge University Press.

Hewstone, M., Jaspars, J. M. F., & Lalljee, M. (1982). Social representations, social attribution and social identity: The intergroup images of 'public' and 'comprehensive' schoolboys. *European Journal of Social Psychology, 12,* 241–269.

Hewstone, M., & Ward, C. (1985). Ethnocentrism and causal attribution in Southeast Asia. *Journal of Personality and Social Psychology, 48,* 614–623.

Higgins, E. T. (1981). The 'communication game': Implications for social cognition. In E. T. Higgins, C. P. Herman, & M. Zanna (Eds.), *Social cognition: The Ontario symposium* (Vol. 1, pp. 343–392). Hillsdale, NJ: Erlbaum.

Higgins, E. T. (1987). Self-discrepancy: A theory relating self and affect. *Psychological Review, 94,* 319–340.

Higgins, E. T. (1996). Knowledge activation: Accessibility, applicability, and salience. In E. T. Higgins & A. W. Kruglanski (Eds.), *Social psychology: Handbook of basic principles* (pp. 133–168). New York: Guilford Press.

Higgins, E. T. (1997). Beyond pleasure and pain. *American Psychologist, 52,* 1280–1300.

Higgins, E. T. (1998). Promotion and prevention: Regulatory focus as a motivational principle. *Advances in Experimental Social Psychology, 30,* 1–46.

Higgins, E. T., Bargh, J. A., & Lombardi, W. (1985). The nature of priming effects on categorization. *Journal of Experimental Psychology: Learning, Memory, and Cognition, 11,* 59–69.

Higgins, E. T., Bond, R. N., Klein, R., & Strauman, T. (1986). Self-discrepancies and emotional vulnerability: How magnitude, accessibility, and type of discrepancy influence affect. *Journal of Personality and Social Psychology, 51,* 5–15.

Higgins, E. T., Roney, C., Crowe, E., & Hymes, C. (1994). Ideal versus ought predilections for approach and avoidance: Distinct self-regulatory systems. *Journal of Personality and Social Psychology, 66,* 276–286.

Higgins, E. T., & Silberman, I. (1998). Development of regulatory focus: Promotion and prevention as ways of living. In J. Heckhausen & C. S. Dweck (Eds.), *Motivation and self-regulation across the lifespan* (pp. 78–113). New York: Cambridge University Press.

Higgins, E. T., & Tykocinski, O. (1992). Self-discrepancies and biographical memory: Personality and cognition at the level of psychological situation. *Personality and Social Psychology Bulletin, 18*, 527–535.

Higgins, E. T., Van Hook, E., & Dorfman, D. (1988). Do self-attributes form a cognitive structure? *Social Cognition, 6*, 177–207.

Hill, C., & Peplau, L. (1998). Premarital predictors of relationship outcomes: A 15-year follow up of the Boston couples study. In T. N. Bradbury et al. (Eds.), *The developmental course of marital dysfunction* (pp. 237–278). New York: Cambridge University Press.

Hill, D., White, V., Marks, R., & Borland, R. (1993). Changes in sun-related attitudes and behaviours and reduced sunburn prevalence in a population at high risk of melanoma. *European Journal of Cancer Prevention, 1*, 447–456.

Hilton, D. J. (1988). Logic and causal attribution. In D. J. Hilton (Ed.), *Contemporary science and natural explanation: Commonsense conceptions of causality* (pp. 33–65). Brighton, UK: Harvester Press.

Hilton, D. J. (1990). Conversational processes and causal explanation. *Psychological Bulletin, 107*, 65–81.

Hilton, D. J. (2007). Causal explanation: From social perception to knowledge-based causal attribution. In A. W. Kruglanski & E. T. Higgins (Eds.), *Social psychology: Handbook of basic principles* (2nd ed., pp. 232–253). New York: Guilford.

Hilton, D. J., & Karpinski, A. (2000). *Attitudes and the implicit associations test*. Ann Arbor, MI: University of Michigan Press.

Hilton, J. L., & Von Hippel, W. (1996). Stereotypes. *Annual Review of Psychology, 47*, 237–271.

Hilton, N. Z., Harris, G. T., & Rice, M. E. (2000). The functions of aggression by male teenagers. *Journal of Personality and Social Psychology, 79*, 988–994.

Himmelfarb, S., & Eagly, A. H. (Eds.) (1974). *Readings in attitude change*. New York: Wiley.

Himmelweit, H. T., Humphreys, P., & Jaeger, M. (1985). *A model of vote choice based on a special longitudinal study extending over 15 years and the British election surveys of 1970–83*. Milton Keynes, UK: Open University Press.

Hinde, R. A. (1982). *Ethology: Its nature and relations with other sciences*. London: Fontana.

Hinkle, S., & Brown, R. (1990). Intergroup comparisons and social identity: Some links and lacunae. In D. Abrams & M. A. Hogg (Eds.), *Social identity theory: Constructive and critical advances* (pp. 48–70). Hemel Hempstead, UK: Harvester Wheatsheaf.

Hitler, A. (1933). *Mein Kampf*. Retrieved November 11, 2003, from http://www.greatwar.nl/books/meinkampf/meinkampf.pdf

Hodges, B. H., Meagher, B. R., Norton, D. J., McBain, R., & Sroubek, R. (2014). *Journal of Personality and Social Psychology, 106*, 218–234.

Hodges, S. D., Klaaren, K. J., & Wheatley, T. (2000). Talking about safe sex: The role of expectations and experience. *Journal of Applied Social Psychology, 30*, 330–349.

Hodson, G., & Dhont, K. (2015).The person-based nature of prejudice: Individual difference predictors of intergroup negativity. *European Review of Social Psychology, 26*, 1–42.

Hoffman, C., Lau, I., & Johnson, D. R. (1986). The linguistic relativity of person cognition: An English–Chinese comparison. *Journal of Personality and Social Psychology, 51*, 1097–1105.

Hoffman, C., Mischel, W., & Mazze, K. (1981). The role of purpose in the organisation of information about behavior: Trait-based versus goal-based categories in person cognition. *Journal of Personality and Social Psychology, 40*, 211–225.

Hoffman, M. L. (1981). Is altruism part of human nature? *Journal of Personality and Social Psychology, 40*, 121–137.

Hofmann, W., De Houwer, J., Perugini, M., Baeyens, F., & Crombez, G. (2010). Evaluative conditioning in humans: a meta-analysis. *Psychological Bulletin, 136*, 390–421.

Hofstede, G. (1980). *Culture's consequences: International differences in work-related values*. Beverly Hills, CA: SAGE.

Hofstede, G. (2001). *Culture's consequences: Comparing values, behaviours, institutions and organizations across nations* (2nd ed.). Thousand Oaks, CA: SAGE.

Hogan, R., & Kaiser, R. (2006). What we know about leadership. *Review of General Psychology, 9*, 169–180.

Hogg, M. A. (1985). Masculine and feminine speech in dyads and groups: A study of speech style and gender salience. *Journal of Language and Social Psychology, 4*, 99–112.

Hogg, M. A. (1992). *The social psychology of group cohesiveness: From attraction to social identity*. London: Harvester Wheatsheaf.

Hogg, M. A. (1993). Group cohesiveness: A critical review and some new directions. *European Review of Social Psychology, 4*, 85–111.

Hogg, M. A. (2000a). Social processes and human behavior: Social psychology. In K. Pawlik & M. R. Rosenzweig (Eds.), *International handbook of psychology* (pp. 305–327). London: SAGE.

Hogg, M. A. (2000b). Social identity and social comparison. In J. Suls & L. Wheeler (Eds.), *Handbook of social comparison: Theory and research* (pp. 401–421). New York: Kluwer/Plenum.

Hogg, M. A. (2000c). Subjective uncertainty reduction through self-categorization: A motivational theory of social identity processes. *European Review of Social Psychology, 11*, 223–255.

Hogg, M. A. (2001). A social identity theory of leadership. *Personality and Social Psychology Review, 5*, 184–200.

Hogg, M. A. (Ed.) (2003). *SAGE benchmarks in psychology: Social psychology*. London: SAGE.

Hogg, M. A. (2006). Social identity theory. In P. J. Burke (Ed.), *Contemporary social psychological theories* (pp. 111–136). Palo Alto, CA: Stanford University Press.

Hogg, M. A. (2007a). Social psychology of leadership. In A. W. Kruglanski & E. T. Higgins (Eds.), *Social psychology: A handbook of basic principles* (2nd ed., pp. 716–733). New York: Guilford Press.

Hogg, M. A. (2007b). Uncertainty-identity theory. *Advances in Experimental Social Psychology, 39*, 69–126.

Hogg, M. A. (2009). From group conflict to social harmony: Leading across diverse and conflicting social identities. In T. Pittinsky (Ed.), *Crossing the divide: Intergroup leadership in a world of difference* (pp. 17–30). Cambridge, MA: Harvard Business Publishing.

Hogg, M. A. (2010). Influence and leadership. In S. T. Fiske, D. T. Gilbert, & G. Lindzey (Eds.), *Handbook of social psychology* (5th ed., Vol. 2, pp. 1166–1207). New York: Wiley.

Hogg, M. A. (2012). Uncertainty-identity theory. In P. A. M. Van Lange, A. W. Kruglanski, & E. T. Higgins (Eds.), *Handbook of theories of social psychology* (Vol. 2, pp. 62–80). Thousand Oaks, CA: Sage.

Hogg, M. A. (2013a). Intergroup relations. In J. Delamater & A. Ward (Eds.), *Handbook of social psychology* (2nd ed., pp. 533–562). New York: Springer.

Hogg, M. A. (2013b). Leadership. In J. M. Levine (Ed.), *Group processes* (pp. 241–266). New York: Psychology Press.

Hogg, M. A. (2014). From uncertainty to extremism: Social categorization and identity processes. *Current Directions in Psychological Science, 23*, 338–342.

Hogg, M. A. (2015). Constructive leadership across groups: How leaders can combat prejudice and conflict between subgroups. *Advances in Group Processes, 32*, 177–207.

Hogg, M. A., & Abrams, D. (1988). *Social identifications: A social psychology of intergroup relations and group processes*. London: Routledge.

Hogg, M. A., & Abrams, D. (1990). Social motivation, self-esteem and social identity. In D. Abrams & M. A. Hogg (Eds.), *Social identity theory: Constructive and critical advances* (pp. 28–47). London: Harvester Wheatsheaf.

Hogg, M. A., & Abrams, D. (1999). Social identity and social cognition: Historical background and current trends. In D. Abrams & M. A. Hogg (Eds.), *Social identity and social cognition* (pp. 1–25). Oxford, UK: Blackwell.

Hogg, M. A., & Abrams, D. (2007). Intergroup behavior and social identity. In M. A. Hogg & J. Cooper (Eds.), *The SAGE handbook of social psychology: Concise student edition* (pp. 335–360). London: SAGE.

Hogg, M. A., & Abrams, D. (Eds.) (2001). *Intergroup relations: Essential readings*. Philadelphia, PA: Psychology Press.

Hogg, M. A., Adelman, J. R., & Blagg, R. D. (2010). Religion in the face of uncertainty: An uncertainty-identity theory account of religiousness. *Personality and Social Psychology Review, 14*, 72–83.

Hogg, M. A., & Blaylock, D. L. (Eds.) (2012). *Extremism and the psychology of uncertainty*. Boston: Wiley-Blackwell.

Hogg, M. A., & Cooper, J. (Eds.) (2007). *The SAGE handbook of social psychology: Concise student edition*. London: SAGE.

Hogg, M. A., Cooper-Shaw, L., & Holzworth, D. W. (1993). Group prototypicality and depersonalised attraction in small interactive groups. *European Journal of Social Psychology, 24*, 452–465.

Hogg, M. A., D'Agata, P., & Abrams, D. (1989). Ethnolinguistic betrayal and speaker evaluations among Italian Australians. *Genetic, Social and General Psychology Monographs, 115*, 153–181.

Hogg, M. A., Fielding, K. S., Johnson, D., Masser, B., Russell, E., & Svensson, A. (2006). Demographic category membership and leadership in small groups: A social identity analysis. *The Leadership Quarterly, 17*, 335–350.

Hogg, M. A., & Gaffney, A. (2014). Prototype-based social comparisons within groups: Constructing social identity to reduce self-uncertainty. In Z. Križan & F. X. Gibbons (Eds.), *Communal functions of social comparison* (pp. 145–174). New York: Cambridge University Press.

Hogg, M. A., & Giles, H. (2012). Norm talk and identity in intergroup communication. In H. Giles (Ed.), *The handbook of intergroup communication* (pp. 373–387). New York: Routledge.

Hogg, M. A., & Hains, S. C. (1996). Intergroup relations and group solidarity: Effects of group identification and social beliefs on depersonalized attraction. *Journal of Personality and Social Psychology, 70*, 295–309.

Hogg, M. A., & Hains, S. C. (1998). Friendship and group identification: A new look at the role of cohesiveness in groupthink. *European Journal of Social Psychology, 28*, 323–341.

Hogg, M. A., Hains, S. C., & Mason, I. (1998). Identification and leadership in small groups: Salience, frame of reference, and leader stereotypicality effects on leader evaluations. *Journal of Personality and Social Psychology, 75*, 1248–1263.

Hogg, M. A., & Hardie, E. A. (1991). Social attraction, personal attraction, and self-categorisation: A field study. *Personality and Social Psychology Bulletin, 17*, 175–180.

Hogg, M. A., Hohman, Z. P., & Rivera, J. E. (2008). Why do people join groups? Three motivational accounts from social psychology. *Social and Personality Psychology Compass, 2/3*, 1269–1280.

Hogg, M. A., & Hornsey, M. J. (2006). Self-concept threat and multiple categorization within groups. In R. J. Crisp & M. Hewstone (Eds.), *Multiple social categorization: Processes, models, and applications* (pp. 112–135). New York: Psychology Press.

Hogg, M. A., Joyce, N., & Abrams, D. (1984). Diglossia in Switzerland? A social identity analysis of speaker evaluations. *Journal of Language and Social Psychology, 3*, 185–196.

Hogg, M. A., Kruglanski, A., & Van den Bos, K. (2013). Uncertainty and the roots of extremism. *Journal of Social Issues, 69*, 407–418.

Hogg, M. A., Martin, R., & Weeden, K. (2004). Leader–member relations and social identity. In D. Van Knippenberg & M. A. Hogg (Eds.), *Leadership and power: Identity processes in groups and organizations* (pp. 18–33). London: SAGE.

Hogg, M. A., Martin, R., Epitropaki, O., Mankad, A., Svensson, A., & Weeden, K. (2005). Effective leadership in salient groups: Revisiting leader–member exchange theory from the perspective of the social identity theory of leadership. *Personality and Social Psychology Bulletin, 31*, 991–1004.

Hogg, M. A., Meehan, C., & Farquharson, J. (2010). The solace of radicalism: Self-uncertainty and group identification in the face of threat. *Journal of Experimental Social Psychology, 46*, 1061–1066.

Hogg, M. A., & Reid, S. A. (2006). Social identity, self- categorization, and the communication of group norms. *Communication Theory, 16*, 7–30.

Hogg, M. A., & Rigoli, N. (1996). Effects of ethnolinguistic vitality, ethnic identification, and linguistic contacts on minority language use. *Journal of Language and Social Psychology, 15*, 76–89.

Hogg, M. A., Sherman, D. K., Dierselhuis, J., Maitner, A. T., & Moffitt, G. (2007). Uncertainty, entitativity, and group identification. *Journal of Experimental Social Psychology, 43*, 135–142.

Hogg, M. A., & Smith, J. R. (2007). Attitudes in social context: A social identity perspective. *European Review of Social Psychology, 18*, 89–131.

Hogg, M. A., Terry, D. J., & White, K. M. (1995). A tale of two theories: A critical comparison of identity theory with social identity theory. *Social Psychology Quarterly, 58*, 255–269.

Hogg, M. A., & Tindale, R. S. (2005). Social identity, influence, and communication in small groups. In J. Harwood & H. Giles (Eds.), *Intergroup communication: Multiple perspectives* (pp. 141–164). New York: Peter Lang.

Hogg, M. A., & Tindale, R. S. (Eds.) (2001). *Blackwell handbook of social psychology: Group processes*. Oxford, UK: Blackwell.

Hogg, M. A., & Turner, J. C. (1985). Interpersonal attraction, social identification and psychological group formation. *European Journal of Social Psychology, 15*, 51–66.

Hogg, M. A., & Turner, J. C. (1987a). Social identity and conformity: A theory of referent informational influence. In W. Doise & S. Moscovici (Eds.), *Current issues in European social psychology* (Vol. 2, pp. 139–182). Cambridge, UK: Cambridge University Press.

Hogg, M. A., & Turner, J. C. (1987b). Intergroup behaviour, self-stereotyping and the salience of social categories. *British Journal of Social Psychology, 26*, 325–340.

Hogg, M. A., Turner, J. C., & Davidson, B. (1990). Polarized norms and social frames of reference: A test of the self-categorization theory of group polarization. *Basic and Applied Social Psychology, 11*, 77–100.

Hogg, M. A., Turner, J. C., Nascimento-Schulze, C., & Spriggs, D. (1986). Social categorization, intergroup behaviour and self-esteem: Two experiments. *Revista de Psicología Social, 1*, 23–37.

Hogg, M. A., & Van Knippenberg, D. (2003). Social identity and leadership processes in groups. *Advances in Experimental Social Psychology, 35*, 1–52.

Hogg, M. A., Van Knippenberg, D., & Rast, D. E., III. (2012a). Intergroup leadership in organizations: Leading across group and intergroup boundaries. *Academy of Management Review, 37*, 232–255.

Hogg, M. A., Van Knippenberg, D., & Rast, D. E., III. (2012b). The social identity theory of leadership: Theoretical origins, research findings, and conceptual developments. *European Review of Social Psychology, 23*, 258–304.

Hogg, M. A., & Vaughan, G. M. (2010). *Essentials of social psychology*. London: Pearson Education.

Hogg, M. A., & Williams, K. D. (2000). From I to we: Social identity and the collective self. *Group Dynamics: Theory, Research, and Practice, 4*, 81–97.

Hohman, Z. P., & Hogg, M. A. (2011). Fear and uncertainty in the face of death: The role of life after death in group identification. *European Journal of Social Psychology, 41*, 751–760.

Hohman, Z. P., & Hogg, M. A. (2015). Fearing the uncertain: Self-uncertainty plays a role in mortality salience. *Journal of Experimental Social Psychology, 57*, 31–42.

Hohman, Z. P., Hogg, M. A., & Bligh, M. C. (2010). Identity and intergroup leadership: Asymmetrical political and national identification in response to uncertainty. *Self and Identity, 9*, 113–128.

Holland, R. W., Verplanken, B., & Van Knippenberg, A. (2002). On the nature of attitude–behavior relations: The strong guide, the weak follow. *European Journal of Social Psychology, 32*, 869–876.

Hollander, E. P. (1958). Conformity, status, and idiosyncracy credit. *Psychological Review, 65*, 117–127.

Hollander, E. P. (1967). *Principles and methods of social psychology*. New York: Oxford University Press.

Hollander, E. P. (1985). Leadership and power. In G. Lindzey & E. Aronson (Eds.), *Handbook of social psychology* (3rd ed., Vol. 2, pp. 485–537). New York: Random House.

Hollander, E. P., & Julian, J. W. (1970). Studies in leader legitimacy, influence, and innovation. *Advances in Experimental Social Psychology, 5*, 34–69.

Hollingshead, A. B. (1996). The rank order effect: Decision procedure, communication technology and group decisions. *Organizational Behavior and Human Decision Processes, 68*(3), 1–13.

Hollingshead, A. B. (2001). Communication technologies, the internet, and group research. In M. A. Hogg & R. S. Tindale (Eds.), *Blackwell handbook of social psychology: Group processes* (pp. 557–573). Oxford, UK: Blackwell.

Hollingshead, A. B., & McGrath, J. E. (1995). Computer-assisted groups: A critical review of the empirical research. In R. A. Guzzo & E. Salas (Eds.), *Team effectiveness and decision making in organizations* (pp. 46–78). San Francisco, CA: Jossey-Bass.

Holloway, S., Tucker, L., & Hornstein, H. A. (1977). The effects of social and nonsocial information on interpersonal behavior of males: The news makes news. *Journal of Personality and Social Psychology, 35*, 514–522.

Holmes, J. G. (2002). Interpersonal expectations as the building blocks of social cognition: An interdependence theory perspective. *Personal Relationships, 9*, 1–26.

Holtgraves, T. (2010). Social psychology and language: Words, utterances and conversations. In S. T. Fiske, D. T. Gilbert, & G. Lindzey (Eds.), *Handbook of social psychology* (5th ed., Vol. 2, pp. 1386–1422). New York: Wiley.

Holtgraves, T. (Ed.) (2014). *The Oxford handbook of language and social psychology*. New York: Oxford University Press.

Holtzworth-Munroe, A., & Jacobson, N. S. (1985). Causal attributions of married couples. When do they search for causes? What do they conclude when they do? *Journal of Personality and Social Psychology, 48*, 1398–1412.

Homans, G. C. (1961). *Social behavior: Its elementary forms*. New York: Harcourt, Brace and World.

Hong, J. S., & Espelage, D. L. (2012). A review of research on bullying and peer victimization in school: An ecological system analysis. *Aggression and Violent Behavior, 17*, 311–322.

Hong, Y.-Y., & Mallorie, L. M. (2004). A dynamic constructivist approach to culture: Lessons learned from personality psychology. *Journal of Research in Personality, 38*, 59–67.

Hong, Y.-Y., Morris, M. W., Chiu, C., & Benet-Martínez, V. (2000). Multicultural minds: A dynamic constructivist approach to culture and cognition. *American Psychologist, 55*, 705–720.

Hoorens, V. (2014). What's really in a name-letter effect? Name-letter preferences as indirect measures of self-esteem. *European Review of Social Psychology, 25*, 228–262.

Hopkins, N., & Moore, C. (2001). Categorizing the neighbors: Identity, distance, and stereotyping. *Social Psychology Quarterly, 64*, 239–252.

Hopkins, N., & Reicher, S. (1997). Social movement rhetoric and the social psychology of collective action: A case study of anti-abortion mobilization. *Human Relations, 50*, 261–286.

Hopkins, N., Reicher, S., & Kahani-Hopkins, V. (2003). Citizenship, participation, and identity construction: Political mobilization amongst British Muslims. *Psychologica Belgica, 43*(1/2), 33–54.

Horai, J. (1977). Attributional conflict. *Journal of Social Issues, 33*, 88–100.

Horgan, J. (2011). The perils of unleashing students' skepticism. *The Chronicle of Higher Education*, 21 January, pp. B6–B7.

Horgan, J. (2014). *The psychology of terrorism*. New York: Routledge.

Hornsey, M. J. (2005). Why being right is not enough: Predicting defensiveness in the face of group criticism. *European Review of Social Psychology, 16*, 301–334.

Hornsey, M. J., Grice, T., Jetten, J., Paulsen, N., & Callan, V. (2007). Group directed criticisms and recommendations for change: Why newcomers arouse more resistance than old-timers. *Personality and Social Psychology Bulletin, 33*, 1036–1048.

Hornsey, M. J., & Hogg, M. A. (2000a). Assimilation and diversity: An integrative model of subgroup relations. *Personality and Social Psychology Review, 4*, 143–156.

Hornsey, M. J., & Hogg, M. A. (2000b). Intergroup similarity and subgroup relations: Some implications for assimilation. *Personality and Social Psychology Bulletin, 26*, 948–958.

Hornsey, M. J., & Hogg, M. A. (2000c). Subgroup relations: A comparison of mutual intergroup differentiation and common ingroup identity models of prejudice reduction. *Personality and Social Psychology Bulletin, 26*, 242–256.

Hornsey, M. J., & Imani, A. (2004). Criticising groups from the inside and the outside: An identity perspective on the intergroup sensitivity effect. *Personality and Social Psychology Bulletin, 30*, 365–383.

Hornsey, M. J., & Jetten, J. (2004). The individual within the group: Balancing the need to belong with the need to be different. *Personality and Social Psychology Review, 8*, 248–264.

Hornsey, M. J., Jetten, J., McAuliffe, B. J., & Hogg, M. A. (2006). The impact of individualist and collectivist group norms on evaluations of dissenting group members. *Journal of Experimental Social Psychology, 42*, 57–68.

Hornsey, M. J., Oppes, T., & Svensson, A. (2002). 'It's OK if we say it, but you can't': Responses to intergroup and intragroup criticism. *European Journal of Social Psychology, 32*, 293–307.

Hornsey, M. J., Spears, R., Cremers, I., & Hogg, M. A. (2003). Relations between high and low power groups: The importance of legitimacy. *Personality and Social Psychology Bulletin, 29*, 216–227.

Hornstein, G. A. (1985). Intimacy in conversational style as a function of the degree of closeness between members of a dyad. *Journal of Personality and Social Psychology, 49*, 671–681.

Hornstein, H. A. (1970). The influence of social models on helping. In J. Macaulay & L. Berkowitz (Eds.), *Altruism and helping behavior* (pp. 29–42). New York: Academic Press.

Horowitz, D. L. (1973). Direct, displaced and cumulative ethnic aggression. *Comparative Politics, 6*, 1–16.

Horowitz, E. L. (1936). The development of attitudes towards the Negro. *Archives of Psychology, 194*.

Horowitz, E. L. (1939). Racial aspects of self-identification in nursery school children. *Journal of Psychology, 7*, 91–99.

Horowitz, I. A., & Bordens, K. S. (1990). An experimental investigation of procedural issues in complex tort trials. *Law and Human Behavior, 14*, 269–285.

Hosie, J., Gilbert, F., Simpson, K., & Daffern, M. (2014). An examination of the relationship between personality and aggression using the General Aggression and Five Factor models. *Aggressive Behavior, 40*, 189–196.

House, R. J. (1977). A 1976 theory of charismatic leadership. In J. G. Hunt & L. Larson (Eds.), *Leadership: The cutting edge* (pp. 189–207). Carbondale, IL: Southern Illinois University Press.

House, R. J. (1996). Path–goal theory of leadership: Lessons, legacy, and a reformulated theory. *The Leadership Quarterly, 7*, 323–352.

House, R. J., Spangler, W. D., & Woycke, J. (1991). Personality and charisma in the U.S. presidency: A psychological theory of leader effectiveness. *Administrative Science Quarterly, 36*, 364–396.

Hovland, C. I., Janis, I. L., & Kelley, H. H. (1953). *Communication and persuasion*. New Haven, CT: Yale University Press.

Hovland, C. I., Lumsdaine, A. A., & Sheffield, F. D. (1949). *Experiments in mass communication*. Princeton, NJ: Princeton University Press.

Hovland, C. I., & Sears, R. R. (1940). Minor studies in aggression: VI. Correlation of lynchings with economic indices. *Journal of Psychology, 9*, 301–310.

Hovland, C. I., & Weiss, W. (1952). The influence of source credibility in communication effectiveness. *Public Opinion Quarterly, 15*, 635–650.

Howard, J. A. (1985). Further appraisal of correspondent inference theory. *Personality and Social Psychology Bulletin, 11*, 467–477.

Howard, J. W., & Rothbart, M. (1980). Social categorization and memory for ingroup and outgroup behavior. *Journal of Personality and Social Psychology, 38*, 301–310.

Howell, D. C. (2010). *Statistical methods for psychology* (8th ed.). Belmont, CA: Duxbury.

Hraba, J. (1972). A measure of ethnocentrism? *Social Forces, 50*, 522–527.

Hraba, J., & Grant, G. (1970). Black is beautiful: A re-examination of racial preference and identification. *Journal of Personality and Social Psychology, 16*, 398–402.

Hudson, N. W., Fraley, R. C., Brumbaugh, C. C., & Vicary, A. M. (2014). Coregulation in romantic partners' attachment styles: A longitudinal investigation. *Personality and Social Psychology Bulletin, 40*, 845–847.

Huesmann, L. R. (1988). An information processing model for the development of aggression. *Aggressive Behavior, 14*, 13–24.

Huesmann, L. R., Eron, L. D., Lefkowitz, M. M., & Walder, L. O. (1984). Stability of aggression over time and generations. *Developmental Psychology, 20*, 1120–1134.

Huesmann, L. R., & Guerra, N. G. (1997). Children's normative beliefs about aggression and aggressive behaviour. *Journal of Personality and Social Psychology, 72*, 408–419.

Huesmann, L. R., & Miller, L. S. (1994). Long-term effects of repeated exposure to media violence in childhood. In L. R. Huesmann (Ed.), *Aggressive behaviour: Current perspectives* (pp. 153–186). New York: Plenum.

Huesmann, L. R., Mois-Titus, J., Podolski, C. L., & Eron, L. D. (2003). Longitudinal relations between children's exposure to TV violence and their aggressive and violent behavior in young adulthood: 1977–1992. *Developmental Psychology, 39*, 201–221.

Hughes, D. J., Rowe, M., Batey, M., & Lee, A. (2012). A tale of two sites: Twitter vs. Facebook and the personality predictors of social media usage. *Computers in Human Behavior, 28*, 561–569.

Hughes, M. T. (1981). To cheat or not to cheat? *Albany Times–Union, 26 July*, pp. B-1, B-3.

Huici, C., Ros, M., Cano, I., Hopkins, N., Emler, N., & Carmona, M. (1997). Comparative identity and evaluation of socio-political change: Perceptions of the European Community as a function of the salience of regional identities. *European Journal of Social Psychology, 27*, 97–113.

Hummert, M. L. (1990). Multiple stereotypes of elderly and young adults: A comparison of structure and evaluations. *Psychology and Aging, 5*, 182–193.

Hummert, M. L. (2012). Communication between age groups. In H. Giles (Ed), *The handbook of intergroup communication* (pp. 223–236). New York: Routledge.

Huston, T. L. (2009). What's love got to do with it? Why some marriages succeed and others fail. *Personal Relationships, 16*, 301–327.

Huston, T. L., Ruggiero, M., Conner, R., & Geis, G. (1981). Bystander intervention into crime: A study based on naturally-occurring episodes. *Social Psychology Quarterly, 44*, 14–23.

Ickes, W., Gesn, P. R., & Graham, T. (2000). Gender differences in empathic accuracy: Differential ability or differential motivation? *Personal Relationships, 7*, 95–109.

Ingham, A. G., Levinger, G., Graves, J., & Peckham, V. (1974). The Ringelmann effect: Studies of group size and group performance. *Journal of Experimental Social Psychology, 10*, 371–384.

Ingoldsby, B. B. (1991). The Latin American family: Familism vs machismo. *Journal of Comparative Family Studies, 23*, 47–62.

Insko, C. A. (1965). Verbal reinforcement of attitude. *Journal of Personality and Social Psychology, 2*, 621–623.

Insko, C. A. (1967). *Theories of attitude change.* New York: Appleton-Century-Crofts.

Insko, C. A., Nacoste, R. W., & Moe, J. L. (1983). Belief congruence and racial discrimination: Review of the evidence and critical evaluation. *European Journal of Social Psychology, 13*, 153–174.

Inzlicht, M., McGregor, I., Hirsh, J. B., & Nash, K. (2009). Neural markers of religious conviction. *Psychological Science, 20*, 385–392.

Inzlicht, M., & Schmader, T. (Eds.) (2011). *Stereotype threat: Theory, process, and application.* New York: Oxford University Press.

Isaacson, W. (2011). *Steve Jobs.* New York: Simon & Schuster.

Isen, A. M. (1970). Success, failure, attention, and reaction to others: The warm glow of success. *Journal of Personality and Social Psychology, 15*, 294–301.

Isen, A. M., Clark, M., & Schwartz, M. (1976). Duration of the effect of good mood on helping: 'footprints on the sands of time'. *Journal of Personality and Psychology, 34*, 385–393.

Isen, A. M., Horn, N., & Rosenhan, D. L. (1973). Effects of success and failure on children's generosity. *Journal of Personality and Social Psychology, 27*, 239–247.

Isen, A. M., & Stalker, T. E. (1982). The effect of feeling state on evaluation of positive, neutral, and negative stimuli when you 'accentuate the positive': Do you 'eliminate the negative'? *Social Psychology Quarterly, 45*, 58–63.

Isenberg, D. J. (1986). Group polarization: A critical review. *Journal of Personality and Social Psychology, 50*, 1141–1151.

Islam, M., & Hewstone, M. (1993). Intergroup attributions and affective consequences in majority and minority groups. *Journal of Personality and Social Psychology, 65*, 936–950.

Israel, J., & Tajfel, H. (Eds.) (1972). *The context of social psychology: A critical assessment.* London: Academic Press.

Ito, T. A., Larsen, J. T., Smith, N. K., & Cacioppo, J. T. (1998). Negative information weighs more heavily on the brain: The negativity bias in evaluative categorizations. *Journal of Personality and Social Psychology, 75*, 887–900.

Ito, T. A., Thompson, E., & Cacioppo, J. T. (2004). Tracking the timecourse of social perception: The effects of racial cues on event-related brain potentials. *Personality and Social Psychology Bulletin, 30*, 1267–1280.

Iyer, A., & Leach, C. W. (2008). Emotion in inter-group relations. *European Review of Social Psychology, 19*, 86–125.

Iyer, A., Schmader, T., & Lickel, B. (2007). Why individuals protest the perceived transgressions of their country: The role of anger, shame, and guilt. *Personality and Social Psychology Bulletin, 33*, 572–587.

Izhaki-Costi, O., & Schul, Y. (2011). I do not know you and I am keeping it that way: Attachment avoidance and empathic accuracy in the perception of strangers. *Personal Relationships, 18*, 321–340.

Izraeli, D. N., & Izraeli, D. (1985). Sex effects in evaluating leaders: A replication study. *Journal of Applied Psychology, 70*, 540–546.

Izraeli, D. N., Izraeli, D., & Eden, D. (1985). Giving credit where credit is due: A case of no sex bias in attribution. *Journal of Applied Social Psychology, 15*, 516–530.

Jacks, Z. J., & Cameron, K. A. (2003). Strategies for resisting persuasion. *Basic and Applied Social Psychology, 25*, 145–161.

Jackson, J., & Harkins, S. G. (1985). Equity in effort: An explanation of the social loafing effect. *Journal of Personality and Social Psychology, 49*, 1199–1206.

Jacobs, D., & Singell, L. (1993). Leadership and organisational performance: Isolating links between managers and collective success. *Social Science Research, 22*, 165–189.

Jacobs, R., & Campbell, D. T. (1961). The perpetuation of an arbitrary tradition through several generations of a laboratory microculture. *Journal of Abnormal and Social Psychology, 62*, 649–658.

Jacobson, D. (1999). Impression formation in cyberspace: Online expectations and offline experiences in textbased virtual communities. *Journal of Computer-Mediated Communication* [online serial], *5*(1). doi:10.1111/j.1083-6101.1999.tb00333.x.

Jacoby, L. L., Kelly, C., Brown, J., & Jasechko, J. (1989). Becoming famous overnight: Limits on the ability to avoid unconscious influences of the past. *Journal of Personality and Social Psychology, 56*, 326–338.

Jahoda, G. (1979). A cross-cultural perspective on experimental social psychology. *Personality and Social Psychology Bulletin, 5*, 142–148.

Jahoda, G. (1982). *Psychology and anthropology: A psychological perspective.* London: Academic Press.

James, W. (1890). *The principles of psychology* (Vol. 1). New York: Holt.

Jamieson, D. W., & Zanna, M. P. (1989). Need for structure in attitude formation and expression. In A. R. Pratkanis, S. J. Breckler & A. G. Greenwald (Eds.), *Attitude structure and function* (pp. 383–406). Hillsdale, NJ: Erlbaum.

Janis, I. L. (1954). Personality correlates of susceptibility to persuasion. *Journal of Personality, 22*, 504–518.

Janis, I. L. (1967). Effects of fear arousal on attitude change: Recent developments in theory and experimental research. *Advances in Experimental Social Psychology, 3*, 167–224.

Janis, I. L. (1972). *Victims of groupthink: A psychological study of foreign policy decisions and fiascoes.* Boston, MA: Houghton Mifflin.

Janis, I. L. (1982). *Groupthink: Psychological studies of policy decisions and fiascoes* (2nd ed.). Boston, MA: Houghton Mifflin.

Janis, I. L., & Feshbach, S. (1953). Effects of fear-arousing communications. *Journal of Abnormal and Social Psychology, 48*, 78–92.

Janis, I. L., & Hovland, C. I. (1959). An overview of persuasibility research. In C. I. Hovland & I. L. Janis (Eds.), *Personality and persuasibility* (pp. 1–26). New Haven, CT: Yale University Press.

Janis, I. L., Kaye, D., & Kirschner, P. (1965). Facilitating effects of 'eating-while-reading' on responsiveness to persuasive communications. *Journal of Personality and Social Psychology, 1*, 181–186.

Janis, I. L., & King, B. T. (1954). The influence of roleplaying on opinion change. *Journal of Abnormal and Social Psychology, 49*, 211–218.

Janis, I. L., & Mann, L. (1977). *Decision making.* New York: Free Press.

Janoff-Bulman, R., & Carnes, N. C. (2013). Surveying the moral landscape: Moral motives and group-based moralities. *Personality and Social Psychology Review, 17,* 219–236.

Jarvis, W. B. G., & Petty, R. E. (1995). The need to evaluate. *Journal of Personality and Social Psychology, 70,* 172–192.

Jaspars, J. M. F. (1980). The coming of age of social psychology in Europe. *European Journal of Social Psychology, 10,* 421–428.

Jaspars, J. M. F. (1986). Forum and focus: A personal view of European social psychology. *European Journal of Social Psychology, 16,* 3–15.

Jellison, J., & Arkin, R. (1977). Social comparison of abilities: A self-presentation approach to decision making in groups. In J. M. Suls & R. L. Miller (Eds.), *Social comparison processes: Theoretical and empirical perspectives* (pp. 235–257). Washington, DC: Hemisphere Press.

Jellison, J. M., & Green, J. (1981). A self-presentation approach to the fundamental attribution error: The norm of internality. *Journal of Personality and Social Psychology, 40,* 643–649.

Jennings, M. K., & Niemi, R. G. (1968). The transmission of political values from parent to child. *American Political Science Review, 62,* 546–575.

Jetten, J., Haslam, C., & Haslam, S. A. (Eds.) (2012). *The social cure: Identity, health and well-being.* New York: Psychology Press.

Jetten, J., Postmes, T., & McAuliffe, B. J. (2002). We're all individuals: Group norms of individualism and collectivism, levels of identification, and identity threat. *European Journal of Social Psychology, 32,* 189–207.

Jodelet, D. (1991). *Madness and social representations.* Hemel Hempstead, UK: Harvester Wheatsheaf.

Johnson, B. T. (1994). Effects of outcome-relevant involvement and prior information on persuasion. *Journal of Experimental Social Psychology, 30,* 556–579.

Johnson, B. T., & Eagly, A. H. (1989). Effects of involvement on persuasion: Meta-analysis. *Psychological Bulletin, 106,* 290–314.

Johnson, D. W., & Johnson, F. P. (1987). *Joining together: Group theory and group skills* (3rd ed.). Englewood Cliffs, NJ: Prentice Hall.

Johnson, E. J., Pham, M. T., & Johar, G. V. (2007). Consumer behavior and marketing. In A. W. Kruglanski & E. T. Higgins (Eds.), *Social psychology: A handbook of basic principles* (2nd ed., pp. 869–887). New York: Guilford Press.

Johnson, K. L., Gill, S., Reichman, V., & Tassinary, L. G. (2007). Swagger, sway, and sexuality: Judging sexual orientation from body motion and morphology. *Journal of Personality and Social Psychology, 93,* 321–334.

Johnson, R. D., & Downing, L. L. (1979). Deindividuation and valence of cues: Effects on prosocial and antisocial behavior. *Journal of Personality and Social Psychology, 37,* 1532–1538.

Johnston, L., & Hewstone, M. (1990). Intergroup contact: Social identity and social cognition. In D. Abrams & M. A. Hogg (Eds.), *Social identity theory: Constructive and critical advances* (pp. 185–210). London: Harvester Wheatsheaf.

Jonas, E., Schimel, J., Greenberg, J., & Pyszczynski, T. (2002). The Scrooge effect: Evidence that mortality salience increases prosocial attitudes and behavior. *Personality and Social Psychology Bulletin, 28,* 1342–1353.

Jonas, K. J., Sassenberg, K., & Scheepers, D. (2010). Self-regulation within and between groups. *Group Processes and Intergroup Relations, 13,* 131–136.

Jones, B., Gray, A., Kavanagh, D., Moran, M., Norton, P., & Seldon, A. (1994). *Politics UK* (2nd ed.). Hemel Hempstead, UK: Harvester Wheatsheaf.

Jones, C. R., Olson, M. A., & Fazio, R. H. (2010). Evaluative conditioning: The "how" question. *Advances in Experimental Social Psychology, 43,* 205–255.

Jones, E. E. (1964). *Ingratiation: A social psychological analysis.* Des Moines, IA: Meredith Publishing Company.

Jones, E. E. (1979). The rocky road from acts to dispositions. *American Psychologist, 34,* 107–117.

Jones, E. E. (1990). *Interpersonal perception.* New York: Freeman.

Jones, E. E. (1998). Major developments in five decades of social psychology. In D. T. Gilbert, S. T. Fiske, & G. Lindzey (Eds.), *The handbook of social psychology* (4th ed., Vol. 1, pp. 3–57). New York: McGraw-Hill.

Jones, E. E., & Berglas, S. (1978). Control of attributions about the self through self-handicapping strategies: The appeal of alcohol and the role of underachievement. *Personality and Social Psychology Bulletin, 4,* 200–206.

Jones, E. E., & Davis, K. E. (1965). From acts to dispositions: The attribution process in person perception. In L. Berkowitz (Ed.), *Advances in experimental social psychology* (Vol. 2, pp. 219–266). New York: Academic Press.

Jones, E. E., Davis, K. E., & Gergen, K. (1961). Role playing variations and their informational value for person perception. *Journal of Abnormal and Social Psychology, 63,* 302–310.

Jones, E. E., & Goethals, G. R. (1972). Order effects in impression formation: Attribution context and the nature of the entity. In E. E. Jones, D. E. Kanouse, H. H. Kelley, R. E. Nisbett, S. Valins, & B. Weiner (Eds.), *Attribution: Perceiving the causes of behavior* (pp. 27–46). Morristown, NJ: General Learning Press.

Jones, E. E., & Harris, V. A. (1967). The attribution of attitudes. *Journal of Experimental Social Psychology, 3,* 1–24.

Jones, E. E., & McGillis, D. (1976). Correspondent inferences and the attribution cube: A comparative reappraisal. In J. H. Harvey, W. J. Ickes, & R. F. Kidd (Eds.), *New directions in attribution research* (Vol. 1, pp. 389–420). Hillsdale, NJ: Erlbaum.

Jones, E. E., & Nisbett, R. E. (1972). The actor and the observer: Divergent perceptions of the causes of behavior. In E. E. Jones, D. E. Kanouse, H. H. Kelley, R. E. Nisbett, S. Valins, & B. Weiner (Eds.), *Attribution: Perceiving the causes of behavior* (pp. 79–94). Morristown, NJ: General Learning Press.

Jones, E. E., & Pittman, T. S. (1982). Toward a general theory of strategic self-presentation. In J. Suls (Ed.), *Psychological perspectives on the self* (Vol. 1, pp. 231–262). Hillsdale, NJ: Erlbaum.

Jones, E. E., & Sigall, H. (1971). The bogus pipeline: A new paradigm for measuring affect and attitude. *Psychological Bulletin, 76,* 349–364.

Jones, E. E., Wood, G. C., & Quattrone, G. A. (1981). Perceived variability of personal characteristics in ingroups and outgroups: The role of knowledge and evaluation. *Personality and Social Psychology Bulletin, 7,* 523–528.

Jones, J. D., Cassidy, J., & Shaver, P. R. (2015). Parents' self-reported attachment styles: A review of links with parenting behaviors, emotions and cognitions. *Personality and Social Psychology Review, 19,* 44–76.

Jones, J. M. (1996). *The psychology of racism and prejudice.* New York: McGraw Hill.

Jones, J. T., Pelham, B. W., Carvallo, M., & Mirenberg, M. C. (2004). How do I love thee? Let me count the Js: Implicit egotism and interpersonal attraction. *Journal of Personality and Social Psychology, 87,* 665–683.

Jones, S. E., & Yarbrough, A. E. (1985). A naturalistic study of the meanings of touch. *Communication Monographs, 52,* 19–56.

Jost, J. T., & Banaji, M. R. (1994). The role of stereotyping in system-justification and the production of false consciousness. *British Journal of Social Psychology, 33,* 1–27.

Jost, J. T., & Hunyadi, O. (2002). The psychology of system justification and the palliative function of ideology. *European Review of Social Psychology, 13,* 111–153.

Jost, J. T., & Kramer, R. M. (2002). The system justification motive in intergroup relations. In D. M. Mackie & E. R. Smith (Eds.), *From prejudice to intergroup emotions: Differentiated reactions to social groups* (pp. 227–246). New York: Psychology Press.

Jost, J. T., & Kruglanski, A. (2002). The estrangement of social constructionism and experimental social psychology: History of the rift and prospects for reconciliation. *Personality and Social Psychology Review, 6,* 168–187.

Jost, J. T., & Major, B. (Eds.) (2001). *The psychology of legitimacy: Emerging perspectives on ideology, justice, and intergroup relations.* New York: Cambridge University Press.

Jost, J. T., & Van der Toorn, J. (2012). System justification theory. In P. A. M. van Lange, A. W. Kruglanski, & E. T. Higgins (Eds.), *Handbook of theories of social psychology.* (Vol. 2, pp. 313–343). London: Sage.

Joule, R.-V., & Beauvois, J.-L. (1998). Cognitive dissonance theory: A radical view. *European Review of Social Psychology, 8,* 1–32.

Jourard, S. M. (1966). An exploratory study of body- accessibility. *British Journal of Social and Clinical Psychology, 5*, 221–231.

Jourard, S. M. (1971). *The transparent self*. New York: Van Nostrand.

Joyce, W. F., Nohria, N., & Roberson, B. (2003). *What really works: The 4+2 formula for sustained business success*. New York: Harper Business.

Judd, C. M., & Park, B. (1988). Out-group homogeneity: Judgments of variability at the individual and group levels. *Journal of Personality and Social Psychology, 54*, 778–788.

Judge, T. A., & Bono, J. E. (2000). Five-factor model of personality and transformational leadership. *Journal of Applied Psychology, 85*, 751–765.

Judge, T. A., Bono, J. E., Ilies, R., & Gerhardt, M. W. (2002). Personality and leadership: A qualitative and quantitative review. *Journal of Applied Psychology, 87*, 765–780.

Judge, T. A., & Cable, D. M. (2004). The effect of physical height on workplace success and income. *Journal of Applied Psychology, 89*, 428–441.

Judge, T. A., & Cable, D. M. (2011). When it comes to pay, do the thin win? The effect of weight on pay for men and women. *Journal of Applied Psychology, 96*, 95–112.

Jung, C. G. (1946). *Psychological types or the psychology of individuation*. New York: Harcourt Brace. (Originally published 1922.)

Jussim, L., Eccles, J., & Madon, S. (1996). Social perception, social stereotypes, and teacher expectations: Accuracy and the quest for the powerful self-fulfilling prophecy. *Advances in Experimental Social Psychology, 28*, 281–388.

Jussim, L., & Fleming, C. (1996). Self-fulfilling prophecies and the maintenance of social stereotypes: The role of dyadic interactions and social forces. In C. N. Macrae, C. Stangor, & M. Hewstone (Eds.), *Stereotypes and stereotyping* (pp. 161–192). New York: Guilford Press.

Kafka, F. (1925). *The trial*. Harmondsworth, UK: Penguin.

Kağitçibaşi, Ç. (2005). Autonomy and relatedness in cultural context: Implications for self and family. *Journal of Cross-Cultural Psychology, 36*, 403–422.

Kahn, A., & Ryen, A. H. (1972). Factors influencing the bias towards one's own group. *International Journal of Group Tensions, 2*, 33–50.

Kahneman, D., & Tversky, A. (1973). On the psychology of prediction. *Psychological Review, 80*, 237–251.

Kanazawa, H., & Loveday, L. (1988). The Japanese immigrant community in Brazil: Language contact and shift. *Journal of Multilingual and Multicultural Development, 9*, 423–435.

Kanouse, D. E., & Hanson, L. R. Jr (1972). Negativity in evaluations. In E. E. Jones, D. E. Kanouse, H. H. Kelley, R. E. Nisbett, S. Valins, & B. Weiner (Eds.), *Attribution: Perceiving the causes of behavior* (pp. 47–62). Morristown, NJ: General Learning Press.

Kanter, R. M. (1977). Numbers: Minorities and majorities. In *Men and women of the corporation* (pp. 206–242). New York: Basic Books.

Kaplan, M. F. (1977). Discussion polarization effects in a modified jury decision paradigm: Informational influence. *Sociometry, 40*, 262–271.

Kaplan, M. F., & Miller, L. E. (1978). Reducing the effects of juror bias. *Journal of Personality and Social Psychology, 36*, 1443–1455.

Karakashian, L. M., Walter, M. I., Christopher, A. N., & Lucas, T. (2006). Fear of negative evaluation affects helping behavior: The bystander effect revisited. *North American Journal of Psychology, 8*, 13–32.

Karau, S. J., & Hart, J. W. (1998). Group cohesiveness and social loafing: Effects of a social interaction manipulation on individual motivation within groups. *Group Dynamics, 2*, 185–191.

Karau, S. J., & Williams, K. D. (1993). Social loafing: A meta-analytic review and theoretical integration. *Journal of Personality and Social Psychology, 65*, 681–706.

Karney, B. R., & Bradbury, T. N. (1995). Assessing longitudinal change in marriage: An introduction to the analysis of growth curves. *Journal of Marriage and the Family, 57*, 1091–1108.

Karniol, R. (1982). Behavioral and cognitive correlates of various immanent justice responses in children: Deterrent versus punitive moral systems. *Journal of Personality and Social Psychology, 43*, 881–920.

Karremans, J. C., Van Lange, P. A. M., & Holland, R. W. (2005). Forgiveness and its associations with prosocial thinking, feeling, and doing beyond the relationship with the offender. *Personality and Social Psychology Bulletin, 31*, 1315–1326.

Kashima, Y. (2005). Is culture a problem for social psychology? *Asian Journal of Social Psychology, 8*, 19–38.

Kashima, Y., & Kashima, E. (1998). Culture, connectionism, and the self. In J. Adamopoulos & Y. Kashima (Eds.) (1999). *Social psychology and cultural context* (pp. 77–92). London: SAGE.

Kasser, T., Koestner, R., & Lekes, N. (2002). Early family experiences and adult values: A 26-year, prospective longitudinal study. *Personality and Social Psychology Bulletin, 28*, 826–835.

Kassin, S. M. (1979). Consensus information, prediction and causal attribution: A review of the literature and issues. *Journal of Personality and Social Psychology, 37*, 1966–1981.

Kassin, S. M., Ellsworth, P. C., & Smith, V. L. (1989). The 'general acceptance' of psychological research on eyewitness testimony. *American Psychologist, 44*, 1089–1098.

Kassin, S. M., & Pryor, J. B. (1985). The development of attribution processes. In J. Pryor & J. Day (Eds.), *The development of social cognition* (pp. 3–34). New York: Springer.

Katsikitis, M., Pilowsky, I., & Innes, J. M. (1990). The quantification of smiling using a microcomputer-based approach. *Journal of Nonverbal Behavior, 14*, 3–17.

Katz, D. (1960). The functional approach to the study of attitudes. *Public Opinion Quarterly, 24*, 163–204.

Katz, D., & Braly, K. (1933). Racial stereotypes of one hundred college students. *Journal of Abnormal and Social Psychology, 28*, 280–290.

Katz, I., & Hass, R. G. (1988). Racial ambivalence and American value conflict: Correlational and priming studies of dual cognitive structures. *Journal of Personality and Social Psychology, 55*, 893–905.

Katz, P. A. (1976). *Towards the elimination of racism*. New York: Pergamon Press.

Kavanagh, P. S., Robins, S. C., & Ellis, B. J. (2010). The mating sociometer: A regulatory mechanism for mating aspirations. *Journal of Personality and Social Psychology, 99*, 120–132.

Kawakami, K., Young, H., & Dovidio, J. F. (2002). Automatic stereotyping: Category, trait, and behavioral activations. *Personality and Social Psychology Bulletin, 28*, 3–15.

Kazdin, A. E., & Bryan, J. H. (1971). Competence and volunteering. *Journal of Experimental Social Psychology, 7*, 87–97.

Keller, P. A., & Block, L. G. (1995). Increasing the persuasiveness of fear appeals: The effect of arousal and elaboration. *Journal of Consumer Research, 22*, 448–459.

Kellerman, A. L., Rivara, F. P., Rushforth, N. B., Banton, J. G., Reay, D. T., Francisco, J. T., et al. (1993). Gun ownership as a risk factor for homicide in the home. *New England Journal of Medicine, 329*, 1084–1091.

Kellerman, B. (2004). *Bad leadership: What it is, how it happens, why it matters*. Cambridge, MA: Harvard Business School Press.

Kelley, H. H. (1950). The warm–cold variable in first impressions of persons. *Journal of Personality, 18*, 431–439.

Kelley, H. H. (1952). Two functions of reference groups. In G. E. Swanson, T. M. Newcomb, & E. L. Hartley (Eds.), *Readings in social psychology* (2nd ed., pp. 410–414). New York: Holt, Rinehart & Winston.

Kelley, H. H. (1967). Attribution theory in social psychology. In D. Levine (Ed.), *Nebraska symposium on motivation* (pp. 192–238). Lincoln, NE: University of Nebraska Press.

Kelley, H. H. (1972a). Attribution in social interaction. In E. E. Jones, D. E. Kanouse, H. H. Kelley, R. E. Nisbett, S. Valins, & B. Weiner (Eds.), *Attribution: Perceiving the causes of behavior* (pp. 1–26). Morristown, NJ: General Learning Press.

Kelley, H. H. (1972b). Causal schemata and the attribution process. In E. E. Jones, D. E. Kanouse, H. H. Kelley, R. E. Nisbett, S. Valins, & B. Weiner (Eds.), *Attribution: Perceiving the causes of behavior* (pp. 151–174). Morristown, NJ: General Learning Press.

Kelley, H. H. (1973). The process of causal attribution. *American Psychologist, 28*, 107–128.

Kelley, H. H. (1979). *Personal relationships: Their structures and processes*. Hillsdale, NJ: Erlbaum.

Kelley, H. H., & Thibaut, J. (1978). *Interpersonal relations: A theory of interdependence*. New York: Wiley.

Kelley, K., Byrne, D., Przybyla, D. P. J., Eberly, C. C., Eberly, B. W., Greenlinger, V., Wan, C. K., & Grosky, J. (1985). Chronic self-destructiveness: Conceptualisation, measurement, and initial validation of the construct. *Motivation and Emotion, 9*, 35–151. ·

Kelley, R. E. (1992). *The power of followership*. New York: Doubleday.

Kellstedt, P. M. (2003). *The mass media and the dynamics of American racial attitudes*. Cambridge, UK: Cambridge University Press.

Kelly, C., & Breinlinger, S. (1996). *The social psychology of collective action*. London: Taylor & Francis.

Kelly, G. A. (1955). *The psychology of personal constructs*. New York: Norton.

Kelman, H. C. (1967). Human use of human subjects: The problem of deception in social psychology. *Psychological Bulletin, 67*, 1–11.

Kelman, H. C. (1976). Violence without restraint: Reflections on the dehumanization of victims and victimizers. In G. M. Kren & L. H. Rappoport (Eds.), *Varieties of psycho history* (pp. 282–314). New York: Springer.

Kelman, H. C., & Hovland, C. I. (1953). 'Reinstatement' of the communicator in delayed measurement of opinion change. *Journal of Abnormal and Social Psychology, 48*, 327–335.

Keltner, D., & Buswell, B. N. (1997). Embarrassment: Its distinct form and appeasement functions. *Psychological Bulletin, 122*, 250–270.

Keltner, D., Gruenfeld, D. H., & Anderson, C. (2003). Power, approach, and inhibition. *Psychological Review, 110*, 265–284.

Keltner, D., & Lerner, J. S. (2010). Emotion. In S. T. Fiske, D. T. Gilbert, & G. Lindzey (Eds.), *Handbook of social psychology* (5th ed., Vol. 1, pp. 317–352). New York: Wiley.

Kelvin, P. (1970). *The bases of social behaviour: An approach in terms of order and value*. London: Holt, Rinehart & Winston.

Kemper, S. (1994). Elderspeak: Speech accommodations to older adults. *Aging and Cognition, 1*, 17–28.

Keneally, T. (1982). *Schindler's ark*. Washington, DC: Hemisphere Press.

Kennedy, J. (1982). Middle LPC leaders and the contingency model of leader effectiveness. *Organizational Behavior and Human Performance, 30*, 1–14.

Kenny, D. A., & DePaulo, B. M. (1993). Do people know how others view them? An empirical and theoretical account. *Psychological Bulletin, 114*, 145–161.

Kenrick, D. T., Li, N. P., & Butner, J. (2003). Dynamical evolutionary psychology: Individual decision rules and emergent social norms. *Psychological Review, 110*, 3–28.

Kenrick, D. T., & MacFarlane, S. W. (1986). Ambient temperature and horn honking: A field study of the heat/aggression relationship. *Environment and Behavior, 18*, 179–191.

Kenrick, D. T., Maner, J. K., & Li, N. P. (2005). Evolutionary social psychology. In D. M. Buss (Ed.), *Handbook of evolutionary psychology* (pp. 803–827). New York: Wiley.

Kernis, M. H., Granneman, B. D., & Barclay, L. C. (1989). Stability and level of self-esteem as predictors of anger arousal and hostility. *Journal of Personality and Social Psychology, 56*, 1013–1022.

Kerr, J. H. (2005). *Rethinking aggression and violence in sport*. London: Routledge.

Kerr, N. L. (1978). Beautiful and blameless: Effects of victim attractiveness and responsibility on mock jurors' verdicts. *Journal of Personality and Social Psychology, 4*, 479–482.

Kerr, N. L. (1981). Social transition schemes: Charting the group's road to agreement. *Journal of Personality and Social Psychology, 41*, 684–702.

Kerr, N. L. (1983). Motivation losses in small groups: A social dilemma analysis. *Journal of Personality and Social Psychology, 45*, 819–828.

Kerr, N. L. (1995). Norms in social dilemmas. In D. A. Schroeder (Ed.), *Social dilemmas: Perspectives on individuals and groups* (pp. 31–47). Westport, CT: Praeger.

Kerr, N. L., & Bruun, S. (1981). Ringelmann revisited: Alternative explanations for the social loafing effect. *Personality and Social Psychology Bulletin, 7*, 224–231.

Kerr, N. L., & Bruun, S. (1983). The dispensability of member effort and group motivation losses: Free rider effects. *Journal of Personality and Social Psychology, 44*, 78–94.

Kerr, N. L., & MacCoun, R. J. (1985). The effects of jury size and polling method on the process and product of jury deliberation. *Journal of Personality and Social Psychology, 48*, 349–363.

Kerr, N. L., Niedermeier, K. E., & Kaplan, M. F. (1999). Bias in jurors vs bias in juries: New evidence from the SDS perspective. *Organizational Behavior and Human Decision Processes, 80*, 70–86.

Kerr, N. L., & Park, E. S. (2001). Group performance in collaborative and social dilemma tasks: Progress and prospects. In M. A. Hogg & R. S. Tindale (Eds.), *Blackwell handbook of social psychology: Group processes* (pp. 107–138). Oxford, UK: Blackwell.

Kervyn, N., Yzerbyt, V., & Judd, C. M. (2010). Compensation between warmth and competence: Antecedents and consequences of a negative relation between the two fundamental dimensions of social perception. *European Review of Social Psychology, 21*, 155–187.

Kesebir, P. (2014). A quiet ego quiets death anxiety: Humility as an existential anxiety buffer. *Journal of Personality and Social Psychology, 106*, 610–623.

Kiesler, C. A., & Kiesler, S. B. (1969). *Conformity*. Reading, MA: Addison-Wesley.

Kihlstrom, J. F. (2004). Implicit methods in social psychology. In C. Sansone, C. C. Morf, & A. T. Panter (Eds.), *The SAGE handbook of methods in social psychology* (pp. 195–212). London: SAGE.

Kilham, W., & Mann, L. (1974). Level of destructive obedience as a function of transmitter and executant roles in the Milgram obedience paradigm. *Journal of Personality and Social Psychology, 29*, 696–702.

Kim, H. S., & Baron, R. S. (1988). Exercise and the illusory correlation: Does arousal heighten stereotypic processing? *Journal of Experimental Social Psychology, 24*, 366–380.

Kim, U. (2000). Indigenous, cultural, and cross-cultural psychology: A theoretical, conceptual, and epistemological analysis. *Asian Journal of Social Psychology, 3*, 265–288.

Kimble, G. A. (1961). *Hilgard and Marquis' conditioning and learning* (2nd ed.). New York: Appleton-Century-Crofts.

Kimmel, P. R. (1994). Cultural perspectives on inter-national negotiations. *Journal of Social Issues, 50*, 179–196.

Kinder, D. R., & Sears, D. O. (1981). Symbolic racism vs. threats to the good life. *Journal of Personality and Social Psychology, 40*, 414–431.

King, M., & Taylor, D. M. (2011). The radicalization of homegrown jihadists: A review of theoretical models and social psychological evidence. *Terrorism and Political Violence, 23*, 602–622.

Kirkpatrick, L. A., & Hazan, C. (1994). Attachment styles and close relationships: A four-year prospective study. *Personal Relationships, 1*, 123–142.

Kirkwood, K. (2012). Defensive doping: Is there a moral justification for 'If you can't beat 'em – Join 'em?'. *Journal of Sport and Social Issues, 36*, 223–228.

Kitayama, S., Markus, H. R., Matsumoto, H., & Norasakkunkit, V. (1997). Individual and collective processes in the construction of the self: Self-enhancement in the United States and self-criticism in Japan. *Journal of Personality and Social Psychology, 72*, 1245–1267.

Kitayama, S., Mesquita, B., & Karasawa, M. (2006). Cultural affordances and emotional experience: Socially engaging and disengaging emotions in Japan and the United States. *Journal of Personality and Social Psychology, 91*, 890–903.

Kitayama, S., Snibbe, A. C., Markus, H. M., & Suzuki, T. (2004). Is there any 'free' choice? Self and dissonance in two cultures. *Psychological Science, 15*, 527–533.

Kitayama, S., & Uskul, A. (2011). Culture, mind, and the brain: Current evidence and future directions. *Annual Review of Psychology, 62*, 419–449.

Kite, M. E., & Johnson, B. T. (1988). Attitudes toward older and younger adults: A meta-analysis. *Psychology and Aging, 3*, 233–244.

Klandermans, B. (1997). *The social psychology of protest*. Oxford, UK: Blackwell.

Klandermans, B. (2002). How group identification helps to overcome the dilemma of collective action. *American Behavioral Scientist, 45*, 887–900.

Klandermans, B. (2003). Collective political action. In D. O. Sears, L. Huddy, & R. Jervis, (Eds.), *Oxford handbook of political psychology* (pp. 670–709). Oxford, UK: Oxford University Press.

Klapp, O. E. (1972). *Currents of unrest*. New York: Holt, Rinehart & Winston.

Klasen, S. (1994). 'Missing women' re-considered. *World Development, 22*, 1061–1071.

Klein, K. J. K., & Hodges, S. D. (2001). Gender differences, motivation, and empathic accuracy: When it pays to understand. *Personality and Social Psychology Bulletin, 27*, 720–730.

Klein, O., & Licata, O. (2003). When group representations serve social change: The speeches of Patrice Lumumba during the Congolese decolonization. *British Journal of Social Psychology, 42*, 571–593.

Klein, O., Spears, R., & Reicher, S. (2007) Social identity performance: Extending the strategic side of SIDE. *Personality and Social Psychology Review, 11*, 28–45.

Klein, S. B., Loftus, J., Trafton, J. G., & Fuhrman, R. W. (1992). Use of exemplars and abstractions in trait judgments: A model of trait knowledge about self and others. *Journal of Personality and Social Psychology, 63*, 739–753.

Klein, W. M. P. (2003). Effects of objective feedback and 'single other' or 'average other' social comparison feedback on performance judgments and helping behavior. *Personality and Social Psychology Bulletin, 29*, 418–429.

Klein, W. M. P., Shepperd, J. A., Suls, J., Rothman, A. J., & Croyle, R. T. (2015). Realizing the promise of social psychology in improving public health. *Personality and Social Psychology Review, 19*, 77–92.

Kleinke, C. L. (1986). Gaze and eye contact: A research review. *Psychological Bulletin, 100*, 78–100.

Klentz, B., & Beaman, A. L. (1981). The effects of type of information and method of dissemination on the reporting of a shoplifter. *Journal of Applied Psychology, 11*, 64–82.

Klineberg, O. (1940). *Social psychology*. New York: Holt.

Klineberg, O., & Hull, W. F. (1979). *At a foreign university: An international study of adaptation and coping*. New York: Praeger.

Klinger, R. L., & Stein, T. S. (1996). Impact of violence, childhood sexual abuse, and domestic violence and abuse on lesbians, bisexuals, and gay men. In R. P. Cabaj & T. S. Stein (Eds.), *Textbook of homosexuality and mental health* (pp. 801–818). Washington, DC: American Psychiatric Press.

Klocek, J., Novoa, C., & Moghaddam, F. (2010). Communication across religions. In H. Giles, S. A. Reid, & J. Harwood (Eds.), *Dynamics of intergroup communication* (pp. 77–88). New York: Peter Lang.

Klohnen, E. C., & Bera, S. (1998). Behavioural and experiential patterns of avoidantly and securely attached women across adulthood: A 31-year longitudinal perspective. *Journal of Personality and Social Psychology, 74*, 211–223.

Kluckhohn, C. (1954). Culture and behavior. In G. Lindzey (Ed.), *A handbook of social psychology* (Vol. 2, pp. 921–976). Cambridge, MA: Addison-Wesley.

Knapp, M. L. (1978). *Nonverbal communication in human interaction* (2nd ed.). New York: Holt, Rinehart & Winston.

Knapp, M. L., Hart, R. P., & Dennis, H. S. (1974). An exploration of deception as a communication construct. *Human Communication Research, 1*, 15–29.

Knee, C. R. (1998). Implicit theories of relationships: Assessment and prediction of romantic relationship initiation, coping, and longevity. *Journal of Personality and Social Psychology, 74*, 360–370.

Knee, C. R., Hadden, B. W., Porter, B., & Rodriguez, L. M. (2013). Self-determination theory and romantic relationships. *Personality and Social Psychology Review, 17*, 307–324.

Knottnerus, J. D., & Greenstein, T. N. (1981). Status and performance characteristics: A theory of status validation. *Social Psychology Quarterly, 44*, 338–349.

Knowles, E. S., & Linn, J. A. (Eds.) (2004). *Resistance and persuasion*. Mahwah, NJ: Erlbaum.

Kochman, T. (1987). The ethnic component in Black language and culture. In M. J. Rotheram (Ed.), *Children's ethnic socialization: Pluralism and development* (pp. 219–238). Newbury Park, CA: SAGE.

Koenig, A. M., & Eagly, A. H. (2014). Evidence for the social role theory of stereotype content: Observations of groups' roles shape stereotypes. *Journal of Personality and Social Psychology, 107*, 371–392.

Koffka, K. (1935). *Principles of Gestalt psychology*. New York: Harcourt, Brace & World.

Kogan, N., & Wallach, M. A. (1964). *Risktaking: A study in cognition and personality*. New York: Holt.

Komorita, S. S., Parks, C. D., & Hulbert, L. G. (1992). Reciprocity and the induction of cooperation in social dilemmas. *Journal of Personality and Social Psychology, 62*, 607–617.

Koneçni, V. J. (1979). The role of aversive events in the development of intergroup conflict. In W. G. Austin & S. Worchel (Eds.), *The social psychology of intergroup relations* (pp. 85–102). Monterey, CA: Brooks/Cole.

Koneçni, V. J., & Ebbesen, E. (1976). Disinhibition versus the cathartic effect: Artifact and substance. *Journal of Personality and Social Psychology, 34*, 352–365.

Konrath, S. H., Chopik, W. J., Hsing, C. K., & O'Brien, E. (2014). Changes in adult attachment styles in American college students over time: A meta-analysis. *Personality and Social Psychology Review, 18*, 326–348.

Koole, S. (2009). The psychology of emotion regulation: An integrative review. *Cognition and Emotion, 23*, 4–41.

Koriat, A., Adiv, S., & Schwarz, N. (2016). Views that are shared with others are expressed with greater confidence and greater fluency independent of any social influence. *Personality and Social Psychology Review, 20*, 176–193.

Korte, C. (1971). Effects of individual responsibility and group communication on help-giving in an emergency. *Human Relations, 24*, 149–159.

Kovera, M. B., & Borgida, E. (2010). Social psychology and law. In S. T. Fiske, D. T. Gilbert, & G. Lindzey (Eds.), *Handbook of social psychology* (5th ed., Vol. 2, pp. 1343–1385). New York: Wiley.

Krahé, B. (2013). *The social psychology of aggression* (2nd ed.). New York: Psychology Press.

Krahé, B. (2014). Media violence use as a risk factor for aggressive behaviour in adolescence. *European Review of Social Psychology, 25*, 71–106.

Krahé, B., Berkowitz, L., Brockmeyer, J. H., Bushman, B. J., Coyne, S. M., Dill, K. E., et al. (2012). Report of the Media Violence Commission. *Aggressive Behavior, 38*, 335–341.

Kramer, R. M., & Brewer, M. B. (1984). Effects of identity on resource use in a simulated commons dilemma. *Journal of Personality and Social Psychology, 46*, 1044–1057.

Kramer, R. M., & Brewer, M. B. (1986). Social group identity and the emergence of cooperation in resource conservation dilemmas. In H. A. Wilke, D. M. Messick, & C. G. Rutte (Eds.), *Psychology of decisions and conflict: Experimental social dilemmas* (pp. 205–234). Frankfurt, Germany: Verlag Peter Lang.

Kraus, S. J. (1995). Attitudes and the prediction of behaviour. A meta-analysis of the empirical literature. *Personality and Social Psychology Bulletin, 21*, 58–75.

Krauss, R. M., & Chiu, C. Y. (1998). Language and social behavior. In D. T. Gilbert, S. T. Fiske, & G. Lindzey (Eds.), *The handbook of social psychology* (4th ed., Vol. 2, pp. 41–88). New York: McGraw-Hill.

Krauss, R. M., Curran, N. M., & Ferleger, N. (1983). Expressive conventions and the cross-cultural perception of emotion. *Basic and Applied Social Psychology, 4*, 295–305.

Kraut, R. E., & Higgins, E. T. (1984). Communication and social cognition. In R. S. Wyer, Jr, & T. K. Srull (Eds.), *Handbook of social cognition* (Vol. 3, pp. 87–127). Hillsdale, NJ: Erlbaum.

Kraut, R. E., & Johnston, R. E. (1979). Social and emotional messages of smiling: An ethological approach. *Journal of Personality and Social Psychology, 37*, 1539–1553.

Kraut, R. E., & Poe, D. (1980). Behavioral roots of person perceptions: The deception judgments of the customs inspectors and laymen. *Journal of Personality and Social Psychology, 39*, 784–798.

Kravitz, D. A., & Martin, B. (1986). Ringelmann rediscovered: The original article. *Journal of Personality and Social Psychology, 50*, 936–941.

Krebs, D. L. (1975). Empathy and altruism. *Journal of Personality and Social Psychology, 32*, 1134–1146.

Krech, D., & Crutchfield, R. S. (1948). *Theory and problems of social psychology*. New York: McGraw-Hill.

Krech, D., Crutchfield, R., & Ballachey, R. (1962). *Individual in society*. New York: McGraw-Hill.

Krizan, A., & Baron, R. S. (2007). Group polarization and choice-dilemmas: How important is self-categorization. *European Journal of Social Psychology, 37*, 191–201.

Križan, Z., & Gibbons, F. X. (Eds.) (2014). *Communal functions of social comparison.* New York: Cambridge University Press.

Kroeber, A. L., & Kluckhohn, L. (1952). *Culture: A critical review of concepts and definitions.* Cambridge, MA: Peabody Museum.

Krosnick, J. A. (1990). Expertise and political psychology. *Social Cognition, 8*, 1–8.

Krosnick, J. A., & Alwin, D. F. (1989). Aging and susceptibility to attitude change. *Journal of Personality and Social Psychology, 57*, 416–425.

Krosnick, J. A., Betz, A. L., Jussim, L. J., & Lynn, A. R. (1992). Subliminal conditioning of attitudes. *Personality and Social Psychology Bulletin, 18*, 152–162.

Krosnick, J. A., Boninger, D. S., Chuang, Y. C., Berent, M. K., & Carnot, C. G. (1993). Attitude strength: One construct or many related constructs? *Journal of Personality and Social Psychology, 65*, 1132–1151.

Krosnick, J. A., Visser, P. S., & Harder, J. (2010). The psychological underpinnings of political behavior. In S. T. Fiske, D. T. Gilbert, & G. Lindzey (Eds.), Handbook of social psychology (5th ed., Vol. 2, pp. 1288–1342). New York: Wiley.

Kruger, J., & Dunning, D. (1999). Unskilled and unaware of it: How difficulties in recognizing one's own incompetence lead to inflated self-assessments. *Journal of Personality and Social Psychology, 77*, 1121–1134.

Kruglanski, A. W. (1975). The endogenous–exogenous partition in attribution theory. *Psychological Review, 82*, 387–406.

Kruglanski, A. W., Chen, X., Dechesne, M., & Fishman, S. (2009). Fully committed: Suicide bombers' motivation and the quest for personal significance. *Political Psychology, 30*, 331–357.

Kruglanski, A. W., & Higgins, E. T. (Eds.) (2007). *Social psychology: Handbook of basic principles* (2nd ed.). New York: Guilford Press.

Kruglanski, A. W., & Mackie, D. M. (1990). Majority and minority influence: A judgmental process analysis. *European Review of Social Psychology, 1*, 229–261.

Kruglanski, A. W., Pierro, A., Mannetti, L., & De Grada, E. (2006). Groups as epistemic providers: Need for closure and the unfolding of group-centrism. *Psychological Review, 113*, 84–100.

Kruglanski, A. W., & Webster, D. M. (1996). Motivated closing of the mind: 'Seizing' and 'freezing'. *Psychological Review, 103*, 263–283.

Kruglanski, A. W., Webster, D. W., & Klem, A. (1993). Motivated resistance and openness to persuasion in the presence or absence of prior information. *Journal of Personality and Social Psychology, 65*, 861–876.

Krull, D. S. (1993). Does the grist change the mill? The effect of the perceiver's inferential goal on the process of social inference. *Personality and Social Psychology Bulletin, 19*, 340–348.

Kuhn, T. S. (1962). *The structure of scientific revolutions.* Chicago: University of Chicago Press.

Kulik, J. A. (1983). Confirmatory attribution and the perpetuation of social beliefs. *Journal of Personality and Social Psychology, 44*, 1171–1181.

Kulik, J. A., Mahler, H. I. M., & Moore, P. J. (1996). Social comparison and affiliation under threat: Effects on recovery from major surgery. *Journal of Personality and Social Psychology, 71*, 967–979.

Kumkale, G. T., & Albarracín, D. (2004). The sleeper effect in persuasion: A meta-analytic review. *Psychological Bulletin, 130*, 143–172.

Kun, A., & Weiner, B. (1973). Necessary versus sufficient causal schemata for success and failure. *Journal of Research on Psychology, 7*, 197–207.

Kunda, Z. (1990). The case for motivated reasoning. *Psychological Bulletin, 108*, 480–498.

Kunda, Z., & Sanitoso, R. (1989). Motivated changes in the self-concept. *Journal of Experimental Social Psychology, 25*, 272–285.

Kurdeck, L. A. (1999). The nature and predictors of the trajectory of change in marital quality for husbands and wives over the first 10 years of marriage. *Developmental Psychology, 35*, 1283–1296.

Kurzban, R., & Leary, M. R. (2001). Evolutionary origins of stigmatization: The functions of social exclusion. *Psychological Bulletin, 127*, 187–208.

Kwon, P. (2013) Resilience in lesbian, gay, and bisexual individuals. *Personality and Social Psychology Review, 17*, 371–383.

LaFrance, M., Hecht, M. A., & Levy-Paluck, E. (2003). The contingent smile: A meta-analysis of sex differences in smiling. *Psychological Bulletin, 129*, 305–334.

LaFrance, M., & Mayo, C. (1976). Racial differences in gaze behavior during conversations: Two systematic observational studies. *Journal of Personality and Social Psychology, 33*, 547–552.

Lakoff, R. (1973). Language and woman's place. *Language in Society, 2*, 45–80.

Lakoff, R. T. (2004). *Language and woman's place: Text and commentaries: Studies in language, gender, and sexuality* (Rev. exp. ed.). Oxford, UK: Oxford University Press.

Lalljee, M. (1981). Attribution theory and the analysis of explanations. In C. Antaki (Ed.), *The psychology of ordinary explanations of social behaviour* (pp. 119–138). London: Academic Press.

Lamarre, P., & Paredes, J. R. (2003). Growing up trilingual in Montreal: Perceptions of college students. In B. Bayley & S. R. Schechter (Eds.), *Language socialization in bilingual and multilingual societies* (pp. 62–80). Clevedon, UK: Multilingual Matters.

Lambert, W. E., Hodgson, R. C., Gardner, R. C., & Fillenbaum, S. (1960). Evaluation reactions to spoken language. *Journal of Abnormal and Social Psychology, 60*, 44–51.

Lambert, W. E., Mermigis, L., & Taylor, D. M. (1986). Greek Canadians' attitudes toward own group and other Canadian ethnic groups: A test of the multiculturalism hypothesis. *Canadian Journal of Behavioural Sciences, 18*, 35–51.

Lambert, W. W., Solomon, R. L., & Watson, P. D. (1949). Reinforcement and extinction as factors in size estimation. *Journal of Experimental Psychology, 39*, 637–641.

Lamm, H., & Kayser, E. (1978). The allocation of monetary gain and loss following dyadic performance: The weight given effort and ability under conditions of low and high intradyadic attraction. *European Journal of Social Psychology, 8*, 275–278.

Lander, E. S., Linton, L. M., Birren, B., Nusbaum, C., Zody, M. C., Baldwin, J., et al. (2001). Initial sequencing and analysis of the human genome. *Nature, 409*, 860–921.

Landman, J., & Manis, M. (1983). Social cognition: Some historical and theoretical perspectives. *Advances in Experimental Social Psychology, 16*, 49–123.

Landry, R., Allard, R., & Deveau, K. (2007). Bilingual schooling of the Canadian Francophone minority: A cultural autonomy model. *International Journal of the Sociology of Language, 185*, 133–162.

Landy, D., & Sigall, H. (1974). Beauty is talent: Task evaluation as a function of the performer's physical attractiveness. *Journal of Personality and Social Psychology, 29*, 299–304.

Langer, E. J. (1975). The illusion of control. *Journal of Personality and Social Psychology, 32*, 311–328.

Langer, E. J. (1978). Rethinking the role of thought in social interaction. In J. H. Harvey, W. I. Ickes, & R. F. Kidd (Eds.), *New directions in attribution research* (Vol. 2, pp. 35–58). Hillsdale, NJ: Erlbaum.

Langer, E. J., Bashner, R. S., & Chanowitz, B. (1985). Decreasing prejudice by increasing discrimination. *Journal of Personality and Social Psychology, 49*, 113–120.

Langer, E. J., Blank, A., & Chanowitz, B. (1978). The mindlessness of ostensibly thoughtful action. *Journal of Personality and Social Psychology, 36*, 635–642.

Langlois, J. H., Kalakanis, L., Rubenstein, A. J., Larson, A., Hallam, M., & Smoot, M. (2000). Maxims or myths of beauty? A meta-analytic and theoretical review. *Psychological Bulletin, 126*, 390–423.

Langlois, J. H., Roggman, L. A., & Musselman, L. (1994). What is average and what is not average about attractive faces? *Psychological Science, 5*, 214–220.

Lansford, J. E., Skinner, A. T., Sorbring, E., Di Giunta, L., Deater-Deckard, K., Dodge, K. A., et al. (2012). Boys' and girls' relational and physical aggression in nine countries. *Aggressive Behavior, 38*, 298–308.

LaPiere, R. T. (1934). Attitudes vs actions. *Social Forces, 13*, 230–237.

LaPiere, R. T., & Farnsworth, P. R. (1936). *Social psychology.* New York: McGraw-Hill.

LaPiere, R. T., & Farnsworth, P. R. (1949). *Social psychology* (3rd ed.). New York: McGraw-Hill.

LaPlace, A. C., Chermack, S. T., & Taylor, S. P. (1994). Effects of alcohol and drinking experience on human physical aggression. *Personality and Social Psychology Bulletin, 20,* 439–444.

Lariscy, R. A. W., & Tinkham, S. F. (1999). The sleeper effect and negative political advertising. *Journal of Advertising, 28,* 13–30.

Larson, J. R., Jr, Foster-Fishman, P. G., & Keys, C. B. (1994). Discussion of shared and unshared information in decision-making group. *Journal of Personality and Social Psychology, 67,* 446–461.

Latané, B. (1981). The psychology of social impact. *American Psychologist, 36,* 343–356.

Latané, B., & Dabbs, J. M., Jr. (1975). Sex, group size and helping in three cities. *Sociometry, 38,* 180–194.

Latané, B., & Darley, J. M. (1970). *The unresponsive bystander: Why doesn't he help?* New York: Appleton-Century-Crofts.

Latané, B., & Darley, J. M. (1976). Help in a crisis: Bystander response to an emergency. In J. W. Thibaut & J. T. Spence (Eds.), *Contemporary topics in social psychology* (pp. 309–332). Morristown, NJ: General Learning Press.

Latané, B., & Rodin, J. (1969). A lady in distress: Inhibiting effects of friends and strangers on bystander intervention. *Journal of Experimental Social Psychology, 5,* 189–202.

Latané, B., Williams, K. D., & Harkins, S. G. (1979). Many hands make light the work: The causes and consequences of social loafing. *Journal of Personality and Social Psychology, 37,* 822–832.

Latané, B., & Wolf, S. (1981). The social impact of majorities and minorities. *Psychological Review, 88,* 438–453.

Latin American Bureau (1982). *Falklands/Malvinas: Whose crisis?* London: Latin American Bureau.

Laughlin, P. R. (1980). Social combination processes of cooperative problem solving groups on verbal intellective tasks. In M. Fishbein (Ed.), *Progress in social psychology* (Vol. 1, pp. 127–155). Hillsdale, NJ: Erlbaum.

Laughlin, P. R., & Ellis, A. L. (1986). Demonstrability and social combination processes on mathematical intellective tasks. *Journal of Experimental Social Psychology, 22,* 177–189.

Laurenceau, J. P., Barrett, L. F., & Pietromonaco, P. R. (1998). Intimacy as an interpersonal process: The importance of self-disclosure, partner disclosure, and perceived partner responsiveness in interpersonal exchanges. *Journal of Personality and Social Psychology, 74,* 1238–1251.

Lavine, H., Huff, J. W., Wagner, S. H., & Sweeney, D. (1998). The moderating influence of attitude strength on the susceptibility to context effects in attitude surveys. *Journal of Personality and Social Psychology, 75,* 359–373.

Lawrence, C., & Andrew, K. (2004). The influence of perceived prison crowding on male inmates' perception of aggressive events. *Aggressive Behavior, 30,* 273–283.

Lazarus, R. S. (1991). *Emotion and adaptation.* New York: Oxford University Press.

Le, B., & Agnew, C. R. (2003). Commitment and its theorized determinants: A meta-analysis of the investment model. *Personal Relationships, 10,* 37–57.

Leana, C. R. (1985). A partial test of Janis's groupthink model: Effects of group cohesiveness and leader behavior on defective decision making. *Journal of Management, 11,* 5–17.

Leaper, C., & Ayres, M. M. (2007). A meta-analytic review of gender variations in adults' language use: Talkativeness, affiliative speech, and assertive speech. *Personality and Social Psychology Review, 11,* 328–363.

Leary, M. R. (1995). *Self-presentation: Impression management and interpersonal behavior.* Madison, WI: Brown & Benchmark.

Leary, M. R. (2010). Affiliation, acceptance, and belonging: The pursuit of interpersonal connection. In S. T. Fiske, D. T. Gilbert, & G. Lindzey (Eds.), *Handbook of social psychology* (5th ed., Vol. 2, pp. 864–897). New York: Wiley.

Leary, M. R., & Baumeister, R. F. (2000). The nature and function of self-esteem: Sociometer theory. *Advances in Experimental Social Psychology, 32,* 1–62.

Leary, M. R., & Kowalski, R. (1995). *Social anxiety.* New York: Guilford Press.

Leary, M. R., Tambor, E. S., Terdal, S. K., & Downs, D. L. (1995). Self-esteem as an interpersonal monitor: The sociometer hypothesis. *Journal of Personality and Social Psychology, 68,* 518–530.

Leary, M. R., & Tangney, J. P. (2012). *Handbook of self and identity* (2nd ed.) New York: Guilford.

Leavitt, H. J. (1951). Some effects of certain communication patterns on group performance. *Journal of Abnormal and Social Psychology, 46,* 38–50.

LeBon, G. (1896/1908). *The crowd: A study of the popular mind.* London: Unwin.

Ledbetter, A. M., Stassen-Ferrara, H. M., & Dowd, M. M. (2013). Comparing equity and self-expansion theory approaches to relational maintenance. *Personal Relationships, 20,* 38–51.

Lee, J. (1993). *Facing the fire: Experiencing and expressing anger appropriately.* New York: Bantam.

Lee, Y. T., & Ottati, V. (1993). Determinants of ingroup and outgroup perceptions of heterogeneity. *Journal of Cross-cultural Psychology, 24,* 298–318.

Lehman, D. R., Chiu, C.-Y., & Schaller, M. (2004). Psychology and culture. *Annual Review of Psychology, 55,* 689–714.

Lemaine, G. (1966). Inégalité, comparison et incomparabilité: Esquisse d'une théorie de l'originalité sociale. *Bulletin de Psychologie, 20,* 24–32.

Lemaine, G. (1974). Social differentiation and social originality. *European Journal of Social Psychology, 4,* 17–52.

Leonardelli, G. J., Pickett, C. L., & Brewer, M. B. (2010). Optimal distinctiveness theory: A framework for social identity, social cognition and intergroup relations. *Advances in Experimental Social Psychology, 43,* 65–115.

Lepore, L., & Brown, R. (1997). Category and stereotype activation: Is prejudice inevitable? *Journal of Personality and Social Psychology, 72,* 275–287.

Lepper, M. R., Greene, D., & Nisbett, R. E. (1973). Undermining children's intrinsic interest with extrinsic reward: A test of the over-justification hypothesis. *Journal of Personality and Social Psychology, 28,* 129–137.

Lerner, M. J. (1977). The justice motive: Some hypotheses as to its origins and forms. *Journal of Personality, 45,* 1–52.

Lerner, M. J., & Miller, D. T. (1978). Just-world research and the attribution process: Looking back and ahead. *Psychological Bulletin, 85,* 1030–1051.

Lesar, T. S., Briceland, L., & Stein, D. S. (1997). Factors related to errors in medication prescribing. *Journal of the American Medical Association, 277,* 312–317.

Leslie, J. B., & Van Velsor, E. (1996). *A look at derailment today.* Greensboro, NC: Centre for Creative Leadership.

Letellier, P. (1994). Gay and bisexual domestic violence victimisation: Challenges to feminist theories and responses to violence. *Violence and Victims, 9,* 95–106.

Leventhal, H., Singer, R., & Jones, S. (1965). Effects of fear and specificity of recommendations upon attitudes and behavior. *Journal of Personality and Social Psychology, 2,* 20–29.

Leventhal, H., Watts, J. C., & Pagano, R. (1967). Effects of fear and instructions on how to cope with danger. *Journal of Personality and Social Psychology, 6,* 313–321.

Levin, D. T. (2000). Race as a visual feature: Using visual search and perceptual discrimination tasks to understand face categories and the cross-race recognition deficit. *Journal of Experimental Psychology: General, 129,* 559–574.

Levine, J. M. (Ed.) (2013). *Group processes.* New York: Psychology Press.

Levine, J. M., & Hogg, M. A. (Eds.) (2010). *Encyclopedia of group processes and intergroup relations.* Thousand Oaks, CA: SAGE.

Levine, J. M., & Moreland, R. L. (1990). Progress in small group research. *Annual Review of Psychology, 41,* 585–634.

Levine, J. M., & Moreland, R. L. (1991). Culture and socialization in work groups. In L. B. Resnick, J. M. Levine, & S. D. Teasley (Eds.), *Perspectives on socially shared cognition* (pp. 257–279). Washington, DC: American Psychological Association.

Levine, J. M., & Moreland, R. L. (1994). Group socialization: Theory and research. *European Review of Social Psychology, 5,* 305–336.

Levine, J. M., & Moreland, R. L. (1998). Small groups. In D. T. Gilbert, S. T. Fiske, & G. Lindzey (Eds.), *The handbook of social psychology* (4th ed., Vol. 2, pp. 415–469). New York: McGraw-Hill.

Levine, J. M., & Moreland, R. L. (2002). Group reactions to loyalty and disloyalty. In E. Lawler & S. Thye (Eds.), *Advances in group processes* (Vol. 19, pp. 203–228). Amsterdam: Elsevier.

Levine, J. M., Moreland, R. L., & Choi, H.-S. (2001). Group socialization and newcomer innovation. In M. A. Hogg & R. S. Tindale (Eds.), *Blackwell handbook of social psychology: Group processes* (pp. 86–106). Oxford, UK: Blackwell.

Levine, J. M., Resnick, L. B., & Higgins, E. T. (1993). Social foundations of cognition. *Annual Review of Psychology, 44*, 585–612.

Levine, M., & Crowther, S. (2008). The responsive bystander: How social group membership and group size can encourage as well as inhibit bystander intervention. *Journal of Personality and Social Psychology, 95*, 1429–1439.

Levine. M., & Manning, R. (2013). Social identity, group processes, and helping in emergencies. *European Review of Social Psychology, 24*, 225–251.

LeVine, R. A., & Campbell, D. T. (1972). *Ethnocentrism: Theories of conflict, ethnic attitudes and group behavior.* New York: Wiley.

Levinger, G. (1980). Toward the analysis of close relationships. *Journal of Experimental Social Psychology, 16*, 510–544.

Levitt, E., & Klassen, A. (1974). Public attitudes towards homosexuality: Part of the 1970 national survey by the Institute for Sex Research. *Journal of Homosexuality, 1*, 29–43.

Levy, B. R. (2009). Stereotype embodiment: A psychosocial approach to aging. *Current Directions in Psychological Science, 18*, 332–336.

Levy, B. R., Zonderman, A., Slade, M. D., & Ferrucci, L. (2009). Negative age stereotypes held earlier in life predict cardiovascular events in later life. *Psychological Science, 20*, 296–298.

Lévy-Bruhl, L. (1925). *How natives think.* New York: Alfred A. Knopf.

Lewin, A. Y., & Duchan, L. (1971). Women in academia. *Science, 173*, 892–895.

Lewin, K. (1936). Some socio-psychological differences between the United States and Germany. *Character and Personality, 4*, 265–293.

Lewin, K. (1943). Forces behind food habits and methods of change. *Bulletin of National Research Council, 108*, 35–65.

Lewin, K. (1947). Frontiers in group dynamics. *Human Relations, 1*, 5–42.

Lewin, K. (1951). *Field theory in social science.* New York: Harper.

Lewin, K., Lippitt, R., & White, R. K. (1939). Patterns of aggressive behavior in experimentally created 'social climates'. *Journal of Social Psychology, 10*, 271–299.

Lewis, A., Snell, S., & Furnham, A. (1987). Lay explanations for the causes of unemployment in Britain: Economic, individualistic, societal or fatalistic? *Political Psychology, 8*, 427–439.

Lewis, A. C., & Sherman, S. J. (2010). Perceived entitativity and the black-sheep effect: When will we denigrate ingroup members? *Journal of Social Psychology, 150*, 211–225.

Lewis, B. (2004). *The crisis of Islam: Holy war and unholy terror.* London: Phoenix.

Lewis, O. (1969). *A death in the Sanchez family.* New York: Secker & Warburg.

Leyens, J.-P., Camino, L., Parke, R. D., & Berkowitz, L. (1975). Effects of movie violence on aggression in a field setting as a function of group dominance and cohesion. *Journal of Personality and Social Psychology, 32*, 346–360.

Leyens, J.-P., Demoulin, S., Vaes, J., Gaunt, R., & Paladino, M. P. (2007). Infrahumanization: The wall of group differences. *Journal of Social Issues and Policy Review, 1*, 139–172.

Leyens, J.-P., Rodriguez-Perez, A., Rodriguez-Torres, R., Gaunt, R., Paladino, M.-P., Vaes, J., et al. (2001). Psychological essentialism and the differential attribution of uniquely human emotions to ingroups and outgroups. *European Journal of Social Psychology, 31*, 395–411.

Leyens, J.-P., Yzerbyt, V. Y., & Schadron, G. (1992). Stereotypes and social judgeability. *European Review of Social Psychology, 3*, 91–120.

Leyens, J.-P., Yzerbyt, V., & Schadron, G. (1994). *Stereotypes and social cognition.* London: SAGE.

Li, N. P., Yong, J. C., Tov, W., Sng, O., Fletcher, G. J., Valentine, K. A., Jiang, Y. F., & Balliet, D. (2013). Mate preferences do predict attraction and choices in the early stages of mate selection. *Journal of Personality and Social Psychology, 105*, 757–776.

Li, Y. J., Johnson, K. A., Cohen, A. B., Williams, M. J., Knowles, E. D., & Chen, Z. (2012). Fundamental(ist) attribution error: Protestants are dispositionally focused. *Journal of Personality and Social Psychology, 102*, 281–290.

Lickel, B., Hamilton, D. L., Wieczorkowska, G., Lewis, A. C., & Sherman, S. (2000). Varieties of groups and the perception of group entitativity. *Journal of Personality and Social Psychology, 78*, 223–246.

Lieberman, M. D. (2000). Intuition: A social cognitive neuroscience approach. *Psychological Bulletin, 126*, 109–137.

Lieberman, M. D. (2010). Social cognitive neuroscience. In S. T. Fiske, D. T. Gilbert, & G. Lindzey (Eds.), *Handbook of social psychology* (5th ed., Vol. 1, pp. 143–193). New York: Wiley.

Lieberman, M. D., Gaunt, R., Gilbert, D. T., & Trope, Y. (2002). Reflexion and reflection: A social cognitive neuroscience approach to attributional inference. *Advances in Experimental Social Psychology, 34*, 199–249.

Liebrand, W., Messick, D., & Wilke, H. (Eds.) (1992). *A social psychological approach to social dilemmas.* New York: Pergamon Press.

Liebrand, W. B. G. (1984). The effect of social motives, communication and group size in an n-person multistage mixed-motive game. *European Journal of Social Psychology, 14*, 239–264.

Lifton, R. J. (1956). "Thought reform" of Western civilians in Communist Chinese prisons. *Psychiatry, 19*, 173–195.

Likert, R. (1932). A technique for the measurement of attitudes. *Archives of Psychology, 22*(140), 44–53.

Lim, R. G., & Carnevale, P. J. D. (1990). Contingencies in the mediation of disputes. *Journal of Personality and Social Psychology, 58*, 259–272.

Limber, J. (1977). Language in child and chimp? *American Psychologist, 32*, 280–295.

Lin, M. H., Kwan, V. S. Y., Cheung, A., & Fiske, S. T. (2005). Stereotype content model explains prejudice for an envied outgroup: Scale of anti–Asian American stereotypes. *Personality and Social Psychology Bulletin, 31*, 34–37.

Lind, E. A., & O'Barr, W. M. (1979). The social significance of speech in the courtroom. In H. Giles & R. N. St Clair (Eds.), *Language and social psychology.* Oxford, UK: Blackwell.

Lind, E. A., & Tyler, T. R. (1988). *The social psychology of procedural justice.* New York: Plenum Press.

Lind, J., & Maxwell, G. (1996). Children's experiences of violence in schools. *Children,* March. Wellington: Office of the Commissioner for Children.

Lindstrom, P. (1997). Persuasion via facts in political discussion. *European Journal of Social Psychology, 27*, 145–163.

Linskold, S. (1978). Trust development, the GRIT proposal, and the effects of conciliatory acts on conflict and cooperation. *Psychological Bulletin, 85*, 772–793.

Linskold, S., & Han, G. (1988). GRIT as a foundation for integrative bargaining. *Personality and Social Psychology Bulletin, 14*, 335–345.

Linssen, H., & Hagendoorn, L. (1994). Social and geographical factors in the explanation of European nationality stereotypes. *British Journal of Social Psychology, 23*, 165–182.

Linville, P. W. (1982). Affective consequences of complexity regarding the self and others. In M. S. Clark & S. T. Fiske (Eds.), *Affect and cognition: The 17th annual Carnegie symposium on cognition* (pp. 79–109). Hillsdale, NJ: Erlbaum.

Linville, P. W. (1985). Self-complexity and affective extremity: Don't put all of your eggs in one cognitive basket. *Social Cognition, 3*, 94–120.

Linville, P. W. (1987). Self-complexity as a cognitive buffer against stress-related depression and illness. *Journal of Personality and Social Psychology, 52*, 663–676.

Linville, P. W., Fischer, G. W., & Salovey, P. (1989). Perceived distributions of the characteristics of ingroup and outgroup members: Empirical evidence and a computer simulation. *Journal of Personality and Social Psychology, 57*, 165–188.

Linz, D., Wilson, B. J., & Donnerstein, E. (1992). Sexual violence in the mass media: Legal solutions, warnings, and mitigation through education. *Journal of Social Issues, 48*, 145–171.

Linz, D. G., Donnerstein, E., & Penrod, S. (1988). Effects of long-term exposure to violent and sexually degrading depictions of women. *Journal of Personality and Social Psychology, 55*, 758–768.

Lippitt, R., & White, R. (1943). The 'social climate' of children's groups. In R. G. Barker, J. Kounin, & H. Wright (Eds.), *Child behavior and development* (pp. 485–508). New York: McGraw-Hill.

Lippman, W. (1922). *Public opinion*. New York: Harcourt and Brace.

Litton, I., & Potter, J. (1985). Social representations in the ordinary explanation of a 'riot'. *European Journal of Social Psychology, 15,* 371–388.

Liu, J. H., Campbell, S. M., & Condie, H. (1995). Ethnocentrism in dating preferences for an American sample: The ingroup bias in social context. *European Journal of Social Psychology, 25,* 95–115.

Liu, T. J., & Steele, C. M. (1986). Attributional analysis and self-affirmation. *Journal of Personality and Social Psychology, 51,* 531–540.

Lock, A. (1980). *The guided reinvention of language*. London: Academic Press.

Lock, A. (Ed.) (1978). *Action, gesture and symbol: The emergence of language*. London: Academic Press.

Lockard, J. S., Kirkevold, B. C., & Kalk, D. F. (1980). Cost–benefit indexes of deception in nonviolent crime. *Bulletin of the Psychonomic Society, 16,* 303–306.

Lockwood, P., Jordan, C. H., & Kunda, Z. (2002). Motivation by positive or negative role models: Regulatory focus determines who will best inspire us. *Journal of Personality and Social Psychology, 83,* 854–864.

Loftin, C., McDowall, D., Wiersema, B., & Cottey, T. J. (1991). Effects of restrictive licensing of handguns on homicide and suicide in the District of Columbia. *New England Journal of Medicine, 325,* 1615–1620.

Loftus, E. F. (1996). *Eyewitness testimony*. Cambridge, MA: Harvard University Press.

Long, G. T., & Lerner, M. J. (1974). Deserving the 'personal contract' and altruistic behaviour by children. *Journal of Personality and Social Psychology, 29,* 551–556.

Long, K., & Spears, R. (1997). The self-esteem hypothesis revisited: Differentiation and the disaffected. In R. Spears, P. J. Oakes, N. Ellemers, & S. A. Haslam (Eds.), *The social psychology of stereotyping and group life* (pp. 296–317). Oxford, UK: Blackwell.

Longley, J., & Pruitt, D. G. (1980). Groupthink: A critique of Janis's theory. In L. Wheeler (Ed.), *Review of personality and social psychology* (Vol. 1, pp. 74–93). Beverly Hills, CA: SAGE.

Lonner, W. J. (Ed.) (1984). Differing views on 'culture.' *Journal of Cross-Cultural Psychology, 15,* 107–109.

Lonsbary, C. E. (2007). Using social norms to reduce academic dishonesty. *Dissertation Abstracts International: Section B: The Sciences and Engineering, 67(7B),* 4159.

Lord, R. G., & Brown, D. J. (2004). *Leadership processes and follower identity*. Mahwah, NJ: Erlbaum.

Lord, R. G., Brown, D. J., & Harvey, J. L. (2001). System constraints on leadership perceptions, behavior and influence: An example of connectionist level processes. In M. A. Hogg & R. S. Tindale (Eds.), *Blackwell handbook of social psychology: Group processes* (pp. 283–310). Oxford, UK: Blackwell.

Lord, R. G., Brown, D. J., Harvey, J. L., & Hall, R. J. (2001). Contextual constraints on prototype generation and their multilevel consequences for leadership perceptions. *The Leadership Quarterly, 12,* 311–338.

Lord, R. G., & Hall, R. (2003). Identity, leadership categorization, and leadership schema. In D. Van Knippenberg & M. A. Hogg (Eds.) *Leadership and power: Identity processes in groups and organizations* (pp. 48–64). London: SAGE.

Lorenz, K. (1966). *On aggression*. New York: Harcourt, Brace and World.

Lorenzi-Cioldi, F., & Clémence, A. (2001). Group processes and the construction of social representations. In M. A. Hogg & R. S. Tindale (Eds.), *Blackwell handbook of social psychology: Group processes* (pp. 311–333). Oxford, UK: Blackwell.

Lorenzi-Cioldi, F., & Doise, W. (1990). Levels of analysis and social identity. In D. Abrams & M. A. Hogg (Eds.), *Social identity theory: Constructive and critical advances* (pp. 71–88). London: Harvester Wheatsheaf.

Lorenzi-Cioldi, F., Eagly, A. H., & Stewart, T. L. (1995). Homogeneity of gender groups in memory. *Journal of Experimental Social Psychology, 31,* 193–217.

Lorge, I., & Solomon, H. (1955). Two models of group behavior in the solution of eureka-type problems. *Psychometrika, 20,* 139–148.

Los Angeles Times. (2017). California secessionists set to take another shot at 'Calexit' ballot initiative. *Los Angeles Times,* 12 May.

Lott, A. J., & Lott, B. E. (1965). Group cohesiveness as interpersonal attraction. *Psychological Bulletin, 64,* 259–309.

Lott, B. E. (1961). Group cohesiveness: A learning phenomenon. *Journal of Social Psychology, 55,* 275–286.

Lowe, K. B., Kroeck, K. G., & Sivasubramaniam, N. (1996). Effectiveness correlates of transformational and transactional leadership: A meta-analytic review. *The Leadership Quarterly, 7,* 385–425.

Lu, L., Yuan, Y. C., & McLeod, P. L. (2012). Twenty-five years of hidden profiles studies in group decision making: A meta-analysis. *Personality and Social Psychology Review, 60,* 103–121.

Luce, R. D., & Raïffa, H. (1957). *Games and decisions*. New York: Wiley.

Lueger, R. J. (1980). Person and situation factors influencing transgression in behavior-problem adolescents. *Journal of Abnormal Psychology, 89,* 453–458.

Luke, M. A., Sedikides, C., & Carnelley, K. (2012). Your love lifts me higher! The energizing quality of secure relationships. *Personality and Social Psychology Bulletin, 38,* 721–733.

Lumsdaine, A. A., & Janis, I. L. (1953). Resistance to 'counterpropaganda' produced by one-sided and two-sided 'propaganda' presentations. *Public Opinion Quarterly, 17,* 311–318.

Luria, A. R. (1928). The problem of the cultural development of the child. *Journal of Genetic Psychology, 35,* 493–506.

Lydon, J., & Dunkel-Schetter, C. (1994). Seeing is committing: A longitudinal study of bolstering commitment in amniocentesis patients. *Personality and Social Psychology Bulletin, 20,* 218–227.

Maass, A. (1999). Linguistic intergroup bias: Stereotype-perpetuation through language. *Advances in Experimental Social Psychology, 31,* 79–121.

Maass, A., & Arcuri, L. (1996). Language and stereotyping. In C. N. Macrae, C. Stangor, & M. Hewstone (Eds.), *Stereotypes and stereotyping* (pp. 193–226). New York: Guilford Press.

Maass, A., & Cadinu, M. (2003). Stereotype threat: When minority members underperform. *European Review of Social Psychology, 14,* 243–275.

Maass, A., & Clark, R. D., III. (1983). Internalisation versus compliance: Differential processes underlying minority influence and conformity. *European Journal of Social Psychology, 13,* 197–215.

Maass, A., & Clark, R. D., III. (1984). Hidden impact of minorities: Fifteen years of minority influence research. *Psychological Bulletin, 95,* 428–450.

Maass, A., & Clark, R. D., III. (1986). Conversion theory and simultaneous majority/minority influence: Can reactance offer an alternative explanation. *European Journal of Social Psychology, 16,* 305–309.

Maass, A., Clark, R. D., III, & Haberkorn, G. (1982). The effects of differential ascribed category membership and norms on minority influence. *European Journal of Social Psychology, 12,* 89–104.

Maass, A., Salvi, D., Arcuri, L., & Semin, G. (1989). Language use in intergroup contexts: The linguistic intergroup bias. *Journal of Personality and Social Psychology, 57,* 981–993.

Maass, A., Suitner, C., Favaretto, X., & Cignacchi, M. (2009). Groups in space: Stereotypes and the spatial agency bias. *Journal of Experimental Social Psychology, 45,* 496–504.

McArthur, L. A. (1972). The how and what of why: Some determinants of consequences of causal attributions. *Journal of Personality and Social Psychology, 22,* 171–193.

McArthur, L. Z. (1981). What grabs you? The role of attention in impression formation and causal attribution. In E. T. Higgins, C. P. Herman, & M. P. Zanna (Eds.), *Social cognition: The Ontario symposium* (Vol. 1, pp. 201–246). Hillsdale, NJ: Erlbaum.

McArthur, L. Z., & Baron, R. (1983). Toward an ecological theory of social perception. *Psychological Review, 90,* 215–238.

McArthur, L. Z., & Friedman, S. A. (1980). Illusory correlation in impression formation: Variations in the shared distinctiveness effect as a function of the distinctive person's age, race, and sex. *Journal of Personality and Social Psychology, 39,* 615–624.

McArthur, L. Z., & Post, D. L. (1977). Figural emphasis and person perception. *Journal of Experimental Social Psychology, 13,* 520–535.

McAuliffe, B. J., Jetten, J., Hornsey, M. J., & Hogg, M. A. (2003). Individualist and collectivist group norms: When it's OK to go your own way. *European Journal of Social Psychology, 33,* 57–70.

McCabe, D. L., Butterfield, K. D., & Trevino, L. K. (2012). *Cheating in college: Why students do it and what educators can do about it.* Baltimore, MD: Johns Hopkins University Press.

McCall, G., & Simmons, R. (1978). *Identities and interactions* (2nd ed.). New York: Free Press.

McCauley, C. (1989). The nature of social influence in groupthink: Compliance and internalization. *Journal of Personality and Social Psychology, 57,* 250–260.

McClintock, C. G., & Van Avermaet, E. (1982). Social values and rules of fairness: A theoretical perspective. In V. Derlaga & J. L. Grzelak (Eds.), *Cooperation and helping behavior: Theories and research* (pp. 43–71). New York: Academic Press

McClure, J. (1998). Discounting causes of behavior: Are two reasons better than one? *Journal of Personality and Social Psychology, 74,* 1–14.

McClure, M., & Lydon, J. E. (2014). Anxiety doesn't become you: How attachment anxiety compromises relational opportunities. *Journal of Personality and Social Psychology, 106,* 89–111.

McConahay, J. G. (1986). Modern racism, ambivalence, and the modern racism scale. In J. F. Dovidio & S. L. Gaertner (Eds.), *Prejudice, discrimination, and racism* (pp. 91–125). New York: Academic Press.

McConnell, A. R., Sherman, S. J., & Hamilton, D. L. (1994). On-line and memory-based aspects of individual and group target judgments. *Journal of Personality and Social Psychology, 67,* 173–185.

McCullough, M. E., Worthington, E. L., & Rachal, K. C. (1997). Interpersonal forgiving in close relationships, *Journal of Personality and Social Psychology, 73,* 321–336.

McDougall, W. (1908). *An introduction to social psychology.* London: Methuen.

McDougall, W. (1920). *The group mind.* London: Cambridge University Press.

McGarty, C., Haslam, S. A., Turner, J. C., & Oakes, P. J. (1993). Illusory correlation as accentuation of actual intercategory difference: Evidence for the effect with minimal stimulus information. *European Journal of Social Psychology, 23,* 391–410.

McGarty, C., & Penny, R. E. C. (1988). Categorization, accentuation and social judgement. *British Journal of Social Psychology, 27,* 147–157.

McGarty, C., & Turner, J. C. (1992). The effects of categorization on social judgement. *British Journal of Social Psychology, 31,* 147–157.

McGillicuddy, N. B., Welton, G. L., & Pruitt, D. G. (1987). Third-party intervention: A field experiment comparing three different models. *Journal of Personality and Social Psychology, 53,* 104–112.

McGinnies, E. (1966). Studies in persuasion: III. Reactions of Japanese students to one-sided and two-sided communications. *Journal of Social Psychology, 70,* 87–93.

McGrath, J. E., & Hollingshead, A. B. (1994). *Groups interacting with technology.* Newbury Park, CA: SAGE.

McGuire, W. J. (1964). Inducing resistance to persuasion. *Advances in Experimental Social Psychology, 1,* 191–229.

McGuire, W. J. (1968). Personality and susceptibility to social influence. In E. F. Borgatta & W. W. Lambert (Eds.), *Hand book of personality: Theory and research* (pp. 1130–1187). Chicago: Rand McNally.

McGuire, W. J. (1969). The nature of attitudes and attitude change. In G. Lindzey & E. Aronson (Eds.), *Handbook of social psychology* (2nd ed., Vol. 3, pp. 136–314). Reading, MA: Addison-Wesley.

McGuire, W. J. (1986). The vicissitudes of attitudes and similar representational constructs in twentieth-century psychology. *European Journal of Social Psychology, 16,* 89–130.

McGuire, W. J. (1989). The structure of individual attitudes and attitude systems. In A. R. Pratkanis, S. J. Breckler, & A. G. Greenwald (Eds.), *Attitude structure and function* (pp. 37–69). Hillsdale, NJ: Erlbaum.

McGuire, W. J., & Papageorgis, D. (1961). The relative efficacy of various types of prior belief-defence in producing immunity against persuasion. *Journal of Abnormal and Social Psychology, 62,* 327–337.

MacKay, N. J., & Covell, K. (1997). The impact of women in advertisements on attitudes toward women. *Sex Roles, 36,* 573–579.

Mackie, D. M. (1986). Social identification effects in group polarization. *Journal of Personality and Social Psychology, 50,* 720–728.

Mackie, D. M., & Ahn, M. N. (1998). In-group and out-group inferences: When in-group bias overwhelms out-group bias. *European Journal of Social Psychology, 28,* 343–360.

Mackie, D. M., & Cooper, J. (1984). Attitude polarization: The effects of group membership. *Journal of Personality and Social Psychology, 46,* 575–585.

Mackie, D. M., Devos, T., & Smith, E. R. (2000). Intergroup emotions: Explaining offensive action tendencies in an intergroup context. *Journal of Personality and Social Psychology, 79,* 602–616.

Mackie, D. M., Hamilton, D. L., Susskind, J., & Rosselli, F. (1996). Social psychological foundations of stereotype formation. In C. N. Macrae, C. Stangor, & M. Hewstone (Eds.), *Stereotypes and stereotyping* (pp. 41–78). New York: Guilford Press.

Mackie, D. M., Maitner, A. T., & Smith, E. R. (2009). Intergroup emotions theory. In T. D. Nelson (Ed.), *Handbook of prejudice, stereotyping and discrimination* (pp. 285–308). New York: Psychology Press.

Mackie, D. M., & Smith, E. R. (2002a). Intergroup emotions and the social self: Prejudice reconceptualized as differentiated reactions to outgroups. In J. P. Forgas & K. D. Williams (Eds.), *The social self: Cognitive, interpersonal, and intergroup perspectives* (pp. 309–326). New York: Psychology Press.

Mackie, D. M., & Smith, E. R. (Eds.) (2002b). *From prejudice to intergroup emotions: Differentiated reactions to social groups.* New York: Psychology Press.

Mackie, D. M., & Worth, L. T. (1989). Processing deficits and the mediation of positive affect in persuasion. *Journal of Personality and Social Psychology, 57,* 27–40.

Mackie, D. M., Worth, L. T., & Asuncion, A. G. (1990). Processing of persuasive in-group messages. *Journal of Personality and Social Psychology, 58,* 812–822.

McKiethen, K. B., Reitman, J. S., Rueter, H. H., & Hirtle, S. C. (1981). Knowledge organisation and skill differences in computer programmers. *Cognitive Psychology, 13,* 307–325.

McKimmie, B. M., Terry, D. J., Hogg, M. A., Manstead, A. S. R., Spears, R., & Doosje, B. (2003). I'm a hypocrite, but so is everyone else: Group support and the reduction of cognitive dissonance. *Group Dynamics: Theory, Research and Practice, 7,* 214–224.

McKinlay, A., & McVittie, C. (2008). *Social psychology and discourse.* Oxford, UK: Wiley-Blackwell.

MacKinnon, D. W. (1933). *The violation of prohibitions in the solving of problems.* Unpublished doctoral dissertation, Harvard University.

McMillen, D. L. (1971). Transgression, self-image, and complaint behaviour. *Journal of Personality and Social Psychology, 20,* 176–179.

McNamara, T. F. (1987). Language and social identity: Israelis abroad. *Journal of Language and Social Psychology, 6,* 215–228.

MacNeil, M., & Sherif, M. (1976). Norm change over subject generations as a function of arbitrariness of prescribed norms. *Journal of Personality and Social Psychology, 34,* 762–773.

Macrae, C. N., & Quadflieg, S. (2010). Perceiving people. In S. T. Fiske, D. T. Gilbert, & G. Lindzey (Eds.), *Handbook of social psychology* (5th ed., Vol. 1, pp. 428-463). New York: Wiley.

Macrae, C. N., Stangor, C., & Hewstone, M. (Eds.) (1996). *Stereotypes and stereotyping.* New York: Guilford Press.

Madden, T. J., Ellen, P. S., & Ajzen, I. (1992). A comparison of the theory of planned behavior and the theory of reasoned action. *Personality and Social Psychology Bulletin, 18,* 3–9.

Maes, M., De Meyer, F., Thompson, P., Peeters D., & Cosyns, P. (1994). Synchronised annual rhythms in violent suicide rate, ambient temperature and the light–dark span. *Acta Psychiatrica Scandinavica, 90,* 391–396.

Maio, G. R. (2010). Mental representation of social values. *Advances in Experimental Social Psychology, 42,* 1–43.

Maio, G. R., & Haddock, G. (2007). Attitude change. In A. W. Kruglanski & E. T. Higgins (Eds.), *Social psychology: Handbook of basic principles* (2nd ed., pp. 565–586). New York: Guilford.

Maio, G. R., & Haddock, G. (2010). *The psychology of attitudes and attitude change.* London: SAGE.

Maio, G. R., & Olson, J. M. (1994). Value–attitude–behaviour relations: The moderating role of attitude functions. *British Journal of Social Psychology, 33,* 301–312.

Maio, G. R., & Olson, J. M. (1995). Relations between values, attitudes, and behavioral intentions: The moderating role of attitude function. *Journal of Experimental Social Psychology, 31,* 266–285.

Maitner, A. T., Mackie, D. M., & Smith, E. R. (2006). Evidence for the regulatory function of intergroup emotion: Emotional consequences of implemented or impeded intergroup action tendencies. *Journal of Experimental Social Psychology, 42,* 720–728.

Major, B. (1981). Gender patterns in touching behavior. In C. Mayo & N. M. Henley (Eds.), *Gender and nonverbal behavior* (pp. 15–37). New York: Springer.

Major, B. (1994). From social inequality to personal entitlement: The role of social comparisons, legitimacy appraisals and group memberships. *Advances in Experimental Social Psychology, 26,* 293–355.

Major, B., & Adams, J. B. (1983). Role of gender, interpersonal orientation, and self-presentation in distributive justice behaviour. *Journal of Personality and Social Psychology, 45,* 598–608.

Major, B., & Heslin, R. (1982). Perceptions of same-sex and cross-sex reciprocal touch: It's better to give than to receive. *Journal of Nonverbal Behavior, 3,* 148–163.

Major, B., & Konar, E. (1984). An investigation of sex differences in pay expectations and their possible causes. *Academy of Management Journal, 27,* 777–792.

Major, B., Quinton, W. J., & McCoy, S. K. (2002) Antecedents and consequences of attributions to discrimination: Theoretical and empirical advances. *Advances in Experimental Social Psychology, 34,* 251–330.

Major, B., & Schmader, T. (1998). Coping with stigma through psychological disengagement. In J. K. Swim & C. Stangor (Eds.), *Prejudice: The target's perspective* (pp. 219–242). San Diego, CA: Academic Press.

Malamuth, N. M. (1981). Rape proclivity among males. *Journal of Social Issues, 37,* 138–157.

Malamuth, N. M., & Donnerstein, E. (1982). The effects of aggressive-pornographic mass media stimuli. *Advances in Experimental Social Psychology, 15,* 104–136.

Malinowski, B. (1927). *Sex and repression in savage society.* New York: Harcourt Brace.

Malkin, P. Z., & Stein, H. (1990). *Eichmann in my hands.* New York: Warner Books.

Malpass, R. S. (1988). Why not cross-cultural psychology? A characterization of some mainstream views. In M. H. Bond (Ed.), *The cross-cultural challenge to social psychology* (pp. 29–35). Newbury Park, CA: SAGE.

Malpass, R. S., & Kravitz, J. (1969). Recognition for faces of own and other race. *Journal of Personality and Social Psychology, 13,* 330–334.

Mandela, N. (1994). *The long walk to freedom: The autobiography of Nelson Mandela,* London: Little, Brown.

Maner, J. K., Luce, C. L., Neuberg, S. L., Cialdini, R. B., Brown, S., & Sagarin, B. J. (2002). The effects of perspective taking on motivations for helping: Still no evidence for altruism. *Personality and Social Psychology Bulletin, 28,* 1601–1610.

Manis, M. (1977). Cognitive social psychology. *Personality and Social Psychology Bulletin, 3,* 550–566.

Mann, L. (1977). The effect of stimulus queues on queue-joining behavior. *Journal of Personality and Social Psychology, 35,* 437–442.

Mann, L. (1981). The baiting crowd in episodes of threatened suicide. *Journal of Personality and Social Psychology, 41,* 703–709.

Mann, L., Newton, J. W., & Innes, J. M. (1982). A test between deindividuation and emergent norm theories of crowd aggression. *Journal of Personality and Social Psychology, 42,* 260–272.

Manning, R., Levine, M., & Collins, A. (2007). The Kitty Genovese murder and the social psychology of helping: The parable of the 38 witnesses. *American Psychologist, 62,* 555–562.

Manstead, A. S. R. (1992). Gender differences in emotion. In A. Gale & M. W. Eysenck (Eds.), *Handbook of individual differences: Biological perspectives* (pp. 355–387). Oxford, UK: Wiley.

Manstead, A. S. R. (2000). The role of moral norm in the attitude–behavior relation. In D. J. Terry & M. A. Hogg (Eds.), (1995). *Attitudes, behavior, and social context: The role of norms and group membership* (pp. 11–30). Mahwah, NJ: Erlbaum.

Manstead, A. S. R., & Parker, D. (1995). Evaluating and extending the theory of planned behaviour. *European Review of Social Psychology, 6,* 69–95.

Manstead, A. S. R., Proffitt, C., & Smart, J. L. (1983). Predicting and understanding mother's infant-feeding intentions and behavior: Testing the theory of reasoned action. *Journal of Personality and Social Psychology, 44,* 657–671.

Manstead, A. S. R., & Semin, G. R. (1980). Social facilitation effects: Mere enhancement of dominant responses? *British Journal of Social and Clinical Psychology, 19,* 119–136.

Mantell, D. M. (1971). The potential for violence in Germany. *Journal of Social Issues, 27,* 101–112.

Marks, G., & Miller, N. (1985). The effect of certainty on consensus judgments. *Personality and Social Psychology Bulletin, 2,* 165–177.

Marks, G., & Miller, N. (1987). Ten years of research on the false-consensus effect: An empirical and theoretical review. *Psychological Bulletin, 102,* 72–90.

Markus, H. (1977). Self-schemata and processing information about the self. *Journal of Personality and Social Psychology, 35,* 63–78.

Markus, H. (1978). The effect of mere presence on social facilitation: An unobtrusive test. *Journal of Experimental Social Psychology, 14,* 389–397.

Markus, H. (2004). Culture and personality: Brief for an arranged marriage. *Journal of Research in Personality, 38,* 75–83.

Markus, H., & Kitayama, S. (1991). Culture and the self: Implications for cognition, emotion, and motivation. *Psychological Review, 98,* 224–253.

Markus, H., & Kitayama, S. (2003). Models of agency: Sociocultural diversity in the construction of action. In V. Murphy-Berman & J. J. Berman (Eds.), *Cross-cultural differences in perspectives on the self* (Vol. 49, pp. 18–74). Lincoln, NE: University of Nebraska Press.

Markus, H., Kitayama, S., & Heiman, R. J. (1996). Culture and basic psychological principles. In E. T. Higgins & A. W. Kruglanski (Eds.), *Social psychology: Handbook of basic principles* (pp. 857–914). New York: Guilford Press.

Markus, H., & Nurius, P. (1986). Possible selves. *American Psychologist, 41,* 954–969.

Markus, H., & Sentis, K. P. (1982). The self in social information processing. In J. Suls (Ed.), *Psychological perspectives on the self* (Vol. 1, pp. 41–70). Hillsdale, NJ: Erlbaum.

Markus, H., & Wurf, E. (1987). The dynamic self-concept: A social-psychological perspective. *Annual Review of Psychology, 38,* 299–337.

Markus, H., Smith, J., & Moreland, R. L. (1985). Role of the self-concept in the social perception of others. *Journal of Personality and Social Psychology, 49,* 1494–1512.

Markus, H., & Zajonc, R. B. (1985). The cognitive perspective in social psychology. In G. Lindzey & E. Aronson (Eds.), *Handbook of social psychology* (3rd ed., Vol. 1, pp. 137–230). New York: Random House.

Marlowe, F., & Wetsman, A. (2001). Preferred waist-to-hip ratio and ecology. *Personality and Individual Differences, 30,* 481–489.

Marques, J. M., Abrams, D., Páez, D., & Hogg, M. A. (2001). Social categorization, social identification, and rejection of deviant group members. In M. A. Hogg & R. S. Tindale (Eds.), *Blackwell handbook of social psychology: Group processes* (pp. 400–424). Oxford, UK: Blackwell.

Marques, J. M., Abrams, D., Páez, D., & Taboada, C. M. (1998). The role of categorization and ingroup norms in judgments of groups and their members. *Journal of Personality and Social Psychology, 75,* 976–988.

Marques, J. M., Abrams, D., & Serodio, R. (2001). Being better by being right: Subjective group dynamics and derogation of in-group deviants when generic norms are undermined. *Journal of Personality and Social Psychology, 81,* 436–447.

Marques, J. M., & Páez, D. (1994). The 'black sheep effect': Social categorisation, rejection of ingroup deviates and perception of group variability. *European Review of Social Psychology, 5,* 37–68.

Marrow, A. J. (1969). *The practical theorist: The life and work of Kurt Lewin.* New York: Basic Books.

Marsh, P., Russer, E., & Harré, R. (1978). *The rules of disorder.* Milton Keynes, UK: Open University Press.

Marshall, T. C., Bejanyan, K., Di Castro, G., & Lee, R. A. (2013). Attachment styles as predictors of Facebook-related jealousy and surveillance in romantic relationships. *Personal Relationships, 20*, 1–22.

Martell, R. F., Parker, C., Emrich, C. G., & Crawford, M. S. (1998). Sex stereotyping in the executive suite: 'Much ado about something'. *Journal of Social Behavior and Personality, 13*, 127–138.

Martin, C. L. (1986). A ratio measure of sex stereotyping. *Journal of Personality and Social Psychology, 52*, 489–499.

Martin, J., Brickman, P., & Murray, A. (1984). Moral outrage and pragmatism: Explanations for collective action. *Journal of Experimental Social Psychology, 20*, 484–496.

Martin, J., & Murray, A. (1983). Distributive injustice and unfair exchange. In K. S. Cook & D. M. Messick (Eds.), *Theories of equity: Psychological and sociological perspectives*. New York: Praeger.

Martin, L. L., & Clark, L. F. (1990). Social cognition: Exploring the mental processes involved in human social interaction. In M. W. Eysenck (Ed.), *Cognitive psychology: An international review* (Vol. 1, pp. 266–310). Chichester, UK: Wiley.

Martin, L. L., & Van den Bos, K. (2014). Beyond terror: Towards a paradigm shift in the study of threat and culture. *European Review of Social Psychology, 25*, 32–70.

Martin, R. (1987). Influence minorité et relations entre groupe. In S. Moscovici & G. Mugny (Eds.), *Psychologie de la conversion*. Paris: Cossett de Val.

Martin, R. (1988). Ingroup and outgroup minorities: Differential impact upon public and private response. *European Journal of Social Psychology, 18*, 39–52.

Martin, R. (1996). Minority influence and argument generation. *British Journal of Social Psychology, 35*, 91–103.

Martin, R. (1998). Majority and minority influence using the afterimage paradigm: A series of attempted replications. *Journal of Experimental Social Psychology, 34*, 1–26.

Martin, R., & Hewstone, M. (1999). Minority influence and optimal problem solving. *European Journal of Social Psychology, 29*, 825–832.

Martin, R., & Hewstone, M. (2003). Social influence processes of control and change: Conformity, obedience to authority, and innovation. In M. A. Hogg & J. Cooper (Eds.), *The SAGE handbook of social psychology* (pp. 347–366). London: SAGE.

Martin, R., & Hewstone, M. (2007). Social influence processes of control and change: Conformity, obedience to authority, and innovation. In M. A. Hogg & J. Cooper (Eds.), *The SAGE handbook of social psychology: Concise student edition* (pp. 312–332). London: SAGE.

Martin, R., & Hewstone, M. (2008). Majority versus minority influence, message processing and attitude change: The source-context-elaboration model. *Advances in Experimental Social Psychology, 40*, 237–326.

Martin, R., & Hewstone, M. (Eds.) (2010). *Minority influence and innovation: Antecedents, processes and consequences*. Hove, UK: Psychology Press.

Martin, R., Hewstone, M., Martin, P. Y., & Gardikiotis, A. (2008). Persuasion from majority and minority groups. In W. Crano & R. Prislin (Eds.), *Attitudes and attitude change* (pp. 361–384). New York: Psychology Press.

Martz, J. M., Verette, J., Arriaga, X. B., Slovic, L. F., Cox, C. L., & Rusbult, C. E. (1998). Positive illusion in close relationships. *Personal Relationships, 5*, 159–181.

Maslach, C. (1979). Negative emotional biasing of unexplained arousal. *Journal of Personality and Social Psychology, 37*, 953–969.

Mason, W., & Suri, S. (2012). Conducting behavioral research on Amazon's Mechanical Turk. *Behavior Research Methods, 44*, 1–23.

Masuda, T., & Nisbett, R. E. (2001). Attending holistically versus analytically: Comparing the context sensitivity of Japanese and Americans. *Journal of Personality and Social Psychology, 81*, 922–934.

Matsui, T., Kakuyama, T., & Onglatco, M. L. (1987). Effects of goals and feedback on performance in groups. *Journal of Applied Psychology, 72*, 407–415.

Matsumoto, D. (2004). Paul Ekman and the legacy of universals. *Journal of Research in Personality, 38*, 45–51.

Matsumoto, D., Frank, M. G., & Hwang, H. S. (Eds.) (2012). *Nonverbal communication: Science and applications*. Thousand Oaks, CA: Sage.

Matsumoto, D., & Hwang, H. S. (2011). Evidence for training the ability to read microexpressions of emotion. *Motivation and Emotion, 35*, 181–191.

Matsumoto, D., & Willingham, B. (2009). Spontaneous facial expressions of emotion of blind individuals. *Journal of Personality and Social Psychology, 96*, 1–10.

Matthews, K. A. (1982). Psychological perspectives on the type-A behavior pattern. *Psychological Bulletin, 91*, 293–323.

Mayer, J. D. (1993). The emotional madness of the dangerous leader. *Journal of Psychohistory, 20*, 331–348.

Mayo, R. (2015). Cognition is a matter of trust: Distrust tunes cognitive processes. *European Review of Social Psychology, 26*, 283–327.

Mazur, A., Booth, A., & Dabbs, J. M. (1992). Testosterone and chess competition. *Social Psychology Quarterly, 55*, 70–77.

Mead, G. H. (1934). *Mind, self and society*. Chicago: University of Chicago Press.

Mead, M. (1928/1961). *Coming of age in Samoa*. New York: Morrow.

Mead, M. (1930/1962). *Growing up in New Guinea*. New York: Morrow.

Medin, D. L., & Ortony, A. (1989). Psychological essentialism. In S. Vosniadou & A. Ortony (Eds.), *Similarity and analogical reasoning* (pp. 179–195). Cambridge, UK: Cambridge University Press.

Medvec, V. H., Madley, S. F., & Gilovich, T. (1995). When less is more: Counterfactual thinking and satisfaction among Olympic medalists. *Journal of Personality and Social Psychology, 69*, 603–610.

Meeus, W., & Raaijmakers, Q. (1986). Administrative obedience as a social phenomenon. In W. Doise & S. Moscovici (Eds.), *Current issues in European social psychology* (Vol. 2, pp. 183–230). Cambridge, UK: Cambridge University Press.

Mehrabian, A. (1972). Nonverbal communication. In J. Cole (Ed.), *Nebraska symposium on motivation* (Vol. 19, pp. 107–162). Lincoln, NE: University of Nebraska Press.

Meindl, J. R. (1995). The romance of leadership as a follower-centric theory: A social constructionist approach. *The Leadership Quarterly, 6*, 329–341.

Meindl, J. R., Ehrlich, S. B., & Dukerich, J. M. (1985). The romance of leadership. *Administrative Science Quarterly, 30*, 78–102.

Meindl, J. R., & Lerner, M. (1983). The heroic motive: Some experimental demonstrations. *Journal of Experimental Social Psychology, 19*, 1–20.

Meleady, R., Hopthrow, T., & Crisp, R. (2013). Simulating social dilemmas: Promoting cooperative behavior through imagined group discussion. *Journal of Personality and Social Psychology, 104*, 839–853.

Mellen, S. L. W. (1981). *The evolution of love*. Oxford, UK: W. H. Freeman.

Menegatti, M., & Rubini, M. (2013). Convincing similar and dissimilar others: The power of language abstraction in political communication. *Personality and Social Psychology Bulletin, 39*, 596–607.

Merei, F. (1949). Group leadership and institutionalization. *Human Relations, 2*, 23–39.

Merritt, A. C., Effron, D., Fein, S., Savitsky, K. K., Tuller, D. M., & Monin, B. (2012). The strategic pursuit of moral credentials. *Journal of Experimental Social Psychology, 48*, 774–777.

Mervis, C. B., & Rosch, E. (1981). Categorization of natural objects. *Annual Review of Psychology, 32*, 89–115.

Messick, D. M. (2005). On the psychological exchange between leaders and followers. In D. M. Messick & R. M. Kramer (Eds.), *The psychology of leadership: New perspectives and research* (pp. 81–96). Mahwah, NJ: Erlbaum.

Metalsky, G. I., & Abramson, L. Y. (1981). Attributional styles: Toward a framework for conceptualization and assessment. In P. C. Kendall & S. D. Hollon (Eds.), *Cognitive–behavioral intentions: Assessment methods* (pp. 13–58). New York: Academic Press.

Meyerhoff, M. (2011). *Introducing sociolinguistics*. New York: Taylor & Francis.

Michelini, R. L., & Snodgrass, S. R. (1980). Defendant characteristics and juridic decisions. *Journal of Research in Personality, 14*, 340–350.

Middlebrook, P. N. (1980). *Social psychology and modern life* (2nd ed.). New York: Alfred A. Knopf.

Middlemist, R. D., Knowles, E. S., & Mutter, C. F. (1976). Personal space invasions in the lavatory: Suggestive evidence for arousal. *Journal of Personality and Social Psychology, 33*, 541–546.

Middleton, D., & Edwards, D. (Eds.) (1990). *Collective remembering*. London: SAGE.

Midlarsky, E., & Bryan, J. H. (1972). Affect expressions and children's imitative altruism. *Journal of Experimental Research in Personality, 6*, 195–203.

Midlarsky, M., & Midlarsky, E. (1976). Status inconsistency, aggressive attitude, and helping behavior. *Journal of Personality, 44*, 371–391.

Mikula, G. (1980). On the role of justice in allocation decisions. In G. Mikula (Ed.), *Justice and social interaction: Experimental and theoretical contributions from psychological research* (pp. 127–166). Bern, Switzerland: Hans Huber.

Mikulincer, M. (1998). Attachment working models and the sense of trust: An exploration of interaction goals and affect regulation. *Journal of Personality and Social Psychology, 74*, 1209–1224.

Mikulincer, M., & Goodman, G. S. (Eds.) (2006). *Dynamics of romantic love: Attachment, caregiving, and sex*. New York: Guilford.

Mikulincer, M., & Shaver, P. (2005). Attachment security, compassion, and altruism. *Current Directions in Psychological Science, 14*, 34–38.

Milardo, R. M., Johnson, M. P., & Huston, T. L. (1983). Developing close relationships: Changing patterns of interaction between pair members and social networks. *Journal of Personality and Social Psychology, 44*, 964–976.

Miles, D. R., & Carey, G. (1997). Genetic and environmental architecture of human aggression. *Journal of Personality and Social Psychology, 72*, 207–217.

Miles, E., & Crisp, R. J. (2014). A meta-analytic test of the imagined contact hypothesis. *Group Processes and Intergroup Relations, 17*, 3–26.

Milfont, T. L., Richter, A., Sibley, C. G., & Fischer, R. (2013). Environmental consequences of the desire to dominate and be superior. *Personality and Social Psychology Bulletin, 39*, 1127–1138.

Milgram, S. (1961). Nationality and conformity. *Scientific American, 205*(6), 45–51.

Milgram, S. (1963). Behavioral study of obedience. *Journal of Abnormal and Social Psychology, 67*, 371–378.

Milgram, S. (1974). *Obedience to authority*. London: Tavistock.

Milgram, S. (1992). *The individual in a social world: Essays and experiments* (2nd ed.). New York: McGraw-Hill.

Milgram, S., & Toch, H. (1969). Collective behavior: Crowds and social movements. In G. Lindzey & E. Aronson (Eds.), *Handbook of social psychology* (2nd ed., Vol. 4, pp. 507–610). Reading, MA: Addison-Wesley.

Milham, J. (1974). Two components of need for approval score and their relationship to cheating following success and failure. *Journal of Research in Personality, 8*, 378–392.

Mill, J. S. (1869). *The analysis of the phenomenon of the human mind*. New York: Kelley.

Millar, M. G., & Millar, K. U. (1990). Attitude change as a function of attitude type and argument type. *Journal of Personality and Social Psychology, 59*, 217–228.

Millar, M. G., & Tesser, A. (1986). Effects of affective and cognitive focus on the attitude–behavior relation. *Journal of Personality and Social Psychology, 51*, 270–276.

Miller, C. E. (1989). The social psychological effects of group decision rules. In P. B. Paulus (Ed.), *Psychology of group influence* (2nd ed., pp. 327–355). Hillsdale, NJ: Erlbaum.

Miller, D. T. (1977). Altruism and the threat to a belief in a just world. *Journal of Experimental Social Psychology, 13*, 113–124.

Miller, D. T., & McFarland, C. (1987). Pluralistic ignorance: When similarity is interpreted as dissimilarity. *Journal of Personality and Social Psychology, 53*, 298–305.

Miller, D. T., & Porter, C. A. (1980). Effects of temporal perspective on the attribution process. *Journal of Personality and Social Psychology, 39*, 532–541.

Miller, D. T., & Porter, C. A. (1983). Self-blame in victims of violence. *Journal of Social Issues, 39*, 139–152.

Miller, D. T., & Ross, M. (1975). Self-serving biases in the attribution of causality: Fact or fiction? *Psychological Bulletin, 82*, 213–225.

Miller, J. G. (1984). Culture and the development of everyday social explanation. *Journal of Personality and Social Psychology, 46*, 961–978.

Miller, N., & Brewer, M. B. (Eds.) (1984). *Groups in contact: The psychology of desegregation*. New York: Academic Press.

Miller, N., Brewer, M. B., & Edwards, K. (1985). Cooperative interaction in desegregated settings: A laboratory analogue. *Journal of Social Issues, 41*, 63–79.

Miller, N., Maruyama, G., Beaber, R. J., & Valone, K. (1976). Speed of speech and persuasion. *Journal of Personality and Social Psychology, 34*, 615–625.

Miller, N. E. (1948). Theory and experiment relating psychoanalytic displacement to stimulus–response generalisation. *Journal of Abnormal and Social Psychology, 43*, 155–178.

Miller, N. E., & Bugelski, R. (1948). Minor studies in aggression: The influence of frustrations imposed by the ingroup on attitudes toward outgroups. *Journal of Psychology, 25*, 437–442.

Miller, N. E., Pederson, W. C., Earlywine, M., & Pollock, V. E. (2003). A theoretical model of triggered displaced aggression. *Personality and Social Psychology Review, 7*, 75–97.

Miller, P. A., & Eisenberg, N. (1988). The relation of empathy to aggressive and externalizing/antisocial behavior. *Psychological Bulletin, 103*, 324–344.

Miller, P. J. E., & Rempel, J. K. (2004). Trust and partner-enhancing attributions in close relationships. *Personality and Social Psychology Bulletin, 30*, 695–705.

Milner, D. (1996). Children and racism: Beyond the value of the dolls. In W. P. Robinson (Ed.), *Social groups and identities: Developing the legacy of Henri Tajfel* (pp. 246–268). Oxford, UK: Butterworth-Heinemann.

Minard, R. D. (1952). Race relations in the Pocahontas coal field. *Journal of Social Issues, 8*, 29–44.

Mischel, W. (1968). *Personality and assessment*. New York: Wiley.

Mischel, W., Ebbesen, E. B., & Zeiss, A. R. (1976). Determinants of selective memory about the self. *Journal of Consulting and Clinical Psychology, 44*, 92–103.

Misumi, J., & Peterson, M. F. (1985). The performance-maintenance (P-M) theory of leadership: Review of a Japanese research program. *Administrative Science Quarterly, 30*, 198–223.

Mita, T. H., Dermer, M., & Knight, J. (1977). Reversed facial images and the mere exposure hypothesis. *Journal of Personality and Social Psychology, 35*, 597–601.

Mitchell, H. E. (1979). *Informational and affective determinants of juror decision making*. Doctoral dissertation, Purdue University.

Mitchell, S. (2002). *American generations: Who they are, how they live, what they think*. Ithaca, NY: New Strategists Publications.

Moghaddam, F. M. (1990). Modulative and generative orientations in psychology: Implications for psychology in the three worlds. *Journal of Social Issues, 46*, 21–41.

Moghaddam, F. M. (1998). *Social psychology: Exploring universals across cultures*. New York: Freeman.

Moghaddam, F. M. (2008). *Multiculturalism and intergroup relations: Psychological implications for democracy in global context*. Washington, DC: American Psychological Association.

Moghaddam, F. M. (2013). *The psychology of dictatorship*. Washington, DC: APA Books.

Moliner, P., & Tafani, E. (1997). Attitudes and social representations: A theoretical and experimental approach. *European Journal of Social Psychology, 27*, 687–702.

Monin, B., & Miller, D. T. (2001). Moral credentials and the expression of prejudice. *Journal of Personality and Social Psychology, 81*, 33–43.

Monson, T. C., & Hesley, J. W. (1982). Causal attributions for behavior consistent or inconsistent with an actor's personality traits: Differences between those offered by actors and observers. *Journal of Experimental Social Psychology, 18*, 426–432.

Monteil, J.-M., & Huguet, P. (1999). *Social context and cognitive performance*. Philadelphia, PA: Psychology Press.

Monteith, M. J. (1993). Self-regulation of prejudiced responses: Implication for progress in prejudice-reduction efforts. *Journal of Personality and Social Psychology, 65*, 469–485.

Montepare, J. M., & Vega, C. (1988). Women's vocal reactions to intimate and casual male friends. *Personality and Social Psychology Bulletin, 14*, 103–112.

Moons, W., Mackie, D. M., & Garcia-Marques, T. (2009). The impact of repetition-induced familiarity on agreement with weak and strong arguments. *Journal of Personality and Social Psychology, 96*, 32–44.

Moore, B. S., Sherrod, D. R., Liu, T. J., & Underwood, B. (1979). The dispositional shift in attribution over time. *Journal of Experimental Social Psychology, 15*, 553–569.

Moradi, B., & Huang, Y. (2008). Objectification theory and psychology of women: A decade of advances and future directions. *Psychology of Women Quarterly, 32*, 377–398.

Moreland, R. L. (1985). Social categorization and the assimilation of 'new' group members. *Journal of Personality and Social Psychology, 48*, 1173–1190.

Moreland, R. L., Argote, L., & Krishnan, R. (1996). Socially shared cognition at work: Transactive memory and group performance. In J. L. Nye & A. M. Bower (Eds.), *What's social about social cognition: Research on socially shared cognition in small groups* (pp. 57–84). Thousand Oaks, CA: SAGE.

Moreland, R. L., & Beach, S. R. (1992). Exposure effects in the classroom: The development of affinity among students. *Journal of Experimental Social Psychology, 28*, 255–276.

Moreland, R. L., Hogg, M. A., & Hains, S. C. (1994). Back to the future: Social psychological research on groups. *Journal of Experimental Social Psychology, 30*, 527–555.

Moreland, R. L., & Levine, J. M. (1982). Socialization in small groups: Temporal changes in individual–group relations. In L. Berkowitz (Ed.), *Advances in experimental social psychology* (Vol. 15, pp. 137–192). New York: Academic Press.

Moreland, R. L., & Levine, J. M. (1984). Role transitions in small groups. In V. Allen and E. van de Vliert (Eds.), *Role transitions: Explorations and explanations* (pp. 181–195). New York: Plenum.

Moreland, R. L., & Levine, J. M. (1989). Newcomers and oldtimers in small groups. In P. B. Paulus (Ed.), *Psychology of group influence* (2nd ed., pp. 143–186). Hillsdale, NJ: Erlbaum.

Moreland, R. L., Levine, J. M., & Cini, M. (1993). Group socialisation: The role of commitment. In M. A. Hogg & D. Abrams (Eds.), *Group motivation: Social psychological perspectives* (pp. 105–129). London: Harvester Wheatsheaf.

Moriarty, T. (1975). Crime, commitment and the responsive bystander: Two field experiments. *Journal of Personality and Social Psychology, 31*, 370–376.

Morley, I. E., & Stephenson, G. M. (1977). *The social psychology of bargaining*. London: Allen and Unwin.

Morley, I. E., Webb, J., & Stephenson, G. M. (1988) Bargaining and arbitration in the resolution of conflict. In W. Stroebe, A. W. Kruglanski, D. Bar-Tal, & M. Hewstone (Eds.), *The social psychology of intergroup conflict: Theory, research and applications* (pp. 117–134). Berlin: Springer-Verlag.

Morris, D. (1967). *The naked ape*. New York: McGraw-Hill.

Morris, D., Collett, P., Marsh, P., & O'Shaughnessy, M. (1979). *Gestures: Their origins and distribution*. New York: Stein & Day.

Morris, M. W., & Peng, K. P. (1994). Culture and cause: American and Chinese attributions for social and physical events. *Journal of Personality and Social Psychology, 67*, 949–971.

Morton, T. A., Hornsey, M. J., & Postmes, T. (2009). Shifting ground: The variable use of essentialism in contexts of inclusion and exclusion. *British Journal of Social Psychology, 48*, 35–59.

Morton, T. L. (1978). Intimacy and reciprocity of exchange: A comparison of spouses and strangers. *Journal of Personality and Social Psychology, 36*, 72–81.

Moscovici, S. (1961). *La psychanalyse: Son image et son public*. Paris: Presses Universitaires de France.

Moscovici, S. (1972). Society and theory in social psychology. In J. Israel & H. Tajfel (Eds.), *The context of social psychology: A critical assessment* (pp. 17–68). New York: Academic Press.

Moscovici, S. (1976). *Social influence and social change*. London: Academic Press.

Moscovici, S. (1980). Toward a theory of conversion behavior. *Advances in Experimental Social Psychology, 13*, 202–239.

Moscovici, S. (1981). On social representation. In J. P. Forgas (Ed.), *Social cognition: Perspectives on everyday understanding* (pp. 181–209). London: Academic Press.

Moscovici, S. (1982). The coming era of representations. In J.-P. Codol & J. P. Leyens (Eds.), *Cognitive analysis of social behaviour* (pp. 115–150). The Hague: Martinus Nijhoff.

Moscovici, S. (1983). The phenomenon of social representations. In R. M. Farr & S. Moscovici (Eds.), *Social Representations* (pp. 3–69). Cambridge, UK: Cambridge University Press.

Moscovici, S. (1984). *Psychologie Sociale*. Paris: Presses Universitaires de France.

Moscovici, S. (1985a). Social influence and conformity. In G. Lindzey & E. Aronson (Eds.), *Handbook of social psychology* (3rd ed., Vol. 2, pp. 347–412). New York: Random House.

Moscovici, S. (1985b). *The age of the crowd*. Cambridge, UK: Cambridge University Press.

Moscovici, S. (1988). Notes towards a description of social representations. *European Journal of Social Psychology, 18*, 211–250.

Moscovici, S. (2000). *Social representations: Explorations in social psychology*. Oxford: Blackwell.

Moscovici, S. (Ed.) (1973). *Introduction à la psychologie sociale* (Vol. 1). Paris: Larousse.

Moscovici, S., & Faucheux, C. (1972). Social influence, conforming bias, and the study of active minorities. *Advances in Experimental Social Psychology, 6*, 149–202.

Moscovici, S., & Lage, E. (1976). Studies in social influence: III. Majority vs minority influence in a group. *European Journal of Social Psychology, 6*, 149–174.

Moscovici, S., Lage, E., & Naffrechoux, M. (1969). Influence of a consistent minority on the responses of a majority in a colour perception task. *Sociometry, 32*, 365–380.

Moscovici, S., Mugny, G., & Van Avermaet, E. (2008). *Perspectives on minority influence*. Cambridge, UK: Cambridge University Press.

Moscovici, S., & Personnaz, B. (1980). Studies in social influence: V. Minority influence and conversion behavior in a perceptual task. *Journal of Experimental Social Psychology, 16*, 270–282.

Moscovici, S., & Personnaz, B. (1986). Studies on latent influence by the spectrometer method: I. The impact of psychologization in the case of conversion by a minority or a majority. *European Journal of Social Psychology, 16*, 345–360.

Moscovici, S., & Zavalloni, M. (1969). The group as a polarizer of attitudes. *Journal of Personality and Social Psychology, 12*, 125–135.

Mosher, D. L., & Anderson, R. D. (1986). Macho personality, sexual aggression, and reactions to guided imagery of realistic rape. *Journal of Research in Personality, 20*, 77–94.

Moskowitz, G. B. (2005). *Social cognition: Understanding self and others*. New York: Guilford Press.

Mowday, R. T., & Sutton, R. I. (1993). Organisational behavior: Linking individuals and groups to organizational contexts. *Annual Review of Psychology, 44*, 195–229.

Mucchi-Faina, A., Maass, A., & Volpato, C. (1991). Social influence: The role of originality. *European Journal of Social Psychology, 21*, 183–197.

Mudrack, P. E. (1989). Defining group cohesiveness: A legacy of confusion. *Small Group Behavior, 20*, 37–49.

Mugny, G. (1982). *The power of minorities*. London: Academic Press.

Mugny, G., & Papastamou, S. (1981). When rigidity does not fail: Individualization and psychologization as resistance to the diffusion of minority innovations. *European Journal of Social Psychology, 10*, 43–62.

Mugny, G., & Papastamou, S. (1982). Minority influence and psychosocial identity. *European Journal of Social Psychology, 12*, 379–394.

Muise, A., Christofides, E., & Desmarais, S. (2014). "Creeping" or just information seeking? Gender differences in partner monitoring in response to jealousy on Facebook. *Personal Relationships, 21*, 35–50.

Mulac, A., Bradac, J. J., & Gibbons, P. (2001). Empirical support for the gender-as-culture hypothesis: An intercultural analysis of male/female language differences. *Human Communication Research, 27*, 121–152.

Mulac, A., Studley, L. B., Wiemann, J. M., & Bradac, J. J. (1987). Male/female gaze in same-sex and mixed-sex dyads: Gender-linked differences and mutual influence. *Human Communication Research, 13*, 323–343.

Mulder, M. (1959). Power and satisfaction in task-oriented groups. *Acta Psychologica, 16*, 178–225.

Mullen, B. (1983). Operationalizing the effect of the group on the individual: A self-attention perspective. *Journal of Experimental Social Psychology, 19*, 295–322.

Mullen, B. (1986). Atrocity as a function of lynch mob composition: A self-attention perspective. *Personality and Social Psychology Bulletin, 12*, 187–197.

Mullen, B., Atkins, J. L., Champion, D. S., Edwards, C., Hardy, D., Story, J. E., & Vanderklok, M. (1985). The false consensus effect: A meta-analysis of 115 hypothesis tests. *Journal of Experimental Social Psychology, 21*, 262–283.

Mullen, B., & Copper, C. (1994). The relation between group cohesiveness and performance: An integration. *Psychological Bulletin, 115*, 210–227.

Mullen, B., & Hu, L. (1989). Perceptions of ingroup and outgroup variability: A meta-analytic integration. *Basic and Applied Social Psychology, 10*, 233–252.

Mullen, B., & Johnson, C. (1990). Distinctiveness-based illusory correlations and stereotyping: A meta-analytic integration. *British Journal of Social Psychology, 29*, 11–28.

Mullen, B., Johnson, C., & Salas, E. (1991). Productivity loss in brainstorming groups. *Basic and Applied Social Psychology, 12*, 3–24.

Mullen, B., & Riordan, C. A. (1988). Self-serving attributions for performance in naturalistic settings: A meta-analytic review. *Journal of Applied Social Psychology, 18*, 3–22.

Mullen, P. E. (1984). Mental disorder and dangerousness. *Australian and New Zealand Journal of Psychiatry, 18*, 8–17.

Mullin, C. R., & Linz, D. (1995). Desensitisation and resensitisation to violence against women: Effects of exposure to sexually violent films on judgments of domestic violence victims. *Journal of Personality and Social Psychology, 69*, 449–459.

Mummendey, A., & Otten, S. (1998). Positive–negative asymmetry in social discrimination. *European Review of Social Psychology, 19*, 107–143.

Mummendey, A., & Wenzel, M. (1999). Social discrimination and tolerance in intergroup relations: Reactions to intergroup difference. *Personality and Social Psychology Review, 3*, 158–174.

Murchison, C. (Ed.) (1935). *Handbook of social psychology.* Worcester, MA: Clark University Press.

Murphy, G., & Murphy, L. B. (1931/1937). *Experimental social psychology.* New York: Harper (rev. ed. published with T. M. Newcomb in 1937).

Murphy, L., & Murphy, G. (1970). Perspectives in cross-cultural research. *Journal of Cross-Cultural Psychology, 1*, 1–4.

Murphy, P., Williams, J., & Dunning, E. (1990). *Football on trial: Spectator violence and development in the football world.* London: Routledge.

Murphy, S. T., Monahan, J. L., & Zajonc, R. B. (1995). Additivity of nonconscious affect: Combined effects of priming and exposure. *Journal of Personality and Social Psychology, 69*, 589–602.

Murray, S. L., & Holmes, J. G. (1997). A leap of faith? Positive illusions in romantic relationships. *Personality and Social Psychology Bulletin, 23*, 586–604.

Murray, S. L., & Holmes, J. G. (1999). The mental ties that bind: Cognitive structures that predict relationship resilience. *Journal of Personality and Social Psychology, 77*, 1228–1244.

Murray, S. L., Holmes, J. G., & Griffin, D. W. (1996). The self-fulfilling nature of positive illusions in romantic relationships: Love is not blind, but prescient. *Journal of Personality and Social Psychology, 71*, 1155–1180.

Murray, S. L., Holmes, J. G., & Griffin, D. W. (2003). Reflections on the self-fulfilling effects of positive illusions. *Psychological Inquiry, 14*, 289–295.

Murstein, B. I. (1980). Love at first sight: A myth. *Medical Aspects of Human Sexuality, 14*(34), 39–41.

Myers, D. G., & Lamm, H. (1975). The polarizing effect of group discussion. *American Scientist, 63*, 297–303.

Myers, D. G., & Lamm, H. (1976). The group polarization phenomenon. *Psychological Bulletin, 83*, 602–627.

Myers, K. K., & Davis, C. W. (2012). Communication between the generations. In H. Giles (Ed.), *The handbook of intergroup communication* (pp. 237–249). New York: Routledge.

Na, J., & Kitayama, S. (2011). Spontaneous trait inference is culture specific: Behavioral and neural evidence. *Psychological Science, 22*, 1025–1032.

Nadler, A. (1986). Help seeking as a cultural phenomenon: Differences between city and kibbutz dwellers. *Journal of Personality and Social Psychology, 51*, 976–982.

Nadler, A. (1991). Help-seeking behavior: Psychological costs and instrumental benefits. In M. S. Clark (Ed.), *Prosocial behavior* (pp. 290–311). Newbury Park, CA: SAGE.

Nadler, A., & Shnabel, N. (2015). Intergroup reconciliation: Instrumental and socio-emotional processes and the needs-based model. *European Review of Social Psychology, 26*, 93–125.

Nahem, J. (1980). *Psychology and psychiatry today: A Marxist view.* New York: International Publishers.

Nail, P. R. (1986). Toward an integration of some models and theories of social response. *Psychological Bulletin, 100*, 190–206.

National Gay and Lesbian Task Force (1990). *Anti-gay violence, victimization & defamation in 1989.* Washington DC: Author.

Neal, D. T., Wood, W., Labrecque, J., & Lally, P. (2012). How do habits guide behavior? Perceived and actual triggers of habits in daily life. *Journal of Experimental Social Psychology, 48*, 492–498.

Neisser, U. (1967). *Cognitive psychology.* Englewood Cliffs, NJ: Prentice Hall.

Nelson, T. D. (2005). Ageism: Prejudiced against our feared future self. *Journal of Social Issues, 61*, 207–221.

Nemeth, C. (1970). Bargaining and reciprocity. *Psychological Bulletin, 74*, 297–308.

Nemeth, C. (1981). Jury trials: Psychology and law. In L. Berkowitz (Ed.), *Advances in experimental social psychology* (Vol. 14, pp. 309–367). New York: Academic Press.

Nemeth, C., & Chiles, C. (1988). Modelling courage: The role of dissent in fostering independence. *European Journal of Social Psychology, 18*, 275–280.

Nemeth, C., Swedlund, M., & Kanki, B. (1974). Patterning of the minority's response and their influence on the majority. *European Journal of Social Psychology, 4*, 53–64.

Nemeth, C., & Wachtler, J. (1983). Creative problem solving as a result of majority vs minority influence. *European Journal of Social Psychology, 13*, 45–55.

Nemeth, C., Wachtler, J., & Endicott, J. (1977). Increasing the size of the minority: Some gains and some losses. *European Journal of Social Psychology, 7*, 15–27.

Nemeth, C. J. (1986). Differential contributions of majority and minority influence. *Psychological Review, 93*, 23–32.

Nemeth, C. J. (1995). Dissent as driving cognition, attitudes, and judgments. *Social Cognition, 13*, 273–291.

Neuberg, S. L., & Fiske, S. T. (1987). Motivational influences on impression formation: Outcome dependency, accuracy-driven attention, and individuating processes. *Journal of Personality and Social Psychology, 53*, 431–444.

Neuberg, S. L., Kenrick, D. T., & Schaller, M. (2010). Evolutionary social psychology. In S. T. Fiske, D. T. Gilbert, & G. Lindzey (Eds.), *Handbook of social psychology* (5th ed., Vol. 2, pp. 761-796). New York: Wiley.

Newcomb, T. M. (1961). *The acquaintance process.* New York: Holt, Rinehart & Winston.

Newcomb, T. M. (1965). Attitude development as a function of reference groups: The Bennington study. In H. Proshansky & B. Seidenberg (Eds.), *Basic studies in social psychology* (pp. 215–225). New York: Holt, Rinehart & Winston.

Ng, B., Kumar, S., Ranclaud, M., & Robinson, E. (2001). Ward crowding and incidents of violence on an acute psychiatric inpatient unit. *Psychiatric Services, 52*, 521–525.

Ng, S. H. (1990). Androgenic coding of man and his memory by language users. *Journal of Experimental Social Psychology, 26*, 455–464.

Ng, S. H. (1996). Power: An essay in honour of Henri Tajfel. In W. P. Robinson (Ed.), *Social groups and identities: Developing the legacy of Henri Tajfel* (pp. 191–214). Oxford, UK: Butterworth-Heinemann.

Ng, S. H., Bell, D., & Brooke, M. (1993). Gaining turns and achieving high influence in small conversational groups. *British Journal of Social Psychology, 32*, 265–275.

Ng, S. H., & Bradac, J. J. (1993). *Power in language.* Thousand Oaks, CA: SAGE.

Ng, S. H., & Liu, J. H. (2000). Cultural revolution in psychology. *Asian Journal of Social Psychology, 3*, 289–293.

Nieburg, H. (1969). *Political violence: The behavioural process*. New York: St Martin's Press.

Niedenthal, P. M., & Beike, D. R. (1997). Interrelated and isolated self-concepts. *Personality and Social Psychology Review, 1*, 106–128.

Niedenthal, P. M., & Brauer, M. (2012). Social functionality of human emotion. *Annual Review of Psychology, 63*, 259–285.

Nier, J. A. (2005). How dissociated are implicit and explicit measures of racial attitudes? A bogus pipeline approach. *Group Processes and Intergroup Relations, 8*, 39–52.

Nisbett, R. E. (2003). *The geography of thought: How Asians and Westerners think differently … and why*. New York: Free Press.

Nisbett, R. E., & Cohen, D. (1996). *Culture of honor: The psychology of violence in the South*. Boulder, CO: Westview Press.

Nisbett, R. E., Krantz, D. H., Jepson, C., & Fong, G. T. (1982). Improving inductive inference. In D. Kahneman, P. Slovic, & A. Tversky (Eds.), *Judgment under uncertainty: Heuristics and biases* (pp. 445–462). New York: Cambridge University Press.

Nisbett, R. E., Krantz, D. H., Jepson, C., & Kunda, Z. (1983). The use of statistical heuristics in everyday inductive reasoning. *Psychological Review, 90*, 339–363.

Nisbett, R. E., & Ross, L. (1980). *Human inference: Strategies and shortcomings of social judgment*. Englewood Cliffs, NJ: Prentice Hall.

Nisbett, R. E., & Wilson, T. D. (1977). Telling more than we can know: Verbal reports on mental behavior. *Psychological Review, 84*, 231–259.

Nisbett, R. E., Zukier, H., & Lemley, R. E. (1981). The dilution effect: Non-diagnostic information weakens the implications of diagnostic information. *Cognitive Psychology, 13*, 248–277.

Noels, K. A., Giles, H., & Le Poire, B. (2003). Language and communication processes. In M. A. Hogg & J. Cooper (Eds.), *The SAGE handbook of social psychology* (pp. 232–257). London: SAGE.

Noels, K. A., Pon, G., & Clément, R. (1996). Language and adjustment: The role of linguistic self-confidence in the acculturation process. *Journal of Language and Social Psychology, 15*, 246–264.

Nolen-Hoeksma, S., Girgus, J. S., & Seligman, M. E. P. (1992). Predictors and consequences of childhood depressive symptoms: Five-year longitudinal study. *Journal of Abnormal Psychology, 101*, 405–422.

Noller, P. (1984). *Nonverbal communication and marital interaction*. Oxford, UK: Pergamon Press.

Noller, P., & Fitzpatrick, M. A. (1990). Marital communication in the eighties. *Journal of Marriage and the Family, 52*, 832–843.

Noller, P., & Ruzzene, M. (1991). Communication in marriage: The influence of affect and cognition. In G. J. O. Fletcher & F. D. Fincham (Eds.), *Cognition and close relationships* (pp. 203–233). Hillsdale, NJ: Erlbaum.

Noor, M., Shnabel, N., Halabi, S., & Nadler, A. (2012). When suffering begets suffering the psychology of competitive victimhood between adversarial groups in violent conflicts. *Personality and Social Psychology Review, 16*, 351–374.

Nordgren, L. F., Banas, K. J., & MacDonald, G. (2011). Empathy gaps for social pain: Why people underestimate the pain of social suffering. *Journal of Personality and Social Psychology, 100*, 120–128.

Norenzayan, A., & Shariff, A. F. (2008). The origin and evolution of religious prosociality. *Science, 322*, 58–62.

Norman, P., & Conner, M. (2006). The theory of planned behaviour and binge drinking: Assessing the moderating role of past behaviour within the theory of planned behaviour. *British Journal of Health Psychology, 11*, 55–70.

North, M. S., & Fiske, S. T. (2013) Act your (old) age: Prescriptive, ageist biases over succession, consumption, and identity. *Personality and Social Psychology Bulletin, 39*, 720–734.

Northouse, P. G. (2009). *Leadership: Theory and practice* (5th ed.). Thousand Oaks, CA: SAGE.

Norton, M. I., Frost, J. H., & Ariely, D. (2007). Less is more: The lure of ambiguity, or why familiarity breeds contempt. *Journal of Personality and Social Psychology, 92*, 97–105.

Norton, M. I., Frost, J. H., & Ariely, D. (2013). Less *is* often more: Additional evidence that familiarity breeds contempt and a call for further research. *Journal of Personality and Social Psychology, 105*, 921–923.

Norton, M. I., Monin, B., Cooper, J., & Hogg, M. A. (2003). Vicarious dissonance: Attitude change from the inconsistency of others. *Journal of Personality and Social Psychology, 85*, 47–62.

Nosek, B. A., & Bar-Anan, Y. (2012). Scientific utopia: I. Opening scientific communication. *Psychological Inquiry, 23*, 217–243.

Nowak, A., Gelfand, M. J., Borkowski, W., Cohen, D., & Hernandez, I. (2016). The evolutionary basis of honor cultures. *Psychological Science, 27*, 12–24.

Nowinski, S. N., & Bowen, E. (2012). Partner violence against heterosexual and gay men: Prevalence and correlates. *Aggression and Violent Behavior, 17*, 36–52.

Nye, C. W., Roth, M. S., & Shimp, T. A. (2008). Comparative advertising in markets where brands and comparative advertising are novel. *Journal of International Business Studies, 39*, 851–863.

Nye, J. L., & Bower, A. M. (Eds.) (1996). *What's social about social cognition: Research on socially shared cognition in small groups*. Thousand Oaks, CA: SAGE.

Oaker, G., & Brown, R. J. (1986). Intergroup relations in a hospital setting: A further test of social identity theory. *Human Relations, 39*, 767–778.

Oakes, P. J. (1987). The salience of social categories. In J. C. Turner, M. A. Hogg, P. J. Oakes, S. D. Reicher, & M. S. Wetherell, *Rediscovering the social group: A self-categorization theory* (pp. 117–141). Oxford, UK: Blackwell.

Oakes, P. J., Haslam, S. A., & Reynolds, K. J. (1999). Social categorization and social context: Is stereotype change a matter of information or of meaning? In D. Abrams & M. A. Hogg (Eds.), *Social identity and social cognition* (pp. 55–79). Oxford, UK: Blackwell.

Oakes, P. J., Haslam, S. A., & Turner, J. C. (1994). *Stereotyping and social reality*. Oxford, UK: Blackwell.

Oakes, P. J., & Turner, J. C. (1990). Is limited information processing capacity the cause of social stereotyping? *European Review of Social Psychology, 1*, 111–135.

Obama, B. (2004). *Dreams from my father: A story of race and inheritance*. New York, NY: Three Rivers Press.

O'Barr, W. M., & Atkins, B. K. (1980). 'Women's language' or 'powerless language'? In S. McConnell-Ginet, R. Borker, & N. Furman (Eds.), *Women and language in literature and society* (pp. 93–110). New York: Praeger.

Ochsner, K. N. (2007). Social cognitive neuroscience: Historical development, core principles, and future promise. In A. W. Kruglanski & E. T. Higgins (Eds.), *Social psychology: Handbook of basic principles* (2nd ed., pp. 39–66). New York: Guilford Press.

Ochsner, K. N., & Lieberman, M. (2001). The emergence of social cognitive neuroscience. *American Psychologist, 56*, 714–734.

O'Connor, J., Mumford, M. D., Clifton, T. C., Gessner, T. L., & Connelly, M. S. (1995). Charismatic leaders and destructiveness: A historiometric study. *The Leadership Quarterly, 6*, 529–558.

O'Connor, S., & Rosenblood, L. (1996). Affiliation motivation in everyday experience: A theoretical perspective. *Journal of Personality and Social Psychology, 70*, 513–522.

Oddone-Paolucci, E., Genuis, M., & Violato, C. (2000). A meta-analysis of the published research on the effects of pornography. In C. Violato, E. Oddone-Paolucci, & M. Genuis (Eds.), *The changing family and child development* (pp. 48–59). Aldershot, UK: Ashgate.

O'Donnell, C. R. (1995). Firearm deaths among children and youth. *American Psychologist, 50*, 771–776.

Ogilvie, C. A., Newman, E., Todd, L., & Peck, D. (2014). Attachment and violent offending: A meta-analysis. *Aggression and Violent Behavior, 19*, 322–339.

Öhman, A., & Soares, J. J. F. (1994). "Unconscious anxiety": Phobic responses to masked stimuli. *Journal of Abnormal Psychology, 103*, 231–240.

Olson, J. M. (1988). Misattribution, preparatory information, and speech anxiety. *Journal of Personality and Social Psychology, 54*, 758–767.

Olson, J. M., & Fazio, R. H. (2002). Implicit acquisition and manifestation of classically conditioned attitudes. *Social cognition, 20*, 89–103.

Olson, J. M., & Zanna, M. P. (1993). Attitudes and attitude change. *Annual Review of Psychology, 44*, 117–154.

Omoto, A. M., & Snyder, M. (2002). Considerations of community: The context and process of volunteerism. *American Behavioral Scientist, 45,* 846–867.

Omoto, A. M., Snyder, M., & Hackett, J. D. (2010). Personality and motivational antecedents of activism and civic engagement. *Journal of Personality, 78,* 1703–1734.

Opotow, S. (1990). Moral exclusion and injustice: An introduction. *Journal of Social Issues, 46,* 1–20.

Oppenheim, A. N. (1992). *Questionnaire design, interviewing and attitude measurement* (2nd ed.). London: Pinter.

Orano, P. (1901). *Psicologia sociale.* Bari, Italy: Lacerta.

Orne, M. T. (1962). On the social psychology of the psychology experiment: With particular reference to demand characteristics and their implications. *American Psychologist, 17,* 776–783.

Ortony, A., & Turner, T. J. (1990). What's basic about basic emotions? *Psychological Review, 97,* 315–331.

Orvis, B. R., Kelley, H. H., & Butler, D. (1976). Attributional conflicts in young couples. In J. H. Harvey, W. J. Ickes, & R. F. Kidd (Eds.), *New directions in attribution research* (Vol. 1, pp. 353–386). Hillsdale, NJ: Erlbaum.

Orwell, G. (1962). *The road to Wigan pier.* Harmondsworth, UK: Penguin.

Osborn, A. F. (1957). *Applied imagination* (Rev. ed.). New York: Charles Scribner's Sons.

Osgood, C. E. (1962). *An alternative to war or surrender.* Urbana, IL: University of Illinois Press.

Osgood, C. E., Suci, G. J., & Tannenbaum, P. H. (1957). *The measurement of meaning.* Urbana, IL: University of Illinois Press.

Oskamp, S. (1977). *Attitudes and opinions.* Englewood Cliffs, NJ: Prentice Hall.

Oskamp, S. (1984). *Applied social psychology.* Englewood Cliffs, NJ: Prentice Hall.

Osterman, L. L., & Brown, R. P. (2011). Culture of honor and violence against the self. *Personality and Social Psychology Bulletin, 37,* 1611–1623.

Ostrom, T. M. (1968). The relationship between the affective, behavioural, and cognitive components of attitude. *Journal of Experimental Social Psychology, 5,* 12–30.

Ostrom, T. M. (1989b). Interdependence of attitude theory and measurement. In A. R. Pratkanis, S. J. Breckler, & A. G. Greenwald (Eds.), *Attitude structure and function* (pp. 11–36). Hillsdale, NJ: Erlbaum.

Ostrom, T. M., & Sedikides, C. (1992). Outgroup homogeneity effects in natural and minimal groups. *Psychological Bulletin, 112,* 536–552.

Oswald, F. L., Mitchell, G., Blanton, H., Jaccard, J., & Tetlock, P. E. (2013). Predicting ethnic and racial discrimination: A meta-analysis of IAT criterion studies. *Journal of Personality and Social Psychology, 105,* 171–192.

Oswald, P. A. (1996). The effects of cognitive and affective perspective taking on empathic concern and altruistic helping. *Journal of Social Psychology, 136,* 613–623.

Otten, S., Mummendey, A., & Blanz, M. (1996). Intergroup discrimination in positive and negative outcome allocations: Impact of stimulus valence, relative group status, and relative group size. *Personality and Social Psychology Bulletin, 22,* 568–581.

Otten, S., & Wentura, D. (1999). About the impact of automaticity in the minimal group paradigm: Evidence from affective priming tasks. *European Journal of Social Psychology, 29,* 1049–1071.

Overall, N. C., Fletcher, G. J. O., & Simpson, J. A. (2006). Regulation processes in intimate relationships: The role of ideal standards. *Journal of Personality and Social Psychology, 91,* 662–685.

Overall, N. C., Fletcher, G. J. O., Simpson, J. A., & Sibley, C. G. (2009). Regulating partners in intimate relationships: The costs and benefits of different communication strategies. *Journal of Personality and Social Psychology, 96,* 620–639.

Overall, N. C., Girme, Y. U., Lemay E. P. Jr, & Hammond, M. D. (2014). Attachment anxiety and reactions to relationship threat: The benefits and costs of inducing guilt in romantic partners. *Journal of Personality and Social Psychology, 106,* 235–256.

Oyserman, D. (2007). Social identity and self-regulation. In A. W. Kruglanski & E. T. Higgins (Eds.), *Social psychology: Handbook of basic principles* (2nd ed., pp. 432–453). New York: Guilford.

Oyserman, D., Coon, H. M., & Kemmelmeier, M. (2002). Rethinking individualism and collectivism: Evaluation of theoretical assumptions and meta-analyses. *Psychological Bulletin, 128,* 3–72.

Pagel, M. D., & Davidson, A. R. (1984). A comparison of three social-psychological models of attitude and behavioral plan: Prediction of contraceptive behavior. *Journal of Personality and Social Psychology, 47,* 517–533.

Paglia, A., & Room, R. (1999). Expectancies about the effects of alcohol on the self and on others as determinants of alcohol policy. *Journal of Applied Social Psychology, 29,* 2632–2651.

Paik, H., & Comstock, G. (1994). The effects of television violence on antisocial behaviour: A meta-analysis. *Communication Research, 21,* 516–546.

Paladino, M. -P., Zaniboni, S., Fasoli, F., Vaes, J., & Volpato, C. (2014). Why did Italians protest against Berlusconi's sexist behaviour? The role of sexist beliefs and emotional reactions in explaining women and men's pathways to protest. *British Journal of Social Psychology, 53,* 201–216.

Palomares, N. A. (2004). Gender schematicity, gender identity salience, and gender-linked language use. *Human Communication Research, 30,* 556–588.

Palomares, N. A. (2012). Gender and intergroup communication. In H. Giles (Ed), *The handbook of intergroup communication* (pp. 197–210). New York: Routledge.

Pandey, J., Sinha, Y., Prakash, A., & Tripathi, R. C. (1982). Right–left political ideologies and attribution of the causes of poverty. *European Journal of Social Psychology, 12,* 327–331.

Pantin, H. M., & Carver, C. S. (1982). Induced competence and the bystander effect. *Journal of Applied Social Psychology, 12,* 100–111.

Paolacci, G., & Chandler, J. (2014). Inside the Turk: Understanding Mechanical Turk as a participant pool. *Current Directions in Psychological Science, 23,* 184–188.

Paolacci, G., Chandler, J., & Ipeirotis, P. G. (2010). Running experiments on Amazon Mechanical Turk. *Judgment and Decision Making, 5,* 411–419.

Papastamou, S. (1986). Psychologization and processes of minority and majority influence. *European Journal of Social Psychology, 16,* 165–180.

Parducci, A. (1968). The relativism of absolute judgments. *Scientific American, 219,* 84–90.

Park, B. (1986). A method for studying the development of impressions of real people. *Journal of Personality and Social Psychology, 51,* 907–917.

Park, B., & Hastie, R. (1987). Perception of variability in category development: Instance- versus abstraction-based stereotypes. *Journal of Personality and Social Psychology, 53,* 621–635.

Park, B., & Rothbart, M. (1982). Perception of outgroup homogeneity and levels of social categorization: Memory for the subordinate attributes of ingroup and outgroup members. *Journal of Personality and Social Psychology, 42,* 1051–1068.

Park, S., & Catrambone, R. (2012). Social facilitation effects of virtual humans. *Human Factors, 49,* 1054–1060.

Parker, D., Manstead, A. S. R., & Stradling, S. G. (1995). Extending the theory of planned behaviour: The role of personal norm. *British Journal of Social Psychology, 34,* 127–137.

Parkinson, B. (1985). Emotional effects of false autonomic feedback. *Psychological Bulletin, 98,* 471–494.

Parkinson, B., & Manstead, A. S. R. (1992). Appraisal as a cause of emotion. In M. S. Clark (Ed.), *Emotion* (pp. 122–149) Newbury Park, CA: Sage.

Parsons, J. E., Adler, T., & Meece, J. L. (1984). Sex differences in achievement: A test of alternate theories. *Journal of Personality and Social Psychology, 46,* 26–43.

Pascoe, E. A., & Richman, L. S. (2009). Perceived discrimination and health: A meta-analytic review. *Psychological Bulletin, 135,* 531–554.

Patch, M. E. (1986). The role of source legitimacy in sequential request strategies of compliance. *Personality and Social Psychology Bulletin, 12,* 199–205.

Patterson, F. (1978). Conversations with a gorilla. *National Geographic, 154,* 438–465.

Patterson, M. L. (1983). *Nonverbal behavior: A functional perspective.* New York: Springer.

Paulhus, D. L., & Levitt, K. (1987). Desirable responding triggered by affect: Automatic egotism. *Journal of Personality and Social Psychology, 52,* 245–259.

Paulhus, D. L., & Williams, K. M. (2002). The dark triad of personality. *Journal of Research in Personality, 36,* 556–563.

Paulus, P. B., Dzindolet, M. T., Poletes, G., & Camacho, L. M. (1993). Perception of performance in group brainstorming: The illusion of group productivity. *Personality and Social Psychology Bulletin, 19,* 78–89.

Pavelchak, M. A., Moreland, R. L., & Levine, J. M. (1986). Effects of prior group memberships on subsequent reconnaissance activities. *Journal of Personality and Social Psychology, 50,* 56–66.

Pawlik, K., & Rosenzweig, M. R. (Eds.) (2000). *International handbook of psychology.* London: SAGE.

Pazda, A. D., Elliott, A. J., & Greitmeyer, T. (2012). Sexy red: Perceived sexual receptivity mediates the red-attraction relation in men viewing woman. *Journal of Experimental Social Psychology, 48,* 787–790.

Pechmann, C., & Esteban, G. (1994). Persuasion processes associated with direct comparative and noncomparative advertising and implications for advertising effectiveness. *Journal of Consumer Psychology, 2,* 403–432.

Pedersen, A., Walker, I., & Glass, C. (1999). Experimenter effects on ingroup preference and self-concept of urban Aboriginal children. *Australian Journal of Psychology, 51,* 82–89.

Pedersen, D. M. (1999). Models for types of privacy by privacy functions. *Journal of Environmental Psychology, 19,* 397–405.

Pedersen, W. C., Vasquez, E. A., Bartholow, B. D., Grosvenor, M., & Truong, A. (2014). Are you insulting me? Exposure to alcohol primes increases aggression following ambiguous provocation. *Personality and Social Psychology Bulletin, 40,* 1037–1049.

Peeters, G., & Czapinski, J. (1990). Positive–negative asymmetry in evaluations: The distinction between affective and informational negativity effects. *European Review of Social Psychology, 1,* 33–60.

Pei, M. (1965). *The story of language* (2nd ed.). Philadelphia, PA: Lippincott.

Peng, K., & Nisbett, R. E. (1999). Culture, dialectics, and reasoning about contradiction. *American Psychologist, 54,* 741–754.

Pennebaker, J. W. (1997). Writing about emotional experiences as a therapeutic process. *Psychological Science, 8,* 162–166.

Penrod, S., & Hastie, R. (1980). A computer simulation of jury decision making. *Psychological Review, 87,* 133–159.

Pepitone, A. (1981). Lessons from the history of social psychology. *American Psychologist, 36,* 972–985.

Peplau, L. A., & Fingerhut, A. W. (2007). The close relationships of lesbians and gay men. *Annual Review of Psychology, 58,* 400–424.

Peplau, L. A., & Perlman, D. (Eds.) (1982). *Loneliness: A sourcebook of current theory, research and therapy.* New York: Wiley.

Peretti-Watel, P., Obadia, Y., Dray-Spira, R., Lert, F., & Moatti, J.-P. (2005). Attitudes and behaviours of people living with HIV/AIDS and mass media prevention campaign: A French survey. *Psychology, Health and Medicine, 10,* 215–224.

Pérez, J. A., & Mugny, G. (1998). Categorization and social influence. In S. Worchel & J. M. Francisco (Eds.), *Social identity: International perspectives* (pp. 142–153). London: SAGE.

Perkins, A. M., Inchley-Mort, S. L., Pickering, A. D., Corr, P. J., & Burgess, A. P. (2012). A facial expression for anxiety. *Journal of Personality and Social Psychology, 102,* 910–924.

Perlman, D., & Oskamp, S. (1971). The effects of picture content and exposure frequency on evaluations of Negroes and Whites. *Journal of Experimental Social Psychology, 7,* 503–514.

Perlman, D., & Peplau, L. A. (1998). Loneliness. *Encyclopedia of mental health* (Vol. 2, pp. 571–581). New York: Academic Press.

Perry, D. G., Perry L., & Boldizar, J. P. (1990). Learning of aggression. In M. Lewis & S. Miller (Eds.), *Handbook of developmental psychopathology* (pp. 135–146). New York: Plenum.

Perry, D. G., Perry, L., Bussey, K., English, D., & Arnold, G. (1980). Processes of attribution and children's self-punishment following misbehaviour. *Child Development, 51,* 545–551.

Peters, K., Morton, T. A., & Haslam, S. A. (2010). Communication silos and social identity complexity in organizations. In H. Giles, S. A. Reid, & J. Harwood (Eds.), *Dynamics of intergroup communication* (pp. 221–234). New York: Peter Lang.

Peters, L. H., Hartke, D. D., & Pohlmann, J. T. (1985). Fiedler's contingency theory of leadership: An application of the meta-analytic procedure of Schmidt and Hunter. *Psychological Bulletin, 97,* 274–285.

Peters, L. H., O'Connor, E. J., Weekley, J., Pooyan, A., Frank, B., & Erenkrantz, B. (1984). Sex bias and managerial evaluation: A replication and extension. *Journal of Applied Psychology, 69,* 349–352.

Peterson, C. (1980). Memory and the 'dispositional shift'. *Social Psychology Quarterly, 43,* 372–380.

Peterson, C., Semmel, A., Von Baeyer, C., Abramson, L. Y., Metalsky, G. I., & Seligman, M. E. P. (1982). The attributional style questionnaire. *Cognitive Therapy and Research, 6,* 287–300.

Peterson, R., & Nemeth, C. (1996). Focus versus flexibility: Majority and minority influence can both improve performance. *Personality and Social Psychology Bulletin, 22,* 14–23.

Pettigrew, T. F. (1958). Personality and sociocultural factors in intergroup attitudes: A cross-national comparison. *Journal of Conflict Resolution, 2,* 29–42.

Pettigrew, T. F. (1971). *Racially separate or together.* New York: McGraw-Hill.

Pettigrew, T. F. (1979). The ultimate attribution error: Extending Allport's cognitive analysis of prejudice. *Personality and Social Psychology Bulletin, 5,* 461–476.

Pettigrew, T. F. (1981). Extending the stereotype concept. In D. L. Hamilton (Ed.), *Cognitive processes in stereotyping and intergroup behavior* (pp. 303–332). Hillsdale, NJ: Erlbaum.

Pettigrew, T. F. (1987). *Modern racism: American Black–White relations since the 1960s.* Cambridge, MA: Harvard University Press.

Pettigrew, T. F. (1998). Intergroup contact theory. *Annual Review of Psychology, 49,* 65–85.

Pettigrew, T. F., & Meertens, R. W. (1995). Subtle and blatant prejudice in Western Europe. *European Journal of Social Psychology, 25,* 57–75.

Pettigrew, T. F., & Tropp, L. R. (2006). A meta-analytic test of intergroup contact theory. *Journal of Personality and Social Psychology, 90,* 751–783.

Petty, R. E., & Cacioppo, J. T. (1979). Issue-involvement can increase or decrease persuasion by enhancing message-relevant cognitive responses. *Journal of Personality and Social Psychology, 37,* 1915–1926.

Petty, R. E., & Cacioppo, J. T. (1981). *Attitudes and persuasion: Classic and contemporary approaches.* Dubuque, IA: Brown.

Petty, R. E., & Cacioppo, J. T. (1986a). *Communication and persuasion: Central and peripheral routes to attitude change.* New York: Springer.

Petty, R. E., & Cacioppo, J. T. (1986b). The elaboration likelihood model of persuasion. *Advances in Experimental Social Psychology, 19,* 123–205.

Petty, R. E., Schuman, D. W., Richman, S. A., & Stratham, A. J. (1993). Positive mood and persuasion: Different roles for affect under high- and low-elaboration conditions. *Journal of Personality and Social Psychology, 64,* 5–20.

Petty, R. E., & Wegener, D. (1998) Attitude change: Multiple roles for persuasion variables. In D. T. Gilbert, S. T. Fiske, & G. Lindzey (Eds.) *The handbook of social psychology* (4th ed., Vol. 2, pp. 323–390). New York: McGraw-Hill.

Pevers, B. H., & Secord, P. F. (1973). Developmental changes in attribution of descriptive concepts to persons. *Journal of Personality and Social Psychology, 27,* 120–128.

Pfau, M., Compton, J. A., Parker, K. A., Wittenberg, E. M., An, C., Ferguson, M., et al. (2004). The traditional explanation for resistance versus attitude accessibility: Do they trigger distinct or overlapping processes of resistance? *Human Communication Research, 30,* 329–360.

Pfau, M., Roskos-Ewoldsen, D., Wood, M., Yin, S., Cho, J., Lu, K. H., et al. (2003). Attitude accessibility as an alternative explanation for how inoculation confers resistance. *Communication Monographs, 70,* 39–51.

Pheterson, G. I., Kiesler, S. B., & Goldberg, P. A. (1971). Evaluation of the performance of women as a function of their success, achievements and personal history. *Journal of Personality and Social Psychology, 19,* 114–118.

Phillips, D. P. (1986). Natural experiments on the effects of mass media violence on fatal aggression: Strengths and weaknesses of a new approach. *Advances in Experimental Social Psychology, 19*, 207–250.

Phinney, J. S., & Rotheram, M. J. (Eds.) (1987). *Children's ethnic socialization: Pluralism and development*. Newbury Park, CA: SAGE.

Piaget, J. (1928). *The child's conception of the world*. London: Routledge & Kegan Paul.

Piaget, J. (1955). *The child's construction of reality*. London: Routledge & Kegan Paul.

Pilger, J. (1989). *A secret country*. London: Vantage.

Piliavin, J. A., & Charng, H.-W. (1990). Altruism: A review of recent theory and research. *Annual Review of Sociology, 16*, 27–65.

Piliavin, J. A., Piliavin, I. M., Dovidio, J. F., Gaertner, S. L., & Clark, R. D., III. (1981). *Emergency intervention*. New York: Academic Press.

Pinker, S. (2011). *The better angels of our nature: The decline of violence and its causes*. London: Allen Lane.

Pinto, I. R., Marques, J. M., Levine, J. M., & Abrams, D. (2010). Membership status and subjective group dynamics: Who triggers the black sheep effect? *Journal of Personality and Social Psychology, 99*, 107–119.

Pittam, J., & Gallois, C. (1996). The mediating role of narrative in intergroup processes: Talking about AIDS. *Journal of Language and Social Psychology, 15*, 312–334.

Pittinsky, T. (Ed.). (2009). *Crossing the divide: Intergroup leadership in a world of difference*. Cambridge, MA: Harvard Business Publishing.

Pittinsky, T. L., & Simon, S. (2007). Intergroup leadership. *The Leadership Quarterly, 18*, 586–605.

Plaks, J., Levy, S. R., & Dweck, C. (2009). Lay theories of personality: Cornerstones of meaning in social cognition. *Social and Personality Psychology Compass, 3*, 1069–1081.

Platow, M. J., Reid, S. A., & Andrew, S. (1998). Leadership endorsement: The role of distributive and procedural behavior in interpersonal and intergroup contexts. *Group Processes and Intergroup Relations, 1*, 35–47.

Platow, M. J., & Van Knippenberg, D. (2001). A social identity analysis of leadership endorsement: The effects of leader ingroup prototypicality and distributive intergroup fairness. *Personality and Social Psychology Bulletin, 27*, 1508–1519.

Platow, M. J., Van Knippenberg, D., Haslam, S. A., Van Knippenberg, B., & Spears, R. (2006). A special gift we bestow on you for being representative of us: Considering leader charisma from a self-categorization perspective. *British Journal of Social Psychology, 45*, 303–320.

Platz, S. J., & Hosch, H. M. (1988). Cross-racial/ethnic eyewitness identification: A field study. *Journal of Applied Social Psychology, 18*, 972–984.

Plous, S., & Williams, T. (1995). Racial stereotypes from the days of American slavery: A continuing legacy. *Journal of Applied Social Psychology, 25*, 795–817.

Pomazal, R. J., & Clore, G. L. (1973). Helping on the highway: The effects of dependency and sex. *Journal of Applied Social Psychology, 3*, 150–164.

Popp, D., Donovan, R. A., Crawford, M., Marsh, K. L., & Peele, M. (2003). Gender, race, and speech style stereotypes. *Sex Roles, 48*, 317–325.

Poppe, E., & Linssen, H. (1999). Ingroup favouritism and the reflection of realistic dimensions of difference between national states in Central and Eastern European nationality stereotypes. *British Journal of Social Psychology, 38*, 85–102.

Popper, K. (1969). *Conjectures and refutations* (3rd ed.). London: Routledge & Kegan Paul.

Postmes, T., & Spears, R. (1998). Deindividuation and anti-normative behavior: A meta-analysis. *Psychological Bulletin, 123*, 238–259.

Postmes, T., Spears, R., & Lea, M. (1998). Breaching or building social boundaries? SIDE-effects of computer-mediated communication. *Communication Research, 25*, 689–715.

Postmes, T., Spears, R., Sakhel, K., & de Groot, D. (2001). Social influence in computer-mediated communication: The effects of anonymity on group behavior. *Personality and Social Psychology Bulletin, 27*, 1243–1254.

Potter, J. (1996). *Representing reality*. London: SAGE.

Potter, J., Stringer, P., & Wetherell, M. S. (1984). *Social texts and context: Literature and social psychology*. London: Routledge and Kegan Paul.

Potter, J., & Wetherell, M. S. (1987). *Discourse and social psychology: Beyond attitudes and behaviour*. London: SAGE.

Potter, J., Wetherell, M. S., Gill, R., & Edwards, D. (1990). Discourse: Noun, verb or social practice? *Philosophical Psychology, 3*, 205–217.

Powell, M. C., & Fazio, R. H. (1984). Attitude accessibility as a function of repeated attitudinal expression. *Personality and Social Psychology Bulletin, 10*, 139–148.

Pratkanis, A. R., & Greenwald, A. G. (1989). A sociocognitive model of attitude structure and function. *Advances in Experimental Social Psychology, 22*, 245–285.

Pratkanis, A. R., Greenwald, A. G., Leippe, M. R., & Baumgardner, M. H. (1988). In search of reliable persuasion effects: III. The sleeper effect is dead. Long live the sleeper effect. *Journal of Personality and Social Psychology, 54*, 203–218.

Pratto, F. (1999). The puzzle of continuing group inequality: Piecing together psychological, social and cultural forces in social dominance theory. *Advances in Experimental Social Psychology, 31*, 191–263.

Pratto, F., Sidanius, J., Stallworth, L. M., & Malle B. F. (1994). Social dominance orientation: A personality variable predicting social and political attitudes. *Journal of Personality and Social Psychology, 67*, 741–763.

Prentice, D. A., & Eberhardt, J. (Eds.) (2008). *Social neuroscience and intergroup behavior*. (Special issue of *Group Processes and Intergroup Relations* – all Vol 11, Issue 2). London: SAGE.

Prentice, D. A., & Miller, D. T. (1993). Pluralistic ignorance and alcohol use on campus: Some consequences of misperceiving the social norm. *Journal of Personality and Social Psychology, 64*, 243–256.

Prentice, D. A., & Miller, D. T. (Eds.) (1999). *Cultural divides: Understanding and overcoming group conflict*. New York: Russell Sage Foundation.

Prentice, D. A., Miller, D., & Lightdale, J. R. (1994). Asymmetries in attachment to groups and to their members: Distinguishing between common-identity and common-bond groups. *Personality and Social Psychology Bulletin, 20*, 484–493.

Prentice-Dunn, S., & Rogers, R. W. (1982). Effects of public and private self-awareness on deindividuation and aggression. *Journal of Personality and Social Psychology, 43*, 503–513.

Price-Williams, D. (1976). Cross-cultural studies. In L. A. Samovar & R. E. Porter (Eds.), *Intercultural communication: A reader* (2nd ed., pp. 32–48). Belmont, CA: Wadsworth.

Prisbell, M. (1985). Assertiveness, shyness and nonverbal communication behaviors. *Communication Research Reports, 2*, 120–127.

Pronin, E., Steele, C. M., & Ross, L. (2004). Identity bifurcation in response to stereotype threat: Women and mathematics. *Journal of Experimental Social Psychology, 40*, 152–168.

Pruitt, D. G. (1981). *Negotiation behavior*. New York: Academic Press.

Pryor, J. B., & Ostrom, T. M. (1981). The cognitive organization of social information: A converging-operations approach. *Journal of Personality and Social Psychology, 41*, 628–641.

Przybyla, D. P. J. (1985). *The facilitating effects of exposure to erotica on male prosocial behavior*. Unpublished doctoral dissertation, State University of New York at Albany.

Purkhardt, S. C. (1995). *Transforming social representations*. London: Routledge.

Pyszczynski, T., Greenberg, J., & Solomon, S. (1999). A dual-process model of defense against conscious and unconscious death-related thoughts: An extension of terror management theory. *Psychological Review, 106*, 835–845.

Pyszczynski, T., Greenberg, J., & Solomon, S. (2004). Why do people need self-esteem? A theoretical and empirical review. *Psychological Bulletin, 130*, 435–468.

Pyszczynski, T. A., & Greenberg, J. (1981). Role of disconfirmed expectancies in the instigation of attributional processing. *Journal of Personality and Social Psychology, 40*, 31–38.

Quattrone, G. A. (1986). On the perception of a group's variability. In S. Worchel & W. Austin (Eds.), *The psychology of intergroup relations* (Vol. 2, pp. 25–48). New York: Nelson-Hall.

Quattrone, G. A., & Jones, E. E. (1980). The perception of variability within ingroups and outgroups: Implications for the law of small numbers. *Journal of Personality and Social Psychology, 38,* 141–152.

Quigley-Fernandez, B., & Tedeschi, J. T. (1978). The bogus pipeline as lie detector: Two validity studies. *Journal of Personality and Social Psychology, 36,* 247–256.

Rabbie, J. M., & Bekkers, F. (1978). Threatened leadership and intergroup competition. *European Journal of Social Psychology, 8,* 9–20.

Rabbie, J. M., & DeBrey, J. H. C. (1971). The anticipation of intergroup cooperation and competition under private and public conditions. *International Journal of Group Tensions, 1,* 230–251.

Rabbie, J. M., & Horwitz, M. (1969). Arousal of ingroup–outgroup bias by a chance win or loss. *Journal of Personality and Social Psychology, 13,* 269–277.

Rabbie, J. M., Schot, J. C., & Visser, L. (1989). Social identity theory: A conceptual and empirical critique from the perspective of a behavioural interaction model. *European Journal of Social Psychology, 19,* 171–202.

Rabbie, J. M., & Wilkens, G. (1971). Ingroup competition and its effect on intragroup relations. *European Journal of Social Psychology, 1,* 215–234.

Rafiq, U., Jobanuptra, N., & Muncer, S. (2006). Comparing the perceived causes of the second Iraq war: A network analysis approach. *Aggressive Behavior, 32,* 321–329.

Ramirez, J., Bryant, J., & Zillman, D. (1983). Effects of erotica on retaliatory behavior as a function of level of prior provocation. *Journal of Personality and Social Psychology, 43,* 971–978.

Randsley de Moura, G., Abrams, D., Hutchison, P., & Marques, J. M. (2011). Leadership deviance. In J. Jetten & M. Hornsey (Eds.), *Rebels in groups: Dissent, deviance, difference and defiance* (pp. 238–258). Oxford, UK: Blackwell.

Rankin, R. E., & Campbell, D. T. (1955). Galvanic skin response to Negro and White experimenters. *Journal of Abnormal and Social Psychology, 51,* 30–33.

Rapley, M. (1998). 'Just an ordinary Australian': Self- categorization and the discursive construction of facticity in 'new racist' political rhetoric. *British Journal of Social Psychology, 37,* 325–344.

Rapoport, A. (1976). *Experimental games and their uses in psychology.* Morristown, NJ: General Learning Press.

Rast, D. E., III, Hogg, M. A., & Giessner, S. R. (2013). Self-uncertainty and support for autocratic leadership. *Self and Identity, 12,* 635–649.

Rauer, A. J., Sabey, A., & Jensen, J. F. (2014). Growing old together: Compassionate love and health in older adulthood. *Journal of Social and Personal Relationships, 31,* 671–696.

Raven, B. H. (1965). Social influence and power. In I. D. Steiner & M. Fishbein (Eds.), *Current studies in social psychology* (pp. 371–382). New York: Holt, Rinehart & Winston.

Raven, B. H. (1993). The bases of power: Origins and recent developments. *Journal of Social Issues, 49,* 227–251.

Raven, B. H., & French, J. R. P. (1958). Legitimate power, coercive power and observability in social influence. *Sociometry, 21,* 83–97.

Ray, M. L. (1988). *Short-term evidence of advertising's long-term effect* (Report no. 88–107). Cambridge, MA: Marketing Science Institute.

Reeder, G. D., & Brewer, M. B. (1979). A schematic model of dispositional attribution in interpersonal perception. *Psychological Review, 86,* 61–79.

Regan, D. T., & Fazio, R. H. (1977). On the consistency of attitudes and behavior: Look to the method of attitude formation. *Journal of Experimental Social Psychology, 13,* 38–45.

Regan, D. T., Williams, M., & Sparling, S. (1972). Voluntary expiation of guilt: A field experiment. *Journal of Personality and Social Psychology, 24,* 42–45.

Regan, J. (1971). Guilt, perceived injustice, and altruistic behaviour. *Journal of Personality and Social Psychology, 18,* 124–132.

Regan, P. C., & Berscheid, E. (1999). *Lust: What we know about human sexual desire.* Thousand Oaks, CA: SAGE.

Rego, A., Vitória, A. Magalhães, A., Ribeiro, N., & e Cunha, M. (2013). Are authentic leaders associated with more virtuous, committed and potent teams? *The Leadership Quarterly, 24,* 61–79.

Regoeczi, W. C. (2003). When context matters: A multilevel analysis of household and neighbourhood crowding on aggression and withdrawal. *Journal of Environmental Psychology, 23,* 457–470.

Reicher, S., Haslam, S. A., & Hopkins, N. (2005). Social identity and the dynamics of leadership: Leaders and followers as collaborative agents in the transformation of social reality. *The Leadership Quarterly, 16,* 547–568.

Reicher, S. D. (1982). The determination of collective behaviour. In H. Tajfel (Ed.), *Social identity and intergroup relations* (pp. 41–83). Cambridge, UK: Cambridge University Press.

Reicher, S. D. (1984). Social influence in the crowd: Attitudinal and behavioural effects of deindividuation in conditions of high and low group salience. *British Journal of Social Psychology, 23,* 341–350.

Reicher, S. D. (1987). Crowd behaviour as social action. In J. C. Turner, M. A. Hogg, P. J. Oakes, S. D. Reicher, & M. S. Wetherell, *Rediscovering the social group: A self- categorization theory* (pp. 171–202). Oxford, UK: Blackwell.

Reicher, S. D. (1996). Social identity and social change: Rethinking the context of social psychology. In W. P. Robinson (Ed.), *Social groups and identities: Developing the legacy of Henri Tajfel* (pp. 317–336). Oxford, UK: Butterworth-Heinemann.

Reicher, S. D. (2001). The psychology of crowd dynamics. In M. A. Hogg & R. S. Tindale (Eds.), *Blackwell handbook of social psychology: Group processes* (pp. 182–207). Oxford, UK: Blackwell.

Reicher, S. D., & Emler, N. (1985). Delinquent behaviour and attitudes to formal authority. *British Journal of Social Psychology, 24,* 161–168.

Reicher, S. D., & Haslam, S. A. (2006). Rethinking the psychology of tyranny: The BBC prison study. *British Journal of Social Psychology, 45,* 1–40.

Reicher, S. D., Haslam, S. A., & Smith, J. R. (2012). Working toward the experimenter: Reconceptualizing obedience within the Milgram paradigm as identification-based followership. *Perspectives on Psychological Science, 7,* 315–324.

Reicher, S. D., & Hopkins, N. (1996a). Seeking influence through characterising self-categories: An analysis of anti-abortionist rhetoric. *British Journal of Social Psychology, 35,* 297–311.

Reicher, S. D., & Hopkins, N. (1996b). Self-category constructions in political rhetoric: An analysis of Thatcher's and Kinnock's speeches concerning the British miners' strike (1984–5). *European Journal of Social Psychology, 26,* 353–371.

Reicher, S. D., & Hopkins, N. (2001). *Self and nation.* London: SAGE.

Reicher, S. D., & Hopkins, N. (2003). On the science of the art of leadership. In D. Van Knippenberg & M. A. Hogg (Eds.), *Leadership and power: Identity processes in groups and organizations* (pp. 197–209). London: SAGE.

Reicher, S. D., Hopkins, N., Levine, M., & Rath, R. (2005). Entrepreneurs of hate and entrepreneurs of solidarity: Social identity as a basis for mass communication. *International Review of the Red Cross, 87,* 621–637.

Reicher, S. D., & Potter, J. (1985). Psychological theory as intergroup perspective: A comparative analysis of 'scientific' and 'lay' accounts of crowd events. *Human Relations, 38,* 167–189.

Reicher, S. D., Spears, R., & Postmes, T. (1995). A social identity model of deindividuation phenomena. *European Review of Social Psychology, 6,* 161–198.

Reicher, S. D., & Stott, C. (2011). *Mad mobs and Englishmen? Myths and realities of the 2011 riots.* London: Constable and Robinson.

Reid, S. A., & Ng, S. H. (1999). Language, power, and intergroup relations. *Journal of Social Issues, 55,* 119–139.

Reid, S. A., & Ng, S. H. (2000). Conversation as a resource for influence: Evidence for prototypical arguments and social identification processes. *European Journal of Social Psychology, 30,* 83–100.

Reis, H. T., Maniaci, M. R., Caprariello, P. A., Eastwick, P. W., & Finkel, E. J. (2011). Familiarity does indeed promote attraction in live interaction. *Journal of Personality and Social Psychology, 101,* 557–570.

Reis, H. T., Maniaci, M. R., & Rogge, R. D. (2014). The expression of compassionate love in everyday compassionate acts. *Journal of Social and Personal Relationships, 31,* 651–676.

Reis, H. T., & Sprecher, S (Eds.) (2009) *Encyclopedia of human relationships.* Thousand Oaks, CA: SAGE.

Reisenzein, R. (1983). The Schachter theory of emotion: Two decades later. *Psychological Bulletin, 94*, 239–264.

Rempel, J. K., Ross, M., & Holmes, J. G. (2001). Trust and communicated attributions in close relationships. *Journal of Personality and Social Psychology, 81*, 57–64.

Renzetti, C. M. (2006). Commentary on Swan and Snow's 'The development of a theory of women's use of violence in intimate relationships'. *Violence Against Women, 12*, 1046–1047.

Reynolds, K. J., Turner, J. C., Haslam, S. A., & Ryan, M. K. (2001). The role of personality and group factors in explaining prejudice. *Journal of Experimental Social Psychology, 37*, 427–434.

Rhodes, G. (2006). The evolutionary psychology of facial beauty. *Annual Review of Psychology, 57*, 199–226.

Rhodes, G., Hickford, C., & Jeffrey, L. (2000). Sex-typicality and attractiveness: Are supermale and superfemale faces super-attractive? *British Journal of Psychology, 91*, 125–140.

Rhodes, G., Sumich, A., & Byatt, G. (1999). Are average facial configurations attractive only because of their symmetry? *Psychological Science, 10*, 52–58.

Rhodes, G., & Tremewan, T. (1996). Averageness, exaggeration, and facial attractiveness. *Psychological Science, 2*, 105–110.

Rhodes, N., & Wood, W. (1992). Self-esteem and intelligence affect influenceability: The mediating role of message reception. *Psychological Bulletin, 111*, 156–171.

Rhodewalt, F., & Strube, M. J. (1985). A self-attribution reactance model for health outcomes. *Journal of Applied Social Psychology, 15*, 330–344.

Rholes, W. S., & Pryor, J. B. (1982). Cognitive accessibility and causal attributions. *Personality and Social Psychology Bulletin, 8*, 719–727.

Rholes, W. S., & Simpson, J. A. (2004). *Adult attachment: Theory, research, and clinical implications.* New York: Guilford Press.

Rholes, W. S., Simpson, J. A., & Blakely, B. S. (1995). Adult attachment styles and mothers' relationships with their young children. *Personal Relationships, 2*, 35–54.

Rholes, W. S., Simpson, J. A., & Friedman, M. (2006). Avoidant attachment and the experience of parenting. *Personality and Social Psychology Bulletin, 32*, 275–285.

Rice, M. E., & Grusec, J. E. (1975). Saying and doing: Effects on observer performance. *Journal of Personality and Social Psychology, 32*, 584–593.

Rice, R. W. (1978). Construct validity of the least preferred co-worker score. *Psychological Bulletin, 85*, 1199–1237.

Rice, R. W., Instone, D., & Adams, J. (1984). Leader sex, leader success, and leadership process: Two field studies. *Journal of Applied Psychology, 69*, 12–31.

Ridgeway, C. L. (2001). Social status and group structure. In M. A. Hogg & R. S. Tindale (Eds.), *Blackwell handbook of social psychology: Group processes* (pp. 352–375). Oxford, UK: Blackwell.

Ridgeway, C. L. (2003). Status characteristics and leadership. In D. Van Knippenberg & M. A. Hogg (Eds.), *Leadership and power: Identity processes in groups and organizations* (pp. 65–78). London: SAGE.

Riess, M., Kalle, R. J., & Tedeschi, J. T. (1981). Bogus pipeline attitude assessment, impression management, and misattribution in induced compliance settings. *Journal of Social Psychology, 115*, 247–258.

Riess, M., Rosenfield, R., Melburg, V., & Tedeschi, J. T. (1981). Self-serving attributions: Biased private perceptions and distorted public descriptions. *Journal of Personality and Social Psychology, 41*, 224–231.

Riggio, H. R. (2004). Parental marital conflict and divorce, parent–child relationships, social support, and relationship anxiety in young adulthood. *Personal Relationships, 11*, 99–114.

Riggio, R. E., & Carney, D. R. (2003). *Social skills inventory manual* (2nd ed.). Redwood City, CA: MindGarden.

Riggio, R. E., Chaleff, I., & Lipman-Blumen, J. (Eds.). (2008). *The art of followership: How great followers create great leaders and organizations.* San Francisco: Jossey-Bass.

Ringelmann, M. (1913). Recherches sur les moteurs animés: Travail de l'homme. *Annales de l'Institut National Agronomique, 2*(12), 1–40.

Riopelle, A. J. (1987). Instinct. In R. J. Corsini (Ed.), *Concise encyclopedia of psychology* (pp. 599–600). New York: Wiley.

Risen, J. L., & Gilovich, T. (2007). Another look at why people are reluctant to exchange lottery tickets. *Journal of Personality and Social Psychology, 93*, 12–22.

Robinson, J. P., Shaver, P. R., & Wrightsman, L. S. (Eds.) (1991). *Measures of personality and social psychological attitudes.* New York: Academic Press.

Robinson, R. J., Keltner, D., Ward, A., & Ross, L. (1995). Actual versus assumed differences in construal: Realism in intergroup perception and conflict. *Journal of Personality and Social Psychology, 68*, 404–417.

Roccas, S., & Brewer, M. B. (2002). Social identity complexity. *Personality and Social Psychology Review, 6*, 88–109.

Rodriguez Mosquera, P. M. (2013). In the name of honor. On virtue, reputation, and violence. *Group Processes and Intergroup Relations, 16*, 271–278.

Roethlisberger, F., & Dickson, W. (1939). *Management and the worker.* Cambridge, MA: Harvard University Press.

Rogers, R. W., & Prentice-Dunn, S. (1981). Deindividuation and anger-mediated interracial aggression: Unmasking regressive racism. *Journal of Personality and Social Psychology, 41*, 63–73.

Rogers, W. S. (2003). *Social psychology: Experimental and critical approaches.* Maidenhead, UK: Open University Press.

Rogoff, B. (2003). *The cultural nature of human development.* Oxford, UK: Oxford University Press.

Rohan, M. (2000). A rose by any name? The values construct. *Personality and Social Psychology Review, 4*, 255–277.

Rohmer, O., & Louvet, E. (2012). Implicit measures of the stereotype content associated with disability. *British Journal of Social Psychology, 51*, 732–740.

Rohrer, J. H., Baron, S. H., Hoffman, E. L., & Swander, D. V. (1954). The stability of autokinetic judgments. *Journal of Abnormal and Social Psychology, 49*, 595–597.

Rokeach, M. (1948). Generalized mental rigidity as a factor in ethnocentrism. *Journal of Abnormal and Social Psychology, 43*, 259–278.

Rokeach, M. (1973). *The nature of human values.* New York: Free Press.

Rokeach, M. (Ed.) (1960). *The open and closed mind.* New York: Basic Books.

Rokeach, M., & Mezei, L. (1966). Race and shared belief as factors in social choice. *Science, 151*, 167–172.

Rommetveit, R. (1974). *On message structure: A framework for the study of language and communication.* New York: Wiley.

Ronay, R., & Von Hippel, W. (2010). The presence of an attractive woman elevates testosterone and physical risk taking in young men. *Social Psychological and Personality Science, 1*, 57–64.

Rosch, E. (1978). Principles of categorization. In E. Rosch & B. B. Lloyd (Eds.), *Cognition and categorization* (pp. 27–48). Hillsdale, NJ: Erlbaum.

Rose, H., & Rose, S. (Eds.) (2000). *Alas, poor Darwin: Arguments against evolutionary psychology.* London: Vintage.

Rosenberg, M. J. (1969). The conditions and consequences of evaluation apprehension. In R. Rosenthal & R. L. Rosnow (Eds.), *Artifact in behavioral research* (pp. 280–349). New York: Academic Press.

Rosenberg, M. J. (1979). *Conceiving the self.* New York: Basic Books.

Rosenberg, M. J., & Hovland, C. I. (1960). Cognitive, affective, and behavioral components of attitude. In M. J. Rosenberg, C. I. Hovland, W. J. McGuire, R. P. Abelson, & J. W. Brehm (Eds.), *Attitude organization and change: An analysis of consistency among attitude components.* New Haven, CT: Yale University Press.

Rosenberg, S., Nelson, C., & Vivekanathan, P. S. (1968). A multidimensional approach to the structure of personality impressions. *Journal of Personality and Social Psychology, 39*, 283–294.

Rosenberg, S., & Sedlak, A. (1972). Structural representations of implicit personality theory. *Advances in Experimental Social Psychology, 6*, 235–297.

Rosenberg, S. W., & Wolfsfeld, G. (1977). International conflict and the problem of attribution. *Journal of Conflict Resolution, 21*, 75–103.

Rosenfeld, H. M. (1965). Effect of approval-seeking induction on interpersonal proximity. *Psychological Reports, 17*, 120–122.

Rosenfeld, D., Greenberg, J., Folger, R., & Borys, R. (1982). Effect of an encounter with a Black panhandler on subsequent helping for Blacks:

Tokenism or conforming to a negative stereotype? *Personality and Social Psychology Bulletin, 8,* 664–671.

Rosenfield, D., & Stephan, W. G. (1977). When discounting fails: An unexpected finding. *Memory and Cognition, 5,* 97–102.

Rosenkoetter, L. I. (1999). The television situation comedy and children's prosocial behavior. *Journal of Applied Social Psychology, 29,* 979–993.

Rosenthal, D. (1987). Ethnic identity development in adolescents. In J. S. Phinney & M. J. Rotheram (Eds.), *Children's ethnic socialisation: Pluralism and development* (pp. 156–179). Newbury Park, CA: SAGE.

Rosenthal, R. (1966). *Experimenter effects in behavioral research.* New York: Appleton-Century-Crofts.

Rosenthal, R., Hall, J. A., DiMatteo, M. R., Rogers, P. L., & Archer, D. (1979). *Sensitivity to nonverbal communication: The PONS test.* Baltimore, MD: Johns Hopkins University Press.

Rosenthal, R., & Jacobson, L. F. (1968). *Pygmalion in the classroom.* New York: Holt, Rinehart & Winston.

Rosenthal, R., & Rubin, D. B. (1978). Interpersonal expectancy effects: The first 345 studies. *Behavioral and Brain Sciences, 3,* 377–386.

Rosenthal, S. A., & Pittinsky, T. L. (2006). Narcissistic leadership. *The Leadership Quarterly, 17,* 617–633.

Rosip, J. C., & Hall, J. A. (2004). Knowledge of nonverbal cues, gender, and nonverbal decoding accuracy. *Journal of Nonverbal Behavior, 28,* 267–286.

Roskos-Ewoldsen, D. R., & Fazio, R. H. (1992). On the orienting value of attitudes: Attitude accessibility as a determinant of an object's attraction of visual attention. *Journal of Personality and Social Psychology, 63,* 198–211.

Rosnow, R. L. (1980). Psychology of rumour reconsidered. *Psychological Bulletin, 87,* 578–591.

Rosnow, R. L. (1981). *Paradigms in transition: The methodology of social enquiry.* Oxford, UK: Oxford University Press.

Ross, E. A. (1908). *Social psychology.* New York: Macmillan.

Ross, L. (1977). The intuitive psychologist and his shortcomings. *Advances in Experimental Social Psychology, 10,* 174–220.

Ross, L., Greene, D., & House, P. (1977). The 'false consensus effect': An egocentric bias in social perception and attribution processes. *Journal of Experimental Social Psychology, 13,* 279–301.

Ross, L., Lepper, M., & Ward, A. (2010). History of social psychology: Insights, challenges, and contributions to theory and application. In S. T. Fiske, D. T. Gilbert, & G. Lindzey (Eds.), *Handbook of social psychology* (5th ed., Vol. 1, pp. 3–50). New York: Wiley.

Ross, L., Lepper, M. R., & Hubbard, M. (1975). Perseverance in self-perception and social perception: Biased attribution processes in the debriefing paradigm. *Journal of Personality and Social Psychology, 32,* 880–892.

Ross, L., & Nisbett, R. E. (1991). *The person and the situation: Perspectives of social psychology.* New York: McGraw-Hill.

Ross, L., & Ward, A. (1995). Psychological barriers to dispute resolution. *Advances in Experimental Social Psychology, 27,* 255–304.

Ross, M., & Fletcher, G. J. O. (1985). Attribution and social perception. In G. Lindzey & E. Aronson (Eds.), *Handbook of social psychology* (3rd ed., Vol. 2, pp. 73–122). New York: Random House.

Rothbart, M. (1981). Memory processes and social beliefs. In D. L. Hamilton (Ed.), *Cognitive processes in stereotyping and intergroup behavior* (pp. 145–182). Hillsdale, NJ: Erlbaum.

Rothbart, M., & John, O. P. (1985). Social categorization and behavioral episodes: A cognitive analysis of intergroup contact. *Journal of Social Issues, 41,* 81–104.

Rothbart, M., & Park, B. (1986). On the confirmability and disconfirmability of trait concepts. *Journal of Personality and Social Psychology, 50,* 131–142.

Rothman, A. J., & Salovey, P. (1997). Shaping perceptions to motivate healthy behaviour: The role of message framing. *Psychological Bulletin, 121,* 3–19.

Rothman, A. J., & Salovey, P. (2007). The reciprocal relation between principles and practice: Social psychology and health behaviour. In A. W. Kruglanski & E. T. Higgins (Eds.), *Social psychology: A handbook of basic principles* (2nd ed., pp. 826–849). New York: Guilford Press.

Rotter, J. B. (1966). Generalized expectancies for internal versus extern control of reinforcement. *Psychological Monographs, 80,* whole no. 609.

Rotter, J. B. (1980). Trust and gullibility. *Psychology Today, 14*(5), pp. 35–38, 40, 42, 102.

Ruback, R. B., & Pandey, J. (1992). Very hot and really crowded: Quasi-experimental investigations of Indian 'tempos'. *Environment and Behavior, 24,* 527–554.

Rubin, A. M. (1978). Child and adolescent television use and political socialization. *Journalism Quarterly, 55,* 125–129.

Rubin, J. (1976). How to tell when someone is saying no. *Topics in Culture Learning, 4,* 61–65.

Rubin, J. (1980). Experimental research on third-party intervention in conflict: Toward some generalizations. *Psychological Bulletin, 87,* 379–391.

Rubin, M., & Hewstone, M. (1998). Social identity theory's self-esteem hypothesis: A review and some suggestions for clarification. *Personality and Social Psychology Review, 2,* 40–62.

Rubin, Z. (1973). *Liking and loving: An invitation to social psychology.* New York: Holt, Rinehart and Winston.

Rubini, M., Menegatti, M., & Moscatelli, S. (2014). The strategic role of language abstraction in achieving symbolic and practical goals. *European Review of Social Psychology, 25,* 263–313.

Ruckmick, C. A. (1912). The history and status of psychology in the United States. *American Journal of Psychology, 23,* 517–531.

Ruddell, R., Thomas, M. O., & Way, L. B. (2005). Breaking the chain: Confronting issueless college town disturbances and riots. *Journal of Criminal Justice, 33,* 549–560.

Rudman, L. A. (1998). Self-promotion as a risk factor for women: The costs and benefits of counterstereotypical impression management. *Journal of Personality and Social Psychology, 74,* 629–645.

Rudman, L. A., & Glick, P. (1999). Feminized management and backlash toward agentic women: The hidden costs to women of a kinder, gentler image of middle managers. *Journal of Personality and Social Psychology, 75,* 1004–1010.

Rudman, L. A., & Glick, P. (2001). Prescriptive gender stereotypes and backlash against agentic women. *Journal of Social Issues, 57,* 743–762.

Rudman, L. A., & Mescher, K. (2012). Of animals and objects: Men's implicit dehumanization of women and likelihood of sexual aggression. *Personality and Social Psychology Bulletin, 38,* 734–746.

Ruggiero, K. M., & Taylor, D. M. (1995). Coping with discrimination: How disadvantaged group members perceive the discrimination that confronts them. *Journal of Personality and Social Psychology, 68,* 826–838.

Ruiz-Belda, M.-A., Fernández-Dols, J.-M., Carrera, P., & Barchard, K. (2003). Spontaneous facial expressions of happy bowlers and soccer fans. *Cognition and Emotion, 17,* 315–326.

Rumelhart, D. E., & Ortony, A. (1977). The representation of knowledge in memory. In C. R. Anderson, R. J. Spiro, & W. E. Montague (Eds.), *Schooling and the acquisition of knowledge* (pp. 99–136). Hillsdale, NJ: Erlbaum.

Rummel, R. J. (1988). *Political systems, violence, and war.* Paper presented at the United States Institute of Peace Conference, Airlie, VA.

Runciman, W. G. (1966). *Relative deprivation and social justice.* London: Routledge and Kegan Paul.

Rusbult, C., Finkel, E., & Kumashiro, M. (2009). The Michelangelo phenomenon. *Current Directions in Psychological Science, 18,* 305–309.

Rusbult, C. E., Martz, J. M., & Agnew, C. R. (1998). The Investment Model Scale: Measuring commitment level, satisfaction level, quality of alternatives, and investment size. *Personal Relationships, 5,* 357–391.

Rusbult, C. E., & Zembrodt, I. M. (1983). Responses to dissatisfaction in romantic involvements: A multi-dimensional scaling analysis. *Journal of Experimental Social Psychology, 19,* 274–293.

Rushton, J. P. (1976). Socialization and the altruistic behavior of children. *Psychological Bulletin, 83,* 898–913.

Rushton, J. P. (1979). Effects of prosocial television and film material on the behavior of viewers. *Advances in Experimental Social Psychology, 12,* 322–351.

Rushton, J. P. (1980). *Altruism, socialisation, and society.* Englewood Cliffs, NJ: Prentice Hall.

Rushton, J. P., & Teachman, G. (1978). The effects of positive reinforcement, attributions, and punishment on model induced altruism in children. *Personality and Social Psychology Bulletin, 4*, 322–325.

Russell, G. W. (2004). Sport riots: A social psychological review. *Aggression and Violent Behavior, 9*, 353–378.

Russell, J. A. (1994). Is there universal recognition of emotion from facial expressions? A review of the cross-cultural studies. *Psychological Bulletin, 115*, 102–141.

Russell, J. A. (2003). Core affect and psychological construct of emotion. *Psychological Review, 110*, 145–172.

Russell, J. A., Bachorowski, J.-A., & Fernandez-Dols, J.-M. (2003). Facial and vocal expressions of emotion. *Annual Review of Psychology, 54*, 329–349.

Russell, J. A., & Fernandez-Dols, J. M. (Eds.) (1997). *The psychology of facial expression: Studies in emotion and social interaction.* Cambridge, UK: Cambridge University Press.

Rutkowski, G. K., Gruder, C. L., & Romer, D. (1983). Group cohesiveness, social norms, and bystander intervention. *Journal of Personality and Social Psychology, 44*, 545–552.

Rutland, A. (1999). The development of national prejudice, ingroup favouritism and self-stereotypes in British children. *British Journal of Social Psychology, 38*, 55–70.

Rutland, A., & Cinnirella, M. (2000). Context effects on Scottish national and European self-categorizations: The importance of category accessibility, fragility and relations. *British Journal of Social Psychology, 39*, 495–519.

Rutte, C. G., & Wilke, H. A. M. (1984). Social dilemmas and leadership. *European Journal of Social Psychology, 14*, 105–121.

Ryan, E. B., Bajorek, S., Beaman, A., & Anas, A. P. (2005). I just want to know that 'Them' is me: Intergroup perspectives on communication and disability. In J. Harwood & H. Giles (Eds.), *Intergroup communication: Multiple perspectives* (pp. 117–137). New York: Peter Lang.

Ryan, E. B., Giles, H., Bartolucci, G., & Henwood, K. (1986). Psycholinguistic and social psychological components of communication by and with the elderly. *Language and Communication, 6*, 1–24.

Ryan, M. K., & Haslam, S. A., (2007). The glass cliff: Exploring the dynamics surrounding the appointment of women to precarious leadership positions. *Academy of Management Review, 32*, 549–572.

Ryan, M. K., Haslam, S. A., Hersby, M. D., & Bongiorno, R. (2011). Think crisis–think female: Glass cliffs and contextual variation in the think manager–think male stereotype. *Journal of Applied Psychology, 96*, 470–484.

Ryan, M. K., Haslam, S. A., & Kulich, C. (2010). Politics and the glass cliff: Evidence that women are preferentially selected to contest hard-to-win seats. *Psychology of Women Quarterly, 34*, 56–64.

Ryan, M. K., Haslam, S. A., Morgenroth, T., Rink, F., Stoker, J., & Peters, K. (2016). Getting on top of the glass cliff: Reviewing a decade of evidence, Explanations, and impact. *The Leadership Quarterly, 27*, 446–455.

Ryan, T. (1985). Human nature and the origins of war. *Hurupaa, 3*, 46–54.

Ryen, A. H., & Kahn, A. (1975). Effects of intergroup orientation on group attitudes and proxemic behavior. *Journal of Personality and Social Psychology, 31*, 302–310.

Sabini, J., & Silver, M. (1982). *The moralities of everyday life.* New York: Oxford University Press.

Sachdev, I., & Bourhis, R. Y. (1993). Ethnolinguistic vitality: Some motivational and cognitive considerations. In M. A. Hogg & D. Abrams (Eds.), *Group motivation: Social psychological perspectives* (pp. 33–51). Hemel Hempstead, UK: Harvester Wheatsheaf.

Sachdev, I., & Bourhis, R. Y. (2005). Multilingual communication and social identification. In J. Harwood & H. Giles (Eds.), *Intergroup communication: Multiple perspectives* (pp. 65–91). New York: Peter Lang Publishing.

Sachdev, I., & Wright, A. (1996). Social influence and language learning: An experimental study. *Journal of Language and Social Psychology, 15*, 230–245.

Sagi, A., & Hoffman, M. (1976). Emphatic distress in the newborn. *Developmental Psychology, 12*, 175–176.

Saint-Blancat, C. (1985). The effect of minority group vitality upon its sociopsychological behaviour and strategies. *Journal of Multilingual and Multicultural Development, 6*, 31–44.

St Claire, L., & Turner, J. C. (1982). The role of demand characteristics in the social categorization paradigm. *European Journal of Social Psychology, 12*, 307–314.

Saks, M. J. (1978). Social psychological contributions to a legislative committee on organ and tissue transplants. *American Psychologist, 33*, 680–690.

Saks, M. J., & Marti, M. W. (1997). A meta-analysis of the effects of jury size. *Law and Human Behavior, 21*, 451–467.

Salovey, P., Rothman, A. J., & Rodin, J. (1998). Health behaviour. In D. T. Gilbert, S. T. Fiske, & G. Lindzey (Eds.), *The handbook of social psychology* (4th ed., Vol. 2, pp. 633–683). New York: McGraw-Hill.

Sampson, E. E. (1977). Psychology and the American ideal. *Journal of Personality and Social Psychology, 35*, 767–782.

San Antonio, P. M. (1987). Social mobility and language use in an American company in Japan. *Journal of Language and Social Psychology, 6*, 191–200.

Sanders, G. S. (1981). Driven by distraction: An integrative review of social facilitation theory and research. *Journal of Experimental Social Psychology, 17*, 227–251.

Sanders, G. S. (1983). An attentional process model of social facilitation. In A. Hare, H. Blumberg, V. Kent, & M. Davies (Eds.). *Small groups.* London: Wiley.

Sanders, G. S., & Baron, R. S. (1977). Is social comparison relevant for producing choice shift? *Journal of Experimental Social Psychology, 13*, 303–314.

Sanders, G. S., Baron, R. S., & Moore, D. L. (1978). Distraction and social comparison as mediators of social facilitation. *Journal of Experimental Social Psychology, 14*, 291–303.

Sanders, G. S., & Mullen, B. (1983). Accuracy in perceptions of consensus: Differential tendencies of people with majority and minority positions. *European Journal of Social Psychology, 13*, 57–70.

Sani, F. (2005). When subgroups secede: Extending and refining the social psychological model of schisms in groups. *Personality and Social Psychology Bulletin, 31*, 1074–1086.

Sani, F., & Reicher, S. D. (1998). When consensus fails: An analysis of the schism within the Italian Communist Party (1991). *European Journal of Social Psychology, 28*, 623–45.

Sani, F., & Reicher, S. D. (2000). Contested identities and schisms in groups: Opposing the ordination of women as priests in the Church of England. *British Journal of Social Psychology, 39*, 95–112.

Sansone, C., Morf, C. C., & Panter, A. T. (Eds.) (2004). *The SAGE handbook of methods in social psychology.* Thousand Oaks, CA: SAGE.

Sansone, C., Weir, C., Harpster, L., & Morgan, C. (1992). Once a boring task always a boring task? Interest as a self-regulatory mechanism. *Journal of Personality and Social Psychology, 63*, 379–390.

Sargant, W. (1957). *Battle for the mind: A physiology of conversion and brainwashing.* Garden City, NY: Doubleday.

Saroja, K., & Surendra, H. S. (1991). A study of postgraduate students' endogamous preference in mate selection. *Indian Journal of Behaviour, 15*, 1–13.

Sassenberg, K. (2002). Common bond and common identity groups on the internet: Attachment and normative behavior in on-topic and off-topic chats. *Group Dynamics: Theory, Research, and Practice, 6*, 27–37.

Sassenberg, K., & Boos, M. (2003). Attitude change in computer-mediated communication: Effects of anonymity and category norms. *Group Processes and Intergroup Relations, 6*, 405–423.

Sato, K. (1987). Distribution of the cost of maintaining common resources. *Journal of Experimental Social Psychology, 23*, 19–31.

Sattler, D. N., & Kerr, N. L. (1991). Might versus morality explored: Motivational and cognitive bases for social motives. *Journal of Personality and Social Psychology, 60*, 756–765.

Saucier, G. (2000). Isms and the structure of social attitudes. *Journal of Personality and Social Psychology, 78*, 366–385.

Saxe, R., Moran, J. M., Scholz, J., & Gabrieli, J. (2006). Overlapping and non-overlapping brain regions for theory of mind and self reflection in individual subjects. *Social Cognitive and Affective Neuroscience, 1,* 229–234.

Scandura, T. A. (1999). Rethinking leader–member exchange: An organizational justice perspective. *The Leadership Quarterly, 10,* 25–40.

Schachner, D. A., Shaver, P. R., & Mikulincer, M. (2005). Patterns of nonverbal behaviour and sensitivity in the context of attachment relationships. *Journal of Nonverbal Behaviour, 29,* 141–169.

Schachter, S. (1959). *The psychology of affiliation.* Stanford, CA: Stanford University Press.

Schachter, S. (1964). The interaction of cognitive and physiological determinants of emotional state. *Advances in Experimental Social Psychology, 1,* 49–80.

Schachter, S. (1971). *Emotion, obesity, and crime.* New York: Academic Press.

Schachter, S., & Burdeck, H. (1955). A field experiment on rumour transmission and distortion. *Journal of Abnormal and Social Psychology, 50,* 363–371.

Schachter, S., & Singer, J. E. (1962). Cognitive, social and physiological determinants of emotional state. *Psychological Review, 69,* 379–399.

Schaller, M., & Crandall, C. S. (Eds.). (2004). *The psychological foundations of culture.* Mahwah, NJ: Erlbaum.

Schaller, M., Simpson, J., & Kenrick, D. (2006). *Evolution and social psychology.* New York: Psychology Press.

Schank, R. C., & Abelson, R. P. (1977). *Scripts, plans, goals, and understanding: An inquiry into human knowledge structures.* Hillsdale, NJ: Erlbaum.

Scheier, M. F., & Carver, C. S. (1981). Private and public aspects of self. In L. Wheeler (Ed.), *Review of personality and social psychology* (Vol. 2, pp. 189–216). London: SAGE.

Scherer, K. R. (1974). Acoustic concomitants of emotional dimensions: Judging affect from synthesised tone sequences. In S. Weitz (Ed.), *Nonverbal communication* (pp. 249–253). New York: Oxford University Press.

Scherer, K. R. (1978). Personality inference from voice quality: The loud voice of extroversion. *European Journal of Social Psychology, 8,* 467–488.

Scherer, K. R. (1986). Vocal affect expression: A review and model for future research. *Psychological Bulletin, 99,* 143–165.

Scherer, K. R., Abeles, R. P., & Fischer, C. S. (1975). *Human aggression and conflict.* Englewood Cliffs, NJ: Prentice Hall.

Scherer, K. R., & Giles, H. (Eds.) (1979). *Social markers in speech.* Cambridge, UK: Cambridge University Press.

Schie, E. G. M., & Wiegman, O. (1997). Children and videogames: Leisure activities, aggression, social integration, and school performance. *Journal of Applied Social Psychology, 27,* 1175–1194.

Schiller, J. C. F. (1882). *Essays, esthetical and philosophical, including the dissertation on the 'Connexions between the animal and the spiritual in man'.* London: Bell.

Schimmack, U., Oishi, S., & Diener, E. (2005). Individualism: A valid and important dimension of cultural differences. *Personality and Social Psychology Review, 9,* 17–31.

Schlenker, B. R. (1980). *Impression management: The self-concept, social identity, and interpersonal relations.* Monterey, CA: Brooks/Cole.

Schlenker, B. R., Dlugolecki, D. W., & Doherty, K. (1994). The impact of self-presentation on self-appraisal and behavior: The roles of commitment and biased scanning. *Personality and Social Psychology Bulletin, 20,* 20–33.

Schlenker, B. R., Weingold, M. F., & Hallam, J. R. (1990). Self-serving attributions in social context: Effects of self-esteem and social pressure. *Journal of Personality and Social Psychology, 58,* 855–863.

Schmader, T. (2002). Gender identification moderates stereotype threat effects on women's math performance. *Journal of Experimental Social Psychology, 38,* 194–201.

Schmader, T., Johns, M., & Forbes, C. (2008). An integrated process model of stereotype threat effects on performance. *Psychological Review, 115,* 336–356.

Schmader, T., & Martens, A. (2005). Knowing is part of the battle: Teaching stereotype threat as a means of improving women's math performance. *Psychological Science, 16,* 175–179.

Schmidt, C. F. (1972). Multidimensional scaling of the printed media's explanations of the riot of the summer of 1967. *Journal of Personality and Social Psychology, 24,* 59–67.

Schmitt, B. H., Gilovich, T., Goore, N., & Joseph, L. (1986). Mere presence and socio-facilitation: One more time. *Journal of Experimental Social Psychology, 22,* 242–248.

Schmitt, M. T., Branscombe, N. R., & Kappen, D. (2003). Attitudes toward group-based inequality: social dominance or social identity? *British Journal of Social Psychology, 42,* 161–186.

Schneider, D. J. (1973). Implicit personality theory: A review. *Psychological Bulletin, 79,* 294–309.

Schneider, D. J., Hastorf, A. H., & Ellsworth, P. C. (1979). *Person perception.* Reading, MA: Addison-Wesley.

Schoebi, D., Karney, B. R., and Bradbury, T. N. (2012). Stability and change in the first 10 years of marriage: Does commitment confer benefits beyond the effects of satisfaction? *Journal of Personality and Social Psychology, 102,* 729–742.

Schoemann, A. M., & Branscombe, N. R. (2011). Looking young for your age: Perceptions of anti-aging actions. *European Journal of Social Psychology, 41,* 86–95.

Schofield, J. W. (1986). Black–White contact in desegregated schools. In M. Hewstone & R. J. Brown (Eds.), *Contact and conflict in intergroup encounters* (pp. 79–92). Oxford, UK: Blackwell.

Schofield, J. W. (1991). School desegregation and intergroup relations: A review of the literature. In G. Grant (Ed.), *Review of research in education* (Vol. 17, pp. 335–409). Washington, DC: American Education Research Association.

Schriesheim, C. A., Castro, S. L., & Cogliser, C. C. (1999). Leader–member exchange (LMX) research: A comprehensive review of theory, measurement, and data-analytic practices. *The Leadership Quarterly, 10,* 6–113.

Schriesheim, C. A., & Neider, L. L. (1996). Path–goal leadership theory: The long and winding road. *The Leadership Quarterly, 7,* 317–321.

Schriesheim, C. A., Tepper, B. J., & Tetrault, L. A. (1994). Least preferred co-worker score, situational control, and leadership effectiveness: A meta-analysis of contingency model performance predictions. *Journal of Applied Psychology, 79,* 561–573.

Schroeder, D. A., Penner, L. A., Dovidio, J. F., & Piliavin, J. A. (1995). *The psychology of helping and altruism.* New York: McGraw-Hill.

Schubert, T. W. (2004). The power in your hand: gender differences in bodily feedback from making a fist. *Personality and Social Psychology Bulletin, 30,* 757–769.

Schul, Y. (1983). Integration and abstraction in impression formation. *Journal of Personality and Social Psychology, 44,* 45–54.

Schul, Y., & Burnstein, E. (1985). The informational basis of social judgments: Using past impression rather than the trait description in forming new impression. *Journal of Experimental Social Psychology, 21,* 421–439.

Schullo, S. A., & Alperson, B. L. (1984). Interpersonal phenomenology as a function of sexual orientation, sex, sentiment, and trait categories in long-term dyadic relationships. *Journal of Personality and Social Psychology, 47,* 983–1002.

Schwab, D. P., & Grams, R. (1985). Sex-related errors in job evaluation: A 'real-world' test. *Journal of Applied Psychology, 70,* 533–539.

Schwartz, N., & Kurz, E. (1989). What's in a picture? The impact of face-ism on trait attribution. *European Journal of Social Psychology, 19,* 311–316.

Schwartz, S. H. (1977). Normative influences on altruism. *Advances in Experimental Social Psychology, 10,* 222–279.

Schwartz, S. H. (1992). Universals in the content and structure of values: Theoretical advances and empirical tests in 20 cultures. *Advances in Experimental Social Psychology, 25,* 1–65.

Schwartz, S. H., & Bardi, A. (1997). Influences of adaptation to communist rule on value priorities in Eastern Europe. *Political Psychology, 18,* 385–410.

Schwartz, S. H., Cieciuch, J., Vecchione, M., Vecchione, E., Fischer, R. et al. (2012). Refining the theory of basic individual values. *Journal of Personality and Social Psychology, 103,* 663–668.

Schwartz, S. H., & David, T. B. (1976). Responsibility and helping in an emergency: Effects of blame, ability and denial of responsibility. *Sociometry, 39,* 406–415.

Schwarz, N. (1996). Survey research: Collecting data by asking questions. In G. R. Semin, & K. Fiedler (Eds.), *Applied social psychology* (pp. 65–90). London: SAGE.

Schwarz, N. (2000). Social judgement and attitudes: Warmer, more social, and less conscious. *European Journal of Social Psychology, 30,* 149–176.

Schwarz, N., & Strack, F. (1991). Context effects in attitude surveys: Applying cognitive theory to social research. *European Review of Social Psychology, 2,* 30–50.

Schwerin, H. S., & Newell, H. H. (1981). *Persuasion in marketing.* New York: Wiley.

Scitovsky, T. (1980). Why do we seek more and more excitement? *Stanford Observer,* October, p. 13.

Searle, A. (1987). The effects of postnatal depression on mother–infant interaction. *Australian Journal of Sex, Marriage & Family, 8,* 79–88.

Searle, J. (1979). *Expression and meaning: Studies in the theory of speech acts.* Cambridge, UK: Cambridge University Press.

Sears, D. O. (1983). The person-positivity bias. *Journal of Personality and Social Psychology, 44,* 233–250.

Sears, D. O. (1986). College sophomores in the laboratory: Influences of a narrow data base on social psychology's view of human nature. *Journal of Personality and Social Psychology, 51,* 515–530.

Sears, D. O. (1988). Symbolic racism. In P. Katz & D. Taylor (Eds.), *Towards the elimination of racism: Profiles in controversy* (pp. 53–84). New York: Plenum.

Sedikides, C. (1993). Assessment, enhancement, and verification determinants of the self-evaluation process. *Journal of Personality and Social Psychology, 65,* 317–338.

Sedikides, C. (1995). Central and peripheral self-conceptions are differentially affected by mood: Tests of the differential sensitivity hypothesis. *Journal of Personality and Social Psychology, 69,* 759–777.

Sedikides, C., & Anderson, C. A. (1994). Casual perceptions of inter-trait relations: The glue that holds person types together. *Personality and Social Psychology Bulletin, 20,* 294–302.

Sedikides, C., & Brewer, M. B. (Eds.) (2001). *Individual self, relational self, and collective self.* Philadelphia, PA: Psychology Press.

Sedikides, C., & Gregg, A. P. (2007). Portraits of the self. In M. A. Hogg & J. Cooper (Eds.), *The SAGE handbook of social psychology: Concise student edition* (pp. 93–122). London: SAGE.

Sedikides, C., & Ostrom, T. M. (1988). Are person categories used when organizing information about unfamiliar sets of persons? *Social Cognition, 6,* 252–267.

Sedikides, C., & Strube, M. J. (1997). Self-evaluation: To thine own self be good, to thine own self be sure, to thine own self be true, and to thine own self be better. *Advances in Experimental Social Psychology, 29,* 209–296.

Sedlovskaya, A., Purdie-Vaughns, V., Eibach, R. P., LaFrance, M., Romero-Canyas, R., & Camp, N. P. (2013). Internalizing the closet: Concealment heightens the cognitive distinction between public and private selves. *Journal of Personality and Social Psychology, 104,* 695–715.

Seeley, E. A., Gardner, W. L., Pennington, G., & Gabriel, S. (2003). Circle of friends or members of a group? Sex differences in relational and collective attachment to groups. *Group Processes and Intergroup Relations, 6,* 251–263.

Segall, M. H. (1965). Anthropology and psychology. In O. Klineberg & R. Christie (Eds.), *Perspectives in social psychology* (pp. 53–74). New York: Holt, Rinehart & Winston.

Seligman, M. E. P. (1991). *Learned optimism: How to change your mind and your life.* New York: Knopf.

Seligman, M. E. P., Abramson, L. Y., Semmel, A., & Von Baeyer, C. (1979). Depressive attributional style. *Journal of Abnormal Psychology, 88,* 242–247.

Seligman, M. E. P., & Csikszentmihalyi, M. (2000). Positive psychology: An introduction. *American Psychologist, 55,* 5–14.

Semin, G. R. (1980). A gloss on attribution theory. *British Journal of Social Psychology, 19,* 291–300.

Semin, G. R. (2000). Language as a cognitive and behavioral restructuring resource: Question-answer exchanges. *European Review of Social Psychology, 11,* 75–104.

Semin, G. R. (2007). Grounding communication: Synchrony. In A. W. Kruglanski & E. T. Higgins (Eds.), *Social psychology: Handbook of basic principles* (2nd ed., pp. 630–649). New York: Guilford Press.

Semin, G. R., & Fiedler, K. (1991). The linguistic category model, its bases, applications and range. *European Review of Social Psychology, 2,* 1–30.

Semmler, T., & Brewer, N. (2002). Effects of mood and emotion on juror processing and judgments. *Behavioral Sciences and the Law, 20,* 423–436.

Senchak, M., & Leonard, K. E. (1993). The role of spouses' depression and anger in the attribution–marital satisfaction relation. *Cognitive Therapy and Research, 17,* 397–409.

Seto, M. C., Maric, A., & Barbaree, H. E. (2001). The role of pornography in the etiology of sexual aggression. *Aggression and Violent Behaviour, 6,* 35–53.

Seuntjens, T. G., Zeelenberg, M., Van de Ven, N., & Breugelmans, S. M. (2015). Dispositional greed. *Journal of Personality and Social Psychology, 108,* 917–933.

Seyfarth, R. M., & Cheney, D. L. (2012). The evolutionary origins of friendship. *Annual Review of Psychology, 63,* 153–177.

Seyranian, V. (2012). Constructing extremism: Uncertainty provocation and reduction by extremist leaders. In M. A. Hogg & D. L. Blaylock (Eds.), *Extremism and the psychology of uncertainty* (pp. 228–245). Boston, MA: Wiley-Blackwell.

Seyranian, V., & Bligh, M. C. (2008). Presidential charismatic leadership: Exploring the rhetoric of social change. *The Leadership Quarterly, 19,* 54–76.

Shackelford, T. K. (2001). Cohabitation, marriage, and murder: Woman-killing by male romantic partners. *Aggressive Behavior, 274,* 284–291.

Shaffer, D. R., Rogel, M., & Hendrick, C. (1975). Intervention in the library: The effect of increased responsibility on bystanders' willingness to prevent a theft. *Journal of Applied Psychology, 5,* 303–319.

Shah, J. Y., Brazy, P. C., & Higgins, E. T. (2004). Promoting us or preventing them: Regulatory focus and manifestations of intergroup bias. *Personality and Social Psychology Bulletin, 30,* 433–446.

Shah, J. Y., Higgins, E. T., & Friedman, R. S. (1998). Performance incentives and means: How regulatory focus influences goal attainment. *Journal of Personality and Social Psychology, 74,* 285–293.

Shamir, B., House, R., & Arthur, M. (1993). The motivational effects of charismatic leadership: A self-concept based theory. *Organization Science, 4,* 1–17.

Shamir, B., Pillai, R., Bligh, M. C., & Uhl-Bien, M. (Eds.). (2006). *Follower-centered perspectives on leadership: A tribute to the memory of James R. Meindl.* Greenwich, CT: Information Age Publishing.

Shapiro, J. R., & Neuberg, S. L. (2007). From stereotype threat to stereotype threats: Implications of a multi-threat framework for causes, moderators, mediators, consequences, and interventions. *Personality and Social Psychology Review, 11,* 107–130.

Shapiro, P. N., & Penrod, S. (1986). Meta-analysis of facial identification studies. *Psychological Bulletin, 100,* 139–156.

Shariff, A. F., Willard, A. K., Andersen, T., & Norenzayan, A. (2016). Religious priming: A meta-analysis with a focus on prosociality. *Personality and Social Psychology Review, 20,* 27–48.

Sharma, N. (1981). Some aspect of attitude and behaviour of mothers. *Indian Psychological Review, 20,* 35–42.

Sharpe, D., Adair, J. G., & Roese, N. J. (1992). Twenty years of deception research: A decline in subjects' trust? *Personality and Social Psychology Bulletin, 18,* 585–590.

Shartle, C. L. (1951). Studies in naval leadership. In H. Guetzkow (Ed.), *Groups, leadership, and men* (pp. 119–133). Pittsburgh, PA: Carnegie Press.

Shaver, P. R., & Mikulincer, M. (2007). Attachment theory and research: Core concepts, basic principles, conceptual bridges. In A. W. Kruglanski & E. T. Higgins (Eds.), *Social psychology: Handbook of basic principles* (2nd ed., pp. 650–677). New York: Guilford Press.

Shaver, P. R., Morgan, H. J., & Wu, S. (1996). Is love a 'basic' emotion? *Personal Relationships, 3,* 81–96.

Shaw, L. L., Batson, C. D., & Todd, R. M. (1994). Empathy avoidance: Forestalling feeling for another in order to escape the motivational consequences. *Journal of Personality and Social Psychology, 67,* 879–887.

Shaw, M. E. (1964). Communication networks. *Advances in Experimental Social Psychology, 1,* 111–147.

Shaw, M. E. (1976). *Group dynamics* (2nd ed.). New York: McGraw-Hill.

Shaw, M. E., Rothschild, G., & Strickland, J. (1957). Decision process in communication networks. *Journal of Abnormal and Social Psychology, 54,* 323–330.

Sheehan, P. W. (1983). Age trends and the correlates of children's television viewing. *Australian Journal of Psychology, 35,* 417–431.

Sheeran, P. (2002). Intention-behavior relations: A conceptual and empirical review. *European Review of Social Psychology, 12,* 1–36.

Sheeran, P., & Taylor, S. (1999). Predicting intentions to use condoms: A meta-analysis and comparison of the theories of reasoned action and planned behavior. *Journal of Applied Social Psychology, 29,* 1624–1675.

Sheeran, P., Trafimow, D., Finlay, K., & Norman, P. (2002). Evidence that the type of person affects the strength of the perceived behavioural control–intention relationship. *British Journal of Social Psychology, 41,* 253–270.

Sheikh, S. (2014). Cultural variations in shame's responses: A dynamic perspective. *Personality and Social Psychology Review, 18,* 387–403.

Sheldon, K. M., Kashdan, T. B., & Steger, M. F. (Eds.) (2011). *Designing positive psychology: Taking stock and moving forward.* New York: Oxford University Press.

Sheppard, J. A. (1993). Productivity loss in performance groups: A motivational analysis. *Psychological Bulletin, 113,* 67–81.

Sherif, M. (1935). A study of some social factors in perception. *Archives of Psychology, 27,* 1–60.

Sherif, M. (1936). *The psychology of social norms.* New York: Harper.

Sherif, M. (Ed.) (1962). *Intergroup relations and leadership: Approaches and research in industrial, ethnic, cultural and political areas.* New York: Wiley.

Sherif, M. (1966). *In common predicament: Social psychology of intergroup conflict and cooperation.* Boston, MA: Houghton Mifflin.

Sherif, M., Harvey, O. J., White, B. J., Hood, W., & Sherif, C. (1961). *Intergroup conflict and cooperation: The robbers' cave experiment.* Norman, OK: University of Oklahoma Institute of Intergroup Relations.

Sherif, M., & Sherif, C. W. (1953). *Groups in harmony and tension: An integration of studies in intergroup relations.* New York: Harper & Row.

Sherif, M., & Sherif, C. W. (1964). *Reference groups.* New York: Harper & Row.

Sherif, M., & Sherif, C. W. (1967). Attitude as an individual's own categories: The social judgement–involvement approach to attitude and attitude change. In C. W. Sherif & M. Sherif (Eds.), *Attitude, ego-involvement, and change* (pp. 105–139). New York: Wiley.

Sherman, D. K., & Cohen, G. L. (2006). The psychology of self-defense: Self-affirmation theory. *Advances in Experimental Social Psychology, 38,* 183–242.

Sherman, D. K., Hogg, M. A., & Maitner, A. T. (2009). Perceived polarization: Reconciling ingroup and intergroup perceptions under uncertainty. *Group Processes and Intergroup Relations, 12,* 95–109.

Sherman, S. J., Presson, C. C., & Chassin, L. (1984). Mechanisms underlying the false consensus effect: The special role of threats to the self. *Personality and Social Psychology Bulletin, 10,* 127–138.

Shibutani, T. (1966). *Improvised news: A sociological study of rumor.* Indianapolis, IN: Bobbs-Merrill.

Shore, T. H. (1992). Subtle gender bias in the assessment of managerial potential. *Sex Roles, 27,* 499–515.

Shorey, R. C., Tirone, V., & Stuart, G. L. (2014). Coordinated community response components for victims of intimate partner violence: A review of the literature. *Aggression and Violent Behavior, 19,* 363–371.

Shotland, R. L., & Heinold, W. D. (1985). Bystander response to arterial bleeding: Helping skills, the decision-making process, and differentiating the helping response. *Journal of Personality and Social Psychology, 49,* 347–356.

Shotland, R. L., & Huston, T. L. (1979). Emergencies: What are they and do they influence bystanders to intervene? *Journal of Personality and Social Psychology, 37,* 1822–1834.

Shotter, J. (1984). *Social accountability and selfhood.* Oxford, UK: Blackwell.

Showers, C. (1992). Compartmentalization of positive and negative self-knowledge: Keeping bad apples out of the bunch. *Journal of Personality and Social Psychology, 62,* 1036–1049.

Showers, C., & Cantor, N. (1985). Social cognition: A look at motivated strategies. *Annual Review of Psychology, 36,* 275–305.

Shrauger, J. S., & Schoeneman, T. J. (1979). Symbolic interactionist view of self-concept: Through the looking glass darkly. *Psychological Bulletin, 86,* 549–573.

Shure, G. H., Meeker, R., & Hansford, E. A. (1965). The effectiveness of pacifist strategies in bargaining games. *Journal of Conflict Resolution, 9,* 106–117.

Shweder, R. A. (1991). *Thinking through culture: Expeditions in cultural psychology.* Cambridge, MA: Harvard University Press.

Shweder, R. A., & Bourne, E. J. (1982). Does the concept of the person vary cross-culturally? In A. J. Marsella & G. M. White (Eds.), *Cultural conceptions of mental health and therapy* (pp. 97–137). Dordrecht: Reidel.

Shweder, R. A., Much, N. C., Mahapatra, M., & Park, L. (1997). The 'big three' of morality (autonomy, community, and divinity), and the 'big three' explanations of suffering. In A. Brandt & P. Rozin (Eds.), *Morality and health* (pp. 119–169). New York: Routledge.

Sidanius, J., Levin, S., Federico, C. M., & Pratto, F. (2001). Legitimizing ideologies: The social dominance approach. In J. T. Jost & B. Major (Eds.), *The psychology of legitimacy: Emerging perspectives on ideology, justice, and intergroup relations* (pp. 307–331). New York: Cambridge University Press.

Sidanius, J., & Pratto, F. (1999). *Social dominance: An intergroup theory of social hierarchy and oppression.* New York: Cambridge University Press.

Sidnell, J. (2010). *Conversation analysis: An introduction.* London: Wiley-Blackwell.

Sidnell, J., & Stivers, T. (2012) (Eds.). *Handbook of conversation analysis.* Boston, MA: Wiley-Blackwell.

Siegel, A. E., & Siegel, S. (1957). Reference groups, membership groups, and attitude change. *Journal of Abnormal and Social Psychology, 55,* 360–364.

Siegman, A. W., & Reynolds, M. A. (1983). Self-monitoring and speech in feigned and unfeigned lying. *Journal of Personality and Social Psychology, 45,* 1325–1333.

Sigall, H., & Ostrove, N. (1975). Beautiful but dangerous: Effects of offender attractiveness and the nature of the crime on juristic judgment. *Journal of Personality and Social Psychology, 31,* 410–414.

Sillars, A. L. (1981). Attributions and interpersonal conflict resolution. In J. H. Harvey, W. J. Ickes, & R. F. Kidd (Eds.), *New directions in attribution research* (Vol. 3, pp. 281–305). Hillsdale, NJ: Erlbaum.

Silvia, P. J. (2006). Reactance and the dynamics of disagreement: Multiple paths from threatened freedom to resistance to persuasion. *European Journal of Social Psychology, 36,* 673–685.

Silvia, P. J., & Phillips, A. G. (2013). Self-awareness without awareness: Implicit self-focused attention and behavioral self-regulation. *Self and Identity, 12,* 114–127.

Simard, L., Taylor, D. M., & Giles, H. (1976). Attribution processes and interpersonal accommodation in a bi-lingual setting. *Language and Speech, 19,* 374–387.

Simmonds, D. B. (1985). The nature of the organizational grapevine. *Supervisory Management,* 39–42.

Simner, M. (1971). Newborn's response to the cry of another infant. *Developmental Psychology, 5,* 136–150.

Simon, B. (2003). *Identity in modern society: A social psychological perspective.* Oxford, UK: Blackwell.

Simon, B., & Brown, R. J. (1987). Perceived intragroup homogeneity in minority–majority contexts. *Journal of Personality and Social Psychology, 53,* 703–711.

Simonton, D. K. (1980). Land battles, generals and armies: Individual and situational determinants of victory and casualties. *Journal of Personality and Social Psychology, 38,* 110–119.

Simonton, D. K. (2003). Qualitative and quantitative analyses of historical data. *Annual Review of Psychology, 54,* 617–640.

Simpson, B., & Willer, R. (2008). Altruism and indirect reciprocity: The interaction of person and situation in prosocial behavior. *Social Psychology Quarterly, 71,* 37–52.

Simpson, J. A. (1987). The dissolution of romantic relationships: Factors involved in relationship stability and emotional distress. *Journal of Personality and Social Psychology, 53*, 683–692.

Simpson, J. A., & Kenrick, D. (1997). *Evolutionary social psychology*. Mahwah, NJ: Erlbaum.

Simpson, J. A., Campbell, B., & Berscheid, E. (1986). The association between romantic love and marriage: Kephart (1967) twice revisited. *Personality and Social Psychology Bulletin, 12*, 363–372.

Sindic, D., & Reicher, S. D. (2008). The instrumental use of group prototypicality judgments. *Journal of Experimental Social Psychology, 44*, 1425–1435.

Singer, J., Brush, C., & Lublin, S. (1965). Some aspects of deindividuation: Identification and conformity. *Journal of Experimental Social Psychology, 1*, 356–378.

Singh, R., Bohra, K. A., & Dalal, A. K. (1979). Favourableness of leadership situations studies with information integration theory. *European Journal of Social Psychology, 9*, 253–264.

Singh, R., & Ho, S. Y. (2000). Attitudes and attraction: A new test of the attraction, repulsion and similarity–dissimilarity asymmetry hypotheses. *British Journal of Social Psychology, 39*, 197–211.

Sinha, D. (1997). Indigenising psychology. In J. W. Berry, Y. Poortinga, & J. Pandey (Eds.), *Handbook of cross-cultural psychology*. Vol. 1: *Theory and method* (2nd ed., pp. 129–169). Boston. MA: Allyn & Bacon.

Sistrunk, F., & McDavid, J. W. (1971). Sex variable in conforming behavior. *Journal of Personality and Social Psychology, 17*, 200–207.

Skevington, S. (1981). Intergroup relations and nursing. *European Journal of Social Psychology, 11*, 43–59.

Skinner, B. F. (1963). Operant behavior. *American Psychologist, 18*, 503–515.

Skowronski, J. J., & Carlston, D. E. (1989). Negativity and extremity biases in impression formation: A review of explanations. *Psychological Bulletin, 105*, 131–142.

Slater, A., Von der Schulenburg, C., Brown, E., Badenoch, M., Butterworth, G., Parsons, S., & Samuels, C. (1998). Newborn infants prefer attractive faces. *Infant Behavior & Development, 21*, 345–354.

Slater, P. E. (1955). Role differentiation in small groups. *American Sociological Review, 20*, 300–310.

Smedley, J. W., & Bayton, J. A. (1978). Evaluative race–class stereotypes by race and perceived class of subjects. *Journal of Personality and Social Psychology, 3*, 530–535.

Smith, B. N., & Stasson, M. F. (2000). A comparison of health behaviour constructs: Social psychological predictors of AIDS-preventive behavioural intentions. *Journal of Applied Social Psychology, 30*, 443–462.

Smith, C. A., & Lazarus, R. S. (1990). Emotion and adaptation. In L. A. Pervin (ed.), *Handbook of personality: Theory and research* (pp. 609–637). New York: Guilford Press.

Smith, C. P. (1983). Ethical issues: Research on deception, informed consent, and debriefing. In L. Wheeler & P. Shaver (Eds.), *Review of personality and social psychology* (Vol. 4, pp. 297–328). Beverly Hills, CA: SAGE.

Smith, E. R. (1994). Social cognition contributions to attribution theory and research. In P. G. Devine, D. L. Hamilton, & T. M. Ostrom (Eds.), *Social cognition: Impact on social psychology* (pp. 77–108). San Diego, CA: Academic Press.

Smith, E. R. (2014). Evil acts and malicious gossip: A multiagent model of the effects of gossip in socially distributed person perception. *Personality and Social Psychology Review, 18*, 311–325.

Smith, E. R., Fazio, R. H., & Cejka, M. A. (1996). Accessible attitudes influence categorization of multiply categorizable objects. *Journal of Personality and Social Psychology, 71*, 888–898.

Smith, E. R., & Zárate, M. A. (1992). Exemplar-based model of social judgment. *Psychological Review, 99*, 3–21.

Smith, M. B., Bruner, J. S., & White, R. W. (1956). *Opinions and personality*. New York: Wiley.

Smith, P. B., & Bond, M. H. (1998). *Social psychology across cultures* (2nd ed.). London: Prentice Hall Europe.

Smith, P. B., Bond, M. H., & Kağitçibaşi, Ç. (2006). *Understanding social psychology across cultures*. London: SAGE.

Smith, P. B., Dugan, S., & Trompenaars, F. (1996). National culture and the values of organisational employees. *Journal of Cross-Cultural Psychology, 27*, 231–264.

Smith, P. B., Misumi, J., Tayeb, M., Peterson, M., & Bond, M. (1989). On the generality of leadership style measures across cultures. *Journal of Occupational Psychology, 62*, 97–109.

Smith, P. M. (1985). *Language, the sexes and society*. Oxford, UK: Blackwell.

Smolicz, J. J. (1983). Modification and maintenance: Language among school children of Italian background in South Australia. *Journal of Multilingual and Multicultural Development, 4*, 313–337.

Sniderman, P. M., Hagen, M. G., Tetlock, P. E., & Brady, H. E. (1986). Reasoning chains: Causal models of policy reasoning in mass publics. *British Journal of Political Science, 16*, 405–430.

Snyder, C. R., & Lopez, S. J. (Eds.) (2009). *Handbook of positive psychology* (2nd ed.). New York: Oxford University Press.

Snyder M. (1974). The self-monitoring of expressive behavior. *Journal of Personality and Social Psychology, 30*, 526–537.

Snyder, M. (1979). Self-monitoring processes. *Advances in Experimental Social Psychology, 21*, 88–131.

Snyder, M. (1981). On the self-perpetuating nature of social stereotypes. In D. L. Hamilton (Ed.), *Cognitive processes in stereotyping and intergroup behavior* (pp. 183–212). Hillsdale, NJ: Erlbaum.

Snyder, M. (1984). When belief creates reality. *Advances in Experimental Social Psychology, 18*, 248–306.

Snyder, M., & Cantor, N. (1998). Understanding personality and social behavior: A functionalist strategy. In D. T. Gilbert, S. T. Fiske, & G. Lindzey (Eds.), *Handbook of social psychology* (4th ed., Vol. 1, pp. 635–679). New York: McGraw-Hill.

Snyder, M., & Gangestad, S. (1982). Choosing social situations: Two investigations of self-monitoring processes. *Journal of Personality and Social Psychology, 43*, 123–135.

Snyder, M., & Miene, P. K. (1994). On the functions of stereotypes and prejudice. In M. P. Zanna & J. M. Olson (Eds.), *The psychology of prejudice: The Ontario symposium* (pp. 33–54). Hillsdale, NJ: Erlbaum.

Snyder, M., & Omoto, A. M. (2007). Social action. In A. W. Kruglanski & E. T. Higgins (Eds.), *Social psychology: Handbook of basic principles* (2nd ed., pp. 940–961). New York: Guilford Press.

Snyder, M. L., Stephan, W. G., & Rosenfield, D. (1978). Attributional egotism. In J. H. Harvey, W. Ickes, & R. F. Kidd (Eds.), *New directions in attribution research* (Vol. 2, pp. 91–120). Hillsdale, NJ: Erlbaum.

Soliz, J. (2010). Family as an intergroup domain. In H. Giles, S. A. Reid, & J. Harwood (Eds.), *Dynamics of intergroup communication* (pp. 181–194). New York: Peter Lang.

Solomon, S., Greenberg, J., & Pyszczynski, T. (1991). A terror management theory of social behavior: The psychological functions of self-esteem and cultural worldviews. *Advances in Experimental Social Psychology, 24*, 93–159.

Solomon, S., Greenberg, J., Pyszczynski, T., & Pryzbylinski, J. (1995). The effects of mortality salience on personally-relevant persuasive appeals. *Social Behavior and Personality, 23*, 177–190.

Sommer, R. (1969). *Personal space: The behavioral basis of design*. Englewood Cliffs, NJ: Prentice Hall.

Sorrentino, R. M., & Field, N. (1986). Emergent leadership over time: The functional value of positive motivation. *Journal of Personality and Social Psychology, 50*, 1091–1099.

Sorrentino, R. M., King, G., & Leo, G. (1980). The influence of the minority on perception: A note on a possible alternative explanation. *Journal of Experimental Social Psychology, 16*, 293–301.

Sorrentino, R. M., & Roney, C. J. R. (1999). *The uncertain mind: Individual differences in facing the unknown*. Philadelphia, PA: Psychology Press.

Spaaij, R. (2014). Sports crowd violence: An interdisciplinary synthesis. *Aggression and Violent Behavior, 19*, 146–155.

Spacapan, S., & Oskamp, S. (Eds.) (1992). *Helping and being helped*. Newbury Park, CA: SAGE.

Sparrowe, R. T., & Liden, R. C. (1997). Process and structure in leader–member exchange. *Academy of Management Review, 22*, 522–552.

Spears, R., & Lea, M. (1994). Panacea or panopticon? The hidden power in computer-mediated communication. *Communication Research, 21*, 427–459.

Spears, R., Lea, M., Postmes, T., & Wolbert, A. (2011). A SIDE look at computer-mediated interaction: Power and the gender divide. In Z.

Birchmeier, B. Dietz-Uhler, & G. Stasser (Eds.), *Strategic uses of social technology: An interactionist perspective of social psychology* (pp. 16–39). Cambridge, UK: Cambridge University Press.

Spence, J. T., Helmreich, R. L., & Stapp, J. (1974). The personal attributes questionnaire: A measure of sex role stereotypes and masculinity–femininity. *JSAS Catalog of Selected Documents in Psychology, 4*, 127.

Spencer-Rodgers, J., Williams, M. J., Hamilton, D. L., Peng, K., & Wang, L. (2007). Culture and group perception: Dispositional and stereotypic inferences about novel and national groups. *Journal of Personality and Social Psychology, 93*, 525–542.

Spitz, R. A. (1945). Hospitalism: An inquiry into the genesis of psychiatric conditions in early childhood. In A. Freud, H. Hartman, & E. Kris (Eds.), *The psychoanalytic study of the child* (Vol. 1, pp. 53–74). New York: International University Press.

Sprecher, S. (1998). Insiders' perspectives on reasons for attraction to a close other. *Social Psychology Quarterly, 61*, 287–300.

Sprecher, S. (2011). The influence of social networks on romantic relationships: Through the lens of the social network. *Personal Relationships, 18*, 630–644.

Sprecher, S., & Fehr, B. (2005). Compassionate love for close others and humanity. *Journal of Social and Personal Relationships, 22*, 629–651.

Srull, T. K. (1983). Organizational and retrieval processes in person memory: An examination of processing objectives, presentation format, and the possible role of self-generated retrieval cues. *Journal of Personality and Social Psychology, 44*, 1157–1170.

Srull, T. K., & Wyer, R. S., Jr. (1986). The role of chronic and temporary goals in social information processing. In R. M. Sorrentino & E. T. Higgins (Eds.), *Handbook of motivation and cognition: Foundations of social behavior* (pp. 503–549). New York: Guilford Press.

Srull, T. K., & Wyer, R. S., Jr. (1989). Person memory and judgement. *Psychological Review, 96*, 58–83.

Stagner, R., & Congdon, C. S. (1955). Another failure to demonstrate displacement of aggression. *Journal of Abnormal and Social Psychology, 51*, 695–696.

Stang, D. J. (1972). Conformity, ability, and self-esteem. *Representative Research in Social Psychology, 3*, 97–103.

Stang, D. J. (1976). Group size effects on conformity. *Journal of Social Psychology, 98*, 175–181.

Stangor, C. (1988). Stereotype accessibility and information processing. *Personality and Social Psychology Bulletin, 14*, 694–708.

Stangor, C. (2016). *Social groups in action and interaction* (2nd ed.). New York: Psychology Press.

Stangor, C. (Ed.) (2000). *Stereotypes and prejudice: Essential readings*. Philadelphia, PA: Psychology Press.

Stanley, D., Phelps, E., & Banaji, M. R. (2008). The neural basis of implicit attitudes. *Current Directions in Psychological Science, 17*, 164–170.

Stasser, G. (1988). Computer simulation as a research tool: The DISCUSS model of group decision making. *Journal of Experimental Social Psychology, 24*, 393–422.

Stasser, G., & Davis, J. H. (1981). Group decision making and social influence: A social interaction sequence model. *Psychological Review, 88*, 523–851.

Stasser, G., & Dietz-Uhler, B. (2001). Collective choice, judgment, and problem solving. In M. A. Hogg & R. S. Tindale (Eds.), *Blackwell handbook of social psychology: Group processes* (pp. 31–55). Oxford, UK: Blackwell.

Stasser, G., Kerr, N. L., & Bray, R. M. (1982). The social psychology of jury deliberations: Structure, process, and product. In N. Kerr & R. Bray (Eds.), *The psychology of the courtroom* (pp. 221–256). New York: Academic Press.

Stasser, G., Kerr, N. L., & Davis, J. H. (1989). Influence processes and consensus models in decision-making groups. In P. B. Paulus (Ed.), *Psychology of group influence* (2nd ed., pp. 279–326). Hillsdale, NJ: Erlbaum.

Stasser, G., & Titus, W. (2003). Hidden profiles: A brief history. *Psychological Inquiry, 14*, 304–313.

Stathi, S., Crisp, R. J., & Hogg, M. A. (2011). Imagining intergroup contact enables member-to-group generalization. *Group Dynamics, 15*, 275–284.

Staub, E. (1974). Helping a distressed person: Social, personality and stimulus determinants. *Advances in Experimental Social Psychology, 7*, 294–341.

Staub, E. (1977). *Positive social behavior and morality: I. Social and personal influences*. New York: Academic Press.

Staub, E. (1989). *The roots of evil: The psychological and cultural origins of genocide and other forms of group violence*. New York: Cambridge University Press.

Staub, E. (1996). Cultural–societal roots of violence: The example of genocidal violence and contemporary youth violence in the United States. *American Psychologist, 51*, 117–132.

Staub, E. (2000). Genocide and mass killings: Origins, prevention, healing and reconciliation. *Political Psychology, 21*, 367–382.

Staub, E. (2010). *The panorama of mass violence: Origins, prevention, healing and reconciliation*. New York: Oxford University Press.

Steele, C. M. (1975). Name-calling and compliance. *Journal of Personality and Social Psychology, 31*, 361–369.

Steele, C. M. (1988). The psychology of self-affirmation: Sustaining the integrity of the self. *Advances in Experimental Social Psychology, 21*, 261–302.

Steele, C. M., & Aronson, J. (1995). Stereotype vulnerability and the intellectual test performance of African-Americans. *Journal of Personality and Social Psychology, 69*, 797–811.

Steele, C. M., Spencer, S. J., & Aronson, J. (2002). Contending with group image: The psychology of stereotype and social identity threat. *Advances in Experimental Social Psychology, 34*, 379–440.

Steele, C. M., Spencer, S. J., & Lynch, M. (1993). Self-image resilience and dissonance: The role of affirmation resources. *Journal of Personality and Social Psychology, 64*, 885–896.

Steinberg, R., & Shapiro, S. (1982). Sex differences in personality traits of female and male master of business administration students. *Journal of Applied Psychology, 67*, 306–310.

Steiner, I. D. (1972). *Group process and productivity*. New York: Academic Press.

Steiner, I. D. (1976). Task-performing groups. In J. W. Thibaut & J. T. Spence (Eds.), *Contemporary topics in social psychology* (pp. 393–422). Morristown, NJ: General Learning Press.

Steir, C. (1978). *Blue jolts: True stories from the cuckoo's nest*. Washington, DC: New Republic Books.

Stenner, K. (2009). Three kinds of 'conservatism'. *Psychological Inquiry, 20*, 142–159.

Stephan, W. G. (1977). Cognitive differentiation in intergroup perception. *Sociometry, 40*, 50–58.

Stephan, W. G. (2014). Intergroup anxiety: Theory, research, and practice. *Personality and Social Psychology Review, 18*, 239–255.

Stephan, W. G., & Rosenfield, D. (1978). Effects of desegregation on racial attitudes. *Journal of Personality and Social Psychology, 36*, 795–804.

Stephan, W. G., & Stephan, C. W. (1984). The role of ignorance in intergroup relations. In N. Miller & M. B. Brewer (Eds.), *Groups in contact: The psychology of desegregation* (pp. 229–255). New York: Academic Press.

Stephan, W. G., & Stephan, C. W. (1985). Intergroup anxiety. *Journal of Social Issues, 41*, 157–175.

Stephan, W. G., & Stephan, C. W. (2000). An integrated threat theory of prejudice. In S. Oskamp (Ed.), *Reducing prejudice and discrimination* (pp. 23–46). Mahwah, NJ: Erlbaum.

Stephan, W. G., & Stephan, C. W. (2001). *Improving intergroup relations*. Thousand Oaks, CA: SAGE.

Stephenson, G. M., Abrams, D., Wagner, W., & Wade, G. (1986). Partners in recall: Collaborative order in the recall of a police interrogation. *British Journal of Social Psychology, 25*, 341–343.

Stephenson, G. M., Clark, N. K., & Wade, G. (1986). Meetings make evidence: An experimental study of collaborative and individual recall of a simulated police interrogation. *Journal of Personality and Social Psychology, 50*, 1113–1122.

Sternberg, R. J. (1988). *The triangle of love*. New York: Basic Books.

Stern, P. C., Dietz, T., & Guagnano, G. A. (1995). The new ecological paradigm in social psychological context. *Environment and Behavior, 27*, 723–743.

Stevens, J. R., Cushman, F. A., & Hauser, M. D. (2005). Evolving the psychological mechanisms for cooperation. *Annual Review of Ecology, Evolution and Systematics, 36,* 499–518.

Stewart, J. E. (1980). Defendant's attractiveness as a factor in the outcome of criminal trials: An observational study. *Journal of Applied Social Psychology, 10,* 348–361.

Stiglitz, J. (2002). *Globalization and its discontents.* London: Penguin.

Stith, S. M., & Farley, S. C. (1993). A predictive model of male spousal violence. *Journal of Family Violence, 8,* 183–201.

Stogdill, R. M. (1948). Personal factors associated with leadership: A survey of the literature. *Journal of Psychology, 25,* 35–71.

Stogdill, R. M. (1974). *Handbook of leadership.* New York: Free Press.

Stone, J. (2003). Self-consistency for low self-esteem in dissonance processes: The role of self-standards. *Personality and Social Psychology Bulletin, 29,* 846–858.

Stone, J., & Cooper, J. (2001). A self-standards model of cognitive dissonance. *Journal of Experimental Social Psychology, 37,* 228–243.

Stone, J., & Fernandez, N. C. (2008). To practice what we preach: The use of hypocrisy and cognitive dissonance to motivate behavior change. *Social and Personality Psychology Compass, 2,* 1024–1051.

Stone, J., Wiegand, A. W., Cooper, J., & Aronson, E. (1997). When exemplification fails: Hypocrisy and the motive for self-integrity. *Journal of Personality and Social Psychology, 72,* 54–65.

Stoner, J. A. F. (1961). *A comparison of individual and group decisions including risk.* Unpublished master's thesis, Massachusetts Institute of Technology, Boston.

Stoner, J. A. F. (1968). Risky and cautious shifts in group decisions: the influence of widely held values. *J Journal of Experimental Social Psychology, 4,* 442–459.

Storms, M. D. (1973). Videotape and the attribution process: Reversing actor's and observer's points of view. *Journal of Personality and Social Psychology, 27,* 165–175.

Storms, M. D., & Nisbett, R. E. (1970). Insomnia and the attribution process. *Journal of Personality and Social Psychology, 16,* 319–328.

Stott, C. J., & Adang, O. M. J. (2004). 'Disorderly' conduct: social psychology and the control of football 'hooliganism' at 'Euro2004'. *The Psychologist, 17,* 318–319.

Stott, C. J., Hutchison, P., & Drury, J (2001). 'Hooligans' abroad? Intergroup dynamics, social identity and participation in collective disorder at the 1998 World Cup finals. *British Journal of Social Psychology, 40,* 359–384.

Stouffer, S. A., Suchman, E. A., DeVinney, L. C., Star, S. A., & Williams, R. M., Jr (1949). *The American soldier. I: Adjustment during Army life.* Princeton, NJ: Princeton University Press.

Strauman, T. J., Lemieux, A. M., & Coe, C. L. (1993). Self-discrepancy and natural killer cell activity: Immunological consequences of negative self-evaluation. *Journal of Personality and Social Psychology, 64,* 1042–1052.

Straus, M. A., Gelles, R. J., & Steinmetz, S. K. (1980). *Behind closed doors: Violence in the American family.* Garden City, NY: Anchor Books.

Straus, M. A. (2001). *Beating the devil out of them: Corporal punishment in American families and its effects on children.* New Brunswick, NJ: Transaction.

Straus, M. A., Sugarman, D. B., & Giles-Sims, J. (1997). Spanking by parents and subsequent antisocial behaviour of children. *Archives of Pediatrics and Adolescent Medicine, 151,* 761–767.

Straus, S., & McGrath, J. E. (1994). Does the medium matter? The interaction of task type and technology on group performance and member reactions. *Journal of Applied Psychology, 79,* 87–97.

Strick, M., Holland, R. W., Van Baaren, R. B., Van Knippenberg, A., & Dijksterhuis, A. (2013). Humour in advertising: An associative processing model. *European Review of Social Psychology, 24,* 32–69.

Strickland, L. H., Aboud, F. E., & Gergen, K. J. (Eds.) (1976). *Social psychology in transition.* New York: Plenum.

Strodtbeck, F. L., James, R., & Hawkins, C. (1957). Social status in jury deliberations. *American Sociological Review, 22,* 713–718.

Strodtbeck, F. L., & Lipinski, R. M. (1985). Becoming first among equals: Moral considerations in jury foreman selection. *Journal of Personality and Social Psychology, 49,* 927–936.

Stroebe, W. (2011). *Social psychology and health* (3rd ed.). Maidenhead, England: Open University Press/McGraw Hill.

Stroebe, W. (2014). Firearm possession and violent death: A critical review. *Aggression and Violent Behavior, 18,* 709–721.

Stroebe, W., & Diehl, M. (1994). Why groups are less effective than their members: On productivity losses in idea-generating groups. *European Review of Social Psychology, 5,* 271–303.

Stroebe, W., Diehl, M., & Abakoumkin, G. (1992). The illusion of group effectivity. *Personality and Social Psychology Bulletin, 18,* 643–650.

Stroebe, W., & Frey, B. S. (1982). Self-interest and collective action: The economics and psychology of public goods. *British Journal of Social Psychology, 21,* 121–137.

Stroebe, W., Lenkert, A., & Jonas, K. (1988). Familiarity may breed contempt: The impact of student exchange on national stereotypes and attitudes. In E. W. Stroebe, A. Kruglanski, D. Bar-Tal, & M. Hewstone (Eds.), *The social psychology of intergroup conflict: Theory, research and applications* (pp. 167–187). New York: Springer.

Stroebe, W., Postmes, T. and Spears, R. (2012). Scientific misconduct and the myth of self-correction in science. *Perspectives on Psychological Science, 7,* 670–688.

Strube, M. J., & Garcia, J. E. (1981). A meta-analytic investigation of Fiedler's contingency model of leadership effectiveness. *Psychological Bulletin, 90,* 307–321.

Strube, M. J., Turner, C. W., Cerro, D., Stevens, J., & Hinchey, F. (1984). Interpersonal aggression and the type A coronary-prone behavior pattern: A theoretical distinction and practical implications. *Journal of Personality and Social Psychology, 47,* 839–847.

Struch, N., & Schwartz, S. H. (1989). Intergroup aggression: Its predictors and distinctiveness from ingroup bias. *Journal of Personality and Social Psychology, 56,* 364–373.

Stryker, S., & Statham, A. (1986). Symbolic interaction and role theory. In G. Lindzey & E. Aronson (Eds.), *The handbook of social psychology* (3rd ed., Vol. 1, pp. 311–378). New York: Random House.

Stürmer, S., & Simon, B. (2004). Collective action: Towards a dual-pathway model. *European Review of Social Psychology, 15,* 59–99.

Sullivan, K. T., Pasch, L. A., Johnson, M. D., & Bradbury, T. N. (2010). Social support, problem solving, and the longitudinal course of newlywed marriage. *Journal of Personality and Social Psychology, 98,* 631–644.

Suls, J., & Wheeler, L. (Eds.) (2000). *Handbook of social comparison: Theory and research.* New York: Kluwer/Plenum.

Suls, J. M., & Miller, R. L. (Eds.) (1977). *Social comparison processes: Theoretical and empirical perspectives.* Washington, DC: Hemisphere Press.

Sumner, W. G. (1906). *Folkways.* Boston, MA: Ginn.

Sundberg, N. D. (1977). *Assessment of persons.* Englewood Cliffs, NJ: Prentice Hall.

Surowiecki, J. (2004). *The wisdom of crowds: Why the many are smarter than the few and how collective wisdom shapes business, economies, societies, and nations.* New York: Doubleday.

Sussenbach, P., & Bohner, G. (2011). Acceptance of sexual aggression myths in a representative sample of German residents. *Aggressive Behavior, 37,* 374–385.

Sussenbach, P., & Bohner, G., & Eyssel, F. (2012). Schematic influences of rape myth acceptance on visual information processing: An eye-tracking approach. *Journal of Experimental Social Psychology, 48,* 660–668.

Sutton, R., & Douglas, K. (2013). *Social psychology.* London: Palgrave Macmillan.

Swann, W. B. (1984). Quest for accuracy in person perception: A matter of pragmatics. *Psychological Review, 91,* 457–477.

Swann, W. B. (1987). Identity negotiation: Where two roads meet. *Journal of Personality and Social Psychology, 53,* 1038–1051.

Swann, W. B., & Bosson, J. K. (2010) Self and identity. In S. T. Fiske, D. T. Gilbert, & G. Lindzey (Eds.), *Handbook of social psychology* (5th ed., Vol. 1, pp. 589–628). New York: Wiley.

Swann, W. B., Gómez, Á., Seyle, D. C., Morales, J. F., & Huici, C. (2009). Identity fusion: The interplay of personal and social identities in extreme group behavior. *Journal of Personality and Social Psychology, 96,* 995–1011.

Swann, W. B., Hixon, J. G., & de la Ronde, C. (1992). Embracing the bitter 'truth': Negative self-concepts and marital commitment. *Psychological Science, 3*, 118–121.

Swann, W. B., Jetten, J., Gomez, A., Whitehouse, H., & Bastian, B. (2012). When group membership gets personal: A theory of identity fusion. *Psychological Review, 119*, 441–456.

Sweeney, P. D., Anderson, K., & Bailey, S. (1986). Attribution style in depression: A meta-analytic review. *Journal of Personality and Social Psychology, 50*, 974–991.

Sweldens, S., Corneille, O., & Yzerbyt, V. (2014). The role of awareness in attitude formation through evaluative conditioning. *Personality and Social Psychology Review, 18*, 187–209.

Swim, J. K. (1994). Perceived versus meta-analytic effect sizes: An assessment of the accuracy of gender stereotypes. *Journal of Personality and Social Psychology, 66*, 21–36.

Swim, J. K., Borgida, E., Maruyama, G., & Myers, D. G. (1989). Joan McKay vs John McKay: Do gender stereotypes bias evaluation? *Psychological Bulletin, 105*, 409–429.

Swim, J. T., Aikin, K., Hall, W., & Hunter, B. A. (1995). Sexism and racism: Old-fashioned and modern prejudices. *Journal of Personality and Social Psychology, 68*, 199–214.

Swim, J. T., & Stangor, C. (1998). *Prejudice from the target's perspective.* Santa Barbara, CA: Academic Press.

Szasz, T. (1970). *The manufacture of madness.* New York: Delta.

Szymanski, K., & Harkins, S. G. (1987). Social loafing and self-evaluation with a social standard. *Journal of Personality and Social Psychology, 53*, 891–897.

Tabachnik, B. G., & Fidell, L. S. (2013). *Using multivariate statistics* (6th ed.). Boston, MA: Pearson.

Taft, R. (1973). Migration: Problems of adjustment and assimilation in immigrants. In P. Watson (Ed.), *Psychology and race* (pp. 224–239). Harmondsworth, UK: Penguin.

Tajfel, H. (1957). Value and the perceptual judgement of magnitude. *Psychological Review, 64*, 192–204.

Tajfel, H. (1959). Quantitative judgement in social perception. *British Journal of Psychology, 50*, 16–29.

Tajfel, H. (1969). Social and cultural factors in perception. In G. Lindzey & E. Aronson (Eds.), *Handbook of social psychology* (Vol. 3, pp. 315–394). Reading, MA: Addison-Wesley.

Tajfel, H. (1970). Experiments in intergroup discrimination. *Scientific American, 223*, 96–102.

Tajfel, H. (1972). Experiments in a vacuum. In J. Israel & H. Tajfel (Eds.), *The context of social psychology: A critical assessment.* London: Academic Press.

Tajfel, H. (1974). Social identity and intergroup behaviour. *Social Science Information, 13*, 65–93.

Tajfel, H. (1978). Intergroup behaviour: II. Group perspectives. In H. Tajfel & C. Fraser (Eds.), *Introducing social psychology* (pp. 423–445). Harmondsworth, UK: Penguin.

Tajfel, H. (1981a). Social stereotypes and social groups. In J. C. Turner & H. Giles (Eds.), *Intergroup behaviour* (pp. 144–167). Oxford, UK: Blackwell.

Tajfel, H. (1981b). *Human groups and social categories: Studies in social psychology.* Cambridge, UK: Cambridge University Press.

Tajfel, H. (1982). Social psychology of intergroup relations. *Annual Review of Social Psychology, 33*, 1–39.

Tajfel, H. (Ed.) (1984). *The social dimension: European developments in social psychology.* Cambridge, UK: Cambridge University Press.

Tajfel, H., & Billig, M. (1974). Familiarity and categorization in intergroup behaviour. *Journal of Experimental Social Psychology, 10*, 159–170.

Tajfel, H., Billig, M., Bundy, R. P., & Flament, C. (1971). Social categorization and intergroup behaviour. *European Journal of Social Psychology, 1*, 149–177.

Tajfel, H., & Fraser, C. (Eds.) (1978). *Introducing social psychology.* Harmondsworth, UK: Penguin.

Tajfel, H., & Turner, J. C. (1986). The social identity theory of intergroup behaviour. In S. Worchel & W. G. Austin (Eds.), *Psychology of intergroup relations* (2nd ed., pp. 7–24). Chicago: Nelson-Hall.

Tajfel, H., & Wilkes, A. L. (1963). Classification and quantitative judgement. *British Journal of Psychology, 54*, 101–114.

Tamir, M., (2016). Why do people regulate their emotions? A taxonomy of motives in emotion regulation. *Personality and Social Psychology Review, 20*, 199–222.

Tanford, S., & Penrod, S. (1984). Social influence model: A formal integration of research on majority and minority influence processes. *Psychological Bulletin, 95*, 189–225.

Tangney, J. P., & Dearing, R. L. (2002). *Shame and guilt.* New York: Guilford.

Tanter, R. (1966). Dimension of conflict behavior within and between nations, 1958–1960. *Journal of Conflict Resolution, 10*, 41–64.

Tanter, R. (1969). International war and domestic turmoil: Some contemporary evidence. In H. D. Graham & T. R. Gurr (Eds.), *Violence in America* (pp. 550–569). New York: Bantam.

Tarde, G. (1890). *Les lois de l'imitation.* Paris: Libraire Felix Alcan.

Tarde, G. (1898). *Etudes de psychologie sociale.* Paris: V. Giard & E. Briére.

Tarde, G. (1901). *L'opinion et la foule.* Paris: Libraire Felix Alcan.

Tarrant, M. (2002). Adolescent peer groups and social identity. *Social Development, 11*, 110–123.

Tausczik, Y., & Pennebaker, J. W. (2010). The psychological meaning of words: LIWC and computerized text analysis methods. *Journal of Language and Social Psychology, 29*, 24–54.

Taylor, A. J. W. (1987). *Antarctic psychology.* Wellington: Science Information Publishing Centre.

Taylor, D. M., & Brown, R. J. (1979). Towards a more social psychology. *British Journal of Social and Clinical Psychology, 18*, 173–179.

Taylor, D. M., & Jaggi, V. (1974). Ethnocentrism and causal attribution in a S. Indian context. *Journal of Cross- cultural Psychology, 5*, 162–171.

Taylor, D. M., & McKirnan, D. J. (1984). A five-stage model of intergroup relations. *British Journal of Social Psychology, 23*, 291–300.

Taylor, D. M., Wright, S. C., & Porter, L. E. (1994). Dimensions of perceived discrimination: The personal/group discrimination discrepancy. In M. P. Zanna & J. M. Olson (Eds.), *The psychology of prejudice: The Ontario symposium* (Vol. 7, pp. 233–255). Hillsdale, NJ: Erlbaum.

Taylor, M. C. (1982). Improved conditions, rising expectations, and dissatisfaction: A test of the past/present relative deprivation hypothesis. *Social Psychology Quarterly, 45*, 24–33.

Taylor, S. E. (1981). The interface of cognitive and social psychology. In J. Harvey (Ed.), *Cognition, social behavior, and the environment* (pp. 189–211). Hillsdale, NJ: Erlbaum.

Taylor, S. E. (1983). Adjustment to threatening events: A theory of cognitive adaptation. *American Psychologist, 38*, 1161–1173.

Taylor, S. E. (1998). The social being in social psychology. In D. T. Gilbert, S. T. Fiske, & G. Lindzey (Eds.), *The handbook of social psychology* (4th ed., Vol. 1, pp. 58–95). New York: McGraw-Hill.

Taylor, S. E. (2003). *Health psychology* (5th ed.). Boston, MA: McGraw-Hill

Taylor, S. E., & Brown, J. D. (1988). Illusion and well-being: A social psychological perspective on mental health. *Psychological Bulletin, 103*, 193–210.

Taylor, S. E., & Fiske, S. T. (1975). Point-of-view and perceptions of causality. *Journal of Personality and Social Psychology, 32*, 439–445.

Taylor, S. E., & Fiske, S. T. (1978). Salience, attention, and attribution: Top of the head phenomena. *Advances in Experimental Social Psychology, 11*, 249–288.

Taylor, S. E., Fiske, S. T., Etcoff, N. L., & Ruderman, A. J. (1978). Categorical and contextual bases of person memory and stereotyping. *Journal of Personality and Social Psychology, 36*, 778–793.

Taylor, S. E., & Koivumaki, J. H. (1976). The perception of self and others: Acquaintanceship, affect, and actor–observer differences. *Journal of Personality and Social Psychology, 33*, 403–408.

Taylor, S. E., Peplau, L. A., & Sears, D. O. (2000). *Social psychology* (10th ed.). Upper Saddle River, NJ: Prentice Hall.

Taylor, S. E., & Thompson, S. C. (1982). Stalking the elusive 'vividness' effect. *Psychological Review, 89*, 155–181.

Taylor, S. P., & Sears, J. D. (1988). The effects of alcohol and persuasive social pressure on human physical aggression. *Aggressive Behavior, 14*, 237–243.

Taynor, J., & Deaux, K. (1973). Equity and perceived sex differences: Role behavior as defined by the task, the mode, and the actor. *Journal of Personality and Social Psychology, 32,* 381–390.

Teger, A. (1970). *Defining the socially responsible response.* Paper presented at the 78th annual meeting of the American Psychological Association.

Teger, A. I., & Pruitt, D. G. (1967). Components of group risk taking. *Journal of Experimental Social Psychology, 3,* 189–205.

Tellis, G. J. (1987). *Advertising exposure, loyalty, and brand purchase: A two-stage model of choice* (Report no. 87–105). Cambridge, MA: Marketing Science Institute.

Tennen, H., & Affleck, G. (1993). The puzzles of self-esteem: A clinical perspective. In R. F. Baumeister (Ed.), *Self-esteem: The puzzle of low self-esteem* (pp. 241–262). New York: Plenum.

Terry, D., Gallois, C., & McCamish, M. (1993). The theory of reasoned action and health care behaviour. In D. Terry, C. Gallois, & M. McCamish (Eds.), *The theory of reasoned action: Its application to AIDS-preventive behaviour* (pp. 1–27). Oxford, UK: Pergamon Press.

Terry, D. J., Carey, C. J., & Callan, V. J. (2001). Employee adjustment to an organizational merger: An intergroup perspective. *Personality and Social Psychology Bulletin, 27,* 267–280.

Terry, D. J., & Hogg, M. A. (1996). Group norms and the attitude–behavior relationship: A role for group identification. *Personality and Social Psychology Bulletin, 22,* 776–793.

Terry, D. J., & Hogg, M. A. (Eds.) (2000). *Attitudes, behavior, and social context: The role of norms and group membership.* Mahwah, NJ: Erlbaum.

Terry, D. J., Hogg, M. A., & White, K. M. (1999). The theory of planned behaviour: Self-identity, social identity and group norms. *British Journal of Social Psychology, 38,* 225–244.

Terry, D. J., Hogg, M. A., & White, K. M. (2000). Attitude–behavior relations: Social identity and group membership. In D. J. Terry & M. A. Hogg (Eds.), *Attitudes, behavior, and social context: The role of norms and group membership* (pp. 67–93). Mahwah, NJ: Erlbaum.

Tesser, A. (1988). Toward a self-evaluation maintenance model of social behavior. *Advances in Experimental Social Psychology, 21,* 181–227.

Tesser, A. (2000). On the confluence of self-esteem maintenance mechanisms. *Personality and Social Psychology Review, 4,* 290–299.

Tesser, A., Gatewood, R., & Driver, M. (1968). Some determinants of gratitude. *Journal of Personality and Social Psychology, 9,* 233–236.

Tesser, A., Martin, L., & Mendolia, M. (1995). The impact of thought on attitude extremity and attitude–behavior consistency. In R. E. Petty & J. A. Krosnick (Eds.), *Attitude strength: Antecedents and consequences* (pp. 73–92). Mahwah, NJ: Erlbaum.

Tesser, A., & Schwartz, N. (Eds.) (2001). *Blackwell handbook of social psychology: Intraindividual processes.* Oxford, UK: Blackwell.

Tesser, A., & Shaffer, D. R. (1990). Attitudes and attitude change. *Annual Review of Psychology, 41,* 479–523.

Tetlock, P. E. (1979). Identifying victims of groupthink from public statements of decision makers. *Journal of Personality and Social Psychology, 37,* 1314–1324.

Tetlock, P. E. (1983). Policymakers: Images of international conflict. *Journal of Social Issues, 39,* 67–86.

Tetlock, P. E. (1984). Cognitive style and political belief systems in the British House of Commons. *Journal of Personality and Social Psychology, 46,* 365–375.

Tetlock, P. E. (1988). Monitoring the integrative complexity of American and Soviet policy rhetoric: What can be learned? *Journal of Social Issues, 44,* 101–131.

Tetlock, P. E. (1989). The structural bases of consistency among political attitudes: Effects of political expertise and attitude importance. Structure and function in political belief systems. In A. R. Pratkanis, S. J. Breckler, & A. G. Greenwald (Eds.), *Attitude structure and function* (pp. 129–151). Hillsdale, NJ: Erlbaum.

Tetlock, P. E. (2007). Psychology and politics: The challenges of integrating levels of analysis in social science. In A. W. Kruglanski & E. T. Higgins (Eds.), *Social psychology: A handbook of basic principles* (2nd ed., pp. 888–912). New York: Guilford Press.

Tetlock, P. E., & Boettger, R. (1989). Accountability: A social magnifier of the dilution effect. *Journal of Personality and Social Psychology, 57,* 388–398.

Tetlock, P. E., & Kim, J. I. (1987). Accountability and judgment processes in a personality prediction task. *Journal of Personality and Social Psychology, 52,* 700–709.

Tetlock, P. E., & Levi, A. (1982). Attribution bias: On the inconclusiveness of the cognition–motivation debate. *Journal of Experimental Social Psychology, 18,* 68–88.

Tetlock, P. E., & Manstead, A. S. R. (1985). Impression management versus intrapsychic explanations in social psychology: A useful dichotomy? *Psychological Review, 92,* 59–77.

Tetlock, P. E., Peterson, R. S., McGuire, C., Chang, S., & Feld, P. (1992). Assessing political group dynamics: A test of the groupthink model. *Journal of Personality and Social Psychology, 63,* 403–425.

Tewari, S., Khan, S., Hopkins, N., Srinivasan, N., & Reicher, S. D. (2012). Participation in mass gatherings can benefit well-being: Longitudinal and control data from a North Indian Hindu pilgrimage event. *PLoS ONE, 7*(10), e47291.

Thakerar, J. N., Giles, H., & Cheshire, J. (1982). Psychological and linguistic parameters of speech accommodation theory. In C. Fraser & K. R. Scherer (Eds.), *Advances in the social psychology of language* (pp. 205–255). Cambridge, UK: Cambridge University Press.

Thatcher, M. (1993). *The Downing Street years.* London: HarperCollins.

Thayer, S. (1986). Touch: The frontier of intimacy. *Journal of Nonverbal Behaviour, 10,* 7–11.

Thibaut, J. W., & Kelley, H. H. (1959). *The social psychology of groups.* New York: Wiley.

Thomas, W. I., & Znaniecki, F. (1918). *The Polish peasant in Europe and America* (Vol. 1). Boston, MA: Badger.

Thompson, J. B. (1990). *Ideology and modern culture: Critical social theory in the era of mass communication.* Stanford, CA: Stanford University Press.

Thompson, L. L. (2015). *The mind and heart of the negotiator* (6th ed.). New York: Pearson.

Thompson, L. L., & Loewenstein, J. (2003). Mental models of negotiation: Descriptive, prescriptive, and paradigmatic implications. In M. A. Hogg & J. Cooper (Eds.), *The SAGE handbook of social psychology* (pp. 494–511). London: SAGE.

Thompson, L. L., Medvec, V. H., Seiden, V., & Kopelman, S. (2001). Poker face, smiley face, and rant 'n' rave: Myths and realities about emotion in negotiation. In M. A. Hogg & R. S. Tindale (Eds.), *Blackwell handbook of social psychology: Group processes* (pp. 139–163). Oxford, UK: Blackwell.

Thompson, L. L., & Pozner, J.-E. (2007). Organizational behavior. In A. W. Kruglanski & E. T. Higgins (Eds.), *Social psychology: A handbook of basic principles* (2nd ed., pp. 913–939). New York: Guilford Press.

Thompson, W. C., Fong, G. T., & Rosenhan, D. L. (1981). Inadmissible evidence and juror verdicts. *Journal of Personality and Social Psychology, 40,* 453–463.

Thompson, W. C., & Fuqua, J. (1998). 'The jury will disregard …': A brief guide to inadmissible evidence. In J. M. Golding & C. M. MacLeod (Eds.), *Intentional forgetting: Interdisciplinary approaches* (pp. 133–154). Mahwah, NJ: Erlbaum.

Thomson, R. (2006). The effect of topic of discussion on gendered language in computer-mediated communication discussion. *Journal of Language and Social Psychology, 25,* 167–178.

Thomson, R., & Murachver, T. (2001). Predicting gender from electronic discourse. *British Journal of Social Psychology, 40,* 193–208.

Thoreau, H. D. (1854/1997). *Walden.* Oxford, UK: Oxford University Press.

Thorndike, E. L. (1940). *Human nature and the social order.* New York: Macmillan.

Thurstone, L. L. (1928). Attitudes can be measured. *American Journal of Sociology, 33,* 529–554.

Thurstone, L. L. (1931). The measurement of social attitudes. *Journal of Abnormal and Social Psychology, 26,* 249–269.

Thurstone, L. L., & Chave, E. J. (1929). *The measurement of attitude: A psychophysical method and some experiments with a scale for measuring attitude toward the church.* Chicago, IL: University of Chicago Press.

Tice, D. M. (1992). Self-presentation and self-concept change: The looking-glass self as magnifying glass. *Journal of Personality and Social Psychology, 63,* 435–451.

Tidwell, N. D., Eastwick, P. W., & Finkel, E. J. (2012). Perceived, not actual, similarity predicts initial attraction in a live romantic context: Evidence from the speed-dating paradigm. *Personal Relationships, 20*, 199–215.

Tiedens, L. Z., & Fragale, A. R. (2003). Power moves: Complementarity in dominant and submissive nonverbal behavior. *Journal of Personality and Social Psychology, 84*, 558–568.

Tilker, H. (1970). Socially responsible behavior as a function of observer responsibility and victim feedback. *Journal of Personality and Social Psychology, 14*, 95–100.

Tindale, R. S., Davis, J. H., Vollrath, D. A., Nagao, D. H., & Hinsz, V. B. (1990). Asymmetrical social influence in freely interacting groups: A test of three models. *Journal of Personality and Social Psychology, 58*, 438–449.

Tindale, R. S., Kameda, T., & Hinsz, V. B. (2003). Group decision making. In M. A. Hogg & J. Cooper (Eds.), *The SAGE handbook of social psychology* (pp. 381–403). London: SAGE.

Tindale, R. S., Meisenhelder, H. M., Dykema-Engblade, A. A., & Hogg, M. A. (2001). Shared cognition in small groups. In M. A. Hogg & R. S. Tindale (Eds.), *Blackwell handbook of social psychology: Group processes* (pp. 1–30). Oxford, UK: Blackwell.

Tindale, R. S., Nadler, J., Krebel, A., & Davis, J. H. (2001). Procedural mechanisms and jury behavior. In M. A. Hogg & R. S. Tindale (Eds.), *Blackwell handbook of social psychology: Group processes* (pp. 574–602). Oxford, UK: Blackwell.

Titus, H. E., & Hollander, E. P. (1957). The California F-scale in psychological research (1950–1955). *Psychological Bulletin, 54*, 47–74.

Toch, H. (1969). *Violent men*. Chicago: Aldine.

Todorov, A., Fiske, S. T., & Prentice, D. A. (2011) *Social neuroscience: Towards understanding the underpinnings of the social mind*. New York: Oxford University Press.

Todorov, A., Mandisodza, A. N., Goren, A., & Hall, C. C. (2005). Inferences of competence for faces predict election outcomes. *Science, 308*, 1623–1626.

Tolan, P., & Gorman-Smith, D. (2002). What violence prevention research can tell us about developmental psychopathology. *Development and Psychopathology, 14*, 713–729.

Tolan, P., Gorman-Smith, D., & Henry, D. (2006). Family violence. *Annual Review of Psychology, 57*, 557–583.

Tolstoy, L. (1869). *War and peace*. Harmondsworth, UK: Penguin.

Tomada, G., & Schneider, B. H. (1997). Relational aggression, gender, and peer acceptance: Invariance across culture, stability over time, and concordance among informants. *Developmental Psychology, 33*, 601–609.

Tomasello, M., & Vaish, A. (2013). Origins of human cooperation and morality. *Annual Review of Psychology, 64*, 231–255.

Tönnies, F. (1955). *Community and association*. London: Routledge & Kegan Paul (originally published in German in 1887).

Tormala, Z. L., Briñol, P., & Petty, R. E. (2007). Multiple roles for source credibility under high elaboration: It's all in the timing. *Social Cognition, 25*, 536–552.

Tormala, Z. L., Jia, J. S., & Norton, M. I. (2012). The preference for potential. *Journal of Personality and Social Psychology, 103*, 567–583.

Tormala, Z. L., & Petty, R. E. (2002). What does not kill me makes me stronger: the effects of resisting persuasion on attitude certainty. *Journal of Personality and Social Psychology, 83*, 1298–1313.

Tormala, Z. L., & Petty, R. E. (2004a). Resistance to persuasion and attitude certainty: The moderating role of elaboration. *Personality and Social Psychology Bulletin, 30*, 1446–1457.

Tormala, Z. L., & Petty, R. E. (2004b). Source credibility and attitude certainty: a metacognitive analysis of resistance to persuasion. *Journal of Consumer Psychology, 14*, 427–442.

Totenhagen, C. J., Butler, E. A., & Ridley, C. A. (2012). Daily stress, closeness, and satisfaction in gay and lesbian couples. *Personal Relationships, 19*, 219–233.

Tourangeau, R., Smith, T. W., & Rasinski, K. A. (1997). Motivation to report sensitive behaviours on surveys: Evidence from a bogus pipeline experiment. *Journal of Applied Social Psychology, 27*, 209–222.

Townsend, S. S. M., Major, B., Gangi, C. E., & Mendes, W. B. (2011). From "in the air" to "under the skin": Cortisol responses to social identity threat. *Personality and Social Psychology Bulletin, 37*, 151–164.

Trafimow, D. (2000). Habit as both a direct cause of intention to use a condom and as a moderator of the attitude–intention and the subjective norm–intention relations. *Psychology and Health, 15*, 383–395.

Trager, G. L. (1958). Paralanguage: A first approximation. *Studies in Linguistics, 13*, 1–12.

Tran, S., & Simpson, J. A. (2009). Pro-relationship maintenance behaviors: The joint roles of attachment and commitment. *Journal of Personality and Social Psychology, 97*, 685–698.

Trawalter, S., Adam, E. K., Chase-Lansdale, P. L., & Richeson, J. A. (2012). Concerns about appearing prejudiced get under the skin: Stress responses to interracial contact in the moment and across time. *Journal of Experimental Social Psychology, 48*, 682–693.

Triandis, H. C. (1971). *Attitude and attitude change*. New York: Wiley.

Triandis, H. C. (1977). *Interpersonal behavior*. Monterey, CA: Brooks/Cole.

Triandis, H. C. (1980). Values, attitudes and interpersonal behavior. In H. H. Howe & M. M. Page (Eds.), *Nebraska symposium on motivation* (Vol. 27, pp. 195–259). Lincoln, NE: University of Nebraska Press.

Triandis, H. C. (1989). The self and social behavior in differing cultural contexts. *Psychological Review, 96*, 506–520.

Triandis, H. C. (1994a). *Culture and social behavior*. New York: McGraw-Hill.

Triandis, H. C. (1994b). Theoretical and methodological approaches to the study of collectivism and individualism. In U. Kim, H. C. Triandis, C. Kağitçibaşi, S. Choi, & G. Yoon (Eds.), *Individualism and collectivism: Theory, methods, and applications* (pp. 41–51). Thousand Oaks, CA: SAGE.

Triandis, H. C., & Davis, E. G. (1965). Race and belief as shared determinants of behavior intentions. *Journal of Personality and Social Psychology, 2*, 715–725.

Triandis, H. C., Lambert, W., Berry, J., Lonner, W., Heron, A., Brislin, R., & Draguns, J. (Eds.) (1980). *Handbook of cross-cultural psychology* (Vol. 1–6). Boston, MA: Allyn & Bacon.

Triandis, H. C., Leung, K., Villareal, M. J., & Clack, F. L. (1985). Allocentric versus idiocentric tendencies: Convergent and discriminant validation. *Journal of Research in Personality, 19*, 395–415.

Tripathi, R. C., & Srivasta, R. (1981). Relative deprivation and intergroup attitudes. *European Journal of Social Psychology, 11*, 313–318.

Triplett, N. (1898). The dynamogenic factors in pacemaking and competition. *American Journal of Psychology, 9*, 507–533.

Trope, Y. (1986). Self-enhancement and self-assessment in achievement behavior. In R. Sorrentino & E. T. Higgins (Eds.), *Handbook of motivation and cognition* (Vol. 2, pp. 350–378). New York: Guilford Press.

Trope, Y., & Gaunt, R. (2007). Attribution and person perception. In M. A. Hogg & J. Cooper (Eds.), *The SAGE handbook of social psychology: Concise student edition* (pp. 176–194). London: SAGE.

Tropp, L. R. (Ed.) (2012). *The Oxford handbook of intergroup conflict*. New York: Oxford University Press.

Trotter, W. (1919). *Instincts of the herd in peace and war*. London: Oxford University Press.

Tsunokai, G. T., McGrath, A. R., & Kavanagh, J. K. (2014). Online dating preferences of Asian Americans. *Journal of Social and Personal Relationships, 31*, 796–814.

Tucker, J. S., Friedman, H. S., Schwartz, J. E., Criqui, M. H., Tomlinson-Keasey, C., Wingard, D. L., et al. (1997). Parental divorce: Effects on individual behavior and longevity. *Journal of Personality and Social Psychology, 73*, 381–391.

Tuckman, B. W. (1965). Developmental sequence in small groups. *Psychological Bulletin, 63*, 384–399.

Tuffin, K. (2005). *Understanding critical social psychology*. Thousand Oaks, CA: SAGE.

Turner, D. D. (2005). Altruism – is it still an anomaly? [Review of *Kindness in a cruel world: The evolution of altruism* by N. Barber. Prometheus: Amherst, NY, 2004]. *Trends in Cognitive Sciences, 9*, 317–318.

Turner, J. C. (1975). Social comparison and social identity: Some prospects for intergroup behaviour. *European Journal of Social Psychology, 5*, 5–34.

Turner, J. C. (1978). Social categorization and social discrimination in the minimal group paradigm. In H. Tajfel (Ed.), *Differentiation between social groups* (pp. 101–140). London: Academic Press.

Turner, J. C. (1980). Fairness or discrimination in intergroup behaviour? A reply to Branthwaite, Doyle and Lightbown. *European Journal of Social Psychology, 10*, 131–147.

Turner, J. C. (1981a). Some considerations in generalizing experimental social psychology. In G. M. Stephenson & J. M. Davis (Eds.), *Progress in applied social psychology* (Vol. 1, pp. 3–34). Chichester, UK: Wiley.

Turner, J. C. (1981b). The experimental social psychology of intergroup behaviour. In J. C. Turner & H. Giles (Eds.), *Intergroup behaviour* (pp. 66–101). Oxford, UK: Blackwell.

Turner, J. C. (1982). Towards a cognitive redefinition of the social group. In H. Tajfel (Ed.), *Social identity and intergroup relations* (pp. 15–40). Cambridge, UK: Cambridge University Press.

Turner, J. C. (1983). Some comments on 'the measurement of social orientations in the minimal group paradigm'. *European Journal of Social Psychology, 13*, 351–368.

Turner, J. C. (1984). Social identification and psychological group formation. In H. Tajfel (Ed.), *The social dimension: European developments in social psychology* (Vol. 2, pp. 518–538). Cambridge, UK: Cambridge University Press.

Turner, J. C. (1985). Social categorization and the self-concept: A social cognitive theory of group behavior. In E. J. Lawler (Ed.), *Advances in group processes: Theory and research* (Vol. 22, pp. 77–122). Greenwich, CT: JAI Press.

Turner, J. C. (1991). *Social influence.* Buckingham, UK: Open University Press.

Turner, J. C. (1999). Some current issues in research on social identity and self-categorization theories. In N. Ellemers, R. Spears, & B. Doosje (Eds.), *Social identity* (pp. 6–34). Oxford, UK: Blackwell.

Turner, J. C. (2005). Explaining the nature of power: A three-process theory. *European Journal of Social Psychology, 35*, 1–22.

Turner, J. C., & Bourhis, R. Y. (1996). Social identity, interdependence and the social group. A reply to Rabbie et al. In W. P. Robinson (Ed.), *Social groups and identities: Developing the legacy of Henri Tajfel* (pp. 25–63). Oxford, UK: Butterworth-Heinemann.

Turner, J. C., Hogg, M. A., Oakes, P. J., Reicher, S. D., & Wetherell, M. S. (1987). *Rediscovering the social group: A self-categorization theory.* Oxford, UK: Blackwell.

Turner, J. C., & Oakes, P. J. (1986). The significance of the social identity concept for social psychology with reference to individualism, interactionism and social influence. *British Journal of Social Psychology, 25*, 237–252.

Turner, J. C., & Oakes, P. J. (1989). Self-categorization and social influence. In P. B. Paulus (Ed.), *The psychology of group influence* (2nd ed., pp. 233–275). Hillsdale, NJ: Erlbaum.

Turner, J. C., & Reynolds, K. (2003). Why social dominance theory has been falsified. *British Journal of Social Psychology, 42*, 199–206.

Turner, J. C., Reynolds, K. J., Haslam, S. A., & Veenstra, K. E. (2006). Reconceptualizing personality: Producing individuality by defining the personal self. In T. Postmes & J. Jetten (Eds.), *Individuality and the group: Advances in social identity* (pp. 11–36). London: SAGE.

Turner, J. C., Wetherell, M. S., & Hogg, M. A. (1989). Referent informational influence and group polarization. *British Journal of Social Psychology, 28*, 135–147.

Turner, M. E., Pratkanis, A. R., Probasco, P., & Leve, C. (1992). Threat, cohesion, and group effectiveness: Testing a social identity maintenance perspective on groupthink. *Journal of Personality and Social Psychology, 63*, 781–796.

Turner, R. H. (1974). Collective behavior. In R. E. L. Faris (Ed.), *Handbook of modern sociology* (pp. 382–425). Chicago: Rand McNally.

Turner, R. H., & Killian, L. (1957). *Collective behavior.* Englewood Cliffs, NJ: Prentice Hall.

Turtle, A. M. (1994). Implications for Asian psychology of the adoption of a stance of theoretical indigenisation. In G. Davidson (Ed.), *Applying psychology: Lessons from Asia-Oceania* (pp. 9–13). Melbourne, Australia: Australian Psychological Society.

Tversky, A., & Kahneman, D. (1974). Judgment under uncertainty: Heuristics and biases. *Science, 185*, 1124–1131.

Tyerman, A., & Spencer, C. (1983). A critical test of the Sherifs' robbers' cave experiments: Intergroup competition and cooperation between groups of well acquainted individuals. *Small Group Research, 14*, 515–531.

Tyler, T. R. (1997). The psychology of legitimacy: A relational perspective on voluntary deference to authorities. *Personality and Social Psychology Review, 1*, 323–345.

Tyler, T. R. (2011). *Why people cooperate: The role of social motivations.* Princeton, NJ: Princeton University Press.

Tyler, T. R., & Jost, J. T. (2007). Psychology and the law: reconciling normative and descriptive accounts of social justice and system legitimacy. In A. W. Kruglanski & E. T. Higgins (Eds.), *Social psychology: A handbook of basic principles* (2nd ed., pp. 807–825). New York: Guilford Press.

Tyler, T. R., & Lind, E. A. (1992). A relational model of authority in groups. *Advances in Experimental Social Psychology, 25*, 115–191.

Tyler, T. R., & Schuller, R. A. (1991). Aging and attitude change. *Journal of Personality and Social Psychology, 61*, 689–697.

Tyler, T. R., & Sears, D. O. (1977). Coming to like obnoxious people when we have to live with them. *Journal of Personality and Social Psychology, 35*, 200–211.

Tyler, T. R., & Smith, H. J. (1998). Social justice and social movements. In D. T. Gilbert, S. T. Fiske, & G. Lindzey (Eds.), *The handbook of social psychology* (4th ed., Vol. 2, pp. 595–632). New York: McGraw-Hill.

Ulman, R. B., & Abse, D. W. (1983). The group psychology of mass madness: Jonestown. *Political Psychology, 4*, 637–661.

Umadevi, L., Venkataramaiah, P., & Srinivasulu, R. (1992). A comparative study on the concept of marriage by professional and non-professional degree students. *Indian Journal of Behaviour, 16*, 27–37.

Underwood, B., & Moore, B. (1982). Perspective-taking and altruism. *Psychological Bulletin, 91*, 143–173.

Unsworth, K. L., & Fielding, K. S. (2014). It's political: How the salience of one's political identity changes climate change beliefs and policy support. *Global Environmental Change, 27*, 131–137.

US Department of Justice. (2001). *Homicide trends in the United States.* Bureau of Justice Statistics. Retrieved 2 January 2002 from http://www.ojp.usdoj.gov/bjs/homicide/homtrnd.htm.

Utz, S., & Sassenberg, K. (2002). Distributive justice in common-bond and common-identity groups. *Group Processes and Intergroup Relations, 5*, 151–162.

Vaes, J., Leyens, J.-P., Paladino, M. P., & Miranda, M. P. (2012). We are human, they are not: Driving forces behind outgroup dehumanization and the humanization of the ingroup. *European Review of Social Psychology, 23*, 64–106.

Valentine, T., Pickering, A., & Darling, S. (2003). Characteristics of eyewitness identification that predict the outcome of real lineups. *Applied Cognitive Psychology, 17*, 969–993.

Valins, S. (1966). Cognitive effects of false heart-rate feedback. *Journal of Personality and Social Psychology, 4*, 400–408.

Valins, S., & Nisbett, R. E. (1972). Attribution processes in the development and treatment of emotional disorders. In E. E. Jones, D. E. Kanouse, H. H. Kelley, R. E. Nisbett, S. Valins, & B. Weiner (Eds.), *Attribution: Perceiving the causes of behavior* (pp. 137–150). Morristown, NJ: General Learning Press.

Van Bavel, J. J., & Cunningham, W. A. (2010). A social neuroscience approach to self and social categorization: A new look at an old issue. *European Review of Social Psychology, 21*, 237–284.

Van Beest, I., & Williams, K. D. (2006). When inclusion costs and ostracism pays, ostracism still hurts. *Journal of Personality and Social Psychology, 91*, 918–928.

Van den Bos, K. (2009). Making sense of life: The existential self trying to deal with personal uncertainty. *Psychological Inquiry, 20*, 197–217.

Van den Ven, N., & Zeelenberg, M. (2015). On the counterfactual nature of envy: "It could have been me". *Cognition and Emotion, 29*, 954–971.

Van der Pligt, J. (1984). Attributional false consensus, and valence: Two field studies. *Journal of Personality and Social Psychology, 46*, 57–68.

Van der Pligt, J., & De Vries, N. K. (2000). The importance of being selective: Weighing the role of attribute importance in attitudinal judgment. *Advances in Experimental Social Psychology, 32*, 135–191.

Van de Vliert, E., Huang, X., & Levine, R. V. (2004). National wealth and thermal climate as predictors of motives for volunteer work. *Journal of Cross-Cultural Psychology, 35*, 62–73.

Van Dijk, T. A. (1987). *Communicating racism: Ethnic prejudice in thought and talk.* Newbury Park, CA: SAGE.

Van Dijk, T. A. (1993). *Elite discourse and racism*. Newbury Park, CA: SAGE.

Van Dijk, T. A., & Wodak, R. (Eds.) (1988). *Discourse, racism and ideology* (special issues of Text, 8, nos 1 and 2). Amsterdam: Mouton de Gruyter.

Van Doorn, A., Zeelenberg, M., & Breugelmans, S. M. (2014). Anger and prosocial behavior. *Emotion Review, 6*, 261–268.

Van Goozen, S. H. M., Cohen-Kettenis, P. T., Gooren, L. J. G., Frijda, N. H., & Van der Poll, N. E. (1995). Gender differences in behaviour: Activating effects of cross-sex hormones. *Psychoneuroendocrinology, 20*, 343–363.

Van Gyn, G. H., Wenger, H. A., & Gaul, C. A. (1990). Imagery as a method of enhancing transfer from training to performance. *Journal of Sport and Exercise Psychology, 12*, 366–375.

Van Knippenberg, A., & Van Oers, H. (1984). Social identity and equity concerns in intergroup perceptions. *British Journal of Social Psychology, 23*, 351–361.

Van Knippenberg, D. (2011). Embodying who we are: Leader group prototypicality and leadership effectiveness. *The Leadership Quarterly, 22*, 1078–1091.

Van Knippenberg, D., & Hogg, M. A. (2003). A social identity model of leadership in organizations. In R. M. Kramer & B. M. Staw (Eds.), *Research in organizational behavior* (Vol. 25, pp. 243–295). Greenwich, CT: JAI Press.

Van Knippenberg, D., Van Knippenberg, B., & Bobbio, A. (2008). Leaders as agents of continuity: Self continuity and resistance to collective change. In F. Sani (Ed.), *Self-continuity: Individual and collective perspectives* (pp. 175–186). New York: Psychology Press.

Van Knippenberg, D., Van Knippenberg, B., De Cremer, D., & Hogg, M. A. (2004). Leadership, self, and identity: A review and research agenda. *The Leadership Quarterly, 15*, 825–856.

Van Lange, P. A. M. (2013). What we should expect from theories in social psychology: Truth, abstraction, progress, and applicability as standards (TAPAS). *Personality and Social Psychology Review, 17*, 40–55.

Van Lange, P. A. M., Balliet, D., Parks, C. D., & Van Vugt, M. (2014). *Social dilemmas: Understanding human cooperation*. New York: Oxford University Press.

Van Lange, P. A. M., Kruglanski, A. W., & Higgins, E. T. (Eds.) (2012). *Handbook of theories of social psychology*. Thousand Oaks, CA: SAGE.

Van Loo, K. J., & Rydell, R. J. (2013). On the experience of feeling powerful: Perceived power moderates the effect of stereotype threat on women's math performance. *Personality and Social Psychology Bulletin, 39*, 387–400.

Van Osch, Y., Zeelenberg, M., & Breugelmans, S. (2016). On the context dependence of emotion displays: Perceptions of gold medalists' expressions of pride. *Cognition and Emotion, 30*, 1332–1343.

Van Overwalle, F., & Siebler, F. (2005). A connectionist model of attitude formation and change. *Personality and Social Psychology Review, 9*, 231–274.

Van Schie, E. G. M., & Wiegman, O. (1997). Children and videogames: Leisure activities, aggression, social integration, and school performance. *Journal of Applied Social Psychology, 27*, 1175–1194.

Van Veelen, R., Otten, S., Cadinu, M., & Hansen, N. (2016). An integrative model of social identification: Self-stereotyping and self-anchoring as two cognitive pathways. *Personality and Social Psychology Review, 20*, 3–26.

Van Vugt, M. (1997). When the privatization of public goods may fail: A social dilemma approach. *Social Psychology Quarterly, 60*, 355–367.

Van Vugt, M., & De Cremer, D. (1999). Leadership in social dilemmas: The effects of group identification on collective actions to provide public goods. *Journal of Personality and Social Psychology, 76*, 587–599.

Van Vugt, M., & Hart, C. M. (2004). Social identity as social glue: The origins of group loyalty. *Journal of Personality and Social Psychology, 86*, 585–598.

Van Vugt, M., Hogan, R., & Kaiser, R. (2008). Leadership, followership, and evolution: Some lessons from the past. *American Psychologist, 63*, 182–196.

Van Zomeren, M., Leach, C. W., & Spears, R. (2012). Protestors as 'passionate economists': A dynamic dual pathway model of approach coping with collective disadvantage. *Personality and Social Psychology Review, 16*, 180–199.

Van Zomeren, M., Postmes, T., & Spears, R. (2008). Toward an integrative social identity model of collective action: A quantitative research synthesis of three socio-psychological perspectives. *Psychological Bulletin, 134*, 504–535.

Vandello, J. A., & Cohen, D. (2003). Male honor and female fidelity: Implicit cultural scripts that perpetuate domestic violence. *Journal of Personality and Social Psychology, 84*, 997–1010.

Vandello, J. A., Cohen, D., Grandon, R., & Franiuk, R. (2009). Stand by your man: Indirect prescriptions for honorable violence and feminine loyalty in Canada, Chile, and the United States. *Journal of Cross-Cultural Psychology, 40*, 81–104.

Vanneman, R. D., & Pettigrew, T. F. (1972). Race and relative deprivation in the urban United States. *Race, 13*, 461–486.

Vaughan, G. M. (1962). The social distance attitudes of New Zealand students towards Maoris and fifteen other national groups. *Journal of Social Psychology, 57*, 85–92.

Vaughan, G. M. (1964). The trans-situational aspect of conforming behavior. *Journal of Personality, 32*, 335–354.

Vaughan, G. M. (1977). Personality and small group behaviour. In R. B. Cattell & R. M. Dreger (Eds.), *Handbook of modern personality theory* (pp. 511–529). London: Academic Press.

Vaughan, G. M. (1978a). Social change and intergroup preferences in New Zealand. *European Journal of Social Psychology, 8*, 297–314.

Vaughan, G. M. (1978b). Social categorization and intergroup behaviour in children. In H. Tajfel (Ed.), *Differentiation between social groups: Studies in the social psychology of intergroup relations* (pp. 339–360). London: Academic Press.

Vaughan, G. M. (1986). Social change and racial identity: Issues in the use of picture and doll measures. *Australian Journal of Psychology, 38*, 359–370.

Vaughan, G. M. (1988). The psychology of intergroup discrimination. *New Zealand Journal of Psychology, 17*, 1–14.

Vaughan, G. M. (2010a). Hate crimes. In J. M. Levine & M. A. Hogg (Eds.), *Encyclopedia of group processes and intergroup relations* (pp. 395–398). Thousand Oaks, CA: SAGE.

Vaughan, G. M. (2010b). Sherif, Muzafer. In J. M. Levine & M. A. Hogg (Eds.), *Encyclopedia of group processes and intergroup relations* (pp. 753–756). Thousand Oaks, CA: SAGE.

Vaughan, G. M. (2010c). Tajfel, Henri. In J. M. Levine & M. A. Hogg (Eds.), *Encyclopedia of group processes and intergroup relations* (pp. 897–899). Thousand Oaks, CA: SAGE.

Vaughan, G. M. (2010d). Territoriality. In J. M. Levine & M. A. Hogg (Eds.), *Encyclopedia of group processes and intergroup relations* (pp. 913–916). Thousand Oaks, CA: SAGE.

Vaughan, G. M., & Guerin, B. (1997). A neglected innovator in sports psychology: Norman Triplett and the early history of competitive performance. *International Journal of the History of Sport, 14*, 82–99.

Vaughan, G. M., Tajfel, H., & Williams, J. (1981). Bias in reward allocation in an intergroup and an interpersonal context. *Social Psychology Quarterly, 44*, 37–42.

Verkuyten, M. (2006). Multiculturalism and social psychology. *European Review of Social Psychology, 17*, 148–184.

Verkuyten, M. (2010). Ethnic communication and identity performance. In H. Giles, S. A. Reid, & J. Harwood (Eds.), *The dynamics of intergroup communication* (pp. 17–28). New York: Peter Lang.

Vermunt, R., Van Knippenberg, D., Van Knippenberg, B., & Blaauw, E. (2001). Self-esteem and outcome fairness: Differential importance of procedural and outcome considerations. *Journal of Applied Psychology, 86*, 621–628.

Verplanken, B., & Aarts, H. (1999). Habit, attitude, and planned behaviour: Is habit an empty construct or an interesting case of automaticity? *European Review of Social Psychology, 10*, 101–134.

Verplanken, B., Aarts, H, Van Knippenberg, A., & Moonen, A. (1998). Habit versus planned behavior: A field experiment. *British Journal of Social Psychology, 37*, 111–128.

Verplanken, B., Hofstee, G., & Janssen, H. J. W. (1998). Accessibility of affective versus cognitive components of attitudes. *European Journal of Social Psychology, 28*, 23–35.

Verplanken, B., & Holland, R. (2002). Motivated decision-making: Effects of activation and self-centrality of values on choices and behavior. *Journal of Personality and Social Psychology, 82*, 434–447.

Vescio, T. K., Hewstone, M., Crisp, R. J., & Rubin, J. M. (1999). Perceiving and responding to multiple categorizable individuals: Cognitive processes and affective intergroup bias. In D. Abrams & M. A. Hogg (Eds.) (1999). *Social identity and social cognition* (pp. 111–140). Oxford, UK: Blackwell.

Vescio, T. K., Sechrist, G. B., & Paolucci, M. P. (2003). Perspective taking and prejudice reduction: The mediational role of empathy arousal and situational attributions. *European Journal of Social Psychology, 33*, 455–472.

Vezzali, L., Hewstone, M., Capozza, D., Giovannini, D., & Wölfer, R. (2014). Improving intergroup relations with extended and vicarious forms of indirect contact. *European Review of Social Psychology, 25*, 314–389.

Vick, S.-J., Waller, B. M., Parr, L. A., Pasqualini, M. C. S., & Bard, K. A. (2007). A cross-species comparison of facial morphology and movement in humans and chimpanzees using the Facial Action Coding System (FACS). *Journal of Nonverbal Behavior, 31*, 1–20.

Vider, S. (2004). Rethinking crowd violence: Self-categorization theory and the Woodstock 1999 riot. *Journal for the Theory of Social Behaviour, 34*, 141–166.

Vignoles, V. L., Chryssochoou, X., & Breakwell, G. M. (2000). The distinctiveness principle: Identity, meaning, and the bounds of cultural relativity. *Personality and Social Psychology Review, 4*, 337–354.

Vine, I. (1983). Sociobiology and social psychology – rivalry or symbiosis? The explanation of altruism. *British Journal of Social Psychology, 22*, 1–11.

Vinokur, A., & Burnstein, E. (1974). The effects of partially shared persuasive arguments on group-induced shifts: A problem-solving approach. *Journal of Personality and Social Psychology, 29*, 305–315.

Vinokur-Kaplan, D. (1978). To have – or not to have – another child: Family planning attitudes, intentions, and behavior. *Journal of Applied Social Psychology, 8*, 29–46.

Visser, P. S., & Cooper, J. (2003). Attitude change. In M. A. Hogg & J. Cooper (Eds.), *The SAGE handbook of social psychology* (pp. 211–231). London: SAGE.

Visser, P. S., & Cooper, J. (2007). Attitude change. In M. A. Hogg & J. Cooper (Eds.), *The SAGE handbook of social psychology: Concise student edition* (pp. 197–218). London: SAGE.

Visser, P. S., & Krosnick, J. A. (1998). Development of attitude strength over the life cycle: Surge and decline. *Journal of Personality and Social and Psychology, 75*, 1389–1410.

Vittengl, J. R., & Holt, C. S. (2000). Getting acquainted: The relationship of self-disclosure and social attraction to positive affect. *Journal of Social and Personal Relationships, 17*, 53–66.

Volk, A. A., Camilleri, J. A., Dane, A. V., and Marini, Z. A. (2012). Is adolescent bullying an evolutionary adaptation? *Aggressive Behavior, 38*, 222–238.

Von Hippel, W., Sekaquaptewa, D., & Vargas, P. (1995). On the role of encoding processes in stereotype maintenance. *Advances in Experimental Social Psychology, 27*, 177–254.

Von Neumann, J., & Morgenstern, O. (1944). *Theory of games and economic behavior*. Princeton, NJ: Princeton University Press.

Vroom, V. H., & Jago, A. G. (1988). *The new leadership*. Englewood Cliffs, NJ: Prentice Hall.

Vygotsky, L. S. (1962). *Thought and language*. New York: Wiley.

Vygotsky, L. S. (1978). *Mind in society*. Cambridge, MA: Harvard University Press.

Wakslak, C. J., Smith, P. K., & Han, A. (2014). Using abstract language signals power. *Journal of Personality and Social Psychology, 107*, 41–55.

Wagner, J., Gerstorf, D., Hoppmann, C., & Luszcz, M. A. (2013). The nature and correlates of self-esteem trajectories in late life. *Journal of Personality and Social Psychology, 105*, 139–153.

Wagoner, J. A., & Hogg, M. A. (2016). Normative dissensus, identity-uncertainty, and subgroup autonomy. *Group Dynamics, 20*(4), 310–322.

Wakefield, J. R. H., Hopkins, N., & Greenwood, R. M. (2012). Thanks, but no thanks: Women's avoidance of help-seeking in the context of a dependency-related stereotype. *Psychology of Women Quarterly, 36*, 423–443.

Walker, I., & Mann, L. (1987). Unemployment, relative deprivation, and social protest. *Personality and Social Psychology Bulletin, 13*, 275–283.

Walker, I., & Pettigrew, T. F. (1984). Relative deprivation theory: An overview and conceptual critique. *British Journal of Social Psychology, 23*, 301–310.

Walker, I., & Smith, H. J. (Eds.) (2002). *Relative deprivation: Specification, development, and integration*. Cambridge, UK: Cambridge University Press.

Walker, L. E. (1993). The battered woman syndrome is a psychological consequence of abuse. In R. J. Gelles & D. R. Loseke (Eds.), *Current controversies on family violence* (pp. 133–153). Newbury Park, CA: SAGE.

Wallace, P. M. (1999). *The psychology of the internet*. Cambridge, UK: Cambridge University Press.

Wallach, M. A., Kogan, N., & Bem, D. J. (1962). Group influence on individual risk taking. *Journal of Abnormal and Social Psychology, 65*, 75–86.

Wallwork, J., & Dixon, J. A. (2004). Foxes, green fields, and Britishness: On the rhetorical construction of place and national identity. *British Journal of Social Psychology, 43*, 21–39.

Walster, E. (1966). Assignment of responsibility for an accident. *Journal of Personality and Social Psychology, 3*, 73–79.

Walster, E., & Festinger, L. (1962). The effectiveness of 'overheard' persuasive communications. *Journal of Abnormal and Social Psychology, 65*, 395–402.

Walster, E., Walster, G. W., & Berscheid, E. (1978). *Equity theory and research*. Boston, MA: Allyn & Bacon.

Walther, E. (2002). Guilty by mere association: Evaluative conditioning and the spreading attitude effect. *Journal of Personality and Social Psychology, 82*, 919–934.

Walther, J. B. (1996). Computer-mediated communication: Impersonal, interpersonal, and hyperpersonal interaction. *Communication Research, 23*, 23–43.

Walther, J. B., Loh, T., & Granka, L. (2005). Let me count the ways: The interchange of verbal and nonverbal cues in computer-mediated and face-to-face affinity. *Journal of Language and Social Psychology, 24*, 36–65.

Walther, J. B., & Parks, M. R. (2002). Cues filtered out, cues filtered in: Computer-mediated communication and relationships. In M. L. Knapp & J. A. Daly (Eds.), *Handbook of interpersonal communication* (3rd ed., pp. 529–563). Thousand Oaks, CA: Sage.

Walton, D., & McKeown, P. C. (1991). Drivers' biased perceptions of speed and safety campaign messages. *Accident Analysis and Prevention, 33*, 629–640.

Walton, G. M., & Cohen, G. L. (2003). Stereotype lift. *Journal of Experimental Social Psychology, 39*, 456–467.

Walumbwa, F. O., Avolio, B. J., Gardner, W. L., Wernsing, T. S., & Peterson, S. J. (2008). Authentic leadership: Development and validation of a theory-based measure. *Journal of Management, 34*, 89–126.

Wänke, M. (2015). It's all in the face: Facial appearance, political ideology and voters' perceptions. In J. P. Forgas, K. Fiedler, & W. D. Crano (Eds.), *Social psychology and politics* (pp. 143–162). New York: Psychology Press.

Wann, D. L., Carlson, J. D., Holland, L. C., Jacob, B. E., Owens, D. A., & Wells, D. D. (1999). Beliefs in symbolic catharsis: The importance of involvement with aggressive sports. *Social Behavior and Personality, 27*, 155–164.

Warburton, W. A., Williams, K. D., & Cairns, D. R. (2006). When ostracism leads to aggression: The moderating effects of control deprivation. *Journal of Experimental Social Psychology, 42*, 213–220.

Warren, P., Richardson, D.S., & McQuillin, S. (2011). Distinguishing among nondirect forms of aggression. *Aggressive Behavior, 37*, 291–301.

Warren, P. E., & Walker, I. (1991). Empathy, effectiveness and donations to charity: Social psychology's contribution. *British Journal of Social Psychology, 30*, 325–337.

Watson, B. M., Gallois, C., Hewitt, D., & Jones, L. (2012). Culture and health care: Intergrou communication and its consequences. In

J. Jackson (Ed.), *The Routledge handbook of intercultural communication* (pp. 512–524). London: Routledge.

Watson, D. (1982). The actor and the observer: How are the perceptions of causality divergent? *Psychological Bulletin, 92,* 682–700.

Watson, J. B. (1913). Psychology as a behaviourist views it. *Psychological Review, 20,* 158–177.

Watson, J. B. (1930). *Behaviorism.* New York: Norton.

Watson, K. (2009) Regional variation in English accents and dialects. In J. Culpeper, F. Katamba, P. Kerswill, R. Wodak, & T. McEnery (Eds.), *English language: Description, variation and context* (pp. 337–357). Basingstoke, UK: Palgrave Macmillan.

Waxman, C. (1977). *The stigma of poverty.* New York: Pergamon Press.

Waytz, A., & Epley, N.'(2012). Social connection enables dehumanization. *Journal of Experimental Social Psychology, 48,* 70–76.

Weary, G., Stanley, M. A., & Harvey, J. H. (1989). *Attribution.* New York: Springer-Verlag.

Weatherall, A. (1998). Re-visioning gender and language research. *Women and Language, 21,* 1–9.

Weaver, A. J., & Kobach, M. J. (2012). The relationship between selective exposure and the enjoyment of television violence. *Aggressive Behavior, 38,* 175–184.

Webb, E. J., Campbell, D. T., Schwartz, R. D., & Sechrest, L. (1969). *Unobtrusive measures: Nonreactive research in the social sciences.* Chicago, IL: Rand McNally.

Webb, T. L., Schweiger Gallo, I., Miles, E., Gollwitzer, P. M., & Sheeran, P. (2012). Effective regulation of affect: An action control perspective on emotion regulation. *European Review of Social Psychology, 23,* 143–186.

Webb, T. L., & Sheeran, P. (2006). Does changing behavioral intentions engender behavior change? A meta-analysis of experimental evidence. *Psychological Bulletin, 132,* 249–268.

Weber, M. (1930). *The Protestant ethic and the spirit of capitalism.* London: Allen & Unwin.

Weber, R., & Crocker, J. (1983). Cognitive processes in the revision of stereotypic beliefs. *Journal of Personality and Social Psychology, 45,* 961–977.

Wegener, D. T., Petty, R. E., & Smith, S. M. (1995). Positive mood can increase or decrease message scrutiny: The hedonic contingency view of mood and message processing. *Journal of Personality and Social Psychology, 69,* 5–15.

Wegner, D. M. (1987). Transactive memory: A transactive analysis of the group mind. In B. Mullen & G. R. Goethals (Eds.), *Theories of group behavior* (pp. 185–208). New York: Springer.

Wegner, D. M. (1995). A computer network model of human transactive memory. *Social Cognition, 13,* 319–339.

Wegner, D. M., Erber, R., & Raymond, P. (1991). Transactive memory in close relationships. *Journal of Personality and Social Psychology, 61,* 923–929.

Weiner, B. (1979). A theory of motivation for some classroom experiences. *Journal of Educational Psychology, 71,* 3–25.

Weiner, B. (1985). 'Spontaneous' causal thinking. *Psychological Bulletin, 97,* 74–84.

Weiner, B. (1986). *An attributional theory of motivation and emotion.* New York: Springer.

Weiner, B. (1995). *Judgments of responsibility.* New York: Guilford Press.

Weiten, W. (1980). The attraction–leniency effect in jury research: An examination of external validity. *Journal of Applied Social Psychology, 10,* 340–347.

Weldon, E., & Weingart, L. (1993). Group goals and group performance. *British Journal of Social Psychology, 32,* 307–334.

Wells, G. L., Memon, A., & Penrod, S. D. (2006). Eye witness evidence: Improving its probative value. *Psychological Science in the Public Interest, 7,* 45–75.

Wells, G. L., & Turtle, J. W. (1988). What is the best way to encode faces? In M. Gruneberg, P. E. Morris, & R. N. Sykes (Eds.), *Practical aspects of memory: Current research and issues* (Vol. 1, pp. 163–168). Chichester, UK: Wiley.

Wenzel, M., Mummendey, A., & Waldzus, S. (2007). Superordinate identities and intergroup conflict: The ingroup projection model. *European Review of Social Psychology, 18,* 331–372.

Wesselmann, E. D., Butler, F. A., Williams, K. D., & Pickett, C. L. (2010). Adding injury to insult: Unexpected rejection leads to more aggressive responses. *Aggressive Behavior, 35,* 232–237.

West, C. (1984). *Routine complications.* Bloomington, IN: Indiana University Press.

West, S. G., Whitney, G., & Schnedler, R. (1975). Helping a motorist in distress: The effects of sex, race and neighbourhood. *Journal of Personality and Social Psychology, 31,* 691–698.

Westie, F. R., & DeFleur, M. L. (1959). Automatic responses and their relationship to race attitudes. *Journal of Abnormal and Social Psychology, 58,* 340–347.

Wetherell, M. (1998). Positioning and interpretative repertoires: Conversation analysis and poststructuralism in dialogue. *Discourse and Society, 9,* 387–412.

Wetherell, M. S. (1986). Linguistic repertoires and literary criticism: New directions for a social psychology of gender. In S. Wilkinson (Ed.), *Feminist social psychology* (pp. 77–95). Milton Keynes, UK: Open University Press.

Wetherell, M. S. (1987). Social identity and group polarization. In J. C. Turner, M. A. Hogg, P. J. Oakes, S. D. Reicher, & M. S. Wetherell, *Rediscovering the social group: A self-categorization theory* (pp. 142–170). Oxford, UK: Blackwell.

Wetherell, M. S. (2012). *Affect and emotion: A new social science understanding.* London: Sage.

Wetherell, M. S., Taylor, S., & Yates, S. J. (2001). *Discourse as data: A guide for analysis.* London: SAGE.

Wetzel, C. G., & Walton, M. D. (1985). Developing biased social judgments: The false consensus effect. *Journal of Personality and Social Psychology, 49,* 1352–1359.

Weyant, J. (1978). The effect of mood states, costs and benefits on helping. *Journal of Personality and Social Psychology, 36,* 1169–1176.

Wheeler, L. (1991). A brief history of social comparison theory. In J. Suls & T. A. Wills (Eds.), *Social comparison: Contemporary theory and research* (pp. 3–21). Hillsdale, NJ: Erlbaum.

Wheeler, L., & Kim, Y. (1997). What is beautiful is culturally good: The physical attractiveness stereotype has different content in collectivist cultures. *Personality and Social Psychology Bulletin, 23,* 795–800.

Whitcher, S. J., & Fisher, J. D. (1979). Multidimensional reaction to therapeutic touch in a hospital setting. *Journal of Personality and Social Psychology, 37,* 87–96.

White, M. (2004). Thirty worst atrocities of the 20th century [electronic version], Retrieved 25 October 2006 from http://users.erols.com/mwhite28/atrox.htm.

White, P. A. (1988). Causal processing: Origins and development. *Psychological Bulletin, 104,* 36–52.

White, P. A., & Younger, D. P. (1988). Differences in the ascription of transient internal states to self and other. *Journal of Experimental Social Psychology, 24,* 292–309.

Whittaker, J. O., & Meade, R. D. (1967). Social pressure in the modification and distortion of judgment: A cross-cultural study. *International Journal of Psychology, 2,* 109–113.

Whorf, B. L. (1956). *Language, thought and reality.* Cambridge, MA: MIT Press.

Whyte, W. F. (1943). *Street corner society* (2nd ed.). Chicago: University of Chicago Press.

Wicker, A. W. (1969). Attitudes versus actions: The relationship of verbal and overt behavioral responses to attitude objects. *Journal of Social Issues, 25,* 41–78.

Wicklund, R. A. (1975). Objective self-awareness. *Advances in Experimental Social Psychology, 8,* 233–275.

Widdicombe, S., & Wooffitt, R. (1990). 'Being' versus 'doing' punk: On achieving authenticity as a member. *Journal of Language and Social Psychology, 4,* 257–277.

Widdicombe, S., & Wooffitt, R. (1994). *The language of youth subcultures.* London: Harvester Wheatsheaf.

Widmeyer, W. N., Brawley, L. R., & Carron, A. V. (1985). *The measurement of cohesion in sports teams: The group environment questionnaire.* London, Ontario: Sports Dynamics.

Wiemann, J. M., & Giles, H. (1988). Interpersonal communications. In M. Hewstone, W. Stroebe, J.-P. Codol, & G. M. Stephenson (Eds.),

Introduction to social psychology (pp. 199–221). Oxford, UK: Blackwell.

Wieselquist, J., Rusbult, C. E., Foster, C. A., & Agnew, C. R. (1999). Commitment, prorelationship behavior, and trust in close relationships. *Journal of Personality and Social Psychology, 77*, 942–966.

Wilder, D. A. (1977). Perceptions of groups, size of opposition and social influence. *Journal of Experimental Social Psychology, 13*, 253–268.

Wilder, D. A. (1984). Predictions of belief homogeneity and similarity following social categorization. *British Journal of Social Psychology, 23*, 323–333.

Wilder, D. A. (1986). Social categorization: Implications for creation and reduction of intergroup bias. *Advances in Experimental Social Psychology, 19*, 291–355.

Wilder, D. A., & Shapiro, P. N. (1984). Role of out-group cues in determining social identity. *Journal of Personality and Social Psychology, 47*, 342–348.

Wilder, D. A., & Shapiro, P. N. (1989). Role of competition-induced anxiety in limiting the beneficial impact of positive behavior by an outgroup member. *Journal of Personality and Social Psychology, 56*, 60–69.

Wilder, D. A., & Simon, A. F. (1998). Categorical and dynamic groups: Implications for social perception and intergroup behavior. In C. Sedikides, J. Schopler, & C. A. Insko (Eds.), *Intergroup cognition and intergroup behavior* (pp. 27–44). Mahwah, NJ: Erlbaum.

Wilkinson, S., & Kitzinger, C. (2006). Surprise as an interactional achievement: Reaction tokens in conversation. *Social Psychology Quarterly, 69*, 150–182.

Williams, A. (1996). Young people's evaluations of intergenerational versus peer under accommodation: Sometimes older is better. *Journal of Language and Social Psychology, 15*, 291–311.

Williams, A., & Nussbaum, J. F. (2001). *Intergenerational communication across the life span.* Mahwah, NJ: Erlbaum.

Williams, E. F., & Gilovich, T. (2012). The better-than-my-average effect: The relative impact of peak and average performance in assessments of self and others. *Journal of Experimental Social Psychology, 48*, 556–561.

Williams, J. A. (1984). Gender and intergroup behaviour: Towards an integration. *British Journal of Social Psychology, 23*, 311–316.

Williams, J. E., & Best, D. L. (1982). *Measuring sex stereotypes: A thirty nation study.* Beverly Hills, CA: SAGE.

Williams, K. D. (2002). *Ostracism: The power of silence.* New York: Guilford Press.

Williams, K. D. (2009). Ostracism: A temporal need-threat model. *Advances in Experimental Social Psychology, 41*, 279–314.

Williams, K. D., Cheung, C. K. T., & Choi, W. (2000). Cyberostracism: Effects of being ignored over the internet. *Journal of Personality and Social Psychology, 79*, 748–762.

Williams, K. D., Harkins, S. G., & Karau, S. J. (2003). Social performance. In M. A. Hogg & J. Cooper (Eds.), *The SAGE handbook of social psychology* (pp. 327–346). London: SAGE.

Williams, K. D., Harkins, S. G., & Karau, S. J. (2007). Social performance. In M. A. Hogg & J. Cooper (Eds.), *The SAGE handbook of social psychology: Concise student edition* (pp. 291–311). London: SAGE.

Williams, K. D., Harkins, S. G., & Latané, B. (1981). Identifiability as a deterrent to social loafing: Two cheering experiments. *Journal of Personality and Social Psychology, 40*, 303–311.

Williams, K. D., & Karau, S. J. (1991). Social loafing and social compensation: The effects of expectations of co-worker performance. *Journal of Personality and Social Psychology, 61*, 570–581.

Williams, K. D., Karau, S. J., & Bourgeois, M. (1993). Working on collective tasks: Social loafing and social compensation. In M. A. Hogg & D. Abrams (Eds.), *Group motivation: Social psychological perspectives* (pp. 130–148). London: Harvester Wheatsheaf.

Williams, K. D., Shore, W. J., & Grahe, J. E. (1998). The silent treatment: Perceptions of its behaviors and associated feelings. *Group Processes and Intergroup Relations, 1*, 117–141.

Williams, K. D., & Sommer, K. L. (1997). Social ostracism by coworkers: Does rejection lead to loafing and compensation? *Personality and Social Psychology Bulletin, 23*, 693–706.

Williams, K. D., & Warburton, W. A. (2003). Ostracism: A form of indirect aggression that can result in aggression. *International Review of Social Psychology, 16*, 101–126.

Williams, L. E., & Bargh, J. A. (2008). Experiencing physical warmth promotes interpersonal warmth. *Science, 322*, 606–607.

Williamson, G. M., & Clark, M. S. (1989). Providing help and relationship type as determinants of changes in moods and self-evaluations. *Journal of Personality and Social Psychology, 56*, 722–734.

Willness, C. R., Steel, P., & Lee, K. (2007). A meta-analysis of the antecedents and consequences of workplace sexual harassment. *Personnel Psychology, 60*, 127–162.

Wills, T. A. (1981). Downward comparison principles in social psychology. *Psychological Bulletin, 90*, 245–271.

Wilpert, B. (1995). Organizational behavior. *Annual Review of Psychology, 46*, 59–90.

Wilson, E. O. (1975). *Sociobiology: The new synthesis.* Cambridge, MA: Harvard University Press.

Wilson, E. O. (1978). *On human nature.* Cambridge, MA: Harvard University Press.

Wilson, J. (2000). Volunteering. *Annual Review of Sociology, 26*, 215–240.

Wilson, M. S., & Liu, J. H. (2003). Social dominance orientation and gender: The moderating role of gender identity. *British Journal of Social Psychology, 42*, 187–198.

Wirth, J., Sacco, D. F., Hugenberg, K., & Williams, K. D. (2010). Eye gaze as relational evaluation: Averted eye gaze leads to feelings of ostracism and relational devaluation. *Personality and Social Psychology Bulletin, 36*, 869–882.

Wishner, J. (1960). Reanalysis of 'impressions of personality'. *Psychological Review, 67*, 96–112.

Wispé, L. G. (1972). Positive forms of social behavior: An overview. *Journal of Social Issues, 28*, 1–19.

Witte, K., Berkowitz, J. M., Cameron, K. A., & McKeon, J. K. (1998). Preventing the spread of genital warts: Using fear appeals to promote self-protective behaviours. *Health Education and Behavior, 25*, 571–585.

Wittenbrink, W., Judd, C. M., & Park, B. (1997). Evidence for racial prejudice at the implicit level and its relationship with questionnaire measures. *Journal of Personality and Social Psychology, 72*, 262–274.

Wittgenstein, L. (1953). *Philosophical investigations.* Oxford, UK: Blackwell.

Wohl, M. J., & Branscombe, N. R. (2008). Remembering historical victimization: Collective guilt for current ingroup transgressions. *Journal of Personality and Social Psychology, 94*, 988–1006.

Wood, G. S. (1982). Conspiracy and the paranoid style: Causality and deceit in the eighteenth century. *William and Mary Quarterly, 39*, 401–441.

Wood, J. V. (1989). Theory and research concerning social comparisons of personal attributes. *Psychological Bulletin, 106*, 231–248.

Wood, W. (2000). Attitude change: Persuasion and social influence. *Annual Review of Psychology, 51*, 539–570.

Wood, W., Lundgren, S., Ouellette, J. A., Busceme, S., & Blackstone, T. (1994). Minority influence: A meta-analytic review of social influence processes. *Psychological Bulletin, 115*, 323–345.

Wood, W., & Neal, D. T. (2007). A new look at habits and the interface between habits and goals. *Psychological Review, 114*, 843–863.

Wood, W., & Quinn, J. M. (2003). Forewarned and forearmed? Two meta-analytic syntheses of forewarnings of influence appeals. *Psychological Bulletin, 129*, 119–138.

Wooffitt, R. (2005). *Conversation analysis and discourse analysis: A comparative and critical introduction.* London: Sage.

Worchel, S. (1979). Cooperation and the reduction of intergroup conflict: Some determining factors. In W. Austin & S. Worchel (Eds.), *The social psychology of intergroup relations* (pp. 262–273). Monterey, CA: Brooks/Cole.

Worchel, S. (1996). Emphasising the social nature of groups in a developmental framework. In J. L. Nye & A. M. Bower (Eds.), *What's social about social cognition: Research on socially shared cognition in small groups* (pp. 261–282). Thousand Oaks, CA: SAGE.

Worchel, S., Andreoli, V. A., & Folger, R. (1977). Intergroup cooperation and intergroup attraction: The effect of previous interaction and outcome of combined effort. *Journal of Experimental Social Psychology, 13*, 131–140.

Worchel, S., Cooper, J., & Goethals, G. R. (1988). *Understanding social psychology* (4th ed.). Chicago: Dorsey Press.

Worchel, S., & Novell, N. (1980). Effect of perceived environmental conditions during cooperation on intergroup attraction. *Journal of Personality and Social Psychology, 38*, 764–772.

Worchel, S., Rothgerber, H., Day, E. A., Hart, D., & Butemeyer, J. (1998). Social identity and individual productivity within groups. *British Journal of Social Psychology, 37*, 389–413.

Word, C., Zanna, M., & Cooper, J. (1974). The nonverbal mediation of self-fulfilling prophecies in interracial interaction. *Journal of Experimental Social Psychology, 10*, 109–120.

Wright, S. C. (2001). Restricted ingroup boundaries: Tokenism, ambiguity, and the tolerance of injustice. In J. T. Jost and B. Major (Eds.), *The psychology of legitimacy: Emerging perspectives on ideology, justice, and intergroup relations* (pp. 223–254). New York: Cambridge University Press.

Wright, S. C., Aron, A., McLaughlin-Volpe, T., & Ropp, S. A. (1997). The extended contact effect: Knowledge of cross-group friendships and prejudice. *Journal of Personality and Social Psychology, 73*, 73–90.

Wright, S. C., Aron, A., & Tropp, L. R. (2002). Including others (and their groups) in the self: Self-expansion and intergroup relations. In J. P. Forgas & K. Williams (Eds.), *The social self: Cognitive, interpersonal and intergroup perspectives* (pp. 343–363). New York: Psychology Press.

Wright, S. C., & Taylor, D. M. (2007). The social psychology of cultural diversity: Social stereotyping, prejudice, and discrimination. In M. A. Hogg, & J. Cooper (Eds.), *The SAGE handbook of social psychology: Concise student edition* (pp. 361–387).

Wright, S. C., Taylor, D. M., & Moghaddam, F. M. (1990). Responding to membership in a disadvantaged group: from acceptance to collective protest. *Journal of Personality and Social Psychology, 58*, 994–1003.

Wrightsman, L. S. (1964). Measurement of philosophies of human nature. *Psychological Reports, 14*, 743–751.

Wundt, W. (1897). *Outlines of psychology*. New York: Stechert.

Wundt, W. (1916). *Elements of folk psychology: Outlines of a psychological history of the development of mankind*. London: Allen & Unwin (German original 1912).

Wyer, R. S., Jr. (1976). An investigation of relations among probability estimates. *Organizational Behavior and Human Performance, 15*, 1–18.

Wyer, R. S., Jr, & Carlston, D. E. (1994). The cognitive representation of persons and events. In R. S. Wyer Jr & T. K. Srull (Eds.), *Handbook of social cognition* (2nd ed., pp. 41–98). Hillsdale, NJ: Erlbaum.

Wyer, R. S., Jr, & Gordon, S. E. (1982). The recall of information about persons and groups. *Journal of Experimental Social Psychology, 18*, 128–164.

Wyer, R. S., Jr, & Gordon, S. E. (1984). The cognitive representation of social information. In R. S. Wyer Jr & T. K. Srull (Eds.), *Handbook of social cognition* (Vol. 2, pp. 73–150). Hillsdale, NJ: Erlbaum.

Wyer, R. S., Jr, & Gruenfeld, D. H. (1995). Information processing in social contexts: Implications for social memory and judgement. *Advances in Experimental Social Psychology, 27*, 49–91.

Wyer, R. S., Jr, & Martin, L. L. (1986). Person memory: The role of traits, group stereotypes, and specific behaviours in the cognitive representation of persons. *Journal of Personality and Social Psychology, 50*, 661–675.

Wyer, R. S., Jr, & Srull, T. K. (1981). Category accessibility: Some theoretical and empirical issues concerning the processing of social stimulus information. In E. T. Higgins, C. P. Herman, & M. P. Zanna (Eds.), *Social cognition: The Ontario symposium* (Vol. 1, pp. 161–198). Hillsdale, NJ: Erlbaum.

Wyer, R. S., Jr, & Srull, T. K. (1986). Human cognition in its social context. *Psychological Review, 93*, 322–359.

Yamagishi, T., & Kiyonari, T. (2000). The group as the container of generalized reciprocity. *Social Psychology Quarterly, 63*, 116–132.

Yancey, G. (2007). Homogamy over the net: Using internet advertisements to discover who interracially dates. *Journal of Social and Personal Relationships, 24*, 913–930.

Yang, K. S. (2000). Monocultural and cross-cultural indigenous approaches: The royal road to the development of a balanced global psychology. *Asian Journal of Social Psychology, 3*, 241–263.

Yang, K. S., & Bond, M. H. (1990). Exploring implicit personality theories with indigenous or imported constructs: The Chinese case. *Journal of Personality and Social Psychology, 58*, 1087–1095.

Yarmouk, U. (2000). The effect of presentation modality on judgements of honesty and attractiveness. *Social Behavior and Personality, 28*, 269–278.

Yates, B. T., & Mischel, W. (1979). Young children's preferred attentional strategies for delaying gratification. *Journal of Personality and Social Psychology, 37*, 286–300.

Ybarra, M., Huesmann, L. R., Korchmaros, J. D., & Reisner, S. L. (2014). Cross-sectional associations between violent video and computer game playing and weapon carrying in a national cohort of children. *Aggressive Behavior, 40*, 345–358.

Young, I., & Sullivan, D. (2016). Competitive victimhood: A review of the theoretical and empirical literature. *Current Opinion in Psychology, 11*, 30–34.

Young, J. L., & James, E. H. (2001). Token majority: The work attitudes of male flight attendants. *Sex Roles, 45*, 299–219.

Younger, J. C., Walker, L., & Arrowood, A. J. (1977). Post-decision dissonance at the fair. *Personality and Social Psychology Bulletin, 3*, 247–287.

Yuki, M. (2003). Intergroup comparison versus intragroup relationships: A cross-cultural examination of social identity theory in North American and East Asian cultural contexts. *Social Psychology Quarterly, 66*, 166–183.

Yukl, G. (2013). *Leadership in organizations* (8th ed.). Upper Saddle River, NJ: Pearson.

Yzerbyt, V., Castano, E., Leyens, J.-P., & Paolino, M. P. (2000). The primacy of the ingroup: The interplay of entitativity and identification. *European Review of Social Psychology, 11*, 257–295.

Yzerbyt, V., & Demoulin, S. (2010). Intergroup relations. In S. T. Fiske, D. T. Gilbert, & G. Lindzey (Eds.), *Handbook of social psychology* (5th ed., Vol. 2, pp. 1024–1083). New York: Wiley.

Yzerbyt, V. Y., Leyens, J.-P., & Schadron, G. (1997). Social judgeability and the dilution of stereotypes: The impact of the nature and sequence of information. *Personality and Social Psychology Bulletin, 23*, 1312–1322.

Yzerbyt, V. Y., Schadron, G., Leyens, J.-P., & Rocher, S. (1994). Social judgeability: The impact of meta-informational rules on the use of stereotypes. *Journal of Personality and Social Psychology, 66*, 48–55.

Zaccaro, S. J. (1984). Social loafing: The role of task attractiveness. *Personality and Social Psychology Bulletin, 10*, 99–106.

Zadro, L., Williams, K. D., & Richardson, R. (2004). How low can you go? Ostracism by a computer lowers belonging, control, self-esteem, and meaningful existence. *Journal of Experimental Social Psychology, 40*, 560–567.

Zahn-Waxler, C., Radke-Yarrow, M., Wagner, E., & Chapman, M. (1992). Development of concern for others. *Developmental Psychology, 28*, 126–136.

Zajonc, R. B. (1965). Social facilitation. *Science, 149*, 269–274.

Zajonc, R. B. (1968). Attitudinal effects of mere exposure. *Journal of Personality and Social Psychology, 9*, 1–27.

Zajonc, R. B. (1980). Cognition and social cognition: A historical perspective. In L. Festinger (Ed.), *Retrospections on social psychology* (pp. 180–204). New York: Oxford University Press.

Zajonc, R. B. (1989). Styles of explanation in social psychology. *European Journal of Social Psychology, 19*, 345–368.

Zanna, M. P. (1993). Message receptivity: A new look at the old problem of open- versus closed-mindedess. In A. A. Mitchell (Ed.), *Advertising exposure, memory and choice* (pp. 141–162). Hillsdale, NJ: Erlbaum.

Zanna, M. P., & Hamilton, D. L. (1972). Attribute dimensions and patterns of trait inferences. *Psychonomic Science, 27*, 353–354.

Zanna, M. P., Kiesler, C. A., & Pilkonis, D. A. (1970). Positive and negative affect established by classical conditioning. *Journal of Personality and Social Psychology, 14*, 321–328.

Zanna, M. P., & Rempel, J. K. (1988). Attitudes: A new look at an old concept. In D. Bar-Tal & A. W. Kruglanski (Eds.), *The social psychology of knowledge* (pp. 315–334). Cambridge, UK: Cambridge University Press.

Zebrowitz, L. A. (1996). Physical appearance as a basis of stereotyping. In C. N. Macrae, C. Stangor, & M. Hewstone (Eds.), *Stereotypes and stereotyping* (pp. 79–120). New York: Guilford Press.

Zebrowitz, L. A., & Collins, M. A. (1997). Accurate social perception at zero acquaintance: The affordances of a Gibsonian approach. *Personality and Social Psychology Review, 1*, 204–223.

Zeelenberg, M., Nelissen, R. M. A., Breugelmans, S. M., & Pieters, R. (2008). On emotion specificity in decision making: Why feeling is for doing. *Judgment and Decision Making, 3*, 18–27.

Zentner, M., & Eagly, A. H. (2015). A sociocultural framework for understanding partner preferences of women and men: Integration of concepts and evidence. *European Review of Social Psychology, 26*, 328–373.

Zhang, S., & Hunt, J. S. (2008). The stereotype rebound effect: Universal or culturally bounded process? *Journal of Experimental Social Psychology, 44*, 489–500.

Zillmann, D. (1979). *Hostility and aggression*. Hillsdale, NJ: Erlbaum.

Zillmann, D. (1984). *Connections between sex and aggression*. Hillsdale, NJ: Erlbaum.

Zillmann, D. (1988). Cognition–excitation interdependencies in aggressive behavior. *Aggressive Behavior, 14*, 51–64.

Zillmann, D. (1996). Sequential dependencies in emotional experience and behavior. In R. D. Kavanaugh, B. Zimmerberg, & S. Fein (Eds.), *Emotion: Interdisciplinary perspectives* (pp. 243–272). Mahwah, NJ: Erlbaum.

Zillmann, D., & Bryant, J. (1984). Effects of massive exposure to pornography. In N. M. Malamuth & E. Donnerstein (Eds.), *Pornography and sexual aggression* (pp. 115–138). New York: Academic Press.

Zimbardo, P. G. (1970). The human choice: Individuation, reason, and order versus deindividuation, impulse, and chaos. In W. J. Arnold & D. Levine (Eds.), *Nebraska symposium on motivation 1969* (Vol. 17, pp. 237–307). Lincoln, NE: University of Nebraska Press.

Zimbardo, P. G. (1971). *The Stanford prison experiment*. Script of the slide show.

Zimbardo, P. G., Ebbesen, E. E., & Maslach, C. (1977). *Influencing attitudes and changing behavior*. Reading, MA: Addison-Wesley.

Zimbardo, P. G., Haney, C., Banks, W. C., & Jaffe, D. (1982). The psychology of imprisonment. In J. C. Brigham & L. Wrightsman (Eds.), *Contemporary issues in social psychology* (4th ed., pp. 230–235). Monterey, CA: Brooks/Cole.

Zimbardo, P. G., & Leippe, M. R. (1991). *The psychology of attitude change and social influence*. New York: McGraw-Hill.

Zimbardo, P. G., Weisenberg, M., Firestone, I., & Levy, B. (1965). Communication effectiveness in producing public conformity and private attitude change. *Journal of Personality, 33*, 233–256.

Zimmerman, D. H., & West, C. (1975). Sex roles, interruptions, and silences in conversation. In B. Thorne & N. Henley (Eds.), *Language and sex: Differences and dominance* (pp. 105–129). Rowley, MA: Newbury House.

Zuckerman, M. (1979). Attribution of success and failure revisited, or: The motivational bias is alive and well in attribution theory. *Journal of Personality, 47*, 245–287.

Zuckerman, M., DePaulo, B. M., & Rosenthal, R. (1981). Verbal and non-verbal communication of deception. *Advances in Experimental Social Psychology, 14*, 1–59.

Zuckerman, M., Lazzaro, M. M., & Waldgeir, D. (1979). Undermining effects of the foot-in-the-door technique with extrinsic rewards. *Journal of Applied Social Psychology, 9*, 292–296.

Zuckerman, M., Miserandino, M., & Bernieri, F. (1983). Civil inattention exists – in elevators. *Personality and Social Psychology Bulletin, 9*, 578–586.

Zukier, H. (1986). The paradigmatic and narrative modes in goal-guided inference. In R. M. Sorrentino & E. T. Higgins (Eds.), *Handbook of motivation and cognition: Foundations of social behavior* (pp. 465–502). New York: Guilford Press.

Zuwerink, J. R., & Devine, P. G. (1996). Attitude importance and resistance to persuasion: It's not just the thought that counts. *Journal of Personality and Social Psychology, 70*, 931–944.

Author index

Subject index